AMERICAN
DECADES
1900-1909

AMERICAN DECADES
1900-1909

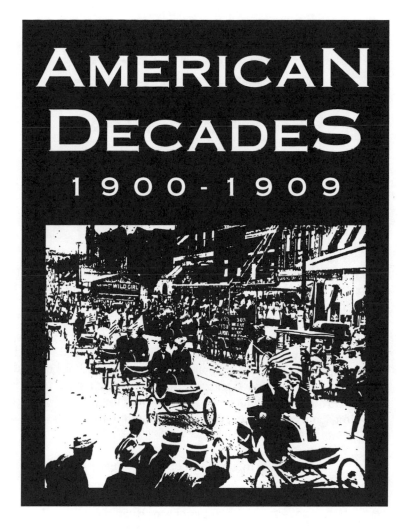

EDITED BY

VINCENT TOMPKINS

A MANLY, INC. BOOK

an International Thomson Publishing company I**T**P®

AMERICAN
DECADES
1900-1909

Matthew J. Bruccoli and Richard Layman, *Editorial Directors*

Karen L. Rood, *Senior Editor*

Printed in the United States of America

The paper used in this publication meets the minimum requirements of American National Standard for Information Sciences-Permanence Paper for Printed Library Materials, ANSI Z39.48-1984. ∞™

Library of Congress Catalog Card Number 95-081586
ISBN 0-8103-5722-4

 Gale Research, an ITP Information/Reference Group Company.
ITP logo is a trademark under license.

10 9 8 7

CONTENTS

INTRODUCTION

The New Century. On 10 April 1899, on the eve of a new century and enthused by his personal triumph with the Rough Riders in the Spanish-American War, a young Theodore Roosevelt called on his fellow Americans to meet the challenges of the dawning age. "The twentieth century looms before us big with the fate of many nations," he said. "If we stand idly by, if we seek merely swollen, slothful ease and ignoble peace, if we shrink from the hard contests where men must win at hazard of their lives and at the risk of all they hold dear, then the bolder and stronger peoples will pass us by, and will win for themselves the domination of the world." While many of Roosevelt's contemporaries worried less about the struggle for world power than about the struggle for daily survival, they would embrace the bold dynamism he brought to the office of the presidency two years later. The United States in the 1900s was a nation sharply conscious of its place on the world stage, even if it was uncertain and divided about the role it would play. Roosevelt's challenge to an older opponent in a debate over war with Spain captured this spirit: "You and your generation have had your chance. . . . Now let us of this generation have ours!"

Growth and Transformation. Americans in the 1900s experienced changes that would have been incomprehensible to earlier generations. The population grew 21 percent in these years, from 75,994,575 to 91,972,266. This growth was driven in large measure by the single greatest influx of immigrants to the United States in its entire history. Between 1901 and 1910 some 8,795,386 immigrants entered the country, more than half of them from eastern, central, and southern Europe. Many of these new Americans, driven from their homelands by violence or poverty and lured by the promise of freedom and opportunity, were drawn to industrial jobs in the Northeast and Midwest, adding velocity to a process of urbanization that was drastically altering the American landscape, American politics, and the way of life of the average person. A nation that was 40 percent urban and 60 percent rural in 1900, the United States by 1910 would be 46 percent urban and 54 percent rural. Like the immigrants from foreign shores, America's internal migrants were drawn from farms and small towns by the lure and luster of the booming cities and by the hope that

a job in one of the nation's factories would provide a better living for their families. The scale and rapidity of these upheavals, and the growing diversity of the American population, left many feeling uneasy and uncertain even as they pursued new opportunities for security and prosperity.

Big Business Consolidates. When Alexis de Tocqueville visited the United States in the 1830s, he wrote regarding the nation's economy that "what most astonishes me . . . is not so much the marvelous grandeur of some undertakings, as the innumerable multitudes of small ones." Had one of his descendants returned seventy years later he surely would have reversed the equation: a nation of small farmers, shopkeepers, and mill owners had become a land of industrial giants whose size dwarfed every other social and political institution. Before the Civil War even the largest manufacturing enterprises — such as the textile mills of Lowell and Lawrence, Massachusetts — were worth less than $1 million, and most manufacturing firms were considerably smaller. When the United States Steel Corporation was formed in 1901, it was capitalized at $1 billion, a sum more than twice the annual budget of the federal government in that year. In transportation, steel, meatpacking, oil refining, and other sectors of the U.S. economy, large corporations dominated relatively new national markets for goods and services. The impact of this consolidation was felt throughout the country, as revolutions in communication and transportation made it possible for businesses to span the continent. Not everyone welcomed this change: local merchants found themselves competing with mail-order houses such as Montgomery Ward and Sears Roebuck; farmers continued to chafe at their dependence on the railroads; city dwellers found themselves at the mercy of monopolistic streetcar and utility companies; and local and state governments struggled to control the behavior and mitigate the impact of towering corporate enterprises. But while some Americans protested the growing power of the trusts, their protest was muted by a rising level of prosperity and material well-being. Despite the disruptions associated with the Panic of 1907, the American economy, as measured by the gross national product, nearly *doubled* during the decade, from $18.7 billion in 1900 to $35.3 billion in 1910.

A World Power. The emergence of the United States as an industrial giant on a par with Germany and Great Britain also sustained the nation's new role in international affairs. The victory of the United States over a decaying Spanish Empire in the Spanish-American War thrust the country into an unaccustomed position as an imperial power. New territories in the Caribbean and the Pacific, a stubborn insurrection against U.S. control in the Philippines, and economic ambitions in China signaled the end of a century of isolationism as official policy. Theodore Roosevelt proved himself to be an activist president abroad as well as at home, reasserting U.S. prerogatives in Latin America, pressing his predecessor's demand for an "Open Door" in China, securing American rights to build the Panama Canal, and sending the U.S. Navy on an around-the-world cruise to signal to the world and to critics of imperialism at home his determination to wield American power abroad.

The Crisis of the 1890s. The last decade of the nineteenth century, despite American triumphs overseas, had been a decade of sometimes violent upheaval and social crises. The worst depression in the nation's history prior to the Great Depression of the 1930s struck in 1893, throwing millions out of work when such things as unemployment insurance and old-age pensions were unheard of. Violent strikes against the Pullman Company in Chicago and Carnegie Steel in Homestead, Pennsylvania, seemed to signal to an anxious middle class a dawning era of bitter class conflict. Government in the nation's cities often made a mockery of the democratic process. Where urban political machines and bosses ruled, votes were bought and sold, insiders reaped windfalls from graft and corruption, and the desperate needs of urban residents for clean air and water, sewer systems, clean streets, and other services were either ignored or contracted to the highest bidder. On the farms of the South and Midwest, populist protest erupted over the power of the railroads, the financiers, and the middlemen who in the eyes of angry farmers were nothing but parasites who fed off their harvests. Together these events suggested a society in peril, and by the turn of the century a host of reformers were busily trying to save America from itself.

An Age of Reform. Reformers dramatically altered American politics and society in the 1900s. Most leaders of what historians refer to as the progressive movement were American-born, urban, and middle class. Many were the sons and daughters of ministers and professionals. They were themselves journalists, lawyers, social workers, politicians, and sometimes businesspeople. The reforms they initiated began in the mid 1890s and achieved their greatest impact during the first two decades of the twentieth century. Their goals were diverse and often contradictory. Some wanted to stamp out vice and corruption in the nation's growing cities: they demanded the prohibition of alcohol, the shutting down of brothels, and the prosecution of crooked cops and politicians. Others were mainly concerned with curbing the power of the trusts and used first state and then federal law to try to restore a competitive economic marketplace. Other reformers wanted to make American society and politics more efficient, to curb the waste of natural resources and human life. Many of the reformers were educated women who believed they had a moral responsibility to put their knowledge to work in the service of society. While reform activities often began as efforts by voluntary associations of individuals (or within professions such as law and medicine), by the time Theodore Roosevelt became president in 1901 most progressives were looking to government as a potential force for change rather than a source of oppression. In the 1900s they achieved major gains in regulating unscrupulous business practices, protecting natural resources and wilderness, reforming city governments across the country, making the electoral process more open, and improving the working conditions of women and children. In these and other areas the progressive legacy would remain powerful for the rest of the twentieth century.

Progressive Beliefs. Despite important differences, progressives shared central beliefs that shaped their activism in the 1900s. They believed that human behavior was shaped by the surrounding environment, and they rejected both the Calvinist doctrine of immutable sin and predestination and the emphasis placed by many nineteenth-century theorists on heredity. They believed that human nature could be improved by changing the conditions under which people lived and worked. They borrowed from the scientific method a belief in experimentation and trial and error. Rather than clinging to unshakable "truths" and immutable laws, they believed that their ideas and values had to withstand the test of experience. While many progressives were nostalgic for an earlier time when it seemed that individuals could control their own destiny, they rejected the "rugged individualism" of earlier generations, believing that cooperation and social control had to replace the survival of the fittest as guiding principles of American society. Many were believers in the "Social Gospel" — which emphasized the need to put Christian principles of human brotherhood, equality, and responsibility for one's fellow human beings into practice. Finally, progressives were firmly convinced that education was the most powerful tool for social change. Following the lead of the philosopher and educator John Dewey, they worked to overhaul the nation's schools so that they would become, as Dewey phrased it, "the deepest and best guarantee of a larger society which is worthy, lovely and harmonious."

The Forces of Tradition. Many Americans embraced the new and the modern and recognized that social and political institutions had to adapt to the changed circumstances of twentieth-century life. But nostalgia for old ways and customs, and strongly held beliefs that the United States was changing in unwelcome and unwanted ways, remained powerful elements in the culture of the 1900s. Religious fundamentalists, of whom there were millions, fiercely resisted any accommodation of empirical science, Darwinian theories of human evolution in particular. In law, the judiciary remained a bulwark of limited government, resisting the efforts of states and the federal government to regulate business but sanctioning government repression of labor unions, especially radical unions such as the Industrial Workers of the World, which judges perceived as a threat to the established social order. In the arts, the 1900s witnessed a fierce and contentious debate between young modernists eager to experiment with new subject matter and novel forms of expression and a strongly entrenched establishment anxious to defend a "genteel tradition" built around "the best that has been thought and said." In politics even the most ardent progressive often simply wanted to return to an imagined simpler past, when neighbors knew one another and social and economic power was localized and personal.

Race. For African Americans, the past was rarely the object of nostalgia, and the future was as much a source of concern as of hope. "The problem of the twentieth century," the African American intellectual, historian, and critic W. E. B. Du Bois wrote in *The Souls of Black Folk* (1903), "is the problem of the color line." Du Bois's prescient remark was born of the bitter experience of African Americans in the decades that followed Reconstruction and in the first decade of the twentieth century. During these years, particularly in the late 1890s and early 1900s, blacks were systematically stripped of their political and civil rights throughout the southern United States. Segregation in public facilities, transportation, and housing, already the norm in much of the South when the Supreme Court declared in 1896 that "separate but equal" facilities did not violate the Constitution, became firmly entrenched in state laws throughout the region (where more than two-thirds of the nation's black population lived in 1900). As blacks began to move north in search of opportunities, they found the doors of some northern communities closed to them altogether. The most extreme form of racial antagonism was violence against individuals and entire communities, an all-too-frequent occurrence in the old century and the new. In the last sixteen years of the nineteenth century there were 2,500 lynchings in the United States; there were 100 in 1900 and 1,100 between the turn of the century and the beginning of World War I. During the 1900s there were race riots in New York City; Brownsville, Texas; Atlanta; Springfield, Ohio; and Springfield, Illinois, the birthplace of Abraham Lincoln. Despite violence and segregation, however, growing African American communities in urban America were finding their voice in churches, schools, colleges, newspapers, and other institutions that would nurture and sustain a persistent demand for equality.

The Culture of Cities. American cities in the 1900s, particularly those in the Northeast and the industrial Midwest, teemed with new inhabitants, new languages, and a new culture. As capitals of the new industrial economy they symbolized its promise and contained many of its problems. Along New York City's Fifth Avenue, on Chicago's Gold Coast, atop Nob Hill in San Francisco, the mansions of a wealthy elite testified to the staggering wealth concentrated in relatively few hands. The crowded tenements of New York City's Lower East Side, the brothels of New Orleans's Storyville, the swarming outdoor markets on Maxwell Street in Chicago's immigrant Jewish neighborhood, typified the lives of the urban working class. New museums, opera houses, and symphony halls housed the high culture of urban elites who had the wealth and leisure time to enjoy them, while baseball parks, saloons, movie houses, and amusement parks such as Dream City (1906) in Pittsburgh and Coney Island in New York were physical emblems of an emerging mass culture. Metropolitan newspapers, locked in a fierce battle for readers, trumpeted the glories and vulgarities, the delights and the dangers of urban life to an eager audience. Skyscrapers and subways were beginning to transform the way cities looked and worked, while streetcars carried the middle class into the expanding suburbs of Boston, Los Angeles, and countless cities in between. Urban schools became central institutions in this decade as they experimented with new forms of education to prepare students for work and citizenship in a complex society and struggled to Americanize immigrant children. For all of their problems, from political corruption to pollution and overcrowding, American cities were magnets, pulling in aspiring artists, steelworkers, shop girls, journalists, and those just plain tired of life on the farm. William Allen White of Kansas, one of the decade's most prominent journalists, captured the nation's ambivalence about its cities when he wrote at the end of the decade that "these cities of ours — spindles in the hands of fate — dirty though they are, and befouled, must keep moving incessantly as they weave the garment."

The Lively Arts. One observer of the artistic and literary scene in the United States at the end of the 1900s is reported to have remarked to a gathering of young artists and intellectuals in New York City that "the fiddles are tuning all over America." There was a palpable sense of excitement in the air as like-minded men and women began to discover one another, to learn that they were not alone in their interest in experimentation with new subject matter and styles. In architecture a distinctively American style was emerging in the Prairie Style houses of Frank Lloyd Wright and the California bungalows of Bernard Maybeck. The Arts and Crafts movement turned up its nose at Victorian ornamentation and championed designs that reflected the ideals of simplicity and craftsmanship. Young American painters and photographers were turning from pastoral scenes to back alleys, tenements, and the boxing ring. Young writers such as Theodore Dreiser — whose *Sister Carrie* (1900) was a frank tale of a young woman's fall from grace and rise to fame — rejected the genteel notion that literature should beautify and uplift and adhered instead to the credo that modern urban life should be portrayed unflinchingly and realistically. In the case of Upton Sinclair's *The Jungle* (1906), life seemed to imitate art, as this fictional portrayal of conditions in the Chicago meatpacking industry revolted consumers and sparked political action.

Invention and Expectancy. Throughout the 1900s Americans in many walks of life seemed animated by the sense that in crossing from one century to the next they had entered a markedly different era. They had only to look about them or read the daily newspaper to see living proof. Orville and Wilbur Wright had taken to the sky in an airplane — and stayed up long enough to demonstrate to the world that flight was no longer a dream. The automobile was becoming a more common sight on city streets and country roads and promised to transform fundamentally patterns of life and leisure, not to mention romance. If one listened closely enough, one could hear radio in the not-so-distant future. That future beckoned, but many believed, like the journalist Herbert Croly, that it would have to be seized and shaped, and would demand fresh approaches and bold action. In *The Promise of American Life* (1909) Croly conveyed this mood when he wrote the following words:

> There comes a time in the history of every nation, when its independence of spirit vanishes, unless it emancipates itself in some measure from its traditional illusions; and that time is fast approaching for the American people. They must either seize the chance of a better future, or else become a nation which is satisfied in spirit merely to repeat indefinitely the monotonous measures of its own past.

ACKNOWLEDGMENTS

This book was produced by Manly, Inc. George Anderson, Philip B. Dematteis, Kenneth Graham, James W. Hipp, and Karen L. Rood were the in-house editors.

Production coordinator is James W. Hipp. Photography editors are Julie E. Frick and Margaret Meriwether. Photographic copy work was performed by Joseph M. Bruccoli. Layout and graphics supervisor is Penney L. Haughton. Copyediting supervisor is Laurel M. Gladden. Typesetting supervisor is Kathleen M. Flanagan. Systems manager is George F. Dodge. Laura Pleicones and L. Kay Webster are editorial associates. The production staff includes Phyllis A. Avant, Ann M. Cheschi, Patricia Coate, Joyce Fowler, Stephanie C. Hatchell, Kathy Lawler Merlette, Jeff Miller, Pamela D. Norton, Emily R. Sharpe, William L. Thomas Jr., and Allison Trussell.

Walter W. Ross and Steven Gross did library research. They were assisted by the following librarians at the Thomas Cooper Library of the University of South Carolina: Linda Holderfield and the interlibrary-loan staff; reference-department head Virginia Weathers; reference librarians Marilee Birchfield, Stefanie Buck, Stefanie DuBose, Rebecca Feind, Karen Joseph, Donna Lehman, Charlene Loope, Anthony McKissick, Jean Rhyne, Kwamine Simpson, and Virginia Weathers; circulation-department head Caroline Taylor; and acquisitions-searching supervisor David Haggard.

AMERICAN DECADES

1900-1909

Wᴏʀʟᴅ Eᴠᴇɴᴛs: Sᴇʟᴇᴄᴛᴇᴅ Oᴄᴄᴜʀʀᴇɴᴄᴇs Oᴜᴛsɪᴅᴇ ᴛʜᴇ Uɴɪᴛᴇᴅ Sᴛᴀᴛᴇs

1900

- World population reaches 1.55 billion.

- Max Planck formulates the quantum theory in physics. He will receive the Nobel Prize for physics in 1918.

- Sigmund Freud publishes *Die Traumdeutung*, later translated as *The Interpretation of Dreams*.

- José Enrique Rodó publishes *Ariel*, a work that heightens anti-U.S. sentiment among South American intellectuals.

- In Japan the Police Regulations of 1900 institute a near-total ban on collective bargaining and the right to strike.

- The Paris Métro (*Chemin de Fer Métropolitain*) opens, with more than six miles of track completed.

- At the Paris Exposition, the elevator is unveiled to the public. An elevator of similar design, first patented by American Charles A. Wheeler in 1892, is installed in Bloomingdale's department store in New York the same year.

1 Jan. A British protectorate is established over northern Nigeria.

20 Jan. John Ruskin, influential English art critic and social reformer of the Victorian era, dies.

31 Jan. John Sholto Douglas, eighth Marquess of Queensbury, dies. Douglas had sponsored a set of rules governing the sport of boxing. Issued in 1867, they became known as the Queensbury rules.

27 Feb. The British Labour Representation Labour Committee, which would soon become the Labour Party, is founded. Ramsay MacDonald is named first secretary.

28 Feb. In South Africa, British forces under the command of Redvers Buller relieve the Boer siege of Ladysmith.

4 Apr. The Prince of Wales narrowly escapes an assassination attempt in Brussels.

7 Apr. The ministers of Germany, France, Britain, and the United States issue an ultimatum to the Chinese government, giving it two months to suppress the Boxer uprising.

14 Apr. The president of France opens the Paris International Exhibition, which covers 547 acres.

22 Apr.	Rabah Zubayr, conqueror of the Sudan, is defeated by French forces in the Battle of Kusseri, in present-day Chad. With this victory, the French unite their colonial possessions in Algeria, West Africa, and the French Congo.
26 Apr.	The Canadian cities of Ottawa and Hull are almost completely destroyed by fire. Fire ravages five square miles of buildings, causes $15 million in damage, and leaves twelve thousand people homeless.
May	The Russians occupy Manchuria, and their forces massacre an estimated forty-five thousand Chinese inhabitants.
17 May	After 217 days, British forces break the siege of Mafeking in the Boer War.
20 May	The second Olympic Games of the modern era open in Paris. More than one thousand athletes from twenty-two nations compete.
24 May	The Orange Free State in southern Africa is annexed by Great Britain.
12 June	The German Reichstag announces a program to expand its naval fleet by thirty-eight battleships over twenty years.
13 June	The Boxer Rebellion intensifies in China and is quickly diverted by the government into an attack against foreigners.
2 July	The maiden voyage of a Zeppelin airship takes place. It features an aluminum hull with sixteen separate compartments filled with hydrogen for buoyancy and two sixteen-horsepower motors. Regular passenger service in dirigibles will not commence until 1910.
29 July	Umberto of Italy, king since 1878, is assassinated and is succeeded by his son, Victor Emmanuel III, who will remain titular ruler of Italy until 1946.
12 Aug.	Wilhelm Steinitz, the world's first acknowledged chess champion, dies.
25 Aug.	Friedrich Nietzsche, German philosopher and poet and bitter critic of Christianity, dies.
31 Aug.	Johannesburg in southern Africa is occupied by British forces. The process of forcing Boers into concentration camps, which continues until 1902, is begun.
18 Oct.	Bernhard von Bülow becomes chancellor of Germany, succeeding Chlodwig Karl Hohenlohe, who resigned two days earlier. Von Bülow's aggressive foreign policy strains Germany's relations with Russia, France, and Great Britain, driving those three countries into closer union.
22 Nov.	English composer Arthur Sullivan, best known for his collaboration with W. S. Gilbert on popular comic operas, including *H.M.S. Pinafore* (1878) and *The Pirates of Penzance* (1879), dies.
30 Nov.	Irish-born writer Oscar Wilde, author of *The Picture of Dorian Gray* (1891) and other works, dies.

1901

- The first Nobel Prizes are awarded for work in physics (Wilhelm Röntgen), chemistry (Jacobus Hendricus van't Hoff), and physiology or medicine (Emil von Behring).

- The Trans-Siberian railway is completed between Moscow and Port Arthur.

- British annexation of Baluchistan, comprising parts of present-day Pakistan and Iran, is completed, effectively extending Britain's empire in India.

1 Jan. The Commonwealth of Australia is officially founded, following an act of the British Parliament (9 July 1900). Edmund Barton will become its first prime minister.

22 Jan. Queen Victoria of Great Britain, after a reign of sixty-four years, dies. Her son Edward VII ascends to the throne.

27 Jan. Italian opera composer Giuseppe Verdi dies.

23 Mar. Emilio Aguinaldo, leader of an insurrection in the Philippines against U.S. rule, is captured. On 19 April he issues a proclamation recognizing U.S. sovereignty.

June The Cuban Congress adopts a new constitution, which grants certain powers to the United States under the terms of the Platt Amendment.

Sept. The Socialist Revolutionary Party of Russia is founded.

7 Sept. The Boxer Rebellion in China ends with the signing of the Peace of Peking between China and major European nations, sometimes called the "Great Powers."

9 Sept. French lithographer and poster artist Henri de Toulouse-Lautrec, famous for his depictions of Paris nightlife in the 1890s, dies.

18 Nov. The Hay-Pauncefote Treaty is negotiated between the United States and Great Britain, providing for the construction of the Panama Canal and ending British treaty rights in the region.

10 Dec. The first Nobel Prize for literature is awarded to French poet and writer Sully Prudhomme.

The first Nobel Peace Prize is awarded to Jean-Henri Dunant, Swiss founder of the International Red Cross, and Frédéric Passy, French founder of the International League of Peace.

1902

- French composer Claude Debussy composes *Pelléas et Mélisande*.
- Joseph Conrad publishes "Heart of Darkness."
- The *Times Literary Supplement* of London is founded.
- In separate experiments, English physicist Oliver Heaviside and British American electrical engineer Arthur Kennelly discover the existence of an electrified layer of the earth's atmosphere, which, by reflecting radio waves, makes radio transmissions across long distances possible.

26 Mar. Cecil John Rhodes, architect of British colonial rule in Africa and wealthy diamond miner, dies. Part of his fortune is used to establish the Rhodes scholarships.

Apr. Under the terms of the Russo-Japanese Convention, Russia agrees to remove its forces from Manchuria.

15 Apr. A peasant uprising in Russia is suppressed by forces of the czar.

20 Apr.	At an exhibition of La Société Nationale des Beaux Arts in Paris, the Art Nouveau style, whose influence will be felt in everything from painting to interior design to the subway entrances of the Paris Métro, is put on triumphant display.
7 May	A volcanic eruption on the island of Saint Vincent, in the Windward Islands, kills an estimated two thousand inhabitants.
8 May	The eruption of Mount Pelée, on the island of Martinique in the Windward Islands, sends a cloud of ash, steam, and gas onto the city of Saint Pierre, killing an estimated thirty thousand people, nearly the entire population of the city.
20 May	Tomás Estrada Palma is elected first president of the independent Republic of Cuba, marking the end of U.S. occupation of the island following the Spanish-American War.
31 May	The Peace of Vereeniging ends the Boer War in South Africa. Britain promises representative government.
18 June	Samuel Butler, the British writer best known for his utopian romance *Erewhon* (1872), dies.
12 July	Arthur James Balfour is named prime minister of Great Britain, succeeding his uncle, Lord Salisbury. After the First World War, he issues the Balfour Declaration, pledging British support for a Jewish homeland in Palestine.
28 Sept.	Emile Zola, a French naturalist writer, dies. Zola's influence was widespread in American fiction at the turn of the century.
Dec.	The Aswan Dam, one of the architetural marvels of the century, is completed in Egypt.
7 Dec.	Great Britain and Germany issue an ultimatum demanding reparations from Venezuela following a violent takeover of the government there in 1899.
10 Dec.	The Nobel Prize for literature is awarded to Theodor Mommsen of Germany.
13 Dec.	Germany and Britain institute a blockade of Venezuela and begin bombarding its forts as punishment for Venezuela's failure to make payments on its international debt.
18 Dec.	In England and Wales the Education Act extends primary education.

1903

- The Krupp Works, a famous armaments factory in Essen, Germany, becomes a public company.

- Norwegian explorer Roald Amundsen begins the first successful voyage through the Northwest Passage, the narrow sea connecting the Atlantic and Pacific Oceans. He completes the journey in 1906.

- Willem Einthoven, a Dutch physiologist, develops the string galvanometer, a forerunner of his electrocardiogram (EKG).

- Russian physiologist Ivan Pavlov reports for the first time on his experiments in behavior and "conditioned reflexes."

- The first Tour de France bicycle race is won by M. Garin of France.

- The Nobel Prize for literature is awarded to Norwegian writer Bjørnstjerne Bjørnson.

Jan. A border dispute between Canada and the United States over Alaska is resolved.

19 Jan. The first radio message is transmitted from the United States to England.

20 Mar. The paintings of Henri Matisse are exhibited at the Salon des Indépendants.

Apr. In a three-day pogrom in Kishinev, Bessarabia, forty-five Russian Jews are killed and fifteen hundred Jewish homes are destroyed.

8 May French painter Paul Gauguin dies in the Marquesas Islands.

11 June Alexander of Serbia and his wife, Draga Mishin, are assassinated by disaffected army officers.

July Pope Leo XIII, elected to the papacy in 1878, dies. He is succeeded in August by Pope Pius X.

17 July American born painter James Abbott McNeill Whistler, who spent most of his life in France and England, dies.

30 July The Russian Social Democratic Party splits into two wings, the Mensheviks and the more radical Bolsheviks, during a meeting in London.

Oct. The Women's Social and Political Union is founded by British feminist Emmeline Pankhurst.

1 Nov. German historian Theodor Mommsen, world-renowned scholar of ancient Rome, dies.

3 Nov. The U.S. warship *Nashville* arrives off the coast of Colón, Colombia. Colombia refuses Theodore Roosevelt's demand for permission to construct the Panama Canal.

6 Nov. Panama declares its independence from Colombia as a U.S. protectorate.

13 Nov. French Impressionist painter Camille Pissarro dies.

18 Nov. The Hay-Bunau-Varilla Treaty between Panama and the United States cedes control of the Panama Canal Zone to the United States.

8 Dec. British philosopher and social theorist Herbert Spencer dies. Spencer is widely credited with disseminating what became known as social Darwinism, the idea that society benefited from living by the rule of "survival of the fittest."

1904

- Joseph Conrad publishes *Nostromo*.

- French sculptor Auguste Rodin creates one of his best-known works, *The Thinker*.

- In Britain the Rolls-Royce automobile company is established.

- Italian Giacomo Puccini composes his opera *Madame Butterfly*.

- In Dublin, Ireland, the Abbey Theatre opens.

- Russian playwright Anton Chekhov writes *The Cherry Orchard*.

- French writer Frédéric Mistral and Spanish writer José Echegaray y Eizaguirre share the Nobel Prize for literature.

- Silicone is developed by F. S. Kipping.

- Sigmund Freud publishes *The Psychopathology of Everyday Life.*

- British scientist John Fleming invents the diode vacuum tube, a crucial step in the development of radio.

- Several industrial cartels merge to form the German Steel Union. With monopoly control of steel markets at home, it sells its products for lower prices on world markets. Its existence aids Germany's expanding military.

8–9 Feb.   The Russo-Japanese War begins when Japanese launch an attack on the Russian fleet. Japan officially declares war on 10 February.

8 Apr.   France and Britain sign the Entente Cordiale after resolving territorial disagreements over Egypt, Newfoundland, Morocco, and Siam. France accepts Britain's position in Egypt, while England allows France and Spain to assert claims in Morocco.

1 May   Czech composer Antonín Dvorák dies.

17 May   A dispute breaks out between the anticlerical government in France and the Vatican.

2 June   A major exhibit of the works of Henri Matisse is staged at Galeries Vollard, Paris.

**1 July–
23 Nov.**   The Summer Olympic Games are held in Saint Louis, Missouri.

2 July   Russian playwright Anton Chekhov dies.

3 July   Theodor Herzl, a leader of the Zionist movement, dies of a heart attack.

4 July   Construction of the Panama Canal begins.

7 July   In France, religious orders are prohibited from teaching by the government.

14 July   Paul Kruger, three-time president of the Boer Republic of Transvaal and foe of British expansion in South Africa, dies.

28 July   Russian Minister of the Interior V. K. Plehve is assassinated.

7 Sept.   The Dalai Lama, spiritual and political leader of Tibet, is forced to sign a treaty granting Great Britain trading rights in three cities. His capitulation follows the capture of Lhasa, the capital of Tibet, by British forces in August.

3 Oct.   In South-West Africa, a rebellion of Hottentots and Herero against German colonial rule begins. It will continue until 1908.

18 Oct.   France establishes Dakar as the capital of its newly reorganized possessions in French West Africa.

21 Oct.   British fishing vessels in the North Sea are mistakenly fired on by the Russian navy. The incident becomes known as the Dogger Bank incident.

1905

- Claude Debussy composes *La Mer.*

- The Fauves (wild beasts), a short-lived group of painters led by Henri Matisse and André Derain, stages an exhibition at the Salon d'Automne in Paris.

- *Die Brüke* (The Bridge), a group of German Expressionist painters explicitly opposed to Impressionism, is formed in Dresden. It disbands in 1913.

- British novelist E. M. Forster publishes *Where Angels Fear to Tread*.

- The Nobel Prize for literature is awarded to Polish writer Henryk Sienkiewicz.

- Sigmund Freud publishes *Three Contributions to the Sexual Theory*.

- The zipper is invented.

- The Trans-Siberian Railroad between Moscow and Vladivostok on the Pacific coast is completed. Construction had begun on Russia's longest rail line in 1881.

- The Mining Act is passed in Japan, limiting the hours of work for women and children and establishing age ten as the minimum age for child laborers. It will be extended by the Factory Act of 1911, though both measures affect only companies employing more than fifteen workers.

1 Jan. The Russian city of Port Arthur is captured by the Japanese.

22 Jan. The "Bloody Sunday" massacre in Saint Petersburg sparks the Russian Revolution of 1905.

17 Feb. Grand Duke Serge, the governor of Moscow, is assassinated in the Kremlin.

3 Mar. Czar Nicholas II of Russia promises religious reforms.

24 Mar. Jules Verne, French pioneer of the genre of science fiction, dies.

26 Mar. British actor Maurice Barrymore, whose children, Lionel, Ethel, and John, will find fame on the American stage and screen, dies.

27 May Japan completely destroys the Russian naval fleet in the Battle of Tsushima, with the loss of only three Japanese torpedo boats.

7 June The parliament of Norway votes to dissolve the union of Norway and Sweden under Oscar II, king of Sweden. Sweden is compelled to agree when a majority of Norwegians approve the dissolution in a plebiscite.

27–28 June The crew of the Russian naval vessel *Potemkin* mutiny in the harbor at Odessa. Soon the entire Russian Black Sea Fleet is immobilized. The mutiny is triggered by political unrest in Russia and anger about the country's recent defeats in the Russo-Japanese War.

30 June Albert Einstein announces his special theory of relativity. On 27 September he issues a second paper on the subject containing his famous formulation, $E=mc^2$. The theory is fully elaborated by Einstein in 1915 as the general theory of relativity.

July Muslims (Maji-Maji) in German East Africa stage an uprising.

3 July Both houses of the legislature in France endorse a law establishing complete separation of church and state.

20 Aug. Chinese nationalist leader Sun Yat-Sen issues his Three People's Principles — nationalism, democracy, and livelihood for the people — in his first public statement of his philosophy after a decade of secret activities.

1 Sept. Alberta and Saskatchewan are made provinces of Canada.

5 Sept.	Under the terms of the Treaty of Portsmouth, brokered by President Theodore Roosevelt, Japan establishes a protectorate over Korea and is granted lease rights to Port Arthur and Sakhalin Island after its victory in the Russo-Japanese War. Roosevelt will receive the Nobel Peace Prize for his efforts.
27 Sept.	Norway gains its independence from Sweden.
Oct.	Under Bolshevik leader Leon Trotsky, the first of the Russian soviets (councils) is created in Saint Petersburg.
17 Oct.	Czar Nicholas II issues the October Manifesto, promising civil liberties and democratic institutions in Russia. The manifesto establishes a constitutional monarchy with an elected Duma (parliament). A general strike in support of the manifesto spreads throughout Russia and lasts until December.
28 Nov.	In Ireland the Sinn Féin (Ourselves Alone) party is established with the goal of ending British rule in Ireland.
4 Dec.	Arthur Balfour, Britain's Conservative prime minister, resigns after his party is split between protectionists and advocates of free trade.
4–5 Dec.	A congress meeting in Vilnius declares Lithuania's independence from Russia.
5 Dec.	All 230 members of the Saint Petersburg soviet are arrested.
9 Dec.	The law in France establishing separation of church and state is officially promulgated.
15 Dec.	Russian troops crush a citizen uprising in Moscow.

1906

- Joseph Thomson discovers gamma rays.

- Frederick Gowland Hopkins discovers vitamins.

- Explorer Roald Amundsen determines the position of the magnetic North Pole.

- Spanish architect Antonio Gaudi begins constructing Casa Milá in Barcelona.

- A test for diagnosing the sexually transmitted disease syphilis is developed by German bacteriologist August von Wassermann and dermatologist Albert Neisser.

- German scientist Walther Hermann Nernst develops the third law of thermodynamics.

- *Tears of Blood* by Yi Injik, generally recognized as the first modern novel in Korean, is published in serialized form in a Korean newspaper.

- Giosuè Carducci of Italy wins the Nobel Prize for literature.

- Le Mans, France, hosts that country's first Grand Prix auto race.

12 Jan.	The Liberal Party wins in a landslide in Britain, and, led by Prime Minister Henry Campbell-Bannerman, inaugurates a period of far-reaching social reforms.
29 Jan.	The king of Denmark, Christian IX, dies.

Feb.	Pope Pius X's encyclical *Vehementer Nos* condemns the separation of church and state in France.
10 Feb.	The HMS *Dreadnought*, prototype of a vastly more powerful warship, is launched by Great Britain.
Mar.	Britain agrees to pay compensation for damages resulting from the Boer War.
7 Mar.	Finland institutes universal suffrage for everyone older than twenty-four, thus becoming the first nation to grant women's suffrage.
10 Mar.	A coal-mine explosion in Courières, France, kills more than one thousand miners.
6 Apr.	Mount Vesuvius erupts, destroying several towns near Naples, Italy.
7 Apr.	France and Spain agree to spheres of influence in Morocco at the Algeciras Conference, which had begun on 16 January.
19 Apr.	French chemist Pierre Curie dies.
6 May	Czar Nicholas II issues the Fundamental Laws, which restore most of the imperial powers he had surrendered in the October Manifesto.
10 May	The first meeting of the Duma, an elected parliament, begins in Russia.
19 May	Jõao Franco, a fervent monarchist, is named prime minister by King Carlos I of Portugal. Franco limits press freedom and suspends parliamentary government.
	The Simplon Tunnel, running 12.3 miles between Brig, Switzerland, and Isella, Italy, opens as the longest railway tunnel in the world.
23 May	Norwegian playwright Henrik Ibsen, whose plays revolutionized modern drama, dies.
June	Several pogroms, targeted at Jews, occur throughout Russia.
July	A peace treaty is negotiated, bringing to an end a war between Guatemala, El Salvador, and Honduras in Central America.
4 July	Britain, France, and Italy agree to guarantee the independence of Ethiopia.
9 July	The Russian Duma is prevented from meeting and martial law is declared.
12 July	Alfred Dreyfus, whose initial trial on treason charges had become a cause célèbre among French intellectuals, is found innocent by France's Supreme Court of Appeals after another trial.
22 July	Nicholas II dissolves the Duma and begins a crackdown on dissenters.
16 Aug.	An earthquake devastates Valparaiso and Santiago, Chile, killing twenty thousand people and causing an estimated $300 million in property damage.
Sept.	The Chinese Imperial Court agrees to the gradual adoption of a constitution.
	An imperial order aims at ending the opium trade in China. Britain cooperates by restricting the flow of the drug into China from India. China, in turn, limits the harvest of poppies, the source of the drug.
29 Sept.	U.S. troops occupy Cuba and repress a liberal uprising against the government of Tomás Estrada Palma.

Oct.	In Cuba a provisional government led by Charles Magoon is put in place by the United States.
1 Oct.	Great Britain, Egypt, and Turkey settle their boundary dispute over the Sinai Peninsula, most of which remained under Turkish control.
18 Oct.	Georges Clemenceau becomes premier of France for the first time. He will remain premier until 1909, when repression of a miners' strike brings down his government.
22 Oct.	French Impressionist master Paul Cézanne dies.
Nov.	Leon Trotsky, one of the leaders of the 1905 Russian Revolution, is exiled to Siberia.
Dec.	Aga Khan forms the All-India Muslim League, demanding representative government and separate electorates for Muslims.
21 Dec.	In Great Britain, the Trade Disputes Act limits the liability of trade unions for damages resulting from strikes and makes picketing legal.
30 Dec.	The shah of Persia, Muzaffer-ed-Din, grants that country its first constitution.

1907

- Austrian Gustav Mahler composes his Eighth Symphony, known as the "Symphony of a Thousand."

- Pablo Picasso paints *Les Demoiselles d'Avignon*, one of the early works of the Cubist movement led by Pablo Picasso and Georges Braque.

- British writer Rudyard Kipling receives the Nobel Prize for literature.

- A secret Russo-Japanese agreement carves up Manchuria into spheres of influence and renders Korea a de facto colony of Japan.

- The *Mauretania* — with a top speed of twenty-five knots, the fastest ocean liner of the era — is launched in Great Britain, ushering in the age of elegant cruise ships.

- Maria Montessori, who had earlier pioneered the education of children with below-normal capabilities, opens in Rome her first school for average children.

1 Jan.	Universal suffrage is instituted in Austria.
14 Jan.	An earthquake strikes Kingston, Jamaica, killing approximately fourteen hundred people.
26 Jan.	The premiere of Irish playwright John Millington Synge's *The Playboy of the Western World* at the Abbey Theatre in Dublin provokes public outrage.
26 Feb.	Louis Botha, a Boer, is elected prime minister of the Transvaal in southern Africa. His government adopts on 22 March the Asiatic Registration Bill, limiting immigration from India.
18 Mar.	French chemist Eugène-Marcelin Bertholet dies. He is best known for his work synthesizing compounds such as alcohol (1855), methane (1858), and benzene (1866).

22 Mar. In Morocco, widespread unrest begins, which will eventually lead to the bombardment of Casablanca and the occupation of that city, as well as Rabat, by French troops.

14 June Women's suffrage is achieved in Norway.

July The Orange Free State is granted autonomous status by Britain in South Africa.

10 Aug. The world's most grueling automobile race to date ends when Italy's Prince Borghese arrives in Paris, having driven eight thousand miles in sixty-two days from Peking (Beijing), China.

31 Aug. An agreement between Russia and Britain carves out defined spheres of influence in central Asia and Persia (Iran).

4 Sept. Edvard Grieg, Norway's foremost classical composer, dies.

6 Sept. Pope Pius X's encyclical *Pascendi Gregis* condemns religious modernism. The pope had broached many of the same themes in an encyclical of 4 July titled *Lamentabili.*

26 Sept. New Zealand, a former British colony, is granted dominion status.

18 Oct. The Second International Peace Conference (which had begun on 15 June) ends without accomplishing its main objective: the reduction of armaments. However, new limits on the use of aerial bombardment, poison gas, and undersea mines are agreed to by the forty-six nations in attendance.

8 Dec. Oscar II, the king of Sweden, dies. His son, Gustav V, succeeds him on the throne.

16 Dec. The "Great White Fleet," a flotilla of sixteen U.S. warships, embarks on a cruise around the world to demonstrate American naval power.

17 Dec. William Thomson, first Baron Kelvin, who developed an absolute scale of temperature (the Kelvin scale), dies. He also consolidated the law of the conservation of energy, one of the basic principles of modern physics.

1908

- Hungarian composer Béla Bartók composes his First String Quartet.

- *Ecce Homo*, the autobiography of German philosopher and poet Friedrich Nietzsche, is published posthumously.

- German writer Rudolf C. Eucken wins the Nobel Prize for literature.

- The first newsreel is shown in a Paris theater by Charles Pathé.

- German chemist Fritz Haber successfully synthesizes ammonia, a breakthrough with major commercial implications.

- German bacteriologist Paul Ehrlich, soon to discover a chemical treatment for syphilis that becomes known as the "magic bullet," shares the Nobel Prize in medicine with immunologist Elie Metchnikoff.

24 Jan. Robert Stephenson Smyth Baden-Powell forms the Boy Scouts.

1 Feb. King Carlos I and Crown Prince Luís Filipe are assassinated in Portugal. Carlos is succeeded by his second son, Manuel II.

20 Feb.	Emilio Marinetti publishes the *Futurist Manifesto*, galvanizing a school of Italian artists fascinated with movement and action and scornful of past artistic achievements.
8 Apr.	Herbert Asquith, chancellor of the exchequer, becomes prime minister of Britain following the resignation of Henry Campbell-Bannerman.
27 Apr.	The fourth Summer Olympic Games of the modern era begin in London and are completed on 31 October.
26 May	Major deposits of oil are discovered in Persia (present-day Iran), igniting an oil boom is southwestern Asia and leading to the discovery of other large oil supplies in the Middle East.
21 June	Russian composer Nikolay Andreyevich Rimsky-Korsakov dies.
24 July	The "Young Turks" force Abdülhamid II, sultan of the Ottoman Empire, to restore the constitution of 1876.
25 July	Louis Blériot achieves the first crossing of the English Channel in a heavier-than-air machine.
Aug.	The first general elections under the supervision of the United States are held in Cuba. Liberal candidate José Gomez is elected president and serves until 1913.
Sept.	In Russia, an Asiatic cholera epidemic claims more than seventy-one hundred lives, close to two thousand in Saint Petersburg alone.
5 Oct.	Bulgaria declares its complete independence from the Ottoman Empire.
6 Oct.	Austria annexes the former Turkish provinces of Bosnia and Herzegovina (setting the stage for events that will spark the First World War six years later).
8 Oct.	Polish-born Hebrew scholar and poet Naphtali Herz Imber, whose hymn "ha-Tiqwa" (also spelled "Hatikvah") later becomes the anthem of the Zionist movement and of the state of Israel, dies.
12 Oct.	The Cape Colony and Natal meet with the former Boer states of the Transvaal and Orange Free State to form the Union of South Africa. The union formally takes effect on 31 May 1910.
18 Oct.	Leopold II gives the Belgian parliament control over the Belgian Congo, which he had held as a personal possession.
14 Nov.	The Chinese government announces the deaths of Kuang Hsü, the Chinese emperor since 1875, and his empress, Tzu Hsi. Hsüan-T'ung, the emperor's infant nephew, becomes the last emperor of the Manchu dynasty.
30 Nov.	The danger of war between Japan and the United States is averted when the Root-Takahira Agreement is signed. The agreement establishes the territorial integrity of China and declares mutual respect for the Pacific possessions of Japan and the United States.
28 Dec.	French Impressionist painter Henri Matisse publishes *Notes d'un peintre* in *La Grande Revue,* setting forth the principles of his art.
	A major earthquake causes widespread devastation in the Italian provinces of Calabria and Sicily, killing eighty-three thousand people.

1909

- Selma Lagerlöf of Sweden is awarded the Nobel Prize for literature.
- Rafael Reyes Prieto is ousted as president of Colombia following his recognition of the independence of Panama in a treaty with the United States.

1 Jan. Astronomers in London report the possibility of another planet in the solar system beyond Neptune.

9 Jan. British explorer Ernest Henry Shackleton misses reaching the South Pole by one hundred miles.

18 Jan. Brewers in New Zealand decide to abolish barmaids and ban women from purchasing alcohol in bars.

9 Feb. A British court rules that a wife is not permitted to divorce her husband, even if her claim is based on desertion.

24 Mar. John Millington Synge, a major figure in the Irish literary awakening at the turn of the century whose *The Playboy of the Western World* had shocked Dublin theater audiences in 1907, dies.

6 Apr. Robert Peary reaches the North Pole, though his achievement will remain in dispute for decades.

10 Apr. British poet Charles Swinburne dies.

13 Apr. Armenians rebel against Ottoman rule following a massacre by the sultan's troops at Adana in southern Turkey.

18 Apr. Joan of Arc is beatified in Rome, bringing her a step closer to canonization as a saint of the Roman Catholic Church.

27 Apr. The "Young Turks" depose Sultan Abdülhamìd II. He is succeeded by Muhammad V, his younger brother.

18 May Sergey Diaghilev's Ballets Russes perform for the first time in Paris.

25 May A Russian court jails the publisher of Tolstoy's "Thou Shalt Not Kill" but declines to prosecute Tolstoy, a devout pacifist.

11 June An earthquake in Provence, in southern France, kills sixty people.

26 June The shah of Persia annuls a new election law and indefinitely postpones adoption of a promised constitution.

24 July Aristide Briand becomes premier of France.

Aug. An uprising in Barcelona, Spain, is put down by government forces. As many as one thousand people die in the fighting.

28 Aug. American Glenn Curtiss wins the first airplane race for the Gordon Bennett Cup in Rheims, France, with an average speed of 47 MPH.

10 Oct. The execution of Spanish anarchist leader Francisco Ferrer ignites protests across Europe.

26 Oct. Former Japanese prime minister Hirobumi Ito is assassinated by a Korean nationalist.

28 Nov. The French national assembly endorses a law granting pregnant women an eight-week leave from their jobs.

17 Dec. King Leopold II of Belgium dies. He is succeeded by Albert I, his nephew.

CHAPTER TWO
THE ARTS

by JANE GERHARD and CYNTHIA MCCOWN

CONTENTS

Sidebars and tables are listed in italics.

1900

Movies

Adventures of Jones (series), produced, directed and acted by James White for Edison; *Battle of Mafeking, Filipinos Retreat from the Trenches,* and *Panorama of the Paris Exposition from the Seine,* filmed and produced by James White for Edison; *Beheading a Chinese Prisoner* and *Chinese Massacring Christians,* produced by Sigmund Lubin; *Cinderella,* produced and directed by Georges Méliès; *The Clown and the Alchemist* and *A Visit to the Spiritualist,* produced and filmed by J. Stuart Blackton and Albert E. Smith for Vitagraph; *The Downward Path,* produced by Wallace McCutcheon and filmed by Arthur Marvin for Biograph; *Faust and Marguerite,* produced and directed by Edwin S. Porter; *Fire Engines at Work, The Gans-McGovern Fight,* and *Something Good — Negro Kiss,* produced by William Selig; *Love in the Suburbs,* filmed by G. W. "Billy" Bitzer for Biograph; *Maude's Naughty Little Brother,* produced and filmed by J. Stuart Blackton and Albert E. Smith for Vitagraph.

Fiction

L. Frank Baum, *The Wonderful Wizard of Oz;* Charles Waddell Chesnutt, *The House Behind the Cedars;* Joseph Conrad, *Lord Jim;* Stephen Crane, *Whilomville Stories,* Theodore Dreiser, *Sister Carrie;* Paul Laurence Dunbar, *The Strength of Gideon and Other Stories;* Finley Peter Dunne, *Mr. Dooley's Philosophy;* Pauline Elizabeth Hopkins, *Contending Forces: A Romance Illustrative of Negro Life North and South;* Booth Tarkington, *Monsieur Beaucaire;* Harriet Prescott Spofford, *Old Madame and Other Stories;* Mark Twain, *The Man that Corrupted Hadleyburg.*

Popular Songs

"A Bird in a Gilded Cage," music by Harry von Tilzer, lyrics by Arthur Lamb; "I Can't Tell Why I Love You, But I Do," music by Charles Previn, lyrics by Gus Edwards; "Rosie, You Are My Posie (Ma Blushin' Rosie)," music by John Stromberg, lyrics by Edgar Smith; "Voodoo Man," music and lyrics by Bert Williams and George Walker.

- The approval of the New York City audience has become the standard by which theater professionals measure their work — the rest of the nation is merely "the Road." More than five hundred New York shows go on the road in 1900.

- *Theatre Magazine,* edited by Arthur Hornblow, begins publication.

- The novelty of the "moving picture" phenomenon of the 1890s has worn off. The public is bored with the uninspired menu of news events, sight gags, panoramas, and camera tricks.

- Eastman Kodak introduces the Brownie Box camera at one dollar; Americans embrace the new hobby of amateur photography.

- The trademark and painting *His Master's Voice* first appears on record labels of the firm that later becomes the Victor Company.

- Brothers James Weldon and J. Rosamond Johnson compose "Lift Every Voice and Sing," a musical inspiration for black Americans.

3 Jan.   Giuseppe Verdi's opera *Aida* (1871) is performed in New York.

5 Feb.   Clyde Fitch's drama *Sappho* premieres in New York; police close it after twenty-nine performances, citing "immorality."

23 Apr.   Buffalo Bill Cody's *Wild West Show* opens at Madison Square Garden.

30 Apr.   Railroad engineer Casey Jones is killed when he jams on the brakes of his wreck-bound train. His passengers' lives are saved, and Jones's exploit becomes the stuff of immediate legend when Wallace Saunders, a black fellow worker, composes a song about him.

May   Poet-dramatist William Vaughn Moody publishes "An Ode in Time of Hesitation" in *Atlantic Monthly* magazine. It is a thoughtful comment on American imperialism.

22 May   Inventor Edwin S. Voter patents the "pneumatic piano attachment"; the Pianola, or player piano, soon becomes popular.

28 May   Posthumous exhibit of American landscape painter Frederic Church's works is mounted at the Metropolitan Museum of Art, New York.

15 June   Ignacy Paderewski, Polish pianist, composer, and statesman, sets up a $10,000 fund for best orchestral works by American composers.

15 Oct.   Mark Twain returns from a nine-year hiatus abroad.

Boston's twenty-five-hundred-seat Symphony Hall opens.

12 Nov.   *Florodora*, one of the most popular stage musicals of the decade, has its debut in New York. It has a run of 505 performances.

16 Nov.   German conductor Fritz Scheel directs the first concert of the newly formed Philadelphia Orchestra at the Philadelphia Academy of Music.

19 Nov.   The Harvard Theatre Collection is opened; it is the oldest dance and theater-research collection in the world.

20 Nov.   Sarah Bernhardt arrives for her first American tour since 1886. At age fifty-six, she plays Hamlet.

1901

Movies   *Bluebeard*, produced by Georges Méliès; *Couche Dance on the Midway* and *Wedding Procession in Cairo*, produced by Sigmund Lubin; *Coaching Party* and *Yosemite Valley*, filmed by Robert K. Bonine for Biograph; *The Finish of Bridget McKeen, Kansas Saloon Smashers*, and *Laura Comstock's Bag-Punching Dog*, filmed and designed by Edwin S. Porter and George S. Fleming for Edison; *In the Forbidden City*, filmed by C. Fred Ackerman for Biograph; *Opening — Pan-American Exposition, President McKinley's Speech at the Pan-American Exposition*, and *Complete Funeral Cortege [McKinley] at Canton, Ohio*, produced by James White for Edison; *Stock Yard Series (Stunning Cattle, Koshering Cattle, Dressing Beef etc.)*, produced by William Selig.

Fiction   Gertrude Bonnin (Zitkala-Sa) *Old Indian Legends*; Charles Waddell Chesnutt, *The Marrow of Tradition*; Paul Laurence Dunbar, *The Fanatics*; Finley Peter Dunne, *Mr. Dooley's Opinions*; Henry James, *The Sacred Font*; Rudyard Kipling, *Kim*; Frank Norris, *The Octopus*; Alice Hegan Race, *Mrs. Wiggs of the Cabbage Patch*.

Popular Songs   "Boola Boola," music and lyrics by Allan M. Hirsch; "Hello Central, Give Me Heaven, For My Mama's There," music and lyrics by Charles K. Harris; "I'm Captain Jinks of the Horse Marines," music by T. MacLaglen, lyrics by William H. Lingard; "Just A-Wearyin' For You," music and lyrics by Carrie Jacobs Bond; "The Maiden With the Dreamy Eyes" and "My Castle on the Nile," music by J. Rosamond Johnson, lyrics by Robert Cole and James Weldon Johnson; "Mighty Lak a Rose," music by Ethelbert Nevin, lyrics by Frank L. Stanton; "Tell Me Pretty Maiden," music by Leslie Stuart, lyrics by Owen Hall and Frank Pixley.

- The American Federation of Musicians passes an antiragtime resolution, calling for "every effort to suppress and discourage . . . such musical trash."

- The Rudolf Wurlitzer Company announces a new coin-operated music machine, the Tonophone.

- Clyde Fitch, the first American playwright to become a millionaire in his profession, has four plays appearing on Broadway simultaneously in 1901.

- Autobiographies of black American leader Booker T. Washington (*Up From Slavery*) and of immigrant reformer Jacob Riis (*The Making of an American)* are published.

- Experimental composer Charles Ives (1874–1954) continues work on his *Songs* and completes his Symphony No. 2; it is not premiered for sixty years.

2 Feb. Giacomo Puccini's opera *Tosca* (1900) debuts in New York.

4 Feb. Clyde Fitch's *Captain Jinks of the Horse Marines* opens on Broadway for 192 performances, making twenty-one-year-old Ethel Barrymore a star.

21 Feb. Vaudeville performers organize and strike to protest the inclusion of moving pictures on vaudeville bills. The Eastern Association of Vaudeville Managers adds more films to replace the striking acts.

13 Mar. Andrew Carnegie, steel baron and philanthropist, gives $2.2 million to fund a New York public library system.

14 Apr. Police enforce New York City's blue laws by arresting actors at the Academy of Music for appearing in costume on Sunday.

1 May The Pan-American Exposition opens at Buffalo, New York.

24 June Pablo Picasso's first exhibition opens at Galeries Vollard, Paris.

29 July Rudyard Kipling, popular chronicler of life in British colonial India, speaks against Britain's conduct of the Boer War.

16 Oct. New President Theodore Roosevelt invites author Booker T. Washington to dinner at the White House. Much of the nation is shocked; within two weeks race riots occur in New Orleans. Thirty-four people are killed.

20 Oct. *The New York Times* celebrates fifty years in publication.

10 Dec. Sweden awards the first Nobel Prizes; French poet Sully Prudhomme is honored for literature.

1902

Movies *Alphonse and Gaston* (series), filmed by Robert K. Bonine for Biograph; *Appointment by Telephone* and *How They Do Things on the Bowery* , filmed by Edwin S. Porter for Edison; *Cake Walking Horse* and *Feeding the Rhinoceros,* produced by Sigmund Lubin; *"Foxy Grandpa"* (series), starring Joseph Hart and Carrie De Mar for Biograph; *The Great Sword Combat on the Stairs* (excerpt from the stage play *A Gentleman of France)*, starring Kyrle Bellew, filmed by J. Stuart Blackton and Albert E. Smith for Vitagraph; *Prizefight in Coontown,* produced by William Selig; *Robinson Crusoe* and *A Trip to the Moon,* produced and filmed by Georges Méliès.

Fiction

Joseph Conrad, "Heart of Darkness"; Arthur Conan Doyle, *The Hound of the Baskervilles;* Paul Laurence Dunbar, *The Sport of the Gods;* Finley Peter Dunne, *Observations by Mr. Dooley;* Hamlin Garland, *The Captain of the Gray-Horse Troop;* Ellen Glasgow, *The Battleground;* Joel Chandler Harris, *Gabriel Tolliver, A Story of Reconstruction;* Pauline Elizabeth Hopkins, *Hagar's Daughter: A Story of Southern Caste Prejudice* and *Winona: A Tale of Negro Life in the South and Southwest;* Henry James, *The Wings of the Dove;* Rudyard Kipling, *Just-So Stories;* Jack London, "To Light a Fire" and *A Daughter of the Snows;* Edith Wharton, *The Valley of Decision;* Owen Wister, *The Virginian.*

Popular Songs

"Bill Bailey, Won't You Please Come Home?," music and lyrics by Hughie Cannon; "Down Where the Wurzburger Flows," music by Harry von Tilzer, lyrics by Vincent P. Bryan; "In the Good Old Summer Time," music by George Evans, lyrics by Ren Shields; "In the Sweet Bye and Bye," music by Harry von Tilzer, lyrics by Vincent P. Bryan; "The Mansion of Broken Hearts," music by Harry von Tilzer, lyrics by Arthur J. Lamb; "Please Go 'Way and Let me Sleep," music and lyrics by Harry von Tilzer; "Under the Bamboo Tree," music by J. Rosamond Johnson, lyrics by Bob Cole.

- For the first time, a well-known stage actor, Kyrle Bellew, agrees to appear in a motion picture.

- *In Dahomey,* a musical written and acted by blacks, scores a hit on Broadway.

- Helen Keller publishes *The Story of My Life.* The autobiography of the twenty-two-year-old woman, blind and deaf since the age of nineteen months, becomes a best-seller.

- *McClure's* magazine begins publishing Ida Tarbell's and Lincoln Steffens's "muckraking" treatments of the oil industry and municipal corruption.

- *Appalachia,* a musical composition by British American Frederick Delius, introduces American folk-song motifs.

- Frederic Remington completes his *Comin' Through the Rye,* a bronze sculptural tribute to the American cowboy.

- Sheet music and player pianos gain nationwide popularity; Broadway scores and ragtime songs reach a wide market.

- Photographer Edouard (later Edward) Steichen opens a one-man show in Paris.

- Works such as *The Hand of Man* and *The Flat-Iron Building* establish Alfred Stieglitz as the foremost art photographer in America.

4 Jan.

The Carnegie Institute is founded for research in the humanities and sciences.

13 Jan.

The well-known British actress Mrs. Patrick Campbell makes her first performance in America.

7 Mar.   J. Pierpont Morgan purchases the Garland collection of oriental porcelain, keeping it in the United States.

18 Mar.   Italian opera singer Enrico Caruso and U.S. recording engineer Fred Gaisberg produce the tenor's first phonograph recording.

16 Apr.   Tally's Electric Theater, the first theater expressly for the purpose of showing motion pictures, opens in Los Angeles.

30 Apr.   Claude Debussy's *Pelleas et Melisande* premieres in Paris with Scots American Mary Garden singing the soprano lead.

1 May   Georges Méliès's science-fiction fantasy film, *A Trip to the Moon*, enchants Paris audiences.

29 Sept.   Emile Zola (b. 1840), whose writing influenced American naturalist writers, dies in Paris.

4 Oct.   Chicago's New Orpheon Theatre opens with the musical *Chow-Chow*.

23 Oct.   Charles Dana Gibson, creator of the "Gibson Girl," whose looks dominate women's fashion in the early part of the decade, accepts a $100,000 contract to draw for *Life* and *Collier's* magazines.

8 Nov.   Barnum and Bailey's Circus ship returns to the United States after a European triumph.

3 Dec.   David Belasco premieres his spectacular melodrama *The Darling of the Gods* in New York at a cost of $78,000.

21 Dec.   Chicago's La Salle Theatre opens.

Guglielmo Marconi sends the first wireless signals across the Atlantic Ocean.

29 Dec.   *The Sultan of Sulu*, a George Ade musical, is one of the few shows to move successfully from Chicago to Broadway. The spoof of U.S. cultural imperialism enjoys an eight-month run.

1903

Movies   *American Soldier in Love and War*, produced by Biograph; *The Divorce*, produced by Wallace McCutcheon and Frank Marion for Biograph; *Don Quixote*, produced by Pathé; *The Great Train Robbery*, starring G. M. Anderson and Justus D. Barnes, produced and filmed by Edwin S. Porter for Edison; *Kit Carson* and *The Pioneers*, starring Kit Carson and produced by Wallace McCutcheon for Biograph; *"I Want my Dinner,"* starring Ross McCutcheon (age two), produced by Wallace McCutcheon and Frank Marion for Biograph; *The Kingdom of the Fairies*, produced by Georges Méliès; *Panoramic View of Multnomah Falls*, produced by William Selig; *Rip Van Winkle*, starring Joseph Jefferson, produced by Biograph; *The Runaway Match; or, Marriage by Motorcar*, produced by British Gaumont; *Sorting Refuse at Incinerating Plant, New York City*, produced and filmed by Edwin S. Porter and J. Blair Smith for Edison; *Uncle Tom's Cabin*, produced and filmed by Edwin S. Porter for Edison.

Fiction   Pauline Elizabeth Hopkins, *Of One Blood, or, The Hidden Self*; Paul Laurence Dunbar, *In Old Plantation Days*; Henry James, *The Ambassadors*; Frank Norris, *The Pit*; Jack London, *The Call of the Wild* and *People of the Abyss*; Kate Douglas Wiggin, *Rebecca of Sunnybrook Farm*.

Popular Songs

"Bedelia," music by Jean Schwartz, lyrics by William Jerome; "Congo Love Song," music by J. Rosamond Johnson, lyrics by Robert Cole; "Dear Old Girl," music by Theodore F. Morse, lyrics by Richard and Henry Buck; "Good-Bye Eliza Jane," music by Harry von Tilzer, lyrics by Andrew B. Sterling; "Ida, Sweet as Apple Cider," music and lyrics by Eddie Leonard; "Something Doing," music by Scott Joplin, lyrics by Scott Hayden; "Sweet Adeline," music by Harry Armstrong, lyrics by Richard H. Gerard; "Under the Anheuser Busch," music by Harry von Tilzer, lyrics by Andrew B. Sterling.

- The sixteen-story Ingalls building in Cincinnati is the first skyscraper built with a reinforced concrete infrastructure.

- Gertrude Stein moves to Paris.

- W. E. B. Du Bois publishes *The Souls of Black Folk*.

- The Manhattan Opera House is completed.

- John Knowles Paine composes an American opera, *Azora*.

- British American designer Frederick Carder founds the Steuben Glass Works. Carder's coloring techniques soon rival Louis Comfort Tiffany's work.

- *The Great Train Robbery*, a twelve-minute, nine-scene film by Edwin S. Porter, shows audiences the potential of the moving picture. Its effective narrative and cinematic techniques make it the most popular movie of the decade and revitalize the motion picture industry.

- Professor George Pierce Baker offers the first playwriting and theater classes at Radcliffe College.

Jan. The first issue of Alfred Stieglitz's photography journal, *Camera Work*, appears.

21 Jan. The musical version of *The Wizard of Oz* debuts on Broadway; it runs for 293 performances.

1 Feb. Eugene Heitler Lehman, son of a Colorado tobacco wholesaler, is the first American recipient of a Rhodes Scholarship.

6 May Emma Lazarus's poem "The New Colossus" (1883) is affixed to the Statue of Liberty.

6 Aug. Twenty-eight circus people are killed when two railroad cars collide in Durand, Michigan.

15 Aug. Publisher Joseph Pulitzer gives $2 million to establish the Columbia University School of Journalism; a portion of the donation is used to establish the Pulitzer Prizes, which are first awarded for literature in 1918.

12 Sept. Scott Joplin's ragtime opera, *A Guest of Honor*, begins a Midwest tour. Internal difficulties cause cancellation in less than six weeks.

13 Oct. Victor Herbert's operetta *Babes In Toyland* opens in New York; it becomes one of the season's biggest hits.

1904

27 Oct.	Richard Jose, onetime minstrel singer, records "Silver Threads Among the Gold" for the Victor Talking Machine Company.
11 Nov.	*Hiawatha,* a cantata composed by English composer Samuel Coleridge Taylor and based on Henry Wadsworth Longfellow's poem, premieres in Washington, D.C.
21 Nov.	Enrico Caruso debuts at the Metropolitan Opera in New York; he appears regularly at the Met until 1920.
30 Dec.	The Iroquois Theatre fire in Chicago claims 602 lives.

Movies
Annie's Love Story, Cowboys and Indians, Barnum's Trunk, and *In the Strike,* produced by Pathé; *Avenging a Crime, or, Burned at the Stake, Just Like a Girl,* and *Trials and Troubles of an Automobilist,* produced by William Paley and William F. Stiener; *The Barber of Sevilla* and *An Impossible Voyage,* produced by Georges Méliès; *Boxing Horses — Luna Park, Coney Island, Elephants Shooting the Chutes at Luna Park, Opening Ceremonies, New York Subway, October 27, 1904,* produced by Edison; *Buster Brown and His Dog Tige* (series), filmed and produced by Edwin S. Porter for Edison; *The Child Stealers,* produced by British Gaumont; *The Ex-Convict,* produced by Edwin S. Porter for Edison; *Girls in Overalls, Tracked by Bloodhounds, or, A Lynching at Cripple Creek,* and *The Hold-Up of the Leadville Stage,* produced by William Selig; *The Hero of Liao-Yang, The Moonshiner, Personal, The Suburbanite,* and *The Widow and the Only Man,* produced by Biograph; *The Kidnapped Child* and *Meet Me at the Fountain,* produced by Sigmund Lubin.

Fiction
Joseph Conrad, *Nostromo;* Paul Laurence Dunbar, *The Heart of Happy Hollow;* Charles Alexander Eastman (Ohiyesa), *Red Hunters and the Animal People;* Henry James, *The Golden Bowl;* O. Henry, *Cabbages and Kings;* Jack London, *The Sea-Wolf;* Gene Stratton Porter, *Freckles;* Edith Wharton, *The Descent of Man.*

Popular Songs
"Alexander, Don't You Love Your Baby No More?" music by Harry von Tilzer, lyrics by Andrew B. Sterling; "Give My Regards to Broadway" and "The Yankee Doodle Boy," music and lyrics by George M. Cohan; "Good Bye My Lady Love," music and lyrics by Joe Howard; "He Done Me Wrong, or, the Death of Bill Bailey," music and lyrics by Hughie Cannon; "Meet Me in St. Louis," music by Kerry Mills, lyrics by Andrew B. Sterling.

- The "kickapoo" dance craze sweeps the nation.

- Chicago's $1 million Orchestra Hall is completed in the French Renaissance style by architect Daniel Burnham.

- Sculptor Augustus Saint-Gaudens creates the General Sherman Memorial for Central Park, New York City.

- The National Academy of Arts and Letters is established; many creative artists oppose its conservative views.

- Ruth St. Denis abandons a theater career to concentrate on achievements in modern dance.

- The first two-sided record disks are put on the American market by Columbia; they retail at $1.50.

5 Jan.	Owen Wister's stage adaptation of *The Virginian*, starring Dustin Farnum, opens in Manhattan. It runs more than seventeen weeks.
17 Jan.	Anton Chekhov's *The Cherry Orchard* debuts in Moscow.
1 Feb.	Enrico Caruso makes his first phonograph recording in the United States.
22 Mar.	The first newspaper color photograph is published by the *London Daily Illustrated Mirror*.
2 Apr.	The musical *Piff! Paff! Pouf!*, starring popular comic actor Eddie Foy, opens on Broadway.
30 Apr.	The Saint Louis World's Fair opens.
23 May	The musical play *The Southerners*, score by black composer Will Marion Cook, premieres in New York with a mixed-race cast.
15 July	Anton Chekhov dies at age forty-four in Badenweiler, Germany.
1 Sept.	Helen Keller graduates from Radcliffe College.
3 Sept.	*Mrs. Wiggs of the Cabbage Patch* opens on the New York stage, proving to be as popular a play as it was a novel.
4 Oct.	French sculptor Frédéric-Auguste Bartholdi, designer of the Statue of Liberty, dies in Paris.

1905

Movies	*Adventures of Sherlock Holmes, Escape from Sing-Sing, Monsieur Beaucaire*, and *The Servant Girl Problem*, produced by Vitagraph; *The Burglar's Slide for Life*, produced by Edison and featuring Mannie the Edison dog; *The Bold Bank Robbery, Dog, Lost, Strayed or Stolen, The Sign of the Cross, A Policeman's Love Affair*, and *Tramp's Revenge*, produced by Sigmund Lubin; *Everybody Works But Father, The Miller's Daughter, On a Good Old Five Cent Trolley Ride*, and *The Whole Dam Family and the Dam Dog*, filmed by Edwin S. Porter for Edison; *The Faithless Lover, A Father's Honor, The Pastry Cook's Practical Jokes*, and *The Mining District*, produced by Pathé; *The Gentle Highwayman, The Lost Child*, and *Tom, and Tom the Piper's Son*, produced by Biograph; *The Launching of the USS "Connecticut,"* filmed by Wallace McCutcheon, G. W. "Billy" Bitzer, and A. E. Weed for Biograph; *The Palace of the Arabian Knights* and *Rip's Dream*, produced by Georges Méliès.
Fiction	Willa Cather, *The Troll Garden*; Charles Waddell Chesnutt, *The Colonel's Dream*; Thomas Dixon, *The Clansman*; Ellen Glasgow, *The Deliverance*; Mary J. Holmes, *Lucy Harding*; Grace King, *Stories from Louisiana History*; Jack London, *White Fang*; Edith Wharton, *The House of Mirth*.
Popular Songs	"Daddy's Little Girl," music by Theodore F. Morse, lyrics by Edward Madden; "Everybody Works but Father," music and lyrics by Jean Havez; "Give My Regards to Broadway" and "Mary's A Grand Old Name," music and lyrics by George M. Cohan; "I Don't Care," music by Harry O. Sutton, lyrics by Jean Lenox; "In My Merry Oldsmobile," music by Gus Edwards, lyrics by Vincent Bryan; "In the Shade of the Old Apple Tree," music by Egbert Van Alstyne, lyrics by Henry Williams; "I Want What I Want When I Want It" and "Kiss Me Again," music by Victor Herbert, lyrics by Henry Blossom; "My Gal Sal," music and lyrics by Paul Dresser; "Wait 'Til the Sun Shines, Nellie," and "What You Gonna Do When the Rent Comes 'Round?" music by Albert von Tilzer, lyrics by Andrew B. Sterling; "Will You Love Me in December as You Do in May?," music by Ernest R. Ball, lyrics by James J. Walker.

- William Randolph Hearst acquires *Cosmopolitan* magazine for $400,000.

- The Institute of Musical Art, later renamed the Julliard School, is established in New York.

- Isadora Duncan opens an academy of modern dance in Berlin.

- *Variety,* the show-business weekly, begins publication in New York.

- Gertrude "Ma" Rainey gains fame as the first black minstrel star to sing "the blues."

- L. A. Coernes's *Zenobia* is the first American opera produced in Europe.

9 Jan.   George Bernard Shaw's *You Never Can Tell* succeeds in New York; three other Shaw plays open in New York this year.

3 May   The Metropolitan Opera chorus strikes.

5 May   The *Chicago Defender,* the first important black newspaper, begins publication.

13 May   Broadway entrepreneur Sam Shubert dies in a railway accident outside Harrisburg, Pennsylvania.

June   The nickelodeon era gets under way when entrepreneur Harry Davis's Pittsburgh movie theater offers continuous showings and frequent program changes. By 1909, eight thousand nickel-admission movie theaters are in operation.

6 June   Real estate at Broadway and Wall Street in New York City is offered at four dollars per square inch.

23 Oct.   Edwin Milton Royle's *The Squaw Man,* a drama attempting serious treatment of the American Indian, premieres in New York City.

31 Oct.   Bernard Shaw's play *Mrs. Warren's Profession* opens and closes in New York; critics call its treatment of prostitution "unfit," "indecent," and "vicious."

The Earl and the Girl, a musical starring Eddie Foy, opens on Broadway.

14 Nov.   David Belasco's atmospheric melodrama *The Girl of the Golden West* opens on Broadway; it plays for three years.

25 Nov.   In New York Alfred Stieglitz inaugurates the first show at the "Little Galleries of the Photo-Secession." The avant-garde gallery soon exhibits a variety of advanced art and come to be known by its address, 291.

23 Dec.   Joseph Stella's drawings of immigrants at Ellis Island are published in *Outlook* magazine.

1906

Movies   *And the Villain Still Pursued Her; or The Author's Dream, Automobile Thieves, Foul Play,* and *The Jailbird and How He Flew,* produced by Vitagraph; *The Bank Defaulter* and *The Secret of Death Valley,* produced by Sigmund Lubin; *The Black Hand, The Lone Highwayman, The Silver Wedding, The Subpoena Server, Trial Marriages,* and *Wanted: A Nurse,* produced by Biograph; *Daniel Boone; or, Pioneer Days in America* and *Kathleen Mavourneen,* filmed by Edwin S. Porter and produced by Edison; *Dream of a Rarebit Fiend,* produced by Edwin S. Porter and Wallace McCutcheon for Edison; *Dr. Dippy's Sanatorium, Mr. Butt-In,* and *Married for Millions,* produced by Biograph; *The Female Highwayman* and *The Tomboys,* produced by William Selig; *The Female Spy,* produced by Pathé; *Humorous Phases of Funny Faces* (animation experiment), filmed by J. Stuart Blackton, produced by Vitagraph; *The Life of Christ,* produced by British Gaumont; *Oh! That Limburger: the Story of a Piece of Cheese* and *Please Help the Blind; or, A Game of Graft,* produced by Vitagraph; *Terrible Kids* and *Three American Beauties,* produced by Edison; *Venetian Tragedy,* produced by Pathé; *World Series Baseball,* produced by William Selig.

Fiction	Rex Beach, *The Spoilers;* Ambrose Bierce, *The Cynic's Word Book;* O. Henry, *The Four Million* and "The Gift of the Magi"; Finley Peter Dunne, *Dissertations by Mr. Dooley;* Mary E. Wilkins Freeman, *By the Light of the Soul;* Upton Sinclair, *The Jungle;* Harriet Prescott Spofford, *Old Washington;* Booth Tarkington, *The Conquest of Canaan;* Owen Wister, *Lady Baltimore.*
Popular Songs	"The Bird on Nellie's Hat," music by Alfred Solman, lyrics by Arthur J. Lamb; "I Just Can't Make My Eyes Behave," music by Will D. Cobb, lyrics by Gus Edwards; "I'm a Yankee Doodle Dandy" and "You're a Grand Old Flag," music and lyrics by George M. Cohan; "Love Me and the World is Mine," music by Dave Reed Jr., lyrics by Ernest R. Ball; "Mandy," music by Bob Cole, lyrics by James Weldon and J. Rosamond Johnson; "Rosalie," music by Jerome Kern, lyrics by George Grossmith; "Virginia Song," music and lyrics by George M. Cohan; "Won't You Come Over to My House," music by Egbert Van Alstyne, lyrics by Harry H. Williams.

- Photographer Arnold Genthe records the aftermath of the San Francisco quake. Although his own studio and library are demolished, his photographs of Chinese immigrant life are saved.

- The American stage is host to foreign talent in 1906: Russian actress and recent immigrant Alla Nazimova debuts in Norwegian playwright Henrik Ibsen's *Hedda Gabler,* and Irish dramatist Bernard Shaw has four plays on Broadway.

- Nickelodeons proliferate across the country; the storefront theaters are expressly for showing films and charge a nickel admission. Among the those who succeed in the nickelodeon business are William Fox and the Warner brothers, who later found the Hollywood movie studios named after them.

- The first radio program of voice and music is broadcast in the United States by R. A. Fessenden.

8 Jan.	Protesters distribute pamphlets at the opening of the play *The Clansman* (based on the novel by Thomas Dixon) at New York's Liberty Theater. The pamphlets call attention to the play's racism; distributors are dispersed by police.
11 Apr.	Russian novelist Maksim Gorky arrives in the United States to raise money for Russia's revolution; Mark Twain heads a funding committee.
14 Apr.	President Theodore Roosevelt publicly chastises "muckrakers." He takes this term from *Pilgrim's Progress,* in which John Bunyan wrote of the man who never looked up to finer things because he was intent on applying his muckrake to the ground.
21 June	In London more than sixty theater people gather to honor Theater Syndicate entrepreneur Charles Frohman.
July	Ruth St. Denis introduces modern dance to the United States; she begins her American tour with the Eastern-inspired *Radha.* The young dancer, who has had little formal training, is praised for her artistic vision.
7 July	Courts rule that Bernard Shaw's play *Mrs. Warren's Profession* is appropriate for New York audiences.
11 Aug.	A patent for a talking film is issued to Eugène Lauste in France.

28 Aug. President Roosevelt proposes that "simplified spelling" be used in federal documents. The proposal, if accepted, would alter the mechanics of American English to achieve a spelling more synchronous with pronunciation; thus, for example, *through* would be spelled *thru*.

17 Oct. A German scientist, Arthur Korn, uses a telegraph wire to send a photographic image over a thousand miles; Korn has built on the work of Italian physicist Luigi Cerebotani.

30 Oct. The U.S. Supreme Court bans "simplified spelling" in federal documents.

3 Nov. French composer Camille Saint-Saëns makes his New York debut.

1907

Movies *All's Well That Ends Well* and *What a Pipe Did*, produced by Selig Polyscope; *An Awful Skate* and *His First Ride*, produced by Essanay; *The Bandit King*, *The Girl from Montana*, and *Western Justice*, directed by G. M. Anderson for Selig Polyscope; *Athletic American Girls*, *"The Bad Man" — A Tale of the West*, produced by Vitagraph; *Bargain Fiend; or, Shopping A La Mode*, starring Florence Lawrence and Florence Turner, produced by Vitagraph; *The Boy, the Bust and the Bath*, produced by Vitagraph; *College Chums*, directed by Edwin S. Porter, produced by Edison; *The Doings of a Poodle* and *The Policeman's Little Run*, produced by Pathé; *Dolls in Dreamland, Crayono*, and *The Tired Tailor's Dream* (all with object animation) directed by Joseph A. Golden, produced by Biograph; *The Hypnotist's Revenge* and *Terrible Ted*, directed by Joseph A. Golden, produced by Biograph; *John D. and the Reporter, The Unwritten Law: A Thrilling Drama Based on the Thaw-White Tragedy, Too Much Mother-in-Law*, and *When Women Vote*, produced by Sigmund Lubin; *The Masher* and *The Matinee Idol*, produced by Selig Polyscope; *The Rivals* and *"Teddy" Bears*, produced by Edison; *The Wrong Flat*, starring William Delany, produced by Vitagraph; *Work for Your Grub*, produced by Filmograph.

Fiction Henry Brooks Adams, *The Education of Henry Adams* (autobiography); F. Marion Crawford, *A Lady of Rome;* Charles Alexander Eastman, *Old Indian Days;* Ellen Glasgow, *The Wheel of Life;* Elinor Glyn, *Three Weeks;* O. Henry, "The Last Leaf"; Frances Little, *The Lady of the Decoration;* George Barr McCutcheon, *Jane Cable;* John Milton Oskison, "The Problem of Old Harjo"; Edith Wharton, *Madame de Treymes;* Kate Douglas Wiggin, *New Chronicles of Rebecca.*

Popular Songs "Harrigan," music and lyrics by George M. Cohan; "Heart of My Heart," music and lyrics by Andrew Mack; "Honey Boy," music by Albert von Tilzer, lyrics by Jack Norworth; "The Little Church Around the Corner," music by Jerome Kern, lyrics by M. E. Rourke; "Marie from Sunny Italy," music by Nick Nicholson, lyrics by Irving Berlin; "School Days," music by Will D. Cobb, lyrics by Gus Edwards.

- Alfred Stieglitz produces his best-known photograph, *The Steerage.*

- Wealthy arts patron and sculptress Gertrude Vanderbilt Whitney opens her Greenwich Village studio to exhibits by fellow artists.

- John Sloan paints *The Haymarket*, *The Wake of the Ferry*, and *The Hairdresser's Window*.

- Hungarian composer Franz Lehar's experimental opera *The Merry Widow* is produced in New York; among its nontraditional elements are the waltz and the cancan.

- The De Forest Radio Company begins New York broadcasts.

- Edwin S. Porter hires D. W. Griffith as an actor at ten dollars a day.

26 Jan.   J. P. Morgan's daughter, a member of the New York Metropolitan Opera Board of Directors, advocates the closing of the Oscar Wilde–Richard Strauss opera *Salome* for indecency.

18 Mar.   In San Francisco the Alcazar Theater, designed by G. H. Corwin, opens; it is one of many theaters that are rebuilt or reopened after the devastating earthquake of 1906.

10 June   In France motion-picture pioneers Auguste and Louis Lumière announce they have developed a method for making color film.

8 July   Florenz Ziegfeld's musical revue, the *Ziegfeld Follies*, opens at the New York Roof Theater; the *Follies* become an annual theater event, continuing until 1927.

24 Aug.   New York galleries are featuring the works of Mary Cassatt, American Impressionist.

7 Sept.   Oscar Hammerstein announces he will build four opera houses in New York City.

8 Nov.   Photographs can now be reproduced by cable, owing to new advances in the field.

3 Dec.   Mary Pickford makes her stage debut in *The Warrens of Virginia*.

1908

Movies   *After Many Years*, *Behind the Scenes*, and *The Fatal Hour*, directed by D. W. Griffith, produced by Edison; *As You Like It*, adapted from William Shakespeare, produced by Kalem; *The Cattle Rustlers* and *The Count of Monte Cristo*, filmed by Francis Boggs for Selig; *A Christmas Carol*, adapted from Charles Dickens, produced by Essanay; *The Cowboy Escapade*, produced by David Horsely's Centaur Film Manufacturing Company; *The Devil* and *Dr. Jekyll and Mr. Hyde*, produced by Edison; *Fireside Reminiscences*, directed by Edwin S. Porter for Edison; *The Girl and the Outlaw*, *The Greaser's Gauntlet*, *The Fight for Freedom*, and *The Red Girl*, directed by D. W. Griffith, produced by Biograph; *Julius Caesar*, *Richard III*, *Romeo and Juliet*, and *Macbeth*, produced by Vitagraph; *The Music Master*, produced by Biograph; *Old Isaacs the Pawnbroker*, scripted by D. W. Griffith, directed by Wallace McCutcheon, produced by Biograph; *Saved by Love*, produced by Edison; *The Welcome Burglar*, directed by D. W. Griffith, produced by Edison.

Fiction   Rex Beach, *The Barrier;* Frances Hodgson Burnett, *The Shuttle;* John Fox Jr., *The Trail of the Lonesome Pine;* Ellen Glasgow, *The Ancient Law;* Zane Grey, *The Last of the Plainsmen;* O. Henry, *The Voice of the City;* Jack London, *The Iron Heel;* Mary Roberts Rinehart, *The Circular Staircase;* Edith Wharton, *The Fruit of the Tree.*

Popular Songs

"I Wonder Who's Kissing Her Now," music by Will M. Hough and Frank R. Adams, lyrics by Joseph E. Howard and Harold Orlob; "Cuddle Up A Little Closer," music by Karl Hoschna, lyrics by Otto Hauerbach; "She Was a Dear Little Girl," music by Ted Snyder, lyrics by Irving Berlin; "Shine On Harvest Moon," music and lyrics by Nora Bayes and Jack Norworth; "Smarty," music by Albert von Tilzer, lyrics by Jack Norworth; "Sunbonnet Sue," music by Will D. Cobb, lyrics by Gus Edwards; "Take Me Out to the Ball Game," music by Albert von Tilzer, lyrics by Jack Norworth; "The Yama Yama Man," music by Karl Hoschna, lyrics by Collin Davis.

- D. W. Griffith directs his first one-reel film, *The Adventures of Dolly;* his cameraman is the expert G. W. "Billy" Bitzer. Griffith directs one hundred films in the next year.

- The Motion Picture Patents Company, the first movie monopoly, is formed. Edison, Lubin, Selig, and other producers believe films should be limited to one reel because audience attention span falters after ten minutes.

- Female ushers, orange drink, and drinking-cup dispensers are introduced at the Shubert-owned Casino Theater.

- Canadian writer Lucy Maud Montgomery publishes the novel soon to be among America's favorites, *Anne of Green Gables.*

- The New Society of American Artists is founded in Paris by Edward Steichen and others.

- Movie actress Florence Lawrence quits Vitagraph Studios and goes to work for Biograph; her salary goes up ten dollars to twenty-five dollars a week.

- The first "documentary" records are released by Edison, who has recorded the campaign speeches of William Jennings Bryan and William Howard Taft.

11 Jan. Italian soprano Louisa Tetrazinni makes her U.S. debut.

14 Jan. A theater fire in Boyertown, Pennsylvania, kills 150.

Feb. "The Eight," painters Robert Henri, George Luks, John Sloan, William Glackens, Everett Shinn, Maurice Prendergast, Ernest Lawson, and Arthur B. Davies, exhibit together in New York, protesting the conservative National Academy of Design.

11 Feb. Thomas Edison and his film-producing partners win a series of patent-infringement lawsuits.

20 Feb. Thomas Edison and Leo Tolstoy exchange gifts: Edison sends Tolstoy a phonograph; Tolstoy later sends Edison a recording of his voice.

Mar. The Original Independent Show, organized in New York, includes works by painters George Bellows, Edward Hopper, and Rockwell Kent.

30 Mar. Tetrazinni signs a five-year contract with Oscar Hammerstein; she appears at the new Manhattan Opera House.

5 May Courts rule that moving pictures be placed under copyright laws; royalties will be paid to the owners of the copyrights.

7 July French courts extend motion-picture copyright laws.

6 Sept. Israel Zangwill's play *The Melting Pot* opens in New York City; the title becomes an internationally recognized description of the United States.

5 Oct. — *The American Idea*, a George M. Cohan musical, opens in New York.

16 Nov. — Italian opera conductor Arturo Toscanini makes his American debut with Verdi's *Aida* at New York's Metropolitan Opera.

22 Dec. — New York's Herald Square Theater is damaged by fire; the successful run of *Three Twins*, starring Bessie McCoy, is halted until a new location is found.

1909

Movies — *The Aborigine's Devotion*, produced by World Pictures; *An Alpine Echo*, produced by Vitagraph; *The Bride of the Lamermoor*, adapted from Sir Walter Scott, produced by Vitagraph; *Brother Against Brother*, produced by Selig; *A Change of Complexion*, produced by the Powers Company; *The Convict's Sacrifice*, directed by D. W. Griffith, starring Stephanie Longfellow, Gladys Egan, James Kirkwood, and Henry Walthall, produced by Biograph; *A Corner in Wheat*, directed by D. W. Griffith, produced by Biograph; *The Escape from Andersonville*, produced by Kalem; *Faust*, produced by Edison; *The Girl Spy*, scripted by and starring in by Gene Gautier, produced by Kalem; *Hiawatha*, produced by Carl Laemmle's Independent Moving Picture Company; *King Lear* and *A Midsummer Night's Dream*, produced by Vitagraph; *The Lonely Villa*, directed by D. W. Griffith, starring Mary Pickford, Gladys Egan, and Adele De Garde, produced by Biograph; *Napoleon, Man of Destiny, The Life of George Washington*, and *The Life of Moses*, produced by Vitagraph; *Pippa Passes*, produced by Biograph; *The Prince and the Pauper*, starring Miss Cecil Spooner in the double role, produced by Edison.

Fiction — Mary Austin, *Lost Borders; The Collected Works of Ambrose Bierce*; Charles Alexander Eastman and Elaine Goodale Eastman, *Wigwam Evenings*; Edith Maude Eaton, "Leaves from the Mental Portfolio of A Eurasian" and *Mrs. Spring Fragrance*; Frank Norris, *The Third Circle* (posthumous); Jack London, *Martin Eden*; Gene Stratton Porter, *Girl of the Limberlost*; Gertrude Stein, *Three Lives*.

Popular Songs — "By the Light of the Silvery Moon," music by Edward Madden, lyrics by Gus Edwards; "Casey Jones," lyrics by Wallace Saunders; "Every Little Movement," music by Karl Hoschna, lyrics by Otto Harbach; "That Mesmerizing Mendelssohn Tune," music and lyrics by Irving Berlin; "Put on Your Old Grey Bonnet," music by Stanley Murphy, lyrics by Percy Wenrich; "Yiddle on Your Fiddle, Play Some Ragtime," music and lyrics by Irving Berlin.

- Modernist poets Ezra Pound and William Carlos Williams publish collections.

- George Bellows paints *Both Members of the Club.*

- D. W. Griffith features sixteen-year-old Mary Pickford in his films. The former Gladys Smith now makes forty dollars a week starring in Biograph pictures.

- "The movies" are now a $40-million-a-year industry employing more than one hundred thousand artists and craftspeople. There are ten thousand moving-picture theaters in the United States.

- W. C. Handy's *Memphis Blues* is the first blues song to be written down.

- Mack Sennett is employed by Biograph as an actor-writer; he tries to convince D. W. Griffith that a film about comic policemen would be successful; years later his Keystone Kops prove him right.

- The first fully animated film is released; Gertie the Dinosaur stars.

19 Jan. Eugene Walter's controversial drama *The Easiest Way,* about a woman who chooses to live "immorally," opens at the Belasco-Stuyvesant Theater in New York. *The New York Times* defends the play.

1 Mar. An adaptation of American author Bret Harte's *The Luck of the Roaring Camp* opens in London.

9 Apr. Enrico Caruso makes a radio broadcast from the Metropolitan Opera House to the home of Lee De Forest, the inventor of the vacuum tube.

1 May The works of American expatriate painter John Singer Sargent are among the most impressive to be seen at the 141st annual Royal Academy of Art Show in London.

15 June The *Ziegfeld Follies* features chorus girls costumed as glittering mosquitoes; Nora Bayes introduces "Shine On Harvest Moon."

11 Oct. George M. Cohan premieres *The Man Who Owned Broadway* at the New York Theater.

28 Oct. The nine-hundred-seat Cort Theater opens in Chicago; the theater's Italianate design is by E. O. Pridmore.

4 Nov. Composer Sergey Rachmaninoff makes his American debut at Smith College.

29 Dec. The first known "goddamn" is uttered on the American stage. Clyde Fitch's *The City* has been banned in Boston but plays in New York without police interference. Several people, including a theater critic, are said to have fainted on hearing the words "You're a goddamn liar."

OVERVIEW

Metaphor for Possibility. Many Americans turned their calendars to 1 January 1900 with confidence in the future and pride in the past. The last years of the 1890s had been stable and productive, at least by comparison with the turbulence and depression of the first half of that decade. Technical achievement and manufacturing efficiency — not to mention the colonial empire gained in the Spanish-American War — had secured for the United States a position as an international power, and U.S. citizens enjoyed the highest standard of living in the world. Most Americans believed the new century would reaffirm the assumptions they brought into it: moral values would remain constant; scientific progress would inevitably benefit society; and tradition would continue to nurture art and culture. Belief that order and opportunity were fixed attributes of American life led those who celebrated the arrival of the first decade of the twentieth century to envision the best of all possible futures.

Looking Backward. If American culture reflected confidence and optimism in the years 1900–1909, it also promoted complacency and mediocrity. The revolution in technology, communications, and transportation had opened the American imagination to the future, but the conservatism born of middle-class comfort closed American eyes to the plight of the poor, the uneducated, and the dispossessed. *Popular culture* was an unknown term, but it was fast becoming a phenomenon. Mass marketing was succeeding on the principle of finding the lowest common denominator of American intellectual life. And the arts and letters "establishment" remained immersed in the romantic idealism and studied refinement of the past. It continued to celebrate the grandeur of nineteenth-century painting, to revere the "genteel tradition" in literature, and to rely on Europe for serious music and theater. Artists, writers, and musicians who dared experiment met with rejection and ridicule.

On the Brink of Modernity. If modernism (that outpouring of talent and experimentation which was to characterize Western cultural achievement for much of the twentieth century) had not quite begun to germinate on American shores, the conditions for growth were favorable. The 1900s are often seen as a fallow season in American artistic life. But 1900–1909 sustained an in-

creasing number of innovators whose accomplishments anticipated America's cultural coming-of-age. These men and women would not only redefine the form and content of art but would also revise the concept of what art *is,* by demonstrating the aesthetic worth of photography and cinema. The arts establishment encouraged reverence for tradition; middlebrow tastes demanded familiarity, morality, and sentiment. Yet an advance guard of writers, painters, architects, and musicians refused to turn back or look away from the realities of twentieth-century life. By the decade's end they had created a small but receptive audience for the sweeping changes of the 1910s and 1920s.

Change and Resistance. In 1900 Theodore Dreiser's frank treatment of sexuality in *Sister Carrie* caused the novel to be suppressed by its publisher; in 1907 the book was republished and won praise for its gritty honesty. When the first exhibition of modern art opened in New York City in 1908, the artists' slum-scene subject matter and loose painterly style appalled conservative critics. But the "Ash Can" exhibit, as it was called, was the first skirmish in the all-out rebellion that was to follow the famous Armory Show of 1913, which introduced European Post-Impressionism and jolted American sensibilities into the modern era. Throughout the decade the Chicago School of architects drew urban eyes upward with steel-skeletoned skyscrapers. Frank Lloyd Wright was building his long, low, environmentally attuned Prairie Style designs. European Art Nouveau, with its characteristic flowing lines and contours, informed American graphic arts and sculpture. In the so-called domestic or decorative arts, the simplicity and quality of the American Arts and Crafts movement signaled a challenge to Victorian elaboration and ornament as design in furniture, ceramics, metalwork, glass, and textiles underwent sweeping change. In music Scott Joplin was "The King of Rag Time" and Ma Rainey sang the blues. But the nation as a whole — which made the now-forgotten romance *To Have and To Hold* a best-seller while Theodore Dreiser's *Sister Carrie* was virtually banned by his own publisher and sang "Boola Boola" while composer Charles Ives labored in obscurity — was overlooking its most creative contributors. Some Americans, such as Gertrude Stein, sought the more liberal climate of Europe in the early

1900s, anticipating the rush of expatriatism in the 1920s. Others found the support of like-minded individuals at home. But the movement away from tradition and gentility had begun.

The Social Impulse. The early 1900s also marked the beginning of the Progressive Era in America. As political progressives resolved to right such prominent national wrongs as poverty and corruption, progressives in the arts sought to bring a new social relevance to their work. Quick brush strokes, stripped-down prose, and improvisational musical riffs stylized the unconventional subject matter that ranged from tenement life to racial pride. Just as the budding arts revolution embraced new style and subject matter, it also brought diversity to its ranks. Blacks, immigrants, and women made their voices heard. African American author W. E. B. Du Bois and performing artists Bert Williams and George Walker, Italian American painter Joseph Stella, and Asian American writer Edith Maude Eaton are only a few of those who broke color, culture, and gender barriers in the early 1900s.

A Stratified Society: City Life. Experimentation flourished in the small art colonies of cosmopolitan urban areas, but tradition and conservatism sustained small towns and rural communities. In general urbanites and rural dwellers — unaffected as yet by the spread of cultural conformity via the airwaves — found few commonalities in their lives. Within the cities cultural gulfs were wide, and the upper class supported the arts. In the turn-of-the-century decade most cities of any size could boast the icons of high culture — an opera house, a symphony orchestra, theaters, libraries, and museums. Middle- to lowbrow tastes supported vaudeville houses, ethnic theaters, dance halls, street entertainers, amusement parks, kinetoscope parlors, and nickelodeons, where the line between arts and entertainment was blurred.

"Highbrow." In places such as New York, Chicago, and San Francisco, the homes of high society were furnished with suitably "high" art. The upper classes spared no expense in filling their mansions — works of art in themselves — with European and Asian antiquities. The wealthy also patronized the performing arts, attending operas and symphonies or entertaining friends at home with full companies of Broadway stars and scenery hired for the night.

"Lowbrow." At the bottom of the economic pyramid were the wage earners who, if they could find work at all, made $1.50 to $5.00 a week. "The arts" were hardly the concern of the labor force in the early 1900s. Any aesthetic enjoyment that was not part of a retained ethnic tradition was a luxury that cost both money and time. If free time was available, the penny arcade, the nickelodeon, or the dance pavilion provided culture and amusement for the cities' poor.

"Middlebrow." The urban middle class benefited both from wealthy patrons' endowment of museums and libraries and from poverty's cheap labor: rare was the middle-class home without printed art reproductions, a well-stocked bookshelf, or at least a cook if not a live-in maid, and thus leisure time to enjoy the arts. The theater was a favorite. Even outside New York, middle-class theatergoers could be assured of seeing touring "stars" depicting romanticized dramatic versions of their own conventional lives. And since vaudeville had ceased presenting risqué humor in the 1890s, the entire family could enjoy the live variety shows. At home, the piano in the parlor and the new, improved phonograph sustained the first popular-music crazes. By countrywide marketing of sheet music and record discs, the tune peddlers of Tin Pan Alley soon had nearly every neighborhood in the nation ringing with "In the Good Old Summertime" and "Bill Bailey Won't You Please Come Home."

Simple Pleasures: Country Life. Popular music and live entertainment found their way to small-town America, but outside the cities life was far more provincial. Appreciation of the arts was the not-very-practical avocation of the educated, a relatively small, though growing, percentage of the population. (Although the number of high schools almost doubled between 1900 and 1909, Americans on average went to school for about six years.) And, educated or not, rich or poor, rural people tended to create their own artistic diversions. A typical town might have its amateur drama group, a band or orchestra, a lending library, and a book club all supporting the "tried and true" traditions of the past. Larger towns on railroad lines were visited by theatrical road companies, and in much of rural America, Chautauqua circuits — traveling versions of the educational programs offered in Chautauqua, New York, every summer since 1874 — introduced artistic awareness via dramatic performances and literary lectures. But the distance between city and country, like the gulf between rich and poor, stratified national tastes.

Communication: Newspapers and Magazines. No method of mass communication yet existed that would provide all parts of the nation with common information and ideas. Television was a science fiction; radio would not be available to most consumers until the 1920s; and the movies, in most people's opinion, had reached their peak as a technological novelty and would go the way of the hand-turned animation toys of the past century. Print was the first medium to reach a national audience. With a steady flow of romantic fiction and serialized adventure, publishing houses capitalized on the nationwide distribution system built up during the last years of the nineteenth century, and by 1900 publishers had discovered the market for color art reproductions as well. The modern metropolitan newspaper, brainchild of William Randolph Hearst and Joseph Pulitzer, was already in its adolescence. With wire associations or press services furnishing the same news, editorials, and pictures to subscribing papers, by the turn of the century even rural readers were able to keep abreast of national events and public opinion. The "Grand Old Magazines" of the late 1800s —

monthlies such as *Harper's*, *The Atlantic*, *Scribner's*, and *Century* — were still-vigorous literary journals with a small, elite readership which enjoyed the best of the older generation: Frederic Remington woodcuts, columns by William Dean Howells, and the more suitable works of Mark Twain. But the circulation of inexpensive magazines such as *McClure's*, *Everybody's*, and *Cosmopolitan* not only brought much of the nation together through exposés of social problems but also provided a forum for writers of distinction, such as Lincoln Steffens, whose *The Shame of the Cities* (1904) created a national outcry for reform. Other periodicals, including the *Ladies' Home Journal* and the *Saturday Evening Post*, published articles, biographies, and commentary designed to appeal to middle-class standards, but they also engaged the talents of writers such as Theodore Dreiser, Ellen Glasgow, Sarah Orne Jewett, and Frank Norris for their fiction columns.

The Best-Seller. Unknown until the advent of mass marketing and cheap binding, the American best-seller was a phenomenon of late-nineteenth- and early-twentieth-century life. The general reading public liked its fiction romantic and sentimental: Anthony Hope's *The Prisoner of Zenda* (1894), Alice Hegen Rice's *Mrs. Wiggs of the Cabbage Patch* (1901), and John Fox Jr.'s *The Little Shepherd of Kingdom Come* (1903) remained popular throughout the decade. Edward Westcott's *David Harum*, a simplistic view of love and heroism, reached the 1.2 million mark by 1909. *The Clansman*, Thomas Dixon's racist depiction of the Old South, on which D. W. Griffith's epic film *The Birth of a Nation* (1915) was based, sold four hundred thousand copies in ten days in 1905. *The Virginian* (1902) by Owen Wister set the fashion of the Western novel and inspired a Broadway hit. Ohioan Zane Grey's trip through the West in 1907 began his long career as a best-selling Western author; many of his novels became motion pictures. Jack London became a millionaire by turning his experiences at sea and in the Klondike into popular adventure novels such as *The Call of the Wild* (1903), *The Sea-Wolf* (1904), and *White Fang* (1906). Copies of Lew Wallace's *Ben-Hur* (1880) and of Horatio Alger's 135 rags-to-respectability tales (written during the last three decades of the nineteenth century) were still enjoying enormous popularity.

Poetry. Two hundred books of poetry were published in 1900 alone, with Robert Service's Alaskan gold-country ballads and James Whitcomb Riley's celebration of Hoosier life in Indiana topping the list of "best-loved" poetry. Paul Laurence Dunbar was the country's most notable African American poet of the era; his dialect verse portrayed human nature over stereotype; and illustrated editions of his work sold in the tens of thousands. Other poets of distinction, notably Harvard alumni William Vaughn Moody, Trumbull Stickney, and George Cabot Lodge, drew a sophisticated readership, but the public admired the rugged or the sentimental voices of the "handyman" poets, "policeman" poets, "vagabond" poets, and the like, who found ready publication in newspapers, magazines, and collections. And although George Santayana and Edwin Arlington Robinson (now considered among the best premodernists) had both produced two collections by 1900, they were still unknown. Americans generally felt that the Golden Age of poetry had passed with Ralph Waldo Emerson, James Russell Lowell, John Greenleaf Whittier, and Henry Wadsworth Longfellow.

The "Grand Old Men" (and Women) of American Letters. In contrast to best-sellers, "high" literature finds a small but elite readership. Most turn-of-the-century writers appealed to one element or the other, with the exception of Mark Twain. One of the most respected and one of the most popular writers this country has produced, Twain, during most of his career, projected the image of the accessible, rough-hewn humorist whose novels and lectures delighted Americans of every walk of life. The first decade of the century was the last of Twain's life, and as he aged he became increasingly dour. His last works were pessimistic, philosophical, and bitter; readers of *Tom Sawyer* would hardly have recognized "Letters from the Earth" (1909) as a work by the same writer. Along with Twain, Henry James, William Dean Howells, Sarah Orne Jewett, and Mary E. Wilkins Freeman were among the living writers who had earned serious critical reputations. But the rapid development of American modernism in the twentieth century brought new styles and sensibilities into literary prominence. James's aristocratic distance contrasted sharply with the gritty naturalism of Dreiser and Frank Norris; Jewett and Freeman's regionalism would be supplanted by Willa Cather and Sherwood Anderson. In his last years Twain became a literary hero to Anderson, H. L. Mencken, Ernest Hemingway, and others for having captured and conveyed the vital tensions in American life between the elite and the popular, the local and the universal.

Tradition and the Individual Talent. Americans in the first decade of the twentieth century, who benefited materially from a technological acceleration previously unknown in human history, were content with, and even contentious about, tradition in the arts. The 1800s had finally produced internationally recognized American writers, painters, and theatrical impresarios; the continuing classical revival in architectural design maintained a tribute to decorum despite nineteenth-century structural advances. Photography, dance, music, and movies were to be part of an artistic revolution not yet imagined by the cult of "high" art. The so-called custodians of culture found security in the evident excellence of the status quo: hope for the future was based on the enduring reputation of the past. But the arrival on the scene from 1900 to 1909 of individual innovators (who understood what certain critics implied when they suggested a "twilight" was approaching in American arts and letters) heralded the dawn of an even finer age of American culture. And while T. S. Eliot did not have this approaching renaissance in mind when he chose "Tradition and the Individual Talent" (1919) as the title for one of his best-known critical works, the phrase is applicable to the state of the arts in the United States at the century's beginning. On the horizon of nineteenth-century tradition were individuals who, separately or as groups and "movements," would bring about a brilliant apogee in the arts of the twentieth century.

Sources:

Frederick Lewis Allen, *The Big Change: America Transforms Itself* (New York: Harper, 1952);

Sean Dennis Cashman, *America in the Age of the Titans* (New York: New York University Press, 1988);

John W. Dodds, *Life in Twentieth Century America*, revised edition (New York: Putnam, 1973);

Henry F. May, *The End of American Innocence*, revised edition (New York: Columbia University Press, 1992);

Kathy Peiss, *Cheap Amusements: Working Women and Leisure at the Turn of the Century* (Philadelphia: Temple University Press, 1986);

David Perkins, *A History of Modern Poetry* (Cambridge, Mass.: Harvard University Press, 1976);

Barbara Rose, *American Art Since 1900* (New York: Praeger, 1968);

Mark Sullivan, *Our Times: Pre-War America*, volume 3 (New York: Scribners, 1930).

TOPICS IN THE NEWS

ART FOR DEMOCRACY'S SAKE

American Impressionism. American artists and their patrons rightly felt proud of the achievements of the past century. Excellent public art institutes existed in New York City, Philadelphia, Detroit, and Chicago, and private collectors had acquired some of the most magnificent of Europe's art treasures. Painters such as George Inness (1825–1894) had moved beyond the Hudson River school by applying a looser brush style to create rich, emotional landscapes. Thomas Eakins (1844–1916), Winslow Homer (1836–1910), John Singer Sargent (1856–1925), and James McNeill Whistler (1834–1903) were living masters of international repute. Eakins's thoughtful, realistic portraits and his vigorous sporting scenes bore the stamp of his intellectual independence, while the vibrant influence of thirty years of French Impressionism could be seen in the works of Homer, Sargent, and Whistler. These painters' reductions of solid objects to broad smudges and misty shadows and their concern with tonality over precision gave their work an enigmatic, romantic quality. It was Mary Cassatt (1844–1926), however, who was identified as the first "pure" Impressionist born on American soil, and her prismatic modeling of shapes into light and color did much to popularize the style in the United States. Cassatt herself, like Sargent and Whistler, chose to live and work in Europe.

The Ten. The Impressionists who remained in America forged a formidable presence. The American Impressionist Establishment. a painters known to themselves and their followers as "The Ten" — had, in the late 1800s, become dissatisfied with the conservatism of dominant American art organizations as well as with their typically huge exhibitions, whose jumble of styles and

Woman with a Red Zinnia, 1890s, by expatriate American Impressionist Mary Cassatt

quality created viewer confusion. They also were concerned that American collectors were buying the works of Parisian painters and ignoring American Impressionism.

The Necklace, circa 1907, by Thomas Wilmer Dewing,
one of "The Ten"

Frank Benson, Joseph De Camp, Thomas Dewing, Childe Hassam, Willard Metcalf, Robert Reid, Edward Simmons, Edmond Tarbell, J. Alden Weir, and John Twachtman (whose death in 1902 brought William Merritt Chase into the fold) all signed an agreement in 1897 to exhibit annually and exclusively as "The Ten" in small, selective venues in New York City. Their independence established, they dominated the young American art scene at the turn of the century.

Regional Flowering. Outside New York City, regional Impressionism grew. The Boston School, the Hoosier School in Indiana, and others in Connecticut and Pennsylvania produced important artists after 1900, as did the art colonies of the West, especially in San Francisco and Taos, New Mexico. Several Chicago-trained painters arrived in Giverny, France, in the early 1900s, and as a result the Art Institute of Chicago was the first American art museum to acquire paintings by Claude Monet.

Stasis. By 1900 Impressionism was no longer a radical departure in the minds of the American art establishment, and although it continued to have its critics throughout the first decades of the century, the style had affirmed its worth and lasting appeal. By the middle of the decade The Ten had successfully "Americanized"

CAMERA WORK

I *saw that what others were doing was to make hard cold copies of hard cold subjects in hard cold light. I did not see why a photograph should not be a work of art, and I studied to learn to make it one.*
— Alfred Stieglitz, 1908

In 1903, after he had broken away from *Camera Notes* because of its increasing conservatism, Alfred Stieglitz set about publication of the photography journal *Camera Work.* His new journal celebrated American and European pictorialist photographers; its stated intention was to "appeal to the ever-increasing ranks of those who have faith in photography as a medium of individual expression, and, in addition, to make converts of many at present ignorant of its possibilities." At first, only photography selected for "individuality and artistic worth" was published. After 1908 the journal invited critical essays from such respected authors as George Bernard Shaw and Gertrude Stein, reproduced works by Pablo Picasso and Auguste Rodin, and provided retrospectives on early photographic pioneers.

Camera Work not only produced quality artwork, but was a work of art in itself. Beautifully rendered halftone prints and photogravures and carefully integrated typeface and initial letters, along with wide margins, gave the journal the look of the best of the pre-Raphaelite designers. *Camera Work* was printed on the finest paper, and copies were often touched up by hand before they were mailed. In addition, Stieglitz designed covers that contributed to the magazine's artistic unity and even judged advertisements on their artistic merit. For over a decade *Camera Work* was the standard against which the art of photography and the craft of printing was measured. In 1924, when England's Royal Photographic Society gave Stieglitz its highest award, the Progress Medal, *Camera Work* was recognized as "the most artistic record of photography ever attempted."

French Impressionism and had established the position, if not the fashion, of the small, independent art show. What, then, was "wrong" with American art? First, after more than one hundred years of political independence, America was still looking to European models for instruction and affirmation. Second, the character of American art institutions, from the rule-bound Society of American Artists (against which The Ten had rebelled) to the exclusivity of The Ten themselves, invited reassessment and reform.

New York Street in Winter, 1902, by Robert Henri, leader of the "revolutionary black gang"

The Eight. The painters who chose to move on did so not from a disagreement with Impressionist philosophy or technique but from a determination to wrest American art from European influence and academic artificiality. The first American artists to attempt both a style and a subject matter suited to the American experience turned back to preimpressionist realism. In addition, they specifically rejected the norms of the various "schools" and the elitism of the academies. Calling themselves "The Eight" in conscious echo of the Impressionist Ten, Arthur Bowen Davies, Robert Henri, William Glackens, Ernest Lawson, George Luks, Maurice Prendergast, Everett Shinn, and John Sloan banded together in rejection of the Eurocentric tastes and undemocratic exhibition policies of the established galleries.

Henri. Robert Henri (1865–1929) was the leader of The Eight, or the "revolutionary black gang" (an epithet coined by critics of the group), which gathered regularly in his studio for discussions of music, literature, and art — and occasional irreverent theatrical parodies of the "living masters." Henri's uncompromising attention to scenes from urban life and his quick, spontaneous technique challenged the "art for art's sake" sensibilities of the early century and encouraged further disparaging references to his circle as "Apostles of Ugliness" and, finally, as the "Ash Can School."

Diversity. All of The Eight were influenced by Impressionism, insisting that realistic subject matter did not dictate realistic detail. And not all of The Eight practiced realism. It is a comment on the group's commitment to inclusion that Davies's dreamlike unicorns, Lawson's land- and cityscapes, and Prendergast's mosaic-inspired abstractions were appreciated as fully as Luks's celebrations of human physicality, Sloan's shops and slums, and Shinn's and Glackens's images of nightlife. Nor were The Eight utterly rejected by the academy. By 1905 each member of the group had been accepted by the Society of American Artists, and Henri, Glackens, and Sloan had won prestige and honors for their work.

The Ash Can Exhibition. For the spring 1907 National Academy of Design exhibition, Henri learned that, despite his having been asked to serve as a judge, his paintings were to be treated as second-rate and that none of his friends' work had been accepted. Henri promptly withdrew from the show. The academy's slight galvanized The Eight, who set about promoting their own, independent exhibition at a New York gallery owned by William Macbeth. The controversial show opened at the Macbeth Gallery in February 1908.

Attacks. Critics descended on the exhibit, complaining in particular about the subject matter: the gritty urban vistas and the coarse faces of tenement dwellers were certainly not fit to hang above the divan, they said, and likened the works to "sores" on canvas and "explosions in a paint factory." The public was especially affronted by George Luks's painting of pigs, and the show was roundly castigated for its disregard of thematic unity.

Realism Triumphs. To the nonconformist Eight, however, opinion was outweighed by fact: the show drew so many viewers that Macbeth ran out of catalogues, and seven paintings found buyers. "Art for life's sake" had achieved a minor triumph. What came to be known in later years as the Ash Can Exhibit had struck a blow against rules and standards and had democratized not only subject matter but exhibition practices. These artists of the vernacular succeeded in promoting the kind of subject matter being treated by naturalist Theodore Dreiser and muckraker Lincoln Steffens. But the lasting significance of the Ash Can School remains in its portrayal of the vitality of the American spirit — a spirit that did not emanate from the ivory towers of high art but rather from the mean streets of urban America. The trend toward revitalized realism dominated avant-garde painting after 1907, culminating in the work of Henri's protégé George Bellows (1882–1925). Bellows's boxing matches and back-alley observations are perhaps the most vigorous and dramatic of the contemporary scenes favored by the realists. Not until the next decade would Americans take up the modernist techniques of Post-Impressionism such as Cubism, Fauvism, and Futurism, and only then after Europe's Post-Impressionists were formally introduced at the Armory Show of 1913.

Photography as Art. The sponsor of the Armory Show, and the individual most responsible for the introduction of modern painting to America, was a photographer, Alfred Stieglitz. His influence on the arts from 1900–1909 and beyond is almost immeasurable. Besides opening Americans' eyes to Georges Braque, Paul Gauguin, Henri Matisse, Pablo Picasso, and later to Georgia O'Keeffe, he pioneered a revolutionary movement to prove photography equal to painting as an art form, nurtured and encouraged scores of young artists, and established *Camera Notes* and *Camera Work,* the first art photography journals.

Photo-Secessionism. Stieglitz had been at the forefront of the "pictorial" photography movement since the 1890s. Pictorial photography, like Impressionist painting, emphasized composition over subject and suggestion over detail. It recognized the camera's ability to elicit mood and to record emotion as effectively as the painter's tools. In 1902, with his friends and fellow photographers Edward Steichen, Gertrude Kasebier, and Clarence White, Stieglitz formed the Photo-Secession, a society of artists dedicated to the advancement of pictorial photography.

Early Efforts. Stieglitz's earlier efforts to bring photography into the realm of art had been somewhat successful, and annual photographic salons had been mounted in New York and Philadelphia in the 1890s. The Philadelphia Photographic Society had even joined with the stiff-necked Pennsylvania Academy of Fine Arts in 1898, and the ensuing exhibits were well received. But in 1900 a third of these exhibits were marked by declining standards and political infighting. The "old school" literalists objected to the hazy, soft-focus effects of the "new school" pictorialists and called the newcomers "fuzzyographers." When the conservative faction won out, Stieglitz and the pictorialists seceded.

Turning Point. The Secessionists' first exhibition, at the National Arts Club Show in New York, was a significant moment in the history of photography; its success placed pictorialism at the vanguard of the art photography movement. The Photo-Secession exhibited from 1902 through 1905 at various galleries throughout the United States, Canada, and Europe. Major talents in addition to Kasebier, White, Steichen, and Stieglitz were Joseph T. Keiley, Frank Eugene Smith, and Alvin Langdon Coburn. Their work not only expanded the boundaries of pictorialism, but their technical innovations in printing and developing resulted in innovative photographic effects.

The 291 Galleries. The Photo-Secessionists were in need of a permanent home, and in 1905 Stieglitz signed a lease on the studio that was to become the hub of avant-garde art in the first decade of the century. The Little Galleries of the Photo-Secession would soon be known simply as 291, the building's Fifth Avenue street number in New York City. As the announcement of its policies indicated, however, 291 would promote "modern art, not necessarily photo-

JOSEPH STELLA: ARTIST OF THE MELTING POT

Joseph Stella arrived in New York City from Naples, Italy, at the age of nineteen to begin his studies in medicine; within two years he had put himself under the tutelage of William Merritt Chase at the New York School of Art. Like Chase, Stella took New York City scenes as his subjects. But Stella moved away from his teacher in the type of scenes he would create. Stella chose as his canvas New York's Lower East Side, the home of recent immigrants, rather than sunny Long Island or stylish Central Park. He became a magazine illustrator in 1905 and for the next several years produced strong, realistic pencil portraits as well as Whistleresque cityscapes. Working for *Outlook* and *Survey* magazines, Stella drew immigrants at Ellis Island, coal miners in West Virginia, steelworkers in Pittsburgh, and crowds at Coney Island. Stella's fascination with industry led him in later years to become associated with the Futurists, but in the first decade of the century he made his mark with works such as *Italian Immigrant* (1907), a tribute to his own relocated countrymen.

graphic." Through its doors from 1905 to 1909 would come the first American exhibitions of Henri Matisse and Henri Toulouse-Lautrec and the first one-woman show (of works by watercolorist Pamela Coleman Smith). Later came the first exhibit of African sculpture and the first children's exhibit. In 1908 the gallery exhibited fifty-eight drawings by Auguste Rodin. Painters John Marin, Marsden Hartley, Max Weber, and Arthur Dove were among 291's frequent visitors and exhibitors. And, although their presence exacerbated the personal and aesthetic differences among them, Robert Henri and members of The Eight could occasionally be found deep in conversation with Stieglitz, Steichen, and the rest of the photo-rebels.

Decisive Victory. Stieglitz himself was influenced by the interchange of ideas that flowed through the Secessionist gatherings and those at 291, and by the end of the decade his own technique had changed: he had moved away from soft-focus approach to create the clear compositions of light and shadow that mark some of his best-known work. But the Photo-Secessionists had never swerved from their basic beliefs — that photography, at its best, was indeed a fine art, and that photography was unique unto itself, not an imitation of other arts. By the end of the decade the photographic image had achieved unquestioned status as a form of artistic expression. With painting and the graphic and cinematic arts, photogra-

FREDERIC REMINGTON (1861-1909)

Frederic Remington's sculpture and paintings are almost synonymous with the spirit of the West in the minds of many Americans. Naturally inclined toward outdoor life, Remington spent little time in formal study. His three years at Yale's School of Art gave him "a smattering" of technique, but he was soon traveling in the West, visiting Indian encampments and detailing cavalry and cowboy life. Remington's magazine work was well known before the turn of the century. His struggle to be appreciated as a serious artist and not simply an illustrator was successful, and by the early 1900s he had achieved celebrity as a talented painter and sculptor. His beautifully balanced sculptures of the early 1900s depicted the action-filled Old West as he remembered it. *The Cheyenne* (1901), *Comin' Through the Rye* (1902–1904), and *Bronco Buster* (1905) are some of his best-known pieces. Remington, who died at age forty-eight of appendicitis, once said, "I knew more about cowboys than I did about drawing." The appreciative viewers of his work felt him to be an expert on both.

phy would go on to shape the vision of the American Century.

Sources:

Sean Dennis Cashman, *America in the Age of the Titans* (New York: New York University Press, 1988);

William H. Gerdts, *American Impressionism* (New York: Abbeville Press, 1984);

William Innes Homer, *Alfred Stieglitz and the Photo-Secession* (Boston: Little, Brown, 1983);

Christina Peterson, *Alfred Stieglitz's Camera Notes* (Minneapolis: Minneapolis Institute of Arts / New York: Norton, 1993);

Barbara Rose, *American Art Since 1900* (New York: Praeger, 1967).

DANCE: BREAKING THE RULES

Strictly Ballroom. The combination of a puritan sense of decency and a Victorian sense of decorum had kept dancing under strict social control in America for two hundred years. To be sure, the lofty European ballet and the antics of "theater people" were tolerated, but Americans in general did not appreciate expressive movement of the body. Until the late nineteenth century, the genteel upper classes considered dancing a "common" amusement, and the public dance halls that peaked in popularity in the first decade of the 1900s were most decidedly for the commoner sort.

The Waltz. The trend toward dining out and night-time entertainment that began in the Gilded Age of the late 1800s had a liberating effect on well-to-do sensibili-

ties. By the turn of the century the annual charity cotillion had given way to the occasional private ball, and the ability to dance was a valued social grace. Still, the waltz (its face-to-face, semiembracing posture was no longer shocking, as it had been when first imported from Europe) was the favored step. Waltzing couples, after all, remained as formal on the dance floor as they did at the punch bowl, with the system of signing dance cards and "saving" dances assuring that partners changed often enough to prevent untoward intimacy.

Ragtime. But the increasingly syncopated beat of popular music inaugurated by ragtime tolled the end of formalism in American social dancing. Ragtime, which had originated in its modern form in the honky-tonks of black America, was now marketed nationally in sheet music and player-piano rolls by the song merchants of Tin Pan Alley. From 1900 on it was heard everywhere. Experimenting with the quick-moving two-step and the shuffle, whites of all classes attempted to emulate the dance steps of blacks as they moved to the "ragged" beat of the new music.

Youth Embraces the Dance Craze. Dancing had never been the pastime of the settled, sedentary older generations, and now young people were discovering attractions in dancing that their parents and grandparents had not: rhythm, expression — and bodily proximity. As a result, more people were dancing, in more places, and in more ways, than ever before. The popularity of the Pianola (the player piano) and the phonograph made dancing in the home an acceptable evening's activity (one print ad of 1906 encouraged young women to "Entertain the Boys" with an Edison Phonograph). Dancing could be done "out" on restaurant rooftop gardens and in hotel ballrooms. The craze spread from big cities to small towns and filtered upward to young marrieds and even to the past-its-prime fortyish set. New dance steps proliferated: by 1907 "ragtime dances" like the one-step, the bunny-hug, the grizzly bear, and the turkey trot were giving palpitations to the dowagers of correctness, who had already been dealt a severe blow by the growing trend away from chaperonage. The dance craze reached its peak toward the end of the decade but would last well beyond it. By the time Irving Berlin's song "Everybody's Doin' It Now" came out in 1911, most of the youth of America had already been "doin'" ragtime dances for many years, and patterns of premarital social interaction had changed for good.

The Culture of the Cakewalk. The black musical spirit of the American South that gave birth to ragtime, the blues, and jazz has an accompanying dance history. African American dance culture originated in the sacred and secular dances of West Africa as well as in European tradition. Slave entertainments frequently involved dancing, and from those early expressions of joy, sorrow, or everyday concerns came the dances that would not only set white youth to "turkey trottin'" in the early part of the century but also to "twistin'" in the 1950s and 1960s.

American youths of every economic class were "dance mad," but the brightly lit dance halls that proliferated in metropolitan areas in the early 1900s were especially popular with young adults of the working classes. For these unmarried men and women, who worked long, hard days and whose wages most often helped support parents and siblings, twenty-five cents or less was well worth the gala evening promised by the dance establishments. Admission to the large halls with their polished floors, lively music, and festive atmospheres meant a respite from the day's labor and the night's boredom. The chance to leave the confines of the family tenement and to spend the evening perfecting the latest dance step was also an opportunity to socialize with members of one's own age group — and of the opposite sex.

Ticket prices were always affordable, but commercial dance halls varied in respectability: some establishments were committed to orderly decorum and advertised lessons in the two-step and waltz, but others promoted more sexually expressive dance styles — often by distributing printed cards with suggestive illustrations—and some were actually brothels. In 1906 "pivoting" and "spieling" were at the height of their popularity; one early observer described the performance of the steps:

> Julia stands erect, with her body as rigid as a poker and with her left arm straight out from her shoulder like an upraised pump-handle. Barney slouches up to her, and bends his back so that he can put his chin on Julia's shoulder and she can do the same by him. Then, instead of dancing with a free, lissome graceful, gliding step, they pivot or spin, around and around with the smallest circle that can be drawn around them.

Performances like Julia and Barney's were attacked because they seemed to lack the self-control and skill needed to achieve the more "proper" form of the waltz; and in fact, the pivot and spiel was a parody of that more genteel dance form. But gentility was no longer the order of the day, and the dance craze was only one more indication that the young generation would not be marching to the staid measures of tradition.

Wringin' and twistin', the buzzard lope, the breakdown, and the pigeonwing all predated the ragtime era. But blacks also danced formally, in learned application of the customs of the dominant culture. Northern blacks of the middle and upper classes sponsored balls and cotillions that were as decorous and as elaborate as those of white society. Along with traditional set-and-figure dances was included — as it was in other areas of black culture like minstrel shows — the cakewalk, a formal, high-stepping movement in which couples paired up and promenaded to a slow but syncopated tune. The irony was never lost on blacks: the cakewalk, which had originated as a slave-time dance contest, was an open parody of the exaggerated mannerisms of southern white socialites. A double irony occurred when, thanks to the popularity of minstrel shows, the cakewalk was heralded as the nation's most fashionable dance from 1900 to 1904.

Theatrical Dance. Basic choreography was an important element in cabaret shows, vaudeville acts, and Broadway revues. Musicals such as *Florodora* (1900), light on plot and heavy on spectacle, were box-office bonanzas. *Florodora,* which featured the high-stepping Florodora Sextette, was so popular that a special train run called "The Florodora Express" deposited theatergoers in Manhattan in time for the curtain. In 1904 another musical, *Piff! Paff! Pouf!,* presented a "Radium Dance," in which chorus girls in luminescent costumes jumped glowing ropes. George M. Cohan, the ultimate Broadway song-and-dance man, seldom resisted adding fancy footwork to the lighthearted plays he wrote, produced, and performed. In 1907 Florenz Ziegfeld presented the first of his "Follies," which starred magnificently clad young women trained in stage movement. Professional ballroom dancers were popular draws in cabarets because they introduced new dance steps. Maurice and Florence Walton, Joan Sawyer and Rudolph Valentino, and Bonnie Glass and Clifton Webb were some of the big names in ballroom dance during the decade.

From Delsartianism to "Dance of the Future." Dance was gaining respectability as an art form as well. A field of study called *expression* (which included a mild form of gymnastic movement, pantomime, and dramatics) had been taught in the United States since the 1820s. Its most popular manifestation was "Delsartianism," named for François Delsarte (1811–1871) and promoted in the United States by actor-director Steele MacKaye (1842–1894). Delsartianism emphasized relaxation, naturalness, and flexibility and was embraced throughout the country by the middle and upper classes as a healthful form of physical culture. Delsartianism helped break down the puritanical and Victorian attitudes Americans had toward the body, but in spite of MacKaye's theatrical applications of the system, it remained essentially an amateur endeavor which, in performance, consisted of statue-posing to music.

Duncan. Isadora Duncan (1878–1927) was the innovator who forged the Delsartian idea into an artistic dance form. Duncan, a native of San Francisco, spent much of her life in Europe, where her bohemian lifestyle and Marxist sympathies were more accepted. Nevertheless, her new theories of dance, as well as her progressive ideas on art in general, education, and women's issues,

Isadora Duncan

influenced American thought for decades. Duncan, who researched all her methods with painstaking care, emphasized the importance of individual expression in dance movement. She rejected the rigidity of classical ballet, although she incorporated ballet into her work and influenced its American future. She called for a dance form that united body and spirit in the manifestation of an "inner music" heard, Duncan suggested, only at the profound center of the being. An eclectic artist, she often based her choreography on literature or classical music, dancing barefoot in loose, flowing costumes. Despite Duncan's lack of popularity in the United States during her lifetime, America was never far from her thoughts. In the emotional culmination of her 1903 essay "The Dance of the Future," Duncan wrote, "I see America dancing. . . . dancing the language of our pioneers, the fortitude of our heroes . . . the justice, kindness, purity of our women. . . . When the Children of America dance in this way, it will make of them Beautiful Beings worthy of the name of Democracy. That will be America dancing."

St. Denis Americanizes an Art. Another product of American Delsartianism was Ruth St. Denis (1878–1968). Although she traveled and toured in Europe, St. Denis, who was more conventional in her personal life than Duncan, did most of her work in the United States. Like Duncan, she rejected the formalism of ballet while still using and influencing its forms, and she, too, devoted much time to academic research of the material that shaped her ideas. Although not the groundbreaker Duncan was, Ruth St. Denis is known as the second great pioneer of American dance.

Beliefs. St. Denis believed the dance to be above all a spiritual art. Drawn at first to Christian Science, St. Denis's also studied yoga and Eastern religious philosophies. It is perhaps a tribute to St. Denis's American sensibilities, however, that one of her most significant spiritual experiences was inspired by an advertising poster. She saw the poster, with its Egyptian motif, in a drugstore while on tour with the theatrical impresario David Belasco. The figure of the goddess Isis, she later wrote, was for her a "universal symbol" that inspired a vision of her next work. The resulting dance piece, finally set in India rather than Egypt, became *Radha,* which she performed to enthusiastic reviews in New York City in 1906. One of St. Denis's major contributions to dance in the United States was simply to popularize it. Her theoretical concerns, inner harmony and spiritual self-improvement, were compatible with American middle-class values. Even her interest in Eastern mysticism followed American thought back to the nineteenth-century transcendentalists. Her triumphant national tour, begun in 1909, enthralled audiences from Boston, Massachusetts, to Chico, California, and created enthusiastic acceptance for modern dance as an art form.

Tap. The purest American dance form to reach the level of art is tap. Developed in the 1800s by African Americans who combined traditional African dances with the Irish jig and the Scottish clog, the intricate figures of tap were perfected and professionalized in the early 1900s. Among the famous tap dancers of the decade were Willie Covan, who began his career before he turned five; Harland Dixon, of the vaudeville duo Dixon and Doyle; Ulysses "Slow Kid" Thompson; and the inim-

LOIE FULLER: BECOMING LIGHT

Loie Fuller's contribution to the dance, and to stage performance in general, is now largely forgotten. In the first decade of the century, however, she was at the apex of her influence; "La Loie" was the darling of Parisian society and a much-admired entertainer of European royalty.

Fuller (1862–1928) began her stage career as a child in Illinois. She performed on the temperance-lecture circuit and in vaudeville until the 1890s when, she recalled, she found a filmy, almost translucent silk skirt in a costume box. As she performed in the costume, lifting its voluminous folds about her body, the audience first whispered, then shouted, its various interpretations: "A butterfly!" "An orchid!" "A spirit!" Loie abandoned acting for dance. Her programs of simple motions and novel lighting effects became nationally famous, and by the turn of the century she was touring Europe.

Experimentation with light and color had become her chief artistic absorption, and, in Paris, Fuller's innovations brought audiences almost to the point of frenzy. For her "Fire Dance" she employed fourteen electricians who bathed the stage in an Impressionist palette of light. Of Fuller's performance (which she danced on a sheet of glass) one reviewer wrote, "luminous streams seemed to flow toward her. With the rhythm of the music the color changed . . . there was a kaleidoscopic vision. Violet, orange, purple, and mauve movements. . . . the hues of the rainbow . . . every fold [of her costume] had its tint and scheme of color intensified . . . until the eye could scarcely bear to look."

Fuller's experimentation with lighting led her to Marie Curie, whom she wrote shortly after the Curies' discovery of radium to inquire how to treat her wings with the substance. The scientist discouraged her. Fuller did, however, experiment with phosphorescent salts mixed with paint for luminescent effects and invented a workable process that was applied both in and out of the theater for many years.

Loie Fuller influenced Isadora Duncan and Ruth St. Denis, both of whom saw her in Paris. Seeing Fuller perform, Duncan wrote in her memoirs, was magical: "Before our very eyes she turned to many-colored and shining orchids, to a wavering flowing sea-flower and at length to a spiral-like lily, all magic of Merlin . . . sorcery of flowing form. What an extraordinary genius. . . . She was one of the first original inspirations of light and changing color — she became light."

itable Bill "Bojangles" Robinson. In 1903 Thomas Edison made a twenty-one-minute film of professional tappers demonstrating time steps, breaks, the strut — and the popular cakewalk.

Sources:

Isadora Duncan, *The Art of the Dance*, edited by Sheldon Cheney (New York: Theatre Arts, 1928);

Lewis A. Erenberg, *Steppin' Out: New York Nightlife and the Transformation of American Culture, 1890–1930* (Westport, Conn.: Greenwood Press, 1981);

Katrina Hazzard-Gordon, *Jookin': The Rise of Social Dance Formations in African-American Culture* (Philadelphia: Temple University Press, 1990);

Paul Magriel, *Chronicles of American Dance* (New York: Holt, 1948);

Thomas L. Morgan and William Barlow, *From Cakewalks to Concert Halls: An Illustrated History of African-American Popular Music from 1895 to 1930* (Washington: Elliott & Clark, 1992);

Nancy Lee Chalfa Ruyter, *Reformers and Visionaries: The Americanization of the Art of Dance* (New York: Dance Horizons, 1979);

Ruth St. Denis, *An Unfinished Life: An Autobiography* (New York: Harper, 1939).

DRAMA: REGARDING BROADWAY

"The Great White Way." By 1900 most of the signs on Broadway had gone electric, and New York City's famous theater district soon became known as "The Great White Way." By 1900 it was the mecca of the American theatrical world: the rest of the country was referred to by people in show business as "the Road." Technically, the New York City theater was as brilliant as its new marquees; artistically, it had not emerged from the nineteenth century's genteel shadow.

Do Not Disturb. Sentimental melodrama passed for legitimate theater. Although they were lavishly produced for maximum appeal, Broadway dramas tended to be thin on plot, weak on character, and heavy on manipulated emotion. The New York City audience in the 1900s was middle class and conservative. Theatergoers who could afford the ever-escalating ticket prices were stubbornly averse to "artiness" and insisted that their expectations regarding decorum be met. They wanted to be driven to tears by the plight of a damsel in distress; they did not wish to be disturbed by plots based on real-world problems. They counted on the presence of a bona fide Broadway star in every production as well as the absence of vulgar language or risqué situations. A play could never cause offense to genteel sensibilities nor suggest that crime paid in any way. It is no wonder that musicals and melodramas were the prime box-office draws of the decade. An occasional London import, such as a Bernard Shaw satire or a J. M. Barrie fantasy, played to appreciative crowds, and a talented group of actors from the Irish National Theatre company was well received on its U.S. tour of 1908, but most popular Broadway drama ran to historical costume pieces, action-adventure Westerns, religious plays, and conventional love stories.

The Syndicate. Commercial theatrical producers were all too happy to accommodate audience demand for spec-

"SINCE YOU WORKED FOR FROHMAN, YOU DON'T KNOW ME ANY MORE"

The pervading influence of Charles Frohman and the Theatrical Syndicate is reflected in this ballad by Thomas J. Grey, a popular "newspaper poet."

'Twas in a crowded railroad train, a soubrette came down
    the aisle,
And she sat beside an actor whom she greeted with a
    smile;
He looked at her with chilly glance and said, 'I guess you
    forget',
And kept looking for his picture in the pink Police Ga-
    zette.
She said, 'Jack dear don't you know me? Just think of days
    of yore?
He threw her a programme and replied, 'I'm with Ethel
    Barrymore,
And I must pick my surroundings, for I'm playing on
    Broadway.'
She just put some powder on her nose and then to him did
    say:

CHORUS
'Since you worked for Frohman you don't know me any
    more,
And I was your sweetheart when you played in repertoire;
Way out in Louisville my love to test —
You had me sew a button on your vest —
Since you worked for Frohman you don't know me any-
    more.'

Source: Alfred L. Bernheim and Sarah Harding, *The Business of the The-atre: An Economic History of the American Theatre, 1750–1932* (New York: Benjamin Blom, 1932), p. 98.

tacle over substance. For them "show business" was no different from any other business. By 1900 Broadway financial backing was almost entirely centralized in a business trust known as the Theatrical Syndicate, headed by entrepreneur Charles Frohman and his fellow theater owners Marc Klaw and Abraham Erlanger. The syndicate would control American theater for the next decade and a half until internal disagreements over money, questionable legal practices, and business rivalry by the Shubert brothers and others weakened its power.

Monopoly. Frohman and his business partners had taken virtual control of Broadway as well as "the road" by offering surefire box-office attractions to theater owners and managers, who in return pledged to book plays and hire artists exclusively through syndicate contracts. Owners who rejected syndicate advances were left to book second- and third-rate shows; managers who failed to sign exclusively with Frohman and his associates were unable to use syndicate-controlled theaters; actors who rebelled were blacklisted. The syndicate also promoted

the star system, which inhibited the development of accomplished drama. Playwrights were commissioned to write vehicles that showcased a certain star's particular abilities, and in doing so subjugated their own talents to the pressure of box-office success. The syndicate was at the height of its power from 1900 to 1909; during the decade it collected 5 to 10 percent of each member theater's gross income and dictated terms to ten thousand members of the theatrical profession. Syndicate-owned plays enjoyed long runs and lucrative road tours, and the syndicate made many actors and playwrights wealthy. Many more were callously exploited by the system and felt a justified resentment toward the monopoly imposed on their art.

Opposition. The syndicate had its enemies, and among them were some of America's best actors and actresses. Minnie Maddern Fiske, a leading lady of the stage and an advocate of realism in acting and playwriting, became an independent producer. She and her husband, Harrison Grey Fiske, brought Henrik Ibsen's modern dramas to the Broadway stage. Arnold Daly (1875–1927) helped establish Bernard Shaw's reputation in the United States by mounting repertory productions of Shaw's work between 1903 and 1905. The talented James O'Neill, father of dramatist Eugene O'Neill, also opposed the monopoly. Relegated to minor theaters, James O'Neill supported his family and made a lifelong career by playing the lead in *The Count of Monte Cristo*. The most effective single response to Frohman and his business partners came from David Belasco (1853–1931), who became the most popular producer-playwright in America during the first decade of the twentieth century. In 1902 Belasco acquired his own theater; he refused to sign with the syndicate, offering high-quality playbills and star players without syndicate backing. The legal battles that ensued resulted in syndicate acceptance of Belasco's terms and signaled the first weakening of the syndicate's grip on show business.

The Shuberts. When the syndicate refused to book Sam and Lee Shubert's productions in 1905 as a punishment for noncompliance with its terms, the brothers decided to branch out on their own. The two men were already successful theatrical producers: since coming to New York City from the "minor leagues" of show business in 1900, they had acquired several theaters and backed many box-office successes despite syndicate control. Now the Shuberts began to mount a massive challenge to Frohman and his associates. They formed an alliance with Belasco, purchased theaters in Philadelphia, and established a New York City–Pittsburgh circuit for their attractions. They gave small theater owners more playbill choices, offered theater managers better terms, and courted the goodwill of other producers. The rivalry was welcomed by those who were feeling the syndicate's artistic and financial muscle, and many producers broke away from the syndicate to shake hands over Shubert contracts instead. In 1905 after Sam Shubert's death in a

CLYDE FITCH: MILLIONAIRE PLAYWRIGHT

In 1902 *Billboard*, the theatrical trades paper, published the following on Clyde Fitch, America's premier playwright:

RESUME

Of the Career of Clyde Fitch, the Playwright

Clyde Fitch, the noted playwright, who has hurried to Berne, Switzerland, for treatment by a noted specialist on appendicitis, in hopes of avoiding an operation, has already accomplished the work of a lifetime, though he has not yet reached the turning post in years. Mr. Fitch's career has been a strenuous one, his rapidity as a playwright having elicited much comment. . . . His literary ability was in no way hereditary, his father having been an army officer who was greatly prejudiced against his son's ambition. . . . Finally, he brought about a compromise between himself and his father, in which it was agreed that if after three years he was not supporting himself with the pen, he should then put aside his ambition and become an architect. The end of the third year approached, and the proceeds from his literary work had failed to materialize. About this time it chanced that he met a friend, who incidentally mentioned that Richard Mansfield was in need of a play. . . . Fitch immediately called upon the actor, and "Beau Brummel" was the result of the conference. Its immediate success assured the sale of future plays, which have been dashed off at the average of two a year ever since.

Clyde Fitch was America's first millionaire playwright, but the judgment of critics is that he bartered his talent to the Syndicate, which employed him; he was, nevertheless, a skillful practitioner with an ear for realistic dialogue and an eye for detailed stage effects. Fitch died in 1909 of the appendicitis he hoped to avoid.

Source: Joseph Csida and June Bundy Csida, *American Entertainment: A Unique History of Show Business* (New York: Watson-Guptill, 1978), p. 123.

train wreck while en route to acquire theater property in Pittsburgh, Jacob Shubert joined Lee in the show-business enterprise. Although in later years the Shubert system became nearly as dictatorial as the syndicate, in the early 1900s the brothers' encroachment on syndicate territory was seen as a positive victory for the theatrical profession against a business conglomerate.

Dramatists. Mass appeal was the mode of the day, but a few American dramatists, whether they worked with commercial producers or not, managed to further the art of drama while they pleased the public. Although these men and women are not remembered as great writers,

they were creative and skillful practitioners. Many addressed contemporary issues and treated characters and plots realistically; others brought about a revival of interest in poetic drama with their literate verse plays. Rachel Crothers (1878–1958), whose long career was just beginning in the early 1900s, took a feminist point of view in *The Three of Us* (1906) and *A Man's World* (1909). Clyde Fitch (1865–1909) was a prolific writer whose finest plays presented realistic human problems through concise characterizations and intense dramatic situations. *The Climbers* (1901), *The Girl With Green Eyes* (1902), and *The City* (1909) are among Fitch's best. William Vaughn Moody (1869–1910), a poet and university professor, wrote poetic dramas with religious themes but is remembered primarily for two prose plays, *The Great Divide* (1906), often called the first modern American drama, and *The Faith Healer* (1909). Moody's student, Josephine Preston Peabody Marks (1874–1922) was another significant poet-dramatist, as was Percy MacKaye (1875–1956). Edward Sheldon (1886–1946) and Eugene Walter (1874–1941) wrote moving character studies; Sheldon's *Salvation Nell* (1908) and Walter's *The Easiest Way* (1909) are both about women who struggle to extract themselves from poverty and abuse. Charles Klein (1867–1915) was an immensely popular playwright whose 1905 hit, *The Lion and the Mouse*, ran for an unprecedented two years on Broadway. Klein's portrayal of monopolistic money interests was inspired by journalist Ida M. Tarbell's exposé of the Standard Oil trust, and the play's main character closely resembled oil baron John D. Rockefeller. The prevailing tendency toward melodrama kept these writers from exploring fully the possibilities of character development and motivation-based action, but through their efforts a tentative modernity, at least, had reached the American stage.

Social Comedy and Farce. Comedy, more often than not, comments on society's faults and foibles. The comedic playwrights of the 1900s were showered with excellent material. William Clyde Fitch earned an international reputation with his comedies of manners and his farces, many of which satirized the American art of social climbing. Plays such as Langdon Mitchell's *The New York Idea* (1907) took aim at marriage and divorce. The erstwhile hero of Winchell Smith and Byron Ongley's *Brewster's Millions* (1906) must spend a million dollars in order to inherit millions more; *The Fortune Hunter* (1909) by Smith and Ongley concerns marrying for money. Inherited wealth created the pivotal situations in Augustus Thomas's farcical *On the Quiet* (1901), which was based on the true story of a young man who secretly married against his family's wishes. Master farceur George Ade spoofed American imperialism in *The Sultan of Sulu* (1902), small-town politics in *The County Chairman* (1903), the importance of college football in *The College Widow* (1904), the value of a college education itself in *Just Out of College* (1905), and the value of success in *Artie* (1907). The satirists of the decade were popular

Ruth St. Denis

Universities and colleges were slow to recognize the teaching of dramatic literature and playwriting as fields of study, but in 1904 Professor George Pierce Baker (1866–1935) began a playwriting class at Radcliffe College. The next year it was offered at Harvard (all-female Radcliffe's brother-school) as "English 47: The Forms of the Drama." Baker's class attracted Eugene O'Neill and Edward Sheldon, among others, before Baker, unable to convince Harvard of the viability of a drama program, moved to New Haven and helped establish the Yale School of Drama. One of Baker's students, Frederick Koch, moved to the University of North Dakota in 1905 to teach theater, and the next year an acting course was taught at the University of Wisconsin. Baylor University in Texas had a technical production course as early as 1901; in fact, the "little theater" movement was to a large degree sponsored by America's colleges and universities; higher education provided virtually the only subsidized theater in the nation — meaning that college and university playhouses were among the few theaters not dependent on box-office receipts for success and could thus provide testing grounds for experimental practices.

because their plays were genial and amusing; they avoided sharp-edged social commentary, and their good-natured jibes at society brought them success at the box office.

Musicals and Operettas. By far the most popular type of Broadway entertainment from 1900 to 1909 was the musical. Although the form did not reach its artistic zenith until the 1940s, musicals, despite their slim plots, often featured lively and engaging tunes, spectacular scenery, pretty girls, and popular comedians. George M. Cohan, Florenz Ziegfeld, Gus and Max Rogers (billed as "The Rogers Brothers"), and the comedy team of Joe Weber and Lew Fields were among those who wrote, produced, and acted in musical shows. Some musicals were based on well-known stories or popular novels: *Chris and the Wonderful Lamp* (1900) and *The Tattooed Man* (1907) were Arabian Nights tales retold; *The Sleeping Beauty and the Beast* (1901) was a hybrid fairy tale from London reworked for the American stage; and *The Wizard of Oz* (1903) was the first of several musical adaptations of L. Frank Baum's best-selling novel of 1900. Victor Herbert's operettas are still remembered and performed: *Babes in Toyland* (1903), *Mlle. Modiste* (1905), and *The Red Mill* (1906) were some of his most prominent stage successes. Gustav Luder was another leading composer of operettas; with Henry Savage and Frank Pixley he wrote *The Prince of Pilsen* (1902), known for the rousing "Heidelberg Stein Song." Most Broadway musicals of the decade, however, were uninspired revues, notable only for their stars — Anna Held, Trixie Friganza, Marie Dressler, Lillian Russell, and Eva Tanguay all became celebrities in the early 1900s — or for the songs

they made famous. "Shine On Harvest Moon" and "In the Good Old Summertime," both introduced in musicals of the decade, are still American favorites.

African Americans on the Stage. It is not surprising that The Great White Way was "white" in more ways than one in the early 1900s. Although white actors frequently put on blackface to play comedic parts, African American performers were not often seen. One musical, *The Southerners* (1904), caused great audience consternation when a black chorus was featured with a white cast. Yet some black actors were able to break through Broadway's wall of prejudice and become headliners. Among them were Bert Williams and his partner George Walker. *In Dahomey* (1903) was the first full-length Broadway musical written and performed by African Americans; Williams and Walker starred as two swindlers who stir up trouble in the African colony of Dahomey (now Benin). The pair took their modest Broadway hit to London, where it enjoyed a seven-month run, and they returned to Broadway with *Abyssinia* (1906) and *Bandanaland* (1908), a solid triumph with a show-stopping cakewalk number. Composer Will Marion Cook and poet Paul Laurence Dunbar collaborated with Williams and Walker. Walker's wife, Ada Overton Walker, not only choreographed and acted, but when her husband became ill, she dressed as his character and took

George M. Cohan, center, singing "Give My Regards to Broadway" in *Little Johnny Jones,* 1904, which he wrote, staged, composed music for, and starred in

his place on the stage. Other African Americans who achieved Broadway success included songwriter-performers Bob Cole and the sibling team of J. Rosamond and James Weldon Johnson. Their first musical was *The Shoo-Fly Regiment* (1907), a critically acclaimed depiction of bravery during the Spanish-American War. The next year the trio presented *Red Moon*, which concerned the betrothal of a beautiful maiden (Abbie Mitchell) of mixed Indian and African parentage. White playwright Edward Sheldon shocked audiences in 1909 with *The Nigger*, a melodrama about a bigoted southern governor who discovers an African American ancestor.

Other Minorities. Asians and Hispanics were virtually nonexistent on the Broadway stage early in the century, although Native Americans were sometimes depicted sympathetically. Edwin Milton Royle's *Squaw Man* (1905) portrayed a doomed romance between an Indian woman and an English soldier. Also in 1905 William C. DeMille treated the same theme in *Strong Heart*, and in 1906 William A. Brady's *The Redskin* featured ten Sioux actors. The plots of David Belasco's drama *The Auctioneer* (1901) and the musical *Sally in Our Alley* (1902), among others, involved Jewish characters. Best remembered for the phrase it introduced into American speech is Englishman Israel Zangwill's comedy-drama of Jewish life, *The Melting Pot* (1909). But in the first decade of the twentieth century, when ethnic and racial stereotyping was common, most minority groups were depicted onstage with something less than dignity. What was worse, genuine artistic talent often went to waste because of

exclusionary hiring practices, despite inroads to equality made by courageous actors, musicians, and writers.

Actors and Actresses. Going to the theater in the early 1900s was a major social event that required formal attire, and the thrill of partaking in the life of the theater, even as a spectator, was enhanced by the promise of seeing a renowned performer in a starring role. The company of leading actresses and actors was sought by socialites; the public clamored to see their favorites in choice parts; and theatrical celebrities could count on loyal audiences late into their careers. Some new stars of the decade came from theatrical royalty: twenty-year-old Ethel Barrymore shot to stardom in 1901 with Fitch's light comedy *Captain Jinks of the Horse Marines*. But Barrymore's father, Maurice, and her mother, Georgianna Drew, were noted thespians of the previous generation; her brother Lionel had distinguished himself in the 1890s; and John, her younger sibling, would make his stage debut in 1903. Maude Adams boosted her celebrity when she played Peter Pan in 1905; the diminutive actress charmed audiences but lived a quiet personal life. Other well-known actors and actresses in a decade of notable talent were Jacob P. Adler, who played a Yiddish-speaking Shylock in *The Merchant of Venice* in 1903; Blanche Bates and Amelia Bingham, who starred in some of the most extravagantly produced plays of the decade; Shakespearean performers Mrs. Leslie Carter, Ada Rehan, and Otis Skinner; and Joseph Jefferson, whose legendary career playing the title character in *Rip Van Winkle* was marked by his naturalistic characterization.

Producer David Belasco

Stage Realism. Acting had not achieved the realism that is now standard on stage and screen, and a present-day theatergoer would be amused by the grandiose gestures, unnatural enunciation, and unabashed exploitation of the actor's "moment" or "point" — a line, phrase, or movement performed specifically to garner thunderous applause — a method employed by many Broadway stars. But realistic set design, for which Belasco in particular was famous, was the phenomenon of the era. The previous century's reliance on painted backdrops gave way to attempts at truth to life. Onstage waterfalls, actual table settings and menu items from a famous Manhattan restaurant, the wallpaper and furnishings from a run-down Bowery boardinghouse, effectively accurate special effects of blizzards and tornadoes, and fourteen-minute sunset-to-sunrise sequences were all among the marvels of the decade's realistic staging.

Premodern. As with so many other businesses in the flush times of the early 1900s, show business was booming. The syndicate, which in every way resembled a trust and whose economic malpractices were evident, was making money like the well-oiled machine it was. Plays were popular entertainment, and American drama was both sumptuous and surprising. Broadway hits enjoyed long runs and lucrative road tours. But the commercial motive on which American theater was being run meant providing popular entertainment rather than relevant

theater and sacrificing dramatic experimentation to box-office profit. American drama was still premodern in the first decade of the century and would not be recognized as a significant artistic force until 1915, when the Provincetown Players and others would inspire the movement away from Broadway and toward the "little" theaters where the art of American drama would experience its first real unfolding.

Dramatic Criticism. A spirit of reform was affecting the country at large in the first years of the 1900s, and American theater was in many ways reforming itself. Realistic drama, naturalistic acting techniques, and advances in scene design and theater architecture were taking hold, while independent producers, as well as ethnic and university theaters, were beginning to contribute to the genesis of modern drama. The "new" discipline of dramatic criticism also did much to stimulate thinking on the state of drama as literature. Although the first publications devoted solely to the theater had appeared in the 1870s, the debut of *Theatre Magazine* in 1900 marked a significant maturation of the genre. Critics such as William Dean Howells, Brander Matthews, Walter Pritchard Eaton, and James Gibbons Huneker were some of the first to set high standards for contemporary American drama in their essays and retrospectives. Press reviewers, among them William Winter and John Corbin, were making serious observations about quality, and the practice of "puffing" (praising) certain plays for pay declined. As criticism grew in stature and authority, American theater began to come of age as an expression of America's cultural vitality.

Sources:

Alfred L. Bernheim and Sarah Harding. *The Business of the Theatre: An Economic History of the American Theatre, 1750–1932.* (New York: Benjamin Blom, 1932);

Oscar G. Brockett and Robert R. Findlay, *Century of Innovation: A History of European and American Theatre and Drama since 1870* (Englewood Cliffs, N.J.: Prentice-Hall, 1984);

Joseph Csida and June Bundy Csida, *American Entertainment: A Unique History of Show Business* (New York: Watson-Guptill, 1978);

Paul Kuritz, *The Making of Theatre History* (Englewood Cliffs, N.J.: Prentice Hall, 1988);

Glenn Loney, *20th Century Theatre*, volume 1 (New York: Facts On File, 1983);

Walter Meserve, *An Outline History of American Drama* (New York: Feedback Theatre Books & Prospero Press, 1994).

LITERATURE: STORMING THE GENTEEL

Genteel. Harvard professor George Santayan used the term *Genteel Tradition* in 1911 to describe the state of American literature and philosophy in the years following the turn of the century. Santayana felt that the prevailing literary mode was insipid and vague. Many others agreed with him. American literature especially poetry, seemed to be deferential to Europe and dedicated to the pursuit of the refined; it had little to do with life-as-lived but rather celebrated the romantic ideal. Mossy banks and sunlit groves proliferated in this

Theatrical star Lillian Russell, best known for her role in comic operas

Harvard professor George Santayana, who defined the Genteel Tradition in American literature

kind of poetry; verses spilled over with "poetic diction"; themes were uplifting; serious challenge to the intellect was rare. But a new generation of writers shattered these conventions in the 1900s, exploring previously forbidden topics and new forms of expression.

Poetry. Poetry was popular with the decade's newspaper and magazine readers. Paul Laurence Dunbar (1872–1906), and James Whitcomb Riley (1849–1916) were among the most accomplished of the popular poets. The title of one of Dunbar's best collections, *Lyrics of Love and Laughter* (1903), suggests the type of poetry the genteel tradition inspired, while Riley is best remembered for poems such as "Little Orphan Annie" and "The Raggedy Man," both published in *Book of Joyous Children* in 1902. T. A. Daly (1871–1949) wrote Irish and Italian immigrant dialect poems; his first collection, *Canzoni* (1906), sold fifty thousand copies. Edwin Markham (1852–1940) was one of the few socially aware poets of the era; the popularity of his sympathetic portrayal of a farmer, "Man with the Hoe" (1899), allowed him the freedom to devote his full time to writing; Markham's "Lincoln, the Man of the People" (1901) praises the abolition of slavery. Much of what Edwin Arlington Robinson (1869–1935) wrote from 1900 to 1909 ("Aunt Imogen," 1902; "Miniver Cheevy," 1907) caused him to be remembered as the first important American poet of the century. Louise Imogen Guiney (1861–1930), Louise Chandler Moulton (1865–1908), and Jessie Rittenhouse (1869–1948) were all poets dedicated to the genteel mode. But Lizette Woodworth Reese (1856–1935) and Anna Hempstead Branch (1875–1937), although traditional, anticipated the Imagist poets of the 1910s and 1920s with their clear, concrete descriptions. In general, however, American poetry from 1900 to 1909 was in what critic Edmund Clarence Stedman (1833–1908) called "a twilight interval." The new age of American poetry did not arrive until after 1912, when the modernist revolution finally succeeded.

Realism. The attempt to present human life as accurately as possible through the arts began as a movement in the 1700s and was an accepted artistic concept by the mid nineteenth century, but artists' definitions of honest portrayal kept evolving. Objectivity and complex characterization coupled with rejection of the idealistic, the sentimental, and the melodramatic were the goals of literary realists. Henry James, William Dean Howells, and Mark Twain were the first to be acknowledged as American realists, and all these were greats on the literary landscape of the 1900s. Though Twain's best work was behind him, he remained a popular and revered figure. James, by the 1900s an established expatriate, wrote three of his major novels during the decade: *The Ambassadors* (1903), *The Golden Bowls* (1904), and *The American* (1907). Edith Wharton (1862–1937), whose style and subject matter were influenced by James, observed the rigidity and hypocrisy of her own upper class with precision and grace in *The House of Mirth* (1905); Jack London's early 1900s adventure novels, including *The Call of the Wild* (1903), were told in gritty detail. In the first decade of the twentieth century fiction writers were intent on honing their skills of observation and their understanding of social problems. Their efforts resulted in increasingly accurate portrayals of believable characters reacting to probable situations, making realism the dominant mode of American literature.

Howells. William Dean Howells (1837–1920), critic, editor, essayist, novelist, and playwright, who has been called the "Father of American Realism," was an important traditional figure in American letters. But Howells, although his work reflected everyday reality, did not begin to approach the accurate portrayals of American society that later writers achieved. Howells's novels had intrigued the reading public with their apparent truth to life in the 1890s; by the turn of the century he was an elder statesman of American literature, concentrating on editing *Harper's Monthly* and writing a column called "The Editor's Easy Chair." In this public forum Howells advocated absolute scientific detachment in the literary examination of life, emphasizing the notion that realistic detail was fundamental to strong writing. Howells's own fictional characters were models for his theory; their behavior was consistently determined by the natural occurrences of daily life, and they responded with the commonplace, ordinary speech that often masks complex psychological reactions. Howells, however, championed only the kind of realism that portrayed "the more smiling aspects of American life." His talent for truthful characterization was undermined by his insistence on limiting his subject matter to the life of the middle class and remaining, literarily, in a bourgeois world of dinner invitations, commuter trains, and shopping trips.

Naturalism. The early-twentieth-century naturalist writers were the most uncompromising of the realists. For them, truly realistic writing excluded everything but the physical world; the only valid perception was sense perception. Naturalist writers subscribed to a philosophy of determinism, insisting that moral choices are nonexistent in a universe ruled by the physical factors of heredity and environment. Trapped in the physical world, the characters in a naturalist tale live more-sordid, more-urgent lives. The smiling aspects of life are overshadowed by the grimmest of realities. Stephen Crane (1871–1900), Frank Norris (1870-1902) and Hamlin Garland (1860–1940) were the first American writers to adopt the naturalistic style, but Theodore Dreiser (1871–1945), whose *Sister Carrie* (1900) was not actively supported by its publisher because of its shockingly naturalistic content, is considered by many the century's best exemplar of the genre.

Norris. Frank Norris (1870–1902) lived the literary life he believed in: he said that the novelist should "sacrifice money, fashion, and popularity for the greater reward of realizing that he has told the truth." Norris's naturalism was influenced by French writer Emile Zola, whose works Norris studied at the University of California: like Zola, Norris suggested that both nature and human behavior should be defined without regard to current Victorian notions of good and evil, and that the question of what it means to be human in an amoral universe should be foremost in the the artist's mind. Norris began a trilogy, three novels on the American West and the growth and distribution of wheat, in 1900. *The Octopus* (1901), which dealt with the stranglehold the railroads had on American wheat farmers, was immediately successful; then followed *The Pit* (1903), another best-seller, which went far to expose the corruption in the American wheat market. A third novel, *The Wolf*, about European wheat consumption, was left unfinished when Norris — whose reputation as a writer was growing rapidly — died at the age of thirty-two of a ruptured appendix.

Naturalistic novelist Frank Norris

Yes, the railroad had prevailed. The ranches had been seized in the tentacles of the octopus; the iniquitous burden of extortionate freight trains had been imposed like a yoke of iron. The monster had killed Harran, had killed Osterman, had killed Broderson, had killed Hooven. It had beggared Magnus and driven him to a state of semi-insanity after he had wrecked his honor in the vain attempt to do evil that good might come. It had enticed Lyman into its toils to pluck from him his manhood and his honesty, corrupting him and poisoning him beyond redemption; it had hounded Dyke from his legitimate employment and had made of him a highwayman and criminal. It had cast forth Mrs. Hooven to starve to death upon the city streets. It had driven Minna to prostitution. It had slain Annixter at the very moment when painfully and manfully he had at last achieved his own salvation and stood forth resolved to do right, to act unselfishly and to live for others. It had widowed Hilma in the very dawn of her happiness. It had killed the very babe within the mother's womb, strangling life ere yet it had been born, stamping out the spark ordained by God to burn through all eternity.

What then was left? Was there no hope, no outlook for the future, no rift in the black curtain, no glimmer through the night? Was good to be thus overthrown? Was evil thus to be strong and to prevail? Was nothing left?

Source: Frank Norris, *The Octopus* (New York: Dougleday, Page, 1901), p. 457.

Socialism and the Novel. Many writers in the early years of the century, particularly those who embraced the tenets of naturalism, also looked upon socialism as a valid means of reform. Their fictional works criticized social and political imbalance in the American way of life; many of their works were not only popular and critical successes but also inspired the public outcries that brought major changes in the American workplace. Jack London (1876–1916) was one of America's best-known adventure writers and socialists in the 1900s. A former manual laborer, seafarer, and vagrant, he seized upon writing as an avenue to middle-class stability. His adventure novels, as he admitted, came from the desire to make money through writing. But his socialist novels (*The War of the Classes,* 1904; *The Human Drift,* 1907) exhibited his loyalty to his working-class origins and demonstrated his profound desire to right the wrongs of American life. Upton Sinclair (1878–1968) was a reform writer whose influence on popular opinion had positive political repercussions. *The Jungle* (1906), his realistic account of working conditions in the Chicago meatpacking industry, won him wide recognition and led to the passage of the country's first pure food laws. In 1908 Sinclair attacked capitalism and urban life in *The Metropolis.*

Women. Regionalists Mary E. Wilkins Freeman (1852–1930) and Sarah Orne Jewett (1849–1909) did their best work in the late 1800s, although Freeman's *By the Light of the Soul* (1906) was well received and in 1908 her novel *The Shoulders of Atlas* won a transatlantic writing contest. Charlotte Perkins Gilman (1860–1935) enjoyed an international reputation as a sociologist and champion of women's rights in the early 1900s; *The Home* and *Human Work* (both 1904) were thoughtful analyses of societal roles. One contemporary of these three well-known writers was Harriet Prescott Spofford, whose *Old Madame and Other Stories* and *Old Washington* appeared in 1900 and 1906, respectively. Although sometimes overlooked in literature courses and anthologies, Spofford published eight books and 374 articles during her long career. The decade also saw the beginning of the writing careers of Mary Austin (1868–1934) and Ellen Glasgow (1873–1945). Austin's *Land of Little Rain* (1903), set in the arid Southwest, was her first and most famous novel; she followed with *Lost Borders* in 1909 and

Edwin Markham, author of "The Man with the Hoe"

wrote on into the 1930s, frequently taking a strong feminist stance in her fiction. Glasgow, a southerner, was told by the first publisher she approached to go home and get married. Glasgow's realistic novels of life in Virginia often dealt with women's roles in southern society. *The Voice of the People* (1900) and *The Deliverance* (1904) were among Glasgow's early novels. (She won the Pulitzer Prize for fiction in 1942.)

Racial Focus. One reason so many writers of the early 1900s — women, African Americans, and Asian Americans in particular — have not been studied in the latter part of the century is that publishing houses were reluctant to risk taking on writers whose subject matter might not appeal to a wide readership. Many talented literary artists were forced to serialize their works in magazines; only recently have reprints of novels by writers such as Pauline Elizabeth Hopkins been made available. Hopkins (1859–1930) was the author of *Contending Forces: A Romance Illustrative of Negro Life, North and South* in 1900; the novel was melodramatic in style but conveyed Hopkins's fierce anger at the victimization of African American women. Hopkins wrote four novels, a play, and numerous short stories during her literary career. Much of her work was published in the *Colored American Magazine,* established in 1900. Charles Waddell Chesnutt (1858–1932) was fortunate in convincing Houghton

Mifflin to publish his first novel, *The House Behind the Cedars,* in 1900; *The Marrow of Tradition* and *The Colonel's Dream* followed in 1901 and 1905, respectively; although *The Marrow of Tradition* impressed William Dean Howells, neither book sold well. In the past twenty-five years, however, Chesnutt has become recognized for his contributions to the African American literary tradition.

Native Americans and the West. The West still held a fascination for Americans, possibly because of a national awareness of the now-vanished frontier. Owen Wister and Zane Grey became best-selling authors with their stories of the "Wild West," and Hamlin Garland (1860–1940) wrote sympathetically about Native Americans in *The Captain of the Gray Horse Troop* (1902). Native Americans themselves, however, were writing prolifically during the first decade of the century, and many whose work has recently been "rediscovered" achieved wide readership and critical acclaim during their lives. Alexander Lawrence Posey's (1873–1908) career as a journalist gained him national recognition; he was the first Native American to establish a daily newspaper, the *Indian Journal.* Taking the pen name Fus Fixico (Heartless Bird), Posey satirized tribal politics in a series of "letters to the editor" from 1902 to 1908. John Milton Oskison (1874–1947), a Cherokee, was a popular regionalist writer who brought scenes of territory life to a national audience during the early 1900s. He worked as an editor for both *The Saturday Evening Post* and *Collier's Weekly* from 1903 to 1910. Oskison's *The Problem of Old Harjo* (1907) is an ironic comment on the good intentions of whites toward Indians. Gertrude Bonnin (1876–1938), a Lakota Sioux also known as Zitkala-Sa (Red Bird), was both a writer and an Indian rights activist. "Impressions of an Indian Childhood," "The School Days of an Indian Girl," and "An Indian Teacher Among Indians" were all published in *The Atlantic Monthly* beginning in 1900. Charles Alexander Eastman (1858–1939) lived in both the white and Indian worlds and throughout his life was conflicted in his loyalties. Also called Ohiyesa, Eastman was the son of a Sioux father and a white mother who led a traditional Sioux life until his newly Christianized father removed him from the reservation. Ohiyesa set down his recollections in *Indian Boyhood* (1902), *Red Hunters and the Animal People* (1904), *Old Indian Days* (1907), and *Wigwam Evenings* (with Elaine Goodale Eastman, 1909). In 1902 Ohiyesa wrote "The Indian no longer exists as a free man. Those remnants that dwell upon the reservations present only a sort of tableau — a fictional copy of the past."

Cultural Variety. American Jewish writer Abraham Cahan (1860–1951) was a novelist, journalist, editor (he headed the *Jewish Daily Forward* from 1903 until 1946), and pragmatic socialist. He examined the American Dream of Success in later works, but in 1905 his historical novel about revolutionary Russia, *The White Terror and the Red,* was praised for its vivid realism. Asian American writer Edith Maude Eaton signed her Chinese name, Sui Sin Far, to her popular short stories that appeared in many magazines during the early 1900s. She and her sister, novelist Winnifred Eaton (Onoto Watanna), were the first known Asian American writers of fiction. Sui Sin Far's short stories, collected as *Mrs. Spring Fragrance* (1912), and her autobiographical essay, "Leaves from the Mental Portfolio of a Eurasian" (1909), express the sense of injustice felt by marginalized Americans.

Dusk or Dawn? Much of the literature written from 1900 to 1909 has been forgotten, but not because it is forgettable literature. Much of what was written during the decade was robust and clear. Social problems were addressed — sometimes with subtle irony, often with forceful statement. Writers of different ethnic and racial backgrounds who held a variety of philosophies contributed generously to the national literary output. The term *twilight*, used by E. C. Stedman to refer to the literary atmosphere of the early 1900s, is as ambiguous as the intermediate state it defines. Twilight can be that period of day between sunset and full night or between sunrise and full day — the question present-day readers will answer for themselves is whether the literary twilight at the turn of the century was a dusk or a dawn.

Sources:

Amy Ling, "Edith Eaton: Pioneer Chinamerican and Feminist," in *American Literary Realism*, 16, no. 2 (1983): 287–298;

David Perkins, *A History of Modern Poetry: From the 1890s to the High Modernist Mode* (Cambridge, Mass.: Harvard University Press, 1976).

Ziegfeld girl Anna Held; she married Florenz Ziegfeld in 1897.

LIVE THEATER VARIATIONS

Vaudeville. Variety entertainment was at the height of its popularity in the United States during the first decade of the century. Vaudeville shows were attended by members of all classes and appeared — via the theatrical chains known as circuits — in nearly every town in the country. American vaudeville had little to do with the French *vaudeville*, a light musical-comedy form. The name *vaudeville* was developed as a means of distinguishing theatrical variety shows from vulgar saloon entertainments, which featured "leg shows" and striptease. Vaudeville shows consisted of eight to ten acts: jugglers, animal acts, acrobats, song-and-dance teams, magicians, ventriloquists, male and female impersonators, skits, recitations, and appearances by celebrities of the day — including criminals, who reflected on their sordid pasts. Many performers who later became film, radio, and television stars (George Burns and Gracie Allen, Jack Benny, Bob Hope, and Milton Berle among them) got their start in vaudeville.

On the Vaudeville Bill. The stars of the vaudeville stage in the early 1900s included Leo Carrillo (1881–1961), a member of one of California's oldest and most respected families, who later became "Pancho" in the 1950s television series *The Cisco Kid*; Julian Eltinge (1883–1941), a female impersonator whose 1907 success as "The Simpson Girl" was a spoof of the famous "Gibson Girl" look; and Eddie Foy (1854–1928) an Irish mimic, pantomimist, and dancer whose courage during the Iroquois Theater fire in 1903 earned him the admiration of his fellow actors. Irene Franklin (1876–1941) was known for her "kid" songs ("I'm Nobody's Baby Now") and adept characterizations of ordinary workingwomen. Ernest Hogan (1859–1909), an African American artist, was confident that vaudeville drew "no color line," until attacked by a New York City mob in 1900; undaunted, he stayed in vaudeville and the next year was commanding the then-impressive weekly salary of $300. Bonnie Thornton (1871–1920), one of vaudeville's first headliners, posed for an Adams Chewing Gum ad in 1900 and became "The Original Tutti Frutti Girl." Al Jolson (1886–1950), Sophie Tucker (1887–1966), and Ed Wynn (1886–1966) all made their vaudeville debuts during the decade.

Eccentrics. Some vaudeville acts were popular for their eccentricity: Blatz the Human Fish ate, read, and played the trombone underwater; Alfred Latell, Animal Impersonator, specialized in bears, goats, and monkeys. Adgie and Her Lions ("once seen, her marvelous work is not forgotten," read the ad) did Spanish dances and performed Delsartian movements, while prohibitionist

Ethnic theater in the United States provided both a profession and a social world for early-twentieth-century immigrants. Cultural and language ties were maintained through the performances and through the act of gathering together to view them. Theatricals provided a festive, nurturing atmosphere, and ethnic theater groups supported other community institutions, from public charities to parochial schools. In the first decade of the century, when immigration was at high tide, ethnic theaters flourished not only in urban areas but also as traveling troupes. Yiddish theater was especially popular in the East, but many other ethic groups also had their own theater troupes. Mexican American repertory companies had been active since the last third of the nineteenth century, and more than a hundred troupes toured Texas, New Mexico, and California during 1900–1909. The best known was the Hernandez-Villalongin Company, which, like other groups of its kind, presented plays from Germany, Italy, France, and Spain as well as works of the Mexican repertoire. Chinese theater, which thrived on the West Coast, was predominantly operatic. Polish American theaters grew up in Cleveland, Detroit, and Milwaukee, and Madame Helena Modjeska (1840–1909), world-renowned Shakespearean actress, appeared many times in Chicago. The Slovakian dramatic society Narod (The Nation) was founded in New York in 1900, the first of many Slovak theatrical organizations active in the decade. Italian American marionette theaters and café entertainments developed in urban centers, and in San Francisco, Italian American theater was among the first to recover from the 1906 earthquake. The actress Antionetta Pisanelli Alessandro, who had arrived in California in 1905, generated the interest of the non-Italian population, and her business acumen led to her sponsorship of nickelodeons, vaudeville troupes, and Commedia dell'Arte (a form of improvisational theater), as well as presentations of Dumas, Goethe, Sardou, and Shakespeare. Immigrant theater in the United States declined as the century wore on and cultural differences became less pronounced, but in the first decade of the century it provided not only an artistic but a social refuge for the thousands of recently arrived new Americans who found theater in their own language to be "reserved seats," where emotions could be released through laughter — and tears: "I go to a heart-rending drama because my boss has deducted a cent-and-a-half [for the piecework I do] and my heart is heavy — and I am ashamed to cry. . . . when I see how Hamlet holds in his hands the skull of his friend . . . and speaks about life and death, I suddenly recall that they have deducted a cent-and-a-half and I cry real tears."

Source: Moishe Nadir, "I, The Theater Goer," in *Ethnic Theater in the United States*, edited by Maxine Schwartz Seller (Westport, Conn.: Greenwood Press, 1983).

Carry Nation took a hatchet to the set at every performance of "Ten Nights in a Barroom." Chung Ling Soo (born W. E. Robinson) caught bullets in his teeth and died in the act.

Powerful Producers. Antonio "Tony" Pastor (1837–1908), a former childhood violin prodigy and circus clown, became "The Father of Vaudeville" when he succeeded in promoting "clean" variety in New York City theaters in the 1880s, attracting a family audience with special matinees and door prizes. But he paid his performers low salaries and was soon overtaken by entrepreneurs Benjamin Keith (1846–1914) and Edward Albee (1857–1930). Keith and Albee introduced the "continuous show," in which a spectator could enter a theater at any time between 9:30 A.M. and 10:30 P.M. to see performances or films. The partners also transformed the tawdry playhouses they acquired into elegant theatrical palaces designed to attract a middle-class clientele. In 1906 the Keith-Albee circuit became the United Booking Office and dominated vaudeville in the eastern United States, while Martin Beck's Orpheum circuit played the West. Other circuits were operated by William Morris, Marcus Loew, Alexander Pantages, and F. F. Proctor. The Theatre Owners Booking Association controlled the African American circuit, and its oppressive tactics soon caused the initials *TOBA* to be interpreted by performers as "Tough on Black Asses." By 1905 vaudeville was a highly organized, nationwide big business, with "big time" or "two-a-day" theaters that presented two variety performances a day, and "small-time" houses that offered three to twelve shows a day. The powerful booking agencies demanded kickbacks, imposed fines, and blacklisted performers in the same manner as the Broadway theater syndicate.

Organized Response. Conditions were indeed tough on most vaudeville performers, who responded by forming actors' unions such as the White Rats (1900), to offset the oppressive operations of the Vaudeville Managers Protective Association. The Colored Vaudeville Benefit Association (1909) was an extension of an earlier

Crystal Hall, on East Fourteenth Street in New York City

African American performers' union formed in 1906. The White Rats failed to sustain their strike against the Eastern Association of Vaudeville Managers in 1901, as racial tension between the essentially segregated groups of actors prevented a united response to the unfair practices of managers and producers.

Minstrelsy on the Wane. Minstrelsy, a variety entertainment that had been popular since the Civil War, was beginning to wane by 1900 but nonetheless remained an important presence on the American stage. Minstrelsy, a combination of sentimental ballads, comic dialogue, and lively dances, is one of only a few authentic American entertainment forms. At the turn of the century, as black minstrels attempted to reclaim aspects of pre–Civil War performances, minstel shows were being staged by whites and blacks, both of whom "blacked up" their faces. The comic stereotyping of African Americans that was the essence of minstrelsy was also part of vaudeville as a whole. Dutch, Irish, Jewish, Swedish, and Italian "comics" were all familiar to audiences of the decade, but the mockery inherent in minstrelsy devolved more significantly on the lives of Americans of African heritage than did the comic presentations of white Americans. Minstrelsy did provide African American performers with an avenue into mainstream American theater, and the minstrel show performed by African Americans was also the first venue in which ragtime, jazz, and blues were performed for white audiences. Lew Dockstadter (a.k.a. George Alfred Clapp, 1856–1925) and his partner George Primrose were the most popular of the white minstrels of the decade; Eddie Cantor and Al Jolson got their initial stage training in minstrelsy and appeared in blackface as late as the 1920s. Many African Americans who performed in minstrel shows, however, soon sought to move away from minstrelsy's degrading stereotypes; Bert Williams and George Walker, Bob Cole, and the Johnson Brothers were among those who moved into vaudeville and from there to Broadway musicals. Gertrude "Ma" Rainey remained with minstrelsy until the 1910s.

Yiddish Theater. Yiddish-language theater, one of the many cultural institutions brought to the United States by European Jewish immigrants, became an important intellectual and social mainstay in the Jewish communities that expanded rapidly in urban America. Nearly a dozen Yiddish theaters flourished in New York City around the turn of the century. Forms and styles ranged from the highest poetic drama to the broadest slapstick and drew audiences from every socio-economic group. "Shund" theater (*shund* meaning rubbish) was the lowest form of popular entertainment and was looked down upon by more-Americanized Jews as "greenhorn" fare. Yet many talented performers began their careers in this variety style. Molly Picon (1898–1992), for example, was one of numerous comedy stars who later became successful on Broadway and in films. Serious-minded theatergoers who demanded more-sophisticated playbills formed groups such as the Progressive Dramatic Club (1902), which sponsored lectures and play readings. Yiddish theater was responsible for the first American performances of the works of Henrik Ibsen and Gerhart Hauptmann in America, and Yiddish translations of Shakespeare and Shaw were frequent attractions. Playwrights such as Sholem Asch (1880–1957), Jacob Gordin (1853–1909), and David Pinsky (1872–1959) all wrote original work during the decade, each realistically depicting the problems and pleasures of Jewish life. Yiddish theater in America tapped into mainstream sensibilities when it addressed

Vaudeville comedian Ed Wynn

assimilation, generational differences, and economic struggles; it touched universal sentiments with its self-deprecating humor. This immigrant theatrical tradition — from dramatic themes to comic "bits" — exerted a far-reaching influence on American entertainment well into the twentieth century.

Sources:

Joseph Csida and June Bundy Csida, *American Entertainment: A Unique History of Show Business* (New York: Watson-Guptill, 1978);

Maxine Schwartz Seller, ed., *Ethnic Theatre in the United States* (Westport, Conn.: Greenwood Press, 1983);

Anthony Slide, *The Encyclopedia of Vaudeville* (Westport, Conn.: Greenwood Press, 1994).

MOVING PICTURES

Chasers. The 1890s had been the decade of the moving picture — or so Americans thought. By 1903 audiences had become used to film technology and bored with the silent newsreels, parlor tricks, sight gags, stage scenes, and "panoramic" vistas that were the subjects of most screenings. Movies were shown at penny arcades on kinetoscopes — hand-turned viewing machines that presented about a half-minute of action. Films were also a staple of vaudeville bills, usually as "chasers" — concluding features meant to head the audience out the door before the next set of live acts began. Even the most rural communities were regularly visited by traveling projectionists. But although exhibitors sometimes provided piano music, accompanying lectures, and off-screen live actors who spoke dialogue, audiences were unimpressed with early-twentieth-century film. Then, in 1903, Edwin S. Porter, a director and cameraman for Thomas Edison's motion picture company, created a twelve-minute Western with continuous action from one scene to the next, as well as flashbacks: *The Great Train Robbery* became the most popular film of the decade in America. Because of Porter and those who hurried to imitate him, "the movies" became, virtually overnight, a booming industry and a budding art form.

The Industry. The Edison Company was producing, patenting, selling, licensing, and exhibiting films across the nation by 1900, but Edison had many eager competitors. Production companies that challenged Edison often found themselves in court, and the years 1900–1903 in particular were marked by litigation, although "out-of-court settlements" — in the form of smuggling, spying, theft, and physical altercations — also often determined ownership and distribution rights. By 1907 there were nine leading companies: Edison, Biograph, Vitagraph, Essanay, Lubin, Selig, Kalem and (from Europe) Méliès and Pathé; their business practices became standard, and the three-part structure of the American film industry — producer, distributor, and exhibitor — was established. In 1908 these nine companies combined to form the Motion Picture Patents Company, a monopolistic trust. Independent producers, among them Carl Laemmle and William Fox, urged fellow producers to join them in resisting the trust; Laemmle and Fox would, in future decades, head Universal Pictures and Fox Studios. Other independents prospered as well: the New York Motion Picture Company would foster the careers of Mack Sennett and Charlie Chaplin; Porter eventually left Edison to found the Rex Company, which would one day become Paramount Studios. Hollywood was not to become synonymous with the motion picture industry until

Edwin S. Porter, standing at left, at the Edison Bronx studio, 1908

the 1910s, but in New York City, Chicago, and elsewhere from 1900 to 1909, the movie industry was thriving.

Storefronts and Nickelodeons. In 1902 the first permanent movie theater in the United States — Thomas Tally's Electric Theater in Los Angeles — opened its doors, featuring a continuous run of films from 7:30 P.M. to 10:30 P.M. and changing its program every four weeks. It was perhaps the best known of the "storefront" movie houses of the decade. Storefront theaters, which operated with minimal overhead (folding chairs, no live acts, and six shows a day) but charged ten-to-twenty-five-cent admission prices, were touch-and-go propositions. Even when featuring such technical wizardry as Georges Méliès's *A Trip to the Moon* (1902), storefront profits fluctuated and eventually fell. In 1905, however, a Pittsburgh storefront opened with plush seats, a piano, frequent program changes, and nickel admission. It was the first film theater to be called a "nickelodeon," and within four years there were over four thousand nickelodeons in the country. By 1908 it was estimated that eighty million nickelodeon tickets were sold every week. The movie theater era had begun.

The Art. The advent of the nickelodeon era created an enormous demand for film, but little demand for film as art. Comedies and melodramas on limited subjects were turned out by the dozens, with few American films of note. Biograph's *Everybody Works but Father* (1905) was based on the popular minstrel song; Edison's *Dream of a Rarebit Fiend* (1906), with its special hallucination effects, took an unprecedented two months to make, and Edison sold 192 copies to distributors in the first year of its release. *The Whole Dam Family and the Dam Dog* (1905) was adapted from a popular picture postcard. Vitagraph produced a fast-paced and violent crime drama called *The Automobile Thieves* (1906), an impressive twenty-three-shot reel. Sigmund Lubin's controversial 1907 film version of the Harry K. Thaw–Stanford White murder case, *The Unwritten Law,* highlighted White's supposed seduction of showgirl Evelyn Nesbitt (later Thaw's wife) and suggested Thaw's vengeful attack on White was justified by spousal prerogative. It was banned in many cities but was the biggest hit of the year in others. Clearly, cinema had a long way to go before it would begin to aspire to becoming an art form. Although in 1907 a French company, Film d'Art, was formed to explore the creative interpretation of the genre, and eventually drew the interest of American producer Adolph Zukor, U.S. studios shied away from the idea of longer or more-serious productions because it was felt that the film audience would not sit through a single picture that was longer than fifteen minutes.

THE IDOL OF THE MIOGRAPH, OR THE UNKNOWN BELOVED

I.

Oh, he's a handsome gallant
He has sweethearts by the score
And ev'ry day and ev'ry night
He always wins some more;
And no wonder, now if you saw him
I know you would agree,
In all the Land from East to West
No finer could you see!

II.

And yet of these admiring maids,
Not any does he know
Not one knows him, nor yet his name,
Still does their rapture flow;
"Oh ain't he swell, gee, but he's great,
Oh, Kid, he sure is fine!"
And from the maidens more refined —
"He simply is divine!"

III.

And so they rave and fast do gaze,
And feast their eyes on him,
Upon his face of beauty rare
His form so tall and slim.
Oh, sometimes he a soldier is
In uniform and sword
And then again in curls and frills
He does the noble lord.

IV.

And now and then he is a monk
In habit and in cowl
But let him be what e're he may
They love him still in all.
His every trick of face they know,
His frown, his smile so bright,
And every turn of foot and hand
As he moves there plain to sight.

V.

And yet not one has heard him speak,
Or seen him in the flesh,
But just the same, with silent spell
He's caught them in his mesh.
Just let some certain places put
A placard at the door,
With magic words "A Miograph"
And they need say no more.

VI.

For if they've but a nickel left,
Out goes each maiden's hand,
They'll enter if the place be packed —
Aye if they've room to stand.
And who you ask, can be this one
Who lures and charms them so —
Why, he's the leading man, you see,
Of a moving picture show.
— *Hortense M. Lanahan, circa 1910*

Infancy. The art and craft of the moving picture that became associated globally with the United States in the later twentieth century was in its infancy from 1900 to 1909. Indoor scenes were static and lifeless; outdoor shots could be ruined by a day of rain or a wayward wind; plots revolved around jealousy, revenge, and innocents in peril — cinematography and screenwriting were as yet unheard-of professions. In 1908 the most important quality a film actor could have was skill at pantomime. Self-respecting theatrical performers and even vaudeville headliners refused to be seen on-screen; actors who did work in movies averaged five dollars a day. But the cinema industry was healthy and growing, despite the economic recession of 1907, and thanks to the creative indi-

viduals who nurtured it, within the next decade cinematic art also thrived.

Morality. Movies were an inexpensive and fascinating amusement for the predominantly working-class audience that frequented the nickelodeons. Upper- and middle-class moviegoers — who generally saw the latest movies at the vaudeville show or between the acts of plays rather than in the nickel theaters — enjoyed a variety of movie types. Westerns, Civil War films, slapstick, and detective pictures were popular, as well as "moral" melodramas such as *The Convict's Sacrifice* (Biograph, 1908) and filmed classics (*A Christmas Carol,* 1908; *Othello,* 1909). Movies could be both entertaining and uplifting;

Movie theater, 1908

and, it was said, motion pictures kept the lower classes away from the saloons. Why, then, did some Americans accuse the movies of fostering immorality? First, unattended children made up a large portion of the audience: working families had quickly discovered the child-care benefits of the nickelodeons, and "order" was a problem in many urban movie houses. Second, the theaters were dark and crowded, frequented as well by "sailors" and "foreigners" (according to an often-quoted *Saturday Evening Post* article), and the back rows were virtual invitations to illicit sexual behavior. Finally, there was the content of the films themselves: more frequent than moral melodramas were vulgar, low comedies, titillating scenes in such films as *The Boy, The Bust, and the Bath* (Vitagraph, 1907) and French films. These last, reported the trade periodical *Moving Picture Magazine* in 1908, were acted with "an abandonment of manner and dress," the sort of thing "Europe may like [but] we don't." By 1909 *Moving Picture Magazine* was proposing that certain distasteful subjects be omitted from films altogether:

prison interiors and prisoners, police stations, sensational crimes, and comedies that degraded people or played on human defects. Reformers bent on rehabilitating the movie-house venue campaigned for lighted theaters, restrooms and nurseries, ushers, and refreshments; those who objected to film content succeeded in instituting a National Board of Censorship in 1909.

The Pioneers. J. Stuart Blackton, G. W. "Billy" Bitzer, Wallace McCutcheon, Edwin S. Porter, William Paley, and James White were all leading filmmakers in the 1900s; under one studio or another they all produced, filmed, and directed many moving pictures, and their remarkable talents laid the groundwork for the flowering of the motion picture as an art form under the second generation of American filmmakers, led by director D. W. Griffith. David Lewelyn Wark Griffith (1875–1948) was a theatrical actor and manager before he entered the movie industry in 1908; he directed his first film, *The Adventures of Dolly,* in that year — one of numerous one-reel pictures he put out weekly. The following year's productions included *A Corner in Wheat* (based on the Frank Norris novel *The Pit*) and *Pippa Passes* (from the poem by Robert Browning). Griffith was experimenting with new techniques, such as the long shot, deep focus, moving camera techniques, cross-cuts, and shifting emotional "beats" or moments, that would make him the first great director of American film. He also insisted on careful casting of actors, a subdued acting style more suitable to film, rehearsals, and ensemble playing. Among the other pictures Griffith made from 1908 to 1909 were melodramas (*The Drunkard's Reformation* and *The Lonely Villa*, both in 1909), American history films (*1776; The Hessian Renegades*, 1908), and moral allegories (*The Devil*, 1909). Within seven years Griffith had produced two great classics of the silent-film era, *The Birth of a Nation* (1915) and *Intolerance* (1916).

Performers. Movies were sold by "brand" name in the early years of the century: moviegoers chose "Edison" or "Biograph" pictures rather than films by a particular director or with a certain performer. Production companies did not allow their actors and actresses to receive name billing, fearing that an interest in the players would detract from interest in the product — the name-brand film. The star system so prevalent in the other theatrical arts did not enter full force into the movie industry until the 1910s. Most film actors were minor stage players glad to have a job and were hired by the day, or at most, the week: Ben Turpin was a weekly performer with Essanay Pictures; D. W. Griffith and his wife, Linda Arvidson, were "day hires" when they first became involved in pictures. Although some were recognized by the public from one film to the next, most movie actors were anonymous faces to those who saw them on the silent screen. Mary Pickford (1893–1979) made her film debut in 1909; audiences loved her, but movie fans who wrote her letters wrote to "The Biograph Comedy Girl." Blanche Sweet, Mae Marsh, and Lillian Gish were all unnamed performers for Griffith in 1908–1909. Florence Turner was "The Vitagraph Girl"; Maurice Costello was "Dimples"; and fan letters came to Charles Inslee, who performed in many Westerns, addressed to "The Indian." By 1909 some companies were issuing group photos of their stock players, and by the first years of the next decade, motion picture companies were beginning to realize the money value of the "movie star." Performers' names and faces appeared in the new fan magazines, on posters and postcards, and even on pillowcases given away as theater door prizes.

Sources:

Eileen Bowser, *The Transformation of Cinema* (New York: Scribners, 1990);

Joseph Csida and June Bundy Csida, *American Entertainment: A Unique History of Popular Show Business* (New York: Watson-Guptill, 1978);

Gerald Mast, *A Short History of the Movies*, revised by Bruce F. Kawin (New York: Macmillan, 1992);

Charles Musser, *The Emergence of Cinema* (New York: Scribners, 1990).

"MY GAL SAL" BY PAUL DRESSER

Ev'ry thing is over and I'm feeling bad,
I lost the best pal that I ever had;
'Tis but a fortnight,
Since she was here,
Seems like she's gone though for twenty year
Oh how I miss her, my old pal,
Oh how I'd kiss her,
My Gal Sal.
Face not so handsome, but eyes, don't you know,
That shone just as bright as they did years ago.
CHORUS
They called her frivolous Sal,
A peculiar sort of a gal,
With a heart that was mellow,
An all 'round good fellow,
Was my old pal.
Your troubles, sorrows and care,
She was always willing to share.
A wild sort of devil,
But dead on the level,
Was My Gal Sal.
Brought her little dainties
Just afore she died,
Promised she would meet me,
On the other side;
Told how I loved her,
She said, "I know Jim,"
Just do your best, leave the rest to him;
Gently I pressed
Her to my breast,
Soon she would take
Her last long rest.
She looked at me and murmured "pal"
And softly I whispered "good bye Sal."

MUSIC: THE POP CENTURY BEGINS

American Original. If any art had come into its own as a purely "American" form by the turn of the century, it was popular music, and popular music was a veritable medley. The rhythms of jazz, the sentimental strains of ballads, the syncopation of ragtime, the poignancy of the blues, the lively melodies of show tunes — all were sung, played, hummed, whistled, recorded, and enjoyed by Americans during the decade. American "popular song" was taking on a character of its own, distinct from the song of other countries. Music was also the basis of a rapidly expanding industry: sheet music, instruments, phonographs, and record cylinders or disks were spreading musical fads countrywide at an unprecedented rate. The ragtime number improvised in a Louisville honkytonk in 1900 was being played in an Omaha parlor by 1902; the catchy tune showcased in a Broadway musical one month was on the lips of the hometown barbershop quartet the next. American popular song and popular culture merged during the decade, and an upbeat tone was set for both.

Tin Pan Alley. The music publishing industry, which had been scattered in several large cities in the late 1800s, was by 1900 centered in New York City on Twenty-eighth Street between Broadway and Sixth Avenue. In 1903 a reporter dubbed the area "Tin Pan Alley" because of the cacophony of sounds emanating from every open window as tunesmiths pounded away at their upright pianos, producing popular songs at assembly-line rates. Musicians played songs for potential performers; arrangers helped composers put their melodies on paper; orchestrators adapted original compositions to numerous orchestrations; and lyricists worked with music writers to "put over" new popular numbers. The sale of sheet music was the goal, and between 1900 and 1909 nearly one hundred Tin Pan Alley songs each sold more than one million copies.

Theme Songs. Tin Pan Alley relied on marketing to the interests of the rapidly expanding national audience. Popular tunes celebrated current events, modern achievements, and popular pastimes: "Meet Me in St. Louis" (1904) and "In My Merry Oldsmobile" (1905) derived from the Saint Louis World's Fair and the increasingly common automobile (airplane, telephone, and telegraph songs were also popular); "Take Me Out to the Ball Game" (1908) remains the best-known baseball song in America. "Kid" songs, such as "School Days" (1907) and "Smarty, Smarty, Smarty" (1908), were favorite vehicles for vaudeville performers. There were temperance songs ("Good Bye Booze," 1901) and drinking songs ("Under the Anheuser Busch," 1904). Songs with women's names in them were especially popular after George M. Cohan wrote "Mary's A Grand Old Name" in 1905. Novelty songs and songs that played on words, such as "Cheyenne" ("shy Ann, shy Ann, hop on my pony," 1906) and "Why Did I Pick a Lemon in the Garden of Love" (1909) were respectable, while others were more salacious: "Be Good" (1907) advised, "If you can't be good, be careful," and "I'd Like to See a Little More of You" (1906) was quite suggestive for an era in which skirts still touched the floor.

Songs of and from African American Life. The enduring appeal in both white and black America of songs about African American life was responsible for the transition from one sort of musical stereotype, the "darky" song, to another, more explicitly racist sort, the "coon"

Advertisement for an Edison phonograph that cost $7.50
(*Harper's,* 13 May 1899)

song. Derived from black minstrelsy and composed by songwriters of both races, the "coon" song, commonly filled with references to chicken and watermelon, was further responsible for the extension of old minstrel stereotypes to Broadway and to Tin Pan Alley. On the other hand, show tunes and Tin Pan Alley–type songs by composers such as Bert Williams and George Walker and Bob Cole and the Johnson Brothers, were superb. "Voodoo Man" and "The Blackville Strutters' Ball" (1900), by Williams and Walker; and "My Castle on the Nile" (1901), "Under the Bamboo Tree" (1902), "Congo Love Song" (1903), and "Mandy" (1906), by Cole and the Johnsons, are among the popular songs of the decade that remained high in the public consciousness for decades to come.

Cole and the Johnsons. Bob Cole (1868–1911) began his early career performing with one of the first African American shows to break from the strict minstrel tradition, "The Creole Show." He then worked with opera singer Sisserietta Jones, whose tour of Europe had earned her comparisons to Italian diva Adelina Patti; hence "Black Patti's Troubadours" was the name of the American stage extravaganza that Cole helped write and produce. Cole's collaboration with James Weldon Johnson (1871–1938) and J. Rosamond Johnson (1873–1954) began around 1900. Rosamond had studied at the New England Conservatory of Music; James, also a poet, had graduated from Atlanta University and had passed the Florida bar in preparation for a legal career. Both brothers' real interest was musical comedy, however, and in 1899 they moved to New York. Together, Cole and the Johnsons wrote more than two hundred songs during their seven-year association; in 1901 they produced a sophisticated vaudeville show and from there broke into Broadway musicals. "Under the Bamboo Tree," one of their first song hits, sold over four hundred thousand copies. Cole died at an early age and Rosamond left show business in the 1930s; James Weldon Johnson became a respected literary figure and civil rights leader after his *Autobiography of an Ex-Colored Man* appeared in 1912; together James and Rosamond wrote "Lift Every Voice and Sing" (1900), considered by many to be the African American national song.

Pluggers. Sheet music was available at music shops, dime stores, and department stores. But in the days before sound systems, there were few ways to assure that significant numbers of the buying public could hear and thus appreciate the new songs that were emerging from Tin Pan Alley. "Pluggers" were singers employed by music publishers not only for their vocal talents but also for their ingenuity, their sales ability, and their personal charm. Pluggers had been used by publishers since the 1890s to put songs over with vaudeville audiences (they would sing along with the vaudeville star and often get audiences to join in), but in the 1900s they invaded department and dime stores, performing for the clientele and persuading customers to purchase the sheet music to their songs. Pluggers also performed at sports events, company picnics, and political gatherings. They would sing from the backs of trucks in crowded neighborhoods. Indeed, any public gathering was a choice venue for these dogged songsters to ply their trade. Plugging became a sophisticated craft, and many pluggers, like Mose Gumble, who sang composer Jean Schwartz's "Bedelia" in 1903, created nationwide "song crazes." Others went on to become songwriters or headliners themselves.

Rag Composers. Ragtime, which first emerged from the Saint Louis, Missouri, area, was the most popular piano rhythm in the 1900s, and after the huge success of "Maple Leaf Rag," Scott Joplin (1868–1917) became the "Ragtime King." Joplin's best rags are known today because of a 1970s revival of interest in the form, but other composers, at least two of whom were Joplin's musical disciples, provided the nation with rags throughout the decade and after. James Scott (1886–1938), former handyman and song plugger, was "discovered" by the owner of the Carthage, Missouri, music store where he worked; among Scott's rags of the decade were "Frog Legs" (1906) and "Great Scott Rag" (1909). Joseph Lamb (1887–1960), a white northerner, began to compose ragtime in 1907 and shortly thereafter met Joplin, who listened to his "Sensation Rag," "Dynamite Rag," and "Old Home Rag" and promoted "Sensation Rag" for publication. Lamb and Scott are considered the two best ragtime

PAUL DRESSER, "BALLAD-MAKER OF A NATION"

He was the brother of a soon-to-be-famous American novelist, but his life took a musical turn. Born Paul Dreiser on 21 April 1857, Paul Dresser, like his younger brother Theodore, was raised in poverty in a strictly religious household. Dresser soon rebelled and ran away to join a blackface minstrel group. Billed as a comic in vaudeville, Dresser began writing songs in the 1880s and became nationally famous after his ballad "On the Banks of the Wabash, Far Away" (1897) attained "hit" status within three months. By the turn of the century, however, Dresser had spent the money he had made writing ballads, and sales of his songs were in decline. By 1905 the publishing house he had started had gone bankrupt. Dresser was subject to depressions, but he was always dressed elegantly in top hat and frock coat even when he owned little more than his pride.

Just when Dresser's career appeared to be over, however, he published "My Gal Sal," a ballad about a madame of an Indiana brothel. The song restored his reputation, but not his fortune. A young singer, Louise Dresser, who had asked Dresser for permission to use his name, introduced the plaintive recollection of a long-lost love in vaudeville, and by the end of 1906 millions of copies of sheet music had been sold. Dresser, however, did not live to enjoy his comeback as a songwriter: he died of a heart attack on 30 January 1906, in poverty.

Dresser was known for his generosity and his extravagance. His brother Theodore wrote this about him in an introduction to his collected songs: "He was, ever full of melodies of a tender . . . nature — that of a ballad-maker of a nation. . . . [his songs were] full of true poetic feeling for the mystery and pathos of life and death, and wonder of waters, the stars, the flowers, the accidents of life, success and failure."

Source: David Ewen, *All the Years of Popular American Music* (Englewood Cliffs, N.J.: Prentice-Hall, 1977).

composers next to Joplin. Harry von Tilzer (born Harry Gumm, 1872–1946) was a prolific composer in every genre of every Tin Pan Alley tune that had a "hit" sound and eventually became the owner of a music publishing business. Von Tilzer was typical of Tin Pan Alley composers who wrote rags along with the other popular material they churned out. His "Good Bye Eliza Jane" (1903) was an early rag that that helped introduce mainstream America to the syncopated beat.

Blues. The blues as an art form was becoming known in the early 1900s, although it had been developing since after the Civil War. The outgrowth of Mississippi Delta field hollers and sorrow songs, the distinctive twelve-bar blues melody, with its repeats and responses, expressed loneliness, woe, humor, and defiance. Although W. C. Handy (1873–1958) first published blues numbers (he wrote his first blues song in 1909), it was Ma Rainey who was considered the bearer of the blues to America through her minstrel performances. Born Gertrude Pridgett (1886–1930), she first appeared in minstrelsy at the age of fourteen; she met and married Will "Pa" Rainey four years later and from then on used the stage name by which she came to be known. She first heard a "strange and poignant" blues song between 1902 and 1904 and immediately reproduced it on the stage, earning the title "Mother of the Blues."

Jazz. It would not be called *jazz* for another fifteen years, and then the term would be coined in Chicago, but what is sometimes called "traditional" jazz had its beginnings in early-twentieth-century New Orleans. The improvisational instrumental form probably originated from parade and funeral music and in the first decade of the century was much indebted to blues and ragtime. Unlike blues and ragtime, however, jazz continued to develop significantly as the century progressed. Among the notable players and composers of the form in the early 1900s were Sidney Bechet, who played clarinet and soprano saxophone; Charles "Buddy" Bolden (1877–1931) and Joe "King" Oliver (1885–1938), both virtuosos on trumpet and cornet; Edward "Kid" Ord, trombonist; and Ferdinand "Jelly Roll" Morton (1885–1942), pianist. Morton's rags and blues tunes incorporated the melodic inventions of Dixieland jazz, and his skillful variations and subtle, intellectual riffs made him one of the greatest piano jazz men in American musical history. Although many white critics remained scornful of jazz, it emerged by the 1920s as a significant American contribution to world music.

Records. Sheet music and player-piano rolls were the primary distribution methods for popular music during the decade, but after 1902, when opera singer Enrico Caruso recorded ten arias for the Gramophone and Typewriter Company of London, the American music industry suddenly realized the commercial possibilities of recorded music. The Victor Talking Machine Company of America bought out Gramophone in 1903, thus acquiring not only Caruso's recordings, but Caruso's contract as well. Thereafter, nearly every major concert and operatic performer made recordings. Singers of popular songs followed, and songs rapidly became identified with vocalists rather than with composers. Former minstrel Richard Jose recorded "Silver Threads Among the Gold" (written by E. E. Rexford and H. P. Danks) in 1903; Irish tenor Chauncey Olcott recorded "When Irish Eyes Are Smiling" (by Olcott, George Graff Jr., and Ernest R. Ball) in 1906; and Broadway songstress Blanch Ring sang "I've Got Rings on My Fingers" (composed by the team of Weston and Barnes, with Maurice Scott) for the Victor Company in 1909. The recording industry quickly expanded; in the early 1900s the record and the record player ceased to be a novelty, becoming a necessity to those who produced American music and to those who wanted to hear it.

Art Music. Popular music became almost synonymous with America in the 1900s, but serious, or "art," music took much longer to find its American soul. Experimental composer Charles Ives (1874–1954), who was not recognized for his symphonies and art songs until after his death, did some of his most important work during the decade. Ives incorporated popular music, military marches, hymns, ragtime, and folk music into his compositions; one of his twenty-seven pieces for piano, written in 1908, is on the subject of baseball, called *Some Southpaw Pitching*. In 1902 British American composer Frederick Delius used American folk-song motifs in his composition *Appalachia;* his 1906 work, *Sea Drift*, was based on Walt Whitman's poems. Edward MacDowell (1860–1908) was considered by many to be the greatest composer of American art music during his lifetime, although much of his work draws from European models. He headed the newly formed music department at Columbia University in New York from its inception until 1904. MacDowell wrote his *Norse Sonatas* and *Celtic Sonatas* in 1900 and 1901. Scott Joplin also composed "serious" music: his opera *A Guest of Honor* was produced in 1903, and he worked on another operatic piece, *Treemonisha*, from around 1905 until his death. In 1905 L. A. Coernes's opera *Zenobia* was the first American opera produced in Europe. Victor Herbert's operettas were popular and critical successes. For the most part, however, American operatic and symphonic artists looked to Europe for their material in the early 1900s, and American orchestras preferred European masters to the works of native composers.

Sources:

David Ewen, *All The Years of American Popular Music* (Englewood Cliffs, N.J.: Prentice-Hall, 1977);

Thomas L. Morgan and William Barlow, *From Cakewalks to Concert Halls: An Illustrated History of African-American Popular Music from 1895 to 1930* (Washington, D.C.: Elliott & Clark, 1992);

Mark Sullivan, *Our Times, 1900–1925*, volume 3 (New York: Scribners, 1930).

HEADLINE MAKERS

THEODORE DREISER

1871-1945

REALIST WRITER

Up from Poverty. Theodore Dreiser's personal experience of poverty, hunger, struggle, and social injustice informed his brand of social realism. Dreiser's America was one beset by class conflict and the ravages of capitalism. His novels were peopled by characters shaped by the difficulties of urban life, not by ideals of the middle class. Critics often dismissed him as being crude and journalistic in his writing; his advocates saw such criticism as a form of class hostility. Whichever side a reader took, few were left indifferent to Dreiser's exploration of crime, capitalism, and sexual passion. Both professionally and personally, Dreiser was an infamous character and an enormously influential figure in American letters for three decades.

Early Life. Dreiser was born in Terre Haute, Indiana, in 1871 into a large, poor Catholic family. His parents, both immigrants, lost their business the year Dreiser was born, and his early years were filled with the daily insecurities of poverty. The family moved frequently, from Terre Haute, to Evansville, to Chicago, and back to rural Indiana. Dreiser's family provided him with the basic materials for many of his fictional families: a warm, forgiving mother, a narrow-minded, disciplinarian father, and fun-loving, wayward children. It also provided a major plot of his fiction: pushing on to new worlds as the old one crashes. Tired of his life at home, the sixteen-year-old Dreiser moved to Chicago and then to Bloomington, where he attended Indiana University for one year in 1889.

Newspaper Reporter. The following year Dreiser returned to Chicago and worked at menial jobs until in 1892, at the age of twenty-one, he landed a job at a local newspaper. He did a stint of reporting in Saint Louis the following year. The daily round of a newspaper reporter brought Dreiser into contact with the underside of urban America, a world of robberies, murders, illegalities, crime, and catastrophe. In 1894 Dreiser moved to Pittsburgh and then to New York City, where he landed a job writing a daily column, which left him free much of the day. Dreiser continued his education by reading at the public library. In 1895 he began editing a magazine, *Ev'ry Month,* to which he contributed editorials, cultural reviews, and book reviews. Two years later, Dreiser left newspaper journalism for the expanding and competitive world of freelance writing. In 1897 he married Sallie White after a lengthy engagement Dreiser bitterly resented.

Sister Carrie. In 1899 Dreiser began his first novel, *Sister Carrie* (1900), his story of individual failure and success in a great American city. Dreiser submitted his manuscript to a new publishing firm, Doubleday, Page. There Frank Norris, a naturalist author, strongly endorsed *Sister Carrie,* and the firm decided to publish it. When Frank N. Doubleday, the firm's principal partner, returned from Europe, he demanded revisions, deeming the novel scandalous and unfit for the reading public. The adventures of Carrie, the heroine of the novel, flew in the face of Victorian morality. Dreiser refused to change his manuscript and refused to break the agreement the firm had made with him. Reluctantly, Doubleday, Page finally agreed to publish *Sister Carrie* but did nothing by way of promoting or advertising the novel, which did not sell. Dreiser's supporters cast him as a martyr to American puritanism, or what they called its narrow-minded hypocrisy toward the gritty reality of American city life.

Editor. Dreiser immediately started work on a second novel, but his progress was slowed by money problems, now that he no longer wrote for magazines, and by the deterioration of his marriage. Dreiser became depressed and roamed the country in search of a cheap room in which to write. By 1903 he was penniless and in New York City, wary of meeting old friends. His brother Paul came to his rescue. Paul, a songwriter who called himself Paul Dresser and is most often remembered for having written "On the Banks of the Wabash," sent Dreiser to a "health camp," where he regained his emotional and physical health. In 1905 Dreiser returned to magazine writing as the editor of the popular monthly, *Smith's* magazine. His success at *Smith's,* and from 1906 to 1907 at the *Broadway Magazine,* was capped in late 1907 when he became editor of a popular women's magazine of the day, Butterick's *Delineator.*

Returning to Fiction. The republication of *Sister Carrie* in 1907 to critical acclaim fueled Dreiser's desire to return to fiction writing. Encouraged by his friendship with critic H. L. Mencken, Dreiser found himself restless from the daily routine of publishing a magazine, yet reluctant to give up the financial success such work entailed. After he started an affair with the daughter of a contributing writer, the *Delineator* fired Dreiser. The affair and its aftermath galvanized him to write, and he published *Jennie Gerhardt* in 1911. The novel was a critical and popular success.

Unleashing. At the age of forty Dreiser entered a remarkably productive phase of his career. He wrote four long novels, *The Financier* (1912), *The Titan* (1914), *The "Genius"* (1915), and *An American Tragedy* (1925), four equally lengthy works of travel narrative and autobiography, two volumes of plays, four collections of short stories, and a volume of philosophical essays. In 1914, with both his marriage and the affair over, Dreiser moved to Greenwich Village in New York City. There he had several romantic relationships, the most important with Helen Patges Richardson, whom he married in 1944, a year before his death.

Offending the Critics. Dreiser's novels continued to generate controversy, particularly his depiction of the sex drive in human experience. Many found *The Financier* and *The Titan* offensive for their representations of sexuality. With *The "Genius"* in 1915, critics felt Dreiser had offended them long enough. In 1915 the New York Society for the Suppression of Vice, led by Anthony Comstock, brought an action to have the novel banned. Dreiser's friend Mencken organized a campaign to force the courts to void any censorship of the novel. This incident confirmed in many people's minds the image of Dreiser as both a champion of artistic freedom and the victim of prudery.

An American Tragedy. For three years, from 1919 to 1922, Dreiser lived in Los Angeles. There he followed the coverage of the sensational murder trial of Chester Gillette, who murdered his fiancée to be free to pursue a wealthier woman. The trial provided Dreiser with the skeleton plot of *An American Tragedy,* considered his masterpiece. Movie and play adaptations brought him needed financial security. In the wake of such success, Dreiser's attention turned to nonfiction writing again. His nonfiction centered on a different kind of American tragedy, this one explicitly social and economic. Like many American writers in the first half of the twentieth century, Dreiser wanted to make the United States a better place to live. At the same time, his realist impulses demanded he acknowledge and expose America's under-

lying social problems. Throughout the 1920s and 1930s, Dreiser's politics became more radical. In November 1927 he visited the Soviet Union, and like many other intellectuals of his day, he was fascinated by the "Russian experiment." Dreiser supported many left-wing causes in such works as *Dreiser Looks at Russia* (1928) and *Tragic America* (1931).

Later Life. The Great Depression wiped out much of Dreiser's personal wealth and that of his publisher, Horace Liveright. Dreiser lost his country home and his New York City apartment. In 1932 he moved to Los Angeles again. There he became even more convinced that the Soviet Union was being sabotaged by capitalist countries. His last nonfiction book, *America Is Worth Saving* (1941), centered solely on Dreiser's political views in support of communism. While in California, Dreiser set out to complete two previously drafted novels, *The Bulwark* (1945) and *The Stoic* (1947), which were posthumously published. Dreiser died in Los Angeles in late December 1945.

Source:
Richard Lingeman, *Theodore Dreiser: An American Journey* (London: John Wiley, 1993).

PAUL LAURENCE DUNBAR

1872-1906

POET, NOVELIST

"Poet Laureate of the Negro Race." Paul Laurence Dunbar was one of America's most popular poets in the 1900s. He was also the first African American poet to achieve national and international fame. Educator Booker T. Washington called him the "Poet Laureate of the Negro Race." One of the most unusual features of Dunbar's poetry was his use of both dialect and standard English, a technique that is no longer as controversial or as startling to readers as it was at the turn of the century. Dunbar's poetry blended the humor, pathos, and determination of African Americans' struggle in and out of slavery. He skillfully used rhythm, satire, narrative, and irony to insist that white Americans see the humanity of a black community they often misunderstood.

Early Life. Dunbar was born in Dayton, Ohio, in 1872 to former plantation slaves. His father, Joshua, and mother, Matilda, taught themselves to read and write, skills that slaves desperately wanted to have but that slave holders regularly withheld and was prohibited by law. When Dunbar was a young boy Matilda taught him to read, and together they cultivated a devotion to literature. Dunbar's parents told him and his brothers about their lives as slaves, and these stories became an important literary resource for Dunbar's poetry.

Getting Started. Dunbar's intelligence and literary talent soon became obvious. In high school he was the only black student in his class. As a senior he was class president, editor of his school's paper, and president of the school's literary club. He was also the class poet, writing and delivering the class poem at graduation in June 1891. At the age of sixteen Dunbar had already published his poetry in the *Dayton Herald*. Encouraged by such successes, Dunbar set out to find work as a journalist when he graduated, but he was denied all but the most menial work. He eventually found work as an elevator operator for four dollars a week; in his free time he read William Shakespeare, John Keats, and Alfred Tennyson and wrote poetry and articles for publication. Invited by his former English teacher, Dunbar gave the opening address to the Western Association of Writers in 1892. His twenty-six-line poem drew the attention of many in the audience, specifically James Newton Matthews, who became one of Dunbar's patrons.

Establishing Ties. Encouraged by Matthews and another admirer, the Hoosier poet James Whitcomb Riley, Dunbar published a small volume of poetry in 1892, *Oak and Ivy*. That volume included Dunbar's first uses of dialect in such poems as "A Banjo Song," as well as standard English, as in "Ode to Ethiopia." Throughout, Dunbar stressed the contributions blacks had made in the building of the United States and their achievements during Reconstruction. Dunbar moved to Chicago in 1893 to work at the World's Columbian Exposition and there met a network of African American artists and intellectuals. Chief among his new acquaintances were Frederick Douglass, Angelina Weld Grimkè, Ida B. Wells Barnett, Hallie Brown, Mary Church Terrell, and fellow poets James D. Corrothers and James Edwin Campbell. At the conclusion of the exposition, Dunbar returned to Dayton and reluctantly resumed his job as an elevator operator.

Arriving. Beset by financial difficulties, Dunbar struggled to make a living. In 1895 *Century* magazine published three poems, "A Negro Love Song," "Curtain," and "The Dilettante." Other important literary magazines and newspapers followed suit, such as *The New York Times, Blue and Gray,* and the *Independent*. He published a second volume of poetry, *Majors and Minors,* in 1896. William Dean Howells, the renowned novelist and critic, reviewed *Majors and Minors* in *Harper's Weekly,* and his praise helped establish Dunbar as an important American poet. Friends directed Dunbar to what would now be called a literary agent, Maj. James B. Pond, who had successfully managed tours for Mark Twain, Frederick Douglass, and George Washington Cable. Pond arranged a series of readings in New York City and located a publisher for Dunbar's poems. Also in 1896 Dunbar published *Lyrics of Lowly Life,* which became his best-selling book, introducing him to a national audience.

International Recognition. In 1897 Dunbar sailed to London and there met the woman who later became his wife, Alice Ruth Moore. U.S. Ambassador John Hay arranged a reading of Dunbar's poetry for some of London's most prominent citizens. After six months in England, and again facing financial ruin, Dunbar returned to the United States and took a job in the Reading Room of the Library of Congress in Washington, D.C. Dunbar enjoyed the security of his work and the vibrant African American community in Washington, which at that time was the largest in the United States. He energetically turned out seven articles, a musical, two collections of short stories, two volumes of poetry, and a novel he had started in London. His royalties, fees, and salary from the Library of Congress gave him financial stability. In recognition of his achievements, Atlanta University bestowed upon him an honorary master of arts degree on 5 June 1899.

Short Stories. In the late 1890s Dunbar began writing short stories about the ongoing problem of racism facing African Americans. In his collection of short stories *Folks from Dixie* (1898) Dunbar dropped the use of dialect that had won him fame from his white audiences. Instead, he used standard English to rekindle African American awareness of the need for solidarity, pride, and, above all, dignity. *Folks from Dixie* won him more critical acclaim. In 1899 Dunbar's delicate health forced him to resign from the Library of Congress. Despite his chronic illnesses, he toured the country giving readings and lectures. After his collection of poems *Lyrics of the Hearthside* (1899) was published, a doctor diagnosed Dunbar as suffering from tuberculosis and advised him to move to the country. In 1900 Dunbar published a book of stories, *The Strength of Gideon and Other Stories,* and his publisher republished eight of Dunbar's poems with a photo essay on southern African Americans. *Poems of Cabin and Field* became widely popular, and other illustrated editions of poems from Dunbar's previous volumes were published: *Candle-Lightin' Time* (1901), *When Malindy Sings* (1903), *Li'l Gal* (1904), *Howdy, Honey, Howdy* (1905), and *Joggin' Erlong* (1906).

Novelist. To support himself, Dunbar also published novels during this period, most notably *The Sport of the Gods* (1902), considered the first major protest novel by a black American writer. In *In Old Plantation Days* (1903) Dunbar took what appeared to many African Americans to be a favorable and romantic view of slavery. Many black critics dismissed the book as a form of Uncle Tomism. White audiences, however, enjoyed the book tremendously. Dunbar's fiction maintained a delicate balance between accommodation and protest, in part to ensure that his work would be published by a predominantly white publishing world. Yet even when his work appeared to accommodate racism, he continued to explore the social, economic, and political conditions facing blacks in the United States at the turn of the century. In 1906 the poet died in his home in Dayton.

Source:
Gayle Addison Jr., *Oak and Ivy: A Biography of Paul Laurence Dunbar* (Garden City, N.Y.: Anchor/Doubleday, 1971).

ISADORA DUNCAN

1878-1927

MODERN DANCER

Innovator of Dance. Isadora Duncan introduced a new, and what many considered radical, style of movement to the American dance world in the 1900s. In an era when American dance was dominated by the formalities of classical ballet, Duncan broke from strictly choreographed steps into flowing, almost spontaneous moves that shocked Victorian audiences with their open sensuality.

Early Life. Duncan was born in 1878 and reared in the San Francisco Bay area. Educated by her freethinking mother, Isadora's upbringing was unique for the period. Comprised of classical music and great poets, her education centered on the arts and the potential of radical expression to change society. This emphasis led Isadora and her three siblings to pursue careers in the theater. As a girl, Duncan enjoyed dancing and motion, and rather than restricting her love of movement, Duncan's mother provided her with encouragement and support. By the time she was a teenager, Duncan had cultivated the fundamentals of what would later would be her contribution to modern dance — a style of dance built on free, natural, expressive movements.

Radical Movement. Duncan's dance inspired much commentary, from critics who viewed it as degenerate and from supporters who viewed it as nothing short of revolutionary. Embraced by a generation of avant-garde poets, painters, and political radicals, Duncan's dance came to symbolize liberation from the stagnant and suffocating traditions of Victorian culture. Like many other innovators, Duncan found Europe to be a much more welcoming place for her than the United States, and she toured Europe extensively throughout the 1900s.

Symbol of Liberation. Duncan boasted that she had been a radical since the age of five, but her political views took a more radical turn when she toured Russia in the wake of the 1905 revolution. There Duncan came to see the possibility of an intimate relationship between revolutionary politics and revolutionary art, and these ideas increasingly shaped her dance. Duncan believed that liberating the body from rigid and highly choreographed dance mirrored the liberation of humanity from the confines of mind-numbing convention and blind obedience to outmoded political systems. From the 1900s on, Duncan became a living symbol of revolt, revolution, women's emancipation, and sexual freedom. Duncan spoke out in support of many radical issues; foremost was the 1917 Bolshevik Revolution in Russia. In 1921 Lenin invited her to establish a school of dance in Moscow. In the Soviet Union Duncan threw herself into creating a politically informed art for the masses. She choreographed dances for the Soviet Union's national anthem, the workers' hymn "The Internationale," as well as for other national peoples' songs, such as Ireland's "Wearin' o' the Green" and France's "Carmagnole."

Expatriate. Through most of the 1900s and 1910s Duncan lived in Europe and the Soviet Union but returned to America to give extended tours benefiting Russian famine relief and other radical causes. On a visit in 1922, when many Americans viewed foreigners and communists with suspicion, immigration officials detained Duncan at Ellis Island in New York City. There officials questioned her about her pro-Bolshevik views. Exposure of her radical politics led the press and conservative civic groups to vilify her as a dangerous radical promoting communism. Newspapers ran headlines that announced Duncan was an "agent of Moscow," and many cities canceled her performances in the wake of such damning press. Finally, deprived of her U.S. citizenship, Duncan fled what she called the "narrow-minded, hypocritical, loathsome United States," vowing never to return. Duncan lived out her life in France, until her death in an automobile accident in 1927.

Sources:
Lillian Loewenthal, *The Search for Isadora: The Legend & Legacy of Isadora Duncan* (Pennington, N.J.: Princeton Book Co., 1993);

Nancy L. Ruyter, *Reformers and Visionaries: The Americanization of the Art of Dance* (New York: Dance Horizons, 1979);

Cynthia Splatt, *Life into Art: Isadora Duncan and Her World*, edited by Spatt, Doree Duncan and Carol Pratl (New York: Norton, 1993).

ROBERT HENRI

1865-1929

MODERN PAINTER

Making Anarchy an Avocation. A revolution in American art circles in 1900 was led by Robert Henri, instigator of what was referred to as "The Eight" and the "revolutionary black gang." Henri, along with John Sloan, William Glackens, George Luks, Everett Shinn, James Preston, Edward Davis, and Charles Redfield, held academic and officially sanctioned art in contempt. They complained that it was cloistered, effete, monotonous, and "fenced in with tasseled ropes and weighed down with . . . bronze plates." These young artistic rebels believed that American art should be public in the broadest sense of the word and have relevance to the people, not just to art experts. According to Henri, American artists had too long been under the sway of the standards and subject matter of

European high art. Henri and The Eight challenged the enshrining of European aesthetics. Following in the footsteps of novelists such as Nathaniel Hawthorne and Herman Melville, and the essayist Henry David Thoreau, who celebrated what they called "an American spirit," Henri turned his artistic vision to native themes. By doing so, he insisted that the unique qualities of America should shape its artists and its art.

Early Life. Robert Henri was born Robert Henry Cozad in Nebraska and studied art at the Pennsylvania Academy of Fine Arts. While there, Henri became fascinated by the realism of his teacher, Thomas Eakins, who counseled his students to study their own country and to "portray its types." To the dismay of the academy, Eakin insisted his students paint from nude models rather than from plaster molds. Eakins's rebelliousness against the decorum of academic art cost him his job but won the admiration of Henri, who continued his studies with Eakins's gifted student Thomas Anshutz. In 1888 Henri left for Paris and enrolled in the bastion of classicism, the Ecole des Beaux-Arts, for two years. While in Paris the radical Henri found Post-Impressionism, the European challenge to academic art, uninteresting.

The Eight. When Henri returned to Philadelphia in 1891, a friend introduced him to two newspaper illustrators, William Glackens and John Sloan. They, along with other renegade artists, made Henri's studio at 806 Walnut Street in downtown Philadelphia a gathering place. At these meetings the group discussed music, literature, art, and, most of all, the stifling confines of the academy. Unlike more-institutional gatherings of artists, such as those of Philadelphia's Tile Club or the Art Club, The Eight's meetings were run in the spirit of a European café — spontaneous and casual discussions. As newspaper artists, Sloan, Glackens, Luks, and Shinn illustrated the city's disasters in quick sketches. Henri found their perspective of the city refreshingly honest. He encouraged them to paint in oil, rather than in charcoal, and to see urban America as a worthy subject of serious art. As a result, The Eight became known for their psychological portraiture, their eye for detail, their sympathy with humanity, and their use of a drab, realistic urban palette.

Return to Paris. In 1898 Henri married and went to Paris for his honeymoon. His compositions from his trip were a series of broadly painted figures that stood in contrast to simple silhouettes, and scenes in which shadow and light figured prominently. While these paintings were rejected by the progressive Salon des Indépendants, the French government purchased one of them, *Snow*, in 1899. When he returned to the United States, Henri and his wife settled in New York City, a place Henri felt was more hospitable to his artistic vision than was Philadelphia. Henri took a job as an instructor at the New York School of Art, or the Chase School. Soon many of his friends joined him. While teaching in New York City, Henri continued to think about, and to challenge, the place of art in the modern world. Henri

believed that art should be socially realistic, and he filled his canvases with unglamorous models and urban action scenes. At the same time, Henri believed the camera freed artists from the obligation to paint realistically. Artists, he felt, should not paint for details but concentrate on the subjective underpinnings of the scene, such as the expression of the model and the feelings the scene inspired.

Gaining a Reputation. In the 1900s The Eight were known as the New York Realists. Many critics found their work to be joyless and unhealthy; others found it a compelling counterpart to the exposé journalism of the muckrakers and the social realism of novelists such as Theodore Dreiser and Frank Norris. Despite their distance from academic art, the conservative National Academy of Design had accepted all of them as members by 1905, a form of official acceptance of which they had been so critical. In 1907 the National Academy of Design appointed Henri a judge for its prestigious spring exhibition. His friends' excitement at finally having one of their own officiate such an exhibit was soon crushed as Henri discovered he had no meaningful say in the evaluation process. The jury gave two of his own paintings a "number two" rating, meaning they were not to be hung on eye level, but either above or below. Henri was furious and quickly withdrew his canvases from the show.

"Apostles of Ugliness." The group met shortly after Henri's resignation and decided to produce an alternative and cooperative exhibition to be financed by the artists themselves. William Macbeth offered them space in his gallery, and Henri, Shinn, Luks, Davies, Lawson, and Maurice Prendergast participated in the show. A newspaper announcing the show referred to the artists as "the apostles of ugliness." The show opened in February 1908 and was a success, selling seven canvases. Critics denounced the show as unfit for civilized viewing. "Is it fine art," one critic asked, "to exhibit our sores?" Henri was singled out for his "streak of coarseness." Despite such criticism, The Eight had made a mark. They had created an alternative to the one-horse art town that New York City had been. Now, at least, those artists whom museums refused to exhibit had a place to display their work.

Establishing a School. In 1909 Henri established his own art school on upper Broadway in New York City, and many of his students followed him there from the New York School of Art, including George Bellows and Edward Hopper. There Henri inspired another generation of modern painters, including Stanton Macdonald-Wright, Patrick Henry Bruce, and Stuart Davis. Henri continued to train his students in his philosophy of freedom of expression. He read out loud from Walt Whitman's *Leaves of Grass*. Henri and his students took to wandering in the streets looking for subjects and turned their sights on the city's new immigrants. They filled their canvases with scenes of Coney Island, Union Square, and the Bowery. Henri painted the rivers in and around New York City and painted them in bleakest winter. For Henri, the New York skyline, with its looming buildings and steel bridges, symbolized the energy of the city. Others labeled the creators of these works the "Ash Can School" for their gritty imagery.

Organizing the Independents. Galvanized by another wave of rejections from the New York art establishment, Henri set out to organize a second group show of independent artists. He timed this show to coincide with the academy's spring exhibition in 1910. When the independents' show opened on West Thirty-fifth Street, Henri's portrait of his wife, which the academy had rejected, hung in the place of honor. The show was large, displaying more than two hundred canvases democratically displayed alphabetically. Within an hour, one thousand people crowded into the gallery, while another fifteen hundred waited outside. A riot squad eventually came to manage the disorderly crowd. Critics continued to see Henri and the show's other artists as vulgar and coarse. But others viewed The Eight's "revolt" a success for injecting a healthy vitality into American art.

Later Life. In his later years Henri continued to teach and to rebel against the boundaries between official and nonofficial art. He wrote a book, *The Art Spirit,* in 1923. Through teaching, he inspired students by demanding innovation in subject matter. He died in New York City in 1929.

Sources:

William Innes Homer, with Violet Organ, *Robert Henri and His Circle,* revised edition (New York: Hacker, 1988);

Barbara Rose, *American Art Since 1900,* revised edition (New York: Praeger, 1975).

Scott Joplin

1868-1917

Ragtime Musician

Early Life. Scott Joplin, the child of a former slave and a freeborn black woman, grew up in Texarkana on the Texas-Arkansas border. His mother took a special interest in her young son's education and cultivated his love of music. As a young man Joplin played music professionally, performing in the Texas Medley Quartette, a local group, and teaching piano, guitar, and mandolin with his brothers, Will and Robert.

Traveling and Touring. Joplin left Texarkana and traveled the country as a musician. He went to Chicago in 1893 to the World's Columbian Exposition, where he, along with other Americans, first heard the new syncopated sounds of ragtime. Ragtime was notable for its "ragged" rhythm. Since its beginnings in the 1880s, ragtime music was an African American musical form, with roots in slavery and complicated African rhythms. It was disseminated and mimicked in blackface minstrelsy and on the vaudeville stage throughout the 1900s and 1910s. Joplin arrived in Saint Louis in 1890, where he came in contact with ragtime pioneer Tom Turpin. In 1895 Joplin reunited with the Texas Medley Quartette in Syracuse, New York, where his waltz songs "Please Say You Will" and "A Picture of Her Face" were published.

Cradle of Classic Ragtime. In 1896 Joplin moved to Sedalia, Missouri, where he attended music classes at the George R. Smith College for Negroes, taught piano and composition to other ragtime composers, and played cornet with several local bands. He played piano at the Maple Leaf Club (after which he named his most famous composition). In Sedalia, Joplin met John Stark, who published many of his compositions.

King of Ragtime Writers. In 1899 Joplin published his first piano compositions, or "rags," "Original Rags" and "Maple Leaf Rag." "Maple Leaf Rag" proved to be popular, and thanks to an attorney friend Joplin obtained a royalty contract that yielded him one cent per copy, an unusual arrangement for the time. Ten years later, "Maple Leaf Rag" was America's most popular piano rag, and Joplin was known as the king of ragtime writers. Joplin's rags were distinctive and caught the attention of audiences with their melodically interesting voices and rich chromatic harmonies. In Joplin's hands, ragtime went from a haphazard and commonplace melody to something more akin to classical music. Joplin and Stark described his work as "classical ragtime" in an effort to distinguish it from other rags.

Operas and Musicals. Joplin wanted to be known not just as a popular songwriter but as a composer of artistic merit. He set out to translate ragtime into operas, musicals, and symphonies. His first attempt, *The Ragtime Dance* in 1899, was a musical production of an African American ball, complete with dancers and a singer-narrator. Joplin's second attempt was an opera, *A Guest of Honor,* staged in Saint Louis in 1903. Neither production met with much success. Joplin continued to move throughout the Midwest, never staying at one address for more than two years. In 1907 Joplin moved to New York City, where he met the ragtime composer Joseph Lamb. Joplin mentored Lamb by promoting his work and introducing him to his publisher, Stark. Encouraged to document his style, Joplin published *School of Ragtime* in 1908, a didactic manual of ragtime music and rhythm.

Later Life. In 1908 Joplin announced he was working on a second opera, *Treemonisha,* which he published himself in 1911. *American Musician and Art Journal* published a favorable review of the opera, but he could not find backers to finance a production. A determined Joplin decided to produce the opera himself at Lincoln Theater in Harlem, New York. With a shoestring budget, Joplin's opera went on without scenery, costumes, or orchestra. Joplin himself played the musical score on the piano. The production received little attention. In 1916 Joplin completed a musical comedy, *If,* and was at work on a ragtime symphony when he died. Interest in Joplin's music in the 1940s and in the 1970s led to a reissue of his compositions and of *Treemonisha.* The public acclaim and official recognition of Joplin's art came in 1976 when he received a posthumous Pulitzer Prize.

Source:
Susan Curtis, *Dancing to a Black Man's Tune: A Life of Scott Joplin* (Columbia: University of Missouri Press, 1994).

JACK LONDON

1876-1916

NATURALISTIC WRITER

Breaking Out. In the 1900s Jack London's naturalistic fiction crashed in on the polite drawing-room stories that had dominated American writing in the late nineteenth century, and left a dramatic mark. His heroes braved the harshest natural elements in Alaska or the open sea and came to see themselves and society with a clarity forged from struggle. London's fascination with the primitive in man, and with the brutal, strong, and simple man of an earlier era, stood in stark contrast to the intellectual and middlebrow heroes of William Dean Howells or Henry James. In creating a compelling portrait of what men learned when stripped of society's comforts, London's short stories and novels introduced a newly masculinized style of writing to American fiction that served as a bridge between the adventure stories of Mark Twain and the war stories of Ernest Hemingway.

Early Life. London was born out of wedlock in San Francisco in 1876. He was named John Griffith Chancy after his biological father, but his mother later changed his name when she married John London, a Civil War veteran. The family moved around northern California in search of work. Throughout London's childhood his mother remained deeply interested in spiritualism and the occult. Her superstitions left London with a permanent disdain for all things spiritual. As a boy London was often lonely, and he turned to books for companionship. He also took odd jobs delivering newspapers, setting pins in a bowling alley, sweeping saloon floors, and doing whatever he could to bring in a few pennies. When he finished grade school in 1889, young Jack went to work full-time in a West Oakland cannery, working for eighteen hours a day at ten cents an hour.

On the Docks. At the age of fifteen London joined with other youths to steal oysters from local fishermen. Fearing that he would end up in prison, London switched sides and joined the California Fish Patrol. He fictionalized many of his experiences on the docks of Oakland in *The Cruise of the Dazzler* (1902) and *Tales of the Fish Patrol* (1905). At eighteen London shipped out as an able-bodied seaman on a sealing schooner heading for the northwest Pacific. He was at sea for seven months. The voyage provided him with materials to write *The Sea-Wolf* (1904) and a short story, "Story of a Typhoon off the Coast of Japan," published in the *San Francisco Morning Call* on 12 November 1893.

On the Road. London disliked working. In his autobiographical *John Barleycorn* (1913), he wrote that he found "the thought of work . . . repulsive. It was a whole lot better to roister and frolic over the world . . . so I headed out . . . East by beating my way on the railroads." London recounted his experiences hoboing in *The Road* (1907). He explained that, as a tramp, he learned how to spin "tales that rang true." When knocking on doors for food, a hobo "out of inexorable necessity" developed the "art of the short-story." Living as a tramp politicized London as well. While on the road, he embraced socialism's philosophy of sharing the wealth. London returned to Oakland determined to lift himself out of poverty and decided to finish his formal education.

The Gold Rush. In 1895 London entered the University of California at Berkeley. Forced to withdraw after his first semester because of financial troubles, he began to pursue his writing career in earnest. Getting little support, London returned to manual labor and in 1897 left for the Klondike gold rush with a friend. There, London reported, he grew up. A bout with scurvy forced him to return to Oakland, but he brought back a wealth of experiences that he turned into successful prose. By 1900 his work was appearing in magazines all over the country, such as the *Atlantic Monthly*, *Cosmopolitan*, and *McClure's*.

Building Fame. In 1900 London published a book of short stories, *Son of Wolf* (1900), and, now famous, he married Bessie Mae Maddern. Critics loved *Son of Wolf*. Tired of sentimental romances, readers responded to the tough realistic portrayal of life in London's stories. In the winter of 1900 London wrote what would become an American classic, *The Call of the Wild*. Published in 1901, it became the nation's best-selling work of fiction. From that point until the end of his life, London was one of the most prolific and widely read writers in the world.

Building a Reputation. While his novels made him famous, London's nonfiction and magazine articles earned him notoriety as a radical. London was a devoted supporter of industrial unions and a fierce critic of corrupt government and monopolies. His lecture tour across the country offered audiences detailed accounts of the evils of capitalism, a system, he explained, that kept half of its population in poverty. Throughout his life, London supported movements for social justice and corporate accountability.

Later Life. While London's success grew, his private life deteriorated. A few years into his marriage, London realized he shared little with his wife. While at Stanford

University to give a lecture, he fell in love with Anna Strunsky, a socialist activist in San Francisco. In 1904 Bessie London filed for a divorce, but Strunsky and London never married. London continued to write prolifically in the 1900s and early 1910s, publishing *Martin Eden* (1907), *The Iron Heel* (1908), *The Cruise of the Snark* (1911), and *Valley of the Moon* (1913), among others. In 1913 London, who was an alcoholic, went into a noticeable physical decline. He finished his last story, "The Water Baby," in October 1916, seven weeks before he died.

Source:
Andrew Sinclair, *Jack: A Biography* (New York: Harper & Row, 1977).

EDWIN STANTON PORTER

1869-1941

DIRECTOR, FILM PIONEER

Innovator. Edwin Porter's curiosity about the mechanics of movies made him one of the most prominent technical innovators in the early years of the American cinema. His interest in the techniques of making images move across the screen led him to push the limits of existing technology to improve the quality of the new medium. His work with Thomas Edison on the mechanics of film, and with several early screen companies as producer and director of films, trained Porter in the full range of skills necessary in the new industry. Throughout the 1900s Porter's expertise made him a pioneer in the history of American cinema.

Early Life. A merchant's son, Porter quit school at the age of fourteen and worked successively in several menial jobs, such as a railway newsboy, sign painter, plumber, telegrapher, theater cashier, tailor, stagehand, and machinist. Looking for direction and a way out of the laboring classes, Porter joined the navy when he was twenty-six. There, he was trained as a machinist. When he returned to civilian life in 1896, Porter worked for Raff and Gammon, the company that marketed Thomas Edison's pioneering Vitascope, the first American movie projector. As part of his job, Porter was involved in the country's first motion-picture screening at New York City's Koster and Bial's Music Hall. Porter was thoroughly captivated by the new medium, and he promptly took a job at Thomas Edison's Menlo Park in West Orange, New Jersey. After three months he and two partners established a franchise to sell Edison's films in the West Indies and South America, and to promote the Projectoscope, an improved film projector. Their venture failed, and Porter returned to New York, where he worked as a projectionist in several local theaters.

Improving the Projector. In 1898 Porter's work on improving the projector resulted in the Beadmell, which gave a brighter and steadier picture than other projectors. He immediately found a financial backer and formed a business manufacturing the Beadmell projector and cameras. At the same time, Porter pursued his love of filmmaking, filming news and cultural events that he sold on a freelance basis to the Edison Company and other clients.

Director-Cameraman. A fire in 1900 destroyed Porter's manufacturing plant. Out of financial necessity, Porter returned to work at the Edison Company, first in the mechanical department designing and building cameras, and later as a combination director-cameraman. Soon Porter was in charge of all the production at Edison's studio on East Twenty-first Street in New York City and directed many of the company's films. Like most directors in the 1900s, Porter organized these early short films around one idea or one situation. He shot them from a static, or unmoving, camera position. But within these constraints Porter began to expand the boundaries of the medium by experimenting with some crude special effects, such as double exposures, matte shots, stop-motion photography, and split screens.

Creating a Plot. In 1903 Porter produced the first of several landmark films in the development of American cinema, both in terms of narrative and technique. *The Life of an American Fireman* (1903) was one of the first films to have a plot that extended beyond one scene. It was also the first film to be created in a cutting room. Porter spliced together scenes and shots from several film reels in an effort to shape a coherent, longer narrative. The material consisted of a mixture of original footage shot by Porter and library stock of fire-fighting scenes. The movie also contained one of the first close-ups in America cinema.

America's First Western. Also in 1903, Porter directed another historic film, *The Great Train Robbery*, considered by many to be America's first Western movie. It was nearly twelve minutes long, boasted a cast of forty (which at the time was considered a large number), and told a cohesive story using new techniques such as intercepting and the panning shot. As with *The Life of an American Fireman*, *The Great Train Robbery* featured what became a famous close-up, in which a cowboy fired his gun into the camera lens at the end of the film. The film told a simple story of a band of villains who sneaked aboard a train, robbed it, and were later chased by a posse on horseback. *The Great Train Robbery* advanced the emerging genre of the story-film considerably. It also helped to establish classic features of the American Western: the chase scene and the dramatic showdown between the hero and villain. It was the country's most famous movie until D. W. Griffith released *The Birth of a Nation* in 1915. Porter continued to work for the Edison Company through 1909. He directed several movies and supervised the production of others. His movies from this period include *The Ex-Convict* (1904), *The Kleptomaniac* (1905), *The Dream of a Rarebit Fiend* (1906), and *"Teddy" Bears* (1907).

The Simplex. The more Porter directed films, the more he realized that he was more interested in the mechanical aspects of motion pictures and in special effects than in directing actors and creating plots. As he got older, Porter preferred to work with another director, which freed him to concentrate on the technical aspects of movie production. Throughout his career he continued to tinker in his workshop with new projectors and cameras. In 1908, while still with Edison, Porter began work on a new projecting apparatus called the Simplex projector.

On His Own. In 1909 Porter left Edison and with a partner established a production company called Defender Pictures. Within a year he left Defender to establish his own company, Rex Films. In 1912 Porter sold his interest in Rex and joined Adolph Zukor to create Famous Players in Famous Plays, the forerunner of Paramount Pictures. At Famous Players, Porter directed and supervised the production of the company's movies. One of the last movies Porter directed was also one of his most successful, *The Eternal City* (1915). He directed only a few more movies after 1915, preferring to devote his energy to the technical innovations sweeping the industry, such as color cinematography, wide-screen projection, and a crude 3-D process. Late in 1915 Porter sold his share of Famous Players and invested his profits in the Precision Machine Corporation, where he produced the Simplex projector. His business thrived until the stock market crash of 1929, when Porter lost his company. He spent his final years in anonymity, seemingly forgotten by the industry he had done so much to shape. Porter died in 1941.

Source:
Charles Musser, *Before the Nickelodeon: Edwin S. Porter and the Edison Manufacturing Company* (Berkeley: University of California Press, 1991).

EDITH WHARTON

1862-1937

NOVELIST

An Elite Upbringing. Edith Wharton, one of the leading American novelists of the 1900s and 1910s, was born Edith Jones to wealthy and conservative parents who were part of New York City's high society. Wharton had the best that money could buy. She was privately tutored, traveled to Europe, and married at the age of twenty-three in 1885 to a member of her family's set, Edward Wharton. However, Wharton disliked playing the role of society matron and hostess in New York City and Newport, Rhode Island, a wealthy summer resort area. A few years into her marriage, she suffered a nervous breakdown. Her doctor suggested that Wharton, who had written and had poems published as a child, should take up writing again as a cure for her nerves.

High Society. Wharton's fiction chronicled the manners of New York City society from the 1840s through the 1930s. Her novels and short stories centered on the conflict between an individual's desires and the constraints of social convention. Wharton's public career began when she started to publish her short stories, three collections of which came out in succession: *The Greater Inclination* (1899), *The Touchstone* (1900), and *Crucial Instances* (1901). Wharton's early writing caught the eye of Henry James, who praised her work for its careful depictions of social situations and its psychological realism. Critics, however, saw her as derivative of James, a criticism that plagued Wharton throughout her career. James and Wharton became fast friends and avid fans of each other's work.

Europe and America. Wharton's yearly travels to Europe shaped much of her fiction. Her first novel, *The Valley of Decision* (1902), was set in Italy on the eve of the Napoleonic invasion. As Wharton explained to her editor, the novel was an attempt to picture Italy at the end of the eighteenth century "when all the old forms and traditions of court life were still preserved, but the immense intellectual and moral movement of the new regime was at work beneath the surface of things," a description she easily might have applied to the world of her youth. *The House of Mirth* (1905) brought Wharton critical acclaim. In this novel Wharton offered a scathing and realistic portrait of what she knew best: New York City society. By showing the wealthy as emotionally frivolous, Wharton shed light on the moral crisis besetting the wealthy in a time of social unrest and upheaval. *The House of Mirth* became a best-seller in 1905 and 1906.

Expatriate. Wharton moved to France in 1907, hoping to find in the exclusive Faubourg Saint-Germain quarter of Paris a literate and sophisticated society she found lacking in America. The same year, Wharton published *Madame de Treymes*, which explored the conflict between American and French high societies, and *The Fruit of the Tree*. While living in France, Wharton discovered the joys of automobile touring and wrote some travel pieces about her tours, most notably *A Motor-Flight Through France* (1908).

Ethan Frome. Wharton wrote prolifically. She published two volumes of short stories before she published her third novel, *Ethan Frome*, in 1911 and her fourth, *The Reef*, in 1913. Throughout this period Wharton struggled with the unhappiness of her marriage. Her husband increasingly suffered from neurasthenia, an emotional and psychological condition akin to hysteria. The two had never had much in common, either in terms of interests or worldview. While working on *Ethan Frome,* Wharton fell in love with an American journalist living in Paris, Morton Fullerton. At the same time, Wharton felt terribly guilty for breaking her marriage vows, which she took seriously. The affair between Wharton and Fullerton was intense and brief, but one of the happiest times of her life. *The Reef,* written in the wake of her affair, chronicled the tortured frustrations of unrequited love.

World War I. In 1912 Wharton left her husband, who was increasingly incapacitated by his mental illness and who had begun embezzling Wharton's trust fund. After her divorce Wharton traveled in Europe until World War I broke out in 1914. She returned to Paris and threw herself into journalism and war charities, organizing, among other things, a workroom for unemployed seamstresses and finding food and lodging for Belgian refugees. Wharton retold her wartime experiences in *Fighting France* and *The Book of the Homeless,* both published in 1915; in the novel *A Son at the Front,* written in 1916 and published in 1923; and in *The Marne* (1918) and in *French Ways and Their Meanings* (1919).

The Age of Innocence. In 1920 Wharton published what would become her best-known novel, *The Age of Innocence.* Set in the old New York City of her youth, the novel explored the European roots of traditional New York City society. Written as the world of civilized manners was giving way to the parties and gin fizzes of the Jazz Age, *The Age of Innocence* faithfully recounted the social rituals of a class now dead and buried, its attendance at the opera, its formal dinners, betrothal visits, and summers in Newport. The innocence Wharton recalled in her novel was as much about the sexual propriety and financial rectitude of her parents' age as it was about their aversion to the uglier side of life. Wharton won a Pulitzer Prize for the book in 1920.

Later Life. Wharton continued her energetic writing schedule, and by 1925 was considered the grande dame of American letters. She had received an honorary doctorate from Yale University and was consistently named as one of the "twelve greatest women in America." Few reviewers gave her negative reviews, but a handful complained that Wharton had nothing new to say. Between 1925 and her death in 1937 Wharton wrote one book of essays on the craft of fiction, five novels, five volumes of short stories, a volume of poems, and her memoirs.

Sources:

Eleanor Dwight, *Edith Wharton, An Extraordinary Life* (New York: Abrams, 1994);

R. W. B. Lewis, *Edith Wharton: A Biography* (New York: Harper & Row, 1975).

BERT WILLIAMS

1874-1922

VAUDEVILLIAN

Pioneer of the Stage. W. C. Fields, star of the silent screen, called Bert Williams "the funniest man I ever saw and the saddest." As a central figure on America's vaudeville circuit, Williams sang, danced, and pantomimed in clubs, cabarets, and theaters across the country. Williams was one of, if not the most, famous African American performers in the 1900s. In an age when the "white vaudeville stage did not welcome black performers," Williams pioneered an important role for black performers who had so profoundly shaped the genre. With unfortunate regularity, he was often the only African American on stage. In the 1900s Williams was the toast of the cities he toured, and in 1904 he played a command performance in England for King Edward VII.

Facing Racism. Racial prejudice shaped Williams's career. Unlike many other blackface performers, Williams did not play for laughs at the expense of other African Americans or black culture. Instead he based his humor on universal situations in which any members of his audience might find themselves. In the style of vaudeville, Williams performed in blackface makeup like his white counterparts. Blackface worked like a double mask for him. It emphasized the difference between Williams, his fellow vaudevillians, and his white audiences. Many white vaudevillians refused to appear on the same bill with Williams, and others complained that his material, which he wrote himself, was better than theirs. Williams, like many black performers, faced discrimination from the hotels and restaurants in which he often performed. Hotels routinely refused to let Williams ride in the same elevators used by their white patrons. He once told a friend how much such seemingly petty discrimination hurt. "It wouldn't be so bad ... if I didn't hear the applause [from his performance] still ringing in my ears."

Early Life. Williams was born in New Providence, Nassau, in the British West Indies, in 1874. He became a showman in 1893, when he joined Martin and Seig's Mastodon Minstrels. While performing with the Minstrels he met African American song-and-dance man George Walker, and the two men teamed up. The twosome debuted in New York's Casino Theatre in 1898 in a short-lived show, *The Gold Bug.* Their act consisted of songs, dance, and quick-paced patter that centered on Walker trying to convince the slower Williams to join him in get-rich-quick schemes. Williams and Walker's popular act continued until Walker's death in 1911.

Ziegfeld Follies. Williams struck out on his own when, in 1909, Walker became too ill to perform. In

1910 Florenz Ziegfeld hired Williams to be one of the stars of *The Ziegfeld Follies*. He performed in the *Follies* almost continually, and his national popularity and fame grew. In 1918 Williams broke another color line when he topped the bill at New York City's Palace. Williams became famous for his pantomimed poker game. In this skit a single spotlight illuminated Williams's head and shoulders as he mimicked all the gestures of the player, from drawing cards to losing the game. The popularity of this skit led to a brief film career in the summer of 1916 when Williams appeared in the film *A Natural Born Gambler*. In addition to the poker-game skit, Williams introduced many popular songs to audiences across the country, such as "You Ain't So Warm," "Nobody," "That's Harmony," and "You Got the Right Church but the Wrong Pew."

Later Life. In 1920 Williams left the *Follies* and signed with another New York company, the Shuberts. On 21 February 1922 Williams collapsed onstage while touring with the production of *Under the Bamboo Tree*. Williams returned to New York City, where he died a month later.

Sources:
Ann Charters, *Nobody: The Story of Bert Williams* (New York: Macmillan, 1970);

Eric L. Smith, *Bert Williams: A Biography of the Black Comedian* (Jefferson, N.C. & London: McFarland, 1992).

PEOPLE IN THE NEWS

Maude Adams, actress, starred in James Barrie's *Peter Pan*, which opened on 6 November 1905 and ran for six months.

On 23 August 1905 director **G. M. Anderson** released *Raffles, Amateur Cracksman*, for Vitagraph Studios; it was the most elaborately produced film to date.

Ethel Barrymore uttered the famous line "that's all there is, there isn't any more" in **Thomas Raceway**'s Broadway show *Sunday*, which premiered 15 November 1904 and ran for ten weeks.

On 4 September 1909 **John Barrymore** appeared in his first nonmusical hit production, Ongley and Smith's *The Fortune Hunter*. The play ran for 345 performances.

Producer-playwright **David Belasco** discovered **Blanche Bates** and starred her in two productions, *Naughty Anthony* and *Madame Butterfly*, in 1900. In 1906 Bates starred in the *Girl of the Golden West*.

On 20 November 1900 French actress **Sarah Bernhardt** arrived in the United States for her first visit since 1896; in 1906 "the Divine Sarah" began an American tour that grossed $1 million — an unprecedented amount of money for the day.

Italian opera star **Enrico Caruso** maded his first recording in the United States on 2 February 1904. On 23 November 1906 Caruso was fined ten dollars for annoying a young lady, Miss Hannah Graham, in the Central Park Zoo monkey house. On 13 August 1908, in London, Caruso's wife ran off with a lover; Caruso said, "It is the very thing I desired."

A major exhibition of American Impressionist **Mary Cassatt**'s work opened in New York City on 24 August 1907. Born in Pittsburgh to a wealthy railroad-owning family, Cassatt had lived in France most of her life. Her "modern madonnas" — paintings of mothers with their children — did much to forward the cause of Impressionism in America.

On 7 November 1904 **George M. Cohan** opened on Broadway in the first show he wrote and staged alone, *Little Johnny Jones;* his song "Give My Regards to Broadway" was an immediate hit.

On 4 January 1906 Berlin police forbade American dancer **Isadora Duncan** to dance in public.

On 18 December 1908 **Thomas Edison** and his partners formed the Motion Picture Patents Company. The incorporation centralized the operation of the "movie business."

On 23 May 1909 police stopped a lecture being given by **Emma Goldman**, anarchist, feminist, and editor of *Mother Earth* magazine. Authorities charged that Miss Goldman digressed from her topic, "Modern Drama, the Strongest Disseminator of Radical Thought," to discuss Joan of Arc.

In 1906 inventor **Eldridge Johnson** introduced the Victrola, the first phonograph with a playback horn located in the body of the machine.

Austrian composer **Gustav Mahler** made his American debut, conducting *Tristan und Isolde* at the Metropolitan Opera House on 1 January 1908.

On 20 February 1909 Italian artist **Filippo Marinetti** published his "Futurist Manifesto," which praises speed, violence, and anarchism; Futurism, although short-lived, influenced American artists such as Joseph Stella in decades to come.

Movie director **Wallace McCutcheon** created the first filmed chase scene in *Personal,* produced by Biograph Studios in June 1904.

On 15 February 1901 temperance advocate **Carry Nation** took a hatchet to saloons in Topeka, Kansas; later in the decade she reprised the role in her vaudeville act, selling souvenir hatchets to audience members.

On 5 March 1900, after twenty-nine performances of Clyde Fitch's play *Sappho,* actress **Olga Nethersole** was arrested for "indecency."

On 22 October 1907 **Ringling Brothers** bought Barnum and Bailey's circus for $410,000.

On 30 October 1905 the New York production of **Bernard Shaw**'s play *Mrs. Warren's Profession,* which deals with prostitution, was halted as unfit for audiences; on 7 July 1906 courts ruled that the content was suitable for performance.

In 1903 singer **Fritzi Scheff** deserted the Metropolitan Opera for Broadway, opening in the musical *Babette.*

In 1903 **Sam** and **Lee Shubert** made their first New York real-estate transaction, purchasing property on Thirty-ninth Street. In 1905 they formed the Shubert Theatrical Corporation, the first serious challenge to the monopoly of the Theater Syndicate.

Ruth St. Denis began her successful U.S. tour with her dance performance of *Radha* in July 1906.

On 15 October 1900 writer **Mark Twain** returned from Europe, telling reporters, "I am absolutely unable to speak of my plans, inasmuch as I have none."

On 26 January 1906 the **Oscar Wilde–Richard Strauss** production of *Salome* was withdrawn from the Metropolitan Opera after one performance. The "dance of the seven veils" and the onstage portrayal of the decapitated head of John the Baptist were too much for New York City audiences to accept.

DEATHS

James Bailey, 59, owner of the Barnum and Bailey Circus, 11 April 1906.

Frédéric-Auguste Bartholdi, 70, creator of the Statue of Liberty, 4 October 1904.

Maurice Barrymore, 57, British American actor, father of John, Lionel, and Ethel, 26 March 1905.

David Braham, 67, songwriter of the 1870s and 1880s, wrote minstrel songs and urban songs, 1905.

Kate Chopin, 54, novelist (*The Awakening*), 22 August 1904.

Frederic Church, 74, landscape artist of the Hudson River School, 4 July 1900.

Stephen Crane, 29, journalist, poet, short-story writer, and novelist (*The Red Badge of Courage*), 5 June 1900.

Jean Margaret Davenport-Lander, 74, first actress to play *Camille* in the United States, 2 August 1903.

Jessie Bartlett Davis, 39, much-admired American actress, 14 May 1905.

Paul Dresser, 49, music publisher, balladeer ("On the Banks of the Wabash," "My Gal Sal"), brother of novelist Theodore Dreiser, 30 January 1906.

Paul Laurence Dunbar, 34, poet, novelist, and short-story writer; significant contributor to the African American poetic tradition, 9 February 1906.

Owen Fawcett, American actor, 21 February 1904.

Clyde Fitch, 44, most popular and successful playwright of his era, first internationally known American dramatist, 4 September 1909.

Wendell P. Garrison, 67, literary editor of *The Nation*, 27 February 1907.

Joel Chandler Harris, 68, southern writer, introduced African folk characters into mainstream American literature (*The Uncle Remus Tales*, 1881–1905), 3 July 1908.

Bret Harte, 66, journalist, short-story writer, celebrated (often sentimentally) frontier life ("The Outcasts of Poker Flat"), 5 May 1902.

James A. Herne, 62, actor-manager-playwright, introduced realism to American drama with *Margaret Fleming* (1890), 2 June 1901.

Bronson Howard, 66, playwright, "Dean of American Drama," 4 August 1908.

Charles H. Hoyt, 41, popular American stage satirist of the late 1800s, 20 November 1900.

Laurence Hutton, 60, drama critic, 10 June 1904.

Joseph Jefferson III, 76, actor-producer, one of the most beloved performers of the nineteenth-century American stage, well-known for his portrayal of Rip Van Winkle, 23 April 1905.

Sarah Orne Jewett, 60, local colorist and short-story writer (*The Country of the Pointed Firs*), 24 June 1909.

Jonathan Eastman Johnson, 82, American painter, 5 April 1906.

Bessie Lamb, 29, vaudeville singer, 30 October 1907.

Olive Logan, 70, American actress and author, 27 April 1909.

Edward MacDowell, 47, composer; introduced Native American and folk themes in his orchestral works, 23 January 1908.

Richard Mansfield, 53, actor-manager, known for lavish melodramas, 30 August 1907.

Ethelbert Nevin, 39, composer, whose musical rendition of Robert Cameron Rogers's poem "The Rosary" remained popular from 1898 to 1925, 1901.

Ada Nielson, 59, actress, 25 January 1905.

Frank Norris, 32, naturalist, novelist (*McTeague, The Octopus, The Pit*), 25 October 1902.

A. M. Palmer, 66, Broadway producer and theatrical manager, 7 March 1905.

Tony Pastor, 71, theater owner, made vaudeville variety a family entertainment, 3 September 1908.

Alexander Lawrence Posey, 35, Native American journalist, humorist, and poet, 1908.

Roland Reed, 49, popular light comedian, 1 April 1901.

Frederic Remington, 48, painter and sculptor of the West; 26 December 1909.

Billy Rice, popular blackface minstrel, 1902.

Hugh C. Robertson, 64, ceramicist, 1908.

Gus Rogers, 49, popular comedian of the Rogers Brothers duo, 19 October 1908.

Sam Shubert, 30, Broadway producer-manager, 12 May 1905.

Lydia Thompson, 72, whose "British Blondes" dancing troupe shocked Victorian moralists, 17 November 1908.

John Twachtman, 49, American Impressionist painter, 1902.

George Walker, African American vaudevillian, 1909.

Lew Wallace, 71, author of *Ben-Hur*, 15 February 1905.

James McNeill Whistler, 69, expatriate American painter (*Arrangement in Grey and Black, No. 1*), 17 July 1903.

Stanford White, 53, architect, 25 June 1906.

PUBLICATIONS

Henry Mills Alden, *Magazine Writing and the New Literature* (New York: Harper, 1908);

Edwin Swift Balch, *Art in America Before the Revolution* (Philadelphia, 1908);

Kenyon Cox, *Old Masters and New: Essays in Art Criticism* (New York: Duffield, 1908);

Walter Pritchard Eaton, *The American Stage of Today* (Boston: Small, Maynard, 1908);

Lewis Charles Elson, *The History of American Music* (New York: Macmillan, 1904);

George William Gerwig, *The Art of the Short Story* (Akron, Ohio: Werner, 1909);

Lawrence Gilman, *Phases of Modern Music* (New York: Harpers, 1904);

Robert Grau, *Forty Years Observation of Music and the Drama* (New York: Broadway, 1909);

Philip Leslie Hale, *Great Portraits, Women* (Boston: Bates & Guild, 1909);

Sadakichi Hartmann, *A History of American Art* (Boston: Page, 1902);

Abby Willis Howes, *A Primer of American Literature* (Boston: D. C. Heath, 1909);

William Lines Hubbard, *The American History and Encyclopedia of Music* (Toledo, N.Y.: Squire, 1908–1910);

David Sherill Hulfish, *The Motion Picture, Its Making and Its Theater* (Chicago: Electricity Magazine, 1909);

Ludwig Lewisohn, *The Modern Novel* (Sewanee, Tenn.: University Press, University of the South, 1909);

Lillie Deming Loshe, *The Early American Novel* (New York: Columbia University Press, 1907);

Loshe, *A Literary History of America* (New York: Scribners, 1907);

Brander Matthews, *The Development of the Drama* (New York: Scribners, 1903);

Hugo Musterberg, *The Priciples of Art Education* (New York: Prang Educational, 1905);

Carleton Eldredge Noyes, *The Enjoyment of Art* (Boston: Houghton, Mifflin, 1903);

Bliss Perry, *A Study of Prose Fiction* (Boston: Houghton, Mifflin, 1902);

F. B. Sanborn, *Recollections of Seventy Years* (Boston: Badger, 1909);

George Santayana, *Interpretations of Poetry and Religion* (New York: Scribners, 1900);

William Edward Simons, *A Student's History of American Literature* (Boston: Houghton, Mifflin, 1909);

William Ladd Taylor, *Our Home and Country* (New York: Moffat, Yard, 1908);

Leon Henry Vincent, *American Literary Masters* (Boston: Houghton, Mifflin, 1906);

American Art News, periodical;

Atlantic Monthly, periodical;

Billboard, periodical;

Camera Work, periodical;

The Century, periodical;

Cosmopolitan, periodical;

Everybody's, periodical;

The Forum, periodical;

Harper's Weekly, periodical;

Life, periodical;

The Literary Digest, periodical;

McClure's, periodical;

Munsey's, periodical;

Musical Times, periodical;

The Nation, periodical;

Scribner's, periodical;

Smith's, periodical;

Variety, periodical.

CHAPTER THREE

BUSINESS AND THE ECONOMY

by LISA MCNARY and STEVE MELLUM

CONTENTS

Sidebars and tables are listed in italics.

1900

10 Jan. The National Civic Federation is established in Chicago to promote labor-management relations with representatives from business, the labor, and the public.

14 Mar. Congress passes the Gold Standard Act to improve the national currency.

18 Mar. Veteran train engineer of the Chicago and New Orleans Limited, John Luther "Casey" Jones, thirty-six, stays at the throttle of the Cannonball Express in an attempt to slow down the six-coach train and spare as many lives as possible. At more than seventy miles per hour, Jones rounds a curve near Vaughan, Mississippi, to find a train stalled on the track in front of him, and the crash is unavoidable. His heroic death would later be immortalized by another railroad worker in the ballad "Casey Jones."

31 Mar. The era of the automobile begins as the first national advertisement for automobiles appears in *The Saturday Evening Post*.

1 May More than two hundred miners are killed in an explosion in Scofield, Utah.

26 May The horsecar era comes to an end as the last horsecar to operate in the United States makes its final run in Washington, D.C.

3 June The International Ladies Garment Workers Union is founded in New York City with a charter by the American Federation of Labor.

17 Sept. The newly formed United Mine Workers (UMW) stages its first strike in Pennsylvania with nearly one hundred thousand miners participating.

29 Oct. With pressure from the Republican Party, the mine owners grant minor pay concessions and the United Mine Workers return to work. Additional negotiations between the mine owners and the UMW continue throughout 1901 on various labor issues.

3 Nov. The first U.S. National Automobile Show opens at New York's Madison Square Garden and lasts a week. The show features fifty-one exhibitors and numerous contests on starting, stopping, turning, and obstacle-course proficiency.

6 Nov. Under the "full dinner pail" slogan as a symbol of prosperity brought about by the Republican Party, Republican candidate William McKinley is reelected president with a percentage of the popular vote exceeding his previous election. Theodore Roosevelt is elected his vice president.

15 Nov. The Carnegie Institute of Technology is founded by steel magnate Andrew Carnegie in Pittsburgh. The institute personifies his belief that contribution to society should be made while donors are living. Carnegie will donate $5.2 million to fund branches of the New York Public Library.

1901

10 Jan. The oil gusher Spindletop blasts near Beaumont, Texas, establishing the petroleum industry in Texas.

25 Feb. Formed from a merger of ten companies, U.S. Steel is established as the world's largest industrial corporation.

9 May The largest single-day decline in the stock market since 1803 occurs, with some stocks dropping twenty points.

6 Sept. President McKinley is shot twice at point-blank range while attending a public reception at the Temple of Music in the Pan-American Exposition in Buffalo, New York. One bullet goes into McKinley's stomach and another hits his breast-plate. Doctors are unable to locate the bullets and close the wounds.

14 Sept. President McKinley, fifty-eight, dies from complications from gangrene from improperly dressed wounds, and Roosevelt is inaugurated as the twenty-fifth president, the youngest to date at the age of forty-two.

1902

19 Feb. The Sherman Antitrust Act is used for the first time against the Northern Securities Company, formed by a railroad merger.

12 May The Anthracite Coal Strike begins and lasts five months, nearly crippling the nation. The United Mine Workers' demands include union representation, wage increases of 20 percent, and eight-hour workdays.

1 June The state of Maryland passes a workers' compensation law, the nation's first.

17 June The National Reclamation Act, also called the Newlands Act as well as the Irrigation Bill, is passed by Congress, authorizing the federal government to build dams in the West for irrigation. The act is considered vital to westward expansion and the farming sector. The first dam to be built under the act is the Roosevelt Dam, located on the Salt River in Arizona.

3 Oct. Representatives of labor and management are invited to Washington by President Roosevelt to confer with him in settling the Anthracite Coal Strike.

16 Oct. A special commission is appointed by Roosevelt to mediate the Anthracite Coal Strike.

21 Oct. The head of the United Mine Workers, John Mitchell, calls off the twenty-three-week strike as negotiations begin, though a settlement is not reached until the following March.

16 Nov. The famous "Drawing the Line in Mississippi" political cartoon appears in the *Washington Post* and the *Washington Evening Star*, depicting Roosevelt's refusal to participate in the staged killing of a bear on a hunting expedition. The cartoon is the impetus for the creation of the teddy bear and the first U.S. manufacturer of toy bears, the Ideal Toy and Novelty Company.

1903

4 Feb. As a result of antitrust investigations, Congress passes the Elkins Act, which regulates interstate commerce activities and is specifically targeted at the railroads.

11 Feb. Congress passes the Expedition Act, giving antitrust suits precedence over other docketed cases.

14 Feb. The Department of Commerce and Labor is created at the cabinet level by Congress. The original act includes a provision for a Bureau of Corporations to investigate the organization, conduct, or management of any company.

25 Feb. The Immunity Provision Act is passed, providing protection for witnesses, especially employees of corporations who are called to testify in antitrust cases.

22 Mar. The Anthracite Mediation Commission appointed by Roosevelt the previous October renders its decision. Concessions are made to both the mine operators and the United Mine Workers.

6 May In a speech at the Grand Canyon, Roosevelt uses the term "Square Deal" publicly for the first time. A term that is used to represent the balancing of interests of business, labor, and the public, the Square Deal will later become Roosevelt's 1904 presidential platform.

14 July Roosevelt settles a union dispute as to whether civil service employees are in a closed or open shop. In the previous weeks William A. Miller had been fired as a foreman in the Government Printing Office when he was expelled from the union, the International Brotherhood of Bookbinders, for openly criticizing their hiring practices. Roosevelt intervened, and his decision made the civil service an open shop, meaning that union membership was not a requirement to be hired because such a requirement was incongruent with the current labor laws of the United States.

8 Aug. Nearly four thousand miners of the Western Federation of Miners walk out in Cripple Creek, Colorado, because of a reduced workday and lowered wages.

4 Sept. Federal troops arrive in Colorado to intervene in the continuing strike, and a few of the mines reopen.

22 Oct. The Electrical Vehicle Company and George B. Selden file suit against the Ford Motor Company for infringement of the Selden patent on engines. The case, known as the Selden Patent Case, will not go to trial for six years.

30 Nov. The U.S. Supreme Court rules in *Atkin* v. *Kansas* that an eight-hour workday for public-works construction workers is constitutional.

17 Dec. The Wright brothers make their first sustained manned flight at Kitty Hawk, North Carolina, creating what will eventually become the airline industry.

1904

7 Feb. The business center of Baltimore burns for more than a day, resulting in $85 million in damage, with more than 140 acres encompassing seventy-five square blocks being destroyed.

14 Mar. The Supreme Court rules in *Northern Securities* v. *United States* that the railroad merger violates the Sherman Antitrust Act of 1890.

30 Apr. The World's Fair, called the Louisiana Purchase Exposition, begins in Saint Louis after a dedication by Roosevelt and is open for seven months.

4 June The Independence railroad station in Colorado is destroyed by an explosion that kills fourteen nonunion miners who were waiting for the train after finishing work at the Findley Mine. The Western Federation of Miners is charged with the crime, though a spy working for the Mine Owners' Association would later confess.

27 Oct. The first rapid transit system, the New York City subway system, opens.

1905

8 Nov. Running on the Square Deal platform, Republican candidate Theodore Roosevelt is elected in his own right as president in a landslide victory with Charles W. Fairbanks, a senator from Indiana, as his running mate.

1 Dec. A publication of the National Association of Manufacturers titled *American Industries* likens union labor's request for a shorter workday to communism.

A fifteen-month strike that began in August 1903 at the gold mine in Cripple Creek, Colorado, by the Western Federation of Miners ends in concessions being made by the Mine Owners' Association, including a three-dollar-a-day minimum wage for an eight-hour day.

8 Jan. A strike lasting more than five months by textile workers in Fall River, Massachusetts, ends successfully, with labor concessions being granted.

30 Jan. The beef trust case, *Swift and Company* v. *United States,* is filed by the Justice Department because of monopolization of the fresh meat market.

23 Feb. The Rotary Club, the first business-related service organization, is founded in Chicago.

17 Apr. The Supreme Court rules in *Lochner* v. *New York* that limiting the maximum number of hours an employee works is unconstitutional.

27 June The Industrial Workers of the World (IWW) is created as a nationwide industrial union. The "Wobblies," as IWW members are called, seek to unite all industrial workingmen in a union.

30 Dec. Former Idaho governor Frank Steunenberg is murdered by a bomb explosion in his home in Caldwell, Idaho. Prominent union organizers from the Western Federation of Miners, including William D. "Big Bill" Haywood, are accused. The case, settled in 1907, becomes one of the most notorious labor trials of the century.

1906

21 Feb. The Heyburn Bill is passed by Congress, regulating the producers and sellers of food.

12 Mar. Trustbusting continues with the U.S. Supreme Court ruling in the case of *Hale* v. *Henkel* that employees called as witnesses in antitrust cases can be forced to testify against their employers.

14 Apr. Roosevelt delivers his infamous "muck-rake" speech in a Washington, D.C., address.

18 Apr. The San Francisco earthquake hits in the morning, destroying the business district and much of the city. More than 500 blocks are gutted in fires erupting after the quake that leave 250,000 people homeless, 25,000 buildings destroyed, and 500 dead.

3 May The advertising age is born with the First Annual Advertising Show opening in New York City.

4 June A specially appointed presidential commission issues the Neill-Reynolds report, documenting the dismal conditions in the meatpacking industry. The commission was appointed as a result of a novel by Upton Sinclair, *The Jungle*, published earlier in the year.

29 June The Hepburn Act, which broadens the powers of the Interstate Commerce Commission (ICC) by overhauling the Interstate Commerce Act of 1887, is passed by Congress.

30 June In response to the Neill-Reynolds report, Congress passes the Meat Inspection Act, which requires federal inspection of all meat involved in interstate and foreign commerce.

The Pure Food and Drug Act, prohibiting the mislabeling or adulteration of food involved in interstate and foreign commerce, is passed.

The Act Defending Right of Immunity revises the Immunity Provision Act of 1903 regarding witnesses testifying in antitrust legislation and applies only to a "natural person" who testifies in "obedience to a subpoena."

12 July The drowned body of factory worker Grace Brown is found in the Adirondacks. Her supervisor from work, Chester Gillette, is convicted. The case provided the inspiration for Theodore Dreiser's novel *An American Tragedy* (1925).

22 July The cable car era comes to an end as the last cable car operating in the United States makes its final run in Chicago.

1907

13 Mar. As the stock market drops, a financial panic begins, resulting in unemployment, high food prices, and bank failures by the end of the year.

An order that segregated Japanese, Chinese, and Korean students is dropped by the San Francisco school board. Originally passed on 11 October 1906, the order is rescinded on condition that a "Gentlemen's Agreement" between the United States and Japan that was passed in August 1900 is enforced. The agreement requires Japan to limit the number of laborers allowed to immigrate to the United States by refusing to issue passports.

29 July William D. "Big Bill" Haywood is found not guilty in the murder of former Idaho governor Frank Steunenberg. Instrumental to the case is a confession from the killer, found to be working for the Mine Owners' Association, that the bomb was planted to frame union organizers, a revelation that shocked the public.

21 Oct. A run on the Knickerbocker Trust Company ruins the bank. In the coming weeks other banks and trusts fail, requiring the infusion of money from the U.S. Treasury and from the private sector under the leadership of J. P. Morgan.

6 Dec. A total of 361 coal miners die in an explosion in Monongah, West Virginia.

19 Dec. A total of 239 coal miners die in an explosion in Jacobs Creek, Pennsylvania.

1908

27 Jan.	The Supreme Court rules in *Adair* v. *United States* that a portion of the Erdman Act of 1898 outlawing yellow-dog contracts is unconstitutional.
3 Feb.	The U.S. Supreme Court issues a unanimous ruling in the Danbury Hatters case, *Loewe* v. *Lawlor*, stating that a nationwide boycott of the industry is a restraint of trade under the Sherman Antitrust Act.
10 Feb.	The Wright brothers sign their first army contract for the delivery of a plane, establishing the record of a bid-to-contract time frame of five days. The conditional contract will be finalized upon successful operation of the plane.
24 Feb.	The U.S. Supreme Court issues a unanimous ruling in the *Muller* v. *Oregon* case, holding that laws limiting the maximum number of hours that women can work to ten hours a day are constitutional.
16 Mar.	The first test of the Elkins Act (1903) occurs in *Armour Packing Company* v. *United States*, which affirms the ICC power to conduct railroad rate investigations.
20 Mar.	Though maintaining his innocence throughout his trial and imprisonment, Chester E. Gillette is electrocuted for the 1906 drowning murder of Grace Brown, his employee and lover.
22 Apr.	Congress passes the Employers' Liability Act for interstate commerce.
30 May	Congress passes the Aldrich-Vreeland Act to correct deficiencies in the banking system that created the Panic of 1907.
26 July	The precursor to the Federal Bureau of Investigation is established as a branch of the Justice Department to investigate organized labor, fight the greed of big business, and prevent thievery of public lands.
1 Oct.	The Ford Motor Company unveils the Model T with a price tag starting at $825, signaling the automobile age for the masses.
3 Nov.	In a narrow victory, Republican candidate William Howard Taft is elected the twenty-seventh president of the United States with only 51.6 percent of the popular vote. In keeping with the tradition against a third term, Roosevelt declined to run for reelection and supported Taft, the secretary of war during the Roosevelt administration.

1909

16 Mar.	After disputes concerning the use of Secret Service agents from the U.S. Treasury for investigations, the Federal Bureau of Investigation is established as a separate division.
28 May	The Selden Patent Case, filed in 1903, opens with complicated arguments over whether the patent on the invention that was not enforced for sixteen years represented a restricted or nonrestricted patent. If a nonrestrictive or broad patent is proved, then royalties on the thousands of cars made since the patent was filed in 1879 would have to be paid to Selden. Selden wins the case, and most established car companies pay the licensing fee. Ford refuses and files an appeal, which he wins in 1910. The case is instrumental in reforming patent laws.

12 July   The Sixteenth Amendment to the Constitution, authorizing income taxes, is passed by Congress.

2 Aug.   The Wright brothers deliver their first plane to Signal Corps at a cost of $30,000.

5 Aug.   The controversial Payne-Aldrich Tariff Act is signed by President Taft in keeping with his campaign promise to reduce tariffs instituted by the Dingley Tariff of 1897.

13 Nov.   More than 250 miners are killed in an explosion at the Saint Paul Mine in Cherry, Illinois.

22 Nov.   A three-month strike by the International Ladies Garment Workers Union begins in New York, with twenty thousand U.S. garment workers protesting.

OVERVIEW

Portrait of America. The first decade of the twentieth-century saw profound change in the makeup of America. According to the twelfth decennial census in 1900, the population was more than seventy-six million, an increase of nearly 21 percent from the 1890 census. The population continued to grow rapidly throughout the decade as nearly nine million immigrants entered the country, with most arrivals coming from Italy, Austria-Hungary, and Russia. The record year for immigrants was 1907, when 1.29 million people entered the United States. By the end of the decade the U.S. population had risen to ninety-one million. One-third of the populace lived in an urban area by the beginning of the century, mostly in the eastern United States, the center of industrialism; New York was the largest city, followed by Chicago and Philadelphia. Agriculture, which had employed the majority of American workers in the nineteenth century, was slowly being replaced by industrial occupations.

Women, Immigrants, and Children. Men and women rarely competed for jobs, primarily because of the sexual division of labor in the workplace. In the industrial sector, for example, men had various opportunities and could claim the jobs that required physical strength while women were confined to low-paying jobs using light machinery. Although by 1910 one-third of the workforce was female, half of women workers were involved in agriculture or in domestic service, leaving little female representation in burgeoning industries. Such white-collar positions open to women — teaching, clerical work, nursing, and retail sales — paid little and carried little prestige. Immigrants were also faced with an uphill climb. But while most immigrants started out in low-ranking and poorly paid jobs, many immigrant men were able to find well-paying craft or union positions by the end of the decade. Children were perhaps the most exploited workers. Until regulation curtailed the practice, child labor was common. In 1900 more than 250,000 children under the age of fifteen worked in factories for minimal pay.

Union and Nonunion Labor. Union wages outpaced nonunion wages by 65 percent in 1900, and this lead was maintained throughout the decade. Average union pay in 1900 was thirty-four cents per hour, compared to non-union, unskilled pay of fifteen cents per hour. By 1909 the average union pay rose to thirty-nine cents per hour, and nonunion pay was nearly eighteen cents an hour. The average workweek in the decade was fifty-three hours. Unskilled laborers faced especially severe hardships, for their income would not support a family of five even if they toiled twelve hours a day, every day of the year.

Home Ownership. Unskilled laborers had little chance of home ownership. They often settled in inner-city tenements or cheap wood-frame homes near the industrial sector and took in boarders for additional income. Semiskilled and skilled laborers could afford modest homes in residential areas, away from the industrial sector and inner city. Mass-manufactured homes became increasingly popular because of their affordability compared to custom-built homes. The entry of Sears Roebuck into the ready-made home market in 1908 made home ownership a viable possibility for many more Americans. Modern Home Number 167, a three-story structure with more than twenty-five hundred feet of living space, cost $754 for the materials and approximately $1,000 more for construction. Heating and plumbing were extra, adding an additional $300 and bringing the total cost to about $2,000. The cost of constructing a home rose only 11 percent throughout the decade, while wages rose 17 percent on average. However, the size of the average home began to decrease dramatically as housing costs escalated in the next decade and wages failed to keep pace with that increase. By 1913 a popular seller was "The Heather," a 320-square-foot home (costing $250 for the materials) that was marketed as a "cozy cottage."

Social Life. Although most cultural activities in the United States were divided along class lines, Americans of all classes were drawn to new diversions. Among the working class, activities such as amusement parks, movie theaters, dance halls, fraternal orders, skating rinks, and spectator sports became popular. With leisure time increasing, the working class also began to take a greater interest in fashion. While the middle and upper classes were enticed by new amusements, they continued to patronize museums, plays, restaurants, university speeches, and other more genteel activities. For all Americans the first decade of the century brought an increasing commercialism of cultural activities as leisure became a marketable commodity.

New Industry. At the beginning of the century the United States had turned away from the isolationism which preceded the Spanish-American War. Now a world power with quickly expanding foreign markets, the United States was considered a major industrial nation. Global expansion meant increased wealth as raw materials became cheaper to acquire, driving prices down and consumption up. The decade saw business prospering in many sectors, including oil, steel, textiles, railroads, and food products. The unprecedented technological progress in the decade was marked by the birth of the automobile and aviation industries as Americans who began the century riding horse-drawn buggies could at the end of its first decade drive cars and begin to dream of someday flying in a plane.

The Progressive Era. The Progressive Era began with Theodore Roosevelt's presidency in 1901 and lasted until the entry of the United States into World War I in 1917. During this period, a prosperous United States witnessed reforms that transformed its economic, social, and political life. Economic reformers sought to regulate trusts and big business, reduce the domination of government by the elite, and reform the fiscal system. The business climate was also affected by social and political reformers, who were concerned with such issues as poverty, health, working conditions, women's rights, the conservation of national resources, election abuses, the power of urban political bosses, and governmental fraud. The spirit of reform gave rise to a separate Progressive Party in 1912 when a split developed within the Republican Party. Led by Roosevelt — who claimed after surviving an assassination attempt that he felt like a "bull moose" — the Bull Moose ticket sustained Roosevelt's advocacy for farmers and industrial workers into the second decade of the century.

The Advent of Professional Managers. With global expansion and increased markets, big business grew, creating a new profession of management, separate from the owners of the business. Thus, the age of the robber baron came to an end as the age of the manager and stockholder took over. The importance of the managerial profession became more recognized in the next decade with the spread of "scientific management" and the publication of the landmark book *Industrial and General Administration* in 1916 by French industrialist Henri Fayol, which laid the foundation of management into the components of planning, organizing, staffing, directing, and controlling. By the 1920s many corporations were requiring professional managers to have college degrees and to go through specialized training programs.

The Rise of Big Business. The first decade of the century saw businesses continue to expand through merging with similar companies (horizontal integration) and taking on additional functions in the production and sale of their products, such as a manufacturer of raw materials becoming involved in marketing the product to consumers (vertical integration). The result was an elimination of competition and a stratification of business enterprises into those that were capital-intensive, such as manufacturers, and those that were not, such as service industries. The overriding concern of the public was that the continued rise of big business through trusts, trade associations, cartels, or pools would destroy America's image as the land of opportunity where success as a self-made business owner was possible. As public unrest grew, the government began to intervene to regulate the proliferation of big business.

Incorporation. With new inventions and discoveries as well as emerging national markets for an array of goods and services, the early 1900s saw the founding of major corporations that have become fixtures of American life: Firestone Tire and Rubber Company (1900), Sylvania Electric Company (1901), United States Steel Company (1901), the American Can Company (1901), the Quaker Oats Company (1901), Monsanto Chemical Company (1901), Philip Morris Corporation (1902), J. C. Penney Company (1902), United States Shipbuilding Company (1902), International Harvester Company (1902), the Pepsi-Cola Company (1902), Texaco, Inc. (1903), the Ford Motor Company (1903), Continental Can Company (1904), Bethlehem Steel Company (1905), Mead Pulp and Paper (1905), Spiegel Catalog (1905), Planters Nut and Chocolate Company (1906), Gulf Oil (1907), American Cyanamid Company (1907), Harley-Davidson (1907), Hershey (1908), AC Spark Plug Company (1908), General Motors Company (1908), and McGraw-Hill Book Company (1909). The overall prosperity of the decade made Americans eager to try new products, especially as companies began to spend more money to advertise their products.

Capital, Labor, and the Public. The century began with a continuing attempt at conciliation between labor and management interests in the spreading of the National Civic Federation, founded in 1898. The goal of the federation was to merge the interests of capital, labor, and the public in working out industrial issues. The federation was run by an executive committee with representatives for all three constituencies. The first president of the federation was an Ohio industrialist and prominent Republican party boss, "Dollar Mark" Hanna. Business representatives included Henry Phipps of U.S. Steel, Francis Robbins of Pittsburgh Coal Company, Frederick Fish of American Bell Telephone Company, and Lucius Tuttle of Boston and Maine Railroad. Union representatives included Samuel Gompers of the American Federation of Labor, John Mitchell of the United Mine Workers, John Tobin of the Boot and Shoe Workers Union, William Mahon of the Amalgamated Association of Street Railway Employees, and Warren Stone of the International Brotherhood of Engineers. The "public" was represented by steel magnate Andrew Carnegie, former U.S. president Grover Cleveland, and banker Isaac Seligman. One major area the federation addressed was wage disputes. However, the success of the federation was short-lived, as interests collided. Many labor members felt their representatives had sold them out on important issues.

Rising Tensions. While the federation made some progress on labor issues, such as the forming of the National Child Labor Committee in 1904 to limit the use of child labor, organized labor grew increasingly uneasy with pay and working conditions as big business grew despite governmental regulation. Throughout the decade the number of organized workers increased, but their progress in gaining concessions was uneven. Business owners, though, became increasingly alarmed at the gains in power made by labor. Many capitalists struck back at the union movement through such owner-operator organizations as the Citizens' Industrial Alliance, the National Council of Industrial Defense, and the American Anti-Boycott Association. The prominent National Association of Manufacturers, founded in 1895, adopted a "Declaration of Labor Principles" at its 1903 convention, designed to weaken the unions. One of the association's strategies was to push for the open shop, meaning that union membership was not required of employees, which was seen by labor as the first step in banning unions from the workplace. The growing tensions in labor relations brought calls for the disputing parties to recognize their mutual interests. The cover of the 1 June 1901 *Harper's Weekly* depicted three figures representing capital, labor, and American commerce and proclaimed, "Come, brothers, you have grown so big that you cannot afford to quarrel."

Labor Strife. Not surprisingly, the first decade was marked by a great deal of labor unrest, including several long and deadly strikes, and government intervention was required in many industries. Several landmark Supreme Court decisions concerning the roles of owners and labor were also handed down. In one ruling, unions became subject to the monopoly provisions of the Sherman Antitrust Act of 1890 and lost many potential gains as a result. An important concession not gained during this era was the legal recognition of unions, thus denying their legal authority to represent workers. While the disparity in lifestyles between owners and workers became publicized through several strikes, notably the Anthracite Coal Strike, and gained some public sympathy for union organizers, union power became increasingly fragmented as worker unity was lost because of factional divisions based on race, nationality, sex, skill, and political ideology.

Legislating Business. While distrustful of organized labor, Americans were also concerned about the proliferation of trusts, agreements made by large corporations for the purpose of controlling the marketplace, which threat-

ened competition. Though the Sherman Antitrust Act had been on the books for nearly a decade, it was not until the Roosevelt administration that cases were pursued against business owners and labor unions. The 1904 *Northern Securities* case involving the dissolution of the Hill-Harriman Railroad established President Roosevelt as a trustbuster, ready to challenge previously unregulated business owners who had accumulated a great deal of economic, social, and political power. Additional legislation came in the regulation of business practices in the areas of transportation, consumer protection, and federal monetary practices.

Panic. The generally optimistic economic tenor of the decade was threatened when the stock market precipitously dropped in 1907. The first overt sign of financial panic was a run on the Knickerbocker Trust Company of New York, which collapsed the bank, but the root causes of the panic ran much deeper, to the weak federal banking and credit system. Confidence was restored because of the intervention of the U.S. Treasury and capitalists under the leadership of J. P. Morgan, who stabilized banks and corporations with an infusion of funds. The panic resulted in legislation to boost the federal fiscal system.

The Horseless Carriage. One of the greatest achievements of this decade was made in the transportation industry, which ultimately built a powerful infrastructure critical to the development of the United States as a world power. By 1900 there were more than fifty manufacturers of self-propelled vehicles, which were known by such names as the horseless carriage, gasoline buggy, locomobiles, motor files, autokinetics, mocoles, and motorrigs. Although automobiles captured the popular imagination, they were hand-crafted and expensive, a product for the elite until Henry Ford introduced the concept of mass production. Progress on mass production began with the Model N car and was perfected on the Model T in 1908, leading to the incorporation of the assembly line by 1913, which dramatically revolutionized the car industry — and subsequently American culture — as the car became a symbol of freedom. Detroit became the center of the car industry early on, and the "Big Three" auto companies — Ford, General Motors, and Chrysler — were all established by the end of the decade. The first car shows and races were held in 1900. As America's fascination with the car grew, so did the number of accidents with pedestrians, carriages, and even trolleys. Legislative acts followed quickly, with the first driving laws and the requirement for automobile plates being passed as early as 1901. By 1903 New York City published the first set of driving regulations, "Rules for Driving." Though by 1900 there were only 144 miles of highway laid in the United States as opposed to 15,000 miles of trolley tracks and 193,000 miles of railroad tracks, the decade belonged to the automobile. The automobile would soon be considered one of the greatest social forces of the century, similar in stature to electricity and the telephone.

The Subway System. The early years of the century also saw the development of the first underground rapid transit system, as excavation began in New York in March 1900 for a subway. Completed in 1904, the subway was the largest in the world and changed the transportation habits of New York City's citizens. Eventually the subway replaced the trolley in the largest metropolitan areas as similar subway systems were planned.

The Airplane. The birth of the airline industry occurred with the Wright brothers' historic flight at Kitty Hawk, North Carolina, in December 1903. The former bicycle mechanics used a twelve-horsepower, chain-driven motorcycle engine to fly 852 feet. By 1905 the Wright brothers had constructed planes capable of flights up to twenty-five miles. A patent on their machine was obtained in 1906. By 1908 the Wright brothers were manufacturing planes for the War Department on government contracts. The airplanes delivered to the U.S. Army in 1909 could fly for an hour at speeds up to 40 MPH with two persons. These continued advancements revolutionized equipment for military combat forces and, later, for domestic transportation. As with automobiles in the early part of the decade, the latter part of the decade was marked by aviation races, tragic accidents, and subsequent legislation to regulate this new and burgeoning transportation sector.

TOPICS IN THE NEWS

"AN AMERICAN TRAGEDY" — 1906

Mill Girl. The story of Grace Brown's life and murder — later immortalized in Theodore Dreiser's novel *An American Tragedy* (1925) — not only brought to public attention the plight of mill girls but also symbolized the dangers inherent in America's transformation from a rural to an industrialized economy. Like many young men and women, Brown left a rural life — in her case, a life on her father's impoverished farm in Otselic, New York — to move to the city to find work. As a young woman in the textile industry in Cortland, New York, she encountered poor working conditions, low wages, and exploitation. Her life was controlled by the factory owners and operators.

Gillette. When he met Grace Brown, Chester E. Gillette, the son of roving evangelical missionary parents who ran a nonaffiliated religious mission out of their home in Kansas City, Missouri, was twenty-two-years old. Gillette had moved to Cortland in 1905 to escape an impoverished, unhappy, and recently troubled life. Although poorly educated and unskilled, Gillette became a supervisor at the shirtwaist factory owned by his paternal uncle. Brown, then nineteen, had worked at the factory for three years. While Brown hoped her romance with Gillette would lead to marriage, Gillette thought it was nothing more than a superficial relationship that passed his time.

Murder on Big Moose Lake. When Brown discovered that she was pregnant, she wrote Gillette several letters, requesting that he marry her. Her pitiful requests became demands as she finally threatened to go to his relatives with her news. Gillette, however, had higher ambitions and hoped to marry a young, rich socialite he had recently met. To extricate himself from the relationship, Gillette used the promise of marriage to lure Brown to the Adirondack Mountains, portraying the trip as a marriage and honeymoon adventure. Arriving by train, they checked into the Glenmore Hotel on Wednesday, 11 July, under the name of "Carl Graham of Albany and Grace Brown of Otselic." After being at the hotel only a matter of minutes, Gillette hired a rowboat to take Brown out on Big Moose Lake. The couple did not return to the hotel. On Thursday, 12 July, searchers found the capsized boat and Brown's body in shallow water. The lake was dragged for a second body until dark, but the only discovery was the retrieval of a man's hat. The coroner, whose suspicions were aroused by Brown's head injuries, suspected murder. The search soon began for Chester Gillette, a.k.a. Carl Graham, and the story started making headlines around the world.

Arrest. Gillette was found and arrested on Saturday, 14 July, at Lake Arrowhead, a resort just twelve miles from Big Moose Lake. He initially denied that he was the person registered as Carl Graham, despite a dozen eyewitness identifications. Brown's father also gave evidence that the last person he had seen his daughter with was

Gillette. After admitting that he was with Brown, Gillette adamantly denied killing her, stating that the boat capsized and he had difficulty saving himself. Despite his story, Gillette was accused of beating Grace Brown unconscious with an oar and throwing her overboard.

Story Crumbles. Many inconsistencies undermined Gillette's testimony. The couple had attracted attention on the train because of their overtly happy behavior, but witnesses at the hotel described Gillette pacing and distant and inattentive to Brown. Gillette had difficulty explaining his not going for help after the "accident" as well as his clothes, which several witnesses had observed were completely dry though he claimed to have swum ashore. Neither could Gillette adequately explain why he had gone to a resort twelve miles from the scene of the accident. Though he steadfastly maintained that he was innocent, Chester Gillette was convicted for the murder of Grace Brown. He was electrocuted at Auburn prison on 20 March 1908.

Sources:

"Gillette Accused of Miss Brown's Murder," *New York Times*, 15 July 1906, p. 5;

H. L. Mencken, Introduction to *An American Tragedy*, by Theodore Dreiser (Cleveland: World, 1948);

"Mystery In Girl's Death," *New York Times*, 14 July 1906, p. 2.

ANTHRACITE COAL STRIKE OF 1902

Coal Shuts Down. The five-month-long Anthracite Coal Strike nearly crippled America. Led by John Mitchell, president of the United Mine Workers, nearly 150,000 miners began their strike on 12 May 1902 after a breakdown in ongoing negotiations that had begun in the aftermath of a brief strike of the year before. The issues of contention included the miners' demands for a reduced workday, better pay, and union recognition.

The "Divine Right" Letter. In July a letter written by a photographer from Wilkes-Barre, Pennsylvania, was sent to George F. Baer, president of the Reading Railroad and spokesman for the mine operators. The letter writer, who asked the Holy Spirit to send "reason to [Baer's] heart," requested that the strike be settled. Baer's response, written on Reading Railroad letterhead and dated 17 July 1902, has come to be known as the "divine right" letter. It clearly revealed the mine operators' contempt for labor:

My dear Mr. Clark:

I have your letter of the 16th instant.

I do not know who you are. I see that you are a religious man; but you are evidently biased in favor of the right of the working man to control a business in which he has no other interest than to secure fair wages for the work he does.

I beg of you not to be discouraged. The right and interests of the laboring man will be protected and cared for

A depiction of a 14 October 1902 meeting at which President Theodore Roosevelt, Secretary of War Elihu Root, and J. P. Morgan planned an arbitration commission to settle the Anthracite Coal Strike (*Harper's Weekly*, 25 October 1902)

— not by the labor agitators, but by the Christian men to whom God in his infinite wisdom has given the control of the property interests of the country, and upon the successful Management of which so much depends.

Do not be discouraged. Pray earnestly that right may triumph, always remembering that the Lord God Omnipotent still reigns, and that His reign is one of law and order, and not of violence and crime.

Public Sentiment. In late July National Guard and cavalry troops were sent to the area after strikers trapped the sheriff and two nonunion men in the Reading Railroad depot. On 29 August Gen. John P. S. Gobin issued shoot-to-kill orders, which caused even further unrest among the strikers. By the time Baer's letter was published in August, the public sentiment had already turned in favor of the strikers. Citizens were without coal, a basic necessity in their lives, and that fact seemed unimportant to the arrogant mine operators, who seemed intent, as one newspaper asserted, upon being "managing directors" of the entire earth.

Intervention. President Theodore Roosevelt was also growing uneasy about the strike as it dragged on. The effects of the work stoppage were being felt well beyond the mines. The price of coal, five dollars per ton when the strike began, was spiraling upward and would reach thirty dollars per ton by the strike's end. As the price rose, businesses and schools closed to conserve fuel, and raids on railroad coal cars began to occur. With no settlement in sight and autumn quickly approaching, Roosevelt realized that suffering would be great if the strike continued much longer. As early as July, Roosevelt had looked into ways to end the strike, and in late September he tried to intervene to bring about a settlement. In early October representatives of the government met with those from labor and management in Washington. Roosevelt's plan was to offer both sides an equal voice, or, in his famous terminology, a "square deal," in the settlement. After describing the potential consequences the strike would cause during the winter, Roosevelt made an impassioned request: "I appeal to your patriotism, to the spirit that sinks personal consideration and makes individual sacrifices for the general good."

Intransigence. John Mitchell, attending the meeting with three UMW district representatives, was the first to speak. He agreed with the president and asked him to appoint a commission to settle the matter, stating that the union would accept the commission's decision if the owners would. But Baer and the mine owners refused to negotiate. Baer at one point referred to the unionists as anarchists, and John Markle, a representative of the independent mine operators, further infuriated the president with his demand that he "squelch" the strikes by the "strong arm of the military at your command." Roosevelt later commented that Baer should have been taken "by the seat of the breeches and the nape of the neck and chucked . . . out of that window." The conference led Roosevelt to believe that the mine operators might be at fault in the strike, and this sentiment was echoed among the American public when news of the conference hit the presses. The failed conference turned the public's attention and sympathy toward the plight of union workers as the strike continued and further coal shortages loomed with winter just ahead. A week after the meeting, Roosevelt openly revealed his intention to threaten the mine operators into a settlement by having the mines run by the army, placing them in receivership, and in effect dislodging the owners from their own businesses. As he worked on this plan, his secretary of war met with J. P. Morgan on 11 October in New York to implement the strikers' request to set up an arbitration panel.

Mediation. The special mediation commission of eight members from varied professions was announced by Roosevelt in mid October, and the strike was called off. Mediation began on 14 November in Scranton, Pennsylvania, and lasted for five months. During the trial-like proceedings more than 558 witnesses were called on the part of labor, nonunion labor, the operators, and the commission, resulting in fifty-six volumes of testimony. Representing the UMW was Clarence Darrow, in a case that was a precursor to his now-famous courtroom defenses. Representing the operators was a former U.S. attorney general, Wayne MacVeagh. For the strikers, economic feudalism was on trial, but to the operators the issue was their right to do as they pleased with their businesses. Darrow questioned the operators' "God-given right to hire the cheapest man they can get" in his ending summation:

> The blunders are theirs because, [in] this old, old strife they are fighting for slavery, while we are fighting for freedom. They are fighting for the rule of man over man, for despotism, for darkness, for the past. We are striving to build up man. We are working for democracy, for humanity, for the future, for the days that will come too

SPINDLETOP

The discovery of the Spindletop oil gusher in 1901 in Beaumont, Texas, occurred after nearly a decade of exploration. After the oil field had been abandoned by Standard Oil prospectors as unproductive, explorers found oil by drilling more than seven hundred feet into a salt dome. The oil gusher established the petroleum industry in Texas, where 491 oil companies were chartered in the next year. Anthony F. Luchrich is credited with the find; he was backed by Pittsburgh financiers John H. Galey and Col. J. M. Guffey. The company formed around the find was originally called Guffey Oil but later became Gulf Oil in 1907 after Guffey was implicated in a financial scandal. The field had more oil than the rest of the United States combined and created the first competition to Standard Oil. The initial burst of oil formed a 160-foot gusher.

The gusher made headlines around the world. Spewing for nine days before it could be brought under control, the well later produced more than one hundred thousand gallons per day. Two fires within the first week of production nearly caused major catastrophes. The smell, soot, and sulfur from the gusher caused a panic among some of the nearby Beaumont population, but a few small investors feared nothing as they knew immediately that they were rich.

Source: William A. Owens, "Gusher at Spindletop," in *Great Stories of American Businessmen* (New York: American Heritage, 1972).

late for us to receive its benefits, but which still will come.

Settlement. The mediation ended in March 1903. Though initially requesting a 20 percent pay raise, union recognition, and an eight-hour day, the union accepted a 10 percent pay increase and a nine-hour day. In part, the better day that Darrow asked for began to dawn slowly with the mediation decision, because the union had begun to win much-needed public support. Initially Roosevelt's intervention in a domestic economic crisis was criticized by the press, but he was given considerable credit when the strike was settled, and later his intervention in the dispute became one of the more celebrated actions of his presidency.

Sources:
Robert L. Reynolds, "The Coal Kings Come to Judgment," in *Great Stories of American Businessmen* (New York: American Heritage, 1972);

Philip Taft, *Organized Labor in American History* (New York: Harper & Row, 1964).

Scene in New York's Little Italy outside the closed Italian Bank in October 1907

FINANCIAL PANIC OF 1907

Economic Reckoning. The relatively prosperous first years of the century came to a halt in 1907 when drains on the money supply revealed a weak national financial infrastructure of banking and credit and precipitated an economic crisis that lasted nearly a year. The money supply was low because of the lack of cash flow from farmers due to a late season and was further drained by overspeculation in copper, money being diverted to the Russo-Japanese War of 1905, the rebuilding of San Francisco after the 1906 earthquake (exacerbated by huge insurance payouts), and the nationwide railroad expansion program. After the stock market fell drastically in March, prices soared, wages decreased, unemployment rose, and many businesses, including banks, failed.

The First Bank Failure. The first bank in trouble was Mercantile National, whose owner, F. Augustus Heinze, was a primary figure in the copper overspeculation. Since there was no central banking system to assist troubled financial institutions in a crisis, the bank turned for assistance to the Clearing House Association, a banking agency that cleared checks. After the bank's collapse on Wednesday, 16 October, the Clearing House Association demanded the resignation of Heinze and those who held controlling shares in the bank. The Clearing House Association also investigated the financial stability of the institution. Although the bank was found to be solvent, the panic had already begun by the time the investigation ended.

Morgan Monitors Situation. J. P. Morgan, founder of J. P. Morgan and Company, was attending a conference of the Episcopal Church in Richmond, Virginia, when the panic began. He was kept apprised of the situation in the early stages and intentionally stayed until the church convention was nearly over in order to prevent further alarm in the press that might affect the already weakening financial sector. Returning to New York by train, Morgan spent the weekend studying the situation and meeting with prominent financial leaders at his library on East Thirty-sixth Street. The situation was becoming increasingly critical as many banks and trusts were already calling in loans to back up cash reserves. By the end of the weekend the media had converged on the library, where they stayed throughout the crisis, pursuing every arriving and departing visitor for information.

Morgan Intervenes. On Monday, 21 October, Morgan asked his daughter, Louisa Morgan Satterlee, to put together a team of bankers whom he could trust for advice as examiners. Four of the members were Thomas W. Joyce of the House of Morgan, Richard Trimble of the United States Steel Corporation, Henry P. Davison of First National Bank, and Benjamin Strong of Bankers Trust Company. Morgan used this advisory team at various points throughout the crisis to gather, interpret, and convey critical data. Morgan went to the Knickerbocker Trust Company of New York, the third largest bank in New York City, which appeared to be in the most trouble. A run on the deposits had already begun that morning, and the long lines served only to induce more anxiety, creating even longer lines as the panic spread. Imminent failure loomed after an examination revealed that only 5 percent of the bank's deposits were held in reserve. The president, Charles T. Barney, was linked to the copper-speculating bankers at the failed Mercantile National and asked to resign. (Barney suffered a nervous breakdown over his resignation and committed suicide on

Morgan's authorization of a bond purchase to support the credit of New York banks during the Panic of 1907

14 November.) An emergency meeting of the Knickerbocker's board was suggested by Morgan to develop a plan to prevent failure, but by the end of the next day the bank had failed, and panic spread throughout the city. The superintendent of banks for the state of New York, Luther W. Knott, resigned after the Knickerbocker failure, realizing the impending doom in the industry. Morgan quickly attempted to set up a group of bankers who would provide aid to carry the weaker financial institutions through the crisis, but other bankers resisted his request.

The Panic Deepens. By Wednesday, 23 October, the second largest trust company, Trust Company of America, was in deep trouble with a run on its deposits. Again Morgan assembled bankers and requested aid, finally receiving it from two national banks, First National and National City, which prevented the bank's failure. Although Morgan publicly urged depositors to keep their funds in the banks, other companies did not fare so well that day: Westinghouse failed, the Pittsburgh Stock Exchange was in suspension, and the panic took on national proportions as western banks withdrew funds vested in

New York banks. But some progress had been made in abating the panic. That evening Morgan realized that it was the trust companies, more than the banks, that faced potential disaster.

The Trusts. By law trust companies could engage in banking but were not subject to the strict regulations with which the national banks had to comply, leaving them more vulnerable to the threat posed by this period of instability and collapse. Meeting with the presidents of the trust companies on Thursday, Morgan urged them to do what they had failed to do only the day before: set up a fund to help institutions through the crisis. They agreed to put up $8.25 million, and Morgan committed to raise $1.75 million for the fund. John D. Rockefeller also agreed to put up $10 million to aid the trust companies. The Bank of England contributed $10 million, which arrived with much fanfare on 4 November via the new ship *Lusitania*.

The Long Week. On the same day Morgan met with the trust company presidents, a fall in the stock market nearly caused it to close its doors for the day. By midday

The Pierpont Morgan Library West Room, circa 1909

there was no money to purchase stocks, and thus there were no sales. Morgan asked the president of the exchange, R. H. Thomas, to keep it open to prevent further panic and managed to procure additional loans from the national banks as lending power for the exchange, which prevented several firms from failing. That evening the talk in the Morgan library centered on the issue of Clearing House Association certificates, a type of temporary loan, that would allow the banks and trusts to stay solvent. These certificates had been issued in previous panics that had created monetary scarcity. Morgan was against the idea, but they were issued and went into effect on 28 October. That same week President Theodore Roosevelt issued a statement of confidence that the panic was temporary and prosperous times would soon return, and Morgan's followers devised plans to handle the press, which had exacerbated the panic in the previous weeks. Every night during the week of 21 October the bankers met at Morgan's library with the objective of planning to get through the next day. When the end of the week came with only eight failures, the press prematurely reported that the crisis was over.

New Problems. The next week on Tuesday, 29 October, Morgan promised the mayor of New York $30 million in bonds at 6 percent interest to keep the city solvent.

Then on 31 October the foreign exchange created a shift in gold from export to import. To restore the import-export balance, grain and cotton shipments to Europe had to be sent immediately. Presidential intervention was required to allow railroads to give favor to one commodity over another, a practice that was otherwise illegal. The following weekend, 2–3 November, the brokerage firm of Moore and Schley ran into credit problems and verged on a collapse that would create problems for the stock market and other weak financial firms.

The Locked Library. To save Moore and Schley, a complicated plan involving the sale of Tennessee Coal and Iron to U.S. Steel was presented to Morgan, who set about to pledge $25 million of his own firm's money to insure the sale. However, his offer was contingent on the trust company heads devising a plan to raise an additional $25 million as emergency funds. With the trust company presidents in the west room of his library and the national bank leaders in the east room, Morgan locked them inside until a viable plan was developed. The trusts' leaders hesitated to commit additional funds without conferring with their directors. Finally, Morgan confronted them with financial documents that proved they were solvent enough to develop the fund. At 4:45 A.M. on 4 November the trust presidents signed the document Morgan had drawn up and were released from the library. The next day the chairman of U.S. Steel, Elbert H. Gary, insisted on President Roosevelt's approval of the terms of the sale to avoid violating antitrust legislation. Roosevelt, who had been hunting in Louisiana during much of the panic, agreed to the antitrust waiver, and Gary called Morgan from the White House to inform him. Moore and Schley had enough money to get them through their credit problems. This news was timed perfectly, as the announcement of the sale was made just as the stock exchange opened, which helped the market stabilize.

Resolution. Morgan's strategic and financial intervention with other capitalists from the private sector and the infusion of funds from the U.S. Treasury finally eased the panic. Confidence was finally restored, though it took several weeks for the crisis to subside fully. Despite some failures, in the end twelve teetering financial institutions were saved. Fortunately, no large banks failed, and the subsequent minor decline in the economy had no major lasting financial effects. In addition to the work of Morgan and his many associates, the support of Treasury Secretary George B. Cortelyou and President Roosevelt were instrumental in resolving the crisis.

Reform. The crisis of 1907 was severe enough that changes in the national financial structure were implemented to avert future panics. The first congressional act passed to correct deficiencies in the banking system was the Aldrich-Vreeland Act in May 1908, which authorized banks to issue bonds based on securities other than federal bonds while imposing a 10 percent tax on them. The aftermath of the crisis also led to the establishment of the National Monetary Commission in 1908, a precursor to the Federal Reserve Bank, which effec-

tively centralized the banking industry in 1913. The United States had been a debtor nation in its early history because of the economic requirements entailed in building a nation, and revamping the financial infrastructure after the Panic of 1907 was critical to the emergence of America as a world financial power and a creditor nation during World War I.

Sources:
Margaret G. Myers, *A Financial History of the United States* (New York: Columbia University Press, 1970);

Herbert L. Satterlee, *J. Pierpont Morgan: An Intimate Portrait* (New York: Macmillan, 1939).

THE LABOR TRIAL OF THE CENTURY

The Bombing. The trial of William D. "Big Bill" Haywood for the murder of former Idaho governor Frank Steunenberg is one of the most notorious trials of this century. The former governor was killed by a bomb

Clarence Darrow (seated second from left), William "Big Bill" Haywood (seated, with moustache), and Haywood's daughter (between them), at Haywood's 1907 trial for the murder of former governor Frank Steunenberg

rigged to the gate in front of his home in Caldwell, Idaho, on 30 December 1905. Shortly before he died from gaping wounds in his back and side, Steunenberg asked, "Who shot me?" There were no witnesses. The next day a reward of $15,000 was offered by the state and the Steunenberg family for the capture of the murderer(s). At the request of Idaho governor Frank R. Gooding, the investigation was headed up by James McPharlan, the head of Pinkerton Security, an established strikebreaking organization.

The Union Accused. Initially a prounion politician, Steunenberg was never forgiven by the Western Federation of Miners (WFM) for calling out federal troops after an uprising at a lead mine in Couer d'Alene in 1899. Union members, imprisoned in bull-pen conditions for months, were left feeling betrayed and bitter. Thus suspicions fell immediately on the WFM. Harry Orchard, a planted spy working for the mine operators, posed as a union member and virtually campaigned for arrest by publicly divulging his knowledge of the crime. Once arrested on 1 January 1906, Orchard reportedly endured ten days of grilling by McPharlan before he confessed to the killing. Orchard stated that as a member of the "inner circle" of the WFM he had been paid $250 by some members to kill Steunenberg. He also admitted that he had committed other crimes for hire on behalf of the union. The three people that Orchard falsely informed on were William D. "Big Bill" Haywood, secretary of the WFM; Charles Moyer, president of the WFM; and George Pettibone, a blacklisted miner. During the next month Orchard and McPharlan created and refined the details of the crime. Orchard was removed from the jail and given a small house to live in, frequently social-izing with McPharlan, who saw this crime as his second career opportunity to discredit the union after his success in disbanding the Molly McGuires in the 1880s. On 17 February 1906 the three WFM members were arrested without a warrant in the middle of the night in Colorado with the permission of the Colorado governor. The accused men were extradited via a special train to Boise, Idaho, where they were jailed for months in the death house section of the prison.

The Trial Begins. The arrests created solidarity in the union movement. Haywood's defense, led by Clarence Darrow and E. F. Richardson of Denver, had the unprecedented support of the WFM, the Industrial Workers of the World, the Socialist Party, the Socialist Labor Party, and the American Federation of Labor. Public sympathy for the defendants was evoked when President Theodore Roosevelt, in an uncharacteristic remark during a presidential address, called the three WFM members "undesirable citizens." The next day thousands of supporters donned placards that read "I am an undesirable citizen." The hoopla was such that Boise was dubbed "Murdertown" because of the industry that had sprung up around the murder and the trial. Initially, several motions were made to release the defendants on writs of habeas corpus, but these pleadings were rejected by the Supreme Court. The trial of Haywood got underway on 9 May 1906.

The Verdict. Under the prosecution led by former governor James Hawley and future U.S. senator William Borah, Orchard was the star of the trial and gave three days of well-rehearsed testimony. In a series of crucial moves, however, Darrow managed to get Orchard to confess that he had perjured himself in previous trials and had in the past admitted to crimes that he never committed. Borah and Darrow were both excellent, articulate attorneys, but Darrow's eloquent eleven-hour summation overwhelmed the prosecution. After nearly three months in trial, Haywood was found not guilty by the twelve jurors on 29 July 1906. In the trial aftermath Moyer was released on bail, and Pettibone was later brought to trial on 26 November 1907 and acquitted on 4 January 1908.

Mine Owners Discredited. Orchard's story soon unraveled, and the involvement of the Mine Owners' Association in framing the union was made public. Many other crimes that had been blamed on the union also came to light as ploys by the operators. For example, it was Orchard who had blown up the train station in Independence, Colorado, and killed fourteen nonunion miners in 1904, an accident initially blamed on the Western Federation of Miners. Though he had committed other crimes for the Mine Owners' Association, the killing of Frank Steunenberg was Orchard's own idea. Ultimately, the duplicity of the mine owners' attempt to discredit the union through conspiracy worked against them in the press. Revelations of their underhanded dealings shocked the public and gave the union movement much needed support in its continuing battle for recognition, a battle it would finally win in 1935 with the passage of the Wagner National Labor Relations Act.

Sources:

Richard O. Boyer and Herbert M. Morais, *Labor's Untold Story* (Pittsburgh: United Electrical, Radio & Machine Workers of America, 1955);

Philip Taft, *Organized Labor in American History* (New York: Harper & Row, 1964).

LEGISLATION AND SUPREME COURT RULINGS

A Decade of Regulatory Change. The years from 1900 through 1909 stand in sharp contrast to the post–Civil War years, when the legislative and judicial branches were uncritical in their support of business efforts to rebuild the country's economic infrastructure. The first decade of the twentieth century saw an extraordinary amount of landmark legislation and Supreme Court rulings aimed at regulating business practices, involving such areas as antitrust laws, fiscal policy, labor disputes, and consumer goods.

Legislation. The legislation passed in the decade that affected business included nine important acts, the earliest of which was the Gold Standard Act (1900). Passed by Congress as a means of developing an efficient national currency, the act established national banks, with capital resources of at least $25,000, in towns of fewer than three thousand inhabitants to finance agrarian demands. The act also included provisions for gold redemptions for monies, the creation of a gold reserve, and bond sale authorization for reserve maintenance. By creating a more efficient, stable national currency, the act was critical to the United States in its expanding role in international finance and commerce.

Regulating the Railroads. The Elkins Act (1903) was drafted to regulate interstate commerce activities and specifically targeted at the railroads as a result of antitrust investigations. The law strengthened the 1887 Interstate Commerce Act and expressly prohibited railroads from deviating from their published rates, a provision designed to prevent the rebating that had become popular in the industry. The act held railroad officials as well as shippers responsible for any infractions. It established the Federal Bureau of Corporations to carry out investigations as a part of the Department of Commerce and Labor. The first major test of the law came with the Supreme Court ruling in *Armour Packing Company* v. *United States* (1908).

Speeding Suits. The Expedition Act (1903) appropriated $500,000 to facilitate the processing of federal antitrust suits, gave antitrust cases precedence over other pending court cases, and allowed appeals to be taken directly to the Supreme Court. This act favored President Theodore Roosevelt's trust-busting stance by moving antitrust cases quickly through the court system.

Guaranteeing Foods. Considered the first federal consumer protection law, the Heyburn Bill (1906) regulated the producers and sellers of food. Specific prohibitions were included against selling diseased, contaminated, or decomposed meats and other foods. The act, supported by the American Medical Association as important to the health and welfare of Americans, also required truth in labeling.

Righting Rates. The Hepburn Act (1906), also called the Railway Rate Regulation Act, broadened the powers of the Interstate Commerce Commission (ICC) by overhauling the Interstate Commerce Act of 1887. The act enabled the ICC to fight the railroad trusts and investigate questionable policies in the industry. The bill's largest impact was allowing the ICC to regulate railroad rates.

Inspecting Meats. In response to the Neill-Reynolds report on conditions in the meatpacking industry, Congress passed the Meat Inspection Act (1906), which required federal inspection of all meat involved in interstate and foreign commerce. Like the Heyburn Bill, this act was considered vital to the health and welfare of the public.

Foods and Drugs. The Pure Food and Drug Act (1906) prohibited the mislabeling or adulteration of food involved in interstate and foreign commerce. The Department of Agriculture was given authority to administer the act. The Meat Inspection Act and the Pure Food and Drug Act were together the strongest regulations Congress had ever imposed on the food industry.

Correcting Deficiencies. Passed to correct deficiencies in the banking system revealed by the financial panic of

Turn-of-the-century sausage makers, among the meat industry workers affected by the Meat Inspection Act of 1906

1907, the Aldrich-Vreeland Act (1908) authorized banks to issue bonds based on securities other than federal bonds but imposed a 10 percent tax on those notes. In order to study the banking and currency system of the United States as well as foreign countries, Congress also established a National Monetary Commission.

Tariffs. The Payne-Aldrich Tariff Act (1909) was passed by Congress and signed by President William Howard Taft in keeping with his campaign promise to reduce tariffs instituted by the Dingley Tariff of 1897. However, it was controversial because tariffs were reduced only on some items (such as hides, which helped the shoe industry), maintained on many items (such as iron and steel), and raised on other goods (such as silk and cotton). The act contained 850 amendments, most of which represented increases.

Supreme Court Rulings. The earliest of the important Supreme Court decisions affecting business in the decade was *Atkin* v. *Kansas* (1903). In this case the Supreme Court ruled that a Kansas law establishing an eight-hour workday for construction workers engaged in public works is lawful and not a violation of "freedom of contract" provided by the Constitution. This ruling distinguished public-sector and private-sector work, which was further ruled on in the 1905 case of *Lochner* v. *New York.*

Applying the Antitrust Act. In the case of *Northern Securities* v. *United States* (1904) the Court ruled in a 5–4 decision that the Northern Securities Company — the merger of the Northern Pacific, Great Northern, and

Burlington Railroads — violated the Sherman Antitrust Act of 1890. The Court ordered the dissolution of the trust. The case represented a cornerstone for the trust-busting stance of the Roosevelt administration in protecting citizens against the power of the trusts. Justice Oliver Wendell Holmes in his first dissent argued that too loose of an interpretation of the Sherman Antitrust Act could encourage government interference in almost any "part of the conduct of life."

Workday Length. In *Lochner* v. *New York* (1905) the Court ruled 5–4 that the state's limitation on the maximum number of hours an employee can work is a violation of the Fourteenth Amendment, which grants the freedom to make contracts. The suit resulted from a Utica bakery owner's breaking a New York law that had limited the working hours of employees to sixty hours in one week or ten hours per day. Justice Holmes wrote a searing dissent in the case that centered on the word *liberty.* Holmes claimed that when the word is used to prevent the state from limiting hours to protect health, then its meaning "is perverted." Holmes further noted that "a constitution is not intended to embody a particular economic theory, whether of paternalism . . . or of *laissez-faire.*"

Compelling Testimony. In *Hale* v. *Henkel* (1906) the Court ruled that employees called as witnesses in antitrust cases can be forced to testify and produce evidence against their employers. The decision strengthened the antitrust stance of the Roosevelt administration.

Stifling Unions. The case of *Adair* v. *United States* (1908) originated when railroad official William Adair fired an employee who belonged to a union. Finding Adair within his rights, the Court ruled that a portion of the Erdman Act of 1898 was a violation of the "freedom of contract" under the constitution. The focus of the case was the section of the law that outlawed "yellow-dog contracts," which as a condition of employment forced employees to agree not to join a union. Building on the *Lochner* decision, the Court similarly upheld the right of the employer to set conditions upon labor, dealing another blow to organized labor.

Antitrust Applied to Labor. In *Loewe* v. *Lawlor* (1908), also known as the Danbury Hatters case, a unanimous Court ruled that a nationwide boycott by the United Hatters of North America in support of workers protesting labor practices in Danbury, Connecticut, at D. E. Loewe and Company constituted a restraint of trade under the Sherman Antitrust Act. The court held that combinations of labor were not different from combinations of business management.

Protecting Women Workers. In *Muller* v. *Oregon* (1908) a unanimous Court ruled that a provision that limits the maximum number of hours that women can work to ten hours a day is constitutional. Reversing the Court's stance established in *Lochner* for male employees, the ruling was based on what the Court saw as the inher-

1908 Ford Model T

ent inequality of women and the necessity for women to be protected by men.

Applying the Elkins Act. The case of *Armour Packing Company* v. *United States* (1908) provided the first test of the Elkins Act (1903), which gave the ICC the power to conduct railroad rate investigations. The ruling of the Court was critical to strengthening the regulation of the railroad industry.

Sources:

Howard B. Furer, *The United States Supreme Court: The Fuller Court, 1888–1910*, volume 5 (Danbury, Conn.: Grolier, 1995);

Oliver Wendell Holmes, *The Dissenting Opinions of Mr. Justice Holmes* (New York: Vanguard, 1929).

THE MODEL T

Motor Car for the Multitude. As the Model T was unveiled to the public in October 1908, Henry Ford, founder of the Ford Motor Company, remarked of his "Tin Lizzie" that it came "in any color you choose, so long as it's black." He also called the automobile "a motor car for the great multitude." The latter statement was an appropriate tribute to the Model T, for mass production lowered its price and made it the first automobile average Americans could afford. The Model T car was not revolutionary, but the process of mass production revolutionized the automobile industry. As a result American life and culture would be transformed as the car became an everyday necessity in a mobile society.

Precursor to the Model T. The Model N cars manufactured in 1906–1907 were the precursor to the Model T and introduced the interchangeable-parts system for large-scale production. The system was implemented under the direction of Walter E. Flanders, a former machine tool salesman and mechanic whom Henry Ford hired as a production manager in 1906. The concept of the static, or stationary, assembly line, where workers moved from car to car as they built them, was also used at this time. With improved production equipment, designs, and manufacturing methods, Ford was the first auto manufacturer that could fill hundreds of orders a day, a contribution recognized when the *Cycle and Automobile Trade Journal* proclaimed the Model N "the most important mechanical traction event of 1906." Sales on the Model N skyrocketed, and the more expensive models, Models K, C, and F, were selling poorly in comparison. Ford realized that progress and profit were in mass production of inexpensive, dependable, and easy-to-drive cars, and the route to that goal was constant simplification, standardization, and efficiency through experimentation and innovation. The result was the Model T.

Features of the Model T. The Model T advertising flyers sent to dealers in March 1908 captured the attention of the public with the slogan "No car under $2,000 offers more, and no car over $2,000 offers more except in trimmings." The Model T had a stout, utilitarian look despite its high roofline. It sported a four-cylinder twenty-horsepower engine, magneto ignition, refined planetary transmission, and tank capacities of ten gallons for the touring sedan and sixteen gallons for the runabout. The Model T was also lighter than other models, had well-placed headlights, good suspension, and a completely enclosed power plant and transmission. By 1909,

The big three automakers — Ford, General Motors, and Chrysler — could have been the big two automakers had Henry Ford agreed to join the GM consortium. In September 1908 William Durant of the Buick Motor Car Company established General Motors Company, a holding company of several smaller car companies. The first merger was with Oldsmobile, and by the end of 1909 Durant had acquired a dozen automobile companies, including Oakland, Rainier, Welch-Pontiac, and Cadillac, as well as two commercial-vehicle producers and ten automotive-parts manufacturers. Durant also wanted to add the Ford line to General Motors and invited Henry Ford to join. Ford, who planned to turn to manufacturing farm equipment, demanded $8 million in cash. Durant agreed to terms stipulating an initial $2 million in cash with the balance to be paid in three years at 5 percent interest. Strapped for working capital after so many acquisitions, Durant's financial advisers at National City Bank of New York insisted that Ford's company was not worth that much money, though the General Motors board had approved the acquisition. Ford refused to take less — a decision that forever changed the face of the automobile industry in America.

Source: Ed Cray, *Chrome Colossus: General Motors and Its Times* (New York: McGraw-Hill, 1980).

Park, Michigan, in 1913. As production increased and prices dropped, consumption increased and profits soared. Though some critics contended that the Model T was produced for too long, consumers bought more than fifteen million cars by the time the Model T went out of production in 1927. The production of the Model T also brought other revolutionary changes to the automobile industry. The Ford Motor Company was a forerunner of in-house manufacturing, which assured the Ford Manufacturing Company of a constant supply of critical auto parts such as the chassis and engine, an especially important element in the efficiency and standardization process used on the Model T.

Creating an Empire. Ford also stirred up controversy in setting the standard for higher wages in the auto industry, paying more than double the going wage rate in order to attract and keep skilled labor. The higher wages in turn created disposable income that workers eventually spent on consumer goods, including cars, which resulted in the further growth of the company. Many social critics, however, contend that the higher wages were more than offset by the demanding, high-production work that the moving assembly line created. While the social consequences of mass production are debatable, there is no doubt that the Model T changed America. Henry Ford's ingenuity as a designer was embodied in the "Tin Lizzie," a car that helped make Ford Motor Company an enduring automobile empire.

Source:
Allan Nevins, *Ford: The Times, The Man, The Company* (New York: Scribners, 1954).

after using red, gray, and black as colors, the Model T was painted green with black trimming and red striping.

New Production Techniques. The revolution, however, was in the process of making Model T. Using the principles of Taylorism, or scientific management, Ford designers vastly improved the efficiency of the assembly line on the Model T by making it movable. No longer did workers have to move from car to car; rather, the car would come to them. The moving assembly line, often referred to as Fordization, became an industrial staple worldwide during the next several years and was one of the major steps in the advancement of the Industrial Revolution. The use of the assembly line made changes and improvements to the model easy to implement; indeed, there were many alterations made through the years, as the initial Model T was far from being a perfect car. The negative side of this revolutionary manufacturing process was the same as it was for scientific management in general: it displaced artisanship and created worker alienation, fatigue, and boredom.

Continuing Innovations. The Model T production rate dropped from 728 minutes when the car was introduced to 93 minutes at the production plant in Highland

RESURRECTION OF THE ANTITRUST MOVEMENT

Economic Impact of Trusts. By 1890, the year the Sherman Antitrust Act was passed, many saw the power of large business monopolies, or trusts, as a serious problem. Encouraged by the expansion of the transportation and communication sectors, trusts had proliferated since the Civil War, resulting in a continual squeezing out of small businesses and a concentration of economic power among fewer, larger businesses. But the effects of trusts were not wholly negative. As opposed to the duplication of efforts inherent in a competitive environment, trusts provided substantial savings and allowed for higher production capacity by assuring that businesses had dependable supplies of critical parts as well as reliable transportation and financing. The savings, however, were not necessarily passed on to the stockholder, working laborers, or the consumer.

Deficiencies of the Sherman Antitrust Act. The Sherman Antitrust Act had deficiencies that were becoming evident at the turn of the century. One major problem was that the act did not define a trust or monopoly. The lack of such a definition left the interpretation of the law up to the judicial branch of the government, which resulted in some contradictory case decisions. Further, violating the Sherman Antitrust Act was only considered a misdemeanor offense, a crime whose punishment was not serious enough to deter those who saw their interests served by trusts.

The Good and the Bad. With the accession of Theodore Roosevelt into the presidency, the antitrust movement gained momentum, though Roosevelt believed it was important to distinguish between good trusts and bad trusts. To Roosevelt, good trusts benefited the public with their infusion of capital and products into the economy. Not coincidentally, many of the people involved with the "good" trusts were friends of Roosevelt and primary contributors to the Republican Party. Bad trusts consisted of greedy financiers interested only in profits at the general public's expense.

The *Northern Securities* Case. Early in his presidency Roosevelt realized that the trust situation had reached a critical point where something had to be done, lest radical reform hurt all trusts, good and bad. In 1902 Roosevelt agreed to the filing of a case against Northern Securities, a huge railroad trust consisting of the Northern Pacific, Great Northern, and Burlington Railroads. The lower court decision against the Northern Securities Company was upheld in 1904 by the Supreme Court. The outcome was met with self-righteous indignation on the part of big business, who saw this move as a violation of their right to conduct their businesses according to their wishes. The response on the part of the public was a mixture of support and relief.

Business on Trial. The *Northern Securities* case was an intentional warning to big business to reform their business practices or have them reformed by government intervention. Many trusts did not heed the warning. Other prosecutions against the trusts followed in the Roosevelt administration. The William Howard Taft administration also vigorously continued prosecution of the trusts in the later part of the decade. In total, during Roosevelt's term the Justice Department filed forty-five antitrust cases. At the time of the *Northern Securities* decision in 1904, there were 318 trusts that had consolidated more than fifty-three hundred businesses. Seven corporations held more than one-third of the working capital in the United States. A much revised business structure was taking shape by the end of the decade. There were two distinct economic business sectors by 1910: small firms competing in enterprises that did not require large capital investments and a few large corporations that controlled the capital-intensive enterprises.

Roosevelt's "Square Deal." In an attempt to provide an equal voice to all of America's constituencies — business, labor, and the public — Roosevelt created a platform for the 1904 presidential race called the "Square Deal," a term taken from gaming. While the Square Deal advocated an even-handed, fair approach to all, it was a nonspecific platform that put forth no tangible idea,

Railroad baron E. H. Harriman, who lost control of the Northern Pacific Railway in 1901 to a holding company controlled by James T. Hill called the Northern Securities Company. President Roosevelt instructed his attorney general to bring suit against the holding company under the Sherman Antitrust Act, which was upheld in 1904 by the U.S. Supreme Court

promise, or theory. The Square Deal promoted only an abstract concept of fairness and promised only conscientiousness on Roosevelt's part.

Defining the Deal. Lest every constituency think that the Square Deal meant that they would always win, Roosevelt used several public addresses first to give substance and later to clarify his meaning of the concept throughout his presidency. At a banquet in Dallas, Texas, on 5 April 1905 Roosevelt stated:

> When I say I believe in a square deal I do not mean, and nobody that speaks the truth can mean, that he believes it possible to give every man the best hand. If the cards do not come to any man, or if they do come, and has not got the power to play them, that is his affair. All I mean is that there shall be no crookedness in the dealing. . . . All any of us can pretend to do is to come as near as our imperfect abilities will allow to securing through governmental agencies an equal opportunity for each man to show the stuff that is in him; and that must be done with no more intention of discrimination against the rich than the poor man, or against the poor man than the rich man; with the intention of safeguarding every man, rich or poor, poor or rich, in his rights, and giving him as nearly as may be a fair chance to do what powers permit him to do; always provided he does not wrong his neighbor.

In advocating fairness to all, Roosevelt managed to rally the disparate constituencies to his side in his presidential election of 1904 and throughout his term. Others saw

Teddy bears offered for sale by a street vendor in 1903

TEDDY ROOSEVELT AND TEDDY BEARS

In November 1902 President Theodore Roosevelt went on a hunting trip in Mississippi. Since he had shot no game throughout the trip, accommodating supporters arranged to have a small, young bear placed in the president's path so he could shoot it. The president refused. Although an avid hunter, Roosevelt thought that shooting such an bear was unsportsmanlike. The press picked up on the story, and a political cartoon by Clifford K. Berryman depicting the incident was printed in the *Washington Post* on 16 November 1902. A redrawing of the cartoon appeared that evening in the *Washington Evening Star*. Both cartoons were called "Drawing the Line in Mississippi" and had a double meaning; not only had Roosevelt drawn the line on sportsmanship but he had also settled a boundary dispute between Louisiana and Mississippi while on this trip. Morris and Rose Mitchom from Brooklyn, New York, who ran a candy store, saw the cartoon and obtained the permission of the president to use one of his many nicknames, "Teddy," on a brown toy bear with movable body parts. The original bear, hand stitched by Rose Mitchom, was called, "Teddy's Bear." Later the name was shortened to "Teddy Bear." Initially the bear was sold at the Mitchoms' store and was an immediate success. The Butler Brothers wholesalers bought the Mitchoms' entire stock and established the Ideal Novelty and Toy Company along with the Mitchoms. By 1903 Teddy Bear mania swept the United States, and it lasted throughout Roosevelt's administration. The teddy bear has remained a popular toy throughout the century.

Source: Pauline Cockrill, *The Teddy Bear Enclyclopedia* (London: Dorling Kindersley, 1993).

Roosevelt's actions as contradictory, especially since he took political contributions from business, labor, and the public, but his landslide victories in presidential elections and his popularity throughout his term in office proved that his pluralistic platform worked. The hallmark of Roosevelt's success was his ability to get various constituencies to compromise.

Commission Appointed to Organize Trust Cases. Despite many successful prosecutions during his administration, Roosevelt as his presidency drew to a close thought that the thrust of the antitrust movement had become disjointed. In many court cases a trust was broken up into smaller companies that were still under the control of the original owners, thus creating a rearrangement rather than a dismantling of the trust. Roosevelt realized that the trust problem would not be permanently or satisfactorily resolved by the sequential prosecution of cases. Instead, he thought that a more organized approach was needed. To regulate business, Roosevelt specifically advocated a commission similar to the Interstate Commerce Commission but having jurisdiction over all businesses engaging in interstate commerce, not just railroads. Big business interpreted this additional governmental regulation as borderline socialism and argued for laissez-faire policies in response. Realizing that big business would invoke any means necessary to avoid regulation, Roosevelt maintained that his idea was not meant to "strangle" business but only regulate trusts and that legitimate businesses need not be concerned. Roosevelt's proposal was partially implemented in 1913 when the Departments of Commerce and Labor became separate.

Sources:
John Morton Blum, *The Republican Roosevelt* (Cambridge, Mass.: Harvard University Press, 1954);

Ernest L. Bogart and Donald L. Kemmerer, *Economic History of the American People* (New York: Longmans, Green, 1942);

Joshua Freeman and others, *Who Built America?: Working People and the Nation's Economy, Politics, Culture, and Society* (New York: Pantheon, 1992);

Charles Morris, *The Marvelous Career of Theodore Roosevelt* (N.p.: Winston, 1910);

Glenn Porter, *The Rise of Big Business, 1860–1910* (New York: Crowell, 1973);

Edwin C. Rozwenc, ed., *Roosevelt, Wilson and the Trusts* (Boston: D. C. Heath).

TAYLORISM AND SCIENTIFIC MANAGEMENT

Principles of Taylorism. Named after its creator, Frederick Taylor, Taylorism is the complete rationalization of all processes involved in the production of a product. The discipline is also referred to as scientific management, since it attempted to make a science out of the management of production processes by defining the "one best way" to do a job. Though the theory evolved

Cooling racks covered with car body parts in a Ford plant.

duction as a moral act that should not waste products or time and engineers as being responsible for the moral good of efficient designs. Scientific management was refined during the next several years, culminating in a landmark work in Taylor's *The Principles of Scientific Management* (1911). Advocates of scientific management such as Frank and Lillian Gilbreth and Henry Gantt expanded the concept in later years through the Taylor Society. Taylorism caught on during a time when America was fascinated by the technological advances of the Industrial Revolution and the emphasis on standardization and mechanization, but the degree to which Americans' lives became scientifically managed at work and at home remains surprising to many social critics. The popularity of Taylorism also fits in with the industrial boom that began in the early 1900s. As markets expanded and productivity demands increased, the need for larger workforces also increased. Scientifically managed work allowed new employees, many of whom were immigrants and women, to be trained quickly, often displacing more skilled labor that was becoming increasingly organized or unionized.

Pig Iron Experiment. One of the most famous applications of scientific management was the pig iron experiment at Bethlehem Steel. After scientifically selecting a worker named Schmidt, analysts examined all aspects of his pig iron loading job. Factors such as bending, lifting, walking, reaching, and rest periods were altered to determine the effects of each on the level of production. Additionally, Schmidt was cajoled into working harder by

through time, there were only a few simple principles in achieving scientific management: shift the responsibility of work organization to management, use scientific methods to establish the one best way to do the work, scientifically select and train workers, and monitor workers to ensure that they are doing their jobs properly and efficiently. The net result was that scientific management required laborers to match the speed of the machinery they used. Scientific management had both good and bad results. The positive side was that production rose by as much as 200 percent, which allowed for more profits and established the United States as a nation with efficient production.

Publication and Spread of the Theory. The theory behind scientific management was first publicly introduced by Taylor in a presentation titled "Shop Management" in 1903 before the American Academy of Mechanical Engineers. The theory essentially exalted pro-

Five-time Socialist presidential candidate (1900, 1904, 1908, 1912, 1920) and American Railway Union president (1893–1897) Eugene V. Debs campaigning

challenging him to live up to his selection as a "high priced man." The experiment was deemed successful since the training enabled Schmidt, who received only a marginal increase in pay, to load forty-seven tons per day when the standard production was only twelve tons in a day. However, much of the literature on the experiment failed to mention that several people dropped out of the experiment before Schmidt was found as a willing, albeit "mentally sluggish," subject.

Shovel Experiments. Equipment also faced scientific analysis. In another famous experiment shovel sizes were analyzed for their optimum output according to the weight of the material being used. Smaller shovels were used for heavier materials and larger shovels were used for lighter materials. An important caveat was that the manager should determine which shovel an employee should use.

Critiques of Taylorism. Scientifically managed work was criticized for having a dehumanizing effect on labor. Before scientific management much of labor remained skilled in spite of the use of machinery, and thus labor exerted considerable influence over the methods of work and levels of production. The time and motion studies required of scientific management routinized all jobs and effectively split off the minds of workers from the labor performed by their hands and backs. Management became thinkers and labor became doers. This division of labor resulted in management's absolute control of employees, easily replaceable workers, fewer skilled workers, and reduced pay for workers.

Specialization. In the scientifically designed system, laborers controlled only the portion of the work that did not require knowledge of production. For example, a job that had required knowledge to perform four separate tasks to set up a piece of machinery, operate it, clean it, and repair it would now be assigned to four separate workers, all of whom would be measured against a time standard. Organized labor vehemently protested the deskilling and displacement of skilled workers, but business owners continued to employ the technique. For the increases in regimented production, labor was given financial incentives, though many thought the trade-off was an uneven one in management's favor. Financial penalties were also put into place for those who could not maintain the benchmark pace established for the scientifically managed job.

Legacy of Taylorism. Although organized labor has protested against scientific management from its inception, the concept's influence has endured. Despite the emphasis in the 1960s placed on job enrichment and job rotation to relieve worker alienation, fatigue, and boredom and the promotion in the 1980s of "quality management" and team building, the principles of Taylorism are still applied, especially in lower-level jobs that are easily routinized. Day in and day out, these repetitive jobs had taken their toll mentally and physically on the workforce of industrial America. One recently noticed effect of scientifically managed work is the occupational hazard of repetitive motion injuries that cost organizations millions of dollars annually in medical bills and lost workdays.

Sources:

Frank Barkley Copley, *Frederick W. Taylor: Father of Scientific Management,* volumes 1 and 2 (New York: Kelley, 1969);

Gareth Morgan, *Images of Organization* (Beverly Hills: Sage Publications, 1986).

WOBBLIES

"One Big Union." The Industrial Workers of the World (IWW), a national industrial union, was formed in Brand's Hall on the North Side of Chicago on 27 June 1905. Leading union officials — including William "Big Bill" Haywood, Eugene Debs, Charles Moyer, Mother Jones, Father Thomas Hagerty, and Daniel De Leon — hoped to accomplish on a national scale what the Western Federation of Miners had done in the West for mining labor. Though the Western Federation of Miners was the largest constituency, other prominent unions that played a role in the IWW formation were the American Labor Union and the Socialist Trade and Labor Alliance. The founding convention, borrowing its symbolism from the American Revolution, was called "The Continental Congress of the Working Class," and Haywood was named chairman. In his opening remarks Haywood incorporated classic Marxist economic theory that became central to the IWW doctrine: "The aims and objectives of this organization should be to put the working class in possession of the economic power, the means of life, in control of the machinery of production and distribution, without regard to capitalist masters."

Syndicalism. The IWW advocated syndicalism, a revolutionary worker-controlled society. This utopian view of the IWW was a backlash against the growing conservatism of the American Federation of Labor (AFL) under Samuel Gompers. Consistently deriding the IWW as leftist agitators, Gompers had an informant inside the IWW to keep him posted of developments. Leaders of the IWW failed to believe that Gompers's craft union structure, which was formed around individual industrial craftsmen such as pipe fitters or boilermakers, would succeed against the powerful and growing trusts, especially in light of several failed strikes — most notably the steel strike of 1901 that ended the union at U.S. Steel. The IWW thought organizing along industrial, rather than craft, lines would result in more power. At the outset the IWW had more than forty trades united. And unlike the AFL, the IWW recruited unorganized workers regardless of job skill, race, or sex. The goal of "one big union" for all industrial workers was the primary aim of the IWW.

Organization. The new union took its organizational scheme from the "Wheel of Fortune," created by Father Hagerty, one of the founders. The IWW was divided into seven divisions: agriculture, mining, transportation, building, manufacturing, public service, and distribution of foodstuffs. Each department was further subdivided into industries and divided further into individual crafts or trades.

Bargaining Strategy. Initially the IWW rejected conventional collective bargaining and arbitration as too indirect. Its direct methods included strikes, boycotts, propaganda, violence, and sabotage to win labor concessions. Strikes of a violent nature were its trademark, and the miners' strike at Goldfield, Nevada (1906–1907), revealed its radical strategies. In addition to their organizing activities, IWW members were also proponents of the First Amendment right to free speech, an advocacy that came about when union members were arrested for speaking out on labor issues. Wobblies, as IWW members were known, would descend on towns that had restricted speech, mounting soap boxes spread out over a town. As soon as one Wobblie was arrested, another would take his place, until the jails and courts were clogged with cases. The strategy was successful in raising the conscience of taxpayers who doubted the wisdom of tax money being spent to keep the Wobblies in jail for crimes as minor as illegal speech. Later the IWW dropped its more radical methods and adopted collective bargaining as a strategy.

Peak. Though hundreds of thousands of union cards were issued, many workers joined the IWW only for short periods of time. At its peak around 1912 — in part because of the notoriety around the textile strike in Lawrence, Massachusetts — the IWW had sixty thousand members, though its labor gains affected the lives of millions of workers indirectly. The most active members were those workers in the areas of mining, construction, lumber, migratory agriculture, and textiles, as well as immigrants and those who had been blacklisted.

Fractious Union. The IWW declined in membership soon after its founding because of the varied interests of its constituents. At its 1906 convention several right-wingers defected over a dispute with Socialist members who advocated revolution. The increased factionalism, as well as the 1907 economic crisis and governmental repression (especially during World War I, when many of its leaders and members were jailed), also added to its decline. In 1907 the backbone of the union, the Western Federation of Miners, defected, leaving the union with fewer than ten thousand actual members. In 1908 the Socialist Laborites who favored Daniel De Leon left the union over the issue of whether the union should pursue a political or economic agenda. Disagreeing with the IWW's lack of affiliation with a political party and its intent to pursue direct economic action by its members as its principal tool, De Leon formed a separate organization. The IWW's utopian stance embodied in the phrase "We shall be all" continued to be one of never making peace with the capitalists, whom it considered enemies of the working class. Despite these serious setbacks in organizing, the IWW has endured as a union.

Sources:

Richard O. Boyer and Herbert M. Morais, *Labor's Untold Story* (Pittsburgh: United Electrical, Radio & Machine Workers of America, 1955);

Opening day on the Plaza at the Saint Louis World's Fair, 30 April 1904

Melvyn Dubofsky, *We Shall Be All: A History of the Industrial Workers of the World* (Chicago: Quadrangle Books, 1969);

Foster Rhea Dulles, *Labor in America: A History* (New York: Crowell, 1949).

THE WORLD'S FAIR AT SAINT LOUIS

The Louisiana Purchase Exposition. Opening on 30 April 1904 with a dedication by President Theodore Roosevelt, the Saint Louis World's Fair lasted for seven months and was then the largest world's fair ever held. There were 187,798 attendees the first day. Officially the fair was named the Louisiana Purchase Exposition to commemorate the one-hundredth anniversary of the Louisiana Purchase from France in 1803. The Olympics were also a part of the fair, and America dominated the medal race. More than twenty million visitors attended throughout the fair's run, and the fair showed a $25 million profit.

Industrial Showcase. World's fairs were the primary venues for exhibiting and introducing new technologies and inventions to the public, celebrating the triumphs of the Industrial Revolution, big business, and a growing economy. The Saint Louis fair stands as a tribute to the Progressive Era and with its elaborate industrial exhibits. Several new products were introduced that remain a part of the American lifestyle. Some of the food debuting included hamburgers by local German immigrants, the ice cream cone by a local pastry maker who made wafer cones when concession stands ran out of dishes, and iced tea when hot fairgoers passed up heated English tea.

Architectural Significance. Costing more than $20 million to erect, the exposition was also noted for its

PEPSI-COLA: WHAT'S IN A NAME?

The Pepsi-Cola Company was founded in 1902, only four years after the elixir's invention in New Bern, North Carolina, by drugstore owner Caleb D. Bradham. The concoction was intentionally created to compete with the many kola nut–derived drinks on the market at the time, especially the Coca-Cola brand. Bradham enjoyed mixing special fountain drinks for his friends at the soda fountain in his drugstore. Originally called "Brad's drink" by Bradham's friends, he renamed it "Pepsi-Cola" for its alleged pharmaceutical qualities. Pepsi derives its name from the ailment it was advertised to relieve: dyspepsia. In modern times, dyspepsia is called indigestion. Early ads for Pepsi-Cola tout this benefit: "Pepsi-Cola: At Soda Fountains. Exhilarating. Invigorating. Aids Digestion."

Sources: Milward W. Martin, *Twelve Full Ounces* (New York: Holt, Rinehart & Winston, 1962);

Adrian Room, *Dictionary of Trade Name Origins* (London: Routledge & Kegan Paul, 1982).

dramatic architectural structures, which housed industrial, agricultural, art, historical, and cultural exhibits as well as buildings from fifty-three states and territories of the United States and fifty-two nations. The layout, with waterways, terraced thoroughfares, and cultivated grounds, was also extraordinary. The central point of the exhibition was Festival Hall, surrounded by the water of the Grand Basin, which had the largest pumping station then ever built, with a capacity of twenty-five million gallons. Yet, the central monument was the commemorative Louisiana Monument with a statue of Peace atop a globe on a tapered obelisk, standing one hundred feet high. Characterized as the "world's university," the focus of the fair was to unite all of the races and nations in one event. In keeping with the tradition of earlier fairs, most of the buildings were razed, with only a few left standing to commemorate the architecture of the period. The only building standing today is the one that houses the Saint Louis Museum of Art.

Sources:
Mark Bennitt, ed., *History of the Louisiana Purchase Exposition* (New York: Arno, 1976);

The World's Fair: The Official Photographic Views of the Universal Exposition Held in Saint Louis, 1904 (Saint Louis: Thompson Publishing, 1904).

HEADLINE MAKERS

ANDREW CARNEGIE

1835-1919

INDUSTRIALIST AND PHILANTHROPIST

Carnegie Steel. Andrew Carnegie, having acquired his wealth during the nineteenth century, spent much of the early 1900s giving away large portions of his fortune to worthy causes. His wealth was primarily built from his domination of the American steel industry by his company, Carnegie Steel. By the turn of the century Carnegie had vertically integrated his holdings from ore to finished products and built his company into one of the world leaders in steel. When J. P. Morgan set up a financing coalition to purchase his business in 1901, Carnegie sold his 58 percent share of Carnegie Steel to the new U.S. Steel Corporation, making him one of the world's richest men.

Industrious Immigrant. Carnegie's prowess in getting wealth and giving it away enriched his adopted nation even more than it did himself. The circumstances of his boyhood fostered both passions. A native of Scotland, Carnegie came to America with his family, looking to fulfill both material ambition and social idealism. Settling in Pittsburgh, young Andrew got his start as a telegrapher, and his work came to the attention of Thomas Scott, the superintendent of the Pennsylvania Railroad's Western Division. He appointed Carnegie his secretary and personal telegrapher. During his twelve years with the Pennsylvania Railroad, Carnegie assimilated the managerial skill, grasped the economic principles, and cemented the personal relationships that enabled him to become a successful manager, capitalist, and entrepreneur. During the depression of the 1870s, with properties cheap and the Bessemer process coming into its own, Carnegie concentrated all his resources and energies in the making of steel. He hired the best people in steel technology and plant management, shrewdly held on to absolute control of his enterprise (the better to plow profits back into capital improvement), and outmaneuvered all his rivals in the field.

Social Concern. Carnegie's family had impressed upon him since he was a child the importance of social justice. With the enormous wealth he had acquired he "felt a moral duty to plow back their money into philanthropy with the same judgment, zeal, and leadership he had devoted to getting rich." He was able to live up to his family's desires. With the $250 million in 5 percent, fifty-year gold bonds he received from the sale of his steel company, Carnegie began to follow the precepts of the famous article he wrote in 1899, "The Gospel of Wealth." His article expressed his opinion that donations should be made during the life of the donor. Carnegie had established standards and routine procedures to handle all requests efficiently and promptly by late 1900 through the creation of the Carnegie Institute of Technology in Pittsburgh.

Making a Difference. Carnegie regarded library giving as his specialty, and he approached it systematically. In the first fifteen years of the century he helped establish 2,811 free public libraries, of which 1,946 were located in the United States. Although Carnegie received some criticism for his devotion to libraries, he was not distracted from building libraries since he felt that no other gifts were as popular or had as direct an impact upon as large a number of people as did his public libraries. Prior to 1880 free libraries were all but nonexistent; however, Carnegie was able to change that by making them almost as much a part of America as schoolhouses or churches. Church organs were another interest of Carnegie's; by his death in 1919 he had given away 4,092 church organs throughout the United States. Education was the biggest beneficiary of Carnegie's fortune. It has been estimated that 80 percent of his fortune went for educational purposes: libraries, colleges and universities, institutions to promote scientific research and the diffusion of knowledge, and individual grants and pensions to college teachers. Carnegie decided to focus his attention on the small colleges and universities. He felt larger institutions had large enough endowments so he concentrated his efforts where he felt he could make the greatest difference.

The Score. Carnegie thoroughly enjoyed the game of philanthropy during the early years when he competed with John D. Rockefeller. The press reported their donation totals each year like box scores. In 1910 the *New York American* reported total lifetime giving by Carnegie at $179,300,000 and Rockefeller at $134,271,000. By 1906 Carnegie was tired of the game and by 1910 he was sick of it. He wrote: "The final dispensation of one's wealth preparing for the final exit is I found a heavy task — all sad. . . . You have no idea the strain I have been under." Most discouraging to him was the fact that no matter how fast he gave during the years from 1901 to 1910, he could not give fast enough. The interest on his bonds kept gaining on his dispersal of the principal. By 1910 he had given away $180 million but he still had almost the same amount left. Carnegie's close friend, Secretary of State Elihu Root, noting his depression, suggested he set up a trust and transfer the bulk of his fortune to others for them to worry about, so he could die happy in a state of grace.

A New Corporation. Carnegie created the Carnegie Corporation of New York in November 1911, and in a series of grants he transferred to it the bulk of his remaining fortune, $125 million. In compliance with his gospel, Carnegie had given 90 percent of his fortune away during his lifetime, but he left other men to worry about its management. At the time of the announcement of the Carnegie Corporation the *New York Herald* ran the final box score on the contest between Carnegie and Rockefeller: "Carnegie, $332 million; Rockefeller, $175 million." It was no longer a contest. The public had lost interest, and so had Andrew Carnegie.

Sources:

Andrew Carnegie, *Autobiography* (Boston: Houghton Mifflin, 1920);

Carnegie, *The Empire of Business* (New York: Doubleday, Page, 1902);

Joseph Frazier Wall, *Andrew Carnegie* (New York: Oxford University Press, 1970).

EUGENE V. DEBS

1855-1926

LABOR ORGANIZER AND SOCIALIST PRESIDENTIAL CANDIDATE

A Political Life. Eugene Debs grew up in the small midwestern city of Terre Haute, Indiana, where his parents, Alsatian emigrants, operated a grocery store. In 1875 he was elected secretary of the Terre Haute lodge of the Brotherhood of Locomotive Firemen. His intelligence and commitment attracted the attention of the brotherhood leaders. By 1881 he was national secretary of the brotherhood, increasingly its spokesman on labor issues, and its most tireless organizer. Debs entered politics as a Democratic candidate for city clerk in 1879. In 1885 he was elected to the Indiana State Assembly.

Union Stand. Debs's evolving views on labor disputes led to his involvement in the strike of the American Railway Union (ARU) in 1894 against the Pullman Company of Chicago. By working intimately with federal authorities, railroad management was able to break the strike. Federal troops occupied Chicago; federal injunctions prevented communication between ARU local unions; and federal judges sentenced Debs and other activists to jail terms. Upon release from jail, Debs had changed some of his views. He questioned the ability of trade unions to compete successfully with the capitalists and their economic power; and, after the 1896 elections, he looked upon socialism as the answer to working people's problems.

Presidential Candidate. Between 1900 and 1920 Debs was the Socialist Party's standard-bearer in five presidential elections. Between campaigns Debs was a tireless speaker and organizer for the party, and he traveled the nation defending workers in their strikes and industrial disputes. In 1905 Debs, William D. Haywood, and others founded the Industrial Workers of the World (IWW), nicknamed the "Wobblies," with the aim of uniting all workingmen and gaining union control of production. Although many workers enthusiastically applauded Debs's vision, relatively few endorsed his political program. He conducted his last campaign for president in 1920 as prisoner number 9,653 in the Atlanta Federal Penitentiary while serving ten years for violation of the Espionage Act, having been arrested after he made a rousing antiwar speech in Canton, Ohio, in June 1918. He received nearly a million votes, and he was pardoned on Christmas Day 1921 by President Warren G. Harding. As the American Socialist Party fragmented in the aftermath of the Bolshevik Revolution, Debs remained with the party he had led for so many years. When he died he was buried in Terre Haute, his home throughout his life.

Sources:

Richard O. Boyer and Herbert M. Morais, *Labor's Untold Story* (Pittsburgh: United Electrical, Radio & Machine Workers of America, 1955);

Eugene Debs, *Debs: His Life Writings and Speeches* (Girard, Kans.: Appeal to Reason, 1908).

HENRY FORD

1863-1947

INDUSTRIALIST

Early Aptitude. Henry Ford did not invent the automobile, but he developed design concepts and production techniques that allowed its manufacture in such high volume and at such low cost as to bring it within reach of the average wage earner. His impact on American life in the twentieth century was enormous. Ford was born on a farm near Dearborn, Michigan. From his earliest days he displayed a marked mechanical aptitude, and all his life he loved working with machinery. In 1879 he became an apprentice in a machine shop in Detroit, repairing watches at night to make ends meet.

Farm to Factory. In 1888 his father gave him a forty-acre tract of land in Dearborn on the condition that he abandon the machinist's trade and return to the farm. Ford built a house on the land and made a small income selling lumber and firewood. But he did not engage in farming and used his spare time to experiment with steam and gasoline engines in a shop attached to the home. In 1891 he left the farm for an engineering job in Detroit. In 1899, with the support of a group of investors, he established the Detroit Automobile Company, capitalized at $150,000. This was the first company organized in Detroit for the manufacture of autos, but after turning out twelve unreliable vehicles, it went out of business in the fall of 1900.

Henry Ford Company. Ford then turned to auto racing and built a racer to gain a wider reputation. The success of his racer revived the enthusiasm of former stockholders and resulted in his firm's reorganization as the Henry Ford Company in November 1901. The firm was capitalized at $60,000, of which more than half was paid in stock. Dissension broke out between Ford and the promoters, and in 1902 Henry M. Leland was brought into the firm as a consulting engineer. Ford resigned, and the firm was then reorganized as the Cadillac Motor Car Company.

Birth of Ford Motor Company. Ford again turned to auto racing and began construction of two racing cars, the *Arrow* and the *999*. With success in racing Ford again turned his attention to creating a model car capable of competing with such popularly priced cars as Oldsmobile. Needing $3,000 in developmental cost, Ford approached Alexander Y. Malcomson, a leading Detroit coal dealer, and in 1902 they formed a partnership to produce a marketable automobile. With demand growing for their model they were able to attract a substantial number of investors, and the Ford Motor Company was incorporated in June 1903 with $150,000 capital. The first Ford automobile, the Model A, was brought out in June 1903, selling for $850. A total of 1,708 sold in the first fifteen months, so a second story was added to the plant. Higher priced B, C, and F models were offered in 1904 and 1905. In early 1905 manufacturing operations were transferred to a newer and larger plant.

Cash Flow Problems. The financial panic of 1907 turned out to be a turbulent summer rather than an extended depression. Makers of expensive cars and ill-financed marginal plants suffered most, but makers of inexpensive cars were also damaged. Since income had dropped, luxuries had to be sacrificed. Fortunately for the Ford Motor Company it had maintained large reserves, but because of the panic and the recent purchases of the Highland Park tract for a new factory and its absorption of the Ford

Manufacturing Company, tremendous strain was put on the cash flow. Ford was forced to postpone paydays several times in the fall of 1907. In order to maintain adequate cash flow, the company turned to its dealers for cash and resorted to paying bills by issuing notes. Ford kept building cars and shipping them to dealers, who had to pay for those cars. This forced the dealers to raise the money for the cars or risk losing their dealership.

Model T. The result of Ford's vision, the Model T was introduced in 1908, combining in a standard utility vehicle the features of lightness, durability, efficiency, interchangeable parts, and low cost. By 1916 the company was able to reduce the price of the car to about $350 because of cost-cutting production methods. From its inception until 1927 the Model T was the sole model sold by the company, and most of the time was available only in black. Ford designed the car for rural America, and it was well suited for travel over poor country roads. It became extremely popular in the untapped market of the Midwest and Plains states and rode the prosperity of agriculture's "golden age" from 1909 to 1916. Production went from 18,664 in 1911 to 78,440 in 1912. By 1913 there were seven thousand dealers affiliated with the company, with at least one in every town with a population of more than two thousand.

Later Years. Although Ford was a mechanical genius, he was otherwise ignorant, narrow, and naive. He published many scurrilous anti-Semitic articles and fought unionization with every weapon at his disposal, including a private police force. Nor would he allow modern management techniques to interfere with his autocratic ways. By the mid 1930s the company was riven by factions, and no one was really in charge. A decade later the Ford Motor Company, once the most prodigious engine of wealth creation in the American economy, was on the brink of ruin, losing $1 million a day. Two years before his death Henry Ford's family finally forced him to cede control to his grandson, Henry Ford II.

Sources:

Henry Ford, *My Life and Work* (Garden City, N.Y.: Doubleday, Page, 1922);

Robert Lacy, *Ford: The Men and The Machine* (Boston: Little, Brown, 1986);

Allan Nevins, with Frank Ernest Hill, *Ford: The Times, The Man, The Company* (New York: Scribners, 1954).

WILLIAM "BIG BILL" HAYWOOD

1869-1928

LABOR LEADER

Out of the Mines. Born in Salt Lake City, Utah, William Haywood experienced a difficult early life, losing his father at the age of three, obtaining minimal formal education, and working for wages as an adolescent. At fifteen he became a miner and in 1896 joined

the Western Federation of Miners (WFM), the era's preeminent radical labor union, in Silver City, Idaho. He served as secretary and president of his local chapter and in 1900 was promoted to the union's general executive board. In 1901 he moved to Denver where he served as editor of the WFM's journal and as secretary-treasurer. Within the radical milieu of the Denver headquarters, Haywood received an education in class struggle and socialism.

IWW Leader. Between 1903 and 1905 Haywood participated in one of the most violent incidents in American labor history. The WFM waged a bitter conflict with mining and smelting corporations in Colorado that degenerated into a war between miners and state militia. Haywood's experiences with "class warfare" in Colorado convinced him that American workers must unite into "one big union." Thus, in 1905 he, along with Eugene Debs, presided at the founding convention of the Industrial Workers of the World (IWW). That convention made Haywood one of the nation's best-known labor radicals, a man described as possessing two rare qualities, "genuine power and genuine simplicity."

Advocate for Revolution. In 1906 Idaho imprisoned Haywood for alleged complicity in the murder of former governor Frank Steunenberg. The ensuing sensational trial, in which he was defended by Clarence Darrow, ended with Haywood's acquittal. He then became a leader of the Socialist Party of America. But in a party opposed to violence and dedicated to respectability, Haywood advised socialists and workers to practice sabotage and risk imprisonment to foster revolution. In 1912 he was recalled from the Socialist Party's National Executive Committee by a vote of its members. The most significant phase of Haywood's career came between 1911 and 1918. He succeeded to the highest office in the IWW and directed the organization's growth among western agricultural, timber, and mine workers during World War I.

Exile. Because strikes threatened the war effort, the federal government arrested all the leaders of the IWW in 1917 and charged them with violating espionage and sedition acts. Haywood and a hundred others went on trial in Chicago. The jury found them all guilty, and the judge sentenced Haywood to twenty years in prison. While released on bail Haywood jumped bond and fled to the Soviet Union. There he led an unhappy life, an alien in Lenin's and Stalin's Russia. He wrote his autobiography, *Bill Haywood's Book* (1929) and died on 18 May 1928 in a Moscow hospital.

Sources:

Richard O. Boyer and Herbert M. Morais, *Labor's Untold Story* (Pittsburgh: United Electrical, Radio & Machine Workers of America, 1955);

William Haywood, *Bill Haywood's Book: The Autobiography* (New York: International, 1929).

ANDREW WILLIAM MELLON

1855-1937

BANKER AND FINANCIER

A Father's Footsteps. Andrew Mellon was the son of Judge Thomas Mellon of Pittsburgh, Pennsylvania, who acquired a great deal of wealth from his legal practice but even more from his investments. Andrew learned a much from his father, and in the early 1870s he started his own lumber and building business in Mansfield, Pennsylvania. Because of the depression of 1873, his company went out of business. Mellon went on to build his financial reputation in his father's bank. By the age of twenty-seven he was running the banking house, and soon thereafter he received ownership of the bank from his father. Mellon built his fortune through his ability to shrewdly judge both businesses and businessmen and his faithfulness in following his father's rule of constantly reinvesting profits in the businesses that generated them.

Ground-Floor Investments. Mellon was able to discover several companies in their infancy and provide them with the capital to become dominant American businesses. One such success was in the newly founded aluminum industry. In 1889 Mellon agreed to give the Pittsburgh Reduction Company $4,000 to meet an overdue note in exchange for stock and expressed his confidence in the company by continued financial support. In 1907 this company became the Aluminum Company of America (Alcoa), having provided aluminum for buildings, boats, automobiles, and the Wright brothers' airplane; by the 1930s Mellon and his brother owned about 33 percent of the company. The oil industry was another success for Mellon. He provided seed money to James Guffey and John Galey for oil explorations at Spindletop Hill, near Beaumont, Texas, where in January 1901 they struck it rich. Within the next year Mellon helped organize the Gulf Refining Company. By 1923 their refinery at Port Arthur was the world's largest, and Gulf was one of the giants of the oil industry. Mellon also invested in the steel industry. He assisted in organizing the Union Steel Company and in 1902 sold it to U.S. Steel for more than $30 million. He also acquired 60 percent ownership in a small steel-fabricating business in the early 1900s. This company, McClintic-Marshall Construction Company, later provided the steel and engineering for the Waldorf-Astoria Hotel, the RCA building in New York City, the George Washington Bridge, and the Golden Gate Bridge in San Francisco. It was merged into Bethlehem Steel in 1931.

The Later Years. In the 1920s Mellon became active in the Republican Party, and in 1921 President Warren G. Harding appointed him secretary of the treasury, a job at which he excelled. Mellon also used his money for philanthropy. He founded the National Gallery of Art in Washington, D.C., assisted the Carnegie Library of Pittsburgh, founded the Mellon Institute, and set up endowments at several universities.

Sources:

Andrew Mellon, *Taxation: The People's Business* (New York: Macmillan, 1924);

Harvey O'Connor, *Mellon's Millions: The Biography of a Fortune* (New York: John Day, 1933).

J. Pierpont Morgan

1837-1913

Banker

To the Bank Born. J. P. Morgan headed J. P. Morgan and Company, the most important force in American finance in the quarter century before World War I, a time when the American economy grew to be the largest and most powerful in the world. Morgan was born into a wealthy banking family in Hartford, Connecticut. His father instilled in him from childhood principles of integrity and trained him early in the business of international banking as it was practiced at the highest levels. Morgan graduated from the university at Göttingen, Germany, in 1857 and immediately went to work on Wall Street. In 1862 he opened his own firm, which eventually became the Morgan Bank. Morgan took over his father's firm when his father died in 1890, and renamed it J. P. Morgan and Company.

U.S. Steel. In 1901 Morgan was instrumental in establishing the United States Steel Corporation. Morgan underwrote a successful public offering of stock in the world's first $1 billion corporation. This offering netted millions for Morgan and paid $492 million to Andrew Carnegie for about $80 million in actual assets in order to eliminate the steel industry's major price-cutter. With the merger of Carnegie's properties and other steel properties, U.S. Steel controlled 65 percent of the U.S. steel-making capacity. Acquiring Carnegie's steel company was vital to Morgan because he saw Carnegie as a disturbing element, not only in steel, but also in the railroad world. On 3 March 1901 the plan of the organization of the U.S. Steel Corporation was made public. The incorporation stabilized the great, widely scattered, uncoordinated domestic steel industry and made it possible for American steel to invade foreign markets.

Morgan's Method. When Morgan backed U.S. Steel he concentrated on eliminating disturbances and selecting the right men to run the corporation. Morgan viewed his enterprise as too important to be subject to the whims of old age, the desire for retaliation, or the health or change in habits of any small group of men. The management had to be conducted at a high level. Constant attention to research and development and the best engineering talent was gathered to ensure that the United States retain its premier standing in the world of steel. The board of directors was made up of some of the most successful businessmen ever organized into a group. Charles M. Schwab was elected president, and Judge Elbert H. Gary was chosen as the chairman of the executive committee. Morgan was represented by Charles Steele on the executive committee and Robert Bacon on the finance committee.

Billion Dollar Steel Trust. Because of the enormous size and wealth generated by U.S. Steel, many politicians attempted to capitalize politically with the "common people" and the "friends of labor" by talking about the "Billion Dollar Steel Trust." It was attacked as a monopoly that was seeking to destroy competition, influence legislation, and control government. Carnegie did not help matters by stating several times that he would soon come back into possession of the Carnegie Steel Company: "Pierpont is not an ironmaster, he knows nothing about the business of making and selling steel. I managed my trade with him so that I was paid for my properties in bonds, not stocks! He will make a fizzle of the business and default in payment of interest. I will then foreclose and get my properties back, and Pierpont and his friends will lose all their paper profits." Carnegie did not realize that Morgan would not have paid him in anything but bonds because he wanted to eliminate him from control and have him as a creditor only and not as a partner. Of course, the event did not turn out as Carnegie predicted.

The Panic. The rhetoric regarding influential, wealthy men such as Morgan was clearly hostile in 1907. In a 4 July address Princeton University president Woodrow Wilson urged an attack on the illegal manipulations of financiers rather than on corporations. In a speech on 20 August President Theodore Roosevelt castigated "malefactors of great wealth." But later in the year Morgan acted single-handedly to avert a financial panic that began on 23 October with a run on New York's Knickerbocker Trust Company and spread to several other banks and trust companies. To calm the panic and shore up the money supply, Morgan obtained pledges from the Bank of England, John D. Rockefeller, and other major financiers. He acted to allow New York City to avoid defaulting on some short-term bonds. He even resorted to locking leading New York trust company presidents in his library overnight in his efforts to negotiate deals to support financial institutions. By taking command and rallying other bankers, Morgan succeeded in restoring confidence. The financial crisis of 1907 eventually led to the creation of the Federal Reserve System in 1913, which made the private manipulation of financial markets such as those represented by Morgan's actions during the panic both unnecessary and unthinkable. Morgan died in Rome, Italy, in 1913.

Sources:

Vincent P. Carosso, *The Morgans: Private International Bankers, 1854–1913* (Cambridge, Mass.: Harvard University Press, 1988);

Herbert L. Satterlee, *J. Pierpont Morgan, An Intimate Portrait* (New York: Macmillan, 1939).

PHILLIP A. PAYTON JR.

1876-

AFRICAN AMERICAN REALTOR

Getting a Start. Phillip A. Payton Jr. was born and reared in Westfield, Massachusetts. He received his education from Livingstone College in Salisbury, North Carolina, and went to New York in 1899 to seek his fortune. Payton's early jobs included being a handyman at six dollars a week, a barber, and a janitor in a real estate office. Intrigued by the boom atmosphere at the turn of the century, Payton entered the real estate business. In an interview he described his first break: "I was a real estate agent, making a speciality of the management of colored tenement property for nearly a year before I actually succeeded in getting a colored tenement to manage," he said, "My first opportunity came as a result of a dispute between two landlords in West 134th Street. To 'get even' one of them turned his house over to me to fill with colored tenants. I was successful in renting and managing this house, and after a time I was able to induce other landlords to . . . give me their houses to manage." In 1904 he organized the Afro-American Realty Company.

A Thriving Business. The Afro-American Realty Company had its beginnings in a partnership of ten blacks organized by Payton. The partnership specialized in acquiring five-year leases on Harlem property owned by whites and subsequently renting them to blacks. Incorporated on 15 June 1904, the company had an estimated capital of $100,000 and was permitted to buy, sell, rent, lease, and sublease real estate in New York City. At first the company had sound support from eminent members of the black community. By 1905 it had assets valued at $690,000 and controlled twenty New York apartment houses, of which six were owned and fourteen held on long-term leases. At its peak Afro-American Realty had leased or mortgaged some twenty-five houses, most of them in Harlem. The paper value of the property was $1.1 million, with annual rental income of $114,500.

Promises to Keep. Payton, however, was under increasing pressure from stockholders in the company who were dissatisfied with his performance. He promised the average investor much more than he was able to fulfill. The prospectus for the Afro-American Realty Company offered profits of 7 to 10 percent, but weekly advertisements omitted the lower figure. Blacks were told that it was their obligation to support this enterprise, which would help end racial prejudice. Such advertising eventually led to Payton being sued by his investors.

Collapse. Because of Payton's speculations, overextension, and the recession of 1907–1908, the company was left with many new tenements, but few tenants. In an attempt to raise additional capital he wrote to Booker T. Washington for a letter of introduction to Andrew Carnegie. Washington refused to intercede, because Payton's business was not a philanthropic matter. Payton went to see Carnegie anyway but won no support. In a final gesture to keep the corporation in business Payton asked Booker T. Washington to underwrite the company's notes due on 1 January 1908. He refused, and the Afro-American Realty Company collapsed, losing all its properties.

Achievements. The Afro-American Realty Company played a significant role in opening homes for blacks in Harlem. Payton owned and managed apartment houses and brownstones in sections never previously rented to black tenants. When the company folded, the buildings were taken over by white owners, but the black tenants remained, laying the foundations of the most famous Negro neighborhood in America.

Source:

Gilbert Osofsky, *Harlem: The Making of a Ghetto* (New York: Harper & Row, 1963).

JAMES CASH PENNEY

1875-1971

CHAIN STORE OWNER

Modest Beginnings. James Cash Penney was born in Hamilton, Missouri. When he was eight years old his father decided that he must begin to buy his own clothes, and he earned enough that year to buy a pair of shoes. He was educated in the public school of his hometown and graduated from high school in 1893. Two years later he began his career as a clerk in a general store in Hamilton. In 1897 he went to Denver, Colorado, where he was a clerk in a department store, later moving to Longmont, Colorado. Penney started a meat and bakery business that was not a success, but as a result he went to work for T. M. Callahan, dry-goods merchant of Johnson and Callahan, whom Penney called "the man who gave me my great opportunity in life."

The Start of a Chain. In 1899 Callahan sent Penney to his store in Evanston, Wyoming, and in 1902 sent him to open a new store in the frontier town of Kemmerer, Wyoming. Penney was given the opportunity to purchase a one-third partnership in the enterprise, which had a capital stock of $6,000. Penney borrowed $1,500, added $500 of his own savings, and on 14 April 1902 opened the Golden Rule store. Opening-day receipts of Penney's first store, open from dawn to midnight, were $466.59. By the end of the first year the store had done $29,000 worth of business. This experience convinced Penney that a chain of similar stores under a partnership-ownership agreement would be successful. The expansion of Penney's company into a national chain was made possible by the developing national transportation and communication infrastructure.

Expansion. By 1907 Penney had acquired forty-eight stores and located his headquarters in New York City. Instead of opening one store at a time, Penney began to purchase whole chains of stores. By 1929 the J. C. Penney Company owned 1,450 stores and had reached annual sales of $209 million. Even during the Depression expansion continued, and the total of stores in the chain rose to 1,600 by 1941. Penney opened an average of one new store every ten days for forty years.

Philosophy. Penney never touched alcohol or tobacco and for many years forbade his employees to do so. He believed "that anyone and everyone has in him the latent capacity to become a human dynamo, capable of accomplishing anything to which he aspires." To his employees he stressed energy, integrity, and loyalty. He made it a policy to offer a new executive less than he had been paid in his previous job, as a test of loyalty and faith — and as a measure of thrift. Late in his life, when his chain had grown to become the nation's fifth largest merchandising operation with annual sales of more than $4 billion, he proclaimed that "the company's success is due to the application of the Golden Rule to every individual, to the public, and to all of our activities." In the early days of J. C. Penney many of his stores had been called Golden Rule stores as part of his philosophy that business had to follow the Golden Rule. Later they were all called J. C. Penney stores. A Democrat and a Baptist, Penney was an ardent supporter of Prohibition. In 1925 he built the Memorial Home Community in Florida at a cost of $1.25 million to house aged religious workers.

Sources:

Norman Beasley, *Main Street Merchant: The Story of the J. C. Penney Company* (New York: Whittlesey House, 1948);

John Brooks, *The Autobiography of American Business* (Garden City, N.Y.: Doubleday, 1974);

J. C. Penney, *50 Years with the Golden Rule* (New York: Harper, 1950);

Penney, *View from the Next Decade: Jottings from a Merchant's Daybook* (New York: Nelson, 1960).

CHARLES MICHAEL SCHWAB

1862-1939

STEEL MANUFACTURER AND FINANCIER

The Beginnings. As a young grocery clerk in Braddock, Pennsylvania, the site of the Edgar Thomson Steel Work of Carnegie Steel, Charles Michael Schwab made the acquaintance of "Captain" William R. Jones. Jones was the plant's general superintendent and got Schwab a job as an engineer's helper at two dollars a day in the early 1880s. From this position Schwab was able to learn a great deal about the steel business. He studied the chemistry and metallurgy of steel late into the night in his chemistry laboratory in his home. Schwab rapidly moved up within Andrew Carnegie's company by using his managerial skills to solve labor and public-relations problems. In 1897 he was appointed president of Carnegie Steel Company, earning more than $1 million a year with bonuses, most of which he reinvested in the firm.

U.S. Steel. In 1900 Schwab sparked J. P. Morgan's interest in the profit potential of a huge new steel combination at a 12 December dinner at the University Club in New York City. He drew up a basic list of companies to be integrated and proposed the financing by which the combination was to be accomplished. Once he had gotten Morgan interested, he encouraged Carnegie to sell after a golf match at St. Andrews. At Morgan's stipulation, Schwab became the first president of U.S. Steel in 1901, at only thirty-nine years of age. Although he was earning $2 million a year in the position, he resigned in 1903 because of difficulties with the board of directors. They had criticized his extended travel and his gambling, and Morgan was also extremely critical of side investments Schwab had made, notably in the United States Shipbuilding Company, which Morgan felt were detracting from his ability to run U.S. Steel in the best interests of the bondholders.

Bethlehem Steel Company. In 1901, as a spinoff of the U.S. Steel formation, Schwab purchased control of the Bethlehem Steel Company. Because of conflicts of interest Schwab suggested that Bethlehem be merged with U.S. Shipbuilding, with Schwab receiving $30 million in securities and a mortgage on the company's property. The new company, however, collapsed in the midst of a financial scandal, with its assets going to Schwab as the largest bondholder. Buying out the other investors, he made U.S. Shipbuilding and Bethlehem Steel into a giant enterprise under his own control, Bethlehem Steel Corporation, in 1904.

Exercising Control. Six weeks prior to Schwab buying controlling interest in Bethlehem Steel, the owners had dismissed Frederick W. Taylor, the controversial pioneer of scientific management. When Schwab took over Bethlehem he discarded almost all of Taylor's policies. Bethlehem was a holding company, not unlike U.S. Steel, and operated seven shipyards and one manufacturing company. Schwab had plans for enlargement so that the plant could produce all types of guns, gun forgings, and tools. In an effort to bring Bethlehem into greater prosperity, Schwab proceeded to sell off its unprofitable properties and invest the proceeds in shipyards, which had the greatest profit potential.

Risking It All. Expansion into the field of commercial steel was foremost among Schwab's plans for the growth of Bethlehem. He decided to risk his fortune and the future of the company on a new and largely untried product. Henry Grey had perfected a new steel beam that could be rolled as a single section instead of being riveted together as conventional beams then were. Into this new concern Schwab poured every penny he owned and every penny he could borrow. He succeeded in bringing the company into a solid competitive position by concentrating on the eastern market and specializing in the new rolled-steel girders, called Bethlehem Beams. The rolled-steel girders were in great demand with the dawning age of the skyscraper.

The Later Years. During World War I, Bethlehem Steel became a major arsenal for the Allied powers. Schwab got huge war contracts from Allied governments, and by the end of the conflict the company had handled orders totaling more than $500 million. After the war Schwab increasingly functioned as an elder statesman of the company, which had by then become a major rival of U.S. Steel, and the senior spokesman for the steel industry as a whole. In his later years he was paid a salary of $250,000 per year for only nominal functions at Bethlehem Steel. Schwab began investing his money in new enterprises. Such ventures as International Nickel, American Steel Foundries, and Chicago Pneumatic Tool, all of which he helped found, were successful. But others, especially those outside the steel industry, turned out badly. He was, indeed, often an "easy mark" for investment capital, and when the Depression hit, his fortune of some $200 million was depleted. He died, insolvent, in New York City in 1939.

Source:
Robert Hessen, *Steel Titan: The Life of Charles M. Schwab* (New York: Oxford University Press, 1975).

FREDERICK WINSLOW TAYLOR

1856-1915

MANAGEMENT CONSULTANT

Obsession with Order. Born into a puritanically disciplined family, Frederick Winslow Taylor became a man preoccupied with control. He had an obsessive-compulsive character and was driven by a relentless need to tie down and master almost every aspect of his life. His activities at home, in the garden, and on the golf course, as well as at work were dominated by programs and schedules, planned in detail and rigidly followed. Even his afternoon walks were carefully laid out in advance. The obsession with order that was manifested later in Taylorism began when he was a child. Childhood friends described the meticulous "scientific" approach that he brought to their games. Before playing baseball he would insist that accu-

rate measurements be made of the field, so that everyone would be in perfect relation. A game of croquet was a subject of careful analysis as Taylor worked out the angles of the various strokes, calculating the force of impact and the advantages and disadvantages of understroke and overstroke. As an adolescent, before going to a dance, he made lists of the attractive and unattractive girls likely to be present, so that he would be sure to spend equal time with each.

Beginnings of Taylorism. During the course of the nineteenth century, unskilled workers and machines had begun to replace skilled craftsmen. Yet because of their specialized knowledge, the more skilled workers continued to exert control over the pace of work, the methods used, and the levels of output. Working as a chief engineer in the Midvale Steel Company in the 1880s, Taylor came to the conclusion that in order to increase production, managers had to take control of the process. Taylor started by doing time studies of each factory job. He observed workers meticulously, analyzing each step in terms of time spent and energy expended, and determined the best method for each task. This standard method would be required of every worker, with scaled piecework rates providing financial incentives for higher output and financial penalties for output below the established benchmarks. Taylor's methods of standardization, close accounting, and managerial control increased production at the Midvale plant.

Bethlehem Steel. Taylor later became involved with Bethlehem Steel, where he worked from 1898 to 1901. With fellow inventor Maunsel White, he developed the Taylor-White process for hardening tool steel, which made him wealthy. He also tried to implement his principles of scientific management at the plant. He introduced a piece-rate system to replace the company's existing day-rate wage system. He applied his time-and-motion study methods to the handling of real materials in the yards and concluded that only 140 men would be needed to do work that had previously required more than 400. To Taylor's dismay, Bethlehem's owners were not pleased. It appeared to Taylor that Bethlehem did not want to alienate the community around its plant. Many of his suggestions, such as increased job specialization, standardization of work procedures, and salary increases for key personnel to reduce turnover, were not adopted. The owners dismissed Taylor in April 1901, six weeks before Charles M. Schwab bought controlling interest in the company. Taylor said that "the moment Schwab took charge of the Bethlehem works in 1901, he ordered our whole system thrown out. He saw no use whatever in paying premiums for fast work; much less in having time study men and slide rule men, 'supernumeraries,' as he called them, in the works at all."

Management Consultant. Since the steel-hardening process had made him independently wealthy, Taylor was able to concentrate on his concept of scientific management throughout the remainder of the decade and entered the management consultant business. His business cards in the early years of consulting read, "Systemizing Shop Management and Manufacturing Cost a Specialty." He visited corporations to promote his system and illustrate how to implement his ideas. While Taylor's methods were not popular with laborers who feared a loss of autonomy and new pressures to produce, management began to embrace Taylor's ideas.

Taylorism. One of Taylor's most important changes in factory management was the elimination of the shop foreman. He proposed instead to form a planning department to administer the factory as a whole and to do so through highly specialized shop bosses, or functional foremen. This would subdivide the activities of the general shift foreman into specialized parts. The planning department was also to supervise job analyses and information, to schedule the flows of current orders, and to set the daily work plan for each operation unit and for each worker in the factory. The planning department was to be in charge of the recruitment and layoff of workers and was to be responsible for the maintenance of the entire planning system. Although his concept of extreme specialization proved unacceptable to most manufacturers, many of his basic concepts were adopted. The weakness of his system was its failure to pinpoint authority and responsibility for completing departmental tasks and for maintaining a steady flow of materials from one stage of the process to the other. No factory owner adopted the Taylor system without modifying it.

The Later Years. Opposition to Taylor's method of scientific management increased during the later years of his life. Owners and managers often refused to institute his entire system, because of its complexity and extreme specialization. He encountered increasing hostility to his system from union workers, who walked out of the shop when scientific management was introduced. In 1911 a strike of molders at the Watertown Arsenal in Massachusetts and an American Federation of Labor campaign against his system led to a congressional investigation of Taylorism. Their conclusions indicated that scientific management was not designed to ensure the best interests of the worker. His management system, nevertheless, profoundly affected American industry, but its impact in practical terms consisted mostly of changes in machine operations, plant layout, and managerial activities.

Sources:

Gareth Morgan, *Images of Organizations* (Beverly Hills: Sage, 1986);

Frederick Winslow Taylor, *Principles of Scientific Management* (New York & London: Harper, 1911).

PEOPLE IN THE NEWS

William Crapo Durant chartered the General Motors Company in 1908. It acquired four motor vehicle firms — Buick, Cadillac, Oakland (later Pontiac), and Oldsmobile — and several parts manufacturers. Durant's bankers told him that Henry Ford's company was not worth the $8 million in cash that Ford demanded, so Ford did not join.

Harvey Samuel Firestone organized the Firestone Tire and Rubber Company in 1900, joining a group that controlled a "crosswire" patent for solid tires. A large order from the Ford Motor Company in 1906 marked the beginning of a long and important business relationship between the companies and led to a personal friendship between the two owners.

In 1903 the Harley-Davidson motorcycle was introduced by Milwaukee draftsman **William Harley**, pattern maker **Arthur Davidson**, mechanic **Walter Davidson**, and toolmaker **William Davidson**. Harley-Davidson produced fifty motorcycles in 1906, incorporated in 1907, and by 1917 produced eighteen thousand motorcycles to become the leading U.S. producer.

In 1903 **Milton Snaveley Hershey** began construction of a new plant in Derry Church, Pennsylvania, for a chocolate factory. Hershey's products dominated the chocolate candy and beverage industry by making milk chocolate affordable for the middle class.

Edward Francis Hutton, a New York stockbroker, founded E. F. Hutton and Company in 1904. His firm was the first to serve California by wire service.

Will Keith Kellogg, backed by **Charles D. Balin,** founded the Battle Creek Toasted Corn Flake Company in 1905. Its corn flakes cartons carried the legend: "None Genuine Without the Signature — W. K. Kellogg," in simulated script. The new company began production at the rate of thirty-three cases a day; by 1909 more than one million cases were being sold a year.

Cyrus Hall McCormick Jr., along with **William Deering** and other leaders of the agricultural implement industry, persuaded J. P. Morgan and Company to underwrite the International Harvester Company in 1902.

The new company controlled about 85 percent of the American harvester and reaper market.

John Mitchell Jr., a black publisher and banker, helped found the Mechanic's Savings Bank in 1902. He abdicated his political leadership in the black community and threw his support to his white associates. He then devoted himself solely to business activities, managing the Mechanic's Bank and editing *The Plant,* a local newspaper started in 1882 by thirteen former slaves.

Cereal manufacturer **Charles W. Post,** along with several others, founded the Citizens' Industrial Alliance, which opposed unionism. This organization was succeeded by the National Trade and Workers Association as a substitute for trade unions.

John D. Rockefeller spent much of the early 1900s devoting his time to philanthropy. He had acquired tremendous wealth in the oil business by making Standard Oil Company one of the most dominant companies in the country. The Standard Oil Company was thought to control 90 percent of U.S. oil-refining capacity and had an annual income of $45 million in 1902.

Novelist **Upton Beall Sinclair** published his book *The Jungle* in 1906. Sinclair lived among the stockyard workers of Chicago in preparation for his book. His hero, Jurgis, is persuaded to immigrate to America and take a job in the stockyards of "Packington." Sinclair was hailed by novelist Jack London, who declared, "What *Uncle Tom's Cabin* did for the black slaves *The Jungle* has a large chance to do for the white slaves of today." With U.S. meatpacking conditions exposed by Sinclair's best-seller, many Americans turned vegetarian, sales of meat products fell off, and Congress was aroused.

Booker T. Washington and others founded the National Business Association in 1900 to assist in the development of small businesses in the black community.

By 1900 **Frank Winfield Woolworth** controlled fifty-nine stores, up from twenty-eight in 1895, with sales more than $5 million. He had long admired the red color of A&P grocery stores, and he painted his store fronts the same color, adding the firm's name in gold letters. By the time of his death in 1919, American sales were more than $119 million in 157 stores. He left a fortune of some $60 million in his estate.

DEATHS

Philip Danforth Armour, 68, meatpacker who was a major supplier of pork during the Civil War and played an important role in the expansion of refrigerated meatpacking, 6 January 1901.

James Anthony Bailey, 58, circus operator and promoter of the Barnum and Bailey Circus, 11 April 1906.

Alexander Johnston Cassatt, 67, railroad executive for Pennsylvania Railroad who was instrumental in solving rebate problems that plagued the railroad industry in the 1890s, 28 December 1906.

Moses Herman Cone, 51, textile manufacturer whose Cone Mills Corporation pursued the development of denim mills, 8 December 1908.

Charles Henry Deere, 70, agricultural implement manufacturer whose father founded John Deere and Company, 29 October 1907.

William Lukens Elkins, 71, public utility and traction entrepreneur, United Gas Improvement Company, 7 November 1903.

Marshall Field, 71, department store pioneer who developed Marshall Field and Company into the largest wholesale and retail dry-goods seller in the world, 16 January 1906.

Edward Henry Harriman, 61, entrepreneur and railway executive who headed Illinois Central, Union Pacific, and Southern Pacific Railroads, 9 September 1909.

Henry Osborne Havemeyer, 60, sugar refiner and entrepreneur whose American Sugar Refining Company grew into a sugar trust that controlled 98 percent of the sugar refining in the United States by the end of the 1890s, 4 December 1907.

Abram Stevens Hewitt, 80, steel manufacturer and politician whose Cooper, Hewitt and Company introduced the Open Hearth furnace and made the first American steel, 18 January 1903.

Cyrus Kurtz Holliday, 73, railroad builder who wrote the charter for Atchison, Topeka and Santa Fe Railroad and served on the railroad's board of directors for forty years, 29 March 1900.

Benjamin Franklin Jones, 78, steel manufacturer and association official, founder of Jones and Laughlin Steel Company, 19 May 1903.

John Leary, 67, entrepreneur and developer associated with Talbot Coal Mines and Lake Shore and Eastern Railroad Company, 8 February 1905.

Emmanuel Lehman, 79, investment banker and financier, founder of Lehman Brothers and Company, 10 January 1907.

Charles Lockhart, 86, pioneer oilman and steel manufacturer who worked with John D. Rockefeller in the early days of Standard Oil Company, 26 January 1905.

John William Mackay, 70, mine operator, financier, founder of Hale and Norcross Mines and Commercial Cable Company, 20 July 1902.

Alexander Majors, 85, expressman and stagecoach operator who established the Pony Express, which only lasted eighteen months, 12 January 1900.

John Augustine McCall, 56, insurance executive with New York Life Insurance Company, 18 February 1906.

William Howe McElwain, 40, shoe manufacturer, founder of W. H. McElwain and Company, 10 January 1908.

Gordon McKay, 82, inventor and shoe machinery manufacturer, 19 November 1903.

Nelson Morris, 69, meatpacker, owner of Nelson Morris and Company, 27 August 1907.

Henry William Oliver, 63, steel manufacturer, iron mine owner, and publisher, 8 February 1904.

James Oliver, 84, plow inventor and manufacturer, president of Oliver Chilled Plow Works, 2 March 1908.

Potter Palmer, 75, merchant, land developer who built the Palmer House and founded dry goods store that became Marshall Field and Company, 4 May 1902.

Charles Elliott Perkins, 66, railroad executive, director of Chicago, Burlington and Quincy Railroad, 8 November 1907.

Ferdinand Schumacker, 86, cereal manufacturer, founder of F. Schumacker Milling and American Cereal Company, 1908.

James Edmund Scripps, 71, newspaper publisher and founder of several papers in Michigan, including *Detroit Evening News,* 29 May 1906.

Quincy Adams Shaw, 83, copper mining entrepreneur associated with Calumet Mining Company, 11 June 1908.

Clement Studebaker, 70, wagon and automobile manufacturer who with older brother, Henry, founded H. and C. Studebaker, 27 November 1901.

Joseph Wharton, 82, zinc and iron manufacturer who for many years was the only U.S. producer of refined nickel; he was associated with Lehigh Zinc Company Bethlehem Iron Company (Bethlehem Steel Company), founded Swarthmore College, and endowed the Wharton School of Finance and Commerce, 11 January 1909.

PUBLICATIONS

James Burrill Angell, *The Age of Quickened Conscience* (Ann Arbor: University, 1908);

John Graham Brooks, *The Conflict Between Private Monopoly and Good Citizenship* (Boston & New York: Houghton Mifflin, 1909);

Andrew Carnegie, *The Empire of Business* (New York: Doubleday, Page, 1902);

Lorin Fuller Deland, *Imagination in Business* (New York: Harper, 1909);

Lawrence Robert Dicksee, *Office Organization and Management Including Secretarial Work* (London: Pitman, 1906);

Morris Friedman, *The Pinkerton Labor Spy* (New York: Wilshire, 1907);

Arthur Twining Hadley, *Standards of Public Morality. The Kennedy Lectures for 1906*, in *The School of Philanthropy Conducted by The Charity Organization Society of the City of New York* (New York: Macmillan, 1907);

George Hall, *The Common Sense of Commercial Arithmetic* (New York: Macmillan, 1901);

Cheesman Abiah Herrick, *Meaning and Practice of Commercial Education* (New York: Macmillan, 1904);

Harlow Niles Higinbotham, *The Making of a Merchant* (Chicago: Forbes, 1906);

Elbert Hubbard, *Helpful Hints for Business Helper* (East Aurora, N.Y.: Roycrofters, 1909);

Jeremiah Whipple Jenks, *Great Fortunes: The Winning: The Using* (New York: McClure, Phillips, 1906);

James Perry Johnston, *How to Hustle* (Chicago: Thompson & Thomas, 1905);

Johnston, *What Happened to Johnston* (Chicago: Thompson & Thomas, 1904);

Orison Swett Marden, *The Young Man Entering Business* (New York: Crowell, 1903);

Morals in Modern Business, Addresses Delivered in the Page Lecture Series, 1908, Before the Senior Class of the Sheffield Scientific School, Yale University (New Haven: Yale University Press, 1909);

Harlow Stafford Person, *Industrial Education: A System of Training For Men Entering Upon Trade and Commerce* (Boston & New York: Houghton, Mifflin, 1907);

Charles Edward Russell, *Lawless Wealth: The Origin of Some Great American Fortunes* (New York: B. W. Dodge, 1908);

Albert Shaw, *The Business Career in Its Public Relations* (San Francisco: Elder, 1904);

Upton Sinclair, *The Industrial Republic: A Study of the America of Ten Years Hence* (New York: Doubleday, Page, 1907);

Samuel Edwin Sparling, *Introduction to Business Organization* (New York: Macmillan, 1906);

Frank A. Vanderlip, *Business and Education* (New York: Duffield, 1907);

Thorstein Veblen, *The Theory of Business Enterprise* (New York: Scribners, 1904);

Henry Alexander Wise Wood, *Money-Hunger: A Brief Study of Commercial Immorality in the United States* (New York: Putnam, 1908);

Gideon Wurdz, *Foolish Finance Company* (Boston: Luce, 1905).

CHAPTER FOUR

EDUCATION

by KEITH WHITESCARVER

CONTENTS

Sidebars and tables are listed in italics.

1900

Mar. The New York City Board of Education makes plans for implementing school baths for students in some schools.

12 May Representatives from thirteen colleges and preparatory schools establish the College Entrance Examination Board.

11 July Renowned progressive educator Francis W. Parker pleads for the centrality of art in education, asserting in a speech to the National Education Association that there is "art in everything."

Sept. Forty-eight students enroll in the new Department of School Administration at Teachers' College, Columbia University.

15 Sept. The Atlanta school system turns away four hundred students because of a lack of space in city schools.

12 Nov. Stanford University President David Starr Jordan ignites a national debate on academic freedom when he dismisses Professor Edward A. Ross for making "radical" political statements.

1901

Jan. Daniel Coit Gilman, president of Johns Hopkins University since its founding, announces his impending retirement.

Bryn Mawr President M. Carey Thomas declares in *Educational Review* that college education for women should be the same as that for men.

June High-school students take the College Board's college entrance examination for the first time.

12 June Pupils at Bunsen School in Belleville, Illinois, go on strike, seeking a shorter school day.

25 June Advocates of the "elective system" in high schools gain a major victory when the Boston School Committee adopts an elective system for all of its high schools. The only requirements for students are courses in hygiene, gymnastics or military drill, and music.

Sept. An international congress of nurses meeting in Buffalo, New York, passes a resolution in favor of the registration and certification of all nurses and the standardization of educational requirements for those entering nursing.

4 Nov. The reform-minded Southern Education Board convenes for the first time.

Dec. Andrew Carnegie announces a gift of $10 million to endow a science research center, the Carnegie Institution of Washington.

1902

- John Dewey's new book, *The Child and the Curriculum*, gives the clearest and best-known explanation of his theory of curriculum.

- Walter Hines Page galvanizes support for southern public-school reform with the publication of *The Rebuilding of Old Commonwealth*.

- Baltimore public schools institute special classrooms for "unmanageable" boys after the Maryland legislature passed a compulsory school-attendance law the previous year.

26 Mar. Rhodes Scholarships are established with a bequest from Cecil John Rhodes.

5 Apr.	Ruling on a suit filed by the Chicago Teachers' Federation, a federal judge in Illinois orders five major utility and street railway companies in Chicago to pay $598,000 in back taxes to the Chicago City Council.
9 June	Woodrow Wilson is selected to be the new president of Princeton University.
July	Emory University Professor Andrew Sledd's article attacking lynching and supporting racial moderation is published in the July issue of *Atlantic Monthly*. School officials subsequently ask for his resignation.
8 Nov.	The Chicago Teachers' Federation joins the American Federation of Labor, becoming the first teachers' union in the United States.

1903

- Chicago's Englewood High School establishes a school lunchroom, the first in the city.

12 Jan.	The General Education Board receives its charter and becomes a clearinghouse for the educational philanthropy of John D. Rockefeller.
Mar.	Philosopher William James complains of the abuses of graduate study in his article "The Ph.D Octopus," published in *Harvard Monthly*.
18 Apr.	With the publication of his book *The Souls of Black Folk*, W. E. B. Du Bois publicly breaks with Booker T. Washington's racial-accommodationist approach to social and educational matters.
19 Oct.	Judge William T. Gary of Augusta, Georgia, draws national attention by stating his opposition to schools for African Americans, claiming that education makes black workers "unfit for the walks of life open to [them]."

1904

- Educational psychologist G. Stanley Hall publishes his pivotal work, *Adolescence: Its Psychology and Its Relations to Physiology, Anthropology, Sociology, Sex, Crime, Religion, and Education*.

- The newly formed National Child Labor Committee lobbies for the passage of laws restricting child labor and mandating compulsory school attendance.

Apr.	John Dewey accepts a professorship at Columbia University, where he will remain until his retirement twenty-six years later.
7 June	The inaugural address of University of Wisconsin President Charles Van Hise states the rationale for the "Wisconsin Idea" of university service.
1 July	Labor leader Margaret Haley implores teachers to organize in a speech at the annual meeting of the National Education Association.
22 Aug.	University of California President Benjamin Wheeler tells women students at his school that they are to prepare for marriage and motherhood and should not try to use a college education for the same purposes as men.
Oct.	In Florida Mary McLeod Bethune founds the Daytona Literary and Industrial Institute for the Training of Negro Girls.

1905

27 Feb. Edwin Dexter reports to colleagues in the National Society for the Scientific Study of Education that 70 percent of male high-school teachers and 53 percent of female high-school teachers are college graduates.

16 Apr. Andrew Carnegie endows the Carnegie Foundation for the Advancement of Teaching with $10 million.

July A National Education Association study of public-school educators in cities finds that 100 percent of district superintendents and 94 percent of all high-school principals are men.

1906

- George Pierce Baker teaches the first drama workshop in the country, English 47, at Harvard University.

- William T. Harris resigns as commissioner of education in his seventeenth year on the job.

Apr. The Massachusetts Commission on Industrial and Technical Education recommends teaching vocational skills to students in the state's public schools.

June John Hope assumes the presidency of Morehouse College, then named Atlanta Baptist College. He is the first African American president of this historically black college.

16 Nov. The initial meeting of the National Society for the Promotion of Industrial Education is held in New York City. The society urges the development and full funding of a comprehensive program of vocational education in the schools.

1907

- William C. Bagley calls for a business approach to education in his widely used textbook *Classroom Management*.

8 Feb. The mayor of Cleveland denounces John D. Rockefeller's gift of $32 million to the General Education Board, charging that the donation was made to perpetuate the privileges of the Standard Oil Company.

12 Mar. Alain Locke becomes the first African American to receive the prestigious Rhodes Scholarship. There will be no other African American recipients of the award for half a century.

Apr. Margaret Sage, widow of financier Russell Sage, establishes the Russell Sage Foundation in honor of her late husband. She stipulates that her endowment of $10 million be used to improve social and living conditions in the United States.

6 May The American School Hygiene Association is organized.

13 June The New York City Board of Education votes to provide free eyeglasses for needy students.

20 July A report by the National Education Association condemns the "deteriorating" behavior of students.

16 Oct. In Hattiesburg, Mississippi, school officials ask the city council to create a separate school for children of immigrants.

20 Nov. The New York City school board bans Christmas carols from the city schools in an attempt to eliminate "sectarianism."

1908

- Sir Robert Baden-Powell publishes *Scouting for Boys* and establishes the Boy Scouts in England. Scouting comes to the United States a little more than a year later when the Boy Scouts of America is chartered.

- Fifty-six students enroll as candidates for Harvard University's newly created degree of master in business administration in the Graduate School of Business Administration.

- Schools in Gary, Indiana, begin operating under William Wirt's "platoon system" of schooling, also known as the "Gary Plan."

Feb.   At the Lowell Institute Lectures in Boston, historian Albert Bushnell Hart expresses dismay about the neglect of black public schools in the South. The lectures are published in 1910 as *The Southern South*.

29 Feb.   Schools for black students in the rural South get a boost when the Anna T. Jeanes Foundation is created with the goal of improving such schools.

4 Mar.   One hundred seventy-four children perish in a fire caused by faulty steam pipes in a school in Collinwood, Ohio.

Apr.   In his article "Why Teaching Repels Men" in *Educational Review* C. W. Bardeen writes that few men enter teaching, because it is a "hireling" profession that "belittles men."

June   The first issue of *School Hygiene* is published.

12 Sept.   The Chicago school board suspends fifty-two students because of their persistence in joining a fraternity. Three days later the fraternity brings suit against the board.

9 Nov.   By a vote of 7–2, the U.S. Supreme Court, in *Berea College* v. *Kentucky*, upholds a Kentucky law prohibiting racial integration in private schools.

Dec.   The U.S. Immigration Commission releases a study showing that 72 percent of New York City schoolchildren are either immigrants or children of immigrants.

31 Dec.   The American Home Economics Association is founded. The organization seeks "to improve the conditions of living in the home, the institutional household, and the community." It aims to advance its purposes by studying problems connected with the household and "by securing recognition of subjects related to the home in the curricula of existing schools and colleges."

1909

23 Jan.   The Federal Commission on Country Life reports to the president that schools fail to provide "good training for country life" and are "largely responsible for ineffective farming, lack of ideals, and the drift to town."

22–24 Feb.   The National Society for the Scientific Study of Education focuses on the subject of sex education at its annual meeting in Chicago.

15 Mar.   Harvard University President Charles W. Eliot announces his plan to create a "five-foot shelf of books" that can provide someone with little formal schooling the essential knowledge necessary to be deemed well-educated.

3 Apr.   In Sayville, New York, a youth is expelled for bringing a revolver to school.

11–13 May   The American Federation of Arts is founded. Organizers support the increased study of art in public schools and the creation of art societies, art schools, and galleries.

19 May   A. Lawrence Lowell succeeds Charles W. Eliot as president of Harvard University.

29 July   Ella Flagg Young becomes the first female superintendent of an urban school system when the Chicago Board of Education appoints her to the post.

Sept.   The Cincinnati public-school system establishes the country's first continuation school, a part-time school for employed children and youth.

13 Sept.   Public School 100, the first public vocational school in the city of New York, opens.

Nov.   The College Entrance Examination Board approves the use of the "Carnegie unit" by its member schools.

18 Nov.   Football is banned from the New York City public-school system.

OVERVIEW

The State of Education. In the first decade of the twentieth century most American children attended schools for no more than a few years, and from their limited education they and their parents were often content if they acquired only the most rudimentary literacy and numeracy skills. During this time American public education suffered from the fact that more than two-thirds of the nation's schools were rural, one-room schoolhouses — the educational equivalent of the horse and buggy; in these rural schoolhouses teachers who usually had little formal education themselves faced the daunting task of instructing students who ranged in age from five to twenty years old. In the typical classroom, memorization, drill, and recitation were the standard teaching methods. Urban schools, by contrast, were usually age-graded and had a longer school year, and urban schoolchildren sat in classrooms with desks bolted to the floor; but here, too, students memorized assigned passages from textbooks and recited them for their teacher. During the decade 1900 to 1909, these well-worn educational practices, familiar to generations of students, were increasingly attacked by critics who adamantly opposed them; in time, pressured by these critics and by sweeping social forces, most schools across America began a process of dramatic change.

Solution to Social Problems. In the decade 1900 to 1909, when many Americans found themselves unsettled by profound changes in American society, the nation's schools faced the growing expectation that they would help address some of the major public concerns. What were the changes causing Americans so much anxiety? First, for at least several decades, the U.S. economy had been rapidly transforming from one based primarily on agriculture and small manufacturing to a new, surging economy powered by the industrial output of large corporations. Second, during the latter decades of the nineteenth century, and accelerating into the twentieth, waves of immigrants were arriving in America, greatly altering the demographic makeup of the nation. As a by-product of these changes, the nation was becoming increasingly urbanized: many Americans left the small farms where they had often lived for years to pursue new opportunities in the cities, while most new immigrants, without the capital to buy land and equipment, settled not in the

countryside but rather in the same rapidly crowding urban areas. Certainly, each of these developments — industrialization, immigration, and urbanization — had started before the decade from 1900 to 1909; nevertheless, each differed enormously in scope and magnitude from earlier years. Facing the combined impact of these dramatic transformations, American political and educational leaders turned to the nation's schools, seeking their help in meeting the radical new challenges to American society.

The Corporate Model. American corporate capitalism, an engine of immense and accelerating power, exerted in the years 1900–1909 a decisive and multifaceted influence on the nation's schools; perhaps the most telling manifestation of this influence was demonstrated when American educators began using the corporate organization model as the model for America's schools. How did this borrowing from the business world work? Under the corporate model, a school system was headed by a superintendent, who acted as the equivalent of the CEO, the chief executive officer, in a corporation. From this school superintendent the lines of authority ran down to supervisors and school principals, who were like middle managers, to, finally, the individual teachers in the classrooms, comparable to workers in a corporation. Oversight responsibilities for the school system rested with a school board that functioned much like the board of a corporation. Furthermore, during this time school efficiency began to be quantified and measured by efficiency experts in much the same way that productivity was studied in the nation's industrial corporations.

Schools and the Economy. Increasingly in the first decade of the twentieth century, the purpose of American schools was seen to be integrally related to the economic well-being of the nation, and school leaders became progressively more concerned with producing qualified workers for the nation's changing workplace. Indeed, during the period 1900 to 1909, there were some people, both inside and outside the educational establishment, who regarded as simply unproductive the act of encouraging students to acquire knowledge for its own intrinsic value. In fact, traditional educators, who sought to educate students for the purpose of, in the language of the day, "developing the faculties of the mind," appeared to many school reformers quaint and irrelevant. In the new social and economic climate, new subjects and new curricula were touted and implemented by modern school administrators who were eager to adapt public education to the new demands confronting it. By the middle of the decade, a coalition of conservative and liberal reformers, pushing for even stronger links between the national educational system and American business, introduced vocational education in the schools; and this strengthening school-business bond intensified to the end of the decade.

Immigration and Schools. By the beginning of the 1900s, foreign peoples were immigrating to the United States in unprecedented numbers, with a majority coming from countries and ethnic groups not widely represented in American society before this time. A majority came from countries and ethnic groups not previously represented in large numbers in American society. In the thirty-year period from 1890 to 1920, approximately 18.2 million newcomers entered the country. Because of this influx of immigrants, schools around the country — especially urban schools — were inundated by immigrant children seeking an education. In 1905 alone, some sixty thousand to seventy-five thousand such children were denied admission to New York City schools because these schools had no space for them. Meanwhile, to help immigrants and their children adjust to American society, educators in urban school systems created special courses to teach English and provide instruction in American political and civic values. In the decade 1900 to 1909, Americanization, the name used to describe this assimilation process, became the watchword for the nation's public schools.

Urbanization and Schools. In nineteenth-century America, rural district schools were governed by well-known community leaders whose decisions regarding hiring and the school curriculum generally reflected local values and local concerns; but in the first decade of the twentieth century the development of large urban school systems brought a dramatic change in school governance. Rapidly, large bureaucracies sprang up, and decision-making became the function of faceless and anonymous managers. These profound changes occurred in the name of expertise and efficiency and undoubtedly had some positive effects; but they greatly reduced the close ties that earlier had existed between schools and their communities. Now new, age-graded schools with lockstep curricula became the norm in nearly all urban areas. Within the educational system, order, regularity, and predictability were gained, but only at the expense of individuality and flexibility.

Emergence of the Modern University. In higher education the decade 1900–1909 witnessed the arrival of a distinctly American educational institution — the modern American university. This new institution was defined not so much by a new building on a new campus as by new conceptions of the nature of higher education. The modern American university offered its students a curriculum that differed from traditional curricula by being more oriented to practical, technological, even economic concerns; the new institution also demonstrated a renewed interest in research and aimed to extend the benefits of education to a greater portion of the population than had its predecessors. In its overall philosophy this new American university still owed much to its European models and influences, but its unique character stemmed mainly from the tumultuous changes shaping America at the turn of the century.

Teachers. The way Americans who wished to enter the teaching profession prepared for a classroom career changed significantly in the decade from 1900 to 1909. In these years teaching, particularly at the elementary level, was a profession reserved primarily for women; indeed, it was one of the few professions open to them. In 1900, 70 percent of all elementary- and secondary-school teachers were female; by the end of the decade this percentage had increased to 79 percent. Whether teachers were women or men, however, the nature of their preparation for teaching was changing dramatically from earlier years. Increasingly, as educational leaders sought to raise the standards of the profession, aspiring educators were expected to spend longer periods of time preparing for their classroom careers. Teacher-education programs were lengthened in many postsecondary institutions; universities and normal schools created new four-year programs that provided aspiring teachers with a theoretical base in educational psychology and in the philosophy and history of education.

Teacher Salaries. By 1910 the average annual salary for American teachers was $485; this average, however, masked great variations that were determined by gender, teaching level, and region. As a case in point, the salaries for New York City, which boasted the nation's best school system, provide an instructive example. In 1900 the salary for a female elementary-school teacher started at $600; for each additional year of experience, her salary increased $40. Male elementary-school teachers started at the same base of $600 but received an extra $150 for each additional year of experience. As a result, a male elementary-school teacher with ten years of experience earned $2,100, while a woman with the same experience and same job earned $1,000. High-school teachers, predominantly male, received higher salaries than elementary-school teachers, while administrators attained the highest pay among school employees. Furthermore, high-school principals in New York City, nearly all of whom were male in 1900, received $5,000 per year, while female elementary-school principals received between $1,750 and $2,500. New York educators ranked at the top of the nation's educational pay scale; by contrast, in rural areas across the country, and especially in the South, educators were paid far less than their colleagues in the cities.

Profile of Schools and School Populations. In 1900, 78 percent of all children from age five to seventeen were enrolled in American schools; by 1910 the percentage had increased only slightly, to 79 percent. In 1905 the average school term lasted 151 days, during which the average student attended 105 days. In this first decade of the twentieth century the large majority of American students were enrolled in public schools; in fact, only 8 percent of all elementary- and secondary-school students attended private schools. Furthermore, very few students attended high school: in 1900 only 11 percent of all children from age fourteen to seventeen were enrolled in high schools, and even fewer graduated. For example, in 1900 a mere 6.3 percent of all seventeen-year-olds were high-school graduates; by 1910 the percentage had increased only slightly, to 8.6. By the end of the decade the average number of school years completed by adults twenty-five and older was slightly more than eight years.

Experiments in Education. The progressive education movement, a complex phenomenon that originated shortly before 1900, flourished in the years 1900–1909 and exerted a decisive influence on later American public education. Facing the radical changes in late-nineteenth-century American society — especially those wrought by industrialization, immigration, and urbanization — members of the progressive education movement believed the nation's schools were obligated to address and adapt to these changes, and, in the process, to achieve a closer integration into the society in which they existed. Furthermore, rejecting both traditional curricula and traditional methods of teaching, progressive educators in this crucial decade developed important new ideas about educational practices — ideas founded on a new understanding of the nature of child development and grounded in new insights suggested by advances in psychology. Most centrally, these new progressive educators advocated moving the child in school from the background to the foreground of classroom life. They assumed this fundamental shift in focus would be accomplished by creating new opportunities to engage the child's cooperation and imagination. Not surprisingly, old-fashioned rote learning was discouraged in the new, child-centered curriculum. Finally, these educators shared a deep belief in the malleability of human nature and the importance of environment in human development; consequently, they exhibited a strong faith in the ability of schools to solve society's problems, if only the proper educational methods were implemented.

TOPICS IN THE NEWS

THE AMERICAN UNIVERSITY

Crystallization of Organization and Purpose. During the final three decades of the nineteenth century, educational leaders in the United States had engaged in acrimonious debate about the fundamental nature and purpose of American higher education; by the early years of the new century, however, these debates had largely ended, and by 1910 a new consensus had been reached on the goals and the structure of the modern American university. The institution that emerged from this long philosophical ferment was uniquely American and differed from its predecessors in three key ways. First, conceding the criticism that the traditional university curriculum had been excessively arcane or simply irrelevant to the changing conditions of American society, schools now exhibited great concern that their curricula reflect practical, "real-world" subjects, such as engineering and accounting. The second difference between the university of 1900–1909 and its predecessors was demonstrated by the fact that many professors showed a new enthusiasm for scholarly and scientific research. Third, the newly focused American university deliberately aimed to extend the benefits of education to more of the population than had its predecessors. In this regard, unlike many earlier colleges and universities, the American university in this decade showed a new appreciation for diversity, an appreciation well expressed by University of Chicago president Harry Pratt Judson, who observed that "the college should (not) aim at any one kind of product. There should be a diversity of results as there is a diversity of natural traits. No college should aim to put its hallmark upon all men in such a sense as to expect that all will be substantially alike." Although the American university owed much to its European models and influences, its new character stemmed primarily from the radically changing American environment of 1900–1909. In a speech in 1907, J. R. Wheeler, a professor at Columbia University, described the multiple purposes of the newly conceived American university as the following: to preserve culture, to share useful knowledge with the public, to act as an agent of social change in the newly created industrial order, and to conduct disinterested research in order to produce new knowledge. Wheeler concluded, "We may seek at times . . . to separate these notions, but

they are really so interwoven in the complete idea of a university that no clear boundary lines can be drawn between them."

The Wisconsin Idea. Perhaps no ideal of the modern American university in this period was more important than service to the community. In his 1904 inaugural address Charles Van Hise, president of the University of Wisconsin, argued that a public university could succeed

---

ACADEMIC FREEDOM AT STANFORD

In 1900 the campus of Stanford University in California found itself bitterly divided by the forced resignation of Professor Edward A. Ross. Stanford President David Starr Jordan had requested the resignation on 12 November at the behest of Jane Lathrop Stanford, the university's benefactor and sole trustee. Mrs. Stanford and Ross first came into conflict in 1896, when, in that election year, Ross worked openly on behalf of Democratic candidates, thereby greatly displeasing Jane Stanford. She subsequently decreed that all faculty members were forbidden to participate in any political activity, and she privately asked President Jordan to fire Ross. President Jordan demurred at that time, but three years later, after Ross made a political speech, Jordan succumbed to pressure and removed Ross from his job. When a popular history professor, George E. Howard, protested the action, Mrs. Stanford demanded that Howard apologize or resign. His resignation upset the campus even more. Five other professors also protested and subsequently resigned. These resignations forced university leaders at Stanford and around the country to ponder the extent to which they believed in academic freedom, the right of members of the academic community to speak their minds on any subject, even if the view expressed was unpopular.

Source: Laurence R. Veysey, *The Emergence of the American University* (Chicago: University of Chicago Press, 1965).

A student room at Princeton in 1906

only if it were open to all, regardless of wealth, and gave back to the public realm dedicated citizens performing service to their society. Accordingly, under Van Hise's guidance, the University of Wisconsin strongly encouraged research that could be applied to the solution of public problems. Furthermore, it provided experts in the physical and social sciences, supplied administrative leadership to state and local government, and furnished extension programs for the state's residents. Under Van Hise the University of Wisconsin soon became the model for other universities, and the "Wisconsin Idea," as the concept came to be known, was duplicated around the country.

Business Models of Organization. As the decade 1900 to 1909 progressed, American universities were increasingly influenced by the business ethos dominant in America's celebrated corporate world. In fact, as time passed, more and more of the nation's universities mimicked corporate organizational models in their own administrations, increasingly approved a new business mentality in their operations, and aggressively recruited their pupils from the growing number of business-minded students. At the same time, because many colleges sought and accepted vast gifts of money, even when strings were attached, philanthropists obtained ever greater influence in school policies. Indeed, some universities, such as Stanford, Clark, and Cornell, owed their very existence to the donations of industrial benefactors. Meanwhile, across

the country the composition of university boards of trustees shifted dramatically from the time when members were primarily clergymen to the time, by 1910, when men from business and nonacademic professions were the norm. Among this new breed of trustees, some were dignified and responsible; some were petty tyrants. Whatever their qualities, their very presence reminded university officials that their institution was expected to reflect "real-world" concerns. Then, too, as the organizational form of universities increasingly resembled the American corporate models, university presidents were often compared to "captains of industry." With the shrewdness of a hard-nosed business leader, one anonymous university president wrote in 1900 that waste in higher education would continue "until the business of education is regarded in a business light, is cared for by business methods."

Critics of the Business Model. Not all who were involved in shaping American universities in the decade from 1900 to 1909 were willing to endorse the business ethos pervading many university administrations. In fact, a small but vocal minority of educators began to speak passionately against the influx of business ideals into higher education. In *The Higher Learning in America*, published in 1915 but written largely before 1910, Thorstein Veblen, the noted scholar and social critic, decried the burgeoning business control of nearly every aspect of university life. Such control, he believed, came

Leland Stanford, founder of Stanford University

Thorstein Veblen, a noted educator and writer who criticized the application of business practices to higher education

at the expense of pure learning. Moreover, according to Veblen, it produced numerous other unfortunate results, including the new affinity of university administrators for expensive buildings, the spread of an administrative bureaucracy, the growth of college athletics and the fraternity system, the development of a curriculum with courses purely vocational, a greater concern for undergraduate education over graduate education, and finally, a competitiveness among universities based solely on prestige. In 1909 another critic, John Jay Chapman, bitterly wrote: "The men who stand for education and scholarship have the ideals of businessmen. They are, in truth, businessmen. The men who control Harvard today are very little else than businessmen, running a large department store which dispenses education to the millions." Indeed, even Andrew S. Draper of Illinois, champion of business influences in American universities, delineated some important reservations. Writing in 1906, Draper said: "Of course the university cannot become a business corporation, with a business corporation's ordinary implications. . . . The distinguishing earmarks of an American university are its moral purpose, its scientific aim, its unselfish public service, its inspirations to all men in all noble things, and its incorruptibility by commercialism."

Sources:

J. David Hoeveler Jr., "The University and the Social Gospel: The Intellectual Origins of the 'Wisconsin Idea,'" *Wisconsin Magazine of History* (Summer 1976): 282–298, reprinted in *ASHE Reader on the History of Higher Education,* edited by Lester F. Goodchild and Harold S. Wechsler (Needham Heights, Mass.: Ginn Press, 1989);

Christopher J. Lucas, *American Higher Education: A History* (New York: St. Martin's Press, 1994);

Laurence R. Veysey, *The Emergence of the American University* (Chicago: University of Chicago Press, 1965).

THE AMERICANIZATION CRUSADE AND THE SCHOOLS

Early Efforts. Most Americans at the turn of the new century believed as an article of faith that the nation's public schools could play a decisive role in helping to assimilate the new immigrants into America's social and political mainstream. This confidence was expressed by a New York City high-school principal, who proclaimed in 1902 that "Education will solve every problem of our national life, even that of assimilating our foreign element." However, faith and rhetoric notwithstanding, American schools did not make vigorous efforts to assimilate, or "Americanize," immigrant children in the first years of the new century, even though thousands of such children were entering the nation's schools. To be sure, school leaders in a few large eastern cities opened special

The Main Hall at Ellis Island, circa 1905. Of the many immigrants who passed through this building during 1900–1909 thousands were children who entered public schools.

night schools with classes in English, and in some locales, civics; but widespread efforts in this direction were simply nonexistent. Nonetheless, the nation's urban schools in the years 1900–1909 were about to undergo a decisive change. Fearful of the growing immigrant population, members of a new movement began voicing great concern about a decline in the "spirit of true Americanism"; they demanded that schools provide classes and curriculum materials to instill American values and "obedience to law" in immigrant children and adults. In their crusade these proponents of Americanization convinced school leaders around the country to shoulder the task of assimilating new immigrant people into the American society. In fact, educational leaders took up the task with such zest that Stanford Professor Ellwood P. Cubberley proclaimed in 1909 that the object of education must be:

> to assimilate and amalgamate these people as a part of our American race, and to implant in their children, so far as can be done, the Anglo-Saxon conception of righteousness, law and order, and popular government, and to awaken in them a reverence for our democratic institutions and for those things in our national life which we as a people hold to be of abiding worth.

A Complex Process. But urban schools across the United States in this decade of 1900–1909 faced a serious, nearly overwhelming challenge: at the same time they were being flooded with thousands of new students, many of whom did not speak more than a few words of English, they were also being asked to fashion these often culture-shocked people into fully assimilated, functioning American citizens. In assessing this huge social task, educators conceptualized the Americanization process as having two distinct strands. One strand was familiar to urban school leaders: schools instructed immigrant children in the skills needed to function in the new world they and their families had recently entered, and, to that end, taught students particular ways of thinking and the basic knowledge required to exist in an interdependent, urban environment. Specifically, students learned such things as how to cope with bureaucratic routine, the need for punctuality, how to fill out forms, and essential academic skills. Most of these skills, however, encouraged students to practice ways of acting and thinking that often contrasted significantly from the rural folk culture of their immigrant homelands. As an important aside, urban schools taught native migrants from the countryside the same adaptive skills. Added to this first strand in the complex process, educators conceived of a second strand in the dynamic of Americanization, one intended to remove from immigrant children all vestiges of their original culture. For this purpose, public schools focused their efforts on eliminating cultural differences and creating in the immigrant child a sense of shame at being "foreign."

A kindergarten group in Richmond, Virginia, during the first decade of the twentieth century

Origins. The Americanization movement developed out of the anxieties some Americans felt about the large numbers of new immigrants arriving in the United States. Already in the 1890s, organizations such as the Daughters of the American Revolution (DAR) had launched campaigns of patriotic education designed to teach "American" values to immigrants. In Buffalo, New York, in 1898, the DAR had begun giving lectures on U.S. history and government to immigrant men who would soon be voting. Other societies, including the Society of Colonial Dames and the Sons of the American Revolution (SAR), spurred additional efforts at assimilation. By 1907 the SAR spent half its annual income on programs providing immigrants information on the United States, as well as practical advice on how to cope with their new American environment. The SAR even received the support of the U.S. Department of Commerce and Labor for a project that printed and distributed in fifteen different languages more than a million copies of a pamphlet extolling the virtues of American patriotism.

School Practices. Using various methods, American public schools in this decade tried to eliminate cultural distinctions and create among their diverse immigrant students a strong sense of their new identity as Americans. Of particular importance in this regard was the teaching of U.S. history, with lessons that emphasized the heroic and romantic aspects of that history and that evidently had a tremendous impact on many young minds. In one autobiography, Russian Jewish immigrant Mary Antin recalled with pride how her teachers' lessons caused her to revere George and Martha Washington. Antin wrote: "Never had I prayed, never had I chanted the songs of David, never had I called upon the Most Holy, in such utter reverence and worship as I repeated the simple sentences of my child's story of the patriot. I gazed with adoration at the portraits of George and Martha Washington, till I could see them with my eyes shut." Furthermore, the textbooks used by immigrants frequently stressed more than basic academic skills. Some prescribed foods to eat, health tips, even how to dress. In New York City schoolteachers began the practice of giving baths to immigrant children. Also, both civics lessons and textbooks provided immigrants with information, sometimes factual, sometimes idealized, on American political life. In *English for Foreigners* (1909) Sara O'Brien instructed students about local politicians with this respectful admonishment: "These men who make and carry out the laws of the city are city officials, and are chosen by the people. The people should choose only honest and unselfish men for these offices." Also, in a section about the American flag, O'Brien closed with a sentence students were instructed to copy: "America is another word for opportunity." A few teachers even went so far as to change students' names to make the names

A school nurse teaching Cincinnati schoolchildren how to brush their teeth, circa 1910

more "American sounding." Thus, "Leonardo" sometimes became "Leonard," and "Rivka" became "Rebecca."

Kindergartens and Americanization. In these years of 1900–1909, some advocates of the growing, but still relatively small, kindergarten movement urged the creation of additional kindergartens to aid in assimilating immigrant youngsters. One kindergarten supporter, James Bruce, urged educators to emphasize Americanization programs in kindergarten because children younger than age six were "still plastic." Children in kindergarten, Bruce argued, "can breathe in the American spirit" through kindergarten's "songs and flag drills, by its elementary practices." Two years after Bruce's statement, in 1909, the founders of the National Kindergarten Association (NKA) declared in their first annual report that public-school systems should start kindergarten programs because kindergartens could be used to promote Americanization. The report stated that public kindergartens were "a philanthropic agent, leading the child gently into right habits of thought, speech, and action from the beginning." Kindergartens would "help in the absorption and amalgamation of our foreign element" and were useful for "social training" and the "development of the citizen-virtues, as well as those of the individual." Partly because of the NKA's linking kindergartens and Americanization, several urban public-school systems around the country established kindergarten programs.

Impact. The Americanization campaign not only became a significant force in education in the early 1900s, but its influence also continued in schools for several decades. Indeed, in the 1910s, with patriotic fervor inflamed by U.S. entry into World War I, the movement increased in momentum and intensity, provoking attacks on "hyphenated Americans." Americanization programs often caused strained relations between immigrant parents and children. As children acquired American tastes and values, conflicts with the older generation were inevitable, even in immigrant families where parents approved of the changes taking place. And many immigrants did approve of the Americanization efforts. A scholar in 1920 reported "if you ask ten immigrants who have been in America long enough to rear families what American institution is most effective in making the immigrant part and parcel of American life, nine will reply the 'public school.'" Not all immigrant families wanted their children to become Americanized or educated, however. Children from Italian neighborhoods in New York City had high rates of truancy, often with their parents' connivance. This fact led a New York City school superintendent to complain in 1905 that southern Italian immigrant parents "are indifferent to the advantages of education for their children." Nevertheless, the Americanization drive reached tens of thousands of new Americans who would in future decades reshape American politics and society.

Sources:

Mary Antin, *The Promised Land* (Princeton, N.J.: Princeton University Press, 1969);

Barbara Beatty, *Preschool Education in America: The Culture of Young Children from the Colonial Era to the Present* (New Haven: Yale University Press, 1995);

Lawrence A. Cremin, *The Transformation of the School: Progressivism in American Education, 1876–1957* (New York: Vintage Books, 1964);

John Higham, *Strangers in the Land: Patterns of American Nativism, 1860–1925,* second edition (New Brunswick, N.J.: Rutgers University Press, 1992);

David B. Tyack, *The One Best System: A History of American Urban Education* (Cambridge, Mass.: Harvard University Press, 1974).

CHANGING CONCEPTIONS OF LEARNING AND TEACHING

Competing Theories of Learning. As the new century began, educators in the United States faced two key questions regarding learning and teaching: 1) How do children learn? and 2) What knowledge is of most value? Disagreements over these fundamental questions consumed both theorists and practitioners, and an intense struggle over competing theories ensued. Eventually, from this intellectual clash, a new way of thinking about learning emerged, one with profound consequences for the future of education in the United States.

The Mind as Muscle. Traditionalists adhered to the theory of mental discipline, which maintained that the human mind was composed of separate and distinct faculties, including reasoning, memory, perception, and imagination. Sometimes referred to as mental disciplinarians, these educators argued that just as physical muscles were strengthened by physical exercise, so the faculties of the mind were strengthened by mental exercise. In their view a student who studied Greek vigorously every day increased his or her memory skills in the same way a weight lifter who worked out daily developed strong biceps and triceps. This theory of learning became the basis for the traditional teaching methods that emphasized frequent drills, tough classroom discipline, and recitation. Just as important, mental disciplinarians argued that only certain subjects, like Latin, Greek, and mathematics, exercised the mind adequately; and, therefore, they resisted changing the standard curriculum to include more-modern subjects.

Opposition to Traditionalists. By the early years of the twentieth century many American educators expressed disdain toward the "mental discipline" theory of learning, dismissing it as old-fashioned and unscientific. These opponents received ammunition for their battle in 1901 when the brilliant psychologist Edward L. Thorndike and his colleague Robert S. Woodworth published a study, "The Influence of Improvement in One Mental Function Upon the Efficiency of Other Functions." Shattering the dominant theory of mental faculties, Thorndike's experiment showed, he wrote, that "Improvement in any single mental function need not improve the ability in functions commonly called by the same name." Indeed, he concluded that improvement in one mental function might actually "injure" other functions. Three years later another psychologist, G. Stanley Hall, published a groundbreaking book, *Adolescence: Its Psychology and Its Relations to Physiology, Anthropology, Sociology, Sex, Crime, Religion, and Education,* a book offering opponents of mental discipline theory a strong rationale for a new, contrasting approach to learning and teaching.

G. Stanley Hall. A developmentalist, Hall believed all individuals advanced through various stages of psychological development and that these stages could be iden-

G. Stanley Hall, an educator and psychologist who focused attention on adolescence as a distinct stage in human development

Harvard President Charles W. Eliot periodically asked audiences at his speeches to imagine a five-foot shelf of books that contained all essential knowledge. Eliot hypothesized that if an individual read these books for fifteen minutes a day, that person would obtain an excellent substitute for a liberal education. Robert Collier, of the publishing house P. F. Collier and Son, told President Eliot that his company would publish such a collection if Eliot would come up with the titles and give both his and Harvard's name to the project. Eliot agreed, and in 1909 the first volumes in the fifty-volume series were published. The books were known collectively as The Harvard Classics, and the series became popular immediately, generating wide acclaim and brisk sales.

Source: Joan Shelley Rubin, *The Making of Middlebrow Culture* (Chapel Hill: University of North Carolina Press, 1992).

tified by the techniques of scientific observation. One such distinct stage, he maintained, was adolescence, a unique period between childhood and adulthood that required special attention and teaching. Hall further argued that traditionalists were wrong in believing all students should receive the same type of education, because, he maintained, such uniformity thwarted the adolescent's natural spontaneity. "The pupil," Hall wrote, "is in the age of spontaneous variation, which at no period of life is so great. He does not want a standardized, over-peptonized mental diet. It palls on his diet." Adolescents, in Hall's view, were miseducated and ill served in the traditional schools that featured a standardized curriculum and constant drill and memorization.

Progressive Education Impulses. By the end of the decade the mental disciplinarians were in full retreat, and educational reformers had succeeded in supplanting traditional methods and theories with new approaches to learning and teaching. Although considerable disagreement existed among these reformers, loosely defined as "progressive educators," they nevertheless shared three common points of agreement. First, they placed great faith in science and supported the scientific study both of the child and the curriculum. Second, they believed in the perfectibility of society and viewed educational institutions as legitimate sources of societal reform. Third, most of them strongly maintained that schools should be child-centered rather than subject-centered. United by these basic views, this shifting coalition of progressive educators dominated American schools and the American curriculum for the next fifty years.

Sources:
Herbert M. Kliebard, *The Struggle for the American Curriculum, 1893–1958* (New York: Routledge & Kegan Paul, 1987);

Arthur Zilversmit, *Changing Schools: Progressive Education Theory and Practice, 1930–1960* (Chicago: University of Chicago Press, 1993).

COLLEGE LIFE

Academic Expectations. Students who graduated from American colleges in the mid nineteenth century generally admitted that course expectations were low and that graduating required little effort; but the academic work required of undergraduates greatly increased from 1865 to 1910; and by the beginning of the new century college entrance requirements had stiffened considerably, especially among elite universities. Indeed, after 1900 it became common for university presidents to attempt to improve the academic performance of their students. Harvard, for example, instituted honors programs, and Princeton, with Woodrow Wilson as president, greatly upgraded its educational quality. Nevertheless, the overall picture for higher education in America in the decade 1900–1909 is mixed. Of the roughly five hundred institutions of higher learning, not even half deserved the title of *college*. Contemporaries noted that only a hundred colleges had standards of sufficient rigor to allow graduates to begin study for a doctorate. Only a dozen universities were considered to be of the "first rank." Moreover, despite the upturn in academic expectations, academic standards often remained surprisingly low. At Yale in

The Senior Debating Society at Kansas State College reading copies of *Roberts' Rules of Order*

1903 many seniors reportedly studied only an hour a day. At Princeton, even during Wilson's tenure, the master's degree was awarded to any graduate who submitted a thesis fifteen to twenty pages long. According to one 1903 article, several students at Harvard received A's in courses they had never attended. By some reports the Harvard undergrads' three-hour cram session with a tutor was sufficient to display mastery of most Harvard course material. In other words, while academic expectations escalated from 1900 to 1910, many observers nevertheless still had strong grounds on which to criticize the lax educational standards prevalent at many colleges and universities.

Training for Careers in the Professions. In the first decade of the twentieth century American universities were attracting increasing numbers of students who were interested in pursuing careers in business and the traditional professions. Although colleges in the United States had always been a training ground for ministry, law, and medicine, it was not until the decade 1900–1909 that obtaining a bachelor of arts degree became a prerequisite for advanced training in these traditional professions. Not until 1901 did one of the country's leading medical schools, at Harvard University, require a bachelor's degree for admission. Meanwhile, as late as 1902 the presidents of Yale and Chicago were still arguing that less than a full bachelor's degree was enough preparation to

be admitted to a professional school. Eventually, however, it was complaints about the quality of medical training, heightened by a study commissioned in 1908 by the Carnegie Foundation for the Advancement of Teaching, that led to dramatic changes in the training for all professional fields. The Carnegie study, known as the Flexner Report, from the name of its chief investigator, Abraham Flexner, caused twenty medical schools in the country, fearful of devastating criticism, to close instantly. Because of the same highly regarded Flexner Report, the standards, practices, and curriculum of many medical schools immediately improved, while other medical schools judged inadequate also eventually closed. During this decade of 1900–1909 the professions outside medicine followed similar, if not as striking, transformations in their training standards. Moreover, by the end of the decade most students interested in pursuing a career in theology, law, or medicine first obtained an undergraduate degree before professional study in their chosen field.

Business Schools and Business Administration. The increasing propensity of college graduates to seek careers in business initially caught American universities by surprise in the years from 1900 to 1909. After all, in earlier years business-minded individuals had frequently belittled the value of a college education. No less a business giant than Andrew Carnegie, the famous steel magnate, wrote in 1902 that young men should avoid college be-

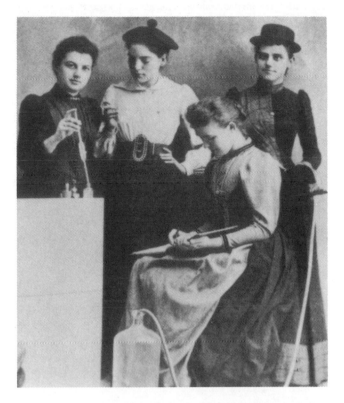

Women in a science laboratory at Wellesley College. Only about a third of American college students were women in 1900–1909.

cause the curriculum unfortunately "injured" them for business. Increasingly, however, business professionals began to appreciate the value of a college degree; and indeed, by middecade, business leaders in Chicago encouraged and partially financed the creation of Northwestern's highly regarded business school. And slowly but surely colleges and universities began to adapt to new conditions and new expectations. At Harvard in 1908 President Charles W. Eliot opened the Graduate School of Business Administration after noting the large proportion of the college's graduates who had chosen business as a career. Nationwide, the demand for instruction and education in business subjects continued to rise. By 1910, of the roughly 150,000 undergraduates in the United States, approximately one-third pursued a classical program of study; the remaining two-thirds pursued vocational programs, such as engineering or accounting, that were specifically geared toward opportunities in business.

Women in Higher Education. Only a minority of students attending American colleges in the years 1900–1909 were women, although three-quarters of all colleges and universities were coeducational at the time. Just 35 percent of undergraduates were female in 1900, and only 39 percent were female in 1910. Even when colleges permitted women to matriculate with men, they frequently treated women as second class citizens. At the University of Wisconsin women had to stand in the classroom until all men were seated. Moreover, few colleges allowed women to participate in extracurricular activities. Expressing a view by no means uncommon in these years, the president of the University of California, Benjamin Wheeler, told women students: "You are not like men and you must recognize the fact. . . . You may have the same studies as the men, but you must put them to different use." Women, Wheeler added, were at the university "for the preparation of marriage and motherhood," and if they applied themselves in studying, they would be "more serviceable as wives and mothers."

Sources:
Patricia Albjerg Graham, "Expansion and Exclusion: A History of Women in Higher Education," *Signs* (Summer 1978): 759–773;

Helen Lefkowitz Horowitz, *Campus Life: Undergraduate Cultures from the End of the Eighteenth Century to the Present* (Chicago: University of Chicago Press, 1987);

Ellen Condliffe Lagemann, *Private Power for the Public Good: A History of the Carnegie Foundation for the Advancement of Teaching* (Middletown, Conn.: Wesleyan University Press, 1983);

Christopher J. Lucas, *American Higher Education: A History* (New York: St. Martin's Press, 1994);

Laurence R. Veysey, *The Emergence of the American University* (Chicago: University of Chicago Press, 1965).

CURRICULUM FOR AFRICAN AMERICANS

The Status of Black Southerners. In the decade from 1900 to 1909, black southerners faced increasing restrictions on all aspects of their lives. Indeed, most educational and economic opportunities that had opened up for blacks in the years immediately following the Civil War had closed by the turn of the century. Moreover, in

PAY DISCRIMINATION IN SOUTHERN CLASSROOMS

Black teachers in the South found that the gap between their salaries and those of their white counterparts increased dramatically during the twenty-year span from 1890 to 1910. In 1890 the salary for black teachers generally was less than that paid white teachers, but the gap was much smaller than it would become later. In 1890 in the states of Louisiana and Mississippi, black teachers earned about 80 percent of the salary of white teachers. In North Carolina and Florida the gap was only 2–6 percent; in Alabama black teachers made slightly more than white teachers.

By 1910 the salary gap between the races increased significantly. Average annual salaries of white teachers more than doubled during the period, while the average salaries of black teachers generally dropped or remained stagnant.

Table: Annual Salaries of Public School Teachers in Selected Southern States (1890–1910)

Alabama

Black teachers	$255–$311
White Teachers	$215–$790

Florida

Black Teachers	$319–$312
White Teachers	$342–$676

Louisiana

Black Teachers	$243–$340
White Teachers	$418–$940

North Carolina

Black Teachers	$204–$268
White Teachers	$207–$506

National Average	$724–$1,102

Source: Robert A. Margo, *Race and Schooling in the South, 1880–1950: An Economic History* (Chicago: University of Chicago Press, 1990).

ETHNIC DIFFERENCES IN HIGH-SCHOOL ENTRY

In Providence, Rhode Island, a port city with many different ethnic groups, rates of high-school entry in 1900 varied among differing ethnic groups. While only 18 percent of all eligible students actually enrolled in high school, some groups were much more likely to enroll than others. Native white children living with parents born in this country were the group most likely to enter high school; Italian immigrants were the least likely. Reasons for the differences between groups were complex, but, in brief, both a student's cultural background and the economic well-being of the student's family played important roles.

Table: Ethnic Differences in High-School Entry, Providence, Rhode Island, 1900

Group	Percent Entering High School
Native whites, native parentage	36
Native whites, Irish parentage	11
Native whites, other parentage	23
Blacks	12
Irish	18
English, Scots, Welsh	8
All other immigrants	13
Total, all groups	18

Source: Joel Perlmann, *Ethnic Differences: Schooling and Social Structure Among the Irish, Italians, Jews, and Blacks in an American City, 1880–1935* (New York: Cambridge University Press, 1988).

---

the period after Reconstruction white southern politicians had succeeded in limiting the political power of blacks — most notably by depriving black men in every southern state of the right to vote. Black political leaders fought to keep or regain some civil and economic rights by trying to convince white politicians that persecuting the black citizenry harmed all of southern society. Their efforts ended in failure, however; and the age of Jim Crow segregation had fully arrived by the first years of the twentieth century.

Booker T. Washington. The most prominent African American at the turn of the century was Booker T. Washington, head of the famous Tuskegee Institute in Alabama. Besides being an educator, the politically astute Washington advised presidents — he once dined with President Theodore Roosevelt — and small-time politicians; he also controlled or influenced much of the limited government patronage available to blacks. In fact, his rivals in the black community feared his power and complained of the "Tuskegee machine" under his control. But Booker T. Washington's prominence and power during these years belied his humble origins. Born into slavery in 1856, he spent his boyhood on his master's small Virginia farm. After emancipation he attended the newly opened

Black students at Tuskegee Institute in Alabama

school for freed people in his West Virginia community. In *Up From Slavery* (1901) Washington eloquently described how education became the key to his rise from obscurity to national prominence. The culmination of his schooling occurred at the Hampton Institute, a black training school headed by Gen. Samuel Chapman Armstrong, a veteran of the Union army. Washington became the Hampton Institute's star pupil, and in 1881 Armstrong recommended him for the principalship of a similar school, the Tuskegee Institute in Alabama. Washington accepted the job and steadily grew in influence and power as head of Tuskegee. Fourteen years later he received national recognition after an electrifying address to Atlanta's Cotton States and International Exposition on 18 September 1895.

The Atlanta Compromise. Washington's speech in Atlanta outlined his views about the ways southern whites and southern blacks should interact in the segregated, Jim Crow South. The two groups, Washington argued, should turn to one another for support in "a way that shall make the interests of both races one." He urged both races to "cast down their buckets" where they were and predicted that everyone would benefit. According to Washington, however, mutual support did not mean full racial integration: "In all things that are purely social we can be as separate as the fingers, yet one as the hand in all things essential to mutual progress." While most in his white audience approved the image of separate fingers, it was the image of the hand, with its reference to mutual progress, that Washington believed most important. Counseling whites to stop their efforts "to curtail the fullest growth of the Negro," he also suggested that blacks should stop agitating for social equality. According to Washington, "The opportunity to earn a dollar in a factory just now is worth infinitely more than the opportunity to spend a dollar in an opera-house." Many whites praised the "Atlanta Compromise," as the speech came to be known, because Washington had proposed that black southerners trade political and social equality for future economic progress. Black reaction, however, was mixed; some blacks feared Washington had conceded too much in his speech. Still, many blacks were pleased to see that whites had praised and supported a highly respected African American leader.

Industrial Training. Under Washington's leadership the Tuskegee Institute in Alabama achieved national renown, and applications for admission remained high throughout the early decades of the twentieth century. During this time Washington's philosophy was strongly reflected in the school's curriculum: Tuskegee emphasized the training of young black men and women in practical, workplace skills. Washington himself argued it was far better for most blacks to learn to make bricks or to cook than to learn "mere book education." While he certainly did not oppose higher education for blacks, he strongly believed the scarce educational resources available to southern blacks should be devoted primarily to industrial education.

W. E. B. Du Bois. Unlike Booker T. Washington in background and temperament, William Edward Burghardt Du Bois offered a starkly different vision of the education blacks should pursue in their quest for economic achievement and full democratic citizenship. Du Bois was born in Great Barrington, Massachusetts, on 23 February 1868. Although growing up black during the later nineteenth century was surely extremely difficult

Agriculture students at Tuskegee Institute

anywhere in the United States, life in western Massachusetts, nevertheless, offered more possibilities for a black child than life in the South did. "Willie," as Du Bois was known to family and friends, thrived in school. His academic achievements in the integrated schools of his town so impressed some people that local Congregational churches pledged to pay for higher education for Willie at Fisk University, a black liberal arts college in Nashville, Tennessee. Du Bois graduated from Fisk in 1888 and then entered Harvard College. A brilliant student, he graduated from Harvard cum laude with his second bachelor's degree in 1890. Eventually Du Bois studied at the prestigious University of Berlin and then again at Harvard, becoming in 1895 the first African American to obtain a Harvard doctorate. His dissertation on the African slave trade was published to acclaim in 1896, and more acclaim followed when his sociological study of blacks in Philadelphia came out in 1899. With the publication of these two works Du Bois was widely recognized as the leading scholar of black America.

Opposition to Washington. In 1903 Du Bois published his most famous book, *The Souls of Black Folk,* a series of personal, historic, and political essays. In an essay titled "Of Mr. Booker T. Washington and Others" Du Bois condemned the so-called "Atlanta Compromise" and split from the accommodationist approach of Washington. Why the breach between the two giants of black America? In the years following the "Atlanta Compromise" speech, Du Bois believed that conditions for blacks in the South had only worsened; the economic advances Washington had hoped for were either agonizingly slow or simply nonexistent. As time passed, Du Bois grew increasingly disillusioned with Washington's approach to

education and social relations, as did a large number of blacks, to whom Du Bois offered an alternative path to follow.

The Talented Tenth. The Washington–Du Bois split over social and political policy was reflected in their vividly contrasting approaches to black education. W. E. B. Du Bois, along with many other highly educated African Americans, thought Booker T. Washington harmed the cause of blacks by not emphasizing the importance of higher education for black people. Not surprisingly, Du Bois adamantly disagreed with Washington's emphasis on industrial training for black southerners at the expense of support for black higher education. Instead, Du Bois argued that educational efforts for blacks should be directed toward advanced schooling for a black "talented tenth." In his influential essay "The Talented Tenth" (1903) Du Bois stated, "The Negro race, like all races, is going to be saved by its exceptional men. The problem of education, then, among Negroes must first of all deal with the Talented Tenth; it is the problem of developing the Best of this race that they may guide the Mass away from the contamination and death of the Worst, in their own and other races."

Common Ground. Although Washington and Du Bois held strongly conflicting views on critical issues, both, in fact, agreed that education was crucial to the future of black Americans. Their differences that seemed so fundamental at the time seem less so in hindsight. Du Bois, after all, recognized the need for some industrial training, just as Washington realized that higher education for some blacks was essential to black progress. In 1904, in a speech in Cambridge, Massachusetts, Washington stated: "We need not only the industrial school, but the college and professional school as well, for a people so largely segregated, as we are, from the body of our people, must have its own professional leaders who shall be able to measure with others in all forms of intellectual life." Still, the differences in emphasis between Washington and Du Bois were real and significant, and the two black leaders remained adversaries until Washington's death in 1915.

Sources:

Edward L. Ayers, *The Promise of the New South: Life After Reconstruction* (New York: Oxford University Press, 1992);

W. E. B. Du Bois, *The Souls of Black Folk* (Chicago: McClurg, 1903);

Louis R. Harlan, *Booker T. Washington: The Wizard of Tuskegee, 1901–1915* (New York: Oxford University Press, 1983);

David Levering Lewis, *W. E. B. Du Bois: Biography of a Race, 1868–1919* (New York: Holt, 1993);

Booker T. Washington, *Up From Slavery* (New York: Doubleday, Page, 1901).

EFFICIENCY AND THE SCHOOLS

An Efficiency Expert and Education. In the first decade of the twentieth century a new system of management that emphasized the most efficient and "scientific" use of resources and labor to increase industrial productivity began taking the American business world by storm. The apostle of this view of efficiency, Frederick W. Taylor, first won renown in the field of engineering. In 1896 the editor of *Engineering Magazine* called Taylor's first paper on scientific management "one of the most valuable contributions that has ever been given to technical literature." As additional publications followed, Taylor was frequently invited to talk to industrial groups; by 1906 his fame was so widespread that he was elected president of the American Society of Mechanical Engineers. At the end of the decade there were few people inside or outside the business world who had not heard about Taylor's exciting ideas about efficiency. Impressed by those ideas, innovators in other fields began to apply Taylor's principles to nonbusiness realms, and, caught up in the excitement, some American educators began advocating new, efficient ways of running and managing the nation's public schools. At the 1908 annual meeting of the National Education Association, Andrew S. Draper gave a talk on "Adaptations of Schools to Industry and Efficiency." In the decade 1900–1909, in a relatively short time, the words "education" and "efficiency" had become inextricably linked in the minds of many school reformers.

Efficiency Comes to Gary, Indiana. In 1908 William Wirt, a school superintendent in Gary, Indiana, set out to create a working model of educational efficiency, one that he could apply to public schools. Not far from Chicago, Gary was a town where, on barren land in northern Indiana, U.S. Steel had built a huge manufacturing complex in 1906. Gary was, in fact, named for Elbert H. Gary, first chairman of the board of U.S. Steel. Because thousands of workers, mostly immigrants, flocked to the city

seeking jobs, most students attending Gary schools were children of laborers, and 57 percent were immigrants. Into this setting came Wirt, who became the city's first school superintendent after convincing the mayor and the three school board members — a civil engineer, a surveyor, and a railroad engineer — that Gary's schools should be engineered for maximum efficiency. Using charts, tables, and figures, Wirt showed how Gary's schools could be run at a low cost, even while incorporating into their classrooms many innovative features. Impressed by his intellect and technically oriented presentation, the school board gave Wirt total control over the development of Gary's new school system.

The Gary Plan. For Gary's schools Wirt quickly developed a unique program to combine the most efficient possible use of resources with an innovative curriculum that merged the community's interests with those of the schools. Wirt urged that the schools in Gary be built near parks and that the city's museums, libraries, and playgrounds be an integral part of the daily school experience. Under Wirt's guidance schools stayed open later than the standard, mid-afternoon end of the school day; they also remained open through most of the year. Extended educational opportunities abounded; parents participated in many school activities; and vocational programs became a staple of the curriculum. In the name of efficiency students were not assigned a permanent desk in a classroom; instead, half the children at any given time were in an academic setting, and half were in shop, a laboratory, the auditorium, or on the playground. Wirt argued that rotating students throughout the "school plant" not only used the facility efficiently, but such a procedure required only half as many classrooms as a traditional, comparably sized school. Finally, the plan saved money. Wirt's program became popularly known as the "Gary Plan," but some who were not convinced of its merits called it the "platoon system."

Model for Other Systems. Reports about the schools in Gary, Indiana, quickly spread through the nation. By combining the ideal of efficiency with other processes favored in progressive education, the Gary Plan resonated with educators and reformers of many political persuasions. Full of curiosity, school officials, reformers, newspeople, and interested citizens converged on the city of Gary to visit its celebrated, innovative schools. Wirt himself was frequently invited to write and speak on his school system that fired so many imaginations. At the height of its popularity 1,068 schools in 202 cities in forty-one states operated under the Gary Plan he developed. Its popularity notwithstanding, however, replications of the plan were not always successful. In some places "Garyized" schools failed to be as efficient or economical as reformers had hoped, and the students' parents were not always enamored with the system. Meanwhile, hoping to improve the famous Gary Plan, some school boards tried triple sessions to gain even greater efficiency in their schools, while omitting some of the curricular innovations. These schools failed quickly and disastrously, the most public failure occurring in the New York City school system. Critics of that system wrote articles with titles such as the "Waste of Triple Sessions" and deplored the administrators' mechanical, businesslike views of education. In time, the celebrated Gary Plan died out among school systems across the country; nevertheless, it left among many educators the enduring legacy of a continued striving for efficiency in the nation's schools.

Sources:

Randolph S. Bourne, *The Gary Schools*, epilogue by Abraham Flexner and Frank P. Bachman, introduced and annotated by Adeline Levine and Murray Levine (Cambridge: MIT Press, 1970);

Raymond E. Callahan, *Education and the Cult of Efficiency* (Chicago: University of Chicago Press, 1962);

Patricia Albjerg Graham, *Progressive Education: From Arcady to Academe* (New York: Teachers College Press, 1967).

HULL HOUSE AND PROGRESSIVE EDUCATION

The Settlement Movement. Originating in Victorian England, but spreading quickly to the United States, the settlement movement was a loose coalition of groups and individuals who sought to relieve the harsh conditions facing factory workers in the crowded English and American cities of the late nineteenth century. The first so-called settlement house opened in London in 1884, when social activist Edward Denison, clergyman Samuel A. Barrett, and historian Arnold Toynbee established a lodge, Toynbee Hall. Believing well-educated people should help close the gap between the society's rich and poor, Denison, Barrett, and Toynbee felt they could promote this purpose by living among poor people, most of whom were factory workers, and making the residence, or "settlement," a center of education. At Toynbee Hall the three men taught classes for the working people of London, hoping to give these people educational weapons to help them fight against their usually despicable living conditions. At the same time, the three men believed they could learn from their working-class students. After visiting Toynbee Hall in 1888, American Jane Addams decided to replicate the English program in Chicago, where her settlement, Hull House, became the third such settlement in the United States. By 1891, six such settlements existed across the country; by 1900 there were more than a hundred; and by 1910 more than four hundred settlement houses had opened.

Hull House. Owing largely to the administrative prowess and successful publicity efforts of the charismatic Jane Addams, Hull House became the best known of the settlement houses in the United States. Addams's Chicago house had two main purposes, the first of which was primarily educational. Hull House residents and volunteers provided numerous programs and services to help their immigrant neighbors; the earliest program offered, a kindergarten begun in 1889, typified the emphasis placed on providing educational opportunities for male

---

AN IMMIGRANT DESCRIBES THE AMERICANIZATION OF HIS NAME

The following extract from Leonard Covello's autobiography, *The Heart is the Teacher*, describes how the author's Italian family reacted to the Americanizing of his name by one of his teachers.

One day I came home from the Soup School with a report card for my father to sign. . . . With a weary expression my father glanced over the marks on the report card and was about to sign it. However, he paused with the pen in his hand.

"What is this?" he said. "Leonard Covello! What happened to the *i* in Coviello?"

My mother paused in her mending. Vito and I just looked at each other.

"Well?" my father insisted. . . . "From Leonardo to Leonard I can follow," he said, "a perfectly natural process. In America anything can happen and does happen. But you don't change a family name. A name is a name. What happened to the *i*?"

"Mrs. Cutter took it out," I explained. "Every time she pronounced Coviello it came out Covello. So she took out the *i*. That way it's easier for everybody."

. . . My mother now suddenly entered the argument. . . . "You must explain this to your teacher," my mother insisted. "It was a mistake. She will know. She will not let it happen again. You will see."

"It was no mistake. On purpose. The *i* is out and Mrs. Cutter made it Covello. You just don't understand!"

"Will you stop saying that!" my mother insisted. "I don't understand. I don't understand. What is there to understand? Now that you have become Americanized you understand everything and I understand nothing."

Source: Leonard Covello, with Guido D'Agostino, *The Heart is the Teacher* (New York: McGraw-Hill, 1958).

---

and female immigrants of all ages. Other programs offered to adults and children included extension classes, lectures, picture exhibitions, a summer school, a laboratory school affiliated with the National College of Education, Sunday concerts, a nursery, a museum of labor that emphasized the ethnic traditions of immigrants' homelands, courses in cooking and housekeeping, and various men's and women's clubs. Eventually Hull House offered classes to teach recent immigrants how to speak, read, and write English; classes in citizenship also became popular. The second principal purpose of Hull House was that of promoting social justice. Settlement residents worked with their immigrant neighbors to seek solutions to the difficult social and economic problems the immigrants frequently faced in the large and growing city. Inspired by the energetic Addams, Hull House residents fought for and achieved many of their goals, which included parks and playgrounds for children, clean and well-lit streets, improved health care, and better working conditions.

Progressive Pedagogy. Basing the teaching and curriculum at Hull House on the ideas of the progressive educator and philosopher John Dewey, Jane Addams was proud that her settlement's educational program supported an unrestricted view of education. Self-expression among children was encouraged, and spirited attempts were made to connect youngsters' school and family lives. Hull House volunteers emphasized the arts in educational programs for all ages, and dancing classes, drama classes, and art and music lessons were a staple of Hull House activities. Addams believed, however, that "the educational efforts of a settlement should not be directed primarily to reproduce the college-type culture but to work out a method and an ideal adapted to adults who spend their time in industrial pursuits." Accordingly, for older students vocational education became a focus of the Hull House curriculum; but it was a vocational education that went beyond the conventional industrial training. Addams maintained that men and women entering the workforce should have an idea of the history and nature of modern, industrial society in urban America, because these workers needed a sense of context that would provide a fuller meaning to their lives. Additionally, Addams sought to furnish adults with meaningful discussions of contemporary issues. "A settlement soon discovers that simple people are interested in large and vital issues," she wrote. In her mind, simple people did not care to hear only about simple things; they wanted to hear of great things, simply told.

Publicizing Progressive Education. Working tirelessly to spread her ideas about education and reform, Jane Addams wrote or edited thirteen books and left in her collected papers more than one thousand articles, speeches, and addresses. Not all these writings concentrated on education, but many did, a fact that reflected Addams's enduring interest in the subject. Besides her work at Hull House, Addams also worked to reform American public schools, not only serving on an ad hoc citizens' school committee in Chicago, but, from 1905 to 1909, serving as an appointed member of the Chicago Board of Education. She also pushed hard for compulsory education laws and, as a member of the National Child Labor Committee, lobbied for laws to end child labor. In 1906 she helped found the National Society for the Promotion of Industrial Education, which helped usher through Congress the 1917 Smith-Hughes Act, supporting vocational education in the nation's high schools. And yet, despite Addams's passionate activism for reform of the formal and public education systems, she nevertheless believed that, ultimately, the nation's

Jane Addams, founder of Hull House

schools and universities played a limited role as agents of social change. It was the settlements, Addams believed, or similar institutions, that provided the driving force that most effectively connected education and social reform. Taken as a whole, the educational philosophy of Jane Addams exemplified the strand of progressivism that viewed education as an essential and powerful instrument for improving American society.

Sources:

Mary Lynn McCree Bryan, "Laura Jane Addams," in *Women Educators in the United States, 1820–1993: A Bio-Bibliographical Sourcebook,* edited by Maxine Schwartz Seller (Westport, Conn.: Greenwood Press, 1994);

Lawrence A. Cremin, *American Education: The Metropolitan Experience, 1876–1980* (New York: Harper & Row, 1988);

Allen F. Davis, *American Heroine: The Life and Legend of Jane Addams* (New York: Oxford University Press, 1973).

NORTHEASTERN PREP SCHOOLS

Prep Schools. At the beginning of the twentieth century America's leading college preparatory schools, although few in number, wielded an impressive influence in American life — particularly in the northeastern United States, where most such institutions were concentrated. The prestige of these preparatory, or "prep," schools — Hotchkiss, Exeter, and Groton, to name a few —

derived largely from the distinguished accomplishments of their graduates, many of whom, especially in the Northeast, became community, state, and national leaders. In 1900 a song from the Choate School summed up the notion that these elite prep schools were the training grounds for future leaders. The song was sung to the tune of "Jingle Bells."

> Let us now explain
> What we mean to be.
> That boy there will be a judge
> And that one a M.D.
> That one's a Diplomat,
> To London he'll be sent,
> And the one who's manliest of all,
> We'll make him President.

Characteristics. Most of the leading prep schools in the United States were founded during the thirty-year period from 1880 to 1910; and among those created in the decade 1900–1909 were Middlesex (1901), Deerfield Academy (1903), and Kent (1906). All these elite, northeastern schools shared four key characteristics. First, all were boarding schools for boys. Second, the objectives of each institution were simultaneously to prepare its students for college success and to build the students' characters. A third common denominator among these schools was that their operating expenses were covered by student tuition and by endowments made by wealthy philanthropists. None of these schools received government assistance, and all were private institutions. Fourth, and perhaps most important, because these schools were expensive to run and therefore charged very high tuitions, their students were almost all sons of wealthy Americans. At a time when two-thirds of all adult male workers in the United States received a yearly salary of $600 or less, these preparatory schools typically levied a tuition greater than $600. Primarily because of such high tuitions, critics charged the prep schools were elitist and, in fact, "class schools." Defenders of these schools pointed with pride to their "independent" nature and claimed that, because they differed in style and curriculum from timid, bureaucratic, public schools, the nation's prep schools had established themselves as the bastions of America's future leadership.

Institutional Connections. In the decade 1900–1909, at the same time prep schools were emerging as a strong institution in the United States, the modern American university was beginning to take its definitive shape and American high schools were surging in number. The simultaneity of these trends is not coincidental. By the end of the nineteenth century, following the decline of the academy — a private secondary school that principally served the economic elites — educators began to search for a new institution to prepare students for college. Critics charged that most of the nation's high schools failed to prepare students adequately for first-rate universities. Indeed, many critics of high schools were

Students in class at Milton Academy

themselves university leaders; and some university presidents, to ensure a body of well-prepared students for their freshman classes, urged the creation of family boarding schools to teach the skills and knowledge necessary for college-level work. During the decade 1900–1909 a large percentage of the students at the leading northeastern universities were graduates of private boarding schools. At Yale in 1907, for example, nearly 40 percent of the freshman class came from the country's top fourteen boarding schools; only 20 percent came from public high schools; the rest came from private day schools. The trend at Yale was repeated in other respected northeastern universities, which, in 1909, drew most of their entering classes from private schools, predominantly boarding schools. At Princeton 78 percent of all entering students in 1909 came from private schools; at Yale, 65 percent; and at Harvard, 47 percent. By comparison only 9 percent of the University of Michigan's entering class of 1909, and just 8 percent of the University of Wisconsin's, had graduated from private schools.

Student and Institutional Origins. The fourteen leading prep schools at the turn of the century fell into three distinct categories. In the first were the oldest boarding schools — Andover, Exeter, and Deerfield — that were comparatively inexpensive and had a student body generally more diverse than that of other prep schools. The second group — St. Paul's, St. Mark's, Groton, St. George's, and Kent — consisted of Episcopalian church schools whose student populations came almost solely from wealthy urban families. The third group consisted of nondenominational boarding schools — Lawrenceville, Hill, Choate, Taft, Hotchkiss, and Middlesex — that also drew their students from wealthy, urban families. The goal of all these schools was perhaps fitly summed up by the son of a St. Paul's School rector, who characterized the schools as "self-sufficient and insular communit[ies], providing for [their] rather narrow clientele just what was expected — a conservative, gentlemanly preparation of body and mind for the Ivy League Colleges and for support of the economic, political, and religious status quo."

Source:
James McLachlan, *American Boarding Schools: A Historical Study* (New York: Scribners, 1970).

SCHOOL REFORM IN THE SOUTH

Lifting "The Forgotten Man." The crippling poverty that devastated the American South after the Civil War and plagued that region for many years afterward had made southern schools, by the late nineteenth century, the least effective in the nation; but in the decade 1900–1909 determined southern progressives made an all-out effort to improve the region's public schooling. Believing that "southern backwardness" in economic and social matters could be eliminated through education, these southern progressives launched their educational campaign after being galvanized to action by the editor of the *Atlantic Monthly*, Walter Hines Page. In his powerful speech titled "The Forgotten Man," delivered in 1897 at the North Carolina State Normal and Industrial College in Greensboro and published separately in 1902, Page had argued that the real victims of southern poverty and underdevelopment were poor white men, women, and children; and furthermore, that the South's appalling underdevelopment had occurred because of the failed policies of both the politician and the preacher. After these failures, Page maintained, "it is time for a wiser statesmanship and a more certain means of grace." His solution? "A public school system generously supported by public sentiment, and generously maintained by both State and local taxation, is the only effective means to develop the forgotten man, and even more surely the only means to develop the forgotten woman."

Northern Support. Although it stirred southern progressives to action, Page's "forgotten man" speech failed to arouse strong support for public schools among the average white voter in his native South. In fact, shortly after Page's speech local referenda in North Carolina on increasing school taxes were defeated nearly everywhere in the state, while voters in only twelve of the state's thirteen hundred districts approved the tax measure. Afterward, one discouraged school reformer wrote, "I lose faith in the political machinery of education" and added, "If we could only do something that would enable men to keep in the field without regard to politics." Nor was the situation in North Carolina unique. In every southern

Southerner Walter Hines Page, an editor and diplomat who was appalled by the state of education in the South

state, school reformers had to fight indifferent voters and uncooperative legislatures. Ironically, however, in Page's adopted North his speech about southern education was a smashing success. There, philanthropists and reformers rallied to the cause of lifting the South's "forgotten man" and "forgotten woman"; and conferences held during the next several years brought together southern reformers and northern philanthropists who shared a deep concern about educational and social conditions in the South. Their discussions culminated in the creation of the Southern Education Board (SEB) in 1901, an organization that directed the educational reform efforts for the region. The first meeting of the SEB was held in New York City — a location that symbolized the importance of northern wealth to the reform movement. Among the SEB's northern benefactors were Wanamaker's department store executive Robert C. Ogden; wealthy capitalist Everit Macy; publisher Frank Doubleday; and oil tycoon John D. Rockefeller. Two years later Rockefeller created and funded the General Education Board (GEB). The two boards essentially acted as one, because Rockefeller placed members of the SEB in key GEB positions. With additional funds from other wealthy industrialists and businessmen, the private Southern Education Board set

A school for black pupils in Henderson, Kentucky

educational policy in the South and managed and distributed a fund of $53 million from 1903 to 1909.

Reform Goals. In the years from 1900 to 1909, the northern businessmen and southern reformers who led the school reform movement in the South shared a common understanding both of the needs of the southern society in these years and also the most desirable means of meeting those needs. First, as one reformer wrote, "The people need leaders to show them the way," and these reformers believed it was their responsibility to convince the southern public to accept and implement the new ideas about schooling and education. Clearly, reform from the top down rather than from the grassroots up was their preferred approach. Second, the reformers saw the educational system in the South not so much as an instrument for creating a learned and intelligent citizenry — the head of the SEB, Ogden, had stated that "learning for its own sake debases" — but rather as an instrument for creating social stability. The reformers wanted to fit individuals "to work under conditions in which they must form their livelihood." Schools, wrote one reformer in 1905, should "educate the children to be law-abiding citizens. The importance of developing a broad and efficient system of drilling the children in the public school to the habits of discipline and the customs of obedience which make for public order cannot be over-emphasized." Third, the reformers linked economic pros-

perity in the South to the development of increased technical skills among the working population. One southern member of the SEB, Charles McIver, stated in 1901 that "machinery has entered all industrial life and modern machinery calls for trained and intelligent operatives." Indeed, a leader of the "New South," Henry Grady, hoped for the advent of a "white Booker T. Washington" who would promote industrial training for poor whites just as Washington championed industrial training for poor blacks. Finally, since they had funds from northern philanthropists, the reformers bypassed state legislatures for the most part and fought their fight for improved schools largely outside the arena of local politics. Money from the SEB was granted directly to southern colleges that trained teachers, as well as to the elementary and secondary schools of the South.

Expansion. In the years 1900–1909, spurred by the infusion of money from the Southern Education Board and the zeal of southern progressives, an extraordinary expansion of public education occurred across the southern states. "These are stirring times," said one reformer, James Y. Joyner. "The forgotten man has been remembered; the forgotten woman has been discovered; the forgotten child shall have his full chance in the South at last, thank God." In the eleven states of the former Confederacy, where reform efforts had been focused, annual expenditures for schools increased by more than $18 million during the period, and the average length of the school term by 1915 was more than thirty days longer than in 1900. Enrollment figures, per-pupil expenditures, teachers' salaries, the number of high schools, and other measures of progress in education also showed steep improvements. By most indications a southern educational awakening occurred during this decade of 1900–1909; and yet, despite this awakening, southern schools continued to lag behind nearly all other schools in the country.

For Middle-Class Whites Only. Moreover, the improvements in education that did occur in the South in these years were not universal. In fact, schools for black students could hardly be said to have improved at all, and schools for the poorest whites improved only marginally. The reasons both groups were excluded from the expansion of educational opportunities were varied, but black students particularly suffered from severe, overt discrimination by whites. James K. Vardaman, later the governor of Mississippi, expressed an extremely racist, but not unusual, viewpoint when he said:

> In educating the negro we implant in him all manner of aspirations and ambitions which we then refuse to allow him to gratify. . . . Yet people talk about elevating the race by education! It is not only folly, but it comes pretty nearly being criminal folly. The negro isn't permitted to advance and their education only spoils a good field hand and makes a shyster lawyer or a fourth-rate teacher. It is money thrown away.

Segregation. Racial discrimination in education varied in its extent from state to state, but it existed everywhere. Educators in North Carolina spent roughly half as much money on black students as they did on whites, while educators in South Carolina spent roughly one-tenth as much. Such discrepancies were possible because the school system was racially segregated throughout the South and because African Americans in that region were shut out from political power and therefore had no voice in educational policy. Southern schools were definitively separate and unequal. Moreover, the progressive educational campaign actually made the gap between black and white schools worse because most of the money and the improvements that resulted from that campaign benefited white schools only. Indeed, the progress white southerners made in education after 1900 came directly and deliberately at the expense of black southerners. Even the reformers of the Southern Education Board, an organization favoring educational improvement for both races, limited the funding of black schools to gain the political support of whites. By compromising itself in matters of race, the Southern Education Board placed a serious blot on the record of its accomplishments.

Plain Folk and Education. Another target population of the reformers, white tenant farmers and mill workers, had their lives only marginally changed by the school reform movement. As schools modernized and transformed in the years 1900–1909 and were removed from local control — or local "politics" — these so-called

---

"plain folk" found the public schools increasingly unsympathetic to their needs and desires. As a result, many were indifferent about schooling. As one woman explained: "Papa was a tenant farmer and him nor Mammy neither one had any learning. All they'd ever knowed was hard work. They didn't believe in education." In the judgment of many of these people, the schools did not teach children how to make a living or how to live, and were, therefore, a waste of time. In the traditional, oral culture of "plain folk," teaching a person how to live and work was the primary purpose of education, and such knowledge could be obtained informally, outside school, where children learned by doing rather than by sitting in classrooms. Specifically, children needed to know how to bridle a mule, plow a field, mix turpentine and tallow — skills not taught in the schools. In fact, many adults in this group thought too much schooling made a person unfit for life — at least for the hard life these people knew. Because of such beliefs, poor whites frequently did not send their children to school; and when their children

---

Robert Wood, who advocated vocational education in public schools

John D. Runkle, president of the Massachusetts Institute of Technology who was impressed by Russian methods of teaching technical education

did attend, the attendance was nearly always sporadic and brief. Literacy skills were usually acquired, but only at the most basic level. Not until compulsory education laws were fully implemented in the southern states after World War II did "plain folk" resistance to school attendance begin to subside.

Sources:

Charles William Dabney, *Universal Education in the South* (Chapel Hill: University of North Carolina Press, 1936);

Louis R. Harlan, *Separate and Unequal: Public School Campaigns and Racism in the Southern Seaboard States, 1901–1915* (Chapel Hill: University of North Carolina Press, 1958);

Neil R. McMillen, *Dark Journey: Black Mississippians in the Age of Jim Crow* (Urbana: University of Illinois Press, 1989);

Theodore R. Mitchell, *Political Education in the Southern Farmers' Alliance, 1887–1900* (Madison: University of Wisconsin Press, 1987);

I. A. Newby, *Plain Folk in the New South: Social Change and Cultural Persistence, 1880–1915* (Baton Rouge: Louisiana State University Press, 1989).

VOCATIONAL EDUCATION

Vocationalism. As American schools underwent intense transformation in the decade of 1900–1909, probably no aspect of their transformation was more fundamental than the introduction of vocational education into the classroom. Increasingly in these years, the nation's schools assumed the task of training workers who could operate productively in the changing economy. This development happened at a time when many Americans thought it appropriate that the public schools should help enhance the nation's economic growth, and the widespread acceptance of vocationalism by the schools meant they were becoming closely aligned with economic concerns. In fact, the philosophical basis for schooling in the United States increasingly changed as vocationalism became more prevalent in the schools. In earlier times workers learned vocational skills from the family, from apprenticeships, or from other less formal arrangements. In the new educational system in the years 1900–1909, however, it was the nation's schools that frequently determined young people's future careers and then carried out career training. In part because of this strong orientation toward vocationalism, schools in this decade were increasingly referred to as "factories." Some educators believed schools should not only help promote American industry but should themselves be organized like a factory.

The Douglas Commission. In Massachusetts in 1906, as many businesspeople looked with dismay at the economic prospects facing their state, the Massachusetts Commission on Industrial and Technical Education, better known as the Douglas Commission, identified four problems in the state's schools that contributed to the state's economic problems. First, the commission found

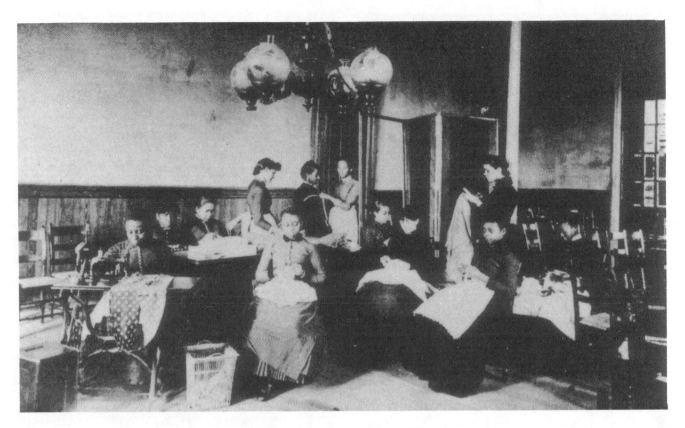

Students in a sewing class at Atlanta University

that most children who left school for employment at age fourteen or fifteen were essentially wasting their time because of their low economic productivity. Second, most children who remained in school nevertheless failed to acquire a sufficient fund of industrial intelligence. Furthermore, according to the commission, Massachusetts's manufacturing, agricultural, and building industries were not competitive with the rest of the world's industries because adequate vocational training among the state's workforce was lacking. Finally, the Douglas Commission concluded that Massachusetts needed an educational system that would strongly emphasize the teaching of industrial intelligence. From their findings the commission recommended that vocational instruction be undertaken in elementary and secondary schools throughout Massachusetts and that another commission be formed to encourage and aid towns in developing independent industrial schools. The state legislature approved these recommendations, and the Douglas Commission report fired interest in vocational education not only among school reformers in Massachusetts but across the nation.

National Movement. The Massachusetts initiative was not unique, however; indeed, a wide range of people throughout the United States championed similar efforts. In 1906, the same year the Douglas Commission published its findings, organizers formed the National Society for the Promotion of Industrial Education, an organization whose sole purpose was to promote the creation of vocational education programs in the nation's schools and to lobby for federal and state financial support for these programs. Meanwhile, across the country progressive social reformers, corporate officers, labor leaders, and academics all found something to like in the movement for vocational education, and few movements in American education have taken so sudden and widespread a hold on school reformers. Even President Theodore Roosevelt wrote in 1907, "We of the United States must develop a system under which each individual citizen shall be trained so as to be effective individually as an economic unit, and fit to be organized with his fellows so that he and they can work in efficient fashion together." Robert Woods, the head of the South End Settlement in Boston, expressed the view of most advocates of vocational education when he wrote, "The truth is that industrial education is coming. Those who do not put themselves in line to reap its advantages may even have some of its force turned against them."

Differentiated Curriculum. A survey completed in 1910 showed that vocational education programs existed in the school systems of twenty-nine states, and as the opportunities for vocational education spread, American teachers were increasingly called upon to sort their students into two distinct groups. In one group were the students who would primarily be taught an industrial curriculum; in the other group were those who would follow an academic curriculum. This fundamental division, moreover, began early in the student's education. In 1908 no less an educational leader than Harvard President Charles W. Eliot stated that "The teachers of the elementary schools ought to sort the pupils and sort them by their evident or probable destinies." In later years special tests would be used as a mechanism for sorting students for the two principal tracks in the schools; but in this early period individual teachers were often asked to determine each student's particular potential. Although sorting was supposed to proceed on a "scientific basis," in fact, vocational tracks frequently became a dumping ground for children who were poor or belonged to an ethnic minority.

First Vocational Schools. Although only a small number of vocational schools opened between 1906 and 1909 and the real explosion in vocational programs occurred later, nevertheless, the model for such schools that formed in these years continued to be the standard model for many later years. In 1909 in Newton, Massachusetts, the Independent Technical School became one of the first vocational schools in the United States, and its curriculum illustrated the wide range of programs that such a school offered. Eventually, the Newton school included a day industrial school for boys, a day industrial school for girls, an evening industrial school for men, a separate evening school for women, a day homemaking school, an evening practical arts school, a continuation school, and an agricultural school.

Sources:

Lawrence A. Cremin, *The Transformation of the School: Progressivism in American Education, 1876–1957* (New York: Vintage, 1964);

Harvey Kantor and David B. Tyack, eds., *Work, Youth, and Schooling: Historical Perspectives on Vocationalism in American Education* (Stanford, Cal.: Stanford University Press, 1982);

Standard Oil magnate John D. Rockefeller, benefactor of many educational enterprises

Marvin Lazerson and W. Norton Grubb, eds., *American Education and Vocationalism: A Documentary History, 1870–1970,* Classics in Education, number 48 (New York: Teachers College Press, 1974).

WEALTH, PHILANTHROPY, AND
EDUCATIONAL POLICY

Private Power for Public Good. In the first decade of the twentieth century, some American businessmen with vast fortunes spent large sums of their wealth to advance their vision of the public good, and their philanthropy exerted a great impact on educational policy in the United States. The two best-known philanthropists of the era were John D. Rockefeller, who had made his fortune by creating the Standard Oil Company, and Andrew Carnegie, whose fortune was made as the head of U.S. Steel. Rather than simply giving charity to people in need, as philanthropists had traditionally done, Rockefeller and Carnegie believed their wealth should be used for a direct attack on the causes of social problems. To that end, both men created large foundations to supervise the distribution of philanthropic resources, foundations that were given broad and flexible mandates to promote the well-being of American society.

Educational Foundations. In 1901 Andrew Carnegie began to establish the famous trusts and foundations that carried his name; and two of these foundations that directly promoted educational advances in the United

States were the Carnegie Institution of Washington (1901), a science research center, and the Carnegie Foundation for the Advancement of Teaching (1905), a pension fund that also provided money for educational studies. During the last years of his life when Carnegie proceeded to give away most of his fortune, he also provided funds to build numerous libraries across America; in addition, he specifically helped improve African American education. During this same decade John D. Rockefeller, who in 1889 had given $600,000 to found the University of Chicago, continued to use his enormous wealth to enhance the state of education in America, forming, among other things, a foundation to address the grave education problems in the American South. In 1903, after Rockefeller had pledged $1 million, Congress chartered the GEB; by 1907 more than $20 million more had been donated to this organization. Finally, on 29 June 1909 Rockefeller signed the deed of trust for the nation's largest foundation, the Rockefeller Foundation, another organization designed to promote educational ventures. Another foundation with an educational policy purpose, the Russell Sage Foundation, opened in 1907 after receiving $10 million from Margaret Sage, the widow of businessman Russell Sage.

General Education Board. While all these foundations helped shape education in the decade 1900–1909, the General Education Board probably had the widest impact on American educational policy; it particularly affected policies in the American South, where the problems facing educators were the most acute in the nation. For all the impact of the GEB, however, its record in these years was mixed. For example, when the GEB accelerated reform efforts in the South, its intention was to focus on the special problems facing southern blacks. In theory, however, the problems of both southern blacks and southern whites were targeted by the board, because,

as John D. Rockefeller Jr. noted, "We [the GEB] soon came to realize that Negro education could not be successfully promoted in the South, except as education for the whites was also promoted." Nevertheless, despite this theory, the fact was that most improvements in southern education in this decade occurred in white schools; moreover, the GEB campaign explicitly helped perpetuate the system of separate and unequal schools for white and black children. In North Carolina, for instance, the GEB supported the educational reform governor, Charles B. Aycock, who successfully disenfranchised the state's black voters and pushed universal education for white children only. Furthermore, while the GEB was willing to fund the Tuskegee Institute and the Hampton Institute, schools that emphasized industrial training for African Americans, it proved unwilling to fund African American colleges. In fact, in December 1903 one GEB member reported the main problem with black colleges in the South was that they emphasized academics rather than practical job training. In sum, the GEB promoted certain reforms in southern education, but its policy clearly favored white education over black education, and vocational training — for black children, at least — over academic knowledge.

Sources:

Robert H. Bremner, *American Philanthropy* (Chicago: University of Chicago Press, 1960);

Raymond B. Fosdick, *The Story of the Rockefeller Foundation* (New Brunswick, N.J.: Transaction Publishers, 1989);

Ellen Condliffe Lagemann, *The Politics of Knowledge: The Carnegie Corporation, Philanthropy, and Public Policy* (Chicago: University of Chicago Press, 1989);

Lagemann, *Private Power for the Public Good: A History of the Carnegie Foundation for the Advancement of Teaching* (Middletown, Conn.: Wesleyan University Press, 1983);

Warren Weaver, *U.S. Philanthropic Foundations: Their History, Structure, Management, and Record* (New York: Harper & Row, 1967).

HEADLINE MAKERS

CHARLES WILLIAM ELIOT

1834-1926

EDUCATOR, COLLEGE PRESIDENT

Educational Leader. Charles W. Eliot was born into an established Boston family on 20 March 1834 and taught chemistry both at Harvard and at the Massachusetts Institute of Technology before being appointed president of Harvard in 1869. When his forty-year tenure as president of Harvard University ended in 1909, he left behind a strong educational legacy that had an enduring impact in the United States. In higher education the innovations he introduced at Harvard influenced institutions of higher education around the country and led to the emergence of the distinctly American university. He also shaped the development of the nation's secondary and elementary schools through his frequent writings and speeches on the subject, his involvement in educational associations, and his membership on various educational reform panels. In 1903, when Eliot was at the height of his influence, the National Education Association (NEA) selected him to be its national president. In an era with little government regulation or control, voluntary organizations like the NEA kept schools and colleges in close contact on policies, programs, and standards and provided forums for discussing educational reforms.

Reforms at Harvard. During President Eliot's administration, Harvard made the transition from a small liberal arts college to a modern university. In 1869, his first year as president, Harvard had roughly one thousand students and sixty professors; forty years later, in 1909, the university was the second largest in the country, with approximately fifty-five hundred students and six hundred faculty. Eliot took great pride in the school's growth, particularly because it was achieved along with Eliot's push to raise entrance requirements at Harvard. In 1897 he wrote, "I find that I am not content unless Harvard grows each year, in spite of the size which it has attained." His principal innovation at Harvard, however, was his introduction of the "elective system," by which he broke with the usual college practice of mandating a set curriculum for all students to follow and allowed Harvard students a greater role in determining their education. Harvard started implementing the elective system with vigor during Eliot's first year as president, and for all practical purposes, requirements for seniors were abolished by 1872. By 1895 the school's only requirements were freshman English and a freshman modern language course. Convinced of the virtues of the elective system, Eliot eventually saw electives as a student "right" and even as the very embodiment of American values. In 1907 he wrote that "The elective system is, in the first place, an outcome of the Protestant Reformation. In the next place, it is an outcome of the spirit of liberty."

Graduate Education. Eliot's second major innovation at Harvard was to bring coherence and purpose to the university's graduate and professional schools. His role in this regard is complex. Although Eliot himself never fully embraced the concept of graduate education, the graduate school at Harvard became the largest and most respected in the United States during his administration. Moreover, from the first year of his presidency Eliot worked to enhance graduate education at Harvard, even while doubting its ultimate utility. Because of the growth of Harvard's graduate school and similar schools at Johns Hopkins, Clark, and Chicago, graduate programs increasingly became a central part of the American university experience. In 1900 graduate studies had become so entrenched in the nation's higher education system that, when the American Association of Universities was founded, the presence of a graduate school became the defining requirement for admission.

Influence on Secondary Schools. Before 1900 Eliot's main influence on secondary education was exerted when he chaired the controversial Committee of Ten on Secondary School Studies. This committee's report in 1894 was frequently misinterpreted as the last-ditch effort of conservative educators to impose the traditional, classical curriculum on high-school students. In fact, however, the committee made a more subtle recommendation about secondary-school standards. Observing that "the secondary schools of the United States, taken as a whole, do not exist for the purpose of preparing boys and girls for colleges," the committee recommended that secondary schools not distinguish between students ending their academic careers at the high-school level and those going on to college. In the committee's view, a sound education good enough for those entering college was also the best education for those ending their studies in high school. At the same time, and seemingly, at first glance, in contradiction, the report urged secondary schools to establish an elective system of courses for their students. In 1894 Eliot, long a proponent of the elective system in the university, pushed mildly for the same system at lower educational levels. A decade later, however, Eliot was a much stronger advocate of electives. After first thinking elective courses should be offered to students at age eighteen, Eliot eventually favored lowering the age to fourteen, then thirteen. In time, he believed electives should begin in kindergarten.

Mental Discipline. How could Eliot urge that elective courses be established in secondary schools, yet, at the same time, advocate a common set of secondary school standards? For Eliot, these two recommendations were not inconsistent because he believed in the theory of "mental discipline," which held that, just like the muscles of the body, the mind had to be exercised to acquire strength. Unlike the majority of mental disciplinarians, however, Eliot did not have a list of preferred subjects for such "exercise." Electives, therefore, he judged appropriate. During the years 1900–1909 supporters of implementing the elective system in secondary schools were always a minority in America; nevertheless, they were a vocal minority and viewed Eliot as their champion.

Linking Higher and Lower Education Levels. Eliot believed advocating school reforms and serving on educational committees were only the first steps to improving the American educational system. Fundamental change, he thought, required creating links between the nation's universities and its public schools. To this end, in his early years at Harvard he encouraged members of the faculty to teach seminars and summer sessions for the benefit of schoolteachers. In the 1890s he went a step further by hiring for Harvard an instructor of pedagogy, Paul Hanus. In 1903 Hanus asked Eliot to create a School of Education that would train professional educators just as the law and medical schools trained professionals for their fields. Eliot, however, was not prepared to adopt this plan, instructing Hanus to "neither talk nor think" about such a school. In fact, the Harvard Graduate School of Education was not created until 1920, at which time Eliot, by then retired as president, gave the school his blessing as a "pioneering" venture. Meanwhile, during Eliot's presidency at Harvard he fostered other connections between the university and the public schools.

School Reform. Eliot strongly encouraged Harvard alumni groups to involve themselves in public-school reform; alumni groups responded to this challenge: for example, the Buffalo Harvard Club successfully lobbied Buffalo, New York, for a more "flexible" curriculum in the city's high schools. At a meeting of the Associated Harvard Clubs in 1908, ten clubs reported their interest in public education issues; to encourage continuing interest, Eliot gave each club a checklist for reforming city school systems. Even Eliot's interest in the women's division of Harvard, the Harvard Annex, later Radcliffe College, was strengthened by his conviction that this school played an influential role in public-school reform. Since many of its graduates chose teaching as their career, Eliot reasoned that these women, having obtained the same excellent education as Harvard men, were helping to upgrade the teaching profession.

Final Years. Eliot's retirement from Harvard in 1909 did not diminish his interest in the issues of American education. Retaining great energy even in his later years, Eliot in 1908 joined the General Education Board, then remained a member of that influential board for nearly a decade. He also served for many years as a member of the Boston Museum of Fine Arts and between 1908 and 1925 was chairman of the museum's Special Advisory Committee on Education. In this position, according to the museum, he "was a leader in bringing about a right and proper system of instruction and training for students of Art." In addition, Eliot served in two associations dealing with preventive medicine, becoming the vice president of one, the National Committee for Mental Hygiene, and the founding president of the other, the American Social Hygiene Committee. The latter was a pioneering organization committed to sex education and the treatment and elimination of venereal diseases. Charles W. Eliot died on 22 August 1926 at his summer home in Maine. He was ninety-two years old.

Sources:

Hugh Hawkins, *Between Harvard and America: The Educational Leadership of Charles W. Eliot* (New York: Oxford University Press, 1972);

Henry James, *Charles W. Eliot: President of Harvard University, 1869–1909* (Boston: Houghton Mifflin, 1930);

Edward A. Krug, *The Shaping of the American High School* (New York: Harper & Row, 1964);

Ralph Barton Perry, "Charles William Eliot," in *Dictionary of American Biography*, edited by Allen Johnson and Dumas Malone (New York: Scribners, 1931).

MARGARET A. HALEY

1861-1939

EDUCATOR, LABOR LEADER

The Chicago Teachers' Federation. Margaret A. Haley headed the most militant teachers' organization in the United States, the Chicago Teachers' Federation (CTF), in the early decades of the twentieth century. Becoming leader of the group in January 1900, she continued in that position until her death thirty-nine years later. As labor advocate and social reformer, Haley fought for the cause of public education in Chicago and battled mightily to improve working conditions and pay for Chicago's elementary-school teachers. Haley's autobiography, *Battleground* (1982), began with the words "I never wanted to fight"; but the slight but fiery "Maggie" never backed away from machine politicians, unscrupulous businessmen, inept school administrators, or anyone who sought to frustrate her efforts to improve schools for students and teachers.

Background. Haley was born in the town of Joliet, Illinois, on 15 November 1861 and spent her early childhood on a farm on the Illinois prairie. At sixteen, to help alleviate her family's financial troubles, Haley went to work as a teacher in a one-room country school. Finding she had a knack for teaching, she moved at age nineteen to Chicago and shortly thereafter began to teach in the urban Chicago public-school system. Securing a job as a sixth-grade teacher, Haley remained in that position until 1900, when, at thirty-eight, she became the business representative for the Chicago Teachers' Federation.

The Tax Fight. Haley's first battle as head of the Chicago Teachers' Federation was waged because of her concern about insufficient revenues for Chicago's public-school system. An agreement between the Chicago Board of Education and the CTF in 1898 promised to grant teachers pay raises in three yearly installments. The board paid the first on time but failed to pay the second and third installments on the agreed dates. Even worse, in late 1899 the board threatened to cancel the earlier raise and close Chicago schools for two weeks because of a lack of funds. Wondering why the city was in such financial straits, Haley discovered that many of Chicago's major corporations were evading city taxes. With proof in hand, Haley and the CTF took five major utility and street-railway companies to court. The corporations lost, and new tax reassessments brought roughly $600,000 in back taxes to the city. Annual revenues available to Chicago increased by $250,000. Haley's fight with corporate scofflaws eventually made more money available for schools and ensured higher salaries for Chicago public-school teachers.

Affiliation with Labor Union. Following the tax fight, Haley urged the Chicago Teachers' Federation to join the most powerful labor union in the city, the Chicago Federation of Labor (CFL). Many people in Chicago — including many in the CTF — opposed such a step. The CTF was a voluntary organization of elementary-school teachers, 97 percent of whom were female; the labor union represented men who were teamsters, carpenters, horseshoers, and other blue-collar workers. Knowing that many teachers were uneasy about joining the union, Haley reminded the women in her organization that they could not legally vote in elections and that in any future political battles they would suffer a decided disadvantage. In Haley's words, "We realized that we had to fight the devil with fire, and, if we were to preserve not only our self-respect but the basic independence of public schools, we must make powerful political alliances." After weeks of deliberation the CTF finally agreed with Haley and joined forces with the labor union on 8 November 1902, thereby uniting the women of the CTF with the two hundred thousand working men of the CFL, all of whom could legally vote. The CTF became the first large body of teachers to affiliate with labor; and, in turn, organized labor became a strong supporter of public education in Chicago.

New Political Battles. After her success in 1902, Haley struggled for the rest of the decade to develop a partnership with working people whose interests included the factory, the home, and the school. During this period the CTF's influence on the civic life of Chicago grew. According to Haley, writing in 1903, "the Federation itself is as much an accepted fact and as essential a part of the business of Chicago now as the Board of Trade, the City Hall, or even the Board of Education itself." In 1905 the CTF energetically campaigned for reform candidate Edward F. Dunne in the city's mayoral election; following Dunne's victory, Chicago's public-school students and teachers continued to make new gains. Under Chicago's charter Mayor Dunne could appoint seven new members to the twenty-one-member school board each year. In his first year three of the seven appointees were women — one of whom was Jane Addams, head of the world-renowned Hull House settlement. In the second year Dunne's appointees were a majority of the board, and these appointees implemented needed reforms in school governance. Although Dunne failed to gain reelection for a second term, Margaret Haley and the CTF remained a vibrant organization fighting for school reform through the rest of the decade. Haley then continued to lead the Chicago Teachers' Federation for thirty more years. In the mid 1930s, she began devoting most of her energy to writing her autobiography, which she hoped would inspire continued faith in the teachers' union movement. Margaret Haley died on 5 January 1939 at the age of seventy-seven.

Source:
Margaret A. Haley, *Battleground: The Autobiography of Margaret A. Haley*, edited by Robert L. Reid (Urbana: University of Illinois Press, 1982).

JOHN HOPE

1868-1936

TEACHER, COLLEGE PRESIDENT

Background. In June 1906 John Hope became the first African American president of Atlanta Baptist College (later renamed Morehouse College), a college for black men. A professor at the institution for eight years, Hope was highly regarded by the white trustees of the college; and as president, he helped build Atlanta Baptist College into one of the most respected black colleges in the United States.

Early Life. John Hope was born in Augusta, Georgia, on 2 June 1868. His father, James Hope, an immigrant from Scotland, had made a small fortune in Augusta as the owner of one of the South's first cotton mills. John's mother, Fanny, was legally black, although both her father and grandfather were white. John, as the son of Augusta's wealthiest and most distinguished white citizen, spent his early years in luxury and safety. Of this time in Augusta, he later wrote: "There was always a choice group, a choice few who defeated circumstances. Then there was the group of people who independent of particular merit on their part, but because of circumstances, their relationships to their masters, received additional money or additional education and were to that extent ahead." Hope belonged in the latter category the first eight years of his life.

Reversal. When John's father died in 1876, the family's financial security and peace suddenly disappeared. The executors of James Hope's will prevented Fanny, his black wife, from inheriting any of the estate and provided her with only a small annuity. As a result, John Hope became, as he later wrote, "only another colored boy," and he was now forced to become one of the "choice few who defeated circumstances." Fortunately, Augusta's black community, with which Hope's family now firmly identified, was one of the more successful of such communities in the South. Blacks in Augusta had established public and private elementary schools, opened a library, and created a literary society, and some blacks were able to send their children to college.

Opportunity. At eighteen, with a $100 gift from a stepbrother, Hope left Augusta to attend school in Worcester, Massachusetts. Even though he had fair skin and blue eyes, Hope insisted on being recognized as a black man by his new classmates. After graduating with honors from Worcester Academy, he enrolled at Brown University in Providence, Rhode Island, in 1890. Following graduation from Brown, Hope returned to his native South and taught for several years at Roger Williams University in Nashville, Tennessee. Then in 1898 the president of Atlanta Baptist College offered Hope a teaching position. Feeling a strong attachment to the Atlanta school — it had actually started as a black school in his hometown of Augusta — Hope accepted the offer, and he and his wife moved to Atlanta. In his first years at the school Hope taught classics, served as the school's bookkeeper, and coached the football team.

Founding. Atlanta Baptist College had been created in 1867 in Augusta by William Jefferson White, a white southerner with a mixed racial background. Before the Civil War White had fallen in love with a black slave in Augusta, Josephine Thomas. When her owner refused to sell her, White married Josephine and proceeded to live on her master's estate as a black man. Sympathetic to slaves, White violated Georgia state law by teaching African American children to read, continuing his teaching even as the Civil War raged around him. After the war White founded a school for blacks, the Augusta Institute. The school moved in 1879 to Atlanta, where it emphasized the training of ministers and became known as the Atlanta Baptist Seminary.

Atlanta Baptist College. The school prospered in Atlanta, enrollments swelled, and in 1897 the school became Atlanta Baptist College. Then in 1899 a contingent of black Baptists petitioned the school's financial backers, the American Baptist Home Missionary Society, to name one of the school's longtime professors, William E. Holmes — an African American — as the new president of the college. To this petition the New York–based missionary society, although a supporter of black schools throughout the South, was not receptive. Two of its representatives, Henry L. Morehouse and General T. J. Morgan, reportedly told Holmes, "Take the college and run it, and pay us a dollar a year." Not having the financial resources for such an undertaking, the humiliated Holmes was forced to withdraw his candidacy, and the presidency of the college continued to be held by a white Canadian, George Sale. After changes in the leadership of the missionary society, John Hope was appointed in 1906 as the first black president of Atlanta Baptist College.

First Crisis. Just months after taking office, Hope faced the first crisis of his presidency. On the evening of 22 September 1906 he and his wife, Lugenia, were startled by the simultaneous sounding of Atlanta's fire alarm, riot call, and militia call. These piercing wails signaled the beginning of the Atlanta Riot, one of the worst race riots in American history. Whipped to a frenzy by weeks of newspaper stories about alleged crimes by African Americans, and prepared, too, by a long history of demagoguery by white politicians, ten thousand white people marauded through the streets of Atlanta for three days, during which large numbers of black people were beaten and even killed. A local newspaper reported that "the sidewalks ran red with the blood of dead and dying negroes." On the first day, during the worst of the riot, President Hope and other professors of Atlanta Baptist College patrolled the grounds of the school, which was located just one mile west of Atlanta's downtown. The following day, as the riot spread southward, professors at other black colleges in Atlanta stood in armed guard at their campuses. While the exact number of deaths from the rioting remains uncertain, at least twenty-five blacks and one white were killed. Then, just one week after the riot, Atlanta Baptist College started the 1906–1907 school year, and many of its students stayed away in fear. Nevertheless, under Hope's firm leadership students gradually began returning to the campus, and within six months the school had enrolled more students than ever.

Intellectual and Civil Rights Leader. Despite its racial unrest, Atlanta was a hub of black intellectual life in the South during Hope's years there and included, besides Atlanta Baptist College, five other black colleges — Atlanta University, Spelman College, Morris Brown University, Clark College, and Gammon Theological Seminary. Hope thrived in this academic climate, where he found intellectual and ideological colleagues, especially in two men, George Towns and W. E. B. Du Bois, both professors at Atlanta University. The three of them agreed the accommodationist approach toward race relations that Booker T. Washington advocated had failed, and all three pressed for economic, political, and social equality for blacks . With passionate eloquence Hope had said in a speech in Nashville in 1896: "If we are not striving for equality, in heaven's name what are we striving for? . . . Yes, my friends, I want equality. Nothing less. I want all that my God-given powers will enable me to get, then why not equality? Now catch your breath, for I am going to use an adjective: I am going to say we demand social equality." During his years in Atlanta, Hope's friendship with the renowned Du Bois was particularly strong and deepened until Du Bois's departure from the city in 1910. Meanwhile, a year earlier, Hope, a lifelong civil rights activist, was the only college president to attend the protest meetings in New York City that led to the founding of the National Association for the Advancement of Colored People; he later became a member of the NAACP's advisory board. In addition, he was a member of the executive committee of the National Urban League and president of the Association for the Study of Negro Life and History, and he worked informally among the business community of Atlanta for improved black-white relations.

Morehouse and Beyond. When Atlanta Baptist College was renamed Morehouse College in 1913, Hope remained as president of the institution. During his tenure superb African American scholars were brought to the campus and student enrollment more than tripled. Then in 1929, twenty-three years after becoming a college president, Hope accepted the presidency of Atlanta University. At this school, which devoted itself to graduate studies, he developed a partnership between Atlanta University and the undergraduate campuses of Morehouse and Spelman. Later, this partnership expanded to include all the city's black colleges. At the same time, Hope attracted a large number of intellectuals to Atlanta University, and the institution received great acclaim for its educational efforts on behalf of blacks. John Hope died of pneumonia on 19 February 1936 at the age of sixty-seven.

Sources:

David Levering Lewis, *W. E. B. Du Bois: Biography of a Race* (New York: Holt, 1993);

Ridgely Torrence, *The Story of John Hope* (New York: Macmillan, 1948).

JULIA RICHMAN

1855-1912

EDUCATIONAL REFORMER, PRINCIPAL, SCHOOL SUPERINTENDENT

Educator of Immigrants. Julia Richman spent her adult life in the New York City school system, working to educate the children of immigrants. As teacher, principal, then school superintendent, Richman developed innovative curricula and programs to teach turn-of-the-century American cultural values to the new immigrants arriving in record numbers. In her 1905 address to the National Education Association (NEA), the nation's leading educational association, Richman stated the philosophy behind her mission to educate immigrant children:

> Ours is a nation of immigrants. The citizen voter of today was yesterday an immigrant child. Tomorrow he may be a political leader. Between the alien of today and the citizen of tomorrow stands the school, and upon the influence exerted by the school depends the kind of citizen the immigrant child will become.

Early Life. Julia Richman was born in New York City in 1855 to Moses and Theresa Melis Richman, Jewish immigrants from Bohemia, in eastern Europe. Her father was a glazier who successfully made the transition from his homeland to the United States. Julia attended public schools in New York and completed her formal education in 1872, graduating from the Female Normal School (later renamed Hunter College of the City University of New York). While still quite young, Julia decided to follow a course different from her siblings and most of her middle-class friends. She wanted to become a teacher of Jewish immigrants from eastern Europe — especially the immigrant children. When only ten years old, she told a friend she eventually expected "all New York to know my name," an expectation later fulfilled. Fresh out of college, she became an elementary schoolteacher. In 1884 she became principal of an elementary school, and in 1889 she was promoted to district superintendent of schools for the Lower East Side of Manhattan, a district in the heart of the European Jewish immigrant community, where she remained the rest of her career.

School Administrator. Julia Richman was many things, but above all she was an innovator. As both principal and superintendent, she initiated new ways of teaching that reflected the special circumstances of immigrant children. One of her innovations was to allow continuous promotion. Under this plan, a student could move up to the next grade level any time during the school year. She argued this procedure kept good students from becoming bored and allowed those held back solely by language barriers to advance quickly once the barriers were overcome. A second innovation was to divide children, based upon teachers' recommendations and classroom tests, into "the brightest material," "medium material," and "the poorest material." Richman then assigned the best teachers to the slowest classes and ordered all teachers to develop lessons appropriate to the capabilities of their students. In a third innovation, she urged schools to classify children based on the students' ability to speak and understand English, thus eliminating age- or academic-ability grading for immigrants. She also created special bilingual classes that provided the advanced student continued academic growth while learning the English language and was one of the first educators to advocate and implement vocational classes for immigrant children. Her goal in all these innovations was to keep children in school longer. To help immigrant parents understand the importance of education and keep them from withdrawing their children at an early age, she created an organization for parents. Further, Richman pushed the school board to create schools for truants and "incorrigible" boys in an attempt to prevent early dropouts. By her argument there were no bad boys, only bad schools, an attitude reflecting the belief of many reformers in the Progressive Era that behavior was shaped largely by environment and education.

Private-Sector Ventures. Richman labored to educate immigrants outside the public schools as well, as a leader of the Young Ladies' Charitable Union (later called the Young Women's Hebrew Association) and a key board member of the Educational Alliance, a settlement house that functioned as both a community center and an educational facility for New York City's immigrant Jews. "English-to-Foreigner" classes at this settlement house were supplemented by similar classes in the public schools. In 1904 the Educational Alliance provided a forum for Jewish parents who were incensed by New York City's board of education. The board had proposed shifting fifteen hundred children from predominantly Jewish schools on the Lower East Side to West Side schools that were less crowded but located in a non-Jewish neighborhood. Two thousand irate parents protested the move and expressed their fears about the long, crosstown trip and the dangers for their children in a hostile, non-Jewish community.

National Fame. Richman became nationally recognized as an expert on the Americanization of immigrants. Urban school leaders faced with educating large numbers of new immigrants consulted her to learn how best to conduct educational programs to "assimilate" the children to American life. Despite her national fame, however, Richman did have critics, who charged that her emphasis on the immigrant child's acquiring American culture encouraged the child to neglect his or her own cultural heritage. Jane Addams and her colleagues at Hull House, for example, offered a contrasting approach to immigrant education. They believed immigrant children brought cultural strengths as well as weaknesses, and ethnic holidays and customs were frequently observed at their settlement. Still, the fact that Richman's ideas stirred some controversy was, for most people, greatly overshadowed by her extraordinary educational contributions; and within the Jewish community Richman had tremendous support for her work in the public schools and her educational activities outside the schools. She also co-authored a book about teaching Jewish ethics and helped edit a weekly magazine for Sabbath schools. Julia Richman died unexpectedly, from complications brought on by appendicitis, at the age of fifty-seven.

Sources:

Selma Cantor Berrol, *Julia Richman: A Notable Woman* (Philadelphia: Balch Institute Press, 1993);

David Tyack, *The One Best System: A History of Urban Education* (Cambridge, Mass.: Harvard University Press, 1974).

M. CAREY THOMAS

1857-1935

COLLEGE PRESIDENT, FEMINIST EDUCATOR

Female Scholar. The life and career of M. Carey Thomas highlighted both the educational limitations and possibilities that women faced at the beginning of the twentieth century. Most Americans at that time felt that educating a young woman beyond elementary school was unnecessary, perhaps even harmful. Her future life as mother and wife required only the most rudimentary level of literacy, according to the opponents of female education. Consequently, high-school attendance for girls was rare, and college opportunities for women were virtually nonexistent. Women who succeeded in going to college had few career options upon graduation and were frequently scorned and belittled by society. Thomas heroically rose above these circumstances and became a scholar of the first rank. Eventually, she also became president of Bryn Mawr, a women's college outside of Philadelphia; at Bryn Mawr she fashioned an institution of high academic standing that offered rigorous undergraduate and graduate study for women.

Background. Martha Carey Thomas was born on 2 January 1857 in Baltimore, Maryland. From an early age her mother and aunt encouraged her educational ambitions and fostered a love of reading. While attending Howland Institute in Utica, New York, as a teenager, Thomas concluded that she wanted to lead the life of a scholar. "I will devote my life to study," she wrote, "and will try to work some good from it." She yearned to enroll in coeducational Cornell University, but her father forbade her, believing that additional schooling would make her unfit for a life as wife and mother. Young "Minnie," as she was known by her family, insisted. She won her mother's support; her father eventually relented; and she enrolled in Cornell in 1875. After receiving her diploma in 1877, Thomas decided to enter graduate school. She was admitted to Johns Hopkins University but was told that, as a female, she could not attend classes. Unable to cope with such restrictions, Carey Thomas, as she now called herself, moved to Europe and received her Ph.D. from the University of Zurich. Returning to the United States at age twenty-six, she applied for the position of president at a planned, but not yet opened, college for women — Bryn Mawr. Her father and three relatives were on the future school's board of trustees, but instead of the presidency, they appointed her dean of faculty and professor of English, judging her too inexperienced for the top position.

Bryn Mawr. Although Thomas did not become its first president, she greatly influenced the development of the school. A contemporary observed that Thomas "practically created Bryn Mawr College." Her main concern from the beginning was to set high, exacting standards. Women at Bryn Mawr would undertake the same course of study as that found at the best men's colleges. Entrance requirements were high. The cornerstone of Thomas's efforts at Bryn Mawr was the creation of a graduate school, a feature not present at any women's college at the time. In 1894 Bryn Mawr's president, James E. Rhoads, announced his resignation. Thomas's longtime companion, Mary Garret, offered the school $10,000 per year if the trustees named Thomas the next president of the school. After much deliberation the trustees accepted the offer and selected Carey Thomas president of Bryn Mawr by a vote of 7–5.

Women and Advanced Education. During her entire career Thomas fought to dispel doubts about women's intellectual capacity and to remove societal barriers to the college-educated woman. In the years from 1898 to 1906, M. Carey Thomas became nationally recognized as the leading spokeswoman for women's higher education. In 1899 she publicly disagreed with Harvard's formidable president, Charles W. Eliot, who had long advocated a distinct curriculum for women that emphasized acquiring "manners." Eliot believed that the world of knowledge existed only for men. Thomas thought this nonsense, and her public remarks to this effect received national newspaper coverage. She firmly believed that women should not take separate courses, such as domestic science or psychology, to prepare for special female roles in life. In 1900 Thomas published her only book, *Education of Women*, in which she noted that the United States had a "larger body of educated women than is to be found in any other country in the world. . . . The higher education of women has assumed the proportions of a national movement still in progress." This book cemented her reputation and presented her views to a worldwide audience.

Elitism and Bigotry. While Thomas became a forceful advocate for women's education, she also had detractors who pointed out her flaws as an educational leader. The deepest flaw was that her college was not for all women. Carey Thomas was an unabashed elitist for her entire life. When she championed the need for education for women, she was thinking of women like herself — privileged, white, and Protestant. Others did not belong at Bryn Mawr, even when their talent was obvious. One exceedingly qualified African American woman, Jessie Redmon Fauset, applied for admission in 1901. Thomas turned down her application and diverted her to Cornell without fanfare. Fauset went on to become one of the leading figures of the Harlem Renaissance. Other potential minority candidates were similarly dissuaded from applying. In 1906 Thomas wrote that she would advise all African Americans to apply "to a college situated in one of the New England states," because they would not be welcome at Bryn Mawr, with its large number of white students from southern and mid-Atlantic states. Thomas was also willing to act deceitfully and clandestinely in order to achieve her ends. In her mind, the ends justified the means, because her goal was always the good of the college. As a result of these flaws, opposition to Thomas began to surface at Bryn Mawr during the decade 1900–1909.

Women's Rights Activist. M. Carey Thomas supported women's rights in areas beyond education. During her first years as president of Bryn Mawr, Thomas hesitated to speak out because she feared offending potential donors to the college or the parents of potential students. In 1906, however, she publicly committed to the cause of women's suffrage when she hosted a benefit at Bryn Mawr for the longtime suffragette Susan B. Anthony. Unlike many of her contemporaries, Thomas did not possess a romantic view of family life and of a woman's role in it. Indeed, she viewed most men with disdain, seeing them as exploiters of women who used the law to further their ends at the expense of women. Gaining the right to vote would allow women to change their condition for the better, according to Thomas. In 1913 Thomas identified herself with *feminism*, a new word that denoted not just legal rights for women but full equality of opportunity. From her public pronouncements and actions in the years from 1906 on, she would be forever known as a feminist. In 1922 Thomas retired from the presidency of Bryn Mawr, and most of her later years were spent traveling overseas. She continued, however, to speak out for feminist causes and women's education. In 1925 she made news again by announcing her support of the Equal Rights Amendment. M. Carey Thomas died in Philadelphia on 2 December 1935 at the age of seventy-eight.

Sources:

Helen Lefkowitz Horowitz, *The Power and Passion of M. Carey Thomas* (New York: Knopf, 1994);

Theodora Penny Martin, "Martha Carey Thomas," in *Women Educators in the United States, 1820–1993*, edited by Maxine Schwartz Seller (Westport, Conn.: Greenwood Press, 1994).

EDWARD LEE THORNDIKE

1874-1949

EDUCATIONAL PSYCHOLOGIST

Scientist of Education. Edward Thorndike influenced the development of American public schooling in the first half of the twentieth century as much as any other individual. During the five decades of his active career, he applied scientific theories and techniques to a wide range of educational problems. Thorndike praised scientific policy making, calling it "the only sure foundation for social progress." In education he focused his science methodology on such diverse issues as learning theory, testing, and school efficiency. He was also a writer of enormous output. During his lifetime Thorndike wrote seventy-eight books and published more than four hundred articles. As a result of his efforts, and the efforts of others taking a similar "scientific" approach, public-school administrators and teachers began applying Thorndike's vision of science in their schools. This new vision was exhibited most dramatically in new attempts to see students as objects to be measured and quantified.

Educational Background. Born on 31 August 1874 in Williamsburg, Massachusetts, Thorndike moved frequently as a child, the son of a Methodist minister who regularly changed pastorates. Young Edward attended elementary and secondary schools in New England before matriculating at Wesleyan University, where he received a bachelor of arts degree. After studying for two years with William James at Harvard, Thorndike received his Ph.D. from Columbia in 1898 at age twenty-three. His dissertation, *Animal Intelligence: An Experimental Study of the Associative Processes in Animals*, was immediately considered a landmark study, and Thorndike's career was launched. He taught for a year at Western Reserve University in Cleveland before moving back to New York to take a position at Teachers' College, Columbia. His work there was so highly acclaimed that Thorndike became a tenured professor of educational psychology before reaching the age of thirty.

Stimulus-Response Theory. As a graduate student at Harvard, Thorndike began the studies of animal learning that led to his theory of connectionism. At the time, his experiments were so controversial that he was refused space on Harvard's campus and had to conduct the experiments in the basement of William James's home in Cambridge. Thorndike's experiments consisted of putting an animal in a "problem box" and then rewarding the animal with a small piece of food if it pressed a lever and escaped. With repetition, the amount of time it took the animal to perform the required task declined. Thorndike called this process learning. Simply stated, Thorndike's theory of learning holds that the application of a given stimulus (S) elicits a response (R). The bond between S and R is "stamped in" by the giving of rewards. Learning, in other words, is enhanced by both repetition and reward.

Application to Education. Thorndike's work had immediate applications to education. Under his model of learning, the basic teaching method required continuous activity. Student learning occurs, he argued, when students respond correctly to a stimulus and are then rewarded. As he wrote in his dissertation: "The best way with children may often be, in the pompous words of an animal trainer, 'to arrange everything in connection with the trick so that the animal will be compelled by the laws of his own nature to perform it.'" A second important aspect of his theory is the notion that teaching precisely what is to be learned is critically important. Furthermore, according to Thorndike's experiments, transfer of learning from one subject matter to another does not take place. This latter idea turned traditional theories of education upside down: older learning theory emphasized the value of learning certain subjects, primarily Latin and Greek, not so much for their own content but because they trained the "faculties of the mind." Critics of the classical curriculum, heartened by Thorndike's work, vigorously renewed their assaults on schools that continued to use the traditional curriculum.

Testing. From the earliest days of his career Thorndike was concerned with mental measurement. In 1901 he offered his services to a school in New York to test and record every pupil on general mental development; in the same year, Thorndike began teaching the nation's first course in educational measurement. In 1904 the publication of his book *Introduction to the Theory of Mental and Social Measurements* made him a leader in the test-and-measurement movement. Needless to say, Thorndike had a nearly boundless faith in the value of quantifying and measuring. He told students at Columbia University in 1921 that the "knowledge of educational products and educational purposes must become quantitative, taking the forms of measurement." The phrase "All that exists, exists in some amount and can be measured" is usually credited to Thorndike. There is some doubt as to whether he actually uttered these words, but whether he did or not, they accurately convey his conviction. In 1909 Thorndike created a rating scale for handwriting, and tests measuring reading comprehension, geography, composition, arithmetic, spelling, and reasoning followed. In his many years of work he developed some of the most widely used tests of aptitude and achievement, and generations of American students took tests that bore his name.

Five-Decade Career. At the close of the first decade of the twentieth century Thorndike was still a relatively young man, one who remained a powerful force in educational circles until his retirement thirty years later. His additional contributions to American education were numerous. With George D. Strayer, he created and shaped the movement to survey and measure school systems during the 1910s and 1920s. He published numerous textbooks used by classroom teachers, and his *Thorndike-Century Junior Dictionary* (1935) became a staple of American classrooms. His laws of learning influenced others to the extent that nearly all aspects of school life, from assessment to course content, were affected by his work. His experiments in adult learning greatly changed the field of adult education when he showed that the ability to learn declined very little with age. Somehow, he also found time to be active in many professional education organizations. Edward Thorndike retired from Teachers' College in 1940 and died of a cerebral hemorrhage on 9 August 1949 at the age of seventy-four.

Sources:

Lawrence A. Cremin, *The Transformation of the School: Progressivism in American Education, 1876-1957* (New York: Vintage, 1964);

Geraldine Jonich, *The Sane Positivist: A Biography of Edward L. Thorndike* (Middletown, Conn.: Wesleyan University Press, 1968);

Clarence J. Karier, *Scientists of the Mind: Intellectual Founders of Modern Psychology* (Urbana: University of Illinois Press, 1986).

PEOPLE IN THE NEWS

From 1905 to 1909 the world-famous leader of the settlement house movement, **Jane Addams**, served as a member of the Chicago Board of Education. Appointed by a reform mayor, Addams was nevertheless unsuccessful in her efforts to change the type of curriculum offered to students in the public schools or the pedagogical practices of the schools' teachers.

In 1904 **Edwin A. Alderman,** after serving as president of the University of North Carolina and Tulane University, started his twenty-seven-year tenure as president of the University of Virginia. As university president, Alderman pushed for educational reform in the elementary and secondary schools of the South.

In 1907 **William C. Bagley** published his popular textbook *Classroom Management,* in which he argued that teachers should run classrooms like a business enterprise. The book went through more than thirty printings during the next two decades and helped define how educators and the public thought of schools and teaching.

In 1906 **George Pierce Baker** originated the prototype for theater-arts programs in American universities when he taught a playwriting class, informally known as "47 Workshop," at Harvard University. Students wrote, produced, and acted their own plays. T. S. Eliot (class of 1909) and Eugene O'Neill (special student 1914–1915) were the most famous course graduates.

Harriet M. Bedell first taught at a Cheyenne mission school in Oklahoma in 1907 and devoted the remainder of her life to the education of Native Americans. Following standard policy of the day, Bedell utilized an academic and industrial curriculum that attempted to suppress Cheyenne culture and encouraged youths to adopt European-centered culture. Eventually she moderated her views, but Bedell always remained convinced that adaptation to the prevailing culture was essential for Native American success.

In October 1904 **Mary McLeod Bethune** founded the Daytona Literary and Industrial Institute for the Training of Negro Girls (later named Bethune-Cookman College) in Florida. Bethune taught the young girls who attended her school basic reading, writing, and arithmetic. She also prepared her students to earn a living in the segregated South, and she stressed the importance of service to the community.

In 1907 **Sophonisba Breckinridge** became director of the Chicago School of Civics and Philanthropy. Supported by a grant from the newly created Russell Sage Foundation, she proceeded to expand the school's Department of Social Investigations. Breckinridge and her colleagues and students conducted investigations of the social problems facing residents living on Chicago's West Side. Their work helped make Chicago a center for research and teaching about social problems.

In 1901 **Nicholas Murray Butler** started his forty-four-year tenure as president of Columbia University. Earlier in his career Butler was instrumental in founding Teachers' College at Columbia University, for many decades the most influential school of education in the country. A leader in educational reform, Butler helped create the College Entrance Examination Board in 1900, and in 1906 he worked for the creation of the

National Society for the Promotion of Industrial Education.

In 1902 **Fanny Jackson Coppin** ended her thirty-three-year career as principal of Philadelphia's prestigious Institute for Colored Youth (ICY). Born into slavery in 1837, Coppin graduated from Oberlin College in 1865. While still a student at Oberlin, Coppin began her work in education: four nights a week she taught the freed people that sought refuge in the city during the Civil War. Upon graduation she continued working toward her most important goals: "to get an education and to teach my people." Coppin moved to Philadelphia and started teaching at ICY, becoming head of the coeducational secondary school in 1869.

In April 1904 education theorist and philosopher **John Dewey** resigned his position at the University of Chicago. Dewey had been engaged in a series of disputes with the university's president, William Rainey Harper, following the merger of Dewey's Laboratory School with the Francis W. Parker School in 1903. Within a month of his resignation, Dewey was offered a professorship at Columbia by its president, Nicholas Murray Butler. Dewey remained at Columbia until his retirement in 1930.

In 1906 **William Torrey Harris** retired from the post of U.S. Commissioner of Education, which he had held since 1889. An educational philosopher as well as a school administrator, Harris insisted that men and women of all social classes were educable and could aid in the creation of a humane and civilized culture. The *Annual Reports* published under his name as commissioner were widely respected both in the United States and abroad.

In 1905 **Winifred Holt** established one of the first educational programs for blind adults. She and two siblings started Lighthouse, the New York Association for the Blind. The organization sought to educate the blind to the fact that they could lead rewarding, self-sufficient lives; it also sought to educate the seeing public about the capabilities of the blind and about blindness prevention. Holt urged policies of inclusion for blind students, but by 1910 only a fraction of the country's blind students were taught in public-school classes.

In 1907 **Marietta Pierce Johnson** started the Organic School in Fairhope, Alabama. A private school that emphasized spontancity and a child-centered curriculum, the Organic School became nationally known as the embodiment of progressive education principles.

In 1904 *Little Citizens*, the first book of former New York City schoolteacher **Myra Kelly**, was published. Kelly's collection of short stories vividly described the classroom experiences of a schoolteacher in Manhattan's Lower East Side, a part of the city teeming with immigrant children. The stories were extremely popular with the American public, and during the next eight years seven other books of Kelly's were published.

"The schoolmaster of American agriculture," **Seaman A. Knapp**, advocated scientific farming as an answer to rural economic distress. He discovered that farmers would adopt scientific methods if one of their neighbors successfully demonstrated the techniques. The U.S. Department of Agriculture adopted his method in 1903, and the idea of scientific demonstrations for agriculture enjoyed enormous success throughout the country.

In 1902 **Walter Hines Page** published a book of essays, *The Rebuilding of Old Commonwealth*, in which he called on southerners to initiate education reform in order to eliminate the region's social and economic problems and to uplift "the forgotten man." He paved the way for subsequent public-school reform efforts in the region.

Francis Wayland Parker died on 2 March 1902, ending his memorable nineteen-year career as director of the Cook County Normal School in Chicago. Parker's innovative instructional and curricular programs illustrated his belief that "the child is the center of all education." His friend John Dewey called him the "Father of Progressive Education."

Lucy Sprague became dean of women at the University of California in 1903. Shocked that some male faculty members viewed women as "inferior beings," Sprague changed the culture of the university in four important ways: she brought women students closer together; she encouraged women to use their moral influence to set standards for campus life; she enhanced women's educational experiences; and she apprised women students of careers outside of teaching.

In 1904 **Richard Welling** organized the National Self-Government Committee and started a national campaign to encourage student governments in the schools. Welling argued that the applied civics lessons learned by students in school would lead to the elimination of corrupt government. School officials agreed, and schools instituted student governments at a phenomenal rate. School administrators, however, never gave students any real power over school life; instead, students learned only the procedural methods of democracy.

In 1909 **Ella Flagg Young** became the first woman superintendent of an urban school system when she was promoted to that position by the Chicago School Board. A longtime Chicago school administrator and strong advocate for teachers and advisory teachers' councils, Young remained in office for six years.

DEATHS

Herbert Baxter Adams, 51, historian, professor of history at Johns Hopkins University, 30 July 1901.

Susan B. Anthony, 86, a leader in the women's suffrage movement; also fought to secure women's rights in education, 13 March 1906.

Henry Barnard, 89, one of the most distinguished educators of the nineteenth century; a nationwide leader in the common-school movement, university president, and first U.S. Commissioner of Education, 21 July 1900.

Ebenezer Don Carlos Bassett, 74, educator and diplomat; former principal of the Institute for Colored Youth in Philadelphia; renowned for being the nation's first African American diplomat, 1908.

Francis L. Cardozo, 66, clergyman, educator, and politician; former school principal; professor of Latin at Howard University; served as both secretary of state and state treasurer in South Carolina's Reconstruction government, 22 July 1903.

Jonas G. Clark, 85, who founded and endowed Clark University in Worcester, Massachusetts, 23 May 1900.

William Hooper Councill, 59, educator; first head of Alabama's State Normal and Industrial School, later renamed the Alabama State Agricultural and Mechanical College for Negroes when, through Councill's efforts, it became a land-grant college, 17 April 1909.

William Howard Day, 75, abolitionist, newspaper editor, educator, former inspector-general for Freedmen's Bureau schools in Maryland and Delaware, 3 December 1900.

Sarah Ann Dickey, 65, teacher, founder and leader of the Mount Hermon Female Seminary, a school for African American women in Clinton, Mississippi, 23 January 1904.

Edward Eggleston, 64, educator, novelist, author of the popular novel of rural schooling *The Hoosier Schoolmaster*, 3 September 1902.

Josiah Willard Gibbs, 64, scientist, professor of mathematics at Yale, 28 April 1903.

Daniel Coit Gilman, 77, first president of Johns Hopkins University, under whose leadership the university became the model for the modern American research university, 13 October 1908.

William Torrey Harris, 74, educator, philosopher, former U.S. Commissioner of Education; known for his innovations in public schools, 5 November 1909.

Frank A. Hill, 61, former secretary of the Massachusetts Board of Education, 12 September 1903.

Christopher Columbus Langdell, 80, legal educator; at Harvard University he originated the case-study method for teaching law, 6 July 1906.

Charles D. McIver, 45, southern school reformer, college president, member of the Southern Education Board, 17 September 1906.

Alice Freeman Palmer, 47, educator, college president, prominent leader in higher education, former president of Wellesley College, and first dean of women at the University of Chicago, 6 December 1902.

Caroline Elizabeth Bushyhead Quarles, 74, Cherokee teacher who helped develop the Cherokee nation's educational system, 23 February 1909.

At his death on 26 March 1902, British-born Cecil John Rhodes, who made a fortune in the diamond fields of southern Africa, bequeathed part of his wealth to an endowment establishing the Rhodes Scholarships for study at Oxford University.

John D. Runkle, 79, professor, president of the Massachusetts Institute of Technology; popularized the Russian idea of industrial training in the United States, 8 July 1902.

Russell Sage, 90, financier, congressman, educational philanthropist, 22 July 1906.

Herbert Spencer, 83, English philosopher; greatly influenced American educational theory and practice by his endorsement of social Darwinism and his affirmation that science was the knowledge of greatest value, 8 December 1903.

David Augustus Straker, 65, politician, educator, lawyer, former dean and professor of law at Allen University in Columbia, South Carolina, 14 February 1908.

Emerson Elbridge White, 73, school superintendent, college president, 21 October 1902.

Marie E. Zakrzewska, 72, founder and president of the New England Hospital for Women and Children, one of the first institutions where female physicians and nurses could obtain clinical training, 12 May 1902.

PUBLICATIONS

Herbert Baxter Adams, *The Church and Popular Education* (Baltimore: Johns Hopkins University Press, 1900);

Jane Addams, *Democracy and Social Ethics* (New York: Macmillan, 1902);

Addams, *The Spirit of Youth and the City Streets* (New York: Macmillan, 1909);

Leonard P. Ayres, *Laggards in Our Schools: A Study of Retardation and Elimination in City School Systems* (New York: Russell Sage Foundation, 1909);

William C. Bagley, *Classroom Management: Its Principles and Techniques* (New York: Macmillan, 1907);

Bagley, *The Educative Process* (New York: Macmillan, 1906);

Edwin C. Broome, *A Historical and Critical Discussion of College Admission Requirements* (New York: Macmillan, 1903);

John Franklin Brown, *The American High School* (New York: Macmillan, 1909);

Sara A. Burstall, *Impressions of American Education in 1908* (London: Longmans, Green, 1909);

Nicholas Murray Butler, *The Meaning of Education* (New York: Macmillan, 1905);

Frank Tracy Carlton, *Economic Influences Upon Educational Progress in the United States* (Madison: University of Wisconsin Press, 1908);

Ellwood Patterson Cubberley, *Changing Conceptions of Education* (Boston: Houghton Mifflin, 1909);

Charles De Garmo, *Principles of Secondary Education* (New York: Macmillan, 1907);

John Dewey, *The Child and the Curriculum* (Chicago: University of Chicago Press, 1902);

Dewey, *How We Think* (Boston: D. C. Heath, 1909);

Dewey, *Moral Principles of Education* (Boston: Houghton Mifflin, 1909);

Edwin Grant Dexter, *A History of Education in the United States* (New York: Macmillan, 1904);

Andrew Sloan Draper, *American Education* (Boston: Houghton Mifflin, 1909);

W. E. B. Du Bois, *The Souls of Black Folk* (Chicago: McClurg, 1903);

Lida Belle Earhart, *Teaching Children to Study* (Boston: Houghton Mifflin, 1909);

Daniel Coit Gilman, *The Launching of a University* (New York: Dodd, Mead, 1906);

G. Stanley Hall, *Adolescence: Its Psychology and Its Relations to Physiology, Anthropology, Sociology, Sex, Crime, Religion, and Education* (New York: Appleton, 1904);

Hall, *Aspects of Child Life and Education* (Boston: Ginn, 1907);

James Parton Haney, *Art Education in the Public Schools of the United States* (New York: American Art Annual, 1908);

Paul Hanus, *Educational Aims and Educational Values* (New York: Macmillan, 1900);

Myra Kelly, *Little Citizens: The Humours of School Life* (New York: McClure, Phillips, 1904);

Kelly, *Wards of Liberty* (New York: McClure, 1907);

Sara R. O'Brien, *English for Foreigners* (Boston: Houghton Mifflin, 1909);

Walter Hines Page, *The Rebuilding of Old Commonwealth* (New York: Doubleday, Page, 1902);

George Herbert Palmer and Alice Freeman Palmer, *The Teacher: Essays and Address on Education* (Boston: Houghton Mifflin, 1908);

Ellen H. Richards and Alpheus G. Woodman, *Air, Water, and Food for Colleges* (New York: John Wiley, 1900);

Julia Richman and Isabel Richman Wallach, *Good Citizenship* (New York: American Book Company, 1908);

David Snedden, *Administration and Educational Work of American Juvenile Reform Schools* (New York: Faculty of Philosophy, Columbia University, 1907);

M. Carey Thomas, *Education of Women*, Monographs on Education in the United States, edited by Nicholas Murray Butler (Albany, N.Y.: J. B. Lyon, 1900);

Edward L. Thorndike, *The Elements of Psychology* (New York: A. G. Seiler, 1905);

Thorndike, *An Introduction to the Theory of Mental and Social Measurements* (New York: Science Press, 1904);

Thorndike, *The Principles of Teaching* (New York: A. G. Seiler, 1906);

Isabel Richman Wallach, *A First Book in English for Foreigners: Designed Especially for Foreigners* (New York: Silver, Burdett, 1906);

Lester Frank Ward, *Applied Sociology* (New York: Ginn, 1906);

Booker T. Washington, *Up From Slavery* (New York: Doubleday, Page, 1901);

Washington and others, *The Negro Problem* (New York: James Pott, 1903);

Owen Wister, *Philosophy Four, A Story of Harvard University* (Philadelphia: Lippincott, 1901);

Ella Flagg Young, *Ethics in the School* (Chicago: University of Chicago Press, 1902);

American Journal of Education, periodical;

Catholic School Journal, periodical;

Child Study Monthly, periodical;

Educational Foundations, periodical;

Educational Review, periodical;

Journal of Education, periodical;

Kindergarten Magazine, periodical;

Normal Instructor, periodical;

Pedagogical Seminary, periodical;

Popular Educator, periodical;

School, periodical;

School Review, periodical;

Southern Educational Review, periodical;

Teachers' College Record, periodical;

Teachers' Magazine, periodical.

FASHION

by JANE GERHARD

CONTENTS

Sidebars and tables are listed in italics.

1900

- The S-curve silhouette is the dominant look in women's fashion.

- Rollin H. White of the White Sewing Machine Company of Cleveland, Ohio, begins marketing a steam-engine automobile, which he calls "The Incomparable White." Stately and powerful, the White becomes the first official presidential car when it is adopted by the William Howard Taft administration.

- The Franklin, Peerless, Stearns, Packard, and Auburn gasoline-powered automobiles are introduced.

- Woods Electrical Car, with enclosed passenger compartment and elevated seat for a footman, sells for $3,000.

- Finnish architect Eliel Saarinen shows the European influence of Louis Sullivan in his designs for the Finnish Pavilion at the Paris Exposition.

3–10 Nov. The first U.S. automobile show, featuring a wide array of steam-, electric-, and gasoline-powered models, opens in Madison Square Garden in New York City.

1901

- A *New York Times* want ad for a dressmaker offers $2.50 per day. An advertisement for women's shirtwaist suits carries prices of $2.25 to $4.50.

- Architects Charles and Henry Greene build one of their first bungalows in Pasadena, California, for David B. Gamble.

- Architect Frank Lloyd Wright delivers his influential lecture "The Art and Craft of the Machine" at Chicago's Hull House.

- Architect Horace Trumbauer completes The Elms, the Newport, Rhode Island, mansion of Philadelphia coal magnate Edward Julius Berwind that is modeled on a French chateau.

- The architectural firm of Babb, Cook, and Willard completes the neo-Georgian mansion of steel magnate Andrew Carnegie on New York City's Fifth Avenue at Ninety-second Street.

- Francis E. and Freelan O. Stanley, forty-seven-year-old identical twins, return to the steam-car business after selling their original designs for a quarter of a million dollars in 1899.

- Ransom E. Olds introduces the Oldsmobile Curved Dash Runabout.

- The Apperson motorcar and the Pierce Motorette are introduced.

22 Jan. Britain's Queen Victoria dies and is succeeded by her son, Edward VII, inaugurating the Edwardian Age in fashion.

Late Oct.–
early Nov. Ransom Olds has Roy Chapin drive his Curved Dash Runabout 820 miles to New York, an unheard-of distance. It takes Chapin seven and a half days and generates fame for the Olds Motor Works.

1902

- The twenty-story, steel-frame Fuller Building, nicknamed the "Flatiron Building" because of its shape, is completed in New York City by Chicago architect Daniel H. Burnham.

- New York architect Stanford White completes Rosecliff, the Newport, Rhode Island, mansion of Mrs. Hermann Oelrichs.

- The architectural firm of Carrère and Hastings completes Whitehall, the seventy-three-room, $2.5 million Spanish-inspired Palm Beach, Florida, mansion of Florida East Coast Railway magnate Henry M. Flagler.

- The Stanley brothers switch their Locomobile from steam to gasoline.

- Ernest Coxhead completes the Wayburn House in San Francisco.

- The Studebaker electric car and the Marmon and Overland gasoline-powered cars are introduced.

4 Mar.   The American Automobile Association is formed to give a national voice to the growing number of local auto clubs. By the end of the decade AAA will have twenty-five thousand members in more than thirty states.

1903

- American women swim in black sleeveless dresses and long, full-length leggings. Men swim in tank tops and knee-length shorts.

- An advertisement in the Columbia, S.C., *State* newspaper offers a "sack business suit; worn by most business men of your acquaintance" for $8.50.

- The Olds Motor Works turns out 4,000 Curved Dash Runabouts, up from 450 in 1901, and shows a profit of $600,000.

- Frank Lloyd Wright modernizes Chicago's Rookery.

- Ninety-three percent of America's 2.3 million miles of roads are little better than plain dirt paths.

- Louis Sullivan completes the Holy Trinity Cathedral in Chicago.

- The Greene brothers build their most famous bungalow, the Bandini bungalow, in Pasadena, California.

- Furniture designer Charles Renne Mackintosh builds a modern, geometric high-back chair that marks a radical break from the historical tastes of the Victorians.

- The Chadwick gasoline-powered car is introduced by engineer Lee Sherman Chadwick; it can reach a speed of sixty miles per hour and sells for $4,000.

- The sixteen-story Ingalls Building, the first skyscraper with a reinforced-concrete skeleton, is completed in Cincinnati. It will be renamed the Transit Building in 1959.

- The Model A Ford is introduced.

Jan.   Henry Martyn Leland unveils the first Cadillac.

23 May   Dr. Horatio Nelson Jackson and mechanic Sewall K. Crocker leave San Francisco in a twenty-horsepower Winton Touring Car; they arrive in New York sixty-four days later, having completed the first coast-to-coast automobile trip. On his return home Jackson is fined for exceeding a six-mile-an-hour speed limit. Within a few weeks a Packard and an Oldsmobile make the same trip.

1904

1 Sept.   Massachusetts issues the first automobile license plate.

- Ford sells fourteen hundred Model A's, calling the car "positively the most perfect machine on the market."

- Millionaire sportsman William Vanderbilt inaugurates the Vanderbilt Cup, a four-hour automobile race on the back roads of Long Island. The race is run every year until 1910, sometimes attracting more than 250,000 spectators.

- The George N. Pierce Company introduces the Pierce Arrow and the luxury Great Arrow; the latter sells for $4,000.

- Ransom E. Olds, having left the Olds Motor Works, founds the R. E. Olds Company; when the Olds Motor Works threatens a lawsuit over the name, Olds changes his company's name to his initials, forming the Reo Motor Car Company. The first Reo car is introduced; it has a steering wheel instead of a tiller.

- Architect Frank Lloyd Wright completes the Martin House in Buffalo, New York.

- Architect Daniel Burnham completes Orchestra Hall and the Railway Exchange Building in Chicago.

13 Aug.   The first Buick is delivered to Dr. Herbert Hills of Flint, Michigan.

1905

- An advertisement in the *Chicago Tribune* offers women's tailor-made suits for $35.

- U.S. automobile production reaches twenty-five thousand units.

- The electric car's share of the automobile market drops to less than 7 percent from its height of 38 percent in 1900.

- William C. Durant takes over the Buick Motor Company; within a year he sells fourteen hundred Buicks to the growing millionaire carriage market.

1906

- Paris designers introduce the Empire dress, a narrower cut, high-waisted dress that does away with the tight curves, luxurious bosoms, and narrow waists of the S-shaped dresses that had dominated women's fashion.

- The Ford Motor Company begins twenty-four consecutive years of industry sales leadership.

- Ford introduces the Model N, a two-passenger runabout with an efficient four-cylinder engine priced at $600. *Cycle and Automobile* magazine proclaims it "distinctively the most important technical event of 1906."

- The Chadwick Six, a six-cylinder car, is introduced by Lee Sherman Chadwick.

- At Ormond Beach, Florida, a Stanley race car captures the world's land speed record at 127 MPH.

1907

- Australian long-distance swimmer Annette Kellerman is arrested for indecent exposure at Revere Beach in Boston for wearing a one-piece bathing suit without a skirt.

- Paris causes a stir by introducing a "short" skirt that ends at the top of the fashionable woman's boot.

- A man's raccoon-fur automobile coat is advertised in *The New York Times* for $47.50, a derby hat for $2.75.

- Architect Daniel Burnham completes the Marshall Field and Company building in Chicago and Union Station in Washington, D.C.

- U.S. automobile production reaches forty-three thousand units.

- Alanson Partridge Brush introduces the Brush Runabout automobile, priced at $500; a Cadillac sells for $800.

1908

- The *San Francisco Examiner* advertises women's "pretty hats for Easter with ribbon" for $6.50.

- U.S. automobile production reaches 63,500 units; there are 200,000 cars on the road.

- Automaker Charles Duryea estimates for *Motor Magazine* that as many as half of the 515 companies that were producing cars in 1900 have gone bankrupt.

- The Hupp Motor Car Company of Detroit introduces the Hupmobile.

- William Durant sells 8,800 Buicks, second only to Ford in market share.

- Louis Sullivan completes the National Farmers Bank Building in Owatonna, Minnesota.

12 Feb. The New York-to-Paris auto race begins; it will proceed through Detroit, Cleveland, Chicago, Salt Lake City, and San Francisco, then via sea to Tokyo, through Vladivostok, Irkutsk, Moscow, Berlin, Bonn, and Brussels. After 169 days and 13,341 miles the lone American entry, a Thomas Flyer driven by George Schuster, is the winner.

12 Aug. The Model T Ford is introduced, priced at $850.

1909

- The Empire line is incorporated into the S-curve silhouette in women's dresses, which are still one piece but now have slightly raised waistlines and long, sweeping trains.

- Women's hats keep getting bigger, with wider brims; these large hats require the longest hatpins in history.

- U.S. automobile production reaches 127,731. The ratio of Americans to automobiles drops from one car for every ninety-five hundred people to one for every two hundred people.

- The Hudson Fulton Exhibition of American furniture opens in the Metropolitan Museum of Art in New York City.

- Charles and Henry Greene establish a trend in American architectural regionalism with the Gamble House in Pasadena, California.

- The world's tallest building (until 1913), the forty-two-story Metropolitan Life Insurance Tower, is completed in New York City by Napoleon Le Brun and Sons.

- Frank Lloyd Wright completes the Frederick G. Robie House, for which he even designs the furniture, in Chicago. Wright closes his studio in the Chicago suburb of Oak Park and departs for Europe, initiating a flurry of activity for Prairie School architects who had long been dominated by his presence.

1 June   Six cars — two Model T Fords, an Acme, an Itala, a Shawmut, and a Stearns — leave New York in the first transcontinental automobile race; one of the Model T's wins, arriving in Seattle on 22 June.

Oct.   The American Ladies Tailors Association exhibition in New York highlights the "suffragette suit," designed in protest against heavy, impractical skirts. It features a jacket with many pockets and a separated skirt with creases and cuffs like those of men's trousers.

OVERVIEW

Modernism and Nostalgia. In fashion and design — clothing, architecture, furniture, interior design, and automobiles — the turn of the century witnessed both a heralding of the new and a reluctance to break with the past. In fashion, men and women remained tied to the formalities of Victorianism even as they complained about them: women who patterned themselves after the Gibson Girl, the national icon of modern young womanhood, still changed their dresses for dinner and would not be caught out of the house without girdles and layers of petticoats. Architecture, furniture, and interior design in America also teetered between old and new: historicism, with its emphasis on styles of the past, was giving way to a new aesthetic of business, commerce, and simplicity. The inventors of the automobile modeled their prototypes on the buggy, envisioning cars quite literally as horseless carriages. Old and new forms clashed and blended as the country headed into the new century.

Fashion. The S-shaped silhouette, formed by a corset, petticoats, and a small, heavy bustle, remained the dominant look for women. At the same time, young women, working women, and those inspired by the Gibson Girl wanted more comfortable and practical clothes. The shirtwaist gradually became acceptable for fashionable women who did not work outside the home. Men's fashions were more practical and comfortable than women's: American men adopted the British tweed or dark-colored jacket over a vest and dark creased pants.

Declining Formality. By the end of the decade the formality of Victorianism was declining: skirts rose to the top of a lady's boot, and the Empire dress, which softened the S-shaped silhouette, became popular. Many younger men adopted the looser-fitting lounge jacket for work and daytime wear, which meant that they had to change clothes only twice a day rather than three or four times. The decade also witnessed growth in national markets, a development that put fashion in the hands of more women in small cities and rural towns across the country. Companies such as Sears, Roebuck mailed catalogues filled with pictures of dresses, petticoats, jackets, and shoes to eager customers. These customers, whose shopping in the late 1880s had been limited to local shops and tailors, could in the 1900s buy a greater range of products through the mail.

The Chicago School. At the turn of the century Chicago architects designed buildings that, for the first time, relied on steel and iron frames rather than masonry to bear the weight of the structure; this innovation, along with the safety elevator and advances in central heating and insulation, made possible the construction of the skyscraper. The Chicago architects did not try to hide their buildings' structures under historical ornamentation. Rather, led by William Le Baron Jenney and Louis Sullivan, they developed a new aesthetic to match their new materials. "Form follows function," Sullivan declared. With this motto he laid the groundwork for modern architecture.

Frank Lloyd Wright. Frank Lloyd Wright, a former student of Sullivan's, applied modern architectural design philosophy to homes. His Prairie Style, supremely represented in the Frederick Robie House (1909) in Chicago, was comprised of long horizontal lines; wide, overhanging eaves; and long bands of windows. The interior space was open and fluid and illuminated by natural light. These homes incorporated elements from the Arts and Crafts movement, such as the use of wood and the stress on craftsmanship, but Wright went beyond the movement with his fascination with structure and the aesthetic possibilities of pure form.

California. California architecture had a national impact in the early 1900s. Charles and Henry Greene of Pasadena and Bernard Maybeck of Berkeley designed homes and commercial buildings that were uniquely suited to their environments. The bungalow style, which had preceded the Greene brothers, was never more lovely than in their hands. Their heavy roofs hung over and sheltered large porches and broke down the line between outside and inside. Maybeck's designs for buildings at the University of California, Berkeley, synthesized modern structures with historic ornamentation. But these regionally distinctive styles faced major challenges from standardized designs in books and from prefabricated house kits sold nationally by Sears, Roebuck and Company; Montgomery Ward; and Aladdin Readi-Cut Homes of Bay City, Michigan.

Interiors. At the turn of the century American taste in interior design vacillated between Victorianism and modernism. Victorian architecture emphasized historical forms, particularly those of Greece, Rome, and Renaissance Europe. Victorian Americans decorated their homes as if they were galleries: each room was filled with objets d'art, wall hangings, carpeting, table covers, lamps, photographs, and heavy drapery. Modern advances in lighting and a rebellion by the young against the dark formality of the Victorian parlor pushed many to replace their parents' clutter with sparer interiors. Brighter lights, coupled with the popularity of white and ivory walls, and a wholesale rejection of oriental rugs marked homes as modern.

Design Trends. The Arts and Crafts movement, which originated in England and became popular in some regions of the United States, emphasized handcraftsmanship and simple forms. Drawing on Japanese and medieval European domestic interior architecture, among other sources, proponents of the Arts and Crafts movement proposed that handmade items replace mass-produced or factory-made pieces. Mission-style furniture, with its broad planes of oak and its simple cushions, became popular. Art Nouveau influenced the designer Louis Comfort Tiffany, whose stained-glass windows, lamp shades, inkwells, wine goblets, and vases used light as an active design element.

The Race to Make a Car. Since the early 1880s mechanics and engineers across the country had worked to produce a reliable mechanized vehicle. In 1900 it was unclear whether steam, electricity, or gasoline would be-come the dominant power source. Early steam engines, such as those developed by Freelan O. and Francis E. Stanley, were powerful and fast but difficult to start. Electric cars were easier to start than either steamers or gasoline (internal combustion) engines, which had to be cranked by hand, but were slower than either of the other two and could only run a short time between battery charges. The gasoline engine, used in such popular cars as the Ford Model A and the curved-dash Oldsmobile Runabout, had emerged as the victor by the end of the decade.

Mass Production. Cars in the early 1900s were hand-made and priced from $800 to $5,000, far out of the reach of most Americans. Henry Martyn Leland found that he could produce his Cadillacs less expensively if he subcontracted the manufacture of the parts out to specialists and assembled the finished product in his own factory. Henry Ford would refine the mass production of automobiles in the 1910s when he perfected the moving assembly line.

Modernism. By the end of the decade it was clear that modernism was here to stay. Middle-class Americans could buy ready-made clothes in stores or through the mail, taking fashion out of the hands of elites. Modern materials and modern aesthetics worked hand in hand to reinvent the look of American cities: buildings were taller and no longer designed to hearken back to the past. Frank Lloyd Wright and the Greene brothers offered new approaches to home design. Henry Ford put the car within the reach of millions of Americans. Victorianism was as outdated as the horse and carriage.

TOPICS IN THE NEWS

AMERICAN WOMEN'S FASHION

Rich and Poor. The new century brought a tremendous influx of immigrants, growth in the economy, and an explosion of new businesses and technologies. Women in the slums of the large cities and those on farms struggled to feed, shelter, and clothe their families, while middle-class women whose husbands worked in business or government offices lived in comfortable homes with hired help. Their children went to schools and enjoyed warm food and new clothes, while children of the poor worked for pennies and attended school erratically. At the other extreme, wealthy women, whose numbers grew in the first decade of the century, had domestic staffs, several homes, and plenty of time to supervise their families' active social lives. The disparity between the working poor and the idle rich had never been more glaring than it was as the new century opened.

European Influence. Paris and London set the fashion trends American women followed, if they could afford to do so, and these trends were tied to the tastes of the French and British upper classes. In America middle-class women copied the Vanderbilts, Astors, and Roosevelts, who, in turn, copied the looks of the European aristocracy. In this way, Paris and London influenced the

The S-shaped silhouette, the dominant look for women in the early 1900s

lacy cotton or linen corset with whalebone stays that produced a clinched, wasplike waist and flat stomach while exaggerating the size of the bust and hips. The bust was further emphasized by a blouse decorated with tucks, frills, braids, and laces. The S shape created an unnatural bend in the back that tilted the woman's upper body forward, while a high, stiff collar drew the head slightly upward. A wide-brimmed hat was worn forward on the head to balance the S shape. Black or tan leather boots fastened with buttons, or pointed suede shoes with low heels, completed the fashionable woman's look.

Undergarments. The S silhouette required much effort to achieve. First, the woman put on a chemise or vest of fine linen, silk, or muslin. Then, with help, she put on the corset, which laced at the back. Next came a corset cover of fine muslin. Next came the petticoats, which rivaled the woman's dress in detail and decorations and were hemmed with ruffles that rustled as the woman moved. After this daily ritual the woman was finally ready to put on her dress.

Narrowing Silhouette. As the decade wore on, skirts narrowed and rose slightly, changing the requirements for undergarments. To produce the narrower hipline, corsets no longer reached above the waist but moved down over the hips. This change required a more flexible structure, so whalebones were replaced by lighter and smaller stays. Ruffled petticoats were replaced by closer-fitting slips.

Hats. No fashionable woman left her house without a hat in the first decade of the 1900s. As the decade opened, women's small hats were lavishly trimmed with feathers, flowers, preserved birds, lace, ribbons, and buckles. So important were feathers to Victorian hat styles that in 1900 the plumage of more than twenty-four thousand egrets was put up for auction in a single month in London — to the despair of the Audubon Society. In 1905 the Sears, Roebuck catalogue offered more than seventy-five types of ostrich feathers for women's hats. Exotic birds were not the only targets of milliners, who also adorned hats with the feathers of purple grackles, red-winged blackbirds, orioles, skylarks, pigeons, doves, thrushes, and wrens. As the decade progressed, women's hats increased in size, became still more lavishly trimmed, and were worn tilted forward or to one side with a face veil. As hats got bigger, women stopped piling their hair in soft buns on top of their heads; instead, they parted it in the center, with curls on the sides and a bun at the back of the neck.

American Innovations. Most women — the rich were the exception — made their own clothes, following standardized patterns sold by companies such as McCall's and Butterick. Professional dressmakers used the same patterns, or else they made dresses to order by copying European originals. The foundations for what would become America's ready-to-wear clothing industry were set in this decade with the immigration of Jewish and eastern

dominant look of American women, even if elite European designers did not directly design for the masses.

The S-Shaped Silhouette. Middle- and upper-class women wore expensive, elaborate, ultrafeminine dresses that produced the fashionable S-shaped silhouette. Based on the figure of the mature and well-built woman, this silhouette comprised a bell-shaped skirt draped over stiff taffeta petticoats; a small bustle gathering a train; and a

The Gibson Girl, the ideal young woman of the early 1900s

European tailors, who applied their skills to making mass-produced shirts, pants, and collars and made New York the center of a burgeoning clothing industry.

The Shirtwaist. The American innovation of well-made ready-to-wear clothes produced a distinctive contribution to fashion: the shirtwaist, a blouse designed to be worn with a skirt. Paris looked down on the shirtwaist, which first appeared in the late nineteenth century, as a fashion disaster; but American women, particularly workingwomen, took to the garment in droves. By 1905 the Sears, Roebuck catalogue offered 150 variations of it, from a plain lawn version priced at 39¢ to one made of taffeta at $6.95. In 1907 a peek-a-boo shirtwaist shocked many conservatives with its eyelet embroidery, which allowed the flesh of the arm to show. By 1910 the national production of shirtwaists was a big business; New York City alone turned out $60 million worth. (On 25 March 1911, 146 people, most of them seamstresses working under sweatshop conditions, would die in a fire at the Triangle Shirtwaist Factory in New York City.)

Simpler Styles. The main advantage of the shirtwaist was its suitability to the active lives most women were leading. Designers used the shirtwaist to offer women a more comfortable range of skirts. At the beginning of the decade women typically wore the shirtwaist with a high-waisted skirt that extended to the floor. Later in the decade more and more women were wearing ankle-length skirts. In 1905 the staid Sears, Roebuck and Com-

pany offered its customers an ankle-length "health skirt," made "expressly for convenience." American women might want to follow European high-fashion trends in the evening, but for the rigors of everyday life they wanted a look that was stylish and functional.

Symbol of the Age. The shirtwaist rapidly became the symbol of a new generation of workingwomen. These young women, called "pink-collar" workers, managed the growing paperwork generated by American businesses. Aided by the invention of the typewriter in 1870, the pink-collar sector of the economy boomed in the first decade of the twentieth century. Where there had been only seven stenographers in America in 1870, in 1900 more than one hundred thousand "lady typewriters" (typists) worked in U.S. businesses. Pink-collar work was much more appealing than factory jobs to many women: in an office a woman could earn ten dollars or more a week, twice what she could make in a clothing sweatshop. In addition to the money, these young women enjoyed a heterosexual social setting outside the supervision of the family. Single secretaries and typists became the age's newest glamour girls, the heroines of serial stories in romance magazines.

The Gibson Girl. From 1890 until World War I many American women from the ages of fifteen to thirty yearned to be like the girls depicted in the magazine illustrations of Charles Dana Gibson. Tall, stately, with soft, wavy hair piled gently on her head and framing her lovely face, the Gibson Girl who appeared in the pages of *Life* magazine was stylishly dressed, assertive, and independent, but not wicked. The era's most famous real-life Gibson Girl was President Theodore Roosevelt's seventeen-year-old daughter, Alice. Spirited and pretty, Alice Roosevelt flouted convention: she spoke her mind, danced until dawn at parties, and, when visiting Hawaii, even did the hula — a dance considered so immodest that most American tourists avoided exposure to it. (Society was so taken with her that a color — "Alice blue" — was named for her.) The Gibson Girl was shaped in part by a new generation of women, both working class and upper class, who sought lives less restricted by social custom and heavy clothing. The real-life Gibson Girl was more than likely a telephone operator or clerical worker in a large city. She embodied the new generation of women influenced by increased job opportunities and the growing suffrage movement. Unlike her mother, the Gibson Girl worked in an office and dated without a chaperon. She also brought a new style sensibility to Edwardian fashion: she dressed in an ankle-length skirt; a blouse with a masculine collar and tie; a wide, stiffened belt tightly encircling a corseted waist; dark, pointed boots; and a straw boater hat.

The Rich Gibson Girl. While workingwomen helped popularize the look of the Gibson Girl, she was also an icon of the rich set's new vision of young womanhood. This idealized woman did not work in an office, no matter how romantic or glamorous the office might be in the decade's magazine fiction. Rather, she was the daughter of a father who could afford the latest looks and gadgets.

Sources:

Madeleine Ginsburg, *Victorian Dress in Photographs* (New York: Holmes & Meier, 1982);

Caroline Rennolds Milbank, *New York Fashion: The Evolution of American Style* (New York: Thames & Hudson, 1989);

Anne V. Tyrrell, *Changing Trends in Fashion: Patterns of the Twentieth Century 1900–1970* (London: Batsford, 1986).

APPAREL FOR MEN

Men's Fashions. For middle- and upper-class men, as for their female counterparts, dress followed rigid rules. In 1901 such men typically changed clothes three times over the course of a day. For the office a man wore a dark frock coat or morning coat, a waistcoat in a contrasting color, and striped trousers. The lounge suit provided a more relaxed alternative for leisure activities: the lounge jacket had short, pointed lapels and was shaped at the waist; the trousers were narrower than those of the business suit and sported a crease down the center of the leg. Following the example set by King Edward VII of Britain, many younger men chose to wear the lounge suit during business hours.

Formal Wear. Also like women, men always changed for dinner, even in their own homes. Dinner wear included a dress coat or the increasingly popular dinner

---

PRICES AT THE PEGUES, WRIGHT DEPARTMENT STORE, JUNCTION CITY, KANSAS, 1909

Ladies' Wear:

Tailor-made suit $10

Skirt $4

Chemise 50¢

Bracelet 35¢

Shoes $1.50

Corset 40¢

Shawl 50¢

Silk petticoat $5

Bead purse 59¢

Men's Wear:

Fancy suit $9

Trousers $1.25

Shirts 50¢

Woolen hose 15¢/pr

Suspenders 25¢/pr

Coat and vest $7

Linen collar 25¢

Hat $2

Work shoes $1.25

Home Furnishings:

Blanket 35¢

Carpet 12¢/yd

Hammock $3.50

Wallpaper 5¢/roll

Forty-two-piece dinner set $2.95

Sheet, double bed 58¢

Dress Goods:

Gingham 12¢/yd

Madras cloth 10¢/yd

Taffeta 85¢/yd

Calico 6¢/yd

Pins 5¢/box

Sewing machine $12

Embroidery 8¢

Silk 50¢/yd

Sewing patterns 10¢

Damask 40¢/yd

The average annual wage in the United States in 1909 for all industries, including farm labor, was $559/yr.

Sources: Ezra Bowen, ed., *This Fabulous Century, volume 1: 1900–1910* (New York: Time-Life Books, 1969), p. 144;

Scott Derks, ed., *The Value of a Dollar: Prices and Incomes in the United States 1860–1989* (Detroit, Washington, D.C. & London: Gale Research, 1994).

jacket. The dinner jacket was closely fitted and fell to the waist at the front and to the knees in back. The lapels were wide and were made of a silk that shone slightly in candlelight. The coat was worn unbuttoned over a low-cut white vest and a stiff, white shirt with three-button cuffs; accessories included a small black bow tie and pointed black leather shoes.

Accessories and Undergarments. Middle- and upper-class office workers wore tunic-style white shirts with stiff, detachable high collars made of white linen or, for the less affluent, celluloid. Silk ties rested under the collar and were tied with a classic triangle-shaped knot. Shirt studs and cufflinks were of mother-of-pearl or onyx. Pocket watches were clipped to a pocket in the vest and the long chain draped across the chest. Hats were silk toppers or felt homburgs in cooler weather, straw panamas in the summer. Men also carried suede, leather, or kid gloves and an umbrella or a walking stick. Older men wore long underwear of knitted wool in winter and wool-and-silk blends or cotton in summer; younger men wore knee-length underpants. Men's knee-high socks were held in place by garters.

Leisure Wear. The loose-fitting, belted tweed Norfolk jacket with box pleats was popular for leisure wear. The jacket was worn over matching trousers or flannels, or over knickerbockers or shorts that tapered just over the knee for golfing, hunting, or shooting. The look was topped with a tweed peaked cap.

The Workingman. Working-class men wore simpler versions of the clothes that upper-class men wore. A typical outfit included a tunic-styled shirt with detachable collar; a vest cut just below the collarbone that reached to the belt and was buttoned tightly with decorated brass buttons; a matching jacket with narrow, high lapels that fell a few inches below the vest; trousers that fit more closely than in previous decades and lacked center creases; and a bowler hat. Workingmen wore detachable scuffs clipped by studs to protect their shirts from ink or city grime. Period photographs show that working-class men shared with their wealthier counterparts a high level of fashion formality.

The Barbershop. In Victorian America the beard had been de rigueur, but by 1906 younger men were rejecting the full beard for a moustache or for no facial hair at all. Whether bearded, moustached, or clean-shaven, men regularly retreated to the neighborhood barbershop, which resembled a men's club. The customers browsed through magazines such as the *Police Gazette*, smoked cigars, and sipped rum while waiting for a fifteen-cent shave. By middecade men no longer were required to part their hair in the center but could part it on the side. They continued to oil the hair to achieve a smooth, dark look.

Sources:
Madeleine Ginsburg, *Victorian Dress in Photographs* (New York: Holmes & Meier, 1982);

Anne V. Tyrrell, *Changing Trends in Fashion: Patterns of the Twentieth Century 1900–1970* (London: Batsford, 1986).

Louis Sullivan's Carson, Pirie, Scott department store building in Chicago, built in 1904

ARCHITECTURE, INTERIOR DESIGN, AND FURNITURE

The Classical Revival. On the eve of the twentieth century American architecture was at a crossroads. Victorian architecture and design were preoccupied with past styles, particularly Greek and Roman classicism. The classical revival in architecture took its lead from the Ecole des Beaux Arts in Paris, where, beginning in the mid nineteenth century, many American architects studied; upon their return to the United States they passed on the Beaux Arts philosophy to their own students. Beaux Arts principles were dominant in American architecture for about a hundred years.

Organic Design. In the late nineteenth and early twentieth centuries Beaux Arts was challenged by two related developments that took their inspiration from organic growth in nature: the Chicago school in architecture and the Arts and Crafts movement. The first, and the most important, architect to employ the organic concept was Louis Sullivan. Sullivan used the term *organic* to mean that a building's structure should be expressed on its exterior, rather than hidden by ornamentation. According to Sullivan, structure and appearance, form and function were part of a single, growing organism. Sullivan's architectural philosophy shaped what came to be called the Chicago school.

The Chicago School. In the wake of the 1871 fire that destroyed much of the city, Chicago rebuilt itself from the ground up. Architects from around the country flocked to the city to participate in an unprecedented opportunity to experiment with the new aesthetics of the period. Sullivan was one of many architects who made names for themselves from the ashes of the fire. Architects of the Chicago school concentrated on office buildings, warehouses, department stores, and other commercial structures; consequently, the style they developed came to be called the Commercial Style. The Chicago school architects rejected the eclecticism of earlier styles, preferring functional designs that subsumed ornamentation and facade to form and structure. Major technological changes developed by Chicago school architects included wide use of the safe elevator, invented by Elisha Graves Otis and first installed in 1857 in a five-story building in New York City, and central heating; these innovations helped make tall buildings possible. Along with new methods of insulation, central heating also permitted the use of large areas of glass in exterior walls of buildings.

Jenney. The father of Chicago's tall buildings was Maj. William Le Baron Jenney, an engineer turned architect who in the late nineteenth century turned away from popular eclectic architecture toward functionality. His Home Insurance Building (1885) in Chicago is often regarded as the first true skyscraper. Jenney was the first architect to use steel framing and the "curtain wall," a sheet of masonry that covered the frame instead of bearing the building's weight. Jenney's "bridge-frame construction," so called because it had previously been used only in bridges, cut months off construction time. It also allowed for larger windows than were possible in masonry buildings, whose lower-floor windows had to be small because of the thickness of the weight-bearing external walls. Jenney's use of steel frame enabled him to invent the "Chicago window," two double-hung windows on either side of a fixed glass panel.

Burnham and Root. Another pioneering Chicago architectural firm was that of Daniel Hudson Burnham and John Wellborn Root, founded in 1873. Their ten-story Montauk Block (1882) was the first building to be referred to as a skyscraper. Their Rookery (1886), built on a site where large numbers of pigeons had roosted, became one of Chicago's favorite and most notable structures. Its large center court filled offices and shops with natural light and pioneered the creation of the glass-enclosed courtyard. Root died in 1891, and Burnham went on to build such notable Chicago buildings as Orchestra Hall (1904), the Railway Exchange Building (now the Santa Fe Building) (1904), and the Marshall Field and Company Building (1907).

Sullivan. Sullivan was the most influential of the Chicago school architects. He set out to prove that buildings could be utilitarian and still maintain a palatial dignity. Buildings, Sullivan insisted, had an overall sense of "Life" that was more than an outgrowth of form. Buildings were simultaneously related to their location, their materials, and the needs of the people who occupied them. Structure, purpose, and beauty could be in harmony, "like a fine sturdy tree," with each branch and leaf fulfilling a specific organic function. "Form follows function," Sulli-

The Fuller Building, nicknamed the "Flatiron Building," designed by Daniel H. Burnham, under construction in New York City in 1901

van's dictum about the relationship of aesthetics and structure, took the Chicago school's principles to new heights. Sullivan believed that organic architecture would lead to a truly original American art form, a prediction that he fulfilled along with his student Frank Lloyd Wright.

Wright. Sullivan's views on the organic relationship of form and function were taken up and extended by Wright, who came to work at Sullivan's office in 1887 and spent the next five years learning from Chicago's foremost architect. In 1892 he left to start his own practice, which would shape American architecture well into the 1950s. In the early years of his career Wright developed the Prairie Style. Based on the open spaces of the prairie, its principles were those of simplicity, wide vistas, freedom of movement, easy accommodation of the ebb and flow of life, quiet domesticity, and generous lighting. The Prairie Style was characterized by horizontal lines, in contrast to the vertical lines favored by the Victorians,

The Frederick C. Robie House in Chicago, an example of Frank Lloyd Wright's Prairie Style

and wide, overhanging eaves. Wright's interiors were more open and spare than those of his predecessors, who preferred deeply ornamental and dense interior decoration. Wright used lead-glass windows, which he frequently designed to interact with the greenery outside. Wright's distinctive style was particularly notable in the Frederick G. Robie House (1909) in Chicago. His designs integrated what historicism separated: process and product, exterior and interior, large-scale elements and the smallest of details.

Pioneer of Modern Interiors. Frank Lloyd Wright not only revolutionized American architecture but also helped transform American interiors with his innovative use of space and light. His interrelated, interlocking rooms, with generous windows and tall ceilings, challenged the distinctions between parlor, sitting room, and dining room. The use of heating techniques designed for industrial buildings enabled him to liberate the house from its dependence on fireplaces and stoves.

Wright's Furniture. Wright frequently designed the furniture for his houses and commercial buildings. For the Larkin Company Administration Building in Buffalo, New York (1904), he designed executive chairs con-

sisting of tubular metal frames and adjustable back panels, a style that would become popular twenty years later. Desks had attached legless steel chairs to make office cleaning more efficient. Wright also introduced the vertically stacked steel filing cabinets that are common in offices today.

Leaving Historicism Behind. The Chicago school and the Prairie Style were remarkable for their break with the historical styles of Victorianism. Their emphasis on simplicity and geometry, function over form, and the beauty of structural elements set the groundwork for modern architecture. Another design trend, which also influenced the emergence of modern architecture, was the Arts and Crafts movement. Arts and Crafts emphasized the artist's involvement in a full range of design, including interiors, furniture, household items, and architecture. It stressed that design stemmed from function, and form from the materials and tools used. Wright shared with the Arts and Crafts movement the ideas of blending function and form, the model of organic unity, and an emphasis on craftsmanship. In the regional architecture of California, the principles of the Arts and Crafts movement were manifested in the Greene brothers' bungalows and the Bay Area Style.

The dining room in the New York City home of Elsie de Wolfe, America's first professional interior designer, in 1896 and after 1898. De Wolfe moved away from the dark, heavy, cluttered look of late Victorianism to a lighter, brighter, airier style.

The Arts and Crafts Movement. Originating in England and popularized by the writings of Charles Locke Eastlake, the Arts and Crafts movement rejected what it viewed as the excesses of the Industrial Revolution, especially the "morally" dishonest ornamentation produced when machines were used to imitate handicraft. In the 1890s the spirit of artisan rebellion came to America. The Arts and Crafts movement advocated stripping away heavy Victorian trappings and returning to the simpler lines of Tudor England. The movement inspired several firms to produce handcrafted furniture, glass, and pottery that was sturdy and simple in style. Taking off from the designs of Wright's Prairie furniture, craftsmen such as Elbert Hubbard of East Aurora, New York; George Niedecken of Milwaukee; and George Grant Elmslie of Chicago helped make the Mission Style popular.

Greene and Greene. Few architects were as devoted to the ideas of the Arts and Crafts movement as the brothers Charles and Henry Greene of California. They conceived their houses as pieces of cabinetwork, extensions of the furniture they also built. Like Wright and Sullivan, the brothers greatly admired Japan, where carpentry was viewed as an art form. They were best known for their bungalows, houses with open spaces, generous eaves that protected the interior against the southern California sun, and colors that blended into the landscape. Valued for their suitability to a warm climate and their blurring of the line between inside and outside, the Greene brothers' bungalows were admired for their elegant craftsmanship and sensitive use of materials such as cobblestones, native plants, and wood.

Bay Area Style. The Bay Area Style was centered in San Francisco, Oakland, and Berkeley, California. The state's informality, its generous climate, and undogmatic clientele inspired architects. Ernest Coxhead in San Francisco designed houses that combined the English manor-house style with modern simplicity, local materials, and attention to craftsmanship. Bernard Maybeck built distinctive redwood houses in Berkeley that used medieval timberwork reduced to a more hospitable domestic scale. John Galen Howard came to Berkeley to design buildings for the University of California. The Hearst Mines Building of 1907, which combined Mediterranean Renaissance style with a metal-framed modern interior court topped by skylight domes, illustrates Howard's eclectic approach.

Victorian Homes. The average American interior in the 1890s resembled a dark, cluttered, late-Victorian art gallery. Middle-class and wealthy Americans filled their sitting rooms and parlors with travel mementos, paintings, sculptures, tapestries, manuscripts, and antiques. Windows were covered by shutters, shades, lace curtains, and heavy draperies; walls by wallpaper or upholstery in heavy, dark patterns; tables by tapestries overlaid with embroidery, crewelwork, or handworked linen. Crocheted doilies protected table coverings from the imprints of pictures, bronze statues, vases, and other bric-a-brac.

Light, Air, and Comfort. By the turn of the century more and more Americans were rejecting the cloistered heaviness of late Victorianism. Elsie de Wolfe, who called herself the first professional interior designer in America, led the charge: she exchanged the dark wall coverings for ones with brighter colors; emphasized wainscoting, doors, ceiling molding, and columns by painting them in contrasting colors; and replaced the gallery-style parlor with one that was brighter and had minimal decoration. She removed the layers of oriental rugs, substituting a single rug of a solid color, and took off the heavy draperies to let in more natural light. De Wolfe introduced beige, ivory, and white to American consumers. These changes, coupled with the brighter electric lighting that became available at the turn of the century, lightened the interior of the post-Victorian home. Stanford White, of the architecture firm McKim, Mead, and White, also made American home interiors lighter, more delicate in detail, and more graceful.

Gustav Stickley and the Mission Style. Gustav Stickley was among the most prominent craftsmen designers. He designed heavy, four-square mission-styled oak furniture in his Craftsman Workshops in Eastwood, a suburb of Syracuse, New York. Stickley's plain and rugged mission furniture was, in his own words, "simple, durable, comfortable and fitted for the place it was to occupy and the work it had to do." The solid oak frames of the Mission Style were a reaction to the fragile veneered furniture that had been popular in the 1880s.

The Colonial Style. Colonial American furniture also became part of the revolt against Victorian eclecticism and mass-market ornament. Colonial America was viewed as a time of heroism, democracy, and craft tradition. The Colonial Style included design motifs and antique pieces of all periods from 1620 to 1830. The study of antiques became popular and culminated in 1909 in the Hudson Fulton Exhibition at the Metropolitan Museum of Art in New York City. The interest in Colonial furniture signified a break from what many Americans viewed as the stultifying hold of high European culture on an "authentic" American culture.

Stylizing the American Past. The Colonial revival and the Arts and Crafts movement were in harmony for a few years, held together by their common disdain for overstuffed Victorian furniture and a desire to return to simpler and more honest times. But by the end of the decade American furniture designers no longer modeled their work on antiques; rather, they turned from an emphasis on the revival of craftsmanship to a new interpretation of the American past. Leading the way toward modern furniture, Frank Lloyd Wright embraced the machine as "a normal tool of civilization." Building on the Arts and Crafts movement and the Colonial revival, Wright moved beyond both into a new synthesis of craftsmanship and the machine.

Art Nouveau. In contrast to the Arts and Crafts movement, Art Nouveau style focused on surface finish, visual effects, and ornamentation. Art Nouveau, which began around 1890 as a reaction of European artists and architects against the influence of the past, would run its course by around 1910. Its major theme was a long, sensitive, sinuous line that evoked comparisons to seaweed, creeping plants, flowing hair, or modern dance. Art Nouveau moved past the highly ornamented forms of historicism toward the simple functionalism of modernism; it was a hybrid form that embraced the modern dictum "form follows function" while employing the lush

HOMES BY MAIL

In the early 1900s it was possible to purchase an entire house by mail order. George F. Barber of Knoxville, Tennessee, began offering such houses in 1886. Montgomery Ward; the Radford Company of Chicago; Aladdin Readi-Cut Homes of Bay City, Michigan; the Farrar Company of Dalton, Georgia; and the R. L. Kenyon Company of Waukesha, Wisconsin, soon followed suit.

Perhaps the largest seller of houses by catalogue was Sears, Roebuck and Company, which first included a "Modern Homes" section in its spring 1908 catalogue. Later that year the firm put out its first *Honorbilt Modern Homes* catalogue, 44 pages and featuring 22 models, ranging from a three-room cottage for $650 to a nine-room Queen Anne–style for $2,500. The longest homes catalogue, 146 pages, appeared in 1918. The cheaper houses were identified by order numbers, the more expensive ones by names such as the Warrenton, the Windmere, the Whitehall, the Magnolia, the Hathaway, and the Chateau.

The firm supplied almost everything the customer needed to erect a house: lumber, roofing, shingles, flooring, lath and plaster, doors, windows, millwork, and paint were shipped by rail; plumbing, heating, and wiring were extra, and the customer provided the building lot and masonry. Blueprints and a 76-page instruction manual were sent by mail. All of the approximately thirty thousand parts (not counting nails and screws) were precut and numbered to correspond to the blueprints. Sears claimed that its smaller houses could be put up in an average of 352 carpenter-hours, as opposed to 583 carpenter hours for a conventional "stick-built" house; a cottage could be erected in an eight-hour day.

Sears offered financing on the houses it sold, sometimes even advancing money to the customer to hire carpenters. This policy ultimately led to the demise of the program: during the Great Depression many borrowers defaulted on their mortgages. Between 1909 and 1934 Sears sold more than one hundred thousand houses for a total of $90 million; profit on the sales was $4.3 million, but losses on the mortgages amounted to almost $7 million, and the firm suffered a public-relations disaster as it foreclosed on homes across the country. The program was ended in 1937. Many of the houses are still standing; in the 1980s a Hathaway that had carried a catalogue price of $1,807 sold for $106,000.

Sources: Thomas J. Schlereth, *Victorian America: Transformations in Everyday Life, 1876–1915* (New York: HarperCollins, 1991);

David M. Schwartz, "Houses That Came in the Mail," *Saturday Evening Post*, 258 (May/June 1986): 52–55, 95–96.

surface decoration of historicism. Predominantly a European design trend, Art Nouveau shaped American styles mainly through the glasswork and metalwork of Louis Comfort Tiffany. While Art Nouveau never reached the level of popularity in America that the Arts and Crafts movement did, it contributed to the development of modernism in design through its belief that work should be of the day and, thus, nonhistorical.

Sources:

Victor Arwas, *Glass: Art Nouveau to Art Deco* (New York: Abrams, 1987);

Jonathan L. Fairbanks and Elizabeth Bidwell Bates, *American Furniture: 1620 to the Present* (New York: Marek, 1981);

Donald Hoffmann, *Frank Lloyd Wright's Robie House: The Illustrated Story of an Architectural Masterpiece* (New York: Dover, 1984);

William Dudley Hunt Jr., *Encyclopedia of American Architecture* (New York: McGraw-Hill, 1980);

George A. Larson and Jane Pridmore, *Chicago Architecture and Design* (New York: Abrams, 1993);

C. Ray Smith, *Interior Design in 20th Century America: A History* (New York: Harper & Row, 1986);

Marcus Whiffen and Frederick Koeper, *American Architecture, 1607–1976* (Cambridge, Mass.: MIT Press, 1981).

AUTOMOBILES

The Horseless Carriage. It was not clear at the turn of the century whether steam, electricity, or gasoline would prove the most efficient power source for automobiles. Americans had been experimenting with mechanized road vehicles since the 1880s; called "horseless carriages," these early cars took many of their design features — high, thin wheels; simple chassis; buggylike interiors; and tillers for steering — from traditional horse-drawn carriages and were nearly indistinguishable from them. Charles E. Duryea of Springfield, Massachusetts; Freelan O. and Francis E. Stanley of Newton, Massachusetts; and Rollin H. White of Cleveland, Ohio, were a few of the more successful mechanics who struggled to build a reliable motorized vehicle in the 1890s.

The Stanley Steamer. As the decade opened, it appeared that steam would win the motorization battle. The Stanley brothers' steam car had no driveshaft, no spark advance to manipulate, no irritating vibration when in motion, and no difficulty racing up any hill. The car, however, carried only a twenty-mile supply of water. An even greater inconvenience than the limited range was the complex procedure for starting the car. The owner had to heat a U-shaped steel pipe on a kitchen stove until it was red-hot, then carry the pipe to the car, insert it in the kerosene burner, and connect it to a fuel valve. Twenty minutes later the water would have heated up enough to raise steam to run the car. While the Stanley Steamer was one of the era's fastest cars and one of the most pleasurable to drive, it was difficult for average Americans to master.

White's Touring Car. The Stanley brothers' major competitor in the steam-engine design race was Rollin H. White of the White Sewing Machine Company. In 1904 the White company pioneered a new look for automobiles: the touring car. The chaises, or bodies, of these cars were lighter in weight and appearance than those of the Stanley Steamers. White's newly designed engine moved the steam from a high-pressure cylinder, where the power was produced, to a low-pressure one, where it recondensed — thereby recycling the steam to extend the car's range. A flash boiler reduced the start-up time. The big, luxurious Whites were powerful and fast and represented the best in steam power in the 1900s. During the William Howard Taft administration a White was chosen as one of the first official White House cars.

Battery-Powered Cars. The electric car also vied for dominance in the early car market. In 1900 the electric car commanded 38 percent of the automotive market. While manufacturers of gasoline and steam cars emphasized power and speed, electric-car makers emphasized the simplicity and elegance of their vehicles. The ease of operating the battery-powered vehicles made them particularly suitable, in the logic of the day, for women. Advertisements frequently pictured the driver of the electric coupe as a well-dressed young matron comfortably manipulating the steering tiller without ruffling her ostrich-plume hat. The electric car required no cranking, no burner, no gear shifting, and no tire changing — the tires were solid rubber. It also offered a quieter ride than early steam and gasoline cars could deliver. Elegant curved-glass windows and luxurious interiors gave this generation of electric cars a style unmatched by steam and gasoline cars. Electric-car manufacturers such as Woods, Baker, Pope-Waverley, Columbian Detroit, and Rauch and Lange also stressed the socially desirable features of their clean, quiet cars. Electric cars were among the era's most expensive vehicles: a Woods electric car, with enclosed riding compartment and seat for a liveried footman, cost $3,000.

Comfort versus Practicality. Despite its luxurious features, the electric car had some nagging problems. It was slow, and its solid-rubber tires made it suitable for driving only on paved roads. More serious were the shortcomings of battery power: batteries were heavy, expensive, and discharged rapidly. A battery in 1900 could run for only twenty miles, and in 1910 for eighty miles. Charging facilities were expensive and were rarely available outside cities. By the end of the decade the electric car was a thing of the past. Americans wanted affordable transportation that could cope with the distances and rudimentary road conditions they faced.

The Oldsmobile. The first American car that met both these needs was built by Ransom Olds in 1896. While most European carmakers were building heavy, powerful, handcrafted, high-priced touring machines, Olds saw that Americans wanted a lightweight, sturdy, economical vehicle capable of handling harsh road conditions and priced close to the cost of a horse and buggy. Olds's major design innovation was the curved dashboard, introduced on his 1901 runabout. The curved dash, gracefully curling

The Oldsmobile Curved Dash Runabout, introduced in 1901

in toward the driver, took automobile design a step away from the dominant horse-and-buggy look. The 1901 Oldsmobile also had shorter wheels and a smaller chaise than a carriage, but it retained the steering tiller. Olds's major business innovation was his use of subcontractors to make the parts for his vehicles: engines, transmissions, wheels, chassis, and bodies were purchased from independent suppliers and assembled at the Oldsmobile factory. Subcontracting kept his costs down and production speed up. Selling for $650, the little curved-dash Oldsmobile, shiny black with red trim, was the buzz of Detroit, the nation's growing automobile production center.

Henry Ford. The first Ford automobile, the Model A, introduced in 1903, was a little two-cylinder, buggy-styled car. Americans loved it, and by October 1904 Ford had sold seventeen hundred. Ford's advertising boasted that the Model A was "positively the most perfect machine on the market." More important, it was affordable, at $850. By the end of the decade Henry Ford was the undisputed king of Detroit.

Driving Fashions. As Americans took to the automobile, they needed appropriate clothes to wear while driv-

ing or riding. In 1904 New York's Saks and Company put out a 270-page catalogue of motoring garb. The main purposes of driving fashions were keeping drivers and passengers free of dust and protecting them from the wind, since most cars were open to the elements. Both men and women wore dusters, long double-breasted coats that fell to the ankle. Long-sleeved and tight-collared, men's dusters were typically of suede or stiff canvaslike materials. Men also wore leather driving gloves, caps, and goggles. Women's dusters were more fashionable then men's: they were tailored, with lapels and open collars; their sleeves bloused at the wrists to keep dust out. Women wrapped their hats in long scarves that were tied closely around the neck and tucked into the duster, and they draped heavy blankets across their laps.

Sources:

Nick Baldwin, G. N. Georgano, Michael Sedgwick, and Brian Laban, *The World Guide to Automobile Manufacturers* (New York & Oxford: Facts On File, 1987);

Stephen W. Sears, *The American Heritage History of the Automobile in America* (New York: American Heritage Publishing, 1977).

HEADLINE MAKERS

DANIEL H. BURNHAM

1846-1912

ARCHITECT AND CITY PLANNER

Forging the Chicago Style. Burnham and Root was one of the most successful architectural firms in America in the late nineteenth century. Daniel Hudson Burnham and John Wellborn Root became partners in 1873 and designed many of Chicago's most notable buildings. Their early works, such as the Montauk Block (1882), the Calumet Building (1884), and the Rookery (1886), had cast-iron interior columns and load-bearing masonry walls. The first building in which they used an all-steel frame was the Rand-McNally Building (1890). Burnham and Root's creative partnership was abruptly ended in 1891 by the death of Root at the age of forty-one. The firm, renamed D. H. Burnham and Company, went on to build many important buildings, such as the Great Northern Hotel (1892) and the Masonic Temple (1892), the tallest buildings of their day, each at twenty stories. The Reliance Building (1895) gained praise with its steel frame and structure-revealing terra-cotta and glass walls.

Early Life and Training. Burnham was born in upstate New York in 1846 and moved to Chicago with his family when he was nine. After graduating from high school, in which his grades were poor except in drawing, Burnham became a store clerk and then a miner in Nevada and ran unsuccessfully for the Illinois Senate before being hired by the Chicago architect William Le Baron Jenney. In 1872 Burnham joined the firm of Carter, Drake and Wight, where he met Root. The following year Burnham, who had had no formal training in architecture, joined the younger but more experienced Root in a new partnership. Within a few years the firm was flourishing.

Burnham and Company. After Root's death D. H. Burnham and Company continued to grow, becoming the largest in Chicago and opening branches in New York and San Francisco. The firm was never again as creative as it had been while Root was alive, adopting various eclectic styles. Even so, it designed several notable buildings, including the Fisher Building (1896), the Field Museum of Natural History (1900), Orchestra Hall (1904), and the Railway Exchange Building (1904), all in Chicago; the Fuller Building (1902) — later known as the Flatiron Building because of its shape — and the Wanamaker department store (1903) in New York City; Union Station (1907) in Washington, D.C.; and Filene's department store (1912) in Boston.

City Planning. In his later years Burnham became interested in city planning. He and Root had designed the master plan for the 1893 World's Columbian Exposition in Chicago — for which Burnham was chief of construction and chief consulting architect — and in 1897 he, Edward H. Bennett, and Jens Jensen began working on a plan for the development of the Chicago lakefront. This collaboration resulted in the construction of Grant Park and other great Chicago parks, beginning in 1904, and in the Chicago Plan of 1909. He also drew up a sweeping plan for the reconstruction of San Francisco after the earthquake and fire of 1906 and made plans for several other cities, including Baltimore, Duluth, and Manila. Burnham died in 1912.

Source:
Thomas S. Hines, *Burnham of Chicago: Architect and Planner* (New York: Oxford University Press, 1974).

IRVING GILL

1870-1936

ARCHITECT

Modern Architect. Though he had no formal training in the field, Irving Gill became a pioneer of modern architecture. Unlike Victorian architects, Gill viewed a building's interior and the surrounding land as integral parts of the architecture. Aesthetically, he rejected the ornamentation and detail work of architectural historicism. He also cared about low-cost housing and about using the most modern materials in his buildings. Gill shared the concern of his fellow California architects, Charles Sumner and Henry Mather Greene, with craftsmanship; but unlike the Greene brothers, who designed intricate, handcrafted details for their buildings, Gill was led by his interest in craftsmanship into modernism — into simplifying his structures almost to the point of abstraction. Also influenced by the simple adobe forms of early California Spanish missions, he used new materials, especially reinforced concrete, to erect buildings with plain, clean surfaces and minimal ornamentation.

Early Life and Training. Gill was born in Syracuse, New York, in 1870. His only early training in architecture came from exposure to his father's work as a building contractor and a brief job in an architect's office. In 1890 he went to Chicago and went to work as a draftsman for the firm of Dankmar Adler and Louis Sullivan; a fellow draftsman there was Frank Lloyd Wright. Vacationing in California in 1892, Gill fell in love with the state and decided to settle in San Diego.

Modernism Adrift. For several years Gill struggled to make a name for himself. His business grew in the early 1900s and hit a high-water mark in 1911. Throughout this period Gill refined his modernist vision of simple, economical concrete houses with little ornamentation and built-in labor-saving devices of his own design such as garbage disposals and vacuum cleaners. Among his better-known buildings were the five-story Wilson Acton Hotel (1908) and the Ellen Scripps House (1916) in La Jolla, California, and the Walter Luther Dodge House (1916) in Los Angeles. Frederick Law Olmsted Jr. and his half brother John Charles Olmsted, son and stepson, respectively, of the landscape architect who had designed New York's Central Park, appreciated Gill's modernism and the importance he placed on landscaping. After 1917, when California tastes turned to the Spanish Colonial style that had been popularized by the Panama Pacific Exposition of 1915, the Olmsteds promoted Gill's flagging business by helping the architect secure work in Newport and Providence, Rhode Island. Collaborating with the Olmsteds, Gill designed the plans for a new industrial town, Torrance, near Los Angeles. Much to Gill's disappointment, of the hundreds of structures he had designed for the town, only a few small buildings, a railroad station, a bridge, and ten houses were built; and the houses were transformed into traditional wooden ones instead of the modern concrete homes he had envisioned.

Later Life. In 1928 Gill married and moved to Palos Verdes, then to Carlsbad, California. In 1929 and 1933 he suffered heart attacks. In the latter year he moved to Lakeside to build an Indian resettlement community at Rancho Barona. He died in 1936, largely forgotten.

Source:
Marcus Whiffen and Frederick Koeper, *American Architecture, 1607–1976* (Cambridge, Mass.: MIT Press, 1981).

CHARLES GREENE

ARCHITECT
1868-1957

Craftsmanship. Charles Sumner Greene and Henry Mather Greene were the foremost American proponents of the Arts and Crafts movement. The movement, which had started in the middle of the nineteenth century in England, promoted the handcrafting of household items out of wood, metals, and textiles. The Greene brothers were deeply committed to the use of craftsmanship in architecture and furniture design during their twenty-one-year joint architectural practice in Pasadena, California. They were also influenced by Japanese domestic architecture and the wooden houses of Switzerland. These interests came together in their exquisite bungalows.

Early Life and Training. Born in Cincinnati in 1868 and 1870, respectively, Charles and Henry Greene grew up in Saint Louis. They attended a high school sponsored by Washington University, where they received training in handcraftsmanship. From 1888 to 1891 they were trained in the Beaux Arts tradition at the Massachusetts Institute of Technology. They established their firm, Greene and Greene, in Pasadena in 1893.

The Bungalow Style. By the 1900s the Greenes' practice was flourishing. Their house designs increasingly took on an open, Japanese feeling that harmonized with the surrounding environment. They also became known for their use of wood, particularly redwood. Their most important homes in the 1900s were designed for L. A. Robinson (1906), Robert R. Blacker (1907), and David B. Gamble (1908) in Pasadena; for William R. Thorsen (1908) in Berkeley; and for Charles M. Pratt (1909) in Ojai, California. These homes, with their large, overhanging roofs; open windows; and horizontal lines reflected the mature vision of the brothers. They conceived of their homes as total environments that included interiors and exteriors, and they often designed gardens and furniture for their clients. Their designs for the Gamble house included furniture, carpets, lighting fixtures, silverware, and linens.

Obscurity. By 1914 the Greene brothers no longer shared the same vision of architecture, and, though they remained close personally, they dissolved their partnership. Charles, who had become interested in philosophy and art, moved to Carmel, California, where he designed a few houses in the Mission Style and wrote about oriental philosophy. Henry stayed in Pasadena, where he designed stucco houses with tile roofs that had little in common with his earlier work with his brother. Both brothers slipped into obscurity.

Revival. After World War II a renewed interest in wood architecture, led by architects in California and the Pacific Northwest, reawakened appreciation for the work of the Greene brothers, who by then had retired. They received praise and prizes from their peers for their accomplishments. Henry Greene died in October 1954; Charles in June 1957.

Source:
Randell Makinson, *Greene and Greene: Architecture as Fine Art* (Salt Lake City, Utah: Peregrine Smith, 1977).

WILLIAM LE BARON JENNEY

1832-1907

ENGINEER AND ARCHITECT

Leader of the Chicago School. Trained as an engineer, William Le Baron Jenney became one of the most influential architects of his time. With his knowledge of structural engineering, he was the first architect to build tall buildings. He and his students, who became known as the Chicago school, used iron and, later, steel skeletons to support their buildings. In time they stopped trying to adapt traditional styles and began to design the exteriors of their buildings to reveal the underlying structure. Jenney's influence on modern architecture came by way of the men who trained and worked under him: Louis Sullivan, Martin Roche, William Holabird, and Daniel Hudson Burnham were the nucleus of the Chicago school.

Early Life and Training. Jenney was born in Fairhaven, Massachusetts, in 1832, the son of the owner of a fleet of whaling ships. After studying engineering for two years at the Lawrence Scientific School of Harvard University, he joined the California Gold Rush of 1849 and then helped to build a railroad in Panama. He entered the Ecole Centrales des Arts et Manufactures in Paris in 1853, graduating three years later. In 1861 Jenney joined the Union army as an engineer, becoming a major and serving on the staffs of generals Ulysses S. Grant and William Tecumseh Sherman.

Chicago. Jenney opened an office in Chicago in 1867. His career was advanced by the fire that destroyed Chicago in 1871: the city had to be almost completely rebuilt, and Jenney's work multiplied. His earliest tall building was the First Leiter Store (1879), in which he used brick columns for the exterior and iron columns for the interior. Jenney's masterpiece, the ten-story Home Insurance Company Building (1885), is considered by some to be the world's first skyscraper. With its frame of cast-iron and wrought-iron columns and wrought-iron and steel beams, it was the first building in which the floors and the exterior masonry walls were supported by a metal skeleton rather than by the masonry itself; it was also the first time Bessemer steel had been used in a building. In 1891 Jenney took William B. Mundie as a partner. His creativity seemed to decline after he designed the Isabella Building (1893) and the Central YMCA Building (1893), both in Chicago. In 1905 Elmer C. Jensen became a partner in the firm, which became Jenney, Mundie, and Jensen. Jenney died in 1907.

Source:
Carl W. Condit, *The Chicago School of Architecture* (Chicago: University of Chicago Press, 1964).

BERNARD MAYBECK

1862-1957

ARCHITECT

Eclectic Style. Bernard Maybeck's eclecticism made him unique in American architecture. In what many consider his best building, the First Church of Christ, Scientist (1910), in Berkeley, California, Maybeck drew on design elements of Byzantine, Romanesque, Gothic, Renaissance, Japanese, and Chinese architecture. A free spirit, he inscribed the initials of his future wife in a monogram that ran around the top of one of his early buildings. He designed his own clothes, including trousers with a high waist that served as a vest.

Early Life and Training. Maybeck was born in New York City in 1862 to German immigrants. His mother wanted Maybeck to become an artist, but he did poorly in school and joined his father as an apprentice woodcarver. At eighteen he went to Paris as an apprentice in furniture design. The shop was across the street from the Ecole des Beaux Arts; this exposure led him to become fascinated with architecture, and he enrolled in the school. From his years in Paris came Maybeck's love of classic Greek, Romanesque, and Gothic forms.

California. Graduating from the Ecole des Beaux Arts in 1886, Maybeck returned to New York and joined the architectural firm Carrère and Hastings. In 1888 Maybeck moved to Kansas City, Missouri, and formed a partnership with James Russell; the following year he left for Berkeley, California, where he worked as an architect, a furniture designer, a wood-carver, and a draftsman. Maybeck's early buildings drew from the Arts and Crafts movement, inspired by William Morris in England with his use of wood and ornate, handcrafted detail. Unlike his fellow California architects Charles and Henry Greene, Maybeck gradually abandoned the simplicities of wood architecture and developed a more complicated and eclectic use of forms and materials. In 1894 he began teaching at the University of California, Berkeley; his courses were the beginnings of the College of Architecture. In his first major building, the university's Hearst Hall (1899), laminated arches made of glued layers of wood eliminated the need for columns in the center of the building. Maybeck continued his innovative approach to structures in his Town and Gown Clubhouse (1899) in Berkeley. He initiated and administered an international competition for a campus master plan that was sponsored and paid for by Phoebe Apperson Hearst; in 1901 John Galen Howard won the competition and replaced Maybeck as professor of architecture. Maybeck also built the Faculty Club (1902) on the Berkeley campus, the Outdoor Art Clubhouse (1905) in Mill Valley, the Hopps House (1906) in Moss Valley, and the Lawson House (1907) and the Chick House (1913) in Berkeley.

Later Life. Maybeck was always a poor manager of money, and his finances took a downturn in the 1910s. He was forced to take a job as a draftsman with one of his former students, Willis Polk. He continued to impress his peers with his designs, particularly those for the Palace of Fine Arts for the San Francisco Panama-Pacific International Exposition in 1915. The palace's structure was formed with three-hinged steel arches that had only been used in a few buildings up to that time. Polk put Maybeck in charge of the work and gave him full credit for it, yet Maybeck continued to work for draftsman wages. The palace was the only building allowed to remain standing after the exposition closed, and it was rebuilt in 1967. After returning to independent practice, he designed the Hearst Memorial Gymnasium for Women (1927) on the Berkeley campus, a twenty-one-level home (1927), automobile showrooms (1928) in Berkeley and San Francisco for Earle C. Anthony, and the campus of Principia College (1938) in Elsah, Illinois. Maybeck slipped into obscurity, but, as with the Greene brothers, a renewed interest in the use of wood in architecture led to a renewed interest in his work. In 1951 Maybeck was awarded the Gold Medal, the highest honor of the American Institute of Architects. He died in 1957.

Source:
Kenneth H. Cardwill, *Bernard Maybeck — Artisan, Architect, Artist* (Santa Barbara, Cal.: Peregrine Smith, 1976).

LOUIS SULLIVAN

1856-1924

ARCHITECT

Chicago's Premier Architect. While not recognized in his own time as a pioneer of modern architecture, Louis Henri Sullivan enjoyed the admiration of his peers during his years as Chicago's premier architect. He was one of the first architects in the late nineteenth century to struggle to free the profession from its adherence to styles of the past, to decoration for its own sake, to masking the functions of buildings in an effort to emphasize their surface effects. His dictum "form follows function" subsumed aesthetics to structure without sacrificing elegance. This dictum became the rallying cry of modern architects, beginning with Sullivan's most famous student, Frank Lloyd Wright. Sullivan's most important work took place between 1880 and 1905, after which he sank into obscurity. Later his reputation was restored by American and European architects who pointed out that Sullivan was the progenitor of architectural modernism. The great American architectural critic Lewis Mumford called him "the [Walt] Whitman of American architecture." The American Institute of Architects awarded Sullivan its Gold Medal in 1946, twenty-two years after his death.

Early Life and Training. Sullivan was born in Boston in 1856 and spent much of his youth on his grandparents' farm near the city. He entered the Massachusetts Institute of Technology in 1872 to study architecture but left after a year for New York City, Philadelphia, and finally Chicago, where he briefly worked for the architect William Le Baron Jenney. He attended the Ecole des Beaux Arts in Paris for six months, returning, disillusioned, to Chicago in early 1875. In 1879 he went to work for Dankmar Adler; in 1881 the two men formed a partnership. The first important building to reflect what would become Sullivan's unique style was the Borden Block (1880), in which he experimented with the structure, form, and ornamentation of tall buildings. One of Sullivan's greatest works was the Auditorium (1890), designed with his partner, Adler. At the time it was completed it was the tallest building in Chicago, and it soon came to be regarded as one of the world's finest opera houses. The Auditorium had five thousand lights and 150 footlights, and could seat four thousand people. Its blend of rational structure and poetic ornamentation elevated Sullivan to international fame. Sullivan went on to design the Garrick Theater in the Schiller Building (1892), the Transportation Building (1893) for the World's Columbian Exposition, and the Stock Exchange Building (1894), all in Chicago. The Wainwright Building (1892) in Saint Louis is believed to be the first tall building to express its steel skeleton in its exterior.

Later Life. After designing the Guaranty (later Prudential) Building (1895) in Buffalo, New York, Adler and Sullivan dissolved their partnership. Sullivan's career took a downturn after the partnership ended; but despite a dwindling clientele, in 1904 he designed what many consider one of his best buildings: the Schlesinger and Mayer store — now the Carson, Pirie, Scott department store — in Chicago won praise for the purity of its exterior. Sullivan also designed a series of bank buildings for small towns in Minnesota, Iowa, Wisconsin, and Ohio; some of these banks are still admired for their forms and ornamentation. The best is the first, the National Farmers (later Security) Bank Building (1908) in Owatonna,

Minnesota. Sullivan became an alcoholic and died, forgotten and in debt, in 1924, his accomplishments not yet fully appreciated.

Source:
Albert Bush-Brown, *Louis Sullivan* (New York: Braziller, 1960).

LOUIS COMFORT TIFFANY

1848-1933

DESIGNER

Decorator to the Wealthy. Louis Comfort Tiffany began his career in the late nineteenth century as what today would be called an interior decorator. While helping wealthy clients coordinate the furniture, wallpaper, tapestries, carpets, and light fixtures in their new homes, Tiffany became interested in the decorative possibilities of leaded-glass windows. Rejecting etched and painted glass, he experimented with colored glass. He found most colored glass too dull for his tastes, so he hired chemists to develop richer and more vibrant colors. He also experimented with different types of glass and with double panes. Tiffany's daring techniques resulted in masterful designs that used light as an active element in a way that was previously unimaginable. Tiffany also experimented with multicolored glass in mosaics, designing large, inlaid murals for the Curtis Publishing Company in Philadelphia and for the National Theater in Mexico City; on the latter project twenty men worked for more than fifteen months to produce two hundred of the three-foot-square panels required for construction.

Early Life and Training. Louis Comfort Tiffany was born in 1848 into a wealthy family. His father, Charles Tiffany, a dealer in fine silver and jewelry, founded Tiffany and Company a year before Louis Tiffany's birth. Tiffany graduated from the Flushing Academy on Long Island at eighteen, then studied with the painters George Innes and Samuel Colman before going to Paris to study under Leon Bailly. After traveling in Europe and Africa, he returned to New York in 1870. The following year he was elected an associate of the National Academy of Design.

Designer and Collector. Tiffany continued as a painter, but his familiarity with America's upper class soon led him into designing their homes. He gathered an army of craftsmen and craftswomen and managed every detail, coordinating furniture, wallpaper, tapestries, carpets, and light fixtures into coherent decorative styles. In the 1880s Tiffany worked for Cornelius Vanderbilt in New York, Potter Palmer in Chicago, and Lily Langtry in London. He decorated several rooms in the White House in 1883. He supplied his clients with the rarest objets d'art money could buy and in the process became a great collector himself.

Glass and Light. Tiffany became interested in the decorative potential of glass in windows, drinking glasses, vases, and lamps. Soon he was designing ornate windows of richly colored glass pieced together with lead. His scenes, illuminated from behind by sunlight or gaslight, shimmered with color. He experimented, together with a chemist, with methods for enhancing the iridescence and colors of glass, creating what became known as Favrile Glass, in which the pigment was injected directly into the molten glass. He formed the Tiffany Glass Company in 1878, which became the Tiffany Glass and Decorating Company in 1892. In the 1900s he began producing bronze-based lamps that supported colorful leaded glass shades. In London he showed a dragonfly-shade lamp of leaded glass and the Nautilus Lamp, consisting of a bronze mermaid base holding up a shade made from a nautilus shell. The Pond Lily Lamp, exhibited in 1902, comprised a cluster of eighteen bronze stems curving upward to form a lily-pad base and terminating in slender decorated shades. Other leaded-glass shades were designed to be suspended from the ceiling. Besides lamps, Tiffany designed domestic tableware in gold or deep blue iridescent glass: liqueur, claret, sherry, champagne, and water glasses; decanters; finger bowls; ice cream plates; pin trays; and salt cellars. His decorative patterns included the Flemish, slightly waisted with an applied band of horizontal parallel glass threads; the Royal, an elegant double-twist stem; the Earl, glass stretched into frills; and the Prime and the Queen, fairly plain patterns with straight stems that were produced in the greatest quantity. Tiffany's Art Nouveau style won him many customers, as well as fifty-four design awards: the latter included the Grand Prix and a Special Diploma at the 1902 First International Exhibition of Modern Decorative Arts in Turin, a Gold Medal at the 1904 World's Fair in Saint Louis, a Medal of Honour at the 1907 Jamestown Exposition, a Grand Prix at the 1909 Seattle Exposition, a Gold Medal at the 1915 Panama-Pacific Exposition in San Francisco, and a Gold Medal at the 1926 Philadelphia Sesquicentennial Exposition.

Later Life. Tiffany's career declined during the 1920s, and by the 1930s he had little left but a warehouse full of unwanted glass. Tiffany died in 1933, a month before his eighty-fifth birthday. While he never again saw his work appreciated as it had been in the first decades of the century, Tiffany's achievements have been reappraised and now are regarded as some of America's foremost design treasures.

Source:
Victor Arwas, *Glass: Art Nouveau to Art Deco* (New York: Abrams, 1987).

FRANK LLOYD WRIGHT

1867-1959

ARCHITECT

Innovator. Frank Lloyd Wright was one of America's — and the world's — most innovative and creative architects. He began his sixty-six-year career copying past styles and went on to play an important part in the establishment of modern architecture. Wright experimented with steel and concrete cantilevers and poured concrete; he was one of the first architects to see the aesthetic value of concrete blocks. He designed buildings of custom-cast blocks with patterns. He also introduced open planning, creating spaces that flowed into each other rather than separating them into distinct rooms. The critic Lewis Mumford said that Wright "altered the inner rhythm of the modern building." Wright was also interested in the creative possibilities of the machine and frequently used factory-manufactured products in his buildings.

Early Life and Training. Wright was born in Richland Center, Wisconsin, in 1867. His mother, who wanted her son to become an architect, began tutoring him in the kindergarten-education techniques of Frederick Froebel when Wright was seven years old. Wright was given a set of blocks, folded paper, and other simple materials, from which he was to design and build model buildings and furniture. In later years Wright claimed that his work with the Froebel system profoundly influenced his architecture. When Wright was sixteen, his father deserted the family. At about the same time, Wright enrolled in the civil engineering program at the University of Wisconsin at Madison. At eighteen he dropped out and worked briefly for a Madison architect, then went to Chicago to work as a designer and draftsman for Louis Sullivan and Sullivan's partner, Dankmar Adler. In 1893 he began his own practice.

The Prairie Style. One of the finest houses Wright designed in what became known as the Prairie Style was the Frederick G. Robie House (1909) in Chicago. Wright said that he wanted to "break the box" of most domestic architecture, and with the Robie House he did so. Designed for a wealthy bicycle manufacturer who was sympathetic to Wright's vision, the Robie House was a long, horizontal structure of brick and wood topped with mammoth overhanging eaves and lighted by long banks of glass windows. Inside, the main floor was a single room broken into subsidiary spaces that merged and overlapped. The delineation of these spaces through light, glass, and color rather than walls was based on Japanese design, long an inspiration to Wright, as it had been to Sullivan. Other notable Prairie houses were those Wright designed for Ward W. Willits in Highland Park, Illinois (1902); for Arthur Heurtley in Chicago (1902); and for Avery Coonley in River Forest, Illinois (1909).

Organic Architecture. The second period of Wright's career lasted from 1909 — in which year Wright, like his father before him, deserted his family (a wife and six children) — to 1944. In these years the architect refined what he called "organic architecture," an aesthetic based on the harmony of nature. In 1911 he designed and built his home and studio, Taliesin (Welsh for "shining brow" and the name of a sixth-century Welsh poet); it would be destroyed by fire twice and rebuilt each time. The Kaufmann House (1937), also called Fallingwater, in Bear Run, Pennsylvania, was built over a waterfall. The geometrical Johnson Wax Company Administration Building (1939) in Racine, Wisconsin, expressed the building's structure in strikingly new ways. Wright designed the campus and buildings for Florida Southern University in Lakeland, Florida, and his own winter house and studio, Taliesin West (1938), in Scottsdale, Arizona, during this period. He also worked on plans for a utopian American city called Usonia.

Late Period. After World War II Wright was swamped with commissions. He built the Unitarian Church (1947) in Madison, Wisconsin; the Beth Shalom Synagogue (1959) in Elkins Park, Pennsylvania; and the H. C. Price Company Tower (1953), a sixteen-story building with professional office spaces and duplex apartments in Bartlesville, Oklahoma — Wright's only free-standing high-rise building. In 1949 the American Institute of Architects awarded Wright its Gold Medal. Wright continued to work until the end of his life. The total number of buildings he produced during his career is unknown but has been estimated as high as six hundred. He died in 1959, the year the revolutionary Guggenheim Museum — which he had begun designing in 1943 — was completed.

Source:
Robert Twombly, *Frank Lloyd Wright: His Life and His Architecture* (New York: Wiley, 1978).

PEOPLE IN THE NEWS

Bragging about the speed of his new Model 10 car, automaker **William "Billy" Durant** explained in 1908 that his car was for "men with real red blood who don't like to eat dust."

Old-time vaudevillians **Gus Edwards** and **Vincent Bryan** captured the nation's mood with their hit 1905 song "In My Merry Oldsmobile"— "It Glides! It Romps!! It Gallops!!!"

Ford's racing cars, the Arrow and 999, with their eighty-horsepower engines, went so fast that they had a tendency to take to the air. Inventor **Henry Ford** described the experience in October 1902: "Going over Niagara Falls would have been but a pastime after a ride in one of them."

Charles Dana Gibson, the illustrator who created the Gibson Girl, continued to be surprised by the notoriety of his heroine. "If I hadn't seen it in the papers," he said in 1906, "I should never have known that there was such a thing as a Gibson Girl."

Henry M. Leland explained his philosophy of car design in 1902: "There always was and there always will be conflict between good and good enough . . . one must sweat blood for a chance to produce a superior product."

Commentator **Robert Sloss** announced in *Outing* in 1909 that it was time to recognize that "woman not only can do but has done with the automobile everything of which man can boast — in some respects she had done it better."

AWARDS

PARIS UNIVERSAL EXPOSITION

1900 — Tiffany and Company wins three Grand Prix medals, ten Gold Medals, ten Silver Medals, and two Bronze Medals; Louis Comfort Tiffany is awarded a Gold Medal.

FIRST INTERNATIONAL EXHIBITION OF MODERN DECORATIVE ARTS IN TURIN, ITALY

1902 — Louis Comfort Tiffany wins the Grand Prix and a special diploma.

SAINT LOUIS WORLD'S FAIR

1904 — Louis Comfort Tiffany wins a Gold Medal.

JAMESTOWN EXPOSITION

1907 — Louis Comfort Tiffany wins a Medal of Honour.

SEATTLE EXPOSITION

1909 — Louis Comfort Tiffany wins a Grand Prix.

DEATHS

Dankmar Adler, 55, architect, former partner of Louis Sullivan in Chicago, 15 April 1900.

William M. Aiken, 53, supervising architect of the U.S. Treasury Department, 7 December 1908.

Frank E. Alden, 49, architect, founding partner of Alden and Harlow in Pittsburgh, Pennsylvania, and designer of the original Carnegie Library, 5 May 1908.

Thomas B. Annan, 67, Saint Louis architect, 12 November 1904.

Mifflin E. Bell, 58, who was appointed U.S. supervising architect by President Chester A. Arthur and later helped design the Illinois capitol, 14 June 1904.

John Bogardus, 74, who designed more buildings in Stamford, Connecticut, than any other architect of his time, 14 June 1903.

Walter Dickson, 69, one of the architects who designed and built the U.S. Immigration Bureau on Ellis Island in New York Harbor, 3 September 1903.

Thomas D. Evans, 59, prominent Pittsburgh, Pennsylvania, architect who designed the Shakespeare Library, 20 April 1903.

Jackson Gott, 82, one of Baltimore's most significant architects, 9 July 1909.

Herbert D. Hale, 43, founding partner of New York City architectural firm Hale and Rogers, 19 November 1909.

Edward S. Hammat, 51, architect whose many works included plans for Saint Augustine College in Raleigh, North Carolina, 24 August 1907.

Joseph C. Hornblower, 60, one of the architects of the Museum of Natural History Building of the Smithsonian Institution, 22 August 1908.

Frank M. Howe, 60, architect who, along with his partners in Van Brunt and Howe, built the Electricity Building at the 1893 World's Columbian Exposition in Chicago, 4 January 1909.

William Le Baron Jenney, 74, Chicago engineer-turned-architect who designed the Home Insurance Building (1885), which many regard as the first skyscraper, 14 June 1907.

George A. Mathews, 43, architect who helped design many of Kansas City's most notable buildings, such as the First Christian Science Church and a factory for Procter and Gamble, 29 September 1903.

John Newton Richardson, 66, architect and engineer who designed the Masonic Temple, the Scottish Rite Temple, and the Jewish Orphanage in Cleveland, Ohio, 6 May 1902.

George Foster Shepley, 42, senior partner in the distinguished Boston architectural firm Shepley, Rutan, and Coolidge, 16 July 1903.

Alfred Stone, 74, founding partner in the Providence, Rhode Island, architectural firm Stone and Carpenter who designed the city's courthouse and public library, 4 September 1908.

Edward H. Swain, 50, San Francisco architect, 10 April 1902.

Stanford White, 52, architect who designed New York's Madison Square Garden (1889), 25 June 1906.

PUBLICATIONS

Maurice Bingham Adams, ed., *Modern Cottage Architecture* (New York: Lane, 1904);

Atlas Portland Cement Company, *Concrete Country Residences* (New York: Atlas Portland Cement, 1906?);

John Cordis Baker, ed., *American Country Homes and Their Gardens* (Philadelphia: Winston, 1906);

Isabel Bevier, *The House: Its Plan, Decoration and Care* (Chicago: American School of Home Economics, 1907);

The Book of a Hundred Houses: A Collection of Pictures, Plans and Suggestions for Householder (Chicago: Stone, 1902);

Helen Churchill Candee, *Decorative Styles and Periods in the Home* (New York: Stokes, 1906);

Oliver Bronson Capen, *Country Homes of Famous Americans* (New York: Doubleday, Page, 1905);

Frank George Carpenter, *How the World Is Clothed* (New York: American Book, 1908);

Chandler R. Clifford, *Period Decoration* (New York: Clifford & Lawton, 1901);

William T. Comstock, ed., *Two-Family and Twin Houses* (New York: Comstock, 1908);

Cyclopedia of Architecture, Carpentry and Building, 10 volumes (Chicago: American School of Correspondence, 1907);

Fred H. Daniels, *The Furnishing of a Modest Home* (New York: Atkinson, Mentzer, 1908);

Daniels, *The Teaching of Ornament* (New York: Witter, 1900);

Harry William Desmond, *Stately Homes in America from Colonial Times to the Present* (New York: Appleton, 1903);

Aymar Embury, *One Hundred Country Houses: Modern American Examples* (New York: Century, 1909);

Margherita Arline Hamm, *Eminent Actors in Their Homes* (New York: Pott, 1902);

William Herbert (Herbert David Croly), *Houses for Town or Country* (New York: Duffield, 1907);

Frederick Thomas Hodgson, *Easy Steps to Architecture and Architecture of Antiquity, for Home Study* (Chicago: Drake, 1907);

Hodgson, *Hodgson's Low Cost American Homes: Perspective Views and Floor Plans of One Hundred Low and Medium Priced Houses* (Chicago: Drake, 1904);

James E. Homans, *Self Propelled Vehicles: A Practical Treatise on the Theory, Construction, Operation, Care and Management of All Forms of Automobiles* (New York: Audel, 1906);

Home Building and Furnishing (New York: Doubleday, Page, 1903);

Charles Edward Hooper, *The Country House: A Practical Manual of the Planning and Construction of the American Country Home and Its Surroundings* (New York: Doubleday, Page, 1905);

Norman M. Isham and Albert F. Brown, *Early Connecticut Houses: An Historical and Architectural Study* (Providence, R.I.: Preston & Rounds, 1900);

Rhys Jenkins, *Motor Cars and the Application of Mechanical Power to Road Vehicles* (New York: Pott, 1902);

Frank Eugene Kidder, *The Architect's and Builder's Pocket-Book* (New York: Wiley, 1904);

Theodore Wesley Koch, *A Portfolio of Carnegie Libraries* (Ann Arbor, Mich.: Wahr, 1907);

Sigmund Krausz, *Krausz's Practical Automobile Dictionary* (New York: Stokes, 1906);

Louis Valcoulon Le Moyne, *Country Residences in Europe and America* (New York: Doubleday, Page, 1908);

Charles Moore, ed., *The Promise of American Architecture: Addresses at the Annual Dinner of the American Institute of Architects, 1905* (Washington, D.C.: American Institute of Architects, 1905);

Jesse Eliphalet Pope, *The Clothing Industry in New York* (Columbia: University of Missouri Press, 1905);

Charles W. Quin, *The Complete House Builder* (Chicago: Donohue, 1904);

William A. Radford, *Radford's Portfolio of Plans: A Standard Collection of New and Original Designs for Houses,*

Bungalows, Store and Flat Buildings, Apartment Houses, Banks, Churches, Schoolhouses, Barns, Outbuildings, etc., Together with Estimates of Cost (Chicago: Radford Architectural, 1909);

S. B. Reed, *Modern House-Plans for Everybody* (New York: Orange Judd, 1900);

G. Woolliscroft Rhead, *The Principles of Design* (New York: Scribners, 1905);

Jaques Denton Snider, *Architecture as a Branch of Aesthetic, Psychologically Treated* (Saint Louis: Sigma, 1905);

Charles Carroll Soule, *Library Rooms and Buildings* (Boston: Published for the American Library Association by Houghton, Mifflin, 1902);

Gustav Stickley, *Craftsman Homes* (New York: Craftsman, 1909);

Russell Sturgis, *A History of Architecture*, 4 volumes (New York: Baker & Taylor, 1906–1915);

Sturgis and others, *A Dictionary of Architecture and Building, Biographical, Historical, and Descriptive*, 3 volumes (New York: Macmillan, 1901–1902);

Louis Sullivan, *Kindergarten Chats on Architecture, Education and Democracy* (New York: Wittenborn, 1901–1902).

Percy Leslie Waterhouse, *The Story of the Art of Building* (New York: Appleton, 1901);

Charles Welsh, ed., *Chauffeur Chaff; or, Automobilia: Anecdotes, Stories, Bon-Mots, also a History of the Evolution of the Automobile* (Boston: Caldwell, 1905);

Edith Wharton and Ogden Codman, *The Decoration of Houses* (New York: Scribners, 1907);

Mabel Hurd Willett, *The Employment of Women in the Clothing Trade* (New York: Columbia University Press, 1902);

A. B. Filson Young, *The Complete Motorist: Being an Account of the Evolution and Construction of the Modern Motor-Car: With Notes on the Selection, Use, and Maintenance of the Same; and on the Pleasures of Travel upon the Public Roads* (New York: McClure, Phillips, 1904);

American Architect, periodical;

American Institute of Architects Quarterly Bulletin, periodical;

Architectural Record, periodical;

Architectural Review, periodical;

Brickbuilder, periodical;

Craftsman, periodical;

Cycle and Automobile, periodical;

Hand Book of Gasoline Automobiles, periodical;

Harper's Bazaar, periodical;

House and Garden, periodical;

House Beautiful, periodical;

Ladies' Home Journal, periodical;

Motor, periodical;

Town and Country, periodical;

Vogue, periodical.

GOVERNMENT AND POLITICS

by JAMES G. LEWIS

CONTENTS

Sidebars and tables are listed in italics.

1900

- Fighting continues in the Philippines as the United States tries to suppress the Filipino rebels led by Emilio Aguinaldo.

- Secretary of State John Hay continues negotiations with countries that have commerce, treaties, and long-term leases with China in an effort to get them to agree to his "Open Door" policy, through which they would support "equal and impartial trade with all parts of the Chinese Empire" and not attempt to prevent trade by other countries within their spheres of influence.

2 Jan.   Secretary Hay announces to the cabinet that he has completed negotiations for the "Open Door" in China.

6 Feb.   Theodore Roosevelt, hero of the Spanish-American War and presently governor of New York, declares that he neither could nor would accept the nomination for the vice presidency on the Republican ticket.

President McKinley appoints William Howard Taft, a U.S. circuit judge, head of the Philippine Commission to establish a civil government in the islands.

6 Mar.   The Social Democratic Party holds its national convention in Indianapolis, Indiana, nominating Eugene V. Debs of Indiana for president and Job Harrison of California for vice president.

14 Mar.   Congress passes the Gold Standard Act, which establishes a set weight for a gold dollar and places all forms of U.S. money on a parity with gold.

24 Mar.   The new Carnegie Steel Company is incorporated in New Jersey in direct defiance of the Sherman Antitrust Law of 1890, which has proven ineffective in preventing the establishment of industrial monopolies. Capitalized at $160 million, the new company is the largest and most controversial incorporation to date.

4 Apr.   Adm. George Dewey, naval hero of the Spanish-American War, announces his willingness to be a candidate for the presidency.

12 Apr.   The Foraker Act confirms the status of Puerto Rico as an unconsolidated territory of the United States, conferring on its citizens substantially the same system of government that England had subjected the American colonies to prior to 1773.

13 Apr.   For the fourth time in eight years the House of Representatives adopts a resolution favoring a constitutional amendment for the election of United States senators by direct vote of the people instead of by state legislatures. The Senate finally concurs in 1911.

30 Apr.   By act of Congress Hawaii is granted territorial standing in the United States, joining Alaska, Oklahoma, New Mexico, and Arizona as American territories. Sanford B. Dole is appointed governor of the new territory.

9 May   A splinter group of the Populist Party meets in Cincinnati, Ohio, nominating Wharton Barker of Pennsylvania for president and Ignatius Donnelly of Minnesota for vice president. On the same day the main branch of the Populist Party meets in Sioux Falls, South Dakota, and once again nominates William Jennings Bryan for president. Joining him on the ticket is Charles A. Town of Minnesota.

14 May   In *Knowlton* v. *Moore* the Supreme Court finds that the inheritance tax, levied for the first time in the United States under the War Revenue Act of 1898, is indeed constitutional.

21 May   Secretary of State Hay informs the Boer envoys from southern Africa that the United States will not recede from its position of strict neutrality during the Boer War.

The House of Representatives passes a bill mandating the eight-hour workday on government contracts — an important victory for labor.

2 June   The Socialist Labor Party convenes in New York and nominates Joseph P. Maloney of Massachusetts for president and Valentine Remmel of Pennsylvania for vice president.

19–21 June   At its national convention in Philadelphia the Republican Party nominates President William McKinley to run for a second term. Despite his earlier denial of interest in the second spot on the ticket, Theodore Roosevelt receives the vice-presidential nomination, which he has in fact encouraged by attending the convention.

20 June   Student revolutionaries in China, seeking to rid their country of all "foreign devils" by force, begin the Boxer Rebellion. Foreign diplomats and residents in Peking remain under siege in the British legation for almost two months.

21 June   Gen. Arthur MacArthur, the military governor of the Philippines, issues a proclamation granting amnesty to Filipino insurgents.

27 June   The Prohibition Party nominates John G. Woolley of Illinois for president and Henry B. Metcalf of Rhode Island for vice president.

3 July   The Chinese revolutionaries are prevented from killing the diplomats trapped in the British legation by the timely arrival of American, British, Japanese, and French troops. In the aftermath of the revolt, Secretary of State Hay issues a second "Open Door" note reiterating the need to protect Chinese territorial integrity and to leave all parts of China open to equal and impartial trade.

4–6 July   Meeting in Kansas City the Democratic Party chooses William Jennings Bryan of Nebraska, already the Populist Party presidential candidate, to head its national slate with Adlai E. Stevenson of Illinois as his running mate.

8 Aug.   Wisconsin Republicans nominate Robert M. La Follette to run for governor on a platform advocating nominations by direct popular vote and the abolition of party caucuses and conventions. He is elected by more than one hundred thousand votes.

8 Sept.   A devastating hurricane kills six thousand people in Galveston, Texas, causing property damage in excess of $20 million. The disorganization that follows leads to the establishment of a commission form of city government, which becomes a model for municipal-government reforms nationwide.

17 Sept.– 25 Oct.   One hundred and twelve thousand anthracite-coal miners in the Northeast go on strike, causing the price of anthracite coal in New York to rise from $1.00 to $6.50 a ton. Acting on behalf of President McKinley, Sen. Mark Hanna mediates a quick settlement.

18 Sept.   The first direct primary in the United States is held in Hennepin County, Minnesota.

6 Nov.   Republican William McKinley easily defeats Democrat William Jennings Bryan in the presidential election. The Republicans hold majorities in both houses of Congress.

29 Dec.   The U.S. State Department announces that negotiations for the purchase of the Danish West Indies (the Virgin Islands) are near completion, but the deal does not go through until 1917.

1901

21 Feb.   Cuba adopts a constitution patterned on that of the United States.

2 Mar.   Congress passes an Army Appropriations Act that includes the Platt Amendment, which establishes continued American domination of Cuban foreign relations. The amendment is abrogated on 29 May 1934.

4 Mar.   William McKinley is inaugurated for a second term as president; Theodore Roosevelt is sworn in as vice president.

23 Mar.   Emilio Aguinaldo, leader of the Filipino rebellion against the United States, is captured by American forces in Luzon.

19 Apr.   The rebellion in the Philippines ends with a proclamation from Aguinaldo.

27 May   The Supreme Court returns verdicts on the first of what are known as the Insular Cases, some fourteen decisions rendered during 1901–1904 that define the application of the Constitution and the Bill of Rights to overseas territories. Declaring that territories acquired as a result of the Spanish-American War are neither foreign countries nor part of the United States, the court rules that "the Constitution follows the flag," but in a later case it says that the privileges of United States citizenship can be granted only by Congress.

6 June   The last of the U.S. volunteer troops leave the Philippines en route to the United States. Only regulars remain in the islands.

10 June   President McKinley issues a statement declaring he has no interest in seeking a third term and would not accept the nomination.

25 July   Against the protests of American commercial interests, President McKinley issues a proclamation establishing free trade between Puerto Rico and the United States. He also installs a civil government there.

5 Sept.   McKinley makes a plea for trade reciprocity, arguing that American industry is strong enough to compete with other countries without tariff protection at home.

6 Sept.   While visiting the Pan-American Exhibition in Buffalo, New York, President McKinley is shot by anarchist Leon Czolgosz.

14 Sept.   President McKinley dies at 2:15 A.M. as a result of his wounds and of inept medical treatment. Theodore Roosevelt takes the oath of office at 3:00 P.M. the same day.

16 Oct.   President Roosevelt invites black leader Booker T. Washington to the White House, outraging southern whites.

4 Nov.   After the exposure of far-reaching corruption in the New York City police department, candidates from the infamous Tammany Hall political machine that has controlled the city for years are beaten by a reform ticket headed by Seth Low, president of Columbia University.

18 Nov.   Great Britain and the United States sign the Hay-Pauncefote Treaty, which authorizes the United States to build, operate, and fortify a canal across the Central American isthmus.

28 Nov.   Alabama adopts a new constitution that effectively disenfranchises blacks (and some poor whites) by including literacy and property tests, as well as a measure known as the "grandfather" clause, which states that a person cannot vote if his grandfather was ineligible. It also denies suffrage to individuals convicted of certain "criminal" acts.

3 Dec.	In his first State of the Union message to Congress, President Roosevelt calls for the regulation of business trusts "within reasonable limits" and becomes the first president to advocate the conservation of natural resources on public land.
16 Dec.	The Senate ratifies the Hay-Pauncefote Treaty.

1902

3 Jan.	The French Panama Canal Company announces that it has decided to offer the canal property and franchises to the United States for $40 million.
24 Jan.	The United States signs a treaty agreeing to purchase the Virgin Islands from Denmark. The U.S. Senate approves the treaty, but the Danish Rigsday rejects it.
6 Mar.	Congress creates the U.S. Bureau of the Census.
8 Mar.	Roosevelt signs the Philippine tariff bill, providing that merchandise coming into the United States from the Philippines should be taxed at a 25 percent lower rate than that levied on merchandise from other countries.
10 Mar.	At President Roosevelt's instigation, Attorney General Philander C. Knox files to dissolve the Northern Securities Company under the Sherman Antitrust Act.
29 Apr.	The Chinese Exclusion Act is extended to prohibit Chinese laborers from coming from the Philippines.
20 May	The United States withdraws its troops from Cuba as the first president of the newly independent nation is installed.
17 June	Following President Roosevelt's suggestion, Congress passes the Newlands Reclamation Act, authorizing the construction of irrigation dams across the West.
28 June	Congress passes the Spooner or Isthmian Canal Act, which authorizes the president to negotiate with France for the purchase of rights to construct a canal in the Colombian province of Panama.
1 July	Congress passes the Philippine Government Act, which authorizes the president, with the advice and consent of Congress, to appoint a commission to run the islands. The act also declares the inhabitants to be citizens of the archipelago, not the United States.
4 July	President Roosevelt signs the Philippine Government Act and grants amnesty to Filipino political prisoners.
11 Aug.	Oliver Wendell Holmes is appointed to the U.S. Supreme Court.
19 Aug.	President Roosevelt begins a speaking tour around New England and the Midwest to spread his message against the irresponsibility of trusts and monopolies to an enthusiastic electorate.
15 Sept.	The United States and Mexico are the first two countries to use the Permanent Court of Arbitration at The Hague to settle an international dispute.
14 Oct.	The Hague Arbitration Court renders its first decision, ruling that Mexico must make back payment of interest on a debt owed to the United States.
21 Oct.	The United Mine Workers anthracite-coal strike, which began on 12 May, ends after the direct intervention of President Roosevelt, who convinces the owners and workers to accept the results of arbitration by a presidential commission.

1903

4 Nov.   In off-year elections both major parties gain seats at the expense of the minority parties, and the Republicans maintain control of both houses of Congress.

11 Jan.   Governor-General William Howard Taft of the Philippines is serenaded by six thousand Filipinos, who beg him not to accept an appointment to the U.S. Supreme Court, which President Roosevelt is reportedly preparing to offer him.

22 Jan.   Colombia and the United States sign the Hay-Herrán Treaty, granting the United States a ninety-nine-year lease on a six-mile-wide zone in which to construct the Panama Canal. The Colombian Senate rejects the treaty on 12 August.

11 Feb.   Responding to popular and presidential pressures, Congress adopts the Expedition Act, which gives priority to the attorney general's antitrust cases in the circuit courts.

14 Feb.   A ninth cabinet-level department, Commerce and Labor, is created. George B. Cortelyou is named its first secretary.

Congress authorizes centralization of the military, creating the General Staff of the Army.

19 Feb.   Congress passes the Elkins Act, which outlaws all rebates on published railroad freight rates. It does not, however, extend to regulation of rates.

23 Feb.   In *Champion* v. *Ames* the Supreme Court upholds a federal law that prohibits lottery tickets from being sent through the mails from one state to another. Arguing that federal police power supersedes the police powers of the states, the court says that the Interstate Commerce Act allows the federal government to prohibit as well as to regulate. The ruling is the basis for later regulation of food, drugs, and other items.

President Roosevelt signs an agreement by which the United States acquires sites for two naval stations in Cuba.

21 Mar.   The Anthracite Coal Strike Commission, created by President Roosevelt to settle the UMW strike, releases a report favorable to the miners on most issues.

27 Apr.   The Supreme Court upholds the clause in the Alabama constitution that can be used to disenfranchise African Americans.

1 May   New Hampshire, after forty-eight years of complete prohibition, institutes a system of licenses for liquor sales.

20 May   Cuba and the United States sign a permanent treaty embodying the provisions of the Platt Amendment.

23 May   Wisconsin becomes the first state to adopt direct primary elections.

26 June   The National Colored Immigration and Commercial Association petitions President Roosevelt and Congress for $100 million to transport African Americans to Liberia.

20 Oct.   A joint commission set up on 24 January by Great Britain and the United States to report on their Alaskan boundary dispute rules in favor of U.S. interests.

2 Nov.	Three U.S. Navy warships are ordered to prevent Colombian troops from landing in the Colombian province of Panama, where Panamians are making plans to secede from Colombia at the urging of Panamanian businessmen, French agents of the Panama Canal Company, and U.S. Army officers.
3 Nov.	Panamanian forces rebel as expected at six in the evening with no bloodshed. Colombia dispatches troops by sea to suppress the revolt, but they are prevented from landing in Panama by the presence of the USS *Nashville* at Colón. The Republic of Panama is proclaimed, and the local fire department becomes the army.
6 Nov.	Secretary of State John Hay recognizes the new Panamanian government.
10 Nov.	Joseph G. Cannon becomes Speaker of the House of Representatives and subsequently becomes one of the most powerful speakers in U.S. history.
18 Nov.	The United States and Panama sign the Hay–Bunau-Varilla Treaty giving the United States permanent rights to a ten-mile-wide canal zone in return for $10 million and an annual payment of $250,000 after nine years.
2 Dec.	Panama ratifies the Hay–Bunau-Varilla Treaty.
10 Dec.	The U.S. Marines formally occupy their first base on Cuba, at Guantánamo Bay.
30 Dec.	A fire at the Iroquois Theater in Chicago kills 588 persons. Public reaction leads to new theater codes in many American cities, including more fire walls and more and better exits.

1904

4 Jan.	The Supreme Court rules in *Gonzalez* v. *Williams* that Puerto Ricans are not aliens and may not be refused admission to the continental United States. The decision does not, however, grant Puerto Ricans the additional privileges of U.S. citizenship.
29 Feb.	President Roosevelt appoints a seven-man Panama Canal Commission to oversee completion of the canal.
14 Mar.	In *Northern Securities Company* v. *United States*, the first case in Roosevelt's campaign to rein in the trusts, the Supreme Court finds that the company violates the Sherman Antitrust Act and orders its dissolution.
5 Apr.	Chicago votes overwhelmingly in favor of municipal ownership of street railways. The measure authorizes the city to construct, own, operate, and lease the railways, but it is never put into effect.
22 Apr.	The Panama Canal property is formally transferred to the control of the United States.
5 May	The Socialist Party holds its national convention in Chicago, nominating Eugene V. Debs of Indiana for president and Benjamin Hanford of New York for vice president.
21–23 June	The Republican Party holds its national convention in Chicago and nominates Theodore Roosevelt for president and Sen. Charles W. Fairbanks of Indiana for vice president.

29 June   The Prohibition Party meets in Indianapolis, Indiana, and nominates Silas C. Swallow of Pennsylvania for president and George W. Carroll of Texas for vice president.

4 July   The Populist Party, meeting in Springfield, Illinois, nominates Thomas E. Watson of Georgia for president and Thomas H. Tibbles of Nebraska for vice president.

6–9 July   Meeting in Saint Louis, Missouri, the Democratic Party nominates Judge Alton B. Parker of New York for president and Henry G. Davis of West Virginia for vice president.

8 Nov.   Theodore Roosevelt is elected president of the United States, defeating his Democratic opponent by more than 2.5 million votes. He takes the electoral college vote 336 to 140. The Republicans increase their majorities in both houses of Congress.

6 Dec.   In his annual message to Congress President Roosevelt announces the Roosevelt Corollary, establishing the principle that since the Monroe Doctrine forbids foreign interference in the Western Hemisphere, the United States has a responsibility to insist on proper redress for wrongs inflicted on a foreign state by any Western Hemisphere nation within the U.S. sphere of influence.

1905

20 Jan.   President Roosevelt invokes the Roosevelt Corollary for the first time as the United States begins to supervise the payment of national and international debts owed by the Dominican Republic.

30 Jan.   In *Swift & Co.* v. *United States* the Supreme Court rules unanimously in favor of the government in its attempt to break up the "Beef Trust"; yet the ruling fails to affect the strongly entrenched meat monopoly.

4 Mar.   Theodore Roosevelt is inaugurated as president. He is the youngest elected president to date.

17 Apr.   In *Lochner* v. *New York* the Supreme Court rules that a state law limiting work hours for bakers to ten per day or sixty per week is unconstitutional. The Court holds that such a law interferes with the right to free contract and is an improper use of police powers. In his dissenting opinion Associate Justice Oliver Wendell Holmes Jr. argues that the Constitution "is not intended to embody a particular economic theory, whether of paternalism . . . or of *laissez-faire.*"

8 June   President Roosevelt urges Japan and Russia, which have been at war since February 1904, to negotiate.

9 Aug.–
5 Sept.   At the invitation of President Roosevelt, Japan and Russia meet for negotiations in Portsmouth, New Hampshire. The final agreement makes Korea a Japanese protectorate and gives Japan the South Manchurian Railway and the southern Liaodong Peninsula. The two countries divide Sakhalin Island in half, and Japan gives up its demand for economic restitution from the Russians. President Roosevelt receives the Nobel Peace Prize for his role as mediator.

6 Sept.   President Roosevelt appoints Charles Evans Hughes to head an investigation of the insurance companies.

1906

12 Mar. The Supreme Court rules in *Hale* v. *Henkel* that witnesses can be compelled to give testimony against their corporations and to produce papers and documents that might prove pertinent to the case. The ruling has a large impact on testimony in antitrust hearings.

28 Apr. The New York State legislature passes a complete legislation package to reform the corrupt life insurance business.

21 May The United States and Mexico reach an agreement over distribution of the waters of the Rio Grande, which are increasingly being diverted into the United States for irrigation.

29 June Congress passes the Hepburn Act, which puts teeth in the Interstate Commerce Act by permitting regulation of rates charged by railroads, pipelines, and terminals. President Roosevelt has strongly endorsed the act and helped guide it through Congress.

30 June Congress passes the Meat Inspection Act, which calls for government inspection of meatpacking plants, and the Pure Food and Drug Act, which prohibits interstate commerce in adulterated or mislabeled food and drugs.

2 Aug. Cuban president Tomás Estrada Palma asks the United States for aid in putting down a rebellion.

14 Sept. President Roosevelt sends Secretary of War William Howard Taft to assess the situation in Cuba.

22 Sept. Sparked by rumors of black men attacking white women, whites riot in the black section of Atlanta, leaving twenty-one people dead, including eighteen African Americans. The city is placed under martial law.

29 Sept. Responding to Taft's call for military intervention, the United States invokes the Platt Amendment and assumes military control of Cuba. Taft serves as provisional governor until 12 October, when he is replaced by Charles E. Magoon. The United States continues to govern Cuba until January 1909.

11 Oct. The San Francisco Board of Education orders segregated schooling for children of Asian descent. Worried about the international consequences of the law, President Roosevelt persuades the board to rescind the order, with the understanding that the White House will attempt to discourage Japanese immigration to the United States.

6 Nov. The Republicans maintain their hold over Congress in the elections. Charles Evans Hughes is elected governor of New York largely on the strength of his investigations into the life insurance corporations.

9–26 Nov. President Roosevelt becomes the first president to take a trip abroad when he travels to Panama to assess progress on the canal project.

1907

26 Jan. Congress passes an act forbidding corporations from contributing to election campaigns of candidates for national offices.

20 Feb. President Roosevelt signs the Immigration Act of 1907, which includes a provision that empowers the president to restrict Japanese laborers from entering the country.

25 Feb. The Senate ratifies the agreement between President Roosevelt and the Dominican Republic that authorizes the United States to supervise Dominican customs until foreign creditors have been repaid.

26 Feb. Congress passes the General Appropriations Bill, which increases annual salaries in the House and Senate to $7,500. Cabinet members and the vice president are paid $12,000.

Congress establishes a commission on immigration to look into the problems created by the flood of unskilled immigrants arriving in the United States each year.

14 Mar. By presidential order the United States excludes Japanese laborers from entering the country.

President Roosevelt appoints the Inland Waterways Commission to study and report on the rivers and lakes of the United States, their relation to forests, traffic congestion, and other matters.

21 Mar. Under the Roosevelt Corollary U.S. Marines are sent to Honduras to help put down a revolution.

15 June–
15 Oct. At the Second Hague Peace Conference, with representatives of forty-six nations in attendance, the United States convinces the participants to forbid war as an instrument for collection of debts.

1 Oct. A downturn in the stock market touches off the Panic of 1907. At the request of the federal government J. Pierpont Morgan and fellow bankers bring $100 million in gold from Europe to restore confidence in the economy and end the currency panic that has caused runs on banks.

16 Nov. Oklahoma becomes the forty-sixth state. Its constitution bans the sale and consumption of alcoholic beverages, reflecting the influence of progressive reformers and conservative religious leaders.

16 Dec.–
21 Feb. 1909 President Roosevelt sends the "Great White Fleet" of sixteen battleships on a world cruise, partly to demonstrate that the United States is an important international power.

1908

3 Feb. In *Loewe* v. *Lawlor* the Supreme Court rules that antitrust laws apply to labor unions as well as capital combinations and declares union boycotting illegal.

24 Feb. In *Muller* v. *Oregon* the Supreme Court rules that an Oregon law setting ten hours as the maximum workday for women in factories and laundries is constitutional and denies that it curtails the liberty of contract guaranteed by the Fourteenth Amendment.

2 Apr. The Populist Party, meeting in Saint Louis, Missouri, nominates Thomas E. Watson of Georgia for president and Samuel W. Williams of Indiana for vice president.

30 Apr. Reflecting a growing trend, 267 Massachusetts towns and cities vote for local prohibition. Worcester, with a population of 130,000, is the largest city in the country to go dry.

10 May   The Socialist Party holds its national convention in Chicago and once again nominates Eugene V. Debs of Indiana for president and Benjamin Hanford of New York for vice president.

13–15 May   The Governors' Conference on Conservation is held to discuss the conservation of natural resources.

28 May   Hoping to set an example for the states, Congress enacts a bill to regulate child labor in the District of Columbia.

30 May   Congress passes the Aldrich-Vreeland Act, which frees banks to issue notes backed by commercial paper and bonds issued by state and local governments. At the same time, archconservative Nelson W. Aldrich is named as head of the National Monetary Commission, set up to review the entire financial structure of the United States.

8 June   At the urging of Gifford Pinchot, head of the U.S. Forest Service, President Roosevelt appoints a fifty-seven-member National Commission for the Conservation of Natural Resources, naming Pinchot as chairman. The commission's job is to compile the first list of all American natural resources.

16–19 June   Holding its national convention in Chicago, the Republican Party nominates Secretary of War William Howard Taft of Ohio for president and Congressman James S. Sherman of New York for vice president.

4 July   At its national convention in New York City the Socialist Labor Party nominates Martin R. Preston of Nevada as its presidential candidate. After Preston is ruled ineligible because he is too young to hold the office, the party selects August Gilhaus of New York as its presidential candidate and nominates Donald L. Munro as his running mate.

7–10 July   Meeting in Denver, the Democratic Party nominates William Jennings Bryan of Nebraska for president and John W. Kern of Indiana for vice president.

15 July   The Prohibition Party nominates Eugene W. Chafin for president at its national convention in Columbus, Ohio. Aaron S. Watkins of Ohio is nominated for vice president.

27 July   The Independence Party nominates Thomas L. Hisgen of Massachusetts for president and John Temple Graves of Georgia for vice president.

14 Aug.   Race riots break out in Springfield, Illinois. Gov. Charles S. Deneen declares martial law, but to little effect. Several African Americans are lynched.

3 Nov.   Republican William Howard Taft wins the presidential election with 1,269,900 more votes than William Jennings Bryan. The Republicans maintain their majorities in both houses of Congress.

21 Dec.   Steel magnate Andrew Carnegie tells the panel at congressional tariff hearings, "Take back your protection; we are now men, and we can beat the world at the manufacture of steel." Yet the bill that results from the hearings includes some of the highest tariffs ever established.

1909

28 Jan.   The military occupation of Cuba ends with the withdrawal of American troops.

4 Mar.   William Howard Taft is inaugurated as the twenty-seventh president of the United States.

23 Mar.   Former president Roosevelt undertakes a scientific expedition to Africa for the Smithsonian Institution, followed by a triumphant tour of European capitals.

9 Apr.   Congress passes the Payne-Aldrich Tariff Act, another high-tariff act that brings no relief to the financially troubled country. Taft signs the bill and, six weeks later, declares it the best tariff law ever passed by Congress.

22 May   President Taft authorizes the opening to settlers of seven hundred thousand acres of land in Washington, Montana, and Idaho.

12 July   Congress proposes the Sixteenth Amendment, which authorizes a federal income tax. It is ratified by the states in 1913.

26 Aug.   Representatives of thirty-seven states attend the first convention of the National Conservation Congress in Seattle.

13 Sept.   President Taft releases a letter exonerating Secretary of the Interior Richard Ballinger of any wrongdoing in his handling of Alaskan coal claims. Taft has felt compelled to take action after Gifford Pinchot, head of the U.S. Forest Service, disobeyed his orders and publicly accused Ballinger of possible illegal involvement in the case. Taft fires Pinchot in January 1910. Coupled with his praise for the tariff fiasco, this controversy diminishes Taft's popularity.

27 Sept.   President Taft puts aside three million acres of oil-rich public land for conservation purposes. Though Taft follows his predecessor's conservation policies with energy, he gets no public acknowledgment for his work.

18 Nov.   Two U.S. warships are sent to Nicaragua following reports that five hundred revolutionaries, including two Americans, have been executed by Nicaraguan dictator José Santos Zelaya.

16 Dec.   U.S. support of rebel-imposed blockade forces, as well as the implied threat of an American intervention, forces President Santos Zelaya of Nicaragua to retire.

OVERVIEW

Pushing for Political Reform. At the dawn of a new century the desire for political change was growing in the United States. Many Americans believed that democracy could be improved, that politics could be freed from the grasp of the corrupt political machines and "bosses" who had controlled the major political parties for the last several decades. Special-interest groups emerged to lead reform movements at the city, state, and federal levels, but there was no cohesive, national agenda, no single source of reform. Reform groups ran the political and socio-economic gamut, as businessmen, unskilled workers, farmers, settlement-house workers, populists, antimonopolists, socialists, and anarchists all worked for reform, and nearly every aspect of life was touched by their efforts. Cleaning up city governments was no longer enough. State governments had granted city charters and were the only entity with legal power to rewrite them. Thus, restructuring and reforming city governments was dependent on similar changes at the state level. After 1903 reformers realized that what they had accomplished on the state level should be repeated on a national level. Corruption, they argued, stretched all the way to Washington, so change had to come there too. Progressives called for national regulation of the railroads and other industries, control over social behavior, and greater control over government through direct primaries and other machinery. The federal government began borrowing the techniques that had worked on the state and local levels: investigate, organize, educate, and legislate. It was a slow process that required a genuine desire to make changes, and opponents fought these reforms every step of the way. Change required public pressure and strong political leadership. Theodore Roosevelt was such a leader, and he was able to mobilize public support for his efforts.

The Trusts. The railroad industry was the first industry to form business trusts, but other industries, such as oil and steel, had followed their lead by the turn of the century. In the 1870s the railroads had decided that the best method of forging an alliance was to turn their stocks over to a "holding company," which would then run the business. In the 1890s — after a U.S. Supreme Court favoring laissez-faire, or "hands-off," economics held that these holding companies, or trusts, were legal — industries from meatpacking to safety-pin manufacturing

borrowed this organizational plan, and trusts quickly came to dominate American industry. Americans held a range of opinions about the trusts. Some favored breaking them up into smaller companies and restoring competition. At the other extreme were those who favored leaving the trusts alone. Those in the middle favored the less radical approach of publicly disclosing the companies' abuses of power and shaming the "bad" trusts into behaving properly. While some states outlawed the activities of interstate trusts in an effort to stop abuses, others — hoping to attract industry — passed laws that favored them. Reformers looked to the federal government for help. Federal antitrust legislation had been passed in 1890, but successful enforcement of it did not come until the 1900s. Debate over how to "bust" the trusts dominated national politics in the first part of the decade, and the question of who should be busted dominated the second half.

The Tariff Issue. An economic depression that began with the Panic of 1893 ended in 1897, and the American economy once again took off. Business leaders unquestionably believed that economic growth resulted from the Republicans' support of high protective tariffs. The Dingley Tariff Act of 1897 placed such high taxes on imported goods that it virtually eliminated foreign competition in the United States. By making products from other countries too expensive for most American consumers, this tariff allowed American companies to dominate the domestic market completely. Little or no competition also meant that American companies could charge exhorbitant prices for their goods, and in some sectors the consolidation of many businesses into a few left only a handful of trusts in control of entire industries. As the trend toward trust formation accelerated in the 1900s, people began to ask why multimillion-dollar companies that controlled entire industries needed tariff protection. Congress provided two chances, in 1901 and 1905, to do something about the tariff, but President Theodore Roosevelt declined to tackle the issue and left it for his successor. Throughout the decade Democrats and Republicans from the West and Middle West joined with rural interests in other areas to call for lowering the tariff as a way to break the trusts, but they did not have control of the White House or Congress. Businessmen in the Northeast and other industrialized regions joined with other conservatives in favor of maintaining the tariff. As the majority party, Republicans realized that they had to modify their support for a high tariff for political reasons, but party members were divided on what industries should remain protected and how far to lower tariff rates. Congress did not address the problem until 1909.

Labor Reform. Companies large and small came under criticism for the way they treated their workers. Unsafe work areas, low wages, long workdays and workweeks, and child labor were just a few of the unjust practices and conditions prevalent in American industry. "Muckraking" journalists wrote exposés revealing horrible working conditions and unsanitary practices in food industries. These investigations into businesses such as the oil trust and meatpacking plants sparked outcries for government intervention to clean up factories and improve working conditions for women and children. Yet the public did not always support labor's efforts to gain higher wages and shorter workdays. Skilled workers had craft unions to protect their interests, but unskilled workers rarely had such protection. They often looked to radical labor unions such as the Industrial Workers of the World (IWW), or "Wobblies," for help. Business leaders generally opposed the formation of labor unions and did not hesitate to use violence to crush them. During the 1880s and 1890s, when a corporation could not end a strike with private troops or Pinkerton detectives, often management could count on government troops to finish the job. Attempting to end such violence the federal government created a bureaucratic mechanism to mediate strikes in 1899. As union organization improved in the 1900s, strikes became more frequent and sometimes more violent than in earlier decades. The growth of radical unions and the increasing success of the Socialist Party in elections created fears of a possible worker revolution. Politicians sought ways to defuse the movement through favorable legislation and direct, personal intervention.

A Power in the Caribbean. During the last quarter of the nineteenth century, the United States had been slowly asserting its limited power in the Caribbean. Having ceased its attempts to take or buy territory there in the 1870s, the nation felt compelled to extend its influence in other ways. In 1895 the government threatened military action if Great Britain and Venezuela did not submit to arbitration to settle a dispute over the boundary between Venezuela and British Guiana (now Guyana), and the United States went to war against Spain in 1898 specifically to liberate Cuba. American dominance of the Caribbean went beyond military strength. Practicing "Realpolitik," American presidents wanted to protect commercial and strategic interests as well as geographic ones. Invoking the Monroe Doctrine, which committed it to opposing European influence in the Western Hemisphere, the United States practiced "Big Stick" and "Dollar" diplomacy to expand American economic dominance

over the region and insure that Latin American countries remained accountable for their actions. This interventionist diplomacy also gained America the right to build and maintain the Panama Canal.

Extending Influence in Asia and Europe. At the end of the Spanish-American War the United States unexpectedly found itself in possession of overseas territory for the first time in its history, and the reelection of William McKinley in 1900 ensured that the country would hold on to the Philippines, Guam, and Wake Island, making the United States a powerful player in Asia, as well as in the Caribbean, where it had acquired Puerto Rico. (In the midst of the war the United States had formally annexed Hawaii, creating a base from which it could assert its growing presence in the Pacific.) Most Americans viewed the former Spanish territories as the spoils of war. Yet the public and the Congress were divided on whether the United States should keep them and how involved in their affairs America should become. Businessmen, who had long considered China a nation of consumers just waiting for American goods, looked at the new acquisitions as stepping-stones to Asian markets. Progressive reformers and Christian missionaries, who saw the inhabitants of these islands as backward peoples desperately in need of democracy and religion, hoped to "civilize" them by bringing them both. Imperialists, who argued that the United States deserved to keep these islands because American men had died taking them, saw the new territories as ideal coaling stations for the U.S. Navy and as forward defenses against the growing Japanese presence in the Pacific. European countries learned that the United States meant to be a player on the world stage when the nation asserted an "Open Door" policy regarding trade with China in 1899 and 1900 and when President Roosevelt mediated the peace negotiations that ended the Russo-Japanese War in 1905.

The Conservation of Natural Resources. A booming economy depended on a continuous flow of natural resources. The United States was blessed with an abundance of coal, oil, iron ore, timber, and other raw materials, but the companies that mined minerals and cut lumber, as well as cattlemen grazing herds, treated the land as if natural resources were inexhaustible. The U.S. Census Bureau announcement in 1890 that the American frontier had closed caused many to rethink their beliefs about inexhaustible supplies of raw materials. Scientists knew these resources were finite, but most people had ignored their warnings as long as there was new land available. While conservationists did not yet fully understand the problems that extraction industries such as mining and lumber created, they knew little good was coming from the practice. They were also aware that individual states could not protect rivers and other waterways from destruction, nor could they manage the difficult task of building irrigation systems to help farmers in the western states. The federal government campaign for scientific management of natural resources became one of the most important crusades of the decade, one that came to represent progressive reform in microcosm.

Political Rights of the Underclasses. Immigration reached a peak during the 1900s. The nearly nine million people who made their way to America during these years came from different regions than earlier immigrants, mostly from southern and eastern Europe and in smaller numbers from Asia. These "new" immigrants encountered a bewildering array of problems. Discrimination was widespread and commonplace. They were often described as the "filthy classes" and blamed for urban problems. Many from eastern Europe had grown up in a different political climate from that of the United States and so became easy prey for clever politicians. Because they lacked work skills they took low-wage jobs and faced hostility from other laborers. Reforms aimed at improving the lives of the middle and working classes often served to undercut the political rights of new immigrants and African Americans. Southern progressives supported the segregation of blacks as a way to reunite a divided white society and bring about desired improvements for it. The direct-democracy movement was as much about removing power from the political bosses as it was about cleaning up the "corrupt" electorate. The targets of this cleanup were the illiterate new immigrants, who often fell prey to the ward and city bosses, as well as African Americans. Yet many urban reformers could not get past their innate prejudices to provide the immigrant population with a better political alternative to "bossism."

The Modern President. Presidential power had long been limited to carrying out the laws passed by Congress and consulting with that body on major foreign-policy decisions. In the late nineteenth century, American political scientists put forward the notion that the chief executive should participate to a greater extent in the creation of legislation and its passage. They argued that he should be a stronger leader, more like the British prime minister. In the 1890s this leadership role for the president slowly became accepted, but not without a struggle. The demands of running two theaters of operation during the Spanish-American War accelerated the modernization of the presidency and the extension of executive power. The telegraph and telephone came into constant use, speeding up the president's communications with his far-flung military commanders. To accommodate the growing demands placed on him, the chief executive's staff nearly doubled and began to assume its modern size and shape. Recognizing that most Americans received their information from the newspapers, the president took newspaper reporters into his confidence to better circulate his policy positions. As the relationship between the president and the press became one of limited cooperation, the president's relations with Congress deteriorated because members of the legislative branch resented their loss of power.

Political Divisions. The presidential election of 1900 created the impression that business was clearly on the side of the Republican Party and that rural and agricultural interests were in the Democrats' camp. But political divisions often depended as much on geography, ethnicity, and economic class as they did on party affiliation, and undercurrents of progressive reform led to a shift in party politics by the end of the decade. Under the leadership of William Jennings Bryan the Democrats shifted from their long-held distrust of government to a positive view of government and the role it could play in society. The party gained the support of organized labor for the first time in 1908 and solidified this marriage of political expediency in the 1910s. The Republicans came under the sway of the "insurgent," or progressive, wing, led by a new generation of reformers, such as Theodore Roosevelt and Robert La Follette. A moderate in 1901–1904, Roosevelt moved to the left of center during his second term. He sowed the seeds of party disintegration during the 1908 election campaign, when he personally selected his successor, the more conservative William Howard Taft. While Roosevelt implied that Taft would continue his policies, Taft did not agree with Roosevelt on the legal powers of the chief executive, and his different approach disappointed the insurgents and brought him closer to the conservatives in the party. During the first year of his administration, factionalism openly broke out and ruptured the Republican Party. Both major parties had to concern themselves with the growing influence of the Socialists, led by Eugene V. Debs. Electoral reforms supported by the Republicans and Democrats took some votes away from the Socialists, but Debs's vision of a better world for the workingman garnered him the largest voter support ever won by a Socialist in 1908. The Democrats and the Republicans alike had to remain accountable to the workingman as long as Debs was on the scene.

TOPICS IN THE NEWS

AMERICA, EUROPE, AND ASIA

The "Open Door" Policy. In 1899, with the European powers effectively carving up a weak China into "spheres of influence" under their financial control and moving on a possible collision course over trade in that Asian nation, Secretary of State John Hay appealed to them to cooperate with each other and the United States. Hay circulated what became known as the "Open Door" notes to Great Britain, France, Russia, Germany, Italy, and Japan, asking them not to erect prohibitive trade barriers and to leave an "open door" for other countries, especially the United States, to trade within their Chinese spheres of influence on an equal basis. They reluctantly agreed. For the time being China maintained the appearance of national integrity, but in reality its sovereignty was a hollow shell. In June 1900 young Chinese nationalists, angry and resentful that their government had succumbed to foreign domination, took matters into their own hands. Calling themselves the Righteous Fists of Harmony (or Boxers), they seized foreign diplomats and residents and herded them into the British legation. Concerned that this action might be used as a pretext for further dismemberment of China, Hay again called for cooperation and coordination in handling the crisis, as well as for an affirmation of Chinese sovereignty. A multinational force put down the rebellion in August and rescued the diplomats.

Pacific Power. At the conclusion of the Spanish-American War, the United States took possession of Wake Island, Guam, and the Philippines. The seizure of these islands touched off a debate over imperialism. Nearly all Americans agreed that the United States was right to liberate the islands from Spain, but they disagreed over the future of American governance in these territories. When President William McKinley, who campaigned on the assertion that the Philippines were not ready for self-government, was reelected in 1900, the debate over imperialism effectively ended. Between 1901 and 1904 Supreme Court rulings in the Insular Cases left to Congress the decision as to what type of government to install in the possessions ceded to the United States by Spain (which also included Puerto Rico) and in the Hawaiian Islands, which had been annexed by the United States during the war. Territorial governments were set up for Hawaii, Wake, Guam, and eventually Puerto Rico. In 1899, while the Filipino insurrection was being suppressed by U.S. troops in some of the bloodiest fighting in American military history, a military governor laid the groundwork for a civil government, headed by Federal Circuit Judge William Howard Taft and the Second Philippine Commission, complete with a judicial branch and plans for a popularly elected legislation. With the capture of rebel leader Emilio Aguinaldo in March 1901, peace was restored and the civil government took over on 4 July 1901. As civil governor of the Philippines Taft acted in a benevolent and judicious manner that won him the praise and admiration of the Filipinos. Overcoming his initial opposition to the American seizure of the islands, Taft became so committed to preparing the Filipinos for self-government that he turned down several offers from President Theodore Roosevelt of an appointment to the Supreme Court, a job to which Taft had long aspired. Finally satisfied with his accomplishments, Taft left the Philippines in 1904 to become Roosevelt's secretary of war.

The Russo-Japanese War. America's chief rival in the Pacific was the emerging power of Japan. Pleased that Japan had so quickly modernized over the preceding half century and had become outwardly western in its ways, many Americans supported Japan in its war with czarist Russia in 1904. The war started after repeated disputes between the two nations over control of Korea and Manchuria, in northern China. Japan won some spectacular early naval and military victories before the war settled into a stalemate. Most American commentators, including President Roosevelt, cheered the "Oriental David" for beating the "Slavic Goliath." As the war dragged on into 1905, however, the president and his advisers became worried that total victory for either of these nations might upset the "balance of power" in the region and threaten the "Open Door" policy in China and endanger the security of the Philippines. Fearing that the war might widen into a world conflict, Roosevelt worked behind the scenes to bring the two powers to the negotiating table. When they agreed to talk, he publicly offered himself as a host, a move that brought him international acclaim and domestic popularity. He urged the belligerents to settle

President Theodore Roosevelt going on board the *Mayflower* in Oyster Bay harbor, 5 August 1905, to meet with Russian and Japanese envoys to the Portsmouth, New Hampshire, peace conference that ended the Russo-Japanese War

matters and also got their respective European allies to pressure them. At a peace conference held in the Portsmouth, New Hampshire, navy yard (9 August–5 September 1905), Japan gained absolute control over Korea, naval bases and economic rights in Manchuria, and half of Sakhalin Island. Russia won the right not to pay the indemnity the Japanese demanded and kept the other half of Sakhalin. Roosevelt's interests were not strictly altruistic: he saw the negotiations as a means of more deeply committing his country to an active role in world affairs and of maintaining the balance of world power. For his efforts Roosevelt was awarded the Nobel Peace Prize in 1906. He was the first American ever to receive it.

The Rising Sun. On 29 July 1905, during negotiations to end the Russo-Japanese War, Secretary of War Taft and the Japanese foreign minister signed a secretly drafted document, the Taft-Katsura Memorandum. Under its terms Japan recognized American sovereignty over the Philippines, and the United States agreed not to oppose Japanese control over Korea. The two nations also agreed to work together to ensure peace in the Far East. Yet such agreements did not lessen tensions between Japan and the United States. In October 1906 the San Francisco school board voted to segregate Japanese students, touching off a crisis that, without the intervention of President Roosevelt, might have led to war. When the Japanese government protested the board's action, politicians and editorial commentators blithely called for war, but the president knew the military was neither large enough nor ready to fight such a prepared and distant opponent without great loss. In February 1907, responding to a Japanese appeal for his intervention, Roosevelt, who privately supported the segregation order, convinced the school board to abandon its plans. Roosevelt's position initially cost him political support in California, but his popularity in the West rose considerably later that month, when the United States and Japan came to a "Gentlemen's Agreement," which severely restricted Japanese immigration to the United States. Although the initial agreement came in February 1907, the basis for effective immigration restriction was not established until February 1908. As Roosevelt explained his position afterward, "Our line of policy must be adopted, holding ever the view that this is a race question, and that race questions stand by themselves." He did not oppose the Californians' intentions; he simply could not support their methods.

The Great White Fleet. Partly to demonstrate that he had not made the agreement out of fear of the Japanese military and partly to impress on the American public the need for constant military preparedness, Roosevelt ordered the navy in December 1907 to send its battleships on a global trip via the Pacific. Dubbed the "Great White Fleet" because of the color of the ships, the squadron was greeted with great enthusiasm wherever it put into port, especially in Japan. Because he was feuding with congress over military size and readiness, the president dispatched the fleet with only enough funding to get to Japan, leaving it to Congress to find the money to bring the fleet back home. Congress grudgingly obliged. (Despite congressional opposition, Roosevelt managed to double the size of the navy during his two terms.) The cruise had two pronounced effects. Roosevelt felt that if America did indeed go to war, the Philippines would be quickly lost because "it forms our heel of Achilles," he wrote Secretary Taft. The imperialist of 1900 had become a realist in 1908 and was privately sounding retreat. Dispatching the fleet was a way to overcome his gloom at this realization. While the fleet was on its worldwide cruise, Japanese officials suggested the two countries attempt to achieve accord on the various issues in the region. The Root-Takahira Agreement, reached in 1908, preserved the status quo in China and reaffirmed their mutual interests in the Pacific.

Dealing with Europe. In April 1905 Roosevelt, who regarded Germany as the prime troublemaker in the world, found himself trying to stabilize European affairs. With the primary goal of weakening the emerging alliance between France and Great Britain against Germany, Kaiser Wilhelm II tried to embarrass France, which was trying to make Morocco a French protectorate, by speaking out in favor of Moroccan independence. He did so hoping to weaken France and escalate the Anglo-French

President Roosevelt reviewing the ships of the "Great White Fleet" during its world cruise

colonial rivalry. Although he claimed that "we have no real interest in Morocco," Roosevelt was concerned about war between France and Germany. Assuring France of American backing, he also pressed them to be conciliatory to the Germans, while privately communicating through highly placed British and German friends that he would not allow the Germans to push the two allies apart. To defuse the Moroccan crisis in a face-saving manner, an international conference was held at Algeciras, Spain, in April 1906. Roosevelt sent a delegation to the conference to assure Britain and France he stood with them and sent word to Berlin that he did not condone German adventurism. The conference ended with France maintaining its interests in Morocco while all parties recognized Moroccan independence and territorial integrity. The Germans took satisfaction in having embarrassed the French and having made them look like aggressors, but the Anglo-French alliance remained unshaken.

Sources:
Howard K. Beale, *Theodore Roosevelt and the Rise of America to World Power* (Baltimore: Johns Hopkins Press, 1956);

John Whiteclay Chambers II, *The Tyranny of Change: America in the Progressive Era, 1890–1920* (New York: St. Martin's Press, 1980).

BIG STICK AND DOLLAR DIPLOMACY

Cuban "Independence." The Teller Amendment, attached to the 1898 declaration of war against Spain, declared that the United States was going to war to gain Cuban independence, not to colonize Cuba. (In contrast, the United States seized Puerto Rico from Spain and made the island a U.S. territory.) As part of the agreement for the withdrawal of American troops at the end of the military occupation in 1902, an independent Cuba was induced to sign a series of provisions, known collectively as the Platt Amendment. Named for its sponsor, Sen. Orville Platt of Connecticut, the amendment declared that Cuba could not make any treaty impairing its sovereignty without consent from the United States, and it allowed the United States to intervene to maintain the independence or political and social stability of Cuba. The amendment also stated that Cuba could not incur any debt it could not repay from current revenues and that Cuba was to lease land to the United States for American naval bases. (The United States still operates a base at Guantánamo Bay as part of this clause.) Diplomatic pressure usually proved sufficient for the American government to get its way with the Cuban government. With Cuba independent in only a formal sense, American troops returned to that nation in 1906 to put down protests by a political party that had lost in recent elections.

Paternalism. Roosevelt practiced "Realpolitik," or the protection of national interests. He learned from his contemporaries to protect not only geographic and racial concerns but also strategic and commercial ones. His paternalistic approach to diplomacy was not restricted to

A Democrat's view of President Roosevelt's "Big Stick" diplomacy (cartoon by Charles R. Macauley for the *New York World*)

fused to ratify the treaty, the president carried it out by executive order, a move that touched off much criticism at home and trepidation throughout Latin America. William Howard Taft continued this sort of diplomacy during his presidency, but his "Dollar Diplomacy" emphasized the protection or extension of American business interests more than Roosevelt had, and Taft did not hesitate to dispatch troops to the Caribbean to ensure these interests. In 1909 Taft had his secretary of state, Philander Knox, persuade American financiers to join a business consortium with Great Britain, France, and Germany to construct a railroad in China. Though American economic expansion at times seemed to follow the pattern of European economic imperialism, American interest in overseas trade rarely led to attempts to impose political control over foreign lands.

Bargaining for Rights. The Spanish-American War emphasized to Americans the need to connect the Atlantic and Pacific Oceans by building an isthmian canal under the control of the United States. The signing of the Hay-Pauncefote Treaty with Great Britain in 1901 cleared the way for America to build and control such a canal as long as all other nations could have equal access to it at all times. The United States had to decide between constructing it in Nicaragua, where the route would be longer but would cross easier terrain, or over a shorter but more difficult route in Panama, then a province of Colombia. Settling on Panama in 1902, Congress paid $40 million to secure the construction lease from the French company that had tried and failed to build a canal in Panama during the 1880s. The next step was to negotiate with Colombia for a transfer of sovereignty over the necessary land. In 1903 the United States and Colombia signed the Hay-Herrán Treaty, granting the United States a ninety-nine-year lease over a six-mile-wide canal zone in return for $10 million and an annual payment of $250,000 beginning nine years after the ratification of the treaty by both nations. Much to the disgust of President Roosevelt and many other Americans, the Colombian Senate rejected the treaty because of concerns over Colombian sovereignty over the zone and hopes for better financial compensation.

Revolution and Construction. Angry over the rejection of the treaty and bitter about many years of mistreatment, Panama revolted against Colombia, as it had more than fifty previous times during the preceding half-century. On 3 November 1903 Panama declared itself an independent republic. Tipped off by the Panamanian agent and former French engineer Philippe Bunau-Varilla about where and when the revolt would occur, Roosevelt hinted that support would be forthcoming and — using an 1846 treaty with Colombia that required the United States to maintain "a free and uninterrupted right of way" across the isthmus as his pretext — the president dispatched the USS *Nashville* and two other ships to help the Panamanians. The presence of the *Nashville* deterred Colombian armed forces from shelling the city of Colón,

Cuba. In 1902–1903 he used a combination of public diplomacy, private pressure, and military muscle to settle a long-running dispute with Great Britain over the boundary between Alaska and Canada. Also in 1902 Roosevelt stepped in to enforce the Monroe Doctrine in an effort to block German, British, and Italian naval intervention in Venezuela to collect debts owed to German banks. Roosevelt persuaded the Europeans to accept the Venezuelans' plea for arbitration. His use of persuasive diplomacy backed by military might in this and other Caribbean crises became known as "Big Stick" diplomacy, a name taken from one of the president's favorite sayings, an African proverb that says "Speak softly and carry a big stick." Exercising his "Big Stick" in 1905, he persuaded France, Belgium, and Italy to let the United States collect debts incurred by citizens of the Dominican Republic.

The Roosevelt Corollary. In his State of the Union Address in December 1904, Roosevelt announced that chronic wrongdoing by Latin American states would compel the United States "to an exercise of an international police power." This amplification of the Monroe Doctrine came to be known as the Roosevelt Corollary. The first use of the corollary came only weeks after it was issued, when the Roosevelt administration negotiated a treaty by which the United States would manage the customhouses of the Dominican Republic and oversee the payment of its foreign debts. When the Senate re-

President Roosevelt operating a large steam shovel during his 1906 visit to the Panama Canal Zone

Consolidation. On 1 January 1901 Andrew Carnegie agreed to sell his steel company for $480 million to J. Pierpont Morgan, who then consolidated that company with his other steel holdings to form United States Steel Corporation, the first company in history capitalized at more than $1 billion. By comparison all U.S. manufacturing combined had only $9 billion in capitalization at that time, and all federal and state government expenditures totaled $1.66 billion in 1902. Through vertical integration of its holdings, U.S. Steel controlled every step in the steelmaking process from mining coal and ore to the making of nails and steel beams. Bringing about 80 percent of all American steel production under one company, U.S. Steel operated with expenses and revenues greater than all but a few of the world's governments. The deal was one of three hundred major consolidations that reshaped the American economy between 1897 and 1903. Those mergers totaled roughly $7.5 billion in capitalization, encompassed an estimated 40 percent of the U.S. industrial output, and effected vast horizontal integrations that brought large segments of industries — sometimes entire industries — under the control of a handful of firms. In railroads, for example, 95 percent of all trackage was controlled by six lines in 1899. Other industries — including aluminum, tobacco, life insurance, sugar, lead, whiskey, plate glass, wire nails, smelting, and coal — underwent consolidations that left them similarly concentrated. Though manufacturers such as Carnegie and John D. Rockefeller personified the trusts in the minds of the general public, the chief catalyst for business consolidation came from financiers and bankers such as Morgan, who sought to eliminate wasteful competition and impose order. These huge companies, popularly known as "trusts," raised fears about the stability of the American economy and the fate of the workers in these industries.

Failed Federal Efforts. The wave of consolidations demonstrated the failure of the vaguely worded Sherman Antitrust Act of 1890, which outlawed illegal combinations in restraint of trade or commerce. During the decade after its passage the federal government did not undertake a vigorous program of prosecution to enforce it. In the one important antitrust case decided by the U.S. Supreme Court in the 1890s, *United States* v. *E. C. Knight Company* (1895), the court ruled against the government, declaring that the Knight sugar manufacturing company, which controlled 95 percent of that industry, did not illegally restrain interstate trade. The decision touched off a wave of consolidations. The Interstate Commerce Act, passed in 1887 to regulate the railroads, proved as ineffective in controlling consolidation in that industry as the Sherman Act had been for American business in general. The Interstate Commerce Commission, created as part of the legislation, quickly proved to be a paper tiger because it could not compel witnesses to

where the ship was docked. Because Colombian troops could not land, they had to march over a much longer overland course. The revolt ended two days later, and the Roosevelt administration granted limited diplomatic recognition of Panama within two hours of the cease-fire and full recognition on 13 November. Within two weeks the two countries had signed the Hay–Bunau-Varilla Treaty, giving Panama the same compensation Colombia had rejected. (After Roosevelt's death, in an effort to repair relations with Colombia, the Senate approved a treaty that called for a payment of $25 million to Colombia. They dared not approve such a measure during Roosevelt's lifetime.) Construction began shortly after the signing of the Hay–Bunau-Varilla Treaty and was not completed until 1914. During construction the work of Drs. Walter Reed and William C. Gorgas of the U.S. Army Medical Department in eradicating yellow fever and malaria saved hundreds of lives. In 1906 President Roosevelt became the first president to leave the country while in office when he visited the canal zone to witness work on what he later called "the greatest task of its own kind that has ever been performed in the world at all." For Roosevelt the canal was the finest accomplishment of his presidency, and his visit was the emotional high point.

Sources:

Howard K. Beale, *Theodore Roosevelt and the Rise of America to World Power* (Baltimore: Johns Hopkins Press, 1956);

David McCullough, *The Path Between the Seas: The Creation of the Panama Canal, 1870–1914* (New York: Simon & Schuster, 1977).

THE NEED FOR FEDERAL ACTION

In his first State of the Union Address, President Theodore Roosevelt explained the need for national antitrust legislation:

The large corporations, commonly called trusts, though organized in one State, always do business in many States, often doing very little business in the State where they are incorporated. There is utter lack of uniformity in the State laws about them; and as no State has any exclusive interest in or power over their acts, it has in practice proved impossible to get adequate regulation through State action. Therefore, in the interest of the whole people, the Nation should, without interfering with the power of the States in the matter itself, also assume power of supervision and regulation over all corporations doing an interstate business.

Source: James D. Richardson, ed., *A Compilation of the Messages and Papers of the Presidents*, 20 volumes (New York: Bureau of National Literature, 1917), XVI: 6647.

---

testify and did not have the power to set rates. Furthermore, the conservative Supreme Court did not support commission findings in most of its cases.

Exposure. The 1900 Republican presidential platform condemned "all conspiracies and combinations intended to restrict business, to create monopolies, to limit production, or to control prices" and favored legislation that would "effectively restrain and prevent all such abuses." In his letter accepting the 1900 Republican nomination, President McKinley elaborated his position on trusts, calling them "dangerous conspiracies against the public good and should be made the subject of prohibitory or penal legislation." In keeping with mainstream Republican thought, including that of his running mate, Theodore Roosevelt, McKinley thought that "publicity will be a helpful influence to check this evil." After becoming president on the assassination of McKinley in September 1901, Roosevelt continued this approach.

Beginnings of Real Regulation. Shortly before President McKinley's death, the stock market and the national economy felt the effects of a merger battle involving the Northern Pacific, the Great Northern, and the Chicago, Burlington, and Quincy Railroads. The protracted struggle involved the financial titans J. P. Morgan, E. H. Harriman, the Rockefellers, and James J. Hill. At stake was control of all railroad lines in the Northwest. The giants finally decided to put their respective stocks into a new holding company, the Northern Securities Company, creating a transportation monopoly. Attorney General Philander Knox estimated that 30 percent of its $400 million in capital stock had been overvalued, a move he thought to be an index to the higher rates the public would be charged. The stock market was again shaken

when Knox announced in 1902 that at the request of the president the government would seek to dissolve the Northern Securities Company under the Sherman Act. Hearing of the announcement, Sen. Mark Hanna remarked, "I warned Hill that McKinley might have to act against his damn company last year. Mr. Roosevelt's done it." The public cheered in March 1904, when the Supreme Court ordered the dissolution of Northern Securities, hailing Roosevelt as "The Trust Buster," which eventually proved to be a bit of a misnomer. While that case slowly proceeded through the courts, Knox also launched a successful attack against the meatpacking industry, or "beef trust." The Sherman Act was alive and well but would need help if it was to remain that way.

Legislative Help. The Northern Securities case showed the president and the attorney general the difficulties of prosecuting trusts in a timely manner. Congress would not give Roosevelt the broad-reaching legislation he desired, but it did pass some measures designed to facilitate enforcement of the Sherman Act. The Expedition Act of 1903 gave precedence on federal-court calendars to cases arising from violations of the Sherman Act or Interstate Commerce Act. After much fighting among conservatives, moderates, and liberals in Congress, they agreed to Roosevelt's proposal to create the Department of Commerce and Labor in 1903 and include within it the Bureau of Corporations, which was authorized to investigate possible violations of antitrust prohibitions. The bureau was established to collect information on business activities, examine their accounting books, and turn the information over to the president for action. If the president and attorney general felt there was a violation of the Sherman Act, the attorney general could then file suit in federal court against the company. Congress also appropriated a special fund of $500,000 for bringing suit against illegal business combinations. The nasty fight over the creation of the Bureau of Corporations helped to induce Roosevelt to back off his pursuit of the trusts until after the 1904 election. In fact, after the "beef trust" suit, no more suits were brought by the government between 1903 and 1905.

Success. During the Roosevelt administration the Justice Department obtained twenty-four indictments against the trusts. The three most significant judicial decisions were the 1905 injunction forbidding the member firms of the beef trust from engaging in certain practices designed to restrain competition; the suit that resulted in the dissolution in 1911 of the Standard Oil Company of New Jersey, which at one point controlled more than 90 percent of the oil refinery business; and the order requiring the reorganization of the American Tobacco Company, found to be an illegal combination that same year. In deciding these cases the Supreme Court formulated what became known as the "rule of reason," which stated that only "unreasonable" combinations in restraint of trade should be prohibited. This rule paralleled Roosevelt's thinking that trusts were a permanent

President Roosevelt as the infant Hercules taking on the "serpents" of Standard Oil, John D. Rockefeller and Henry H. Rogers, after the Roosevelt administration acted against Standard Oil for receiving secret freight rebates of nearly $1 million a year from the railroads (cartoon by F. A. Nankivell, *Puck*, 23 May 1906)

fixture in the economic world and that one could differentiate between good and bad trusts. In 1906 and 1907 Roosevelt reversed his earlier opposition to requiring interstate corporations to obtain federal licenses and to report annually on the kinds and amounts of business done. It was not until the 1910s that the federal government required federal licensing of businesses.

Taft and the Trusts. President Taft continued the suits started during the Roosevelt administration and declared in a 1908 speech before his inauguration that he would continue enforcing the Sherman Act pending the passage of improved legislation. Taft believed in a more judicial approach than Roosevelt. He wanted legislation that would outlaw every combination of capital in interstate commerce and would spell out exactly what actions businessmen could follow so that there would be no more misunderstanding, but Congress balked at passing such laws. By the end of his administration Taft had shifted to a policy of seeking the destruction of all trusts, but Congress rejected his demands for the necessary legislation. The ability to break up trusts ultimately remained with the courts. The higher courts also refused to sanction extreme penalties imposed on railroads or shippers found guilty of violating the law by the lower courts. In 1907 the higher courts set aside the decision of Judge Kenesaw M. Landis, who had imposed a record fine of more than

Railroad Regulation. By 1900 the demand for regulation had risen from municipal and state levels to the national level, and businessmen found it in their best interests to join the effort. Disliking the state-by-state, hodgepodge of regulations governing interstate businesses, they had come to believe that federal regulation had the advantage of uniformity. Railroads were among the first to seek out federal regulation. Railroad owners had long resented the practice of paying rebates (or kickbacks) to the various trusts to carry their goods and saw that the best way to stop such practices was to cooperate with the federal government. Instead of scrapping the existing legislation, President Roosevelt wanted Congress to pass additional laws that would strengthen the Sherman and Interstate Commerce Acts, adding greater deterrents to crime and compensating for the rulings of the conservative courts, which had limited the Commerce Commission's powers. Railroad owners willingly threw their support behind the Elkins Act of 1903, which made the recipient as well as the grantor of a rebate liable to prosecution. The act also declared that an agent or official of the railroad should be held responsible for any deviation from regular published rates. Not wanting to lose the support of businessmen before heading into the 1904 elections, Roosevelt then eased off railroad reform until after the election.

More Transportation Regulation. Still not wanting to destroy the trusts or have the government take control of the rail lines — as the populist wing of the Democratic Party wanted — Roosevelt pursued legislation that would establish government regulation over interstate shipping. Passage of the Hepburn Act in 1906 achieved his goal of significantly strengthening the Interstate Commerce Commission (ICC). The ICC gained jurisdiction over express companies, ferries, and pipelines, and it was given the power to reduce unreasonably high and discriminatory rates, subject to judicial review. The act placed the burden of proof in all legal disputes on the carrier and not the commission; it established a uniform system of accounting to be used by carriers; and it forbade the railroads to transport commodities in the production of which they were themselves interested. This last item helped break the stranglehold some lines had on the coal industry.

Consumer Protection. Businessmen pursued regulation in consumer protection, but as with railroad regulation, they were simply catching up to popular opinion when they entered the fray. Anger toward meatpackers flared up in 1905 with the publication of Upton Sinclair's *The Jungle*, his fictionalized account of life in the stockyards and processing plants of Chicago. Written as a socialist attack on big business, the book spurred the president to call for a thorough probe of the industry. Two Department of Agriculture investigators supported Sinclair's findings, reporting that "the stockyards and

Upton Sinclair's investigation into meatpacking plants revealed horrifying working conditions. For example, some men "worked in tank rooms full of steam," where "there were open vats near the level of the floor." In such rooms workers often "fell into the vats; and when they were fished out, there was never enough of them left to be worth exhibiting, — sometimes they would be overlooked for days, till all but the bones of them had gone out to the world as Durham's Pure Leaf Lard!"

Other workers told Sinclair stories of appalling sanitary practices:

> With one member trimming beef in a cannery, and another working in a sausage factory, the family had a first-hand knowledge of the great majority of Packingtown swindles. For it was the custom, as they found, whenever meat was so spoiled that it could not be used for anything else, either to can it or else to chop it up into sausage. With what had been told them by Jonas, who had worked in the pickle rooms, they could now study the whole of the spoiled-meat industry on the inside, and read a new and grim meaning into that old Packingtown jest — that they use everything of the pig except the squeal.

A stunned nation demanded reform and regulation, and shortly after Sinclair's exposé was published Congress responded with the Pure Food and Drug Act and the Meat Inspection Act.

Source: Upton Sinclair, *The Jungle* (New York: Doubleday, Page, 1906).

sold in interstate commerce and had been stalled in the House since December 1905. Small operators who relied on preservatives and cheapeners in their products opposed this bill as well. Roosevelt signed the bill into law on the same day as the meat-inspection law.

Sources:

Lewis L. Gould, *The Presidency of Theodore Roosevelt* (Lawrence: University Press of Kansas, 1991);

Samuel P. Hays, *The Response to Industrialism, 1885–1914,* second edition (Chicago: University of Chicago Press, 1984);

Thomas K. McCraw, *Prophets of Regulation: Charles Francis Adams, Louis D. Brandeis, James M. Landis, Alfred E. Kahn* (Cambridge, Mass.: Harvard University Press, 1995);

Robert H. Wiebe, *Businessmen and Reform: A Study of the Progressive Movement* (Cambridge, Mass.: Harvard University Press, 1962).

CITY AND STATE REFORMS

Few Are Immune. Reformers in major cities at the turn of the century faced widespread problems. It seemed as if no city were immune to corruption and graft. Geography played no favorites. Reporters and journalists found city councils for sale as well as mayors protecting criminals or keeping company with criminal elements in Jersey City, Milwaukee, San Francisco, and many other major cities. Men with names such as "Hinky Dink" Kenna and "Bath Tub" John Coughlin and political machines such as Tammany Hall in New York City supplied the necessary votes on election day to keep their systems operating. Franchises for streetcars, water and sewage, gas, and electricity were sold to private companies — often run by the corrupt politicians or their friends — with fifty-year leases that allowed them to set rates without interference. The police and other civil servants employed to protect the public interest were no less corrupt, taking kickbacks or payoffs for favorable treatment. Underpaid policemen could expect to supplement their pay with bribes from saloon keepers or the owners of brothels. The true victims in all these crimes saw their paychecks covering less and less of their bills as they watched the cost of their household utilities rise, their children's schools fall apart, the streets remain unpaved and littered with trash, and their water become contaminated. All the while these private citizens felt they had no say in the matter.

Sources of Corruption. In a search for the sources of these problems, descendants of early immigrants often blamed the large number of recent immigrants from southern and eastern Europe. Immigration from abroad and migration from the farm to the city grew at a tremendous rate during the 1900s, causing cities to expand at a rate their governments could not handle. In such urban areas the melding of different cultures and languages created a large, fragmented society that would be difficult to govern in any era, let alone one in which municipal governments operated much as they had in the early 1800s. Often ignorant of democratic ways, immigrants from southern and eastern Europe made easy prey for political bosses, who often understood immigrants' needs

packing houses are not kept even reasonably clean, and that the method of handling and preparing food products is uncleanly and dangerous to health." Sen. Albert J. Beveridge of Indiana, who had set the investigation in motion by giving Roosevelt a copy of Sinclair's book to read, worked with the investigators and the department to prepare a meat-inspection law. To pressure Congress into passing the law, Roosevelt threatened to disclose his findings publicly. The Senate complied, but conservative allies of the meatpackers in the House threatened to kill the measure. Small meatpackers disapproved of the measure because the new regulations would drive up operating costs and put them out of business. After a month of wrangling and posturing, the House finally passed a compromise version, which the Senate and president approved on 30 June 1906. The law called for the inspection of sanitary conditions in packing plants engaged in interstate commerce and for the inspection of the meat they sold. The pressure for meat inspection also gave momentum to the Pure Food and Drug Bill — which forbade the adulteration or fraudulent labeling of food and drugs

In 1907 sociologist Edward A. Ross tried to make it clear that old ideas about morals were not adequate for a system of social morality in the industrial age. New sorts of sins were being ignored, and reformers found themselves doing battle with a new kind of criminal:

The immunity enjoyed by the perpetrator of new sins has brought into being a class for which we may coin the term *criminaloid*. . . . Do we not hail him as "a man who does things," make him director of our banks and railroads, trustee of our hospitals and libraries? . . . Not to bribe, but to employ and finance the briber; not to lie, but to admit to your editorial columns "paying matter"; not to commit perjury, but to hire men to homestead and make over to you claims they have sworn were entered in good faith and without collusion; not to cheat, but to promise a "rake-off" to a mysterious go-between in case your just assessment is cut down; not to rob on the highway, but to make the carrier pay you a rebate on your rival's shipments; not to shed innocent blood, but to bribe inspectors to overlook your neglect to install safety appliances: such are the ways of the criminaloid. He is a buyer rather than a practitioner of sin, and his middlemen spare him unpleasant details.

Source: Edward Alsworth Ross, *Sin and Society* (Boston: Houghton, Mifflin, 1907).

better than the social workers and reformers, who were the bosses' sworn enemies. Urban political machines provided many "services," such as feeding hungry families, posting bail for children, giving families hams and turkeys at holiday time, and fighting to protect their native customs. In exchange the machines expected loyalty on election day. The close link between businessmen and politicians made fighting corruption difficult. Investigations revealed how extensive contract padding, personal graft, protection peddling, and collusion between city officials and utilities had become. Many city and state politicians were on business payrolls. To end corrupt practices reformers would have to gain control of city hall.

Interest in Reform Grows. Critics of municipal corruption had been heard since the end of the Civil War, but reform movements during the Gilded Age had proven short-lived and ineffective at best. The reform impulse emerged as a topic of national discussion in the 1890s. Within five years of its founding in 1895, the *Journal of American Sociology* had published thirteen scholarly articles critical of some phases of urban living. Popular magazines reached broader audiences with similar articles, helping to feed interest in reform. While these articles spoke about the problem of municipal governments, college-educated men and women began moving to inner-city neighborhoods with hopes of alleviating the problems by establishing settlement houses. Reformers such as Jane Addams, Florence Kelley, and Lillian Wald learned firsthand the impact graft and corruption had on their immigrant neighbors, and they sought to change or pass laws on child labor, workmen's compensation, and other social-welfare issues. In 1895 such social critics came together with civic leaders to form the nonpartisan, reform-minded National Municipal League. Instead of seeking reform through social-welfare laws, they emphasized honest, efficient government and called for changing the deficient government structure through direct-democracy techniques. By the end of the century, like-minded groups such as municipal-ownership leagues, city clubs, and direct-legislation leagues sprang up across the nation, calling for new city charters or different forms of city government.

Stronger Mayors. These forces converged at almost the same time. As part of its push to restructure municipal governments in some cities, the National Municipal League got its wish for stronger or broader powers for city mayors, who had typically been little more than figureheads. Samuel "Golden Rule" Jones served four terms as mayor of Toledo, Ohio, where he bucked the expectations of the Republican machine that supported him in his first election in 1897. Declaring "Each individual must rule himself" and calling every citizen of Toledo a "member of the family," he instituted broad, sweeping reforms. He took clubs away from the city police; established a free lodging house for tramps, free kindergartens, playgrounds, and night schools; constructed a municipal golf course; and set a minimum wage of $1.50 a day for municipal common labor at a time when the prevailing wage was one dollar or less. To Jones, an ethical anarchist, public ownership was the only economic system consistent with Christian ethics, whose political expression was democracy. Other reform-minded mayors included James D. Phelan of San Francisco, Mark M. Fagan of Jersey City, Seth Low of New York City, and Tom Johnson of Cleveland, Ohio.

Reforming City Governments. In 1902 Lincoln Steffens shocked the nation with his *McClure's Magazine* series "The Shame of the Cities," in which he exposed the extent of the graft and corruption in several major cities, blaming a quiescent voting public for its tolerance of such activities. Readers discovered that their city was not unique in suffering at the hands of the corrupt political machines. In reaction to Steffens's revelations goodgovernment forces mobilized in many cities, attacking corruption and demanding reform. At the heart of the problem were corrupt businesses that were essentially holding city services hostage. After cities instituted "gas and water socialism" by establishing municipal ownership of utilities, services improved as rates for water, sewage, electricity, and streetcars dropped. The drive to restructure the city government of Galveston, Texas, received an unlikely boost from a September 1900 hurricane that decimated the city. To deal with the disaster a nonpartisan administrative commission was appointed in 1901 to replace the mayor and elected city commission. Des Moines, Iowa, instituted a modified form of commission government in 1907, and hundreds of cities adopted similar plans by the end of the next decade. Staunton, Virginia, refined this form of government in 1908, when it appointed a city manager responsible to an elected council. The city-manager plan gained widespread acceptance — especially in the South and Midwest — after Dayton, Ohio, adopted it in 1914. Other measures enacted around the country included the election of councilmen or aldermen from the city at large instead of from individual districts; reducing state interference in city affairs; making administrative appointments according to civil-service rules; and the creation of juvenile courts. Together, social reform — such as that championed by "Golden Rule" Jones and Jane Addams — and structural reform — as advocated by the National Municipal League — furthered the cause of good government.

A "Laboratory of Democracy." By the end of the nineteenth century, reformers recognized that city reform could take place only after a good housecleaning on the state level. State politicians were no less unethical than their city counterparts, often exercising tight control over the fate of their constituents. Along with the power to grant utility franchises and other contracts, state governments often had other means of exercising control over cities, such as the ability to change city charters. Robert M. La Follette led reform efforts on the state level in Wisconsin. Attacking collusion and the railroads, La Follette captured the governor's mansion in 1900 and remained there for the next six years. After the regular wing of his Republican Party in the state legislature rejected his bills to regulate the railroads and to create a direct primary in 1901, "Battlin' Bob" began a slow struggle to clean up state government. First he worked to get a reform majority in the legislature. Once in place, these reformers helped him to enact a direct primary law, to establish an efficient railroad-rate commission, and to increase taxes on railroads and corporations substantially. They passed a civil-service act, an antilobbying law, a conservation and water-power franchise act, and a state banking-control measure. La Follette also supported a state income tax, the first of its kind, which was passed after he left the governorship for a seat in the U.S. Senate in 1906. La Follette's "laboratory of democracy," as Theodore Roosevelt called it, demonstrated to the rest of the nation that government could be responsive to the voters' desires. La Follette's use of academic experts to draft legislation assured the passage of carefully conceived measures. Other midwestern states, including Iowa and Minnesota, quickly followed suit by overthrowing their corrupt political machines and electing reform governors.

Contradictions in the South. While Midwest reformers attacked conservative corporation politics, a similar

A GROWING MENACE

Editorial cartoon on the widespread practice of vote buying, circa 1905

movement sprouted up in the agricultural South. Like the citizens of the corn and wheat states, southerners wanted to restore direct democracy, but in the South progressivism and racism went hand in hand. The agrarian revolt of the 1890s, which saw many blacks and poor whites uniting in support of the Populists, left whites unsettled because black voters held the balance of power. Conservative whites vowed never again to allow blacks such leverage. Starting in 1890, southern states sought to exclude blacks (and some poor whites) from the ballot by statutory or constitutional means. At the same time state legislatures enacted "Jim Crow" legislation that relegated blacks to separate and inferior public services and permitted their exclusion from facilities such as theaters, restaurants, and hotels. With the race problem "settled," whites then undertook measures to help bring the South out of its social, economic, and political isolation. Acts strictly regulating railroads and other monopolistic corporations, improvements for public schools, and laws banning the leasing of convicts to private contractors swept through the majority of southern states. Reforms helped to cut illiteracy rates for whites in half between 1900 and 1920 and virtually eliminated yellow fever and hookworm, diseases that had been widespread in the South. Yet any benefits blacks received from reform legislation were mostly incidental, never direct.

Reform in the Western States. Long-standing party factionalism within the Republican Party helped bring reformers to power in many western states. Tapping into the antimonopoly, antilabor feelings prevalent there, progressive reformers pleased middle-class voters by successfully attacking railroad, timber, and mining corporations while also stemming the rising radical labor movement. Such reform worked most effectively in urban California, where progressive Republican Hiram Johnson and his followers smashed the railroad trust that dominated state politics and Union Labor Party control of San Francisco on their way to capturing the state legislature and governor's mansion. The greatest successes for western progressives stemmed from passage of democratic, antiinstitutional legislation that created the initiative, the referendum, the recall, and the direct election of senators. Several western states returned power to the voters with these techniques. The initiative, which was first adopted by South Dakota (1898), permits voters to initiate, or propose, a law. Also passed in South Dakota in 1898, the referendum allows voters to reject a law passed by the state legislature. In 1903 Los Angeles made public officials more responsive to the people's will by passing the recall, which allows voters to remove an elected official before his or her term expires. Prior to changes in election laws state legislatures selected each state's U.S. senators. Inevitably, political machines or businesses dictated who became a senator. The West again led the way in changing this practice, and by 1909 twenty-nine states selected senators by popular ballot. The ratification of the Seventeenth Amendment in 1913, providing for direct election of senators in all states, was simply an acknowledgment of the inevitable.

Eastern Reforms. Though not as spectacular or passionate as their western or southern counterparts, eastern progressives met with success as well. The majority of their reform efforts went into solving urban problems. Lacking the populist roots of the West and South, eastern progressivism tended to be more conservative and drew on diverse, often conflicting sources. Urban, foreign-stock reformers worked more on social-welfare legislation while old-stock suburban progressives preferred to work toward direct democracy through election laws. Massachusetts continued in its long-established role as a reform leader, especially in natural resource conservation. Little known when he began his investigation in 1905, Republican Charles Evans Hughes rose quickly to national prominence as the lead counsel for the New York legislative committee examining the leading American insurance companies. Hughes's revelations of graft and corporate greed led to much-needed financial reforms and to his election as governor of New York in 1906 on a modest reform platform. His fight with the regular Republicans limited his effectiveness during both his two-year terms.

Sources:

Arthur S. Link and Richard L. McCormick, *Progressivism* (Arlington Heights, Ill.: Harlan Davidson, 1983);

William L. Riordan, *Plunkitt of Tammany Hall: A Series of Very Plain Talks on Very Practical Politics,* edited by Terrence J. McDonald (Boston: Bedford Books of St. Martin's Press, 1994);

Robert H. Wiebe, *The Search for Order, 1877–1920* (New York: Hill & Wang, 1967).

THE CONSERVATION CRUSADE

Origins of the Movement. Concern over the consumption of natural resources and its impact on the land began in the middle of the nineteenth century. Transcendentalist writers Henry David Thoreau and Ralph Waldo Emerson called attention to the destruction of nature in their native New England. Landscape painters of the Hudson River School, including Thomas Moran and Frederic Church, depicted idyllic wilderness scenes in the Adirondacks and the Rockies, evoking a yearning for romantic natural vistas by then under threat of destruction. Lumbermen had cleared eastern forests and were moving westward at a rapid pace, leaving behind barren lands subject to injurious soil erosion. In 1894 fear of watershed destruction and soil erosion in the Adirondacks led the New York State legislature to pass a "Forever Wild" constitutional amendment, which banned any logging within the Adirondack State Park. By the turn of the century lumbering was the second largest industry in the country, and statistics showed that annual timber consumption was still rising. Also during the late nineteenth century western farmers and ranchers competing for water had tangled in shooting wars over water rights. Neither private corporations nor individual western states could afford to finance the desperately needed irrigation systems to resolve the problem of water shortages. The 1890 census report announcing the closure of the frontier caused many Americans to become concerned about the depletion of natural resources through the increasing demands of industry and agriculture. To maintain economic growth and stave off destructive competition would necessitate the conservation of natural resources.

Government Intervention. Many scientists and progressive reformers alike believed that the federal government should encourage rational, planned management of public lands through regulations that ensured efficient and wise use. The Forest Reserve Act of 1891 laid the groundwork by authorizing the president to set aside public land as forest reserves for protection of watersheds, but it did not specify what to do with such reserves, most of which lay west of the Mississippi River. Western lumbermen, miners, and legislators resented having the land "locked up" and left unavailable for development. Those favoring preservation demanded that the land be left alone and never developed, but utilitarians (later known as conservationists) favored scientifically managed development and worked for the passage of the Forest Management Act of 1897, which spelled out how the

President Roosevelt at Yosemite Falls, 17 May 1903, during a western tour designed to mobilize support for his conservation programs

reserves should be used, partially but not entirely correcting the oversight in the Forest Reserve Act. By placing the forest reserves under the control of the Interior Department, which included no foresters, rather than in the Agriculture Department, which had foresters, the Forest Management Act left the forests without proper supervision and subject to continued plundering.

Coming Together. The conservation movement got a much-needed boost when Theodore Roosevelt entered the White House. To many Americans Roosevelt personified the conservation movement. He was a respected naturalist and ornithologist, passions he popularized while in the White House. He taught the nation respect for nature and wildlife. While hunting in 1902 he refused to shoot a young bear cub, which editorial cartoonists called "Teddy's bear" — a name soon given to a stuffed bear that became extremely popular. While governor of New York (1899–1900), he invited an acquaintance, Gifford Pinchot, chief of the U.S. Bureau of Forestry, to Albany to discuss conservation matters. Pinchot and Roosevelt found much common ground — patrician backgrounds, a love of the outdoors and the sporting life,

and a desire to better the lives of their fellow citizens. The two men became good friends and close allies in the fight to save American natural resources from improper consumption. During his brief service as vice president, Roosevelt remained active in the growing conservation movement, often meeting with Pinchot and other experts to discuss issues and plan for the future.

Conservation Legislation. Shortly after becoming president in September 1901, Roosevelt called Pinchot to the White House to help prepare the conservation section of his first State of the Union Address and set an agenda for proper management of natural resources. At the urging of Pinchot and Frederick Newell of the U.S. Geological Survey, Roosevelt requested legislation to transfer the forest reserves to the Agriculture Department and to create a reclamation bureau in the Interior Department, but Congress passed only the latter. Six months after taking office, Roosevelt signed a bill creating the Bureau of Reclamation to oversee construction of irrigation systems in sixteen western and southwestern states. Financing for the irrigation system was to come from the sale of public lands in the same region. The system, in other words, would pay for itself while bringing water to the arid region. After the mixed results of 1902, Roosevelt eased off the volatile political issue of conservation until after the 1904 elections.

The Square Deal. Elected president in his own right in 1904, Roosevelt made conservation one of the central issues of his Square Deal, educating Americans about conservation by writing many articles for popular magazines and several forewords for books by naturalist and scientist friends. Though he was friends with the naturalist John Muir, founder and president of the Sierra Club, he rejected as impractical Muir's position favoring aesthetic preservation of all natural or wild areas. Instead Roosevelt threw his support behind Pinchot's program of utilitarian conservation. In 1905 Roosevelt finally convinced Congress to transfer the forest reserves to the Department of Agriculture and to create the U.S. Forest Service to run the National Forests, the new name Pinchot wanted for the forest reserves. (They were officially given this name in 1907.) Like many Americans, Roosevelt supported the preservation and protection of natural oddities and wonders. He urged Congress to pass the Antiquities (or National Monuments) Act of 1906, which allows the president to set aside scientifically or historically important areas such as the Grand Canyon for protection. Pinchot advised Roosevelt to appoint commissions to investigate conservation matters and gain public support for more legislation. Roosevelt focused national attention on the conservation crusade in 1907, when he appointed the Inland Waterways Commission to design multiple-purpose development of river basins. The next spring the Governors Conference on Conservation, held at the White House, brought increased publicity for the cause. Inspired by the success of the meeting, Pinchot and Roosevelt continued establishing commis-

The 1905 proposal calling for the construction of a dam in Hetch Hetchy Valley of Yosemite provoked a furious reaction from naturalist John Muir, founder and president of the Sierra Club, who summed up the position of many preservationists. The proposal created a deep rift in the conservation movement and ended the friendship of Muir and Gifford Pinchot:

The proponents of the dam scheme bring forward a lot of bad arguments to prove that the only righteous thing to do with the people's parks is to destroy them bit by bit as they are able. Their arguments are curiously like those of the devil, devised for the destruction of the first garden. . . . These temple-destroyers, devotees of ravaging commercialism, seem to have perfect contempt for Nature, and, instead of lifting their eyes to the God of the mountains, lift them to the Almighty Dollar. Dam Hetch Hetchy! As well dam for water-tanks the people's cathedrals and churches, for no holier temple has ever been consecrated by the heart of man.

Source: John Muir, *The Yosemite* (New York: Century, 1912).

---

sions, including the National Conservation Commission and the Country Life Commission, charging them with investigating ways to "conserve," or save, people and society.

Growing Opposition. Many westerners and congressmen were displeased that Pinchot, a "lowly" bureau chief, had the president's ear. By 1907 Pinchot's conservation crusade expanded from timber to include coal and mineral lands, oil reserves, and water-power sites, bringing him into more and more conflicts. Pinchot wanted the Forest Service to spearhead government conservation efforts. Through the enforcement of government regulations and issuance of leasing fees, the Forest Service controlled all mining, grazing, and lumbering operations within the two hundred million acres of the National Forests. The appointment of James R. Garfield, a close friend of Pinchot and the president, as secretary of the interior in 1907, gave Pinchot an important ally at a critical point in conservation history. Together the two administrators decided which tracts of land to withdraw from the public domain for managed development and submitted their plans to a cooperative president. The withdrawal of potential water-power sites for municipal and agricultural use meant the land could not be used for anything else. Thus, it was not surprising that Pinchot, the Forest Service, and President Roosevelt all became targets of western hostility. Western cities and farmers in need of water for irrigation supported the expanding program, but many farmers, miners, lumbermen, and ranch-

ers resented the government presence because they could no longer exploit resources on government land for free.

Congress Fights Back. Western congressmen increasingly attacked Pinchot and resented the president's use of "dictatorial" powers to withdraw huge tracts of land without congressional approval. Caught off guard by Roosevelt's use of the executive order and resentful of Pinchot's growing power, Congress sought ways to strike back. At the end of 1906 Pinchot's proposal to make the Forest Service financially independent of congressional appropriations gave his enemies on Capitol Hill the opportunity they wanted. In 1907 Sen. Charles W. Fulton of Oregon succeeded in attaching a rider reasserting congressional control of all Forest Service revenues to a Department of Agriculture appropriations bill. More important, the rider forbade the withdrawal of land in six western states without the consent of Congress. Convinced that it would be unwise to veto such an appropriations bill over the forest-reserve issue, the president decided to sign the bill, but while waiting for it to arrive from Congress, he ordered Pinchot and the Department of the Interior to submit their requests for more land withdrawals, an order with which they happily complied. Before signing the agriculture bill, Roosevelt withdrew seventeen million additional acres, thereby establishing or enlarging thirty-two National Forests. Led by a combination of conservative Republicans and western leaders, Congress retaliated by refusing to fund the work of Roosevelt's many conservation commissions after 1908. This action and Fulton's amendment restored the political equilibrium.

The Paradigm of Progressive Reform. The conservation movement serves as one of the best examples of how political reform worked during the Progressive Era. Early efforts on local and state levels met with little success. Protecting watersheds was one conservation effort that exceeded state boundaries. Moving cautiously after the 1904 election, President Roosevelt set up investigative commissions and then used the information gathered to educate the public. If the public had not understood the problem, they would have been unlikely to support the necessary conservation measures. Articles about conservation by Roosevelt, Pinchot, and others flooded the popular press. Pinchot also designed teaching materials for schoolchildren. Private conservation organizations sponsored informative meetings, helped raise public awareness, and bombarded Congress with letters. By 1905 pressure from all sides forced Congress to transfer the national reserves to the Department of Agriculture and create the Forest Service. Graduates of new forestry schools — mostly from middle- and upper-middle-class backgrounds — flocked to Washington to join the crusade. Like Pinchot, these foresters believed that scientific management was the best hope for saving forests. By 1909 a decentralized, yet highly efficient, bureaucracy oversaw two hundred million acres of federal land. After the Governors Conference of 1908, many individual states

Two powerful conservative Republicans: Joseph G. Cannon of Illinois, Speaker of the House of Representatives (1903–1911), and Nelson W. Aldrich of Rhode Island, U.S. senator (1881–1911) and son-in-law of Standard Oil magnate John D. Rockefeller

copied the federal model, establishing state forests, forest services, and conservation boards. While states struggled to catch up to federal activity, conservation on the federal level expanded its focus to include the health of children, waste in war, and civic beautification. The Country Life Commission, for example, wanted to stop the disintegration of rural life, which reformers considered of vital importance to the survival of America. Yet problems plagued conservation efforts. New projects or commissions began work before the government had a chance to assess the benefits created by earlier ones. Underfunded and understaffed, new federal agencies often had to rely on companies to police themselves. As a consequence, agencies and companies developed close working relationships that limited the effectiveness of regulation. In the end the movement was less a grassroots effort than an attempt by progressives to make the federal government carry out the conservationist agenda.

Sources:

Lewis L. Gould, *The Presidency of Theodore Roosevelt* (Lawrence: University Press of Kansas, 1991);

Samuel P. Hays, *Conservation and the Gospel of Efficiency: The Progressive Conservation Movement, 1890–1920* (Cambridge, Mass.: Harvard University Press, 1959);

Roderick Nash, *Wilderness and the American Mind,* third edition, revised (New Haven: Yale University Press, 1982).

DIVISIVE PARTY POLITICS

Growing Executive Power. During the first decade of the twentieth century, the presidency underwent dramatic changes. In office from 1897 until his death on 14 September 1901, William McKinley had quietly expanded the chief executive's power during the Spanish-American War, making policy decisions regarding the Philippines without consulting Congress. Strong support in Congress for the expansion of American international influence muted any congressional opposition to McKinley's actions. He reorganized the executive branch and increased the size of his staff to handle his increasing responsibilities. McKinley was also more involved than previous "caretaker" presidents in the creation and passage of legislation, actively leading his party and the government. He presided over a victory in the Spanish-American War and a strong economic recovery, both of which helped to generate public confidence in his administration.

A Prototypical President. When Vice President Theodore Roosevelt became president in September 1901, the nature of the office quickly came to reflect his own character. Congress and the nation at large knew within a few months that great change was afoot. Journalist Ray Stannard Baker captured Roosevelt's essence: "The President ran full-speed on all the tracks at once." In his December 1901 State of the Union message Roosevelt reaffirmed his promise to continue McKinley's programs, but he also established an agenda that was clearly his own. He called for regulation of the trusts, addressed the tariff issue, and spoke to other typical Republican concerns, but he set himself apart from his predecessors with his genuine concern for the plight of labor, his call for strengthening the peacetime military, and his discussion of needed conservation measures. His belief that the chief executive should do as much as the law and Congress allowed — that is, be a strong executive — served as a model for later presidents. At times his actions challenged the constitutional limits of his presidential powers. In contrast, McKinley and Roosevelt's successor, William Howard Taft, believed in a more restrained approach to the presidency. Taft felt his role as president was to consolidate Roosevelt's gains, placing them on a more solid judicial footing, but Taft failed to be a dynamic and aggressive leader like Roosevelt, thus losing the support of the progressive wing of the Republican Party and the 1912 presidential election to Democrat Woodrow Wilson.

How Roosevelt Worked. To achieve some of his goals Roosevelt borrowed an idea used by Gov. Robert La Follette of Wisconsin. He appointed experts to executive commissions that investigated various problems and then drew up the necessary legislation. Often Roosevelt himself had a hand in drafting the bills or maneuvering them through Congress. If Congress balked at his suggestions, which happened more frequently in the final years of his presidency, Roosevelt did not hesitate to use his office as a "bully pulpit," as he called it, to take his opponents to task. He publicized issues by meeting with reporters on a regular basis, made speaking tours around the country to spread his message, and even wrote articles for popular magazines to get the word out. He met frequently with a select group of trusted young subordinates, including Gifford Pinchot and James R. Garfield, with whom he discussed policy matters while engaging in horseback riding or tennis. Dubbed the "Tennis Cabinet," Roosevelt's inner circle of informal advisers who carried out his goals generated resentment from conservatives during the president's second term. Though he did not hesitate to use government patronage to assure electoral victory in 1904, Roosevelt's earlier tenure as civil-service commissioner (1889–1895) influenced him to make appointments based on the merits of the candidate rather than on the repayment of political debts. For instance, he selected Oscar Straus to become his secretary of commerce and labor not to garner the Jewish vote but because Straus was the best available man for the job.

Placating the Right. Roosevelt's strong will and independent streak, popular with the general public, did not sit well with the conservatives on Capitol Hill, and after 1906 these qualities served only to alienate them. Chief among Roosevelt's "stand-pat" political opponents was Speaker of the House Joseph Cannon, who was determined to regain for the House some of the prestige and power lost to the Senate and the president under his predecessor. Rough and crude whereas Roosevelt was polished and sophisticated, "Uncle Joe" Cannon, a Republican from Illinois, brought such a conservative, "stand-pat" philosophy to the lower house that pundits

---

THE WORST TRUST OF ALL

David Graham Phillips's "The Treason of the Senate," a series of articles published in *Cosmopolitan* magazine, prompted President Theodore Roosevelt to attack the muckrakers. This excerpt comes from Phillips's profile of Sen. Nelson W. Aldrich, a Republican from Rhode Island:

The greatest single hold of "the interests" is the fact that they are the "campaign contributors" — the men who supply the money for "keeping the party together," and for "getting the vote". . . . Your candidates get most of the money for their campaigns from the party committees; and the central party committee is the national committee with which congressional and state and local committees are affiliated. The bulk of the money for the "political trust" comes from "the interests." "The interests" will give only to the "political trust." And that means Aldrich and his Democratic (!) lieutenant, [Arthur P.] Gorman of Maryland, leader of the minority in the Senate. Aldrich, then, is the head of the "political trust" and Gorman is his right-hand man.

Source: David Graham Phillips, "Aldrich, The Head of It All," *Cosmopolitan*, 40 (April 1906): 628–638.

---

quipped that had he been in on the Creation he would have voted against the Lord on chaos. With "Cannonism" controlling all legislative matters in the House, and conservative senators Nelson W. Aldrich of Rhode Island, Orville Platt of Connecticut, John C. Spooner of Wisconsin, and William B. Allison of Iowa controlling the "Millionaires' Club," Roosevelt had a dangerous political tightrope to walk during his first few years in office. To help soothe the worried right wing of his party, he populated his cabinet with conservatives such as Elihu Root and William Howard Taft. With his eye on 1904, he sought the congressional conservatives' cooperation from the outset and dared not challenge them until after the election. The conservatives did not care for the president's expansive use of executive power during his second term, nor for his conservation campaign, and they detested the push for federal direct-democracy legislation like that already enacted by some states.

Left of Center. On Roosevelt's political left within his party were progressive Republicans led by La Follette and other midwesterners. Roosevelt was closer to this wing of the party than to the conservatives, agreeing especially with the methods they employed to design reform legislation, but he did not fully embrace their desire to destroy the trusts and seize the railroads. Recognizing that the voting public was shifting in the progressives' direction, the president led them as far to the left as he felt was feasible. As he and the progressives further distanced themselves from conservative Republicans, Roosevelt managed to hold the party together during his presidency through sheer force of personality. Taft had neither Roosevelt's political acumen nor his dominant personality, and he damaged himself politically before his inauguration when he tacitly promised to carry out Roosevelt's program. After 1909 the progressives split with Taft and mainstream Republicans over issues such as the Payne-Aldrich Tariff Act of 1909, Taft's failure to carry out Roosevelt's conservation program and his dismissal of its leader, Gifford Pinchot, in January 1910, and his inability to end "Cannonism."

Disorganized Democrats. Throughout the decade, the Democrats suffered from party factionalism that left them effectively on the sideline. This problem was longstanding: though roughly equal to Republicans in electoral strength, Democrats occupied the White House for only eight years during the period from the Civil War to the election of Woodrow Wilson in 1912. Eastern Democrats, with their mostly urban, immigrant base, tended to be more conservative on issues such as tariffs, trusts, and electoral and social reform than southern and western Democrats, who were mostly rural and agrarian and opposed the trusts and consolidation but did not want a large federal bureaucracy regulating them. Westerners, of whom there were relatively few, opposed the protective tariff, while southerners usually favored it because it reduced foreign competition to foodstuffs and cotton grown in the South. At the center of party power and controversy stood the "Great Commoner," William Jennings Bryan of Nebraska, supported largely by the rural, populist wing of the party. His vitality just barely held the Democrats together through these lean political years. The conservative, urban wing opposed Bryan's nomination in 1900 and 1908, believing that his radical platforms would not win them the White House. Toward the end of the decade, state elections reflected a growing disenchantment with the conservative-dominated Republicans, bringing Democrats and progressive Republicans together in a search for greater reforms.

Tariff Divisions. Tariffs provided a substantial portion of government revenue before the creation of the federal income tax in 1913. In 1902 customs duties accounted for $243 million of the $653 million collected in taxes. Economic conservatives revered the high tariff as the foundation of a strong American economy, but its opponents argued it was the tool of the trusts. President McKinley tried to circumvent high tariff rates through reciprocity agreements with trade partners, but he had limited success. Theodore Roosevelt continued this program but avoided tackling the high tariff, leaving the political "time bomb" for his successor. The divisive issue was so volatile that in 1902 David Henderson, Cannon's predecessor as Speaker of the House, claimed he had not "truly represented" his Iowa constituents, who wanted to lower the tariff, and consequently declined his party's nomination for an eleventh term. The tariff debate split the country more along sectional and economic lines than along party lines. Most in the Midwest and West supported lowering or eliminating it as an antitrust move, while southern and eastern businessmen wanted to maintain the high rates to protect raw materials and finished products from foreign competition. The working class opposed the high tariff because it kept consumer prices artificially high.

Taft and Tariff Reform. In 1909 Taft called a special session of Congress to deal with the tariff problem. Believing that lower rates would generate competition naturally and thus weaken the trusts, he favored lowering rates from the all-time high of 57 percent. The House passed a bill lowering rates on most items and placed coal, iron ore, and animal hides on the list of goods that were tariff-free. The Senate bill (sponsored by the protectionist Nelson W. Aldrich, who also happened to be the son-in-law of John D. Rockefeller) added 847 amendments to the Payne bill, almost all of which increased rates. Midwestern progressive Republicans, led by Robert La Follette, fought the bill and managed to get a reduction on some duties with Taft's support. Though the bill lowered tariffs somewhat, the Payne-Aldrich Tariff, which removed coal and iron ore from the free list and established rates at an average of 40 percent, was decidedly protectionist. Hoping for party harmony Taft accepted the bill and declared it "the best bill that the Republican party ever passed." Instead of keeping the party together he aggravated a growing rift.

Sources:
John Whiteclay Chambers II, *The Tyranny of Change: America in the Progressive Era, 1890–1920* (New York: St. Martin's Press, 1980);

George E. Mowry, *The Era of Theodore Roosevelt and The Birth of Modern America, 1900–1912* (New York: Harper & Row, 1958).

INDUSTRIALISM AND GOVERNMENT

The Effects of Industrialism. As industries consolidated at the turn of the century, factories grew larger and more dangerous. By 1900 industrial accidents killed thirty-five thousand workers each year and maimed five hundred thousand others, and the numbers continued to rise. The general public became concerned with industrial accidents only when scores of workers were killed in a single widely reported incident, such as the many coal-mine explosions or the tragic Triangle Shirtwaist Company fire in 1911. The average workday varied from industry to industry, but most laborers worked ten-hour days, six days a week for wages that barely covered the cost of living for a family of four. To make ends meet many of these families had little choice but to send their children, sometimes as young as six, to work in the factories. Wages generally rose during the first decade of the twentieth century, but these increases were outpaced by inflation, making it more expensive to live. At the first sign of economic trouble owners did not hesitate to slash wages or lay off workers. The loss of skilled jobs to automation, the institution of "Taylorism," or scientific

An October 1903 magazine illustration of the meeting at which President Roosevelt intervened in the dispute between coal-mine owners and the United Mine Workers (UMW). Roosevelt is seated in a wheelchair because he had been injured in a recent carriage accident. UMW head John Mitchell is seated on the president's left; George F. Baer, spokesman for the mine owners, is standing at right.

management, and the hiring of new immigrants at lower wages added to the plight of the working class.

Labor Organizes. In response to the rise of the trusts at the end of the nineteenth century, membership in the American Federation of Labor (AFL), a union for skilled workers formed in 1886, grew rapidly from 256,000 members in 1897 to 1,676,000 in 1904. More-radical and politically active trade unions often had even larger memberships, mostly because they were not as exclusionary as the AFL and because they also welcomed unskilled labor. One of the most radical, the Industrial Workers of the World (IWW), founded in 1905 and popularly known as the Wobblies, recruited primarily among the unskilled immigrants but also competed with the AFL to attract skilled laborers. Less radical than the Wobblies and more successful at recruiting supporters, socialists gained political strength throughout the decade because of growing numbers of immigrants and disenchanted unskilled laborers. The lack of real class conflict in the United States and the electoral reforms of the era undercut their efforts on a national level. Despite growing union activism, the vast majority of workers remained unorganized during the decade.

Strikes and Government. With the violent labor strikes of the 1890s still a vivid memory, the rise of labor unions after 1900 gave the average American cause for concern. In the first decade of the twentieth century there were three times as many strikes as in the 1890s, and they resulted in far more violence than in previous years. In a country with generally conservative political and social views about labor, most Americans abhorred such violence and sided with business. Trying to prevent legislation to provide job security, guarantee a minimum wage, or ensure the safety of the workplace, most businessmen and conservatives argued that wages were set by the marketplace and that higher wages and worker protection would lead to higher prices for consumers. Government had long supported business, using court injunctions and armed troops to put down strikes and break unions. In the 1890s, ruling that unions operated as "combinations in restraint of trade," the federal government used the Sherman Antitrust Act against unions more often than against businesses. Tacit government support of racist hiring policies in the northwestern states hindered labor efforts to gain legislation ending discriminatory practices.

Progressive Efforts. During the first decade of the century several states passed legislation helpful to labor, such as laws establishing a minimum wage for women, maximum work hours, and workmen's compensation, and abolishing child labor and convict leasing. Groups such as the National Child Labor Committee, the Woman's Trade Union League, and the National Consumers League spearheaded the drives for many of these measures. Ironically, organized labor opposed minimum-wage laws for women because it preferred to win such measures through collective bargaining or strikes, rather than through legislation. Business had to persuade labor to accept workmen's compensation plans, which unions opposed because the benefits were not very generous and many sorts of workers were excluded. Businessmen wanted the plans to protect themselves against the large payments that courts sometimes awarded in injury cases. Only when the loopholes in state laws became apparent to reformers did they lobby for federal legislation, most of which did not come until the 1910s.

Progressive Paradox. The federal government was generally unsupportive of trade unions during Roosevelt's first term. Congress failed to follow the lead of the states that passed sweeping labor legislation, and the conservative federal courts overturned some state laws regulating employment. Instead, Congress passed legislation affecting workers in the District of Columbia, which was under its jurisdiction, and hoped that states would follow the example. As the decade progressed and justices were replaced, the Supreme Court became less conservative and began upholding some labor-friendly laws, as in the case of *Muller* v. *Oregon* in 1908, where they ruled that limiting women's work hours was a valid exercise of a state's police powers.

Roosevelt's Strike Mediation. In 1900 the United Mine Workers (UMW) led a walkout of anthracite-coal miners in the Northeast, calling for better wages, shorter hours, and union recognition. Acting on behalf of President McKinley, whom the UMW had asked to mediate between workers and owners, Sen. Mark Hanna met with J. Pierpont Morgan and quickly settled the strike in the crucial industry, minimizing the damage to President McKinley's reelection bid. The agreement ran only until April 1902. In May of that year John Mitchell, head of the UMW, led the miners out on strike once again. The strike dragged on through the summer with a minimum of hope for resolution but with little violence. As winter approached and coal supplies dwindled to dangerous levels, President Roosevelt felt compelled to intervene. In October he invited both sides to discuss matters in Washington, becoming the first president to mediate a labor dispute personally. The groundwork for this action had been laid by President McKinley, who had obtained from Congress an administrative structure for government mediation. Instead of sending in federal troops to crush the strike and force the miners back to work, Roosevelt threatened to use those troops to operate the mines and turn over any profits to the government. Though the threatened action most likely was unconstitutional, the bluff worked. Morgan and other financiers pressured the owners to agree to arbitration by a presidential commission and to let the men return during the deliberations.

The commission agreed that the miners should have shorter hours and a 10 percent wage increase (not as great a raise as they had demanded) and recommended maintaining an "open shop." The principle of the "open shop" — which means union and nonunion workers can be employed in an industry under the same contract — was later used to dilute the power of organized labor, but in this instance, when the commission went along with the owners' adamant refusal to recognize the UMW, the decision precluded discrimination against union members. Roosevelt's actions set a new precedent for the chief executive. The iron-fisted strike-breaking tactics of the past would be tolerated no longer by labor or capital.

Sources:

Melvin Dubofsky, *Industrialism and the American Worker, 1865–1920* (Arlington Heights, Ill.: Harlan Davidson, 1985);

Lewis L. Gould, *The Presidency of Theodore Roosevelt* (Lawrence: University Press of Kansas, 1991).

JIM CROW, NATIVISM, AND RACISM

Jim Crow Matures. By 1900 southern segregationists had completed much of their legislative agenda. Through legal devices such as poll taxes, literacy tests, and the grandfather clause (which denied suffrage to anyone whose grandfather had been ineligible to vote) voter rolls had been reduced, and the disfranchisement of blacks was virtually complete. The Supreme Court tacitly approved the creation of a separate society with its 1896 decision in *Plessy* v. *Ferguson*, which upheld the Louisiana law requiring "separate but equal" railroad facilities for blacks and whites. Starting around 1900, this notion of "separate but equal" was quickly applied to all facets of southern life, though never with any effort to make things equal. By 1915, for example, South Carolina was spending twelve times as much per capita for the education of white children as it did for black children. Throughout the South movie theaters, water fountains, hotels, restaurants, and swimming pools were segregated or declared off limits to blacks. Laws legislating this separation of the races, named Jim Crow laws, relegated blacks to an inferior status socially and to second-class status legally.

Southern Paradoxes. Southerners effectively used progressive arguments for their actions. Jim Crow laws were extreme examples of social-control legislation, laws in which the government dictated how citizens should act. To southern progressives the new election laws were a means of cleaning up a corrupt electorate. By preventing poor whites as well as blacks from voting, the poll tax and other laws restricting suffrage kept corrupt white politicians from obtaining their votes through bribery or intimidation. The all-white primaries furthered this aim as well. Use of the Australian secret ballot, which listed the candidates by name instead of by party, required the voter to be able to read in order to vote. It mattered little to progressives if illiterate voters happened to be blacks or poor whites, because this and other measures took power away from the hated political machines. Segregation

Booker T. Washington arriving for dinner at the White House, 16 October 1901

would allow the reconciliation of a white society divided after the tumultuous, divisive populist campaigns of the 1890s, and, reformers argued, it would minimize contact with "deceptive" and "corrupting" Negroes. With blacks eliminated from the picture, such reformers believed, whites could join together to begin reforming and improving (white) society.

Northern Views. Racism was not restricted to the South during the Progressive Era. It was simply more blatantly displayed in the South than in the North. Race riots and lynchings, commonly associated with the South, occurred in the North as well — and riots with nearly the same frequency. In the North segregation came about more by custom, geography, and economics (de facto segregation) than by law (de jure segregation). Confronted with such intense repression and racism, blacks listened to the opposing arguments of the two leading black leaders, Booker T. Washington and W. E. B. Du Bois. Washington, the "Wizard of Tuskegee," recommended that blacks temporarily acquiesce to the loss of their political rights and concentrate on improving their economic independence. Whites supported Washington's conciliatory, gradual approach. Du Bois, a Harvard-educated black intellectual, advocated immediate direct action to obtain civil rights and economic equality.

Roosevelt and the "Negro Problem." President Roosevelt's "Negro policy" reflected the broader opinions of most national leaders of his time. Shortly after taking over the presidency in 1901, he invited his friend Booker T.

Washington to an informal dinner at the White House to discuss southern patronage jobs. As a leader of the southern wing of the Republican Party, Washington held great influence over the rank-and-file membership, which was predominantly black. When news of the event hit southern newspapers, segregationists and critics widely denounced Roosevelt's invitation as "the most damnable outrage that has ever been perpetrated by any citizen of the United States." The invitation was a personal gesture done for political reasons. Roosevelt, like so many others of his time, felt that "as a race and in the mass" African Americans were "altogether inferior to whites," not social and intellectual equals. Yet black Republicans remained politically important because of their voting strength in some states, and Roosevelt needed them if he was to be elected in 1904. After the visit, their political collaboration continued. The president never apologized for the invitation, but he never repeated the action or invited other blacks to the White House for dinner. His successor, William Howard Taft, wanted even less to do with African Americans and did virtually nothing during his four-year term to aid them.

The Brownsville Affair. As the 1904 election drew near, President Roosevelt publicly shifted his position on the "Negro problem" in an effort to court the southern white vote. After the election he became increasingly critical of African Americans who failed to take control of their own condition and improve their lot in life. At the same time he came to rely increasingly on white southern

Democrats for advice on racial matters. The events of August 1906 demonstrated just how far he had shifted. Roosevelt received information on 15 August alleging that on the previous day black soldiers of the First Battalion of the Twenty-fifth Infantry, stationed at Brownsville, Texas, had shot up the town, killing one bartender and wounding a policeman. Roosevelt ordered an investigation, during which the twelve soldiers suspected of doing the shooting were at no time presumed innocent or provided with legal representation. The inquiry assumed the guilt of the men and simply sought to prove their involvement despite indications of their possible innocence. Investigators ignored contradictory testimony from eyewitnesses, and the available evidence did not support the official version. On 5 November 1906 Roosevelt issued orders that all the soldiers of the three affected companies be discharged and barred from holding any future governmental position. Among the 170 men discharged were six who had been awarded the Medal of Honor and some veterans of the Spanish-American War. A Congress disenchanted with Roosevelt launched an investigation into the affair in an effort to embarrass the president, keeping the incident in the news for the next two years, but they failed to overturn the finding.

Immigration Restriction. Immigration to the United States reached its zenith, 8.2 million people, between 1900 and 1909, with "new immigrants" from southern and eastern Europe outnumbering earlier immigrants from northern and western Europe by nearly three to one. The West Coast battled Asian immigrants, even though their total numbers did not exceed 172,000 for 1900–1909 or 300,000 over the thirty years between 1880 and 1909. Nevertheless, white American laborers felt threatened by the "yellow peril" and demanded appropriate action from their government. Chinese immigration was virtually nonexistent after passage of the Chinese Exclusion Act of 1882, which banned the immigration of Chinese laborers. In 1902 the Roosevelt administration supported measures that tightened the restrictions the Chinese already faced, a move that brought the president much popular support on the West Coast, especially in California. Nativists seeking to keep out more than just the Chinese proposed literacy tests for entry into the United States and sought to limit immigrant voting rights through similar measures. These measures failed, but they came before Congress many times during the next three decades. The president did support the Naturalization Act of 1907, which tightened procedures for becoming a U.S. citizen. The wording of the measure, supported by organized labor but opposed by big business, explicitly limited the number of unskilled laborers coming into the country. In the aftermath of the fight over this act, the president appointed the Dillingham Commission to probe the issue of immigration restriction as a national policy. Its report, issued in 1911, lent weight to the movement to restrict immigration.

The "Gentlemen's Agreement." Unlike the Chinese, most of whom arrived in poverty, many Japanese came to America with sufficient funds to purchase farmland. Predictably, Americans viewed the immigrant Japanese much as they did their country of origin: as ambitious, aggressive, and a little too successful. Xenophobic nativists sounded the alarm. In 1905 they formed the Asiatic Exclusion League in San Francisco, and in 1906 they persuaded the city school board to restrict Japanese pupils to attendance at segregated Chinatown schools. The Japanese community attacked the racism of the California politicians and protested to the Japanese government to intervene on their behalf. (In 1906 only ninety-three of the twenty-five thousand students in San Francisco were Japanese.) The Japanese government pointed out the folly of segregation to President Roosevelt, who himself called the measure a "wicked absurdity." Hoping to avoid an embarrassing international incident that might to lead to war, Roosevelt pressured the school board into rescinding its directive. In return the Japanese government agreed to a Gentlemen's Agreement in 1907, by which it pledged to refuse exit visas to laborers wishing to immigrate to the United States and Hawaii. The anti-Japanese rioting in San Francisco on 20–21 May 1907 rekindled the flame and again created a war scare. The riots were put down by local officials, but they had international ramifications, including Roosevelt's decision to send the navy on a Pacific cruise.

Sources:
Alan Kraut, *Huddled Masses: Immigrants in American Society, 1880–1921* (Arlington Heights, Ill.: Harlan Davidson, 1982);
Arthur S. Link and Richard L. McCormick, *Progressivism* (Arlington Heights, Ill.: Harlan Davidson, 1983).

THE MCKINLEY ASSASSINATION

Security Concerns. On 5 September 1901, Presidents' Day, President William McKinley, who was visiting the Pan-American Exposition in Buffalo, New York, delivered a speech that clearly set forth his position on the controversial issue of tariffs and trade reciprocity and laid out a new direction for the GOP during his second term. As part of his visit he had also scheduled a public reception at the Temple of Music on the afternoon of 6 September. Although the president was guarded by three members of the Secret Service, four special agents, and several soldiers, his secretary, George Cortelyou, believed that it would be difficult to ensure McKinley's safety at so public a gathering and asked the president to cancel the reception. McKinley brushed aside his secretary's apprehensions.

The Shooting. Before the reception a crowd gathered under a blazing sun, hoping to see the president and shake his hand. He arrived promptly at four o'clock. The public was admitted to the building two abreast and then formed into single file. As the line moved along, the Secret Service men tried to catch a glimpse of each person before he or she reached the president. At around seven

Born in 1873, the fourth child of Polish immigrants, Leon Czolgosz became interested in socialism while working in a Cleveland wire mill. As he became more and more resentful of social injustice, he grew to hate the American system of government and to believe that all rulers were the enemies of the people. He became strongly attracted to the doctrines of anarchism, which hold that the perfection of humanity will not be attained until all government is abolished and each individual is left absolutely free. Czolgosz adopted the minority position within the anarchist movement: that violence and terrorism are acceptable means of bringing about this freedom.

Testimony at his trial and subsequent research have suggested that Czolgosz suffered from severe clinical depression. He quit his job in 1898, returned to his family's farm, and took to his bed for weeks at a time, becoming increasingly withdrawn and irritable. His thinking and perception of reality deteriorated. In spring 1901 he returned to Cleveland, where he sought out Emma Goldman and other anarchists, but his superficial understanding of their beliefs and his vague revolutionary talk arose suspicion among those he contacted. He then inexplicably moved to Buffalo, returning briefly to Cleveland in late August. Back in Buffalo he heard of McKinley's impending visit and made plans to assassinate him.

In a statement he gave to police after his arrest Czolgosz explained Goldman's influence on his thinking and revealed his mental deterioration:

> During the last five years I have had as friends anarchists in Chicago, Cleveland, Detroit and other Western cities, and I suppose I became more or less bitter. Yes, I know I was bitter. I never had much luck at anything, and this preyed upon me. It made me morose and envious, but what started the craze to kill was a lecture I heard some time ago by Emma Goldman. She was in Cleveland, and I and other anarchists went to hear her. She set me on fire.
>
> Her doctrine that all rulers should be exterminated was what set me thinking, so that my head nearly split with pain. Miss Goldman's words went right through me, and when I left the lecture, I had made up my mind that I would have to do something heroic for the cause I loved.

Despite Czolgosz's assertion that he acted alone, his statement fed public fears of a broad conspiracy against the government. Police arrested Goldman and other anarchists, but they were unable to uncover any evidence that anyone had helped Czolgosz to plan the assassination.

Source: Margaret Leech, *In the Days of McKinley* (New York: Harper, 1959).

---

minutes past four, Leon Czolgosz, a short, slender young man with a bandaged hand worked his way through the line, patiently waiting his turn. When Czolgosz reached McKinley, he brushed aside the president's hand and fired two shots from a .32-caliber Iver-Johnson revolver. The first shot hit a button. The second entered McKinley's stomach, felling him. After a moment of stunned silence, the crowd pounced on Czolgosz as the president pleaded to Cortelyou, "Don't let them hurt him." McKinley's thoughts then turned to his frail wife: "My wife, be careful, Cortelyou, how you tell her — oh, be careful." As Czolgosz was subdued and taken into custody, the president was taken to the emergency hospital on the exposition grounds. The doctor who performed emergency surgery there did not find the bullet, and because of his improper medical procedures the president died a week later, in the early morning hours of 14 September.

Swift Justice. The day after the shooting newspapers across the country revealed that Czolgosz was an anarchist, but testimony at his trial — which was held on 23 September, just nine days after McKinley's death — revealed little else about the assassin. He refused to take the stand, was found guilty, and was sentenced to death by electrocution. On the morning of 29 October, while he was being strapped into the electric chair at Auburn Prison, he declared: "I killed the President because he was the enemy of the good people — the good working people. I am not sorry for my crime." After his execution the government had doctors examine his brain before turning the body over to his family. At that time medical science hypothesized that a criminal's brain had a distinctive shape, but Czolgosz's brain did not support their theory.

A Cowboy President. When told of McKinley's death Sen. Mark Hanna, a conservative Republican, exclaimed, "Now that damned cowboy is president." Czolgosz's crime had catapulted the young, energetic, progressive Republican Theodore Roosevelt into the White House. Roosevelt carried out McKinley's plans to make the Republican Party more socially beneficent — though without his predecessor's subtlety — and he built on McKinley's modest successes in modernizing the presidency. The new president largely ignored the public outcry against anarchists that followed the assassination, believing correctly that claims of a conspiracy were mostly unfounded. He did, however, support the portions of the

President William McKinley arriving for a reception at the Pan-American Exposition on 6 September 1900, a few minutes before he was mortally wounded by an assassin

Immigration Act of 1903 that virtually barred anarchists from entering the country. After the assassination of a third president within forty years, President Roosevelt ordered the Treasury Department to assign Secret Service agents to protect the president on a permanent basis.

Source:
Margaret Leech, *In the Days of McKinley* (New York: Harper, 1959).

NATIONAL POLITICS: THE 1900 REPUBLICAN CONVENTION

A Successful Incumbent. As the sitting president, William McKinley faced no challenge for the Republican nomination. The prospering economy, his deft handling of the Spanish-American War and its aftermath, and his statements about containing the trusts helped his popularity immensely — as had his successful use of the press and his many speaking trips across the country. After March 1900 he followed tradition and withdrew from the public eye, retiring to the White House for the spring and for the summer to his home in Canton, Ohio, where he received visitors and dealt with a growing crisis in China. His friend Sen. Mark Hanna, who had run McKinley's successful campaign four years earlier, was again selected as head of the Republican National Committee.

Seeking a Running Mate. The only question facing the Republicans who met in Philadelphia on 19–21 June was who would be McKinley's running mate. The death of Vice President Garrett Hobart in 1899 had left open the second spot on the ticket. (Prior to passage of the Twenty-fifth Amendment to the Constitution in 1967, there was no provision for filling the vacancy if a vice president died in office.) The prospective vice-presidential candidate needed to be an easterner to balance the ticket, and several names had been mentioned prior to the convention. Secretary of War Elihu Root was McKinley's first choice, but the problems the administration faced in the Philippines and Cuba in late 1899 convinced McKinley that Root should remain in his cabinet post. The president next favored his former secretary of the interior, New Yorker Cornelius N. Bliss, but he listened to other suggestions as well.

Candidate Roosevelt? Of the many names mentioned for the vice-presidential slot, only one aroused Republican interest. The popularity of the young governor of New York, Theodore Roosevelt, had steadily increased since he arrived in Albany in 1898 and made him an early favorite for the vice presidency. Though he already had a lengthy career in politics by the tender age of forty-one, he had ridden into the governor's mansion on the basis of his heroics in Cuba during the Spanish-American War. Unfortunately, he had announced to the press in February that "*under no circumstances* could I or would I . . . accept the nomination for the Vice-presidency." Yet as the possibility that he might not gain a cabinet post or another prominent position in McKinley's administration dawned on him, Roosevelt began privately repudiating his denial of vice-presidential ambitions while trying to maintain his lack of interest publicly. In an effort to get him out of the Empire State, his Republican opponents in New York whipped up support for him. Much to Hanna's chagrin, McKinley offered no opinions about possible candidates, nor could Hanna get the president to squelch the "draft Roosevelt" movement. Roosevelt's appearance as a New York delegate at the convention in Philadelphia convinced the rank and file that he wanted the vice presidency, and they enthusiastically obliged. Hanna, who distrusted Roosevelt's ambitions and disliked his relatively progressive political views, prophetically exclaimed, "Don't you realize there is only one heartbeat between that madman and the presidency?" As tradition dictated, McKinley did not attend the convention. On 12 July 1900, the day he was formally notified of

Republican campaign poster, 1900

his party's nomination, he delivered a short acceptance speech from his front porch in Canton, Ohio, and issued a formal letter of acceptance in September.

NATIONAL POLITICS: THE 1900 DEMOCRATIC CONVENTION

Few Surprises. The Democrats gathered in Kansas City on 4 July, and to no one's surprise they nominated the charismatic William Jennings Bryan, who had been their candidate four years earlier, on the first ballot. As his running mate they chose Adlai E. Stevenson of Illinois, who had been vice president during Grover Cleveland's second term and who shared Bryan's belief that the nation should abandon the gold standard for silver. The only suspense at the convention pertained to which issue would be given greater weight in the party platform: an attack on expansionism or a restatement of the 1896 pledge to free coinage of silver. The debate was short, and expansionism won out. Attacking the foreign policies of the McKinley administration, the Democrats declared that "imperialism growing out of the Spanish war, involves the very existence of the Republic, and the destruction of our free institutions. We regard it as the paramount issue of this campaign." They called for the establishment of a stable form of government and independence for the Philippines to be followed by protection of the new nation from outside interference. This course was what the Republicans had planned for Cuba and were considering for the Philippines as well. At

Bryan's insistence the platform also included a reaffirmation of the party's support for the coinage of silver.

NATIONAL POLITICS: THE 1900 ELECTIONS

The Republican Platform. Shortly after the Democrats issued their platform, Republican newspapers began discussing the GOP platform adopted in Philadelphia. The Republican platform was interesting for what it did not include as much as for what remained. Senator Hanna's pet project of subsidies for enlarging the merchant marine, which would help overseas business expansion, had been dropped because of midwestern opposition. A statement affirming that Congress has power over territories that belong to the United States had been left out. Other controversial issues, such as a statement about civil-service reform, were also removed to prevent injury to Republican chances. McKinley, who had favored all three proposals, expressed his support for the most important, stating that Congress has "full legislative power over territory belonging to the United States" and adding, "This doctrine, first proclaimed in the cause of freedom, will never be used as a weapon of oppression." He also reasserted the Republican position backing the gold standard.

The Republicans' Real Positions. McKinley's formal letter of acceptance, issued in September to be used by Republican campaigners, addressed other issues at length. He explained the actions he took to resolve the

Senate	56th Congress	57th Congress	Net Gain/Loss
Democrats	26	31	+5
Republicans	53	55	+2
Other	8	4	-4

House	56th Congress	57th Congress	Net Gain/Loss
Democrats	163	151	-12
Republicans	185	197	+12
Other	9	9	0

Governors	1898	1900	Net Gain/Loss
Democrats	14	17	+3
Republicans	26	27	+1
Other	5	1	-4

Boxer Rebellion in China and the threat it posed to American lives. He again chastised Bryan and the Democrats for their position on silver, calling their support of the issue "financial heresy." He found the nation's economic situation to be excellent, called for an expanded merchant marine, an isthmian canal, and lower taxes. The party platform, written by Hanna and edited by McKinley, had condemned trusts that restricted business, limited production, created monopolies or controlled prices, and favored legislation to restrain and prevent these abuses. In this letter McKinley went further by calling trusts "dangerous conspiracies against the public good" that should be subject to prohibitory legislation. Like his running mate, he thought "publicity will be a helpful influence to check this evil."

Foreign Policy. When the Democrats decided to emphasize expansionism in their platform, they made foreign policy the main issue of the campaign. Their objections to the seizure and control of territory was out of step with the beliefs of most Americans at the time. That the Democrats implicitly condemned taking over the Philippines proved ironic, for Bryan had helped negotiate the peace treaty. While the Democrats called for the establishment of a protectorate in the Philippines — that is, installing a government there that remained answerable to the United States — Republicans argued that the Filipinos could not yet properly govern themselves and that to make the islands a protectorate would lead to anarchy. When McKinley brought up these points, especially Bryan's participation in the peace treaty, in his acceptance letter, he clarified the differences between himself and his opponent while skillfully undermining the idea of a protectorate. The Democrats had little choice but to concede the issue.

Contrasting Campaign Styles. With the debate over foreign policy effectively over by mid September, the Democrats turned to the only issue left, the economy. Their pleas were ignored in those prosperous times. Criticism of McKinley's handling of the trusts was quickly rebuked with reminders of the Democrat Cleveland's failure to do any better. Once again, the Democrats had little money and relied heavily on Bryan's oratorical skills to get out their message. They also suffered from factionalism in key states. Faced with only one perceived threat to Republican chances — general apathy — Hanna raised only $2.5 million for the campaign, compared to $7 million in 1896. The majority of that money came from wealthy and business donors, helping to solidify the identification of his party with the nation's wealthy. Millions of pamphlets and press releases blanketed the countryside, and Hanna and Roosevelt barnstormed the country speaking on behalf of McKinley and the party. The campaign completed Roosevelt's emergence as a national figure. By mid October, the election was a foregone conclusion.

Another Republican Victory. Though voter turnout was lower than in previous elections (owing in part to the certainty of the results and a general decline in partisan politics), McKinley's margin of victory was impressive. Some of the previous elections had been decided by as few as two hundred thousand votes. McKinley received 7,218,491 popular votes (51.7 percent) to Bryan's 6,356,734 (45.5 percent). He won by 292 to 155 in the electoral college. The Republicans captured six more governorships, including the one in Bryan's home state of Nebraska, than they had in 1896. Republican domination over Congress continued as well, with a margin of forty-six in the House and twenty-four in the Senate. McKinley took the results as the people's endorsement of his party's policies and as a sign of growing political consensus. "I can no longer be called the President of a party," he declared, "I am now the President of the whole people."

Sources:

Paul Boller Jr., *Presidential Campaigns* (New York: Oxford University Press, 1989);

Lewis L. Gould, *The Presidency of Theodore Roosevelt* (Lawrence: University Press of Kansas, 1991);

Gould, *The Presidency of William McKinley* (Lawrence: University Press of Kansas, 1980);

Walter La Feber, "Election of 1900," in *History of American Presidential Elections, 1789–1968*, edited by Arthur M. Schlesinger Jr., volume 3 (New York: Chelsea House, 1971), pp. 1877–1962.

NATIONAL POLITICS: THE 1902 ELECTIONS

Breaking with Tradition. As the off-year elections got under way, the new president, Theodore Roosevelt, planned to make a series of speeches. Roosevelt's active participation in the campaign was an innovation, and to quell criticism that a sitting president was supposed to be above party politics, the White House told reporters that

Senate	57th Congress	58th Congress	Net Gain/Loss
Democrats	31	33	+2
Republicans	55	57	+2
Other	4	0	-4

House	57th Congress	58th Congress	Net Gain/Loss
Democrats	151	178	+27
Republicans	197	208	+11
Other	9	0	-9

Governors	1900	1902	Net Gain/Loss
Democrats	17	19	+2
Republicans	27	26	-1
Other	1	0	-1

while his speeches would be "along Republican lines, so far as they may relate to politics, they will not be political speeches." Yet it came as no surprise that Roosevelt's speeches were indeed political. As he did for his entire presidency, Roosevelt avoided the tariff issue almost completely in these speeches and concentrated on the trust issue. While touring New England, where he spoke of the use of publicity as a way to control the trusts, he narrowly escaped death when a trolley struck his horse-drawn carriage in Pittsfield, Massachusetts, injuring Roosevelt and other passengers and killing a Secret Service agent. The president suffered assorted injuries to his face and bruises on one leg.

National and State Results. The accident helped the president's popularity — and along with it Republican chances. The mishap — combined with his involvement in settling the anthracite-coal strike and his antitrust campaign — contributed to a good voter turnout. Redistricting after the 1900 census helped both major parties to gain seats in both houses. The Republicans picked up eleven House seats, while the Democrats gained twenty-seven, and each party gained two seats in the Senate, but the GOP maintained its majority in both houses. Third-party candidates were shut out. The Democrats maintained control of southern governorships.

NATIONAL POLITICS: THE 1904 REPUBLICAN CONVENTION

The Benefits of Incumbency. Political events in the early part of 1904 — especially Senate approval of the Hay–Bunau-Varilla Treaty, Roosevelt's greatest foreign-policy triumph to date — bolstered the president's election chances. In March Roosevelt openly courted Union

Army veterans, traditionally a powerful block of Republican voters, by having the Pension Bureau issue an order lowering the age at which Union veterans could receive benefits. That same month his trust-busting program, which worried conservative Republicans and their wealthy supporters, gained a boost when the Supreme Court handed down a decision favoring the government in the Northern Securities case. His efforts to emphasize conservation were gaining support as well. The last part of his "Square Deal" — the friendliness toward organized labor that he demonstrated by how he had settled the anthracite-coal strike in 1902 — rounded out the successes of his first term.

The Convention. The death of Sen. Mark Hanna in February 1904 removed any threat of opposition to Roosevelt's nomination. Roosevelt struggled to find a replacement for Hanna as chairman of the Republican National Committee. After being turned down by three different men, including Elihu Root, Roosevelt asked the man he had wanted all along, George B. Cortelyou, secretary of commerce and labor. With Roosevelt's nomination assured, the only drama centered around who would be his running mate. That question was resolved just prior to the convention, which opened in Chicago on 21 June, when Sen. Charles W. Fairbanks of Indiana emerged as the vice-presidential front-runner. As soon as his name was placed in nomination at the convention, his only rival withdrew as a candidate. Fairbanks's nomination provided geographical balance for the ticket and satisfied the conservative wing of the party. The platform endorsed Roosevelt's "Square Deal," as he called his domestic program. The Square Deal promised that the federal government would treat everyone — labor and capital, Jew and Gentile, black and white, immigrant and native — equitably and equally. Roosevelt intended to achieve this goal through progressive legislation and actions.

Excitement at Last. On the second day of the convention, a clerk read aloud a news bulletin from Washington, D.C. It reported that the U.S. State Department had sent a message to the U.S. consul in Morocco that stated, "We want either Perdicaris alive or Raisuli dead." The delegates erupted in cheers, the only genuine emotion expressed during the entire convention. On 18 May 1904 Ion Perdicaris and his stepson had been kidnapped from their home by a bandit known as Raisuli and were being held for ransom. Because Perdicaris was believed to be an American citizen, the American press and public as well as the president protested his seizure. To support the diplomatic protest Roosevelt decided to dispatch to Tangier U.S. warships that were en route to Europe. As negotiations dragged on, Roosevelt sent more ships and flirted with the possibility of landing U.S. Marines at Tangier. The telegram read to the convention was intended to pressure the Moroccan government and influence Raisuli, but by the time it was delivered, Perdicaris, who turned out to be a citizen of Greece, had already

President Roosevelt and his running mate, Charles W. Fairbanks, during the 1904 election campaign

been set free. Roosevelt's willingness to use American military power in foreign affairs proved important in the long run.

NATIONAL POLITICS: THE 1904 DEMOCRATIC CONVENTION

Conservative Reemergence. After the defeat of William Jennings Bryan in 1900, the conservative wing of the Democratic Party emerged as the dominant force in the party. Casting about for a candidate, Democrats first considered asking Grover Cleveland to run for a third term, but Bryan's opposition and memories of Cleveland's mixed record quickly ended that boom. They then looked for someone not associated with the factionalism of the 1890s. The conservatives pushed aside maverick publisher William Randolph Hearst, turning instead to Judge Alton Brooks Parker of New York. They theorized that he could carry New York, and, if he could pick up just a few more states to go along with the Solid South, the Democrats could reclaim the White House. Silence on the issues was the key to winning the nomination, Parker's managers felt, so much so that he was called the "enigma from New York" by some members of the press. The strategy worked, and the judge swept the nomination rather easily.

A Conservative Convention. The platform reflected the conservatives' sway over the party, further angering Bryan and his supporters, who failed to get a tougher antitrust plank and a strong commitment to tariff reform. Parker completed the push to the right when he sent the convention a telegram stating his monetary views. As president, he said, he would take the position that the gold standard was "firmly and irrevocably established." If the delegates did not approve this policy, he would not run. The "gold telegram," as it came to be called, set off an intense debate, led by Bryan, the silverite. The convention responded to Parker's message by remaining silent on the money issue. As his running mate, the convention selected West Virginia millionaire Henry Gassaway Davis. His backers hoped that he would bring balance to the ticket and his bankroll to the campaign. Much to their disappointment, the eighty-two-year-old brought neither. At the end of the convention, hopes ran high among the party faithful. The Democratic South most assuredly provided 150 electoral votes. They expected Parker to carry his home state, along with Connecticut and New Jersey. Three border states — West Virginia, Maryland, and Delaware — brought them within sight of the necessary 239 votes needed to win. They hoped that the party could carry Indiana to put them over the top. With money expected from Davis and other eastern conservatives, the Democrats believed their sane and calm alternative to Roosevelt would become the next president.

Judge Alton B. Parker (far right) receiving formal notification that he has received the Democratic presidential nomination (*Harper's Weekly,* 20 August 1904)

NATIONAL POLITICS: THE 1904 ELECTIONS

The Invisible Candidates. Parker's bold statement of his position on the gold standard led many Democrats to believe that they had indeed found a candidate aggressive enough to take on Roosevelt. That hope quickly dissipated with the reading of his acceptance speech in August. He spoke out for self-government in the Philippines and said that the states had all the power needed to regulate trusts. The rest of his remarks listlessly ran through a litany of Democratic positions. Parker's decision to run a front-porch campaign, as McKinley had done in 1896, showed how little energy his campaign had. It was difficult to reach his hometown of Esopus, New York, and the voters stayed away. The Democratic National Committee had money to spend on the campaign, but it did so inefficiently, further hurting the party's chances. In taking a conservative stance on the issues, Democrats conceded the middle and left of the political spectrum to Roosevelt and the Republicans. The Republicans, on the other hand, could not unleash their best campaign weapon because of tradition. According to long-standing political custom, the incumbent president should not actively campaign for votes. With Roosevelt off the stump the Republicans lacked their best speaker. He could give one speech accepting the nomination and outline his positions in his acceptance letter, but that was the extent of his public participation in the race.

An Uninspiring Race. Given the candidates' absence from the public eye, there was little to inspire the voters or arouse their interest. Parker seemed dull in comparison to the charismatic president. Not only had the Democrats conceded much political ground, they also allowed the Republicans to make inroads into traditional Democratic constituencies, such as Catholics and Jews as well as German Americans and Irish Americans. Only Socialist Party candidate Eugene V. Debs, who campaigned actively, caused much of a stir. Toward the end the campaign became somewhat lively when Parker charged that

Senate	58th Congress	59th Congress	Net Gain/Loss
Democrats	33	33	0
Republicans	57	57	0
Other	0	0	0

House	58th Congress	59th Congress	Net Gain/Loss
Democrats	178	136	-42
Republicans	208	250	+42
Other	0	0	0

Governors	1902	1904	Net Gain/Loss
Democrats	19	20	+1
Republicans	26	25	-1
Other	0	0	0

Cortelyou was using information he had obtained as secretary of commerce and labor to induce the trusts to finance Roosevelt's election. The trusts were "being allowed to buy protection," Parker claimed. In addition to the charges he had aired publicly, Parker had been told by wealthy Democrats that Roosevelt had asked prominent businessmen to contribute to Republican coffers. Parker received no specific information, and his informants swore him to secrecy. Indeed, the president's campaign had received $250,000 from railroad baron E. H. Harriman and $100,000 from Standard Oil. The White House responded angrily, releasing a press statement calling the accusations "unqualifiedly and atrociously false." Parker could not provide evidence of the charge, and the issue died out the week before the election.

National and State Results. The election marked the beginning of a trend in twentieth-century presidential politics — a decreasing concern with party positions and a growing interest in the merits and personalities of the candidates. The change resulted in part from election-law reforms and changes in campaign styles. The election also demonstrated the growing influence of special-interest groups in politics. As a charismatic and fascinating candidate, Roosevelt faced little competition in this sort of election. His margin of victory, 7.6 million votes (56.4 percent) to Parker's 5 million (37.6 percent), was greater than McKinley's four years earlier. Roosevelt's 336 electoral votes was the highest total to that time. He carried thirty-three of forty-five states, and by picking up Missouri he was the first Republican to crack the Solid South in a generation. Most worrisome to the two major parties was the strong showing of the Socialist Debs, who garnered around 400,000 votes, a huge increase over his 1900 total. The increase in votes for the Socialist Party reflected the subtle shift in the focus of national politics. The federal government no longer could concern itself only with the promotion of economic growth. Now it had to decide the extent to which it should intervene in the regulation and supervision of a growing industrial society. The Republicans maintained their hold over Congress once again with comfortable margins in both houses, but Democrats won the governorships of Colorado, Massachusetts, and Minnesota.

Sources:
Paul Boller Jr., *Presidential Campaigns* (New York: Oxford University Press, 1989);

Lewis L. Gould, *The Presidency of Theodore Roosevelt* (Lawrence: University Press of Kansas, 1991);

William H. Harbaugh, "Election of 1904," in *History of American Presidential Elections, 1789–1968*, edited by Arthur M. Schlesinger Jr., volume 3 (New York: Chelsea House, 1971), pp. 1965–2146.

NATIONAL POLITICS: THE 1906 ELECTIONS

Republican Concerns. The contentious 1906 session of Congress left the Republican Party in some disarray. The division of the party in the debate over tariff reform was compounded by wrangling over the Hepburn Act to

Senate	59th Congress	60th Congress	Net Gain/Loss
Democrats	33	31	-2
Republicans	57	61	+4
Other	0	0	0

House	59th Congress	60th Congress	Net Gain/Loss
Democrats	136	164	+28
Republicans	250	222	-28
Other	0	0	0

Governors	1904	1906	Net Gain/Loss
Democrats	20	21	+1
Republicans	25	24	-1
Other	0	0	0

strengthen the ICC and other regulatory laws. GOP infighting left the Democrats gleeful about their prospects that fall. Their success hinged to a great extent on William Jennings Bryan's ability to keep the two wings of their party together. He positioned himself to the left of Roosevelt — and for another run at the White House — by asking if Roosevelt had "the courage to be a reformer" and by defining the Democrats as the true defenders of property because they accumulated wealth "honestly." The Democrats hoped to use these themes to make gains in Congress. In 1906, when congressional Republicans spurned organized labor's push for federal laws that benefited and protected them, Samuel Gompers, president of the AFL, urged the 1.7 million members of his union to work for the defeat of Republican candidates who had opposed their demands. To help his party, the president gladly pitched in by making the election another referendum on his personal popularity and his regulatory program. By mid October, the momentum had shifted back to the Republicans.

National and State Results. Despite Roosevelt's growing optimism about election day, the Republicans lost twenty-eight seats in the House, dropping their majority to fifty-eight. They did pick up four seats in the Senate. Republican dominance over Congress continued, and they won the governorships of the key states of New York, Massachusetts, and Ohio but suffered setbacks in Rhode Island and North Dakota. The president's announcement on the day before the election of the dismissal of 170 African American soldiers in the wake of the Brownsville Affair had little influence on voting. The

Republicans' success was widely attributed to the popularity of the president.

NATIONAL POLITICS: THE 1908 REPUBLICAN CONVENTION

Changing of the Guard. Despite Roosevelt's pledge not to seek another term, conservative Republicans feared a third-term movement for the popular president at the convention. Sticking to his promise, Roosevelt made every effort to ensure that delegates elected to the convention supported the nomination of his friend and hand-picked successor, Secretary of War William Howard Taft. Roosevelt's support made Taft's collection of delegates prior to the convention relatively easy. Progressive Republicans supported Taft as the president's heir apparent, further helping his cause. The administration's control of the seating process at the convention virtually sealed the deal. When two hundred disputed delegates gave their support to Taft, his two rivals, Vice President Charles Fairbanks and Sen. Joseph Foraker of Ohio, were essentially defeated before the convention opened in Chicago on 16 June. The wrangling over selection of Taft's running mate during the convention reflected the tension between conservatives and progressives. Neither the president nor the candidate got the vice presidential candidate they wanted. After Sen. Jonathan P. Dolliver of Iowa, Gov. Charles Evans Hughes of New York, and Sen. Albert J. Beveridge of Indiana turned down the second spot on the ticket, the progressives were left empty-handed, opening the way for the conservatives. They succeeded in gaining the nomination for James S. Sherman, a New York congressman solidly in the right wing of the party.

The Platform. Taft and Roosevelt had better success with the party platform, which supported further strengthening of the Interstate Commerce Act, reform in the Sherman Antitrust Act, and development of a system of postal savings banks. For the first time in several elections, the party took a stand on the tariff issue, demanding a special session of Congress immediately after the presidential inauguration to deal with the revision of the tariff. The platform did not say in which direction the tariff should be revised, but the very existence of the plank demonstrated the growing pressure within the party to take action. Taft interpreted the plank to mean a revision downward, which aligned him with the progressives in his party. Along with Taft's promise of progressive legislation, the plank was enough to silence the midwestern Republicans who wanted drastic tariff reduction. On the other hand, the conservatives, who supported a high tariff, prevented Roosevelt from getting a provision limiting the use of back-to-work injunctions in labor disputes. Roosevelt's idea did not go as far as labor leader Samuel Gompers wanted, but it was still more than Joseph Cannon and the conservatives would tolerate. In the end the platform made the vague promise to

Democratic campaign poster, 1908

"uphold at all times the authority and integrity of the courts." Taft's acceptance of this compromise alienated labor. Nonetheless, the platform pleased Roosevelt and Taft alike.

NATIONAL POLITICS: THE 1908 DEMOCRATIC CONVENTION

The Return of the Great Commoner. William Jennings Bryan returned to the helm of his party in 1908. He had staked out his position two years before in a speech leaving little question that he was trying to reclaim the political left from Roosevelt and the progressive Republicans. In this two-hour speech he dedicated six paragraphs to the railroad question. Viewing them as monopolies, he said that if proper, effective railroad regulation could not be obtained, the government should treat the railroads as public property and ultimately take them over. The Republican press acted as if the entire speech were about railroads. They substituted "immediately" for "ultimately," making the proclamation seem more extreme than it really was. Congressional Republicans responded to Bryan's criticism by passing the Hepburn Act, and southern states rejected his argument because it went counter to their states' rights philosophy of restricting the power of the federal government. Bryan quickly dropped the issue, but his opponents did not. The remainder of his speech did little to inspire his followers or appease the conservatives within his party. Yet regardless of how the Democrats felt about the speech, Bryan was still the man to beat for the nomination in 1908.

The Convention. Having not recovered from the disaster in the previous election, the conservative wing of the party stood little chance of stopping Bryan's nomination. In fact, he received it on the first ballot. The instant his name was mentioned before the convention, which opened in Denver on 7 July, the delegates broke out into frenzied dancing in the aisles and cheers of "Bryan! Bryan! Bryan!" that lasted for an hour and a half, the longest ovation in political history to date. The convention also concurred with Bryan's choice of a running mate, John W. Kern of Indiana. The conservatives unsuccessfully protested the "radical" platform, which called for antiinjunction legislation, a plank that garnered Bryan an endorsement from the AFL. Bryan maintained the position on the railroads that he had laid out two years before and also called for dissolution of trusts that controlled 50 percent or more of the American marketplace, government-guaranteed bank deposits, and a gradual elimination of the protective tariff, which should be replaced by a tariff for revenue only. After three previous tries on the issue, the Democrats finally dropped silver from the platform.

NATIONAL POLITICS: THE 1908 ELECTIONS

The Bryan Campaign. As the campaign got under way, Bryan ran in his usual style. He attacked the Republicans for stealing many of his platform ideas from previous years. He argued that he was the rightful successor to Roosevelt because he was more progressive than Taft and could carry out better reforms than his Republican opponent. The Panic of 1907 left the Republicans unable to promote themselves as the party of prosperity, but Bryan did not capitalize on the issue. He campaigned on so many issues that his message failed to reach the public in an effective manner, and he unsettled many middle-class voters by adopting as his campaign slogan, "Shall the People Rule?" — a question whose strong socialist undertones were repellent to many middle- and upper-class Americans. The Democrats also remained outside mainstream political feelings by adhering to their support for states' rights. In the end his ideas proved too radical for most voters, including labor, despite the endorsement of the AFL.

Taft's Lackluster Effort. Docile by nature and overshadowed by a much-loved, charismatic president, Taft did little to invigorate the voters on his own. After the convention he took a two-month vacation before hitting

Senate	60th Congress	61st Congress	Net Gain/Loss
Democrats	31	32	0
Republicans	61	61	0
Other	0	0	0

House	60th Congress	61st Congress	Net Gain/Loss
Democrats	164	172	+8
Republicans	222	219	-3
Other	0	0	0

Governors	1906	1908	Net Gain/Loss
Democrats	21	21	0
Republicans	24	24	0
Other	0	0	0

the campaign trail. His speeches lacked the fire of either his predecessor or his opponent, but the crowds proved large and warmly receptive to him nonetheless. He campaigned on the theme of continuity. His administration, he said, would not try anything radical and destructive. Rather, it would continue Roosevelt's policies. Roosevelt tried to stay out of the fight, so that Taft could emerge in the public eye his own man, but he felt compelled to issue a constant stream of press releases because of Taft's apparent reluctance to mix it up with Bryan. At one point the president was receiving more campaign press coverage than the candidate. The action picked up in mid September with newspaper publisher William Randolph Hearst's revelation that Bryan's campaign treasurer, Charles N. Haskell, had accepted money from Standard Oil while governor of Oklahoma, thus linking him to the hated oil trust. Roosevelt called for Haskell to step down. Public pressure soon became such that he had little choice.

National and State Results. By October Roosevelt's actions had combined with errors by the Democrats to push voters to Taft, setting up yet another Republican victory. Taft handed Bryan the worst of his three defeats, winning by 7.6 million to 6.4 million votes, or by a margin of more than 1.2 million votes. He gained nearly 50,000 more votes than Roosevelt had received in 1904, and won an astounding 159 more electoral votes than Bryan (321–162). Bryan's total popular vote was lower than in 1896, despite the increase in the nation's population. Eugene V. Debs increased his vote total by only 20,000 over 1904, garnering slightly more than 420,800 votes, 3 percent of the total. State elections reflected the growing partisanship that would soon divide the majority party. The Republicans lost the governorships of Ohio, Indiana, Minnesota, and North Dakota, all of which voted for Taft. Progressive Republicans, who had previously defeated conservatives in Republican primaries, swept into the governorships of Wisconsin, Iowa, Nebraska, and Kansas. The results showed that midwestern voters had separated themselves from the conservative wing and standpat Republicanism, as symbolized by Speaker Cannon in the House and Nelson Aldrich in the Senate.

Sources:

Paul Boller Jr., *Presidential Campaigns* (New York: Oxford University Press, 1989);

Paolo E. Coletta, "Election of 1908," in *History of American Presidential Elections, 1789–1968,* edited by Arthur M. Schlesinger Jr., volume 3 (New York: Chelsea House, 1971), pp. 2049–2131;

Lewis L. Gould, *The Presidency of Theodore Roosevelt* (Lawrence: University Press of Kansas, 1991).

HEADLINE MAKERS

WILLIAM JENNINGS BRYAN

1860-1925

DEMOCRATIC PRESIDENTIAL CANDIDATE, 1896, 1900, 1908

SECRETARY OF STATE, 1913-1915

"The Great Commoner." Best known for his three unsuccessful campaigns for the presidency of the United States (1896, 1900, and 1908), for his tireless advocacy of the rights of the "common man," and for his participation in the Scopes "Monkey" Trial in 1925, William Jennings Bryan is also notable for his exemplary leadership of the faltering Democratic Party during the first decade of the twentieth century.

Background. Born in Salem, Illinois, on 19 March 1860, Bryan inherited from his parents a fervent Protestant faith and an intense commitment to the Democratic Party. After earning an A.B. (1881) and an A.M. (1884) at Illinois College and a law degree from Union Law School in 1883, he married Mary Elizabeth Baird in 1884. In 1887, seeing no political future for himself in Illinois, he set up a law practice in Lincoln, Nebraska. In 1890, when the new Populist Party disrupted Nebraska politics, Bryan ran for Congress as a Democrat and was elected. He was reelected in 1892. In Congress he earned respect for his oratorical skills and became a leader among free-silver Democrats, who came predominantly from rural, agricultural parts of the country and viewed the unlimited coinage of silver as a way of relieving farm debts. He also championed a federal income tax to offset losses from lowering import tariffs, a move that brought him close to the Populists. In 1894 the "Boy Orator of the Platte," as he had become known, led Nebraska Democrats to support the state Populist Party, and he embarked on a speaking tour that gained him a national reputation, but he lost his bid for a Senate seat.

The "Cross of Gold." During the platform debate over the free-silver issue at the 1896 Democratic convention Bryan delivered one of the greatest political speeches ever given. Speaking in defense of western and southern rural interests, he proclaimed: "You come to us and tell us that the great cities are in favor of the gold standard, we reply that the great cities rest upon our broad and fertile prairies. Burn down your cities and leave our farms, and your cities will spring up again as if by magic; but destroy our farms and the grass will grow in the streets of every city in the country." He then compared the silver struggle to the American Revolution before moving to his conclusion: "Having behind us the producing masses of this nation and the world, supported by the commercial interest, the laboring interests, and the toilers everywhere, we will answer their demand for a gold standard by saying to them: You will not press down upon the brow of labor this crown of thorns." Raking his hand down his temples, he thundered, "You shall not crucify mankind upon a cross of gold." His speech touched off a half-hour of cheering and demonstrating. This "Cross of Gold" speech won him the Democratic presidential nomination and the leadership of his party for the next four presidential elections. He also received the nomination of the Populist Party. His great oratory and unprecedented eighteen thousand miles of travel proved too little against the overwhelming Republican machine, and he lost to William McKinley in 1896 and again in 1900. Bryan's 1896 campaign marked a long-term shift within the Democratic Party from a Jacksonian commitment to minimal government toward a positive view of government.

Campaigning for Reform. Bryan served as a colonel in a Nebraska regiment during the Spanish-American War, but after the war he opposed McKinley's Philippine policy as imperialism. The 1900 presidential election brought the debate over American imperialism to the fore, causing many Americans to question and rethink what they wanted from their foreign policy. After his loss to McKinley in 1900, Bryan launched a newspaper, *The Commoner* (an allusion to his nickname, "The Great Commoner"), and made frequent speaking tours — advocating greater popular participation in government decision making, opposing monopolies, and proclaiming the importance of faith in God. Having lost twice, he stepped aside in 1904, only to watch the conservative eastern wing take the party down to an even greater defeat. His 1908 campaign — run under the slogan "Shall the People Rule?" — helped propel the reform movement and put pressure on the conservative-minded William Howard Taft to be more progressive as president. By 1920 the Democratic-Populist campaign platforms that Bryan had championed for three decades had been largely adopted, changing forever the way the public viewed their government.

"King Maker." After his 1908 loss he became the "king maker" of the party and worked for Woodrow Wilson's nomination and election in 1912. His efforts were rewarded with an appointment to the post of secretary of state. As secretary, he promoted conciliation, or cooling-off, treaties, in which the parties agreed to allow a year of independent fact-finding on their disputes before going to war if they could not resolve their differences. When the European war broke out in 1914, Bryan, like Wilson, was committed to neutrality. Trying to avoid having the nation drawn into war, he exceeded Wilson in advocating restrictions on American citizens and businesses. When Wilson began to adopt a hard line against German submarine warfare, which was costing American lives, Bryan resigned in protest over the president's move away from neutrality.

The Scopes "Monkey" Trial. After leaving the administration, Bryan worked for peace, Prohibition, and woman suffrage, and he increasingly criticized the teaching of evolution. In 1925 he entered the public arena for the last time when he joined the prosecution in the trial of John Scopes, a Tennessee schoolteacher charged with violating state law by teaching evolution. During what the press called the "Monkey Trial," Scopes's attorney,

Clarence Darrow, called Bryan to the witness stand and humiliated him by confusing him and revealing his ignorance of science and archaeology. The two-hour examination was carried live over national radio. Bryan died shortly after the trial. Though not regarded as a deep or original thinker, Bryan is respected for his sincere belief in equality and in helping to improve the lives of common citizens.

Sources:

Robert W. Cherny, *A Righteous Cause: The Life of William Jennings Bryan* (Boston: Little, Brown, 1985);

Lawrence W. Levine, *Defender of the Faith* (Cambridge, Mass.: Harvard University Press, 1965).

ROBERT M. LA FOLLETTE

1855-1925

GOVERNOR OF WISCONSIN, 1901-1905

U.S. SENATOR, 1906-1925

"Battlin' Bob." With his election as governor of Wisconsin in 1900, Robert La Follette emerged as one of the most impassioned American progressives, battling the entrenched power of the corrupt political "machine" by putting into practice his "Wisconsin Idea" of entrusting his administration to nonpartisan civil servants drawn largely from the University of Wisconsin faculty. Largely because of Lincoln Steffens's articles about his efforts in *McClure's Magazine* he was soon marked as a rising star in the nationwide progressive movement, earning him the nickname "Battlin' Bob."

Background. La Follette was born into a poor but respectable farming family in pioneer Dane County, Wisconsin, on 14 June 1855. Despite their poverty, La Follette's family managed to scrape together enough money to send him to the University of Wisconsin. His love of oratory and the need to perform drew him to the stage, but fearing he could not support a family as an actor, he turned to law. After graduation in 1879, he stayed at the university to study law and was admitted to the bar in 1880. Within a year he had been elected district attorney of Dane County, Wisconsin, and married Belle Case, with whom he subsequently had four children, including two sons, Robert M. Jr. and Philip Fox, who followed their father into politics. Driven by ambition and local popularity, Robert La Follette Sr. was elected to the first of three terms in Congress in 1884 as a more or less orthodox Republican. After his district unseated him in 1890, he spent the next eight years in private practice in Madison, where populist rumblings could be heard. During this period La Follette gained an understanding of what he described as the sinister alliance between the "interests" (Wisconsin's lumber and railroad corporations) and the "bosses" (the majority-party leaders, predominantly the Republicans) who worked together to "cheat" the people — the farmers, workers, and small businessmen. La Follette became the popular champion of "the people" as he crisscrossed the state on a speaking campaign that finally landed him in the governor's mansion in 1900, after two unsuccessful tries. His election signaled the temporary defeat of the Republican machine in Wisconsin.

Fighting for Reform. While trying to reform state government, La Follette was engaged in a continual struggle against a conservative legislature and a Republican political machine dominated by "the interests." La Follette's strength came from his seemingly infinite energy, his firm belief in the need to restore representative democracy, and his willingness to borrow ideas such as railroad taxes and direct primaries from other states and adapt them for Wisconsin. Not until around 1903 did he, and the rest of the country, recognize that there was a nationwide reform movement afoot. Once he recognized this upsurge of progressivism La Follette, like other insurgent governors, decided to take his program to Washington and try to make it a national one. Elected to the Senate in 1905, he never became a successful insider despite his long tenure there. He had the same problems he had while governor — an unwillingness to compromise and an ideology far to the left of the general public.

Progressive Candidate. Never a team player in the Senate, La Follette did well at independently and uncompromisingly fighting for progressive legislation on the floor of the Senate and on the nationwide lecture circuit. In 1912 he was the leading candidate of progressive Republicans who unsuccessfully attempted to take away the Republican presidential nomination from the incumbent William Howard Taft. After the Progressives formed their own party, La Follette hoped to be their candidate to oppose Taft, but his presidential ambitions sustained a setback when Theodore Roosevelt reentered the national political scene. La Follette lost his supporters when rumors spread that he had suffered a "nervous breakdown" while giving a long, rambling speech on 3 February 1912, and the Progressive Party nomination went instead to Roosevelt. After progressive Democrat Woodrow Wilson won the election, La Follette supported his domestic programs but broke with him over American entry into World War I. La Follette was vilified and ostracized for his position and nearly expelled from the Senate. After the war, he was forgiven and assumed a new role — the respected elder of a progressive movement that went into an eclipse during the administrations of Warren G. Harding and Calvin Coolidge. In 1924 La Follette ran for the presidency on the Progressive Party ticket, polling almost six million of the nearly thirty million votes cast, but he carried only one state, Wisconsin, for a total of thirteen electoral votes. The campaign took its toll on his health, and he died of a heart attack on 25 June 1925.

Source:
David P. Thelen, *Robert M. La Follette and the Insurgent Spirit* (Boston: Little, Brown, 1976).

GIFFORD PINCHOT

1865-1946

HEAD OF THE FORESTRY DIVISION, U.S. DEPARTMENT OF AGRICULTURE, 1898-1901

HEAD OF THE BUREAU OF FORESTRY, 1901-1905

HEAD OF THE U.S. FOREST SERVICE, 1905-1910

A Valued Adviser. The most influential of the small group of close friends who advised President Theodore Roosevelt on conservation issues, Gifford Pinchot made conservation one of the leading causes of the Progressive Era. In the course of his career he slowly expanded the nation's concept of conservation from protection of forest resources to the conservation of human society itself.

Background. Born on 11 August 1865 at his maternal grandfather's summer home in Simsbury, Connecticut, Gifford Pinchot, the son of a wealthy New York merchant and land speculator, spent much of his childhood abroad with his parents and three siblings. After graduation from the prestigious Phillips Exeter Academy in 1884, he enrolled at Yale University. His maternal grandfather, who had achieved even greater wealth in Manhattan real estate and construction than Pinchot's father, promised to leave his entire fortune to young Gifford if he would enter the business after he graduated from Yale in 1889. Instead, he followed his father's advice and decided to become a forester. His father had seen the great working forests of Europe and anticipated the need for such scientific management of American woodlands in the near future. There were no schools of forestry in the United States, and Pinchot naively shared the American conception of a forester that came from the tales of Robin Hood, a man prancing about in the forest looking after the king's animals while wearing green stockings and leather cap. (In fact, students at the first forestry schools in the United States often formed Robin Hood Societies, with members appearing in pictures dressed like that legendary outlaw.) Pinchot learned differently in Europe, where he went after graduation in 1889. There he studied at the French Forest School in Nancy and went to Germany to meet Sir Dietrich Brandis, former head of forestry in British India and one of the leading foresters of the age. Pinchot returned to the United States in late 1890, and in February 1892 he took a job supervising forestry work at George W. Vanderbilt's sprawling Biltmore Estate in Asheville, North Carolina. Vanderbilt wanted to try scientific management in his private forest, the first attempt of its kind in the United States.

Forester-Politician. Achieving modest success in North Carolina, Pinchot opened a consulting office in New York City, hoping to attract the attention of the wealthy landowners of the Adirondacks. He became deeply involved in the forest conservation movement emerging in the early 1890s, serving on several government-appointed investigative committees. In 1898 President William McKinley invited him to take the position of chief of forestry in the Division of Forestry, then part of the Department of Agriculture. He replaced Bernhard Fernow, a German-born forester whose work in the division had done much to promote conservation. Two years later Pinchot's father and mother joined him in establishing and endowing the Yale University School of Forestry, where Pinchot began delivering a series of annual lectures in 1903. Pinchot's close friendship with President Roosevelt, who took office in September 1901, proved crucial to the survival of the conservation movement. In the Forest Service he built a strong bureaucracy that became a model of efficiency and professionalism. He urged Roosevelt to appoint many conservation commissions and then, to insure they carried out his vision, had himself appointed to them as secretary, the most powerful position on such commissions. Pinchot zealously carried out conservation policies, exerting strict control over all mining, grazing, and lumbering in the two hundred million acres of National Forests and withdrawing from the public domain large tracts of western land to manage resources that had previously been exploited for free.

Making Enemies. Bernhard Fernow and Pinchot had quickly taken a disliking to one another while working together on various forestry committees, and Fernow was only the first of many enemies Pinchot made because of differences of opinion over the goals of conservation. Pinchot's friendship with the naturalist John Muir ended in 1905, when Muir, who believed in preservation of America's scenic resources in their pristine natural states, opposed the construction of a dam in Hetch Hetchy Valley in Yosemite National Park, while Pinchot favored the dam because it would provide water for the city of San Francisco. He made many other enemies who believed he erred too much on the side of conservation. The uncompromising power with which he controlled grazing, lumbering, and mining activities on government land led to cries of "Pinchotism" from western newspapers and citizens. Western congressmen resented the power held by this mere bureau chief and tried cutting off funding for some of his commissions and to the Forest Service itself, but Pinchot and Roosevelt's efforts to publicize their efforts had helped create a conservation-minded public, ensuring that the federal government would always have a hand in regulating the development of natural resources. In 1907 Congress finally succeeded in reining in Pinchot by attaching to an Agriculture Department appropriations bill a rider forbidding the Forest Service to withdraw land in six western states without the approval of Congress. Pinchot's downfall came in January 1910, when he was dismissed from the Forest Ser-

vice after publicly accusing Interior Secretary Richard Ballinger of illegal actions in permitting the development of Alaskan coal lands under federal protection. The "Ballinger-Pinchot Affair" hurt President Taft politically and widened the split within the Republican Party between conservatives and Roosevelt Republicans, or the "insurgents," who supported Pinchot.

Outside Looking In. After his dismissal Pinchot continued to exert influence over forestry and conservation. Over the next decade he served another term as president of the Society of American Foresters (1910–1911), which he had founded in 1900 and headed until 1908. From 1910 until the mid 1920s he was president of the National Conservation Association, which he had formed in 1909 to further his conservation goals. He also wrote books on forestry and conservation, including *The Fight for Conservation* (1910) and three editions of *The Training of a Forester*, the first appearing in 1914. From 1920 to 1922 he was the commissioner of the Pennsylvania Department of Forestry, and later he served as secretary of the Department of Forests and Water in that state. As governor of Pennsylvania in 1923–1927 and 1931–1935, he carried out a progressive agenda in a time of political conservatism and became known as the "governor who got the farmers out of the mud" because of his extensive rural road-building program. Toward the end of his life Pinchot espoused the belief that conservation of global resources was the foundation for world peace. He served as an informal conservation adviser to President Franklin Roosevelt and worked on the president's behalf to put together a World Conservation Conference. Roosevelt's death put a temporary halt to the plan, but a few days before Pinchot's death, President Harry S Truman submitted the plan to the United Nations. Pinchot's plan for a meeting on global conservation became a reality after his death on 4 October 1946.

Sources:
M. Nelson McGeary, *Gifford Pinchot: Forester-Politician* (Princeton: Princeton University Press, 1960);

Gifford Pinchot, *Breaking New Ground* (New York: Harcourt, Brace, 1947);

Harold T. Pinkett, *Gifford Pinchot: Private and Public Forester* (Urbana, Chicago & London: University of Illinois Press, 1970).

THEODORE ROOSEVELT

1858-1919

PRESIDENT OF THE UNITED STATES, 1901-1909

A Modern President. As president, Theodore Roosevelt embodied the new century, full of boundless energy and endless possibilities. His dynamic personality overshadowed the accomplishments of both his predecessor, William McKinley, and his successor, William Howard Taft.

Roosevelt's youthful vigor and active lifestyle personalized the presidency to an extraordinary degree. Public focus shifted away from the party to the man in office, as Roosevelt continued McKinley's efforts to modernize the presidency and aggressively exercised his executive powers instead of playing the part of "caretaker president." Roosevelt used the office as his "bully pulpit," lecturing his fellow citizens on moral, ethical, and political issues. America's power and presence on the world stage expanded further under Roosevelt's "Big Stick" diplomacy, while his writings and speeches also had a major impact on domestic issues. By the time he left office, the presidency had been permanently transformed.

Background. Theodore Roosevelt was born on 27 October 1858 in New York City to Theodore Roosevelt Sr., a wealthy glass importer, and Martha Bulloch Roosevelt, a southerner whose relatives had fought for the Confederacy in the Civil War. The elder Theodore Roosevelt hired a substitute to serve in his place during that war — an action that influenced his son to seek active duty in times of military crises. Young Theodore was a sickly child. Afflicted with asthma, he was forced to spend much time indoors during his young years, but his illness did not prevent him from becoming an expert amateur naturalist. He began collecting and embalming animals, a passion he maintained the rest of his life. He also became a voracious reader. At thirteen he was given glasses to correct his poor eyesight, which fueled his enthusiasm for collecting and reading. Yet his illness also aroused a desire to strengthen his body, fostering a life-long love of sports and what he later called "the strenuous life." Encouraged by his father, he took up sports such as boxing, swimming, horseback riding, calisthenics, and shooting, eventually overcoming his asthma.

Harvard, Marriage, and Politics. Until he entered Harvard University in 1876, Theodore (who did not like to be called "Teddy") was privately educated by tutors. At Harvard he briefly considered becoming a naturalist or scientist before deciding to study history. His father's death from cancer in early 1878 came as a severe blow, but he managed to enjoy his remaining time in college. In the fall of his junior year, he met Alice Hathaway Lee, a delicate seventeen-year-old from a well-to-do Boston family. After a persistent courtship, she finally agreed to marry him and did so on his twenty-second birthday. After graduation in 1880, Roosevelt studied law at Columbia University, invested in cattle ranching in the Dakota Territory, and wrote *The Naval War of 1812* (1882), the first of his many books on subjects such as history, politics, and nature. Elected to the New York State Assembly as a Republican in 1881 and reelected in 1882 and 1883, he sponsored legislation to improve the working conditions of cigar makers in New York City, opposed railroad baron Jay Gould, and even tangled with Gov. Grover Cleveland. Roosevelt's splashy entrance into politics caused some problems with the Republican leadership, but from the beginning of his political career he cultivated the press, helping to shape his image and get his message out.

Tragedy and Decisions. The year 1884 was one of immense struggle for Roosevelt. His wife died only hours after giving birth, and his mother died of typhoid fever in the same house on the same day. Roosevelt left his daughter, named Alice after her mother, in the care of his sister while trying to get his life back together. After creating a memorial for his wife, he never mentioned her again and never allowed anyone else to discuss her in his presence. That same year James G. Blaine received the Republican presidential nomination. When Blaine, who was disliked by eastern Republicans for his financial dealings and close association with the party's conservative faction, received the nomination, some of Roosevelt's friends urged him to join them in bolting the party to support the Democratic nominee, Grover Cleveland. In the end he and his friend Henry Cabot Lodge from Massachusetts decided that staying in the party was the best thing for their political careers. After his wife's death, Roosevelt began dividing his time between New York and his Dakota ranch. He ended up losing most of his investment in the ranch, some 20 percent of his estate; yet as Lewis L. Gould has noted, "The gains in his physical well-being, emotional release, and political appeal lasted throughout his life." In Dakota he battled storms, punched cattle, killed grizzlies, and served as deputy sheriff — in all, collecting enough experiences to fill three new books.

Fighting Corruption. In 1886 New York City Republicans asked him to run for mayor against land reformer Henry George and Democrat Abram S. Hewitt. He finished a poor third but served the purpose of keeping the office from George. That December he married a childhood sweetheart, Edith Kermit Carow. After the hard winter of 1886–1887 he had lost most of his Dakota investment, and in 1892 he gave up ranching for good, settling with his wife and daughter at Sagamore Hill, in Oyster Bay, Long Island. After Benjamin Harrison was elected president in 1888, he appointed Roosevelt to the Civil Service Commission. During his six years at this post he learned about national politics and party patronage from the inside. In 1895 he asked for and received an appointment as one of four New York City police commissioners. His nighttime undercover expeditions around Manhattan to find on-duty policemen sleeping or drinking in saloons became the stuff of legend and great copy for the press. His effectiveness in cleaning up the department helped to create a new image for the city police, "New York's Finest," but his vigor in enforcing unpopular prohibition laws that closed saloons on Sunday met with resistance.

War. The election of Republican William McKinley to the White House in 1896 brought Roosevelt an appointment as assistant secretary of the navy, which he helped to modernize in preparation for war with Spain. Though in favor of overseas expansion and a greater role for the United States in world affairs, he did not hasten the war with Spain, as some biographers have asserted. He did not have a large role in the conduct of McKinley's diplomacy, nor did he create the tensions that led to the Spanish-American War of 1898. On 25 February 1898 he sent a telegram ordering Adm. George Dewey, in the event of hostilities with Spain, to bottle up the Spanish navy in Asia and then attack the Philippines. Yet the order stemmed from war plans dating back to 1895 and was part of the ongoing preparations for war at that time. Once the war began, Roosevelt volunteered immediately, entering the army as a lieutenant colonel in a volunteer regiment commanded by Col. Leonard Wood. The mix of western cowboys, eastern aristocrats, and Indians in the regiment made great copy for the newspapers, which were soon calling it "Roosevelt's Rough Riders." After a month's training, they landed in Cuba to oust the Spanish. In July, during the American assault on the San Juan Heights around the city of Santiago, Roosevelt, who had been promoted to colonel, led his men, including some African American troops, in attacks on Kettle and San Juan Hills, killing at least one Spaniard. The experience became "the great day of my life," and he long believed afterward that he deserved the Medal of Honor. The war in Cuba ended shortly thereafter, and he returned home in August 1898 to popular acclaim and a nomination as the Republican candidate for governor of New York. A narrow margin of victory and the tenuous support of party regulars did not keep him from carrying out policies such as conservation and the use of publicity to regulate corporate power. Feeling the pressure from campaign contributors, party leaders maneuvered to get Roosevelt out of New York and onto the national ticket as President McKinley's running mate in 1900. Little did they know that the assassination of the president in September 1901 would elevate Roosevelt to the presidency six months into McKinley's second term.

The Roosevelt White House. Roosevelt's actions as chief executive — both official and unofficial — made great newspaper copy. His energy seemed boundless. He hiked, camped, hunted, and played tennis with almost reckless enthusiasm. He had little respect for a man who refused to join him in such pursuits. The president's practice of jujitsu sparked a national rage for the martial art, and after his refusal to shoot a small bear on a November 1902 hunting trip in Mississippi, a toy manufacturer created one of the most popular toys of all time by naming a stuffed bear the "Teddy Bear." Roosevelt's young family also became a great political asset for him, capturing the nation's attention and holding it for eight years. Edith Roosevelt often commented that the president was simply the oldest of her children. He was frequently found playing cowboys and Indians with his children and their friends or helping them feed their veritable zoo of pets. His eldest daughter, Alice, so entranced "high society" that a shade of blue was named for her and quickly became fashionable. When she married Congressman Nicholas Longworth on 17 February 1906 in a White House ceremony, the wedding made international news. A learned couple, the Roosevelts entertained a wide array of people at the White House, all of whom could expect to hear the president speak knowledgeably on almost any topic.

Retired from Politics? After two successful terms in office, Roosevelt "retired" from the political limelight and went off to Africa for some big-game hunting and then to Europe for a triumphant tour of European capitals. But he was never far from the eye of the press. Disapproving of his successor's efforts as president, Roosevelt reentered the political fray in 1912. He first tried to recapture the Republican nomination, but he was outmaneuvered by President William Howard Taft. Disenchanted Progressives turned to Roosevelt after their original choice, Robert La Follette, appeared physically unable to carry out the campaign. "Feeling fit as a bull moose," Roosevelt picked up the banner of progressivism and launched one of the most successful third-party campaigns in U.S. presidential election history against his old friend Taft. His candidacy as the Progressive "Bull Moose" Party nominee split the Republican vote, enabling Woodrow Wilson to become the first Democrat to occupy the White House in sixteen years. Roosevelt remained in the political spotlight during World War I, criticizing President Wilson's position of neutrality during the period before the United States entered the war and actively campaigning for Wilson's Republican opponent, Charles Evans Hughes, in 1916. After the United States finally entered the war in 1917, he quickly volunteered to lead troops into combat, a request the president rebuffed. Frustrated, Roosevelt went to South America to search for the source of the Amazon River. He discovered a new river but also suffered great physical distress and illness that hastened his death. The loss of one of his sons during the war was a blow from which he never recovered. He died quietly in his sleep on 6 January 1919.

Sources:

Paul Russell Cutright, *Theodore Roosevelt: The Making of a Conservationist* (Urbana: University of Illinois Press, 1985);

Lewis L. Gould, *The Presidency of Theodore Roosevelt* (Lawrence: University Press of Kansas, 1991);

William Henry Harbaugh, *Power and Responsibility: The Life and Times of Theodore Roosevelt* (New York: Farrar, Straus & Cudahy, 1961).

WILLIAM HOWARD TAFT

1857-1930

SECRETARY OF WAR, 1904-1908

PRESIDENT OF THE UNITED STATES, 1909-1913

Reluctant Politician. Few Americans had heard of William Howard Taft when President Theodore Roosevelt appointed him to replace Elihu Root as secretary of war in 1904. In 1908, when conservative Republicans championed him as their presidential candidate, Taft's family and friends had to persuade him to run. He aspired to a seat on the Supreme Court, but his wife had greater ambitions for him. A large man given to lethargy, he did not have the drive or the skill to be a truly successful politician. "Politics, when I am in it, makes me sick," he exclaimed.

Background. Born on 15 September 1857 into a midwestern, staunchly Republican family of moderate wealth and some legal and political distinction near Cincinnati, Ohio, William Howard Taft was indoctrinated early with the conservative attitudes frequently found among members of the upper middle class. At Yale University he was exposed to the laissez-faire teachings of William Graham Sumner. After graduating as salutatorian from Yale University in 1878, he attended Cincinnati Law School, graduating in 1880. Except for his work in his father's law firm and as a part-time newspaper reporter in 1880 and his private law practice in 1883–1885, all the positions Taft held until he was elected president were appointive: assistant prosecuting attorney of Hamilton County, Ohio (1881–1882); collector of internal revenue for the First Ohio District (1882–1883); assistant county solicitor of Hamilton County (1885–1887); judge of the Superior Court of Cincinnati (1887–1890); solicitor general of the United States (1890–1892); U.S. Circuit Court judge (1892–1900); president of the Second Philippine Commission (1900–1901); first civil governor of the Philippines (1901–1904); and secretary of war (1904–1908).

A Cabinet Post. Having already turned down an appointment to the Supreme Court, the job he really wanted, because of his sense of obligation to complete the work he had started as civil governor of the Philippines, Taft accepted the post of secretary of war in 1904 only because it would allow him to continue exerting control over activities in the Philippines. Powerful conservative Republicans welcomed his appearance in the cabinet as a counterbalance to Roosevelt's progressive leanings. Based on his success as civil governor of the Philippines, they bandied about his name as a possible challenger to Roosevelt for the Republican presidential nomination in 1904, but Roosevelt's popularity and his control of the party apparatus squelched the idea. Taft did a commendable job in the cabinet, traveling the world on missions to Japan, the Vatican, Cuba, China, Russia, and the Panama Canal Zone. Ignoring Taft's recent statements, which made him sound like a Roosevelt Republican, conservatives embraced him as the nominee in 1908 to block Roosevelt from seeking a third term, an event they feared even though the president had promised not to do so after the 1904 election. Elected to the presidency by a comfortable margin, Taft turned back toward his conservative roots just as the country veered to the left. His battles with the Republican insurgents on issues such as tariff reform and conservation split the party and opened the way for the Democrats to win the White House in 1912.

Judicial Temperament. As a judge Taft was a moderate on labor and social issues and a conservative on financial ones, and his judicial background influenced his philosophy about the role of the chief executive. He rejected Roosevelt's stretching and testing the limits of executive action, and he resented Roosevelt's fostering of this practice in his subordinates. As he wrote after his single term as president, "the President can exercise no power which cannot be reasonably and fairly traced to some specific grant of power or justly implied or included within such express grant as necessary and proper to its exercise. Such specific grant must be either in the Constitution or in an act of Congress passed in pursuance thereof." This philosophy was more in line with the nineteenth-century "caretaker" concept of the presidency than with ideas about the office in the Progressive Era. Yet Taft also met congressional attempts to encroach on his executive power with stiff rebukes. In spite of his conservative outlook, Taft's judicial approach allowed him to do more "trust busting" than the "Trust Buster" himself, to withdraw more public lands from development in four years than Roosevelt had in eight, and to enact more social-welfare legislation than his two predecessors. During World War I Taft served as head of the quasi-judicial War Labor Board. In 1921 Taft realized his lifelong dream when he was named Chief Justice of the Supreme Court, a post he held until his death on 8 March 1930. As chief justice he again proved somewhat more progressive than conservative, thus remaining something of an enigma in American political history.

Source:
Paolo E. Coletta, *The Presidency of William Howard Taft* (Lawrence: University Press of Kansas, 1973).

BOOKER T. WASHINGTON

1856-1915

AFRICAN AMERICAN POLITICAL LEADER AND EDUCATOR

Up from Slavery. Booker T. Washington was the most influential African American political, social, and educational leader of the 1900s. As head of the Tuskegee Institute and founder of the National Negro Business League he shaped an accommodationist strategy to cope with segregation and discrimination and became the center of a fierce debate among black leaders and intellectuals. He was born the son of a slave woman and a white father, whose identity he never learned, on a small farm in western Virginia in 1856. As a child Washington, who was taught the virtues of frugality, cleanliness, and personal morality, worked in a salt furnace and as a houseboy for a white family. In 1872 he entered Hampton Institute, graduating in 1875. There he formed one of the central ideas of his life: if African Americans were to be accorded equality and respect by whites, they would have to demonstrate their usefulness and establish their autonomy in concrete and unmistakable ways.

Tuskegee. This idea shaped the guiding principles of the Tuskegee Institute, which Washington founded in 1881. The school instructed its students in academic subjects, but it primarily emphasized training in carpentry, masonry, agriculture, cooking, and other basic skills. Washington shaped the curriculum at Tuskegee around manual training, not because he accepted the notion that blacks were inferior to whites but because he believed that the black community would have to establish a firm economic foundation before demanding political equality. Washington's ideals attracted the financial support of several northern white philanthropists, whose contributions helped to fund the dramatic expansion of Tuskegee in the 1880s and 1890s. The school was even accepted by most white southerners, despite their hostility to education for African Americans.

Washington and Jim Crow. In the 1890s and 1900s, as Washington's influence was reaching its peak, southern politics and government were being transformed by new legislation mandating separation of the races and disenfranchising black voters. These "Jim Crow" laws were advocated by white Democrats, who had controlled the region since the end of Reconstruction. Since virtually all southern blacks voted for the Republican Party — the party of Abraham Lincoln and *not* the party of most former slaveowners — disenfranchising black voters solidified Democratic control of the South and made it clear to disgruntled poor southerners that racial solidarity was the foremost political issue of the era. Washington's critics believed that in his 1895 address at the Cotton States and International Exposition in Atlanta, he signaled to both whites and blacks his acceptance of segregation and political repression when he said, "In all things purely social we can be as separate as the five fingers, yet one as the hand in all things essential to mutual progress." In the same address he advised black southerners to stay in the region rather than seeking opportunity in northern cities. When a year after Washington's Atlanta address the Supreme Court upheld the legality of segregated facilities, Washington seemed fully in step with white opinion and the political reality of the New South.

Republican Leader. Washington's prominence among whites, and a war chest he assembled at Tuskegee from funds donated by northern benefactors, made him an intimidating presence in black politics in the 1900s. His stature as a political leader with the power to influence federal patronage was immensely augmented in 1901, when Theodore Roosevelt invited Washington to dine with him at the White House. Southern Democrats were outraged, and blacks across the country were delighted at this signal that Roosevelt did not side with segregation. Despite the uproar that followed Washington's visit with the presidents, both Roosevelt and his successor, William Howard Taft, continued to consult with Washington throughout the 1900s on political appointments and policy issues touching on the race issue. While on the surface Washington seemed content to build his influence, he in fact was working behind the scenes throughout the 1900s to fight segregation, not through the ballot box but through establishing the economic importance of the black community to southern businessmen. He quietly supported boycotts of segregated streetcar lines, and he proclaimed that he did not "favor the Negro's giving up anything which is fundamental and which has been guaranteed to him by the Constitution."

Opposition. Despite these sentiments, Washington found himself confronted by increasingly vocal opposition from other African Americans in the 1900s, particularly those outside the rural South. The leading spokesman for an alternative black political strategy was W. E. B. Du Bois, who admired Washington's achievements but disagreed with his tactics. Du Bois argued that the only appropriate response to disfranchisement was to demand equality and to fight for it at the polls when possible and in the courts when necessary. While he shared Washington's aspirations for black economic independence (a goal Washington advanced in the 1900s through the National Negro Business League), Du Bois believed that African Americans were equally in need of a cadre of leaders with college educations and professional training. As an alternative to Washington's "Tuskegee Machine" Du Bois helped to organize the Niagara Movement in 1905 and the National Association for the Advancement of Colored People (NAACP) in 1909. While Du Bois's willingness to battle prejudice directly left an important legacy, so too did Washington's quiet diplomacy and emphasis on the need for the economic autonomy and independence of African Americans.

Sources:

Edward L. Ayers, *The Promise of the New South: Life After Reconstruction* (New York: Oxford University Press, 1992);

Louis R. Harlan, *Booker T. Washington: The Making of a Black Leader, 1856–1901* (New York: Oxford University Press, 1972);

Harlan, *Booker T. Washington: The Wizard of Tuskegee, 1901–1915* (New York & Oxford: Oxford University Press, 1983);

Booker T. Washington, *Up From Slavery: An Autobiography* (New York: Doubleday, Page, 1901).

PEOPLE IN THE NEWS

Albert J. Beveridge, a freshman senator from Indiana, made his first speech as a U.S. senator on 9 January 1900. Having just returned from a visit to the front lines in the Philippine Islands, where American troops were fighting Filipino insurrectionists, he chastised the Democrats for wanting to give up the islands and praised the Republican effort to establish and maintain control over them.

On 5 December 1904 it was announced that Sen. **Francis Marion Cockrell** of Missouri would retire after twenty-nine years of service and would take with him the last pair of cowhide boots worn in the Senate. After Cockrell's retirement, President Theodore Roosevelt appointed him to the Interstate Commerce Commission.

Secret Service agent **William Craig** was killed and President Roosevelt suffered an injured leg when the carriage in which they were riding was struck by a trolley car near Pittsfield, Massachusetts, on 3 September 1902.

Minutes after San Francisco was hit by a devastating earthquake early on 18 April 1906, Gen. **Frederick Funston,** one of the heroes of the Filipino Insurrection and commander at the Presidio in San Francisco, acting without orders from Washington, marched his troops into the city and quickly established martial law to combat looting and general anarchy. His quick thinking was subsequently praised by city leaders and citizens.

Democrat **William Goebel,** governor-elect of Kentucky, was shot and mortally wounded in an ambush on 30 January 1900. The oath of office was administered to him as he lay in bed the next day, and he died on 3 February. Several leading state Republicans were arrested, tried, and convicted of complicity in Goebel's murder.

Congressman **J. Thomas Heflin** (D–Ala.) was indicted for assault on 11 May 1908 by a federal grand jury in Washington, D.C., for shooting Lewis Lundy, an African American, and accidentally wounding another man during a streetcar fight several weeks earlier. Hef-

lin claimed the shooting was in self-defense and the indictment was quashed a few months later.

In November 1907 government prosecutor **Frank B. Kellogg** filed papers under the Sherman Antitrust Act, which led to the 1911 government-ordered dissolution of Standard Oil of New Jersey, an action that broke up the oil monopoly.

Roy Knabenshue's dirigible balloon flight around the dome of the U.S. Capitol on 15 June 1906 caused so many representatives and senators to leave their desks to watch the spectacle that for an hour both houses lacked a quorum.

On 3 August 1907 U.S. District Court Judge **Kenesaw Mountain Landis** levied the largest fine to date — in excess of $29 million — against the Standard Oil Company of Indiana for accepting rebates in violation of the Elkins Act of 1903. The decision and fine were overturned on appeal. The publicity generated by the ruling was an important factor in the selection of Landis as the first baseball commissioner in 1920.

Nicholas Longworth, a young congressman from Cincinnati, Ohio, married **Alice Lee Roosevelt,** the president's eldest daughter, on 17 February 1906 in a White House ceremony. Many of the female guests wore dresses and overcoats of "Alice blue," named for the second most popular member of the first family.

On 19 November 1903 Kansas prohibitionist **Carry Nation** called at the White House and was refused an opportunity to see President Theodore Roosevelt. She then went to the Senate gallery, where she sold miniature hatchets, began a tirade, was arrested, and was fined twenty-five dollars.

On 25 January 1900 the House of Representatives refused to allow congressman-elect **Brigham H. Roberts** of Utah to occupy the seat to which he had been elected because he was a Mormon who practiced polygamy.

On 15 November 1906 Mayor **Eugene Schmitz** of San Francisco and political boss **Abe Ruef** were indicted on five counts of extortion. **Hiram Johnson,** who took over as the lead prosecutor after the first one was injured in an attack, was elected governor of California on a progressive platform in 1910.

On 21 April 1902 Brig. Gen. **Jacob H. Smith** was put on trial in Manila on charges that he had instructed a subordinate to "kill and burn and make Samar a howling wilderness." The court-martial recommended that the general be "admonished." Both Secretary of War Elihu Root and President Roosevelt were sympathetic to the conditions of war that provoked the orders, but Smith was ordered to retire from active service.

Oscar S. Straus was appointed secretary of commerce and labor on 12 December 1906, becoming the first Jew to hold a cabinet post.

DEATHS

Henry C. Adams, 55, Republican representative from Wisconsin (1903–1906), 9 July 1906.

Robert Adams Jr., 57, minister to Brazil (1889–1890); Republican representative from Pennsylvania (1893–1906), 1 June 1906.

Russell A. Alger, 69, Union Army veteran; secretary of war (1897–1899); Republican senator from Michigan (1902–1907), 24 January 1907.

William B. Allison, 79, Republican representative (1863–1871) and senator (1873–1908) from Iowa; Senate majority leader (1897, 1904–1906, 1907–1908), 4 August 1908.

William B. Bate, 78, Mexican War and Confederate veteran; Democratic senator from Tennessee (1887–1905), 9 March 1905.

Vincent Boreing, 63, Union Army veteran; Republican representative from Kentucky (1899–1903), 16 September 1903.

Abraham L. Brick, 47, Republican representative from Indiana (1899–1908), 7 April 1908.

Marriott Brosius, 58, Republican representative from Pennsylvania (1889–1901), 16 March 1901.

William J. Bryan, 31, Democratic senator from Florida (1907–1908), died three months after filling the vacancy caused by the death of Stephen Mallory, 22 March 1908.

Henry Burk, 53, Republican representative from Pennsylvania (1901–1903), 5 December 1903.

Robert E. Burke, 53, Confederate Army veteran; Democratic representative from Texas (1897–1901), 5 June 1901.

George A. Castor, 50, Republican representative from Pennsylvania (1904–1906), 19 February 1906.

Charles A. Chickering, 56, Republican representative from New York (1893–1900), 13 February 1900.

Frank G. Clarke, 50, Republican representative from New Hampshire (1897–1901), 9 January 1901.

Cassius M. Clay, 92, abolitionist and minister to Russia (1861–1869), 22 July 1903.

Grover Cleveland, 70, twenty-second and twenty-fourth president of the United States (1885–1889, 1893–1897); the only president to serve two nonconsecutive terms, 24 June 1908.

Jay Cooke, 84, banker and railroad owner whose sale of Union treasury bonds helped to finance the Civil War; the collapse of his economic empire touched off a nationwide depression in 1873, 16 February 1905.

Jacob D. Cox, 71, secretary of the interior (1869–1870); Republican representative from Ohio (1877–1879), 4 August 1900.

George W. Croft, 57, Confederate Army veteran; Democratic representative from South Carolina (1903–1904), 10 March 1904.

Rosseau O. Crump, 57, Republican representative from Michigan (1895–1901), 1 May 1901.

Amos J. Cummings, 60, Union Army veteran; Democratic representative from New York (1887–1902), 2 May 1902.

Francis W. Cushman, 42, Republican representative from Washington (1899–1909), 6 July 1909.

William D. Daly, 49, Democratic representative from New Jersey (1899–1900), 31 July 1900.

Robert C. Davey, 55, Democratic representative from Louisiana (1893–1895, 1897–1908), 26 December 1908.

Cushman K. Davis, 62, Union Army veteran; governor of Minnesota (1874–1875); Republican senator from Minnesota (1887–1900); member of peace commission that negotiated an end to the Spanish-American War (1898), 27 November 1900.

David A. De Armond, 65, Democratic representative from Missouri (1891–1909), 23 November 1909.

Reese C. De Graffenreid, 43, Democratic representative from Texas (1897–1902), 29 August 1902.

Charles T. Dunwell, 56, Republican representative from New York (1903–1908), 12 June 1908.

Sydney P. Epes, 44, Democratic representative from Virginia (1897–1898, 1899–1900), 3 March 1900.

William H. Flack, 45, Republican representative from New York (1903–1907), 2 February 1907.

Robert H. Foerderer, 43, Republican representative from Pennsylvania (1901–1903), 26 July 1903.

John H. Gear, 75, governor of Iowa (1878–1881); Republican representative (1887–1891, 1893–1895) and senator (1895–1901) from Iowa; assistant secretary of the treasury (1892–1893), 14 July 1900.

Geronimo, 80, respected leader of the Chiricahua Apache tribe, 17 February 1909.

John B. Gordon, 73, Confederate Army officer; Democratic senator from Georgia (1873–1880, 1891–1897); governor of Georgia (1886–1890), 9 January 1904.

Arthur Pue Gorman, 67, Democratic senator from Maryland (1881–1899, 1902–1903); Senate minority leader (1889–1893, 1895–1898, 1903–1906); Senate majority leader (1893–1895), 4 June 1906.

Daniel L. D. Granger, 56, Democratic representative from Rhode Island (1903–1909), 14 February 1909.

Wade Hampton, 84, Confederate army officer; governor of South Carolina (1876–1879); Democratic senator from South Carolina (1879–1891), 11 April 1902.

Marcus A. Hanna, 65, Republican senator from Ohio (1897–1904); Republican National Committee chairman (1896, 1900) who engineered William McKinley's successful 1896 and 1900 election campaigns, 15 February 1904.

Alfred C. Harmer, 74, Republican representative from Pennsylvania (1871–1875, 1877–1900), 6 March 1900.

Benjamin Harrison, 67, twenty-third president of the United States (1889–1893), 1 March 1901.

John Hay, 66, novelist and historian; personal secretary to President Abraham Lincoln; secretary of state (1898–1905) who wrote the "Open Door" notes regarding trade with China, 1 July 1905.

Abram Hewitt, 80, iron manufacturer; Democratic representative from New York (1875–1879, 1881–1886); reform mayor of New York City (1887–1888), 18 January 1903.

Robert R. Hitt, 72, first secretary of legation and chargé d'affaires ad interim in Paris (1874–1881); assistant secretary of state (1881); Republican representative from Illinois (1882–1906); member of the commission to establish a government in the Hawaiian Islands (1898), 19 September 1906.

George F. Hoar, 77, Republican representative (1869–1877) and senator (1877–1904) from Massachusetts; member of the electoral commission to settle disputes over presidential-election results (1877); a leading anti-imperialist, 30 September 1904.

Rockwood Hoar, 51, Republican representative from Massachusetts (1905–1906); son of George F. Hoar, 1 November 1906.

John H. Hoffecker, 72, Republican representative from Delaware (1899–1900), 16 June 1900.

Oliver O. Howard, Union Army officer; head of the Freedmen's Bureau (1865–1874), which helped freed blacks and poor whites in the postwar South; helped to establish Howard University (1867), 26 October 1909.

John J. Ingalls, 66, Republican senator from Kansas (1873–1891); president pro tempore of Senate (1887–1891), 16 August 1900.

Martin N. Johnson, 59, Republican representative (1891–1899) and senator (1909) from North Dakota, 21 October 1909.

John H. Ketcham, 73, Union Army veteran; Republican representative from New York (1865–1873, 1877–1893, 1897–1906); commissioner of the District of Columbia (1874–1877), 4 November 1906.

James H. Kyle, 47, Independent senator from South Dakota (1898–1901), 1 July 1901.

Francis R. Lassiter, 43, Democratic representative from Virginia (1900–1903, 1907–1909), 31 October 1909.

Asbury C. Latimer, 56, Democratic representative (1893–1903) and senator (1903–1908) from South Carolina, 20 February 1908.

Fitzhugh Lee, 69, Confederate Army officer; governor of Virginia (1886–1890); U.S. Army officer who fought in Cuba during the Spanish-American War (1898); military governor of Havana (1899); author of a biography of his uncle Robert E. Lee (1894) and *Cuba's Struggle Against Spain* (1899), 29 April 1905.

Stephen D. Lee, 74, decorated Confederate Army veteran, who at age thirty became the youngest officer in the C.S.A. to attain the rank of lieutenant general, 29 May 1908.

Rufus E. Lester, 68, Confederate Army veteran; Democratic representative from Georgia (1889–1906), 16 June 1906.

Henry Demarest Lloyd, 56, political economist and author of several books, including *Wealth Against Commonwealth* (1894), 29 September 1903.

William F. Mahoney, 48, Democratic representative from Illinois (1901–1904), 27 December 1904.

Stephen R. Mallory, 59, Confederate Navy veteran; Democratic representative (1891–1895) and senator (1897–1907) from Florida, 23 December 1907.

Benjamin F. Marsh, 65, Union Army veteran; Republican representative from Illinois (1877–1883, 1893–1901, 1903–1905), 2 June 1905.

William McKinley, 58, twenty-fifth president of the United States (1897–1901), 14 September 1901.

Anselm J. McLaurin, 61, Confederate Army veteran; Democratic senator from Mississippi (1894–1895, 1901–1909); governor of Mississippi (1895–1900), 22 December 1909.

James McMillan, 64, Republican senator from Michigan (1889–1902), 10 August 1902.

Adolph Meyer, 65, Confederate Army veteran; Democratic representative from Louisiana (1891–1908), 8 March 1908.

John H. Mitchell, 70, Republican senator from Oregon (1873–1879, 1885–1897, 1901–1905), 8 December 1905.

James M. Moody, 44, Spanish-American War veteran; Republican representative from North Carolina (1901–1903), 5 February 1903.

John T. Morgan, 82, Confederate Army veteran; Democratic senator from Alabama (1877–1907), 11 June 1907.

Peter J. Otey, 61, participant in the capture of John Brown (1859); Confederate Army veteran; Democratic representative from Virginia (1895–1902), 4 May 1902.

Norton P. Otis, 64, Republican representative from New York (1903–1905), 20 February 1905.

William H. Parker, 61, Union Army veteran; representative from South Dakota (1907–1908), 26 June 1908.

George R. Patterson, 42, Republican representative from Pennsylvania (1901–1906), 21 March 1906.

Edmund W. Pettus, 86, Mexican War and Confederate Army veteran; Democratic senator from Alabama (1897–1907), 27 July 1907.

John M. Pinckney, 59, Confederate Army veteran; Democratic representative from Texas (1903–1905), 24 April 1905.

Orville Platt, 77, Republican senator from Connecticut (1879–1905); Senate majority leader (1902–1903); best known for sponsoring the Platt Amendment, 21 April 1905.

Rufus K. Polk, 35, Spanish-American War veteran; Democratic representative from Pennsylvania (1899–1902), 5 March 1902.

Fitz-John Porter, 78, Union Army officer; court-martialed in 1863 for failure to follow orders at the Second Battle of Manassas and exonerated by a military review board headed by John Schofield in 1879, 21 May 1901.

John Wesley Powell, 68, naturalist and explorer who led the first scientific expedition into the Grand Canyon (1869); director of the U.S. Bureau of Ethnology (1879–1902) and director of the U.S. Geological Survey (1880–1894), 23 September 1902.

Llewellyn Powers, 71, Republican representative from Maine (1877–1879, 1901–1908); governor of Maine (1896–1900), 28 July 1908.

Redfield Proctor, 76, Union Army veteran; governor of Vermont (1878–1880); secretary of war (1889–1891); Republican senator from Vermont (1891–1908); a supporter of the conservation movement, 4 March 1908.

Matthew S. Quay, 70, Republican senator from Pennsylvania (1887–1899, 1901–1904), 28 May 1904.

Thomas B. Reed, 63, Republican representative of Maine (1877–1899), Speaker of the House during the Fifty-first, Fifty-fourth, and Fifty-fifth Congresses, 7 December 1902.

John N. W. Rumple, 61, Union Army veteran; Republican representative from Iowa (1901–1903), 31 January 1903.

Charles A. Russell, 50, Republican representative from Connecticut (1887–1902), 23 October 1902.

Joshua S. Salmon, 56, Democratic representative from New Jersey (1899–1902), 6 May 1902.

John M. Schofield, 74, U.S. Army officer, commanding general (1888–1895); recommended Pearl Harbor as the site for a naval base, 4 March 1906.

Carl Schurz, 77, Republican senator from Missouri (1869–1875); secretary of the interior (1877–1881); one of the leading liberal Republicans in the 1872 challenge to Ulysses Grant's renomination, 14 May 1906.

William J. Sewall, 66, Union Army veteran and recipient of the Congressional Medal of Honor (25 March 1896) for his gallant efforts at the Battle of Chancellorsville; Republican senator from New Jersey (1881–1887, 1895–1901), 27 December 1901.

Albert D. Shaw, 59, Union Army veteran; Republican representative from New York (1900–1901), 10 February 1901.

John L. Sheppard, 50, Democratic representative from Texas (1899–1902), 11 October 1902.

John Sherman, 77, Republican representative (1855–1861) and senator (1861–1877, 1881–1897) from Ohio; Senate minority leader (1893–1895); Senate majority leader (1895–1897); secretary of the treasury (1877–1881); secretary of state (1897–1898); a leading Republican on financial issues and sponsor of the Sherman Antitrust Act, 22 October 1900.

Franz Sigel, 77, Union Army officer best known for losing the Battle of New Market (1864) to Confederate troops augmented by Virginia Military Institute cadets, 21 August 1902.

William W. Skiles, 54, Republican representative from Ohio (1901–1904), 9 January 1904.

Campbell Slemp, 67, Confederate Army veteran; Republican representative from Virginia (1903–1907), 13 October 1907.

George W. Smith, 61, Republican representative from Illinois (1889–1907), 30 November 1907.

J. William Stokes, 47, Democratic representative from South Carolina (1895–1901), 6 July 1901.

Charles W. Thompson, 43, Democratic representative from Alabama (1901–1904), 20 March 1904.

Thomas H. Tongue, 58, Republican representative from Oregon (1897–1903), 11 January 1903.

Lew Wallace, 77, Union Army officer who sat on the military court that tried the conspirators in the assassination of President Abraham Lincoln (1865); governor of New Mexico Territory (1878–1881); minister to Turkey (1881–1885), author of *Ben Hur* (1880) and other novels, 15 February 1905;

Joseph Wheeler, 69, Confederate Army officer who fought in more than four hundred engagements; Democratic representative from Alabama (1881–1896); U.S. Army officer in the Spanish-American War, who served in Cuba and the Philippines, 26 January 1906.

William Pinkney Whyte, 83, Democratic senator from Maryland (1868–1869, 1875–1881, 1906–1908); governor of Maryland (1872–1874), 17 March 1908.

Ariosto A. Wiley, 59, Spanish-American War veteran; Democratic representative from Alabama (1901–1908), 17 June 1908.

Richard A. Wise, 57, Republican representative from Virginia (1898–1899, 1900), who twice won office by successfully contesting the election of William A. Young, 21 December 1900.

Carroll Wright, 69, prominent economist and statistician; commissioner of labor (1885–1905); member of the U.S. Anthracite Strike Commission (1902), 20 February 1909.

PUBLICATIONS

Albert J. Beveridge, *The Russian Advance* (New York & London: Harper, 1903);

John Burroughs, *Camping and Tramping with Roosevelt* (Boston & New York: Houghton Mifflin, 1907);

John H. Clifford and Marion M. Miller, eds., *The Works of Abraham Lincoln*, 4 volumes, with introductions and articles by Theodore Roosevelt (New York: Newton & Cartwright, 1908);

Oscar King Davis, *William Howard Taft, The Man of the Hour* (Philadelphia: P. W. Ziegler, 1908);

Marshall Everett, *Complete Life of William McKinley and Story of His Assassination* (Cleveland: N. G. Hamilton, 1901);

Samuel Fallows, ed., *Life of William McKinley, Our Martyred President* (Chicago: Regan Printing, 1901);

William Bayard Hale, *A Week in the White House with Theodore Roosevelt* (New York: Putnam, 1908);

Murat Halstead, *The Illustrious Life of William McKinley, Our Martyred President* (Chicago, 1901);

Halstead, *Victorious Republicanism and Lives of the Standard Bearers, McKinley and Roosevelt* (Chicago: Republican National Publishing, 1900);

Marcus A. Hanna, *Mark Hanna: His Book* (Boston: Chapple, 1904);

John Hay, *Memorial Address on the Life and Character of William McKinley* (Washington, D.C.: U.S. Government Printing Office, 1903);

L. T. Hobhouse, *Democracy and Reaction* (London: Unwin, 1904; New York: Putnam, 1905);

Frederick Howe, *The City: The Hope of Democracy* (New York: Scribners, 1905);

Francis E. Leupp, *The Man Roosevelt* (New York: Appleton, 1904);

Alfred Henry Lewis, ed., *A Compilation of the Messages and Speeches of Theodore Roosevelt, 1901–1905*, 2 volumes (Washington, D.C.: Bureau of National Literature and Art, 1906);

Alexander K. McClure, *The Authentic Life of William McKinley, Our Third Martyred President, Together* with a Life Sketch of Theodore Roosevelt (Philadelphia, 1901);

Joseph Hampton Moore, *With Speaker Cannon Through the Tropics: A Descriptive Story of a Voyage to the West Indies, Venezuela, and Panama, Containing the Views of the Speaker upon Our Colonial Possessions, The Panama Canal, and Other Governmental Problems* (Philadelphia: Book Print, 1907);

Edward Leigh Pell, James W. Buel, and James P. Boyd, *A Memorial Volume of American History: McKinley and Men of Our Times* (Saint Louis: Historical Society of America, 1901);

Jacob Riis, *Theodore Roosevelt, The Citizen* (New York: Macmillan, 1904);

Theodore Roosevelt, *The Philippines: The First Civil Governor* [and] William Howard Taft, *Civil Government in the Philippines* (New York: Outlook, 1902);

Roosevelt, *The Roosevelt Doctrine, Being the Personal Utterances of the President on Various Matters of Vital Interest,* edited by E. E. Garrison (New York: R. G. Cooke, 1904);

Roosevelt, *The Roosevelt Policy: Speeches, Letters, and State Papers, Relating to Corporate Wealth and Closely Allied Topics,* 2 volumes (New York: Current Literature, 1908);

Roosevelt, *The Strenuous Life: Essays and Addresses* (New York: Century, 1901);

Roosevelt, *The Works of Theodore Roosevelt,* Elkhorn Edition, 26 volumes (New York: Scribners, 1906–1910);

Carl Shurz, *To the Independent Voter: An Open Letter* (New York: Parker Independent Club, 1904);

Moorfield Storey, *Secretary Root's Record. "Marked Severity" in Philippine Warfare: An Analysis of the Law and Facts Bearing on the Action and Utterances of President Roosevelt and Secretary Root* (Boston: Printed by G. H. Ellis, 1902);

John W. Tyler, *The Life of William McKinley, Soldier, Statesman and President* (Philadelphia & Chicago: P. W. Ziegler, 1901);

Woodrow Wilson, *Constitutional Government in the United States* (New York: Columbia University Press, 1908);

Wilson, *A History of the American People,* 5 volumes (New York: Harper, 1902).

LAW AND JUSTICE

by ROBERT J. ALLISON

CONTENTS

Sidebars and tables are listed in italics.

1900

- Carry Nation begins raiding saloons in Kansas.

- Twenty-five law schools form the Association of American Law Schools; membership requires that students have high-school diplomas, take a two-year course of instruction, and have access to a library containing the federal and state law reports.

14 Mar.   Congress passes the Currency Act, making gold the standard for all U.S. currency.

30 Apr.   Congress passes an act establishing the territory of Hawaii.

14 June   President William McKinley appoints Sanford B. Dole, Honolulu-born son of American missionaries, as the first governor of Hawaii.

Nov.   The International Ladies' Garment Workers' Union is formed. The average worker in the garment industry earns thirty cents each day and works seventy hours per week.

Cuba, occupied by American troops after expulsion of Spanish forces, holds a convention to draw up a constitution.

29 Dec.   The United States and Denmark conclude negotiations for the United States to purchase the Danish West Indies. Congress does not allocate money for the purchase until 1917.

1901

2 Mar.   Congress adopts the Platt Amendment, a series of provisions that the United States insists Cuba add to her constitution, giving the United States the right to intervene in Cuba. Cuba's ability to form alliances with other countries is restricted.

3 Mar.   U.S. Steel, the first billion-dollar corporation, is formed, primarily from Carnegie Steel; J. P. Morgan is among the organizers.

23 Mar.   The U.S. Army captures Filipino insurgent leader Emilio Aguinaldo in Isabela, Luzon.

19 Apr.   The United States declares war in the Philippines is over.

27 May   The Supreme Court decides the first of the "Insular Cases," which declare that some, but not all, provisions of the U.S. Constitution and laws apply in former Spanish colonies that are now American territories (Puerto Rico, the Philippines, Guam).

June   Alabama adopts a new state constitution disenfranchising black citizens.

6 Sept.   President William McKinley is shot at the Pan-American Exposition in Buffalo, New York. The assailant is Leon Czolgosz, an anarchist.

14 Sept.   President McKinley dies; Theodore Roosevelt becomes president.

23 Sept.   Leon Czolgosz goes on trial for murdering President McKinley. He is convicted and dies in the electric chair in October.

Nov.   Northern Securities Company is incorporated in New Jersey as a holding company to control the stock of the Northern Pacific; the Great Northern; and Chicago, Burlington, and Quincy railroads.

1902

- Supreme Court Associate Justice Horace Gray dies; Oliver Wendell Holmes Jr. is appointed to the Supreme Court, where he serves until 1932.

- Two hundred fourteen people are lynched in the United States during the first two years of the twentieth century.

10 Mar. The United States charges the Northern Securities Company with violating the Sherman Antitrust Act.

29 Apr. Congress amends the Chinese Exclusion Act to prohibit Chinese people in the Philippines from entering the United States.

12 May Anthracite coal miners in Pennsylvania ask for an eight-hour workday and 20 percent wage increase. When mine owners refuse to submit to arbitration, miners go on strike. The strike lasts through October, severely limiting the nation's coal supply.

20 May The United States accepts Cuba's independence.

28 June Congress authorizes the building of a canal across Panama, pending negotiations with France and Colombia.

1 July Congress passes a law recognizing the Philippines as an unincorporated territory of the United States, entitling citizens of the Philippines to some protections of the U.S. Constitution. The president is authorized to appoint a commission to govern the islands. On 4 July President Roosevelt appoints a civil government and grants amnesty to political prisoners.

16 Oct. President Roosevelt appoints Judge George Gray to head the Anthracite Coal Strike Commission to resolve the strike.

21 Oct. After the commission decides in favor of the coal miners, John Mitchell of the United Mine Workers declares the coal strike over.

1903

- Associate Justice George Shiras Jr. retires; William R. Day is appointed to the Supreme Court.

5 Jan. In *Lone Wolf* v. *Hitchcock* the Supreme Court rules that Congress has absolute control over Indian land, even through Congress is abrogating a prior treaty by taking it.

19 Feb. Congress passes the Elkins Act, sponsored by West Virginia Republican Stephen Elkins, which makes it illegal for railroads to give rebates on published fares to favored customers.

Oregon passes a law limiting women in hazardous occupations to a ten-hour workday; the law is later challenged in *Muller* v. *Oregon*, decided in 1908.

23 Feb. In *Champion* v. *Ames* the Supreme Court rules that Congress can prohibit lottery tickets from being sent through the mail; this is an expansion of federal police powers.

9 Mar. In *Brownfield* v. *South Carolina* the Supreme Court upholds the murder conviction of John Brownfield, a black defendant, despite the fact that blacks, who make up 80 percent of the population in the county, were excluded from the jury.

21 Mar. In a victory for the United Mine Workers, the Anthracite Coal Strike Commission decides that mines cannot refuse to hire union members or nonunion members.

1904

9 Apr. Federal circuit court judge Amos Thayer rules that Northern Securities Company violates the Sherman Antitrust Act. J. P. Morgan and James J. Hill appeal the case to the U.S. Supreme Court.

27 Apr. The Supreme Court, in *Giles* v. *Harris*, rules that Alabama's state constitution, which requires a literacy test for voters, does not discriminate on the basis of race.

1 May After forty-eight years of Prohibition, New Hampshire decides to allow liquor sales in state-licensed stores.

23 May Wisconsin holds the nation's first direct, statewide primary election to choose candidates for office.

4 Jan. The Supreme Court rules that citizens of Puerto Rico are neither aliens nor citizens of the United States; they cannot be refused admission to the United States, but they are not guaranteed all civil rights of American citizens.

14 Mar. In the *Northern Securities* case the Supreme Court rules that Northern Securities Corporation violates the Sherman Antitrust Act and orders it dissolved.

Aug. Race riots break out in Statesboro, Georgia.

Sept. Race riots break out in Springfield, Ohio.

9 Sept. New York City uses its first unit of mounted police.

21 Sept. A woman is arrested for smoking in an open automobile on Fifth Avenue in New York City.

19 Oct. Consolidated Tobacco Company and American & Continental Tobacco merge to form American Tobacco Company.

24 Oct. In *McCray* v. *United States* the Supreme Court rules that Congress can put a prohibitive tax on oleomargarine. The tax, passed under pressure from the dairy industry, was not designed for revenue but to make margarine nearly as expensive as butter.

21 Dec. James R. Garfield, federal commissioner of corporations, recommends that corporations involved in interstate trade be placed under federal control.

1905

- Pennsylvania forms a state constabulary, a special unit also called the coal and iron police, to fight unions.

- The Association of American Law Schools requires that member schools have a three-year course of instruction.

30 Jan. In *Swift & Co.* v. *United States* the Supreme Court rules that the beef trust violates the Sherman Antitrust Act; Justice Holmes introduces the idea that interstate commerce is a stream involving different actions, including manufacturing and processing.

20 Feb. In *Jacobsen* v. *Massachusetts* the Supreme Court rules that states may require vaccinations.

17 Apr.   In *Lochner* v. *New York* the Supreme Court rules that a New York law restricting bakers to a sixty-hour workweek interferes with their liberty to make contracts.

27 June   The Industrial Workers of the World (IWW) is formed in Chicago by western miners, socialists, and anarchists. The IWW is open to all working people and is committed to the overthrow of capitalism.

9 July   Facing a rising tide of racism and lynchings, black leaders including Ida B. Wells-Barnett, Monroe Trotter, and W. E. B. Du Bois meet at Niagara Falls, Canada, to discuss strategy. This "Niagara Movement" opposes the policies of Booker T. Washington and pushes for full political and civil rights.

Aug.   Nashville, Tennessee, imposes Jim Crow laws requiring blacks to ride on the outside platform of streetcars. Blacks boycott the streetcar lines but are not successful in forcing the city to rescind the segregation ordinance.

30 Dec.   Former Idaho governor Frank Steunenberg is killed by a bomb; it is suspected that members of the IWW killed him in retaliation for his crushing of an 1899 strike.

1906

- Supreme Court Associate Justice Henry Brown retires; Attorney General William H. Moody is appointed to the Supreme Court.

- Mississippi bans convict labor.

Jan.   The beef-trust trial opens in Chicago.

31 Jan.   The Niagara Movement is incorporated in Washington, D.C.

15 Feb.   Idaho authorities arrest IWW leader William "Big Bill" Haywood in Colorado and charge him with the murder of former governor Steunenberg.

21 Feb.   The Senate passes the Pure Food and Drug Act in response to reports of adulterated foods and patent medicines.

12 Mar.   In *Hale* v. *Henkel* the Supreme Court rules that witnesses can be compelled to testify and to produce evidence against their corporations.

17 Mar.   In a speech at the Gridiron Club, President Roosevelt compares investigative journalists to the the "Man with the Muckrake" in John Bunyan's *Pilgrim's Progress:* so busy pointing out faults, these journalists never look up to see the progress brought by the system they attack.

11 June   Congress passes the Federal Employers' Liability Act, which makes employers engaged in interstate commerce liable for the death or injury of a worker on the job.

29 June   Congress passes the Hepburn Act, giving the Interstate Commerce Commission (ICC) the authority to set rates charged by railroads, pipelines, and terminals.

30 June   Congress passes the Pure Food and Drug Act and the Meat Inspection Act.

June   The Niagara Movement, black leaders who met the previous year at Niagara Falls, meets in Harper's Ferry, West Virginia.

Aug.   Race riots break out in Brownsville, Texas; President Roosevelt suspends a battalion of black soldiers from Fort Brown after the riot.

22 Sept.	Race riots in Atlanta kill twenty-one people, eighteen of whom are black; the city is placed under martial law.
29 Sept.	The United States and Cuba invoke the Platt Amendment; the United States assumes military command of Cuba under the provisional governorship of William Howard Taft.

1907

	• The American Bar Association sets up a special committee "To Suggest Remedies and Formulate Proposed Laws to Prevent Delay and Unnecessary Cost in Litigation."
26 Jan.	Congress prohibits corporate contributions to candidates for national office.
13 Mar.	The stock market crashes; President Roosevelt later suspends the Sherman Antitrust Act to allow businesses to recover.
14 Mar.	Under provisions of the new Immigration Act signed on 20 February, President Roosevelt bars Japanese immigrants from entering the United States.
15 Apr.	In *Patterson* v. *Colorado* the U.S. Supreme Court upholds the conviction of a publisher whose newspaper carried cartoons criticizing the state supreme court. Justice Holmes rules that the First Amendment guarantee of "freedom of the press" means the traditional common-law protection against prior restraint. Justice John Marshall Harlan dissents, arguing that freedom of the press is protected against state infringement by the Fourteenth Amendment and that a free press means freedom from all legislative restraint.
June	The Niagara Movement meets in Boston's Faneuil Hall.
28 July	An Idaho jury acquits Bill Haywood.
17 Sept.	The new Oklahoma Constitution forbids convict labor and the manufacture or sale of alcohol; Oklahoma enters the Union on 16 November.
Dec.	Samuel Gompers defies a court order and encourages a boycott against Buck's Stove and Range Company.

1908

	• Disclosures about the treatment of convicts from Oklahoma in Kansas prisons set off an uproar about prison conditions.
	• The Boston Watch and Ward Society prosecutes book salesmen for distributing the racy novel *Three Weeks* by Elinor Glyn.
6 Jan.	The Supreme Court, in *Adair* v. *United States,* strikes down the Federal Employers' Liability Act and holds that protecting all workers on railroads is not a regulation of interstate commerce; Congress prepares a new liability law for railroad employees involved in interstate commerce.
15 Jan.	Louis D. Brandeis argues *Muller* v. *Oregon* in the U.S. Supreme Court.
3 Feb.	In *Loewe* v. *Lawlor* the Supreme Court rules that striking workers violated the Sherman Antitrust Act by calling for a boycott against a Danbury hat manufacturer.
20 Feb.	The Illinois Supreme Court rules that picketing is illegal.
24 Feb.	In *Muller* v. *Oregon* the U.S Supreme Court upholds Oregon's ten-hour workday law for women.

22 Apr.	Roosevelt signs the new Employers' Liability Act.
30 Apr.	Worcester, Massachusetts, population 130,000, becomes the largest dry city in the country. Seventeen other Massachusetts cities and 249 towns also vote to prohibit the sale of alcohol.
28 May	Congress passes the Child Labor Law for the District of Columbia, prohibiting labor of children.
	The American Bar Association adopts a canon of professional ethics.
8 June	President Roosevelt appoints a fifty-seven-member National Commission for the Conservation of Natural Resources.
Aug.	The Niagara Movement meets in Oberlin, Ohio.
14 Aug.	Race riots break out in Springfield, Illinois.
Oct.	The New York State Court of Appeals upholds an eight-hour workday.
Nov.	New York district attorney William T. Jerome investigates lawyers who extort property from poor clients.
9 Nov.	In *Twining* v. *New Jersey,* the U.S. Supreme Court rules that states do not have to guarantee a right against self-incrimination.
Dec.	In *Gompers* v. *Buck's Stove and Range Company* a federal district court in Washington, D.C., says a boycott organized by the American Federation of Labor violated the Sherman Antitrust Act and holds in contempt of court Samuel Gompers and other labor leaders who supported the boycott.
24 Dec.	The New York Society for the Prevention of Crime persuades Mayor George McClellan to revoke 550 movie-theater licenses. To renew licenses theaters must agree not to show movies on Sundays or to show immoral films.

1909

•	U.S. Supreme Court Associate Justice Rufus Peckham dies; Horace Lurton is appointed to the Supreme Court.
2 Jan.	Alabama and Mississippi adopt Prohibition laws.
15 Feb.	Idaho adopts the local option on Prohibition; South Carolina blocks Prohibition.
30 Apr.	Learned Hand is appointed to the federal district court for southern New York, the beginning of a half century of distinguished service as a federal judge.
30 May	In response to increasing racial tensions, white liberals, including Oswald Garrison Villard, Mary White Ovington, and Florence Kelley, convene a National Conference on the Negro; it merges with the Niagara Movement in 1911 to form the National Association for the Advancement of Colored People (NAACP).
12 July	Congress submits to the states a constitutional amendment allowing a federal income tax; it is ratified as the Sixteenth Amendment in February 1913.
Sept.	New York's Triangle Shirtwaist Company fires women for trying to organize a union. Women in the clothing industry earn four dollars to six dollars a week, working sometimes eighty hours each week.
4 Sept.	The Tennessee chancery court upholds the state Prohibition law.

4 Nov. In an Oklahoma case the U.S. district court rules that the state cannot seize interstate shipments of liquor.

22 Nov. In response to police arresting picketers and their supporters at the Triangle Company, women call for a general strike, with twenty thousand to thirty thousand women walking off their jobs. The strikers stay out until February, when the companies agree to some of their demands: reduced hours (to about fifty each week) and increased wages; but the companies do not recognize the union.

28 Nov. Voters in Alabama reject a Prohibition amendment to the state constitution.

15 Dec. Voters in Worcester, Massachusetts, approve reopening of regulated saloons.

16 Dec. The Indiana Supreme Court upholds the local option law.

OVERVIEW

Changing Population. During the years 1900 to 1909 the United States was fast becoming an industrial society, yet its laws were based on an ideal of an agrarian society. American society was changing tremendously. Between 1901 and 1909 more than eight million immigrants came to the United States, more than twice the amount in the previous decade and more than in any previous decade in American history. By 1910 one of every seven Americans had been born in another country. Even those Americans born in the United States might have felt they now lived in a different country. In 1860 five of every six Americans had lived on a farm. By 1910 nearly half of the American people lived in cities, which had grown rapidly since the Civil War. With a population of thirty million in 1860, the United States had sixteen cities with more than fifty thousand people in them. By 1910 there were ninety million Americans and more than one hundred cities of more than fifty thousand people, and three cities had populations of one million or more.

Economic Change. The economy, whose growth was once fueled by millions of farmers, merchants, and mechanics, now was dominated by a handful of corporations led by men who were shrewd enough to see the changes that would be brought by industrialization and centralization and who were able to exploit these changes. Between 1899 and 1909 the number of American businesses engaged in manufacturing dropped from more than half a million to 240,000. But the number of workers employed in manufacturing increased; the capital invested in these factories doubled; and the value of their products grew from $13 billion to $20 billion. Financiers created holding corporations, which existed only to "hold" the stock of other companies, those that actually manufactured goods or shipped them. The idea of a holding company was new, but it grew rapidly. By 1902 some two hundred of these companies were worth more than $10 million each. These new corporate organizations meant that wealth was concentrated into fewer hands. For example, by 1906 seven men controlled 85 percent of American railroads. Novelist William Dean Howells lamented, "The struggle for life has changed from a free fight to an encounter of disciplined forces, and the free fighters that are left are ground to pieces between organized labor and organized capital."

American Law and the Changing Society. Some lawmakers tried to restore the "free fight" to American life, but others regarded any attempt by the state to regulate economic activity as inherently unfair. For much of American legal history, the basic assumptions were that all men were equal before the law and that the government, either federal or state, should not regulate economic activity. To do so would be to give an unfair advantage to one side or another. But governments had in fact given advantages to some groups: railroads, for example, were private industries that had brought the public the benefit of transportation, yet they had also been given generous land grants and subsidies to encourage their growth. In the 1880s some states had tried to regulate the rates railroads could charge, and Congress established the Interstate Commerce Commission (ICC) to suggest rates for the railroads. The ICC actually had little power to regulate railroads, even if the men appointed to it had been inclined to do so. In 1890, fearing that large holding companies would buy up all the available independent companies, Congress passed the Sherman Antitrust Act, which banned "combinations or contracts in restraint of trade." No president until Theodore Roosevelt made much use of the Sherman Act in combating large trusts: in 1895 Attorney General Richard Olney said he would not prosecute "under a law which I believe to be no good."

Tradition and the Law. Olney, though he was a former railroad lawyer, was not simply an apologist for big business. Like many other political and business leaders in the late nineteenth century, he believed that the government should not interfere in the economy. Many lawyers and judges in this era believed that law flowed from the customs and traditions of a society and that legislatures could not make laws that violated those customs or traditions. The law could not correct social problems. So when legislatures, responding to pressure from working people, reformers, farmers, and consumers, tried to regulate working hours, child labor, and railroad rates, the courts rejected these attempts to interfere in the natural order. And while the courts were reluctant to uphold the Sherman Act against corporations, it had no such qualms about using it against organized labor. Nor did the courts or governments have qualms about using violence against labor unions: in 1902 labor unions, in fact, were regarded as contrary to the American idea of free competition and individual enterprise. During a 1902 coal miners' strike the president of the Philadelphia and Reading Railroad said that workers should not seek protection in unions or in legislation but in "the Christian men to whom God in His infinite wisdom, has given control of the property interests of the country."

State Laws and Labor. Attempts by the states to regulate working hours or working conditions were resisted as fiercely by the courts as they were by employers. Under the Fourteenth Amendment to the U.S. Constitution states could not deprive any person of life, liberty, or property without due process of law. In case after case the courts interpreted this to mean that states could not limit an individual's liberty to make a contract and that when a state tried to set limits to the number of hours a person worked in a day or a week, the state was infringing on his or her liberty. In *Lochner* v. *New York* (1905) the court found that the state of New York had no compelling interest to deprive bakers of their "right" to work more than sixty hours each week. Though in 1908 the court found that Oregon could limit the working hours of women to ten each day, it based its ruling on the belief that women occupied a special place in society and needed the law to protect them. Most men, even in dangerous occupations, were considered to be able to protect themselves. Though some states, including Colorado, tried to protect mine workers, for example, by restricting their working day to eight hours, the mine owners in Colorado ignored the law. The miners at Cripple Creek, Colorado, went on strike in 1903 and 1904, led by the Western Federation of Miners. The mine owners hired a private police force to drive out the union leaders and force the miners back to work, using violence and intimidation. The union leaders in 1905 formed the Industrial Workers of the World (IWW), committed to forming one big union of all working people that would fight, violently if necessary, not only against employers but against all allies of the bosses, including governments and courts.

Labor and the Law. The courts were reluctant to acknowledge the change in economic or working conditions. Having grown up in an era when an employer not only knew all of his employees but was also their neighbor and often their relative, judges were slow to understand the dramatic change in the workplace. Workers and employers were no longer equal in bargaining for wages, working hours, and the amount of work an employer expected in return. A flood of immigration meant that more hands were available if one man, woman, or child's proved unwilling. Every year half a million American workers were injured on the job and thirty thousand died. The United States led the industrial world in the number of industrial accidents every year. Under the common law a man, woman, or child who took on a dangerous job was presumed to know the risks and so could not collect compensation for an injury. Congress tried to rectify this, passing the Federal Employers' Liability Act in 1906. This law covered only railroads that were engaged in interstate commerce, which is subject to congressional regulation according to Article I, section 8 of the Constitution. But in 1908 the Supreme Court ruled the law unconstitutional. The court, however, did not speak with a clear voice: two justices ruled the law unconstitutional; three others concurred in the result but not in the reasoning; two dissented in part and concurred in part; and Oliver Wendell Holmes, the justice most willing to defer to the legislature, dissented. (Congress passed a similar law, applying specifically to railroad workers involved in interstate commerce, after the court struck down this first law. In 1909 Montana also replaced the common law idea of presumed risk with a law mandating employer liability, and other states followed.) In 1908 the court also struck down a law that forbade railroads to fine or fire workers who joined unions. It was up to an employer and employee, the Court ruled, to make a contract, and these so-called yellow-dog contracts (according to the unions, only a yellow dog would sign such a contract) were as valid as any other. Second, the court found that regulating contract conditions for railway employees did not have a direct relationship to interstate commerce.

Labor and the Sherman Act. In 1894 Eugene Debs led a strike by the American Railway Union against the Pullman Company, successfully shutting down American railroads. The Supreme Court found that Debs had violated the Sherman Act by restraining trade between the states. The court used the Sherman Act against labor unions more vigorously than it did against corporations. In 1901 hatmakers in Danbury, Connecticut, struck against their employer, the Dietrich E. Loewe Company. Supporters of the striking workers called for a national boycott of Loewe's hats, which was so successful that the National Association of Manufacturers supported Loewe's legal challenge to the boycott. In 1908 the Supreme Court ruled that this boycott was a conspiracy in restraint of trade and thus illegal under the Sherman Act. Union members were assessed court costs and damages, which amounted to more than $250,000.

Courts and Injunctions. Debs had been charged with contempt of court in 1895 after he ignored an injunction issued by a federal court. The injunction was a sweeping one, issued under the terms of the Sherman Act, which prohibited combinations or conspiracies in restraint of trade, and Congress's mandate to see that the mails be delivered. This injunction, which directed strikers to go back to work, was ignored. By ignoring the injunction Debs and the American Railway Union defied federal law, and President Grover Cleveland dispatched federal troops and marshalls to enforce the law. Similar injunctions would be issued in other strikes, always against the unions or the strikers. The courts, state and federal, generally operated to protect property interests. It was easier for a company facing a strike to convince a judge to issue an injunction than it would be to rally public opinion against workers. Union leaders chafed at this "government by injunction," and some, like the IWW, saw the courts working together with the corporations to prevent workers from organizing. Even more-moderate union leaders found themselves in trouble for violating injunctions. In 1906 the metal polishers' union went on strike against the Buck's Stove and Range Company. Like the Danbury hatters, the strikers called for a boycott of the Buck's Stove and Range Company. James W. Van Cleave, the company president, was also the president of the National Manufacturers Association and understood current thinking on the law. He went to court and convinced a judge to issue a sweeping indictment not only against the boycott but against any discussion of the strike either in the press or in public meetings. Samuel Gompers, the head of the American Federation of Labor (AFL) and one of the more conservative union leaders, ignored the injunction and spoke out in support of the boycott and striking workers. He was sentenced to one year in jail. His conviction was affirmed by the federal circuit court in Washington, D.C., as the boycott violated the Sherman Act, and Gompers's advocacy was part of a conspiracy to restrain trade, the court ruled. This ruling led the relatively conservative AFL to take a more vigorous political role.

The Commerce Clause in Transition. The Constitution gives Congress the power to regulate interstate commerce. But the Constitution does not specify what commerce is or how it can be regulated. The Sherman Act was an attempt to regulate interstate commerce, but in 1895 the Supreme Court distinguished between "direct commerce" and "indirect commerce," ruling that though one company controlled 85 percent of American sugar manufacturing, it was not engaged in interstate commerce because it was manufacturing sugar, not selling it across state lines. In the 1908 Danbury hatters case, though, the Court ruled that strikers who organized a boycott against a hat manufacturer were in fact restraining interstate commerce. This was not just a cynical attempt by the Court to bolster corporate power and to punish workers. The Court was changing its definition of interstate commerce. In 1905 the United States sued the Swift and Armour companies, which controlled 60 percent of American beef production. The companies claimed that they were simply running stockyards in Chicago and thus, like the sugar trust in 1895, were not involved in interstate commerce. Justice Holmes, speaking for the Court, said that "commerce among the states is not a technical legal conception, but a practical one, drawn from the course of business." Swift and Armour were engaged in different activities: regulating prices, shipping cattle, and running stockyards and slaughterhouses. Each of these component parts by itself was not necessarily either illegal or subject to congressional regulation. But taken together they formed a "current of commerce among the states," and so Swift's activities were subject to the Sherman Act.

Clarence Darrow: Lawyer of the Decade. Clarence Darrow of Chicago was the most famous lawyer of his time. During the years 1901 to 1910 Darrow grew famous as a courtroom maestro, using eloquence and passion to stir jurors. He typically defended unpopular people and causes: he had been a railroad lawyer in the 1890s but switched sides to defend Eugene Debs during the Pullman Strike. An ally and law partner of Illinois governor John Peter Altgeld, an outspoken liberal, Darrow was involved with the radical and reform activities in Chicago. He represented the coal miners during the 1902 strike and in 1907 defended Bill Haywood at his murder trial.

Darrow and Changes in the Law. Darrow was a great lawyer. But most lawyers by 1900 were not courtroom artists. The work of lawyers was changing, from defending clients in a courtroom and trying to convince a jury of impartial men of the facts, to working in offices and helping clients negotiate through the intricate details of the law. Darrow was an intellectual who wrote novels and gave lectures on modernist playwright Henrik Ibsen in his spare time. He was also involved in politics, serving in the Illinois legislature and actively supporting the Democratic Party. Lawyers would continue to engage in politics, but the role of lawyers as public citizens, enlightened men able to discuss a broad variety of topics, was all but gone by the time Darrow arrived at the bar. Unlike contemporary members of the legal profession, he was a lawyer in the way Daniel Webster or Thomas Jefferson had been lawyers.

Probation and Indeterminate Sentences. According to the new system, lawyers were not supposed to be mere technicians; the law itself was supposed to be more scientific. This new scientific approach to the law is best illustrated by the change from fixed sentences for specific crimes to allowing judges to determine the appropriate sentence for a particular offender. Reformer Roland Molineux compared the practice of setting a certain sentence for a specific crime to sentencing "the lunatic to three months in the asylum, or the victim of small pox to thirty days in the hospital." In the first decade of the twentieth century the concept of probation and parole were introduced into the American legal system, and by the end of the decade they were both widely used as alternative means of treating offenders. Instead of mandating how many years in prison a criminal should serve to atone for a specific crime, new legal codes left it to a judge to set a maximum and minimum term for a specific individual and then to allow a parole board to review each prisoner's conduct and whether the prisoner was "cured" of his impulse toward crime. The purpose of jail was not to punish but to cure. Judges and prison wardens were to be less interested in punishing crime than in reforming individual criminals. In 1900 six states had some form of probation, but by 1915 thirty-three did, and virtually every state had probation for juvenile offenders. After 1900 state legal codes allowed judges to impose maximum and minimum sentences rather than specifying exact terms for certain offenses. The criminal justice system's interest was supposed to turn from the offense to the offender. Its first task, according to some reformers, was to diagnose each case.

The Path to the Law. The way men became lawyers was also changing (though the fact that most lawyers were men was not). Traditionally, a young man who wanted to be a lawyer would go to work for a lawyer. In return for copying documents and writing out letters, briefs, and reports, all by hand, he would be allowed to study the law books: the eighteenth-century William Blackstone, nineteenth-century commentaries on Blackstone, and the statute books of his own state. After a year or two of this apprenticeship the candidate would take a bar exam, usually an oral quiz administered by a judge. If the judge deemed the candidate worthy, he would give him license to practice law. But in 1870 the invention of the typewriter began to change this system. With a typewriter a skilled typist could type in an hour a manuscript that would have taken the fastest clerk half a day to write by hand. By the end of the century lawyers no longer needed clerks for the drudgery of copying and writing. Women seemed to be faster typists than men, and so women replaced men as the clerks and secretaries to lawyers and other men of business. Women were not expected to become lawyers — in fact, they were forbidden by law to do so. They were expected to remain as clerks or secretaries until they retired or married. Lawyers no longer needed clerks, but young men still wanted to become lawyers. Instead of apprenticing themselves to older, established lawyers, young men now would have to go to law school.

The Study of Law. The way law was taught changed in the decades between the Civil War and 1920. Since the law had been regarded as a craft, one that could be learned through an apprenticeship, it had not been necessary under the traditional system of reading law for a prospective lawyer to have a college degree or even a high-school diploma. In 1904 future Supreme Court justice Hugo Black arrived at Tuscaloosa, Alabama, to begin his studies at the University of Alabama. He was not qualified to enter the academic department, the equivalent of an undergraduate college, so he instead entered the law school. Law schools in the first decade of the century raised their standards, but the movement to do so was controversial. The central issue, often obscured behind other equally contentious points, was defining the purpose of studying law. In the first decade of the century the Association of American Law Schools (AALS) was formed for this purpose and to make sure all law schools adhered to a certain set of standards. Typically, the schools that belonged to the AALS followed the "case method" of legal study: by considering actual cases, law students would discover the legal philosophy that generated solutions. This was more than simply learning the law; proponents of the case method recommended that legal studies take at least three years of full-time work. On the other hand, in this decade other law schools, not affiliated with the AALS, emerged to train in the law men and women who had not been to college. These law schools often were run by practicing lawyers (the faculty at the AALS schools tended to be full-time teachers) who used their offices at night to train prospective lawyers. These schools focused on the practical rather than philosophical questions of law.

Conclusion. Just as the country was changing, the law was changing. But lawyers and judges did not always welcome the changes in their society or their profession. In this decade of tremendous change, some embraced progress without fully understanding all of its implications. One of President William McKinley's reelection buttons showed black smoke pouring from a factory chimney. For McKinley the smoke was a symbol of progress. During the decade that began with his reelection, Americans began to understand the cost of this industrial progress, as courts and legislators grappled with the exploitation of women, children, men, and the environment; the rise of corporate power; an increasingly violent labor movement; lynchings of black Americans and mob violence directed against them; and a host of other evils either brought on by industrialization or made more glaring by it. McKinley himself, a gentle and compassionate man, probably did not consider all the consequences of progress. His murder by anarchist Leon Czolgosz in September 1901 may have been one of those consequences.

TOPICS IN THE NEWS

THE DILEMMA OF SECOND-CLASS CITIZENS: RACE RIOTS AND CIVIL DISORDER

Second-Class Citizens. In August 1900 a white New York City policeman, Robert Thorpe, died after a fight with Arthur Harris, a black man. The next day mobs of whites set out to avenge his death by attacking blacks. Some black leaders in New York City charged that the police instigated these attacks. Harris was ultimately convicted of Thorpe's murder, and an investigation by the police cleared officers of charges of brutality. Whites and blacks perceived the situation differently, and it seemed impossible that the two would recognize this difference. In 1896 the Supreme Court had ruled in *Plessy* v. *Ferguson* that states could treat blacks separately but equally, at least in principle. Southern states took steps to disenfranchise blacks, and in northern states restrictive housing covenants and other ordinances restricted where they could live. In 1904 the Maryland legislature passed a law disenfranchising black voters, and though the governor vetoed the act, it still sent a message that blacks were not entitled to full citizenship rights. Blacks were forbidden to move into many towns in Ohio and Indiana.

Brownsville, Texas. The fact that black Americans were held to a different standard of justice than white Americans was borne out in the aftermath of a 1906 riot near Fort Brown, Texas. That August some soldiers from the Twenty-fifth Regiment, an all-black regiment stationed at Fort Brown, Texas, were involved in a riot in Brownsville. One citizen was killed; one was wounded; and the police chief was injured. The commander of Fort Brown prevented violence from escalating. After an investigation President Theodore Roosevelt determined that all members of the regiment had to be disciplined and so dishonorably discharged every soldier in that regiment and disqualified all from further service either in the military or in the civilian branches of government. Sen. Ben Tillman of South Carolina, a racist demagogue, denounced Roosevelt's action as an "executive lynching," and other, more sincere critics charged that Roosevelt had punished the soldiers because they were black. John Milholland of the Constitution League argued that the soldiers were deprived of their rights, but in January 1907 a Senate investigation approved the president's conduct.

W. E. B. Du Bois, seated, with, from left, F. H. M. Murray, L. M. Hershaw, and William Monroe Trotter at the 1906 Niagara Movement meeting at Harpers Ferry, West Virginia

In 1909 Sen. Joseph Foraker of Ohio succeeded in having a court of inquiry set up to determine each individual soldier's case and to reinstate those not involved in the riot. Not until 1972, though, were the dishonorable discharges rescinded by Congress.

Political Rights and the Atlanta Riots. Booker T. Washington had urged blacks not to agitate on political questions. Washington, the president and founder of Tuskegee Institute in Alabama, emerged as the leading spokesman for black America. He urged blacks to work toward economic power, but not to agitate for political rights or social equality. Other blacks, like Ida Wells-Barnett, James Weldon Johnson, Monroe Trotter, and W. E. B. Du Bois, believed political agitation was essential. In 1905 the more radical leaders met at Niagara

Falls, Canada, to discuss ways to improve the lives of black Americans and to free them from the specter of lynch law. Each year, as "the Niagara Movement," they reconvened in a place resonant with the history of the abolitionists: Harpers Ferry, West Virginia; Boston's Faneuil Hall; and Oberlin College in Ohio. The issue of black suffrage touched off in Atlanta in 1906 one of the decade's most severe riots. Georgia was following other states in considering ways to take the vote away from blacks. After months of agitation on this political question, led by Hoke Smith, candidate for governor, and former governor Tom Watson, both of whom urged that the vote be taken away from blacks, Atlanta's newspapers published false reports of black men attacking white women. White mobs formed and attacked every black person they found. In four days of rioting twenty-one people, most of them black and many of them substantial citizens, were killed and many more injured.

Springfield, Illinois. In 1908 racial violence struck in the hometown of Abraham Lincoln. A white woman, Mrs. Earle Hallam, accused George Richardson, a black man, of dragging her from her bed and raping her. When Hallam testified before a grand jury, though, she recanted her charge against Richardson. She had been beaten by a white man, with whom she had sexual relations, but she declined to name him. It was a sordid episode for her, and to escape her shame she had accused Richardson. Though she now withdrew her charge, the white community was enraged. To protect Richardson, the authorities had put him on an outbound train. When a white mob discovered him gone, it went on a rampage. The mob destroyed a restaurant whose owner had driven Richardson to the train and then set out to find more weapons. They broke into stores to seize guns, axes, knives, and kerosene. They burned a barber shop and lynched the barber, a black man, and were about to burn his body when the state militia, called from neighboring Decatur, fired on them to disperse. The next night the mob resumed its violence, lynching an eighty-four-year-old black man who had lived with his wife, a white woman, for thirty quiet years. The mob pursued one black man into a crowd in front of the courthouse, where Eugene Chafin, the presidential candidate of the Prohibition Party, was speaking. When Chafin tried to protect the man, he was smashed in the face with a brick. It took five thousand state militia to restore order. Two men were lynched; two whites were killed; and seventy people were injured.

Founding of the NAACP. That this racial violence had happened within a few blocks of Abraham Lincoln's house, and less than two miles from his grave, in the year before the centennial of his birth shocked white America, which had not taken a keen interest in the problems of black Americans. In May 1909 a National Conference on the Negro convened. Though sponsored by whites, including Jane Addams, Oswald Garrison Villard (editor of the *Nation* and grandson of abolitionist William Lloyd

Garrison), and William English Walling, who had investigated the Springfield, Illinois, riot, the conference also invited participants from the Niagara Movement. Out of this conference emerged the National Association for the Advancement of Colored People (NAACP), with Moorfield Storey, a prominent white Bostonian, as its head. W. E. B. Du Bois, the only black person in a prominent position in the organization, was named as editor of the NAACP newspaper, *The Crisis*. The NAACP would combat lynching, though lynching would never become a federal crime. The NAACP also began a long legal campaign against segregation, culminating in 1954 when the Supreme Court reversed *Plessy* v. *Ferguson* and ruled that separate but equal is inherently unequal.

Sources:

John Hope Franklin and Alfred A. Moss Jr., *From Slavery to Freedom: A History of African Americans* (New York: McGraw-Hill, 1994);

Richard Kluger, *Simple Justice: The History of Brown v. Board of Education and Black America's Struggle for Equality* (New York: Knopf, 1975);

Nell Irvin Painter, *Standing at Armageddon: The United States 1877–1919* (New York: Norton, 1987).

INSANITY AND GUILT: THE TRIALS OF HARRY THAW

Thaw Murders White. On 25 June 1906 Harry K. Thaw shot Stanford White three times with a pistol. White died almost immediately, and Thaw raised the pistol above his head and walked out of the rooftop restaurant at Madison Square Garden in New York City. Thaw rejoined his wife, Evelyn Nesbit Thaw, and two friends and volunteered to them that he had just killed White, whom he said had ruined his life.

Thaw's Mental Instability. These facts were never in dispute. But for the next two years, during two sensational, highly publicized trials, virtually every other fact concerning Thaw, White, and Evelyn Nesbit Thaw would be bitterly disputed. Stanford White, at age fifty-four, was one of the country's leading architects; in fact, his architectural firm had designed Madison Square Garden. Harry K. Thaw, twenty years younger than White, was the son of a Pittsburgh coke and railroad magnate. With tremendous family resources, Thaw had never settled down. In fact, the record of his life revealed great mental instability, and insanity seemed to recur in his family. His mother recalled that as a baby he would cry uncontrollably; his first-grade teacher remembered that hardly a day went by without Thaw creating a scene; the headmaster of his boarding school remembered his bulging eyes, his nervous habits, and his propensity to howl. In 1897 he had a nervous breakdown in Monte Carlo, and two years later in London a doctor said he suffered "acute insanity, or sub-acute mania." Thaw was also sadistic: he rented rooms in a brothel, ostensibly to train girls for the stage. Instead, he beat them with whips. He also whipped Evelyn Nesbit before their marriage. In Paris in 1904 he attempted suicide, and apparently by that time he had also become addicted to cocaine. His

Harry K. Thaw, second from right, during his first trial for the murder of Stanford White

family fortune allowed the episodes to be either hidden (during his trial for the murder of White, his family paid the brothel keeper $40,000 to keep quiet and paid Evelyn Nesbit Thaw $200,000, with a tacit promise of more, for her testimony) or dismissed as eccentricities.

Thaw's Paranoia. Evelyn Nesbit Thaw had been Stanford White's lover. White had seduced Evelyn Nesbit when she was sixteen. Thaw developed a passionate hatred for the architect, whom he accused of ruining Evelyn. Thaw also believed that the influential White was having him followed. Anthony Comstock, founder of the Society for the Suppression of Vice, a group committed to eradicating immorality, recalled that Thaw had visited him in 1904 to discuss White's career as a libertine. What impressed Comstock most about the visit, however, was not the bizarre stories of White's libidinous parties, but Thaw's insistence that White was having him followed and that White had conspired with a gang of New York thugs to kick Thaw to death. When Thaw drew up his will, on the day he married Evelyn Nesbit, he set aside $50,000 from his estate to investigate the circumstances of his death, should he die from other than natural causes, and another $7,500 to be used by anyone who had been wronged by Stanford White to bring suit against the architect.

The First Trial. At his trial Thaw resolutely denied that he was insane. Instead, the defense strategy was to show that Thaw had been enraged on hearing of Stanford White's seduction of his wife. His "insanity" was a temporary fit, caused by White's "blackguardism." Thaw's family engaged San Francisco criminal lawyer Delphin Michael Delmas, "the Napoleon of the Western Bar," for a fee of $100,000 to lead the defense team. Delmas had defended nineteen men charged with murder, and all had been acquitted. The defense turned on Evelyn Nesbit Thaw's story of her seduction by White and the profound impact her revelation had upon her husband's mental state. One doctor, who visited Thaw in the Tombs (New York City's infamous jailhouse) eight times between the murder and the trial, reported that Thaw had suffered a "brain explosion or mental storm," which led him to murder White. Though the psychological evidence was inconclusive — other witnesses attested that Thaw was rational and lucid — this testimony popularized the term *brainstorm*. Using the press to rouse public sympathy for the Thaws, the defense put White's character on trial. District Attorney William Travers Jerome, frustrated by the defense's ability to keep evidence of Thaw's mental instability out of court, called for a Commission of Lunacy to investigate whether Thaw was insane. The commission found Thaw sane, and the trial resumed. In his summation to the jury, Delmas said, "If Thaw is insane, it is with a species of insanity that is known from the Canadian border to the Gulf. If you expert gentlemen ask me to give it a name, I suggest that you label it *dementia Americana*. It is that species of insanity that inspires every American to believe that his home is sacred. It is that species of insanity that persuades an American that whoever violates the sanctity of his home or the purity of his wife or daughter has forfeited the protection of the laws of this state or any state." On 12 April 1907 the jury declared it could not reach a verdict: seven members found Thaw guilty of first-degree murder, five found him not guilty by reason of insanity.

Thaw's Second Trial. Thaw was kept in prison to await his second trial, which began on 6 January 1908. This time the prosecution set out to prove Thaw was sane, rational, and therefore responsible for his actions. The defense, this time led by New York lawyer Martin Littleton, argued that Thaw was in fact insane. In the second trial the defense introduced evidence of Thaw's mental instability, having doctors from France and England, as well as Thaw's teachers and others who had known him, testify as to periods of irrationality. District Attorney Jerome attacked this strategy, especially the psychological experts (called "alienists" because of their study of mental alienation), whose "theories" he said had brought "shame and disgrace" to the court of law. "Did you ever hear of a lawyer," he asked, "who couldn't get some expert to take any side of a question?" On 1 February 1908 the jury found Thaw not guilty by reason of

The 1898 invasion of Puerto Rico during the Spanish-American War brought to the fore the problem, highlighted in the Insular Cases, of the reach of American laws.

insanity. He was committed to the state asylum for the criminally insane at Matteawan, New York.

Thaw's Later Career. Thaw was surprised that he did not go free. He immediately asked his lawyers to enter a plea for a writ of habeas corpus. This attempt, and three successive ones, failed, as the state supreme court heard evidence of Thaw's mental instability and so deemed him a potential menace to society. In 1908 Evelyn Nesbit Thaw filed for an annulment, having been given a settlement by the Thaw family and now having evidence that her husband was not of sound mind at the time of their wedding. At his next habeas corpus hearing Evelyn testified that Harry had threatened to kill her when he got out. The U.S. Supreme Court refused to release Thaw in December 1909, and he remained in the state asylum until August 1913, when he escaped to Canada. He was apprehended there and during a long extradition dispute emerged once again as a popular hero. He was returned to New York by order of the U.S. Supreme Court in December 1914, where he was granted a new trial. This time he was acquitted, declared sane, and set free. He lived until 1947, spending his last years in and out of trouble with the law for his erratic behavior, which included kidnapping and whipping teenage boys, beating up women, and assaulting waiters. At the time of his release

in 1915, the *New York Sun* wrote, "In all this nauseous business we don't know which makes the gorge rise more, the pervert buying his way out, or the perverted idiots that hail him with wild huzzas."

Source:
Gerald Langford, *The Murder of Stanford White* (Indianapolis: Bobbs-Merrill, 1962).

THE INSULAR CASES: THE CONSTITUTION FOLLOWS THE FLAG

Acquisition of an Empire. By 1900 the United States had acquired Hawaii, Guam, the Philippines, and Puerto Rico and was maintaining a protectorate over Cuba. What would be the legal status of the people of these places? Were they subjects or citizens? What relationship would they have with the United States? What rights would they have? None of these questions had a clear answer, nor were all Americans comfortable with the idea of being an imperial power. In 1900 the Democratic Party, with William Jennings Bryan again its presidential nominee, tried to make imperialism an issue in the campaign. Imperialism, Democrats argued, was a ploy by wealthy capitalists to distract American workers from domestic problems and to exploit cheap overseas labor. These new territories would require a large military force —

in fact, a U.S. army of sixty-five thousand would spend three years suppressing the Filipino leader Emilio Aguinaldo's movement against American rule — and this would mean higher taxes. But the issue itself was too complicated to use in a political campaign. Some Americans did not like imperialism because it would change the nature of their republican government, others because they feared that the people of the colonies might try to join American society.

The Problem of Cuba. The United States had entered the war with Spain for the purpose of freeing Cuba from Spanish colonialism. The United States disavowed any interest in keeping control of Cuba after the war. In November 1900 a constitutional convention in Cuba drew up a plan of government modeled on that of the United States. The United States now feared Cuban independence, and Sen. Orville Platt of Connecticut proposed an amendment, actually formulated by Secretary of War Elihu Root, giving the United States the right "to intervene [in Cuba] for the preservation of Cuban independence, the maintenance of a government adequate for the protection of life, property, and individual liberty, and for discharging the obligations with respect to Cuba imposed by the Treaty of Paris on the United States." The U.S. Army under Gen. Leonard Wood governed Cuba until 1902, when it turned power over to the Cuban government. In 1906 the United States intervened in Cuba, establishing a provisional government that remained until 1909. American political and military intervention in Cuba continued until 1934, when the United States and the government of Cuba abrogated the Platt Amendment. But American economic intervention continued: Americans had investments in Cuba valued at $50 million in 1898; by 1930 these investments were valued at $1.5 billion. American control of the sugar industry and of gambling interests undermined Cuba's economic independence, ultimately helping to provoke the Cuban revolution of 1959.

The First Insular Cases. In 1900 Congress passed the Foraker Act providing for self-government for Puerto Rico. Under the law, sponsored by liberal Republican Joseph Foraker of Ohio, Puerto Rico's people would elect an assembly, and the president of the United States would appoint an executive council and a governor. The United States would be allowed to collect duties on some goods imported from the island. But in 1901, in *DeLima* v. *Bidwell,* the Supreme Court ruled that Puerto Rico was not a foreign country, and therefore tariff laws did not apply to Puerto Rican sugar brought into the United States. By terms of the Treaty of Paris, which ended the war with Spain, Puerto Rico was no longer a foreign country. However, Justice Henry Brown wrote, the treaty gave Congress the power to determine how the island would be governed. So while the tariff on sugar did not apply to Puerto Rico, other special duties mandated by the Foraker Act were constitutional. This rather complicated legal doctrine reflects the ambiguity Americans felt

in establishing colonies. Congress would have power over the people of these colonies, the court said, but that power would not be unlimited. Some "natural rights enforced in the Constitution" could not be abridged, even by Congress. Among these rights were freedom of speech, property, and religion.

Limits to Freedom. Having established that people in colonies enjoyed some fundamental rights, because "the Constitution follows the flag," the court heard more cases coming from Hawaii, Alaska, and the Philippines. In these cases the court ruled that if a territory was incorporated, its people enjoyed all the constitutional rights guaranteed to citizens of the United States. Alaska, for example, which had been purchased from Russia in 1867, had been incorporated as a territory. Alaskans thus were entitled to the procedural rights guaranteed in the Constitution: trial by jury, grand jury indictment, and counsel. Hawaii, the Philippines, and Puerto Rico were not incorporated, and so their people were not entitled to grand jury indictments or trial by jury. In another 1901 case the Court ruled that though Cuba was occupied by an American army and governed by an American general, Cuba was still an independent country. The United States was merely acting as a guardian or protector of the country until Cuba could establish a stable government. The court balanced the issues of self-government and imperialism, maintaining that the United States could acquire territories but that the people in the territories would have some fundamental rights. These careful decisions caused humorist Finley Peter Dunne's character, Mister Dooley, to remark, "No matther whether th' constitution follows th' flag or not, th' supreme coort follows th' ilictin returns."

Sources:

Philip S. Foner, *The Spanish-Cuban-American War and the Birth of American Imperialism, volume 2: 1898–1902* (New York: Monthly Review Press, 1972);

George Fredrickson, *The Black Image in the White Mind: The Debate on Afro-American Character and Destiny, 1817–1914* (Middletown, Conn.: Wesleyan University Press, 1971);

Laurence M. Friedman, *A History of American Law* (New York: Simon & Schuster, 1985);

Alfred H. Kelly, Winifred Harbison, and Herman Belz, *The American Constitution: Its Origins and Development,* sixth edition (New York: Norton, 1983).

LABOR ON TRIAL: THE MURDER OF FRANK STEUNENBERG

Frank Steunenberg Murdered. In 1899 Idaho governor Frank Steunenberg had called for federal troops to suppress a strike by miners in Couer d'Alene. After breaking the strike, Steunenberg and the legislature worked to break the union, passing a law that forbade miners to organize unions. Though Steunenberg retired from politics, he was still a hated figure to miners and to organized labor. On the evening of 30 December 1905, as Steunenberg opened the front gate to his home in Caldwell, Idaho, a bomb exploded, killing him.

Charles Moyers, Big Bill Haywood, and George Pettibone, who were acquitted of conspiracy in the assassination of former Idaho governor Frank Steunenberg

Confession of Harry Orchard. Police arrested Harry Orchard, who had been living in Caldwell under the name of T. S. Hogan. Orchard claimed to have been a bomber for the Western Federation of Miners (WFM), and he confessed to a grisly series of bombings aimed at police officers and strikebreakers. He claimed to have planted a bomb at the Cripple Creek, Colorado, mine during a strike there in 1903, and in 1904 he said he had shot a deputy sheriff and later killed fourteen strikebreakers by planting a bomb at the Independence, Colorado, train station. He had also been part of a plot to kill three state officials in Colorado. All of this violence, he said, was done under orders from the WFM. Specifically, he named Bill Haywood, the WFM's treasurer; Charles Moyer, its president ; and George Pettibone, a Denver merchant sympathetic to the WFM. These three, he claimed, had hired him to kill Frank Steunenberg. Idaho officials, eager to put the WFM out of business, released Orchard after he had implicated the union leaders in Steunenberg's death. On 15 February 1906 Idaho officials arrested Haywood, Moyer, and Pettibone and brought them to Boise for trial.

Clarence Darrow Comes to Idaho. Clarence Darrow, one of the nation's leading lawyers and the most prominent labor lawyer in the country, came to Idaho to defend Haywood, Moyer, and Pettibone. First, before their trial started, Darrow challenged the fact that they had not been extradited from Colorado. None of the three had been in Idaho when Steunenberg was murdered; therefore Idaho police should not have gone to Colorado to arrest them. The legal thing to do would have been to extradite them. Idaho, though, argued that the three had "conspired" in the murder and so were "present" in the state so far as they had a role in the conspiracy to commit murder. Darrow lost this round of his defense, and the trial of the three union men entered its second phase.

Trial of Steve Adams. Under Idaho law, no one could be convicted of a crime on the uncorroborated testimony of an accomplice. The state needed to produce evidence other than Harry Orchard's testimony to convict Haywood, Moyer, and Pettibone. Steve Adams, a miner, had been implicated by Orchard in other crimes and had confessed to the murder of Fred Tyler but had not been involved in Steunenberg's murder. Under pressure from the state, which promised not to prosecute Adams for Tyler's death if he testified against Haywood, Adams had corroborated Orchard. Darrow was convinced, though, that Adams had been pressured to implicate Haywood. Darrow visited the miner in jail and convinced him to withdraw his confession. He would defend Adams, he promised, if the state indicted him. Once Adams withdrew his testimony, he was charged with murder in the death of Fred Tyler. Darrow defended Adams so effectively against a charge to which he had already confessed that the jury could not reach a verdict. Adams was free, and Idaho's case against Haywood was severely weakened.

Trial of Bill Haywood: Political Context. Haywood's trial began on 9 May 1907. James H. Hawley was the prosecutor, assisted by William E. Borah, recently elected to the U.S. Senate from Idaho. Though the prosecution did not want to inject politics into the case, which they said was a simple murder, they did see Haywood and the others as trying to upset the established order through any means. Haywood himself was a founder of the Industrial Workers of the World (IWW) and had advocated violence as a tactic for strikers who were the victims of violence. On the eve of the trial President Roosevelt described the defendants as "undesirable citizens." Darrow and the defense, on the other hand, argued not only that Haywood had not been involved in Steunenberg's killing, but that the union leader was on trial for his political beliefs. President Roosevelt said that Haywood and the IWW represented "a revolt against economic and social injustice" only in the way "that we thus describe a band of road agents who rob a coach." All expected Haywood to be convicted, and most of the establishment would have applauded. For the radical press, Haywood's conviction would be further proof that no union man could receive a fair trial in an American court, that the judicial system operated to suppress the working people.

A Sensational Trial. The trial created great excitement both internationally and in the United States. It was the first trial covered by newspaper wire services, with reporters coming to Idaho and filing their reports over the telegraph wires to papers around the globe. Celebrities, too, visited the courtroom. Actress Ethel Barrymore, who knew how to set a stage, noted that Darrow "had all the props, an old mother in a wheelchair and a little girl with curls draped all around Haywood. I don't know whether she was his daughter or just one of Mr.

Darrow's props." Despite Darrow's props and his legal skill, all expected Haywood to be convicted; Steunenberg was a well-respected local citizen, and the jury was made up of men who had known him well.

Darrow's Closing Argument. The crux of the defense's argument was that Harry Orchard was a liar. The prosecution called on the jury to avenge Steunenberg's death and to beat back the forces of violence and anarchy. Darrow called on the jury to look beyond the facts of the case, to the importance their verdict would have in the nation and the world. "I speak for the poor, for the weak, for the weary, for that long line of men who, in darkness and despair, have borne the labors of the human race," Darrow told the jury. "Their eyes are on you twelve men of Idaho tonight. If you should decree Bill Haywood's death, in the railroad offices of our great cities men will applaud your names. . . . In every bank in the world, where men hate Haywood because he fights for the poor and against that accursed system upon which the favored live and grow rich and fat," they would "receive blessings and unstinted praise." But "Out on our broad prairies where men toil with their hands, out on the wide ocean where men are tossed and buffeted on the waves, through our mills and factories, and down deep under the earth, thousands of men, and of women and children will kneel tonight and ask their God to guide your hearts — these men and women and these little children, the poor, the weak, and the suffering of the world, are stretching out their helpless hands to this jury in mute appeal for Bill Haywood's life." Darrow's partner in the defense, Edmund Richardson, doubted that this heartfelt plea would convince twelve Idaho farmers that Bill Haywood was innocent. They had known Steunenberg, and Darrow's speech would have found a better reception at a labor rally than in an Idaho courtroom. Darrow's eloquent plea, Richardson said, "was enough to hang any man regardless of his innocence or guilt."

Haywood Acquitted. The jury deliberated for twenty hours and then, on 28 July 1907, acquitted Bill Haywood. Though most jurors believed Haywood had been involved in a conspiracy to kill Frank Steunenberg, the prosecution had not presented enough evidence to establish his guilt beyond a reasonable doubt. It was a victory for Darrow, helping to establish his reputation as one of the country's premier criminal and labor lawyers. The state brought Pettibone to trial, but in January 1908 he too was acquitted. Harry Orchard, who had been promised immunity for testifying against Haywood and the others, was found guilty of Steunenberg's murder and sentenced to death. His sentence was commuted, and he died in prison in 1954. The acquittal of Haywood was a victory for the labor movement and for Darrow but also a victory for the system of justice. The radical press had argued that men like Haywood could never receive a fair trial; the fact that the jury had acquitted Haywood seemed to prove them wrong. Haywood himself grew increasingly bitter about American society, and his continued advocacy of violence alienated many in the labor movement. Charged with sedition during World War I, Haywood fled the country while free on bail. In 1921 he arrived in the Soviet Union, dying there in 1928. He is buried in the Kremlin.

Sources:

Philip S. Foner, *History of the Labor Movement in the United States, volume 4: The Industrial Workers of the World, 1905–1917* (New York: International Publishers, 1965);

Walter Lord, *The Good Years: From 1900 to the First World War* (New York: Harper, 1960);

Kevin Tierney, *Darrow: A Biography* (New York: Crowell, 1979).

LOCHNER V. NEW YORK (1905)

Background. A changing economy, moving toward larger industries and complicated corporate structures, meant that workers lost significant control over their work. Though the court in the 1890s had allowed corporations to expand, the courts had not been friendly to workers who tried to form unions. Working people were expected to negotiate individually for their wages and working hours. Courts used injunctions to prevent workers from striking, and the courts were equally skeptical of state attempts to improve working conditions. In 1885 the Supreme Court had struck down a New York law that regulated working conditions for cigar makers. Working in their tiny tenement apartments, cigar makers rolled tobacco into cigars. Often the entire family, women and young children, spent long hours rolling cigars for which they were paid by the piece. This kind of work, often the only kind available to an unskilled immigrant, paid a tiny amount and posed significant health risks to the worker and his family. The law, sponsored by assemblyman Theodore Roosevelt, prohibited this kind of work. But the Supreme Court in 1885 ruled that New York could not regulate these working conditions, as to do so violated the cigar maker's and his employees' liberty to make a contract. In 1898 the court upheld a Utah law that limited the working hours of miners, because the court recognized the hazards of mining: more than two thousand miners would die in mine accidents between 1900 and 1909. Though labor was much weaker than business, workers and middle-class reformers pressured legislatures to restrict working hours in hazardous occupations. In 1897 New York's legislature, recognizing that breathing flour dust contributed to lung disease, limited bakers in "biscuit, bread, or cake bakery, or confectionary" factories to sixty hours of work each week.

Lochner and the Court. Joseph Lochner owned a bakery in Utica, New York. Lochner's bakers worked more than sixty hours a week. He was arrested and fined fifty dollars. He appealed his conviction, but the state appeals court, in an opinion written by Alton B. Parker, affirmed his guilt. The state could regulate the working hours of bakers in order to protect the health and safety of citizens.

Oliver Wendell Holmes, a dissenter from the Supreme Court ruling in *Lochner* v. *New York,* in 1909

Lochner Challenges the Law. One of Lochner's employees studied law and urged him to appeal the case to the U.S. Supreme Court. The New York law, he said, violated the U.S. Constitution. The Fourteenth Amendment says no state can deprive any person of equal protection, and no state can deprive any person of life, liberty, or property without due process. Because the New York law did not apply to bakers in hotels or restaurants, it denied all bakers equal protection. Because the law restricted the number of hours bakers could work, it limited their liberty to make contracts with their employers. The U.S. Supreme Court had said that the liberty to make contracts was a fundamental liberty covered by the Fourteenth Amendment.

The Supreme Court Rules. The Supreme Court overturned Lochner's conviction. The state law violated Lochner's freedom to make contracts with his employees. Justice Rufus Peckham ruled that the state had no reasonable ground to interfere with a baker's working hours and that bakers could protect themselves without help from the state. A state could only restrict working hours or regulate working conditions when it could prove that its regulation was fair, reasonable, and appropriate. Peckham did not understand baking to be a particularly hazardous occupation. Doctors would likely not recommend working in a bakery as a way to improve one's health, but that did not mean the state could restrict the hours bakers could work. Nor did the state show that by restricting working hours of bakers would the bread they produced be healthier. There was, then, no compelling reason for the state to limit bakers to sixty hours of work, and to do so violated their liberty to work longer hours if they desired. There had to be more than a small amount of possible ill health before the state could interfere with economic liberty.

Justice Holmes Dissents. Oliver Wendell Holmes disagreed with the court's decision, and he wrote one of the most famous dissents in the court's history. "This case is decided upon an economic theory which a large part of the country does not entertain," Holmes wrote. Justice Peckham and the majority had struck down the New York law because it violated their belief in laissez-faire economics. "A constitution," Holmes wrote, "is not intended to embody a particular economic theory, whether of paternalism and the organic relationship of the citizen to the State or of laissez-faire. It is made for people of fundamentally differing views, and the accident of our finding certain opinions natural and familiar or novel and even shocking ought not to conclude our judgment . . . whether . . . the[y] conflict with the Constitution of the United States." The court's role was not to decide how laws squared with the judges' ideologies or economic or political theories. If a majority of New Yorkers thought bakers should only work sixty hours each week, it was not up to the court to tell them otherwise. The court should defer to the legislature and not impose its own political, economic, or ideological views. Referring to the nineteenth century's leading proponent of a free marketplace and unlimited competition, Holmes wrote, "The Fourteenth Amendment does not enact Mr. Herbert Spencer's Social Statics." It was not up to judges to decide if a law was appropriate, nor was it up to judges to interpret the law based on their own limited understanding of the workplace. Judges should not interpose their own ideologies between the people and their lawmakers.

Reactions to *Lochner.* Holmes was an admirer of Spencer, and his dissent in the *Northern Securities* case suggests that he was a supporter of a free marketplace. The issue was not whether he agreed with a particular law, but whether the legislature had the power to enact a certain law. The *Lochner* case brought up two fundamental issues in American constitutional history: the power of the state to limit liberty and the role of the courts in interpreting legislation. *Lochner,* even as it rejected the New York law, did suggest that the state could pass reasonable laws that limited liberty. The majority had simply not accepted New York's regulation of bakers as reasonable. Holmes had accepted the evidence as reasonable and thought that the other judges had interjected their own views into the cases. There was no fundamental legal principle involved, but merely a difference of opinion. Three years later New York lawyer Learned Hand asked in an article whether unelected judges should be able to veto legislation based on their own social or polit-

ical views rather than on fundamental principles of law. "Whether it be wise or not," Hand wrote, for the court to "veto . . . legislation with whose economic or political expediency it totally disagrees, is a political question," and he warned that if the court continued to involve itself in political questions, the judges would find their power limited. Their unlimited power to restrain political majorities could not survive in a democratic state, "while the court retains the irresponsibility of a life tenure." The people, frustrated by judges who made political decisions, would subject the judges themselves to the political process. If the court continued to thwart laws that the majority of the people supported, the people would find a way to limit the court's power.

Sources:

Liva Baker, *The Justice from Beacon Hill: The Life and Times of Oliver Wendell Holmes, Jr.* (New York: HarperCollins, 1991);

Gerald Gunther, *Learned Hand: The Man and the Judge* (New York: Knopf, 1994);

Paul Kens, *Judicial Power and Reform Politics: The Anatomy of Lochner vs. New York* (Lawrence: University Press of Kansas, 1990).

LYNCHING AND LAWLESSNESS

Lynching. Nothing illustrates the failure of American justice better than the persistence of lynching and of race riots in the first decade of the twentieth century. More than twenty-five hundred people, most of them black men, had been lynched between 1886 and 1889; there were more than one hundred lynchings in 1900 and again in 1901. Between 1885 and 1905 there were more lynchings in the United States than there were legal executions. One proposed solution to this crisis was to make lynching a federal crime: at that time it was punishable only in state courts, where blacks were often excluded from juries and where few witnesses were willing to testify against leaders of mobs. Another solution, presented by defenders of "Southern justice," was to repeal the Constitution's Fifteenth Amendment. Some whites charged that the problem stemmed from blacks having the right to vote. Remove political equality, and whites would no longer feel threatened by blacks and perceive a need to kill them.

Patterns of Lynchings. All lynchings were different but followed certain patterns. For instance, in Missouri one Sunday afternoon in 1901 a white woman was found murdered. Within hours of her discovery a mob of whites seized three black men, two of them elderly, and tortured them to death before hanging them. The mob then burned five black families out of their homes. Thirty other families took to the woods until the mob's thirst for vengeance was abated. None of the victims, either the three murdered men or the homeless families, had any connection with the murdered woman. But the mob had decided to punish black people for an offense against a white woman, and the law could not stop them. None of the leaders of the lynch mob was punished, since no one would dare testify against them. Lynching was not con-

Thomas Nast cartoon captioned "The Christian (?) Turks/'Reforming' colored voters in the South."

fined to the South or to rural areas. In 1904 a white police officer in Springfield, Ohio, fought with a black man. During the struggle the black man killed the officer. He was arrested and put in jail. A mob gathered, broke into the jail, murdered the man, then hung his body from a telephone pole and shot bullets into it. The mob then ransacked the black section of town, as lynch mobs commonly turned on other blacks, even in a case like this one, which arose out of a specific incident.

Reasons for Lynching. Apologists for the lynch mob sometimes argued that mobs were swift to punish rapists and that lynching served as an extralegal way to protect white women from black men. Lynching, it was said, was "the only successful method of dealing with a certain class of crimes." But Ida B. Wells-Barnett, a black woman who had begun her career as a Memphis journalist and had become a crusader against lynching, showed that most lynchings were not in response to rapes. The *Chicago Tribune* published an annual report on lynchings, noting the alleged crime for which a victim was executed. Of more than 500 victims of lynching between 1896 and 1900, 96 had been accused of rape, 179 of murder. Nearly half the victims, 229, were lynched for "crimes" such as giving evidence in court, writing letters, registering to vote, making insulting statements, race prejudice, or simply "unknown crime."

Statesboro, Georgia, 1904. Apologists for the lynch mob argued that the law was not effective in punishing criminals, that only an enraged citizenry could preserve public order. Journalist Ray Stannard Baker's 1908 book, *Following the Color Line,* suggested that whites turned to

lynching when they lost faith in the system of justice to punish crime. But often a lynch mob acted when the law was working to punish a convicted criminal. In 1904 two black men were arrested in Statesboro, Georgia, for a particularly gruesome mass murder of a white farmer, his wife, and their three children. The accused were kept in Savannah, about fifty miles away, to allow tempers to cool. After two weeks the accused were brought to Statesboro for trial and were found guilty. As the judge pronounced their sentence, death by hanging, a mob stormed into the courtroom, seized the men, dragged them outside, and burned them alive. As the convicted men were roasting alive, the mob turned on other blacks, singling out anyone perceived to be a threat to the white order. In this case, as in many lynchings, the punishment was not merely intended for the accused: the mob would use the lynching as the starting point for a general riot and attack on any black person it could find.

The Supreme Court and Lynching. Lynching was not a federal crime, but a Chattanooga case came before the Supreme Court in 1906. Ed Johnson, a black man, had been convicted of raping a white girl. A lower court refused to hear his appeal, but Justice John Marshall Harlan granted Johnson a stay of execution and allowed him to appeal his case to the U.S. Supreme Court. On the night before his scheduled execution, before the justices could hear his appeal, Johnson was kidnapped from the jail, dragged six blocks by a mob, and hung from a bridge over the Tennessee River. The rope snapped, but the mob retrieved Johnson and hung him again, making sure he was dead by shooting at his body. The next day in Washington, Chief Justice Fuller called the justices to an emergency meeting. Johnson's lynching was an attack on the dignity and power of the Court. Two months later the Supreme Court charged Chattanooga sheriff John Shipp with contempt for failing to protect Johnson. Shipp responded that the Supreme Court did not have jurisdiction over his jail. This angered the justices, and Oliver Wendell Holmes wrote an opinion for the Court insisting that it did have jurisdiction to punish contempt against the judicial power of either the United States or the state of Tennessee. "The power and dignity of this court are paramount," Holmes said, and Johnson's lynching was "murder by a mob, and was an offense against the United States and this court." The Court appointed an investigator, who in 1909 reported that Shipp had not adequately defended the prisoner. Three years after Johnson's lynching, the Supreme Court sentenced Sheriff Shipp to ninety days in jail. This was a defense of judicial power, and though it was the strongest statement the Court would make against lynching, it was not going to stop the mobs.

Sources:
Liva Baker, *The Justice from Beacon Hill: The Life and Times of Oliver Wendell Holmes, Jr.* (New York: HarperCollins, 1991);

Jacqueline Jones Royster, *The Anti-Lynching Campaign of Ida B. Wells, 1892–1900* (New York: St. Martin's Press, 1996).

Carry Nation in jail after her arrest for smashing a saloon

PROHIBITION AND THE TEMPERANCE MOVEMENT

Prohibition in Kansas. At the end of the nineteenth century six states (Iowa, Maine, New Hampshire, Vermont, Kansas, and Rhode Island) were officially "dry," which meant it was illegal to manufacture or sell alcohol in them. In 1888 the Supreme Court ruled that states could not prohibit the sale of alcohol that came into a state in its original package: this, said the Court, would interfere with Congress's power to regulate interstate commerce. Though a state banned alcohol, hotels and clubs could sell alcohol by the bottle. A state that wanted to prevent alcohol abuse, then, could not completely control drinking. After the Court made this ruling, the liquor interest pushed to have all state laws limiting alcohol sales repealed. This move by the liquor interest, seemingly supported by the U.S. Supreme Court, came at a time when many Americans felt powerless to control the new economic forces that governed their society.

Alcohol as a Social Problem. By 1909 there were more saloons in the United States than there were schools, libraries, or churches. There was one saloon for every three hundred Americans, and these saloons were concentrated in cities. Medical evidence that alcohol was seriously harmful underscored a perception of its ill effects. Adding to the social problem was a political one: most taverns were controlled by brewers or the liquor trust. Many in the era came to consider those two as an

interest group, like the railroads, insurance companies, or other manufacturers, more concerned with profit than with public welfare. The Anheuser-Busch company controlled 65 percent of Saint Louis's taverns, and 90 percent of the saloons in Minneapolis were controlled by that city's liquor interest.

Opposition to Alcohol. In opposition to the liquor interest were different temperance organizations, each with its own methods and agenda. The Methodist Church was active in agitating against alcohol. The Prohibition Party, formed in 1872, received at least a quarter of a million votes in every election from 1888 to 1908. The Woman's Christian Temperance Union (WCTU), founded in 1874, and the Anti-Saloon League, founded in 1895, sought legal limits to alcohol sales and worked to convince individuals to give up drinking. The WCTU was a women's organization, and women were thought to have a special interest in restricting alcohol consumption. In fact, one argument against giving women the right to vote was that they would use it to enact Prohibition laws. Though the Methodists, the Anti-Saloon League, and the WCTU operated through education and lobbying, one Kansas woman, whose first husband had died of alcoholism, decided to take direct action against the liquor interests. Since saloons were illegal under Kansas law, Carry Nation in 1900 decided it would be legal to destroy them. A tall, muscular woman (about six feet tall and weighing 175 pounds), Carry Nation dressed in a black and white church deaconess uniform and carried an ax into local saloons and hotels, destroying the decor, furnishings, and most important, the hated bottles and kegs. Confinement to jail (on a charge of destroying property) only confirmed her views on the rightness of her cause. After her release she continued her campaign through Kansas and then through the rest of the United States, paying her fines with fees collected from public lectures and the sale of hatchets. For ten years she campaigned against alcohol with persistence and drama until, worn out from touring and smashing, she died in 1911. Her epitaph at Belton, Missouri, reads, "She hath done what she could."

The Temperance Movement Grows. Carry Nation was one colorful figure in the temperance movement, but to many advocates of Prohibition she was something of an embarrassment. Other advocates of temperance worked less dramatically, but perhaps more effectively, in convincing voters to ban alcohol. Eighteen Massachusetts cities, including Worcester, the state's second largest, and 249 towns went dry in 1908. Temperance and Prohibition were among the most important reforms of the Progressive Era, and after the 1912 election, in a stunning victory for progressive ideals (Wilson and Roosevelt, both running as progressives, received nearly two-thirds of the vote), Congress overturned the Supreme Court ruling of 1888 and allowed dry states to forbid the sale of alcohol, even in its original containers. Within three years nineteen states were officially dry. The United States adopted Prohibition as a wartime measure in 1917, as a way to save grain, but after the war national Prohibition was quickly established by a constitutional amendment.

Sources:

Ruth Bordin, *Frances Willard: A Biography* (Chapel Hill: University of North Carolina Press, 1986);

Bordin, *Women and Temperance: The Quest for Power and Liberty, 1873–1900* (Chapel Hill: University of North Carolina Press, 1981);

Nell Irvin Painter, *Standing at Armageddon: The United States 1877–1919* (New York: Norton, 1987).

REVIVING THE SHERMAN ACT: THE NORTHERN SECURITIES CASE

Roosevelt and Corporations. Theodore Roosevelt was no enemy of big business. However, he believed it was important to demonstrate that the federal government could enforce the law. Roosevelt did not want to go to court every time a corporation violated the law: that would be bad for the government and bad for business. It would be more effective, he believed, to have boards like the Interstate Commerce Commission to regulate corporations. In 1903 his administration created a bureau of corporations, which he hoped would be able to regulate big business. Roosevelt also believed the federal government should have the power to charter corporations, which would give these regulatory boards more control over illegal practices. All of this was not because Roose-

A cartoon, by Bartholomew in the Minneapolis *Journal*, depicting the Sherman Antitrust law being resurrected by President Roosevelt

velt did not like corporations. He believed a bureau of corporations should set out clear rules, which all parties would understand before they created a corporation. This way the government would not have to take them to court after the fact. This would be more effective for government and more efficient for business.

Northern Securities Case. But before Congress would create a bureau of corporations or a Securities and Exchange Commission to regulate the marketplace, large companies instead tried to buy one another up, to drive competitors out of business, and otherwise manipulate the nation's economy. In his first months in office Roosevelt watched a display of this kind of corporate behavior, and he determined to use the Sherman Act to protect the public from unscrupulous practices. The case involved four railroads that crossed the northern plains: the Great Northern and the Northern Pacific, which both ran from Minneapolis to the Pacific; the Union Pacific, from Omaha to Ogden, Utah; and the Chicago, Burlington, and Quincy, crossing the prairies of Illinois and Minnesota and running parallel to the Union Pacific to the Rockies. Though the railroads ran through the west, they were controlled by men in New York. J. P. Morgan, New York financier, owned the Northern Pacific; James J. Hill owned the Great Northern; and E. H. Harriman owned the Union Pacific. All three men eyed the Burlington, and in 1901 Hill and Morgan, who had learned to cooperate, bought it. Hill and Morgan now could drive Harriman out of business. But Harriman struck back. By May 1901 he had nearly bought a majority of the Great Northern stock. Hill nearly lost his own railroad, and before he could get it back he had to buy up every share he could find. Other investors, not knowing why the Great Northern's stock was climbing, tried to buy it, selling off other stocks to finance the purchase of Great Northern. A contest among three men for a railroad in Minnesota created a panic on Wall Street and bankrupted thousands of unsuspecting investors. None of the three tycoons won the struggle for the Great Northern. On 31 May, Hill and Harriman signed a peace agreement, which called for a new board of directors of the Northern Pacific, one of whom would be Harriman. To prevent another hostile takeover, they created the Northern Securities Company, a holding company, which would control the stocks of the Northern Pacific, the Great Northern, and the Burlington. Northern Securities, incorporated in New Jersey in November 1901, was worth so much — $400 million — that no one would ever be able to buy it. Morgan and Hill believed their investment was safe.

Northern Securities and the Sherman Antitrust Act. Was this holding company a "combination in restraint of trade," which the Sherman Act of 1890 prohibited? The American economy had been changing since the Civil War, and combinations like this one were not new. Between 1897 and 1904 more than four thousand companies had combined to form 257 corporations. Though this concentration seemed to violate the Sherman Act, the Supreme Court did not interpret the law that way. In 1895 the Court had limited the scope of the Sherman Act, ruling in the case of *U.S.* v. *E.C. Knight Company* that although the Knight company had formed a trust that controlled 95 percent of American sugar manufacturing, it was not a combination in restraint of trade. Manufacturing, according to the Court, was not commerce. The only cases in which the Court had found unreasonable combinations in restraint of trade involved labor unions, not businesses or trusts. In the same year that the court had found E. C. Knight Company innocent of violating the Sherman Act, it found that labor leader Eugene Debs's strike against the Pullman Company did violate the Sherman Act. Presidents Cleveland and McKinley had been reluctant to use the Sherman Act against corporations. But President Theodore Roosevelt believed differently. Not only did he believe that the Northern Securities Company violated the Sherman Act, he was determined to prove that the U.S. government could prevent such combinations. Hill, Morgan, and Harriman had acted, Roosevelt said, "in an open and above-board fashion, acting under what they, and most members of the bar, thought to be the law." Roosevelt wanted to make clear what this law meant and also make clear that the U.S. government would enforce the law. He asked Attorney General Philander Knox to look into the Northern Securities Company. In March 1902 Knox filed suit against Northern Securities in federal court in Saint Paul, Minnesota, claiming it was an unreasonable combination in restraint of trade, and thus illegal under the Sherman Antitrust Act.

Morgan Protests. J. P. Morgan, who had contributed generously to the 1900 Republican campaign, felt deeply wounded by the lawsuit. Roosevelt's action was a surprise: the federal government had only filed eighteen suits under the Sherman Act, and during McKinley's administration more business combinations had been formed than at any other time in history. No wonder Morgan felt betrayed. Why had he not been told in advance? he asked the president. If he had done something wrong, he told Roosevelt, "send your man to my man and they can fix it up." He was worried that the administration might next turn on his other interests. Would it do so, he asked? "Certainly not," Roosevelt began to reassure him, then added, "unless we find out that in any case they have done something wrong." Hill and his friends called on Ohio senator Mark Hanna, close adviser to the late president McKinley. But Hanna would not help them: "The Senate passed the Sherman Antitrust Law; how can I take it off the books?"

The Trial. In the trial at Saint Paul, Morgan's lawyer, Francis Lynde Stetson, argued that the Great Northern and the Northern Pacific had not formed the Northern Securities Company to restrain trade but to prevent future hostile takeovers. The railroads had not really been competitors, anyway, even though they ran parallel to one another: only 2 percent of their business competed directly with each other. The Northern Securities Company itself, Stetson argued, did not run railroads at all; it merely held stock in companies that ran the railroads. Men who owned stock in a baseball team, he said in an analogy, did not actually play baseball, and men who owned stock in railroads did not actually run trains. Thus they were not involved in interstate commerce. The government maintained that the Northern Securities Company had been set up to restrain competition and that it was engaged in interstate commerce. On 9 April 1903 district court judge Amos Thayer agreed with the government. "These railroads are, and in public estimation have ever been regarded, as parallel and competing lines." The creation of the Northern Securities Company destroyed every motive for competition and the court had to conclude that the company's creators intended to do so. Their intention was more important than any actual reduction in competititon.

The Supreme Court. In December 1903 the Supreme Court heard the case. Arguing for the Northern Securities Company, John G. Johnson tried to distinguish between an actual reduction in competition, which would be a crime under the Sherman Act, and the mere possibility of such a reduction. "Few of us have a desire to commit murder, but many of us use a razor, which gives us the power to commit murder," he said. Could a company be punished for having the power to do something, even if it did not do so? To deprive them of their property by dissolving Northern Securities violated their Fifth Amendment rights. Attorney General Knox would have none of this. "The Securities Company is guilty of the jority, Justice John Marshall Harlan affirmed that the Northern Securities Company was a combination in restraint of trade. By its very existence the company was "a menace to, and a restraint upon, that freedom of commerce which Congress intended to recognize and protect. . . . If such a combination be not destroyed . . . the entire commerce . . . between the Great Lakes and the Pacific . . . will be at the mercy of a single holding corporation." In a dissenting opinion Oliver Wendell Holmes Jr., appointed to the Court by Roosevelt, disagreed with Harlan. Combinations and contracts in restraint of trade, Holmes said, had particular common law meanings, neither of which applied in this case. Further, combinations had to be unreasonable to be illegal, and Holmes did not see the Northern Securities Company as an unreasonable creation. All railroads, in a sense, were monopolies, since no more than one railroad company could run trains over the same set of tracks. Monopolies and large corporations, Holmes argued, were not the result of criminal intent but the results of a changing economy. As the economy became more efficient, larger corporations and monopolies were inevitable.

Result of the Decision. Despite Holmes's dissent, the verdict showed that the federal government would use the Sherman Act to break up some monopolies and trusts that operated to restrain trade. Roosevelt did move against some of the larger trusts: the beef trust, the tobacco trust, and Standard Oil, though he preferred using administrative boards to resolve these problems. Make it clear what the law is, Roosevelt argued, and have some administrative board that can approve a merger or combination before it happens, to spare both business and the government the expense of going to court. Though Roosevelt wanted regulation rather than litigation, his administration filed forty-four antitrust suits, double the number filed by all previous administrations, and William Howard Taft, his successor, would file eighty suits. The Sherman Act was on the books, and Roosevelt was determined to enforce it. Roosevelt, along with Holmes, and probably most Americans, realized that large corporations were a permanent feature of the economy. The government should try to regulate rather than abolish them.

Source:
R. W. Apple Jr., "The Case of the Monopolistic Railroadmen," in *Quarrels That Have Shaped the Constitution*, edited by John A. Garraty (New York: Harper & Row, 1962).

mischief the law is designed to prevent — namely, it brings transportation trade through a vast section of a country under the controlling interest of a single body. . . . To deny that this is a combination challenges common intelligence. To deny that it is in restraint of trade challenges the authority of this court."

Verdict. In March 1904 the Court agreed with the government and ordered the Northern Securities Company dissolved. Speaking for the five justices in the ma-

WOMEN, LOUIS BRANDEIS, AND THE LAW: MULLER V. OREGON (1908)

Oregon and the Ten-Hour Day. In 1903 Oregon forbade women employed outside the home to work longer than ten hours a day. Massachusetts had been the first state to pass such a law (1874), and by 1903 twenty states had done so. States acted to protect women from overwork but also to give them sufficient time to do household chores, which most Americans still believed were

Louis Brandeis, lawyer for the plaintiffs in *Muller* v. *Oregon*

the responsibility of women. In 1895 the Illinois Supreme Court had found an eight-hour workday for women unconstitutional on the grounds that it infringed on women's liberty to make contracts. The U.S. Supreme Court's 1905 decision in *Lochner* suggested that it might also find such laws protecting women unconstitutional.

Curt Muller Breaks the Law. Curt Muller owned the Grand Laundry in Portland, Oregon. On 4 September 1905 his foreman, Joe Haselbock, required Mrs. E. Gotcher to work longer than ten hours. Muller was arrested, convicted, and fined ten dollars. He appealed his case, believing, in the wake of *Lochner,* that the state could not regulate working hours. His lawyers reasoned that while the law prevented people from making contracts, it did not apply to all people similarly situated (men in the same occupations were allowed to work longer than ten hours), and the kinds of work it restricted were neither illegal, immoral, nor dangerous to the public health. The state could restrict those occupations but had no valid reason to restrict other occupations.

Louis D. Brandeis Takes the Case. Florence Kelley of the National Consumers' League supported the ten-hour workday. The National Consumers' League was a middle-class reform organization dedicated to improving working conditions for American workers. The Consumers' League came to the defense of the Oregon law and set out to find a lawyer who could assist the Oregon attorney general in preparing a case. Kelley first approached New York lawyer Joseph Choate, a leading constitutional lawyer. But Choate said he could not see why "a big husky Irishwoman should not work more than ten hours if she so desired." Kelley next turned to Boston lawyer Louis D. Brandeis, a corporate lawyer with a growing national reputation as a consumer advocate. Brandeis agreed to cooperate with the Oregon attorney general in defending the state law.

The Brandeis Brief. In *Lochner* the court had found no evidence that baking was a hazardous occupation that the state had an interest in restricting. Brandeis accepted the *Lochner* ruling as the basis for his defense of Oregon. Arguing that a "judge is presumed to know the elements of law, but there is no presumption that he knows the facts," Brandeis set out to prove that the state did have an interest in promoting the health and safety of working women. His brief in *Muller* v. *Oregon* (1908) set out the law and his argument in seventeen pages, then devoted ninety-five pages to evidence that the health and safety of women were at risk if they worked long hours outside the home. His evidence demonstrated that the state did have an interest in protecting the health of women, since women would bear the next generation. Much of the evidence Brandeis presented addressed the issue of women's health, both physical and moral. The manager of a print shop, for example, was quoted as saying, "Girls must sit at the 'case.' . . . Female compositors, as a rule, are sickly, suffering much from back ache, headache, weak limbs, and general 'female weakness.' " Married women had to cook meals and clean house for their husbands, and single girls also had to do their own household chores. Women who worked long hours were believed to be more likely to seek entertainment in saloons than were women whose work schedules did not leave them exhausted after ten hours. All of these arguments relied on a basic assumption that women were different from men and required special protection. In *Lochner* the Court had insisted that bakers did not need the state to protect them. Brandeis argued that women did need protection, but this was an idea the Court would have accepted without discussion. The importance of his brief in *Muller* was that he presented sociological data rather than simply presenting the Court with the law.

Importance of the Brandeis Brief. This was an innovation in the law. Brandeis presented the court with facts and with sociological evidence that demonstrated that the state did have an interest in restricting working hours. The National Consumers' League was so impressed with Brandeis's brief that the league printed it for mass distribution in support of its campaign to limit women's working hours. The Court found it equally convincing and ruled that Oregon could limit women's working hours. The following year Brandeis argued a similar case in

Illinois, which had ruled such a law unconstitutional in 1895. That state's supreme court was convinced by Brandeis's evidence and upheld a state law restricting the workday for women to ten hours.

Sources:

Louis D. Brandeis and Josephine Goldmark, *Women in Industry* (New York: National Consumers' League, 1908);

Alpheus T. Mason, *Brandeis: A Free Man's Life* (New York: Viking, 1946);

Mason, "The Case of the Overworked Laundress," in *Quarrels That Have Shaped the Constitution*, edited by John A. Garraty (New York: Harper & Row, 1975).

HEADLINE MAKERS

CHARLES EVANS HUGHES

1862-1948

LAWYER, REFORMER, CHIEF JUSTICE OF THE SUPREME COURT

New York Lawyer. Charles Evans Hughes was the son of a minister from Glens Falls, New York. After graduating from Brown University he received a law degree from Columbia in 1884, and for the next twenty-two years practiced law in New York City, except for two years (1891–1893) spent as a law professor at Cornell University. Even when he practiced law, though, Hughes also taught, either the law or the Bible. To prepare themselves for the bar exam many young New York City law school graduates attended the evening drill sessions Hughes conducted at Columbia; and at both Cornell and the Fifth Avenue Baptist Church he offered a Sunday class on the Old Testament prophets. (When Hughes's workload overwhelmed him he turned the class over to John D. Rockefeller Jr.) As president of the Baptist Social Union he scandalized some New York City Baptists by inviting Booker T. Washington to speak at a dinner and then seating Washington and his wife at the head table. Aside from small events like this one, Hughes worked successfully behind the scenes, establishing a reputation among lawyers, but not among the general public, for dedication and hard work. When his wife asked why she saw all of his associates, but not Hughes, written about in the newspapers, he responded, "My dear, you must know that I have a positive genius for privacy."

Gas Investigation. This privacy would end in 1905. That spring the state legislature launched an investiga-

tion of the companies delivering natural gas to New York City. The legislature was trying to set fair rates for the companies to charge and needed a lawyer able to master the intricacies of both the gas business and the regulatory process. Though at first Hughes declined, he ultimately accepted the assignment. In June 1905, after a few months of intense investigation, he wrote a report that recommended establishing a public service commission to regulate the gas business. He declined an offer to serve as the commission's chairman, sailing instead for Europe to join his family on their annual holiday.

Insurance Investigation. Back in New York City another investigation was about to begin. The *New York World* was charging that insurance companies like the Equitable Life Assurance Society were speculating with policy funds — "gambling with the people's money" — for their own gain. State regulators, the *World* charged, had not only failed to regulate the industry but in fact had been paid off by the insurance companies. The Republicans in the legislature were sensitive about this, since the regulators were also Republicans. They would have to investigate both the regulators and the insurance companies and needed a counsel who was not connected to the Republican leadership, who could understand the complexities of the insurance industry, and whom the people would trust. In Europe, Hughes received a cable that the legislature needed him. He returned home to serve as counsel to an investigation that would last from September to December 1905. "The time for rumors and the sensational reporting of conjectures had passed," Hughes wrote, "and now evidence must be produced and the actual situation fully ascertained in a responsible manner."

Hughes Examines the Witnesses. Each day the committee held hearings and Hughes questioned the witnesses. Compared by observers to "a teacher finding a mild enthusiasm in leading a child to concede the irrefutable verities of mathematics," Hughes patiently and thoroughly questioned some of the nation's leading business figures. The revelations were shocking, and often as much a shock to Hughes as to the committee and the public. The insurance companies had misused their funds, paid off political allies, lobbied against "undesirable" legislation, and used large sums of money to influence the political process. Hughes, a hardworking man with a deep respect for the law and for public morality, found all these practices deeply disturbing. However, he did not harass the witnesses, but simply asked penetrating questions that exposed a lurid tale. Newspaper readers who had read the sensational allegations of muckrakers in the *World* now had the stories confirmed by the sober Hughes.

Insurance Influence. Hughes exposed a pattern of corruption involving the insurance companies as well as business and political leaders. When he asked financier E. H. Harriman if he did not have undue influence through his connection with Gov. Benjamin Odell, Harriman objected: it was the governor's connection with me, Harriman said, that gave *him* influence. One morning Hughes questioned insurance executive George Perkins about a $48,000 payment given out by New York Life. No one could explain where the money had gone. Over lunch Perkins warned Hughes to think carefully before he prodded him further: the money had gone to Theodore Roosevelt's 1904 election campaign. Hughes would want to consider carefully, Perkins said, if that information should be made public knowledge. "After lunch," Hughes responded, "I'm going to ask you what was done with that $48,000, and I expect a candid answer."

The Republicans and the Investigation. The investigation was most damaging to New York's Republicans. In October the party leaders tried a bold move to get Hughes off the panel and to prevent a seemingly inevitable defeat at the polls. New York City's Republican Party nominated Hughes for mayor. He declined, and the Republicans lost. But the party leaders knew their regular candidates were too tarnished by corruption to win the next year's governor's race and kept Hughes in mind, though President Roosevelt joked that the Republicans had been so damaged by Hughes's investigation that at the next state convention he would receive only two votes: President Roosevelt's and his secretary's. Hughes continued his investigation, denying any desire to seek office, and even declined a nomination for a federal judgeship (he said he could not afford the small salary it paid). At the conclusion of the investigation Hughes drafted a report calling for reforms to prevent the kinds of abuses he had uncovered: insurance companies could not make political contributions; companies had to pay dividends every year; companies had to adopt a standard policy form; and all annual reports had to be made public. In 1906 the New York Republicans nominated Hughes for governor. Hughes was the only Republican to win statewide office in New York, defeating publisher William Randolph Hearst.

Reform Governor. As governor for three years, Hughes initiated several reforms in New York State. Though he now had to work with an often stubborn Democratic legislature, he wielded his executive power against corruption. After investigating corruption in Manhattan and the Bronx, he removed the presidents of those boroughs, and he appointed new personnel to existing state commissions. He successfully campaigned to strengthen the Public Service Commission, giving it broader regulatory powers. The utilities and other businesses subject to regulation opposed this, often arguing that it should be up to the courts, not an unelected commission, to set rates and determine business practices. Hughes disagreed. At one public meeting a lawyer, who had formerly represented many of the utilities, rose to criticize Hughes's reform moves but explained that he spoke as a private citizen and not as the representative of any particular interest. Hughes responded that *he* did represent a particular interest: the public.

Hughes and the Courts. As governor of New York during this campaign to strengthen the state public service commission, Hughes made his most-remembered statement: "We are under a Constitution, but the Constitution is what the judges say it is." This statement is among the most misconstrued in American history. Hughes did not mean that the judges can determine, based on their own understanding, what the Constitution means. Instead, he was debating the broader issue of regulation. "Let us keep the courts for the questions they were intended to consider," he said, and give power to regulate corporations and set utility rates to administrators directly accountable to the public. "I have the highest regard for the courts. . . . I reckon him one of the worst enemies of the community who will talk lightly of the dignity of the bench. We are under a Constitution, but the Constitution is what the judges say it is, and the judiciary is the safeguard of our liberty and of our property under the Constitution. I do not want to see any indirect assaults upon the courts." Hughes did not want to see judges burdened with "questions of administration" that they were not prepared to answer. This is similar to the argument Herbert Croly would make in his influential 1909 book, *The Promise of American Life,* that administrators and experts, above "the realm of partisan and factious political controversy," would come to occupy the position of respect and independent authority "traditionally . . . granted to a common law judge." So Hughes's statement, instead of a glib call for judge-made law, was a defense of judicial independence. This statement acquired great importance in 1910, when Hughes became a justice of the U.S. Supreme Court. Resigning from the Court in 1916 to run for, and nearly win, the presidency, Hughes returned to the Court as chief justice in 1930, serving for twelve years. He died on 27 August 1948.

Sources:

Samuel Hendel, *Charles Evans Hughes and the Supreme Court* (New York: King's Crown, 1951);

Charles Evans Hughes, *The Autobiographical Notes of Charles Evans Hughes,* edited by David J. Danelski and Joseph S. Tulchin (Cambridge, Mass.: Harvard University Press, 1973).

WILLIAM TRAVERS JEROME

1859-1934

DISTRICT ATTORNEY, CIVIC REFORMER

Background. William Travers Jerome, New York's district attorney for much of the decade, was born in New York City. After attending a private preparatory school in Switzerland, he studied at Amherst College for three years before moving on to Columbia Law School, where he received his law degree in 1884. Three years after being admitted to the bar in New York, he was appointed an assistant district attorney. An appointment like this insured a steady income, but it depended on party loyalty: a political appointee had to be absolutely loyal to the party organization that appointed him. In this case, Jerome owed his position to the Democrats, and in return he was expected to be loyal to their organization, known as Tammany Hall. But in 1890 he joined the People's Municipal League, a reform organization, and returned to private practice.

Reformer. Jerome maintained his interest in political affairs. In 1894 he served as an assistant counsel to a legislative committee looking into corruption in city government, and he himself served as counsel to the anti-Tammany Hall Committee of 70. William L. Strong, who ran for mayor in 1894 and defeated the Democratic candidate, rewarded Jerome for his campaign assistance by making him a judge on the court of special sessions, where he served until 1901. In 1901 Jerome ran for district attorney of New York City.

Crusading Candidate. Jerome knew how to manage a campaign. Money from gambling, he knew, came from the poor and subsidized other criminal activities. Gambling and prostitution both flourished under Tammany Hall's control of New York City. Though Tammany and the police force maintained they could not uncover gambling dens, Jerome knew that in fact these vices were protected, if not encouraged, by the political machine. In a daring series of raids, Jerome, using a hatchet to break down doors, invaded gambling dens, accompanied by reporters and his own magistrates. Pulling a Bible from his pocket, he swore in witnesses and held trials on the spot. Jerome raided one popular gambling den next door to Tammany's headquarters, demonstrating that the Democratic machine protected vice. More important, the raids showed Jerome to be a man of action, and he was easily elected.

District Attorney. Jerome proved more than just an able candidate: as district attorney, he considerably improved the office's efficiency, hiring a dynamic staff, speeding up prosecution, and collecting more on forfeited bonds, thus increasing the office's income. To keep his office close to the city's poor, Jerome opened a branch office in the Lower East Side, where poor immigrants could come with their complaints about corrupt police, their worries about daughters forced into prostitution, or other problems. When he realized that witnesses caught in gambling raids would be reluctant to testify against the men who ran the rings if the witnesses later would have their own testimonies used against them, Jerome sponsored a state law giving them immunity. He also sponsored a new, tougher law against gambling, which the legislature passed in 1904. Nicknamed somewhat ironically "New York's Carry Nation" — though Jerome broke up gambling dens with the same moral fervor Carry Nation used on saloons, he was known as a drinker — and "Cigarette Willy," Jerome made for a good story.

Reelection and Loss of Power. In 1905, again demonstrating his independence, Jerome ran for reelection without the support of either political party. He won by an overwhelming margin. Yet in his second term he could not sustain the dynamic popularity or effectiveness of his first. In 1904 he had successfully prosecuted some corrupt labor leaders, yet he did not pursue the contractors who had bribed the union men. In his campaign in 1901 he had pledged to investigate the Metropolitan Street Railway, a huge corporate entity that not only ran the trolleys and streetcar lines but issued stocks and bonds that turned out in 1907 to be virtually worthless. When the Metropolitan went bust, thousands of shareholders lost their life savings. Jerome was attacked for not having investigated this corporation, for being less interested in the crimes of wealth, in the speculators who gambled with stocks and bonds and other people's fortunes, than in the men shaking dice in back rooms. Though an investigation in 1908 cleared Jerome of any impropriety, his political career was ruined. Much of the damage was done by the same newspapers that had helped propel him into the spotlight. He retired at the end of 1909. His distant cousin Winston Churchill thought Jerome might have become president of the United States "had he wished to pay the price." Instead Jerome left public life, having set the pattern of a tough, crusading district attorney, seeking out crime and putting criminals in jail. Investments in the technicolor process of making movies ensured a comfortable retirement. He died on 13 February 1934.

Source:

Richard O'Connor, *Courtroom Warrior: The Combative Career of William Travers Jerome* (Boston: Little, Brown, 1963).

FRANCES (ALICE) KELLOR

1873-1952

LAWYER AND SOCIOLOGIST

Childhood. Alice Kellor was born in Columbus, Ohio. When her father abandoned the family, she moved with her mother to Coldwater, Michigan. Her mother worked as a laundress, and Alice helped her in this. Though she was a good student, she could not afford to stay in high school, so she dropped out to help support the family. The Eddy sisters, two spinsters in town, took an interest in Alice and sent her to adult education classes and finally to Cornell University, where, now calling herself Frances after one of the sisters, she received a law degree in 1897.

Studies of the City. After Cornell, Kellor went to Chicago, combining her scholarly zeal with a keen interest in social problems. With a scholarship from the Chicago Women's Club she studied southern penal systems, especially the treatment of women prisoners and the racial discrepancies in punishment. Her first book, *Experimental Sociology, Descriptive and Analytical: Delinquents* (1902), used the empirical methods of sociology to address a complicated social problem and in this way was a model for later studies, relying on statistics more than on anecdotes or impressions. From Chicago Kellor went to New York City, where she conducted a study of southern black women who had been lured to the city by promises of good jobs at good wages. Kellor detailed the corrupt practices of employment agents who charged these workers for their transportation but then did nothing to secure them the kinds of jobs they had expected to find. Some employment agencies, she found, not only failed to deliver what they had promised but were in fact luring women into prostitution.

Blacks and Immigrants. She expanded her focus, as the problems these women faced in the city were similar to the problems immigrants from other countries faced, arriving in a land that promised work but offered none. Her book *Out of Work* (1904) resulted in stricter laws governing employment agencies. In 1905 she set up the Association for the Protection of Negro Women and the Inter-Municipal Committee on Household Research. In the latter she drafted legislation to combat the kinds of social ills her research uncovered and lobbied the legislature, or Congress, to enact the laws. Frances Kellor's career was dedicated to solving problems through the law, either by changing it or by using it more effectively.

Reform Administration. In 1906 President Roosevelt began calling for Kellor's advice on how the federal government could help solve the problems of immigrants. Her notion that the government, either state or federal, had a positive role in shaping the lives of people found a sympathetic ear in the president. By careful research into living and working conditions experts could plan effective and efficient ways of improving people's lives. Too much had been left to accident or chance; sociological research now allowed shapers of public policy to determine what needed to be done. Kellor was given a chance to do more than study problems when Governor Hughes in 1908 appointed her to the newly established New York State Commission on Immigration. She investigated the slums and tenement housing that were home to the state's immigrants, examining the labor camps and the educational system. This was a continuation of her earlier study of exploited immigrants, but this time she undertook her research on behalf of the state of New York. At the end of this study, the legislature established a permanent Bureau of Industries and Immigration, and Kellor was its first director. She was the first woman to head a state bureau, and under her leadership the state began regulating banks, steamship lines, and lodging houses that catered to immigrants.

Kellor's Legacy. Kellor's belief in a positive role for an enlightened state made her a close ally of Theodore Roosevelt, and in 1912 she campaigned for his election on the Progressive ticket. She became involved in other reform activities, especially in trying to foster cooperation between different ethnic groups. Later in life her work in creating dialogues between people with profoundly different interests led her to become a mediator and to advocate arbitration and mediation as alternatives to legal or even physical confrontations. Her books on arbitration in the 1930s became the standard works in the field, as her sociological studies in the 1900s had been. She died on 4 January 1952.

Sources:

John Higham, *Strangers in the Land: Patterns of American Nativism* (New Brunswick: Rutgers University Press, 1955);

Ruth Rosen, *Lost Sisterhood: Prostitution in America, 1900–1918* (Baltimore: Johns Hopkins University Press, 1982).

BEN B. LINDSEY

1869-1943

JUDGE

Background. Ben B. Lindsey understood what it was like to be a troubled youth. His father, a Confederate veteran, had moved the family to Colorado when Ben was eleven and committed suicide five years later. Ben left school to support his family, working simultaneously as a janitor, a newspaper carrier, and an office boy to a lawyer. Overwork and despair drove Ben to attempt suicide at nineteen, though his failure inspired him to change direction. He began to read law, and though not a high school graduate, at age twenty-five he was admitted to the Colorado bar.

Lindsey's Awakening. In 1899 Lindsey became a public guardian and administrator, a minor position in Colorado's rudimentary public welfare system. Two years later he was appointed a county judge. He later recalled a case from about this time of a young boy caught stealing coal. Under common law, children older than the age of seven could be tried as adults and after age fourteen would be sent to prison if found guilty. Lindsey sentenced this young offender to reform school. The boy's mother became hysterical and had to be removed from the court. Curious, Lindsey put the boy on probation and that evening paid a call on the family. He found the boy and his parents living in a shack, where the father was dying from lead poisoning. The man had become sick working in the mines, but since men who undertook hazardous occupations were presumed to know the risks, there was no employer liability, nor was there compensation for disabled workers. The only person being punished was the boy who had stolen coal to keep his dying father warm.

Lindsey's Campaign. This visit confirmed a suspicion Lindsey, with other progressive reformers, had long entertained: at the root of many crimes was an economic injustice. To prevent crime, judges like Lindsey would have to combat the injustice. Lindsey knew he alone could not rework the social and economic systems, but he could change the nature of his court. For the next twenty-six years Lindsey would preside over the Juvenile and Family Court of Denver, and he became the nation's leading exponent of the juvenile court movement.

Rise of Juvenile Courts. Cook County, Illinois, established the first juvenile court in 1899. Begun by Judge Richard Tuthill, the Cook County court was the model that other courts followed. Tuthill's court also published a magazine, the *Juvenile Court Record,* to bring attention to the idea of juvenile justice. Lindsey, a genius at self-promotion, did even more to promote both the idea of juvenile courts and his own image as the movement's leader. Other states followed the lead of Cook County and Denver, establishing special court systems for children who committed crimes as well as for children deemed "incorrigible" or delinquent. Juvenile court proceedings were not trials: there was no jury, and the court was less concerned with the offense than it was with the offender. By enlisting social workers as well as police officers, proponents of juvenile courts hoped to reform young people before they became criminals. Offenders would be put on probation and under the care of social workers, rather than in jail. Young offenders, Lindsey believed, had to be treated differently from adults. This was a novel idea, but it spread quickly, largely through the agitation of sociologists, social workers, and reformers such as Cook County's Richard Tuthill and Julian

Mack. Lindsey proposed a law to make adults legally responsible for contributing to the delinquency of minors. Colorado's law was the first in the nation, but within two decades thirty-nine states had followed suit.

Lindsey and Other Problems. Lindsey's crusade did not stop with the juvenile courts. He hoped to eliminate most social problems, which he saw based in economic injustice or moral hypocrisy. Lincoln Steffens profiled Lindsey in *McClure's* in 1906, calling him "The Just Judge," and Lindsey became an ally of progressive reformers such as Jane Addams, Jacob Riis, Robert La Follette, and Tom Johnson. Ultimately his campaign on behalf of children and adolescents led him to make radical attacks not only on economic injustice but on the structure of the family. His advocacy of companionate marriages and liberal divorce laws cost him his judgeship in Colorado, though ultimately he would be restored to the good graces of that state's citizens. He died on 26 March 1943.

Sources:

Charles Larsen, *The Good Fight: The Life and Times of Ben B. Lindsey* (Chicago: Quadrangle, 1972);

David J. Rothman, *Conscience and Convenience: The Asylum and its Alternatives in Progressive America* (Boston: Little, Brown, 1980).

ALTON BROOKS PARKER

1852-1926

JUDGE, PRESIDENTIAL CANDIDATE

Candidacy. Alton Parker's nomination for president in 1904 shows how the political process worked. Party nominees were chosen by party leaders. Candidates generally would not seek office by asking voters for support. Instead, a candidate or his political allies would make connections with party bosses in different states to secure their support. In Wisconsin, South Dakota, and Oregon insurgents were trying to break the control of party bosses by having primary elections to nominate candidates for state office; but for president the choice would still be made in party caucuses, which were easily manipulated by the bosses. Among the Democrats there was great fear as the election of 1904 loomed. The party was divided into two wings: its last president, Grover Cleveland, represented the probusiness, conservative party. Its most recent presidential nominee, William Jennings Bryan, who had twice lost the election to William McKinley, was a westerner, allied with the more radical populists of the prairies, the South, and the far West. As the party prepared for the 1904 election, the eastern leaders organized to wrest control from the more radical westerners. Once they resumed their control of the party, all they needed was a candidate. The choice fell on Alton B. Parker, chief justice of New York's Court of Appeals.

Background. Alton Parker, like Charles Evans Hughes, was born in upstate New York. The son of a farmer, Parker could not afford college and so at the age of sixteen began teaching school in his hometown of Cortland. In his spare time he studied law in a local law office before he had enough money to go to the Albany Law School, from which he graduated in 1873. Opening a practice in the Hudson River city of Kingston, he came to public attention for an assessment case he handled on behalf of Ulster County against the city. He was elected to county surrogate in 1877 and reelected in 1883, and both times he was the only Democrat to win a county office. This brought him to the attention of state leaders, who sent him as a delegate to the national convention in 1884. President Cleveland offered Parker the post of assistant postmaster general, which was an important position for distributing patronage. Parker declined, though he did consent to serve as state party chairman. He was a loyal party worker and organizer and was rewarded with an appointment to a vacant seat on the third district of New York's Supreme Court. He moved up in 1889 to the second division of New York's Court of Appeals. Then in 1897, when New York's Democrats were on the verge of complete defeat, he was elected chief justice of the state's Court of Appeals, the highest judgeship in the state. He was the only Democrat to win statewide office in New York that year.

Liberal Judge. Parker was a rare judge for his time. Most American judges were not friends of labor. Parker, however, upheld the right of unions to strike and their right to a closed shop: unions could make union membership a requirement for employment. The prevailing judicial wisdom was that this violated freedom of contract, but Parker upheld the rights of workers to negotiate such contracts. In an 1896 antitrust case Parker ruled that the "reasonableness" of a combination was irrelevant: under common law no person or corporation had the right to restrain trade at all. Perhaps his most famous case was in *People* v. *Lochner,* though it would not have been notable in 1904. He upheld the conviction of Joseph Lochner, owner of a Utica bakery, for requiring his employees to work more than sixty hours in a week. The next year the Supreme Court ruled that New York's law forbidding bakers to work sixty hours was unconstitutional, as it infringed on bakers' liberty of contract. Parker simply upheld the law as a valid exercise of the state's police power, its power to protect the health and safety of its citizens. Like Oliver Wendell Holmes, Parker did not believe judges should dictate what the legislature could do.

Candidate Parker. Parker's judicial record was of little importance to the Democratic leaders who nominated him for president. What mattered was that he had been loyal to the party, that he was from New York, that he had not been involved in any scandals, and that he was not William Jennings Bryan, nor was he the other possible candidate, publisher William Randolph Hearst, who frightened the party's conservative wing even more than did Bryan. The fact that Parker was unknown to most Americans, and probably to many New Yorkers, counted less than the fact that he was acceptable to the Democratic leadership. He conducted his campaign in the traditional way, by staying at home and issuing addresses to visiting delegations. These addresses, then printed in newspapers throughout the country, did impress those who read them with Parker's sincere honesty, but they roused little enthusiasm for the man. This could have been deliberate: the Democrats presented Parker as an alternative to President Roosevelt, and part of his appeal as an alternative may have been his inability to stir public interest. Though Parker had a solid record as a liberal judge, the Democrats presented him as a conservative friend of business, unlike the increasingly progressive Roosevelt. Toward the end of the campaign Parker ventured out onto a campaign trip, in which he discarded the role the party tried to write for him. Parker charged that the large corporations, far from being against Roosevelt, were in fact contributing large amounts to his campaign. After the election, Parker charged, Roosevelt would deliver favors to these trusts and special interests. When the Republicans demanded proof of Parker's charges, he could produce none. Roosevelt was elected with a higher percentage of the popular vote (56.4 percent) than any president up to that point in history, and with Parker the Democrats received the lowest percentage of votes in their history (37.6 percent).

After the Election. After the election, it turned out that Parker had been right. The insurance investigation conducted by Charles Evans Hughes showed large corporate contributions to Roosevelt. Parker's defeat weakened the Democratic leaders who had pushed his nomination, and in 1908 William Jennings Bryan was once again the nominee. After Bryan's loss, the party sought out a progressive leader who could unite both factions of the party and found him in New Jersey governor Woodrow Wilson. Alton Parker went back to the practice of law. In 1907 he represented American Federation of Labor president Samuel Gompers in the contempt case brought against him for the Buck's Stove and Range Company strike, and in 1915 he represented the Danbury hatters before a U.S. congressional investigation. In 1912 he was temporary chair of the Democratic National Convention, where he opposed Woodrow Wilson's nomination. He died on 10 May 1926.

Source:
Irving Stone, *They Also Ran: The Story of the Men Who Were Defeated for the Presidency* (Garden City, N.Y.: Doubleday, 1949).

ROSCOE POUND

1870-1964

LAW PROFESSOR

Youthful Brilliance. Roscoe Pound, who would become one of the twentieth century's most influential legal thinkers, was something of a child prodigy. He was already reading when he was three, and his mother taught him German when he was six. His first real passion was botany, and when he turned fourteen he entered the University of Nebraska in his hometown of Lincoln. After graduating with a degree in botany he studied law with his father, a local lawyer, and then spent a year at Harvard Law School. Convinced the law was not for him, he was willing and able to both practice and teach law while he pursued a doctorate in botany. He returned to Lincoln where he wrote his dissertation, "Phytogeography of Nebraska" (1898), while practicing law, serving as an assistant professor in the College of Law and teaching Roman law in the Latin department. In 1903 he became dean of the College of Law. Two years later he abandoned academia temporarily, and botany permanently, to become a practicing lawyer.

Pound and Sociological Jurisprudence. Trained in both science and the law, Pound approached the two disciplines as similar. Law schools and academic training for lawyers were replacing the traditional routes to the profession, and academic lawyers saw themselves as social scientists. At the 1906 meeting of the American Bar Association Pound gave an influential address, "The Causes of Popular Dissatisfaction with the Administration of Justice." He attacked contemporary trial procedures — which emphasized lawyers as adversaries contesting over the truth — for creating a "sporting theory of justice," and he argued that many disputes would be better settled by administrative boards than by courts. Judges were not trained to be sociologists, were not in touch with new economic or social conditions, yet continued to treat complicated economic relationships, such as the relationship between a railroad and its employees, as though both parties "were farmers haggling over the sale of a horse." Judges and courts needed to recognize changes in society and needed to understand sociology and economics as well as the law.

Pound and Mechanical Jurisprudence. Pound attacked what he called "Mechanical Jurisprudence," brought on because judges, trained in the common law, were unwilling to uphold statutes that went beyond what the common law envisioned. Liberty, the judges insisted, included the liberty to make contracts, and any legislative attempt to restrict this liberty (such as a sixty-hour week for bakery workers or requiring workers to join unions)

violated a common law doctrine. Courts were also restricted by the sharp line between law and fact: juries could determine facts, but it was up to the judge to apply the law. The line between law and fact, Pound argued, was increasingly artificial, as common law notions that once had clear meanings, such as combinations in restraint of trade, were becoming more complicated and confusing.

Pound and Administrative Law. Pound, like other progressive reformers, proposed administrative boards and other nonjudicial ways of regulating economic affairs. When the state attempted to regulate working hours or other conditions and the court struck down the regulations because they violated "liberty of contract," the end result would not be as damaging for labor or business as it would be for the courts. The legislatures would "learn how to comply with the letter of the decisions and to evade the spirit of them," and the "evil of those cases will live after them in impaired authority of the courts long after the decisions themselves are forgotten."

Pound and Changes in the Law. The substantive doctrines of the common law, Pound emphasized, had changed by the twentieth century. Judges, trained in Blackstone, were not qualified to pass judgment on technological problems. In two law review articles, "Mechanical Jurisprudence" and "Liberty of Contract," Pound made the intellectual case for the kind of fact-based law Louis Brandeis had helped to shape in the *Muller* case. In the absence of the kind of sweeping changes Pound and other reformers proposed, an attention to fact and to social conditions could help judges more effectively mete out justice.

Pound's Later Career. Pound as a legal philosopher outshone Pound the lawyer; and Pound the law professor outshone both. After a few years in legal practice he became a professor of law at Northwestern University, then at the University of Chicago, and in 1910 at Harvard, where he would spend the rest of his career as both a teacher (in 1910 he became the Joseph Story Professor of Law) and as dean of the law school (1916–1936). He became more conservative in his later years, and he wrote his most influential essays before he was forty. But his work in the first decade of the century so changed the legal profession, and so influenced the study and practice of the law, it is inconceivable anything else could have matched their importance. He advised the Nationalist Chinese regime of Chiang Kai-shek and became Harvard's first University Professor in 1937. By the time Pound arrived at Harvard, the leaders of the profession were coming to accept his ideas, and young lawyers and philosophers of the law were prepared to take his ideas far beyond his own application of them. He died on 1 July 1964 at the age of ninety-four.

Source:
Morton J. Horwitz, *The Transformation of American Law, 1870–1960: The Crisis of Legal Orthodoxy* (Cambridge, Mass.: Harvard University Press, 1992).

WILLIAM MONROE TROTTER

1872-1934

THE GUARDIAN OF BOSTON

Background. William Monroe Trotter's father, James Monroe Trotter, was an imposing man. A musician and soldier, he had succeeded Frederick Douglass as recorder of deeds in the District of Columbia and so had been one of the highest-ranking black officials in nineteenth-century America. William Monroe Trotter, who usually went by his middle name, was born on a farm in Ohio but grew up in Hyde Park, Massachusetts, a suburb of Boston. The only black in his high school class, he was elected class president. He entered Harvard in 1891. After college he worked negotiating real estate mortgages and seemed destined to become one of Boston's most successful businessmen.

Call to Action. But in 1901 Trotter launched a newspaper devoted to the cause of civil rights for blacks. He was moved to start his paper by the rising tide of racial hatred in the country. He blamed Booker T. Washington for this worsening racial climate, and through his paper, *The Guardian*, Trotter blasted Washington and the Washington program. Trotter regarded Washington as a hypocrite who urged other Negroes not to push for social equality, while he himself was having dinner at the White House, and not to demand their right to vote, while he himself not only voted but was consulted by the president. While white Americans applauded Booker T. Washington as the representative Negro, black people throughout the country were being murdered for trying to vote. Washington, Trotter declared, was building a monument for himself at Tuskegee and declaring that black men and women had no need for higher education or for any education beyond manual labor. Trotter, a Harvard graduate and the son of a successful public official, disdained this kind of philosophy. Trotter's *Guardian*, bitterly critical of Washington, became popular among northern, more-educated blacks and other urban reformers.

The Riot. In July 1903 Booker T. Washington visited Boston, where he was scheduled to address a public meeting at a Boston church. This would be a rare event for Washington: he was to speak to a black audience in a black church in the North. Washington usually addressed white audiences on trips to the North, as he generally made his trips to raise money for Tuskegee. William H. Lewis, a black lawyer in Boston, presided at the meeting (Lewis later would be appointed assistant attorney general by President Taft). Trotter attended the meeting to ask Washington about voting rights. At the meeting friends and foes of Washington got into a shouting match, which turned into a fracas, at the end of which Trotter was in jail for disturbing the peace. His coeditor, George Washington Forbes, a Mississippi-born graduate of Amherst, left the paper when Washington filed a libel suit against him, and Trotter found himself isolated. During his month in jail Trotter read W. E. B. Du Bois's *Souls of Black Folk* and found himself closely allied with Du Bois's philosophy. "Read the book," he told his friends.

Personality Clashes. Trotter emerged from jail with a renewed respect for Du Bois. Du Bois saw in the riot and Trotter's jail sentence an ominous sign. He disagreed with Washington's whole philosophy, and while he did not always agree with Trotter, he saw that Washington had too much power as a white-anointed "leader of his race." As a result of this Du Bois put out a call for black leaders other than Washington and his forces to form an organization that would specifically push for political equality. This became the Niagara Movement, which Trotter and Ida B. Wells-Barnett helped to launch. Trotter and Du Bois became allies, but the two had such strong personalities a close working relationship was impossible. Trotter distrusted the white liberals involved with the National Association for the Advancement of Colored People (NAACP), instead creating his own National Equal Rights League. But Trotter's skills as a journalist, his independence, and his ferocious tenacity were not the skills required to build an organization. One ally said, "It is impossible for a man with ideas and opinions of his own, for a man with personality and individuality, to get along with Trotter." Trotter supported liberal Republican Joseph Foraker for president in 1908, and in 1912 he and Du Bois both supported Woodrow Wilson. At a White House meeting with other black leaders Trotter and Wilson began shouting at one another, resulting in the whole group being ejected from the office. On his own initiative Trotter sailed for the Versailles conference in 1919 to have a racial equity clause written into the treaty: Wilson was promoting self-determination for European ethnic groups, and Trotter believed the same right should be extended to Africans. He died on 7 April 1934.

Sources:

W. E. B. Du Bois, *The Autobiography of W. E. B. Du Bois* (New York: International Publishers, 1968);

Stephen R. Fox, *The Guardian of Boston: William Monroe Trotter* (New York: Atheneum, 1970).

PEOPLE IN THE NEWS

In 1906 **Harvey Humphrey Baker,** a special justice on the Brookline, Massachusetts, Police Court, was appointed Boston's first juvenile court judge. Eager to resolve the problems of youth through the juvenile court system, Baker also advocated clinics where social workers and others could try to resolve the more "baffling cases" of troubled youth.

In 1903 **Simeon E. Baldwin,** a Connecticut lawyer and a founder of the American Bar Association, attended an international congress on prisons in Budapest. The following year he was vice president of the Universal Congress of Lawyers and Jurists in Saint Louis, and in 1905 he was president of both the Association of American Law Schools and the American Historical Association.

In 1908 **Kate Barnard,** Oklahoma's commissioner of prisons, investigated prisons in Kansas, where some Oklahoma prisoners were being held. Shocking revelations of conditions in Kansas penitentiaries led to revelations from other states about their treatment of prisoners.

In May 1906, anarchist **Alexander Berkman** was released after fourteen years in prison for a botched attempt to assassinate industrialist **Henry Clay Frick.**

In 1908 **Godfrey Lowell Cabot** became a member of the board of the Boston Watch and Ward Society, and led the society to prosecute purveyors of books it deemed offensive. Cabot immediately launched a campaign against the novel *Three Weeks* by **Elinor Glyn.** Cabot led the society for the next thirty years.

On 9 November 1908 **Edward Ward Carmack,** advocate of Prohibition and a former congressman and senator from Tennessee, was murdered on the street in Nashville by **Duncan B. Cooper** and **Robin Cooper,** political supporters of Gov. **M. R. Patterson.** Carmack had run against Patterson for governor, and when he was murdered Carmack was campaigning against both Patterson and the liquor interests. The Coopers were each sentenced to twenty years in prison, but Governor Patterson pardoned Duncan Cooper; Robin Cooper's conviction was reversed, and the state did not prosecute him again. However, the legislature passed Prohibition over Governor Patterson's veto in 1909.

In 1905 **Charles Waddell Chesnutt** returned to his Cleveland law practice after taking five years off to write novels, *The House Behind the Cedars* (1900), *The Marrow of Tradition* (1901), and *The Colonel's Dream* (1905), on the themes of race, the law, and history in America.

In April 1905 former president **Grover Cleveland** wrote in the *Ladies' Home Journal* that "sensible and responsible women" will not want to vote. "The relative positions to be assumed by man and woman in the working out of our civilization were assigned long ago by a higher intelligence than ours."

In September 1901 Russian-born anarchist **Emma Goldman** was arrested after **Leon Czolgosz,** assassin of President **William McKinley,** suggested that her lectures and ideology had influenced his attack on the president. She was released after a few weeks.

In October 1902 U.S. Circuit Judge **George Gray,** former senator from Delaware and a member of the Permanent Court of Arbitration at The Hague, was named by President **Theodore Roosevelt** to be chairman of the commission to arbitrate the coal strike. Gray's successful settlement led to his appointment to resolve other labor disputes.

In May 1901 Albany lawyer **Billings Learned Hand** investigated a riot that broke out during a strike against a streetcar company. In April 1909 Hand was appointed to the U.S. District Court for Southern New York.

In February 1907 **Oliver Wendell Holmes Jr.** ruled in *Georgia* v. *Tennessee Copper Co.* that the state has an interest "in all the earth and air within its domain. . . . It is a fair and reasonable demand on the part of sovereign that the air over its territory should not be polluted on a great scale by sulphurous acid gas, that the forests on its mountains . . . should not be further destroyed or threatened by the act of persons beyond its control, that the crops and orchards on its hills should not be endangered from the same source."

In 1900 **Timothy Hurley,** administrator of the Cook County, Illinois, juvenile court, began publishing the *Juvenile Court Record,* a journal advocating juvenile courts and publicizing their success.

In 1906 **O. Edward Janney,** a Baltimore doctor and Quaker leader, gave up his medical practice to organize the National Vigilance Committee for the Suppression of White Slavery. Janney was also active in the Baltimore Society for the Suppression of Vice.

In 1909 **Mary Harris "Mother" Jones,** a union organizer for the United Mine Workers in 1900 and 1902, who had led a 1903 miners' strike in Colorado, persuaded President **William Howard Taft** to investigate the case of Mexican revolutionaries imprisoned in the United States.

In 1907 federal district judge **Kenesaw Mountain Landis** fined Standard Oil of Indiana $29 million in an antitrust suit, a judgment later overturned by the U.S. Supreme Court. Landis, with a "piercing eye, a scowl, and a rasping voice," had been appointed a judge by President **Theodore Roosevelt;** during World War I he sentenced **Bill Haywood** of the Industrial Workers of the World (IWW) to twenty years in prison. In 1921 he became the first commissioner of Major League Baseball.

In 1907 Nashville lawyer **Luke Lea** began publishing the *Nashville Tennessean* to advocate Prohibition. Lea became active in politics, successfully brought Prohibition to Tennessee, and was elected to the U.S. Senate in 1911.

In 1903 President Roosevelt appointed **William Henry Lewis** to be assistant U.S. attorney for Massachusetts. Lewis, born in Virginia, had practiced law in Boston since his graduation from Harvard Law School in 1895. After four years he became the assistant U.S. attorney for all of New England, and in 1911 he became the assistant attorney general of the United States, the first black to hold a subcabinet position.

In 1905 **Julian Mack** resigned after two years on the Cook County juvenile court to become a state appeals court justice. Mack, a lawyer, community activist, and Zionist leader, remained involved with the problems of young offenders, and in 1909 he would attend the White House Conference on Children. This conference led to the establishment of a federal Children's Bureau.

In 1903, outraged by lynching, mob violence, and legal means used to take away civil and constitutional rights of African Americans, wealthy New Yorker **John Milholland** formed the Constitution League.

In January 1901 the Supreme Court ruled that **C. F. W. Neely,** a postal official in the U.S. military government of Cuba, could be extradited back to Cuba to stand trial for corruption. Despite Cuba's occupation by the United States, Justice **John Marshall Harlan** wrote, Cuba continued to be a foreign country, and it would be returned to its inhabitants when they had established a stable government.

In 1906 **Thomas Osborne,** mayor of Auburn, New York, told the National Penal Association that a prison must be an institution where every inmate must have the largest practical amount of individual freedom, because "it is liberty alone that fits men for liberty." Osborne continued to advocate prison reform and in 1913 became head chair of the state commission on prison reform, beginning his term by serving one week in the Auburn penitentiary.

On 23 September 1900 millionaire **William M. Rice,** eighty-four-year-old founder of Rice University in Texas, was murdered by his valet, **Charles F. Jones,** in his Madison Avenue, New York City apartment. Jones murdered Rice under instructions from lawyer **Albert T. Patrick,** who had forged a will for Rice naming himself beneficiary. New York district attorney **William T. Jerome** prosecuted Patrick for first-degree murder; Jones was freed for giving evidence against his accomplice. Patrick was convicted in April 1902 and sentenced to the electric chair; one governor commuted Patrick's sentence, and in 1912 another pardoned him. Freed after ten years, Patrick went west to resume the practice of law.

In 1909 **Clifford G. Roe,** a Chicago assistant district attorney and crusader against prostitution, was appointed a special prosecutor to investigate the "white slave trade." Roe's investigation into the recruitment of women into prostitution led to the first American law against "white slavery" and ultimately to the Mann Act of 1910, which prohibited transporting women across state lines for purposes of prostitution.

In 1906 President Roosevelt appointed Chicago lawyer **Edward W. Sims** to be U.S. attorney for Chicago. Sims, who had been a lawyer in the Commerce and Labor Department and had investigated the Alaska seal fisheries for the administration, successfully prosecuted the Standard Oil Company during his term as U.S. attorney.

In 1907 **Warren Spaulding,** a Massachusetts reformer and advocate of probation as an alternative to prison, told the state Conference on Charities that the system of justice must approach each defendant as an individual. It was imperative, he said, to diagnose each case to determine what led the accused to his conduct. The first step in treating illness was to diagnose the ailment; diagnosis must also be the first step "in the treatment of badness."

In 1906 New York lawyer **Henry L. Stimson** was appointed by President **Theodore Roosevelt** as U.S. attorney for the southern judicial district of New York. Stimson reorganized the office, bringing in a talented staff, including **Thomas D. Thacher** and future Supreme Court justice **Felix Frankfurter.** He successfully prosecuted the paper trust and other violators of the antitrust acts. Stimson later served as secretary of state under President **Herbert Hoover** (1929–1933) and secretary of war under President **Franklin Roosevelt** (1940–1945).

On 15 May 1900, Judge **William Howard Taft** of the U.S. circuit court resigned to become a member of the Philippine Commission. In July 1901 be became civil governor of the Philippines. His major problems were putting down the Aguinaldo insurrection and settling the issue of church lands (he conferred with **Pope Leo XII** to reach a settlement in 1902). He became U.S. secretary of war in February 1904, and smoothed over American relations with Cuba in 1906. In 1908, though his one ambition was to be on the U.S. Supreme Court, he was elected president. He supported an amendment to allow Congress to levy an income tax and increased litigation against trusts violating the Sherman Act.

In December 1904 **Richard Tuthill,** the first judge of the Cook County Juvenile Court, opened the Illinois State School at Saint Charles. The old John Worthy School was more a prison than a school, and its location in a complex with the city's poorhouse and workhouse, surrounded by bars, gangs, and thugs, did little to encourage its inmates to reform. Tuthill pushed for a new school in the open country, where boys could learn agriculture and other vocational arts, free of the temptations of the city.

In 1902 Oregon adopted the initiative petition and popular referendum for making laws and amending the state constitution. **William U'Ren,** a blacksmith who had studied law and had begun publishing a newspaper, promoted the idea of direct democracy that citizens of South Dakota had adopted in 1898 and U'Ren in 1900 had read about in accounts of Switzerland's direct democracy. In 1904 U'Ren led a successful campaign for Oregon to adopt the primary election, instead of a party caucus, to choose candidates for office.

DEATHS

William Boyd Allison, 81, senator from Iowa instrumental in establishing the Interstate Commerce Commission in 1887, 4 August 1908.

John Peter Altgeld, 55, former governor of Illinois who wrote *Our Penal Machinery and its Victims* (1884), pardoned the three surviving men convicted in the 1886 Haymarket bombing, and protested President Cleveland's use of federal troops against Pullman strikers (1894), 12 March 1902.

Susan B. Anthony, 86, leader of the woman suffrage movement who was arrested in 1872 for voting in Rochester, New York, convicted, and refused to pay a $100 fine; she argued that laws were meaningless if they contradicted what was right, 13 March 1906.

Robert Charles O'Hara Benjamin, 45, West Indian–born lawyer and teacher who practiced law throughout the United States and fought for legal and political rights for blacks; he was murdered for registering black voters, October 1900.

James Coolidge Carter, 77, one of New York's leading lawyers; he vigorously opposed an attempt to codify New York laws in 1880s because he believed that law emerged from society and custom, not from the legislature, 14 February 1905.

James Clagett, about 70, lawyer who practiced throughout the West; he was a delegate from Montana to Congress, served in Nevada's territorial legislature, and presided at Idaho's constitutional convention, 1901.

Grover Cleveland, 71, former district attorney of Erie County, mayor of Buffalo, governor of New York (1882–1884), and president of the United States (1885–1889, 1893–1897); as president he used federal troops to put down the 1894 Pullman strike; he advised President Roosevelt on the 1902 coal miners' strike; he was appointed a trustee of Equitable Assurance Company after the 1905 scandal, 24 June 1908.

Charles Francis Donnelly, 71, Irish-born Boston lawyer, counsel to the Catholic Church in Massachusetts; he chaired the state Board of Health, Lunacy, and Charity and proposed giving alcoholics the same treatment as the mentally ill, 31 January 1909.

Ignatius Donnelly, 69, land speculator and Populist leader in Minnesota; he wrote books on the world of the future, including *Caesar's Column: A Story of the Twentieth Century* (1891), and was Populist candidate for vice president in 1900, 1 January 1901.

William Maxwell Evarts, 83, the "Prince of the American bar"; he successfully defended both President Andrew Johnson in his 1868 impeachment trial and Rev. Henry Ward Beecher in his 1874–1875 adultery trial; he also served as U.S. secretary of state and senator from New York, 28 February 1901.

John Brown Gordon, 71, Georgia lawyer, senator, and railroad developer who was active in restoring "home rule" after Reconstruction, 9 January 1904.

Laura De Force Gordon, 78, one of California's first two women lawyers (1879) and one of the first women admitted to practice before the U.S. Supreme Court (1887); she was a newspaper publisher before successfully suing for admission to law school, 6 April 1907.

Horace Gray, 74, U.S. Supreme Court justice, 15 September 1902.

Andrew Haswell Green, 83, New York lawyer and commissioner of Central Park who revised state tax laws in 1881 and in 1897 drafted a report to consolidate Queens, Kings, Richmond, and New York Counties into New York City; he was murdered on his doorstep by an insane man who mistook him for someone else, 13 November 1903.

Galusha Aaron Grow, 84, Speaker of the U.S. House (1861–1863) and Homestead Act sponsor, 31 March 1907.

John A. Halderman, 75, Kansas lawyer and politician who as American consul to Siam introduced postal and telegraph systems and suppressed liquor traffic, 21 September 1905.

George Harding, 75, patent lawyer whose first patent case involved Samuel F. B. Morse's telegraph; he used models to demonstrate workings of telephones, reapers, and blast furnaces, 17 November 1902.

John Innes Clark Hardy, 89, Philadelphia judge and professor of law who established law of equity in Pennsylvania and wrote many books on law, 29 December 1905.

Nathaniel Harrison Harris, 66, San Francisco lawyer who had also practiced in Mississippi and South Dakota, 23 August 1900.

Benjamin Harrison, 67, Indiana lawyer and politician; after a term as president (1889–1893) he wrote books on the U.S. Constitution and championed the rights of people in the Philippines and Puerto Rico, 13 March 1901.

Henry Baldwin Harrison, 80, Connecticut lawyer and politician who in 1854 proposed a state personal liberty bill to nullify the federal Fugitive Slave Act, after the Civil War championed the rights of blacks to vote, and chaired the state legislature's committee on railroads, 29 October 1901.

Samuel Dexter Hastings, 86, Massachusetts lawyer, abolitionist, and advocate of prohibiting liquor and tobacco, 26 March 1903.

David Bremner Henderson, 65, New York lawyer and Speaker of the U.S. House of Representatives (1899–1903), 25 February 1906.

William Wirt Henry, 69, grandson of Patrick Henry; he practiced law and wrote history in Richmond, Virginia, 5 December 1900.

Robert Andrews Hill, 89, U.S. district judge in Mississippi (1868–1891) who urged the state to rescind laws in conflict with federal laws, such as those barring blacks from voting, 2 July 1900.

Walter Barnard Hill, 54, one of Georgia's leading lawyers who at age twenty-one had helped revise Georgia's legal code, 28 December 1905.

Henry Hitchcock, 72, first dean of Saint Louis Law School, president of the American Bar Association (1889–1890), 18 March 1902.

George Hoadly, 76, professor at Cincinnati Law School (1864–1887) and governor of Ohio (1883–1885) before becoming a New York corporate lawyer, 26 August 1902.

George Frisbie Hoar, 78, senator from Massachusetts and chairman of the judiciary committee, 30 September 1904.

James Stephen Hogg, 54, Texas lawyer and former governor; as state attorney in the 1880s he had acted against insurance and railroad companies, 3 March 1906.

George Frederick William Holls, 46, New York lawyer specializing in international law; he attended New York's 1894 constitutional convention and the 1899 Hague peace conference, 23 July 1903.

Isabella Beecher Hooker, 84, founder of the Connecticut Women's Suffrage Association in 1870; she presented a bill, which passed in 1877, to the state legislature

making husbands and wives equal in property rights, 25 January 1907.

William F. Howe, 74, lawyer nicknamed "Habeas Corpus Howe" because he specialized in homicide cases and used theatrics and legal skill to win acquittals in the face of imposing evidence; he helped revise New York's penal code in 1882, 1 September 1902.

William Wirt Howe, 75, lawyer, writer, justice of the Louisiana Supreme Court, and U.S. attorney for eastern Louisiana, 17 March 1909.

Richard Bennett Hubbard, 68, lawyer nicknamed the "Demosthenes of Texas"; he served as U.S. attorney for west Texas and American minister to Japan in the 1880s, 12 July 1901.

Robert William Hughes, 80, Virginia newspaper editor and federal judge who edited U.S. circuit court *Reports,* 10 December 1901.

Edward Christopher James, 59, New York lawyer, 24 March 1901.

Lucy Bagby Johnson, 72, woman thought to be the last slave to be returned to the South under the Fugitive Slave Law, her January 1861 trial enraged Cleveland; she returned to the city after the war, 1906.

Henry Demarest Lloyd, 56, lawyer, writer, and reformer who helped Clarence Darrow present the miners' case during the 1902 coal strike, 28 September 1903.

Josephine Shaw Lowell, 61, founder of the Consumers' League; her report on the poor law in Westchester County, New York, led to her 1876 appointment to the state Board of Charities, from which she resigned to spend more time attacking the problems of industrial workers; she wrote *Public Relief and Private Charity* (1884) and *Industrial Arbitration and Conciliation* (1893), 12 October 1905.

Louis Emory McComas, 61, justice of the District of Columbia Supreme Court (1892–1899), lecturer on law at Georgetown, and drafter of an organic law for the Philippines and Puerto Rico, 10 November 1907.

Johann Most, 50, anarchist expelled from his native Austria who spent two years in prison in America in the 1880s for inciting violence and one year in Blackwell's Island penitentiary after President William McKinley's assassination, 17 March 1906.

Rufus W. Peckham, 70, associate justice of the U.S. Supreme Court since 1896; as a district attorney in Albany, New York, he had prosecuted train robbers, 24 October 1909.

Wheeler Peckham, 72, brother of Justice Rufus Peckham and founder and president (1892–1894) of the Bar Association of New York; his own appointment to the Supreme Court in 1894 was blocked by New York senators, 27 September 1905.

Orville Hitchcock Platt, 77, Connecticut patent, real estate, and corporate lawyer who offered an amendment to the Cuban constitution, which restricted Cuba's ability to form alliances, and chaired the U.S. Senate patent committee and judiciary committees, 21 April 1905.

John Henniger Reagan, 86, Texas lawyer and judge before the Civil War, and the Confederacy's postmaster; he helped write state constitutions of 1866 and 1875 and headed the state railroad commission (1891–1903), 6 March 1905.

John Sherman, 77, Ohio lawyer and politician who dominated American politics after the Civil War; to garner support for the 1890 antitrust law, sponsors attached his name to it, 22 October 1900.

Thomas Jefferson Simmons, 68, chief justice of the Georgia Supreme Court, 12 September 1905.

Charles Henry Simonton, 74, federal district and circuit court judge in South Carolina who lectured on federal courts in 1896, 25 April 1904.

Elizabeth Cady Stanton, 86, writer and sponsor of the 1848 Seneca Falls Convention for women's political rights; she worked to pass New York's married women's property act in 1848, 26 October 1902.

Albion Winegar Tourgee, 77, judge in North Carolina during Reconstruction who in the *Plessy v. Ferguson* case (1896) argued that segregation of races violated the Fourteenth Amendment, 21 May 1905.

John Louis Waller, 57, former slave born in Missouri; as American consul at Tamatave, Madagascar, he was arrested in the 1895 French invasion of that island, charged with passing secrets to the Malagasy resistance, but released after pressure from the U.S. government, 13 October 1907.

Stephen Mallory White, 48, California lawyer and politician who fought corruption and corporations, 21 February 1901.

Marshall Jay Williams, 65, chief justice of the Ohio Supreme Court and first dean of Ohio State University College of Law, 7 July 1902.

William Lyne Wilson, 57, classical scholar from West Virginia who as congressman supported income tax and opposed trusts and monopolies, 17 October 1900.

PUBLICATIONS

Simeon Baldwin, *The American Judiciary* (New York: Century, 1905);

John W. Burgess, *The Civil War and the Constitution* (New York: Scribners, 1901);

Burgess, *Reconstruction and the Constitution 1866–1876* (New York: Scribners, 1902);

Benjamin Cardozo, *Jurisdiction of the Court of Appeals of the State of New York* (Albany, N.Y.: Banks, 1903);

Herbert Croly, *The Promise of American Life* (New York: Macmillan, 1909);

George B. Davis, *The Elements of International Law* (New York: Harper, 1900);

Davis, *The Elements of Law: An Introduction to the Study of the Constitutional and Military Law of the United States* (New York: Wiley, 1904);

Ernst Freund, *Constitutional Aspects of the Ten Hour Law* (Springfield: Illinois State Journal, 1909);

Freund, *Empire and Sovereignty* (Chicago: University of Chicago Press, 1903);

Freund, *Labor Legislation in the 46th General Assembly of Illinois* (Springfield: Illinois Department of Labor, 1909);

Freund, *The Police Power* (Chicago: Callaghan, 1904);

Leonard F. Fuld, *Police Administration: A Critical Study of Police Organizations in the United States and Abroad* (New York: Putnam, 1909);

John Chipman Gray, *The Nature and Sources of the Law* (New York: Columbia University Press, 1909);

Hutchins Hapgood, ed., *The Autobiography of a Thief* (New York: Fox, Duffield, 1906);

George Frederick William Holls, *The Peace Conference at The Hague and its Bearings on International Law and Policy* (New York: Macmillan, 1900);

William Draper Lewis, ed., *Great American Lawyers*, 8 volumes (Philadelphia: Winston, 1907–1909);

Edward A. Ross, *Sin and Society: An Analysis of Latter-Day Iniquity, With a Letter from President Roosevelt* (Boston: Houghton Mifflin, 1907);

David Y. Thomas, *A History of Military Government in New Acquired Territory of the United States* (New York: Columbia University Press, 1904);

Arthur Train, *The Prisoner at the Bar: Sidelights on the Administration of Criminal Justice* (New York: Scribners, 1906);

Thomas Travis, *The Young Malefactor: A Study in Juvenile Delinquency, Its Causes and Treatment*, introduction by Ben B. Lindsey (New York: Crowell, 1908);

Two Centuries Growth of American Law, 1701–1901 (New York: Scribners, 1901);

Charles Warren, *History of the Harvard Law School and of Early Legal Conditions in America*, 3 volumes (New York: Lewis, 1908);

John H. Wigmore, *A Treatise on the System of Evidence in Trials at Common Law, Including the Statutes and Judicial Decisions of all Jurisdictions of the United States*, 4 volumes (Boston: Little, Brown, 1904–1905);

Delos Wilcox, *The American City: A Problem in Democracy* (New York: Macmillan, 1904);

William F. Willoughby, *State Activities in Relation to Labor in the United States* (Baltimore: Johns Hopkins University Press, 1901);

Willoughby, *Territories and Dependencies of the United States: Their Government and Administration* (New York: Century, 1905);

Woodrow Wilson, *Constitutional Government* (New York: Columbia University Press, 1908);

Frederick H. Wines, *The New Criminology: An Essay Read Before the Social Science Section of the International Congress of Arts and Sciences, at St. Louis, Sept. 23, 1904* (New York: Kempster, 1904).

LIFESTYLES AND SOCIAL TRENDS

by ALANA J. ERICKSON, DAVID MCLEAN, and JAMES G. LEWIS

CONTENTS

Sidebars and tables are listed in italics.

1900

- The census reports a population of 75,994,575.

- The divorce rate reaches one in twelve marriages.

- Illiteracy in the United States is reduced to a new low of 10.7 percent of the population.

- Excavation begins on the New York City subway system, which will become the most extensive system in the United States.

- Cocaine, a small but vital ingredient of Coca-Cola (to which the soft drink owes its name), is removed from the formula. Coca-Cola continues to advertise itself as a stimulant, although caffeine is now the agent of wakefulness.

- The tobacco industry produces four billion cigarettes, which remain less popular than cigars, pipes, and chewing tobacco.

- Eight thousand passenger automobiles are registered in the United States. Of these, half are of European manufacture.

- The International Ladies Garments Workers Union is founded in New York City. Its membership is composed primarily of Jewish and Italian immigrants. Reformer Jacob Riis reports that women laboring in their homes for the garment industry make at most thirty cents a day.

- The number of telephones in use reaches 1,335,911.

Mar. The Good Roads Campaign begins, in an effort to macadamize the dirt roads that prevail in rural areas and make them safe for automobiles. There are approximately ten miles of paved roads in the United States at the beginning of the decade.

5 Mar. Symphony Hall in Boston opens to the public. Designed by the architectural firm of McKim, Mead, and White, the building costs $750,000.

15 Apr. One of the earliest automobile road races in America is run at Springfield, N.Y., on Long Island. The fifty-mile race is won by A. L. Riker, driving an electric car, in a time of two hours, three minutes.

June Carry Nation throws rocks at saloons in Kiowa, Kansas, thus marking the start of her militant and well-publicized campaign against liquor.

16 Oct. The Automobile Club of America gathers for the first time. On 3–10 November it holds the first auto show in the United States, in Madison Square Garden.

1901

- The Socialist Party of America is formed. The socialist movement draws significant suppport from the growing immigrant population.

- The National Bureau of Standards is established to make weights and measures of consumer products more consistent.

- Jessie Field founds the predecessors of the 4-H Club, the Boys Corn Club and Girls Home Club, in Shenandoah, Iowa.

- Booker T. Washington founds the National Negro Business League, dedicated to creating a prosperous, autonomous black economic sector.

- Albert Paine's play *The Great White Way* is published, giving the new Times Square theater district its nickname.

- King Camp Gillette begins manufacturing the modern safety razor.

1902

Mar. A group of New York conservationists proposes that the Hudson River Palisades be set aside as a park. The Rockefeller family, which owns most of the land, eventually throws its weight behind the scheme, after adding a parkway to the original proposal.

12 Mar. A $5.2 million gift from Andrew Carnegie endows the New York City public library system. Carnegie's gift provided for the construction of thirty-nine branch libraries.

5 Sept. The Pan-American Exposition, a celebration of the United States' global economic power, opens in Buffalo, New York. President William McKinley is shot at the Exposition on 6 September by immigrant anarchist Leon Czolgosz and dies 14 September.

16 Oct. New president Theodore Roosevelt causes a national controversy when he dines with black leader Booker T. Washington at the White House.

- The first public-school nursing system is organized by Lillian Wald and Lina Rogers.

- Ragtime music, particularly that of composer and pianist Scott Joplin, is all the rage.

- Oregon adopts the statewide initiative and referendum system, extending direct popular rule for the first time, at the instigation of Gov. William S. U'Ren. It becomes known as the Oregon System.

29 Apr. The Chinese Exclusion Act, originally adopted in 1882, is extended to ban the immigration of Chinese laborers from the Philippines. The measure is strongly supported by politicians and trade unions on the West Coast.

12 May A bitter and violent anthracite coal strike begins in Pennsylvania, affecting 140,000 miners. Miners' demand an eight-hour workday and a 20 percent pay increase. President Theodore Roosevelt appoints a commission to arbitrate the dispute on 16 October, and on 21 October John Mitchell, the United Mine Workers' president, declares the strike at an end.

15 June The New York Central Railroad makes the trip from New York to Chicago in twenty hours.

1903

- Edwin S. Porter's *The Great Train Robbery* is screened. It is the first American film with a plot and features the first movie close-ups. It is also considered by many to be the first Western.

- The National Women's Trade Union League is founded by both women trade unionists and middle-class settlement-house women to encourage female workers to join unions and to carry out a campaign of public information. Its ranks are open to anyone "who will declare himself or herself willing to assist those trade unions already existing, which have some women workers, and to aid in the formation of new unions of women wage earners."

- The Williamsburg Bridge, spanning the East River, opens in New York City.

- Theodore Roosevelt makes Pelican Island off the Florida coast the first federal wildlife sanctuary.

1 May	New Hampshire creates a licensing system for the sale of liquor, ending a forty-eight-year ban on alcohol.
4 July	President Roosevelt inaugurates the first Pacific communication cable by sending a message around the world and receiving it twelve minutes later.
26 July	Dr. Horatio Nelson Jackson and Sewall K. Crocker complete the first cross-country automobile trip when they arrive in New York City. Their trip had begun on 23 May in San Francisco.
30 Dec.	A fire in the Iroquois Theatre in Chicago kills 602 patrons and leads to the adoption of new safety codes for theaters in cities across the country.

1904

- Sophonisba Breckinridge is the first woman to receive a law degree from the University of Chicago.

- Phonograph rolls, a new use of one of Thomas Edison's inventions for sound recording, become a popular form of entertainment in American homes.

- The first automobile road maps are published, essential in an age before highways are numbered and towns marked with signs.

- The first automobile speed limits are adopted in New York State, establishing top speeds of ten miles per hour in densely populated areas and twenty miles per hour in rural areas.

- Saint Louis hosts the Louisiana Purchase Exposition, a world's fair marking the one-hundredth anniversary of the Louisiana Purchase.

- Sapolio soap becomes a popular name brand and an early example of the growing influence of advertising campaigns on public consumption.

- The National Child Labor Committee is founded in New York City by social workers Florence Kelley and Lillian Wald. It will agitate for stronger child-labor laws at the state level and for national legislation covering industries engaged in interstate commerce.

- Black blackface vaudevillians Bert Williams and George Walker teach the popular cakewalk dance to the Prince of Wales.

11 Mar.	The Morton Street Tunnel, the first Hudson River tunnel for railroad traffic between New York and New Jersey, is completed. William Gibbs McAdoo, president of the New York and New Jersey Railroad, is the first man to cross under the river.
15 Apr.	Andrew Carnegie gives $5 million to establish a hero fund to honor those who put themselves at risk to save others.
23 May	Steerage rates on transatlantic steamships are cut to ten dollars per person as shipping lines from Belgium, France, Germany, and the Netherlands intensify their competition with British ships for the lucrative business of ferrying immigrants to the United States.
15 June	The *General Slocum,* a pleasure steamboat, burns in the Hell Gate passage of New York City's East River, killing more than one thousand of the eighteen hundred picnickers aboard, mostly immigrant women and children.

Oct.	The New York City Young Men's Christian Association opens a training school for chauffeurs.
27 Oct.	The first completed segment of the New York City subway system, running from the Brooklyn Bridge to 145th Street, is opened to the public.
2 Nov.	Evangeline Booth becomes the first commander of the Salvation Army in the United States.

1905

- Population density in the worst New York City slums climbs to one thousand people per acre.

- Seventy-eight thousand passenger automobiles are registered in the United States.

- W. E. B. Du Bois and William Monroe Trotter found the Niagara Movement, forerunner of the National Association for the Advancement of Colored People (NAACP).

- The Rotary Club begins in Chicago as a volunteer community-service organization. The club is founded by a Chicago attorney, Paul Percy Harris, and takes its name from the practice of gathering in the offices of individual members on a rotating basis.

- Novocaine, a nonaddictive relative of cocaine, is produced for the first time as a painkilling medicine.

- Comedians Fatty Arbuckle and Harry Bulger, along with actor John Mason, become the first popular entertainers to appear in cigarette advertisements when they sing the praises (in print) of Murad Cigarettes.

- Designer Elsie de Wolfe gets her first interior decorating commission, for the Colony Club in New York City. She revolutionizes interiors, freeing them from Victorian darkness. She also begins tearing stoops off New York City brownstones in the name of modernity.

- Portland, Oregon, hosts the 1905 World's Fair.

- Madame C. J. Walker (Sarah Breedlove) perfects and markets a hair straightener for black women. The success of the product makes Walker a prominent businesswoman in the black community.

- Joan Cuneo is the only woman to compete in the first Glidden Cup, a one-thousand-mile automobile tour.

- Thomas Dixon publishes *The Clansman*, which romanticizes the origins of the Ku Klux Klan and is later made into a controversial 1915 film, *Birth of a Nation*, by D. W. Griffith.

- The first nickelodeon opens, in Pittsburgh, Pennsylvania.

- June Wallace Nutting opens a Southbury, Connecticut, workshop specializing in colonial reproduction furniture and "colonial" photographs, signaling the growing popularity of a colonial revival in architecture and interior decoration.

7 June	The highest price paid for real estate is established when No. 1 Wall Street, in New York City, a 1,250-square-foot plot, is sold for $700,000.

1906

18 June   The Twentieth Century Limited begins train service between Chicago and New York, boasting a travel time of only eighteen hours between the two cities.

- *Little Nemo in Slumberland,* Winsor McKay's popular comic strip, is first published in syndication.

- Inventor Ward Stone Ireland introduces the stenotype for "machine shorthand." It is later joined by the stenograph, and both devices become essential equipment for creating courtroom transcripts.

- President Theodore Roosevelt dedicates Devils Tower in Wyoming as the first national monument in the United States.

28 Jan.   Ruth St. Denis begins her style of interpretive dance with "Radha." The type is now known as modern dance.

18 Apr.   An earthquake strikes San Francisco at 5:13 A.M., followed by three days of fire. Hundreds are killed; thousands injured; and since the city is largely destroyed, more than two hundred thousand people are left homeless.

30 June   The Pure Food and Drug Act is signed into law, along with the Meat Inspection Act, to prevent what had been rampant adulteration of food and medicines and lax quality control. Manufacturers now also have to list accurately the ingredients of their products, though enforcement remains inadequate.

July   New Jersey passes the first law requiring the licensing of automobile operators.

14 Aug.   Black soldiers stationed outside Brownsville, Texas, are involved in a riot in which one person is killed and one is wounded. The entire regiment is court-martialed and dishonorably discharged by Theodore Roosevelt despite conflicting testimony and slender evidence. In 1972 Congress restores members of the regiment, most of whom had died by then, to good standing.

22 Sept.   A violent race riot begins in Atlanta, Georgia, when newspapers publish dubious reports of assaults on white women by black men. Four blacks are killed and many more are injured.

12 Dec.   Theodore Roosevelt appoints Oscar S. Straus as secretary of commerce and labor. Straus is the first Jewish American to hold a cabinet position.

24 Dec.   Reginald Aubrey Fessenden broadcasts both words and music on the radio for the first time from Brant Rock, Massachusetts. His only listeners are radio operators on fishing and military boats at sea.

1907

- Florenz Ziegfeld's musical stage extravaganzas, the Follies, begin in New York City.

- "Animal dances" such as the Turkey Trot, Kangaroo Hop, and Grizzly Bear have their heyday.

- Suffragist Harriet Stanton Blatch founds the Equality League of Self-Supporting Women to organize working-class support for women's suffrage.

- The Chicago School of Civics and Philanthropy is founded by Sophonisba Breckinridge and Julia Lathrop to teach the new profession of social work. The school is later renamed the University of Chicago School of Social Service Administration.

- The first Carnegie Arbitration Conference on world peace is held at Lake Mohonk, New York.

- Lee De Forest begins regular radio broadcasts from lower Manhattan.

- Canada Dry Ginger Ale is first produced.

- The Pittsburgh Survey, the first large social-science survey of urban living conditions, is sponsored by the new Russell Sage Foundation.

20 Feb. The Immigration Act of 1907 gives the president the power to restrict the immigration of laborers from Japan. On 14 March Theodore Roosevelt issues an executive order to this effect.

14 Mar. Theodore Roosevelt creates the Inland Waterways Commission, headed by Theodore E. Burton, to oversee the nation's commercial water routes and promote conservation measures.

26 Apr. The Jamestown Tercentennial Exposition in Jamestown, Virginia, opens, to celebrate the three-hundredth anniversary of the English colonization of Virginia.

May The first taximeter cabs to be put into service in the United States arrive in New York City from Paris.

Miss Anna M. Jarvis holds the first Mother's Day observance in Grafton, West Virginia.

30 June Immigration to the United States peaks at almost 1.3 million entrants in fiscal year ending 30 June.

12 Sept. The world's largest steamship, the *Lusitania*, completes its initial voyage, having set a new speed record of five days from Ireland to New York.

17 Sept. Oklahoma, which will become the forty-sixth state on 16 November, adopts a constitution that includes prohibition of alcohol.

1908

- The Singer Building, the first true skyscraper (forty-seven stories, 612 feet), is completed in New York City. It will be eclipsed as the world's tallest building less than a year later by the Metropolitan Life Tower, with a height of seven hundred feet and fifty stories.

- Airplane advertising is used for the first time, to promote a Broadway play.

- For twelve dollars, emigrants can travel in steerage from Genoa, Italy, to New York City.

- General Electric patents the electric iron and toaster.

- The "directoire" or "sheath" dress arrives from Paris. The first woman in Chicago to wear one has to be rescued from the crowd by police, but despite difficulties in walking, slim dresses without petticoats become popular. Also popular is the song "Katie Keith, she wears a sheath / With very little underneath." The first fishnet stockings arrive from Paris in this year as well.

- John P. Harris and Harry Davis, who had launched the first nickelodeon, in Pittsburgh, Pennsylvania, in 1905, now own about eight hundred nickelodeons in the United States, usually located in storefronts.

- The first animated cartoon, "Gertie the Dinosaur," by Winsor McKay, is screened.

21 Jan. New York City passes the Sullivan Ordinance, which prohibits females from smoking cigarettes.

12 Feb. A twenty-thousand-mile New York to Paris automobile race begins in Times Square with six entrants. The U.S. entry, a Thomas, wins on 31 July 1908.

30 Apr. Worcester, Massachusetts, becomes the largest "dry" city in the country when it passes a Prohibition ordinance. It is joined by seventeen other cities and 249 towns in Massachusetts. Worcester's action resulted in the closing of seventy-six saloons and the unemployment of two thousand men.

13–15 May Theodore Roosevelt hosts a conservation conference at the White House, attended by the governors of forty-four states and territories, to promote the protection of natural resources.

28 May Child-labor legislation is adopted for the District of Columbia. Advocates of the measure work to make it a model for similar legislation in the states.

17 Sept. The first airplane fatality occurs when Lt. Thomas W. Selfridge dies after a plane piloted by Orville Wright (who is seriously injured) crashes.

Dec. The American Red Cross sells $135,000 worth of Christmas Seals to raise money to fight tuberculosis.

24 Dec. The licenses of 550 nickelodeons are revoked on the grounds of immorality, that is, being open on Sundays and allowing sexual activity by audiences.

1909

- Only eleven states require automobile operators to have licenses.

- The invention of Bakelite plastic is announced by Leo H. Baekeland, a Belgian-born American inventor. The new product will lead to affordable plastic containers and appliances.

- A White House Conference on the Care of Dependent Children is held, and leads to the establishment of the Children's Bureau in 1912.

- The Alaska-Yukon-Pacific Exposition opens in Seattle, Washington.

- Henry Ford introduces the Model T automobile, which costs about $850 and comes in one color, black.

- Rube Goldberg's "Foolish Questions" in the *New York Evening Mail* is popular. Goldberg is best known for drawing nonsensical machines that solve a problem in an unnecessarily elaborate way.

27 Sept. President Taft sets aside three million western acres for national park land.

12 Feb. William English Walling, Mary White Ovington, and Oswald Garrison Villard found the National Association for the Advancement of Colored People (NAACP) in Ovington's New York City apartment. W. E. B. Du Bois signs the organizing document, as do Jane Addams, John Dewey, and William Dean Howells.

7 Mar. This day is designated as Arbor Day by the state of California in honor of its native son, the botanist Luther Burbank.

9 June– 6 Aug. Alice Huyler Ramsey becomes the first woman to drive cross-country, from New York to San Francisco.

2 Aug.   The Philadelphia mint issues the Lincoln penny to replace the Indian head penny, which had been in circulation for half a century.

24 Nov.   The "Uprising of the Thirty Thousand," a garment workers' strike, erupts in New York City. It is the first female-dominated (more than 80 percent of strikers are women) mass action. After fourteen weeks the workers win. The victory establishes the International Ladies Garment Workers Union as a force with which to be reckoned.

OVERVIEW

Entering the New Century. In some ways the 1900s were the last decade of the nineteenth century. The opulence and self-confidence of the wealthy, which had suffered a temporary, if severe, setback in the depression of 1893–1894, were back on display in Newport, Rhode Island, and other watering holes of the well-heeled members of high society. At the other end of the social spectrum, the everyday lives of working men and women were shaped by many of the same social forces that had changed the United States so dramatically in the decades after the Civil War. Big business grew even bigger, and the distance between rich and poor seemed just as great as it had during the 1890s, when social strife and violent clashes between labor and capital broke out with frightening regularity. Many of the habits, customs, and mores of the nineteenth century shaped patterns of behavior and belief in the new decade as well.

Changes in American Life. However, enormous changes were under way during the 1900s. The population grew substantially (by sixteen million from seventy-five million between 1900 and 1910), in large part because of the hundreds of thousands of immigrants who arrived every year on American shores. The process of urbanization, already well established in the nineteenth century, continued unabated, bringing millions of Americans into contact with complete strangers and reshaping the way they worked and lived. Women entered the workforce in increasing numbers as manufacturing and retailing expanded. The automobile, which in 1900 was an expensive commodity available only to the rich, was by 1909 becoming a method of travel available to the ordinary American at a reasonable price. The Wright brothers, who had started out as bicycle mechanics, successfully flew an airplane for the first time when they soared above the dunes for two minutes at Kitty Hawk, North Carolina, in 1903. The motion picture industry, though in its infancy during this decade, signaled the arrival of a new form of entertainment that would alter the way Americans spent their leisure hours. Household appliances, some of them newly invented, became accessible and affordable to a growing middle class. The vacuum cleaner was invented, and more and more homes had iceboxes, phonographs, telephones, and electric lights.

The Religion of Consumption. Earlier generations of Americans had embraced moderation, self-denial, thrift, and enterprise as a code of behavior for individuals and for society. But in the 1900s this "Protestant ethic," as the German sociologist Max Weber called it, was under assault. Simon N. Patten, one of the decade's most popular economists, argued that surplus wealth created energy, which could then be used in consumption, which then stimulated production and created more surplus wealth as society progressively improved. Patten thought women stored energy and men spent it, and that those who disagreed with him were afraid of consumption, or spending. "The habits, instincts, and feelings we have inherited from our forefathers are no longer safe guides for us to follow," Patten wrote in 1901. Where previous theorists saw scarcity as the iron law of economics, Patten and others preached a gospel of abundance and promised that Americans could spend their way to the promised land. All of this was set in the context of a changing economy, and it required both the manufacture and the eager purchase of goods by consumers. "Don't postpone your happiness," the trade magazine *Thought and Work* advised Americans in 1904. This was the decade when the department store emerged as the major retail force, and as a potent symbol of an economy that had grown proficient in the manufacture and delivery of consumer goods. Previously, there had been dry-goods stores where people bought material for making clothes at home. They went elsewhere for candles, for lamps, for carpets, and for other goods. Now ready-to-wear clothing, along with a huge variety of household goods, was available under one roof, or from a single catalogue. The new religion was a success, the department store its new cathedral.

Anxieties. There was another side to America, however, one full of fear and anger. Because so much wealth and power were concentrated in the trusts and large corporations, laborers had little control over how, when, and for how long they did their jobs. There were numerous acrimonious strikes during this decade; the distance between capital and labor had never seemed so great. Many of these battles were fought over such bread-and-butter issues as wages and hours, but something equally important was at stake: how much control, collectively and individually, workers would have over their lives. These kinds of concerns propelled many workers into radical political and social organizations, from the Socialist Party to the Industrial Workers of the World (IWW). Even for the well-to-do, it was an anxious time. One of the most talked-about ailments among the middle and upper classes of the 1900s was neurasthenia, a kind of nervous exhaustion that struck at those overcome by the frenetic pace of modern living. The "cures" sometimes involved using electricity, a use of technology to master human frailty. Women who were deemed to be suffering from neurasthenia were often confined to their homes to take the "rest cure."

Progress for Women. Since an 1848 conference in Seneca Falls, New York, many American women had been writing, speaking, and protesting in favor of equal political and social rights for women. This battle continued on many fronts in the 1900s, a time that also saw divisions appear within the ranks. Women made important gains within professions such as law and medicine, though they remained a small minority. In the 1900s women forced open the doors of some of the nation's most prestigious colleges and graduate schools, but also used women's colleges such as Bryn Mawr as a training ground for their strengthening push for suffrage. By 1910 women made up 40 percent of undergraduates in American colleges and universities. In the growing field of social work, women such as Jane Addams, Lillian Wald, and Florence Kelley were the acknowledged leaders. For working-class women there were battles of a different sort: for just wages, reasonable hours, safe working conditions, and recognition from the male-dominated trade unions. For black women these struggles were intensified by the blight of racism, even among those who proclaimed themselves allies and friends. Although women were divided in the 1900s, they were also forging personal and institutional bonds that would serve them well in future decades.

The New Immigrants. By 1910 nearly one-seventh of the population of the United States was foreign-born. In cities such as Cleveland, Chicago, New York, Philadelphia, Pittsburgh, and Saint Louis, immigrants and the children of immigrants made up the majority of the population. The United States had for decades absorbed substantial numbers of immigrants, but the quantity and diversity of the immigrant population in the 1900s created additional social and political tensions. Suddenly, on the streets of some American cities it was as common to hear Czech, Polish, or Russian being spoken as it was to hear English. Urban schools faced the challenge of teaching not only language skills and the three R's, but survival skills to children unaccustomed to city life. Municipal services were stretched beyond the breaking point. Labor unions struggling to gain better wages and shorter hours found their battle made more difficult by the steady flow of cheap labor from overseas. And urban political bosses quickly established a system of patronage and informal social services in return for immigrant loyalty at the polling stations on election day. Immigrants helped to make the neighborhood saloon a prominent feature on city streets, and a favorite target of temperance crusaders. Tensions over ethnicity, politics, jobs, and religion contributed to a steady growth in hostility toward immigrants during the 1900s.

Strategies for Improvement. A large group of Americans, primarily businessmen, believed that the cure for the country's problems lay in propagating middle-class values of efficiency and hard work. In business Frederick Taylor's theories of management found eager ears. Jobs were broken down into their component parts; a new class of middle managers and engineers took over day-to-day operations, animated by the belief that the company was a machine that could be run as a set of well-oiled parts. On another front, middle-class reformers began to establish themselves in immigrant communities in settlement houses so they could teach new arrivals how to be Americans. What these two strategies had in common was a belief that life was a struggle for integrity, morality, and success, a struggle people were capable of winning — if they conformed to middle-class standards.

Preparing for the Future. If there was discontent during this decade, there was also the prevailing feeling that change equated with improvement and progress. Americans faced the future with confidence. Their country was a major world power. The cities, despite their many problems, symbolized through their skyscrapers and symphony halls, their streetcars and subways, their movie houses and amusement parks, that a distinctive American culture was coming of age. Some of the leading manufacturers of the world were American, and entrepreneurs such as Henry Ford were using new production techniques to usher in an age of automobility for the masses. A fundamental optimism created a feeling that Americans were in control of their destiny, and that the future belonged to Americans to shape as they wished. As one prominent reformer of the decade recalled in his memoirs, "We felt that the world had been wished onto our shoulders."

Global Superiority. Indeed, some authors believe that behind the global expansion of the United States was the need to prove its superiority. In controlling the Philippines and parts of Latin America, the United States placed itself on a par with the European powers. But there was also a fear of "race suicide," most eloquently expressed in the 1907 "Gentlemen's Agreement" in which the United States and Japan agreed to exclude the Japanese from immigrating. This was also a time of racial ferment. The cakewalk, a dance that had begun in black communities in the previous decade, gained widespread popularity among whites. Ragtime was increasingly popular, as well, and black vaudevillian performers were among the most famous comedians in the world. Yet in 1900 New York City witnessed a huge race riot. There were also riots in Atlanta; Springfield, Illinois; and other cities.

TOPICS IN THE NEWS

EXPOSITIONS, FAIRS, AND AMUSEMENT PARKS

Decade of Fairs. American cities in the 1900s were engaged in a fierce competition for prestige and status, and civic boosters looked to world's fairs as one vehicle for attracting press attention, visitors, and new business. Thanks to the stylistic and popular success of the 1893 World's Columbian Exposition in Chicago, promoters in the 1900s sought to imitate it across the United States. The 1901 Exposition in Buffalo, New York, (where President William McKinley was assassinated); the 1904 Saint Louis exposition; the 1905 Portland, Oregon, World's Fair; the 1907 Jamestown (Virginia) Tercentennial; and the 1909 Seattle fair were among the major spectacles of the decade. Fairs attempted to educate and entertain their visitors. They usually featured displays of the latest technological marvels, from railroad locomotives to dynamos to new household gadgets. Countries from around the world often mounted exhibits designed to reflect their own technological and industrial achievements and distinctive cultural heritage. The fairs and expositions of the 1900s prominently featured the new role of the United States as an imperial power. For example, the Philippines Reservation at the 1904 Louisiana Purchase International Exposition in Saint Louis displayed twelve hundred Filipinos living under "primitive" conditions. The exhibit was intended as a clear demonstration of their need for the missionary and educational influence of the United States. A similar display was organized for the 1909 Seattle World's Fair.

Impact. Fairs usually lasted for about six months. After they were over, often at least one of the fair buildings was turned into a museum, allowing the impact of the event to linger afterward, in a sense becoming a permanent world's fair. Newspapers and magazines spread the cultural influence of the fairs, as did the strenuous merchandizing of fair-related products. Sometimes seemingly trivial innovations had long-term consequences. For example, it was during the Saint Louis World's Fair of 1904 that people first ate hot dogs and ice cream cones as they walked. They were the world's first "fast food."

Amusement Parks. One of the most popular attractions at the Columbian Exposition was the Midway Plaisance, a raucous and eclectic collection of exotic entertainments, restaurants, shops, and theaters featuring everything from the giant wheel designed by George W Ferris to belly dancers and a "World Congress of Beauty." The legacy of the Midway was a new form of popular entertainment for the urban masses, and it inspired permanent amusement parks around the United States, where factory workers, secretaries, clerks, and other urban workers could spend what leisure time they had pursuing idle pleasures and inexpensive thrills.

Coney Island. The most spectacular of the new parks was Coney Island, located on Long Island, New York, nine miles from Manhattan. Coney Island had wide, sandy beaches on the Atlantic Ocean, which had made it a resort destination since the early 1800s. By the 1890s there were hotels, restaurants, roller coasters, and public ocean swimming, or bathing, as people then called it. Coney Island came into its own as a major working-class mecca during the 1900s, after three large amusement areas opened there. In 1897 George Tilyou opened Steeplechase Park, where customers could ride mechanical horses on a rail around the perimeter of the park, sometimes going as high as thirty-five feet in the air. This was a thrilling novelty at the time, and it attracted thousands of riders. Inspired by Tilyou's success, Frederic Thompson and Elmer "Skip" Dundy opened Luna Park in 1903 on the site of the old Sea Lion Park. The old, slower-paced Coney Island was literally replaced by the new, exciting resort. Luna Park quickly became known as "the Heart of Coney Island." It featured minarets and spires, and at night the bold park structures were illuminated by more than a million light bulbs, an exciting innovation during an age when electricity was in its youth. Finally, in 1904 William H. Reynolds opened Dreamland, with wide boulevards and murals of such marvels as the destruction of Pompeii. It completed a triumvirate of attractions that drew hundreds of thousands of visitors daily from May through September.

A Seaside Mecca. The crowds traveled to Coney Island by steamboat, railroad, elevated train, horsecars, bicycles, and even automobiles later in the decade. The

A section of the 1904 Louisiana Purchase Exposition

most popular way to go, however, was the trolley, in large part because the price had dropped to five cents in 1895, making a trip to Coney Island affordable for just about everyone. To attract customers, the parks often offered combination prices, like Steeplechase Park's 1905 offer of twenty-five rides for twenty-five cents. Many people saved their money to be able to go even once a month. It attracted factory workers, salespeople, secretaries, even the new middle class. In return for the price of admission, the new resort promised safe, respectable fun, in the open air.

New Mores. Since so many kinds of people patronized the new amusement parks, they became a place for immigrants to learn about the way Americans behaved in a setting entirely different from the school, settlement house, or factory. The taboos of genteel society began to crumble in these settings as single men and women met each other there without chaperones. The rides encouraged physical intimacy; the sign for Coney Island's Cannon Coaster shouted: "WILL SHE THROW HER ARMS AROUND YOUR NECK AND YELL? WELL, I GUESS, YES!" Swimmers wore very little clothing by contemporary standards — yet another way in which moral strictures were challenged.

Decline. Coney Island's heyday lasted only through the 1900s. Motion pictures and other new forms of popular entertainment offered stiff competition by providing exotic locales and vicarious excitement closer to home. In 1911 Dreamland suffered a disastrous fire. Luna Park's Skip Dundy died in 1907; his partner died in 1919; and

the park faded slowly until it, too, burned in the 1940s. Only Steeplechase Park remains in the 1990s, with the Cyclone rollercoaster and without the Steeplechase Race — a reduced version of its previous glory.

Sources:

Burton Benedict, *The Anthropology of World's Fairs* (Berkeley: University of California Press, 1983);

John F. Kasson, *Amusing the Millions: Coney Island at the Turn of the Century* (New York: Hill & Wang, 1978);

Robert W. Rydell, *World of Fairs: The Century-of-Progress Expositions* (Chicago: University of Chicago Press, 1993).

HOME LIFE

The Family. Most American families in the 1900s were large by the standards of the late twentieth century, but their size was already diminishing. The birthrate in the United States in 1900 was 32.3 births per thousand people. A century earlier it had been 55 births per thousand people. The average number of children per family was 3.56. Poorer families tended to have more children, since they often needed the income their offspring could provide. Life expectancy was low, and it varied significantly by class, race, and sex. The life expectancy for white women in 1900 was 48.7 years; for nonwhite women it was 33.5 years. For white men in that year the average life expectancy was 46.6 years, compared to 32.5 years for nonwhite men. Short life expectancy and high infant mortality meant that many families had to cope with the loss of a child or a parent. For the average

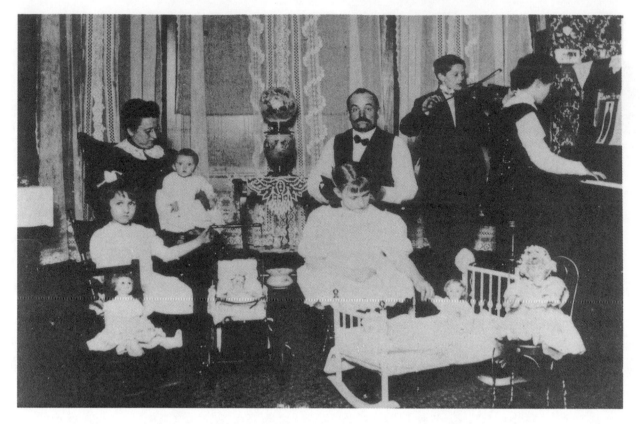

A typical "evening at home" in middle-class Chicago in the early 1900s

working family, loss of income because of the injury or illness of a wage earner could prove catastrophic.

Keeping House. Household chores such as cooking and cleaning, which fell on the shoulders of mothers and daughters in working-class families and to hired domestic servants in the homes of the upper middle class and the well-to-do, became easier, though still laborious, in the 1900s. Women cooked on unregulated stoves that burned coal or wood. They had to guess at cooking times and feed the fire while preparing meals. Cleaning was hard toil, and new products such as Sapolio, a scouring soap, were eagerly welcomed by consumers during this decade. Only the middle class and the wealthy were likely to have indoor-plumbing facilities: in 1907–1908 Robert Coit Chapin observed that only one in twenty-five of the poorest New Yorkers had bathrooms, and of the working poor only one-third had a toilet in their apartment buildings. Laundry was by far the most arduous task, and it took all day to do. Most women did their washing in tubs that had to be hauled into the kitchen. Clothes were soaked, scrubbed, and rinsed several times according to the amount of dirt on them, then boiled, starched, wrung out, and hung to dry. The water for this had to be boiled and poured each time. One popular option in cities was sending clothes out to power laundries; by 1909 even some of the poorest slum dwellers used them. There were some improvements in the process during this decade: Lux, in 1906, became the first laundry soap to be sold in

flakes, not bars. Among other conveniences were iceboxes, which most urban dwellers had by the 1900s, largely because it had become possible during the 1890s to manufacture ice cheaply and reliably. Canning was improved, too, lowering the price of canned goods and allowing the housewife to opt out of home canning. And the development of large food processing companies and the rapid spread of chain grocery stores such as A&P in the first two decades of the twentieth century transformed marketing by increasing the awareness of national brands and threatening the survival of local merchants.

Electricity. The spread of electricity, and with it of new electric appliances, helped to make some household jobs easier. David Kenney patented the electric vacuum cleaner in 1907, and the Hoover vacuum cleaner was patented in 1908. Vacuuming promised to replace the arduous task of sweeping floors and beating rugs to remove dust and dirt. These new appliances remained out of the reach of most Americans during this decade, since they were expensive to purchase and operate. But electric appliances were marketed as basic requirements of the "modern" home, and in the 1910s and 1920s the use of small and large appliances followed the spread of electricity across the country.

Source:
Susan Strasser, *Never Done: A History of American Housework* (New York: Pantheon, 1982).

IMMIGRATION

A Land of Immigrants. In 1885 the Protestant writer and orator Josiah Strong noted in his popular tract *Our Country* that "America, as the land of promise to all the world, is the destination of the most remarkable migration of which we have any record. During the last four years we have suffered a peaceful invasion by an army more than twice as vast as the estimated number of Goths and Vandals that swept over Southern Europe and overwhelmed Rome. . . . A study of the causes of this great world movement," he continued, "indicates that as yet we have seen only beginnings." Whatever one might think of Strong's equation of immigrants with an invading army, he was perceptive in recognizing that a migration of unprecedented scope was under way, a migration that would continue until the eve of World War I. Immigration not only transformed American society in the 1900s, but became a focal point for widespread anxiety about the nation's future, about the growth of cities and slums, and about what exactly it meant to be an American. Immigration was not, of course, a new phenomenon in the American experience. From the early seventeenth century to the Civil War, American culture, religion, and society had been shaped by successive waves of immigration from Europe, Africa, Asia, and Mexico. But the immigration of the 1900s was different in several significant ways.

Scale. Never before had the United States absorbed so many newcomers in such a short period of time. Between 1865 and 1915 some twenty-five million immigrants arrived in America, more than four times the number that arrived in the fifty years before the Civil War. In the decade before 1914 immigrants were arriving at the rate approaching one million per year. In the 1900s more than eight million newcomers flocked to the United States. Most were processed at Ellis Island, New York, where an impressive new complex of buildings was completed in 1901. Immigrants were registered in the Great Hall, a room two hundred feet long and one hundred feet wide. Other facilities included a shower facility that could handle eight thousand bathers a day, restaurants, railroad-ticket offices, a laundry, and a hospital. During the peak years of immigration, approximately 80 percent of arrivals were processed without difficulty.

Origins. These decades also witnessed an important shift in the origins of the nation's immigrants. Throughout most of the nineteenth century the vast majority of immigrants came from northern and western Europe: the British Isles, Scandinavia, and Germany. But beginning in the 1880s and 1890s the contribution of these regions, in both absolute and relative terms, began to decline, and the flow of newcomers from southern and eastern Europe — Russia, Poland, Italy, Greece, and the Austro-Hungarian Empire — increased dramatically. From 1900 to 1909 there were more than 2 million Austro-Hungarian immigrants (which at the time included much of central and eastern Europe), nearly 2 million from Italy, and 1.5 million from Russia. By comparison, there were 1.7 mil-

A tenement district on Hester Street in New York City in the early 1900s

lion immigrants during the decade from Great Britain, Ireland, Scandinavia, Germany, and France *combined*. Immigration from China, which had supplied many of the laborers for the construction of railroads in the western United States, was reduced to a trickle after the Chinese Act of 1882.

Destination. Earlier waves of immigrants had, for the most part, settled in rural America and the nation's interior, with the major exception being the Irish who came in the 1840s and 1850s. Germans had settled on farms in the Midwest or in cities such as Milwaukee, Saint Louis, and Cincinnati. Almost all Scandinavians had settled farms in Midwest and the Plains states. The new immigrants, most of them unskilled and from rural backgrounds, lacked the capital to settle on farms of their own. They were drawn by economic necessity, and by the growth of ethnic enclaves, to the cities. This concentration made them a more visible presence in American life and would eventually contribute to a rising tide of nativism and xenophobia.

The Image of America. Immigrants came to the United States in the 1900s for a variety of reasons. The United States enjoyed a reputation as a country relatively free from religious persecution and political oppression. There was no officially established church, no national police, no compulsory military service, and no overt restriction on land ownership or university enrollment. The constitution guaranteed individual liberties. While there were many exceptions to this benign image, particularly

SPELLING SIMPLIFICATION

During this decade, with its emphasis on order and efficiency, the spelling of the words in English language came to seem cumbersome and overly complex. Not only was it difficult for immigrants to learn to spell in English, but it was a challenge for native speakers as well. Why, people wondered, should the letters *ough* have several different pronunciations? Why not spell words the way they sounded? Andrew Carnegie, among others, supported a move to simplify spelling. They founded the Spelling Reform Association, which promoted the cause of rational spelling. The movement went so far that in August 1906 President Theodore Roosevelt ordered the government to simplify three hundred words in official publications. *Theatre* became *theater; centre* became *center.* Other changes included eliminating the u's in *colour, honour,* and *rumour,* altering *omelette* to *omelet, catalogue* to *catalog,* and removing traces of the French origins in several other words. Some changes did not take, like the changes from *phoenix* to *phenix* and *surprise* to *surprize,* but many more did. The press enjoyed poking fun at the movement, suggesting names like Andru Karnegie and Rusevelt. The Supreme Court refused to change its spelling, and Congress was so irritated by the order that they completely ignored it. Despite all this, most of the changes eventually took hold, shaping our written language today.

for blacks and Asian Americans, this reputation for tolerance and freedom drew many who were plagued by ethnic or religious persecution in their homelands. The United States also had a reputation as place where economic opportunities were more numerous. Despite the harsh conditions of labor in the nation's mines, factories, slaughterhouses, and railroads, there were jobs and at least some opportunities for advancement. The reputation of the United States for tolerance and economic opportunity was spread by many means in communities across Europe, Asia, and elsewhere. Steamship companies, who were engaged in fierce competition for immigrant business, promoted the bounty of America and the opportunities awaiting anyone willing to work. They used guidebooks, posters, poems, and paid agents to sing the praises of the United States. Equally important were the communications among friends and within families and communities. Often this took the form of someone who had gone to the United States to work for a period of time and returned to his or her community. But letters were especially important in shaping the expectations and decisions of immigrants. Of those arriving at the port of New York in 1908–1910, 92 percent said they were joining relatives or friends who had sent for them. Mary Antin, a Russian Jewish immigrant who came to the United States with her family while still a child, recalled in her memoir that in Russia "America was in everybody's mouth. Businessmen talked of it over their accounts; the market women made up their quarrels that they might discuss it from stall to stall; people who had relatives in the famous land went around reading their letters for the enlightenment of less fortunate folk. . . . all talked of it, but scarcely anyone knew one true fact about this magic land."

"Birds of Passage." Those who did know something about it were the young male immigrants whom American officials referred to as "birds of passage." These immigrants left families behind to come to the United States in search of work, usually during the summer months. In the period from 1908 to 1914, officials recorded 6.7 million arrivals and a little more than 2 million departures. They found jobs as outdoor laborers on farms, in mining camps, and on construction sites. When work was scarce, as it was following the Panic of 1907, they were sometimes stuck without enough money to pay their fare home. Eventually many of these young migrant workers settled in the United States, becoming citizens, and bringing over their families. Their migration and settlement were particularly sensitive to changing economic conditions and opportunities.

Immigrant Communities. Even though immigrants were by definition uprooted, many quickly established new ties in their new surroundings. Shaped in large measure by the need for cheap housing, ethnic neighborhoods also reflected the desire of many first-generation immigrants to maintain connections to their country of origin. They were knit together by bonds of language, religion, and ethnic identity that was often also regional. Though it was rare for an ethnic group to monopolize an entire neighborhood, each group occupied particular blocks or streets. There immigrants could buy familiar food, speak their native language, and find that customs and traditions still had relevance. Mutual-aid societies such as the Sons of Italy provided basic services such as life insurance. Churches were crucial anchors in ethnic neighborhoods, with the parish priest functioning as spiritual leader, social worker, and mediator between old customs and the demands of what was for many newcomers a bewildering urban world. Most ethnic groups had their own newspapers that preserved their language and published news from the old country. Saloon keepers and ethnic politicians helped immigrant workers find jobs and resolve disputes. And those immigrants who came with some money in their pockets, or with valuable skills, opened small grocery stores, butcher shops, boardinghouses, and other institutions that knit ethnic communities together.

Theodore Roosevelt, standing, and Booker T. Washington, seated right, in Tuskegee,
Alabama, 24 October 1905

Nativism. Those who hired immigrant men, women, and children to work in the mills and mines, in sweatshops, and on the docks welcomed the steady supply of cheap labor. But increasing numbers of Americans in the 1900s resented their new neighbors. Native-born workers were threatened by intense competition for jobs that drove down wages and made successful strikes difficult. Others felt that the ethnic diversity of the new immigrants was diluting the power and cultural influence of those whose ancestry was northern or western European. Municipal reformers decried the ease with which blocs of immigrant voters were manipulated by corrupt bosses who traded services for votes. From all of these groups the call for restriction of immigration would swell to a chorus by the 1910s, and their goal would be achieved with the passage of the Immigration Restriction Acts of 1921 and 1924. But by then the immigration of the 1900s had already indelibly transformed American society.

Sources:

David Brody, *Workers in Industrial America: Essays on the Twentieth-Century Struggle* (New York: Oxford University Press, 1980);

Joshua Freeman and others, *Who Built America? Working People and the Nation's Economy, Politics, Culture, and Society* (New York: Pantheon, 1992);

John Higham, *Strangers in the Land: Patterns of American Nativism, 1860–1925* (New York: Atheneum, 1955);

Alan Kraut, *The Huddled Masses: The Immigrant in American Society, 1880–1921* (Arlington Heights, Ill.: Harlan Davidson, 1982).

RACE RELATIONS

The Color Line. Race relations in the United States reached a new low in the first decade of the new century. By 1900 Native Americans had been reduced to dependency, stripped of much of the land granted to them by treaty and left to defend themselves against further encroachment by mining companies and land speculators. On the West Coast Asian Americans continued to encounter resentment and misunderstanding. Relations between whites and blacks were marked by two unavoidable phenomena: violence and segregation. The decade began with a race riot in New York City and saw subsequent riots in Atlanta in 1906 and in Springfield, Illinois, in 1908. In the latter incident two blacks were lynched, four whites were killed, seventy people were injured, and a force of five thousand militiamen was required to restore order in the birthplace of Abraham Lincoln. A regiment of black soldiers was summarily and dishonorably discharged from the U.S. Army after its role in a riot in Brownsville, Texas, in August 1906. Lynchings of blacks were frighteningly common, though on the decline by comparison with the last two decades of the nineteenth century: there were one hundred such incidents in 1900 alone, and eleven hundred between 1900 and the beginning of World War I.

Jim Crow. Segregation, long the practice in most parts of the country, was written into law in southern states during the 1890s and 1900s. Known as Jim Crow laws,

THE NAACP

The National Association for the Advancement of Colored People (NAACP) was founded in 1909 by a group of black and white reformers. Its roots were in the Niagara Movement, founded in July 1905 by W. E. B. Du Bois and twenty-nine other educated professional black men. They held annual meetings for five years, and their purpose was to protest white America's treatment of black people. Unlike Booker T. Washington, who acquiesced in the separate-but-equal doctrine the Supreme Court had handed down in *Plessy* v. *Ferguson* (1896), the Niagara men wanted an integrated society achieved by agitation and legislation. They became convinced that protest would be effective only if it were interracial. After the Springfield, Illinois, riots in 1908, a small group of white reformers — Oswald Garrison Villard, Joel Spingarn, and Mary White Ovington among them — decided that the gradualism advocated by Washington would not work, and they joined with Du Bois's group to form the NAACP in 1909. Its purpose was to use publicity and litigation to force an end to racial discrimination. Most of the NAACP members were black, but its funding came mostly from wealthy whites, and the only black among its official leaders was Du Bois—a situation that did not change until the 1920s. But the principles laid down at its beginning eventually bore fruit, especially the commitment to working for change in the courts, which resulted in the 1954 *Brown* v. *Board of Education* Supreme Court school desegregation decision.

Source: *Black Leaders of the Twentieth Century* (Urbana: University of Illinois Press, 1982).

these statutes, and the social practices they inscribed, required separate facilities in transportation, accommodations, education, and entertainment. There were separate railroad cars for blacks, usually just behind the engine car, which meant that the passengers had to contend with the heat and dirt from the coal-burning locomotives. Schools were separate, and most white reformers ignored black institutions. This was often true in the North as well, even though there were not many laws on the books mandating it. Throughout the South in the 1900s, the process of depriving black citizens of their constitutional rights continued as the doctrine of white supremacy held sway. The extreme prejudice among some whites was conveyed by J. K. Vardaman, a U.S. senator and later governor from Mississippi, who declared that he was "just as opposed to Booker T. Washington as a voter, with all his Anglo-Saxon re-enforcements, as I am to the coconut-headed, chocolate-colored, typical little coon,

Andy Dotson, who blacks my shoes every morning. Neither is fit to perform the supreme function of citizenship." Through such devices as poll taxes, grandfather clauses, and literacy tests, blacks were deprived of the right to vote throughout the South, a right they would not regain in large numbers until 1965.

Two Approaches. In response the black community tried two different approaches. One was led by Booker T. Washington, head of the Tuskegee Institute in Alabama and the most prominent black figure of the decade of the 1900s. Washington preached a doctrine of accommodation and self-help, arguing that blacks should not demand social or political equality until they had established their economic strength. In 1895 he delivered a famous address at the Atlanta Exposition in which he advocated economic cooperation between the races and social separation. Other blacks disagreed with him. They favored integration, and demanded both social equality and the protection of the law against segregation and violence. The most prominent spokesman for this position was W. E. B. Du Bois, who began the Niagara Movement in June 1905 after the Springfield riots. His purpose was to convince whites that blacks deserved to be received fully into American society. In a manifesto written by Du Bois — and issued by the Niagara Movement after its 1906 convention in Harpers Ferry, West Virginia — he decried the poison of racism and the new segregation laws in America: "Never before in the modern age has a great and civilized folk threatened to adopt so cowardly a creed in the treatment of its fellow-citizens, born and bred on its soil. Stripped of verbose subterfuge and in its naked nastiness, the new American creed says: fear to let black men even try to rise lest they become the equals of the white." The Niagara Movement would by the end of the decade lead to the founding of the National Association for the Advancement of Colored People (NAACP).

Patterns of Black Life. Blacks faced persistent problems in the 1900s, and their communities were evolving in significant ways as they sought improved educational opportunities, better housing and jobs, and safety from mob violence. At the beginning of the decade two-thirds of the nation's black population of ten million lived in the rural South. Most worked as farm laborers, sharecroppers, and tenant farmers in an agricultural economy that was growing steadily worse, on land that was exhausted from intensive cultivation. The average farm worker in South Carolina in 1902 was paid $10.79 per month, while his counterpart in New York garnered $26.13. Even though blacks comprised half of the population of the South in 1900, there were just more than 150,000 black-owned farms, compared to more than a million owned by whites. Given these conditions, many rural blacks were joining the flight to the city. By 1900 seventy-two American cities had black populations of at least five thousand; Washington, Baltimore, New Orleans, Philadelphia, New York, and Memphis all had black populations that exceeded fifty thousand. Even

PUBLIC REACTION TO A LYNCHING

In a 1905 article journalist Ray Stannard Baker described a lynching in Springfield, Ohio. His series of articles on lynching in the North and the South provoked criticism not merely of lynch mobs but of law officers who failed to stop them. Baker's articles were collected in his *Following the Color Line* (1908):

They murdered the Negro in cold blood in the jail doorway; then they dragged him to the principal business street and hung him to a telegraph-pole, afterward riddling his lifeless body with revolver shots.

That was the end of that! Mob justice administered! And there the Negro hung until daylight the next morning — an unspeakably grisly, dangling horror, advertising the shame of the town. His head was shockingly crooked to one side, his ragged clothing, cut for souvenirs, exposed in places his bare body: he dripped blood. And, with the crowds of men both here and at the morgue where the body was publicly exhibited, came young boys in knickerbockers, and little girls and women by scores, horrified but curious. They came even with baby carriages! Men made jokes: A dead nigger is a good nigger. And the purblind, dollars-and-cents man, most despicable of all, was congratulating the public: It'll save the county a lot of money!

Significant lessons, these, for the young!

But the mob wasn't through with its work. Easy people imagine that, having hanged a Negro, the mob goes quietly about its business; but that is never the way of the mob. Once released, the spirit of anarchy spreads and spreads, not subsiding until it has accomplished its full measure of evil.

Source: Ray Stannard Baker, "What Is Lynching? A Study of Mob Justice, South and North," *McClure's*, 24 (February 1905): 422–430.

University to train a new generation of leaders, scholars, and artists; founding innumerable small businesses in urban neighborhoods; and through the churches maintaining a powerful sense of community that would sustain decades of protest and progress.

Sources:

W. E. B. Du Bois, *The Souls of Black Folk* (Chicago: McClurg, 1903);

John Hope Franklin and Alfred A. Moss Jr., *From Slavery to Freedom: A History of African Americans* (New York: McGraw-Hill, 1994);

Jacqueline Jones, *Labor of Love, Labor of Sorrow: Black Women, Work and the Family from Slavery to the Present* (New York: Basic Books, 1985);

David Levering Lewis, *W. E. B. Du Bois: Biography of a Race, 1868–1919* (New York: Holt, 1993);

C. Vann Woodward, *The Strange Career of Jim Crow*, third revised edition (New York: Oxford University Press, 1974).

THE SETTLEMENT HOUSE MOVEMENT

Origins and Aims. In order to address the problems faced by the urban poor, many of whom were new Americans, progressive reformers organized schools and settlement houses. The idea behind settlement houses was that social reform had to begin with individuals, who needed help to overcome conditions created by circumstances that were beyond their control. To that end, reformers had to live in the neighborhoods of their clients so that they could truly understand their needs. Stanton Coit brought the settlement house idea to New York City in 1886, when he opened the Neighborhood Guild. Although the guild failed soon afterward, it inspired the College Settlement (1889), founded by graduates of the "Seven Sisters" women's colleges. Among the best known of the dozens of settlement houses founded in the late nineteenth and early twentieth centuries were the Hull House in Chicago, the Henry Street Settlement in New York City, and James Reynolds's New York University Settlement. College-educated middle-class people, especially women, were attracted to settlements because they offered a way to be useful in a time when opportunities for educated women were constricted. Workers tended to be in their twenties or thirties, and were often inspired by the message of the Social Gospel to carry Christian principles of equality and mutual responsibility into poor neighborhoods. Some did not stay long, but there was a constant stream of eager recruits. Settlement houses spread widely in the 1900s, and most large cities in the United States had more than one by the end of the decade.

Settlement Activities. Settlement houses provided a variety of educational activities for poor tenement dwellers, and also Americanized them. There were sewing classes, cooking classes, housekeeping classes, English classes, kindergarten classes — all geared either to help women gain job skills or to educate their children. Settlement workers also helped to disperse middle-class standards of cleanliness and behavior to new arrivals. They provided recreational and cultural activities as an alterna-

---

in cities with well-established black populations, however, discrimination in employment and housing posed major obstacles to black workers. Black women, more than 50 percent of whom were employed by 1910, found work in low-paying jobs as domestics, seamstresses, or as laundry workers. Black men had a somewhat wider range of choices, but often found themselves in menial jobs in factories, on the railroads, in mines, or in the construction trades. Many trade unions refused to admit blacks. The American Federation of Labor, which in 1890 had declared its unwillingness to admit unions that discriminated on the basis of race, quietly reversed its position by the turn of the century, even though this step weakened its effectiveness. Skilled black artisans could command only two-thirds of the wages of their white counterparts. In the face of these long odds, blacks, occasionally with the assistance of white philanthropists, were establishing institutions to improve black schools; using black colleges such as Morehouse College and Howard

A settlement house in Pittsburgh, Pennsylvania, where youths learned to weave

tive to the local saloon. Hull House in Chicago staged drama productions, and Henry Street Settlement in New York had plays and playgrounds. Since the middle-class reformers went to their clients and lived among them, they were better able to understand their needs.

Henry Street. One of the best examples of the role that settlement houses played in the broader progressive reform movement, and of the aims of those who staffed them, is the Henry Street Settlement and its founder, Lillian Wald. Wald grew up in Rochester, New York, in a comfortable middle-class home and trained as a nurse at New York Hospital. After attending New York City's Woman's Medical College, Wald found her life's calling in 1893 when she attended a sick woman in a tenement. Appalled at the bad conditions in the slums, she decided to pursue public-health nursing. In 1893 she established the Nurses' Settlement on Henry Street on New York City's Lower East Side. Before Wald established Henry Street she, like many of the other middle-class women drawn to settlement work, was astonishingly naive about the living and working conditions of the working class. She recalled in her memoirs a visit from a downstairs neighbor during her days as a visiting nurse. The neighbor, a young immigrant woman, wanted help in organizing a trade union, and Wald admitted that "even the term was unknown to me. . . . The next day I managed to find time to visit the library for academic information on the subject of trades unions." But what Wald lacked in worldliness she quickly made up through sympathy and intelligence. By the 1900s the Henry Street Settlement featured a visiting-nurse service and full settlement facilities. Inspired by Wald's example, people in other cities established visiting-nurse systems as well.

Activism. For Wald and those she influenced, the goal was not simply to cure the sick but to attack the conditions and habits that spread disease and poor health, and the settlement houses became a base for broader activities on the state and national level. Through her exposure to poor families Wald became committed to child welfare. With Florence Kelley she founded the National Child Labor Committee in 1904 and lobbied for legislation regulating children's work. The federal Children's Bureau was established in 1912 at their suggestion. Many settlement-house workers became strong advocates of municipal reform, after witnessing firsthand the problems of corruption, graft, and inefficiency that plagued city governments. In a time when the cities were overflowing with needy dwellers, settlement houses provided a useful way to expose rich and poor, immigrant and native-born, to each other, and settlement house workers functioned as effective advocates for necessary social legislation.

Sources:

Jane Addams, *Twenty Years at Hull House* (New York: Macmillan, 1910);

Allen F. Davis, *Spearheads for Reform: The Social Settlements and the Progressive Movement, 1890–1914* (New York: Oxford University Press, 1967).

R. L. Duffus, *Lillian Wald, Neighbor and Crusader* (New York: Macmillan, 1938);

Lillian Wald, *The House on Henry Street* (New York: Holt, 1915).

SOCIAL WELFARE

A New Profession. Prior to the 1900s what we now know as social work was done by amateurs, well-intentioned women and men who lacked formal training but possessed a desire to help those they viewed as less fortunate than themselves. But in the 1900s the field was transformed by the application of new knowledge and methods to the problems of poverty, vice, disease, alcoholism, and other social ills. Many of these new approaches were generated by social scientists such as Edward A. Ross at the University of Wisconsin, who had been trained in Europe, and in turn trained a young generation of men and women in economics and sociology. While many were educated at what were still known as schools of philanthropy, social workers made every effort to distance themselves from their roots in the voluntaristic tradition of the rich helping the poor. Instead, they saw themselves as professional investigators equipped with tools that nineteenth-century charitable organizations did not possess.

Middle-Class Values. Social workers were mainly middle-class whites. During this decade it was one of the few occupations in which men and women had relative parity. And although one of their motives was to control those they aided and mold them into more-acceptable behavior, social welfare reformers did much to improve people's health and well-being. They also tried to teach people how to keep house and how to stretch their budgets to ensure that they had healthy meals. They brought women and children out for seaside or lakeside excursions, providing a rare escape from the often confining existence in urban tenements. But even those social workers most attuned to objective social science and most willing to defend the character of the urban poor sometimes slipped into old patterns. Lillian Wald, founder of the Henry Street Settlement House in New York City, while rejecting the anti-immigrant sentiment of many native-born Americans, nonetheless held "coming-out parties" for the daughters of her immigrant neighbors when they turned eighteen.

The Pittsburgh Survey. In spite of their cultural blinders, social workers made substantial contributions to an improved understanding of urban life. Their main method was to gather statistics on slums, and the most famous effort was the 1907 Pittsburgh Survey, which was carried out primarily by New York City social workers with funding from the new Russell Sage Foundation. Workers fanned out in ethnic communities and looked at housing conditions, counted members of the household, and asked questions about employment and income, housekeeping standards, diet, clothing, education, and recreational activities. Statistical evidence was accompanied by hundreds of photographs of workers and their families by Lewis Hine. His photographs portrayed the mostly immigrant workers as proud individuals willing to do their part to provide for themselves. In the Pittsburgh Survey and other similar efforts the work was mostly descriptive and was used to advocate reforms. After seeing families where every member had to work in order to pay the rent and buy food, reformers used this information to lobby state legislators to adopt minimum-wage laws and maximum-hour laws. They used the information about housing to try to change laws regarding the size and type of buildings that could be erected. They worked with doctors to encourage states and municipali

A child worker at the Turkey Knob Mine in West Virginia; the 1908 photograph by Lewis Hine is typical of his work recording poverty and working conditions in the United States.

ties to undertake vaccination programs using the information they gathered about the spread of disease.

Housing Reform. One of the consequences of the rapid and largely unplanned urbanization of the late nineteenth century — and one of the major challenges for social workers and urban reformers — was the prevalence of substandard housing with inadequate provision for light, air, privacy, and sanitation. Urban tenements were built to make use of most of the plot of land upon which they stood, resulting in dark and airless rooms. Tenements were crowded, often fitting large families into two rooms, one for sleeping and the other for cooking, socializing, and work. Most lacked indoor plumbing. In 1901 New York City passed a Tenement House Law, which became a model for other cities. Builders had to use larger lots and create large courtyards for tenements, which would ensure that some sunlight and air reached dwelling spaces. In addition, indoor plumbing was mandated, as was fireproof construction. These innovations materially improved the lives of thousands of city dwellers, though the demand for housing would continue to outstrip the supply in most American cities.

Sources:
John D. Fairfield, *The Mysteries of the Great City: The Politics of Urban Design, 1877–1937* (Columbus: Ohio State University Press, 1993);

Joshua Freeman and others, *Who Built America? Working People and the Nation's Economy, Politics, Culture and Society,* volume 2 (New York: Pantheon, 1992);

Mel Scott, *American City Planning Since 1890* (Berkeley: University of California Press, 1969);

Robert H. Wiebe, *The Search for Order, 1877–1920* (New York: Hill & Wang, 1967).

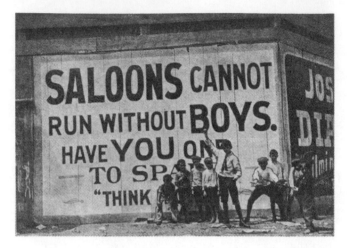

Billboard in Wilmington, Delaware, circa 1908. The last three lines read "HAVE YOU ONE / TO SPARE? / 'THINK IT OVER.' "

TEMPERANCE AND PROHIBITION

New Concerns. Temperance was a prominent issue in American reform movements throughout the nineteenth century, but it took on new urgency during the decade of the 1900s as part of the effort by the progressives to exert social control. Progressives blamed the "liquor trust" for promoting alcohol use and abuse and thus tied the growing crusade for Prohibition to the larger goal of curbing the influence of big business.

Saloons. There was some truth to the charges by temperance crusaders: in 1900 brewers controlled two-thirds of bars and saloons in the Midwest. These saloons were gathering places for the urban working class, where machine politicians could find their constituents and cajole them for their votes. Indeed, urban working-class voters were known as "wets" and strongly opposed any kind of Prohibition. Many first- or second-generation immigrants drank as part of their customary recreation, and they would not accept government interference in their personal lives.

Reformers. For reform-minded Protestant elites, the gathering of the "lower orders" in taverns and saloons was dangerous and corrupt, and when mixed with politics was yet another reason to prohibit alcohol sales. Reformers thus argued that consumption of alcohol was bad for the body *and* for the body politic. In pamphlets churned out by the thousands they decried the role of alcohol in domestic abuse, in the disintegration of families, and in the waste of hard-earned wages.

Problems in the Workplace. Employers increasingly joined the ranks of antialcohol crusaders, for the consequences of drunkenness in the workplace were more severe than ever before. A hungover worker was much more likely to be hurt in the new mechanized factory than would a nineteenth-century artisan who worked with hand tools. Henry Ford, Henry Clay Frick, and other industrialists insisted that their employees be teetotalers, as much out of the hope for increased productivity as out of a desire to protect their workers from injury.

New Tactics. The two best-known organizations promoting temperance and Prohibition were the Woman's Christian Temperance Union (WCTU), founded in 1874, and the American Anti-Saloon League (ASL), founded in 1895. The WCTU had initially focused on a campaign of persuasion, hoping to convince the individual drinker to give up liquor; the ASL focused on closing bars and saloons, and after 1910 also advocated prohibition of the manufacture, sale, and consumption of alcohol.

The Role of Women. Women played a major role in the Prohibition campaign, and the brewers and distillers of alcohol in turn provided significant financial backing to opponents of women's suffrage, fearing that if women gained the vote they would put them out of business. Activists such as Carry Nation used more confrontational methods than before, attacking saloons with bricks and hatchets. By 1907, when Oklahoma included Prohibition in its new state constitution, several states had gone dry. The tide was beginning to turn. The ASL proposed a constitutional amendment in 1914, and anti-German (that is, antibeer) sentiment during World War I helped set the stage for the Eighteenth Amendment's passage in 1919.

Sources:

Paul Boyer, *Urban Masses and Moral Order in America, 1820–1920* (Cambridge, Mass.: Harvard University Press, 1978);

Sean Dennis Cashman, *America in the Age of the Titans: The Progressive Era and World War I* (New York: New York University Press, 1988);

Norman H. Clark, *Deliver Us From Evil: An Interpretation of American Prohibition* (New York: Norton, 1976);

Mark Thornton, *The Economics of Prohibition* (Salt Lake City: University of Utah Press, 1991).

TRANSPORTATION

Streetcars. The electric streetcar was the most influential transportation alternative in the 1900s. Cities expanded along streetcar routes, and they enabled skilled workers to move further from their workplaces and out of slums and permitted middle-class families to move to new suburban neighborhoods. The streetcar network was so complete that it was possible to travel from New York City to Portland, Maine, via streetcars. The explosive growth of Los Angeles in the 1900s would have been impossible without the streetcar. Pacific Electric, a streetcar company founded by railroad magnate Henry E.

The poor condition of roads, such as this one in North Carolina, was the motivation behind the first Good Roads Movement.

Huntington in 1901, was by 1920 moving a quarter of a million riders a day across more than a thousand miles of track, making Los Angeles a suburban city, and a planner's nightmare, almost from its inception.

Automobiles. Just as the train and steamboat revolutionized travel in mid-nineteenth-century America, the automobile begin to change everyday life in America dramatically in the 1900s. Motoring became a middle-class pursuit during this decade, especially after the 1909 introduction of the more affordable Ford Model T. In 1900 most cars cost about $1,000, well out of reach for the average American. The 1909 Model T still sold for $850. The growing population of the automobile was reflected in car registrations: in 1900 there were 8,000, and in 1906 there were more than 106,000 cars registered in the United States. Once new assembly-line practices perfected by Henry Ford and others made automobiles more affordable, they had a telling impact on life in rural America, where distances were often long and travel was difficult. Automobiles brought rural Americans closer to their neighbors, to markets, to towns. Rural doctors were able to reach their patients more quickly and cover more territory. Those who could afford the purchase price of an automobile also became more likely to rely more heavily upon stores and less on homemade products, since journeys to stores were now much easier. Women gained some independence, too, first driving electric cars (which did not have the crank starter). After the crankless self-starter was invented in 1906, women and men were equally competent to start and drive automobiles. Many thought that the advantages brought by the automobile

would help keep the farm population from continuing to drop (it went from 64 percent of the population in 1890 to 54 percent in 1910).

Good Roads. The car changed the physical shape of the country as well, since automobiles required better roads than horse-drawn carriages. The first Good Roads movement began in this decade, and macadam, or pulverized stone bonded with cement or asphalt, spread across America, eliminating the threat of becoming stuck in deep mud. New businesses would follow the car and the highway into the countryside: service stations, restaurants, and accommodations for the increasing number of Americans who used their cars and their leisure time for motor touring. In fact, the car changed American life perhaps more than any other technology of the twentieth century. It made possible a dispersal of population and businesses out of crowded urban neighborhoods — and into rapidly expanding suburbs — even as it brought rural Americans into closer contact with towns, stores, and an array of goods and services that had previously been out of reach.

Sources:
Robert Fishman, *Bourgeois Utopias: The Rise and Fall of Suburbia* (New York: Basic Books, 1987);

Kenneth Jackson, *Crabgrass Frontier: The Suburbanization of the United States* (New York: Oxford University Press, 1985);

Peter J. Ling, *America and the Automobile: Technology, Reform and Social Change* (Manchester, U.K.: Manchester University Press, 1990);

Virginia Scharff, *Taking the Wheel: Women and the Coming of the Motor Age* (New York: Free Press, 1991).

Maternalism. Though widely excluded from the male-dominated political parties, fraternal organizations, and trade unions, women found other ways of influencing public policy, making great strides by the first decade of the twentieth century but often at high cost to themselves. Through their own labor organizations, volunteer groups, and pressure groups they won broader and greater rights for working-class women and their children. Drawing on the widely held belief in the moral superiority of women, their wisdom and special responsibility in dealing with family issues, middle-class reformers developed a "maternalist" vision of women's political role. They expanded the nineteenth-century cult of domesticity — the belief that a woman's proper sphere was the home — to legitimize their efforts to influence public-policy issues that affected the family, including prostitution and abuse of the family by male alcoholics, as well as economic and health provisions for children, mothers, and working women. Early feminists used many other strategies, but the maternalist approach became dominant. By promoting the maternalist view, however, its supporters undercut the emerging theory that women were equal to men and instead fell back on the long-held belief that women were different from men and needed special protection.

Pressure Groups. Middle-class women affected change through their volunteer organizations and the settlement houses. By turn of the century, members of the moral voluntarist groups of the 1880s and 1890s — including the Woman's Christian Temperance Union, the General Federation of Women's Clubs, the National Federation of Day Nurseries, the National Congress of Mothers, and the National Association of Colored Women — and workers from Hull House and other settlement houses were beginning to create issue-oriented pressure groups. Few social problems escaped examination and promotion by women's groups. As settlement house workers had done in the 1890s, the pressure groups gathered data and used it to formulate social-welfare programs and legislation. Reformers no longer viewed working women and their children as morally inferior, but rather as victims caught up in the problems of an urban, industrial environment. Maternalist groups provided some services for these dependents, and joined with other reformers to lobby municipal, state, and federal politicians for public funding for social welfare. As with other progressive reform efforts, the struggle was slow and difficult. The first federal social legislation was not passed until the 1910s.

The Fight for Suffrage. Women reformers recognized early on that the best way to ensure the success of their social-welfare programs was by gaining the right to vote. The arguments in support of women's suffrage varied considerably, but most hearkened back to the cult of domesticity. As the traditional housekeepers, Jane Addams proclaimed in 1906, women were better suited than

Rose Schneiderman, center, leading a demonstration of the Women's Trade Union League

men for the civic housecleaning needed to sweep out the political scoundrels. Because of their different life experiences, reformers argued, women could best protect their own interests and those of their children if they had the right to vote, whether they were working women subject to exploitation without protection, or mothers looking after their children's educations. As guardians of social morality, women understood the need for social-welfare legislation far better than men. Suffragists also argued that the vote would allow women to carry out their traditional role of motherhood better: only a mother who exercised her own rights and responsibilities and participated fully in a democracy as a citizen could truly teach citizenship to her children.

Racism and Suffrage. As the fight for suffrage moved from the periphery to the mainstream of women's organized activities, suffrage advocates sought the support of the white middle class by falling back on old appeals. The most destructive argument for allowing women the right to vote came from those who blatantly appealed to white supremacy. As early as 1893 they argued that allowing white females to vote would not increase the number of "undesirable" voters because there are "more women who can read and write than the whole number of illiterate male voters," be they black or foreign-born. In other words, even if women were granted suffrage, illiteracy would still prevent "undesirables" from voting. As segregation became the norm in the South, racism became increasingly accepted in arguments for women's voting rights. Southern suffragist Belle Kearney proclaimed to the National American Woman Suffrage Association convention in 1903 that "The enfranchisement of women would insure immediate and durable white supremacy, honestly attained." The presence of southern white suffragists in the movement made the participation of black women nearly impossible. Consequently, they created their own local suffrage groups, which, in an instance of bitter irony, pursued the same goals and used many of the same arguments as white women in fighting for their rights. Despite the Herculean efforts of all involved, only eight sparsely populated western states had granted the right to vote to women by 1913.

Women and Labor. As female factory workers tried to organize themselves and improve conditions in their workplaces, they received little support from the male unions. The American Federation of Labor (AFL), in particular, excluded women from many trades and did not want to organize workers in the unskilled positions that most women held. Working women instead turned to middle-class women reformers for help. A new generation of immigrant women from southern and eastern Europe, imbued with a variety of radical traditions, provided the women's rights movement with a new constituency and a greater sense of urgency and militancy.

Trade Unionism. Women from the three economic classes came together in an effective alliance when they formed the Women's Trade Union League (WTUL) in 1903. The league's dual goal was organizing working women in the trade-union movement and integrating working women's concerns into the women's rights movement. In 1908 the Supreme Court upheld *Muller* v. *Oregon*, which set a maximum number of hours a woman could work. The justices rendered their decision based on the maternalist arguments presented in support of the law, but they just as easily could have ruled against it. After that decision the emphasis of trade-union activities rapidly shifted away from the progressives' pursuit of state legislation, such as protective laws, to more-direct, militant action. The "Uprising of the Thirty Thousand," the 1909 strike by the International Ladies Garment Workers Union (ILGWU), accelerated the shift. The ILGWU carried out the strike with the help of the WTUL and women of the Socialist Party. In the end industry won, but the women scored a tactical victory. After the tragic Triangle Shirtwaist Company fire in 1911 in New York City killed 146 women in one of the factories that had rejected the workers' demands for safe conditions, public outrage led to reforms such as safety codes for the workplace. Their 1909 strike established the ILGWU as a major union, which — together with a similar men's garment industry union, the Amalgamated Clothing Workers — helped to revive industrial unionism. Though the memberships of both the ILGWU and the WTUL were largely female, the top leadership in both was virtually all male.

Sources:
John Whiteclay Chambers II, *The Tyranny of Change: America in the Progressive Era, 1890–1920* (New York: St. Martin's Press, 1980);

Melvin Dubofsky, *Industrialism and the American Worker, 1865–1920* (Arlington Heights, Ill.: Harlan Davidson, 1985);

Arthur S. Link and Richard L. McCormick, *Progressivism* (Arlington Heights, Ill.: Harlan Davidson, 1983).

THE WORLD OF WORK

American Industry. The continuing Industrial Revolution made the workplace of the 1900s a starkly different place from that of the mid nineteenth century, and within the decade itself the nature of industrial work changed even more. First, the scale of industrial enterprises continued to increase: in the early twentieth century the old industrial giants of the Gilded Age — plants that manufactured steel, iron rails, and other railroad equipment — would be dwarfed by enormous factory complexes sometimes employing fifteen thousand to twenty thousand workers and producing automobiles, farm machinery, electrical equipment, and textiles. Second, within the new factories the skills of the nineteenth-century artisan were being replaced by machines that could be tended by workers with much less training and experience. Where artisanal skills had once given workers a degree of control over the pace and method of work, machines — along with efficiency experts such as Frederick Winslow Taylor and Frank and Lillian Gilbreth — were reducing many jobs to a series of repetitive motions. Finally, more and more Americans were employed in white-collar positions, from supervisory and clerical personnel in business

Child laborer in the early 1900s

John Spargo's investigations of child labor nationwide helped to draw attention to the problems it created and fueled the push for child-labor laws. In this passage he describes boys working in the coal mines:

Work in the coal breakers is exceedingly hard and dangerous. Crouched over the chutes, the boys sit hour after hour, picking out the pieces of slate and other refuse from the coal as it rushes past to the washers. From the cramped position they have to assume, most of them become more or less deformed and bent-backed like old men. When a boy has been working for some time and begins to get round-shouldered, his fellows say that, "He's got his boy to carry round wherever he goes." The coal is hard, and accidents to the hands, such as cut, broken, or crushed fingers, are common among the boys. Sometimes there is a worse accident: a terrified shriek is heard, and a boy is mangled and torn in the machinery, or disappears in the chute to be picked out later smothered and dead. Clouds of dust fill the breakers and are inhaled by the boys, laying the foundations for asthma and miners' consumption. . . .

I could not do that work and live, but there were boys of ten and twelve years of age doing it for fifty and sixty cents a day. Some of them had never been inside of a school; few of them could read a child's primer. True, some of them attended the night schools, but after working ten hours in the breaker the educational results from attending school were practically *nil*.

Source: John Spargo, *The Bitter Cry of the Children* (New York & London: Macmillan, 1906), pp. 166–167.

and industry, to professionals like lawyers, doctors, and engineers, to the thousands of people working in the booming retail sector.

Child Labor. The exploitation of child labor was a major preoccupation of progressive reformers in the 1890s and 1900s. Children worked on family farms, as "breaker boys" in coal mines, in sweatshops, and in textile mills. Boys sold newspapers and shined shoes on street corners. Many children did piecework (in which wages were based on the number of items produced) that was performed in the home, making costume jewelry and clothing, among other items. By 1900 twenty-eight states had some child-labor legislation on their books, but the trend toward regulation became stronger during this decade, especially after the 1904 formation of the National Child Labor Committee (NCLC) by a group of influential social reformers. Lewis Hine took stark photographs of grimy and exhausted children working in mines and factories, and the NCLC used its influence to display them widely. "No anonymous or signed denials can contradict proof given with photographic fidelity," Hine wrote. The efforts of the NCLC paid off in 1908, when the first national child-labor law was passed, but child

labor would remain an issue well beyond the decade of the 1900s as abuses were continually uncovered.

Women's Work. Women were in the workforce in greater numbers as well; by the end of the decade they would make up more than 21 percent of wage earners. They worked as typists in corporations, as telephone operators, and as salesclerks in department stores. They also worked in factories, particularly in the garment industry in the North and the tobacco industry in the South. They had long hours — the average workweek was at least fifty-four hours long, since most laborers worked at least nine hours a day, Monday through Saturday. In 1905 attorney Louis Brandeis, with the aid of research by his sister-in-law Pauline Goldmark, argued successfully before the Supreme Court, in *Muller* v. *Oregon*, that women needed to be protected from exhaustion and that legislation limiting their hours of work was constitutional. This was the first step down the road toward legislation protecting worker health and safety, though it was premised on the argument that women needed time and energy to maintain their households. Minimum-wage laws followed, as did workmen's compensation for injury, and other kinds of protection for workers.

Sources:
Mimi Abramovitz, *Regulating the Lives of Women* (Boston: South End Press, 1988);

James R. Green, *The World of the Worker: Labor in Twentieth-Century America* (New York: Hill & Wang, 1980);

David Montgomery, *The Fall of the House of Labor* (New York: Cambridge University Press, 1987).

HEADLINE MAKERS

JANE ADDAMS

1860-1935

REFORMER; PEACE ACTIVIST; FOUNDER OF HULL HOUSE

Background. Jane Addams was best known for her role as a leader of the settlement-house movement in the United States and as the founder of Hull House in Chicago. But she was also a prominent peace activist, an ardent campaigner for women's suffrage, and one of the intellectual leaders of the progressive movement. Born to a wealthy businessman and Illinois state senator and his wife, she graduated from Rockford (Illinois) Seminary in 1881. Addams then attended the Women's Medical College in Philadelphia, but after a year she had to drop out for health reasons. For seven years she searched for something meaningful to do with her life, and finally found it on a trip to Europe. For young women of Addams's background, a trip to Europe was intended as the capstone of their cultural education, the final preparation for lives as wives, mothers, and club women. But Addams, as she recalled in her autobiography, *Twenty Years at Hull House* (1910), rejected "the assumption that the sheltered, educated girl has nothing to do with the bitter poverty and the social maladjustment which is all about her, and which, after all, cannot be concealed, for it breaks through poetry and literature in a burning tide which overwhelms her; it peers at her in the form of heavy-laden market women and underpaid street laborers, gibing her with a sense of her uselessness."

Hull House. While in London, Addams visited Toynbee Hall, one of the world's first settlement houses, where educated men and women lived in a slum neighborhood in order to be on the spot to help the neighbor-

hood residents. She decided to open such a house in Chicago. With her friend Ellen Gates Starr she bought the old Hull mansion on South Halsted Street, and moved in on 18 September 1889. It soon became the most important settlement house in the United States. Eventually, it had thirteen buildings, a staff of sixty-five, and an annual budget of $100,000. Addams made Hull House a center of political, cultural, and educational activities in the neighborhood. Hull House sponsored lecturers (among them John Dewey, a personal friend of Addams, and Frank Lloyd Wright) and encouraged its immigrant neighbors to maintain their ethnic traditions even as it helped them through the process of assimilation. Well into the 1920s Addams was among the most famous American women and an acknowledged leader in the growing field of social work.

Progressive Reformer. Addams was an engaging public speaker, a tireless fund-raiser, and a prolific author, and she put all of these talents to use in the service of a variety of progressive causes. Among her ten books and five hundred articles were *Democracy and Social Ethics* (1902) and *Twenty Years at Hull House* (1910). Addams was a strong defender of organized labor and women's suffrage. In part because of her influence, Illinois passed a Factory Act in 1893, and she also lobbied heavily for the national Child Labor Act. Addams's influence was widespread. She was one of the leading figures in the Progressive Party, and an important supporter of Theodore Roosevelt's 1912 Bull Moose presidential campaign.

Peace Activist. When World War I began, Addams remained more firmly committed than ever to her pacifist principles. She was the chair of the Women's Peace Party and president of the 1915 International Conference of Women in The Hague. She was criticized severely in some quarters: the Daughters of the American Revolution revoked her membership because of her opposition to American involvement in the war. However, her lifetime of efforts on behalf of world peace were recognized in 1931, when she shared the Nobel Peace Prize with Nicholas Murray Butler.

Sources:

Jane Addams, *The Second Twenty Years at Hull House* (New York: Macmillan, 1930);

Addams, *Twenty Years at Hull House* (New York: Macmillan, 1910);

Allen F. Davis, *American Heroine: The Life and Legend of Jane Addams* (New York: Oxford University Press, 1973).

WILLIAM EDWARD BURGHARDT DU BOIS

1868-1963

AUTHOR, EDITOR, ACTIVIST

Student. W. E. B. Du Bois was born in Great Barrington, Massachusetts, in 1868 and educated until the age of sixteen in a small local school of some twenty-five students and two teachers. They were humble origins for a man who would not only become a major voice for the advancement of blacks in the decade of the 1900s but would become an international figure of the twentieth century, active until his death in 1963 in Accra, Ghana. Du Bois's father left home when Du Bois was just a year old. He was raised by his mother, Mary Du Bois, until his 1885 departure for Fisk University, an all-black college in Nashville, Tennessee. While at Fisk he founded the *Fisk Herald,* the college newspaper, but more importantly observed for the first time life in the American South, where the great majority of blacks lived in the nineteenth century. During two of his summers at Fisk he walked at length around the countryside looking for a school in which he could teach. The experience of living among and observing rural southern blacks would form the core of his most enduring book, *The Souls of Black Folk* (1903). He received his degree from Fisk in 1888 and then attended Harvard University. At Harvard he studied under William James and George Santayana, but for the most part he lived a segregated life, socializing primarily in Boston's black community. He received a B.A. in philosophy from Harvard in 1890, and his graduation speech on the position of blacks in American society attracted attention. He remained at Harvard, finishing his Ph.D. in 1895 after a two-year stint at the University of Berlin in Germany. His dissertation, "The Suppression of the African Slave Trade 1638–1870," became his first published book and established Du Bois as a major voice in the history profession.

Professor. In 1894, while still completing his doctoral work, Du Bois began his teaching career at Wilberforce University in Ohio. The all-black college was a religious institution, and Du Bois found its strictures confining. In 1896 he obtained a fifteen-month appointment to the University of Pennsylvania in Philadelphia. While living in the city's Seventh Ward slums, he began his sociological studies of American blacks. Du Bois was convinced that prejudice was the result of ignorance and that sociological study that destroyed stereotypes and myth would gradually remove barriers. He also developed his concept of the "talented tenth," the idea that if 10 percent of blacks could achieve higher education, they could then begin the process of lifting poor and rural blacks out of poverty and inequality. Du Bois's time in Philadelphia resulted in his first work of sociology, *The Philadelphia Negro* (1898). By the time the book appeared, Du Bois had moved on to a position as professor of economics and history at Atlanta University, where he remained until 1910. The years in Atlanta were productive for Du Bois. He was helping to develop the new field of sociology and inventing the field of black studies. While in Atlanta he edited the annual *Publications,* which summarized the department's work. He published *The Souls of Black Folk* in 1903, written as a direct response to the philosophy of Booker T. Washington, then the most influential black man in the country.

Activist. Although he remained a professor through the first decade of the new century, Du Bois's greatest work in the period was as an activist. He became an antilynching activist, but his emergence as a leader of black opinion in the 1900s resulted primarily from his debate with Booker T. Washington. Blacks were divided during the decade. Conservatives like Washington, who had grown up in the shadow of slavery and racism in the South, believed in slow progress, built through technical training and manual labor while tacitly accepting a lower position in American society. Washington's position seemed the path of least resistance in a dangerous racial climate. In 1905 Du Bois and others formed the Niagara Movement at Niagara Falls. Du Bois became the movement's general secretary, and the group issued demands for political and social equality while deriding Washington's policy of appeasement. The following year Du Bois began publishing *The Moon,* which lasted a year. From 1907 to 1910 he edited *Horizon,* the magazine of the Niagara Movement. His biography of militant abolitionist John Brown appeared in 1909, a book Du Bois would later consider his best written work. The Niagara Movement formed the core of what in 1909 became the National Association for the Advancement of Colored People (NAACP), a group of blacks as well as liberal whites determined to combat segregation and racial violence. In 1910 Du Bois left Atlanta University to become the director of publications and research for the NAACP. In his autobiography he wrote that "My career as a scientist was to be swallowed up in my role as master of propaganda. This was not wholly to my liking." Yet, since his early sociological studies, Du Bois had come to realize that numbers and facts were not enough to combat racism. Civil rights would only be obtained through public demands.

The Crisis. Du Bois became editor of the NAACP's magazine, *The Crisis,* in November 1910, where he remained for twenty-four years. Through *The Crisis* Du Bois became a leading black voice on all subjects, political and social. *The Crisis* exploded in popularity from a circulation of one thousand in 1910 to thirty thousand just three years later. Du Bois also became more internationally active. In 1911 he joined the Socialist Party, but left it the following year. He published a novel, *The Quest of the Silver Fleece,* in 1911 and that same year attended the first Universal Races Congress in London. In 1918 he traveled to France to observe the status and treatment of black soldiers and caused a furor the following year when he published an army memo he had obtained that urged the degrading treatment of black soldiers. He was, however, on record as supporting the war, causing conflict with other NAACP members who wanted to concentrate on the situation in America. In 1919, 1921, and 1923 he attended Pan-African congresses in Europe. And though he disagreed with militant Marcus Garvey's attempt to create an autonomous black Africa and have American blacks immigrate to it, Du Bois did take a strong anti-imperialist stance. While at *The Crisis* Du Bois published the work of nascent Harlem Renaissance writers who would thrive, some under Du Bois's patronage, in the 1920s and 1930s.

Atlanta Again. In 1934 Du Bois, at age sixty-six, left the NAACP and *The Crisis* after conflicts with organization leader Walter White. He returned to Atlanta University as chairman of the Sociology Department, where he resumed his career as a teacher as well as a sociologist, while remaining an international spokesman against racism. In 1935 he published an academic work, *Black Reconstruction,* which attempted to refute the claims of white historians that black politics in Reconstruction had been corrupt and inefficient. He also traveled extensively, visiting Nazi Germany, the Soviet Union, China, and Japan. Du Bois founded *Phylon,* a quarterly humanities journal in 1940, and edited it for four years. Du Bois's politics, though he was member of no party, had always been controversial. In 1926 he had visited the Soviet Union for six weeks as a guest of the Communist leadership. His outspokenness regarding American capitalism, about which he felt some ambivalence and eventually distaste, gave him a strong affinity with the leftist movements around the world. He would eventually run into trouble during the McCarthy years before finally joining the Communist Party of America in 1961 at the age of ninety-two. In 1944 he abruptly left Atlanta University and returned to the NAACP as a director of special research. Despite his advancing years he remained active, publishing *Color and Democracy: Colonies and Peace* (1945), attending a Pan-African Congress in 1945, and publishing *The World and Africa* in 1947.

Exile. Du Bois's activism for the cause of peace and equality became a source of trouble. After being dismissed again from the NAACP in 1949, he joined the Council of African Affairs. He ran for the U.S. Senate in New York on the American Labor Party ticket in 1950, and was indicted in 1951 as an "unregistered foreign agent." He was tried and acquitted of the charges but had his passport revoked, which prevented him from traveling between 1952 and 1958. The final years of Du Bois's life were celebratory, however. He had published *In Battle for Peace: The Story of My 83rd Birthday* in 1952, unable to imagine that he would live for another eleven years. He did, however, and even embarked on a world tour in 1958 and 1959, which included his being awarded the Lenin Peace Prize by the Soviet Union in 1959. In 1961, at the request of President Kwame Nkrumah, Du Bois moved to Ghana to edit the *Encyclopedia Africana.* Two years later, just prior to his death, one of America's most influential voices for peace and equality during the twentieth century became a citizen of Ghana.

Sources:

Virginia Hamilton, *W. E. B. Du Bois: A Biography* (New York: Crowell, 1972);

David Levering Lewis, *W. E. B. Du Bois: Biography of a Race 1868–1919* (New York: Holt, 1993).

CHARLOTTE PERKINS GILMAN

1860-1935

FEMINIST WRITER AND LECTURER

Background. Charlotte Perkins Gilman, one of the most prominent lecturers and social critics of the 1900s, was born in Hartford, Connecticut, into one of the most intellectually prestigious families in the United States. Her father was the nephew of Henry Ward Beecher and Harriet Beecher Stowe, and was the brother-in-law of Edward Everett Hale. Gilman had a difficult childhood. Her father left the household in 1866, and Gilman grew up fatherless with her mother dependent on family members for support. Gilman later recalled her great-aunt Harriet Beecher Stowe fondly and early on chose her as a role model. Although she had a somewhat limited formal education, Gilman was a voracious reader from the age of fifteen. At seventeen she requested from her distant father Frederick Perkins, author of *The Best Reading* (1877), a list of books to read. He replied with a long list of nonfiction titles on evolution, anthropology, and ethnology. In 1880, at the age of twenty, Gilman completed two years of study at the Rhode Island School of Design in Providence. Her modest education was over. She began earning a living as a freelance commercial artist, but in 1882 she met Charles Walter Stetson, an aspiring artist. After much reluctance and inner struggle she married Stetson in 1884; she gave birth to a daughter, Katherine, the following year. Marriage and motherhood had an immediate and devastating effect on Gilman. She broke down, depressed and hysterical, mortified that she had given up her freedom. She traveled to Utah and California to visit friends and family in late 1885 and recovered almost instantly. When she returned home in 1886, she again succumbed to despair. A year later she visited the famous physician S. Weir Mitchell in Philadelphia. He did not take her condition seriously and simply ordered her to "Live as domestic a life as possible," a common "cure" for women of the nineteenth century. Gilman skirted the edge of madness all summer, and finally, in October 1887, she traveled with her daughter and mother to Pasadena, California, separated from her husband and truly free for the first time in her adult life.

Writer and Activist. In the West she began writing articles and poems for the *Pacific Monthly* and *Pacific Rural Press.* She was then and would remain a didactic writer, believing that to instruct was the true role of the writer. She was deeply influenced by Edward Bellamy's *Looking Backward* (1888). Bellamy's conception of a socialist, utopian future swept the country in the form of the Nationalist movement. Gilman became an active Nationalist, joining a Nationalist Club and contributing to the *California Nationalist* and the *Nationalist* magazines. Her poem "Similar Cases," which parodied social conservatism, appeared in the *Nationalist* in 1890 and became a minor classic, attracting the notice of William Dean Howells, among others. In a sense, the poem launched her lecturing career. She began giving public lectures on Nationalism and at Nationalist meetings, a period which peaked in 1891 and 1892. She also published in Bellamy's *New Nation.* But the phase passed. Nationalism declined and Gilman stepped away from it. In the meantime she had sued for divorce, which was finally granted in 1894.

The Yellow Wallpaper. In January 1892 Gilman published "The Yellow Wallpaper" in the *New England Magazine.* The story, a harrowing account of a woman's spiral into madness and hysteria based on Gilman's own illness, caused an instant controversy while also being hailed as a masterpiece of horror fiction worthy of Edgar Allan Poe. To this day the story remains Gilman's most widely known work. Gilman's first book, a collection of poetry titled *In This Our World,* appeared in 1893 and was received well in both the United States and the United Kingdom. Another controversy followed in 1894, when Gilman, feeling the need to "serve" by writing full-time, gave up motherhood. She sent her nine-year-old daughter to the East to live with Walter Stetson and his new wife. This decision provoked a public scandal. Though she privately grieved over the decision, she worked harder at her writing. She edited and published a weekly magazine, *Impress,* for twenty weeks. She also became more active in women's political issues, helping to organize a Woman's Congress in San Francisco. She met suffragists Anna Howard Shaw, Susan B. Anthony, and Jane Addams, who would become a close friend.

Women and Economics. The 1890s were a busy decade for Gilman and culminated with the publication of *Women and Economics* in 1898. She had spent the previous three years in constant travel, including a stay at Addams's Hull House in Chicago. She had lectured on women's issues and testified before the House Judiciary Committee hearings on suffrage. In 1896, at a Women's Congress in Washington, D.C., she met Lester Ward, a reform Darwinist who had attacked Herbert Spencer's doctrine of social Darwinism. Ward's work had a major impact on Gilman and her social writings. Another influence came from the Fabian movement in England. Gilman traveled there for a Socialist Congress in 1896 and met with George Bernard Shaw, Sidney Webb, and William Morris. She later contributed to the monthly *American Fabian.* By 1897 she had decided to write a long essay about economics and sexual repression. The result, written in just five weeks, was *Women and Economics* (1897). The book won great acclaim, with reviewers comparing it to John Stuart Mill's *The Subjection of Women* (1869) The book outlined marriage as an economic transaction forced by circumstance, not a natural arrangement that could not be undone. It also questioned the idea of motherhood as something sacred, considering it instead an occupation. The book was radical and well received and opened Gilman's most productive period.

1900s. As the new century opened, Charlotte Perkins Gilman (she had married her cousin Houghton Gilman in 1900) was among the leading lights of American intellectuals. The decade would prove to be her most productive, though much of her lasting work was by then done. She published *Concerning Children* in 1900, *The Home* in 1903, *Human Work* in 1904, *The Man-Made World* in 1910, and also that year her first novel, *What Diantha Did.* She became a regular contributor to the *Saturday Evening Post, Harper's Bazaar, Scribner's, Appleton's,* and the *Woman's Home Companion.* She also became a regular speaker at suffrage conventions. Among her most radical ideas was the socialization of housekeeping proposed in *The Home.* Gilman argued that the home should be without a kitchen, or at least only a kitchen staffed by hired workers. While asserting the positive aspects of the home, she criticized the subjection of women that resulted from the kitchen. Following Bellamy's model in *Looking Backward,* Gilman imagined a socialized kitchen replacing a private one, serving the needs of many at lower cost to all. The book is among her most coherent of the period and was critically acclaimed, in contrast to ambivalent reviews of *Concerning Children* and *Human Work.* Gilman seemed to be at her height of pricking contemporary mores.

Forerunner and Beyond. Gilman took on a new challenge in 1906, even as her celebrity began to wane. She began the incredible task of single-handedly writing, editing, and publishing a magazine called *Forerunner.* The venture would last more than seven years, and even though the circulation was never more than about fifteen hundred, Gilman had subscribers all over the world. In *Forerunner* Gilman wrote political essays, sociology, poems, serialized novels, book reviews, and contemporary news. She was a one-woman tour de force, and in eighty-six issues of the magazine she wrote an estimated twenty-eight full-length books of prose. Included in *Forerunner* were *What Diantha Did*, *The Man-Made World*, and three romances — *Moving the Mountain* (1911), *Herland* (1915), and *With Her in Outland* (1916). Unfortunately, Gilman exhibited some unattractive beliefs in *Forerunner*, beliefs that seem incongruous with modern progressive stances. She at times exhibited racist opinions regarding Jews and blacks and endorsed "race-improvement" via birth control, eugenics, and sterilization of the "unfit," ideas to which many progressives gave serious consideraton at the time. She ceased producing *Forerunner* in 1916 and at sixty-six slowed down her work. In 1922 Carrie Chapman Catt ranked her at the top of her list of a dozen prominent American women. Through the 1920s Gilman wrote an autobiography, contributed an occasional essay, and wrote a detective novel. She committed suicide in 1935, two years after being diagnosed with breast cancer. She had disappeared from the public eye, and her work was only rediscovered in the 1960s with the advent of the modern women's movement.

Sources:

Ann J. Lane, *To Herland and Beyond: The Life and Work of Charlotte Perkins Gilman* (New York: Pantheon, 1990);

Gary Scharnhorst, *Charlotte Perkins Gilman* (Boston: Twayne, 1985).

EMMA GOLDMAN

1869-1940

FREETHINKER, ANARCHIST, SOCIAL CRITIC

Anarchist Background. Emma Goldman was born in Kovno, Russia; she immigrated to the United States in 1885. After working in Rochester, New York, for a few months, she moved to New Haven, Connecticut. There she became acquainted with political radicals, and she was deeply impressed by the anarchists involved in the 1886 Chicago Haymarket Square bombing. By 1889 Goldman was a confirmed anarchist, and she moved to New York City at a time, as she recalled in her memoirs, when her "entire possessions consisted of five dollars and a small handbag." In partnership with another Russian immigrant, Alexander Berkman, whom she called Sasha, Goldman helped plan the attempted assassination in 1892 of Henry Clay Frick, an associate of Andrew Carnegie whom labor activists held responsible for a pitched battle between striking steelworkers and Pinkerton detectives at Homestead, Pennsylvania. For her role in the failed attempt she served a year in jail. By 1901 Goldman had a reputation as a violent political revolutionary. When President William McKinley was assassinated, Goldman was im-

plicated when the gunman, Leon Czolgosz, told police that he had been inspired by Goldman.

Social Views. Goldman's anarchism was part of a broad critique of American society, and her views on sex, marriage, and family life were every bit as controversial as her political beliefs. In 1906 she began to edit the journal *Mother Earth*, in which she proclaimed her desire to abolish all government, and with it the oppressive Victorian restrictions on personal freedom. Goldman was an early advocate of birth control, which in the 1900s one could not discuss in print without being censored. She hated the institution of marriage, saying that it enslaved women, and she encouraged women to express themselves freely sexually. An effective and frequent public speaker, Goldman routinely scandalized America during the 1900s. In 1917 she was arrested for interfering with the military draft, and after two years in prison she was deported to Russia. She disliked the Soviet Union and spent the rest of her life living in several countries.

Source:

Emma Goldman, *Living My Life* (New York: Knopf, 1931).

HENRY EDWARDS HUNTINGTON

1850-1927

STREETCAR MAGNATE, RAILROAD EXECUTIVE, FINANCIER

Apprentice. Henry Edwards Huntington was born to Solon and Harriet Huntington in Oneonta, New York, in 1850. Huntington attended a local public school, finishing at age seventeen. He traveled in 1869 to Cohoes, New York, to work for his brother-in-law at a hardware store. His uncle Collis Huntington was a successful businessman living in New York City, and in 1870 Henry (known as Edward to intimates) moved there to find work. After a one-year stint working as a hardware wholesaler, Huntington accepted the first of many business opportunities from his Uncle Collis. He moved to Coalsmouth, West Virginia, and managed a sawmill owned by his uncle. In 1873 Huntington married Mary Prentice and bought half of the sawmill from his uncle, the other half having been purchased by Gen. Richard Franchot, a Civil War veteran and associate of Collis Huntington. Henry Huntington continued to run the mill, which served as his apprenticeship as a businessman.

Railroad Man. In 1881 Collis Huntington offered his nephew a new position overseeing track expansion for the Chesapeake, Ohio and South Western Railroad Company. Huntington accepted the job. He would spend the rest of his working days involved with railroad construction and management. He moved to Kentucky and worked the next four years as head of railroad construction. In 1885 he became superintendent of the Kentucky Central Railroad Company, which offered him the chance of managing the operation. The company was only modestly successful, though Huntington did supervise the construction of an important railroad bridge between Covington, Kentucky, and Cincinnati, Ohio. The position served as a preparatory course for the next phase of Huntington's career. By 1891 Collis Huntington had focused on the West, where he had speculated shortly after the Gold Rush of 1849. He was a major owner of the Southern Pacific Railroad, the massive monopoly that controlled most of the transportation in booming California. In 1892 Huntington traveled to San Francisco to become the first assistant to the president of Southern Pacific. The president was Collis Huntington.

California. The 1890s were a difficult time for the Southern Pacific Railroad. The company had become a symbol of corporate monopoly and greedy owners battling one another for control. Collis Huntington was at the center of the controversy, thus putting Henry Huntington in a difficult situation upon arrival. He was well received, however, thanks to his genial personality and strong work ethic. Working for the Southern Pacific was a high profile job, but Huntington even managed to impress a skeptical San Francisco press. He survived the deep depression of 1893 and a massive strike by railroad workers in 1894, standing up to and triumphing over the union. He also began traveling extensively throughout California. He was enamored of the Golden State, especially the south, which was still relatively undeveloped. Los Angeles did double in population between 1890 and 1900, from fifty thousand to one hundred thousand, but Huntington saw the potential of the Los Angeles basin and would have a huge impact on its growth. By 1895 and 1896 southern California was seen as Huntington's "hobby," as he began looking to invest. Electric rail had arrived in American cities during the 1880s, and Huntington was deeply impressed by San Francisco's trolley-car system and how it was changing the face of urban life as well as advancing growth of the city's environs. In 1898, now determined to move to southern California, Huntington purchased the Los Angeles Railway Company, a bankrupt rail company that had been incorporated in 1895. In January 1899 he resigned as director of the Southern Pacific. He was elected as the first vice president of the railroad in June of that year, but refused the position. In August 1899 Collis Huntington died. He left Henry a large portion of his massive fortune with the expectation that he would become the president of the Southern Pacific. Huntington wanted the presidency and was bitterly disappointed when it was instead given to E. H. Harriman. He sold out his portion of the railroad and moved south permanently, determined to build an urban transit system.

Los Angeles. Huntington did not invest heavily in an electric rail system around Los Angeles in order to sell fares to the locals. Railroads were not the end but a means to an end. That end was real estate development. Huntington bought choice, undeveloped land and used the rail system in order to create communities that would grow, bringing people to purchase his land. He would even supply water to the new communities at a loss in order to entice buyers of his lucrative real estate properties. His Pacific Electric Railway Company covered southern California with railroad tracks in the first ten years of the twentieth century. In 1898 the Los Angeles Railway had some fifty miles of track laid. By 1910 there were 918 miles of track — 350 in the city proper and 568 "interurban," connecting Los Angeles to nearby suburbs — crisscrossing the Los Angeles basin. The big red trolley cars became famous for their speed and reliability. By 1910 it was the best urban rail system in the world. Huntington laid track with remarkable speed, leading to equally remarkable growth in the small rural areas around Los Angeles. Rail lines connected Huntington Beach, Whittier, Pomona, San Pedro, Newport, Sierra Madre, Covina, Watts, Redondo, Pasadena, Altadena, Santa Monica, San Bernardino, and other towns with Los Angeles. Huntington was hailed as a hero in the Los Angeles press, and towns would give him depots and land for rail lines for nothing in order to be connected. Huntington was not only changing the face of Los Angeles, but he was changing the way people viewed urban and suburban life. California had among its attributes an abundance of open land. Huntington's rail lines and streetcar suburbs offered people a way to escape life in the crowded cities while still being able to work in the city. The city and its surrounding area boomed. Between 1900 and 1910 the population of Los Angeles more than tripled from 102,000 to 319,000. The figure would be at 500,000 before 1920. Huntington's fortune also boomed because of his extensive landholdings and their subsequent sales.

The Library. In 1910 Huntington sold the interurban lines of the Pacific Electric to the Southern Pacific. He retained control of the city lines in Los Angeles, but many saw the change as a disaster. "A calamity has befallen Los Angeles in this change," wrote the *Los Angeles Express*. Some worried that Huntington had lost interest in southern California. The fears were unfounded. Huntington shifted his focus to other speculations. His library became a primary concern. He had always been a great buyer of books, but after 1910, with his astounding wealth, he began to accumulate an enormous library. He had a preference for books and manuscripts from England and the United States and for the works of English painters. The collection was initially kept at his house in New York and then at his estate in San Marino. The estate became in 1919 the Henry E. Huntington Library and Art Gallery, with five trustees appointed to care for it. It was deeded to the state of California after Huntington's death following prostate surgery in 1927. At the time, the collection was valued at $30 million, and an endowment of $8 million was left for upkeep of the library. Huntington was mourned by the city he had helped build. He had written in a letter in 1906 that "I must confess that the progress and prosperity of Los Angeles and its environs is quite a hobby of mine. I feel myself vitally interested in it, as I indeed am and must be — proud of it, in fact . . . I do want to be known as one of the good people who are responsible for it, who believe in it, and who are ready to pin their money to their faith every time."

Sources:

Kenneth T. Jackson, *Crabgrass Frontier: The Suburbanization of the United States* (New York: Oxford University Press, 1985);

James Thorpe, *Henry Edwards Huntington: A Biography* (Berkeley: University of California Press, 1994).

FLORENCE KELLEY

1859-1932

SOCIAL REFORMER

At the Vanguard. As a single mother, a socialist, and a sociologist working for suffrage, women's rights, and urban reform in Chicago and New York, Florence Kelley was at the vanguard of several reform movements. For thirty-four years, after she helped to found it in 1899, she served as the head of the National Consumers' League (NCL), the single most effective lobbying agency for protective labor legislation for women and children.

Background. The daughter of Quaker abolitionist William Darrah Kelley — a founding member of the Republican Party, a Radical Reconstructionist, and a U.S. congressman from Philadelphia — Florence Kelley combined the firsthand education acquired from her father with the tradition of female political activism she inherited from her great-aunt Sarah Pugh, a leading abolitionist. After she graduated from Cornell University in 1882, Kelley discovered that women of her generation had no real opportunity to locate work commensurate with their talents. In September 1883 she went to the University of Zurich where she studied government and law and came into contact with European socialism. Translating several major works by Karl Marx and Friedrich Engels into English gave her a solid grounding in European socialist thought. Her translation of Engels's *Condition of the Working Class in England in 1844* (1887) is still the preferred scholarly version. In Zurich she also met Lazare Wishnieweski, a Polish socialist medical student, whom she married in 1884. By the time they arrived in New York City in 1886, they had one child, and two others followed in quick succession. In 1891 Kelley fled with her children to Chicago to escape her physically abusive husband.

Settlement Houses. In Chicago Kelley joined Jane Addams and other women working at Addams's Hull House and became deeply involved in the work of the settlement house. Such settlements allowed women to learn the intricacies of state, city, and ward-level politics. After she prepared a special report for the Illinois State Bureau of Labor on the conditions of child labor in Chicago sweatshops, Kelley was appointed the first state factory inspector in Illinois in 1893, and the lessons she learned became part of the lessons offered to the Hull House community. During the same period she studied law at Northwestern University so that she could conduct her own court battles. Kelley's routine of investigation, organization, education, and legislation was widely adopted by other progressive reformers.

Protective Laws for Women. Relying on her own extensive research, Kelley published leaflets and persuaded many states to pass laws restricting the number of hours women could work. In 1893 she convinced the Illinois legislature to pass an eight-hour-workday law for women, but the Illinois Supreme Court struck it down two years later. After it was established in 1899, the NCL supported women's strikes nationwide. In 1908 Kelley and her close friend and ally Josephine Goldmark prepared the statistics and arguments that future Supreme Court justice Louis D. Brandeis (Goldmark's brother-in-law) presented to the Supreme Court when he represented Oregon in *Muller* v. *Oregon*, defending Oregon's right to set a ten-hour limit on the workday of women employed in factories and laundries. The well-known "Brandeis Brief," which Goldmark actually wrote, proved to the Supreme Court's satisfaction that long hours were harmful to the well-being of women. Basing their decision on this sociological evidence instead of legal precedent, the court upheld the Oregon law, and most states enacted similar laws during the next decade.

Campaigning for Reform. In 1899 Kelley had moved to the Henry Street settlement house in New York City and become secretary-general of the NCL. She helped to establish sixty-four local consumers' leagues, traveling extensively among them each year to promote the policies of the national board. In 1909 Kelley introduced the social experiment of the minimum wage to the United States, and during the next decade she worked for suffrage and with Addams for peace. When America became involved in World War I, Kelley and Addams continued their campaign and were publicly vilified for their efforts. Their adherence to peace led to a split between them and the mainstream suffrage movement, which supported the war effort. In 1921 Kelley helped to create and guide through Congress the Sheppard-Towner Maternity and Infancy Protection Act, which for the first time allocated federal funds for health care. She considered this act her most important social contribution.

Sources:

Allan Davis, *Spearheads for Reform: The Social Settlements and the Progressive Movement, 1890–1914* (New York: Oxford University Press, 1967);

Kathyrn Kish Sklar, *Florence Kelley and Women's Political Culture: Doing the Nation's Work, 1820–1940* (New Haven: Yale University Press, 1992).

JOHN MUIR

1838-1914

NATURALIST, FOUNDER OF THE SIERRA CLUB

Background. John Muir was the most influential and best known advocate of wilderness protection during the 1900s. He was born in Scotland and immigrated to the Wisconsin frontier in 1849. Self-educated, he later attended the University of Wisconsin from 1860 to 1863. Muir became interested in botany, and he took walking trips around the Midwest and Canada. After an industrial accident in 1867, he decided to devote himself to "the study of the inventions of God." In 1868 he first visited California's Yosemite Valley, where he remained for six years. After spending years away from it, Muir returned to the valley in 1889 to find it spoiled by logging and sheep grazing. In 1890 he helped to win passage of the Yosemite National Park Act.

National Influence. By 1900 he had helped found the Sierra Club (1892) and was busy raising public awareness of the need to protect America's wilderness lands. In 1901 he published *Our National Parks,* and two years later went on a camping trip in California with President Theodore Roosevelt. It was on this trip that Muir was able to influence public policy the most. Roosevelt was moved to add 148 million acres to the national forest lands, and he also doubled the number of national parks and created sixteen national monuments. One of them, a stand of redwood near San Francisco, was later named the Muir Woods National Monument.

Preservation Versus Conservation. Theodore Roosevelt was a personal friend of Muir's, and declared in 1908 that in the nation's park's "all things wild should be protected and the scenery kept wholly unmarred." But as president he was torn between Muir's belief in preservation — the notion that wilderness should be protected simply for its beauty and wonder — and conservation, advocated by chief forester Gifford Pinchot, who thought more in terms of the wise use of natural resources than about "Nature." Conservationists advocated such measures as the 1902 Newlands Act (named for Francis G. Newlands, representative from Nevada), which required that the money from the sale of public lands be used to build dams and irrigation for the approximately five hundred million open acres in the West that were mostly arid land. While preservationists and conservationists often cooperated in the effort to establish parks and national forests, their differences in principle came to a head in the great battle of John Muir's life, the struggle to save the Hetch Hetchy Valley in Yosemite National Park.

Hetch Hetchy. In 1900 the city of San Francisco announced its desire to create a reservoir in the Hetch Hetchy Valley, one hundred fifty miles away in the Sierra Nevada mountains, by constructing a hydroelectric dam on the Tuolomne River. Because the valley was located in a national park, the secretary of the interior blocked the plan. Following the devastating earthquake and fire of 1906, the city tried again and was granted permission by the Interior Department, with the backing of Pinchot. Muir swung into action. Since the plan would require congressional approval, he hoped to block the measure in Congress by gathering public support. He denounced advocates of the project as "Temple destroyers, devotees of raging commercialism," who "seem to have a perfect contempt for Nature, and instead of lifting their eyes to the God of the Mountains, lift them to the Almighty Dollar." Muir put his heart and soul into the effort for more than a decade, but advocates of urban growth finally prevailed in 1913, when Congress approved the dam. A year later, worn out and disheartened, Muir died of pneumonia, but not before making wilderness protection a national issue.

Sources:

Stephen R. Fox, *The American Conservation Movement: John Muir and His Legacy* (Madison: University of Wisconsin Press, 1981);

Samuel P. Hays, *Conservation and the Gospel of Efficiency* (Cambridge, Mass: Harvard University Press, 1959);

Roderick Nash, *Wilderness and the American Mind* (New Haven: Yale University Press, 1967);

Elmo R. Richardson, "The Struggle for the Valley: California's Hetch Hetchy Controversy, 1905–1913," *California Historical Society Quarterly,* 38 (1959): 249–258.

CARRY NATION

1846-1911

TEMPERANCE ADVOCATE

Background. Carry Nation was the most famous prohibition activist during the 1900s. Born poor in Garrard County, Kentucky, Carry had little education and married young. Soon she discovered that her husband was an alcoholic, so she left him and returned home. He died six months later, and she married David Nation in 1877. After several moves the couple arrived in Medicine Lodge, Kansas, where Nation began to crusade against liquor. She helped found the local chapter of the Woman's Christian Temperance Union, and in 1899 closed a saloon by leading a prayer vigil in it. This did not work with the other bars in town, so Carry soon adopted more dramatic methods. In 1900 she began to throw bricks at saloons, causing considerable damage. Soon she had a full arsenal of weapons, including the famous hatchet.

"Joint Smasher." Almost six feet tall and powerfully built, Carry had the strength to attack saloons physically. Her methods brought her national attention when she wrecked the bar of Wichita's Hotel Carey and was jailed for two weeks. Thereafter, she was arrested frequently. In order to pay her fines, she lectured widely, spreading the Prohibition gospel far and wide. She also published her autobiography, *The Use and Need of the Life of Carry A. Nation,* in 1904 and sold miniature hatchets that said "Carry Nation, Joint Smasher." In 1910 she was beaten badly by the female owner of a Montana saloon and collapsed while speaking not long after. Six months later, she was dead, having given the Prohibition movement in the United States a critical amount of publicity during her lifetime.

Source:
Carry Nation, *The Use and Need of the Life of Carry A. Nation* (Topeka, Kans.: F. M. Steves, 1904).

SIMON PATTEN

1852-1922

ECONOMIST

Unlikely Beginning. The turn of the twentieth century witnessed a major change from the economic theories that had dominated the nineteenth century. At the forefront of these new economic theories of consumerism, prosperity, and abundance was an unlikely "revolutionary." Simon N. Patten, by all accounts, was a lonely, solitary figure who insisted on social betterment. He was a farmer who settled in and helped revolutionize the business economy of the cities. He was a monastic and somewhat ascetic figure, yet insisted that happiness could be gleaned by all through materialism and consumerism. But he was also regarded as a fine teacher and a brilliant thinker, a man who discarded what he believed to be the limiting factors of the old economics and saw that something good could and would happen in the United States in the new century.

Education. Patten was born in Cossumyuna, New York, in 1852, but shortly after his birth, his family moved to a farm near Sandwich, Illinois. His mother died of typhoid fever when Patten was four. His father became a successful farmer, was an elder in the United Presbyterian Church, and served in the Illinois legislature as well as in the Union army during the Civil War. Patten attended a local public school and at seventeen entered the Jennings Seminary in nearby Aurora, Illinois. He graduated in 1874 and returned to the family farm. He entered Northwestern University in 1875 but almost immediately quit in order to travel to Germany, where a close friend, Joseph French Johnson, was studying at the University of Halle. Germany had a major impact on Patten's subsequent thinking about economics. Among his teachers was Johannes Conrad, one of the driving minds behind the industrialization of Germany. Patten was also impressed by Germany's mature economy, with its ability to satisfy a high level of consumerist demands. He graduated from Halle in 1878 with a Ph.D. and returned to Illinois.

The Premises of Political Economy. Patten found only disappointment upon his return. He worked on the farm for a year. He tried to study law in Chicago but developed terrible eye troubles that prevented him from reading. For the next two and a half years he remained inactive, but on a trip to Philadelphia he received successful treatment for his eyes. The cure gave him a renewed interest in life, and upon his return to Sandwich he became a teacher in the local district school. He subsequently became a superintendent of schools in Rhodes, Iowa. In the meantime, after his vision was restored, Patten began work on his first book. *The Premises of Political Economy* was published in 1886. The book was an adaptation of John Stuart Mill's thinking to fit the economic situation in America, and led to Patten's appointment to a position at the Wharton School of Economics at the University of Pennsylvania. Patten traveled to Philadelphia and never saw his family again. He would remain at the Wharton School until 1917 and make it the most influential center of economic theory in the United States.

Economic Abundance. Patten was an economic optimist. To him the theories that had dominated the nineteenth century — the theory of scarcity, the fixed-wage-fund law, the law of diminishing returns — were not to be applied in the United States. In all of these theories the dominant note was one of fierce competition for limited resources. As the population grew, these theories held, pressure on the supply of basic necessities created scarcity, even as desperate competition for work drove down wages. Patten, on the other hand, believed that man was the limiting factor and that man could intelligently find a way to sustain and even increase abundance. Patten saw at the turn of the century that a new business culture was developing, and he embraced it fervently. He thought a society's culture should fit its economic character. Thus, as the country prospered, as it produced and accumulated wealth, the culture of America should emphasize the possibilities of abundance. This would be done by changing people's attitudes about consumerism and materialism, creating a consumer culture that explicitly rejected the nineteenth century's emphasis on restraint and self-denial, the idea that luxuries were immoral. Patten acknowledged the necessity of that old thinking but clearly saw that times had changed and that a new abundance would define the future.

A New Morality. Patten carried his argument even further. Business not only was to create material wealth but was also to redefine morality. The market and contemporary corporate capitalism were not only useful, they were moral. They were moral because of the prosperity they brought to so many, because of their betterment of society as a whole, because of "elimination of the unsocial capitalists and the increasing control of each industry by a social group." Hedonism in the individual, the preference for consumption, overwork, or production, was a positive force, one that should be harnessed for the good of all, Patten thought. The more people consumed, the happier they would become and the less they would want. Patten believed that the banker, serving the public, cooperating with business, transcending national or local limits, was the leader of this new morality. In fact, individuals, now endowed with more capital, would follow the virtue of the banker and his budgets. Surplus wealth could be used to create a better society with amenities like libraries, museums, and civic centers, available to all. Though in a sense Patten was a laissez-faire capitalist, even to the point of supporting the existence of monopolies, he was no social Darwinist. He believed in the betterment of all and was a seminal writer on the new field of sociology. He simply believed that the market was the tool to social betterment, not political or labor strife.

Professor. Patten's theories had a major impact on not only the economic theory of the 1900s but on its practice. The Wharton School, the first business-oriented institution in an academic institution in the United States, became the think tank that would influence not only economists and sociologists, but practicing politicians.

"Patten men," loyal students, apostles of a new economic gospel, left the Wharton School determined to teach Americans how to crave consumer goods. Patten had a long, fruitful career. Among his influential books were *The Development of English Thought* (1899), *The Consumption of Wealth* (1901), *The New Basis of Civilization* (1907), and *Product and Climax* (1909). In addition Patten helped found the American Economic Association and served as its president in 1908 and 1909. His ideas for the betterment of urban planning, especially in the areas of recreation, helped redefine life in urban centers. He married in 1903, but the marriage ended unhappily six years later. Patten remained at the Wharton School until 1917, when he was forced to retire. The university cited his age (sixty-seven), but Patten insisted that he was being forced out because of his pacifist beliefs on the verge of the entry of the United States into World War I. Late in life he published a book of poems, *Folk Love* (1919), and a novel, *Mud Hollow* (1922), neither of which was well received. He died in 1922 at Brown's-Mills-in-the-Pines, New Jersey, after suffering two strokes. A former student, Rexford Tugwell, who served in the Franklin Roosevelt administration, wrote that Patten had exerted "a greater influence than was ever exerted by any other teacher, with the possible exception of John Dewey, I believe, or William James, in American academic history."

Source:
William Leach, *Land of Desire: Merchants, Power, and the Rise of a New American Culture* (New York: Random House, 1993).

PEOPLE IN THE NEWS

In 1908 **Grace Abbott** became director of the Immigrant's Protective League (1908–1917). She called for regulation of employment agencies, compulsory education, and open immigration. She later served as director of the Children's Bureau in the U.S. Department of Labor.

In 1909 **Alva Erskine Smith Vanderbilt Belmont,** inheritor of two of the largest fortunes in the United States, lent her name and financial support to striking garment workers in New York City. She was also an active member of the Congressional Union, an important suffrage organization in the 1900s.

In 1900 **Carrie Chapman Catt** was elected president of the National American Woman Suffrage Association, and would remain a prominent leader of the movement into the 1920s.

In 1909 **Herbert David Croly** published *The Promise of American Life,* in which he advocated a platform of reform and administration he called the "New Nationalism." The term, and the book, caught the attention of former president Theodore Roosevelt, who incorporated Croly's ideas into his 1912 presidential campaign.

Joan Cuneo, the first eminent woman race driver, entered her first race in 1905, and in 1907 completed a fifteen-hundred-mile round trip.

In 1908 **Josephine Clara Goldmark** provided pathbreaking sociological research that helped convince the Supreme Court to uphold legislation limiting the working hours of women in *Muller* v. *Oregon.* She also served as research director for National Consumers' League.

In 1904 **Helen Keller,** an early and illustrious advocate of improved education for the blind and deaf, graduated from Radcliffe College. She was the author of *The Story of My Life* (1902) and *Optimism* (1903), among other works.

In 1901 **Seth Low,** after serving as president of Columbia University, was elected mayor of New York City on a reform platform. Low was a prominent advocate of improved municipal government, particularly as president of the National Civic Federation.

In 1909 **Mary White Ovington,** a social worker, helped to establish the National Association for the Advancement of Colored People (NAACP).

In 1903 **Rose Schneiderman,** a labor activist, took a leading role in establishing the Women's Trade Union League, an organization that brought together settlement workers, suffrage advocates, and trade-union organizers.

Throughout the 1900s **Mary Church Terrell,** founding president of the National Association of Colored Women (1896), was a leading black spokeswoman and organizer on behalf of civil rights and women's suffrage.

DEATHS

Herbert Baxter Adams, historian whose students included Woodrow Wilson and Frederick Jackson Turner who helped organize the American Historical Association (1886), 30 July 1901.

Daniel Agnew, 93, Pennsylvania Supreme Court judge who found local dry laws constitutional, 9 March 1902.

Susan Brownell Anthony, 86, reformer and founder of the women's suffrage movement in the United States, 13 March 1906.

Caroline Astor, 78, socialite, founder of the "Four Hundred," 30 October 1908.

Harriet Hubbard Ayer, 54, first woman to make fortune in the cosmetics industry, 1903.

Frank C. Bangs, 74, humorist, lecturer, 12 June 1908.

Josephine Abiah Penfield Cushman Bateham, 71, influential advocate of Sunday closing laws (blue laws), 15 March 1901.

John Bidwell, 80, former Prohibition Party presidential candidate, 4 April 1900.

Calamity Jane, 51, cowgirl, adventurer, 1 August 1903.

Julia Colman, 80, Woman's Christian Temperance Union officer, influential writer and editor, 10 January 1909.

Jane "Jennie June" Cunningham Croly, 72, newspaper reporter and clubwoman, 1902.

Rev. Theodore Ledyard Cuyler, 87, well-known Presbyterian preacher, writer, and ardent temperance worker, 26 February 1909.

Nathan Smith Davis, 87, physician, sanitary reformer, and antialcohol advocate, 16 June 1904.

Noah Davis, 83, New York attorney and temperance advocate who linked drinking and crime, 20 March 1902.

Mary Mapes Dodge, 74, author of *Hans Brinker, or the Silver Skates* (1865), 21 August 1905.

Ignatius Donnelly, 69, Republican and Populist politician and reformer, author of social commentary novel *Caesar's Column* (1891), 1 January 1901.

Marshall Field, 70, merchant, developed one of the first department stores in the United States, 16 January 1906.

Rev. Charles Henry Fowler, 70, Methodist minister, foreign missionary, Prohibition advocate, 20 March 1908.

Helen Mar Jackson Gougar, 63, teacher, writer, WCTU and Prohibition Party activist, 6 June 1907.

Edward Everett Hale, 87, reformer, author of "The Man Without a Country," 10 June 1909.

William Torrey Harris, 74, educator, writer, 5 November 1909.

Samuel Dexter Hastings, 86, merchant, politician, antislavery and temperance reformer, 26 March 1903.

Oliver Otis Howard, 78, commissioner of U.S. Freedmen's Bureau 1865–1876, 26 October 1909.

Mary Hannah Hanchett Hunt, 75, national temperance worker and health-education reformer, 24 April 1906.

Chief Joseph of the Nez Perce tribe, 64, who said in 1877, "I will fight no more forever," 1904.

Samuel Porter Jones, 58, Methodist evangelist who preached all over the country on moral and temperance issues, 15 October 1906.

Leslie Enraught Keeley, 67?, successful promoter of the Keeley (or Gold) Cure for alcoholism, 21 February 1900.

Mary Ashton Livermore, 83, teacher, suffragist, Massachusetts WCTU president, 23 May 1905.

Henry Demarest Lloyd, 56, publicist, social reformer, author of the influential book *Wealth Against Commonwealth* (1894), 28 September 1903.

Helena Modjeska, 58, actress, 8 April 1909.

Francis Murphy, 71, temperance evangelist whose "Murphy Movement" got tens of thousands to take the "Murphy Pledge," 30 June 1907.

Frederick Law Olmsted, 80, urban planner, designer of Central Park, Boston's Emerald Necklace, and other parks, 28 August 1903.

Hiram Price, 87, president of Anti-Saloon League of America, 30 May 1901.

Esther Pugh, 73, national WCTU treasurer, 28 March 1908.

Carl Schurz, 76, reformer, champion of civil service reform, 14 May 1906.

Samuel R. Scottron, household goods manufacturer, encourager of black inventors, 1905.

Henrietta Skelton, 57, national WCTU lecturer and organizer, German-language temperance worker, 22 August 1900.

Elizabeth Cady Stanton, 87, leading suffragist and peace activist, 1902.

Sarah Hackett Stevenson, 66, nurse, educator, first head of WCTU's National Temperance Hospital, 14 August 1909.

Eliza Daniel "Mother Stewart" Stewart, 96, radical dry crusader, antislavery activist, first chairwoman of the national WCTU, 8 August 1908.

Eliza Jane Trimble "Mother Thompson" Thompson, 89, Ohio temperance reformer; instigator of 1873–1874 "Hillsboro uprising" involving praying at saloons, 3 November 1905.

Isabelle Urquhart, 42, actress, 7 February 1907.

Zarelda Gray Sanders Wallace, 84, temperance activist, suffragist, March 1901.

Annie Turner Wittenmyer, 73, first president of national WCTU, president of Non-Partisan (antisuffrage) WCTU, 2 February 1900.

PUBLICATIONS

Brooks Adams, *America's Economic Supremacy* (New York: Macmillan, 1900);

Henry Adams, *The Education of Henry Adams* (Wahington, D.C.: Privately printed, 1907);

Jane Addams, *Democracy and Social Ethics* (New York: Macmillan, 1902);

Addams, *Newer Ideals of Peace* (New York: Macmillan, 1907);

Addams, *The Spirit of Youth and City Streets* (New York: Macmillan, 1909);

James Lane Allen, *The Reign of Law* (New York: Macmillan, 1900);

Susan B. Anthony, Elizabeth Cady Stanton, Matilda Joslyn Gage, eds., *The History of Woman Suffrage*, 4 volumes (Rochester, N.Y.: Susan B. Anthony, 1887–1902);

Ray Stannard Baker, *Following the Color Line* (New York: Doubleday, Page, 1908);

Baker (as David Grayson), *Adventures in Contentment* (New York: Doubleday, Page, 1907);

Charles W. Chesnutt, *The Marrow of Tradition* (Boston: Houghton Mifflin, 1901);

Charles H. Cooley, *Human Nature and the Social Order* (New York: Scribners, 1902);

Cooley, *Social Organization: A Study of the Larger Mind* (New York: Scribners, 1909);

Herbert David Croly, *The Promise of American Life* (New York: Macmillan, 1909);

Thomas Dixon Jr., *The Clansman: An Historical Romance of the Ku Klux Klan* (New York: Doubleday, Page, 1905);

W. E. B. Du Bois, *The Souls of Black Folk* (Chicago: McClurg, 1903);

Charles William Eliot, *The Religion of the Future* (Boston: J. W. Luce, 1909);

Richard T. Ely, *The Coming City* (New York: Crowell, 1902);

Ely and George Ray Wicker, *Elementary Principles of Economics* (New York: Macmillan, 1904);

Charlotte Perkins Gilman, *Concerning Children* (Boston: Small, Maynard, 1900);

Joseph H. Greer, *True Womanhood* (Chicago: Columbia, 1903);

Greer, *The Wholesome Woman* (Chicago: Atheneum, 1902);

Florence Kelley, *Some Ethical Gains Through Legislation* (New York: Macmillan, 1905);

Henry Demarest Lloyd, *A Country Without Strikes* (New York, 1900);

Lloyd, *Man, The Social Creator* (New York: Doubleday, Page, 1906);

George Horace Lorimer, *Letters from a Self-Made Merchant to His Son* (New York: Grosset & Dunlap, 1902);

Charles Eustace Merriman, *Letters from a Son to His Self-Made Father* (Boston & Manchester: New Hampshire Publishing, 1903);

Simon Nelson Patten, *Heredity and Social Progress* (New York: Macmillan, 1903);

Patten, *The New Basis of Civilization* (New York: Macmillan, 1907);

Whitelaw Reid, *Careers for the Coming Men* (Akron, Ohio: Saalfield, 1904);

Reid, *Problems of Expansion* (New York: Century, 1900);

Edward A. Ross, *Sin and Society* (Boston: Houghton Mifflin, 1907);

Ross, *Social Control* (New York: Macmillan, 1901);

Upton Sinclair, *The Industrial Republic* (New York: Doubleday, Page, 1907);

Sinclair, *The Jungle* (New York: Doubleday, Page, 1906);

Rev. Sylvanus Stall, D.D., *Self and Sex* (Philadelphia: Vir, 1903);

Lester Frank Ward, *Applied Sociology* (New York: Ginn, 1906);

Booker T. Washington, *Up From Slavery* (Garden City, N.Y.: Doubleday, 1901).

CHAPTER NINE

MEDIA

by NANCY BERNHARD

CONTENTS

Sidebars and tables are listed in italics.

1900

- Lincoln Steffens joins *McClure's* as managing editor.

- Arthur Brisbane, editor, launches William Randolph Hearst's *Chicago American* newspaper.

- Herbert Croly founds the *Architectural Record*.

- Frank Munsey changes title of *Puritan Magazine* to *Junior Munsey*.

- The first volume of *Who's Who in America* is published.

- McClure Phillips, book publisher, is founded.

- C. M. Clark, the only turn-of-the-century Boston publishing house owned by a woman, is launched.

- The Supreme Court of Illinois rules that the Associated Press wire service is a public utility and must not discriminate among subscribers. The AP declares bankruptcy in Illinois and reincorporates in New York.

Nov. Walter Hines Page founds the public-affairs monthly *World's Work* to promote business and good labor relations.

1901

- *House and Garden* is founded.

- *Appeal to Reason*, a socialist paper, is founded by J. A. Wayland in Girard, Kansas.

- Irvin S. Cobb becomes editor of the *Paducah* (Ky.) *News-Democrat*.

- Upton Sinclair founds Sinclair Press to publish his own books.

- Frank Munsey buys the *New York Daily News* and the *Washington Times;* a year later he buys the *Boston Journal* and, in 1908, the *Baltimore Evening Times.*

- *The Guardian*, a militant black paper, is founded in Boston by William Monroe Trotter with George Forbes.

29 June The trade journal *Editor and Publisher* is founded in New York by James B. Shale, publisher of the *McKeesport* (Pa.) *News,* to crusade against the abuses of press agentry, bad advertising, and fraudulent information.

1 July Aldoph S. Ochs becomes majority stockholder of *The New York Times.*

5 Sept. Leon Czolgosz shoots President William McKinley at Buffalo, New York. The rumor circulates that the assassin carried a copy of Hearst's virulently anti-McKinley *New York Journal* in his pocket.

24 Oct. Eastman Kodak incorporates in Trenton, New Jersey. George Eastman consolidates most British and U.S. manufacturers of photographic equipment. His big seller is the Brownie Box camera, which sells for one dollar.

Nov. *The New York Times* marks its fiftieth anniversary.

12 Dec. Guglielmo Marconi sends the letter *S* two thousand miles across the Atlantic from Cornwall, England, to Saint John's, Newfoundland.

1902

- The B. W. Huebsch publishing company is launched.
- Norman Hapgood becomes editor of *Collier's Weekly*, a position he will hold until 1912.
- E. W. Scripps founds the Newspaper Enterprise Association, a news syndicate for his papers.
- The first installment of Ida Tarbell's "The History of the Standard Oil Company" appears in *McClure's*.
- The *South Atlantic Quarterly* is founded.

Sept. *McClure's* publishes Lincoln Steffens's "The Tweed Days in St. Louis."

Oct. *Junior Munsey* is merged into *Argosy Magazine*.

1903

- *Redbook* is founded.
- The Bobbs-Merrill publishing company is founded in Indianapolis.
- Abraham Cahan assumes complete control of the *Jewish Daily Forward*.
- Jampes Palmer Knapp founds *Associated Sunday Magazine*, the first newspaper magazine supplement.
- Gilbert Grosvenor becomes editor of *National Geographic*, a position he holds until 1954.
- The "Nantucket Limerick" comes into vogue in newspapers. (There once was a man from Nantucket / Who kept all his cash in a bucket; / But his daughter, named Nan, / Ran away with a man, / And as for the bucket, Nantucket.)
- *Everybody's Magazine*, founded as an adjunct to Wanamaker's Department Store in 1899, is purchased by Erman Jesse Ridgway and becomes a leading muckraking journal.

Jan. The groundbreaking issue of *McClure's* magazine publishes articles by Ida Tarbell, Ray Stannard Baker, and Lincoln Steffens and establishes the substance, form, and style of muckraking.

Feb. The *Ladies' Home Journal* becomes the first American magazine to reach one million paid subscriptions.

22 Feb. Marconi publishes a newspaper on the Cunard liner *Etruria*, the first printed at sea.

29 Mar. Regular telegraph service begins between New York and London on Marconi's wireless.

15 Aug. Joseph Pulitzer gives $2 million to Columbia University to begin a school of journalism.

1904

- Lincoln Steffens publishes *The Shame of the Cities*, a collection of his articles on municipal corruption.
- The University of Illinois institutes the first four-year journalism curriculum, directed by Frank W. Scott.

1905

May	Edward Bok of the *Ladies' Home Journal* declares editorial war on patent medicines.
Dec.	The first radio transmission by Reginald Fessenden of music (from Brant Rock, Massachusetts) takes place.
	The new *New York Times* building opens on Longacre Square in midtown Manhattan, which becomes known as Times Square.

- W. D. Moffat leaves Charles Scribner's Sons to form the publishing company Moffat Yard with Robert Yard.

- Chicago's *Defender* is founded by Robert S. Abbott to decry racial injustice.

- Sime Silverman founds *Variety* as a weekly theatrical trade journal.

Jan.	*National Geographic* magazine publishes eleven pages of photographs of the Tibetan capital, Lhasa.
15 May	Charles Alexander launches the monthly *Alexander's Magazine* for black readers.
Oct.	Samuel Hopkins Adams's series on patent medicines, "The Great American Fraud," begins appearing in *Collier's*.

1906

- W. E. B. Du Bois publishes *Moon Illustrated Weekly* from a small print shop in Memphis.

- Lee De Forest patents the triode vacuum tube, a critical development in broadcasting, amplification, high-fidelity music systems, public address systems, and sound film.

Feb.	Upton Sinclair publishes *The Jungle*, a novel depicting horrifying conditions in the meatpacking industry and spurring the passage of the Meat Inspection Act. Also in 1906, Congress passes the Pure Food and Drug Act and the Hepburn Act, enlarging regulation over the railroads. Muckraking journalists are given credit for creating public demand for all of this legislation.
Apr.	Mitchell Kennerley announces his book publishing imprint of American authors and English imports.
14 Apr.	President Theodore Roosevelt makes a speech in Washington, D.C., condemning those journalists who, by consistently exposing corruption and abuse, miss the larger social picture. He introduces the term "muckraking."
18 Apr.	A major earthquake and fire destroy much of San Francisco, but the following day the city's three newspapers join forces and print a single edition across the bay in Oakland.
Oct.	Ida Tarbell, Lincoln Steffens, and Ray Stannard Baker leave the staff of *McClure's* to take over the *American Magazine*. They are joined by John S. Phillips, Finley Peter Dunne, and William Allen White. The magazine soon fails.
21 Nov.	Reginald Fessenden, using a high-frequency alternator built by Ernst F. W. Alexanderson, sends the first voice radio transmissions, covering the eleven miles between Plymouth and Brant Rock, Massachusetts.
24 Dec.	Fessenden's Christmas Eve broadcast (from Brant Rock) of Handel's "Largo," himself on violin playing Gounod's "O Holy Night," followed by Christmas wishes is picked up by ships in the West Indies. He also established two-way wireless communication with Scotland this year.

1907

- W. E. B. Du Bois establishes *Horizon* magazine, intended to spread the views of the Niagara Movement of black intellectuals.

- The George H. Doran publishing company is launched.

- E. W. Scripps founds the United Press Association, a commercial wire service, by combining two regional news services in the Midwest. The UP soon has bureaus in many foreign capitals and news exchanges with leading foreign newspapers.

23 Jan. The "Trial of the Century" begins in New York, where millionaire Harry K. Thaw is charged with the murder of world-famous architect Stanford White over the honor of Thaw's wife, showgirl Evelyn Nesbit. Irvin S. Cobb labels Hearst reporter Annie Laurie (Winifred Black) and her associates "Sob Sisters" for their melodramatic coverage.

Apr. Ray Stannard Baker's pathbreaking series on race, "Following the Color Line," begins appearing in the *Atlantic Monthly*.

1908

- P. F. Volland Company is founded in Chicago to publish greeting cards; later they begin publishing children's books.

- Mary Baker Eddy founds the *Christian Science Monitor* to "injure no man, but to bless all mankind" and achieves a national circulation of more than 150,000 with no sensationalism of any kind.

- The University of Missouri founds the first separate School of Journalism, with Walter Williams as dean.

Winter Oliver K. Bovard (OKB) becomes managing editor of the *St. Louis Dispatch*.

1909

- The Macaulay Company, a publisher, is founded.

- Sigma Delta Chi is founded at DePauw University as a professional fraternity for journalists.

- William Randolph Hearst founds the International News Service, the third major U.S. press assocation after the Associated Press and the United Press.

- James H. Anderson founds the New York *Amsterdam News* in Harlem, which would become one of the nation's largest and most influential black newspapers.

- *La Follette's Weekly* is founded by Robert La Follette in Madison, Wisconsin, to further progressive reform.

- The first radio station with a regular series of programs is begun by Charles D. "Doc" Herrold of San Jose, who powers his station by illegally tapping into the streetcar lines of the Santa Fe Railway.

23 Mar. Former president Theodore Roosevelt leaves for a hunting trip in Africa. *Scribner's* pays him $500,000 for his account of the trip.

9 Apr. Enrico Caruso broadcasts from the Metropolitan Opera House in Manhattan to the house of Lee De Forest.

3 May The first wireless press message is sent from New York City to Chicago.

Sept. During the first week of the month, both Frederick Cook and Robert E. Peary make claims to have reached the North Pole the preceding April. Most scientists come to believe that Peary was the actual winner, and his account of his journey appears in *The New York Times* from 8 to 11 September.

15 Nov. Herbert Bayard Swope takes a job as a reporter for the *New York World*.

OVERVIEW

Big Business. During most of the nineteenth century, a newspaper or a magazine could be started with a little borrowed cash and a lot of hard work. Most publications expressed the views and preferences of their publishers and editors: it was the age of personal journalism. By 1900 it took at least a million dollars to launch a newspaper in New York City, and most publications were affected by business concerns. So began the age of corporate journalism. What had been a personal, local, and literary enterprise became steadily more bureaucratic, national, and professional throughout the twentieth century. In 1900 there were 2,226 dailies with a combined circulation of 15.1 million in the United States.

Big Questions. Rapid growth in population, resources, and power had turned the United States into a decidedly industrial nation by the turn of the century, but basic questions about the character of the nation remained unanswered. What role would the United States play in world politics? How could unrestricted economic individualism be reconciled with the goals of social reformers who crusaded against the ills of capitalism? How many people would benefit from the wealth generated by the nation's prodigious natural resources? Would the government guarantee living and working conditions, educational opportunities, health, and security? And not least, what was the role of the press in monitoring business and government? These questions were discussed and answered in the pages of the nation's newspapers and magazines.

The Spirit of the Reformer. To many observers, the most pressing problem facing the American nation at the turn of the century was the concentration of economic power in the hands of a few huge corporations, known as the trusts. Between 1898 and 1904, 5,300 individual companies combined into just 318 trusts. Aided by corrupt politicians, the trusts accrued power for themselves at the expense of thousands of American workers, some of whose wages did not sustain their families. Newspapers and magazines took up the challenge of exposing the trusts and cleaning up the political machines that smoothed their way. These "people's champions" campaigned for a more equal distribution of wealth, for the rights of the worker and the farmer, and for honesty in government. Wealthy Americans distrusted the publishers of the dailies crusading for reform, while the larger public also attacked the publishers for their wealth and privilege.

The Illustrated Weekly. American manufacturers introduced a wide new array of consumer products in this era and needed to publicize them. Old-style religious and literary magazines were not a suitable outlet for the splashy advertisements these products required. During the first decade of the twentieth century, half the space of the general-circulation weeklies was filled with ads, driving down their price and driving up their circulation. This circumstance, along with innovations in printing technology in the 1880s and 1890s, made the magazine a dominant mass medium of this period, before the introduction of movies or radio. The cost of producing a weekly magazine with pictures dropped steadily. In 1893 *McClure's* debuted at fifteen cents a copy. In 1903 *Collier's* sold for just five cents, compared with twenty-five cents for one of the older publications such as *Harper's* or the *Century*. The *Saturday Evening Post,* purchased in 1897 by Cyrus H. K. Curtis and edited from 1899 until 1937 by George Horace Lorimer, became the largest-circulation weekly in the nation, reaching one million in 1908. Lorimer, aiming at the middle-class businessman and his family, attracted famous writers such as Joseph Conrad, O. Henry, Jack London, Stephen Crane, and Bret Harte.

Investigative Zeal. Cheap and well produced, *Collier's, McClure's, Everybody's, Arena,* and *Cosmopolitan* pioneered a new kind of magazine journalism. They exposed the monopolistic and abusive practices of the trusts in oil, insurance, railroads, and food production and brought to light the deep corruption in municipal, state, and federal government. Groundbreaking journalists, such as Ida Tarbell, Lincoln Steffens, Ray Stannard Baker, and David Graham Phillips, became celebrities in their own right. Mr. Dooley, the wisecracking saloon keeper created by another muckraker, Finley Peter Dunne, commented, "Time was whin th' magazines was very ca'ming to th' mind. Th' idea ye got fr'm these publications was that life was wan glad, sweet song . . . But now, when I pick up my fav'rit magazine, what do I find? Iv'rything has gone wrong . . . Here ye arre! Last edition! Just out! Full account iv th' Incalculated!"

A Name for the New Investigative Journalism. President Theodore Roosevelt enacted a series of moderate reforms to curb the worst abuses of the trusts. He appreciated the work of responsible journalists in bringing problems to public attention, but he railed against those who, driven by sensationalism, sullied the reputation of all businessmen and politicians. On 14 April 1906 he delivered a speech at the new House Office Building in Washington, D.C. Roosevelt cited a passage from John Bunyan's *Pilgrim's Progress* (1678) as a metaphor for the journalists determined not to see any good anywhere: "the Man with the Muckrake, the man who could look no way but downward with the muckrake in his hand, who was offered a celestial crown for his muckrake, but would neither look up nor regard the crown he was offered, but continued to rake to himself the filth of the floor." The speech won headlines everywhere, and conservative papers fastened onto the label "muckraker" as a derogatory term for reformist journalists. It could be a good term or a bad term: to muckrake meant to investigate and to expose. Critics and supporters alike dubbed muckraking a "literature of exposure," with a "perspective of revolt" and irreverence toward all authority. Muckraking diminished through the decade, and historians give the date of its death as 1912, when *McClure's,* which had pioneered the movement, joined the trend to publish more fiction after the magazine changed hands.

The Ladies. Not every publication was swept up in the spirit of muckraking. While the long-standing leader in women's magazines, the *Ladies' Home Journal,* did publish important exposés, it also published fiction by William Dean Howells, Mark Twain, Sir Arthur Conan Doyle, and Sarah Orne Jewett. Its longtime editor, Edward Bok, aspired to improve home life in America with advice on everything from marriage to nutrition to architecture. His campaigns to beautify American neighborhoods and to clean up American morality proved popular and influential. He joined forces with the Woman's Christian Temperance Union to attack patent medicines, which often contained high percentages of alcohol and narcotics. In 1901 *Good Housekeeping* inaugurated the Good Housekeeping Institute, which conducted experiments to evaluate a range of household products and practices. In 1900 *McCall's* and the *Woman's Home Companion* already contained the "service" departments familiar to readers of today's women's magazines: beauty, children, home, food, and features.

Color. The first decade of the twentieth century brought the flowering of two kinds of color in American publishing. First, a humorous blend of folklore and political commentary known as the "colyum" made its way into the newspapers. Writers such as Bert Leston Taylor, George Ade, and Don Marquis made their names writing verses and telling stories. More literally, color printing became technologically and financially viable at this time. It began in earnest with the introduction of color supplements to the Sunday papers, filled with cartoons and comic strips. A new kind of artistry combined political commentary, zinging wit, and draftsmanship, and the modern comic strip was born. Both kinds of color added fuel to the circulation wars between the papers in big cities, with writers and artists constantly being lured from one paper to another. And both kinds of color led people who had never bought a newspaper before, especially children, to become regular readers.

TOPICS IN THE NEWS

BOOK PUBLISHING

Publishers Modernize. During the nineteenth century, most book publishers in America believed theirs was an ivory-tower profession, bearing the cultural and social responsibility of providing Americans with works of literary distinction or political and philosophical distinction, whether such volumes returned a profit or not; but in the decade 1900 to 1909, shocked by the collapse of two of the nation's oldest and most formidable houses, Harper and Appleton, publishers grew progressively less genteel and more aggressively profit-oriented and business-minded. In the very first year of the decade, the venerable institutions of Harper's and Appleton did not disappear from the American publishing scene, but only because they were rescued from bankruptcy by Wall Street financiers. In the process, Wall Street found the publishers' idealism quaint and their mismanagement maddening; and in the following years a much more fiscally minded generation of managers moved into the industry to work alongside the high-minded editors and proprietors. As a result, although many major houses, like Scribners, Putnam's, and Dutton, continued to be owned by the families whose names they bore, they began rapidly transforming their business and marketing methods and dramatically expanding into large-scale businesses of the twentieth century.

Growth and Expansion. In this dynamic and turbulent period, more and more books were mass-produced, a feat made possible by the fact that printing and binding were becoming progressively mechanized. In 1900 *Publishers' Weekly* noted that the capacity of bookprinting houses and binderies in New York alone was estimated to be one hundred thousand volumes per week. The same publication observed that the publishing industry was developing in other ways: in the single year 1900, for example, more than seven thousand new books, mainly by American writers, had been published by nearly six hundred publishers. By 1907, despite the panic of that year, the number of new books published had risen to 9,620, the largest number ever recorded. As the decade proceeded, new publishing houses, such as Doubleday, Page and Company sprang up — mainly in New York City — and traditional houses, such as Scribners, incorporated. At the same time, to increase markets and guard their balance sheets, the new breed of profit-oriented publishers saw to it that the distribution of their titles became more national and even international, as American books appeared in homes and bookstores in Europe, Canada, and Mexico. And in this important transitional decade, as the business grew and redefined itself, New York City became the undisputed capital of the publishing world.

Fiction Predominates. Meanwhile, the boom in fiction publishing that had begun after the Civil War showed no signs of abating, and while biography, history, economics, and poetry continued to sell, fiction became the great mainstay of the industry. Sales of novels of all types climbed higher and higher, with best-sellers enriching author and publisher alike. In 1900 Mary Johnston's *To Have and To Hold*, a historical novel about colonial Virginia, sold more than 250,000 copies in six months. For perspective, consider that an analyst a few years later recalled that, as recently as the late 1890s, a book was considered highly successful if it sold 25,000 copies. Then in 1904, according to the annual listing in *The Bookman*, a top best-seller was *Rebecca of Sunnybrook Farm*, by Kate Douglas Wiggin; in later years writers such as Upton Sinclair and Booth Tarkington enjoyed huge sales; in 1908 Mary Roberts Rinehart, one of the most popular authors of the time, published yet another best-seller, *The Circular Staircase*. In this same year, of 9,254 new titles published, 1,458 were works of fiction; these numbers represented a constant trend during this time, and if they were to include fiction for children, they would be much larger. During these years America's taste for fiction, especially popular fiction, seemed insatiable. High-brow publishers took pains to distinguish melodramatic and sensationalistic novels from the more worthy and realistic "literature," such as that advocated by William Dean Howells, and written by Henry James, Edith Wharton, and Stephen Crane. Publishers generally vied for successful fiction writers by offering large advances and royalty rates as much as 20 percent of sales, and devoted great energy to wooing the reading public by spending ever larger sums on advertising and promotion. Even as rates for ads placed in books and magazines skyrocketed, one noted publisher estimated in 1904 that even small publishers spent $50,000 a year on advertising. Indeed, in 1909 Henry Holt, a longtime giant in the business, complained that with so much competition for fiction readers, marketing and advertising costs had made it difficult to clear a profit on a book.

Authors' Rights. In the nineteenth century, publishers generally treated their authors with little consideration; but in the years 1900–1909 American writers, aided by a new cadre of literary agents, began to demand better compensation and more control over their work. Quickly gone were the days when Henry Holt had refused to give his authors written contracts and declared that royalties in excess of 10 percent were "immoral." In the past, both publishers and editors had changed manuscripts to suit their own tastes, without consulting the person whose name would appear on the book. This practice, too, stopped, as the growing number of literary agents worked ever more aggressively to protect the integrity of the authors' works, and, of course, ensure their authors' largest advances and highest royalties. In addition, the first decade of the twentieth century saw the first bidding wars between houses for the works of popular authors, a practice appalling to traditional publishers, who yearned for the years when, at least in their memories, a loyalty existed between publisher and author, and business was conducted on a more gentlemanly basis. In the new commercial climate of the early 1900s, Charles Scribner II, a titan of the industry, was aghast that he might be forced to pay more than "whatever the book is fairly worth." Despite his resistance to such new methods, however, he managed to assemble an impressive literary stable at Scribners, whose authors included Edith Wharton, Thomas Nelson Page, and Richard Harding Davis.

Revolts against Commercialization of Literature. Between 1900 and 1909, the dramatic and accelerating commercialization of the book industry provoked strident protests from some publishers, especially older ones, who, keeping a nineteenth-century ideal of the nature and purpose of publishing (which one had likened to teaching and even the ministry), felt their traditionally honorable profession was being corrupted. These men — there were very few women in publishing management at this time — were repelled by the growing and seemingly irreversible dominance of economic issues in the publishing business. They disliked the new literary agents, the bidding wars for books, the huge advances paid to authors, the excesses of advertising, the cutthroat competition for readers, the sheer yearly volume of new and frequently undeserving books. One prominent publisher contemptuous of such trends was Henry Holt; writing in 1907, he particularly vented his spleen against literary agents, charging that they had "forced over-production by selling several of an author's books before they were written, and dazzling him with forced earnings from forced work, followed by inferior earnings from inferior work." Holt then declared, on a larger point: "It would be an immense gain for the cause of literature and to the

---

SALESMANSHIP ON PAPER

Riddle, circa 1901:

"Why is the merchant who doesn't advertise like a man in a rowboat?"

"Because he goes backward, I suppose."

"No; because he has to get along without sales."

After a couple of decades when advertising used enticing impressions and images to draw buyers to a product, it returned to the language of the hard sell at the turn of the century. In 1904 an enterprising copywriter arrived at the Chicago offices of the eminent Lord and Thomas advertising agency. He sent up a note that said, "You do not know what real advertising is. If you want to know, let me come up and tell you." An executive named Albert Lasker was sent to receive the visitor, one John E. Kennedy. The two spoke until three o'clock in the morning, when Kennedy was made the firm's new chief copywriter.

"Advertising," Kennedy told Lasker, "is salesmanship-on-paper." Forget pretty and diverting ads, he said. Tell the customer in reportorial prose the hard facts that a skilled salesman would convey in person. Treat the customer sensibly, as if he or she was uneducated but smart. And so began a new phase in advertising style, which was actually another turn in an old cycle that would continue to turn throughout the twentieth century.

Source: Stephen Fox, *The Mirror Makers: A History of American Advertising and Its Creators* (New York: Morrow, 1984).

---

profit of all worthy authors . . . if the 'commercial enterprise' that has come in from Wall Street . . . were taken out of the publishing business — if the competition consisted simply in selecting books wisely, making them tastefully and honestly, informing the interested public of their existence and supplying them to whatever legitimate demand they might effect through their own merit." Another publisher who disdained business trends in this decade was Walter Hines Page, former editor of the *Atlantic,* who wrote in *A Publisher's Confession* (1905) that publishing was "the worst business in the world," and that every successful publisher "could make more money going into some other business." Why, then, do people continue to become publishers? According to Page, the genuine publishers "every year invest in books and authors that they know cannot yield a direct or immediate profit . . . because they feel ennobled by trying to do a service to literature."

Joseph Pulitzer first conceived the idea of a professional school of journalism in the early 1890s, but the trustees of Columbia University rejected his plan. By 1903 the university had accepted his gift of $2 million, but debate within the newspaper profession raged over the wisdom of this approach. Many reporters believed that news talent was born rather than made. Influential educators asserted that a course in liberal arts and experience on a college newspaper would suffice as formal training. Reporters of the hard-knocks school dismissed the idea of journalism education, saying it would create a two-tiered profession. Pulitzer countered that he had never met a born editor and proposed courses in law, ethics, truth and accuracy, the liberal arts, statistics, science, principles of journalism, and news. Conceding that some people had an innate "news instinct," Pulitzer nonetheless believed that education would keep that instinct from overriding the "restraints of accuracy and conscience." The groundbreaking ceremony was held in 1904, and the Columbia School of Journalism officially opened in 1912.

Source: Marion Marzolf, *Civilizing Voices: American Press Criticism, 1880–1950* (New York: Longman, 1991).

Adolph S. Ochs, publisher of *The New York Times* from 1896 until his death in 1935

Doubleday, Page and Company. On January 1 1900 a new house made its debut in New York City. Frank Doubleday, who had left Scribners after a tempestuous relationship with Scribner and briefly gone into business with magazine and newspaper publisher Frank McClure, decided to form a partnership with Walter Hines Page. A deeply committed professional and a prodigy of energy, Page's aim was nothing less than the promotion of social democracy, education, science, sanitation, and dignity. Combining forces, the two men founded Doubleday, Page and Company, establishing their offices in Union Square, an area of New York rapidly becoming the heart of the publishing district. In the following years, these two publishers brought the new house to rapid prominence. Frank Doubleday was tall, zestful, charismatic, and very commercially astute. He pioneered advertising techniques for his company's books by, for example, placing his ads in newspapers and particularly in magazines, whose readers he judged more likely to be Doubleday patrons. He was fascinated by the challenges of book advertising. He observed: "Each book is its own individual advertising problem, and when you have made a success with one you have hardly any definite principle to put into words or guide you in advertising the next." Besides starting a chain of bookstores, he took mail-order and subscription selling of books far beyond their nineteenth-century dimensions. Both he and his partner,

meanwhile, encouraged the seeking out of writers of merit and importance and the forming of long and fruitful relationships. In the course of the decade, Doubleday, Page and Company set a new standard among successful New York publishers, and the only thing more impressive than its list of authors — which included Joseph Conrad, Booth Tarkington, Sir Arthur Conan Doyle, O. Henry, Edna Ferber, and Joel Chandler Harris — was its profit statement.

Sources:

Mark Sullivan, *Our Times: The United States, 1900–1925*; volume 1, *The Turn of The Century;* volume 2: *America Finding Herself;* and volume 3: *Pre-War America* (New York: Scribners, 1927, 1930);

John Tebbel, *Between Covers: The Rise and Transformation of Book Publishing in America* (New York: Oxford University Press, 1987);

Tebbel, *A History of Book Publishing in the United States,* volume 2: The Expansion of an Industry, 1865–1919 (New York & London: Bowker, 1975).

CITY LIFE AND THE TWO JOURNALISMS

An Urban Nation. In 1790 less than 5 percent of the U.S. population lived in cities of more than twenty-five hundred people. By 1920 more than 50 percent lived in cities. As the nation became increasingly urban and mobile, people knew fewer of their neighbors personally, and the daily newspaper's importance as the main source of community information and identity grew. Two distinct kinds of journalism evolved to meet the needs of city dwellers. The first, epitomized by the "Old Gray Lady," *The New York Times,* adhered to a policy of strict factuality. *The New York Times* aspired to strict objectivity and took a tone of scrupulous dispassion. Its readers were largely upper-middle-class people who needed accurate information for their businesses and who preferred the paper's cultivated tone. The second style, known vari-

Galveston, Texas, on 9 September 1900, the day after the city was devastated by a hurricane and flood that caused more than five thousand deaths

ously as the New Journalism, yellow journalism, entertainment journalism, or the "use-paper," targeted a much broader audience of urban workers. Papers, including Joseph Pulitzer's *New York World* and William Randolph Hearst's *New York Journal,* sought to entertain their readers with stories rather than inform them with strictly construed facts.

The Honor of Adolph Ochs. When he purchased the bankrupt *New York Times* in 1896, Adolph Ochs was the publisher of the *Chattanooga Times.* His initial innovations, lists of the out-of-town businessmen arriving and leaving, real estate transactions, court cases, and market prices, made *The New York Times* indispensable to the city's growing class of professionals. He added a Sunday magazine and book-review section. He promised dignified language, calm headlines, and intelligent discussion. Before settling on the slogan "All the News That's Fit to Print," he considered "It Does Not Soil the Breakfast Cloth," meaning both that he used a less smeary ink than his competitors and that he insisted on good taste. In 1898 he lowered the paper's price to a penny, and the circulation tripled within a year. Circulation jumped past one hundred thousand in 1901, and advertising lineage doubled. In 1904 Ochs built the Times Tower in midtown Manhattan and hired Carr Van Anda as managing editor, two moves that supported the reputation of the *Times* as the newspaper of record for the twentieth century. But nothing created the lustrous image of the *Times* as much as the veneration accorded its publisher. Ochs was seen as a man of impeccable morals and judgment.

The Newspaper Wars Continue. During the late 1890s a famous circulation battle between the New York papers of Hearst and Pulitzer resulted in a series of escalating stunts and increasingly sensationalized features. The war culminated in 1898, when the papers fanned the flames of actual battle between the United States and Spain. By 1900 the competition had moderated. Sexy sensationalism lost its edge because people had heard it

all before. Now the papers reached for a smart, "seen-it-all" sophistication. Pulitzer left the working-class audience to Hearst and fashioned his *World* as a liberal organ. Each paper, and their many competitors and imitators, vied to be seen as the champion of the common man and woman. In politics, this meant crusading against the power of big corporations and corrupt politicians. It also meant luring readers with juicy stories about murders and sexual scandals, color pictures, comic strips, and celebrity writers. Most immediately for the urban populace, it meant stories and columns that illuminated the confusing new fashions and manners that prevailed in the city. New Yorkers alone had fifteen papers to choose from, as they rode the subways to work or walked the crowded downtown streets. Both informational journalism and story journalism helped their readers to accommodate to city life in the dawning twentieth century.

Source:
Michael Schudson, *Discovering the News: A Social History of American Newspapers* (New York: Basic Books, 1978).

THE GALVESTON FLOOD

Disaster. On 7 September 1900 hurricane-force winds and rain whipped the states on the western end of the Gulf of Mexico. A storm surge smashed into the city of Galveston, Texas, on the north end of Galveston Island. The four bridges connecting it to the mainland were swept away; most of the city's buildings were destroyed; and five thousand of its forty thousand residents died. Survivors waited through the night on rooftops. The rest of the world waited days for news of Galveston's fate, so cut off was the city and the region by severed telegraph lines, flooded roads, and impassable railroad tracks. Militiamen with bayonets patrolled the streets to keep scavengers and newspaper reporters away.

Annie Laurie to the Rescue. Winifred Black, a reporter for the *Denver Post* and special contributor to the Hearst papers who wrote under the name Annie Laurie,

On 18 January 1904 the cornerstone to a new headquarters and printing plant for *The New York Times* was laid in midtown Manhattan, on Longacre Square, where several new subway lines would converge. A replica of Giotto's Florentine Tower, the building soared 375 feet and delved several stories below street level.

In the move from the paper's old Park Row address, not one of five thousand pieces of linotype was lost. The first paper to come off the new presses, which could print and fold 144,000 copies of a sixteen-page paper in an hour, rolled off on 2 January 1905. The celebration marking the move began on New Year's Eve, when publisher Adolph Ochs proposed to drop an enormous lighted ball to mark midnight, beginning a famous tradition to mark the New Year. Longacre Square soon became known as Times Square.

Sources: Meyer Berger, *The Story of the New York Times, 1851–1951* (New York: Simon & Schuster, 1951);

Elmer Davis, *History of the New York Times, 1851–1921* (New York: New York Times, 1921).

Winifred Sweet Black, who reported the Galveston hurricane devastation for the Hearst papers under the pseudonym Annie Laurie

was the first reporter to arrive on the scene. Dressed as a boy, she sneaked onto the boat that met the relief trains coming from Houston. After twenty-four hours she filed stories for the Hearst syndicate describing the terrible stench of decaying bodies and the need for disinfectant. "In pity's name, in America's name, do not delay one single instant. Send this help quickly or it will be too late!" She related the story of a man who floated all night on a piece of his roof with his wife and mother, kissing them good-bye because he did not think he could hold on. When he awoke, he was alone on the raft and did not know when they had died. She described vast pyres where thousands of bodies were cremated. The tiniest details moved her: a baby's shoe, a piece of a woman's dress, letters.

Hearst Promotes Charity. The staff and readers of Hearst's *San Francisco Examiner, Chicago American,* and *New York Journal,* where Laurie's stories appeared, hurried to fill trains with supplies, relief workers, and money. The three trains raced across the country to see which would arrive first, the name Hearst blazing in banners on their sides. In New York the publisher himself organized a charity bazaar at the Waldorf-Astoria Hotel and several theatrical benefits featuring Broadway stars. The *Journal* carried a daily list of contributions led by Hearst's own $1,000. Critics charged that the good Hearst did in Galveston was tainted by the magnate's shameless self-promotion: he had his eye, as many Americans knew, on the White House.

Relief. With the help of Galveston's police chief, Annie Laurie took over a school building that had survived the flood and turned it into a hospital, quickly spending the initial $60,000 Hearst forwarded to her on blankets, cots, pillows, and cookstoves. Her stories eventually raised more than $350,000 in contributions from Hearst readers. She also found permanent homes for forty-eight orphans, proving her talent as a tireless organizer as well as a vivid and stirring reporter.

Sources:

Madelon Golden Schlipp and Sharon M. Murphy, *Great Women of the Press* (Carbondale: Southern Illinois University Press, 1983);

W. A. Swanberg, *Citizen Hearst* (New York: Scribners, 1961).

THE HEYDAY OF THE FOREIGN-LANGUAGE PRESS

A Nation of Immigrants. In 1900, 46 percent of the nation's population was composed of first- or second-generation immigrants. Beginning in 1896 immigrants from southeastern European countries outnumbered those from northwestern European countries, bringing with them a diversity of languages and cultures that America had never before experienced. Many of these new Americans could not read at all, and most of them could not read English but were eager to learn. In the last decades of the nineteenth century, most foreign-language papers were run by intellectuals or clergy on the European model of dedication to one religion or ideology. In the first decade of the twentieth century all this changed. More than one thousand foreign-language papers operated, the number peaking at thirteen hundred in 1914. More than 140 of these were dailies, and 40 percent were in German. German-, Polish-, and Yiddish-language papers claimed circulations of one million readers in each language; the Italian papers reached about seven hundred thousand; and the Swedish, five hundred thousand. The single largest daily was the German *New Yorker Staats-Zeitung*, with a quarter of a million readers.

Learning to Assimilate. Innovators such as Abraham Cahan of the Yiddish *Jewish Daily Forward* and Charles Barsotti of the Italian *Il Progresso* brought the conventions of Pulitzer's New Journalism to their readers: an emphasis on features and plenty of pictures. While foreign-language papers printed news from the home countries of their readers and news from within their ethnic communities, they also provided advice for successful assimilation into American culture. They carried news about employment opportunities and proper behavior on the job and articulated a sense of ethnic identity and pride consonant with successful adjustment to life in America. An enthusiastic promoter of Italian culture and Italian-American pride, Barsotti raised statues of famous Italians all around New York City: Verrazano in Battery Park, Garibaldi in Washington Square, Columbus in Columbus Circle, Dante at Broadway and Sixty-third Street, Verdi at Broadway and Seventy-third Street.

Success Means Failure. The growing number of foreign-language publications early in the century does not indicate how volatile the industry was. For every one hundred papers that started, ninety-three stopped. As each generation of immigrants passed into the mainstream of American culture, the need for an "immigrant" press diminished. After World War I newly restrictive policies abruptly arrested the flow of immigration. By 1960 there were half the number of foreign-language publications that there had been in 1914. A more appropriate term for those remaining would be *ethnic* papers, since the readers were no longer necessarily first- or second-generation immigrants. The flowering of the immigrant press between 1900 and 1930 remains one of the most understudied areas of American history.

Source:
Sally M. Miller, ed., *The Ethnic Press in the United States: A Historical Analysis and Handbook* (Westport, Conn.: Greenwood Press, 1987).

NEWSPAPERS AT SEA

With the advent of wireless telegraphy, oceangoing ships could communicate with stations on either side of the Atlantic. For five dollars, the Marconi Company's station on Nantucket Island, Massachusetts, would report the arrival of ships to their steamship companies. In 1901 the *New York Herald* contracted with Marconi to lease the services of the Nantucket station in order to gather the news from Europe as quickly as possible. The desire of the *Herald* for news from any incoming ship conflicted with the Marconi Company's policy of noncommunication with any ship that did not lease its services.

Marconi also provided news service in the opposite direction, providing news from shore to passengers on ships. While transmission grew less reliable with distance and the telegraph operators' prose showed considerably less color than that of newspaper writers, passengers enjoyed the novelty of news produced at sea. On 22 February 1903 when the Cunard liner *Etruria* arrived in New York harbor, it carried the first oceangoing newspaper produced from wireless reports from Great Britain. The ship also carried a famous passenger, Guglielmo Marconi.

Source: Susan J. Douglas, *Inventing American Broadcasting: 1899–1922* (Baltimore: Johns Hopkins University Press, 1987).

"LET MUNSEY KILL IT!": THE BIRTH OF THE NEWSPAPER CHAIN

A Businessman's Vision. In 1890 New York had fifteen English-language daily newspapers. By 1932 it had half that number. The twentieth-century trend toward newspaper consolidation began in earnest during the century's first decade. Frank A. Munsey did as much as any other person to bring this about. His own rags-to-riches tale began when he started a children's magazine, the *Golden Argosy*, and proceeded to build a publishing empire with *Munsey's*, an illustrated general-interest weekly that had a circulation of 650,000 in 1900. A shrewd businessman with no sentimentality toward the traditions of newspaper publishing, Munsey saw chaos and disorder in an industry that he believed had 60 percent too many products. He dreamed of a chain of five hundred newspapers. In addition to creating vast economies of scale, this enterprise would employ the greatest minds in every field, dispensing wisdom from a central facility, with local coverage left up to each outlet. "The combined genius of the men in control would be the most uplifting force the world has ever known," he exclaimed.

Munsey Fails. Munsey became known as the Grand High Executioner, and the slogan "Let Munsey Kill It!" was a familiar refrain around flagging papers, as he bought and consolidated property after property. In the first two decades of the century, Munsey bought and sold at least fifteen newspapers in Boston, New York, Philadelphia, Baltimore, and Washington, D.C., but only a few remained profitable. *Saturday Evening Post* publisher Cyrus H. K. Curtis attempted consolidation of Philadelphia's industry, and Herman Kohlstaat of Chicago made similar moves. Newspapermen blamed these businessmen for ruining a noble profession with crude commercial interests. When Munsey died in 1925, William Allen White of the *Emporia Gazette* commented: "Frank A. Munsey contributed to the journalism of his day the talent of a meatpacker, the morals of a money-changer and the manners of an undertaker. He and his kind have about succeeded in transforming a once-noble profession into an eight percent security. May he rest in trust!"

Scripps Starts Small. Other entrepreneurs, away from the vast urban centers of the East, found greater success with chain journalism. Edward W. Scripps started the first successful chain when he launched the *Cleveland Penny Press* in 1878. Scripps seldom bought established properties. He looked for growing industrial cities in the Midwest and created new papers. If they showed a profit in the first ten years, he gave 49 percent of their stock to their editor and business manager. If not, he closed them. In 1902 Scripps began a feature and illustration syndicate to supply his growing empire. In 1907 he organized the United Press Association as a competitor to the Associated Press wire service.

Gannett's Gradual Growth. In upstate New York Frank E. Gannett bought a partial interest in the *Elmira Gazette* in 1906 and then merged it with the *Elmira Star*. In the 1910s he bought two papers in Ithaca and combined them, and in the 1920s acquired others in Rochester, Utica, and in other northeastern states, laying the groundwork for the largest chain in the country. Munsey's vision for economies of scale and standardization of quality were fulfilled by other men, who started small and built their empires from scratch.

Steady Consolidation. In the 1900s ten chains controlled just thirty-two dailies. (In the 1990s Gannett publishes more than one hundred dailies.) Critics continue to debate the pitfalls of chain journalism: standardization, a corporate editorial slant, and lack of local control. While the growth of chains and syndicates reduced diversity in American publishing, it undeniably improved the quality of small papers in remote locales. In any case, the first decade of the twentieth century brought the techniques and practices of modern financial management to an in-

A 1901 *New York Journal* political cartoon by Frederick Burr Opper depicting William McKinley put "on ice" for the presidential campaign by Vice President Roosevelt, bottom center, to the chagrin of McKinley's powerful supporters, the trusts and big-business advocate Sen. Marcus Hanna

dustry that had long been run by gentlemen publishers and editors luxuriously detached from the balance sheet.

Sources:

Edwin and Michael Emery, *The Press and America: An Interpretive History of the Mass Media,* fourth edition (Englewood Cliffs, N.J.: Prentice-Hall, 1978);

John Tebbel, *The Compact History of the American Newspaper* (New York: Hawthorn Books, 1963).

THE NEW YORK JOURNAL AND THE ASSASSINATION OF WILLIAM McKINLEY

Hatred of the Trusts. The most volatile political issue at the turn of the century was the growing power of enormous corporations. Prominent publishers, including Joseph Pulitzer and William Randolph Hearst, used their papers to campaign against the trusts as the enemy of their readers, the common people. The reelection in 1900 of Republican president William McKinley meant that little would be accomplished to curb the centralization of economic power that came, the trusts' opponents argued, at the expense of the industrial worker and the farmer.

The *Journal* Cartoonists Get Rough. Hearst's *New York Journal* had an outstanding staff of political cartoonists, an art form just then coming into its own. Homer Davenport began in 1900 to draw President McKinley as the stooge of the millionaire industrialist Mark

Hanna, drawn wearing a suit of dollar signs. McKinley and his longtime patron were portrayed as the bullying, criminal, scornful agents of the trusts. Davenport's new colleague, Frederick Burr Opper, started a series called "Willie and his Papa," with McKinley depicted as a small son to the trusts, attended by a nursemaid resembling Hanna. McKinley's vice-presidential nominee, Theodore Roosevelt, was shown as a show-off playmate stealing Willie's limelight and making him cry. Respected *Journal* editor Arthur Brisbane pronounced McKinley "the most hated creature on the American continent."

An Incendiary Rhyme and a Provocative Editorial. On 4 February 1900 the governor-elect of Kentucky, William Goebel, was shot dead in an election dispute. Famous story writer Ambrose Bierce of the *Journal* penned a harsh quatrain:

> The bullet that pierced Goebel's breast
> Can not be found in all the West,
> Good reason, it is speeding here
> To lay McKinley on his bier.

Hearst began to regret the virulence of his papers' assaults on the president and sent his associate James Creelman to Washington to apologize for the personal nature of the attacks. But on 10 April 1901 the *Journal* again became vicious. An editorial against McKinley, probably written by Brisbane, ended with the shocking sentiment "If bad institutions and bad men must be got rid of only by killing, then the killing must be done." When this line came to Hearst's attention, he called an immediate stop to the presses. It did not appear in later editions, but Hearst's enemies filed it away.

Shots in Buffalo. Public sentiment against the trusts grew so volatile that even McKinley had begun to consider some limited moves against them. On 5 September 1901 he stopped at the Pan-American Exposition in Buffalo to give a speech. The next day he graciously held a reception to shake the hands of hundreds of citizens. One half-mad twenty-eight-year old, Leon Czolgosz, concealed a pistol under a handkerchief and shot the president twice. McKinley lived nine days before he died on 14 September. Vice President Roosevelt, vacationing at a remote spot in the Adirondacks, could not be reached for several hours.

Hearst Burned in Effigy. The publisher learned of the shooting in Chicago and said quietly to editor Charles Edward Russell of the *American*, "Things are going to be very bad." All of his papers took a sorrowful, solicitous, hopeful stance while waiting for news of McKinley's fate. When the president died, Hearst's enemies reprinted the cartoons, the poem, and the editorial that seemed to incite assassination. It was widely believed that Czolgosz was carrying a copy of the *Journal* in his pocket when he shot the president, but that story is apocryphal. Nonetheless, the Hearst papers were widely boycotted, and their publisher was burned in effigy along with anarchist

Emma Goldman, whose lecture Czolgosz cited as his true inspiration for the assassination. Hearst punished none of the writers or cartoonists but soon changed the name of the *Journal* to the *American*. A cloud hovered over his empire for about a year, but by 1902 he was popular enough to win election to the House of Representatives from New York.

Sources:
Edwin and Michael Emery, *The Press and America: An Interpretive History of the Mass Media,* fourth edition (Englewood Cliffs, N.J.: Prentice-Hall, 1978);

W. A. Swanberg, *Citizen Hearst* (New York: Scribners, 1961).

PATENT-MEDICINE ADVERTISEMENTS

The Poison Trust. The 1900 census reported that eighty million Americans spent a total of $59 million each year on patent medicines. More of that money went to pay the cost of advertising in newspapers and magazines and on billboards than into either production costs or profit. These tonics, elixirs, and syrups contained up to 80 percent alcohol and often had morphine, cocaine, or the heart stimulant Digitalis as a basic ingredient. Naturally they sold well. Paine's Celery Compound, Burdock's Blood Bitters, Doctor Pierce's Favorite Prescription, and Colden's Liquid Beef Tonic promised to cure maladies ranging from a baby's fussiness to cancer. Many people trusted these nostrums as an inexpensive alternative to visiting doctors, and even church publications printed their advertisements.

Protests Grow. In 1892 Edward Bok, editor of the influential *Ladies' Home Journal,* had decreed that his magazine would no longer accept ads for patent medicines. By 1904, when the industry's success showed no signs of flagging, he began to print the contents of some of the most popular cures. He ran incorrect information about Doctor Pierce's Favorite Prescription and was forced to print a retraction and pay damages, but he continued his editorials, calling upon all decent people to boycott the medicines. He appealed to the temperance

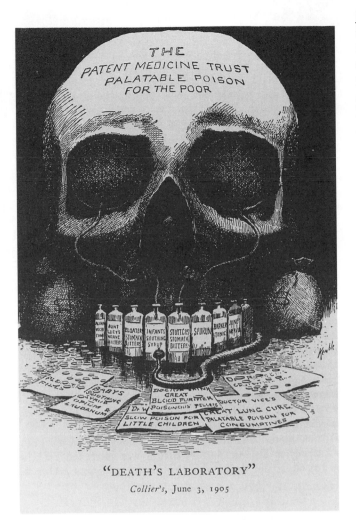

THE
PATENT MEDICINE TRUST
PALATABLE POISON
FOR THE POOR

Cartoon indicting the patent-medicine industry that appeared as a full page in the 3 June 1905 issue of *Collier's* magazine

journalist, Samuel Hopkins Adams, to continue researching patent medicines. In June 1905 *Collier's* printed a full-page cartoon labeled "Death's Laboratory," showing a death's-head with medicine bottles as teeth, suggesting that the remedies poisoned children. On 7 October 1905 Adams's long-awaited series began to appear under the headline "The Great American Fraud." With documents, illustrations, and wit, Adams made a devastating case against the noxious cures. *Collier's* was criticized for joining the ranks of irresponsible muckrakers, but the magazine's popularity picked up, encouraging Hapgood to pursue other important investigations.

The Pure Food and Drug Act of 1906. While bills proposing to regulate the food and drug industries had been proposed for many years in Congress, the work of the muckrakers in 1904–1906 created an irresistible public demand for action. The early 1906 publication of Upton Sinclair's novel *The Jungle*, detailing the horrifying conditions in Chicago's meatpacking plants, dominated the headlines. President Roosevelt joined the American Medical Association, the Woman's Christian Temperance Union, and the National Consumer's League in fighting for this bill. The legislation required the label of any product to list harmful ingredients such as alcohol or narcotics, but it did not require disclosure of other ingredients. While an important step, the Pure Food and Drug Act ensured only minor improvements. Within a few years Samuel Hopkins Adams was again publishing articles on patent medicines, condemning the government for its failure to enforce the Pure Food and Drug Act.

Sources:

Samuel Hopkins Adams, *The Great American Fraud* (book reprint) (Chicago: American Medical Association/Colliers, 1907);

David Mark Chalmers, *The Muckrake Years* (New York: Van Nostrand, 1974);

Louis Filler, *The Muckrakers* (University Park: Pennsylvania State University Press, 1976).

THE MURDER OF STANFORD WHITE

The Murder of the Century. On 25 June 1906 world-famous architect Stanford White, forty-seven, took in a show at the rooftop café of Madison Square Garden, a complex he had designed. Harry Thaw, heir to a Pittsburgh railroad fortune, killed him with three shots from a pistol. Thaw's beautiful young wife, the model and actress Evelyn Nesbit Thaw, had carried on an affair with White and had told her husband that the architect had raped her when she was a virgin of sixteen.

A Morality Tale. The incident provided sensational fodder for New York's fifteen newspapers. William Randolph Hearst's *Evening Journal* pinpointed what the case seemed to reveal about the city's rich: "The flash of that pistol lighted up an abyss of moral turpitude, revealing powerful, reckless, openly flaunted wealth." The circulation of Joseph Pulitzer's *World* jumped one hundred thousand the first week after the murder. Photographs of Nesbit, a poor girl from Pittsburgh who had become a

movement to fight them as if they were cocktails, which indeed many were. Bok hired a young lawyer and journalist named Mark Sullivan to check his facts and carry on the research. Lydia Pinkham's remedy for women had been a staple of the patent-medicine market for several decades, and the ads invited women to write to Pinkham for advice. Sullivan took a photograph of her tombstone in Lynn, Massachusetts, showing that Pinkham had been dead for more than twenty years. He interviewed people in the industry and described how they laughed, passing around letters to nonexistent quacks from sick and desperate people. Sullivan published two articles in the *Ladies' Home Journal*, but Bok felt that the bulk of his research was not appropriate for his audience. Sullivan sent it along to *Collier's*.

"The Great American Fraud." Editor Norman Hapgood at *Collier's* appreciated the fine investigative work of distinguished muckrakers such as Lincoln Steffens and Ida Tarbell but wanted nothing to do with their sensationalistic imitators. He recognized the value of Sullivan's research and assigned an experienced health

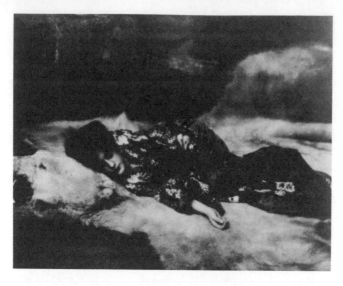
Evelyn Nesbit posing in Stanford White's studio

sensation for her perfect features and versatile image, had previously appeared in hundreds of newspapers and magazines. She was immortalized as a Gibson Girl, one of illustrator Charles Dana Gibson's icons of American beauty. The papers portrayed her as a tragic innocent caught between White, a man of voracious appetites for everything beautiful, and Thaw, an obsessed and vindictive eccentric. Even the staid *New York Times* gave the affair extensive coverage, its high-minded publisher, Adolph Ochs, explaining that White's stature and Thaw's social prominence gave the case "sociological" import. Within a week of the murder, Biograph had produced a motion picture dramatizing the tale.

The Defendant's Public Relations Machine. The entire Thaw family fortune was mobilized to portray young Harry as a hero who had nobly slain a predatory fiend. The family hired an early practitioner of public relations, who wrote a book titled *A Woman's Sacrifice.* They paid to mount a play called *For the Sake of Wife and Home,* where a character named Shaw shoots a notorious scoundrel called Black for ruining a young woman. While Thaw dined in prison on squab and champagne from Delmonico's restaurant, the public, by a margin of two to one, expressed approval of his crime.

"The Girl in the Velvet Swing." The trial of Harry K. Thaw began on 23 January 1907. The public had to be banned from the New York courtroom to accommodate hundreds of reporters and illustrators. Thaw's attorneys claimed that their client was not guilty by reason of temporary insanity, hinging their entire case on the testimony of Evelyn Nesbit Thaw and what she had told her husband about her relationship with White. Her witness-stand accounts of how White pushed her on a red velvet swing in his office and forced her to drink champagne until she blacked out and how she awoke, naked and terrified in his bed, sold millions of papers.

The "Sob Sisters." A panel of famous women reporters — including Dorothy Dix, Ada Patterson, Annie Laurie, and Nixola Greeley-Smith — who sat at a central table in the courtroom, milked the story for all it was worth. Irvin Cobb, reporter and humorist for the *World,* dubbed these women, who turned America's courtroom dramas into titillating serials for the yellow press, "Sob Sisters." Laurie, who would write more than sixteen thousand articles in her forty-seven-year career, resented the name and said, "I'd rather smell the printer's ink and hear the presses than go to any grand opera in the world." Cobb himself was appalled by the parade of paid witnesses called by the defense, dubbing one "Dr. J. Mumble Viceversa."

Thaw Later Released. The first trial ended in a hung jury. In the second trial Thaw's lawyers altered their strategy to say that Thaw was thoroughly rather than temporarily deranged, and he was committed to a facility for the criminally insane. He was released after seven years, at which time his marriage was promptly dissolved. When she was near death in 1967, Evelyn Nesbit claimed that Stanford White was the only man she had ever loved.

Sources:

Carl Charlson, *Murder of the Century,* PBS;

Gerald Langford, *The Murder of Stanford White* (Indianapolis: Bobbs-Merrill, 1962);

Michael Macdonald Mooney, *Evelyn Nesbit and Stanford White: Love in the Gilded Age* (New York: Morrow, 1976).

THE RACE TO THE NORTH POLE

An Accident Brings Peary to the *Times*. By 1908 an American explorer, Comdr. Robert E. Peary, had made several attempts to reach the North Pole. The *New York Herald* had subsidized his previous expeditions in return for the exclusive rights to his story. In 1908, seeking funding for another attempt, Peary discovered that his contacts, the financial officer William Reick and the city editor Charles M. Lincoln, now worked for *The New York Times.* Peary then asked to see the new city editor, who told him that the public was tired of Arctic adventures. Discouraged, Peary walked from downtown all the way to the new midtown headquarters of the *Times. Times* publisher Adolph Ochs and managing editor Carr Van Anda shared a boyish enthusiasm for the scientific exploration of remote places, and in short order the paper paid Peary $4,000 for the exclusive New York rights to his story. The *Times* would also distribute the story for him elsewhere at no cost. Peary departed New York harbor on 6 July 1908 and dispatched letters on his progress from Newfoundland and Labrador. Then he disappeared.

Cook Makes a Claim. On 1 September 1909 the world was inspired to learn that Dr. Frederick A. Cook of Brooklyn, a surgeon on two previous Peary expeditions, had reached the North Pole on 21 April 1909. He claimed to have buried an American flag in a metal tube at the top of the world. The *New York Herald,* as it turned

The Robert E. Peary party at the North Pole on 6 April 1909

out, had paid Cook $25,000 for his exclusive. The *Times* scavenged overseas papers for its own coverage and gave it full play, but Van Anda felt Cook's account lacked proof.

Suspicion Grows. Correspondents in London began to doubt that Cook could have crossed from Cape Columbus to the pole in thirty-five days, as he claimed. A U.S. Navy admiral who had been on a previous attempt contradicted Cook's descriptions of the far northern terrain. When Cook reached Copenhagen, the British reporter Philip Gibbs interviewed him, and Cook claimed that all his written records of the expedition had been shipped directly from Greenland to the United States. He conceded that the only witnesses on the last leg of his journey were Eskimos unschooled in scientific documentation. The interview, which politely called Cook's claims "inconclusive," was reprinted in the *Times*.

Peary Surfaces with His Own Claim. On 6 September 1909, more than a year after he sailed from New York, a telegraph message from Commander Peary in Indian Harbor, Labrador, contained the message "G.O.P.," the prearranged signal that he had achieved the pole. The date he gave was 6 April 1909, two weeks before Cook's claim. Celebrating in Copenhagen, Cook was generous. "Two records are better than one," he cabled the *Times*. When told of Cook's claims, Peary became angry and

said that the Eskimos who accompanied Cook told him that the doctor had not gotten far enough north to lose sight of land. Scientists and explorers, as well as newspapers, began to take sides. Cook versus Peary became the most celebrated scientific controversy of the decade. In October Cook's guide, Edward N. Barrill, swore that Cook's claim was false.

Two Scoops. The dimensions of the *Times* scoop, and its increase in circulation, were enormous, as scientific and public opinion weighed in on Peary's side. His vivid account ran in the paper for four days, from 8 to 11 September 1909. He said that his second-in-command, a Cornell engineer named Ross G. Marvin, had died on the ice on 10 April 1909, just days after reaching the pole. The Peary story solidified the reputation of *The New York Times* as the leader in accuracy and enterprise in news gathering, a standard that had long been set by the *Herald*. Seventeen years later the *Times* got a second scoop on the Peary expedition from Peary's son and the commander of his boat on the 1909 expedition. The reporter George Palmer Putnam found out that Marvin had not drowned as Peary first reported but that their Eskimo guides had murdered him.

Source:
Meyer Berger, *The Story of the New York Times: 1851–1951* (New York: Simon & Schuster, 1951).

THE SAN FRANCISCO EARTHQUAKE AND FIRE

490 City Blocks Ruined. On 18 April 1906 a major earthquake shook the city by the bay, and by the following day a massive fire had consumed the remaining downtown structures. The entire business district was destroyed; an estimated 700 people had died, including 270 inmates of an insane asylum; and 300,000 were left homeless. Estimates of the property damage reached $500 million.

The Local Papers Do Not Miss a Day. The buildings housing the city's newspapers, the *Examiner*, the *Call*, and the *Chronicle*, all burned. At the *Chronicle* twenty linotype machines crashed several stories through the flames to the basement. The three papers joined forces the first day after the disaster and printed a combined edition across the bay in Oakland called the *California Chronicle-Examiner*. Manufacturers speedily shipped new presses out. William Randolph Hearst, who owned the *Examiner*, commandeered a press just shipped to a Salt Lake City paper by doubling its price. He also added a dollar a week to the salary of every employee on the paper to help with their added expenses.

Creative National Coverage. While some reporters rushed to the scene (Annie Laurie in Denver received a one-word telegram from Hearst: "GO."), others had to cover the story from a distance. The *New York American* used a retouched photograph of the great Baltimore fire of 1904 and received a barrage of reproaches from its

San Francisco after the earthquake on 18 April 1906 (photograph by Arnold Genthe)

rivals. Will Irwin of the *New York Sun*, who had been a reporter and editor of the *San Francisco Chronicle* from 1900 to 1904, wrote a story titled "The City That Was" completely from memory, and it became an instant classic of newspaper journalism. It read, in part:

> The old San Francisco is dead. The gayest, lightest hearted, most pleasure loving city of the western continent, and in many ways the most interesting and romantic, is a horde of huddled refugees living among ruins. It may rebuild; it probably will; but those who have known that peculiar city by the Golden Gate and have caught its flavor of Arabian Nights feel that it can never be the same. It is as though a pretty, frivolous woman had passed through a great tragedy. She survives, but she is sobered and different. If it rises out of the ashes it must be a modern city, much like other cities and without its old atmosphere.

Although the story appeared without a byline, as was the custom of the day, word quickly spread of Irwin's authorship, and newspapers around the country reprinted it. In all, the tragedy in San Francisco demonstrated the newfound ability of the press to create an instant national story from a local event.

Sources:
Frank Luther Mott, *American Journalism: A History, 1690–1960* (New York: Macmillan, 1962);

W. A. Swanberg, *Citizen Hearst* (New York: Scribners, 1961).

SUNDAY COLOR COMICS

Art, Commerce, and the Color Press. Between 1895 and 1905 the comic strip coalesced as a new art form and newspaper feature. The gradual improvement of color presses throughout the 1890s led publishers, in their frantic circulation wars, to introduce color supplements to their Sunday papers. Only the doggedly serious *New York Times* refrained from adding comics. In order to meet the demand from readers, most papers reprinted art from humor magazines such as *Puck* and *Life*. Some political cartoonists began to draw weekly features, but most of the strip artists came to the new form directly.

Hogan's Alley. Richard Felton Outcault began his career doing technical drawings for Thomas Edison. In 1896 Outcault began drawing a weekly feature for Pulitzer's Sunday *World* titled *Hogan's Alley*. In choosing the subject of a poor urban neighborhood, Outcault followed the literary realists and progressive reformers of the day. His drawings were funny, but they also aimed to stir the reader's conscience. *Hogan's Alley* was not a comic strip but a packed single frame. One character, a jug-eared toddler in a stained nightdress, captured the public's imagination.

The Yellow Kid. The color yellow had given press operators a big headache because it took too long to dry

THE OPEN-AIR SCHOOL IN HOGAN'S ALLEY.

Hogan's Alley comic strip in the *New York World* by George B. Luks, drawn after the strip's creator, Richard Felton Outcault, was hired away by the Hearst chain. The message on the Yellow Kid's shirt, bottom right, refers to the feud between Hearst and *World* publisher Joseph Pulitzer.

and inevitably smudged. When Pulitzer's operators developed a fast-drying yellow, they tried it out on the large expanse of the shirt of an elf in the step, and thus gave birth to the Yellow Kid. The character was so popular that Pulitzer used the kid's likeness on promotions for the *World* and it spawned a merchandising frenzy: Yellow Kid cigarettes, a magazine, even a Broadway musical. He also gave his name to the circulation wars between Pulitzer and Hearst and defined an era in newspaper publishing, that of yellow journalism. Outcault migrated between the *World,* the *Journal,* and the *New York Herald,* setting off lawsuits as to who retained the rights to the Yellow Kid.

Buster Brown. By 1902 *Hogan's Alley* had run its course. Outcault, feeling pressure from social critics who complained that the Sunday comics were too crude, created a new strip centered around an upper-class rascal named Buster Brown. Buster terrorized servants, wrecked society balls, frightened the elderly, and created continual pandemonium. Buster had a dog named Tige and a sister, Mary Jane, based on Outcault's daughter. Each misadventure ended with Buster delivering a homily on what he had done wrong and what he had learned. Outcault derived these nuggets from the writings of Ralph Waldo

Emerson, Henry David Thoreau, and Henry George, which he kept in his studio. The move from Hogan's Alley to Buster's opulent home reflected the artist's own social ascent. He grew wealthy leasing the Buster Brown character to manufacturers. In 1906, after a chance meeting with William Randolph Hearst in Stratford-upon-Avon, Outcault switched employers once again to the Sunday *Journal* and again was taken to court over the rights to his creation. This time, he got to keep Buster's likeness, but the *Herald* got to keep Buster's name.

The Katzenjammer Kids. German-born Rudolph Dirks began drawing Hans and Fritz for the *Journal* in 1897 when he was just twenty years old. These pranksters spoke in pidgin German and were meant to attract German American readers. *Katzenjammer* literally means "howling cats" but colloquially refers to a hangover. Dirks's true innovation was the comic strip. He abandoned the static vignette in favor of evolving stories with developing characters. He also was a master at the placement of speech balloons, which were not yet widely used. (The Yellow Kid's remarks, for example, had been printed on his shirt.) When the United States went to war with Germany in 1917, the strip's name was briefly changed to *The Shenanigans Kids.*

Opper's *Happy Hooligan.* The most prolific and humanistic turn-of-the-century cartoonist was Frederick Burr Opper. He not only drew some of the most successful comic strips; he also illustrated children's books and drew political and magazine cartoons. His scathing political cartoons about Theodore Roosevelt so delighted the president that he kept them in a scrapbook. Opper's respectability quieted the funnies' critics, and beginning in 1899 he was known as the "dean" of the comic artists, even though he worked for the notoriously sensational Hearst. His *Happy Hooligan* (along with *Gloomy Gus and Montmorency*), *Maud the Mule,* and *Alphonse and Gaston* strips lasted into the 1930s and became indelible parts of American culture.

Sources:
Stephen Becker, *Comic Art in America* (New York: Simon & Schuster, 1959);
Richard Marschall, *America's Great Comic Strip Artists* (New York: Abbeville Press, 1989).

THEODORE ROOSEVELT SUES JOSEPH PULITZER FOR LIBEL

Questions over the Panama Canal. On 4 November 1903 a small revolution established the state of Panama, formerly part of the nation of Colombia. Two United States warships, the *Nashville* and the *Dixie,* sailed offshore to deter interference by the Colombian military. The new state of Panama was far more receptive than Colombia had been to American plans to complete the long-stalled Panama Canal, a project begun by a French syndicate and now secretly backed by wealthy American investors. President Roosevelt privately expressed reservations over the way the project's future had been se-

Cartoon in the *Cleveland Plain Dealer* ridiculing the feud between President Theodore Roosevelt and Joseph Pulitzer, publisher of the *New York World,* whom the president had sued for libel

cured, but publicly he defended every action taken by his government. William Nelson Cromwell, a handsome and influential New York lawyer, had spread his clients' money liberally in the Congress, including $60,000 to the Republican campaign fund in 1900.

Threat of Political Blackmail. Shortly before the 1908 election, Panamanians disgruntled over their small share of the profits going to the canal's overseas investors threatened to expose the part played by powerful Republicans. Roosevelt's handpicked successor was William Howard Taft. Taft's brother Charles and Roosevelt's own brother-in-law, Douglas Robinson, had each gained a fortune when the United States paid $40 million, supposedly to buy out the French syndicate that had begun the canal. Cromwell, the lawyer who brokered the deal with the French and guided the canal legislation through the Congress, gave the story to Pulitzer's *World,* including his own denial, in order to forestall a political scandal. The story was repeated by the *Indianapolis News,* secretly owned by Vice President Charles W. Fairbanks, who was furious that Roosevelt had backed Taft for the Republican nomination for the presidency.

The President Strikes Back. Roosevelt heatedly denied all charges of impropriety. The *World* began to trace the $40 million paid by the U.S. government and ran a story claiming that the money had gone not to the French government as alleged, but to a dummy corporation

fronting for J. P. Morgan and Company. It suggested that people close to the president had profited richly and implicated American greed in the Panamanian revolution. The paper accused the president of deliberate lies. Pulitzer himself, cruising the Atlantic on his yacht, was shocked to learn that his *World* had printed the allegations against Charles Taft and Douglas Robinson based only on the statements of their lawyer, Cromwell. Roosevelt demanded that the district attorney of New York prosecute Pulitzer for libel. Although the district attorney felt that he too had been unfairly attacked in Pulitzer's papers, he declined to indict, but Roosevelt found more willing prosecutors. He told one U.S. district attorney, "I do not know anything about the law of criminal libel, but I should dearly like to invoke it against Pulitzer, of the *World.*"

The Grand Jury Convenes. On 17 February 1909 a District of Columbia grand jury indicted Pulitzer, his editors Caleb Van Hamm and Robert Hunt Lyman, as well as Pulitzer's corporation, for five counts of criminal libel against Theodore Roosevelt, J. P. Morgan, Douglas Robinson, Charles P. Taft, Elihu Root (the secretary of state), and William Nelson Cromwell. Similar indictments were issued against the *Indianapolis News.* The *World* took an unrepentant editorial stance. Its editorial director, Frank I. Cobb, wrote, "Long after Mr. Roosevelt is dead, long after all the present editors of this paper

Theodore Roosevelt revolutionized the relationship between the president and the press. He took reporters into his confidence, treated them as professionals, and used them much to his advantage. Previously, all presidential announcements were carefully guarded until the day of official release. Roosevelt gave them to the press days in advance, with prohibition on publication until the release date, so that full analysis could accompany the statement.

Roosevelt also invited correspondents he particularly liked, including *The New York Times* Washington bureau chief Richard Oulahan, known as the "fair-haired," to talk with him during his morning shave. They could not quote him directly without his consent. In this way, Roosevelt adopted a technique pioneered by James G. Blaine, known as the "trial balloon." He could get public reaction to a policy without tying his name to it. When the new West Wing of the White House opened in 1902, Roosevelt designated an official press room. He understood that a colorful president could lead public opinion and force the unruly Congress to follow his lead.

Source: Donald Ritchie, *Press Gallery: Congress and the Washington Correspondents* (Cambridge, Mass.: Harvard University Press, 1991).

A single issue of a magazine rarely changes the shape of journalism, but in January 1903 *McClure's* did just that. Three long, detailed, and pathbreaking articles on the relationship between business, labor, and government appeared together in the preeminent reformist magazine. Its editor, Samuel S. McClure, contributed an editorial that marked the advent of muckraking as a coherent movement in investigative journalism, although that term would not be used by Theodore Roosevelt for three more years. His "Concerning Three Articles in this Number of McClure's, and a Coincidence that May Set Us Thinking" noted the corruption common to corporations in Ida Tarbell's "The History of the Standard Oil Company," labor unions in Ray Stannard Baker's "The Right to Work," and city government in Lincoln Steffens's "The Shame of Minneapolis."

Who is left, McClure asked, to uphold the law when businessmen, workingmen, politicians, and citizens all disregard it for their own benefit? "There is no one left: none but us all," he answers. The public would pay the price for such thoroughgoing dishonesty. "And in the end the sum total of the debt will be our liberty."

Source: Louis Filler, *The Muckrakers* (University Park: Pennsylvania State University Press, 1976).

---

are dead, *The World* will still go on as a great independent newspaper, unmuzzled, undaunted and unterrorized." The old and sickly but still fierce Pulitzer cruised the Atlantic outside the three-mile territorial limit to avoid arrest.

A Victory for Freedom of the Press. In 1909 a federal judge dismissed the case against the *Indianapolis News,* citing clear improprieties in the Panama Canal affair. The *World* decided to challenge the government's jurisdiction in its case rather than to fight the charges themselves. But when a New York judge dismissed the charges against the paper in January 1910 as "opposed to the spirit and tenor of legislation for many years," Pulitzer was not satisfied. He kept needling his opponents to appeal the case to the Supreme Court, so that it might end with a resounding affirmation of the freedom of the press. On 3 January 1911 the Court handed down a decision that did exactly that. The *World* commented that the victory was so sweeping "no other President will be tempted to follow in the footsteps of Theodore Roosevelt, no matter how greedy he may be for power, no matter how resentful of opposition." This prophecy would prove to be short-lived, as American involvement in World War I brought new government efforts to curtail press freedom.

Source:
W. A. Swanberg, *Pulitzer* (New York: Scribners, 1967).

THE WIRELESS TELEGRAPH

Marconi Sends an *S*. By the turn of the century, reporters had long made use of telegraph wires to transmit news to their papers. Innovations in the development of "wireless telegraphy," or radio, as it came to be known, proceeded rapidly in the first decade of the twentieth century. Wireless pioneer Guglielmo Marconi announced on 15 December 1901 that he had transmitted the letter *S* across two thousand miles from Cornwall in England to Newfoundland, Canada. While the press lionized Marconi as a heroic, humble, and tireless genius, his competitors pointed out that this feat was unverifiable. Only Marconi and his assistants had witnessed it.

The New World Sends Greetings to the Old. On 21 December 1902 Marconi succeeded in sending a full message twenty-three hundred miles from the governor general of Canada to King Edward VII. In January 1903 he transmitted "most cordial greetings" from President Theodore Roosevelt to the British monarch. By the end of that year he had inaugurated regular transatlantic commercial service. By 1907 the cost of ten cents a word far undercut the twenty-five cents that the cable telegraph companies charged. Press clients received a discount rate of five cents a word, and in 1907 *The New York Times* inaugu-

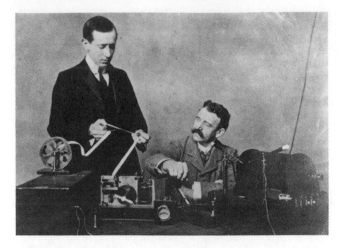

Guglielmo Marconi reading a wireless message, with his assistant George Kemp, circa 1900

in the development of tuning devices to better isolate and use the spectrum of electromagnetic waves. His chief competitors, Americans Lee De Forest and Reginald Fessenden, concentrated on different aspects of wireless technology. De Forest advanced the technology of reception with his invention of the three-element grid audion tube, or triode, announced to the public in October 1906. This was the forerunner of the vacuum tube, which became central to all broadcast reception later in the century. Meanwhile, Fessenden concentrated on transmission.

The Human Voice Takes to the Air. In October 1906, over the eleven miles between his laboratories in Brant Rock and Plymouth, Massachusetts, Fessenden sent the first radio transmissions of voice and music, rather than just the dots and dashes of telegraphy. Like Marconi, Fessenden conceived of radio broadcasting as a way to improve point-to-point communications — in effect, to invent wireless telephone service. On Christmas Eve 1906 he broadcast a recording of Handel's "Largo," himself on violin playing "O Holy Night," and himself singing and making a speech. Startled shipboard telegraph operators as far away as the Caribbean reported receiving the spotty transmissions. This is considered the first radio broadcast in history. It would be left to later innovators to reconceive the technology for uses other than point-to-point communication.

Source:

Susan J. Douglas, *Inventing American Broadcasting, 1899–1922* (Baltimore: Johns Hopkins University Press, 1987).

rated a special Sunday section called the "Marconi Transatlantic Wireless Department," with news from its London correspondent. No longer was the flow of news physically restricted by the speed of ships or the laying down of cables.

The Limits of Marconi's Vision. Marconi conceived the future of wireless telegraphy as a series of improvements on point-to-point communication, and he hoped to establish a monopoly in that industry. His innovations came primarily

HEADLINE MAKERS

ABRAHAM CAHAN

1860-1951

EDITOR AND NOVELIST

An Exiled Russian Radical. Born in Lithuania, Abraham Cahan immigrated to New York in 1882 to escape persecution for his socialist views. A fiery speaker, he helped to organize the first Jewish tailors' union on the Lower East Side in 1884. Cahan dominated the intellectual and public life of the rapidly expanding Jewish immigrant community on the Lower East Side of New York City from 1900 to 1920 as editor of the *Jewish Daily Forward.* He was brilliant, with a grim temperament, and could be

quite spiteful. He both symbolized and shaped the power of the immigrant press at a time when 20 percent of the nation's population was foreign born.

The *Forward*. The Yiddish-language daily the *Jewish Daily Forward* was founded on 22 April 1897 with Cahan as editor. He soon resigned over conflicts with its publishers about who wielded ultimate control of the paper. The publishers wanted the paper to be an outlet for socialism, while Cahan would have patterned it after the papers of Pulitzer and Hearst. He went to the *New York Commercial Advertiser,* where his editor was Lincoln Steffens. When Steffens left to become an editor at *McClure's* in 1901, Cahan lost interest and began writing fiction. In 1902 Cahan was rehired by the *Forward,* with the mandate of telling stories rather than spouting socialist ideology. Circulation soared, but some intellectuals accused him of low taste and vulgarity, and he was once again forced out after six months. In 1903 he returned with assurances of complete control.

Yellow Journalism for Jews. Cahan remained at the helm of the *Forward* for more than forty years, aiming it at an audience of laborers and housewives. He wanted to provide them with useful information and compelling stories in which they recognized themselves rather than with anti-capitalist dogma. The introduction of a sports page to the *Forward* caused quite a stir. In 1906 he inaugurated the famous "Bintel Brief" (Bundle of Letters) feature, with letters from readers sharing their views and tales on subjects ranging from marriage to proper American behavior. Illiterate people sometimes visited the paper's offices to dictate their stories. Cahan remained a socialist but was never dogmatic. His politics aimed at practical improvements in the lives of his readers. He crusaded first and foremost for better working conditions in the garment industry, where many Jewish immigrants worked.

Literary Achievements. Cahan published his first short story, "A Providential Match," in 1895 and attracted the interest of *Atlantic* editor and novelist William Dean Howells. Howells helped Cahan to find a publisher for his first novel, *Yekl: A Tale of the Ghetto* (1896). In 1913 *McClure's* serialized his autobiography, and in 1917 he published a fictionalized version of it called *The Rise of David Levinsky.*

Political Trouble during the War. The constituency of the *Forward,* many of whom had fled persecution in czarist Russia, tended to support the Germans after the outbreak of World War I in Europe. This unpopular position endangered the paper's third-class mailing privileges, and Cahan soon backed off. When the United States entered the war and the Russian Revolution took the Russian army out of it, circulation soared to over two hundred thousand. While Cahan initially supported the goals of the Bolshevik Revolution, by the late 1920s he became one of Joseph Stalin's harshest critics. In the 1920s the *Forward* added Los Angeles and Boston editions, and by the 1930s it was far removed from its radical socialist beginnings. Cahan died in 1951 at the age of ninety-one.

Source:
Jules Chametzky, *From the Ghetto: The Fiction of Abraham Cahan* (Amherst: University of Massachusetts Press, 1977).

DOROTHY DIX

1861-1951

ADVICE COLUMNIST

"Mother Confessor to Millions." Elizabeth Meriwether Gilmer started her column "Dorothy Dix Talks" in New Orleans in 1896. It lasted until her death in 1951, making her probably the best-known woman writer of her era. William Randolph Hearst lured her from New Orleans to his *New York Journal* at the turn of the century, and with his syndication operations, her readership eventually reached some sixty million throughout the world.

Poor in the New South. Elizabeth Meriwether grew up in a poor but cultivated Tennessee family after the Civil War. When she was twenty-one, she married her stepmother's brother, a charming but emotionally unstable man who could not hold a job. The marriage was unhappy, but they never divorced. Faced with the need to support her family, she began to work as a freelance writer. Eliza Nicholson, publisher of the *New Orleans Picayune,* recognized the thirty-three-year-old's abilities and hired her as a "Gal Friday" to the paper's sharp editor, Maj. Nathaniel Burbank. She graduated from the obituaries and drudge stories of the cub reporter to her own straightforward column of advice to women, called "Sunday Salad." Her down-to-earth style brought a barrage of letters.

Sob Sister Extraordinaire. Her first story for Hearst was to cover the saloon-busting tour through Kansas of temperance leader Carry Nation in 1901. "What a waste of good liquor," Dix wrote, in the voice of an inveterate southern belle. She became a favorite with Hearst's brilliant editor Arthur Brisbane, who helped sharpen her prose. He asked in 1902, "Did any man ever make a quicker success in the newspaper business than Dorothy Dix?" She covered titillating murder trials, including the Harry K. Thaw trial, and became the most dogged of the "Sob Sisters," wrangling interviews from victims, perpetrators, and their families. By 1917, at age fifty-five, she ceased work as a reporter to concentrate on her column and sermonettes.

The Hall-Mills Case. In 1926 Dix was persuaded to cover one last trial, that of a New Jersey minister's wife accused of killing her husband and his church-choir lover. The jury shared Dix's sympathies, and the woman was acquitted.

Everyone's Problems. People wrote to Dorothy Dix about universal difficulties: interfering parents, unfaithful spouses, recalcitrant children, romance, religion, etiquette, and recipes. She urged spouses to work out their disagreements, children to listen to their parents, and young men and women to hold to their ideals. She was an early advocate of the Nineteenth Amendment. If possible, she thought, women should stay home with young children, but as she herself had learned, having a vocation is crucial in case of need. She continued to dictate her column until she died in 1951 at the age of ninety. She allowed no one to carry on under the name Dorothy Dix.

Sources:
Harnett T. Kane and Ella Bentley Arthur, *Dear Dorothy Dix: The Story of a Compassionate Woman* (Garden City, N.Y.: Doubleday, 1952);
Madelon Golden Schlipp and Sharon M. Murphy, *Great Women of the Press* (Carbondale: Southern Illinois University Press, 1983).

WILLIAM RANDOLPH HEARST

1863-1951

EDITOR, PUBLISHER, POLITICIAN, COLLECTOR

Empire. Born to a family fortune made in mining, William Randolph Hearst built one of the largest communications empires in U.S. history. His assets, estimated at between $200 million and $400 million, included sixteen daily newspapers with a combined circulation of more than five million, the International News Service, King Features, the *American Weekly* Sunday supplement, *Cosmopolitan, Harper's Bazaar,* and *Good Housekeeping.* He also amassed one of the finest private art and antique collections in the world.

A Rich Kid's Diversion Turns to Serious Business. Young Hearst was thrown out of Harvard University in his junior year for a series of practical jokes. He distributed chamber pots to faculty members with their names inserted on the bottoms and tethered a jackass in the home of one professor, with a note that read, "Now there are two of you." He then went to work at Joseph Pulitzer's *World.* He admired both its sensationalism and its idealism. His father, who served as a U.S. senator from California, had purchased the *San Francisco Examiner* to further his political ambitions. Young Hearst proposed to take it over and turn it into a real newspaper, increase circulation, subscribe to the telegraph service of the *New York Herald,* and clean up California with campaigns against the influence of Southern Pacific Railroad magnates Leland Stanford and Collis P. Huntington. He was twenty-four years old.

Talent Raids. In 1895 he bought the *New York Journal,* a morning paper. Within a year it was second only to the *World* in circulation. By offering salary increases, he raided the *World* and other papers, hiring away many of its star reporters, editors, and artists, including Arthur Brisbane, Richard Outcault, and Solomon Carvalho. His art department created cartoon characters such as the Katzenjammer Kids, Foxy Grandpa, Alphonse and Gaston, and Happy Hooligan. The next year Hearst added the *Evening Journal* and bought the *New York Morning Advertiser* to secure its Associated Press franchise. His publishing tactics infuriated Pulitzer, who accused Hearst of pandering to the lowest tastes of his readers.

"I'll Furnish the War." When a conflict with Spain over Cuba threatened to turn into war in 1898, Hearst used his papers to incite bloodthirst. He sent the artist Frederic Remington to Cuba to draw the coming conflict, but Remington cabled him that all seemed quiet. Hearst cabled back, "You furnish the pictures and I'll furnish the war." While Hearst's excessive jingoism contributed to public support of hostile action against Spain, most historians agree that the publisher did not actually cause the war.

Political Ambitions. Hearst harbored political ambitions and set his eye on the White House. He supported Democrat William Jennings Bryan in 1900 and hoped to be Bryan's running mate in 1904. Since the Democratic convention was scheduled for Chicago, the party wanted a sympathetic newspaper in that city. Hearst dutifully bought the *Chicago American* and was rewarded with the presidency of the National Association of Democratic Clubs, a high-profile national position in the party. He ran for Congress from New York in 1902 and won by a margin of three to one, but the victory was marred when a fireworks accident at his Madison Square Garden celebration killed eighteen people and injured many others. In Congress he worked against railroad trusts and for public ownership of railroads, telegraphs, and mines. He also supported the eight-hour workday, a graduated income tax, and more money to schools and the U.S. Navy. In 1904 Hearst polled second in the balloting for the Democratic presidential nomination and then won reelection to Congress. He ran unsuccessfully for governor of New York in 1906 and mayor of New York City in 1909.

Later Exploits. During World War I Hearst got into trouble for his anti-British sentiments, which were construed as pro-German. While his personal popularity plummeted, he continued to expand his empire to twelve newspapers by 1919, including the *Boston Daily Advertiser,* the *Washington Star,* the *Chicago Herald,* the *Wisconsin News,* and the *San Francisco Call.* He lived in semiseclusion at his famous California castle, San Simeon, until his death in 1951 at age eighty-eight.

Source:
W. A. Swanberg, *Citizen Hearst* (New York: Scribners, 1961).

JOSEPH PULITZER

1847-1911

NEWSPAPER EDITOR AND PUBLISHER

Beginnings. Born in Hungary in 1847, Joseph Pulitzer immigrated to Boston to serve in the Union army during the Civil War. After becoming a U.S. citizen in 1867, he worked for various German newspapers and became involved in Republican Party politics, campaigning for *New York Tribune* publisher Horace Greeley for president in 1872. But he soon became disenchanted with politics and the party. He began his newspaper empire with the *St. Louis Staats-Zeitung* and the *Post and Dispatch* in the 1870s, serving as publisher, editor, and business manager. In 1883 he bought the *New York World* from tycoon Jay Gould. The *World* became the strongest voice of the Democratic Party in the United States, crusading for the "people" against the powerful "interests," but Pulitzer did not always conform to party policies.

The Mastermind of the Modern Newspaper. Pulitzer created the New Journalism that dominated his age, establishing the model for the big-city daily in the twentieth century. His papers covered crime, sponsored and publicized stunts by its own staff, ran sensational features and more pictures than any other paper, and carried on crusades against corruption in government and business. Pulitzer conceived of news as stories that entertained the ordinary person rather than as strictly factual information. He also revolutionized advertising, linking its price to circulation and standardizing rates. In 1887 he inaugurated the *Evening World* and in 1890 opened the famed World Building on Park Row in downtown Manhattan, in its day the tallest and grandest structure in the city.

War with Hearst. The famous rivalry between the *World* and William Randolph Hearst's *Journal* began in 1896. Hearst raided the *World* for talent by greatly outpaying Pulitzer. Their competitive flag-waving is sometimes cited as a cause of the Spanish-American War. The war sobered Pulitzer, and after it ended, he returned the *World* to its former balance and always resented the tendency of critics to lump his papers together with Hearst's under the term *yellow journalism.*

Into the Twentieth Century. By 1900 Pulitzer had long since put aside his own political ambitions and wanted his papers to serve as schoolmasters and provocateurs. He cheered the reformist Republican president Theodore Roosevelt and relentlessly attacked New York City's Tammany Hall machine. In 1904 he endowed with $2 million the first professional school of journalism in the nation at Columbia University. Despite his belief that there was no substitute for practical experience in the world, he believed that labor combined with learning was unbeatable. His estate also endowed the prestigious Pulitzer Prizes. Despite the reputation of his papers for sensationalism, after his death his name became synonymous with the highest standards of journalistic excellence. He died aboard his yacht in Charleston harbor in October 1911.

Source:
W. A. Swanberg, *Pulitzer* (New York: Scribners, 1967).

LINCOLN STEFFENS

1866-1936

MUCKRAKER

A Privileged Boyhood. When they had a son the year after the assassination of Abraham Lincoln in 1865, Lincoln Steffens's parents named their child in honor of the fallen leader. Steffens grew up in Sacramento with all the privileges of wealth. He loved horseback riding, literature, and writing and attended the University of California, Berkeley. Afterward he went to Germany to study philosophy and then to Paris to study psychology. When he arrived home with a new wife, he found that his father expected him to make his own living immediately. He secured a job covering Wall Street for the *New York Evening Post.*

Business and Politics Mix. Covering the financial community, Steffens observed the strong and corrupt connections between powerful business interests and government at every level. He admired the men who, having been drawn into a corrupt system, used their knowledge to help clean it up. His greatest scorn was reserved for alleged reformers who lacked both the information and the character to follow through on their promises. Covering police headquarters, he got a first-hand education in the workings of the Democratic Tammany Hall political machine and the close ties that bound Tammany, the police, and criminal syndicates. At police headquarters he also met the legendary reporter Jacob Riis and the energetic police commissioner, Theodore Roosevelt. Steffens soon went to the *New York Commercial Advertiser* as city editor.

A Move to *McClure's*. S. S. McClure asked Steffens to cover Roosevelt's exploits as a Rough Rider during the Spanish-American War for *McClure's* magazine. In 1901 Steffens accepted *McClure's* offer of the managing editorship of the magazine, where Ida Tarbell and Ray Stannard Baker were already on the staff. With their solid educations, literary aspirations, and investigative zeal, these three young reporters revolutionized journalism.

The Shame of the Cities. Steffens pursued the story of municipal corruption, and successful reform, in Saint Louis, Minneapolis, Pittsburgh, and Chicago. The most startling aspect of his exposés was the participation of each city's "best" citizens in elaborate systems of graft and payoffs. He wrote, "the source and sustenance of bad government [are] not the bribe taker, but the bribe giver, the man we are so proud of, the successful businessman." He chastised the apathetic public for failing to demand more principled government and cited a blind civic- and commercial-spiritedness for tolerating businesslike thievery. After publishing his municipal investigations in book form as *The Shame of the Cities* (1904), Steffens moved on to the shame of the states.

It Works. Writing as a freelance journalist after 1906, Steffens became interested in radicals and revolution. He covered the Mexican Revolution of 1910–1917 and the Russian Revolution of 1917. After a visit to the new Soviet Union, he made the memorable observation, "I have seen the future, and it works." His 1931 autobiography is a classic of Progressive Era and journalism history. He died in 1936.

Sources:
David Mark Chalmers, *The Muckrake Years* (New York: Van Nostrand, 1974);

Louis Filler, *The Muckrakers* (University Park: Pennsylvania State University Press, 1976);

Ellen Fitzpatrick, *Muckraking: Three Landmark Articles* (New York: Bedford Books/St. Martin's Press, 1994);

Justin Kaplan, *Lincoln Steffens, A Biography* (New York: Simon & Schuster, 1974);

Lincoln Steffens, *Autobiography* (New York: Harcourt Brace, 1931).

IDA TARBELL

1857-1944

MUCKRAKER

Born in an Oil Boom. Ida Tarbell was raised in northwest Pennsylvania at a time when the discovery of oil was transforming the region into an industrial hub. While many people made fortunes, including her father (who invented a storage system for oil), Ida remembered the terrible accidents, explosions, and fires that claimed many lives and the environmental devastation drilling caused. With her family's new wealth came access to books and magazines, and Ida grew up reading the popular magazines of the day. The only woman in her class at Allegheny College, she trained for a teaching career but soon grew bored with it. In 1882 she took a job with a monthly magazine *The Chautauquan.*

From Social Issues to Biography. She wrote on the great reform movements of the 1880s and 1890s: temperance, antimonopoly crusades, housing reform, the eight-hour workday, and other labor issues connected with the Knights of Labor. Her interest in women's roles in social change led her to research a biography of Madame Roland and her part in the French Revolution. In France she decided to try to make her living as a freelance writer for American newspapers and magazines, which were then undergoing a boom of their own as printing technologies brought down costs. She sold stories on French culture and politics to *McClure's* and *Scribner's.* A biographical series on Napoleon for *McClure's,* richly illustrated with portraits, became a sensation. Her series on Abraham Lincoln, which drew on prodigious research, boosted the magazine's circulation by more than one hundred thousand. She became a contributing editor in 1896.

History of the Standard Oil Company. When *McClure's* suggested that Ida commence major research into John D. Rockefeller's powerful holding company known as Standard Oil, her father, who had fallen on hard times, warned her against it. He said Standard Oil would ruin the magazine. For five years she searched the public record: court documents, congressional investigations, newspaper accounts, pamphlets put out by reformers. What was envisioned as a three-part series turned into nineteen articles that ran for more than two years.

Published as a book in 1904, *The History of the Standard Oil Company* constituted a devastating exposé of how Rockefeller had used ruthless measures to drive his competitors out of business and secure a monopoly. One Standard Oil executive, Henry H. Rogers, who had been an independent oil refiner and was forced to join the company, met with Tarbell for a period of more than two years and introduced her to others high in the corporate structure. As the series began to appear, other "victims" contacted Tarbell with their own evidence of Standard Oil's domination.

Plus and Minus. Never a radical, Tarbell tried to see both sides of every story. She concluded the series by reflecting on the "legitimate greatness" of Standard Oil, the intelligence, organization, and vision it represented. But she found the cost of its success too great: the power it amassed, like all absolute power in history, was used against the public. In further articles on Rockefeller, she called such tactics "Commercial Machiavellianism." In 1906, with Lincoln Steffens and Ray Stannard Baker, Tarbell set out to launch the *American Magazine,* but it failed. She continued to write as a freelance journalist well into the twentieth century, traveling to Italy to write on the ascendant Benito Mussolini, whom she found "gallant" but a "fearful despot." She never became an advocate of women entering public life, finding their domestic role, which she never performed, more crucial. She died in 1944 in a hospital near her Connecticut farm at the age of eighty-six.

Sources:

Kathleen Brady, *Ida Tarbell: Portrait of a Muckraker* (New York: Seanew Putnam, 1984);

David Mark Chalmers, *The Muckrake Years* (New York: Van Nostrand, 1974);

Louis Filler, *The Muckrakers* (University Park: Pennsylvania State University Press, 1976);

Ellen Fitzpatrick, *Muckraking: Three Landmark Articles* (New York: St. Martin's Press, 1994).

IDA B. WELLS-BARNETT

1862-1931

JOURNALIST FOR RACIAL JUSTICE

Early Adversity. When a yellow fever epidemic claimed the lives of sixteen-year-old Ida Wells's parents, she determined to keep her brothers and sisters together. She taught in a one-room school near Holly Springs, Mississippi. She soon moved the family to Memphis, in order to take a teacher's examination and find a better job. Riding the Chesapeake and Ohio Railroad to her job, she refused to sit in the smoky, dingy car reserved for African Americans and filed suit against the railroad for not providing "separate but equal" accommodations. Wells won her case and $500 in damages, but in 1887 the Supreme Court of Tennessee reversed the decision. As a teacher, she began to write for the black church weekly *Living Way* under the pseudonym "Iola" and soon realized that she loved journalism.

A Crusader for Equality. Encouraged by the eminent Frederick Douglass, in 1889 Wells accepted the editorship of a small Memphis paper that she renamed *Free Speech.* She attacked the inferior condition of black schools, and in 1892 her articles about the lynching of three grocery-store operators who had been kidnapped from the city jail brought trouble from Memphis whites. While she was on a lecture tour in the East, a mob destroyed the *Free Speech* offices.

New York, London, Chicago. To avoid harm in the aftermath of this incident, she took a job with T. Thomas Fortune's *New York Age,* a leading black newspaper. Wells soon owned one-fourth of the paper and made it her mission to inform the world about lynching. In 1893 and 1894 she made a well-publicized tour of the British Isles and began to organize antilynching committees in Europe and (northern) North America. She decided to settle in Chicago, where she published an influential book, *A Red Report: Tabulated Statistics and Alleged Causes of Lynching in the United States, 1892–1893–1894.* There she married Ferdinand Lee Barnett, a lawyer and founder of Chicago's first black newspaper, the *Conservator.*

Prepared. In 1901 the Barnetts became the first black family to buy a house east of State Street in Chicago. Their neighbors turned their backs and slammed their doors to humiliate them. When young neighborhood toughs stood jeering outside her house, Ida Wells-Barnett let them know that she kept a pistol and knew how to use it. As she often said in her antilynching campaigns, it was necessary to fight fire with fire. She told her young harassers that if she were to die by violence, she would take some of her persecutors with her.

A Family and a League. During the first decade of the twentieth century, Wells-Barnett dedicated herself to raising four children; in 1910 she founded a Negro Fellowship League in the roughest section of Chicago. Modeled on her friend Jane Addams's Hull House, it provided counseling, job services, religious services, recreation, and cheap housing. She chided middle-class blacks, and particularly clergy, for their unwillingness to help the poorest members of the community. She campaigned for women's suffrage and participated in the founding of the National Association for the Advancement of Colored People (NAACP) in 1909 but soon found the organization too accommodationist.

Legacy. Until her death in 1931 at age sixty-nine, Wells-Barnett continued to agitate for social justice. She set up black women's clubs and even ran, unsuccessfully, for the state Senate. Her husband became the first black appointed as an assistant state's attorney in Chicago and

served for fourteen years. In 1940, after her enthusiastic civic campaign, the Chicago Housing Authority honored her by changing the name of a new forty-seven-acre housing complex to the Ida B. Wells Garden Homes.

Source:
Madelon Golden Schlipp and Sharon M. Murphy, *Great Women of the Press* (Carbondale: Southern Illinois University Press, 1983).

WILLIAM ALLEN WHITE
1868-1944
EDITOR AND PROPRIETOR, EMPORIA GAZETTE

What's the Matter with Kansas? As a young reporter, William Allen White saw both sides of the radical populism that swept his home state of Kansas. He understood the plight of the poor farmer and workingman but disdained the abilities and the motivations of the movement's leaders. In 1895 at the age of twenty-five, after working as a reporter in larger cities, he bought his hometown paper, the *Emporia Gazette.* He used it to promote the town's fortunes, attract business, and herald the reform wing of the Republican Party. In 1896 he published a scathing editorial against the populist presidential candidate William Jennings Bryan titled "What's the Matter with Kansas?" This editorial brought him national attention and invitations to write for the *Saturday Evening Post* and *McClure's.* It also was credited with helping to secure victory for William McKinley over Bryan.

Common Sense and Respectability. The circulation of the *Gazette* never exceeded eight thousand, but White's talent brought him international recognition. He was a lifelong Republican who exemplified respectable, middle-class, progressive liberalism. He attacked the populists as much because they took such a disapproving tone about American life as for their ideology. He much preferred constructive criticism and became a close companion and backer of Republican reformer Theodore Roosevelt. White was more sympathetic to the aggressive muckrakers than Roosevelt. He welcomed Ida Tarbell to *Emporia* in 1905. But like the president, White held that business plutocracy was at the root of political corruption.

"Mr. Republican." As his nickname attests, White was linked throughout the early twentieth century with the struggle to control the Republican Party. He helped Roosevelt to found the Progressive Party in 1911 and championed independent newspapers against the growth of chains and conglomerates. He won the Pulitzer Prize in 1923 for a prolabor editorial called "To an Anxious Friend" and again in 1946. Perhaps his most famous editorial, "Mary White," came in 1921, when his daughter was killed at the age of seventeen in a horseback riding accident. Later in the century he became a charismatic leader of the American Society of Newspaper Editors, arguing that commercialism had dangerously degraded the quality of journalism. Press critic Gilbert Seldes judged him "the most outstanding figure in American journalism."

Sources:

Sally Foreman Griffith, *Hometown News: William Allen White and the Emporia Gazette* (New York: Oxford University Press, 1989);

Gilbert Seldes, *Lords of the Press* (New York: Messner, 1938).

PEOPLE IN THE NEWS

Robert S. Abbott, the child of former slaves, founded the *Chicago Defender* on a shoestring budget in 1905. Its masthead carried the motto "American race prejudice must be destroyed!"

In his *Chicago Record* column "Stories of the Streets and of the Town," distinctively midwestern humorist and fablist **George Ade** immortalized the vernacular in such pieces as "The Fable of the Good Fairy of the Eighth Ward and the Dollar Excursion of the Steam Fitters."

Known as the "dean of American magazine editors," **Henry Mills Alden** reigned at *Harper's* from 1869 to 1919. He gave special attention to American writers and to burgeoning social problems, and *Harper's* became the most widely circulated periodical in the country.

One of the most famous muckrakers, **Ray Stannard Baker** wrote about industry and labor for *McClure's,* where he was associate editor from 1899 to 1905. His groundbreaking article "The Right to Work" appeared in its January 1903 issue.

In 1901 **Charles Walker Barron** bought the Dow-Jones Company from founder Charles Dow and thus became the publisher of the *Wall Street Journal.* He revolutionized economic reporting by moving beyond simple figures and making it accessible to the general reader. He campaigned against irresponsible speculation and for honest investment policies.

Frederick G. Bonfils and **Harry H. Tammen,** known as "Bon" and "Tam," bought the *Denver Post* in 1895 and turned it into a sensational success. Its circulation in the 1900s was more than that of its three competitors combined. In 1907 they were shot by their own lawyer but were saved from further injury by a beautiful "Sob Sister," Polly Pry, who grabbed the gun.

Peter F. Collier founded the general weekly that bore his name in 1888, and after 1895 he changed its emphasis from fiction to news and public affairs. He died in 1909 and was succeeded by his son Robert, who continued the muckraking tradition.

Publisher **Gardner Cowles** bought a majority interest in the *Des Moines Register and Leader* in 1903 and in 1908 added the *Des Moines Tribune.* Its daily circulation grew from 14,000 to more than 350,000, and 425,000 on Sunday, becoming the base property of one of the twentieth century's great media empires.

Cyrus H. K. Curtis bought the oldest weekly in the United States, the *Pennsylvania Gazette,* once operated by Benjamin Franklin, in 1897 and renamed it the *Saturday Evening Post.* Under the editorship of **George Horace Lorimer,** it attained a circulation of 500,000 within five years, reached one million in 1908, and became one of the most profitable and popular publications in United States history.

In 1893 Chicago newspaperman **Finley Peter Dunne** created the philosophical saloon keeper Mr. Dooley. In 1900 he moved to New York to join the staff of *Collier's.*

Frank E. Gannett founded what was to become the largest newspaper chain in the country. In 1906 he bought an interest in the *Elmira Gazette* and later merged it with the *Elmira Star.* During the next three decades he bought several other newspapers in upstate New York, establishing his headquarters in Rochester.

Lewis W. Hine began to take photographs in 1903 at the suggestion of a friend. From 1907 to 1914 he photographed scenes of child labor for the National Child Labor Committee, often in secret. His work helped to bring about legislative reform of working conditions for children.

The living embodiment of a tough, incorruptible, cigar-smoking editor, **James Keeley** of the *Chicago Tribune* reinvented the paper for the urban twentieth century by offering its harried and alienated readers useful advice and a sense of community.

In 1902, late in his eventful life as a frontiersman and sheriff, **William B. "Bat" Masterson** became a sportswriter and then sports editor of the *New York Morning Telegraph*.

St. Clair McKelway was editor in chief of the *Brooklyn Eagle* from 1884 until his death in 1915. It flourished as a local paper but also covered national news.

In 1905 **William V. McKean's** *Philadelphia Bulletin* became the leading paper in Philadelphia. When he bought it in 1895, it was thirteenth out of thirteen in circulation. By treating the city as a collection of distinct urban villages, McLean built the paper into one of the most successful and prestigious in the country.

Publisher **Frank A. Munsey** led the trend to ten-cent magazines in the 1890s. *Munsey's* was the first general illustrated monthly to reach half a million in circulation. It specialized in articles on royalty, celebrities, industrialists, and statesmen and ran pictures of nude and seminude women. During the 1900s Munsey also bought and sold more than a dozen newspapers, including the *New York Tribune*. He tried (and failed) to improve the quality of journalism by targeting the largely Republican business class.

Frank Ward O'Malley ("O'Malley of the *Sun*"), ace reporter, covered New York for fourteen years, "thirteen of which were spent in Jack's restaurant." His writing was both funny and dramatic. One of his most famous pieces, "A Policeman Walks East to his Death," described the killing of cop Gene Sheehan from the point of view of Sheehan's mother.

Richard F. Outcault, cartoonist for the *New York World* and later the *New York Journal*, introduced the character Buster Brown in 1902. Outcault had created the *Yellow Kid* comic that gave yellow journalism its name and touched off a great newspaper rivalry.

Jacob Riis was a crusader against urban slum conditions. Beginning in 1890 with the publication of *How the Other Half Lives*, he became New York's "most useful citizen." In the 1900s he no longer wrote or photographed for the newspapers but continued to publish books, including *The Battle of the Slum* (1902) and *Children of the Tenements* (1903).

In his column "Just for Georgia," which ran in the *Atlanta Constitution* from 1890 to 1927, **Frank L. Stanton** lovingly depicted the Old South, complete with "cracker" and African American dialects. While he condemned lynching in a famous piece called "They've Hung Bill Jones," he often glorified plantation life.

Banker and founder of the *Chicago Daily News*, **Melville Stone** served as general manager of the Associated Press from 1893 to 1921. A 1900 court decision ruled that the AP was a public utility and could not refuse subscribers. The organization dissolved in Illinois and reorganized in New York.

Bert Leston Taylor ("B.L.T.") began his "A Line o' Type or Two" column for the *Chicago Journal* for thirty dollars a week. The *Chicago Tribune* lured him away with sixty dollars a week. In 1903 the *New York Telegraph* induced another move, and in 1905 he became an editor at the humor magazine *Puck*. In 1909 he returned to Chicago, the city he loved, at a yearly salary of $10,000 with the *Chicago Tribune*.

Charles H. Taylor served as manager, editor, and publisher of the *Boston Globe* between 1873 and 1921. He emphasized unbiased reporting, local events, and working-class issues and courted women and children as readers. His innovations upset traditions in the 1870s but set standards for twentieth-century reporting.

DEATHS

Thomas Bailey Aldrich, 70, editor of various national magazines, including the *Atlantic,* who introduced literary realism to adolescent fiction, 19 March 1907.

Henry Brown Blackwell, 84, editor, with his wife Lucy Swope, of the national woman's suffrage paper, the *Woman's Journal,* 7 September 1909.

Henry Chadwick, 83, the first baseball writer for *The New York Times* and the *Brooklyn Eagle,* 20 April 1908.

Francis Pharcellus Church, 66, editor of the *Galaxy* (1870–1895), a New York answer to the *Atlantic.* He also wrote editorials for the *New York Sun,* including one with the immortal line, "Yes, Virginia, there is a Santa Claus," 11 April 1906.

Peter Collier, 59, founder in 1888 of the weekly that bore his name. In 1895 he changed its emphasis from fiction to public affairs, 1909.

Stephen Crane, 28, war correspondent, novelist and poet, 5 June 1900.

Jane Cunningham Croly (Jennie June), 72, the first woman to write a daily newspaper feature and the first to syndicate one; the wife of newspaperman David Croly and mother of *New Republic* editor Herbert Croly, 23 December 1901.

Amos J. Cummings, 60, managing editor of the *New York Sun* who served contemporaneously in the House of Representatives for fifteen years, 3 May 1902.

Collin M. Daggett, 70, frontier journalist, founder of *Golden Era* and editor of the *Territorial Enterprise,* 12 November 1901.

Mary Mapes Dodge, 74, editor of the first American children's magazine, *St. Nicholas: Scribner's Illustrated Magazine for Girls and Boys,* 21 August 1905.

Wendell P. Garrison, 66, editor of *The Nation* for forty-one years, 27 February 1907.

Richard Watson Gilder, 65, editor of *Scribner's,* later renamed *Century Illustrated Monthly Magazine,* 18 November 1909.

E. L. Godkin, 70, conservative, combative editor of the *New York Evening Post* and *The Nation* from 1865 to 1899, 21 May 1902.

Murat Halstead, 78, war correspondent, political reporter, and editor of the *Cincinnati Commercial;* also a prominent Republican, 2 July 1908.

Joel Chandler Harris, 59, creator of humorous "Negro" folktales told through "Uncle Remus," spent twenty years writing for the *Atlanta Constitution,* 3 July 1908.

Bret Harte, 65, beginning with his dispatches for the *Overland Monthly* attained great success as a chronicler of western life, 5 May 1902.

Evan P. Howell, 65, from 1876 to 1897 served as editor in chief of the *Atlanta Constitution,* 6 August 1905.

John Foster Kirk, 80, scholarly editor of *Lippincott's* magazine for sixteen years who shunned the new and popular, 21 September 1904.

John Armoy Knox, 56, cracker-barrel humorist for *Texas Siftings* in the 1880s and 1890s, 18 December 1906.

Sara Jane Clarke Lippincott (Grace Greenwood), 80, wrote political letters from Washington, D.C., to *The New York Times* during Reconstruction, 20 April 1904.

Henry Demarest Lloyd, 55, editorial writer for the *Chicago Tribune* who was a forerunner of the muckrakers in his defense of unpopular reformers and attacks on Standard Oil, 1903.

William V. McKean, 82, editor in chief of the *Philadelphia Ledger* from 1864 to 1891 who was known for insistence on fairness and accuracy, 29 March 1903.

Thomas Nast, 60, political cartoonist, artist, and Civil War correspondent for *Harper's Weekly,* 7 December 1902.

Crosby S. Noyes, 83, editor in chief of the *Washington Evening Star* from 1867 to 1908 who with objectivity fought yellow journalism, 21 February 1908.

Oswald Ottendorfer, 74, proprietor of the foremost German-language daily, the *New Yorker Staats-Zeitung,* from 1859 to 1900, 15 December 1900.

Emil Preetorius, 78, dean of German American newspapermen, co-owner with Carl Schurz of the *St. Louis Westliche Post,* 19 November 1905.

Julian Ralph, 49, esteemed and gifted correspondent for the *New York Sun* who "could write 5,000 words about a cobblestone," 20 January 1903.

Henry Romeike, 48, founded the press clipping bureau for prominent people who wanted to follow their own news coverage, 3 June 1903.

Carl Schurz, 77, editor and co-owner with Emil Preetorius of the *St. Louis Westliche Post*, 14 May 1906.

James E. Scripps, 71, with his sister Ellen and half brother Edward started the first American newspaper chain, 29 May 1906.

Albion W. Tourgee, 67, colorful novelist who also published and edited *Our Continent* and *Basis: A Journal of Citizenship*, 21 May 1905.

Henry Villard, 65, famous Civil War correspondent for the *New York Sun*, railroad financier, and publisher of the *New York Evening Post* and *The Nation*, 12 November 1900.

Josiah Flint Willard (Josiah Flynt), 37, lived with and wrote about the tramps that traveled the rails and lived on the streets, later worked on Tolstoy's estate, 21 January 1907.

Benjamin Wood, 79, editor of the widest-circulation daily of the nineteenth century, the *New York Daily News*, 1869–1900, 21 February 1900.

PUBLICATIONS

George W. Alger, "The Literature of Exposure," *Atlantic Monthly*, 96 (August 1905): 210–213;

Alger, "Sensational Journalism and the Law," *Atlantic Monthly*, 91 (February 1903): 145–151;

Edith Baker Brown, "A Plea for Literary Journalism," *Harper's Weekly*, 46 (25 October 1902): 1558;

O. F. Byxbee, *Establishing a Newspaper* (Chicago: Inland Printers, 1901);

F. M. Colby, "Attacking the Newspapers," *Bookman*, 15 (August 1902): 534–536;

Lydia Kingsmill Commander, "The Significance of Yellow Journalism," *Arena*, 34 (August 1905): 151;

Charles B. Connolly, "Ethics of Modern Journalism," *Catholic World*, 75 (July 1902): 453–462;

Herbert Croly, *The Promise of American Life* (New York: Macmillan, 1909);

Finley Peter Dunne, "Mr. Dooley on an Editor's Duties," *Harper's Weekly*, 45 (3 August 1901): 770;

Dunne, "Mr. Dooley on the Magazines," *American Magazine*, 68 (October 1909): 539–542 ;

Dunne, "Mr. Dooley on the Power of the Press," *American Magazine*, 62 (October 1906): 607;

A. E. Fletcher, "The Ideal Newspaper," *Independent*, 52 (29 March 1900): 771–774;

Charles E. Grinnell, "Modern Murder Trials and Newspapers," *Atlantic Monthly*, 88 (November 1901): 662–673;

Richard A. Haste, "The Evolution of the Fourth Estate," *Arena*, 41 (March 1909): 352;

Nevada Davis Hitchcock, *What a Reporter Must Be: Helps to Succeed in Newspaper Work* (Cleveland: Ralph Hitchcock, 1900);

Hamilton Holt, *Commercialism and Journalism* (Boston: Houghton Mifflin, 1909);

Will Irwin, "The New York *Sun*," *American Magazine*, 67 (January 1909): 301;

Arthur Reed Kimball, "The Invasion of Journalism," *Atlantic Monthly*, 86 (July 1900): 119–124;

Charles Edward Kloeber Jr., "The Press Association," *Bookman*, 20 (November 1904): 196–212;

Thomas W. Lawson, "The Muck-Raker," *Everybody's*, 15 (August 1906): 204–208;

A. Maurice Low, "Tabloid Journalism: Its Causes and Effects," *Forum*, 31 (March 1901): 56–61;

Rollo Ogden, "Some Aspects of Journalism," *Atlantic Monthly*, 98 (July 1906): 13–20;

Julian Ralph, *The Making of a Journalist* (New York: Harper, 1903);

James Edward Rogers, *The American Newspaper* (Chicago: University of Chicago Press, 1909);

Ellery Sedgwick, "The Man with the Muck Rake," *American Magazine*, 62 (May 1906): 111–112;

Upton Sinclair, "The Muck Rake Man," *Independent*, 65 (3 September 1908): 517–519;

Charles Emory Smith, "The Press: Its Liberty and License," *Independent*, 55 (11 July 1903): 1371–1375;

Lincoln Steffens, "The New School of Journalism," *Bookman*, 18 (October 1903): 173–177;

Steffens, *The Shame of the Cities* (New York: P. Smith, 1904);

John Swinton, "Newspaper Notoriety," *Independent*, 53 (24 January 1901): 211–213;

Charles Whibley, "The American Yellow Press: A British View," *Bookman*, 25 (May 1907): 239–243;

Henry Loomis Wilson, "American Periodicals," *Dial*, 28 (1 May 1900): 349–352.

CHAPTER TEN

MEDICINE AND HEALTH

by A. J. WRIGHT

CONTENTS

Sidebars and tables are listed in italics.

1900

- U.S. Army Yellow Fever Commission, headed by Dr. Walter Reed, identifies the *Aedes aegypti* mosquito as the carrier of the disease.

- Dr. John Edward Summers Jr. publishes the first account in America of a choledochoenterostomy, or surgical creation of an artificial anus.

- Dr. Eugene Lindsay Opie discovers the relationship between degeneration of the islets of Langerhans (the special cells of the pancreas that secrete insulin) and diabetes.

- Dr. Ludvig Hektoen creates one of the earliest experimental disease models, for cirrhosis of the liver.

- Biochemist Otto Knut Olof Folin begins work on the chemistry of urine; his methods will be adapted in a decade to study blood and tissues.

- Dr. Walter B. Cannon persuades Harvard Medical School to begin use of the case method of teaching.

- The first caesarean section in Wyoming is performed by Dr. C. Dana Carter.

- Sen. Jacob H. Gallinger introduces a bill to regulate medical research on humans in the District of Columbia; the bill is defeated in Congress.

- Dr. Ernest Amory Codman begins his work on diseases and injuries of the shoulder.

- Dr. George Blumer demonstrates that trichinosis, a disease caused by a worm infecting undercooked pig meat, is more widespread in the United States than previously believed.

6 Mar. The body of a Chinese laborer is discovered in the Globe Hotel's basement in the Chinese district of San Francisco. Local officials find that he died of bubonic plague. The outbreak of the disease will last for four years and kill more than one hundred people.

1901

- The U.S. Army Nurse Corps is given permanent status by an act of Congress.

- Physician-dentist Dr. William Herbert Rollins announces that his research on guinea pigs shows that X rays could cause death.

- Dr. Jay Frank Schamberg describes a progressive noninflammatory skin disease that later will be named after him.

- The Rockefeller Institute for Medical Research is organized.

- Dr. Arthur Robertson Cushny begins his important work on mechanisms of kidney secretion.

- The American Medical Association's House of Delegates approves a radical reorganization plan.

Mar. The U.S. Commission to Investigate Plague, headed by Dr. Simon Flexner, confirms presence of the disease in San Francisco.

3 Mar. Congress passes the Sundry Civil Appropriation Act, which includes a $35,000 budget for the Hygienic Laboratory, a part of the U.S. Marine Hospital Service. The laboratory is the forerunner of the National Institutes of Health.

1902

- At the annual medical association meeting in Georgia, Dr. H. F. Harris reports on his diagnosis of pellagra in a poor farmer. Within six years pellagra, a serious disease resulting in most cases from particular dietary deficiencies, will be identified as a major medical problem in many parts of the South.

- Sen. Jacob H. Gallinger reintroduces his bill to regulate medical research on humans in the District of Columbia; the bill fails to pass a second time.

- Congress passes the Biologics Control Act to regulate vaccines and antitoxins.

- The first perineal prostatectomy is performed at Johns Hopkins Hospital in Baltimore by Dr. Hugh Hampton Young.

- The McCormack Institute for Infectious Diseases is founded in Chicago.

- Dr. John Miller Turpin Finney performs the first standard surgical procedure for duodenal ulcer relief.

- Dr. Isaac Arthur Abt begins almost forty years of editorship of the *Yearbook of Pediatrics.*

May At the Pan-American Sanitary Congress, Dr. Charles Wardell Stiles of the U.S. Public Health Service identifies the hookworm parasite devastating the South.

1903

- Dr. Arnold Schwyzer performs the first surgical removal of a foreign body from the lung.

- Dr. Frederick George Novy establishes the first unit to fight rabies in the United States in Ann Arbor, Michigan.

- The first survey on tuberculosis, a disease common in congested urban neighborhoods, is conducted by Homer Folks and others in New York City.

- Based on research by chemist Edwin Freemont Ladd, the North Dakota legislature passes a Pure Food and Drug Law.

1904

- Dr. Hugh Hampton Young performs the first radical operation on a cancerous prostate gland.

- Dr. John LaRue Robinson founds the first general hospital in Nevada — People's Hospital.

- Dr. Joseph Erlanger does important studies on kidney output in persons afflicted with albuminuria.

- The Rockefeller Institute for Medical Research opens.

Mar. The National Association for the Study and Prevention of Tuberculosis is founded by Homer Folks, Dr. Lawrence Flick, and others; it becomes the model for subsequent private health associations.

1905

- The American Medical Association, the Association of American Medical Colleges, and the Southern Medical College Association form the Council on Medical Education to begin reforms in the nation's medical schools.

- Dr. Louis Blanchard Wilson develops a method for quick and accurate laboratory analysis of surgical tissue specimens.

- The Long Island Society of Anesthetists, forerunner of the American Society of Anesthesiologists, is founded in New York.

- Dr. Ludvig Hektoen demonstrates that measles can be transmitted from one human to another.

- Dr. Arthur Douglass Hirschfelder is appointed director of the physiological laboratory at Johns Hopkins Medical School; two other clinical research facilities are also established — the first such divisions in the United States.

- The last yellow fever epidemic in the United States hits New Orleans.

1 Apr. Standard diphtheria antitoxin is introduced.

1906

- A pathologist at the University of Chicago, Dr. Howard Taylor Ricketts, begins work that will identify infected ticks as the cause of Rocky Mountain spotted fever.

- The Meat Inspection Act is passed by Congress after widespread public concern over unsanitary conditions in the meatpacking industry.

- Drs. Milton Joseph Rosenau and John F. Anderson publish the first of their landmark studies on anaphylaxis, or hypersensitivity.

- Yale University economist J. Pease Norton recommends a federal department of health to address such problems as the high costs of illness and premature death.

- The first biochemical research facility in the United States is established at Johns Hopkins Medical School with Dr. Carl Voegtlin as director.

- The American Society of Biological Chemists is established by physiological chemist Russell Henry Chittenden and others.

- Medical societies in Oklahoma and Indian Territory are merged into a single society.

- In Baltimore the Babies' Milk Fund Association is organized by Dr. James Hall Mason Knox Jr. to give milk to infants in low-income families.

- Dr. Emanuel Libman begins work on use of blood cultures to diagnose subacute bacterial endocarditis, a disease attacking heart valves and previously identifiable only at autopsy.

- A state medical publication for Nebraska is proposed by Dr. Francis A. Long.

30 June • President Roosevelt signs the Pure Food and Drug Act.

1907

- Bernarr Macfadden is arrested for mail distribution of obscene materials — a magazine issue explaining to men how venereal disease is contracted.

- Dr. E. I. McKesson promotes using a blood pressure test in conjunction with surgical anesthesia.

- The Rockefeller Institute for Medical Research opens a facility in New Jersey to breed animals for laboratory research. Arsonists will destroy it two years later.

- Drs. C. C. Guthrie and F. H. Pike conduct successful experiments using plasma and serum to replace blood during surgery.

- Using frog embryos, Dr. Ross G. Harrison of Johns Hopkins Medical School performs the first successful tissue culture.

- The Council on Medical Education asks the Carnegie Foundation to study medical education in the United States. Carnegie hires Abraham Flexner, a layman, to conduct the landmark study, which is completed two years later and published in 1910.

- Dr. S. Josephine Baker begins a hygiene program for children at the New York City Department of Health.

- Serum treatment for epidemic spinal meningitis is developed by Dr. Simon Flexner and others.

- Dr. Robert Tait McKenzie of the University of Pennsylvania becomes the first professor of physical therapy in an American university.

- Dr. Ross G. Harrison performs pioneering work in the exploration of the relationship between nerve cells and nerve fibers.

- Dr. James Ewing and others found the American Association for Cancer Research.

- Dr. Charles Solomon Caverly and others found the Vermont Tuberculosis Sanitarium.

1908

- Drs. E. Zeh Hawkes and Edward Wharton Sprague perform the first blood transfusion in New Jersey.

- Dr. David Marine begins publication of his research on the role of iodine in thyroid function, which is important for normal body growth.

- Dr. David Linn Edsall gives the first description of "heat cramps," a severe reaction in workers exposed to intense heat.

- The American Society for Clinical Investigation, the first organization devoted to patient research, is founded.

- The first National Conference on Pellagra is held in Columbia, South Carolina.

- Clifford Whittingham Beers and Drs. Adolph Meyer and William H. Welch found the Connecticut Society for Mental Hygiene, the world's first mental health organization.

1909

- Dr. Yandell Henderson of Yale University publishes his landmark paper on the relationship of carbon dioxide, shock, and heart rate.

- The American Medical Association creates the Council on the Defense of Medical Research; Harvard physiologist Walter B. Cannon is appointed director.

- The Committee of One Hundred on National Health issues a report recommending a federal department of health.

- Philanthropist Nathan Straus establishes the first tuberculosis prevention facility for children, in Lakewood, New Jersey.

- At the University of Wisconsin Dr William Snow Miller develops a seminar on medical history that becomes the model for other universities.

- Dr. Frederick Parker Gay publishes the first English translation of Jules Bordet's classic *Studies in Immunity*.

- Dr. James Grassick founds the North Dakota Tuberculosis Association.

- Dr. John Howland performs landmark studies showing the poisoning of the liver by the anesthetic gas chloroform. These studies resulted in the gradual decrease in the use of this agent.

- The College of Medical Evangelists is founded by Seventh-Day Adventists in Loma Linda, California.

- Walter B. Cannon, chair of the American Medical Association's Council on the Defense of Medical Research, circulates a proposed set of guidelines to all U.S. laboratories and medical schools using animals in research.

- The National Association for the Study of Pellagra is founded, and South Carolina physician James Babcock is elected president.

Oct. The Rockefeller Foundation creates the Rockefeller Sanitary Commission to alert southerners to the hookworm problem.

OVERVIEW

Medicine and Health at the Beginning of the Century. In the first decade of the twentieth century medical practice in the United States remained much as it had been throughout the nineteenth century — a curious mixture of the effective and what is now known to be the ridiculous. Luckily, the ratio of the former to the latter had been changing toward more effective patient care. General public health was also improving. Urban clean-water supplies and the disposal of human, animal, and industrial wastes had increasingly come under the control of public health agencies in the preceding century. Sanitation engineering had developed as a specialty to aid these efforts. Vaccinations for some diseases were becoming widespread.

Nineteenth-Century Medicine. When chemist Charles Eliot became president of Harvard University in 1869, he proposed radical changes in the medical school. Eliot wanted to raise admission standards to weed out the kind of undesirable students that often filled classes and to extend the training period to include more laboratory experience in the curriculum. Faculty members such as famed surgeon Henry Bigelow objected, wondering why a system that worked so well needed changing. Eliot told him, "I can answer Dr. Bigelow's question very easily; there is a new President." Within two years Eliot's changes were being implemented. Improvements in medical practice throughout the nineteenth century were driven by this kind of individual determination. Institutional structures now taken for granted — sophisticated offices and hospital-based clinical care, extensive education and certification of doctors and other health care personnel, and medical practice supported by extensive basic research — simply did not exist. Yet signs of development were under way.

Advances in Patient Care. In the one hundred years after 1800 health care had improved enormously in the United States. The discovery in the 1840s that inhalation of ether and chloroform gases could ease the pain of surgery provided relief to thousands of patients and meant surgeons could perform longer and more complicated operations. The antiseptic methods of Englishman Joseph Lister, used to prevent surgical wound infection, reached America in the 1870s. Sterile conditions in oper-

ating room equipment and personnel prevented the spread of infections that doctors and nurses had previously carried from patient to patient on filthy hands, instruments, and clothing.

Improved Equipment and Research. Medical equipment had become more sophisticated by 1900. Following the development of the stethoscope early in the century, other diagnostic tools like the laryngoscope, improved microscopes, the medical thermometer, and the X ray had appeared. The hypodermic syringe and anesthesia machines greatly increased the accuracy of drug administration. Imitating developments in Europe, some American physicians were turning to laboratory research to improve medical care. Specialists such as physiologists explored the newly discovered cellular causes of some diseases and bacterial and viral causes of others. Chemists developed more sophisticated drugs, and pharmacologists worked to understand their actions in the human body.

Evolving Professionalism. In addition to hospitals, medical schools, and private practice, physicians could find employment with life insurance firms, railroads and other industries, the military, and newly developing government health agencies. Women and blacks were trained as physicians in significant numbers. Nursing had developed as a profession, and many doctors were beginning to specialize in areas other than general medicine or surgery. In order to improve their status in society, doctors formed the American Medical Association in 1848. Other organizations and many medical journals appeared after the Civil War. A few full-time faculty appeared at medical schools. After essentially abandoning the practice earlier in the century, states began to strengthen medical licensing laws to weed out unqualified physicians. A few efforts, such as Eliot's at Harvard, were made to improve medical education.

Continuing Problems. Despite these vast areas of progress by 1900, many problems remained. Most medical schools operated primarily for the benefit of their physician-owners and lacked libraries, laboratories, or even much clinical experience for students. Hospitals were few in number, located only in the largest urban areas, and served primarily the poor. Most surgeries were still done in the home. The nation was flooded with ineffective and sometimes dangerous patent medicines sold directly to the public by charlatans. Diseases such as yellow fever, typhoid fever, tuberculosis, pellagra, and hookworm ravaged entire communities. Government support of health care initiatives was weak at best.

Reform and Dedication. In the first decade of this century many of these problems were attacked with renewed energy. The ineffectual American Medical Association reorganized itself and aggressively pursued medical education reform and the exposure of health quackery. Largely successful campaigns were begun against yellow fever, pellagra, and hookworm. A public education crusade on the causes and prevention of tuberculosis became a model for subsequent efforts with other diseases. While medical practice in the first years of the twentieth century was certainly primitive by modern standards, in the midst of human failings and misunderstandings many men and women dedicated their lives to improving the nation's health care.

TOPICS IN THE NEWS

THE AMERICAN MEDICAL ASSOCIATION REORGANIZES

Organizational Weakness. In 1846 and 1847 physicians held meetings in New York City and Philadelphia to discuss the creation of a national medical association. The new organization, the American Medical Association (AMA), held its first meeting on 2 May 1848 in Baltimore. Yet despite more than fifty years of existence the AMA remained a weak organization in 1900, reflecting the medical profession's lack of institutional control over itself. The AMA's strength lay in the East and Midwest, but its complicated method of granting membership based on attendance at annual meetings severely limited the organization's base and its prospects for expansion. Only a small percentage of eligible physicians bothered to attend meetings and thus join the AMA. The group did publish a prominent weekly journal, but not even all AMA members subscribed. Internal problems kept the AMA from effectively addressing important professional issues raised by poor medical education, competing health philosophies, and increasing specialization among physicians.

Reorganization Begins. At the June 1900 annual meeting in Atlantic City the AMA initiated its self-reform movement. A committee that became the Committee on Organization was formed and included a prominent member from each state. At this same meeting the group also created the Special Committee on Reorganization made up of just three men: Joseph N. McCormack of Kentucky, P. Maxwell Foshay of Ohio, and George H. Simmons of Illinois. These physicians formulated and presented the renewal plan that was approved by the attending delegates at the AMA's 1901 meeting.

Membership Growth. The changes recommended by the special committee not only revised the AMA's constitution to allow broader membership but also urged a reorganization plan for state and local medical societies that would strengthen their ties to each other and to the AMA. In support of these efforts McCormack wrote many articles and crisscrossed the country on a speaking tour that lasted most of a decade. As a result, an organi-

zation with only eighty-four hundred members in 1900 grew to more than seventy thousand in 1910.

PURE FOOD AND DRUG ACT OF 1906

As the twentieth century began, Americans were increasingly concerned with their food and drug supplies. The safety of patent medicines, or nostrums, sold directly to the public and containing "secret" ingredients such as alcohol was questioned in popular magazines and medical journals. In February 1906 Upton Sinclair finally found a publisher for *The Jungle*, his novel of lower-class life in Chicago that contained pages exposing the horrors of the meatpacking industry. President Theodore Roosevelt chose two men, U.S. labor commissioner Charles P. Neill and New York reformer James B. Reynolds, to investigate Sinclair's charges. These impartial observers confirmed everything: the sale of rancid meat, workers suffering from active tuberculosis, the appearance of foreign matter in the processed meat. Under pressure from business interests, Roosevelt refused to release the report, but Sinclair wrote a letter to *The New York Times*, and public reaction was immediate.

Two bills to regulate food and drugs had passed the House in previous years, but the Senate had taken no action on them. Several states regulated food and drugs in some ways, but state laws had no effect on interstate trade. Sinclair's book and the Neill-Reynolds corroboration provided the spark needed to get a national food and drug bill passed by Congress. Roosevelt signed the bill into law on 30 June 1906. The task of getting a law had been accomplished, but the even more difficult task of enforcement lay ahead.

Source: Arlene Finger Kantor, "Upton Sinclair and the Pure Food and Drug Act of 1906," *American Journal of Public Health*, 66 (1976): 1202–1205.

New Power. Energized by its reorganization, the AMA moved quickly on several fronts after 1900. In 1904 the Council on Medical Education was created to begin reform efforts. The Committee on Medical Legislation acted forcefully in support of the 1906 Pure Food and Drug Act and subsequent attempts to pass similar legislation in each state. The Council on Pharmacy and Chemistry was formed in 1905 to test the claims of proprietary medicines prescribed by doctors and patent medicines sold directly to the public. By the end of the decade the AMA had become one of the most powerful professional associations in the United States, with the ability to grant admission to the profession, set standards for medical practice, sanction its members, and shape a wide range of legislation affecting the public health.

Sources:

James G. Burrow, *AMA: Voice of American Medicine* (Baltimore: Johns Hopkins University Press, 1963);

Morris Fishbein, *A History of the American Medical Association, 1847–1947* (Philadelphia: Saunders, 1947).

DIVERSITY IN THE MEDICAL PROFESSION: AFRICAN AMERICAN PHYSICIANS

Pioneering Physicians. The first black physician in the United States is generally considered to be James Derham, who was born a slave in Philadelphia in 1762. Derham learned medicine under his owner, prominent physician Dr. James Kearsley Jr. At the close of the Revolutionary War Derham was sold to Dr. Robert Dove of New Orleans and continued his apprenticeship. Derham apparently developed a lucrative practice in that city. In 1837 James Smith became the first black American physician to obtain a medical degree, which he received from the University of Glasgow in Scotland. Ten years later David Smith became the first black U.S. medical school graduate when he finished at Rush Medical College in Chicago. Until the end of the Civil War most blacks in the United States were slaves. However, several hundred thousand, mostly in the northeastern states, were free and could obtain an education. Thus, several black males obtained medical degrees in the United States before the war. In 1864 Rebecca Lee became the first black female to receive such a degree when she graduated from the New England Female Medical College (now Boston University School of Medicine).

Medical Education. After 1865 several for-profit and religious medical schools were opened to serve the former slaves from the South. The earliest of these institutions was Howard University in Washington, D.C., which first accepted students in 1869. By 1900 a dozen other such colleges were operating in Louisiana, Tennessee, North Carolina, Kentucky, Maryland, and Pennsylvania. Most black physicians in practice in the United States before 1920 graduated from one of these schools. Only four survived until 1910, and only Howard and Meharry Medical College in Nashville (opened in 1876) remain in

Dr. Mathilde Evans, who opened the first hospital for blacks in Columbia, South Carolina

existence today. In 1895 black physicians founded a professional organization, the National Medical Association. Both the group and its journal continue to flourish.

Individual Achievements. Despite being confined primarily to segregated institutions and medical schools, black physicians during the first decade of this century have an impressive record of achievement. The black hospital movement that lasted for several decades gained its initial momentum during this period. These facilities were needed to offer care to black patients who would not be admitted to white hospitals. Dr. Aaron M. Moore raised funds among whites to open Lincoln Hospital in Durham, North Carolina, in 1901. Six years later Dr. Eugene T. Hinson and Algernon Brashear founded Mercy Hospital, the second oldest black facility in Philadelphia. From 1899 to 1901 Dr. Alonzo C. McClennan edited one of the earliest black medical publications in Charleston, South Carolina, the monthly *Hospital Herald*. In 1908 Drs. John A. Kenney and Charles V. Roman founded the *Journal of the National Medical Association*. Chicago surgeon Dr. Daniel H. Williams developed in 1904 a suturing (stitching) method for ruptured spleens. Many physicians also began long careers of service to their local black communities, including Dr. George C. Hall in Chicago (1900–1930) and Dr. Benjamin J. Covington in Houston (1903–1961).

After 1909. In the 1890s a young black doctor in Kentucky observed that "As a physician I am well received by my white professional brother. We ride in the same buggy, consult together, and read each other's books. I have a few white patients, but most of them are colored." This cordial segregation continued throughout most of this century for black physicians. Blacks were not admitted to many medical schools until well after World War II, and their numbers remain small at many institutions. Just before and after 1900 blacks had to create their own medical institutions — schools, local and national associations, hospitals, and journals. The need for this separate system has only in recent years begun to dissipate.

Sources:

M. O. Bousfield, "An Account of Physicians of Color in the United States," *Bulletin of the History of Medicine*, 17 (January 1945): 61–84;

Todd L. Savitt, "Entering a White Profession: Black Physicians in the New South, 1880–1920," *Bulletin of the History of Medicine*, 61 (Winter 1987): 507–540.

Two students from the Woman's Medical College of Pennsylvania pursuing their study of anatomy in their boardinghouse room

DIVERSITY IN THE MEDICAL PROFESSION: WOMEN PHYSICIANS

Determined Women. In 1900 more than seven thousand female physicians were practicing in the United States. More than one hundred of these doctors were African Americans. These women comprised about 5 percent of all doctors, and that percentage remained steady until increases began in the 1960s. Elizabeth Blackwell, the first woman in the United States to receive a medical degree, began her studies at Geneva Medical College in upstate New York in October 1847. Her admission had been a fluke. The college faculty opposed the idea and put it to a vote of the students on the assumption they would agree. The students considered the matter a joke, and all voted for her. Two years later Blackwell graduated at the top of her class. Blackwell's younger sister Emily was not so lucky: she had to apply to eleven schools before Rush Medical College in Chicago admitted her in 1852. In the meantime, the Woman's Medical College of Pennsylvania had opened in Philadelphia in October 1850 and graduated its first class of eight women in December 1851, even though male medical students in the city attempted to disrupt the ceremony. Before the end of the century nineteen medical colleges for women were founded.

Social Context. In the mid nineteenth century most male physicians were opposed to the medical education of females. Women were considered temperamentally and physically incapable of success in any male-dominated sphere of life; domestic matters in the home were the proper realms of female activity. Yet women were beginning to assert themselves in various ways in public life. In the early 1840s Dorothy Dix began her crusade for the humane treatment of the insane. In 1848 the first women's rights conference was held in Seneca Falls, New York; two years later a National Woman's Rights Convention took place in Worcester, Massachusetts. The Confederacy granted official status to female nurses in 1862. Victoria Woodhull ran for president of the United States in 1870. Three years later the Woman's Christian Temperance Union was founded to fight the evils of alcohol consumption, and the first national meeting of women ministers convened. Women working to give females the vote founded the Equal Rights Party in 1884. Despite male resistance, many women were moving out of the home and into civic life during the century. By 1900 objections were still voiced, but women were prominent in many areas once exclusively male.

Buying an Education. By the early 1890s women could attend some of the same medical schools as men; photographs of medical students from the period often include several females. At nineteen such coeducational schools women made up 10 percent or more of the student body in the 1893–1894 school year. This situation developed because women were willing to pay the price — literally. As early as 1848 Harriot Hunt had applied to Harvard University Medical School. Hunt was denied admission, even though she had more than a decade of medical practice following her medical training as an apprentice to an older male physician. Hunt's reapplication in 1850 was also refused. Elite medical schools did not admit women until much later in the century. By 1890 the new Johns Hopkins University in Baltimore needed funds badly. School officials announced they would accept women to the medical school if wealthy women donated half a million dollars to the university's endowment. The money was raised, and women entered the medical school. Other prestigious institutions began to admit women, and by 1900 only two of the medical colleges for women were still open.

THE MOTHER OF ANESTHESIA

On 16 October 1846 dentist William Morton administered ether anesthesia to surgical patient Edward Gilbert Abbot in the operating theater of the Massachusetts General Hospital in Boston. In attendance at this first successful public demonstration of anesthesia were surgeon John Collins Warren, other physicians, and several medical students. While the idea of using anesthetics to relieve pain during surgery quickly spread around the world, for the next five decades the administration of anesthetics was mostly handled either by medical students or physicians poorly trained in the procedure. Most physicians simply were not interested in serving as anesthetists. By the end of the nineteenth century, however, a few physicians were suggesting in the medical literature that anesthetics should be administered by medical personnel specifically trained to do so.

In America Alice Magaw, a nurse, was one of the first individuals to administer anesthetics full-time. Magaw went to work at St. Mary's Hospital (later the famed Mayo Clinic) in Rochester, Minnesota, in 1893. By 1906 Magaw had given more than fourteen thousand anesthetics for two brothers, Drs. William W. and Charles H. Mayo, and other hospital surgeons. Not a single death among all those cases could be attributed to anesthesia. Between 1892 and 1906 Magaw authored five articles documenting her work. She was a pioneer for women in an era when physicians were almost 95 percent male. Dr. Charles Mayo called her the "Mother of Anesthesia."

Source: Marianne Bankert, *Watchful Care: A History of America's Nurse Anesthetists* (New York: Continuum, 1989), pp. 28–38.

Individual Achievements. As the twentieth century began, most female physicians operated private practices with mostly women and children patients or worked on hospital staffs. Yet many women contributed to the clinical or research aspects of medicine during the decade. Dr. Dorothy R. Mendenhall, a Johns Hopkins graduate, demonstrated in 1901 that Hodgkin's disease (a form of cancer) was not a type of tuberculosis as was believed at the time. The first African American female doctor in Columbia, South Carolina, Dr. Mathilde A. Evans, opened the first hospital for blacks in the city and several clinics. In 1907 Dr. Martha Wollstein and Dr. Simon Flexner finished the first experimental analysis of polio in the United States. Several women, such as Dr. Alice Hamilton and Dr. Lydia M. DeWitt, were beginning distinguished careers on medical school faculties.

After 1909. Although the proportion of women doctors did not change in the next few decades, thousands of women physicians continued to enter medical schools, establish careers, and contribute to medical advancement. Acceptance of women by male doctors, however, was slow. Some women entered new specialties, such as anesthesiology, that would not be as attractive to male physicians until after World War II. In the early twentieth century women physicians published widely in the medical press, taught at prestigious medical schools, and performed important basic research in laboratories. At the end of the century women physicians are prominent in all aspects of medical practice and research, and some 50 percent of U.S. medical students are women.

Source:
Ruth J. Abram, ed., *Send Us a Lady Physician: Women Doctors in America, 1835–1920* (New York: Norton, 1985).

HOOKWORM IN THE SOUTH

The Southern Disease. Hookworm is an aggressive intestinal parasite that causes physical and mental underdevelopment and other symptoms such as dry hair, ulcered shins and feet, protruding shoulder blades and stomachs, and a general lack of energy. The hookworm contaminates soil through unsanitary privies or outhouses; primarily, victims become infected by walking through larvae-rich soil in bare feet. The disease was common in the rural American South after the Civil War. This "germ of laziness" or "ground itch" created a southern stereotype: poor, barefoot, lazy, deformed, and mentally deficient.

First Known American Cases. The parasite was first identified in Europe in the mid 1800s. A few American physicians suspected its presence in the United States as well, but the first confirmed case was not reported until Philadelphia physician Abe Blickhalm published an account in 1893. Other cases from Richmond and New Orleans soon appeared, and in 1901 Dr. Allen J. Smith diagnosed a sailor in Galveston, Texas. Smith believed this hookworm was a different species from the European parasite.

Recognition. One man, Dr. Charles Wardell Stiles, was primarily responsible for identifying the American hookworm and alerting the nation to its devastating effects. Born in North Carolina, Stiles became a zoologist with the Department of Agriculture's Bureau of Animal Industry. Even before Blickhalm's report in 1893, Stiles noticed that the symptoms of the hookworm disease he saw in animals were similar to those of many poor whites in the rural South. Stiles and Smith traded information via correspondence, and Stiles made a trip through the Gulf-Atlantic states to confirm his theory. In May 1902 Stiles, then the chief of the Division of Zoology of the U.S. Public Health Service, reported to the Pan-American Sanitary Congress that he had found the "germ

Dr. Charles Wardell Stiles (center, by tent post) at a North Carolina field clinic for hookworm

of laziness" and that hookworm disease was common in the American South.

Reactions. Stiles's announcement produced swift reactions. Some physicians and public officials praised the zoologist for pinpointing the cause of a serious health problem. Many southerners, however, were indignant and disgusted by the idea that their fellow citizens were infested with worms. Newspapers in the North and South turned the situation into an excuse for mocking editorials and cartoons.

Eradication. Stiles was convinced that an education campaign could solve the hookworm problem, but it took several years of effort on his part before he could convince any authorities to implement such a program. In 1908 Stiles was appointed by President Theodore Roosevelt to the Country Life Commission, a group formed to suggest ways to improve farm life. Through this appointment Stiles met Walter Hines Page, a crusading southern journalist. Page had connections at the General Education Board, a philanthropy funded by industrialist John D. Rockefeller. In October 1909 Rockefeller donated $1 million to fund the Rockefeller Sanitary Commission. This commission cooperated by invitation with state boards of health in creating education and eradication programs that helped hundreds of thousands of hookworm disease sufferers in the southern states. The commission operated until the end of 1914, by which time hookworm control was well advanced in those states. More than twenty years after

Stiles's first suspicions about the "germ of laziness," his untiring efforts finally produced results.

Sources:

Mary Boccaccio, "Ground Itch and Dew Poison: The Rockefeller Sanitary Commission 1909–14," *Journal of the History of Medicine and Allied Science,* 27 (January 1972): 30–53;

James H. Cassedy, "The "Germ of Laziness" in the South, 1900–1915: Charles Wardell Stiles and the Progressive Paradox," *Bulletin of the History of Medicine,* 45 (1971): 159–169;

John Ettling, *The Germ of Laziness: Rockefeller Philanthropy and Public Health in the New South* (Cambridge, Mass.: Harvard University Press, 1981).

HUMAN SUBJECTS IN MEDICAL RESEARCH

A Growing Debate. Humans had served as experimental subjects in medical research long before 1900. In 1799 and 1800 more than forty volunteers participated in extensive trials on the effects of inhaling nitrous oxide gas. In 1803 Englishman Thomas Percival wrote a classic text on medical ethics in which he discussed experimentation on patients. Contributing to the increase in this type of research was the acceptance in the United States, beginning in the 1880s, of the germ theory of disease causation, which required more research with both animals and humans. Basic research of all kinds was also beginning in American medical schools. In the closing decades of the nineteenth century many examples of research on hospital patients in the United States and Europe were publicized, and opposition to such work developed among both medi-

Anatomy lab at the Philadelphia College of Osteopathy in 1908

cal professionals and laymen. Many antivivisectionists who were critical of experimentation on animals soon joined this debate.

Human Vivisection. The word *vivisection* means to cut open a living human or animal. Around the turn of the century the term *human vivisection* came to mean any experimental procedure that did not offer direct benefit to a patient's health. Organizations such as the American Society for the Prevention of Cruelty to Animals and the American Humane Society, founded just after the Civil War, expanded their concerns from animals to children and adult human experimentation. In 1901 novelist Elizabeth Ward told Massachusetts legislators that "Dog or man, cat or baby, it does not matter so much — the fashion is to slice. Human vivisection follows animal vivisection naturally and easily, secretly or openly." The antivivisectionists were convinced that vulnerable animals and humans — such as children, hospital patients, and the institutionalized insane — were equally subject to exploitation by uncaring physician-researchers.

Professional Concerns. Throughout the first decade of the twentieth century Dr. Albert T. Leffingwell worked tirelessly at reform efforts and favored legal limits on animal research. In 1900 and 1902 Sen. Jacob H. Gallinger introduced a bill to regulate medical experiments on people in the District of Columbia, but the bill was defeated both times. Dr. William W.

Keen, then president of the American Medical Association, and other physicians objected to such restrictions. They believed human vivisection was rare and could be regulated by the medical profession itself. Attempts to pass legislation similar to Gallinger's on the state level were made during the decade in Maryland and Illinois. The opening in 1904 of the Rockefeller Institute for Medical Research heightened public concern about medical research on animals. Three years later the institute opened a New Jersey facility for breeding laboratory animals; arsonists destroyed it in 1909. The continuing campaign against animal and human experimentation led the American Medical Association to form the Council on the Defense of Medical Research in 1908. Harvard physiologist Walter B. Cannon was appointed head of the council and spent almost twenty years defending medical research involving animal and human subjects.

The Debate Continues. The use of humans and animals as subjects for medical experimentation has often provoked controversy in the twentieth century. Nazi medical "experiments" in the 1940s, the infamous Tuskegee syphilis study that lasted from the 1930s until the 1960s, and other notorious examples have resulted in strong institutional controls in the United States over humans as subjects in medical and scientific research. While there is continuing pressure by the animal rights movement to ban animal experimenta-

Cartoon titled "Only a Step," reflecting a deep distrust some felt toward medical scientists at the beginning of the twentieth century.

tion and there remain concerns that scientists are too quick to involve human subjects, doctors and medical researchers have successfully defended the practice of vivisection and the autonomy of physicians in the laboratory and the operating room that was first meaningfully challenged at the beginning of the century.

Source:
Susan E. Lederer, *Subjected to Science: Human Experimentation in America before the Second World War* (Baltimore: Johns Hopkins University Press, 1995).

MEDICAL EDUCATION REFORM

Nineteenth-Century Education. Medical schools proliferated in America during the nineteenth century; between 1810 and 1875 at least seventy-three such institutions opened for business. Most of these schools were proprietary, meaning they were owned by one or more physicians who operated them in order to make a profit. Both entrance and graduation requirements were low. Classes consisted solely of lectures by professors. Clinical, laboratory, and library resources were either inadequate or, most often, nonexistent. Those who could not afford even these rudimentary medical schools could apprentice themselves to established physicians and then call themselves doctors.

Early Reform Efforts. Throughout the nineteenth century many doctors condemned the quality of medical education in the United States. At an 1846 meeting in New York City, where more than one hundred physicians had gathered to form a national association, a committee was appointed to study and recommend changes in medical education. Although sweeping reforms were suggested, just two schools adopted them and then only until their enrollment began to decline. By 1900 more than 150 medical schools were operating in the country, but the vast majority put student fees ahead of educational standards. Yet change was slowly coming. In 1870 the president of Harvard University, Charles W. Eliot,

The Pure Food and Drug Act of 1906 included among its goals the regulation of the flood of "patent" medicines that were marketed with outrageous claims and dangerous ingredients. Charged with enforcing the new law was a man who had been instrumental in its passage, Harvey W. Wiley, chief of the Department of Agriculture's Bureau of Chemistry. Wiley chose a headache remedy called Cuforhedake Brane-Fude, which Robert N. Harper had been making since 1888, as his first test case.

Brane-Fude was a combination of several compounds and a large amount of alcohol, a standard ingredient for patent medicines of the day. After the 1906 law passed, Harper tried to comply with its provisions and changed his medicine's label. Wiley believed the change was insufficient, since the label continued to claim the medicine was "harmless" and had "no . . . poisonous ingredients of any kind." Wiley also felt the name falsely told the buyer that the medicine was a "cure for headache" and "brain food" — claims that Harper could not prove. The trial jury agreed, and President Roosevelt urged a jail sentence for Harper to make an example of him. The presiding judge disagreed and fined Harper $700. Since Harper had made an estimated $2 million from the sale of his product, the fine damaged him very little. Ironically, Harper enjoyed a measure of public sympathy thanks to Roosevelt's heavy-handed interference.

Source: James Harvey Young, *The Medical Messiahs: A Social History of Health Quackery in Twentieth-Century America* (Princeton: Princeton University Press, 1967), pp. 3–12.

strengthened requirements in the medical department. Other universities soon followed. In 1893 Daniel Coit Gilman, the visionary president of Johns Hopkins University, opened a medical school that for the first time required a bachelor's degree for admission. The following year the National Association of Medical Colleges was formed.

True Reform Begins. In 1900 delegates to the American Medical Association's annual meeting voted to require that new members have a medical degree with four years of training, and a permanent committee on education was appointed four years later. By 1905 the AMA, the Association of American Medical Colleges, and the Southern Medical College Association were ready to join forces. Together these groups created the Council on Medical Education. The following year the council reported that 20 percent of existing medical schools were completely inadequate and named five states with especially poor schools. In 1907 the council requested a detailed inquiry by the Carnegie Foundation, which then hired Abraham Flexner, a Johns Hopkins graduate and the author of a study of American colleges. Flexner spent almost two years evaluating U.S. medical schools and published his harsh conclusions in 1910.

The Flexner Report. Flexner found appalling conditions in many of the nation's medical schools, and his report described the details. Laboratories advertised in school catalogues did not exist. Dissecting rooms were filled with the stench of corpses that were not disinfected. Supposed libraries had no books; many listed faculty members did no teaching. Flexner's report cast a harsh light on the difference between medical school claims and the reality of their facilities.

Flexner's Legacy. After his report appeared, Flexner persuaded the Rockefeller Foundation to fund schools that had met his standards; $50 million was eventually invested by the foundation. Other philanthropies imitated the practice, and as some schools were strengthened, inferior schools began to close. Between 1906 and 1920 at least seventy-six institutions shut their doors; by 1930 only sixty-six medical schools remained in the United States. The efforts of Flexner and his predecessors caused proprietary schools to disappear from medical education — and thus in the long run helped improve patient care. An unintended result of these reform efforts was the closure of some schools that admitted significant numbers of blacks and women.

Sources:

Abraham Flexner, *Medical Education in the United States and Canada: A Report to the Carnegie Foundation for the Advancement of Teaching* (New York: Carnegie Foundation, 1910);

R. P. Hudson, "Abraham Flexner in Perspective: American Medical Education, 1865–1910," *Bulletin of the History of Medicine*, 46, no. 6 (1972): 545–561;

Steven Charles Wheatleys, *The Politics of Philanthropy: Abraham Flexner and Medical Education* (Madison: University of Wisconsin Press, 1988).

PELLAGRA IN THE SOUTH

American Outbreak. Pellagra is a disease caused by a diet deficiency of nicotinamide, a B vitamin, and results in dermatitis (inflammation of the skin), diarrhea, dementia, and often death. Today the disease is rare even in undeveloped countries. First identified in Spain in 1735 by Don Pedro Casal, physician to King Philip V, pellagra was for many years thought to be nonexistent in America. Yet from about 1900 until the 1940s an epidemic swept through the country that accounted for more than three million cases and one hundred thousand deaths.

Growing Awareness. In 1902 Dr. H. F. Harris reported a single case of pellagra in a Georgia farmer at the state's annual medical association meeting. Alabama physician George H. Searcy published in 1907 a description of eighty-eight cases at the state's insane asylum. The

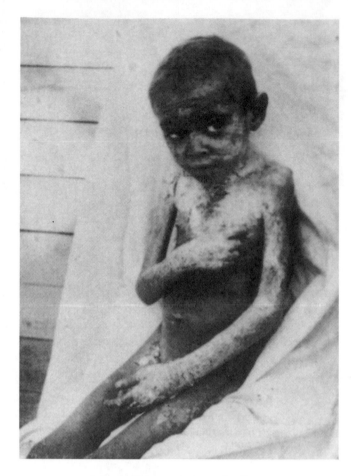

A boy with a severe case of pellagra

following year Dr. James Babcock identified cases among the insane in South Carolina. Later in 1908 the first National Conference on Pellagra was held in Columbia, South Carolina, with more than seventy physicians in attendance. The next year more than four hundred doctors attended, and Babcock was elected first president of the National Association for the Study of Pellagra. By 1924 pellagra was being reported in thirty-six states and the District of Columbia, with 90 percent of the cases in nine southern states. Four southern states known to have high disease rates did not bother to report that year.

Dietary Causes. Throughout the four-decade epidemic, pellagra was most prevalent in the southeastern United States. In that region large numbers of people subsisted on a "Three M" diet of fatty meat, cornmeal, and molasses. The disease appeared at the same time that a change in corn milling technology made the meal less prone to decay but removed vital nutrients. Southern insane asylums provided their inmates with a diet heavy in cornmeal — thus many cases developed in those institutions. Rural people who ground their own corn were much less likely to develop the dietary deficiency.

Southern Reaction. By the second decade of this century the spreading epidemic of pellagra began to panic the populace. Dr. Joseph Goldberger of the federal Hygienic Laboratory initiated a series of studies across the South and began to suspect a dietary cause for the disease. Politicians such as Georgia's senator Tom Watson and many physicians protested that a monotonous diet among southern poor could not be the cause. South Carolina Congressman James F. Byrnes branded publicity about a famine or plague in his state an "utter absurdity." Despite Goldberger's untiring efforts, pellagra persisted in the United States for more than a decade after his death in 1929.

A Familiar Pattern. The pellagra epidemic has interesting parallels with AIDS in the 1980s and 1990s. Isolated reports appeared over several years until an epidemic was finally recognized. Politics and cultural factors were also important in reactions to the disease and impediments to a cure. White political, business, and cultural leaders in the South were embarrassed that poverty among whites in their region gained national attention. State government officials were at first reluctant to act, but the continuing publicity and the eventual realization that the pellagra problem was real forced them to take action.

Sources:
Alfred Jay Bollet, "Politics and Pellagra: The Epidemic of Pellagra in the U.S. in the Early Twentieth Century," *Yale Journal of Biology and Medicine,* 65 (May–June 1992): 211–221;

E. W. Etheridge, *The Butterfly Caste: A Social History of Pellagra in the South* (Westport, Conn.: Greenwood Press, 1972);

D. A. Roe, *A Plague of Corn: The Social History of Pellagra* (Ithaca: Cornell University Press, 1973).

PLAGUE IN SAN FRANCISCO

Two Outbreaks. Bubonic plague is a disease caused by the *Yersinia pestis* bacillus and is most often transmitted from rats to humans by infected fleas; symptoms include virulent fever and swollen lymph nodes. Known since biblical times, bubonic plague has swept through various regions of the world during the last fifteen hundred years. At least four widespread outbreaks — pandemics — have occurred as well as many local outbreaks, or epidemics. In the first decade of this century, the disease struck San Francisco twice. The second of these two epidemics suggested how effective a coordinated public health campaign could be, but the first showed how political meddling could lead to deadly results.

Death in Chinatown. On 6 March 1900 the body of a Chinese worker was discovered in the Globe Hotel basement. The dead man was one of more than eighteen thousand Chinese and almost two thousand Japanese who lived in a fourteen-block area of San Francisco. At this time the city was California's major city, and the area known as Chinatown was among its important tourist attractions. When the assistant city physician, Dr. Frank P. Wilson, performed an autopsy, he discovered symptoms that suggested plague. He notified the city health officer, Dr. A. P. O'Brien, and bacteriologist Dr. Wilfred H. Kellogg. These men confirmed the discovery and con-

---

TYPHOID MARY

Mary Mallon was a thirty-one-year-old immigrant from northern Ireland who spent much of the first decade of the twentieth century cooking for wealthy families in New York. Mary had eight jobs in seven years, and typhoid fever — a disease that results in the inflammation of the small intestine, fever, coughing, abdominal pain, and diarrhea — followed in her path. Although never sick herself, she spread the disease in the households where she worked and beyond. At least fifty-three cases and three deaths can be attributed directly to Mary Mallon, but she may have been responsible for fourteen hundred cases in Ithaca, New York, in 1903. Epidemics of the disease at the time could cause thousands of cases and many deaths.

Mary Mallon was the first carrier of typhoid to be identified. Public health officials persuaded her to enter Riverside Hospital in the Bronx section of New York City in 1907, and she became infamous in the newspapers of the day. She was released in 1910 and promised to stop working as a cook but quickly disappeared. Around 1914 she was located again and quarantined for life in the hospital. Officials built a cottage for her on the grounds, and she died there on 11 November 1938.

Source: Richard Gordon, "Typhoid Mary: Death on a Plate," *Great Medical Disasters* (New York: Stein & Day, 1983), pp. 77–80.

---

tacted Dr. Joseph J. Kinyoun, the chief quarantine officer of the U.S. Marine Hospital Service in San Francisco. After O'Brien recommended a quarantine of twelve blocks in Chinatown, the head of the city's board of health, Dr. John M. Williamson, ordered police to surround the area, and a search for more cases began. When the Marine Hospital Service's surgeon general, Walter Wyman, was informed of the situation, he recommended further aggressive measures, including inoculation of all Chinese with a plague vaccine. In 1900 only twenty-two cases of the plague were documented, though many other victims were never found because of deliberate efforts to hide them.

Political Reaction. On 19 February 1904 the last case of plague in the city's first outbreak of the decade was confirmed. During the four years of the endemic a pitched battle over control of the disease took place between medical officials on one side and most public officials, businessmen, and news outlets on the other. San Francisco's mayor James Phelan and his successor E. E. Schmitz, governor Henry Gage, and American and Chinese business leaders all denied the existence of the disease. Gage declared that plague "did not nor ever did exist in California." One city newspaper mocked

Kinyoun's efforts in verse. Because of public pressure, the initial quarantine did not last three days. One newspaper, the *Examiner*, did accept the plague reports. Because that paper was part of a chain owned by William Randolph Hearst, the news quickly spread around the country.

Federal Response. To break this impasse, Surgeon General Wyman sent a prominent surgeon, Joseph H. White, to assess the situation. White recommended the appointment of a blue-ribbon panel, and Drs. Simon Flexner, L. F. Barker, and Frederick G. Novy were chosen as members of this "Commission for the Investigation of the Existence or Non-Existence of Plague in San Francisco." This committee confirmed the existence of plague in the city in March 1901. Their report was largely ignored; Governor Gage even appointed his own committee — loaded with prominent newsmen and business leaders — which failed to find any evidence of plague. Antiplague efforts were left to San Francisco health officials and the Marine Hospital Service.

The Tide Turns. Despite one hundred confirmed cases by the end of 1902, Governor Gage denied that the plague was a threat in his final legislative message as governor in January 1903. Fortunately, he was soon succeeded by George C. Pardee, a physician who declared himself ready to cooperate with local and federal health authorities. Early in 1903 an emergency conference convened in Washington, D.C., to discuss the plague problem. Calls were made for a complete quarantine of California. Such talk finally convinced the business community that further action was needed, and an extensive eradication effort was finally mounted. Decaying buildings in Chinatown were either demolished or repaired to eliminate the rat infestation. By early 1904 the plague had subsided.

Second Outbreak. In April 1906 an earthquake devastated San Francisco and provided excellent conditions for another plague epidemic. A little more than a year later two city physicians diagnosed several cases of the disease. This time the mistakes of the earlier outbreak were not repeated. Under the auspices of the Citizens' Health Committee local, state, and federal health and political officials together with business leaders immediately recognized the presence of the disease and began aggressive measures to fight it. An extraordinary voluntary education and eradication campaign aided the official efforts. By the time a final report was issued in March 1909, this second effort was a credit to the city and a model for action in the face of public health emergencies. Two more outbreaks in 1919 and 1924 received similar responses.

Sources:

Loren George Lipson, "Plague in San Francisco in 1900," *Annals of Internal Medicine,* 77 (August 1972): 303–310;

Guenter B. Risse, " 'A Long Pull, a Strong Pull, and All Together': San Francisco and Bubonic Plague, 1907–1908," *Bulletin of the History of Medicine,* 66 (Summer 1992): 260–286.

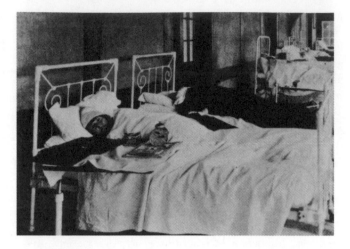

Tuberculosis sanatorium in the Adirondack Mountains of New York State

THE TUBERCULOSIS MOVEMENT

Background. Tuberculosis is a bacterial infection contracted by humans either through inhaling the bacteria or by eating meat from infected animals. Common symptoms are coughing, fatigue, and weight loss. Aging, poor nutrition, or other stresses on the body can free the bacteria, and clinical, or "open," tuberculosis results. Most frequently attacked are the lungs. As the victim coughs, the tubercles (nodules that the body forms around the bacteria as a defense mechanism) burst and particles are exhaled or released in sputum. Open cases can carry and spread the disease for months or years. Tuberculosis was long thought to be hereditary, but around 1880 the German Robert Koch discovered its bacterial cause. Today the disease can be controlled with drugs.

Tuberculosis in the 1900s. An ancient disease, tuberculosis was long known as "consumption," since victims appeared to be consumed by their sickness. In 1900 the standard treatment was fresh air, proper nutrition, and rest — a therapy only the wealthy could afford. Since the disease spread slowly, tuberculosis did not create as much fear as yellow fever, cholera, or typhoid. Yet tuberculosis was the cause for more than 10 percent of U.S. disease mortality in 1908. The public health effort against tuberculosis had begun in New York City in 1889 when that city's board of health issued a report outlining its causes and methods of treatment. Acknowledging that the disease was primarily spread from person to person, this report recommended disinfecting the living quarters of victims. The health board also printed a circular for public distribution; this tactic was imitated in the same year in Rhode Island and Maine and subsequently in many other states and cities. A more comprehensive attack on the disease began in 1892, when Hermann M. Biggs became chief of the pathology lab at New York City's board of health. Biggs recommended a series of strict measures designed to identify, treat, and control the disease.

Jacob Riis, the journalist who suggested Christmas Seals be used to fund the campaign against tuberculosis

Sanatorium Movement. In the 1880s a wealthy tuberculosis specialist in New York, Edward L. Trudeau, popularized in the United States the sanatorium treatment method begun in Germany. These facilities were built in rural areas and featured fresh air, regular and varied diets, rest, and moderate exercise. Trudeau's sanatorium in the Adirondack Mountains accepted some poor and middle-class patients. Although it was not the first such facility in the United States, Trudeau's sanatorium attracted national attention and initiated a method of treatment that seemed to work, especially with early cases.

Organizing to Educate. The measures developed and promoted by Biggs and Trudeau demonstrated that tuberculosis could be treated and even prevented. But these measures required an aggressive campaign of public education, and another physician took up that challenge. Unlike many other doctors, Lawrence F. Flick had quickly accepted that tuberculosis was contagious. By 1892 he had persuaded a few friends, other physicians, and public health officials to help him form the Pennsylvania Society for the Prevention of Tuberculosis. This organization was the first voluntary tuberculosis organization and also the first devoted to a single disease. Until 1900 Flick's group operated alone, but in that year another organization appeared in Toledo, Ohio, and a statewide body formed in Ohio the following year. Local and state organizations began to form elsewhere. Lawyer Clark Bell attempted to organize a national group in 1900, but it dissolved over the issue of whether non-physicians could participate. Finally, led by Flick, approximately one hundred doctors and laymen met in Philadelphia in March 1904 and formed the National Association for the Study and Prevention of Tuberculosis.

Public Awareness. The campaign to inform the populace about tuberculosis emphasized that the disease could be prevented and its spread contained while stressing its human costs as well as its great economic harm to the nation. Families were devastated if the father died or became too sick to work; orphanages were crowded with children whose parents had both died or could no longer care for them. Many forms of publicity were used to spread these messages, including newspaper articles, public lectures and meetings, exhibitions, and band concerts. One of the most effective methods of raising public awareness of the disease was through the sale of Christmas Seals.

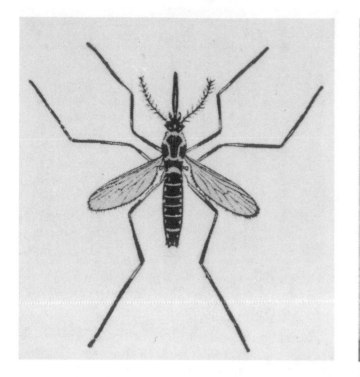

The female *Aedes aegypti* mosquito, transmitter of yellow fever, and Dr. Jesse William Lazear, a member of Walter Reed's team who died in the test of the mosquito hypothesis

Christmas Seals in the United States. The idea of a stamp sold to raise money for a charitable cause originated in Denmark. American journalist Jacob Riis suggested in 1907 that such stamps be adopted here. The president of the Delaware Anti-Tuberculosis Society liked the idea, and that group quickly raised $3,000 selling the stamps. The practice was soon incorporated into the campaigns of other local, state, and finally national tuberculosis organizations. Christmas Seals not only helped groups raise money to continue and expand their activities but also provided educational and publicity opportunities.

Results of the Tuberculosis Campaign. Tuberculosis continued to ravage many Americans until after World War II, but efforts to educate the public on a national scale that began just after 1900 improved or saved many thousands of lives. Like other public health campaigns of the Progressive Era, the crusade against tuberculosis marshaled the forces of experts with the authority to demand improvements in the often abysmal living conditions of the nation's teeming cities. In addition, strategies the tuberculosis movement implemented during that decade became the model for many other health movements in America during this century. The National Association for the Study and Prevention of Tuberculosis survives today as the American Lung Association.

Source:
Michael E. Teller, *The Tuberculosis Movement: A Public Health Campaign in the Progressive Era* (Westport, Conn.: Greenwood Press, 1988).

YELLOW FEVER

Yellow Fever in the United States. Before the twentieth century the acute viral disease yellow fever was one of the most feared diseases in the United States, especially in the Southeast. Victims suffered high body temperatures, headaches, liver damage and resulting jaundice, and internal bleeding that caused discharge from the nose and mouth, bloody stool, and black vomit. Death could follow in one day or two weeks, and reported mortality rates often reached 50 percent of known cases. Between the mid 1600s and 1905 yellow fever epidemics ravaged many cities along the coastal and lower Mississippi Valley regions of North America. During those years more than 230 major epidemics were recorded. The country's earliest outbreaks appeared in Spanish Florida and the Northeast; as populations grew in the lower Atlantic and Gulf Coast states, yellow fever followed. Transmitted by the bite of the female *Aedes aegypti* mosquito, the disease typically developed in the summer and early fall and spread rapidly. By November or December yellow fever would disappear. By the mid 1820s quarantine measures and improvements in sewerage and water drainage effectively eliminated yellow fever from the cooler northern states. Warmer cities from South Carolina to Louisiana continued to endure epidemics until 1905, when the final outbreak in the United States hit New Orleans.

Response to Yellow Fever. Yellow fever caused more panic on a national scale than any other disease except Asiatic cholera, which threatened many areas untouched by the fever. Outbreaks of the fever were swift and unpredictable: a community free from yellow fever for a few years might be struck several years in a row. In efforts to respond to the epidemics, many communities formed temporary boards of health with powers to quarantine the sick. These boards were among the few cooperative health efforts undertaken by American governments in the nineteenth century and became a model for the permanent public health institutions that were established in the 1900s and 1910s.

Attempts to Find a Cause. Before the Civil War yellow fever was widely believed to develop spontaneously from filthy conditions. During the 1850s some southern physicians began to suspect that the disease arose from a transportable agent. By the 1870s most American doctors accepted the idea that a microscopic agent was involved. In that decade the search began for a microbe in the blood of yellow fever victims. In the 1880s researchers in Brazil and Mexico announced that they had found the agent, but investigation proved these reports to be false.

The Cause Is Found. In 1881 Dr. Carlos Finlay published his idea that a mosquito was the carrier agent for yellow fever. But like Dr. Josiah Nott, who had suggested a similar theory in 1848, Finlay was not able to develop irrefutable proof. In June 1900 Finlay began advising the U.S. Army Yellow Fever Commission, which had been formed in response to noncombat deaths among military personnel during the Spanish-American War and the subsequent U.S. Army occupation of Cuba. Dr. Walter Reed, chairman of the four-man team, was at first skeptical of Finlay's mosquito theory. After two members of his group were bitten by mosquitoes and contracted yellow fever, however, Reed was convinced. He established a quarantined camp and quickly confirmed Finlay's idea.

Controlling the Fever. By early 1901 Dr. William Gorgas, chief U.S. Army sanitation officer, began to rid Cuba of the mosquito and thus of yellow fever. While more than one hundred thousand people are estimated to have died in the United States alone through the New Orleans outbreak in 1905, by the end of the first decade of the twentieth century yellow fever had been eradicated from most parts of the world. In their continuing attempts to control mosquito and other insect pest populations, officials would employ increasingly toxic chemicals, including DDT, which would create environmental hazards that were exposed by Rachel Carson in the 1960s.

Sources:

John Duffy, "Yellow Fever in the Continental United States During the Nineteenth Century," *Bulletin of the New York Academy of Medicine,* 44 (1968): 687–701;

K. David Patterson, "Yellow Fever Epidemics and Mortality in the United States, 1693–1905," *Social Sciences and Medicine,* 34 (1992): 855–866;

Margaret Warnert, "Hunting the Yellow Fever Germ: The Principles and Practice of Etiological Proof in Late Nineteenth-Century America," *Bulletin of the History of Medicine,* 59 (Fall 1985): 361–382.

HEADLINE MAKERS

JOHN J. ABEL

1857-1938

PHARMACOLOGIST

Far-Ranging Education. Descended from German immigrants, John Jacob Abel was born near Cleveland on 19 May 1857, the son of farmer George M. Abel and his wife Mary. At age nineteen he entered the University of Michigan, where he received his Ph.D. in 1883. Abel spent the following year conducting graduate research in biology at Johns Hopkins University in Baltimore. In 1884, at the age of twenty-seven, Abel embarked on a study trip to Europe that lasted seven years. During his time abroad Abel trained under the biggest names in pharmacology of that era, including the Germans Bernhard Naunyn, Felix Hoppe-Seyler, and Oswald Schmiedeberg. While on the Continent he received an M.D. from the University of Strasbourg in 1888.

Return to the United States. When he returned to his native country, Abel was offered a faculty position at the University of Michigan. Before Abel could establish a department of pharmacology as he was hired to do, Dr. William Osler asked him to accept the chair of pharmacology at Johns Hopkins. Abel arrived in Baltimore in the fall of 1893. In the late nineteenth century pharmacology was just beginning to develop as a specialty. The rise of chemistry in the first half of the century had demonstrated that organic compounds could be synthesized in the laboratory. Experimentation by European researchers had led to a developing understanding of the body's metabolizing such foreign substances as drugs. As the century came to a close, European investigation focused on how specific drugs worked in the body even as pharmacological studies were in their infancy in America.

Father of American Pharmacology. Abel spent the next thirty-nine years at Johns Hopkins and during those decades helped create the discipline of pharmacology in the United States. Unlike many medical school faculty of his day, whose lectures were based on textbook material, Abel taught his students from original research published in journals and by using laboratory experiences. In December 1900 Abel lost an eye in a lab explosion, but that did not stop his drive to establish pharmacology as an independent discipline in medical schools. He was instrumental in 1905 in the founding of the American Society of Biological Chemists and its *Journal of Biological Chemistry.* Four years later he was also involved in establishing the American Society for Pharmacology and Experimental Therapeutics and what later became the *Journal of Pharmacology and Experimental Therapeutics.* Both journals continue publication today. During the decade Abel also continued his important research on hormones, which he had begun in the late 1890s. He had identified the first adrenal hormone, epinephrine, in 1897. Abel published a simple method for preparing the hormone and its derivatives in 1902. Also called adrenaline, this hormone is important in various nervous system functions.

Abel's Legacy. Abel's many contributions to medicine after the decade included a method of demonstrating the presence of amino acids in the blood and the suggestion for an artificial kidney. His discipline of pharmacology has risen to become one of the most important fields in American medicine. Abel died on 26 May 1938.

Sources:

A. McGehee Harvey, "Pharmacology's Giant: John Jacob Abel," *Johns Hopkins Medical Journal,* 135 (1974): 245–258;

John Parascandola, *The Development of American Pharmacology: John J. Abel and the Shaping of a Discipline* (Baltimore: Johns Hopkins University Press, 1992).

WILLIAM CRAWFORD GORGAS

1845-1920

ARMY SURGEON AND SANITATION EXPERT

Army Doctor. William Crawford Gorgas was born on 3 October 1845 in Mobile, Alabama. His father, Josiah, served as chief of ordnance for the Confederate army during the Civil War and later as a college president. His mother, Amelia, was a member of a prominent Mobile family. Gorgas received a bachelor's degree from the University of the South in 1875 and four years later finished his M.D. at Bellevue Hospital Medical College in New York. After a year as an intern at Bellevue, Gorgas entered the military as a first lieutenant at a salary of $1,500 per year. He remained in the U.S. Army Medical Corps until the year before his death.

Yellow Fever. During the next two decades Gorgas rotated through remote military posts in the United States, including forts in Texas, North Dakota, and Florida. Gorgas had his first contact with yellow fever in 1883 while stationed at Fort Brown, Texas, located on the Rio Grande River. Some twenty-three hundred sufferers from the disease were quarantined at the fort, and Gorgas was under orders not to have contact with any of them. Nevertheless, Gorgas undertook an autopsy on a fever victim and was promptly placed under house arrest by the fort commander. The arrest order was soon overturned, and Gorgas was assigned to care for the yellow fever patients. One victim who came under his care was Marie Doughty, the sister-in-law of a fort officer. Marie became so ill that Gorgas had a grave prepared for her. Although she lived, Gorgas contracted the disease, and the pair recovered together. The two were married in the fall of 1884. The immunity to yellow fever that Gorgas developed at Fort Brown would prove useful later in his career.

Assignment to Cuba. Just after the close of the Spanish-American War in 1898, Gorgas was sent to Cuba as chief sanitary officer. American troops in Havana were suffering not only from yellow fever but also typhoid and dysentery. Gorgas, who thought yellow fever developed from filthy conditions, cleaned up the city. Typhoid and dysentery rates declined; but as twenty-five thousand people from Spain entered Cuba, yellow fever rates began to rise.

Cuba and Panama. As the situation in Havana worsened, U.S. Army surgeon general George M. Sternberg appointed Dr. Walter Reed and three others to a commission to study the yellow fever epidemic. Once they demonstrated the relationship between *Aedes aegypti* mosquito and yellow fever, Gorgas cleaned Havana of larvae breeding grounds. His success in Cuba led to his assignment to the Panama Canal Project, where his work began in March 1904. During the next decade Gorgas implemented the sanitation lessons he learned in Cuba. His efforts reduced the death rate from all diseases among canal workers in Panama below that of any American state or city.

Later Life. By the time the Panama Canal was completed in 1914, Gorgas was sixty-eight years old. Despite his age, President Woodrow Wilson appointed him surgeon-general of the U.S. Army, and Gorgas supervised a medical corps that during World War I grew from 435 to more than 32,000 physicians. Three days after the war ended Gorgas retired and began a private effort with the International Health Board to rid the world of yellow fever. Gorgas died on 3 July 1920 and is buried in Arlington National Cemetery.

Source:
John M. Gibson, *Physician to the World: The Life of General William C. Gorgas* (Tuscaloosa: University of Alabama Press, 1989).

BERNARR ADOLPHUS MACFADDEN

1868-1955

ADVOCATE OF "PHYSICAL CULTURE" AND PUBLISHER

Early Life. Born 16 August 1868 in Mill Spring, Missouri, Bernarr Macfadden was the son of farmer William McFadden and his wife, Mary. Bernard (who later changed the spelling of his first and last names) received only a grade-school education. By the time he was eleven, his parents had divorced and then died — his father from alcoholism and his mother from tuberculosis. After a brief period spent with farmer relatives, Macfadden left home and worked a series of odd jobs that included farm laborer, delivery boy, printer's assistant, bookkeeper, and bill collector. Years later he would observe about this period that he "had no chance to indulge in those exercises so necessary to the health of boys of that age.... At the age of sixteen I was a complete wreck. I had the hacking cough of a consumptive; my muscular system had so wasted that I resembled a skeleton; my digestive organs were in a deplorable condition." He consulted various doctors but found little help and quickly developed a hatred of the medical profession and its reliance on prescription drugs.

Transformation. Macfadden bought a pair of dumbbells and began a daily schedule of exercise that he maintained for the rest of his life. By the age of eighteen he was calling himself a "professor of kinesitherapy" and teaching gymnastics at schools in Missouri and Illinois. His regimen soon expanded to include long walks, semi-vegetarian eating habits, fresh air, cold baths, and minimal clothing. Macfadden called his methods "physical culture" and put them on display, along with his exercise equipment, at the Chicago World's Fair in 1893.

Building an Empire. In the late 1890s Macfadden left the Midwest and moved to New York City. In 1898 he began publication of *Physical Culture,* a monthly magazine that by 1900 sold thousands of copies at fifteen cents an issue. Macfadden used this success to establish the Physical Culture Publishing Company, which became in subsequent decades the nucleus of a publishing empire. Other magazines and books on such topics as marriage, muscle development, and male diseases poured from the presses. In Chicago; Battle Creek, Michigan; and other cities Macfadden established "healthatoriums," luxurious health spas where he trained new teachers of his methods. He also opened twenty restaurants that served vegetarian meals.

Macfadden and the Law. His magazine *Physical Culture* relentlessly promoted Macfadden's health and fitness ideas. Many issues featured scantily clad men and women photographed as they exercised. In the early twentieth century such pictures were considered scandalous and quickly caught the attention of postal authorities, who began to monitor the magazine. A 1907 issue containing an article on venereal disease transmission provided officials with the evidence they needed. Macfadden was arrested, tried for obscenity, convicted, and sentenced to two years in prison and a $2,000 fine. Subscribers and other supporters deluged President William H. Taft with letters, and Taft granted Macfadden clemency.

Macfadden after 1909. His brush with the legal system did not stop Macfadden. In 1911 he began publication of a massive five-volume *Encyclopedia of Physical Culture,* one of more than a hundred books he wrote during his lifetime. He traveled to England in 1913 to spread his ideas. A relentless self-promoter, he included in his trip the gimmick of a search for England's "perfect woman." By the 1920s Macfadden's ideas and publications were so popular that medical critics took note. In 1925 Dr. Morris Fishbein, editor of the official journal of the American Medical Association, included Macfadden's physical culture in his book *The Medical Follies.* Eleven years later one of the American Medical Association's foremost critics of medical quackery, Dr. Arthur J. Cramp, attacked Macfadden in *Nostrums and Quackery and Pseudo-Medicine.* Nothing slowed Macfadden down; by the 1930s his magazines — which then included such tabloid titles as *True Story, True Romances,* and *Photoplay* — and his sensationalistic newspapers reached some forty million readers. One of his protégés, Charles Atlas, was the hero of every male who perceived himself as a weakling. Another student, Jack La Lanne, built a physical fitness empire of his own.

The Bubble Bursts. By the eve of World War II several circumstances combined to weaken Macfadden's power. He had spent enormous sums on unsuccessful political campaigns. He was a vocal admirer of Benito Mussolini, the fascist dictator of Italy and ally of Hitler. In 1941 stockholders in his company accused him of personal use of corporate funds and forced Macfadden to relinquish control. By 1950 he had sold all his publications, but he continued his self-promotion. He earned a pilot's license at age sixty-three and celebrated several birthdays in his eighties with parachute jumps from airplanes. Macfadden died of a blood clot in the brain on 12 October 1955 in Jersey City, New Jersey.

Macfadden's Legacy. In 1989 Macfadden Holdings, the corporate child of his original company, bought the tabloid newspapers *National Enquirer* and *The Star.* Macfadden himself might have approved, for he had built his empire promoting both the healthy and the sensational.

Source:

David Armstrong and Elizabeth Metzger Armstrong, *The Great American Medicine Show* (Englewood Cliffs, N.J.: Prentice Hall, 1991), pp. 203–214.

WALTER REED

1851-1902

ARMY SURGEON AND PATHOLOGIST

Early Career. Born in Belroi, Virginia, on 13 September 1851, Walter Reed was the son of Methodist minister Lemuel S. Reed and his wife, Pharaba. Reed received his first medical degree from the University of Virginia in 1869 and a second degree from Bellevue Hospital Medical College in New York City the following year. After a two-year internship in Brooklyn, he served in two public health posts in New York City until 1875. In that year he joined the U.S. Army Medical Corps and rotated through various U.S. posts — including Fort Apache, Arizona — until being named to the just-opened Army Medical School's faculty in 1893. Prior to this assignment, Reed spent two years studying pathology under the famed Dr. William Welch at Johns Hopkins University in Baltimore. Much of this work involved laboratory research on hog cholera and typhoid fever. His studies of microscopic bacteriology under Welch were useful in his academic post in Washington, D.C.

Academic Career. Reed spent much of the final decade of his life doing original laboratory and clinical work related to bacterial diseases. He published journal articles as well as books on typhoid and yellow fevers. Especially important were his studies of typhoid, a disease that killed American soldiers in Cuba during the 1898 Spanish-American War at a rate fifty times greater than combat injuries. As chairman of a typhoid commission, Reed demonstrated that filthy camp conditions were ideal for the flies that carried the infected fecal matter.

Yellow Fever Conquered. Reed's greatest triumph also took place in Cuba. During the American army's occupation of the island beginning in 1898, yellow fever appeared among the troops with increasing frequency. As early as 1848 Alabama physician Josiah Nott theorized that mosquitoes were the carriers — or vectors — of yellow fever. A physician in Cuba, Carlos Finlay, attempted to revive the mosquito theory fifty years later. No one listened, despite the fact that Ronald Ross had just proven in 1897 that some species of mosquito carried malaria. Army surgeon general Sternberg named Reed to lead a commission to Cuba to study yellow fever. Elaborate quarters were constructed to provide controlled conditions for the commission members to experiment upon themselves and keep detailed records. This effort produced convincing proof that the *Aedes aegypti* mosquito was responsible for yellow fever transmission, though it cost some members of Reed's team their lives.

Glory Cut Short. Following Reed's discovery the U.S. Army under Chief Sanitary Officer William Gorgas quickly implemented a vigorous mosquito extermination program in Cuba, and for almost a year not a single case of the fever appeared on the island. After five exhausting trips to Cuba, Reed returned to the United States expecting to be named surgeon general. Instead, he died of appendicitis on 23 November 1902 at the age of fifty-one.

Source:
William Bennett Bean, *Walter Reed: A Biography* (Charlottesville: University Press of Virginia, 1982).

PEOPLE IN THE NEWS

In 1900 Dr. **John Auer** begins a decade of work with Dr. **Samuel J. Meltzer** on the use of artificial ventilation and anesthesia during surgical operations in which the chest is open.

In 1908 Dr. **Sara Josephine Baker** becomes head of the Division of Child Hygiene within the New York City Health Department. She remains in the post for fifteen years.

Orthopedic surgeon **Edward Hickling Bradford** convinces state authorities to open the Massachusetts Hospital School for Crippled Children in Canton in 1904.

Dr. **Will Henry Chase** helps establish Alaska's first medical society in 1906 and the future state's first hospital two years later.

In August 1909 Dr. **Alfred Einstein Cohn,** a specialist in cardiovascular diseases, brings the first electrocardiograph to the Western Hemisphere at Mount Sinai Hospital in New York City.

In 1906 Dr. **Arthur Joseph Cramp** organizes the American Medical Association's Bureau of Investigation to research fraud and quackery in medicine.

Ohio surgeon **George Washington Crile** develops blood-transfusion methods and pioneers their use in surgery beginning in 1905.

Famed Johns Hopkins University surgeon **William Stewart Halsted** publishes one of the most famous of his many works, an article titled "The Training of a Surgeon," in *American Medicine* in 1904.

Physician and patent medicine king **Samuel Brubaker Hartman** convinces fifty members of the U.S. Congress to endorse his popular product Peruna in 1903 and 1904.

Alabama surgeon **Luther Leonidas Hill,** who had performed the first successful heart suture operation in the United States, publishes a report of seventeen cases in *Medical Record* in 1900.

As dean of faculty at Amherst College in Massachusetts for twelve years beginning in 1898, Dr. **Edward Hitchcock** implements his idea of the importance of physical education for college students. His programs at Amherst are imitated at many other colleges around the country.

A pathfinder among American pharmacologists, Dr. **Reid Hunt** begins a decade as chief of the Division of Pharmacology at the U.S. Public Health Service in 1904.

Pharmacist and drug manufacturer **John Uri Lloyd** emerges as prominent supporter of the movement against impure drugs that leads to passage of the federal Pure Food and Drug Act in 1906.

Dr. **Franklin Henry Martin,** a specialist in surgical gynecology, starts the journal *Surgery, Gynecology and Obstetrics* in 1905. He will serve as its editor for three decades.

In the early years of the decade Louisiana surgeon Dr. **Rudolph Matas** continues his innovative use of cocaine as an anesthetic that he began in 1886.

In 1902 military surgeon **Walter Drew McCaw** begins an eleven-year tenure as chief of the museum and library division of the U.S. Army Surgeon General's office in Washington, D.C., which evolves into the world's greatest medical library, the National Library of Medicine.

Dr. **Anita Newcomb McGee** plays a major role in the organization of a permanent U.S. Army Nurse Corps in 1901.

Physician and pharmacologist Dr. **Samuel James Meltzer** demonstrates in 1905 that magnesium salts can produce a state of unconsciousness and muscle relaxation in humans and thus could be used in the treatment of tetanus.

In 1900 bacteriologist **Charles Edward North** begins his thirty-year campaign to persuade dairymen to improve the sanitation of milk. Infant mortality caused by raw milk will eventually be eliminated.

One of America's greatest physicians, **William Osler,** begins publication of his seven-volume opus, *Modern Medicine, Its Theory and Practice,* in 1907.

In 1901 Dr. **Francis Randolph Packard** publishes his monumental *History of Medicine in the United States,* which sparks the development of medical historiography in America.

Surgeon **Roswell Park,** who had played a major role in bringing antiseptic surgical techniques from Europe to the United States, treats President William McKinley after he is shot at the Pan-American Exposition in Buffalo, New York, in 1901.

Dr. **William Allen Pusey** develops techniques for using X rays in the treatment of Hodgkin's disease and various skin diseases.

In 1903 Dr. **Niles Oliver Ramstad** cofounds the second oldest group medical practice in America in Bismark, North Dakota, and starts a hospital in that city two years later.

In 1908 military physician **Frederick Fuller Russell** begins to demonstrate the value of typhoid fever vaccination, first in the army and then in the civilian population.

Biologist **William Thompson Sedgwick** continues his studies of sewage disposal that make him a leader in sanitation engineering in the United States.

In 1901 Dr. **Torald Hermann Sollmann** begins a career of more than four decades at what is now Case Western Reserve University in Ohio and publishes the first extensive American pharmacology text. Sollmann and Dr. John Jacob Abel are probably the only two men who can truly be called "fathers" of pharmacology in the United States.

Beginning in 1906 Dr. **Howard Taylor** engages in five years of research on the group of diseases bearing his name and on the tick-borne Rocky Mountain spotted fever.

Beginning in 1904 Dr. **Bertha Van Hoosen** experiments with the use of "twilight sleep," a method of childbirth anesthesia using morphine and scopolamine. Three years later she begins a series of public lectures for women on hygiene.

Pathologist **William Henry Welch** continues his spectacular career at Johns Hopkins University. Among his innovations is the first pathology course in the United States based in a laboratory.

DEATHS

Dr. **Edmund Andrews**, 80, surgeon who developed many instruments and pioneered the use of nitrous oxide/oxygen mixture and blood transfusion, 22 January 1904.

Wilbur Olin Atwater, 63, agricultural chemist who researched heat-energy potential and caloric values of foods, 22 September 1907.

Dr. **Frederick Jones Bancroft**, 69, pioneer Colorado physician who organized a medical department at the University of Denver, 16 January 1903.

Dr. **Roberts Bartholow**, 73, physician who made an early study of electrical stimulation of the brain, 10 May 1904.

Dr. **John Janvier Black**, 72, prominent physician in the treatment of tuberculosis in Delaware, 27 September 1909.

Dr. **Nathan Bozeman**, 80, physician responsible for many advances in gynecology and obstetrics, 16 December 1905.

Dr. **John Hill Brinton**, 75, surgeon who was active in the Civil War, first curator of the Army Medical Museum, and organizer of a major medical history of the war, 18 March 1907.

Dr. **Charlotte Amanda Blake Brown**, 58, strong supporter of public health measures and women in medicine, 19 April 1904.

Dr. **Samuel Clagett Busey**, 73, pioneer in pediatric medicine in the District of Columbia, 12 February 1901.

Dr. **James Carroll**, 53, physician who worked under Dr. Walter Reed on the Army Yellow Fever Commission and allowed himself to be bitten by a carrier-mosquito to help prove insect transmission, 16 September 1907.

Dr. **Julian John Chisolm**, 73, pioneer in ophthalmology and local and general anesthesia during and after the Civil War, 2 November 1903.

Dr. **Victor H. Coffman**, 69, Civil War surgeon and the first American to remove a tumor from a thyroid gland, 4 August 1908.

Dr. **Richard Beverly Cole**, 72, early medical pioneer in San Francisco, 15 January 1901.

Dr. **Jacob Mendez DaCosta**, 67, physician who influenced the emergence of internal medicine as a specialty and wrote the classic text *Medical Diagnosis* (1864), 11 September 1900.

Dr. **Israel Thorndike Dana**, 77, prominent medical organizer in Maine, 13 April 1904.

Dr. **Nathan Smith Davis**, 87, a founding member of the American Medical Association (1847) and first editor of its journal (1883–1888), 16 June 1904.

Dr. **Charles Denison**, 64, physician who developed improvements in many medical instruments and promoted Colorado's climate as a cure for tuberculosis, 10 January 1909.

Dr. **James Anthony Dibrell Jr.**, 58, prominent Arkansas surgeon and state and local medical organizer, 11 November 1904.

Dr. **Sarah Read Adamson Dolley**, 80, third American woman medical college graduate (1851), 27 December 1909.

Dr. **Joseph Eastman**, 60, surgeon and innovator in techniques and instruments, 5 June 1902.

Dr. **John Johnson Elwell**, 80, physician-lawyer who wrote the first book on medical malpractice (1860), 13 March 1900.

Dr. **Christian Fenger**, 62, prominent brain surgeon known as the "father of modern pathological surgery," 7 March 1902.

Dr. **William Henry Fitzbutler**, 59, one of the first black physicians to practice in Kentucky (1872), 28 December 1901.

Dr. **Eugene Foster**, 53, Georgia advocate of municipal sanitation, 23 January 1903.

Dr. **George Ryerson Fowler**, 58, well-known surgeon and author of a classic text, *Treatise on Surgery* (1906), 6 February 1906.

Dr. **Alonzo Garcelon**, 93, prominent advocate of public health and sanitation in Maine, 7 December 1906.

Dr. **Albert Leary Gihon,** 69, senior medical officer in the navy, where he advocated preventive medicine and recording vital statistics, 17 November 1902.

Daniel Coit Gilman, 77, president of Johns Hopkins, where he established one of the earliest modern research universities in America by building a hospital (1889) and medical school (1893) and by assembling a prominent medical faculty, 13 October 1908.

Dr. **Cordelia Agnes Greene,** 74, early female medical school graduate who championed health measures among women and children, 28 January 1905.

Dr. **William Alexander Hammond,** 72, physician who contributed to the development of neurology in America and wrote the first textbook on the topic (1871), 5 January 1900.

Dr. **William Tod Helmuth,** 69, one of the leading homeopathic surgeons in America from the 1860s until his death, 15 May 1902.

Dr. **Philo Oliver Hooper,** 69, medical pioneer in Arkansas, 29 July 1902.

Dr. **William Travis Howard,** 86, developer of many gynecological instruments, 31 July 1907.

Dr. **Edward Watrous Jenks,** 70, gynecologist and medical organizer in Detroit, 19 March 1903.

Dr. **George Augustus Ketchum,** 81, first physician to use large doses of quinine for yellow fever (1846) who helped organize the Medical Association of the State of Alabama and that state's medical college, 29 May 1906.

Dr. **Levi Cooper Lane,** 72, surgeon who performed the first vaginal hysterectomy in the United States and pioneered improvements in harelip treatment, 18 February 1902.

Dr. **Jesse William Lazear,** 34, member of Dr. Walter Reed's Army Yellow Fever Commission who died after allowing himself to be bitten by an infected mosquito, 25 September 1900.

Mary Ashton Rice Livermore, 84, Civil War nurse and activist in women's rights and public sanitation movements, 23 May 1905.

Dr. **Hannah E. Myers Longshore,** 82, first female physician in Philadelphia, 18 October 1901.

Dr. **James Brown McCaw,** 83, a founder of the Medical Society of Virginia and editor of many medical journals, 13 August 1906.

Dr. **Hunter Holmes McGuire,** 65, prominent Confederate medical leader and Gen. Stonewall Jackson's personal physician, 19 September 1900.

Dr. **Marie Joseph Mergler,** 50, second woman named to the staff of Chicago's Cook County Hospital (1882) and one of the best-known women physicians of her day, 17 May 1901.

Dr. **Robert Wood Mitchell,** 72, national leader in public health, 2 November 1903.

Dr. **Edward Mott Moore,** 88, prominent surgeon and medical educator, 3 March 1902.

Dr. **Henry Rinaldo Porter,** 55, prominent military surgeon of the 1870s who became famous for gallantry during the Little Big Horn battle in the Montana Territory (1876), 3 March 1903.

Dr. **George Edward Post,** 71, medical missionary in the Middle East for fifty years, 29 September 1909.

Dr. **Samuel Smith Purple,** 78, founding member of the New York Academy of Medicine and generous contributor to its library, 29 September 1900.

Dr. **Walter Reed,** 51, military physician who headed the Army Yellow Fever Commission and planned the laboratory and field experiments that identified the *Aedes aegypti* mosquito as the carrier of the disease, 22 November 1902.

Dr. **James Theodore Reeve,** 72, public health advocate in Wisconsin, 4 November 1906.

Dr. **Robert Reyburn,** 76, prominent black physician in Washington, D.C., and one of the attending physicians to President James Garfield after an assassination attempt (1881), 25 March 1909.

Dr. **Lewis Albert Sayre,** 80, known as the "father of American orthopedic surgery," 21 September 1900.

Dr. **Nicholas Senn,** 64, pioneer in abdominal and plastic surgery and the early use of X rays in the treatment of leukemia, 2 January 1908.

Dr. **Furman Jeremiah Shadd,** 56, prominent black physician in Washington, D.C., 24 June 1908.

Dr. **Edward Oram Shakespeare,** 54, innovator in ophthalmology and typhoid fever research, 1 June 1900.

Dr. **George Frederick Shrady,** 70, plastic surgery innovator and well-known medical journal editor, 30 November 1907.

Dr. **Alexander Johnston Chalmers Skene,** 63, pioneer in gynecology, 4 July 1900.

Dr. **Samuel Edwin Solly,** 61, early supporter of climatological treatment for tuberculosis, 18 November 1906.

Dr. **Edward Robinson Squibb,** 81, physician who developed and refined a manufacturing process for many drugs and was a prolific author and supporter of pure food and drug laws, 25 October 1900.

Dr. **William L. Steele,** 76, pioneering physician in Montana and advocate of public health improvements, 16 May 1909.

Dr. **Sarah Ann Hackett Stevenson,** 40, first woman physician at Chicago's Cook County Hospital (1881), 14 August 1901.

Dr. **Alfred Stille,** 87, a founder of the American Medical Association and widely known educator and author, 24 September 1900.

Dr. **Theodore Gaillard Thomas,** 72, prominent gynecologist and author on medicine, 28 February 1903.

Dr. **William Woodbury Watkins,** 55, organizer of the medical profession in Idaho, 4 August 1901.

Dr. **Conrad Wesselhoeft,** 68, homeopathic practitioner and educator who tried to adapt homeopathy to modern advances, 17 December 1904.

Dr. **William Riddick Whitehead,** 70, developer of instruments and techniques for cleft-palate surgery, 13 October 1902.

Dr. **Thomas Dudley Wooten,** 77, medical educator and organizer who served as president of the University of Texas, 1 August 1906.

Dr. **Morrill Wyman,** 91, pioneering surgeon who also wrote important works on building ventilation, 30 January 1903.

Dr. **Marie Elizabeth Zakrzewska,** 72, founder of a Boston hospital that trained women physicians, 12 May 1902.

PUBLICATIONS

Albert Abrams, *Diseases of the Heart* (Chicago: Engelhard, 1900);

Samuel Hopkins Adams, *The Great American Fraud* (New York: Collier, 1905);

James M. Anders, *A Text-book of the Practice of Medicine* (Philadelphia & New York: W. B. Saunders, 1903);

Frank Billings, *General Medicine* (Chicago: Year Book, 1901);

John Janvier Black, *Forty Years in the Medical Profession, 1858-1898* (Philadelphia: Lippincott, 1900);

Eugene Wilson Caldwell and William Posey, *The Practical Application of the Roentgen Rays in Therapeutics and Diagnosis* (New York: Saunders, 1903);

J. M. G. Carter, *Lectures on Diseases of the Stomach* (Saint Louis: Fortnightly, 1902);

Charles Value Chapin, *Municipal Sanitation in the United States* (Providence, R.I.: Snow & Farnham, 1901);

Eugene Fauntleroy Cordell, *The Medical Annals of Maryland, 1799–1899* (Baltimore: Press of Williams & Wilkins, 1903);

Thomas Stephen Cullen, *Cancer of the Uterus* (New York: Appleton, 1900);

Ronald G. Curtin, *A Study of Ancient and Modern Secret Medical Fraternities* (Philadelphia, 1907?);

Nathan Smith Davis, *History of Medicine* (Chicago: Cleveland Press, 1903);

Lavinia Lloyd Dock, *History of Nursing* (New York: Putnam, 1907);

Max Einhorn, *Diseases of the Intestines* (New York: Wood, 1900);

Palmer Findley, *Diagnosis of Diseases of Women* (Philadelphia: Lea, 1903);

Lawrence Francis Flick, *Consumption, a Curable and Preventable Disease* (Philadelphia: McKay, 1903);

Dr. George Ryerson Fowler, *Treatise on Surgery* (Philadelphia: Saunders, 1906);

John William Fyfe, *Specific Diagnosis and Specific Medication* (Cincinnati: Scudder Brothers, 1909);

Cordelia Agnes Greene, *The Art of Keeping Well; or, Common Sense Hygiene for Adults and Children* (New York: Dodd, Mead, 1906);

Charles Hazzard, *The Practice and Applied Therapeutics of Osteopathy,* revised edition (Kirksville, Mo.: Journal Printing, 1905);

Fernand Henrotin, *Democracy of Education in Medicine* (Chicago: R. R. Donnelley, 1903);

Woods Hutchinson, *Instinct and Health* (New York: Dodd, Mead, 1908);

Edwin Oakes Jordan, *Textbook of General Bacteriology* (Philadelphia: Saunders, 1908);

William W. Keen, *Addresses and Other Papers* (Philadelphia & London: Saunders, 1905);

John Harvey Kellogg, *Rational Hydrotherapy* (Philadelphia: Davis, 1901);

Howard Atwood Kelly, *Walter Reed and Yellow Fever* (Baltimore: Standard, 1906);

Henry Koplik, *Diseases of Infancy and Children* (New York: Lea, 1902);

Albert E. Leach, *Food Inspection and Analysis*, revised edition (New York: Wiley, 1909);

Lorenzo B. Lockard, *Tuberculosis of the Nose and Throat* (Saint Louis: Mosby, 1909);

Franklin Paine Mall, *A Study of the Causes Underlying the Origin of Human Monsters* (Philadelphia: Wistar Institute, 1908);

Charles Wells Moulton, ed., *The Doctor's Who's Who* (New York & Akron: Saalfield, 1906);

Eugene Lindsay Opie, *Diseases of the Pancreas* (Philadelphia: Lippincott, 1902);

William Osler, *Modern Medicine, Its Theory and Practice*, 7 volumes (Philadelphia: Lea, 1907);

Francis Randolph Packard, *History of Medicine in the United States* (Philadelphia: Lippincott, 1901);

Henry B. Palmer, *Surgical Asepsis: Especially Adapted to Operations in the Home of the Patient* (Philadelphia: Davis, 1903);

The Aesculapian, periodical;

American Journal of Anatomy, periodical;

American Medicine, periodical;

The Antiseptic, periodical;

Journal of Infectious Diseases, periodical;

Journal of the American Osteopathic Association, periodical;

Journal of the Association of Military Surgeons of the United States, periodical;

Journal of the National Medical Association, periodical;

Medical Library and Historical Journal, periodical;

Military Surgeon, periodical;

Surgery, Gynecology and Obstetrics, periodical.

RELIGION

by DAVID MCLEAN and MONICA SIEMS

CONTENTS

Sidebars and tables are listed in italics.

1900

- Katherine August Westcott Tingley founds a utopian settlement at Point Loma, California, which includes a theosophical school and an artistic community.

- Congregationalist preacher and Social Gospel theologian Washington Gladden runs for city council in Columbus, Ohio, and wins a two-year term.

- Baptist Temple in Philadelphia, the church that launched what would become Temple University, is the largest congregation in the United States. The Baptist Temple was an "institutional church" that provided a range of social as well as religious services.

- Julia A. J. Foote, the first woman deacon in the African Methodist Episcopal Zion Church, is ordained an elder.

- Reverdy C. Ransom, pastor of the Bethel African Methodist Episcopal Church in Chicago, establishes the Institutional Church and Social Settlement on Dearborn Street near Thirty-ninth Street. The church, modeled on Jane Addams's Hull House, was the first of its kind for blacks.

25 Jan. The House of Representatives votes 268–50 to unseat Congressman-elect Brigham H. Roberts of Utah because of his having three wives and an undetermined number of children. The Mormon church had officially prohibited polygamy in 1890.

31 Aug. The Lott Carey Baptist Home and Foreign Mission, a group that had separated from the National Baptist Convention, U.S.A., Inc., establishes a Women's Auxiliary that is instrumental in enlisting black Baptist youths to work for the cause of foreign missions.

15 Sept. Nannie Helen Burroughs founds the Women's Auxiliary Convention of the National Baptist Convention, U.S.A., Inc. She gives an influential speech titled "How the Sisters are Hindered From Helping."

18 Dec. The Colored Men's Branch of the YMCA in New York City, founded by Baptist pastor Charles Thomas, is accepted as a regular branch.

1901

- The American Federation of Catholic Societies is formed to coordinate the efforts of lay organizations devoted to social reform.

- Jacob Beilhart founds the communal Spirit Fruit Society with ten members. In 1914 the society moves to Santa Clara County, California, where it lasts until 1930.

- John Alexander Dowie's Christian Catholic Church purchases sixty-six hundred acres on the shore of Lake Michigan and founds the city of Zion, Illinois.

- Henry McNeal Turner, bishop of the African Methodist Episcopal Church, founds *Voice of the People,* a periodical devoted to the church and to black activism.

1 Jan. Agnes Ozman receives baptism of the Spirit in Topeka, Kansas, and allegedly begins speaking in tongues, the first modern instance of the phenomenon known as glossolalia.

14 Mar. The governor of Utah vetoes a bill aimed at relaxing the prosecution of polygamy cases.

29 Dec. Alma White, the wife of a minister, founds her own Holiness Church after she is forbidden by the Methodists to hold revival meetings. Begun as the Methodist Pentecostal Church and later renamed the Pillar of Fire Church, by 1936 it will have forty-six congregations, $4 million in assets, and more than four thousand members. White later becomes the first female bishop of any Christian church.

1902

- Baptist leader Lucy Peabody becomes chairman of the new Committee on the United Study of Missions, a position she will hold until 1929.

- Solomon Schechter arrives in New York to take over the presidency of the Jewish Theological Seminary, becoming a major figure in Conservative Judaism.

- William James publishes *The Varieties of Religious Experience,* a pioneering work in the psychological study of religion.

- The last of a series of prophetic conferences originally organized by Dwight L. Moody in 1880 is held in Northfield, Massachusetts.

- The National American Woman Suffrage Association sets up a Committee on Church Work to help promote the cause of suffrage within male-dominated religious bodies.

- The Christian Union, a Holiness group in Appalachia that had been reduced to about twenty members, reorganizes itself as the Holiness Church at Camp Creek in order to provide organizational stability and prevent "fanaticism" and loss of membership.

4 July Swami Vivekananda, who had spoken at the World's Parliament of Religions in Chicago in 1893 and founded the Vedanta Society, the first Hindu mission in the United States, dies in India.

1903

- George A. Coe, professor of philosophy at Northwestern University; John Dewey, professor of philosophy at the University of Chicago; and others establish the Religious Education Association, an interfaith group devoted to designing morally responsible but not doctrinally specific curricula.

- William Walker Atkinson, a proponent of New Thought, adopts the name Swami Ramacharacka and begins publishing works that popularize Hinduism.

- Former professional baseball player and YMCA lecturer Billy Sunday is ordained a Presbyterian minister. His independent revivalistic career begins soon after.

- Eliza Healy, known as Sister Mary Magdalene, becomes principal of a school in Saint Albans, Vermont. At the same time, she is named superior of the convent, becoming the first black nun to hold so high a position.

- The Seventh-Day Adventists move their national headquarters to Washington, D.C.

28 July Pope Leo XIII dies in Rome. He is succeeded by Giuseppe Melchiorre Sarto, who takes the name Pius X.

1904

- Archbishop Patrick J. Ryan establishes the Catholic Missionary Society of Philadelphia. Among its first acts is the opening of Madonna House, a settlement house primarily for Italian Catholic immigrants.

- Western Theological Seminary in Chicago (now Seabury-Western in Evanston) is closed but is later reopened and reenergized by Charles Palmerston Anderson, the bishop of Chicago. By 1910 the seminary is flourishing.

- Evangeline Booth becomes field commander for the Salvation Army, a post she would hold until 1934.

7 Sept. The Polish National Catholic Church comes into existence when a group of parishes meets in Scranton, Pennsylvania, to establish a synod that is independent of the Roman Catholic Church.

1905

- A Catholic priest from Michigan forms the Church Extension Society, dedicated to raising the funds needed to build churches in sparsely populated areas of the South and West.

- The liberal, ecumenical Protestant journal *Christian Century* begins publishing.

- John Wilbur Chapman, a former associate of Dwight L. Moody, begins the Chapman Simultaneous Evangelistic Campaign, or "Chapman Brigade," a massive revival effort.

- Prominent Catholic Maria Longworth Nichols Storer, in her efforts to have Archbishop John Ireland of Saint Paul appointed to the cardinalate, alleges that President Theodore Roosevelt had promised to recommend him to the Vatican. Roosevelt rebukes her and dismisses her husband, U.S. ambassador Bellamy Storer. The Storers later circulate unfavorable accounts of Roosevelt to the press.

- Pogroms in Russia lead to a massive wave of Jewish immigration to the United States.

- English revivalist F. B. Meyer, a central figure in the great Welsh Keswick revival of 1903, gives a series of lectures in Los Angeles. His visit encourages a number of Holiness believers to pray for a massive Pentecostal revival.

- Former pastor Thomas Dixon Jr. publishes *The Clansman*, adding fuel to the nascent Ku Klux Klan revival.

18 June The Federation of American Zionists adopts a resolution at its eighth annual convention stating that Palestine would be the best place to establish a Jewish colony. Their position affirms the platform of the International Zionist Congress, which had previously declined a British offer to help establish a colony in East Africa.

- African Methodist Episcopal preacher Reverdy C. Ransom gives a famous speech, "The Spirit of John Brown," at the second annual meeting of W. E. B. Du Bois's Niagara movement. According to Du Bois, Ransom's eloquence "led to the eventual founding of the National Association for the Advancement of Colored People."

1906

- John A. Ryan, a Catholic priest, publishes *A Living Wage*, which fuels the minimum-wage-law movement.

- Theodor Herzl, the Hungarian Jew who founded modern political Zionism with his book *The Jewish State*, dies at the age of forty-six.

- The Seventh-Day Adventists establish the College of Medical Evangelists (later Loma Linda University) in Loma Linda, California.

9 Apr. The Pentecostal movement has its official beginning when William J. Seymour, a Holiness preacher from Texas, receives baptism in the Holy Spirit and launches the Apostolic Faith Gospel Mission on Azusa Street in Los Angeles.

18 Apr. The San Francisco earthquake adds fervor to revivalist and Pentecostal movements throughout California.

24 Sept. Riots occur in Brownsville, Georgia, after the Atlanta press urges disfranchisement of Negroes and the revival of the Ku Klux Klan.

1907

- Walter Rauschenbusch publishes *Christianity and the Social Crisis*, a seminal work in the Social Gospel movement.

- The First Presidency of the Church of Jesus Christ of Latter-Day Saints publishes *An Address: The Church of Jesus Christ of Latter-Day Saints to the World*, affirming the patriotism of American Mormons and renouncing all "quasi-political notions of kingdom."

- Some congregations in southern Illinois, upset by the liberalism being taught at the University of Chicago, split from the Illinois Baptist Convention and join the Southern Baptist Association.

- The Catholic Board for Mission Work among Colored People is founded. The board funds nuns and lay teachers in black schools in the South.

- The Church of Christ (Holiness), U.S.A., is founded by Charles Price Jones. Jones and Charles H. Mason had founded the Church of God in Christ in 1894, but after Mason's conversion to Pentecostalism, Jones split off to found the new Holiness denomination.

- Black Primitive Baptists meet in Huntsville, Alabama, to form the National Primitive Baptist Convention of the U.S.A. The convention establishes a Sunday school union and publishing board, a National Women's Auxiliary Convention, and an industrial and theological college at Winston-Salem, North Carolina.

6 Jun. Dropsie College for Hebrew and Cognate Learning, a postgraduate college for rabbinical and biblical studies, is chartered in Philadelphia.

8 Sept. - Pope Pius X issues the encyclical *Pascendi dominici gregis,* condemning theological modernism.

1908

- *The Christian Science Monitor* begins publishing.

- Mary Lewis Tate, a self-appointed preacher since 1903, speaks in tongues after experiencing a miraculous recovery from illness. She subsequently founds the Church of the Living God, the Pillar and Ground of Truth, a Pentecostal denomination in Alabama.

- W. O. Fuller, the only black charter member of the Fire-Baptized Holiness Church in Georgia, breaks off with a substantial number of black members to form the Colored Fire-Baptized Holiness Church (now the Fire-Baptized Holiness Church of God of the Americas). The split occurs because of the rise of Jim Crow laws, which make it increasingly difficult for the church to find places to hold interracial services.

- William J. Seymour of the Azusa Street Mission and Charles H. Mason hold revival services in Washington, D.C., leading to the founding of the Apostolic Faith Church of God.

- A black Catholic priest, Father John Dorsey, with three white priests and several black laymen, forms the Knights of Peter Claver in Mobile, Alabama. Modeled on the Knights of Columbus, the new fraternity is named for a Spanish Jesuit saint who, in the seventeenth century, had cared for sick slaves arriving on ships in Cartagena, Colombia.

13 Apr. The New England Methodist Episcopal Conference votes to remove its ban on dancing, card playing, and theatergoing.

26 May Mirza Ghulam Hazrat Ahmad, founder of the Ahmadiyya movement, one of the first Islamic missions to come to the United States, dies in Pakistan.

29 June Pope Pius X issues the encyclical *Sapienti Consilio,* declaring that the United States is no longer a missionary area, thereby removing the American church from the jurisdiction of the Congregation for the Propagation of the Faith in Rome.

2 Dec. The Federal Council of Churches of Christ in America, representing thirty-three Protestant denominations and twelve million church members, is established in Philadelphia. The council adopts a Social Creed, calling for a series of labor reform measures.

27 Dec. Dressed in white gowns "made specially for the occasion," followers of doomsday prophet Lee J. Spangler sit atop a mountain in Nyack, New York, awaiting the end of the world.

1909

- *The Reference Bible* edited by Cyrus I. Scofield, an extremely popular resource for the doctrines of dispensational premillennialism, is published.

- Amzi C. Dixon, pastor of the Moody Church in Chicago, meets layman Lyman Stewart and agrees to help him publish *The Fundamentals,* the classic statement of conservative Protestantism that first appeared in 1910.

- Unitarian educator Charles W. Eliot steps down as president of Harvard University, which he had substantially liberalized and secularized. Shortly before leaving, he writes an essay titled "The Religion of the Future," in which he predicted that secular benevolent societies would provide the model for a substantially modified twentieth-century Christianity.

- Jehovah's Witnesses establish their world headquarters in Brooklyn, initially occupying the former parsonage of nineteenth-century Congregationalist preacher Henry Ward Beecher.

**26 Jan.–
17 Feb.**   The "Chapman Brigade" holds 990 services in Boston alone.

OVERVIEW

Coming to Maturity. As "the American century" dawned, the country's religious bodies faced a distinctly modern world, one in which the United States would often take center stage. If the Civil War had represented the growing pains of the nation's adolescence, the twentieth century clearly saw America attaining maturity. The country still faced a long and difficult task of defining what its role in the world should be, and its churches likewise had to clarify their place in a changing society. Economic, social, and intellectual trends that had begun shortly after the Civil War continued to transform American society, often in ways that challenged traditional religious values. Many religious leaders observed an increasing secularization that threatened the effectiveness of churches both in shaping public policy and in maintaining the loyalty of their members. Many theologians wrestled with two parallel concerns: if, and how, the churches should adapt to keep up with the spirit of the times; and if, and how, the conditions of the times should be altered to bring them more into keeping with the ideals of the churches. Many debates that had started in the 1870s on a theoretical level played themselves out in practical terms in the early 1900s. Through new faith ideals, as well as renewed commitments to some old ones, American religion began the process of putting on a new face to meet the new century.

Imperialism and World Missions. Some religious leaders entered the twentieth century filled with confidence and optimism, inspired to a new faith in Manifest Destiny by America's recent victory in the Spanish-American War. Many believed that the Protestant faith, to which the majority of Americans adhered, could join the principles of democratic government as an American export for the great benefit of humanity worldwide. Nothing illustrated this sentiment as much as the enthusiastic drive to send Protestant missionaries to the newly acquired and predominantly Catholic Philippines. Although this plan caused considerable consternation among American Catholics, the belief that America had a special place in the destiny of the world, religiously as well as politically, continued to inspire massive foreign missionary movements. In 1900 John R. Mott, director of the Student Volunteer Movement, wrote confidently of *The Evangelization of the World in This Generation.*

Many other American religious leaders also had their gazes firmly fixed on foreign shores. They saw a grand opportunity to share the values, success, and grandeur of a rapidly maturing America and thought it a Christian duty to spread the gospel to unenlightened peoples around the globe.

A Social Critique. Others, however, focused their attention within America's borders and found much less cause for optimism. Such voices cautioned against both political and religious imperialism, especially when, as they saw it, America did not have its own house in order. In their eyes the ideals that the United States was packaging for export had hardly found wholesale distribution at home, and these dissenting voices predicted failure for missionary enterprises that only thinly veiled the hypocrisy of preaching Christian brotherhood abroad while practicing rugged individualism at home. They advocated a broad application of the principles of Christian love to the nation's growing ranks of laboring poor as a prerequisite to the evangelization of the world. Proponents of a social gospel, these religious leaders preached the need for economic reforms to relieve the distress of workers and to correct the excesses of capitalism. Others took their concerns to the streets, operating rescue missions and relief organizations. Still others increased their emphasis on moralism, focusing on the individual rather than the system and joining in crusades such as the ongoing drive for temperance. The churches had gone out into the world to an unprecedented degree, a move that attracted considerable opposition. The battle that ensued was over no less than the true meaning and application of the term *Christian.*

Diversity. For some, religion had ventured so far into the secular realm as to be unrecognizable. This feeling may have been heightened by the number of new religious forms that prospered in America, challenging the strength of the old-line Protestant core. While the traditional mainline denominations — Methodists, Baptists, Lutherans, Presbyterians, Episcopalians, Congregationalists, and Disciples of Christ — taken together maintained a substantial numerical dominance, other religious bodies would as much as quintuple their membership during the course of the century's first decade.

Roman Catholicism, Eastern Orthodoxy, Judaism, and some Asian religions enjoyed a high rate of growth through the massive immigration of 1900 through 1910. Sectarian movements that had been born in the late nineteenth century, including Mormonism, Christian Science, Seventh-Day Adventism, and Jehovah's Witnesses, continued to attract new members and to mature on the institutional level, commanding public attention as their leaders lectured, published, and established national and world headquarters. When in 1902 the American philosopher William James published the Gifford lectures he had delivered in Edinburgh as *The Varieties of Religious Experience,* many could find in the title a theme that increasingly characterized the religious life of America. Ethnic tensions wracked many religious bodies, while some mainline Protestants launched new efforts at ecumenical union in the hope that a unified front would help them preserve what they could of Protestant cultural dominance.

The Debate within Protestantism. Protestant unity was hard to come by, however, as the early decades of the twentieth century would see the crystallization of two opposed camps within Protestantism. What would soon become known as the Fundamentalist and Modernist parties were at the turn of the century merely loosely arrayed groups of conservative and liberal theologians, with the liberals especially being concentrated within a handful of the country's most prestigious seminaries and divinity schools. Nineteenth-century debates about Darwinism and biblical literalism had quieted somewhat, but the larger issue of what, or whether, doctrinal sacrifices to the spirit of the times were acceptable continued to vex the country's leading religious minds. As American philosophers embraced a new method known as pragmatism, many liberal religious leaders also started to evaluate their theologies on the basis of results in gaining and keeping members. Relaxing their demands for unconditional truth and looking at religious doctrines as evolving over time in response to social circumstances, these theologians set off a conservative backlash. Religious conservatives responded by becoming increasingly strident in matters of dogma, developing doctrinal "tests" to measure the depth of a person's faith. In a decade of rapid social change, the religious middle ground was quickly shrinking. Where some saw an opportunity for faith, others saw a threat to it. And while most Protestants agreed that the Kingdom of God was coming soon, the difference between pre- and postmillennial thought only heightened the dispute between those who saw an almost unlimited sphere for human action and those who held fast to their faith in an absolutely sovereign God. Liberal postmillennialists sought to remake the world in the image of God's Kingdom, while conservative premillennialists focused on prophetic images from the Bible that only God could make real.

Pentecostalism. One of the more extreme reactions to the perceived social decline came in the form of the Pentecostal movement that was born with the new century. Deeply concerned with the imminent millennial future, Pentecostalists focused equally on the restoration of the biblical past, in which gifts of prophecy, healing, and speaking in tongues were granted to the first Christian disciples. Although it drew heavily on doctrines that had grown up in England, Pentecostalism was an American religious innovation, one that spoke particularly to the country's contemporary social situation. In dramatic outpourings of religious enthusiasm, even the most socially displaced persons could directly experience the feeling of spiritual empowerment. Despite meeting with substantial opposition and controversy, this new religious form would endure as a permanent feature of the American religious landscape.

Roman Catholicism. The Roman Catholic Church in America entered the twentieth century with the problems of the nineteenth century still demanding its attention. Though nativist and anti-Catholic institutions had passed their peak in America some decades before, the sentiments that they had embodied had not vanished entirely, so Catholics still worked to shed the image of blind obedience to papal authority that they retained in the eyes of Protestant America. Despite papal censures in the 1890s, some of the church's most prominent leaders, notably archbishops James Cardinal Gibbons and John Ireland, continued to pursue a liberal program of shaping a Catholicism that would embrace the best aspects of American society. In 1907 they would face another setback when Pope Pius X issued an encyclical condemning "modernism," a theological program that largely corresponded to the liberal Protestant trends of accepting biblical criticism, doctrinal relativism, and evolution. The pope's rebuke, however, applied more directly to European theologians than to American prelates, who were largely known for their focus on the practical matters of building churches and serving their flocks.

The Catholic Mission. As well as producing its share of social activists to respond to the crises faced by large numbers of immigrant Catholic laborers, the American Catholic Church quickly adapted to the change from being a "mission territory" to being a missionizing one. In June 1908, the pope removed the Catholic Church in the United States from the jurisdiction of the Society for the Propagation of the Faith in Rome. Just five months later at a missionary conference in Chicago Archbishop James Quigley spoke of galvanizing "the missionary sentiment now being awakened in the Catholic clergy and people, to the end that all may realize their common duty of preserving and extending the Church of Christ." In many ways American Catholicism was coming of age just in time to meet new pressures and challenges offered by the twentieth century. The largest single denomination in the United States, it also, despite the ethnic tensions that continued to trouble it from within, had come close enough to the Protestant mainstream to accept a full share in the social and missionary activism that characterized so many of the nation's other religious bodies.

Judaism. The history of Judaism in the United States has largely been the story of the development of the three major "denominations" of Reform, Orthodox, and Conservative, the latter two taking shape primarily in the twentieth century. Large numbers of Orthodox Jews arrived in America in the late nineteenth and early twentieth centuries, fleeing state-sponsored violence in eastern Europe, especially Russia. They stood in stark contrast to the highly assimilated Reform Jews who had previously constituted the majority of the nation's Jewish population, which stood at about one million at the turn of the century. The result of the new influx was the development of conflicts parallel to those in American Catholicism and Protestantism — tensions concerning ethnicity, Americanization, and theological modernism. Conservative Judaism, especially as articulated by Romanian-born Solomon Schechter at Jewish Theological Seminary in New York, emerged as a compromise position between Orthodoxy and Reform. Although he had been trained in all the methods of scriptural criticism being taught in the "science of Judaism" that had taken shape in Germany, Schechter argued in 1901 that the revelation of the Torah was so central to Judaism that Jews had been "slain by the hundreds and thousands rather than become unfaithful to it." In the years to come Judaism would also make its voice heard on the major social questions of the day, demonstrating, as Catholicism did, the place it had established as a religious force in America.

Blacks. Though mostly Protestant, blacks had their own religious development that often paralleled but was separate from that of the white American churches. The major denominations were still split along racial lines, and even many white churches still had separate northern and southern federations, showing that Civil War–era disunity persisted. New denominations, such as those associated with Pentecostalism, sometimes began as multiracial movements but often found that outside pressures forced them to develop as segregated institutions, especially in the South, where Jim Crow laws were on the rise. Segregation did not imply weakness, however, and black churches continued to both multiply and divide at this time. The National Baptist Convention U.S.A., Inc., the largest black denomination, and its splinter group, the Lott Carey Baptist Home and Foreign Missionary Convention, both established Women's Auxiliaries in the first year of the century, and these women became instrumental in recruiting volunteers for the churches' foreign mission efforts. By 1903 the National Baptist Convention was stressing the need for world missions, with a special emphasis on sending representatives to Africa. At home the churches were equally active, again mirroring the activities of their white counterparts. The first black branch of the YMCA and the first black institutional church were both established in 1901, demonstrating the involvement of black churches in social reform and rescue efforts. Despite the strictures of segregation, black churches found ample opportunities to make their presence felt in the lives of their members as well as in the larger communities of which they were a part.

Women. American women at the turn of the century were still largely restricted from enjoying full participation in their churches. Exceptions came mostly within traditionally marginalized religious bodies. Black churches demonstrated an impressive willingness to place women in positions of leadership. Even as Nannie Helen Burroughs gave a speech titled "How the Sisters are Hindered from Helping," she was taking the helm of the newly created Women's Auxiliary Convention of the National Baptist Convention U.S.A., Inc. At the same time, the African Methodist Episcopal Zion Church promoted the first woman deacon it had ever ordained, Julia A. J. Foote, to the rank of elder. Other black churches also ordained women as deaconesses, giving them a role that did not yet exist in most white Protestant churches. Women also found opportunities for leadership in the new Pentecostal movement as preachers and healers, some carrying over from their earlier days as itinerant Holiness preachers, a position that had placed them just as squarely on the religious fringe. But perhaps the most important avenue for religious involvement for women came in the field of social reform. The Salvation Army had many women in its top positions, including Evangeline Booth, field commander for the United States and daughter of the Army's founder. The Woman's Christian Temperance Union continued its crusade against both personal drunkenness and the liquor trade, finding its most extreme expression in the hatchet-wielding antics of Carry Nation, who claimed that conversations with Jesus Christ formed the basis for her work. Often slighted, women nonetheless found ways to serve, and perhaps ultimately save, the whole community.

Challenges and Changes. Empowerment certainly represents one of the more salient themes of early-twentieth-century American religion. Theologians felt unprecedented freedom to adapt their dogmatic heritage to the needs of a new time, and preachers felt a new calling to take their ministry out into the streets where people needed them. Ethnic minorities arrived determined to exercise the freedom of religion that so many had been denied in their homelands. Women and blacks found a host of ways to overcome the barriers that blocked their progress. The rising lament of the mainstream's conservative core, that religion was becoming unrecognizable, is easy to understand, but it is difficult to fathom if and how traditionalists believed they could stem the tide of changes, some of which had begun in the 1870s and many of which crested in the 1900s. A new century had dawned, and many believed that the millennium was not far behind it. The changes occurring in American religion were as unstoppable as they were dramatic.

TOPICS IN THE NEWS

IMMIGRATION AND NEW ETHNIC DIVERSITY

The Golden Door. Between 1900 and 1910 nearly nine million people arrived in the United States from foreign shores, marking the country's all-time peak of immigration. The numbers had been steadily climbing since the Civil War, and at the same time the ethnic makeup of the immigrants had been changing considerably from northern and western European to southern and eastern European. Asian immigration was also a significant factor in America's evolving religious composition, for though the Japanese and Chinese communities of the West Coast were small, their thriving presence contributed substantially to American religious diversity with varieties of Buddhism and Shinto, among other traditions. Clearly the nation's white, Anglo-Saxon Protestant core population found itself increasingly surrounded by people whose languages, customs, and religious beliefs and practices varied substantially from the American mainstream, and immigration continued to outpace assimilation vastly. As the twentieth century began, the United States could point to a greater variety in religious belief and practice than it had ever possessed before. But at the same time, it could look at the ways in which that diversity was causing the nation and its established religious bodies to creak and groan under the weight of the "huddled masses" who were flooding through the "golden door" mentioned on the Statue of Liberty's pedestal.

Ramifications. Not surprisingly, the opening decade of the twentieth century witnessed occasional outbursts of nativistic fervor as those born in America fought to maintain their privileged place in society. For some ethnic groups, the story of their early years in the United States abounds with instances of prejudice and persecution. Moreover, many ethnic groups experienced internal disputes over the desirability, pace, and extent of assimilation. Often new arrivals would begin to attend churches established by their countrymen who had arrived in America decades before, only to find that the new country had occasioned changes in doctrine and practice that the newer immigrants found unacceptable. Some immigrants would become bitterly disappointed when, upon

CHURCH MEMBERSHIP AT THE TURN OF THE CENTURY

In 1900 the population of the United States stood at seventy-six million. An estimated twenty-six million, almost exactly one-third of the total, officially belonged to a church. The top eight denominations and their membership at this time were as follows:

Roman Catholics	8,000,000
Methodists	5,500,000
Baptists	4,000,000
Presbyterians	1,500,000
Lutherans	1,000,000
Disciples of Christ	1,000,000
Episcopalians	600,000
Congregationalists	600,000

These statistics already reflected major changes in America's religious makeup since the original colonies had been settled mostly by Congregationalists and Episcopalians. These changes had occurred largely because of immigration, especially Catholic, and liberalization within Protestantism. The seven Protestant denominations listed above, however, still represented the mainstream of American religiosity, and although very few individual religious bodies would mount any sort of serious numerical challenge to this mainstream, the dizzying array of new religions and sects, with ethnic variations on some of the old, combined to serve notice to the old Protestant establishment that the ground was continuing to shift beneath its feet.

Source: Edwin Scott Gaustad, *A Religious History of America,* revised edition (San Francisco: HarperCollins, 1990).

Immigrants arriving in Manhattan in 1905

attempting to exercise their newly found religious freedom, they found themselves beset with pressures to adopt English as their language of worship and adjust their customs to the prevailing tastes of American society. Many religious bodies would experience schisms along ethnic lines as this issue of assimilation or "Americanization" was negotiated by their members. The late nineteenth century had seen this process repeated over and over in Protestant denominations, with one, Lutheranism, ending the century with no fewer than twenty-four distinct organizations in this country.

Asian Beginnings. Perhaps no story better illustrates the extremes of prejudice immigrants sometimes faced as well as the perseverance they could demonstrate than that of the Chinese and Japanese immigrants who arrived in Hawaii and on the West Coast in the nineteenth and early twentieth centuries (forming one of the few major waves of United States immigration that did not start on the East Coast and gradually move westward). Chinese laborers had been arriving in California to work on the railroads since the 1840s, and the Chinatowns that sprang up in California's cities during subsequent decades revealed the presence for the first time of ethnic Buddhism on American soil. But by 1902 a series of legislative steps had already been taken to effectively prevent further Chinese immigration, so the development of that tradition would be severely hampered until much later in the century when immigration laws were finally relaxed

for all nationalities. Somewhat more successful in establishing a presence were the Japanese, especially after 1899 when the annexation of Hawaii provided a logical jumping-off point for increased settlement in California. Japanese immigrants to that state established institutions from both of Japan's major religious traditions, Buddhism and Shinto, which have endured to the present day, despite the "Gentlemen's Agreement" of 1907 whereby laws enacting segregation of Asian students in California schools were scrapped in favor of tighter controls on Japanese immigration.

Buddhism. Replicating Japan's own variety and diversity, the Japanese American tradition of Buddhism consisted of more than one branch. Pure Land (also known as Jodo Shinshu) Buddhism, a major nonmeditative strand, had made its presence felt in 1899, when two priests from Japan established the Buddhist Mission of North America, an organization that would continue to grow in numbers of both temples and members and, in 1942, be renamed the Buddhist Churches of America. Although over time the services held at these Buddhist churches would become more "Americanized," the presence of the tradition often served as a vehicle for maintaining Japanese identity, even among the American-born. The other major type of Buddhism practiced by Japanese immigrants at the beginning of this century was a meditative branch of Zen Buddhism known as Rinzai Zen. Founded in Japan in the twelfth century, this variety

Orthodox Jewish immigrant

of Buddhism focuses on the attainment of enlightenment as a sudden, dramatic event. To achieve enlightenment, the believer learns to meditate on the meaning of *koans* — puzzling questions such as "What is the sound of one hand clapping?" — which are meant to jolt one out of his or her normal mode of consciousness. Rinzai Zen was first brought to America by Soyen Shaku, who had attended the World's Parliament of Religions in Chicago in 1893. He returned to America, and through a series of lectures in 1905 and 1906 he familiarized many Americans in major cities with Zen. When he returned to Japan, he selected three disciples to continue the work of establishing Rinzai Zen in America. That work went on in fits and starts as the disciples at various points in their careers postponed their mission efforts or returned to live in Japan. It was not until much later in the century that Soyen Shaku's best-known disciple, D. T. Suzuki, would bring Rinzai Zen into wide public awareness through his writings and lectures.

Shinto. Asian religions in America are often distinguished by whether they are "ethnic," that is, practiced primarily by immigrants and their descendants, or "export" varieties, those that are adopted primarily by non-

Asian Americans. While Pure Land Buddhism has remained mainly ethnic in this country, Zen has crossed over and become a significant export tradition as well. Through their efforts Shaku and Suzuki managed to reach a wide non-Asian audience while also establishing institutions in areas where Japanese immigrants concentrated. Another group of Japanese religious bodies remained almost exclusively ethnic in America: the forms of Shinto, Japan's indigenous, nature-centered religion, which arrived with many of the immigrants (many of whom would also have practiced some form of Buddhism). Some forms of Shinto have left few institutional traces as they center not on congregational life but in private households and seasonal community festivals. Two Shinto sectarian movements, however, were established in California within the first decade of the century. The Taishakyo sect was represented by the North American Shinto Church, founded in San Francisco in 1904, and the Tenrikyo sect made inroads after 1896 through the work of independent preachers in San Francisco as well as Los Angeles, where an official religious fellowship was established in 1903. These institutions, since joined by many others, have survived until the present, providing ample testimony of the presence of Japanese Americans and their determination to preserve their beliefs and customs even as their countrymen found the famous golden door locked tight against them.

Ethnic Tensions within Roman Catholicism. The Roman Catholic Church in America provides perhaps the prime example of an established religious body dealing with ethnic tensions caused by the rapid immigration of the early twentieth century. Despite its centralized, hierarchical power structure (and perhaps in some ways because of it), the Catholic Church could not escape the tendency toward ethnic schism that had plagued so many Protestant denominations in prior decades. In the late nineteenth century a controversy over "Americanism" in terms of language, worship, leadership, and education had swept through the Catholic Church, its first major battles being fought between Irish Catholics, who held a disproportionate number of seats in the hierarchy, and the Germans who had begun to arrive in droves after 1850 and now constituted a formidable presence. Irish and German attitudes toward temperance and the clergy differed as considerably as their languages did, and many German Catholics resented the fact that their parishes and dioceses were often led by Irish clergymen. In the first decade of the twentieth century this controversy, deemed settled by a 1895 papal encyclical condemning Americanism, would be replayed by other new arrivals such as the Italians and especially the Poles, who did not shy away even from schism in order to exercise their right to worship as they wished.

The Polish National Catholic Church. Many of the ethnic tensions in Catholicism stemmed from Irish control of the hierarchy and a traditional lack of deference to the clergy among other ethnic groups. Immigrants from countries with long histories of anticlericalism, such as Italy and Germany, perhaps had an inherent tendency to revolt against Irish dominance. In cities with large Polish concentrations controversy often ensued over the ownership of church property and the input of lay trustees in directing church affairs. Many Polish immigrants hoped that in America they could democratize the system of church patronage they had known in Poland, where wealthy nobles gained a voice in church governance in exchange for their financial support. After arriving in America, these immigrants became deeply frustrated when the established hierarchy would not allow such developments. Milwaukee, Chicago, and Scranton, Pennsylvania, were the sites of the most heated conflicts. In Milwaukee the bishop against whom Polish priests struggled was a German who had been appointed to the post after a prior Irish-German controversy there. In these and other cities, predominantly Polish churches would break away from the diocese to become independent parishes; it was at a conference of such parishes in Scranton in 1904 that the Polish National Catholic Church was established, declaring its independence from Rome. Francis Hodur, a priest from Scranton, was named the first bishop, and the synod adopted a platform calling for democracy in church governance. The new church attracted only about 5 percent of the Polish population, but even where they did not opt for schism, Polish parishioners often lobbied heavily for parish committees made up of lay people to give them a voice in church governance. Similar episodes occurred in other eastern European Catholic communities. A group of Slovak women in Bridgeport, Connecticut, resentful over their lack of influence in the selection of their pastor, chose a surprising and effective means of making their voices heard: they chased their priest into the rectory, which they threatened to destroy until the police intervened. Like these women, other ethnic Catholics chose not to form independent churches but remained within the established church while fighting for what they considered their due. They would clearly have an impact on Catholic parish governance as the twentieth century progressed.

Eastern Orthodoxy. The immigration of the early twentieth century would also occasion a massive increase in the number of Eastern Orthodox Christians in the United States, another tradition with a variety of forms. The two major ethnic forms of Orthodoxy in America at the turn of the century were Russian and Greek. Russian Orthodoxy had been present in the United States since the mid eighteenth century, starting in Alaska and slowly making inroads down the West Coast, but it was the large influx of Russian immigrants to the East Coast early in the early 1900s that brought Orthodoxy to the notice of mainstream America. The Russian Orthodox Church in America, which had just less than twenty thousand members in 1906, increased to nearly one hundred thousand by 1916. The Russian church's prominence caused some tension with the Greek Orthodox immigrants who

were beginning to arrive at the same time. In 1900 Archbishop Tikhon of the Russian church had celebrated a liturgy in Greek for immigrants in Chicago; when he performed a similar service in New York in 1904, the Greeks reacted by forming a Hellenic society to safeguard the "self-sufficiency" of Greeks in matters of belief and worship. Sporadic efforts would be made in subsequent decades to unite Orthodox Christians of different ethnic backgrounds into a single church, but given the disparate backgrounds of church members and the fact that no centralized authority structure had ever governed Orthodoxy in Europe, such efforts were undertaken to almost no avail. Some of the ethnic churches would experience schisms within their own ranks in America, further hampering any drive toward unity. The growth of the Russian and Greek branches, along with the arrival of Ukrainians, Syrians, and many others after 1900 meant that Orthodoxy would contribute a substantial number of streams to the pool of religious diversity in twentieth-century America.

The Uniates. Another ethnic group that experienced turmoil after the turn of the century were the Christians known as Carpatho-Rusyns, ethnic Ukrainians who came from the Hungarian border regions. Although they allowed their priests to marry and used the Byzantine rather than the Latin rite in their liturgies, these Uniates, as they were known, had been technically attached to the Roman Catholic Church, which granted them special exceptions. In the United States, however, their relations with the Catholic Church would sour dramatically, causing many of them to change their allegiance to Russian Orthodoxy. Many Catholic dioceses could not support a parish specifically for their Uniate congregants, who found, as the Germans and Poles had before them, that the Vatican could be very slow to respond to requests for accommodation in their local parish life. The Uniates, moreover, aroused some considerable hostility among the American Catholic clergy, who rejected their acceptance of clerical marriage and the interest they shared with their fellow eastern European immigrants in lay ownership of church property. As there were perhaps as many as 250,000 Uniates in this country at the turn of the century, the potential for conflict clearly existed. In 1891 Archbishop John Ireland of Saint Paul, Minnesota, had angrily dismissed a Uniate priest who had been called to serve at a Ukrainian Catholic church in Minneapolis. The priest refused to yield to the archbishop and accepted the pastorate in defiance of Ireland's wishes. He eventually took his congregation over to the Russian Orthodox Church. Dozens of parishes would follow suit in the subsequent twenty years, finding themselves uncomfortable even in predominantly Polish or Slovak churches of the Latin rite. America had challenged the Uniates to change their customs, but the bonds of tradition had proved too strong and resulted in substantial Catholic defections to Orthodoxy.

A RIOTOUS FUNERAL

The striking appearance and practices of Orthodox Jews caused consternation in the larger American community as well as among Reform Jews. In July 1902 after the death of Jacob Joseph, chief Orthodox rabbi of New York, some fifty thousand mourners followed his coffin in its procession from his home to the cemetery. *The New York Times* reported that "most of the men wore long beards. They were of the type of Russian Jew, so familiar to those who have visited the east side." As they passed a printing factory on the Lower East Side, chanting and lamenting, the factory workers began to yell, jeer, and throw buckets of water as well as iron debris onto the mourners from second-story windows. When the procession's leaders went into the factory foreman's office to complain, he drew a pistol on them and ordered them out. Or so ran the mourners' version of the story. The factory owner claimed that as his employees were returning from lunch they became entangled in fights already going on among the mourners, who were armed with umbrellas and soon unleashed a barrage of stones against the factory building. In any case the police were called in, applied force to the rioters, and arrested some Jews, thus sending the battle of blame into the courts. For Orthodox Jews the incident was an egregious violation of their freedom of religion: "Talk of Russia, where the Jew is said to be oppressed!" said one. "There never was such an outrage on our race as that which happened this afternoon." For others the combination of the Jews' unfamiliar customs and their powerful presence in New York was simply too much to bear quietly. "Even if the rioting had not marred the solemnity of the funeral procession," the *Times* reported, "the last honors to Chief Rabbi Jacob Joseph would have been a conspicuous event in the history of east side celebrations.... Never had ... there been another opportunity since those Jews came to number hundreds of thousands in this city for them to unite in a public observance that appealed so strongly to every one of them."

Sources: Martin E. Marty, *Modern American Religion, Volume 1: The Irony of It All, 1893–1919* (Chicago: University of Chicago Press, 1986);

"Riot Mars Solemn Procession," *New York Times*, 31 July 1902, p. 1.

Tension in American Judaism. While not technically causing schism, as there was no central established body from which to break away, ethnicity played a major role in the shaping of American Judaism in the early twentieth century. During the nineteenth century American Judaism had been dominated by German Jews who, in their homeland, had experienced the emancipation of Jews from their urban ghettos and had been profoundly influenced by the Enlightenment. In America these immigrants and their descendants shaped the Reform wing of Judaism, in which beliefs and practices had been liberalized and Americanized to a substantial extent. At the turn of the twentieth century Jews from eastern Europe began to arrive in large numbers, with massive waves of immigration following pogroms, outbreaks of state-sponsored violence against Jews, that occurred in Russia in 1881, 1891, and 1905. The conservatism, Yiddish language, and visible ritual life of these new Jewish arrivals were an embarrassment to many Reform Jews, just as the near-total absence of those same features in the latter constituted an outrage in the minds of many of the Orthodox immigrants.

Conservative Judaism and Ethnicity. The new arrivals from eastern Europe wished to take advantage of the religious freedom guaranteed them in America by practicing their religion in traditional ways but without fear of reprisal or persecution. The value placed by the Reform Jews on assimilation, then, was little short of incomprehensible to them. But besides helping to ensure that Judaism in America would never constitute a unified, monolithic entity, the tension between Reform and Orthodoxy also played a role in shaping the third major branch of American Judaism, the Conservative movement. Centered at the Jewish Theological Seminary in New York, which was under the direction of Solomon Schechter from 1902 to 1915, Conservative Judaism sought to tread a middle path between the Reform and the Orthodox branches of the religion. Thanks to religious liberty, Schechter argued, "we Jews need not sacrifice a single iota of our Torah"; but on the other hand neither was there anything in the Torah to prevent Jews from embracing "what is desirable in modern life." For Schechter and Conservative Judaism it was most important that the Jewish *people* should craft a new consensus about what could change and what should remained essential in their faith. With his notion of a "catholic Israel," Schechter thus paved the way for Judaism itself to be regarded as an ethnicity superseding the national origins of its adherents. Although Reform Jews had explicitly repudiated ethnic and national aims in their Pittsburgh Platform of 1885, the call to Jewish nationhood had gained a new resonance in 1896 when a Hungarian Jew named Theodor Herzl published *The Jewish State*, thus launching modern political Zionism. Schechter and other Conservative Jews would provide one of the earliest groundswells of support for Zionism in the United States, richly illustrating the extent to which ethnic identity and its implications were transforming the American religious landscape.

Sources:
Sydney E. Ahlstrom, *A Religious History of the American People* (New Haven: Yale University Press, 1972);

Catherine L. Albanese, *America: Religions and Religion,* second edition (Belmont, Cal.: Wadsworth, 1992);

Jay P. Dolan, *The American Catholic Experience* (Garden City, N.Y.: Doubleday, 1985);

Edwin Scott Gaustad, *A Religious History of America,* revised edition (San Francisco: HarperCollins, 1990);

C. Carlyle Haaland, "Shinto and Indigenous Chinese Religion," in *Encyclopedia of the American Religious Experience,* edited by Charles H. Lippy and Peter Williams (New York: Scribners, 1988);

Martin E. Marty, *Modern American Religion, Volume 1: The Irony of It All, 1893–1919* (Chicago: University of Chicago Press, 1986);

Charles S. Prebish, "Buddhism," in *Encyclopedia of the American Religious Experience,* edited by Charles H. Lippy and Peter Williams (New York: Scribners, 1988).

LIBERAL PROTESTANT THEOLOGY

The Continuation of a Trend. Liberal Protestant theology at the turn of the century represented a movement that had already gained a large measure of self-confidence and was now putting down deeper and more extensive roots as well as finding new spheres for the practical application of its major beliefs. The debate over Darwinian evolution had crested in the late nineteenth century, and it would not resurface with the same intensity until the Fundamentalist-Modernist disputes of the 1920s. Most of the liberal-conservative disagreements of the early twentieth century came down to the question of how the Bible was to be interpreted, with the liberals exercising ever more freedom in allegorizing the Scriptures to make them applicable to the present day and the conservatives growing ever more intransigent in their insistence on a literal reading of the Bible. The more strident the conservatives became, however, the more they risked alienating the ranks of middle-class Christians who identified with the progressive movement in American politics.

An Institutional Base. Political progressivism thus represented a close corollary to theological modernism, and both movements attracted the same kinds of adherents — largely urban, middle-class individuals who had some exposure to liberal and/or secular institutions of higher learning. It was in such institutions, both liberalized seminaries and secular universities, that liberal theology found a home and a power base. From their positions on the faculty of schools such as the University of Chicago and its Divinity School, Harvard University, Boston University, and a host of Protestant seminaries, modernist theologians published prolifically and implemented many of their ideas about education, ecumenism, and social reform. The early decades of this century, then, saw liberal ideas being expressed through a growing number of organizations and institutions.

Christian Nurture. One of the areas in which liberal theology had the greatest effect in the early 1900s was religious education. The Religious Education Association, founded in 1903 by George A. Coe of Northwestern University and the famous humanist philosopher John Dewey at the University of Chicago, provided the basis

AN ECUMENICAL WARNING

Liberal and conservative Protestants were facing off against each other on many related issues in the early 1900s. The heresy trial of Episcopal priest Algernon S. Crapsey in New York in 1906 illustrated how several theological questions functioned simultaneously in the growing debate. The church court that tried Crapsey found him guilty of contradicting avowals he had made at his ordination, including his affirmation that the Bible is the word of God and his pledge to uphold the doctrines expressed in the Apostles' Creed, the Nicene Creed, and the Episcopal Book of Common Prayer. Crapsey was dismissed from his post for not adhering to biblical literalism and for adopting a scientific mentality that questioned creedal statements about the resurrection of Jesus and the virgin birth as well as for challenging the Episcopal Church's unique statement of theological truth. Crapsey's lawyer, Edward Shepard, saw in the verdict a trend toward religious exclusivism and censorship that could seriously threaten the church's influence in modern society. Pleading the case for more freedom of expression and a more ecumenical theology, Shepard did not hesitate to make this threat clear to the leaders of the Protestant Episcopal Church. "If they shall take the narrow, sectarian view of the work of the Church which the majority of this court has taken, then, of course, the future of the Protestant Episcopal Church is merely the future of a single Christian sect in our country, and far from the most important one."

Sources: "Dr. Crapsey a Heretic; Court for Suspension," *New York Times,* 16 May 1906, p. 9;

Winthrop Hudson and John Corrigan, *Religion in America,* fifth edition (New York: Macmillan, 1987).

for Sunday school curricula that focused on the humanity and social activism of Jesus and introduced high-school students to historical and critical methods of Bible study. Coe, Dewey, and colleagues such as Newman Smyth in New Haven thus secularized even Sunday schools, but they still felt they were preserving the churches' essential task of turning out good citizens with a strong sense of moral responsibility. They focused on ethical and practical, rather than doctrinal, concerns and continued to shape educational programs in Protestant seminaries in ways that reflected this new agenda. By the turn of the century Harvard Divinity School had created a social ethics department through the efforts of Francis Greenwood Peabody, a Unitarian minister who had become the

Newman Smyth, a radical ecumenicist

first professor of that subject in an American theological school. The men at the forefront of this liberal trend in religious education all acknowledged a debt to Horace Bushnell, the nineteenth-century Congregational pastor whose influential book *Christian Nurture* (1847) had stressed the need for an educational program that would foster moral, as well as intellectual, development. In the 1900s a new generation of liberals would build on Bushnell's legacy by establishing new seminary programs to address the moral demands posed by an increasingly secular society.

Ecumenism. Another major outlet for liberal Protestant thought in the early 1900s was the continuing drive toward ecumenical union between the churches. Ecumenism became an increasingly popular topic as churches faced what they perceived as their diminishing influence in the larger culture and wondered how best to respond with an effective public presence. Many liberals became involved in efforts to improve society and looked to ecumenical cooperation as the best means of coordinating and carrying out major social and missionary programs. Proponents of ecumenism favored a variety of options, ranging from a federation of churches to an

actual "organic" merger, or the dissolving of denominational boundaries. Federationists, while opposing "creedal rigidity" and claims of absolute truth on the part of any single denomination, nonetheless recognized denominational distinctions as insurmountable. Shailer Mathews of the University of Chicago Divinity School was one of the leading exponents of such a view. More radical in their ecumenism were men such as Newman Smyth, who saw the cultural dominance of American Protestantism passing with the times. But rather than look for ways in which Protestants could regain their privileged position, Smyth saw instead the perfect opportunity to create an even greater religious establishment. He even went so far as to suggest that the long-standing breach between Protestantism and Roman Catholicism might be healed along with Protestant denominational divisions. Smyth's *Passing Protestantism and Coming Catholicism* (1908) set forth his vision for the new, unified church. Although the number of Catholic theological modernists in America was small and their work had been censured by the pope in 1907, Smyth still felt that liberal Protestants could learn much from a collaboration with their Catholic fellow travelers. He especially hoped to see the new church recognize that religious doctrines evolve over time in response to specific social contexts, a fact that would place serious limits on the possible truth claims of church creeds and foster theological relativism.

Federationists and Social Action. Smyth's radical views placed him in the minority of liberal Protestants, however, and in the same year that he published *Passing Protestantism* the federationists won the day. Following up on a resolution adopted at the 1905 Interchurch Conference on Federation, delegates from thirty-three denominations voted in 1908 to establish the Federal Council of Churches of Christ in America. The federationists' practical motives for ecumenical union were clearly illustrated by the speed with which the new council addressed the major social concerns of the day. At their first meeting council members voiced their support for a statement on "The Church and Modern Industry," which, closely following an earlier Methodist Social Creed, gave strong support to a host of labor-reform proposals. Through religious education, federation, and their commitment to social action, many prominent Americans had crafted a Protestantism that has maintained a highly visible presence in modern society. While secular detractors could not argue with their effectiveness, opposition to the social emphasis of the federationists soon began to grow within the Christian community. Liberal Christianity might be influential in society, conservatives would say, but is it Christianity? Over time, the middle would largely disappear from American Protestantism as the liberals turned more and more toward practical and social concerns and the conservatives became more and more appalled at the theological changes that often accompanied that shift. The lines for a prolonged and often ugly religious battle in America were being drawn.

Sources:

Sydney E. Ahlstrom, *A Religious History of the American People* (New Haven: Yale University Press, 1972);

William R. Hutchinson, *The Modernist Impulse in American Protestantism* (Cambridge, Mass.: Harvard University Press, 1976);

William R. Miller, ed., *Contemporary American Protestant Thought, 1900–1970* (Indianapolis: Bobbs-Merrill, 1973).

MILLENNIALISM

The Thousand-Year Reign. As conservative Protestants became ever more strident in their insistence on the inerrancy of Scriptures, millennial speculation could not help but enjoy a renewed vigor as well. The term *millennialism* comes from the last book of the Bible, Revelation, and refers specifically to the thousand-year reign of peace that is predicted in connection with other events of the apocalypse, or "end days," of human time. In a general sense millennialism includes a wide range of beliefs about the establishment of the kingdom of God on earth. Since its inception America has proved itself to be a fertile ground for the proliferation of variant and often competing millennial visions. Many of the most vigorous religious movements at the turn of the century were steeped in millennialism, even if their doctrines remained somewhat vague and confusing. The growing sectarian movements Seventh-Day Adventism and Jehovah's Witnesses were based in large part on the millennial beliefs of their founders, Ellen G. White and Charles Taze Russell, respectively. In the dawning days of Protestant Fundamentalism, however, a veritable cottage industry arose devoted to the precise interpretation of Revelation and other biblical prophecies, and timetables of history bafflingly rich in detail were crafted from some of the most obscure passages in Scripture. The first decade of the twentieth century truly marked a sort of millennial dawn over the American religious landscape.

Conflicting Visions. The two major divisions in American millennial speculation — pre- and postmillenialism — take their names from their views on when the Second Coming of Jesus will occur, whether his advent will be before or after the thousand-year period. Underlying this distinction are vastly differing views on the role of human beings in the unfolding of the apocalyptic drama. For the premillennialist the timetable includes a period of tribulation, characterized in part by worsening social conditions, before the return of Jesus to establish the kingdom of God. The postmillennialist view, on the other hand, holds that human efforts to perfect society will bring about the beginning of the millennium, and that only after humans have established the kingdom on earth will Jesus return.

Postmillennialism. In the first decade of the twentieth century, the most visible adherents of postmillennial views were the social gospelers. Men such as Walter Rauschenbusch advanced the belief that a reformed social

Postmillennialist Walter Rauschenbusch

order would evolve into the kingdom of God. Reflecting the social gospel's roots in liberal theology, this doctrine was based on an allegorical interpretation of scriptural passages referring to the kingdom. Other liberal theologians, notably Arthur Cushman McGiffert of Union Theological Seminary in New York, defined the kingdom in terms very similar to Rauschenbusch's. McGiffert wrote in 1909 that "the kingdom of God was the burden of his preaching, not a kingdom lying in another world beyond the skies but established here and now" and characterized by "the control of the lives of men and of all their relationships one with another and of all the institutions in which those relationships find expression by the spirit of Jesus Christ who has shown us what God is and what he would have this world be." For liberal Protestants and social reformers, the kingdom of God came about through human, not divine, intervention in society.

Premillennialism. In stark contrast to the postmillennialist view, premillennialists believed the establishment of the kingdom would be a cataclysmic, supernatural event, utterly transforming or entirely eliminating human social systems. Understandably, then, millennialism would be one of the many factors that served to widen the gulf between liberal and conservative Protestants. Again

After 1907 Cyrus Ingerson Scofield not only worked on his famous *Reference Bible* but also promulgated dispensationalist doctrines through his Correspondence Bible School. One of the classic statements of his beliefs is the essay "Rightly Dividing the Word of Truth," first published in 1907. In the essay Scofield lays out his complex vision of humankind's dispensational past, present, and future. Time is divided into the following seven dispensations, each characterized by a new "test" of humankind from God and ending with humankind's "utter failure" to meet the challenge.

I. *Man Innocent* — Beginning with creation, this dispensation lasted until the fall of Adam and Eve.

II. *Man Under Conscience* — From the expulsion of Adam and Eve from the Garden of Eden through a period of increasing wickedness despite humanity's newly acquired knowledge of good and evil until the great Flood.

III. *Man in Authority over the Earth* — From the Flood to the building of the tower of Babel, an act of human arrogance that resulted in the "Confusion of Tongues" and the dispersion of humanity across the globe.

IV. *Man Under Promise* — Beginning with the covenant made between God and Abraham this dispensation ends with the punishment of the Israelites through their slavery in Egypt.

V. *Man Under Law* — This dispensation includes the giving of the Law to Moses, its desecration, and the Babylonian Exile of 587 B.C. It extends to the return of the Jews to Palestine and the crucifixion of Jesus.

VI. *Man Under Grace* — The present dispensation, which is near its end. The only age focused on the Christian church rather than on the nation of Israel, this dispensation begins with the "sacrificial death of the Lord Jesus Christ," with its promise of salvation for all who will believe. It will end in a time characterized by "an unbelieving world and an apostate Church."

VII. *Man Under the Personal Reign of Christ* — The thousand-year rule of Christ prophesied in Revelation is to be preceded by the "descent of the Lord from Heaven, when the sleeping saints will be raised" and together with believers then living caught up "to meet the Lord in the air" (the rapture) and a seven-year period of tribulation. The millennium will begin with "the personal return of the Lord to the earth in power and glory." At the end of the thousand years Satan will be unchained long enough to muster his forces for the final battle between good and evil (Armageddon), the dead shall be raised and judged, and then a "new heaven and a new earth" shall be established for all eternity.

Source: C. I. Scofield, "Rightly Dividing the Word of Truth," in *The Holy Bible*, a reproduction of the first Scofield Reference Bible (Grand Rapids, Mich.: World Publishing, n.d.).

the issue of biblical literalism provided much of the basis for the dispute. Opposing the notion that the Second Coming would not happen until after the world "has submitted to the spiritual reign of Christ for one thousand years," premillennialist Cyrus Ingerson Scofield argued in 1907 that "It would be impossible to 'watch' and 'wait' for an event which we knew could not occur for more than one thousand years," appealing to the plain sense of scriptural injunctions to be prepared for the return of Jesus.

Premillennial Tribulations. Literal interpretations, however, proved to be tricky business when dealing with prophetic Bible books such as Daniel and Revelation, and premillennialists experienced their share of internal dispute. One of the most prominent examples was the rift that took shape in 1901 and 1902 over the timing of the Second Coming, the "rapture," in which the saints (individuals who had been saved) would be taken up to meet Jesus in midair, and the period of tribulation. Scofield was a staunch "pretribulationist" who believed that the

rapture would precede the tribulation, which would in turn be followed by the Second Coming. Robert Cameron headed up the posttribulationist party, which rejected the doctrine of the rapture and looked for the appearance of Jesus after the tribulation. The dispute escalated into a schism in 1902, when Cameron wrote an eight-part series, "To the Friends of Prophetic Truth," in which he charged that pretribulationism had sprung "from the lips of a heretic" and was "supported by the testimony of demons." Despite Cameron's harsh accusations, the majority of America's premillennialists in the early 1900s adhered to the pretribulationist view. But this division even within premillennialism provided further evidence that the kingdom of God was a hotly contested place.

Postmillennialism and World Missions. Most millennialists shared at least one thought in common — they agreed that the worldwide spreading of the gospel was a necessary prerequisite to the establishment of the kingdom of God. But here again they differed dramatically on the question of what result to expect from their missionary efforts. Postmillennialists were more likely to look for the conversion of the world as a sign of the gradual development of the kingdom on earth. Their ambition, of course, left them vulnerable to disappointment when actual gains were modest or when an even worse fate befell mission efforts. The Boxer Rebellion of 1900 in China, after which many American missionaries were left dead or missing, fed into a developing view that missions faced no less than a "crisis" situation and needed to reevaluate their goals and expectations. Liberals such as William Newton Clarke began articulating such a view at the turn of the century. Clarke saw contemporary social conditions as posing a serious challenge to evangelical optimism but advocated "patience" in missionary endeavors rather than their suspension.

Spreading the Word. Premillennialists contrastingly saw the task of world evangelization as a pressing need, because of their underlying belief in the imminence of the Second Coming. There was urgency in the efforts of groups like the Student Volunteer Movement, whose slogan was "the evangelization of the world in this generation," the title of director John R. Mott's book of 1900. Perhaps of necessity, however, given their restricted time frame, premillennialist missionaries did not measure their goals in such comprehensive terms as the postmillennialists did. Critics of the movement, in fact, pointed out the paradoxical nature of massive missionary efforts undertaken with no real expectation of success. But premillennial evangelists pointed out that the only burden on them was to provide all the peoples of the world with *access* to the gospel. Whether or not they accepted it was considered largely beyond the responsibility, or even concern, of the evangelist. Even Mott, perhaps the most tireless worker in the world missionary field, observed that "We have no warrant for believing that all who have the Gospel preached unto them will accept it. . . . We are not responsible for the results of our work, however, but for our fidelity and thoroughness." As Scofield explained, "It is . . . sometimes said that [the second] coming cannot occur until after the world has been converted by the preaching of the Gospel," but this view is "wholly erroneous," because "The purpose of God in this dispensation is declared to be, not the conversion of the world, but to 'gather out of the Gentiles a people for His name.'" Again Scofield appealed to the literal sense of relevant scriptural passages that provided the justification for the seemingly contradictory premillennialist missionary program.

Dispensationalism. The strain of premillennialism that Scofield embraced was one of the most detailed systems of millennial speculation ever to take hold in America. Known as dispensational premillennialism, it had its roots in the teachings of an Englishman, John Nelson Darby, who had toured the United States in the 1870s. Darby taught that history could be seen as the succession of various ages, or dispensations, each of

which was characterized by a different relationship between human beings and God. The present time marked for him the penultimate dispensation, that which directly preceded the return of Christ and the subsequent millennium, both of which were expected to occur soon. Darby's teaching gained popularity in America not only through his lectures here but also through the influence of the late nineteenth century's most prominent revivalists. Foremost among these was Dwight L. Moody, the Chicago-based preacher who himself had lectured in England, where he had been exposed to the new doctrines. His Moody Bible Institute and the many Bible and prophetic conferences he organized became the primary vehicles for transmitting dispensationalist teachings in this country. The Student Volunteer Movement was an outgrowth of one of Moody's conferences, which accounts for the premillennial overtones in its mission statements, despite the fact that Mott himself never explicitly advocated any millennial beliefs.

The Scofield Bible. The dispensationalist lineage of Scofield is much easier to trace; at the turn of the century he was serving as pastor of the "Moody Church" in East Northfield, Massachusetts. He would later produce the most enduring statement of dispensational premillennialism in America, *The Scofield Reference Bible*. First published in 1909, the *Reference Bible* was a heavily annotated and cross-referenced edition of the King James translation. The *Reference Bible* explained the progress of the dispensations that had already passed and provided detailed explanations of the prophecies regarding the dawning of the millennium. It went through a second edition in Scofield's lifetime, and another revision in 1966 helped ensure its continuing influence beyond dispensationalist circles into the sphere of conservative Protestantism as a whole. Dispensationalism also exerted a profound influence on the burgeoning Pentecostal movement in the first decade of this century, expanding both the reach and the variety of millennial thinking still further in American religion. As the 1900s began, vast numbers of Americans clearly believed that, somehow or other, "Jesus is coming soon."

Sources:
Sydney E. Ahlstrom, *A Religious History of the American People* (New Haven: Yale University Press, 1972);

William R. Hutchinson, *The Modernist Impulse in American Protestantism* (Cambridge, Mass.: Harvard University Press, 1976);

Charles H. Lippy, "Millennialism and Adventism," in *Encyclopedia of the American Religious Experience*, edited by Lippy and Peter Williams (New York: Scribners, 1988);

George M. Marsden, *Fundamentalism and American Culture: The Shaping of Twentieth Century Evangelicalism, 1870–1925* (New York: Oxford University Press, 1980);

Ernest Sandeen, *The Roots of Fundamentalism: British and American Millenarianism, 1800–1930* (Chicago: University of Chicago Press, 1970);

C. I. Scofield, *Rightly Dividing the Word of Truth* (Oakland, Cal.: Western Book and Tract, n.d.);

Timothy P. Weber, *Living in the Shadow of the Second Coming: American Premillennialism, 1875–1982* (Grand Rapids, Mich.: Academie Books, 1983).

Holiness evangelist Maria B. Woodworth-Etter

THE PENTECOSTAL MOVEMENT

The Latter Rain. Among the many different events that millennialists had come to hope for and expect, one was a repeat of the Pentecost described in the biblical book the Acts of the Apostles. In Acts 2, the original twelve disciples of Jesus had gathered for the Jewish holiday of Shavuoth, or in the Greek, Pentecost, the commemoration of the giving of the Law to Moses. The Holy Spirit then descended on them in the form of a strong wind and tongues of fire that came to rest on their heads. The Spirit bestowed upon the apostles several gifts, or *charisms*, including the ability to speak in other languages (the "gift of tongues"), to heal, and to prophesy. The early twentieth century saw the beginnings of what would become an extensive charismatic movement in American religion as Protestants of many hues looked for these gifts

to be replicated among present-day believers. This "latter rain" of the Spirit would be a clear indication of the imminence of the Second Coming of Jesus, and the Pentecostal movement would represent its most dramatic expression.

Holiness. The Holiness movement that had flourished in nineteenth-century America provided the broad precedent from which the Pentecostal movement arose. Primarily a Methodist phenomenon, Holiness centered around the doctrine of sanctification that had been promulgated by Methodism's founder, John Wesley. For Wesley, conversion was a necessary but not a sufficient indicator of a full Christian life. To achieve that full life, a believer needed to experience a "second blessing," sanctification, whereby all remaining traces of sin would be cleansed from his or her soul. The doctrine of sanctification allowed for a wide variety of interpretation, and throughout the nineteenth century revivalist preachers often focused less on the attainment of perfect sinlessness and more on sanctification as an endowment of the Holy Spirit that enabled the believer to serve God more fully. Within Holiness circles, then, sanctification became synonymous with baptism in the Holy Spirit, a necessary follow-up to the baptism in water that accompanied conversion.

A "Tremendous Lot of Fanaticism." The Holiness movement had grown up within the major Protestant denominations, especially through the immensely popular Methodist revivals of the early nineteenth century. But as the movement progressed, the entrenchment of middle-class sensibilities in the denominations led many disillusioned Holiness believers to leave the established churches in favor of loosely organized associations and camp meetings. Their exit was not always voluntary, for as much as they frowned on the complacency of middle-class churchgoers, they were themselves scorned for the intense emotionalism that often accompanied the Holiness experience. One prominent Holiness evangelist, Maria B. Woodworth-Etter, wrote vividly of the scenes she encountered at camp meetings in the 1880s: people shouting, screaming, and fainting; miraculous healings; and, possibly as early as 1890, people speaking in "unknown languages." Even within the Holiness movement itself, there were disputes over what ought to be the boundaries of "liberty in the Spirit"; one preacher bemoaned the "tremendous lot of fanaticism" evident at many camp meetings. But many Holiness believers continued to look precisely to those emotional outbursts for proof of the experience of sanctification. Predominantly lower class and by the end of the century predominantly unchurched, these believers would provide the nascent Pentecostal movement with the bulk of its members.

The Apostolic Faith. Other important precedents for the Pentecostal movement were the Keswick doctrines (named for Keswick, England, where a series of Bible conferences were held) and the Apostolic Faith founded by Charles Fox Parham. The Keswick doctrines, which

Specimen of Agnes Ozman's handwriting, which she claimed to have been inspired by God.

baptism received by Jesus's disciples. When he returned on 30 December, he claimed that each of his students had individually reached the conclusion that speaking in tongues provided definitive proof that the believer had received the Spirit. Parham's students then began to pray in earnest that this proof might be manifested among them. Their prayers were answered on the first day of 1901, when Agnes Ozman, after asking Parham to lay his hands on her in prayer, suddenly broke out praising God in "several languages." For the next three days she claimed to speak and write only Chinese, a language of which she had had no previous knowledge. Other students followed suit in a massive "outpouring of the Spirit" on 3 January, during which some even claimed to see tongues of fire descending as they had on the original Pentecost. Parham himself spoke in Swedish and other languages, firmly establishing the Pentecostal doctrine that the gift of tongues provided the only real proof of the baptism they sought.

From Topeka to Los Angeles. The bloom came quickly off the rose for most of Parham's students who had experienced the new Pentecost; most of them had abandoned his school, which had moved to Kansas City, by the end of the year. Furthermore, unfavorable news coverage and unsuccessful mission efforts in Kansas City and Lawrence, Kansas, seemed to spell a quick end to Parham's Apostolic Faith. By 1903 he had shifted his focus back to works of healing and set up a tent meeting in Galena, Kansas, where a months-long revival yielded large audiences, hundreds of converts, and some cases of speaking in tongues. Parham then moved through the tristate area where Kansas, Missouri, and Oklahoma meet, establishing several Apostolic Faith missions before heading south to the rapidly growing Houston area. In 1905, after healing the wife of a prominent lawyer (whose suit for injuries in a streetcar accident had been widely publicized), Parham was able to establish a Bible college similar to Bethel, where prophecy and messages in tongues were interpreted as teachings direct from the Holy Spirit. Among the students at the Houston school was William J. Seymour, a black Holiness preacher who had come to Parham's school after hearing Parham's governess speak in tongues at a Negro mission. While at Parham's school, Seymour met Miss Neeley Terry, a member of a Holiness mission in Los Angeles. It was in response to an invitation from her that Seymour asked Parham's blessing to carry the work to Los Angeles, even though he himself had not yet received the baptism and the gift of tongues. Though Parham was reluctant, he agreed, and in January 1906 Seymour set off to become the semiofficial founder of the Pentecostal movement from his headquarters on Azusa Street.

included dispensational premillennialism and a distinction between sanctification and baptism in the Spirit, were embraced in America by Dwight L. Moody and Reuben A. Torrey. For these revivalists, sanctification was a gradual development toward perfection (though that goal could never be reached in this life), and baptism in the Spirit represented a special endowment of power for service in the worldwide revival the Keswick adherents expected to coincide with the turning of the twentieth century. This revival would represent a second Pentecost, providing evidence for the nearness of the millennium. Between 1903 and 1905 revivals had broken out at local levels in Wales, England, India, Norway, and elsewhere, while hopeful people everywhere prayed earnestly that the sparks of revival would spread quickly. People were also praying for revival in Los Angeles, and 1906 would see the fulfillment of those prayers when a disciple of Parham's Apostolic Faith would arrive there to establish a mission.

The Spirit Falls on Topeka. After falling out with the Methodist Church in which he was a minister, Parham had worked as an independent Holiness preacher and healer in Kansas. In October 1900 he founded the College of Bethel in Topeka, where students prayed, fasted, studied the Bible, and experienced healings, all in anticipation of receiving baptism in the Spirit and thus attaining the fulfillment of the Christian life. Parham became especially concerned with distinguishing the true baptism from the experience of sanctification, and it appears that by the end of 1900 he had formulated the doctrine that was to undergird the entire Pentecostal movement. Leaving for a brief mission campaign in December of that year, Parham instructed his students to study the text of Acts 2 to discern what it provided as evidence of the

The Azusa Street Revival. Seymour's mission on Azusa Street has historically been regarded as the cradle of the Pentecostal movement, and many of the early leaders of the worldwide movement had direct or indirect connections to it. Of course in the early days few would

One of the notable features of the early Pentecostal movement was the degree of racial and ethnic diversity, as well as gender equity, among its membership and its leadership. The welcoming of minorities and members of the lowest social classes — groups often termed "the disinherited" — played a significant role in its early success, and the movement's leaders did not hesitate to make the most of their inclusiveness. Just as the original Pentecost of Acts 2 resulted in the apostles evangelizing citizens "from every nation under heaven," so in the Pentecostal movement did "Ethiopians, Chinese, Indians, Mexicans and other nationalities worship together," proclaimed the first issue of *The Apostolic Faith*, the newspaper of the Azusa Street Mission. Many more ethnic groups than that author named were also involved, as were women (reflecting tendencies toward gender equality that were already present in both black churches and the Holiness movement). As one observer noted, "No instrument that God can use is rejected on account of color or dress or lack of education."

Source: Robert Mapes Anderson, *Vision of the Disinherited: The Making of American Pentecostalism* (Peabody, Mass.: Hendrickson, 1979).

have predicted the sweeping influence Seymour's humble mission would eventually exert. After being barred from Neeley Terry's mission for preaching unorthodox beliefs about the baptism, Seymour began participating in prayer meetings in the homes of adherents of Holiness churches or Keswick-style revivals. Parham had sent reinforcements from Houston in early April, including a woman known for her ability to induce the gift of tongues in others with the touch of her hands, and shortly thereafter Seymour and others finally received the baptism during a house meeting. One of the participants in this meeting subsequently spoke in tongues during a service at her church, and the resulting burst of interest enabled Seymour to rent an abandoned African Methodist Episcopal church on Azusa Street for his meetings. Although meetings went on at the mission twenty-four hours a day, progress remained slow, largely because of the Pentecostal insistence that the mission be completely directed by the Spirit, which precluded advertising and formal organization. But the lasting impact of the Apostolic Faith Gospel Mission, as it was known, would come not from its own size or permanence but rather from the ranks of converts that took the message and experience of Azusa Street back to their hometowns across the country and around the world.

The Spread of Pentecostalism. One of the tasks for which Pentecostalists in the 1900s believed they were fitting themselves by receiving the baptism and the gift of tongues was the worldwide spread of the gospel thought to be a necessary precedent for the Second Coming. Indeed, one of the main reasons Parham settled on glossolalia (speaking in tongues) as the sure mark of baptism came from his belief that this gift would allow Christians to proclaim the gospel throughout the world in the native languages of the people they visited without needing any formal training to do so. Seymour and the other elders who ran the Azusa Street mission dispatched many missionaries into the worldwide field, but virtually all of them were forced to return, admitting failure after a short time. More significant would be the efforts of preachers who traveled throughout the United States, spreading the Pentecostal message largely in Holiness circles and most successfully in the South.

Internal Obstacles. In becoming established as a religious force, the Pentecostal movement faced substantial obstacles. Foremost among these was the Pentecostals' own reluctance to establish or build permanent churches, because of their firm belief in the imminent end of the world. Reflecting the tendencies of the antecedent Holiness movement, Pentecostalism flourished in individual congregations, camp meetings, and a host of publications devoted to spreading the movement's core message about the second Pentecost and the imminent return of Jesus, but the movement lacked structural cohesion. The Assemblies of God, the largest Pentecostal denomination, came into existence when a group of local churches associated in 1914, only to experience considerable stress in its first two years over doctrinal issues. And aside from contentiousness, Pentecostal leaders had to deal with other problems as well; Parham himself was indicted by civil authorities in Texas on undisclosed charges late in 1906 and accused of sodomy by opponents. Seymour and others who had come into the movement under Parham's influence were forced to try to repudiate him but defend the movement at the same time.

Opposition. As might be expected, the dramatic displays of speaking in tongues brought ridicule and hostility down on the movement at the hands of the press. Even the mainstream Holiness movement rejected the extremes to which the Pentecostals carried their principles, as did the Fundamentalist wing emerging within the mainline denominations. In 1906 the executive committee of the South California Holiness Association voted to prohibit its members from either speaking in tongues or encouraging the practice on camp grounds, and other Holiness leaders made much more intemperate statements regarding the "Holy Ghost bedlam" witnessed at Pentecostal meetings. In many Holiness churches, the acceptance of the Pentecostal message by some of the members often occasioned a schism. Given its internal problems and such strong opposition, the Pentecostal movement threatened to fall apart almost as soon as it had begun. The Azusa Street revivals had petered out by 1908, and with few exceptions the initial fervor was never

Charles Fox Parham (center, seated) and his followers in Houston (1905)

matched again. Clearly Pentecostalism had an uphill battle to survive, but it did and continues to prosper. Pentecostal denominations have grown slowly and steadily over the decades, and in almost any American city one can find at least one church where the gifts of the Holy Spirit are still being poured out.

Sources:

Robert Mapes Anderson, *Vision of the Disinherited: The Making of American Pentecostalism* (Peabody, Mass.: Hendrickson, 1979);

Grant Wacker, "Pentecostalism," *Encyclopedia of the American Religious Experience,* edited by Charles H. Lippy and Peter Williams (New York: Scribners, 1988).

SOCIAL CHRISTIANITY, CHRISTIAN SOCIALISM, AND THE SOCIAL GOSPEL

The Social Crisis. American society at the turn of the century stood in the middle of a process of industrialization and urbanization that had begun after the Civil War and would continue until the Great Depression. The gap between upper and lower classes was widening throughout this period, as immigration swelled the ranks of the laboring class while industrialists and financiers — some soothed by the late-nineteenth-century liberal Protestant Gospel of Wealth, which made poverty a sin and prosperity a Christian duty — consolidated their monopolies and raised their profit margins. Labor unions were just

beginning to gain a foothold, often being born into an atmosphere of strikes and violence. No safeguards existed to prevent industrialists from demanding long hours and dangerous work, and labor abuses of the sort documented by immigrant journalist Jacob Riis were in abundance. The churches of America could look out their front doors and see immigrant families living in poverty and squalor. Ministers began to ask challenging questions about their Christian duty to rescue and elevate such souls, and few religious people could ignore the plight of the urban working class. But at the same time, there was great disagreement over the proper response to the perceived social crisis. The social reform efforts that were being designed and implemented at the turn of the century constitute the broad category of Social Christianity, which can be subdivided into those who felt reform was best undertaken at the level of the individual and those who sought change at the level of the socioeconomic system.

Christian Socialism. Many who favored systematic change spoke fervently of the need to introduce a morally based cooperative element into capitalism but nonetheless took pains to distance themselves from political socialism. Some, however, were not at all shy about using the term *socialist* to describe themselves, even when their

Father John A. Ryan, Catholic advocate of a social gospel

The Social Gospel. The advocates for a social gospel, less extreme than the Christian socialists but still committed to reform at the institutional level, included a variety of preachers and theologians who devoted themselves assiduously to the task of defining what would constitute a truly Christian social order. One of the most celebrated early proponents of this movement begun in the 1880s was Washington Gladden, a Congregationalist pastor who worked in Massachusetts and then, from 1882 to 1914, in Columbus, Ohio. Gladden championed the cause of organized labor, called for public ownership of utilities, and propounded — in many of the three dozen books he authored — the need for cooperation (including between labor and management) to replace competition as the driving force of the capitalist engine. In 1900 Gladden ran for a seat on the Columbus City Council, and during his two-year term he gained insight into the ways in which local governments could address the social problems of their constituents.

Leaders. The social gospel found another tireless crusader in Walter Rauschenbusch, a Baptist minister who served at a German church in the Hell's Kitchen district of New York City and later enjoyed a long career as a professor at Rochester Seminary (later Colgate-Rochester Divinity School). In a series of influential books, starting with *Christianity and the Social Crisis* in 1907, Rauschenbusch set forth his vision of the kingdom of God, which he believed could be realized on earth by Christianizing the social order. Francis Greenwood Peabody, a professor of social ethics at the Harvard Divinity School, sought to educate both undergraduate and graduate students in issues pertaining to "the social question," and Rauschenbusch pointed to Peabody's major work, *Jesus and the Social Question* (1900), as a particularly masterful treatment of the topic. Among Catholics, the foremost theologian of the social gospel was John A. Ryan, a priest whose doctoral dissertation for Catholic University, *A Living Wage,* was published in 1906 with an introduction by prominent economist Richard T. Ely. Ryan became a professor at Catholic University and continued to agitate not only for the minimum wage but also for the eight-hour day, regulations on the labor of children and women, workmen's compensation, and arbitration in labor disputes, thus addressing many of the social ills that social gospelers targeted for reform.

Legacy. Although it has been estimated that the message of the social gospel was embraced by perhaps only one-third of even the liberal theologians within Protestantism, the legacy of its great spokesmen can be traced not only through the history of theology but also through the growing concern many churches would exhibit throughout the twentieth century for social justice and social reform. Perhaps this concern was nowhere more evident than at the founding, in 1908, of the Federal Council of Churches, an ecumenical body composed of thirty-three Protestant denominations that adopted a "Social Creed" calling for the abolition of child labor,

denominational bodies turned decidedly unreceptive to their work. These politically active Christians included William Dwight Porter Bliss, a former Congregationalist and Episcopalian, who adopted British Christian Socialist ideas and in 1906 joined the Christian Socialist Fellowship founded by Vida Scudder. He also joined the burgeoning Socialist Party, as did George Herron, a former Congregationalist pastor who gave the nominating speech for Eugene V. Debs's presidential bid in 1904. In 1909 a previously existing group, the Catholic Socialists of Chicago, founded the Catholic Socialist Society, which was affiliated with both the Christian Socialist Fellowship and the Socialist Party, despite the pope's repeated denouncements of socialism on the grounds that it violated the sanctity of private property. Even these self-styled socialists, however, were careful to distinguish their views from those of Karl Marx. They spoke more generally of cooperative economic ventures that valued the well-being of all above the profit of a few, and, of course, they sought an economic system that would be grounded in Christian love. But perhaps because of their willingness to become involved in the wider world of socialist politics, the sphere of influence of these radical reformers, both within and outside of the churches, remained small.

Salvation Army "slum sisters," appointed to live among and serve the poor

regulations on women's labor, a six-day workweek, and conciliation and arbitration in labor disputes. Clearly one feature of twentieth-century American religion would be a belief on the part of the churches that they could and must speak out about the morality of the existing social order.

Individual Salvation. Proponents of the most conservative form of social Christianity inverted the formula of the social gospelers and argued that the salvation of individuals preceded the salvation of society both chronologically and in importance. Many church leaders felt that the proper way for religious organizations to address the "social crisis" was simply to do the job they were meant to do more thoroughly and conscientiously. A purified social order would be the result, not the starting point, for such efforts; the focus was firmly on rescuing the individual, removing him or her from detrimental social conditions, rather than removing those conditions from society. Examples of this approach to social Christianity took

the form of various social service agencies. Urban rescue missions, settlement houses, Young Men's and Young Women's Christian Associations, and institutional churches (which offered educational and recreational programs in addition to liturgies and often had a gymnasium and other buildings attached to the main church) had sprung up in response to urbanization in the late nineteenth century, and they maintained a visible presence into the twentieth. Ongoing crusades for temperance also played a significant role in the overall effort to redeem the individual. Many denominations began to extend their reaches so far into the social sphere through rescue and relief efforts that departments of social action or other formal organizations were founded to coordinate these activities.

The Social Mission. Social service organizations sometimes became denominations unto themselves, the most prominent example being the Salvation Army, which often incurred criticism on the grounds that its soldiers focused too much on physical redemption and not enough on the spiritual salvation its name implied. Such criticism may or may not have been justified; certainly Evangeline Booth, the Salvation Army's U.S. commander from 1904 to 1934, resented the charge that her organization was religiously suspect. What it illustrates, however, is the extent to which even conservative religious bodies had thrown their church doors open and carried their message out into the secular world, rather than waiting for individuals to renounce the world and come in to them. Writings from this period often evoked the image of lost souls wandering by the doors of a church where a service or a revival was in progress; the question, either implied or stated, was, what must the church do to reach those wanderers? Increasingly, religious leaders had come to the conclusion that the church must go out to them and make them receptive to the gospel by providing for their most pressing physical needs. Almost across the board Christianity had become a truly social phenomenon.

Sources:

Aaron I. Abell, *American Catholicism and Social Action: A Search for Social Justice, 1865–1950* (Garden City, N.Y.: Hanover House, 1960);

Sydney E. Ahlstrom, *A Religious History of the American People* (New Haven: Yale University Press, 1972);

Edwin Scott Gaustad, *A Religious History of America*, revised edition (San Francisco: HarperCollins, 1990);

William R. Hutchinson, *The Modernist Impulse in American Protestantism* (Cambridge, Mass.: Harvard University Press, 1976);

Charles H. Lippy, "Social Christianity," in *Encyclopedia of the American Religious Experience*, edited by Lippy and Peter Williams (New York: Scribners, 1988);

Martin E. Marty, *Modern American Religion, Volume 1: The Irony of It All, 1893–1919* (Chicago: University of Chicago Press, 1986).

HEADLINE MAKERS

EVANGELINE CORY BOOTH

1865-1950

SALVATION ARMY LEADER

Born with the Army. Evangeline Cory Booth was born in London on Christmas Day, 1865, the year that her father, William, a pawnshop worker, began the East London Revival Society, later called the Christian Mission and subsequently known as the Salvation Army. Her life would never veer from the mission of the Army, which followed from her father's Christian principles and compassion for the poor. She was named Evelyne and was called Eva. Years later, at the suggestion of Frances E. Willard of the Woman's Christian Temperance Union, she took a longer, fuller name, choosing Evangeline because it suited her work of saving souls as well as feeding them. Evangeline devoted her life to the Army, as had her brothers, Ballington, Bramwell, and Herbert, and her sister, Emma, though she served longer than any of her siblings. At fifteen she became a sergeant in the Army and for the first time wore its characteristic bonnet. She sold *War Cry* in the street. At eighteen she worked in the Marylebone district of London, singing, selling matches, and dressed in rags in order to blend in with London's outcast poor. Although never formally educated, she would take the Salvation Army and its "active Christianity" through a world war to its greatest heights around the world.

Canada. At the age of thirty Booth left England for Canada to become field commissioner for the Canadian branch of the Salvation Army, which had begun in Canada in 1882 when two converts from England happened to meet in London, Ontario. By the time of Evangeline's arrival in 1895 to replace her brother Herbert (who was on his way to Australia to help establish the Army), the Army in Canada had some three hundred stations scattered through the country. Her experiences in Marylebone and in the "Torquay Wars," a Salvation Army clash with the citizens of Torquay, England, in 1888 that had seen Army members jailed for unlawful marches, made Canada at first seem too respectable to her. But she was soon traveling from Toronto to the gold boom towns such as Dawson City and to Alaska, where conditions were hard and plenty of souls needed converting. She worked among pioneers and native peoples alike for nine years "of the most arduous toils in my experience," as she was to write in 1928. But her greatest work lay ahead.

The United States. In late 1903 Emma Booth, Evangeline's sister and the commander of the Salvation Army in the United States, died in New York City. Seventy-five thousand people passed her open casket. The New York *Daily News* said that the funeral was the "largest held in the city for a woman, and that the crowd which followed her to the grave was the largest which ever attended any public funeral except that of General Grant." Evangeline had large shoes to fill, but her father insisted she could do it. "Your career has been a remarkable one, but destiny, unless I am mistaken, has something in store for you more wonderful still," he wrote to her a year later on the commencement of her term as commander. He proved to be a prophet. In 1904 the Salvation Army in New York held assets valued at $1.5 million. By the time of her retirement as commander in 1934, the organization possessed $48 million in property and $35 million in its accounts. The Army grew from 696 stations to more than 1,600. Startled by the poverty when she arrived in immigrant New York, she began bread lines and organized efforts to feed schoolchildren. She announced donation drives and exceeded her goals. The Salvation Army provided emergency disaster relief and helped hospitals and the elderly. Booth was a powerful orator who championed the causes of women's rights and the drive toward prohibition. She gained an acceptance for her charitable endeavors from those who did not believe in the Army's salvation of souls, thus broadening the base of support. In 1912 her father William Booth died in London and was succeeded by the second general of the Army, Bramwell Booth, her eldest brother.

France. World War I saw an expansion of Salvation Army activities and popularity. By the war's end both the group and Evangeline Booth were immensely popular, especially with anyone who had served in France during the war. The Army had held its International Congress in London in the summer of 1914 with forty thousand Salvationists from fifty countries attending. The war began shortly thereafter, and Booth began coordinating the Salvation Army's activities to support the Allies and then the Americans once the United States had entered the war in 1917. The Army trained men and women to serve at or near the front lines, opening canteens and helping with the wounded. The Army gained great support with a program of lending money to troops unconditionally. The Salvation Army was seen as so valuable that many Salvationists were excused from their military duty in order to continue their work for the organization. When the war ended, the Army and Booth received nothing but praise from such dignitaries as General Pershing, British prime minister Lloyd George, President Woodrow Wilson, former president Theodore Roosevelt, and Gen. Leonard Wood. An enormous postwar program to aid the Salvation Army brought in $15 million. In October 1919 Evangeline Booth was given a Distinguished Service Medal by President Wilson. The Army had never been so popular on so many fronts. Evangeline

Booth remained commander of her father's Army in the United States for another fifteen years after the war.

General Booth. In the 1920s the Army was marked by political infighting. In 1922 Bramwell Booth had tried to remove Evangeline as commander after she had an operation on her throat. His plan was to divide the U.S. Salvation Army into three commands with separate commanders. The move caused an uproar among the people of America, and Bramwell had to take the defensive quickly. The organization's confidence in General Booth wavered, and in 1929 he was replaced. Edward J. Higgins then became the first elected general of the Salvation Army. Throughout the controversy Evangeline Booth's popularity continued, and in 1934 she was elected general of the Salvation Army, a position she held for one term of five years. She retired in 1939 and subsequently died in 1950 at the age of eighty-five. She had traveled a long way from selling her father's newspaper on the streets of London. She had met presidents, received honorary degrees from universities, and been given the Vasa Gold Medal by the king of Sweden. But her triumph was in her service. Her words in a 1914 interview summed up her life's work: "I'm for the man who, after we picked him up from the gutter, falls again and again. God help him, he is only weak and very human. After many struggles he may finally win . . . Oh, the task that is set for us, and ways, through God, in which we can help!"

Source:
P. W. Wilson, *General Evangeline Booth of the Salvation Army* (New York: Scribners, 1948).

MARY BAKER EDDY

1821-1910

FOUNDER OF THE CHURCH OF CHRIST, SCIENTIST

Youth. Mary Baker Eddy, the founder, matriarch, and "pastor emeritus" of the Church of Christ, Scientist (more commonly known as Christian Science), was born in 1821 on a farm in Bow, New Hampshire, the youngest of six children of Mark and Abigail Baker. She was a sickly child who suffered from an unknown nervous disorder that sent her into hysterical seizures. The result of her poor health was a spotty education, though she did study Hebrew, Greek, and Latin with her older brother Albert. She had a traditional religious upbringing that led her into membership of the Congregational Church in Sanbornton Bridge, New Hampshire (now Tilton), where the family had moved during her childhood. At the age of twenty-one Mary Baker married George Washington Glover, a builder who moved to Charleston, South Carolina. The marriage was the beginning of a long period of difficulty for the frail young woman. Glover died of illness within months of the marriage, leaving a pregnant, impoverished wife to be supported by a local Masonic lodge. She returned home in 1844 and gave birth to her only son, George.

Desperate Years. In New Hampshire she taught school periodically but essentially had no means of support except her family. Years passed in inertia. She gave up her son, then four years old, to a former nurse who had married and moved away. Her contact with George through the years would be infrequent and strained. Mary Glover's health continued to decline, with continuing nervous problems and depression, but in 1853, ten years after her first husband's death, she married Dr. Daniel Patterson, a homeopath and dentist. The couple lived in several small villages in New Hampshire for nine years before Patterson, on a visit to the Civil War battlefield of Bull Run, was taken prisoner by Confederate forces and sent to a prison camp. Mrs. Patterson was forced to return to her family, living as an invalid. She was thirty-two years old, but the turning point in her life was just ahead.

Quimby. In 1862 Mary Patterson consulted with Dr. Phineas Parkhurst Quimby, a mental healer from Portland, Maine. Within three weeks she had regained her health and proclaimed so in a letter to the *Portland Courier*. Quimby became her physician, her guiding light, and a profound influence on what would become Christian Science. Quimby died in 1866, the same year that Mary Patterson separated from Daniel Patterson, who had been released from his captivity and returned home. Quimby's death left her feeling desolate, in need of a new source of strength and inspiration.

Science and Health. That inspiration came sooner than anyone could have expected. Within weeks of Quimby's death, Eddy (the name she took when she married Asa Gilbert Eddy in 1877) sustained a back injury in a fall on ice. Laid up in bed, she took to reading the Bible assiduously, and "on the third day," by her account, the Scriptures opened up to her a revelation. Her cure was instantaneous, and her next task was to elaborate the principles by which her healing had taken place. During the next decade, prolonged introspection and prolific writing culminated in *Science and Health* (1875), which joined the Bible as the bedrock of Christian Science beliefs. Those beliefs centered on illness and healing and included her famous tenet that physical matter is illusory. It followed that physical illness must also be an illusion, what she regarded as the result of mistaken belief. All that truly existed in the universe was Mind, and the secret to wellness was to discipline the individual mind to bring it into harmony with the infinite Mind as it had been revealed through the example of Jesus Christ. Throughout her life Eddy would continue to revise and expand *Science and Health*, including adding *A Key to the Scriptures*, which guided its readers to the Christian Science principles Eddy found expressed in the Bible. By the time of her death in 1910, subsequent editions of the book had sold about four hundred thousand copies.

Building a Church. The thirty-five years of Eddy's life following the publication of *Science and Health* were spent first in spreading her church and then strengthening it internally from the seclusion of her private home. The first formal organization of her students came in 1876 when they took the name of the Christian Scientists' Association, and full religious establishment came soon after with the chartering of the Church of Christ, Scientist in 1879. The next few years saw a remarkable spread and growth in the church, so that by 1886 a national association was founded to coordinate the activities of all member congregations. In the meantime Eddy founded her Massachusetts Metaphysical College for the training of Christian Science practitioners in 1881. By 1889 she had retired from the day-to-day operations of the church and moved into a home in Concord, New Hampshire, which she named Pleasant View, but she did not cease her efforts to stabilize the church's institutional structures. One step in this direction was the 1892 abolition of the national association, in favor of a small board of directors who would have control in all matters of property, doctrine, and the training of practitioners. Through them and through a continuing stream of publications, Eddy's voice would continue to be heard and heeded in Christian Science until her death.

Not New Thought. Despite her church's remarkable growth, Eddy's twilight years saw their share of dissent and struggle as well. She continued to deny allegations that her teachings were merely a reworking of Quimby's, insisting that her revelation had been unique and original. Her church also suffered defections, even among her most prominent students, to the New Thought movement, which took its doctrines from another disciple of Quimby's, Warren Felt Evans. New Thought followers also believed in the power of mind over matter and focused on healing illness by restoring harmony between the human mind and the divine mind. Eddy had an authoritarian streak that alienated many students, and in her declining years she developed a reputation for eccentricity that verged on paranoia. Later editions of *Science and Health* began to explore the notion of "malicious animal magnetism," a mental force that could be projected onto others to blunt their healing powers and possibly even cause them physical harm. Firmly believing that she had enemies who wished her harm, Eddy allegedly gathered groups of her students around her when she traveled to form a physical shield against any projection of this "m.a.m." and engaged others to ward off such projections through prayer. In 1906 rumors of her death prompted a frail Eddy to summon nine reporters to her home for an interview so she could set the public record straight on that and other issues. Eddy and the religion she founded remain controversial, but her life certainly reveals a singular woman with an extraordinary drive to promulgate the truth she felt had been revealed to her, the vision of reality and wellness contained in the notion of "Divine Science."

Source:
Robert David Thomas, *"With Bleeding Footsteps": Mary Baker Eddy's Path to Religious Leadership* (New York: Knopf, 1994).

WASHINGTON GLADDEN

1836-1918

CONGREGATIONAL MINISTER

Roots. Solomon Washington Gladden, the "Father of the Social Gospel" and one of the most influential clergymen in America during the late nineteenth and early twentieth centuries, was born in Pottsgrove, Pennsylvania, in 1836. His father died when Washington was six years old, resulting in his being raised by his uncles on a farm in Oswego, New York, a part of the country that had been swept by religious revivals in the 1830s. At sixteen Gladden began working for the *Oswego Gazette,* the first of many affiliations with newspapers throughout his career. He attended Oswego Academy and in 1856 enrolled at Williams College, graduating in 1859. He was soon married and licensed to preach. He had led a rather ordinary life in his first twenty-four years. But Gladden was no ordinary man.

Clergyman and Author. In 1860 he became pastor of the First Congregational Church in Brooklyn where, later that year, he was ordained. A second position took him to Morrisania, New York, for five years (1861–1866), and he then moved on to North Adams, Massachusetts. During these years Gladden was influenced by the work of Horace Bushnell, a Congregational pastor in Hartford, Connecticut, who had pushed the idea of transcending conflict through a theology that rose above the factiousness of denominational forces. The work influenced Gladden greatly. A basic tenet of his social gospel would be the importance of putting moral and practical solutions above theological debate. While in Massachusetts Gladden began his prolific and influential literary career by writing for New York's *Independent* and *Scribner's Monthly.* In 1868 he published the first of his many popular books, *Plain Thoughts on the Art of Living.* In 1871 he became an editorial staff member of the *Independent,* a position he quit four years later because he found the paper's advertising dishonest. He moved to Springfield, Massachusetts, in 1875 to serve the North Congregational Church, staying there for seven years.

Labor and Capital. Early in his life Gladden had become interested in the struggle between labor and capital, a student not only of labor rights and relations but of economics as well. His seven years in the industrial city of Springfield confirmed his support for workers against what Gladden saw as the immoral forces of capital. Support of labor unions became a tenet of his social gospel thought, and he later advocated public ownership of utilities and cooperative management of industries, although he disavowed socialism. His criticism of capitalism grew stronger during the years as he furthered his study of workers' rights and taxation. Books with titles such as *Tools and the Man* (1893) and *Social Salvation* (1902) presented his views of how churches should deal with economic injustices.

Columbus. Gladden's greatest work and greatest fame came during his years with the First Congregational Church, Columbus, Ohio. From 1882 until his death in 1918, Gladden worked in the church as his writing increased, his popularity bloomed, and his influence grew. He wrote popular books of contemporary theological criticism, all the while preaching the gospel of a socially active church. He was a firm believer in civic organizations, and in 1900, tired of remaining unheard, he ran for city council in Columbus and was elected to a two-year term. He had recognized that public organizations did not function well because the individuals most suited for the task of leadership by and large refused to take the responsibility of doing so. He hoped to impress on people, through his words and example, the notion that public service was not only a respectable option but could also be a Christian duty. His *Applied Christianity: Moral Aspects of Social Questions* (1886) explained his philosophy of social activism and the role of religion in fostering the development of a moral social order.

Gladden's Legacy. Washington Gladden was a fair and highly scrupled voice at a time of great conflict not only within and between churches but also between social classes, immigrants, and early labor forces and capital. He authored thirty-eight books and fourteen hundred articles and lectured widely, spreading his words of reconciliation, progress, and compassion. His unswerving dedication to applying his principles to all the major social issues of his day placed him firmly in American religious history as the major force in the awakening of the Protestant conscience in America. He died on 2 July 1918.

Source:
Jacob H. Dorn, *Washington Gladden: Prophet of the Social Gospel* (Columbus: Ohio State University Press, 1967).

JOHN IRELAND

1838-1918

ARCHBISHOP OF SAINT PAUL

Social Gospel. John Ireland, the first archbishop of Saint Paul, Minnesota, was very much a man of his times, and in regard to the Catholic Church, perhaps a man of the future. Along with James Cardinal Gibbons, John L. Spalding, John Keane, and Denis O'Connell, Ireland was instrumental in bringing the Catholic Church to prominence as a political as well as a social force in the United States. Ireland was frank, energetic, progressive, and controversial not only within the church in America but within the church worldwide. The Vatican paid attention to John Ireland, who insisted that his faith not only adapt itself to this new land but also to the times. He was interested in what the church was, its ancient rites and stature, but also interested in what it could do. "Church and age!" he proclaimed. The age was one of social concerns, and Ireland confronted them despite the controversy involved in doing so. He believed in just wages for workers, workers' rights against the forces of capital, desegregation, separation of public schools from religious doctrine, and reform in urban life. He was a social liberal who championed a more "democratic" church for Americans while they retained their ties to Rome.

American. "I am an American citizen," he would sometimes say to open his lectures. But he had been born in Kilkenny, Ireland, in 1838, the son of a carpenter. The family was part of the great Irish immigration to the United States during and after the Irish potato famine of the 1840s. John Ireland arrived in America in 1849 and moved to Saint Paul in 1853. The local bishop, Joseph Crétin, noted the intelligence of the teenage Ireland and sent him to the Séminaire de Meximieux in France and later to the Scholasticat à Montbel. He returned to Saint Paul in 1861 and was ordained. Within months he had joined the Union army, serving the Fifth Minnesota Volunteers. Two years later, after an illness at Vicksburg, he left the army and returned to Saint Paul, where he became pastor of the cathedral in 1867. His life of social activism then truly began.

Crusader. Although he never fully supported the drive toward Prohibition, Ireland believed strongly in temperance. He began organizing temperance societies in order to help working people while also attacking the organized liquor trade. Temperance would remain one of his main themes, though on this issue he was in the minority among American Catholics. He spoke at conventions of the Catholic Total Abstinence Union and pushed temperance in his newspaper, *The Catholic Bulletin.* In 1879 Ireland promoted a plan to colonize the still sparsely populated areas of Minnesota. He procured railroad land and allowed colonists to purchase it cheaply through his Catholic Colonization Bureau. He had been made coadjutor bishop at the urging of Bishop Thomas Grace, with rights to succession upon Grace's death. In 1884 he succeeded Grace and became even more active, always urging the involvement of others as well. He was active in such organizations as the Minnesota State Historical Society, the Saint Paul Law and Order League, the American Civic Federation, and the Saint Paul Catholic Historical Society, which he founded. He was also instrumental, along with John J. Keane, in the founding of Catholic University in Washington, D.C., in 1889.

Controversies. In May 1888 Bishop Ireland became Archbishop Ireland when the diocese of Saint Paul became an archdiocese with five suffragan bishops. He was already nationally known, and the next two decades saw him involved in controversies both in America and with the Vatican. He clashed with German Catholics over the use of German in American churches and parochial schools. Ever insistent on Americanizing the church, Ireland believed English should be the sole language used in worship and education. Over labor issues he, along with Gibbons, Keane, and O'Connell, clashed with Canadian bishops and the Vatican when an incipient labor organization, the Knights of Labor, was condemned as a secret society. Through the American bishops' progressive lobbying efforts, Catholic workers were given the right to join such organizations. Ireland also clashed over the issue of parochial schools. In 1891 he organized an experiment in which Catholic schools were turned over to two Minnesota towns, Faribault and Stillwater. The towns ran the schools and allowed for religious education after school hours. Protestants condemned the experiment while American Catholics split over the issue. The Vatican declared that the plan could be "tolerated," but nonetheless it was eventually abandoned.

The Blizzard. Ireland's activities forced the Vatican to pay attention to him. Along with other progressive Catholics, he felt the sting of rebuke when a papal encyclical of 1895 condemned a host of propositions known collectively as "Americanism." But Ireland remained undaunted. He did not hesitate to employ backroom diplomacy through his friend Denis O'Connell at the Vatican, nor to bring the issues facing the Catholic church into the wider public eye via the mainstream media. It was not without reason that his allies and detractors alike referred to him as "the consecrated blizzard of the Northwest."

Church and State. Ireland was active in the political realm as well. In the early 1890s he denounced Tammany Hall in New York and was denounced by conservative Archbishop McQuaid of Rochester for interfering in local politics (among other sins). He opposed the mobilization for the Spanish-American War, but once hostilities began he voiced his support for the effort. However, when the United States emerged victorious and began to consider launching massive Protestant missionary efforts among the Catholic inhabitants of the Philippines, Ireland lodged strenuous objections. He saw no easier way for the United States to lose the respect of the islands' residents than by having a host of Protestant missionaries arrive and tell them "that their historic faith is wrong." As on the school question, in this issue Ireland expressed his devotion to the principle of separation of church and state — which in order to be fully realized often entailed the removal of the distinctly Protestant undertones that ran through America's government and public schools. With such separation achieved, Ireland believed the Catholic Church in America would have an opportunity for unprecedented vitality as it exerted its influence in every sphere of the lives of Catholic citizens. As a man who believed in a socially active church, Ireland used his position to comment upon and participate in the daily operations of his country as well as his church.

Builder. Although he might fairly be labeled an activist, progressive, or politician, Ireland believed that all of his efforts should be directed toward the growth of the church in America, a goal that he fostered in deeds as well as words. In 1885 he established Saint Thomas Seminary (later called Saint Thomas College) in Saint Paul. In 1894 he established the Saint Paul Seminary, and a decade later he helped found the College of Saint Catherine. In 1907 work on the new Saint Paul Cathedral began, and a year later Ireland laid the cornerstone of the Basilica of Saint Mary in Minneapolis. Although many of his personal aspirations for the church had been frustrated by his superiors' inaction and rebuke, by the time of his death in 1918 at the age of eighty, Ireland could point to an ample number of physical and doctrinal landmarks in the church that bore his personal stamp.

Source:
Marvin O'Connell, *John Ireland and the American Catholic Church* (Saint Paul: Minnesota Historical Society Press, 1988).

WILLIAM JAMES

1842-1910

PHILOSOPHER AND PSYCHOLOGIST

Crisis. "In general I dreaded to be left alone. I remember wondering how other people could live, how I myself had ever lived, so unconscious of that pit of insecurity beneath the surface of life," William James wrote in *The Varieties of Religious Experience* (1902). He was recalling a time that was evidently a turning point in his young life, a period of crisis in 1869 and 1870 that led him to seriously contemplate suicide but ultimately helped him articulate a defining theme and one of the legacies of his work. Twenty-eight years old at the time, James had finished his medical degree at Harvard in June 1868 but had yet to settle into a direction for the course of his life. This personal confrontation with nihilistic despair gave rise to what he would later call the "will to believe." In his diary of April 1870, James described what would be for him the philosophy that kept him alive and working: "I will go a step further with my will, not only act with it, but believe as well; believe in my individual reality and creative power." The crisis passed. James had pushed himself to act, and the result would be astonishing.

Education. He was born into one of the most original and intellectually gifted families of the nineteenth century. His brother, Henry, would become a great novelist, one who would set the standards for what the art of the novel could become. His father, Henry James Sr., was, William wrote in an 1865 letter, "the *wisest* of all men whom I know." The elder James was a man of deep religious conviction and liberal idealism. He believed in human experience and in society and held that the value of a man's life was in his participation in the world. His books included *Society — the Redeemed Form of Man* (1879) and *Social Significance of Our Institutions* (1861). Henry James Sr.'s religious beliefs represented an eclectic mix of various nineteenth-century currents, including the occult and spiritualist teachings of Emanuel Swedenborg. The result of these beliefs for his children was a strange mixture of formal schooling, rootlessness, and worldly experience as an education. William James's education was characterized by drift, from New York to Geneva to England to Paris to Boulogne to Bonn, where he saw the best of European art and society while receiving private tutoring as well as formal training at several schools. At the age of eighteen he returned to Newport, Rhode Island, where a course of life for this budding genius was to be chosen.

Decisions. He chose painting. In the fall of 1860 he began studying under the tutelage of William M. Hunt. He quit a year later, convinced that great art was beyond him. The choice then was to pursue his other passion — science — and in 1861 James entered the Lawrence Scientific School, a part of Harvard University. He concentrated on chemistry, anatomy, and physiology for three years before entering the Harvard Medical School in 1864. He interrupted his studies a year later for a nine-month stint with the Thayer expedition, which, under the leadership of Louis Agassiz, collected zoological specimens in the Amazon basin. He interrupted his studies a second time in April 1867 to travel to Germany, in part for his failing health but also out of indecision. He read voraciously in Germany, took cures in Divonne and Teplitz, and returned to Harvard in 1868. He finished his medical degree the following spring but then slipped into his crisis period, though he continued his wide reading and philosophical explorations.

Teacher. With his crisis passed and his will to believe reinvigorating him, James began teaching physiology at Harvard College in the fall of 1872. He would remain with the university for his entire career, though not with physiology. The course of his teaching career illustrated not only the depth of James's abilities but also the breadth. He taught comparative physiology and then began exploring the psychological implications of physiology. After teaching a course on the "Philosophy of Evolution," he advanced to become an assistant professor of philosophy (1880) and a chaired professor of that discipline in 1885. He had meanwhile begun what is considered the first American laboratory of psychology in 1876 and in time became a full professor of psychology (1889). He remained remarkably open to new ideas and explored them himself in essays published through the 1880s in

Mind and *Critique Philosophique.* Throughout the 1880s James built his reputation and cultivated professional friendships. He met Europeans such as Charles Renouvier, whose *Traité de Psychologie Rationelle* (1912) had profoundly influenced him as a young man. Among others of his circle of friends and acquaintances were Ernest Mach, Carl Stumpf, Shadworth Hodgson, George Croom Robertson, James Sully, Leslie Stephen, Frederick Pollock, Henry Sidgwick, and Théodore Flournoy, who became one of his most intimate friends. The decade of writing, teaching, and travel culminated with James's first book, *The Principles of Psychology* (1890), a book that was to have a profound impact on the intellectual climate of the day.

Writer. Capturing the state and position of psychology at the time of its publication, *The Principles of Psychology* was in a sense a declaration of independence for the young "science" of psychology. James's arguments, augmented by his experience in physiology and clinical psychology, pulled psychology away from the field of philosophy, declaring it to be a subject unto itself. James's style also set the book apart. Comprehensible to nonprofessionals since he had dared to be humorous and to use plain language, James's book was a popular as well as a professional success for the forty-eight-year-old author. The final twenty years of his life would be remarkably productive, as though his accumulation of experience, ideas, and practice reached critical mass in 1890 and exploded into a flurry of activity. A briefer version of *The Principles of Psychology* appeared in 1892 and became the most widely used text on the subject. In 1899 his *Talks to Teachers on Psychology* appeared, giving rise to the subject of educational psychology.

Philosopher. In the meantime James had also published an important book on a different subject. *The Will to Believe and Other Essays On Popular Philosophy* had appeared in 1897. *The Will to Believe* was the culmination of James's philosophical explorations during the previous two decades and remains the most concise expression of his philosophical worldview. Essays such as "The Sentiment of Rationality," "The Will to Believe," and "The Moral Philosopher and the Moral Life" reveal James's engagement with the philosophical pragmatism of Charles Sanders Peirce. In defining both truth and morals in the terms of propositions to be proved or disproved by experience, James was aligning himself not only with a new school in philosophical thought but with a method of intellectual inquiry that was to gain wide application in other scientific and educational arenas. In James most of the nineteenth century's major currents of thought coalesced and found expression in a way that suggested fruitful intellectual endeavors ahead. His own endeavors would run the gamut from neurological psychology to psychical research. Clearly, for James, nothing in the world of human experience was closed to inquiry. Few who followed him could match his intellectual versatility.

Lecturer. The final decade of James's life, the first in the twentieth century, was spent in traveling, lecturing, writing, and also fighting to recover from sporadic ill health. In 1901 and 1902, having recovered from another bout with illness, he presented the Gifford lectures in Edinburgh, which became *The Varieties of Religious Experience,* among James's most popular books. Many people found that James's work strengthened or affirmed their religious faith, despite its scientific approach. The key to this success was James's pragmatic willingness to allow for the limited truth of any religious belief that had a positive effect on the life of the believer. In 1906 James visited Stanford University as a guest lecturer, giving a series of talks that was published posthumously as *Some Problems of Philosophy* (1911). Later that year he lectured at the Lowell Institute in Boston, lectures that were published in 1907 as *Pragmatism,* which remains the definitive popular statement of that movement's principles. James had meanwhile become an outspoken critic of what he saw as a growing American imperialism. The Spanish-American War and America's involvement in the Philippines led him to complain that America had betrayed its original ideals for the sake of "bigness and greatness." In 1907 James retired from Harvard. The following year he gave a series of lectures in Oxford that would become *A Pluralistic Universe* (1909). He was elected to the French Academy of Moral and Political Sciences and the Prussian Academy of Sciences, along with being given many honorary degrees. He died on 26 August 1910 in Chocorua, New Hampshire. He had, forty years before, convinced himself that life was worth living. He lived it as few in American intellectual history ever have.

Sources:
Gay Wilson Allen, *William James: A Biography* (New York: Viking, 1967);

John J. McDermott, ed., *The Writings of William James: A Comprehensive Edition* (New York: Modern Library, 1967).

CHARLES TAZE RUSSELL

1852-1916

FOUNDER OF JEHOVAH'S WITNESSES

Multimedia. At the time of his death from heart failure on 31 October 1916, Charles Taze Russell, the founder and soul of the Jehovah's Witnesses, was among the most widely read columnists in America. The new century had brought with it new technologies, and Russell, who began spreading his faith in the 1870s via publication and public speaking, had taken full advantage of the chance to "harvest" followers, as he referred to his work. His newspaper columns and sermons had expanded by 1913 to some two thousand newspapers with an estimated readership of fifteen million. His own publication *The Watch Tower*

referred to it as "newspaper gospelling," but his word had found other avenues besides the printed page. An example of Russell's innovation and forward thinking for spreading his word was his "Photo-Drama Creation." This multimedia event begun in 1914 was quickly taken overseas as a means of astounding audiences with technology while also preaching Russell's interpretation of the Bible. "Photo-Drama" managed to put words to moving pictures, incorporating phonographic recordings and silent films, and combine artwork, music, and preaching to dazzle the audience. But the core of Russell's work was always his message, a message he had searched hard to find, interpret, and spread.

Youth. "Pastor Russell," as he was known in later life, was born near Pittsburgh in 1852 to Joseph and Eliza Russell, both of Scots-Irish heritage. Russell was raised in a Presbyterian household though in his teens joined a Congregationalist church for a time. His mother had died when Russell was nine, and by age eleven he was working in his father's clothing business. By the age of fifteen, however, Russell had rejected traditional Christian churches because of his repulsion at the idea of predestination and eternal torment. He dabbled with oriental religions for a time in his late teens but he later claimed to have found the road toward his faith when he chanced upon a Second Adventist service in 1869. The seventeen-year-old Russell was deeply impressed by the millennialism preached by Rev. Jonas Wendell and decided that he could only find his faith in studying the Bible directly.

Influences. Wendell was not the only source of influence for Russell. From about 1870 to 1875 Russell studied the Bible fervently with the help of George W. Stetson, pastor of the Advent Christian Church in Edinboro, Pennsylvania, and George Storrs, publisher of *Bible Examiner* magazine and author of *Six Sermons,* a book that reached a circulation of two hundred thousand. Storrs's theology, his rejection of the Trinity, his reliance on the Bible, and his belief in a mortal soul that could achieve immortality through atonement strongly influenced Russell, but it was his later association with Nelson H. Barbour that would have the biggest impact on Russell's career. Barbour was the publisher of the *Herald of the Morning,* a religious periodical that Russell first read in 1876 when he was twenty-three years old. Barbour convinced Russell that the "harvest period" had begun, that Christ had already returned to earth in an invisible form in the autumn of 1874, and that the work for gathering souls should begin. Russell became devoted to preaching as well as writing and publishing to spread the good news. "I therefore at once resolved upon a vigorous campaign for the Truth," he later wrote.

Writer. In 1877 Russell published *The Object and Manner of Our Lord's Return.* That same year he and Barbour published *Three Worlds, and the Harvest of This World.* In these books Russell presented his carefully rendered interpretation of the Bible and the idea that Christ

had already returned. In order to spread the word on a more regular basis, Russell and Barbour began publishing *Herald of the Morning* again in 1877, but a schism soon developed. They parted in 1878, and Russell had his name removed from the *Herald.* He began to publish his own journal in July 1879. Six thousand copies of the first issue of *Zion's Watch Tower and Herald of Christ's Presence* were printed. By 1914 *The Watch Tower* was printing fifty thousand copies of each issue. Russell continued to preach and write, producing *Food for Thinking Christians* in 1881, which upon republication in 1886 was known as the *Millennial Dawn.* During the next two decades, Russell published six volumes of *Millenial Dawn,* of which some five million copies circulated worldwide.

Spreading the Word. The final thirty years of Russell's life consisted primarily in organizing and enlarging his following. In 1880 he announced that he would visit towns in Pennsylvania, New Jersey, Massachusetts, and New York in an effort to enlarge his flock. These were the first of his extensive travels throughout Canada, Europe, the Orient, the United States, and even Palestine. His "London Tabernacle" became a major center in Europe, while his fervent support for a Jewish return to Palestine made him famous in the nascent Zionist movement. Upon his return to New York in 1910 he was given a huge ovation by New York's Jewish community in a gathering at the Hippodrome. Russell had moved his headquarters to Brooklyn in 1908, creating the "Brooklyn Tabernacle," and located the church headquarters in a building named "Bethel," which means "House of God."

Transcending Scandal. His life was not without scandal, though the negative publicity seemed to have no lasting affect on his popularity. In 1909 his wife of thirty years filed for divorce, charging Russell with immoral conduct with women in the church. Russell appealed the divorce five times but was rejected each time. Another scandal involved the selling of a dubious "Miracle Wheat" at his church in Brooklyn. The expensive wheat, said to have miraculous properties, had been donated to the Watch Tower Society by two students. Russell sold the grain for a dollar a pound, raising $1,800 for the church, though the *Brooklyn Daily Eagle* presented the case as a fraud. Russell sued the newspaper in 1911 but lost the case. It did not seem to matter. Russell continued his work, which gained a measure of validity in 1914 with the outbreak of World War I. Russell had for years predicted that 1914 would mark the end of the genteel times and that heaven was imminent after a period of chaos. The war seemed to be the chaos expected, and many anticipated the coming of heaven. Though heaven did not immediately follow, Russell's prophecy was taken to have come to fruition. His sudden death in 1916 shocked and saddened his congregation, now worldwide.

Sources:

Jehovah's Witnesses: Proclaimers of God's Kingdom (Brooklyn: Watch Tower Bible & Tract Society of New York, 1993);

M. James Penton, *Apocalypse Delayed: The Story of Jehovah's Witnesses* (Toronto: University of Toronto Press, 1985).

SOLOMON SCHECHTER

1850-1915

SCHOLAR AND PRESIDENT OF THE JEWISH THEOLOGICAL SEMINARY

Humble Beginnings. Solomon Schechter was born in or about 1850 in the village of Fokshan (Focsani), Romania. His father was a ritual slaughterer, and the family adhered to the Hasidic sect of Judaism that Schechter would come to disavow as a young scholar. From his early years Schechter, who would become a giant among scholars of Judaism, was recognized as an *Iluy,* the Hebrew word for a wonder child of learning. His early education, administered by his father, centered on religious texts. At the age of ten Schechter attended a Talmudic college in Piatra, Romania. By sixteen he was in the rabbinical school at Lemberg, where he studied with Rabbi Joseph Saul Nathanson, the great scholar of the Talmud. Schechter returned to Fokshan and remained until 1875. His parents had arranged a marriage, as was the custom, but the marriage failed, ending in divorce within a year. In 1875 Schechter left Romania for good, traveling to Vienna, the cultural hub of central Europe. He received his rabbinical diploma in 1879, but he never practiced the functions of a rabbi. Instead he became a scholar whose thought would influence Judaism greatly in the new century.

A Scholar Emerges. Schechter lived and studied in Vienna for four years. He attended the Jewish *Bet ha-Midrash,* or house of study, which charged poor students no fees. It was there that he synthesized his previously unfocused study and became an outstanding scholar under the tutelage of three great teachers, Adolph Jellinek, Isaac Hirsch Weiss, and Meir Friedman. In 1879 Schechter traveled to Berlin to study at the German "Academy for Jewish Science," which had been founded only eleven years before. He studied with Israel Lewy and Pincus Friedrich Frankl, to whom Schechter would dedicate his first book in English, *Studies in Judaism* (1896). Schechter made two discoveries in Berlin that would affect him deeply. The first was the critical and historical approach to Judaism that was still relatively new. The Bible was being as much examined as revered, and Schechter would come to take controversial stands on points of historical veracity, such as questioning the actual existence of Moses and concluding that Solomon did not write Ecclesiastes. His second discovery was that Germany's intellectuals were aggressively applying scientific methods to support anti-Semitism. Schechter had seen plenty of anti-Semitism in Romania, but seeing it so entrenched among the educated led him to leave Germany. In 1882 at the suggestion of Frankl, Schechter traveled as a tutor with Claude Goldsnid Montefiore to London. He was expected to stay a year. He stayed for twenty.

England. Although he arrived in London with little knowledge of English, Schechter found a culture that would allow him to pursue his work. The British Museum and Oxford's Bodleian Library contained a massive number of ancient books and manuscripts. Schechter also enjoyed the intellectual freedom the country afforded and felt little of the anti-Semitism in academic circles that he had encountered in Germany. He quickly began embracing English culture, literature, and language. He joined a small group of fellow scholars — including Moses Gaster, Israel Zangwill, Israel Abrahams, Lucien Wolf, and Asher Myers — who were keeping Jewish scholarship alive in England. They called themselves "The Wanderers" and would have an enduring influence on the English-speaking Jewish world. Schechter married Mathilda Roth, a native of Breslau, in 1887. He continued his study of manuscripts, teaching and writing in London until 1890, when a readership in Talmud and rabbinical literature opened at Cambridge University. He took the post and entered his most fruitful scholarly period.

Genizah. Schechter traveled a great deal during the 1890s, visiting Italy for library study, Philadelphia and Baltimore for lectures, and Palestine to see his twin brother, who had settled there. His journey to Cairo in 1896 profoundly affected his life. Having identified a fragment of a manuscript as an original piece of the oldest book of the Apocrypha, Schechter was convinced that a treasure of manuscripts must lie in Genizah (or burial place) in the Egyptian city. Although the Genizah had been known about for a century and some of its pieces had filtered into private collections, no one had systematically explored its contents. "All I wanted was to empty the Geniza," he wrote when he was done. "In this I have succeeded." The arduous work underground, lasting months, would be detrimental to his health. "He has been choked with dust and bad air and has worked like a horse. He wishes he had a respirator," wrote a friend to Mrs. Schechter. He emerged with more than fifty thousand manuscripts and fragments in Hebrew and Arabic, the largest collection ever found by one man. He found the remaining chapters of Ecclesiasticus, which he published in 1899 as *The Wisdom of Ben Sira, Portions of the Book Ecclesiasticus from Hebrew Manuscripts in the Cairo Genizah Collection.* The discovery made him world famous and led to the final stage of his career.

America. In 1901 Schechter was invited to become president of the Jewish Theological Seminary in New York, a post he would hold from 1902 until his death in 1915. Jews, especially those from eastern Europe, had poured into the United States during the previous twenty years, creating a large Jewish community in New York.

Schechter desired to work within such a community after years of living in a small, isolated Jewish group. It was in New York that Schechter would have his greatest impact on Jewish thought and practice. He reorganized the seminary and within six years made it a center of contemporary scholarship with a star faculty.

Conservative Movement. Developing and organizing Conservative Judaism was Schechter's great work in America. He was able to find the center in the debate between the devotional Orthodox Jews and the iconoclastic Reform Jews who were questioning all aspects of the faith. The Conservative Judaism Schechter championed was a devotional doctrine in practice but one that kept Judaism contemporary. He bridged the gap between Western and Eastern Jewry with his notion of a "catholic Israel" (K'lal Yisrael), a Jewish option for the twentieth century. He believed that Judaism for each age was what that age made of it without abandoning ancient traditions. "Conservative Judaism united what is desirable in modern life with the precious heritage of our faith . . . that has come down to us from ancient times," he wrote. In 1913 he helped found the United Synagogue of America, a union of twenty-two congregations that had broken free of Orthodox Judaism. Schechter felt that the survival of Judaism in America depended on its adaptability to the emerging culture in the new century. Schechter also continued his own scholarly work, publishing the important two-volume *Some Aspects of Rabbinic Theology* in 1909 and *Documents of Jewish Sectaries* in 1910. He died in November 1915.

Sources:

Norman Bentwich, *Solomon Schechter: A Biography* (Cambridge: Cambridge University Press, 1938);

Martin E. Marty, *Modern American Religion*, volume 1 (Chicago: University of Chicago Press, 1986).

WILLIAM JOSEPH SEYMOUR

1870-1922

PENTECOSTAL PREACHER

Background. William Joseph Seymour was born in Louisiana in 1870, the son of recently freed slaves Phyllis Salabarr and Simon Seymour. Few particulars are known of his early life, except that he received scant formal education and reported having had visions of God as a young man. He was associated with the Evening Light Saints, a Holiness group that believed in faith healing and total sanctification. In 1895 Seymour arrived in Indianapolis and worked as a waiter. He joined the Methodist Episcopal Church there but in 1900 moved to Cincinnati, Ohio, and affiliated himself with the Church of God in Anderson, Indiana, a group that had an interracial membership. After a bout with smallpox, which caused him to lose his left eye, Seymour became ordained as a Church of God minister in 1902 and began his career as an evangelist.

Preparation. He settled in Houston, where his family then lived. It was there he met Charles F. Parham, who had founded the first Pentecostal Bible school in Topeka, Kansas. Having witnessed Parham's governess speak in tongues at a Negro mission, the first time he had ever seen glossolalia, Seymour had asked to be admitted to Parham's Houston school. Parham's initial reluctance was because of racial considerations as he feared provoking his white students, but he eventually admitted Seymour, who did not actively seek the full Pentecostal experience of speaking in tongues. Seymour also met Neeley Terry in Houston. She had come from Los Angeles, where she followed Sister Hutchinson, an itinerant evangelist who had a storefront mission there. Terry would lead Seymour, backed by Parham's money, to Los Angeles in January 1906. Seymour would start a ministry that would shake the world.

Azusa Street. Within a week of arriving Seymour had alienated his new congregation with the message of the Pentecost. He was locked out. It took months for him to convert the leaders of the group and attend prayer meetings. On the evening of 9 April 1906 Seymour's preaching evoked speaking in tongues among the congregation at a meeting in a home on Bonnie Brae Street. Three nights later Seymour himself received the baptism in the Spirit and began speaking in tongues. Within days the group had moved into a building on Azusa Street. A mixed-race congregation began to attend, and on 18 April, the same day as the San Francisco earthquake, the *Los Angeles Times* ran a story about Azusa Street. The story, along with the aftereffects of the earthquake, brought a flood of people to the mission. Within months Seymour had ordained ministers, raised other congregations, and was publishing *The Apostolic Faith*.

New Messengers. People from around the country came to experience the revival. In 1907 the mission officially became the Azusa Street Apostolic Faith Mission of Los Angeles. That year and the next saw even more success for the mission. Those who had come to Los Angeles returned home carrying the Pentecostal message. Charles H. Mason, founder of the Church of God in Christ, came and took the message to churches in the Southeast. Ira Campbell took the movement to Akron, Cleveland, Pittsburgh, and other places. Glenn A. Cook spread the word to Indianapolis. Parham, encouraged by Seymour's success, sent more missionaries out, though shortly thereafter he was humiliated by civil charges brought against him. Seymour and the Azusa Street Mission repudiated him, and Seymour was left to carry on the work alone.

Decline. Though Azusa Street was the longest continuous revival in American religious history, Seymour's fame was essentially short-lived as a series of problems developed. An administrative assistant stole Azusa's mailing list, damaging the mission's nationwide impact. In 1911 William Durham, a white man, left the mission over racial conflicts as well as doctrinal ones. Seymour alienated his group by building a "throne" for himself. Traditional Christians had opposed the revival from the beginning, and the mission's energy could not be sustained. By 1913 Seymour had only about twenty members in his congregation. He spent the final nine years of his life traveling and speaking to black audiences. He wrote *Doctrines and Discipline* (1915), a handbook for his faithful followers. He died of a heart attack in 1922, leaving his work to his wife, Jennie Moore, who continued it until her death in 1936, even after losing the Azusa Street Mission in 1931.

Sources:

Robert Mapes Anderson, *Vision of the Disinherited: The Making of American Pentecostalism* (Peabody, Mass.: Hendrickson, 1979);

J. Gordon Melton, ed., *Religious Leaders of America* (Detroit: Gale Research, 1991).

ELLEN GOULD HARMON WHITE

1827-1915

COFOUNDER OF SEVENTH-DAY ADVENTISTS

Visions. Ellen Gould Harmon White's childhood is remarkable not for any particular accomplishment or intimation of her future but instead for the fact of her survival. She was born Ellen Gould Harmon in Gorham, Maine, in 1827. At age nine she was seriously injured when a classmate threw a stone at her, hitting her in the head and knocking her to the ground. Ellen lay unconscious for three weeks, and afterward, her face somewhat disfigured and her constitution weakened, she was unable to obtain a formal education. Her life changed when at age fourteen she dreamed of Christ and consulted Elder Stockman, Portland Adventist, who told her that she had been chosen as a messenger for God. She found her faith and expression for it in the then-popular evangelist William Miller, who taught his followers that Christ would return on 22 October 1844. Miller's followers were deeply disappointed when the day passed uneventfully, though Ellen retained her faith. Two months later she had the first of her more than two thousand visions, in which God's messages were communicated through her to individuals and congregations in the form of prophecy, censure, or praise. Reports were that she stopped breathing during these visions and that her eyes remained open.

Publishers. In 1846, not quite nineteen years old, Ellen married Rev. James White, an Adventist minister from Palmyra, Maine. They were very poor and neither was in good health, but their faith and their work sustained them. White began to write down her visions with a vigor she had not previously possessed. Three years later the Whites began the first of their many publishing projects together, creating the periodical *The Present Truth*, an eight-page semimonthly. White had seen the need for publication in a vision that would later expand to show her a future of faith-spreading international publishing ventures. The Whites moved to Rochester, New York, where they had secured a printing press. They met Uriah Smith, who would oversee much of their publishing work, such as *The Review and Herald*, a weekly magazine that grew out of *The Present Truth*. By 1855 conditions had improved financially for the Whites, who moved to Battle Creek, Michigan, to continue their publishing work in a building given to them by friends and followers. Smith continued to put out *The Review and Herald* almost single-handedly. Ellen White's first book, *Christian Experiences and Views*, appeared in 1851. She would write more than three dozen in her life, which when combined with her diaries and notebooks totaled more than one hundred thousand pages of work.

1860. In the early years of their marriage the Whites became convinced that Scripture dictated Saturday as the Sabbath day, thus leading to the adoption of the name "Seventh-Day Adventists" around 1860. The Seventh-Day Adventists were a scattered, unorganized group of congregations in 1860, but largely through the work of James White, a general conference for the emerging church was organized. Twenty delegates came to Battle Creek in 1863 and offered the presidency of the group to James White, but he refused. The year 1860 also saw publication of what may be Ellen White's greatest work, *The Great Controversy*, a book that grew out of a vision she had in Lovett's Grove, Ohio, in 1858. The vision revealed the cosmic war between good and evil and the imminent Second Coming of Christ. Another great vision occurred in June 1860 when she was shown the connection between physical health and spirituality. She quickly issued a series of sixty-four-page pamphlets titled *Health, or How to Live*. But 1860 was not all good news for the Whites. In December their fourth son, Henry, died suddenly at the age of three months.

Health. The work caught up to James White. In 1864 he suffered a serious illness. Though he was nursed back to health, the illness had an affect on the Whites' future. On Christmas Day 1865 a vision inspired Ellen White to establish a health institute for the sick as well as a place to teach preventive medicine. The Western Health Reform Institute (later the Battle Creek Sanitarium) opened the following year, the first in a series of Seventh-Day Adventist clinics around the world. By the time of Ellen White's death, there would be thirty-three such sanitariums and hundreds of treatment rooms worldwide. The success of the Western Health Reform Institute made White even more popular. She was a mesmerizing speaker who in the 1860s and 1870s drew some of the largest crowds of the age. She became a temperance advocate and also disavowed meat, coffee, tea, and many drugs. White never claimed status as a prophet, however, nor did she push her views on others; instead, she requested Bible study from her followers.

Travels. In August 1881 James White died. He and Ellen White had been partners in work and marriage for thirty-five years. James White in his later years had been a major force in establishing Battle Creek College (later Andrews University) as well as the Review and Herald Publishing Association and the Pacific Press Publishing Association. The sanitarium had succeeded under his guidance. As a result of his death, Ellen White took on even more work. She began pushing international mission programs, the establishment of a college in the West, and overseas publishing ventures. She traveled abroad herself, to Europe from 1885 to 1889 and to Australia in 1891, where she lived for nine years. In 1901 she returned to the United States and at the age of seventy-four continued speaking publicly in the American South, where she established the Southern Publishing Association in Nashville, Tennessee. In 1903 White moved the denominational headquarters from Battle Creek to Washington, D.C. She founded the College of Medical Evangelists at Loma Linda, California, in 1909. Between 1900 and 1915, the tireless White resided in Saint Helena, California, where she finished ten books while carrying out her other work. "Your work," she wrote that the Lord had told her, "is to bear My word. Strange things will arise, and in your youth I set you apart to bear the message to erring ones, to carry the word before unbelievers, and with pen and voice to reprove from the Word actions that are not right." Ellen White lived by his word as she believed it and carried it faithfully. When she died in 1915, she had an estimated 135,000 followers.

Source:
Rene Noorbergen, *Ellen G. White: Prophet of Destiny* (New Canaan, Conn.: Keats, 1972).

PEOPLE IN THE NEWS

The Tantrik Order in America was founded in 1909 by **Pierre Bernard,** who took for himself the title of Oom the Omnipotent. In 1910 two women would complain to New York City police that Bernard was keeping them against their will for his "orgies."

The first step toward the canonization of the first American Catholic saint was taken in 1909, when Italian-born **Mother Francis Xavier Cabrini** became a naturalized citizen of the United States. The superior of the Missionary Sisters of the Sacred Heart, Mother Cabrini had been highly active in relief work among immigrants in New York's "Little Italy" since 1889. The continuation and expansion of that charitable work until her death in 1918 would be recognized by an unusually quick beatification (1938) and canonization (1946).

Dr. **Algernon S. Crapsey,** an Episcopal priest in Rochester, New York, was brought up before an ecclesiastical court on charges of heresy in 1906. The church alleged that in a series of sermons published as *Religion and Politics* (1905) Crapsey had impugned and denied the doctrines that Jesus Christ is God and Savior of the world as well as the doctrines of the Resurrection and the Virgin Birth. He was found guilty and dismissed from the ministry.

During the coal strike of 1902 in Wilkes-Barre, Pennsylvania, Catholic priest **John J. Curran** became known as "the miners' friend" for his support of the striking workers and his efforts on their behalf. He joined forces with John Mitchell, who led the United Mine Workers of America, and ultimately took the issue of the strike to President Theodore Roosevelt, urging him to bring about a settlement.

In 1904 former Congregationalist minister **George D. Herron** gave the nominating speech for presidential candidate Eugene V. Debs at the Socialist Party convention in Chicago. His socialist ideas had previously given rise to an experiment in communal living in Georgia (1896–1900), but in 1901, after a divorce and remarriage, he had been shunned by his church for being a "free lover."

Francis Hodur, a Polish American Catholic priest in Scranton, Pennsylvania, rose to unexpected prominence in religious leadership (despite having been excommunicated from the Roman Catholic Church in 1897) when he was named bishop of an independent synod of Polish Catholic churches in 1904. In 1907 the Scranton-based synod merged with a similar group in Chicago to form the Polish National Catholic Church, of which Hodur was elected bishop. He retained this position until his death in 1953.

Comanche chief **Quanah Parker** rode in the inaugural parade for President Theodore Roosevelt after his election in 1904. Quanah, who lived on the Comanche reservation in Indian Territory (Oklahoma), was a shrewd businessman, highly assimilated into American society, who enjoyed good relations with many government officials. His standing would allow him to become one of the central figures in the incorporation of the pan-Indian Peyote Road religious movement as the Native American Church before his death in 1911.

Reverdy C. Ransom, a minister in the African Methodist Episcopal Church, preached a series of sermons in 1903 against crime and corruption in the Chicago area, naming names. Although a dynamite explosion soon thereafter destroyed his office, he was ultimately successful in closing down many gambling and racketeering houses in the city.

On 28 December 1908 *The New York Times* reported that **Lee J. Spangler,** known as "The Prophet," was missing from Nyack, New York. He had apparently "left town under the shadow of darkness" that morning, after his prophecy that the end of the world would occur on 27 December failed to come true. A group of his followers, all women, had gotten up at dawn on the 27th, dressed in white robes, and ascended South Mountain to wait for "the trumpet call of the angel," but, as the newspaper stated, "after a while they got tired, as nothing happened. Then they dispersed."

DEATHS

Francis Ellingwood Abbot, 66, cofounder in 1867 of the Free Religious Association, 23 October 1903.

Benjamin William Arnett Jr., 68, seventeenth bishop of the African Methodist Episcopal church and self-educated editor of *The Budget* (1881 1904), 9 October 1906.

Josephine Abiah Penfield Cushman Bateham, 71, social activist who headed the Woman's Christian Temperance Union's Department for the Suppression of Sabbath Desecration, 15 March 1901.

Joseph A. Beebe, 70, bishop of the Colored Methodist Episcopal Church, 6 June 1903.

Jacob Beilhart, 41, founder of the communal Spirit Fruit Society, which lasted from 1901 until 1930, 24 November 1908.

Mary Lucinda Bonney, 84, Baptist laywoman and Indian rights activist as head of Women's National Indian Association, 24 July 1900.

Margaret McDonald Bottome, 78, president and organizer of the International Order of the King's Daughters and Sons, 14 November 1906.

George Quayle Cannon, 74, editor, writer, leading member of the Church of Jesus Christ of Latter-day Saints who was once jailed for polygamy, 12 May 1901.

William Colley, 62, organizer of the National Baptist Foreign Mission Convention of the United States, 24 December 1909.

Michael Augustine Corrigan, 62, conservative Catholic archbishop of New York, 5 May 1902.

Malinda Elliott Cramer, 62, founder of Divine Science Federation International, a splinter group from the Christian Scientists, 2 August 1906.

William Saunders Crowdy, 61, founder in 1896 of the black Jewish group Church of God and Saints of Christ, 4 August 1908.

Richard De Baptiste, 69, popular black preacher and president of the Consolidated American Baptist Convention, 21 April 1901.

Abby Morton Diaz, 83, New Thought lecturer, feminist, and writer, 1 April 1904.

John Alexander Dowie, 59, faith healer and founder in 1896 of the Christian Catholic Church and in 1901 of the town of Zion, Illinois, as a communal settlement, 9 March 1907.

George Park Fisher, 82, dean of Yale Divinity School and Congregational church historian, 20 December 1909.

Randolph Sinks Foster, 83, bishop of the Methodist Episcopal Church who wrote the six-volume *Studies in Theology*, 1 May 1903.

Emanuel Vogel Gerhart, 86, prominent theologian in the German Reformed Church, 6 May 1904.

Geronimo, 79, Chiricahua Apache holy man, healer, and war chief, 17 February 1909.

William Samuel Godbe, 69, founder in 1870 of the Church of Zion, a Mormon splinter group, 1 August 1902.

Frederick William Grant, 68, leader of the Plymouth Brethren and author of *The Numerical Bible* series, 25 July 1902.

Edward Everett Hale, 87, minister of the American Unitarian Association and author of *The Man Without a Country*, 10 June 1909.

Thomas Lake Harris, 82, Spiritualist leader and founder of the Brotherhood of the New Life, 23 March 1906.

James Augustine Healy, 70, first black bishop in the Roman Catholic Church, 5 August 1900.

John Holdeman, 68, founder of the Church of God in Christ, Mennonite, 10 March 1900.

Henry Ritz Holsinger, 72, founder of Brethren Church in Ashland, Ohio, and publisher of *Christian Family Companion*, 12 March 1905.

Moses Hull, 71, leading Spiritualist writer and publisher of *The New Thought*, 10 January 1907.

William Reed Huntington, 70, Episcopal minister in New York City and author of *A Short History of the Book of Common Prayer*, 26 July 1909.

Sheldon Jackson, 75, Presbyterian missionary to Alaska and the western United States, 2 May 1909.

Samuel Porter Jones, 59, popular evangelist of the Methodist Episcopal Church, South, 15 October 1906.

Martin Wells Knapp, 48, founder of the International Holiness Union and Prayer League, 7 December 1901.

Charles Cardwell McCabe, 70, bishop of the Methodist Episcopal Church who oversaw the church's expansion into the West, 19 December 1906.

William Leroy Pettingill, 39, fundamentalist minister and author of the Simple Studies series, 15 September 1905.

Piapot, 92, traditional religious leader of the Cree Indian tribe and Sun Dance organizer, 1908.

Hiram Rhoades Revels, 78, educator, U.S. senator, minister of the African Methodist Episcopal Church, and president of Alcorn University, 16 January 1901.

Ann Eliza Worcester Robertson, 79, missionary to the Creek Indians and Bible translator, 19 November 1905.

Ira D. Sankey, 68, hymn writer for Dwight L. Moody, 14 August 1908.

Theodore Lorenzo Seip, 61, educator and minister of the General Council of Lutheran Churches in America, 28 November 1903.

Joseph Augustus Seiss, 81, educator, minister of the General Council of Lutheran Churches in America, and author of *The Apocalypse,* a series of lectures given in 1865, 20 June 1904.

Uriah Smith, 70, pioneer Seventh-Day Adventist and editor of the *Review and Herald,* 6 March 1903.

Smohalla, 92?, founder of the Washani (Dreamer) religion, a Native American millennial movement, 1907.

Lorenzo Snow, 87, fifth president of the Church of Jesus Christ of Latter-day Saints who was once arrested for polygamy, 10 October 1901.

Elizabeth Cady Stanton, 86, president of the National American Woman Suffrage Association and editor of *The Woman's Bible,* 26 October 1902.

Eliza Allen Starr, 77, Roman Catholic author and artist who wrote *Pilgrims and Shrines* (1881), 7 September 1901.

John Henry Wilbrandt Stuckenberg, 68, pioneering sociologist and theologian of the General Synod, Lutheran Church, 18 May 1903.

Thomas DeWitt Talmage, 70, popular preacher, columnist, and editor of *Frank Leslie's Sunday Magazine,* 12 April 1902.

Isaac Taylor Tichenor, 77, missionary secretary for the Southern Baptist Convention (1881–1900), 2 December 1902.

Henry Clay Trumbull, 73, Congregationalist minister and popularizer of Sunday schools, 8 December 1903.

Milton Valentine, 81, educator and theologian of the General Synod, Lutheran Church, 7 February 1906.

Aaron Wall, 71, founder of the Defenseless Mennonite Brethren in Christ of North America, 6 August 1905.

Isaac Mayer Wise, 81, rabbi and founder of Reform Judaism, the Central Conference of American Rabbis, and Hebrew Union College, 26 March 1900.

Annie Turner Wittenmyer, 72, first president of the Woman's Christian Temperance Union who founded and edited the journal *Christian Women,* 2 February 1900.

Henry Wood, 75, popular metaphysical and New Thought author who in 1903 published *The New Thought Simplified,* 28 March 1909.

PUBLICATIONS

Francis Ellingwood Abbot, *The Syllogistic Philosophy*, 2 volumes (Boston: Little, Brown, 1906);

Lyman Abbott, *The Great Companion* (New York: Grosset & Dunlap, 1904);

Abbott, *The Life and Literature of the Ancient Hebrews* (Boston: Houghton Mifflin, 1901);

Abbott, *The Other Room* (New York: Macmillan, 1903);

William Walker Atkinson, *Advanced Course in Yogi Philosophy and Oriental Occultism* (Chicago: Yogi Publication Society, 1904);

Atkinson, *The Law of the New Thought* (Chicago: Psychic Research, 1902);

Atkinson, *Reincarnation and the Law of Karma* (Chicago: Yogi Publication Society, 1908);

Kate Waller Barrett, *Some Practical Suggestions on the Conduct of a Rescue Home* (Washington, D.C.: National Florence Crittenton Mission, 1903);

Louis S. Bauman, *The Faith Once for All Delivered to the Saints* (Winona Lake, Ind.: Brethren Missionary Herald, 1909);

Pierre Bernard, *In Re Fifth Veda* (New York: Tantrik Order in America, 1909);

William Edward Biederwolf, *The Growing Christian* (Chicago: Winona Lake Publishing, 1903);

Charles Albert Blanchard, *Modern Secret Societies* (Chicago: National Christian Association, 1903);

Evangeline Cory Booth, *Desperation* (New York: Salvation Army, 1904);

Booth, *Love Is All* (New York: Press of Reliance Trading, 1908);

Borden Parker Bowne, *Studies in Christianity* (Boston: Houghton Mifflin, 1909);

Henry Harrison Brown, *Art of Living*, 25 volumes (San Francisco: "Now" Company, 1902);

Paul Carus, *The Dharma* (Chicago: Open Court Publishing, 1906);

Thornton Chase, *The Baha'i Revelation* (New York: Baha'i Publishing, 1909);

William Newton Clarke, *The Christian Doctrine of God* (New York: Scribners, 1909);

George Albert Coe, *Education in Religion and Morals* (New York: Fleming H. Revell, 1904);

Coe, *The Spiritual Life: Studies in the Science of Religion* (New York: Eaton & Mains, 1900);

Wilberforce Juvenal Colville, *Universal Spiritualism* (New York: R. F. Fenno, 1906);

Malinda Elliot Cramer, *Divine Science and Healing* (San Francisco: C. L. Cramer, 1907);

Algernon Sidney Crapsey, *Religion and Politics* (New York: T. Whitaker, 1905);

Arthur L. Cross, *The Anglican Episcopate and the American Colonies* (New York: Longmans, Green, 1902);

William Saunders Crowdy, *The Bible Gospel Told: The Revelation of God Revealed* (Washington, D.C.: Church of God & Saints of Christ, 1902);

John Alexander Dowie, *Zion's Conflict with Methodist Apostasy* (Chicago: Zion Publishing House, 1900);

W. E. B. Du Bois, *The Negro Church* (Atlanta: Atlanta University Press, 1903);

Du Bois, *The Souls of Black Folk* (Chicago: McClurg, 1903);

William Porcher Dubose, *The Gospel in the Gospels* (New York: Longmans, Green, 1907);

Mary Baker Eddy, *Rudimental Divine Science* (Boston: Christian Science Publishing Society, 1908);

James Arthur Edgerton, *Glimpses of the Real* (Denver: Reed, 1903);

John Murphy Farley, *The Catholic Church, the Teacher of Mankind*, 3 volumes (New York: Office of Catholic Publications, 1905);

Frank H. Foster, *A Genetic History of the New England Theology* (Chicago: University of Chicago Press, 1907);

George Berman Foster, *The Finality of the Christian Religion* (Chicago: University of Chicago Press, 1906);

James Gibbons, *Discourses and Sermons for Every Sunday and the Principal Festivals of the Year* (Baltimore: John Murphy, 1908);

Washington Gladden, *The Church and Modern Life* (Boston: Houghton Mifflin, 1908);

Gladden, *Social Salvation* (Boston: Houghton Mifflin, 1902);

Charles Leroy Goodell, *Pastoral and Personal Evangelism* (New York: Fleming H. Revell, 1907);

George Angier Gordon, *The New Epoch for Faith* (Boston: Houghton Mifflin, 1901);

Gordon, *Religion and Miracle* (Boston: Houghton Mifflin, 1909);

Edward Everett Hale, *Memories of a Hundred Years*, 2 volumes (New York: Macmillan, 1902);

Hutchins Hapgood, *The Spirit of the Ghetto* (New York: Funk & Wagnalls, 1902);

Newell Dwight Hillis, *The Influence of Christ on Modern Life* (New York: Macmillan, 1901);

Jesse Lyman Hurlbut, *Hurlbut's Handy Bible Encyclopedia* (Philadelphia: Winston, 1908);

Henry Eyster Jacobs, *Summary of the Christian Faith* (Philadelphia: General Council Publishing House, 1905);

William James, *The Varieties of Religious Experience* (New York: Longmans, Green, 1902);

Charles Edward Jefferson, *The Character of Jesus* (New York: Crowell, 1908);

Henry Churchill King, *Rational Living* (New York: Macmillan, 1905);

King, *Reconstruction in Theology* (New York: Macmillan, 1901);

Martin Wells Knapp, *Holiness Triumphant* (Cincinnati, Ohio: God's Bible School Book Room, 1900);

John Benjamin Lawrence, *A New Heaven and a New Earth* (New York: American Press, 1906);

Charles Webster Leadbeater, *An Outline of Theosophy* (Chicago: Theosophical Book Concern, 1903);

Henry Pereira Mendes, *The Jewish Religion Ethically Presented* (New York, 1905);

Joanna Moore, *In Christ's Stead* (Chicago: Woman's American Baptist Home Mission Society, 1903);

John R. Mott, *The Evangelization of the World in This Generation* (New York: Student Volunteer Movement for Foreign Missions, 1900);

Albert Henry Newman, *A Manual of Church History*, 2 volumes (Philadelphia: American Baptist Publication Society, 1900–1903);

James Martin Peebles, *Reincarnation: or, the Doctrine of the Soul's Successive Embodiments* (Battle Creek, Mich.: Peebles Medical Institute, 1904);

William Leroy Pettingill, *God's Prophecies for Plain People* (Philadelphia: Philadelphia School of the Bible, 1905);

Pettingill, *Simple Studies in Daniel* (Philadelphia: Philadelphia School of the Bible, 1909);

Arthur Tappan Pierson, *The Bible and Spiritual Criticism* (New York: Baker & Taylor, 1905);

Pierson, *Forward Movements of the Last Half Century* (New York: Funk & Wagnalls, 1900);

Pierson, *The Modern Mission Century* (New York: Baker & Taylor, 1901);

James Morgan Pryse Jr., *Reincarnation in the New Testament* (New York: Theosophical Publishing, 1900);

Walter Rauschenbusch, *Christianity and the Social Crisis* (New York: Macmillan, 1907);

Seth Cook Rees, *Miracles in the Slums* (Chicago: Published by the author, 1905);

Brigham Henry Roberts, *New Witnesses for God, II and III* (Salt Lake City, Utah: Deseret News, 1909);

John Augustine Ryan, *A Living Wage* (New York: Macmillan, 1906);

Ira D. Sankey, *My Life and the Story of the Gospel Hymns and Sacred Songs and Solos* (Philadelphia: Sunday School Times, 1906);

Solomon Schechter, *Some Aspects of Rabbinic Theology* (New York: Macmillan, 1909);

Soyen Shaku, *Sermons of a Zen Buddhist Abbot* (Chicago: Open Court Publishing, 1906);

Hannah Whitall Smith, *The Unselfishness of God and How I Discovered It: My Spiritual Autobiography* (New York: Fleming H. Revell, 1903);

Newman Smyth, *Passing Protestantism and Coming Catholicism* (New York: Scribners, 1908);

Smyth, *Through Science to Faith* (New York: Scribners, 1902);

Josiah Strong, *The Challenge of the City* (New York: Eaton & Mains, 1907);

J. H. W. Stuckenberg, *Sociology: The Science of Human Society*, 2 volumes (New York: Putnam, 1903);

Jabez Thomas Sunderland, *The Spark in the Clod: A Study of Evolution* (Boston: Beacon, 1902);

Lindsay Swift, *Brook Farm: Its Members, Scholars, and Visitors* (New York: Macmillan, 1900);

Worth Marion Tippy, *The Socialized Church* (New York: Eaton & Mains, 1909);

Rueben Archer Torrey, *How to Work for Christ* (Chicago: Fleming H. Revell, 1901);

Milton Valentine, *Christian Theology*, 2 volumes (Philadelphia: Lutheran Publication Society, 1907);

Henry Clay Velder, *The Baptists* (New York: Baker & Taylor, 1903);

Anna White and Leila S. Taylor, *Shakerism: Its Meaning and Message* (Columbus, Ohio: Press of F. J. Fleer, 1904);

Ella Wheeler Wilcox, *The Heart of New Thought* (Chicago: Psychic Research, 1902);

Stephen Samuel Wise, *The Improvement of the Moral Qualities* (New York: Columbia University Press, 1902);

Henry Wood, *The New Old Healing* (Boston: Lothrop, Lee & Shepard, 1908);

The Apostolic Faith, periodical;

Banner of Light, periodical;

The Budget, periodical;

The Catholic World, periodical;

Christian Century, periodical;

Christian Science Monitor, periodical;

The Continent, periodical;

The Dawn, periodical;

Harvard Theological Review, periodical;

Jewish Quarterly Review, periodical;

The Messenger, periodical;

New Thought Magazine, periodical;

Outlook, periodical;

Quarterly Review of the Evangelical Lutheran Church, periodical;

The Scroll, periodical;

Serving-and-Waiting, periodical;

Suggestion, periodical;

Voice of the People, periodical;

The Watch Tower, periodical;

Weekly Prophet, periodical.

CHAPTER TWELVE

SCIENCE AND TECHNOLOGY

by THOMAS GLICK

CONTENTS

Sidebars and tables are listed in italics.

1900

- Thomas Alva Edison invents the nickel-alkaline storage battery.
- Gregor Mendel's forgotten laws of genetics are independently rediscovered by three European biologists.
- The modern pendulum seismograph for the detection of earthquakes is invented in Germany.
- Sigmund Freud publishes *On the Interpretation of Dreams* in German.

2 July   First Zeppelin dirigible flies in Germany.

14 Dec.   German physicist Max Planck announces the basis of quantum theory: light rays are not continuous but are emitted in discrete amounts called quanta.

1901

- Congress establishes the National Bureau of Standards.
- Dutch biologist Hugo de Vries publishes the first volume of his theory of genetic mutation.
- The hormone adrenaline is isolated by Japanese American chemist Jokichi Takamine and chemist-pharmacologist John Jacob Abel.
- Freud publishes *The Psychopathology of Everyday Life*, explaining "Freudian slips" of the tongue.
- Wilbur and Orville Wright begin glider flights to observe and master the aerodynamics of flying.
- General Electric founds the first corporate research laboratory.
- John D. Rockefeller establishes the Rockefeller Institute for Medical Research in New York City.
- Andrew Carnegie announces his intention to donate $10 million to promote scientific research.

Apr.   Thaddeus Cahill exhibits his electric typewriter at the Pan-American Exhibition in Buffalo.

12 Dec.   Guglielmo Marconi receives the first transatlantic radio communication.

1902

- Dupont and Parke-Davis companies establish research laboratories.
- Charles Steinmetz patents the magnetite lamp.
- The vacuum cleaner and power lawn mower are invented in England.
- German Arthur Korn invents the photofax machine to transmit news photographs by telegraph.
- French auto manufacturer Louis Renault invents the drum brake; Englishman Frederick W. Lanchester invents the disc brake.
- Russian physiologist and psychologist Ivan Pavlov discovers conditioned reflexes.
- German chemist Richard Zsigmondy invents the ultramicroscope, making possible the observation of the individual particles of colloidal solutions.

- British physicists Ernest Rutherford and Frederick Soddy explain radioactivity as a transformation or disintegration of the structure of atoms.

1903

- The U.S. Navy buys German "Slaby-Arco" radio sets to equip its battleships and tests them in maneuvers.

- Reginald A. Fessenden discovers the electrolytic radio detector, capable of receiving the human voice.

- Edison perfects the electroplating technique of making master record molds.

- The safety razor is invented.

- Willem Einthoven, the Dutch physiologist who invented the string galvanometer, defines its application for electrocardiograms.

- English philosopher Bertrand Russell publishes *The Principles of Mathematics*, an attempt to reduce pure mathematics to a limited number of logical concepts.

Jan. President Theodore Roosevelt, from a Marconi station in Wellfleet, Massachusetts, exchanges greetings with England's King Edward VII via a wireless telegraph.

7 Oct. Samuel P. Langley's airplane, launched from a houseboat, fails to fly. Langley's plane will fail a second time nine days before the Wrights' success.

17 Dec. The Wright brothers fly successfully at Kitty Hawk, North Carolina.

1904

- French physicist Jules-Henri Poincaré delivers a lecture on the principles of mathematical physics at the International Congress of Arts and Sciences in Saint Louis.

- Englishman John A. Fleming invents the diode vacuum tube.

- Charles D. Perrine discovers the sixth moon of Jupiter.

- Japanese physicist Hantaro Nagaoka proposes a model of the structure of the atom by comparing the motion of electrons to that of the rings of the planet Saturn.

- The U.S. Panama Canal project gets under way.

- The United Engineering Society is established.

- Invented in Germany, the phonograph record quickly replaces Edison's wax cylinder.

20 Dec. George Ellery Hale and the Carnegie Institution establish Mount Wilson Observatory near Pasadena, California. Hale becomes the observatory's first director.

1905

- Albert Einstein publishes four significant scientific papers. Two were on the special theory of relativity (in one he showed that because of the constancy of the speed of light, time passes at different rates for objects in motion; in the second he stated the relationship between mass and energy); the third was on Brownian movement; the fourth (for which he later won the Nobel Prize) was on the photoelectric effect.

- German physicist Philipp Lenard wins the Nobel Prize for the discovery of cathode rays.

- English physiologist Ernest Starling coins the term *hormone* to describe chemical messengers produced by the endocrine glands.

- Freud publishes *Jokes and their Relation to the Unconscious* and *Three Essays on the Theory of Sexuality,* both in German. The latter was considered perverse and shocking by German medical opinion.

- The German navy launches its first U-boat submarine.

30 Aug.   Path of solar eclipse passes through Spain.

1906

- Thaddeus Cahill invents the telharmonium, a kind of telephonic organ.

- J. J. Thomson wins the Nobel Prize in physics for the discovery of the electron.

- The Nobel Prize for medicine is shared by Camillo Golgi of Italy and Santiago Ramón y Cajal of Spain for the neuron theory.

24 Dec.   The first radio broadcast originates from Brant Rock, Massachusetts.

31 Dec.   De Forest invents the triode vacuum tube.

1907

- De Forest develops the triode radio tube.

- The first helicopter flight occurs in France.

- Albert Michelson wins the Nobel Prize in physics, becoming the first American Nobel laureate, for his measurements of the speed of light.

14 Jan.   Telharmonic Hall opens in New York City.

1908

- George Ellery Hale discovers magnetic fields in sunspots.

- G. H. Hardy works out a mathematical law governing the frequency of a dominant genetic trait in successive generations (Hardy-Weinberg law).

- Ernest Rutherford of England wins the Nobel Prize in chemistry for his studies of radioactivity.

- Heike Kamerlingh Onnes, Dutch specialist in low-temperature physics, produces liquid helium in his laboratory.

- The first tractor with moving treads is introduced by the Holt Company of California.

- The electric razor is introduced.

- Henry Ford introduces the Model T, or "Tin Lizzie," the most popular of early motorcars.

- Edison unveils his concrete house.

7 Dec.   A sixty-inch reflecting telescope is installed at Mount Wilson Observatory.

21 Dec.   Wilbur Wright wins the Michelin Cup in France by flying 77 miles in 2 hours, 20 minutes.

1909

- Wilhelm Johannsen introduces the terms *gene, genotype,* and *phenotype.*

- German evolutionary biologist August Weismann publishes his *Theory of Selection.*

- German chemist Wilhelm Ostwald wins the Nobel Prize in chemistry for his studies of catalysis.

- Guglielmo Marconi and Karl F. Braun share the Nobel Prize in physics for wireless telegraphy and the radio.

6 Apr. U.S. Navy commander Robert Peary reaches the North Pole.

29 June John D. Rockefeller charters the Rockefeller Foundation.

25 July Louis Blériot flies across the English Channel.

Sept. In his only visit to the United States, Freud lectures at Clark University in Worcester, Massachusetts.

24 Nov. The fiftieth anniversary of the publication of Charles Darwin's *On the Origin of Species* and the centennial year of Darwin's birth are both marked by commemorative celebrations in the United States and England.

OVERVIEW

Technology for a Whole Century. In the first decade of the twentieth century three of the inventions that would dominate the century technologically were either invented or underwent their early development: the automobile, the airplane, and the radio. The automobile and the roads that paved its way would change the face of the country and the daily habits of Americans perhaps more than any other invention. The airplane became a kind of royal road for technological innovation, the breakthrough that suggested the unlimited possibilities of the future. In the first decade flying captured the popular imagination more than any other innovation, in spite of its having no practical effect on most people's lives at the time. The radio was, after the telegraph and telephone, the leading edge of the communications revolution, more revolutionary than its antecedents because it did not require wires.

Heightened International Communication. One of the characteristics of new and important technologies is that invention is followed by one or two decades of intense international communication as the best engineers and inventors from different countries exchange ideas while fine-tuning and building upon the original idea. This happened in the case of the automobile, a German invention, which Henry Ford improved on with the help of some ideas from France (note the prevalence of French terms used to describe basic features of the early motorcar: *automobile, chassis, garage, chauffeur*). The invention of the airplane was a race between the Wright brothers and foreign, mainly French, aeronauts. The key to creating consumer demand (when the early consumers were mainly governments or governmental agencies) was Wilbur Wright's exhibition tour of France in 1908. The pedigree of radio was also culturally complex: the Italian inventor Guglielmo Marconi received important experimental help from the English physicist Oliver Lodge; but Nikola Tesla, a Croatian-born immigrant to the United States, claimed that he was the real inventor. America's most famous inventor, Thomas Alva Edison, openly acknowledged his dependence on a transatlantic network of electrical engineers at the time when the electric power industry was in its phase of initial consolidation and expansion.

Infant Science. In contrast to the feverish activity on many different fronts of technology, American science was underdeveloped at the turn of the century. In the 1860s there had been only about two thousand American scientists in all fields. Growth came slowly, particularly in theoretical areas. The public universities favored teaching science from a practical viewpoint, looking to support engineering and agriculture in particular. Modern centers of experimental physics were established at Johns Hopkins University by Henry A. Rowland and at Case Institute of Technology by Albert Michelson. Yet by century's end there were only two hundred physicists in the entire United States, virtually all of them experimentalists. Government-sponsored efforts, such as the U.S. Geological Survey, the Naval Observatory, and the Smithsonian Institution, would be instrumental in promoting the growth of science.

Ideas from Abroad. Although American science was undeveloped in comparison to Europe, the United States nevertheless provided an ample audience for new concepts arriving from European research fronts. The rediscovery of Mendel's laws of heredity by three Europeans quickly created a new science of genetics that was closely followed in the United States, not only by biologists but by plant and animal breeders. Einstein's theory of relativity was known to American physicists, its development having been presaged by American contributions to the study of the velocity of light. Sigmund Freud introduced his new theory of psychology — psychoanalysis — personally in a celebrated visit to Massachusetts. Astronomers, as perhaps no other group of American scientists, participated fully in the programs of the world community of astronomers and made important contributions from their home observatories, made possible in great part by the appearance of the first foundations with serious interests in promoting scientific research. The foundations would change the nature of the scientific enterprise in the United States during succeeding decades.

A Different Kind of Science. A more forward-looking view of science arose in the 1870s and 1880s, especially at Johns Hopkins, a new university where laboratories and departments were modeled after those in Europe that encouraged research for its own sake, not just for practical concerns. By the end of nineteenth century science was increasingly focused on original research projects, a trend that was enhanced by the foundations established to promote just such a new orientation. Thus the present system of support for science and its typical form of organization around specific research projects was put in place in the first decade of the twentieth century.

TOPICS IN THE NEWS

THE AIRPLANE

Antecedents. Aviation in the United States began with the enthusiasm for ballooning in the years before the Civil War. There were some three thousand balloon ascents by 1859. Both the Union and Confederate armies used balloons for reconnaissance during the war. The Union effort, headed by Thaddeus Lowe, used tethered balloons to observe enemy movements which were then telegraphed to field officers. At the Saint Louis Exhibition of 1904 prizes that were offered for navigable airships drew ninety-seven entrants with dirigibles and similar machines. One of these was Roy Knabenshue, who piloted a sixty-two-foot dirigible over New York City in 1905. A second airship competition held in Saint Louis in 1907 again reflected the national fascination with large airships. Many Americans believed that dirigibles held the key to future air travel.

Early Experiments. The major precursor of American aeronautical engineering was Samuel P. Langley, director of the Smithsonian Institution, who in 1891 asserted, "Mechanical flight is possible with engines we now possess." Beginning in 1887 he had experimented with large model airplanes (weighing as much as thirty pounds), using twisted-rubber motors in order to test various wing designs. He eventually settled on a tandem model with two sets of wings, one behind the other, with twin propellers in between. One of these, his model 5, with a twelve-foot wingspan and a one-horsepower steam engine, flew three thousand feet along the Potomac on 6 May 1896. In the same year, a French-born engineer named Octave Chanute began experimenting with manned gliders, a necessary step in learning how to maneuver a winged aircraft. Chanute perfected a two-wing glider, called the double-decker, which proved to be the origin of early biplanes. In the fall of 1896 it registered glides as long as 256 feet in trials on the Indiana shore of Lake Michigan. Activities like these created a journalistic frenzy, with reporters constantly asking inventors when flight would at last be achieved. Finally in the fall of 1903

The 7 October 1903 launching of Samuel P. Langley's airplane, which twice failed to achieve manned flight before the success of the Wright brothers on 17 December 1903

Langley built an airplane called the *Aerodrome* with a five-cylinder engine. Twice Charles M. Manly attempted to fly the plane, which was catapulted into the air from a houseboat on the Potomac River, and twice he had to be pulled from the river. Nine days after the second failure, Wilbur and Orville Wright achieved manned flight at Kitty Hawk, North Carolina. The Wright brothers, by focusing on the interaction between wing and air currents, solved the practical problems of flight before they attempted to put a motor on their glider. Langley and others who assigned priority to the motor all failed.

The AEA. In 1907 Alexander Graham Bell, attracted to the exciting new field of aeronautical technology, formed the Aerial Experiment Association for the express purpose of "getting into the air." Of the four other members, two — Thomas Selfridge and Glenn Curtiss — would make marks in aeronautical history. (Selfridge became the first American aviation casualty when he

The Wright brothers achieved the first manned flight of a power-driven, heavier-than-air machine. Piloted by Orville Wright, the plane remained aloft fifty-nine seconds, reaching an altitude of only fifteen feet and traveling less than three hundred yards.

crashed to his death while flying with Orville Wright in 1908.) Bell himself had become obsessed with an original wing design he had conceived by building kites made of cells in the form of tetrahedrons. This made for a very light and strong wing. Bell considered the Wrights' plane to be dangerous because it required high speeds to take off and maintain flight. He aimed at designing a manned flying kite that would travel at no more than 10 to 15 MPH. His prototype failed, however, and the AEA turned to biplanes. Curtiss flew the *White Wing* successfully in a series of flights in July and August 1908. The Wright brothers began to think their patent had been infringed.

Aerial Competition. Curtiss, in partnership with Alexander Herring, then built a new biplane on his own. This plane, the *Golden Flier,* caused a sensation when Curtiss flew it before a large, paying crowd in New York in June 1909. Later that summer in France, at the end of August, he faced the Wrights' flier (piloted by French aviators trained by the Wrights) at Rheims. The occasion was the Gordon Bennett trophy for the two fastest laps around a ten-kilometer course. Curtiss arrived with his *Reims Racer* equipped with a V-8 engine built for speed tests. He beat all rivals handily, completing the twenty-kilometer race at an average speed of 47 MPH. By the end of the decade both Curtiss and the Wrights, soon to be joined by Glenn Martin, were producing airplanes for military and civilian use. The first decade of the century had set the stage for the vast expansion of airplane production ushered in by World War I.

Sources:

Roger E. Bilstein, *Flight in America: From the Wrights to the Astronauts* (Baltimore: Johns Hopkins University Press, 1984);

Fred Howard, *Wilbur and Orville: A Biography of the Wright Brothers* (New York: Knopf, 1987).

ANTIVIVISECTIONISM

Vivisection and Experimental Medicine. Virtually all advances in physiology and endocrinology in the late nineteenth and early twentieth centuries were based on vivisection — the experimental use of living animals to observe physiological processes under laboratory conditions. The most successful forms of vivisection began with the French physiologist Claude Bernard, who discovered the liver's glycogenic function by severing a rabbit's cerebellar peduncle nerve and noting the abnormally high levels of sugar (glycosuria) that resulted. In endocrinology at the turn of the century, the chemical actions of the ductless glands were studied by extirpating the gland and observing the resultant metabolic changes in the animal subjects. The procedure led in 1901 to the isolation of adrenaline (epinephrine) by Japanese American chemist Jokichi Takamine and Johns Hopkins Medical School chemist-pharmacologist John Jacob Abel.

Organized Opposition to Vivisection. The rise of the movement to curtail the experimental use of animals paralleled the successes of vivisection and advances in physiology, pathology, and bacteriology in the third quarter of the nineteenth century. In England an Antivivisection Act was passed by Parliament in 1876. In 1883 the

An antivivisectionist cartoon, captioned "The Little Boy Who Never Grew Up"

Walter B. Cannon, who spearheaded the American Medical Association's defense of animal experimentation

American Antivivisection Society was founded in Philadelphia. Such societies joined with state chapters of the American Society for the Prevention of Cruelty to Animals to lobby legislatures. A major battle was launched in Boston, an important center of medical research in 1896, when a bill was introduced in the state legislature to restrict experimentation on animals in medical schools. Abbott Lawrence Lowell of Harvard led the charge on the medical side by saying that someone ought to speak on behalf of "the people whose children die by the thousands in the warm weeks of summer. . . . It is for them that the scientific biologists are at work." The hearings convinced the antivivisectionists that they were combating an entrenched intellectual elite, while the medical community, which had organized a Committee on Experimental Biology in 1903 to promote their cause, was afraid that new methods of treating human subjects was the real target.

Laboratory Conditions. The agitation was strong enough to stimulate medical schools to investigate the nature of animal research and evaluate the conditions under which laboratory animals were kept. Walter B. Cannon of Harvard Medical School wrote to experimentalists throughout the country to find out how animals were cared for and whether medical schools had done anything to educate the public concerning the need for vivisection. Percy Dawson of Johns Hopkins replied that

although conditions in American laboratories were generally good and physiologists strove to avoid inflicting pain, nevertheless "it is probable that although animals are usually well treated in the operating room, their quarters are often very miserable and the care of the animals before they reach the operating table much worse than should be." Dawson concluded that some control over these animals should be instituted.

The AMA Gets Involved. In 1908 the American Medical Association, mindful that the problem was a national one, formed a special defense committee to support research and explain to the public the need to use animals. Named chairman, Cannon held that antivivisectionists were ignorant both of medical research and of the actual laboratory conditions and procedures against which they were complaining. He continued to gather information and, at the same time, to write a model code of laboratory rules. By 1910 Cannon's rules had been adopted in laboratories at thirty-seven medical schools and research institutes, including the largest ones.

Cannon versus James. In May 1909 William James, philosopher, former physiologist, and one of the most influential American academics, published a letter in the *New York Post* arguing that scientists could not be counted on to police themselves and attacking as irresponsible the notion that scientists had the right to en-

Naval officers and sailors who observed the 1905 total eclipse in Spain

gage in animal experimentation without any public accountability. James had long expressed distaste for animal experimentation. Cannon rejoined that James had "confused a protest by medical men against special legislation directed at them and an assumption commonly made that they object to any control of their work." Cannon thought that no special legislation aimed at research scientists was required because general laws against cruelty to animals were already on the books.

Significance of the Debate. The antivivisection debate of the first decade of the twentieth century stands out because it seemed to threaten the unprecedented advances in medical science made in the previous quarter century. The biomedical leadership regarded the antivivisection movement with horror because experiments with live animals accounted for most of the physiological knowledge of the digestive, cardiovascular, and nervous systems. Without animal research it was feared that progress would be slowed. Such a concern was prudent, for

looking ahead a decade or two, the research that led to the discovery of insulin and its effective treatment of diabetes could not have been accomplished without vivisection. On the other hand, antivivisectionism can also be seen as a movement in favor of the public promotion and awareness of standards of medical ethics and their extension into the laboratory. In that sense the antivivisection debate presaged public debates over genetic research and bioengineering.

Source:
Saul Benison, A. Clifford Barger, and Elin L. Wolfe, *Walter B. Cannon: The Life and Times of a Young Scientist* (Cambridge, Mass.: Harvard University Press, 1987).

ASTRONOMY: 1905 SOLAR ECLIPSE

Photography and Eclipse Observations. Since the middle of the nineteenth century solar eclipses had attracted intense interest among astronomers. The invention of photography and its application to astronomical observations made it possible to record with great precision the solar phenomena that eclipses revealed. Although some primitive daguerreotype photographs had been made of both the sun and the moon in the 1840s, the crucial breakthrough came with Englishman Warren de la Rue's invention of the photoheliograph, a photographic telescope with a fast shutter that could be used to map the surface of the sun.

Solar Prominences. The first significant riddle that astronomical photography resolved concerned the existence of solar prominences, protuberances from the sun's outer edge that had long puzzled astronomers. It was not clear whether they were physical features of the sun or merely optical illusions. De la Rue took his photoheliograph to Spain, which offered the best view of the solar eclipse of 1860, an event that attracted many European astronomers, including Angelo Secchi, the second pioneer of photographic astronomy. Secchi compared his observations with de la Rue's photographs and confirmed that the prominences seen during the eclipse were real.

The Eclipse of 1905. The path of totality of the eclipse again passed through Spain 30 August 1905, which created a scientific tourist attraction for hundreds of astronomers. The United States was represented by three separate teams, two of which were dispatched by the navy. The third, representing the Lick Observatory in California, was headed by the country's leading observational astronomer, William Wallace Campbell. One navy team, with a forty-foot telescopic camera, was stationed in Daroca and included the director of the University of Virginia's McCormick Observatory, Samuel Mitchell. The team included some thirty-five individuals, including the astronomers and their support staff. In his account of the expedition Mitchell described the hard work involved in building sheds to protect the telescopes, in mounting spectroscopes, and establishing a meteorological observatory. On several nights before the eclipse the astronomers had to stay up all night in order to fine-tune their instrumentation.

Results. Since observations must be concentrated in the tiny window of time bracketing the totality of the eclipse, eclipses do not generally produce startling new findings. Rather, they contribute to the slow building of a cumulative data bank that aids in understanding the physical and, through spectroscopy, chemical phenomena observed. (The results of the solar eclipse of 1919 that confirmed the predictions of Einstein's general theory of relativity was a dramatic exception to the rule of slowly gathered cumulative results.) The most fortunate solar astronomers tried to view as many eclipses as they could afford: Campbell witnessed eight solar eclipses between 1898 (India) and 1922 (Australia). Thus the American teams gathered data about the prominences and the solar corona, ultraviolet radiation, polarization phenomena (measured by a photopolarimeter), and the chemical composition of the sun. The 1905 eclipse was significant in the history of American astronomy because of the large number of personnel participating in an international scientific project. More than any other single

---

PEARY AT THE POLE

When Commander Robert Edwin Peary reached the North Pole he knew that, in order to establish that he had accomplished the feat, he would have to make and record accurate observations of his geographical position. These observations he recorded in his log. On 6 April 1909 he wrote: "The Pole at last. The prize of three centuries. My dream and goal for twenty years. Mine at last!" When he wanted to record some geographical observations, however, he found that the sky was overcast, so he pressed on with his instruments and a team of dogs for about ten miles, to a place where the sky had cleared. He took his observations and wrote: "When I had taken my observations, at Camp Jesup in the Western Hemisphere at noon of April 6th, Columbia meridian time, the sun had been in the south. When I had taken my observations at midnight between the 6th and 7th, at the end of my ten-mile march, in the Eastern Hemisphere, the sun was in the South at that point — but to those at the camp on the other side of the world, only ten miles away, it was in the North." The opposite orientations to the sun proved that he had indeed found the pole.

He then retraced his steps some eight miles toward the pole and on noon of 7 April took another set of observations: "I had now taken thirteen single, or six and a half double, altitudes of the sun, at two different stations, in three different directions, at four different times, and to allow for possible errors in instruments and observations, had traversed in various directions an area of about eight by ten miles across. At some moment during these marches and countermarches, I had for all practical purposes passed over the point where north and south and east and west blend into one."

Sources: William Herbert Hobbs, *Peary* (New York: Macmillan, 1936);

Robert E. Peary, *The North Pole* (Washington, D.C.: F. A. Stokes, 1910).

---

event, it marked the coming of age of American astronomy.

Sources:
Rebecca R. Joslin, *Chasing Eclipses: The Total Solar Eclipses of 1905, 1914, 1925* (Boston: Walton, 1925);

Samuel Alfred Mitchell, *Eclipses of the Sun* (New York: Columbia University Press, 1923).

THE AUTOMOBILE

The Invention of the Automobile. Although some steam-driven vehicles were built in England, France, and the United States in the early nineteenth century, the

Henry Ford's first automobile, the Quadricycle, which he drove through the streets of Detroit on 6 June 1896

prototypes of the modern motorcar were built by the Germans Gottleib Daimler and Karl Benz. Daimler first used his gasoline engine in a four-wheeled vehicle in 1886. The two men licensed their vehicles for production in France during the 1890s.

Ford. Born on a farm in Dearborn, Michigan, in 1863, Henry Ford saw his first horseless carriage (a steam-driven one) at the age of twelve and never forgot the tremendous impression it made on him. His earliest automotive projects were aimed more at developing a practical tractor than a pleasure vehicle. Ford established himself in Detroit in 1891, where he was employed by the Edison Illuminating Company, and soon began to tinker with automobile engines. Ford did not invent the motorcar, nor was he the first American to build one, but he was instrumental in the development of the private automobile. Early American models were behemoths, car-

riages designed for the wealthy. From the beginning Ford had a different idea: to produce a practical, sturdy vehicle within reach of the common man. He built his first car, the Quadricycle, in 1896.

The First Model A. Ford's work to engineer a more efficient motor led in 1902 to an engine with two cylinders set vertically instead of horizontally; this increased its power and reduced wear. The first engine to be produced by the Ford Motor Company was designed and assembled by Ford and his staff, but its parts were manufactured by the machine shop of John and Horace Dodge. The Model A's wooden body was purchased from a carriage company. By early 1904 the company was making twenty-five cars daily. (This first Model A should not be confused with the second, more famous one of 1927.)

The Model N. In the early days of the automobile, innovations were tried out in car races, with each succes-

Model Ks driving in front of Ford's Piquette Avenue plant

sive race producing faster times. At such a race in 1905, Ford noticed that French cars were lighter and stronger than American entries, including his own Model K, a powered-up six-cylinder racing machine. The French used an alloy of vanadium and steel, unknown in the United States, and difficult to produce because it required very high furnace temperatures. Ford convinced a steel company in Ohio to experiment with and later to manufacture vanadium steel exclusively for his company. The new steel was introduced with Ford's Model N in January 1906. Meanwhile, he had established the Ford Manufacturing Company to make his own engines and chassis. The Model N was envisioned as a mass-production vehicle, but without a movable assembly line (not introduced until 1913), assembly entailed an unavoidable bottleneck. So many workers were required that it was impossible to hold the price to the announced figure of $450.

The Model T. The four cylinders for the Model N's engine were cast separately and then bolted together. For the Model T, Ford wanted all four cast together in a single block and so devised what is still the basic design of the internal combustion engine. A magneto vastly simplified the electrical system, and Ford and his top engineer, Charles Sorensen, developed a new transmission with three pedals, one for forward motion, one for back, one as a brake. The Model T was a huge success, nicknamed the "Tin Lizzie" by loyal consumers. The company sold ten thousand in the first year (ending 30 September 1909). By the end of World War I half the automobiles in the world were Model Ts.

The Competition. Ford's most serious early competitors were the Duryea brothers, who built the first workable American automobile in 1893, and Ransom Eli Olds, whose first "Merry Oldsmobile" — a four-passenger two-seater — went on the market in 1896. In 1899 he established his own plant in Detroit, the Olds Motor Works. There he turned out the first mass-produced motor vehicle in the United States, the "curved dash" Oldsmobile runabout. Not all early automobile manufacturers put their faith in gasoline engines. Starting in 1897, the Stanley brothers of Newton, Massachusetts, manufactured a steam-driven car, the famous Stanley Steamer. All told, between 1900 and 1908, 502 automobile companies were started, of which 302 had failed. By 1908 David D. Buick's company was the leading car producer. In that year William C. Durant engineered a merger of three independent companies, Buick, Olds, and Cadillac, to form the General Motors Company. The year also saw the first car manufactured by Walter Chrysler. So by the end of the decade the Big Three automobile companies — Ford, General Motors, and Chrysler — had all been established.

Popular Adoption of the Motorcar. The impact of the automobile was felt immediately in many areas of life. Horse-drawn transportation entered a period of rapid decline. Owners of urban livery stables converted their properties into parking garages and began to rent automobiles. Fewer horses meant less manure to soil the streets, so the automobile was hailed as healthier mode of transportation. The car was also viewed as more reliable than the horse, especially after 1906 when most of the problems that had caused mechanical breakdowns in early autos had been solved. Doctors, who immediately saw the advantage of the motorcar for making house calls, were proportionally the largest group of early owners. Among early specialized motor vehicles were street-cleaning vehicles (1905), post-office mail cars (1909), ambulances, and milk delivery trucks. The military use of autos lagged: not until 1909 were motor vehicles used in military maneuvers. Throughout the decade a series of improvements in car design provided continual stimulus to public interest and rising sales: the wider French-style tonneau body (1901); the steering knuckle, which enabled the front wheels to turn without turning the entire axle (1902); running boards (1903); shock absorbers and the h-slot gearshift (1904); and tire chains (1905) are some examples.

Sources:

Frank Donovan, *Wheels for a Nation* (New York: Crowell, 1965);

James J. Flink, *America Adopts the Automobile, 1895–1910* (Cambridge, Mass.: MIT Press, 1970);

Henry Ford, *My Life and Work* (Garden City, N.Y.: Doubleday, 1922);

Robert Lacey, *Ford: The Men and the Machine* (Boston: Little, Brown, 1986).

BIOLOGY: BEGINNINGS OF BIOENGINEERING

Background. Scientific interest in bioengineering preceded the late-twentieth-century interest in biotechnology that is centered on genetics and on the possibility of altering the genetic makeup of cells and organisms. The early history of bioengineering in the United States is associated with Jacques Loeb. Born in Germany in 1859, Loeb immigrated to the United States in 1891, where he taught biology at the Universities of Chicago and California and from 1910 until his death in 1924 at the Rockefeller Institute.

Loeb and Parthenogenesis. Parthenogenesis is the process whereby an egg is induced to develop into an organism without having been fertilized. Both Loeb and Thomas Hunt Morgan, the most prominent American geneticist, had experimented with sea urchin eggs. Morgan had induced them to segment by immersing them in a solution of inorganic salts, although they failed to produce larvae. Loeb, using a variation of the same procedure, was able to raise larvae, a result he announced in 1899. The news caused a sensation, and Loeb was a finalist for the first Nobel Prize in physiology, awarded in

Jacques Loeb, a pioneer of bioengineering

1901. American newspapers played up the story and throughout the first decade of the twentieth century painted Loeb as a new Dr. Frankenstein, a man who boasted of the ability to control life and reproduction. In a 1902 interview Loeb asserted that he "wanted to take life in my hands and *play* with it." He wanted to handle life in the laboratory "as I would any other chemical reaction — to start it, stop it, vary it, study it under every condition, to direct it at my will!"

Creating Life. Ancient and medieval thinkers, misinterpreting the appearance of living creatures from microscopic eggs or larvae, believed that life could generate itself spontaneously. Then in a famous series of experiments in the 1870s, Louis Pasteur demonstrated that fermentation would not take place in an atmosphere that was free of all microorganisms, putting an end to the long debate over spontaneous generation but also stimulating scientists to speculate about the origins of life. Loeb believed that life could be engineered, and the notion of creating life in a test tube originated in an interview given by Loeb in 1899. Because of his experiments Loeb asserted, "we have drawn a great step nearer to the chemical theory of life and may already see ahead of us the day when a scientist, experimenting with chemicals in a test tube, may see them unite and form a substance which shall live and move and reproduce itself."

Loeb's Legacy. Loeb influenced several important American scientists, in particular the behavioral psychologists John B. Watson and B. F. Skinner, who believed that behavior could be predicted and controlled without reference either to instincts or to the structure of the brain. Watson wanted to control behavior and believed its explanation or interpretation was irrelevant to that objective, much as Loeb was uninterested in biological theory. (Loeb was an evolutionist but always stressed that he was most interested in *future* evolution, something that could be brought about by the active intervention of biologists in the processes of life.) Gregory Pincus, who developed the birth control pill, was also under the spell of Loeb's mystique when in the 1920s and 1930s he experimented on artificial parthenogenesis in mammals and even claimed to have produced it in rabbits. "Loeb," Pincus said, "stopped too soon." In this light, in vitro fertilization, wherein mammalian — including human — eggs are fertilized artificially in a test tube, can be seen as a logical extension of Loeb's view of artificially engineered reproductive processes.

Source:
Philip L. Pauly, *Controlling Life: Jacques Loeb and the Engineering Idea in Biology* (Berkeley: University of California Press, 1990).

BIOLOGY: MENDELIAN GENETICS

Mendel and His Rediscovery. Gregor Mendel was an Austrian monk who, as a result of experimentation in plant hybridization between 1856 and 1863, discovered that certain parental characteristics are dominant in the next generation and others are what he called recessive (that is, they do not appear but can be passed on to the next generation). Moreover, he found that such parental traits segregate themselves in a precise numerical ratio. Thus, if *A* represents a dominant round seed shape and *a* a recessive angular shape, then one-quarter of the progeny will have the dominant (*AA*), one-quarter the recessive (*aa*), and one-half will have a dominant and a recessive (*Aa* or *aA*), what is now called a heterozygous combination. Mendel's work was scarcely noted at the time. It was not until 1900 that three European biologists, Hugo de Vries, Karl Correns, and Erich von Tschermak independently rediscovered Mendel's "principle of segregation." In 1909 the Danish biologist Wilhelm Johannsen coined the terms that became standard: *gene* to represent the unit of heredity, *genotype* to designate the genetic makeup of an organism, and *phenotype* to denote the actual appearance of the organism.

Mendelism in the United States. American curiosity about genetics was first evinced by farmers interested in breeding. With the foundation of agricultural experimental stations and the establishment of agricultural colleges in the decades after the Civil War, agricultural scientists were naturally interested in the improvement of varieties of plants and animals through hybridization (or crossing, as it was then called) and selection ("breeding from the best"). In 1899 some American professors, including Liberty Hyde Bailey of Cornell University's agricultural college, attended the first International Conference on Hybridization in London. Then in 1903 Bailey and others

WAS BURBANK REALLY A SCIENTIST?

The horticultural methods of plant breeder Luther Burbank, famous for his spectacular new varieties of fruit, attracted the interest of professional biologists. In 1905 the Carnegie Institution, a foundation interested in backing useful scientific projects, looked into Burbank's methods and results. The institution's president, Robert S. Woodward, went so far as to visit Burbank's farm. Burbank, Woodward reported to his board, "is like a mathematician who never has to refer to his formulas; all information he possesses he can summon in an instant for his use. . . . He is not a trained man of science; he lacks knowledge of the terminology of modern science. He often expresses himself in a way quite offensive to many scientific men, if due allowance is not made; but he is a man who unconsciously works by the scientific method to the most extraordinary advantage. I think anybody who goes to his orchards and sees what he has produced and who studies Mr. Burbank as I have done will admit at once that he is a most unusual man." Woodward thought Burbank's work was valuable for all humanity. Andrew Carnegie himself agreed but urged that scientists be kept away from him.

The following year, the institution sent the pioneer geneticist George H. Shull to interview Burbank. Shull found that Burbank's notions of science were largely preconceptions. In particular, Burbank held on to ideas that contemporary genetic science had discredited, such as the notion that alterations in the environment directly cause genetic change through the inheritance of acquired characteristics : "He holds that nothing but acquired characters may be inherited and is thus led to attribute every variation to environmental causes in a more definite way than observations would warrant. Again, without knowing just what the various scientists and philosophers have learned or taught, he takes sides strongly, — *against* Weismann, Mendel, and De Vries, and *with* Darwin, and the modern opponents of mutation and Mendelism." The scientists' bottom line on Burbank was that he was a pragmatic plant breeder with scant capacity for understanding what he had really done.

Source: Nathan and Ida H. Reingold, *Science in America: A Documentary History* (Chicago: University of Chicago Press, 1981).

with similar interests founded the American Breeders' Association to promote the scientific approach to breed-

Thomas Hunt Morgan, whose work with fruit flies made an important contribution to evolutionary theory

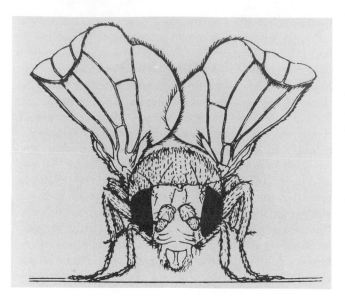

The common fruit fly, which quickly became the chosen subject for genetic experimentation

ing. From the beginning, members of the association were interested both in Mendel's laws and in de Vries's theory of mutation, which stressed the importance of sharp, discontinuous changes in heredity. Between 1903 and 1909 as many as one-fifth of the papers presented at the annual meeting of the association discussed Mendel's ideas, and at the 1907 meeting George H. Shull gave a paper praising de Vries's theory and stressing its significance to breeders. The reason for the strong, early interest in Mendel is clear: his laws made it possible to predict the probable outcomes of specific breeding strategies. In 1910 the association began publication of the *American Breeders' Magazine*, the first American journal devoted to genetics. In 1912 the association was reorganized as the American Genetic Association, and the journal became the *Journal of Heredity*.

X and Y Chromosomes. The new attention given to Mendel's work stimulated microscopic research into the structure and function of chromosomes. In 1902 two graduate students at Columbia University, zoologist Walter Sutton and botanist W. A. Cannon, first suggested that the division of chromosomes might be the mechanism that explained Mendelian segregation. Around the same time, Clarence E. McClung, then at the University of Kansas, discovered the role of the X chromosome in the determination of sex. It had been understood by scientists for some years that chromosomes appeared to be paired. McClung argued that gender is the only hereditary characteristic that divides organisms into two equal groups. McClung thought the X chromosome, which was unpaired, was an "accessory" chromosome that determined gender (he thought wrongly that the presence of the X chromosome in a sperm would produce a male offspring; in fact it denotes a female). In 1905 E. B. Wilson at Columbia and Nettie Stevens at Bryn Mawr, working independently, demonstrated that all eggs have a single X chromosome, while a sperm may carry an X or a Y; female animals generally have two X chromosomes, males one X and one Y.

Enter the Fruit Fly. The common fruit fly, *Drosophila melanogaster,* has proven to be the classic organism used for genetic experimentation because its reproductive cycle is short (ten days to three weeks), it has large numbers of offspring (one hundred to four hundred or more), and it has only a few chromosomes. During the first decade of the twentieth century, it became the laboratory subject of choice for genetic experiments. The first American biologist to use the fruit fly for genetic research was William E. Castle, at Harvard in 1901. Other pioneer experimenters, such as William Moenkhaus at Indiana and Frank Lutz at Cold Spring Harbor (the Carnegie Institution's laboratory of experimental evolution), learned of the fruit fly from Castle. The greatest experimental geneticist of the first half of the twentieth century, Thomas Hunt Morgan, then at Columbia University, heard about the technique from Lutz in 1906 and passed it on to several of his students, including Stevens. In addition to its utility in research, *Drosophila* also proved to be an ideal teaching instrument: fly colonies were easy to maintain, lent themselves to classroom demonstration, and used little laboratory space.

Fruit Flies and Mutation. Morgan first saw the relationship of fruit flies to genetic research in 1907, when he began to suspect that it would be easy to induce mutations in them and so test de Vries's theory. The idea was to subject the flies to extremes of temperature, centrifuging, and finally the application of X rays. But Morgan's real interest in this line of research began in 1909 when he thought that fruit flies would be ideal subjects on which to test Charles Darwin's ideas about natural selection. In order to show this, he needed to re-create natural situations in the laboratory, wherein variations, produced by mutation, would occur with the same incidence as they did in nature. By linking de Vries's notion of mutation with Darwin's concept of variation, Morgan invented a line of experimental research that is now called microevolution. When combined with the statistical study of selection developed by R. A. Fisher and Sewall Wright, the new genetics led directly to the so-called synthetic theory of evolution that has dominated biological thinking since the 1930s. This neo-Darwinian view of evolution understands natural selection as acting on gene pools, rather than on individuals, and therefore represents a recasting of Darwin's theory in terms of Mendelian genetics.

Sources:

Peter J. Bowler, *The Mendelian Revolution* (Baltimore: Johns Hopkins University Press, 1989);

Barbara A. Kimmelman, "The American Breeder's Association: Genetics and Eugenics in an Agricultural Context," *Social Studies of Science*, 13 (1983): 163–204;

Robert E. Kohler, *Lords of the Fly: Drosophila Genetics and the Experimental Life* (Chicago: University of Chicago Press, 1994);

T. H. Morgan, *The Genetics of Drosophila* (The Hague: M. Nijhoff, 1925).

Albert Einstein, whose revolutionary theories invigorated scientific debate

EINSTEIN'S SPECIAL THEORY OF RELATIVITY

A New Idea. The German Jewish theoretical physicist Albert Einstein formulated the special theory of relativity in 1905. Relativity is that area of physics that has to do with how observers in motion with respect to the phenomenon observed can account for their observations given that two different frames of reference (that of the observer and that of what is observed) are involved. Einstein labeled his 1905 theory "special" because it dealt with a limited range of phenomena, namely uniform linear motion at constant but high velocities. The consequences of special relativity became cornerstones of twentieth-century physics and displaced some of the central tenets of Newtonian physics that had been pillars of scientific thought for two centuries.

Einstein's Discoveries. First, Einstein showed that time, space, and matter are interdependent, as expressed in the famous formula $e = mc^2$, where e is energy, m is mass, and c is the speed of light. The mass of material objects is determined by their energy; if they give off energy, their mass decreases. Mass increases with velocity and since the velocity of light is so great, a small mass traveling at the speed of light is equivalent to a vast amount of energy. (Atomic energy is an example of the special theory but was not based on it.) Second, time is not absolute: it depends on the circumstances of the observers. Third, there are no privileged observers: what one person sees or measures may not be what another person measures, even if both think they are measuring the same phenomenon, especially if one is moving faster than the other. For example, according to the special theory, a person on a moving train and another on an adjacent embankment do not see the same light signal on the railroad station at the same time and thus cannot say that the two observations were simultaneous. Fourth, space is not absolute; it is only a conventional way of describing the relationships of objects. Fifth, as American physicist Albert Michelson had already demonstrated, the ether, an invisible substance that supposedly filled the entire universe and through which light waves were propagated, does not exist.

Fun and Games. The theory gave rise to all kinds of widely discussed paradoxes that delighted Einstein and his supporters and enraged physicists opposed to the theory. The most famous was the "twin paradox" of the space traveler. An astronaut travels through space at speeds approaching that of light for many years. When he returns to Earth, he finds his twin brother to be an old man while he has hardly aged at all. Einstein's theory explained that at very high speeds time slows down.

The American Debate. There were few theoretical physicists in the United States when Einstein published his theory. Most physicists were experimentalists and were hostile to the theory that struck many of them as hopelessly abstract and counter to intuition and common sense. Moreover, they were committed to Maxwell's principles of electrodynamics, which purported space to be filled with aether. The first Americans to comment on relativity were Gilbert N. Lewis, professor of physical chemistry at MIT, and his student, Richard C. Tolman. In a paper published in 1909 they argued that Einstein's theory was both practical and based on empirical evidence. Other American scientists, with considerably less understanding, ridiculed special relativity, attacking it as metaphysical and unrelated to observation. Many were bothered by the counterintuitive nature of the theory and asserted that if a scientific theory were true, it would be, almost by definition, comprehensible to everyone. Tolman, on the other hand, always responded to such doubts by reasserting his conviction that Einstein's hypotheses could be tested by experiment. Both Einstein's early supporters and detractors in the United States, therefore, appealed to American scientific traditions of practicality and experimental verification.

The General Theory. In 1914 Einstein broadened his concepts to include nonlinear motion in a general theory of relativity. This introduced his famous theory of curved space. When certain predictions contained in the theory were later verified (as when observations during the solar eclipse of 1919 confirmed that light rays emitted by stars bent when passing through the gravitational field of the sun), many scientists who previously had been skeptical now accepted the special theory as well. Einstein won the Nobel Prize in 1921, not for relativity — still considered too controversial — but for another of his discoveries of 1905, the photoelectric effect.

Delayed Acceptance of Relativity. The first book in English on special relativity was published by mathematician Robert D. Carmichael of Indiana University in 1912. At the same time, physicist Percy W. Bridgman began to work out the role of relativity in the philosophy of modern physics. But, perhaps because of the difficulty of the theory and its lingering aura of controversy, coverage of the theory in textbooks was sparse. Prior to World War II most American textbooks simply presented special relativity as a theory suggested by the Michelson-Morley experiment, which was understood as having proven that the speed of light was invariant. Such discussions were wrong on two counts: first, Michelson-Morley measured the speed of light but made no claims regarding its invariance; second, Einstein was in all likelihood unaware of that famous experiment when he conceived his theory.

EDISON'S CONCRETE ARCHITECTURE

In 1906, four years after he had founded the Edison Portland Cement Company at Stewartsville, New Jersey, Thomas Edison announced that his solution to the problem of the housing shortage and inner city slums was the reinforced concrete house, which, if he had his way, could be built in a week. Edison thought he might be able to pour an entire house in one operation. Houses could then roll off a production line and be sold at a low price. Such houses could be built almost entirely of fire-resistant materials, thus also saving the cost of fire insurance.

Edison identified bentonite clay as a substance that had the binding and stability requirements suitable to such monumental concrete structures and determined that more than one structure would have to be built on a single site in order to save on construction costs. All architectural and decorative features, from staircases to exterior flourishes, were included in the mold, and colors were added to the concrete mix to avoid any separate painting of the structure.

After years of hoopla Edison had failed to produce a single house. Finally two houses were cast in Montclair, New Jersey (they remain standing today), but Edison decided that the process was too grandiose and complex. He then designed a smaller, two-bedroom model with a front porch, weighing 250,000 pounds, some 200,000 less than the Montclair prototypes. This house was built in South Orange, New Jersey, in 1910. Edison's ideas for the utility of concrete extended even to household furnishings. He boasted that a line of furniture made from a kind of foamy concrete would cost half as much as wood and outlast the marriages of their buyers. In 1911 he actually molded some prototypes, including cabinets, a bathtub, and even a piano! Edison's cement business was to have some great achievements, including the building of Yankee Stadium, and several successful Edison houses were built in Union, New Jersey, in 1917, but the idea never caught on. In spite of the longevity of those houses that were built, Edison, at least in the area of design, was a prophet without honor.

Source: Michael Peterson, "Thomas Edison's Concrete Houses," *The American Heritage of Invention and Technology,* 11 (Winter 1996): 50–56.

Source:
Thomas F. Glick, ed., *The Comparative Reception of Relativity* (Dordrecht, Netherlands: D. Reidel, 1987).

Participants in the September 1909 celebration at Clark University: (front row) Sigmund Freud, G. Stanley Hall, C. G. Jung; (second row) A. A. Brill, Ernest Jones, Sandor Ferenczi

FREUD COMES TO AMERICA

A New Approach to Psychology. Sigmund Freud, an Austrian Jewish psychiatrist who fashioned a dynamic theory of psychology of human behavior based on the workings of the unconscious mind, achieved world prominence by virtue of his highly publicized visit in September 1909 to Clark University in Worcester, Massachusetts. Clark had built a strong psychology program under president and leading psychologist G. Stanley Hall, who invited Freud to lecture as part of the festivities celebrating the twentieth anniversary of the university's founding. Freud's trip to Clark was his only trip to the United States.

Psychoanalysis. Freud had first set forth his concepts of psychoanalysis in his famous book *On the Interpretation of Dreams*, published in German in 1900. He explained how conscious thoughts — particularly those that are unpleasant or threatening — are repressed, only to reappear in a person's unconscious mind where they are revealed, in distorted form, in dreams. The analysis of first his own and then his patients' dreams gave Freud a key to understanding how the unconscious works — specifically by mechanisms of repression, wish fulfillment, condensation (whereby one word or image replaces another similar one: the origin of most "Freudian slips"), and displacement (the exaggeration of unimportant details, which gives dreams their absurd quality). Freud

discovered that by examining patients' dreams, the analyst could help them to reconstruct their past emotional lives in order to understand events or thoughts that may have led to their distress. Freud further found that many of the thoughts repressed by his patients had to do with sexual matters, a finding that scandalized many European physicians, who feared that Freud was simply encouraging his patients' "perversity." For ten years Freud kept his ideas confined to a small circle of colleagues and disciples, not wishing to confront a hostile medical establishment openly.

Freud in America. Hall's invitation provided Freud with a platform to discuss his concepts openly and an audience to approve, he hoped, his view of the mind. Those who heard Freud's "Five Lectures on Psychoanalysis" included the top echelon of American psychiatry: James Jackson Putnam, chief of psychiatry at Massachusetts General Hospital; William James, professor of psychology at Harvard (who said he had come "to see what Freud was like"); Edward Bradford Titchener; Adolf Meyer; and A. A. Brill. Other intellectuals such as Franz Boas and Emma Goldman, socialist leader and feminist activist, were also present. When Freud was awarded an honorary degree, he stood out among the ordinary crowd of professors "like a giant among pygmies," Goldman later recalled.

The Clark Lectures. The lectures offered a synthesis of Freud's psychological system. The first was on his pioneering work on hysteria, a nervous disorder believed at the time to be confined to women, which he treated by simply having patients discuss their symptoms, causing them to subside. The second was on his discovery of the mechanism of repression in the course of treating hysterical patients. The third dealt with his new techniques, such as analysis of dreams and slips of the tongue. The fourth, on the sexuality of children and the Oedipus complex (the attraction of children to their parent of the opposite sex), shocked some members of the audience. The final lecture focused on the demands that civilization places on emotional life and the creative results that can result from meeting the demands of reality, and even — as in the case of artists — fleeing from reality into fantasy.

Impact of Freud's Visit. Freud's visit had an electrifying effect on American psychology and psychiatry. Some of the psychiatrists present immediately became influential supporters of psychoanalysis. Putnam, for example, soon afterward established a psychoanalytic service at his own hospital. Meyer had already expressed disillusion with the prevailing style of diagnosis and treatment in psychiatry, which presumed that emotional disorders had physical causes, even if they were unknown, and concentrated on the physical rather than the psychological symptoms of mental disease. The treatments available — bed rest, electric shock, and other therapies that did not directly address the patients' emotional state — were ineffectual, and Freud's "talking cure" and other new techniques seemed a promising way out of a medical impasse. For Meyer, Freud's interpretation of the symbolism contained in dreams made sense of symptoms, such as those of schizophrenia, that previously had no explanation. Psychologists saw an opportunity to broaden into practical and therapeutic areas a field that up to then had been purely academic.

Freud's Social Message. Freud promoted the idea that the values of "civilized morality" (often called "Victorian morality") were at the root of many emotional disorders because they caused sexuality and sexual desires to be repressed rather than acknowledged. Such repressed feelings were the most immediate cause of neurosis. Freud's message struck just as Victorian morality was coming under attack from a variety of groups, from the Purity Crusaders who attacked the sexual double standard by calling for the legalization of prostitution, to those — such as the British sexual reformer Havelock Ellis, whose books were widely read in the United States in the first decade of the century — who promoted a healthier attitude toward sexual hygiene and sexual education. Freud and psychoanalytic theory provided such reformers with a theoretical justification for their social programs. The Kinsey Reports of the 1940s and 1950s on sexual behavior of American women and men confirmed that the sexual behavior of Americans actually changed around this time, in part as a result of the popularization of Freud's ideas on the relationship between sexual repression and emotional disorder.

Source:

Nathan G. Hale Jr., *Freud and the Americans: The Beginnings of Psychoanalysis in the United States, 1876–1917* (New York: Oxford University Press, 1971).

THE RADIO

Early History. Radio waves were discovered in 1887 when the German physicist Heinrich Hertz produced electromagnetic waves from an oscillating circuit connected to an induction coil. The waves traveled with the speed of light and could be detected (that is, received) with a simple wire loop. "Hertzian waves," as they came to be called, were promptly studied by physicists in laboratories around the world. One of these experimenters, the Italian Augusto Righi, introduced the phenomenon to his friend Guglielmo Marconi. In 1894 Marconi experimentally transmitted Hertzian waves around his own house and estate. In 1895 he tied a telegraph machine into a circuit and found he could send Morse code signals through the air: he had invented wireless telegraphy. Unable to interest the Italian government in his invention, he moved to England and established the Marconi Wireless Telegraph Company (1897–1900). Aided by the English physicist Oliver Lodge, Marconi learned how to transmit waves of definite length and devised receivers that could be tuned to receive waves of specific length — the origins of radio, although neither man recognized it at the time. Marconi built a transmitter in Cornwall and a receiving antenna first on Cape Cod then in Newfoundland, where, on 12 December 1901 he received the first transatlantic wireless message, in Morse code, an event that made him famous.

American Pioneers of Radio. Marconi had demonstrated wireless telegraphy to officials of the U.S. Navy in 1899, and the navy secretary announced in 1900 that the invention would be adopted for ship-to-ship and ship-to-shore communications if the level of interference could be reduced. At this point the American engineer Lee De Forest produced a design that he claimed reduced interference with mechanically tuned transmitters and receivers. He received a contract from the U.S. Signal Corps in 1902. Marconi would only lease, not sell, his instruments to the navy, which finally purchased a competing German system in 1903. These early instruments were true wireless telegraphs: they could only receive dots and dashes produced by electrical oscillations and could not transmit the human voice. In 1902 Reginald A. Fessenden of the University of Pittsburgh invented a signal detector called the hot-wire barretter and in 1903 a "liquid barretter" (later known as the electrolytic detector) that could "hear" sounds. The problem was that the transmitted voice could scarcely be heard because low-frequency transmissions were drowned out by static. Fessenden then went to work on a high-frequency alternator to

Reginald Fessenden (center) and his coworkers at Brant Rock, Massachusetts, the site of the first radio broadcast

resolve the problem. The year 1903 witnessed open competition between the systems of Marconi, Fessenden, and De Forest, spawning a seemingly endless series of patent infringement suits.

From Wireless Telegraphy to Radio. The Marconi Company of America began to build wireless telegraph stations as early as 1902. The next year, from its station in Wellfleet, Massachusetts, President Theodore Roosevelt exchanged greetings with King Edward VII of England. By 1904 the U.S. Navy had twenty shore wireless stations in operation, and twenty-four of its ships carried wireless equipment. In 1903 Fessenden had ordered a ten-thousand-cycle alternator from General Electric. The project was designed by Ernst Alexanderson and took three years to complete because Fessenden wanted an armature built out of a material other than iron, which he did not believe suitable for high-frequency operations. The alternator was installed at Brant Rock on the Massachusetts coast, and on Christmas Eve 1906 voice messages and violin music were transmitted — the first radio broadcast. The voices were heard through telegraph headsets and had the same sound quality as audible Morse code vibrations. By 1907 Fessenden was broadcasting experimentally to New York and Washington.

The Audion and the Crystal. In 1906 De Forest achieved a major breakthrough with the invention of the triode vacuum tube or audion. The two-electrode vacuum tube was invented by John A. Fleming, following up on a phenomenon discovered and described — but never used — by Thomas Alva Edison, who noticed that such a tube allowed the current to flow in one direction only. This property was subsequently called the Edison effect, and using it, Fleming devised a tube in which frequencies could be reduced to the point where the audible effects of the waves could be received. De Forest found on 31 December 1906 that if a third electrode were added, the signals were received with great clarity and strength. In the same year, army general Henry Dunwoody discovered that Carborundum crystals could detect electric currents. This was the origin of the inexpensive crystal receiver that some years in the future would be used by thousands of listeners to build homemade radio sets.

Beginnings of Broadcasting. In 1910 retailer John Wanamaker installed the Marconi apparatus in his stores in New York and Philadelphia to provide entertainment for customers. In April 1912 David Sarnoff, future president of the Radio Corporation of America (RCA), received wireless telegraph messages from the *Titanic* as the

A De Forest Audion

giant ship sank after colliding with an iceberg. Sarnoff then broadcast these messages by voice to the Wanamaker stores, causing a sensation and arousing the public's awareness of the possibilities of radio for the dissemination of news and entertainment. In 1916 Sarnoff proposed to the Marconi Company that it manufacture what he called a "Radio Music Box." With their antennae these first sets would cost around seventy-five dollars each.

Commercial Broadcasting Stations. In 1919 an agreement was reached between General Electric and the Marconi Company to merge radio operations as RCA, which became a communications giant. Its rival was Westinghouse Electric, which in November 1920 began operation of the first commercially successful broadcasting station, KDKA (the commercial successor of the company's experimental station) in Pittsburgh. KDKA then delivered a long series of radio firsts, including the first broadcast of a boxing match on 11 April 1921 and the first play-by-play broadcast of a baseball game on 5 August 1921. The radio broadcasting age had begun.

Source:
Gleason L. Archer, *History of Radio to 1926* (New York: American Historical Society, 1938).

MARCONI AND TESLA

Nikola Tesla was a Croatian-born inventor who immigrated to the United States in 1884. He worked for Thomas Edison for a few years but then left to work on alternating current electrical systems, while Edison was still insistent on direct current. In 1893 he gave a famous lecture in Saint Louis in which he predicted wireless telegraphy based on the spark transmission that Guglielmo Marconi and others were soon to use (a technology that was superseded when the vacuum tube was invented). He refused, however, to admit the potential application of Hertzian (radio) waves.

Marconi, credited with the discovery of radio telegraphy in 1895, always denied he had ever heard of the system that Tesla had described in his 1893 lectures. There were suits and countersuits between the two inventors for patent infringement. H. Otis Pond, one of Edison's engineers was with Tesla in December 1901 when Marconi received the first transatlantic signal.

"Looks like Marconi got the jump on you," said Pond.

"Marconi is a good fellow," Tesla replied, "Let him continue. He is using seven of my patents!"

In a 1904 article in *Electrical World and Engineering*, Tesla predicted that radio would eventually "prove very efficient in enlightening the masses, particularly in still uncivilized countries and less accessible regions, and that it will add materially to general safety, comfort, and convenience, and maintenance of peaceful relations." People carrying portable receivers in their pockets "will record the world's news or such special messages as may be intended for it. Thus the entire earth will be converted into a huge brain, capable of response in every one of its parts." Tesla's notion of the world as a giant, unified brain is the cybernetic equivalent of what Marshall McLuhan would later describe as the "global village" that would result from the communications revolution.

Testifying in one of a long series of patent-infringement suits in 1910, Professor Michael Pupin of Columbia University stated that when Marconi was "a mere strip of a lad working for Signor Righi in Italy he grounded both wires out of curiosity in an experiment to see what would result and he produced wireless waves without ever fully realizing the full significance of it." Tesla, he said, gave radio to the world. Although Marconi's original patent was eventually disallowed in 1943, the fact remains that Marconi went on to develop wireless telegraphy, while Tesla failed to follow up on his inspiration of 1893.

Sources: Margaret Cheney, *Tesla: Man Out Of Time* (Englewood Cliffs, N.J.: Prentice-Hall, 1981);

Marshall McLuhan, *Understanding Media: The Extensions of Man* (New York: McGraw-Hill, 1964);

Nikola Tesla, *My Inventions* (Zagreb: Nikola Tesla Museum, 1977).

SCIENCE AND THE NEW FOUNDATIONS

A New Kind of Patronage. Modern American science, especially that carried out in major universities and hospitals, has been highly dependent not only on government support but on the aid of large philanthropic organizations known as foundations. Until the first decade of the twentieth century, however, American scientists either worked in universities or in some cases government bureaus, both of which supported research on a modest level. If they conceived of projects that were out of the ordinary, scientists either had to find a private donor or put up the money themselves. In 1902 the Carnegie Institution was founded by Andrew Carnegie; then in 1909 John D. Rockefeller established the Rockefeller Foundation. Both organizations believed that promising scientific ideas and capable scientists ought to be supported substantially, but there were no precedents to guide either the new foundations or the scientists themselves in spending the relatively vast sums now available to them.

The Carnegie Institution. Andrew Carnegie, a steel magnate and follower of Herbert Spencer's doctrine of progress as an immutable law of nature, caused a sensation in late 1901 when he announced that he intended to donate $10 million to promote scientific research. He was disturbed by the undistinguished place held by the United States in the ranks of world science and was aware that few American universities could boast the solid research tradition common to so many European institutions. No one knew exactly what he had in mind or what to make of his statement of his own goals: "To discover the exceptional man, inside or outside of schools, and enable him to make the work for which he seems specially designed his life work." How was one to identify the "exceptional" person with promise in science? The grants were to be funneled through the Carnegie Institution, which, beginning in 1903, distributed about $100,000 annually to individual scientists. The instant availability of money caused an immediate change in the way universities projected their budgets. For the first time, college administrators began to set their budgetary sights on foundations, and the support of the new foundations contributed to a growing infrastructure to sustain research on American campuses.

The Carnegie Institution and Astronomy. Astronomy was one of the first scientific fields that the Carnegie Institution addressed, appointing a commission whose leading lights were George Ellery Hale and William Wallace Campbell. Whether through Hale's influence or some other's, the institution's early goal became the establishment of an astrophysical observatory to study solar radiation, solar spectroscopy, and other problems in stellar research that could be advanced by a large reflecting telescope. The institution was directly responsible for the construction of the Mount Wilson Observatory in California, with Hale as its first director.

Andrew Carnegie, whose generous financial support contributed to the shaping of a new era of funding for scientific research in America

Rockefeller. The Rockefeller Foundation really dates to 1901, when millionaire oilman John D. Rockefeller established the Rockefeller Institute for Medical Research (now Rockefeller University) in New York City. In 1903 he established the General Education Board to promote progress in education, particularly in the southern states. From the GEB emerged the Rockefeller Sanitary Commission in 1909, whose main objective was to eradicate hookworm. In 1905 Frederick Gates, Rockefeller's top aide on charitable gifts, suggested the establishment of a corporate philanthropy that would concern itself with a range of problems. John D. Rockefeller Jr. liked the idea, and the Rockefeller Foundation was chartered in 1909.

Hookworm. Hookworm is a parasitic disease usually acquired by walking barefoot on soil infected by the worm. Zoologist Charles W. Stiles convinced a Rockefeller official that this worm was the cause of endemic disease in the South because of environmental conditions peculiar to the area. The General Education Board then established a commission to study hookworm headed by Dr. Simon Flexner, who concluded that a practical solution could be found, and the Rockefeller Sanitary Commission, headed by Stiles, was founded. The sanitary commission found that 90 percent of children in rural areas of the South were infected by hookworm, the eradication of which required an extensive campaign of public education. In the following years, under the auspices of the foundation's International Health Board (established in 1916), the campaign was carried worldwide.

Administering Science. Foundations, although a kind of philanthropy, were from their inception run like businesses, and scientific decisions were frequently made according to a corporate model. While many of the early foundation officials with responsibility for scientific projects were scientists who had turned to administration, their superiors were men with business experience. The corporate approach to science was later to have an enormous impact on the development of "big science" in the United States. On the other hand, the two foundations also emerged out of a personal style of charity characteristic of the nineteenth century, which also influenced their early managerial styles. Working largely through personal contacts, the Carnegie and Rockefeller scientist-administrators felt confident in identifying worthy projects and the "exceptional" scientists appropriate to carry them out.

Sources:

Robert E. Kohler, *Partners in Science: Foundations and Natural Scientists, 1900–1945* (Chicago: University of Chicago, 1991);

Nathan and Ida H. Reingold, *Science in America* (Chicago: University of Chicago Press, 1981).

THE SUBMARINE

Early Notions. The concept of the submarine is an old one and appears always to have been linked to military uses. As long ago as the fifteenth century the Italian engineer Roberto Valturio designed (but probably never built) a submarine powered by paddle wheels. In the seventeenth century the Dutch engineer Cornelius Drebbel built a diving bell that was open at the bottom and held several passengers. Both the English natural philosopher John Wilkins and the Frenchman Marin Mersenne speculated on whether a ship might be made to navigate underwater. In the eighteenth century David Bushnell of Connecticut built a submarine named the *Turtle* that was used during the Revolutionary War to attack a British ship in New York harbor in August 1776. Jules Verne, of course, popularized the concept in his famous novel *Twenty Thousand Leagues Under the Sea* (1873).

The First Holland Models. John P. Holland made his first design for a submarine in 1873, shortly after arriving in Boston from his native Ireland. His earliest design was a one-man boat, fifteen feet long, which was operated with pedals and equipped with air reservoirs divided by oiled silk panels. His first model with a metal hull, Holland's Boat No. 1, was probably the smallest submarine ever built, only fourteen and a half feet long. The pedals were replaced by a gasoline engine. It sank immediately at its first launch, and Holland found it was difficult to ignite the gas engine under pressure. But he had a successful short test in June 1878,

Submarine inventor John P. Holland aboard his ninth model in 1898

submerging for an hour. In May 1879 work began on his second submarine, called the *Fenian Ram*. Thirty-one feet long, the *Fenian Ram* displaced nineteen tons and achieved a surface speed of 9 MPH with a two-cylinder engine. The *Fenian Ram* was a three-man vessel, carrying the captain, an engineer to monitor the pressure valves, and a gunner to operate a pneumatic gun that could shoot a torpedo some three hundred yards. The *Fenian Ram* made successful trial runs between 1881 and 1883.

The Race for an Effective Boat. Holland was an astute engineer and early on discarded the idea of the operator wearing a pressurized diving suit in favor of pressurizing the whole hull. In figuring out the hydrodynamics of diving he observed porpoises and tried to emulate their motions, much as early aviators observed the flight of birds; and indeed Holland once designed a steam-powered flying machine. In the 1880s French, English, and Russian inventors were also experimenting with submarines, and Holland knew he had to have a machine that would interest the U.S. Navy. In 1888 the navy convoked an open competition for a submarine torpedo boat that could attain speeds of fifteen knots on the surface and eight knots submerged, and could stay submerged for two hours. Holland's model won, having been judged better than that of his closest rival, the Swedish torpedo inventor Thorsten Nordenfeldt. Holland won again the following year.

Holland's Government Contract. In 1893 Holland founded the John P. Holland Torpedo Boat Company to

The *Protector,* the third design of Holland's chief competitor, Simon Lake

manufacture submarines for the navy. Holland began construction on his fifth ship, the *Plunger,* in August 1895. It was eighty-five feet long, steel hulled and steam-powered for surface cruising, with an auxiliary electric motor to run the boat when submerged. The space occupied by its enormous boiler was only one of the ship's problems, and the *Holland VI* soon followed. Meanwhile a debate developed in governmental circles over how much money the navy should invest in the untried boat. Alfred Thayer Mahan, whose influential book *The Influence of Sea Power Upon History* had been published in 1890, was one of Holland's supporters. The war with Spain in 1898 lent added urgency to the development of a practical submarine. In June and July of that year the *Holland VI* made her first successful trial runs, but the navy insisted on substantial modifications that dragged on into 1899. The key demonstration took place on the Potomac in March 1900 before a large group of politicians and officers including Adm. George Dewey. The submarine's outstanding performance led the navy to purchase it in April. Most of the crucial technical problems of submarine design, such as the regulation of submersion by activating ballast tanks, were solved quite early. Designing adequate power and electrical systems proved more difficult than the hydrodynamic problems.

The Dawn of the Submarine Age. In spring 1901 the Electric Boat Company launched a rival submarine, the *Fulton,* which soon after proved its ability to remain submerged for up to fifteen hours. The pace of submarine-building activity was increasing. In 1902 Simon Lake — Holland's archrival — launched his third submarine model, the *Protector,* and the following year Union Iron Works of San Francisco built two subs, the *Grampus* and the *Pike.* The English had built a variant of Holland's design in the winter of 1901, and the French were also active. In 1904 the Japanese government bought two Holland submarines and five more from Electric Boat. (These were supposed to serve in the Russo-Japanese War but the Japanese had already destroyed the enemy fleet before the subs were delivered.) Holland himself had withdrawn from public life by the end of the decade, although he did produce some sketches in 1907 for a passenger version of his boat. The submarine was not to be proven in war until World War I.

Source:
Richard Knowles Morris, *John P. Holland, Inventor of the Modern Submarine* (Annapolis, Md.: United States Naval Institute, 1966).

HEADLINE MAKERS

LUTHER BURBANK

1849-1926

HORTICULTURIST

Background. Luther Burbank was an American original: largely self-taught, he was an inventor and tinkerer by temperament but worked in the organic, rather than the mechanical, world and had an immense influence on academic botany and genetics. Born in Lancaster, Massachusetts, Burbank's first job was with the Ames Plow Company in Worcester (1864–1867). Then he attended the Lancaster Academy for a year, during which he first read Charles Darwin's *On The Variation of Animals and Plants Under Domestication* (1868), a book that exercised a profound influence on his career. Burbank learned from Darwin the methods of artificial selection that breeders use to develop desirable characteristics in domestic plants and animals. On his family's farm in Lunenburg, Massachusetts, he developed the Burbank potato, an immensely popular and economically important variety, the antecedent of the Idaho potato. In 1875 he moved to California where he established a fruit and vegetable farm in Santa Rosa in 1876. There he began experimenting with a variety of techniques such as grafting, hybridization, and cross-breeding in order to create new varieties of fruits and ornamental flowers. For the next twenty-five years he devoted himself mainly to experimentation with plant varieties, developing improved stocks of peach, pear, prune, blackberry, plum, tomato, and other plants, which he sold to commercial growers.

Burbank's Method. Burbank worked by trial and error. He would cross-pollinate the flowers of two trees by hand and plant all the resulting seeds. He would then select the dozen or so most promising seedlings to cross with other plants. With fruit trees he would graft cuttings from his seedlings to mature trees in order to obtain fruit sooner. He kept records that were haphazard and unsystematic (in those cases when he kept any records at all) and claimed to work by instinct alone according to prin-

ciples he learned from Darwin's books. With berries he practiced selection on a massive scale, sometimes growing thousands of bushes and discarding all but a few from his breeding pool. Burbank had no use either for Mendelian genetics or for Hugo de Vries's theory of mutation. He believed that de Vries, who visited Burbank's operation and praised it highly, had erred in mistaking certain hybrids for mutants. In one of his few published writings, an article titled "The Training of the Human Plant," he outlined his own theory of heredity, which was very much in the line of American neo-Lamarckian biology of the second half of the nineteenth century. Like the neo-Lamarckians, Burbank assumed the inheritance of acquired characteristics. He believed that if a plant should produce an uncommonly good fruit owing to its having been provided with the proper environment and care, the qualities of that fruit would be passed along to its descendants. "Environment is the architect of heredity," he wrote, "*all* characters which are *transmitted* have been acquired." Among Burbank's many "new creations" were the Royal and Paradox walnuts, the Primus berry — a cross between a raspberry and a dewberry — the Van Deman quince, the Paradox berry (something like a boysenberry), the "New Japan" mammoth chestnut, and the Golden plum.

A National Figure. Burbank became known through his plant catalogues (the most famous was the 1893 catalogue titled *New Creations in Fruits and Flowers*), through the word of mouth of satisfied customers, and through flamboyant press reports that kept him in the news throughout the first decade of the century. He was made an honorary member of the American Breeders' Association, even though most of the other members accepted Gregor Mendel's genetic principles. From 1904 through 1909 Burbank received several grants from the Carnegie Institution to support his ongoing research on hybridization. He was supported by the practical-minded Andrew Carnegie himself, over those of his advisers who objected that Burbank was not "scientific" in his methods.

Later Life. In 1912 Burbank participated in the creation of the Luther Burbank Press to promote his discoveries. Burbank had by then become a nationally prominent figure. The press and the associated Luther Burbank

Society published a twelve-volume set titled *Luther Burbank; His Methods and Discoveries and Their Practical Applications* (1914–1915) setting out the results — so it was claimed — of more than one hundred thousand experiments. In the 1920s Burbank became a kind of cult figure, visited by yogis and others who claimed that his findings substantiated their theories. He became a spokesmen for "free thinkers" and was widely attacked as antireligious. His legacy is mixed. On the one hand, his rejection of modern genetics caused him to be identified as a horticultural quack; on the other, his notion of developing plants and fruits to meet the demands of market taste was far in advance of his times. Burbank died of a heart attack 24 March 1926.

Source:
Peter Dreyer, *A Gardener Touched With Genius: The Life of Luther Burbank* (Berkeley: University of California Press, 1985).

LEE DE FOREST

1873-1961

RADIO PIONEER

Childhood and Education. Born in Council Bluffs, Iowa, Lee De Forest was raised in Alabama, where his father was president of Talladega College. He studied engineering at Yale University's Sheffield Scientific School and then continued as a graduate student in physics. His favorite teacher was J. Williard Gibbs, but Gibbs was a theoretician who could not instruct in practical matters. While in graduate school De Forest read Nikola Tesla's lectures on high-voltage, high-frequency electric current phenomena, because he intended to ask Tesla for a job. Tesla's laboratory in New York, De Forest later explained, "was a fabulous domain into which all ambitious young electric students aspired to enter and there remain." In 1896 he met Tesla at his laboratory. De Forest's principal interest was radiotelegraphy, and his 1899 doctoral thesis on "Reflection of Hertzian Waves from the Ends of Parallel Wires" was a means for advancing his understanding of the phenomena involved.

Wireless Telegraphy. In 1901 De Forest devised a telegraph transmitter that replaced the clumsy spark coil and supplied a steady, high-frequency spark. "From the start I had the aim in view," he later admitted, "to make my name at least rank with that of Marconi." He then launched the De Forest Wireless Telegraph company. He wanted to use "Hertzian waves" to make a "telephone" without wires. De Forest sent radio equipment and two operators to China in 1904 to report the Russo-Japanese War. An operator on ship was to send wireless messages to a receiver on the mainland.

The Triode. In 1906 De Forest applied for a patent for the triode vacuum tube, in which a third electrode is inserted between the anode and the cathode to control and amplify the current. The triode not only proved to be an effective high-frequency oscillator but also was the model for all successive electronic amplifiers. De Forest, however, did not appreciate the potential of his invention until 1912, when he found that a triode connected in a line between a transmitter and a receiver could amplify voice currents, making quality long-distance radio transmission possible. The triode became standard equipment when Irving Langmuir of General Electric perfected a method of obtaining the greatest vacuum possible in radio tubes.

Pioneering Efforts. In the summer of 1908 De Forest made a celebrated trip to Paris where he broadcast recorded music from the Eiffel Tower. In the winter of 1909–1910 De Forest began to broadcast operas from the Metropolitan Opera House, the fulfillment of one of his great dreams. He was especially proud to have broadcast Enrico Caruso singing Canio in Puccini's opera *I Pagliacci*. De Forest's career, however, was not without controversy. Early companies pirated technical secrets with brazen impunity, and De Forest, like other early radio inventors, became enmeshed in an interminable series of patent infringement suits that reached a feverish pitch in 1912 and 1913. Stock in radio companies soared upward and then plummeted, in part because it was difficult to appraise which technology was most promising. In March 1912 De Forest's arrest for stock fraud and brief imprisonment destroyed his company's reputation.

Broadcasting Innovations. In 1916 De Forest put the triode to work as a transmitter, initiating scheduled radio transmission for the first time. In that year he started an experimental broadcasting station in the Bronx, New York. He hired a singer named Vaughn de Leath, the first woman to sing into a De Forest microphone, who subsequently had a long career in broadcasting and was known as the "Original Radio Girl." De Forest then pioneered radio news, broadcasting hourly news bulletins of the presidential election of 1916. Acting as radio's first announcer, De Forest signed off by announcing that Charles Evans Hughes had won the election, only to find out in the morning that Woodrow Wilson had been reelected!

Later Life. In 1917 De Forest sold all of his audio patents to the American Telephone and Telegraph Company for $250,000. In the early 1920s he developed a sound process for motion pictures called Phonofilm. It was done with an audion amplifier tube that permitted a camera to project sound-modulated light onto a sound track one-eighth inch wide. The process was a technical success, but, according to De Forest, Hollywood was too committed to silent film to take any interest in Phonofilm. He struggled on, slowly expanding his network of Phonofilm theaters. A film called *Retribution,* produced originally in Swedish with De Forest's process in 1924, was the first talking picture, two years before Al Jolson's *Jazz Singer*. The film companies eventually backed two rival systems, Western Electric's synchronized disk and RCA/General Electric's sound-on-film. De Forest lost out in 1929 when his patent was ruled invalid. Lee De Forest died in Hollywood on 30 June 1961.

Sources:

Gleason L. Archer, *History of Radio to 1926* (New York: American Historical Society, 1938);

Lee De Forest, *Father of Radio: The Autobiography of Lee de Forest* (Chicago: Wilcox & Follett, 1950).

THOMAS ALVA EDISON

1847-1931

INVENTOR

Life and Legend. The story of Thomas Edison's youth was retold many times around the beginning of the twentieth century and was embroidered with anecdotes that lent a Horatio Alger quality to his biography. His background and many inventions made Edison the best-known scientific figure of the 1900s, a figure of near mythic proportions in a decade fascinated with new technologies. Edison worked as a youth on a train where he set up a chemistry laboratory and printing press on which he published a weekly paper for travelers. He was said to have been taught telegraphy as a reward for saving the life of a telegraph operator's son (the story was only partly true). After working for more than a decade as a telegraph boy, he launched his career as an inventor at the age of twenty-eight with a series of innovations that transformed telegraphy: first the duplex telegraph, which could transmit two messages simultaneously, one in each direction, and then the multiplex, which transmitted four messages, two in each direction. He sold the multiplex to Western Union in 1876 and with the proceeds established a "factory for inventions" at Menlo Park, New Jersey.

The Phonograph. Fame came the following year, 1877, with the invention — by pure chance — of the phonograph. Edison had just devised a "repeater," a rotating disk on which telegraph signals could be recorded and saved. He then wanted to extend the process to create a similar repeating mechanism for Alexander Graham Bell's telephone. When the machine produced semi-human noises, it occurred to him to shout "Halloo!" into its diaphragm while the apparatus was recording on a cylinder covered with tinfoil. When the machine repeated the word, he was astounded. The phonograph caused a sensation in part because it was so simple: it was completely mechanical, with no electrical components. News of the invention spread rapidly. Edison demonstrated it in January 1878 at the Royal Institution in London and later to President Rutherford B. Hayes at the White House. It made him a public figure instantly and created the legend of the "Wizard of Menlo Park," even though the machine was not immediately commercialized. Edison at first envisioned the phonograph as a dictaphone, with business applications only; he thought those who wanted to record music were silly.

The Light Bulb. Edison put the phonograph aside for a while and plunged into the development of an incandescent light. Streets and large halls were already illuminated electrically with arc lamps that produced a brilliant light when the current passed between two electrodes. But arc lamps could not be used domestically. The problem of finding a manageable household light bulb involved searching for a material to serve as a filament that would light without burning up or melting. Edison first saw that a filament could be prevented from burning by enclosing it in a glass bulb from which the air had been evacuated (thus creating a vacuum inside the bulb). Since he was building generators at the same time and trying to conceive of how a lighting *system* might work, it occurred to him that several hundred low-resistance light bulbs would require huge generators while high-resistance bulbs would require less current and operate more efficiently. This conceptual breakthrough permitted Edison to develop an efficient electrical system that could distribute current from a central station and at considerable distances — an impossibility under the prevailing illumination systems of high current and low resistance, which lost power over all but the shortest distances. Edison then needed only to find a filament that would glow a long time without burning out. He found the substance by trial and error, experimenting with dozens of different substances before finally narrowing the list down to carbonized paper or cotton thread. Finally, on 22 October 1879, his famous bulb no. 9 stayed lit for fifteen hours. On 1 November he applied for a patent on a light bulb with a carbon filament.

A New Year's Eve to Remember. Edison immediately set out to electrify the entire town of Menlo Park. Passengers on the New York–Philadelphia train were astonished to see the town lit up at night, and on New Year's Eve 1879 three thousand persons came on special trains to view the spectacle. Stock shares in the Edison Electric Company soared.

Expansion and Diversification. In the 1890s and 1900s Edison was primarily occupied with designing and building electrical systems for the companies using his system. In 1887 Edison built a laboratory in Orange, New Jersey, claiming it was a unique facility even though Bell had set up a similar industrial laboratory for the expanding telephone industry in 1881. Indeed because of the nature of electricity, every electrical inventor had a laboratory. Edison's Orange facility dwarfed them all, however, both in size and number of employees. There he worked out a whole series of commercial phonographs throughout the 1890s, in 1896 introducing the first model designed to play prerecorded cylinders.

Motion Pictures and X Rays. Motion pictures interested Edison as an analogue to the phonograph: a device that would store pictures as the "talking machine" stored sounds. His first models actually combined pictures and sound in a cylinder format, but he soon turned to film. The chief technical problem that Edison had to solve was how to get a filmstrip to move through a camera; having solved it by devising sprockets, he applied for patents on a machine to take pictures and another to view them in 1891. Marketing began in 1893 when he sold kinetoscope viewers to amusement parlors. To produce the films he constructed a film studio, a "revolving photographic building" covered with tar paper, nicknamed the Black Maria (1893). Soon after Wilhelm Roentgen's discovery of X rays in 1895, Edison went into action, learned to replicate Roentgen's experiments, and produced a device for taking X-ray pictures called the fluoroscope all within two weeks of learning of the discovery by telegraph. X rays proved difficult to control, and one of Edison's assistants, Clarence Dally, was an early casualty of radiation poisoning. Edison eventually lost out to General Electric in marketing X-ray machines.

Edison and the Automobile. Edison's first project of the new century, suggested by the growing popularity of automobiles, was the development of a storage battery in 1900. The project was a difficult one because the complexity of chemical reactions that took place in battery cells made the analysis of the different experimental substances intricate. He finally settled on a model using mainly nickel hydrate for the positive electrode and iron oxide for the negative. Used to power electric automobiles, Edison's battery went into production in 1903, but these first batteries leaked and were generally unreliable. By summer 1905 Edison claimed he had made more than ten thousand experiments on the battery and had redesigned it completely. Then in 1908 he found that adding lithium hydroxide substantially increased the life of the battery: this was an important, wholly empirical discovery, and Edison had no notion of why it worked. He also experimented with steel and concrete construction techniques for low-cost housing and built several prototypes.

Edison and Science. Edison developed virtually all of his inventions on a trial-and-error basis. But as electronics became more sophisticated and required training in mathematics, physics, and formal engineering, he was unable to keep up. During World War I the navy consulted him about possible methods of detecting submarines and he proved unable to conceptualize the problem adequately. He always proclaimed his opposition to what he mocked as "the-o-ret-ical" science. His last great project, which he began in 1920, was the search for an indigenous plant species that could produce rubber for automobile tires. True to his ways, he examined more than fifteen thousand different plant species, all in vain. Edison died 18 October 1931.

Sources:

Robert Freidel and Paul Israel, *Edison's Electric Light: Biography of an Invention* (New Brunswick, N.J.: Rutgers University Press, 1987);

Matthew Josephson, *Edison: A Biography* (New York: McGraw-Hill, 1959);

André Milliard, *Edison and the Business of Invention* (Baltimore: Johns Hopkins University Press, 1990);

Wynn Wachhorst, *Thomas Alva Edison: An American Myth* (Cambridge, Mass.: MIT Press, 1981).

GEORGE ELLERY HALE

1868-1938

ASTROPHYSICIST

Early Life. Born in Chicago, George Ellery Hale developed an early interest in astronomy. While still in high school he was fascinated with solar spectroscopy, a method of determining the chemical components of the Sun through the observation of its light. He was a physics major at Massachusetts Institute of Technology but spent his spare time at the Harvard Observatory working as an unpaid assistant. Among the many phenomena that interested him were solar prominences, clouds of gas above the surface of the Sun, which up to that time had only been observed and photographed during eclipses. At the age of twenty-one he devised an instrument, which he called the spectroheliograph, to photograph them in the light of day.

Astrophysics. In 1892 Hale became associate professor of astrophysics at the University of Chicago. Until the late nineteenth century, astronomers had been mainly interested in observing the motion of celestial bodies. Those few who were interested in their physical nature were astrophysicists. For Hale and others the main method of research was spectrography, a field that required a physics laboratory in which to make spectrographic analyses under controlled conditions to compare with observational results. Astrophysics also required larger reflecting telescopes than were currently in use, because in order to measure stellar spectra, especially the vast spectrum of the sun, an instrument with a capacity to gather large quantities of light was required. In 1892 Hale convinced an industrialist, Charles T. Yerkes, to build an observatory with a telescope that surpassed all others in focal length and light-gathering power. The Yerkes Observatory opened in 1897 in Williams Bay, Wisconsin, with Hale as its first director. It was an entirely new kind of installation, a physics laboratory as well as an observatory with a forty-inch reflecting telescope.

Mount Wilson. But Hale was not satisfied and immediately began searching for an even more powerful instrument. He approached the Carnegie Institution soon after it was established in 1902 and won the promise of $100,000 to build a sixty-inch telescope on top of Mount Wilson near Pasadena, California. Observation began there in 1904 with a twelve-inch solar telescope borrowed from the Yerkes Observatory. Hale was able to discover that sunspots are cooler than other regions of the sun and also possess intense magnetic fields. These were the most significant discoveries regarding sunspots since Galileo had first discovered them in the seventeenth century.

New Research. In 1907 he designed and had built in Mount Wilson's instrumentation shop a heliomicrometer with which he could establish the positions of flocculi, or calcium clouds, observable on the sun. He found that the stars rotate in a way different from that of planets: bodies made of gas, like the sun, turn faster at their equators than they do at their poles. In 1908 the sixty-inch telescope was set up. Hale then shifted the focus of his research from the sun to other stars to broaden his understanding of stellar evolution. Thus he found characteristics in red stars similar to those he found in sunspots. Hale was regarded by his main backer, the Carnegie Institution, as running the best kind of scientific program, one with highly focused objectives and strong leadership.

Cal Tech. In 1906 Hale was named a trustee of a small school in Pasadena called Throop Polytechnic Institute. He moved immediately to transform it from a local vocational school into a small, select institute of advanced science, concentrating on electrical engineering and a few basic science disciplines. This modest college eventually evolved into a great scientific university, the California Institute of Technology. Hale was involved with selecting the first few presidents and with planning the new campus, where building began in April 1909. His grand design for scientific education was to make Cal Tech into one of three great regional science centers along with the University of Chicago and MIT.

A Bigger and Better Telescope. As early as 1906, two years before the sixty-inch telescope was installed on Mount Wilson, Hale was already discussing plans for an even bigger instrument, a one-hundred-inch telescope that would gather more than twice the light of the sixty-inch model and permit the observation of much smaller objects. It would, he said, "enormously surpass all existing instruments in the photography of stars and nebulae, thus giving new information on their chemical composition and the temperature and pressures in their atmospheres." A glass disk for such a telescope was cast for Hale in France in 1907 but proved defective. Toward the end of the decade Hale, who was plagued by headaches (for him the prelude to a nervous breakdown), had to give up observational astronomy almost completely. The one-hundred-inch telescope was finally inaugurated in 1917.

Last Years. In 1923 Hale resigned as director of Mount Wilson and devoted his time to a solar laboratory at Cal Tech named in his honor. From around 1928 on,

he devoted much of his energy to a grandiose project, the building of a two-hundred-inch telescope. This was the instrument that when finally built was installed on Mount Palomar. But Hale did not live to witness the realization of his dream. He died in Pasadena 21 February 1938.

Source:
Helen Wright, *Explorer of the Universe: A Biography of George Ellery Hale,* second edition (Woodbury, N.Y.: American Institute of Physics, 1994).

G. STANLEY HALL

1844-1924

PSYCHOLOGIST

Education. G. Stanley Hall was one of the first American "scientific" psychologists. Along with William James and others he established psychology as an academic discipline in the United States. After receiving his education from Williams College and the Union Theological Seminary, he became a philosophy instructor at Antioch College, where in 1872 he read Wilhelm Wundt's book on physiological psychology and decided to redirect his efforts. Psychology had been considered a branch of philosophy until Wundt began to study the physiology of the nervous system, the localization of functions in the brain, and the physiology of sense perception. Hall returned to graduate school and received his doctorate under James at Harvard in 1878.

Experimentalist. At Harvard, Hall performed experiments in the line of Wundt's famous research on reaction time. He was especially interested in the way perceptions were registered by muscles and also studied the visual perception of color. His view of mind at this time was based on Charles Darwin's concepts of adaptation: the mind is the faculty that mediates between human beings and their environment. After graduate school Hall spent a year in Berlin, studying the physiology of the muscular system and reflex action in Emil Dubois-Reymond's laboratory. At the same time, he consulted the famous physiologist Hermann von Helmholtz on color perception. Hall was now convinced that psychology was completely based in physiology and that experiments could be formulated to learn how sensations give rise to perceptions and emotions.

Hall's New Psychology. In 1884 Hall set up an experimental psychology laboratory (the first in the United States) at Johns Hopkins University, affiliated with the biology department. There he investigated motor sensations of the skin, the perception of rhythm, and other aspects of physiological psychology. But he also developed an interest in the unconscious mind, specifically hypnosis, and as a result grew increasingly disenchanted with this completely somatic approach to psychology, the processes of which now seemed to him to require more complex explanations than those offered by physiology. In 1888 Hall was named president of Clark University, a new institution in Worcester, Massachusetts, that offered graduate study only and was able to build a strong psychology department quickly. In the 1890s he began to focus on the psychology of children as the basis for developmental psychology, using a questionnaire to gather information about how children saw their world. In Darwinian theory children were thought to be like contemporary primitive people or like the remote ancestors of civilized people. In 1898 Hall wrote a pioneering study on the child's sense of self, which he argued developed unconsciously from two distinct tendencies, one that focuses on mother and home, the other on society.

Hall and Freud. Hall's new interests were parallel to those of Sigmund Freud, the Austrian psychiatrist whose papers on hysteria Hall had read in the 1890s. Freud spoke for the many psychiatrists who had found that the currently recommended physical therapies, such as bed rest and electrical shock, seemed unable to cure the majority of neuroses that doctors had to confront. In the first decade of the twentieth century Hall turned to the psychology of adolescence, which heightened his awareness of the role of sexuality in development — another point of contact with Freud, as was Hall's increasing focus on instinctual behavior and how society acts to repress it. All of these new interests led him to invite to Freud to come to Clark for the twentieth-anniversary celebration in 1909. Freud's lectures confirmed Hall's support for psychotherapy and his emphasis on the significance of the unconscious. He now believed that unconscious complexes "dominate psychopathic symptoms and also our normal life."

Hall and American Psychology. After Freud's visit Hall became a prominent American proponent of psychoanalysis and Freudian psychology. As a spokesman for Freud he played a powerful role in turning American psychology away from both philosophy and physiology and toward the dynamic approach that Freud brought to the study of mind and the emotions, despite the resistance of many American psychologists to Freud's and Hall's emphasis on sexuality. At Clark he organized a Dream Club where students discussed their dreams and applied Freud's ideas about the unconscious to them. Hall was the most influential American psychologist of his time. He started the *American Journal of Psychology* in 1887 and founded the American Psychological Association in 1892. He died on 24 April 1924.

Source:
Dorothy Ross, *G. Stanley Hall: The Psychologist as Prophet* (Chicago: University of Chicago Press, 1972).

ALBERT ABRAHAM MICHELSON

1852-1931

PHYSICIST AND FIRST AMERICAN NOBEL PRIZE WINNER

Background. Albert Abraham Michelson was born in Prussia, in 1852, immigrating with his family at the age of four first to Panama and then to San Francisco, where his father became an itinerant merchant serving the mining camps of the Gold Rush days. He was sent to boarding school where he developed an interest in science and, after an interview in 1869 with President Ulysses Grant, was appointed to the Naval Academy at Annapolis. Upon graduation he was named physics instructor at the academy. He became interested in the speed of light and how to measure it accurately. As a result he was granted a leave of absence, which permitted him to spend 1880 to 1882 in Europe, much of the time in the physics laboratory of Hermann von Helmholtz in Berlin.

The Velocity of Light. The problem of measuring the speed of light had both practical and theoretical aspects. Under the then-current theory, space was filled with an invisible substance known as the ether, through which light waves were thought to be propagated. Michelson's working hypothesis was that inasmuch as the ether is at rest and the earth moves through it, the speed of light on the earth's surface should be affected by the density and flow of the ether. In Helmholtz's laboratory (and with the financial assistance of Alexander Graham Bell) he designed an instrument called the interferential refractometer (later shortened to interferometer), which he could use to test the existence of the ether by comparing beams of light reflected in opposite directions.

The Michelson-Morley Experiment. In 1881 Michelson resigned from active duty in the navy and was appointed professor of physics at the Case Institute of Applied Science in Cleveland, Ohio. In 1885 he began a collaboration with physicist Edward W. Morley of Western Reserve University to test for the relative motion of the earth with respect to a presumably stationary ether. The experiment was painstaking because of the problems arising from measuring an extraterrestrial phenomenon under terrestrial conditions. The interferometer had to be carefully mounted on a sandstone slab that rested on a mercury bearing. The results of the experiments were negative: no difference in the velocity of light could be detected no matter how a light beam might be rotated with respect to the ether.

Michelson in Chicago. Having become an internationally recognized expert in precision measurement, Michelson was named chairman of the Department of Physics at the University of Chicago in 1893. There he built new precision instruments and turned to spectroscopy, the measurement and analysis of stellar spectra to determine the chemical components of stars. In 1899 he gave the Lowell Lectures at Harvard in which he stated that the more important fundamental laws and facts of physical science have all been discovered, and these are now so firmly established that the possibility of their ever being supplanted in consequence of new discoveries is exceedingly remote. In retrospect, Michelson's remarks constitute an odd capstone to the Newtonian era, just before the quantum and relativity revolutions broke upon the complacent world of academic physics.

Einstein, Michelson, and Relativity. In 1905 Albert Einstein demonstrated in the special theory of relativity that the speed of light was constant and therefore the ether did not exist. Einstein was later unable to recall whether he had read or heard of the Michelson-Morley experiment before then, but in light of his theory it quickly became apparent that Michelson and his colleague had in fact demonstrated the nonexistence of the ether even though they had not recognized it. Toward the end of his life Michelson spoke fondly of "the beloved old aether" and remained skeptical of Einstein's theory, although open to its possibility. In 1907 he became the first American to win the Nobel Prize, awarded to him for his invention of precision optical instruments and for the various experiments he had conducted with them.

Last Years. Michelson returned to the navy during World War I and contributed to a variety of technical projects, especially the optical range finder. In the 1920s he supervised experiments at Mount Wilson Observatory in California, including an optical determination of the velocity of light between two mountain peaks (Mount Wilson to Mount San Antonio). He died in Pasadena on 9 May 1931.

Source:

Loyd S. Swenson Jr., *The Ethereal Aether: A History of the Michelson-Morley-Miller Aether-Drift Experiments, 1880–1930* (Austin: University of Texas Press, 1972).

ROBERT EDWIN PEARY

1856-1920

ADMIRAL AND ARCTIC EXPLORER

Background. Born in Cresson, Pennsylvania, Robert Edwin Peary studied civil engineering at Bowdoin College in Maine, graduating in 1876. In 1879 he joined the U.S. Coast and Geodetic Service as a draftsman, and he signed up with the navy as a civil engineer in 1881. In 1884 and 1885 he was sent with a navy expedition to survey prospects for an interoceanic canal in Nicaragua, where he devised locks of a great height for the proposed channel. He returned to Nicaragua in 1887 in charge of new canal surveys. When Congress finally opted for a Panama site in 1902, Peary's surveys were forgotten.

Greenland. Peary's first northern expeditions were to Greenland. In 1886 he set out to cross the island from the western coast on a one-man sled of his own design, achieving greater penetration of the inland ice cap than ever before and greater elevation (2,125 feet). The area he explored around Mount Wistar has ever since been called Peary Land. He realized that a party equipped with snowshoes and skis could use the ice cap as an "imperial highway" to reach the eastern coast. On a second expedition in 1892 he crossed the island northeastward from Whale Sound. This sled trip made him a world figure. Another land crossing in 1895 confirmed that Greenland was an island. On summer trips in 1896 and 1897 he excavated meteorites at Cape York and studied the peculiar wind system of the island.

Still Heading North. Peary was granted a leave from the navy to explore the Arctic from 1898 to 1902. By 1900 he had lost all but two of his toes to frostbite, making all exploration physically difficult for him. In 1900 and 1902 he made two great sledding expeditions northward, reaching Lockwood's Island, thought to have been the northernmost site in Greenland, on 8 May 1900. Realizing there was still more land to the north, he pressed on to Cape Jesup, confirming the glacial origin of so-called floeberg ice, chunks that are too small to be icebergs. In 1902 he tried unsuccessfully for the pole and established a new "farthest north" at 84°17′ on 14 April. He was turned back by impossible conditions and returned to naval duty.

The North Pole. Peary had all but given up his dream of reaching the pole, but Robert F. Scott's Antarctic expedition of 1905 encouraged him to try again. He designed a new polar steamship, named the *Roosevelt* after the exploration-minded American president, to provide a winter base and left on his seventh Arctic expedition on 16 July 1905. The route to the North Pole followed the north coast of Grant Land to Cape Moss and thence across sea ice directly to the pole, some 450 miles further on. On 21 April 1906 a new farthest north was established at 87°6′, but the entire party was forced to head south to hunt game to provision the ship. The seventh expedition ended in late autumn 1906 when the *Roosevelt* was crippled in an ice pack and was forced to head south for repairs. The eighth and last expedition sailed from New York on 6 July 1908. Under Peary's plan there were five cooperating but independent teams, four of which were supporting parties that went back and forth with supplies. The objective was to place the main team on an advanced base at 87°47′, 150 miles from the pole. Peary reached the pole on 6 April 1909, and took a comprehensive set of astronomical readings to establish his position. He was made rear admiral by an act of Congress in 1911, but only after submitting to cross-examination by a congressional committee, some of whose members were skeptical of his claims.

Last Years. Peary became an active member of the Aero Club of America and when World War I began in 1914 campaigned tirelessly for the creation of an American air force. He died of pernicious anemia on 20 February 1920.

Sources:
J. Gordon Hayes, *Robert Edwin Peary: A Record of his Explorations, 1886–1909* (London: Grant Richards, 1929);

William Herbert Hobbs, *Peary* (New York: Macmillan, 1936).

CHARLES PROTEUS STEINMETZ

1865-1923

ELECTRICAL ENGINEER

Early Life in Europe. Charles Proteus Steinmetz was born in Breslau, Germany (now Wroclaw, Poland), in 1865. He was educated at the University of Breslau, whose physics department had a solid reputation in electrophysics, and was a doctoral candidate in mathematics. Felix Auerbach, his professor of mathematical physics, encouraged all of his students to develop mathematical theories of how specific pieces of electrical equipment work. Steinmetz was forced to leave Breslau because of his socialist politics and went to Zurich, Switzerland, where he enrolled for a semester of engineering at the Polytechnic Institute. While there he published his first two articles on electrical engineering: one on the resistance of conductors, the other a mathematical theory of the transformer. When the Breslau police issued a warrant for his arrest in 1889, he decided to immigrate to the United States.

First Years in America. In the 1890s American electrical engineering was entering its golden age: the electric illuminating and power industries were in their infancy, as was the telephone. The radio would soon be developed. Steinmetz's training in mathematics and his interest in mathematical physics were virtually unrivaled in the American electric world and assured him a rapid rise in the industry. He was hired as an engineer by Eickemeyer and Osterheld, a company based in Yonkers, New York, that made ironclad DC (direct current) dynamos and that was then developing electric streetcar and elevator motors based on Eickemeyer's design. Steinmetz worked on all of the company's electrical projects, but particularly on the development of a practical alternating current motor. Steinmetz developed several single-phase AC induction motors, one of which became General Electric's standard fan motor when Steinmetz joined that firm in 1893. The papers he wrote in Yonkers were landmarks in the fusion of technology with science in the electrical industry, a movement that presaged the immi-

nent end of the tinkering phase of American technology. To develop electrical theory intelligible to other engineers, Steinmetz had to shift from differential equations, the kind of mathematics favored by physicists, to the graphical analysis that engineers used (which had been pioneered by English civil and mechanical engineers in the previous two decades).

The Law of Hysteresis. Steinmetz began attending meetings of the American Institute of Electrical Engineers and the New York Mathematical Society and published two papers on synthetic geometry in the *American Journal of Mathematics*. Steinmetz's early fame in American technology and science was based on his research in two areas: magnetic hysteresis and alternating current electricity. Hysteresis refers to the tendency of materials to resist being magnetized or demagnetized. The phenomenon plagued both DC and AC systems, because it caused the iron cores of electrical equipment to overheat. Steinmetz derived a mathematical equation to describe hysteresis as a naturally occurring phenomenon, which has subsequently been called the law of hysteresis. One reason for his success was that he understood the electrical characteristics of common laboratory instruments such as the galvanometer, wattmeter, and differential magnetometer better than most and so secured more-accurate readings. The research involved four thousand separate observations during a period of two years. Steinmetz drew some fire from the physics community by comparing his law to Newton's law of gravitation.

General Electric. In late 1892 General Electric bought out Eickemeyer's company and so acquired the services of Steinmetz. This was a critical moment in the electrical industry. By now it was clear that AC systems would win out over Thomas Edison's original DC concept. GE needed to position itself to compete with the rival Westinghouse Electric Company, and both firms were hiring college-educated engineers. Steinmetz was assigned to GE's plant in Lynn, Massachusetts, where he worked in the Calculating Department, a kind of internal consulting unit. There his work on induction led to his first patents on methods of reducing induction in power transmission lines. He also developed a breakthrough technique of analyzing AC electrical circuits with complex numbers: he was not the first engineer to do this, but he developed the method more comprehensively. By showing how advanced algebraic techniques could be applied to practical problems such as transformers, circuits, and transmission lines, Steinmetz laid the foundations for modern electrical engineering. He presented these methods in a series of textbooks beginning with *Theory and Calculation of Alternating Current Phenomena* in 1897 and continuing through the first two decades of the twentieth century. They exercised tremendous influence over the electrical engineering curriculum throughout the United States.

Engineer and Teacher. The Calculating Department, with Steinmetz at its head, was moved to Schenectady,

New York, in 1894. In effect, he was GE's chief engineer; all of the company's design calculations were under his control. As GE built electric power plants around the world, Steinmetz's department was charged with designing all of the equipment (alternators, motors, transformers, and so forth) associated with these installations. This meant a flood of patent applications for Steinmetz. GE allowed him to publish his research (which he did in twelve books and 150 articles on AC systems alone) as long as he did not disclose "proprietary" details. In 1902 he was named head of the Electrical Engineering Department at Union College, in which capacity he was able to perfect his pedagogical approach to the subject.

The Steinmetz Legend. Steinmetz was physically deformed, about four feet tall, and spoke English with a thick German accent. According to a GE official who interviewed him 1892: "I was startled . . . by the strange sight of a small, frail body surmounted by a large head, with long hair hanging to the shoulders, clothed in an old cardigan jacket, cigar in mouth, sitting cross-legged on a laboratory work table." Scientifically trained, he developed an influential philosophy of engineering that was based on a distinction between rational equations, derived from basic physical principles, and empirical equations, based on experimental research. Steinmetz liked to work with rational equations but understood that engineers, who frequently had to confront real technical problems for which no physical solution was readily available, must also use empirical formulas. In 1922 when he succeeded in creating lightning under laboratory conditions, the press hailed him as a modern Jove and elevated him to the status of wizard shared by Edison and Albert Einstein, who seemed able to command nature to do their will. He died 26 October 1923.

Source:
Ronald R. Kline: *Steinmetz: Engineer and Socialist* (Baltimore: Johns Hopkins University Press, 1992).

WILBUR AND ORVILLE WRIGHT

1867-1912; 1871-1948

PIONEER AVIATORS

The Bicycle Shop. Wilbur Wright was born on a farm in Indiana in 1867. His brother, Orville, was born in 1871, after the Wright family had moved to Dayton, Ohio. Their father was a bishop of the United Brethren

in Christ and edited and published several church papers. The Wright brothers' first enterprise was a print shop, which they ran from 1889 until 1892, when they joined in the national obsession for bike riding and bought a bicycle shop. In 1895 they began to manufacture bicycles. The Wrights became interested in aeronautics in 1899 and immersed themselves in the available literature. From their analysis of a long line of failed attempts with heavier-than-air machines they concluded that the first step would be to master the principles of flight by observation and then by using gliders. Only then, they believed, could one think about combining an engine with the wing structure.

Kitty Hawk. Between 1899 and 1903 the brothers achieved a series of conceptual and technical breakthroughs that made flight possible. The first was the recognition in 1900 of the desirability of "wing-warping," the twisting of the wing tips (eventually by attaching wires to them) so that flight could be adjusted to changing air patterns without requiring the pilot to shift his weight. At the end of 1901 they determined that the published figures for the lift and drag coefficients required to design effective wings were wrong and built a wind tunnel to achieve the correct measurements. By the fall of 1902 they had built a new glider based on their discoveries, adding a rudder to control the aerodynamic effects of wing warping. They experimented with gliders each fall on the beach at Kitty Hawk, North Carolina, where the winds were both powerful and constant, and there they made the first tests of a redesigned glider with a twelve-horsepower engine and propellers turned with bicycle chains. On 17 December 1903 the Wrights' plane flew — 852 feet in fifty-nine seconds.

Wilbur in France. The brothers spent the next few years refining the Wright Flyer and unsuccessfully attempting to find a financial backer or to sell their machine to some government. Their 1908 model had a more powerful motor, together with control levers and seats for the pilot and one passenger. To pursue the best opportunities for commercial success, Wilbur departed for France, arriving in Paris on 29 May. On 8 August he flew before a select crowd at Le Mans, near Paris, and caused a sensation by his seemingly effortless flight with beautifully banked turns. The French pioneer aviators realized that they had been beaten by the Americans. On 21 December he won the Michelin Cup by completing a 77-mile flight in 2 hours, 20 minutes. Orders for flyers began to come in.

Breakthrough. In the summer of 1909 the brothers fulfilled a contract by submitting to a series of tests and performing demonstrations for the Army Signal Corps. The tests met the corps's specifications and resulted in the War Department's purchase of the U.S. Army's first airplane for $30,000. Additional orders would follow in the 1910s, as the military began to realize some of the potential uses in warfare of the Wrights' invention.

The Last Exhibition. In September 1909 Orville traveled to Germany where, at Temeplhof field in Berlin, as many as two hundred thousand people came to see him fly. On 18 September he broke his own endurance record for a two-man flight by flying for an hour and thirty-five minutes. On the same day he set an unofficial altitude record of 500 meters, more than twice the existing record of 155 meters. Meanwhile, Wilbur remained in the United States training officers to operate the Army Flyer.

The Battle with Curtiss. As the decade ended, the Wrights played out a classic patent war that had come to typify most of the extraordinary series of inventions of the late nineteenth and early twentieth centuries. Thomas Edison was challenged on the light bulb and had to prove his priority, as Henry Ford did over certain features of his early automobile models. Such litigation was only to be expected in view of the large numbers of inventors and entrepreneurs that such inventions attracted. The Wrights' problem was with Glenn Curtiss, a member of Alexander Graham Bell's Aerial Experiment Association. The Wrights alleged that the ailerons (movable flaps on the trailing edge of an airplane wing) of Curtiss's *Golden Flier* infringed the wing-warping concept described in their basic patent. The Wrights filed their suit on 18 August 1909. *Wright* v. *Curtiss,* later recognized as a classic patent case, was tried in New York on 14 and 15 December 1909 before a judge who had found against Henry Ford in a similar suit in 1900. (Henry Ford sided with Curtiss because he believed that overly broad patents, such as the one the Wrights held, stifled innovation.) The judge found for the Wrights, asserting that ailerons were the functional equivalent of the wing warp even though structurally dissimilar.

The Partnership Ends. On 28 May 1912 Wilbur died of typhoid fever. The brothers had been close friends and partners in all they did. Shortly before his death, Wilbur explained that "My brother Orville and myself lived together, played together, worked together, and in fact thought together." Orville continued in aviation as president of the Wright Company, which produced a succession of new models until 1915, when he sold the firm. He maintained a laboratory in Dayton and served as consulting engineer for a new aircraft company called Dayton-Wright. He continued to be the elder statesman of American aviation until his death on 30 January 1948.

Sources:
Fred Howard, *Wilbur and Orville: A Biography of the Wright Brothers* (New York: Knopf, 1987);

Robert Wohl, *A Passion for Wings: Aviation and the Western Imagination, 1908–1918* (New Haven: Yale University Press, 1994).

PEOPLE IN THE NEWS

General Electric engineer **Ernst Alexanderson** designed a ten-thousand-cycle alternator for the first successful radio transmission at Brant Rock, Massachusetts, in 1905.

Wilbur O. Atwater of the U.S. Department of Agriculture invented the respiratory calorimeter in 1904.

In 1909 Belgian-born chemist **Leo Hendrik Baekeland** announced the development of Bakelite, a condensed resin that became a standard insulation product.

Edward Binney, a Pennsylvania chemist, developed the Crayola crayon in 1902.

In 1903 **Percy Brown** established a radiology department, using new X-ray technology, at Children's Hospital in Boston.

Thaddeus Cahill exhibited his electric typewriter at the Pan-American Exhibition in Buffalo in 1901.

In 1906 **Willis H. Carrier** invented air conditioning.

In 1908 **Frederick G. Cottrell** patented the electrolytic precipitator, an air purifying device that removes particulate materials from factory smokestacks.

In 1901 **Reginald Fessenden,** an engineering professor at the University of Pittsburgh, invented a high-frequency alternating current generator.

Yale physics professor **Josiah Willard Gibbs** published *Elementary Principles in Statistical Mechanics* (1902), which became a classic college textbook.

Ross G. Harrison, experimental embryologist at Johns Hopkins University, published reports in 1907 on his studies of live animal nerve tissue, cultivated in vitro under laboratory conditions.

William James, professor of psychology at Harvard, published *Pragmatism* (1907), a major statement of philosophical empiricism.

Based on an inference drawn from observations of radio waves, **Arthur E. Kennelly,** professor of engineering at Harvard University and former assistant of Thomas Edison, and Oliver Heaviside of England discovered the ionosphere in 1902.

Percival Lowell in 1901, 1903, and 1905 observed the planet Mars from his observatory in Flagstaff, Arizona.

Geneticists **Clarence McClung, Nettie M. Stevens,** and **E. B. Wilson** in 1905 identified the X and Y chromosomes as the genetic mechanism for sex differentiation in mammals.

In 1905 **Dayton Miller** and **Edward Morley** again attempted to detect the presence of aether in space by devising ether drift experiments in Cleveland.

In 1907 **Robert Millikan** began a series of experiments that led to the determination of the charge on the electron.

In 1907 **Thomas Hunt Morgan,** geneticist at Columbia University, began genetic experiments with the fruit fly.

Edward Charles Pickering, director of Harvard University's observatory at Arequipa, Peru, published the first photographic map of the entire sky in 1903.

In 1902 **Vlademar Poulsen,** Danish immigrant scientist, invented the arc generator, which transmitted continuous waves for wireless telegraphy and radio.

Francis Peyton Rous started experimentation in 1909 at the Rockefeller Institute on the chicken sarcoma, caused by a "filterable agent" that later proved to be a virus — a crucial experiment in the history of virology.

In 1908 **Elmer A. Sperry** introduced the gyrostablizer, which was quickly adopted by the U.S. Navy.

Almon B. Strowger, an undertaker by profession, invented the dial telephone in 1905.

Walter S. Sutton, a graduate student at Columbia University, published an important research paper in 1903 on the relationship of the pairing of chromosomes to random genetic recombination.

In 1903 **Frank Bursley Taylor** of the U.S. Geological Survey explained in a privately printed book his theory that planetary bodies, including the Moon, may have originated as comets.

In 1903 **Nikola Tesla** filed patents describing the use of tuned circuits to control mechanical devices at a distance, a basic principle of robotics.

Geneticist **Edmund B. Wilson** established the relationship between meiosis (reproductive cell division) and Gregor Mendel's laws of heredity in 1902.

DEATHS

Timothy Field Allen, 65, botanist, studied mainly *Characeae,* a group of algae, 5 December 1902.

Philip Danforth Armour, 69, meatpacking pioneer who adopted assembly-line methods for processing meat, 6 January 1901.

Wilbur Olin Atwater, 63, director of the first agricultural experiment station at Middletown, Connecticut, from 1875 to 1877, inventor (with E. B. Rosa) of the Atwater-Rosa calorimeter, 22 September 1907.

Hans Herman Behr, 86, entomologist and botanist, studied butterflies of California, 6 March 1904.

Alexander Melville Bell, 86, father of Alexander Graham Bell and founder of the scientific study of speech who devised a physiological alphabet that visually represented the sounds of the human voice, 7 August 1905.

Lorin Blodget, 78, climatologist, conducted early research on atmospheric physics, 24 March 1901.

Henry Carrington Bolton, 60, chemist, researched compounds of uranium, 19 November 1903.

DeWitt Bristol Brace, 42, physicist who studied the factors affecting the velocity of light propagated through matter, 2 October 1905.

William Keith Brooks, 60, invertebrate marine zoologist, 12 November 1908.

Lafayette Houghton Bunnell, 79, explorer who discovered and named the Yosemite Valley, 21 July 1903.

James Carroll, 53, bacteriologist, the second in command on Walter Reed's yellow fever expedition to Cuba, whose research showed that the agent that caused the fever was a filterable virus, 16 September 1907.

John Henry Caswell, 63, mineralogist, specialist in micropetrography and the first to identify phonolite in the United States, 16 October 1909.

William Francis Channing, 81, inventor of electric fire-alarm telegraph, the antecedent of all electric fire-alarm systems, 19 March 1901.

Henry Cadwalader Chapman, 64, anatomist who studied primates, especially the gorilla and chimpanzee, 7 September 1909.

James Graham Cooper, 72, naturalist who studied the geographical distribution of plants and animals mainly on the West Coast, 19 July 1902.

Thomas Craig, 45, mathematician who conducted studies of linear differential equations and hydrodynamics, 8 May 1900.

Richard John Gatling, 85, inventor in 1862 of the rapid-fire gun subsequently named after him, which was used by the Union army during the Civil War, 26 February 1902.

Augustin Gattinger, 78, botanist who studied the flora of Tennessee, 18 July 1903.

Josiah Williard Gibbs, 64, theoretical physicist who did important research on thermodynamic equilibrium, 28 April 1903.

Oliver Wolcott Gibbs, 86, pioneer chemist who studied complex inorganic acids, 9 December 1908.

Augustin Radcliffe Grote, 62, entomologist who studied butterflies, especially noctuid moths, 12 September 1903.

Asaph Hall, 78, astronomer at the U.S. Naval Observatory who discovered the two satellites of Mars in 1877, 22 November 1907.

William Harkness, 66, astronomer, Transit of Venus commissioner of the Naval Observatory for the transits of 1874 and 1882, 24 February 1903.

John Bell Hatcher, 43, paleontologist who did research on vertebrate fossils of the United States, including the first fossil specimen of *Tricerotops,* and studied mammalian fossils in Patagonia, 3 July 1904.

Clarence Luther Herrick, 46, neurologist and second president of the University of New Mexico, 15 September 1904.

George Washington Hough, 73, astronomer who discovered 627 double stars and also became an expert on the topography of Jupiter, 1 January 1909.

Oliver Payson Hubbard, 91, chemist who worked with Charles Goodyear on experiments leading to the vulcanization of rubber, 9 March 1900.

Alpheus Hyatt, 64, zoologist and paleontologist who formulated, along with E. D. Cope, a neo-Lamarckian law of acceleration to account for evolution, 15 January 1902.

Edward James Keeler, 43, astrophysicist and director of the Lick Observatory, known for his many photographs of nebulae, 12 August 1900.

Clarence Rivers King, 59, geologist who led the U.S. geological exploration of the fortieth parallel from 1867 to 1878 and promoted a neocatastrophist theory to modify Charles Darwin's account of evolution, 24 December 1901.

Samuel Pierpont Langley, 72, astrophysicist whose experiments on aerodynamics led to his 1891 prediction that mechanical flight was feasible using engines currently available, 22 February 1906.

Jesse William Lazear, 34, bacteriologist and member of United States Army Yellow Fever Commission who did research on the hematozoa of malaria and died in the field, 26 September 1900.

Joseph Leconte, 78, naturalist who studied both geology, writing a textbook in 1878, and physiology, particularly the glycogenic function of the liver, 5 July 1901.

J. Peter Lesley, 84, geologist who became famous for his study of Appalachian coal beds and iron deposits, 1 June 1903.

Ross G. Marvin, 34, professor of civil engineering at Cornell and chief scientist on Robert Peary's polar expedition, died after being shot by an Eskimo, 10 April 1909.

Thomas Meehan, 75, botanist, author of *The Natural Flowers and Ferns of the United States* (1878–1880), 19 November 1901.

Simon Newcomb, 74, professor of mathematics and astronomy at Johns Hopkins University, expert in celestial mechanics, especially the Earth's effects on the motion of the Moon, 11 July 1909.

Alpheus Spring Packard Jr., 66, geologist and entomologist who described approximately fifty new genera and 580 species of invertebrates, 14 February 1905.

John Wesley Powell, 68, explorer and geographer who studied the geology of the American West, 23 September 1902.

Temple Prime, 71, conchologist, expert on mollusks, 25 February 1903.

Walter Reed, 51, head of the U.S. Medical Corps in Cuba that confirmed the transmission of yellow fever by mosquitoes, 22 November 1902.

Ogden Nicholas Rood, 71, physicist, specialist in optics who did research on chromatics and the polarization of light, 12 November 1902.

Henry Augustus Rowland, 53, physicist, best known for his development of concave diffraction gratings for the mapping of solar spectra, 16 April 1901.

Edward Augustus Samuels, 72, ornithologist, author of *The Birds of New England* (1867), 27 May 1908.

Charles Anthony Schott, 75, geophysicist, chief of the U.S. Coastal Service, who participated in the triangulation of North America, 31 July 1901.

Nathaniel Southgate Shaler, 65, geologist specializing in the reclamation of arid lands by irrigation and a popular writer on human interaction with the physical environment, 10 April 1906.

Edward Robinson Squibb, 81, chemist with research in percolation who established Squibb Laboratories in 1852, 25 October 1900.

Richard B. Warder, 57, German-trained physical chemist who studied atomic motion in liquid molecules, 23 July 1905.

Charles Tyson Yerkes, 68, entrepreneur and businessman who pioneered electric traction streetcars in Chicago in the 1880s, 29 December 1905.

PUBLICATIONS

Aero Club of America, *Navigating the Air: A Scientific Statement of the Progress of Aeronautical Science up to the Present Time* (New York: Doubleday, Page, 1907);

Alphonse Berget, *The Conquest of the Air: Aeronautics, Aviation, History, Theory, Practice* (New York: Putnam, 1909);

Arthur Bird, *Looking Forward: The Phenomenal Progress of Electricity in 1912* (Northamptom, Mass.: Valley View, 1906);

H. A. Bumstead and R. G. Van Name, eds., *The Scientific Papers of J. Williard Gibbs*, 2 volumes (New York: Longmans, Green 1906);

Luther Burbank, *The Training of the Human Plant* (New York: Century, 1907);

A. Frederick Collins, *Wireless Telegraphy: Its History, Theory and Practice* (New York: McGraw, 1905);

C. Field, *The Story of the Submarine* (Philadelphia: Lippincott, 1907);

Josiah Williard Gibbs, *Elementary Principles in Statistical Mechanics* (New York: Scribners, 1902);

Grove Karl Gilbert and others, *John Wesley Powell, A Memorial* (Chicago: Open Court, 1904);

Augustus Gottinger, *The Flora of Tennessee and a Philosophy of Botany* (Nashville, 1901);

George Ellery Hale, *The Study of Stellar Evolution* (Chicago: University of Chicago Press, 1908);

Granville Stanley Hall, *Adolescence: Its Psychology, and Its Relation to Physiology, Anthropology, Sociology, Sex, Crime and Religion* (New York: D. Appleton, 1904);

Hall, *Youth, Its Education, Regimen and Hygiene* (New York: D. Appleton, 1906);

Gardner Dexter Hiscox, *Gas, Gasoline and Oil Vapor Engines* (New York: N. W. Henley, 1900);

Edwin J. Houston, *Electricity in Everyday Life*, 3 volumes (New York: Collier, 1905);

Frederick Remsen Hutton, *The Gas-Engine*, second edition (New York: John Wiley, 1904);

William James, *Pragmatism* (New York: Longmans, Green, 1907);

Herbert Spencer Jennings, *Behavior of the Lower Organisms* (New York: Columbia University Press, 1906);

Arthur E. Kennelly, *Wireless Telegraphy: An Elementary Treatise* (New York: Moffatt, Yard, 1906);

Oliver Lodge, *The Ether of Space* (New York: Harper, 1909);

Percival Lowell, *The Evolution of Worlds* (New York: Macmillan, 1909);

Lowell, *The Solar System* (Boston: Houghton Mifflin, 1903);

Charles Edward Lucke, *Gas Engine Design* (New York: Van Nostrand, 1905);

Graham Lusk, *The Elements of the Science of Nutrition*, second edition (Philadelphia: W. B. Saunders, 1909);

Hiram S. Maxim, *Artificial and Natural Flight* (New York: Whittaker, 1909);

Domenico Mazzotto, *Wireless Telegraphy and Telephony* (New York: Whittaker, 1906);

Albert A. Michelson, *Light Waves and Their Uses* (Chicago: University of Chicago Press, 1903);

Simon Newcomb, *The Reminiscences of an Astronomer* (Boston: Houghton Mifflin, 1903);

Max Planck, *Treatise on Thermodynamics* (New York: Longmans, 1903);

Edward Bagnall Poulton, *Charles Darwin and the Origin of Species; addresses . . . in America and England in the Year of the Two Anniversaries* (New York: Longmans, Green, 1909);

Nathaniel Southgate Shaler, *The Autobiography of Nathaniel Southgate Shaler* (Boston: Houghton Mifflin, 1909);

Hugo de Vries, *The Mutation Theory. Experiments and Observations on the Origin of Species in the Vegetable Kingdom*, 2 volumes (Chicago: Open Court, 1909–1910);

de Vries, *Plant Breeding: Comments on the Experiments of Nilsson and Burbank* (Chicago: Open Court, 1907);

de Vries, *Species and Varieties: Their Origin by Mutation* (Chicago: Open Court, 1905);

H. G. Wells, *The War in the Air* (New York: Macmillan, 1908);

Edmund Beecher Wilson, *The Cell in Development and Inheritance*, second edition (New York: Macmillan, 1900);

Edwin Bidwell Wilson, *Vector Analysis Founded Upon the Lectures of J. Williard Gibbs* (New Haven: Yale University Press, 1901);

Harry Egerton Wimperis, *The Internal Combustion Engine* (New York: Van Nostrand, 1909);

Aero Club of America, periodical;

American Breeders' Association Reports, periodical;

Automobile Club of America Annual Yearbook, periodical;

Journal of Experimental Zoology, periodical;

Motor World, periodical.

CHAPTER THIRTEEN

SPORTS

by ADAM HORNBUCKLE

CONTENTS

Sidebars and tables are listed in italics.

1900

29 Jan.	Byron Bancroft "Ban" Johnson forms the American League by expanding the former minor Western Association to include major eastern cities. The new league quickly becomes a threat to the dominant National League.
19 Apr.	James J. Caffrey of Hamilton, Ontario, wins the fourth annual Boston Marathon with a time of 2:39:44.0.
3 May	Jimmy Boland rides Lieutenant Gibson to victory in the twenty-sixth annual Kentucky Derby.
20 May– 28 Oct.	Paris hosts the Summer Olympic Games, called the International Meeting of Physical Training and Sport, as an adjunct to the Paris Exhibition.
12–15 June	The first Grand American Championship for shooting clay targets, won by Rollo O. "Pop" Heikes of Dayton, Ohio, is held in Queens, New York.
8–10 Aug.	The United States defeats Great Britain, three matches to one, in the first Davis Cup Challenge tennis tournament.
Sept.	The Brooklyn Dodgers win 82 games, losing 54, to capture the National League pennant.
5 Oct.	Harry Vardon of Great Britain wins the sixth annual U.S Open Golf Tournament, held at the Chicago Golf Club.

1901

8–11 Jan.	The American Bowling Congress holds the first National Bowling Championship in Chicago in which forty-one teams, representing seventeen cities from nine states, compete for a purse of $1,592.
19 Apr.	James J. Caffrey of Hamilton, Ontario, wins the fifth annual Boston Marathon in 2:29:23.6.
29 Apr.	Jimmy Winkfield rides His Eminence to victory in the twenty-seventh annual Kentucky Derby.
12 May	Joe Gans captures the lightweight boxing title, which he will hold until 1908.
15 June	Willie Anderson defeats Alex Smith in a play-off round by one stroke to win the U.S. Open Golf Tournament, held at the Myopia Hunt Club in South Hamilton, Massachusetts.
21 Aug.	Joe "Iron Man" McGinnity, pitcher for the Baltimore Orioles, is expelled from major-league baseball for stepping on umpire Tom Connolly's toes, spitting in his face, and punching him. McGinnity is reinstated because of fan support.
Sept.	The Pittsburgh Pirates, with 90 wins and 49 losses, take the National League pennant, while the Chicago White Sox, with 83 wins and 53 losses, capture the first American League pennant.
28 Sept.– 4 Oct.	The U.S. yacht *Columbia* successfully defends the America's Cup against the British challenger, *Shamrock II*.
18 Dec.	Joe Walcott wins the welterweight boxing title by knocking out Rube Ferns in the fifth round.

1902

1 Jan. Michigan defeats Stanford 49–0 in the first Tournament of Roses Association football game. The Rose Bowl would become an annual event beginning in 1916.

19 Apr. Samuel A. Mellor of Yonkers, New York, wins the sixth annual Boston Marathon with a time of 2:43:12.0.

3 May Jimmy Winkfield rides Alan-a-Dale to his second consecutive victory in the Kentucky Derby.

8 Aug. The United States, led by William A. Larned, defeats Great Britain, three matches to two, to win a second consecutive Davis Cup tennis challenge.

Sept. The Pittsburgh Pirates, with 103 wins and 36 losses, win the National League pennant, while the Philadelphia Athletics, with 83 wins and 53 losses, win the American League pennant.

11 Oct. Laurie Auchterlonie wins the U.S. Open Golf Tournament at the Garden City Golf Club on Long Island, New York.

1903

- The Portage Lakers of Houghton, Michigan, the first professional hockey team formed in the United States, win 24 of 26 games in their first year. They are champions of the International Hockey League.

20 Apr. John C. Lorden of Cambridge, Massachusetts, wins the seventh annual Boston Marathon in 2:41:29.8.

22 Apr. Jack Root wins the light heavyweight boxing title over Charles "Kid" McCoy.

2 May Hal Booker rides Judge Himes to victory in the twenty-ninth annual Kentucky Derby.

27 June Willie Anderson defeats David Brown by two strokes to win a second U.S. Open Golf Tournament.

8 Aug. Great Britain defeats the United States four matches to one to win the third Davis Cup tennis challenge.

13 Aug. Frankie Nell wins the bantamweight boxing title.

14 Aug. Jim Jeffries defeats James J. Corbett, thus retaining his world heavyweight boxing title.

**22 Aug.–
2 Sept.** The U.S. yacht *Reliance* successfully defends the America's Cup against the British yacht *Shamrock III.*

1–13 Oct. Boston defeats Pittsburgh five games to three in the first World Series played between the National League and American League champions.

4 Nov. Bob Fitzsimmons wins the light heavyweight boxing title, outpointing George Gardner in twenty rounds.

Harvard Stadium, the first stadium built for football and the largest reinforced steel structure in the world, is formally opened.

1904

- The Gold Cup, the premier event of the American Power Boat Association, is held for the first time on the Hudson River.

1905

Jan.	Henry Ford sets a world land-speed record of 91.37 MPH.
22 Feb.	The National Ski Association holds the first national ski jumping championship in Ishpeming, Michigan.
19 Apr.	Michael Spring of New York City wins the eighth annual Boston Marathon in 2:38:04.4.
30 Apr.	Aaron "Dixie Kid" Brown defeats Joe Walcott for the welterweight boxing championship.
2 May	Frankie Prior rides Elwood to victory in the Kentucky Derby.
5 May	Denton T. "Cy" Young pitches baseball's first perfect game under modern pitching rules, not allowing any opposing player to reach first base.
1 July– **23 Nov.**	Saint Louis holds the Summer Olympic Games in conjunction with the Saint Louis World's Fair.
9 July	Willie Anderson wins his third U.S. Open Golf Tournament.
Fall	John McGraw, manager of the New York Giants, calls off the World Series between the Giants and the Boston Red Sox.

•	American May G. Sutton wins the Wimbledon singles title and becomes the first foreigner to win the British championship.
5 Apr.	Yale wins the first intercollegiate wrestling tournament against Columbia, Penn, and Princeton.
19 Apr.	Frederick Lorz of Yonkers, New York, wins the ninth annual Boston Marathon in 2:38:25.0.
10 May	Jack Martin rides Agile to victory in the thirty-first annual Kentucky Derby.
3 July	Marvin Hart wins the world heavyweight boxing championship by knocking out Jack Root in the twelfth round.
22 Sept.	Willie Anderson wins his fourth U.S. Open Golf championship, held at the Myopia Hunt Club in South Hamilton, Massachusetts.
Oct.	President Theodore Roosevelt hosts a conference of academic and athletic officials from Harvard, Princeton, and Yale to curb the brutality of college football.
9–14 Oct.	The New York Giants of the National League defeat the Philadelphia Athletics of the American League four games to one in the second World Series.
5 Dec.	Columbia and Cornell tie, 2–2, in the first intercollegiate soccer match.
20 Dec.	Bob Fitzsimmons is knocked out by Philadelphia Jack O'Brien in the light heavyweight title bout. O'Brien holds the title until his retirement in 1912.
	The Intercollegiate Athletic Association of the United States is founded in New York with sixty-two institutions to establish rules and requirements for intercollegiate athletics.

1906

- Daniel J. Kelley sets a new world record of 9.6 seconds in the 100-yard dash.

26 Feb. Swimmer Charles M. Daniels equals the world record of 57.6 seconds for 100 yards to become the first American to swim the distance in less than 60 seconds.

19 Apr. Timothy Ford of Cambridge, Massachusetts, wins the tenth annual Boston Marathon in 2:45:45.0.

22 Apr.– 2 May Athens hosts the Summer Olympic Games to celebrate the tenth anniversary of their revival.

2 May Roscoe Troxler rides Sir Huon to victory in the thirty-second annual Kentucky Derby.

23 May Frank Gotch defeats Tom Jenkins for the heavyweight wrestling title.

25 May *Tamerlane*, a thirty-eight-foot yawl, wins the first Bermuda Race, organized by Thomas Fleming Day, editor of *Rudder* magazine.

11–24 June *Lurline* wins the first Trans-Pacific Race from Los Angeles to Honolulu.

29 June Alex Smith defeats brother Willie in the U.S. Open Golf Tournament.

9–14 Oct. The Chicago White Sox of the American League defeat the Chicago Cubs of the National League four games to one in the World Series.

29 Dec. The Intercollegiate Athletic Association of the United States is renamed the National Collegiate Athletic Association (NCAA).

1907

- Hawaiian George Douglas Freeth introduces surfing to the U.S. mainland at Redondo Beach, California.

7 Feb. Asario Autio wins the first national cross-country skiing championship.

19 Apr. Thomas Longboat wins the eleventh annual Boston Marathon in 2:24:20.8.

6 May Andy Minder rides Pink Star to victory in the Kentucky Derby.

21 June Alex Ross wins the U.S. Open Golf Tournament in Philadelphia.

8–12 Oct. The Chicago Cubs of the National League defeat the Detroit Tigers of the American League four games to none in the World Series.

28 Nov. John Hayes wins the first Yonkers Marathon in New York.

1908

- Irving Brokaw, who studied figure skating in Europe, returns to the United States and begins to promote the sport.

14 Feb.– 30 July A U.S. team wins the automobile race around the world sponsored by *The New York Times* and the Paris *Le Matin*.

22 Feb. Stanley Ketchel knocks out Jack Sullivan for the middle heavyweight title, in twenty rounds, in San Francisco.

3 Apr. Frank Gotch defends his world heavyweight wrestling championship against George Hackenschmidt, who quits after two rounds.

20 Apr. Thomas P. Morrissey of Yonkers, New York, wins the twelfth annual Boston Marathon in 2:25:43.2.

27 Apr.– **31 Oct.**	London holds the Summer Olympic Games as an adjunct to its World's Fair.
30 Apr.	Abe Attell wins the featherweight boxing title.
5 May	Arthur Pickens rides Stone Street to victory in the thirty-fourth annual Kentucky Derby.
4 July	Oscar "Battling" Nelson knocks out Joe Gans in seventeen rounds for the lightweight title.
8 Aug.	Fred McLeod wins the U.S. Open Golf Tournament by one stroke over Willie Smith at the Myopia Hunt Club in South Hamilton, Massachusetts.
7 Sept.	In Los Angeles Billy Papke knocks out Stanley Ketchel in the twelfth round for the middle heavyweight boxing championship.
Fall	The National Collegiate Athletic Association assumes control of college basketball rules from the Amateur Athletic Union and the Springfield, Massachusetts, YMCA.
	The college of Washington and Lee begins the practice of identifying football players with numbered jerseys.
2 Oct.	Addie Joss, of the Cleveland Indians, pitches a perfect game against the Chicago White Sox.
10–14 Oct.	The National League's Chicago Cubs defeat the Detroit Tigers of the American League four games to one in the World Series.
21 Nov.	Cornell University wins the first ICAA cross-country championship.
26 Dec.	Jack Johnson becomes the first black world heavyweight boxing champion, defeating Tommy Burns in fourteen rounds in Sydney, Australia.

1909

	• Ralph Rose becomes the first shot putter to throw the sixteen-pound weight beyond 50 feet, with a throw of 51 feet.
	• The United States wins the Westchester Cup, polo's most prestigious trophy, from Great Britain.
15 Mar.	Edward P. Weston, age seventy, completes a walk from New York to San Francisco in 107 days, 7 hours.
19 Apr.	Henri Renaud of Nashua, New Hampshire, wins the thirteenth annual Boston Marathon in 2:53:36.8.
3 May	Vincent Powers rides Wintergreen to victory in the thirty-fifth annual Kentucky Derby.
1–29 June	The first transcontinental automobile race is held from New York City to Seattle.
24 June	George Sargent wins the U.S. Open Golf Tournament with the decade's best score of 290 strokes.
23 Aug.	Glenn H. Curtiss wins the Bennett Cup and the Prix de la vitesse at the first International Aviation Meet at Rheims, France, setting a new speed record of 43.34 MPH.

4 Sept.   After platform diving is added to the events at the men's national swimming championship, George Gaidzik wins the title. He captures the next two as well.

Fall   The value of the field goal in football is reduced from four to three points.

8 Oct.   The Pittsburgh Pirates of the National League defeat the Detroit Tigers of the American League four games to three to win the World Series.

OVERVIEW

Roosevelt as Symbol. More than any athlete of the 1900s, Theodore Roosevelt epitomized the sporting character of the decade. In 1900, the year before he became the twenty-sixth president of the United States, he encouraged Americans to act aggressively and confidently but with a sense of fair play: "In life, as in a football game, the principle to follow is: Hit the line hard: don't foul and don't shirk, but hit the line hard." Roosevelt believed that participation in "vigorous, manly sports" was so important in the development of character and the preparation of young men for leadership roles in business and politics that he called Ivy League presidents and athletic officials to the White House in 1905 to discuss ways to reduce the high rate of injury and death in college football. Although Roosevelt's football summit did not lead to immediate reform of the game — as injury and death continued to haunt the college game throughout the decade — it did lead to the formation of organizations such as the National Collegiate Athletic Association. The NCAA and other governing bodies legislated sportsmanship within college sport and took other measures to insure the safety of football and other sports.

The Boxing Paradox. Throughout the decade sports culture promoted a conflicted character that was both aggressive and gentlemanly. No sport demonstrated this contradiction better than boxing, or prizefighting, as it was commonly known during the late nineteenth and early twentieth centuries. While boxing attracted its chief promoters and participants from underprivileged classes denied access to traditional means of employment because of ethnicity and race, the sport also enticed interest from society's most respectable elements. For proponents of boxing such as Roosevelt, who had practiced the "manly art" as a student at Harvard, the sport offered an appropriate means for building character, instilling confidence, and improving physical dexterity. The critics of the ring, however, saw boxing as a senseless, brutal activity that bred immorality and crime. Although certain cities such as New Orleans legalized boxing under the Queensbury Rules, which limited rounds to three minutes and required pugilists to wear gloves, prizefighting remained illegal in most states until the next decade.

Racism. The triumphs of Jack Johnson and other African American boxers dramatized the racial tensions bound up in American attitudes toward sports. Most white American males, who saw the heavyweight champion as the symbol of athletic superiority, were stunned when Johnson became the world's first African American heavyweight boxing champion after his resounding defeat of Canadian boxer Tommy Burns in 1908. Most whites continued to believe that African Americans were their inferiors, and resentment toward Johnson intensified as several "Great White Hopes" failed to win back the title. While boxing promoters did not systematically exclude African Americans from the sport, major league baseball, YMCA basketball leagues, and thoroughbred horse racing had erected barriers against the participation of African Americans before the turn of the century. Perhaps no other sport was more affected by racism than baseball, whose mid-nineteenth-century organizers had decided that only Caucasians could uphold the gentlemanly conduct of the game. In part because of such barriers, African American athletes and sports promoters organized their own teams and leagues to realize, if only partially, the rewards of competition.

Baseball. Although baseball would not confront its racism and desegregate until 1947, the game faced serious management and labor problems during the early 1900s. Once these were resolved, the path was open toward establishing a truly national game. In 1900 Byron Bancroft "Ban" Johnson expanded the minor Western League to include major eastern cities and renamed it the American League, declaring it to be a major league in competition with the established National League. Johnson formed the American League to halt the National League's practice of drafting minor league players without adequately reimbursing the minor league teams fairly for the players' worth. After a year of luring players away from the National League with greater salaries, the American League agreed with its rival to respect each other's team rosters. The two leagues also established a three-man National Commission to govern the game and settle disputes with the minor leagues. After 1903 major league baseball came of age in the United States, as the nation became obsessed each year with the outcome of the World Series and formulated a mythology about the unique American origins of the game.

English Traditions. Baseball, like most sports in America during the 1900s, could trace its roots to England. While baseball and football had evolved into wholly distinct sports from their English counterparts, rounder and rugby, other sports such as golf, tennis, track and field, rowing, and yachting developed in America without many recognizable changes. Throughout the nineteenth century and the early 1900s, English-born athletes dominated many of these transplanted sports, especially golf. In tennis, however, American men defeated Britain twice in the newly established Davis Cup Challenge Tournament. In 1905 May G. Sutton became the first American to capture a Wimbledon singles tennis title. Moreover, American yachtsmen continued to outperform their English counterparts in defense of the America's Cup.

Basketball. Of the sports that were popular during the century's first decade, only basketball was originally American. James Naismith, a physical education instructor in Springfield, Massachusetts, developed basketball in the winter of 1891 to replace the gymnastics and calisthenics routinely practiced during the months between the end of football in the fall and the beginning of baseball in the spring. The YMCA used basketball to increase membership and promote spiritual growth through physical activity. Basketball spread throughout the nation's colleges and universities, challenging football as the main campus sport. Basketball, moreover, became the foremost sport for women after Senda Berenson, a physical education instructor at Smith College, developed a separate set of rules for a unique women's game in 1892. For social reformers active in the urban settlement house move-ment, basketball was the chief recreational vehicle for cultural assimilation of immigrants.

The Rise of Professionalism. While basketball remained a largely amateur sport in the 1900s, baseball was developing its modern professional structures and resembled a business in its bureaucratic organization, team ownership, and labor relations. Other sports began to show signs of an evolving professionalism as well. Boxing promoters and participants certainly profited from their sport. Throughout the decade professional football teams flourished throughout western Pennsylvania and Ohio. Similarly, Philadelphia witnessed a surge in professional basketball teams. Houghton, Michigan, sported the nation's first professional ice hockey team during the early 1900s. The end of the decade witnessed a boom in professional marathon races, spawned by the controversial outcome of the 1908 Olympic marathon, in which American Johnny Hayes won as the result of the disqualification of Italian Pietro Dorando.

Olympic Games. Baron Pierre de Coubertin, a wealthy French nobleman, revived the Olympic Games in the 1890s, and three official Olympic Games were held during the 1900s. Hosted by Paris in 1900, Saint Louis in 1904, and London in 1908, Olympic Games were staged as adjunct events to World's Fairs. American athletes, especially track-and-field performers, dominated these contests, demonstrating the physical superiority of the nation's athletes even as Theodore Roosevelt was asserting American military strength and diplomatic influence abroad through his policies as president. In the first decade of what has been called America's century, sports were becoming ever more central to the nation's cultural life and were increasingly shaping not only the country's view of itself but also the way the nation was perceived abroad.

AMERICA'S CUP

Origin. Although yacht racing in America began informally with the Dutch burghers of New Amsterdam, the first recorded race featured John Cox Stevens's *Wave* defeating John Cushing's *Sylph* in 1835. Stevens, a wealthy New Jersey real estate broker and sports promoter, spearheaded the organization of the New York Yacht Club in 1844. As commodore of the New York Yacht Club, he organized a syndicate of five other club members that commissioned William H. Brown in 1850 to construct a yacht "to race against the best the British had to offer." Following the design by George Steers, Brown finished *America* in 1851, in time for Stevens to accept an invitation from the Royal Yacht Squadron to enter its race around the Isle of Wight. Pitted against seventeen seasoned British boats, *America* started poorly but finished with a commanding lead and won the hundred-guinea cup offered by the Royal Yacht Squadron. In response to the win by *America,* the *Spirit of the Times* observed that "old England was no match for young America." Stevens accepted the cup and kept it on display at his Annandale, New Jersey, estate. After his death in 1857, it became a trust of the New York Yacht Club "as a permanent challenge cup, open to competition by any organized yacht club of any foreign country."

The Lipton Era. American yachtsmen, by 1899, had defended the cup successfully against two Canadian and eight British challenges. In 1895 Lord Dunraven's charge that the interference of spectator boats caused his *Valkyrie II* to lose to J. P. Morgan's *Defender* led to such acrimony between England and the United States that the New York Yacht Club did not expect to receive another English challenge for the cup until the next century. However, in 1899 the Yacht Club received a challenge from Sir Thomas Lipton, the Scottish-bred Irish tea merchant. Lipton's challenge was the first of five that the New York Yacht Club would accept from him during the next thirty-one years. Lipton, who had amassed a great fortune first as a grocer and meatpacker and then as a tea merchant, became enthralled with sailing through his friendship with Edward, Prince of Wales (soon to become King Edward VII). Despite his lack of racing experience, Lipton announced to his friends in

Reliance leads *Shamrock III* in the 1903 America's Cup.

1898 that "I think I'll have a shot at the ould mug," meaning the America's Cup. A shrewd businessman and artful self-promoter, he recognized that competing in the America's Cup would bring great publicity to himself and his tea business. Although Lipton failed to bring the cup back to Britain, his convivial character and raffish charm erased the bitterness of earlier races and ushered in an era of warm feelings and friendly but intense competition between American and English yachtsmen.

Shamrock* versus *Columbia. The New York Yacht Club scheduled the 1899 America's Cup for early October, but dense fog and calm winds delayed the competition until the middle of the month. Lipton's boat, *Shamrock,* built by William Fife, a third-generation Scottish shipbuilder, was more "a pure racer than a practical yacht," with so much play in her towering 140-foot steel mast that "she wore out six separate suits of sails in her first year." Rather than sail the *Shamrock* across the Atlantic for the event, Lipton towed her with his steamship, *Erin.* The American boat, *Columbia,* was the third America's Cup defender designed and built by Nathanael Herreshoff. Commissioned by a syndicate led by J. P. Morgan, *Columbia,* "the largest and costliest vessel ever designed for sport," according to the *New York Journal,* won the first race by more than ten minutes. Strong gusts during the second day snapped the topmast of the *Shamrock* and carried away her topsail, causing Captain Archie Hogarth to retire her from the race. Although *Shamrock* performed magnificently in the third race, clipping along at thirteen knots in a strong northerly gale, *Columbia* was even faster, finishing the course more than six minutes ahead of the challenger. Once again, an American yacht defended the cup. Gracious in defeat, Lipton announced at a farewell banquet that "I shall be back." New York high society, charmed by the jovial tea baron who had entertained them lavishly on the fully appointed *Erin,* heralded him as "the world's best sportsman."

Shamrock II versus *Columbia.* Lipton, as promised, returned in 1901 to challenge for the America's Cup. His second boat, *Shamrock II,* was designed and built by George Watson, the architect of Dunraven's *Valkyrie.* Described by the marine editor of the *Scientific American* as "the most refined form ever seen in a Cup challenger," *Shamrock II* was much longer than her forerunner and "had a nearly flat body with a keel so deep and narrow it resembled a fin." *Columbia,* the 1899 defending champion, was selected to race *Shamrock II,* since it had outperformed the *Constitution,* a new racer designed by Herreshoff. Having the opportunity to race against *Columbia* again delighted Lipton, who believed that the radical design of *Shamrock II* insured his victory. In fact, he had the support of many Americans, including Thomas F. Day, the editor of *The Rudder,* America's foremost yachting journal, who wrote that he "would like to see Sir Thomas Lipton win. As it is, the contest is too one-sided, but if the Cup could be passed and repassed across the ocean it would be better for yachting on both sides." Although *Shamrock II* performed better than her predecessor and at times led *Columbia* by nearly a minute at the halfway point, *Columbia* emerged triumphant in three consecutive races to retain the America's Cup for the New York Yacht Club. After the third race, Lipton implied that he would return for a third challenge as he reminded his adoring American fans that "the shamrock has three leaves."

Shamrock III versus *Reliance.* In 1903 Lipton returned for a third attempt at bringing the America's Cup, now dubbed the Lipton Cup, back to England. As the toast of

Sir Thomas Lipton aboard the steamship *Erin,* from which he watched his yachts challenge the Americans

the nation, he dined at the White House with President Theodore Roosevelt and visited Boston, where he praised Boston Tea Party revolutionaries for dumping three shiploads of tea into the harbor, because "it wasn't Lipton's." His boat, *Shamrock III,* resembled its predecessors in shape and size, "following the evolutionary trend toward light and lively vessels with large amounts of sail." In designing the American craft, Herreshoff took full advantage of the gray areas in the New York Yacht Club's specifications for racing vessels, especially those regarding the shape of the hull and displacement, to develop "the biggest, fastest sloop ever to race for the America's Cup." His final product, *Reliance,* with its shallow hull and massive sails, was described as nothing more than a "skimming-dish," whose sole purpose was to race. *Reliance,* wrote Thomas Day in *The Rudder,* "is an overgrown, ugly brute." With 16,160 square feet of sail area, 2,000 more than *Shamrock III, Reliance* was penalized with a one-minute, fifty-seven-second handicapped start but easily overtook the British challenger to defend the America's Cup in three straight races. Lipton later remarked that he considered the defeat by the *Reliance* as "the greatest disappointment of my life," and, although he was not a gambling man, he added that he would have been "willing to bet the *Erin*" that *Shamrock III* would win the series.

Close of the Lipton Era. As a result of the 1903 America's Cup series, the New York Yacht Club issued new specifications for racing yachts, collectively called the Universal Rule. By setting limits on minimal displacement, standardizing hull shape and size, and penalizing excessive sail area, highly specialized, unseaworthy "skimming dishes" such as *Reliance* were outlawed. Ironically, the Universal Rule, intended to produce "a wholesome type of yacht," was formulated by the iconoclastic Herreshoff, who smashed the old rules with *Reliance.* The Universal Rule, which defined boats in different classes designated by letters of the alphabet, was quickly adopted for yacht races throughout the United States. European yachting organizations adopted similar measures under the International Rule, which defined boats according to a metric formula. Controversy ensued over the applicable rules in 1907, when Lipton issued another challenge for the America's Cup with the proviso that both boats meet the specifications of the Universal Rule. The New York Yacht Club maintained that in its selection of a defending craft, it should not be limited by any regulation. Lipton withdrew his challenge and did not issue another until 1912, but the club had not changed its position. The club accepted Lipton's unconditional challenge in 1913, but the series scheduled for 1914 was postponed because of the outbreak of World War I. Lipton raced for the cup twice more, in 1920 and 1930 with *Shamrock IV* and *Shamrock V,* but he never succeeded in wresting the "ould mug" away from his American competitors.

Sources:

John Rousmaniere, *America's Cup Book, 1851–1983* (New York: Norton, 1983);

A.B.C. Whipple, *The Racing Yachts* (Alexandria, Va.: Time-Life Books, 1978).

BASEBALL: BIRTH OF THE MODERN GAME

Beginnings. Americans had played games that were in some ways similar to baseball since the colonial era. In the 1840s and 1850s affluent New York merchants and businessmen began to form baseball clubs. Alexander Cartwright in 1845 organized the most prominent of these clubs, the New York Knickerbockers. Under Cartwright baseball became standardized: he placed the bases ninety feet apart in the shape of a diamond, positioned the pitching mound forty-five feet from home plate, limited teams to nine players, and forbade throwing the ball at the base runner. The Civil War disseminated Cartwright's game throughout the nation as Union and Confederate soldiers alike routinely played baseball. In 1869 the Cincinnati Red Stockings emerged as the first professional team, and in 1876 eight professional teams formed the National League. NL team owners agreed not to place more than one team in a single city and not to play teams from other leagues. Team owners — like their counterparts in late-nineteenth-century American indus-

try — imposed strict order upon their workers, the players. Their chief weapon was the reserve clause, which restricted the movement between teams of players in search of higher salaries.

Opposition to the National League. In the 1880s and 1890s the NL faced opposition from upstart rival leagues and players organizing for salary reform. In 1880 the NL dismissed the Cincinnati team for selling beer and playing on Sunday. Cincinnati and other teams excluded from the NL formed the American Association (AA) in 1881. By charging twenty-five-cents admission, serving beer, and offering Sunday play, the AA challenged the NL for baseball hegemony. In 1882, after signing the National Agreement, the AA and NL agreed to respect each league's territorial and reserve clause rights. Problems in leadership, however, splintered the AA, and its Brooklyn and Cincinnati clubs joined the NL in 1890. The year 1890 also saw the rise of the Players' League (PL), organized by John Montgomery Ward, former New York Giants star shortstop, attorney, and advocate of players' rights and salary reform. The PL, a private and cooperative enterprise in which players and owners shared team management and profits, drew attendance from the AA and the NL. By the end of the 1890 season, however, the PL folded as the NL offered attractive bribes to its financial backers. The AA surrendered to the NL in 1891, as the NL absorbed four franchises and bought out four others.

National League Troubles. Despite the demise of its rivals the 1890s brought more troubles to the NL. The league navigated much of the decade without a strong leader as Albert G. Spalding, who had led the NL against the PL in 1890, retired as president of the Chicago club in 1891. As a result of its buyouts of the PL and the AA, the NL accumulated great debts, which the league could not immediately settle because of a downturn in the national economy, poor attendance because of the public disillusionment with the game, and increasing competition from other forms of public entertainment. Fans refused to attend games at home or on the road involving teams such as Louisville and Saint Louis, which consistently vied for last place. Even the New York Giants, the mainstay to the success of the NL, failed to field a strong team in the 1890s. To increase fan interest and profitability, the team owners wrestled with the decision to reduce the number of teams or form two six-team divisions. In 1900 the league returned to an eight-team circuit composed of Boston, Brooklyn, Chicago, Cincinnati, New York, Philadelphia, Pittsburgh, and Saint Louis.

Challenge of the American League. In 1900 Byron Bancroft "Ban" Johnson, the president of the minor Western Association (WA), changed the name of his organization to the American League and declared it a major league. Johnson's actions stemmed from resentment of the NL's practice of drafting players from the WA and not reimbursing the teams fairly for the players' worth, thus causing instability throughout the league.

BASEBALL ATTENDANCE

Although there are no statistics available for the years prior to 1901, baseball historians and statisticians agree that attendance at baseball games boomed during the 1900s. In 1901 attendance was 3.6 million, an average of 225,000 for the sixteen major league teams. By 1910, the first decade of play by both the American and National Leagues, attendance had doubled to 7.2 million. The primary causes for this increase were the effective control of vulgarity and unseemly behavior on the field, a series of outstanding pennant races, and huge popular interest in the World Series. During the 1900s the New York Giants drew the greatest number of fans, 4,977,481, with 910,000 in 1908.

Year	American League	National League
1901	1,683,584	1,920,031
1902	2,206,454	1,683,012
1903	2,344,888	2,390,362
1904	3,024,028	2,664,271
1905	3,120,752	2,734,310
1906	2,938,076	2,781,213
1907	3,398,764	2,640,220
1908	3,611,366	3,512,108
1909	3,739,570	3,496,420

Source: Hy Turkin and S. C. Thompson, *The Official Encyclopedia of Baseball*, eighth revised edition (South Brunswick & New York: A. S. Barnes / London: Thomas Yoseloff, 1976).

Johnson declared war on the NL, first by establishing AL franchises in Cleveland, Baltimore, and Washington, cities that the NL abandoned when it returned to its original eight-team circuit. Next, Johnson raided NL team rosters, luring seventy-four players to the AL with the promise of better pay. Napoleon Lajoie, an established NL superstar with the Philadelphia Phillies, jumped to the AL Philadelphia Athletics in 1901 and led the fledgling league in batting (.422), home runs, doubles, scoring, RBIs, and slugging. The high-caliber play of Lajoie and others established the credibility of the AL and boosted attendance at AL games over NL contests in 1902. In 1903 the AL established a franchise in New York City, the Highlanders, which later became the Yankees. With New York replacing Baltimore, the AL matched the NL with eight teams, with others located in Boston, Philadelphia, Washington, Detroit, Cleveland, Chicago, and Saint Louis.

A New National Agreement. By 1903 the AL had demonstrated its competitiveness against the NL for the baseball dollar. In that year the leagues negotiated a settlement to limit their competition and promote cooperation for the profitability of the teams. The outcome of these negotiations, the National Agreement, became the foundation of "Organized Baseball," ending nearly two decades of league and franchise instability. The leagues agreed to recognize each other's reserve clauses and established a three-man National Commission to govern the game. The National Commission, which consisted of the NL and AL presidents and a third individual selected by them, would serve as a judicial body to resolve disputes between the major leagues and the controversies involving the minor leagues. The National Agreement incorporated the existing minor league structure. In 1901 the minor leagues had formed the National Association of Professional Baseball Leagues to insulate themselves from the contentious AL and NL. The NAPBL created a hierarchy of minor leagues (A through D), which set salary limits and permitted higher leagues to draft players from lower ones. The National Agreement recognized the territorial monopolies of the minor leagues, granted teams reserve rights to players, and set up a system by which the major leagues could draft minor league players.

Sources:
Benjamin G. Rader, *Baseball: A History of America's Game* (Urbana & Chicago: University of Illinois Press, 1992);

David Quentin Voigt, *American Baseball: From the Gentleman's Sport to the Commissioner System* (University Park & London: Pennsylvania State University Press, 1992).

BASEBALL: EARLY POWERS

Summary of the Decade. During the 1900s no single team dominated, although several teams captured consecutive league pennants during two- or three-year periods. After the Brooklyn Dodgers won the National League pennant in 1900, the Pittsburgh Pirates claimed it three straight years, from 1901 to 1903. In 1909 the Pirates returned to the top of the National League as well as all of baseball by winning the World Series. After Pittsburgh, the New York Giants, led by John J. McGraw, claimed two National League titles in 1904 and 1905 and the World Series in 1905. The Chicago Cubs won three consecutive pennants from 1906 to 1908. In 1908 the Cubs became the first team to win two consecutive World Series titles. Only two American League teams won two or more consecutive pennant races during the decade. The Boston club, who changed their name from the Beaneaters to the Red Sox in 1904, captured the American League title in 1903 and 1904. The Beaneaters, led by legendary pitcher Cy Young, claimed the first, albeit unofficial, World Series title in 1903. From 1907 to 1909 Detroit, powered by the irascible Ty Cobb, claimed the pennant. The Chicago White Sox, in 1901 and 1906, and the Philadelphia Athletics, in 1902 and 1905, also garnered American League titles.

M. BROWN.   J. PFEISTER   A. HOFMAN   C.G. WILLIAMS   O. OVERALL.   E. REULBACH.   J. KLING.
H. GESSLER.   J. TAYLOR.   H. STEINFELDT.   J. McCORMICK.   F. CHANCE.   J. SHECKARD.   P. MORAN.   F. SCHULTE.
C. LUNDGREN.   T. WALSH.   J. EVERS.   J. SLAGLE.   J. TINKER.

CHICAGO NATIONAL LEAGUE BALL CLUB 1906

Winners of three consecutive National League pennants beginning in 1906 and the first team to win back-to-back World Series, the Chicago Cubs have not been the champions of baseball since 1908.

Pittsburgh. In addition to winning four National League pennants, the Pittsburgh Pirates also finished second in 1900, 1905, 1907, and 1908; third in 1906; and fourth in 1904. Pittsburgh's success stemmed in part from the contributions of Fred Clarke, who played left field and managed the Pirates from 1900 to 1915. One of history's finest defensive players, Clarke handled nearly five thousand chances and led the league in fielding percentage nine times. Clarke's major league career began with the Louisville Colonels in 1894, where he became the manager in 1897, before the slumping organization merged with Pittsburgh in 1900. Pittsburgh's strength throughout the decade hinged on a powerful batting contingent, which included Clarke, Clarence Beaumont, and Honus Wagner. Shortstop Wagner led the league in batting average seven times and in RBIs four times during the decade. Slugger Thomas W. Leach led the league in home runs in 1902. Moreover, the Pirates' bullpen was one of the decade's best, as Sam Leever led the league in wins in 1901, 1903, and 1905; Jack Chesbro, in 1902; and Howie Camnitz, in 1909. Although losing the first World Series to Boston, five games to three, in 1903, Pittsburgh defeated Detroit, four games to three, to win the series in 1909.

New York. In 1904 and 1905 the New York Giants replaced Pittsburgh as the National League champion. The Giants, who finished eighth and last in 1900 and 1902, and next to last in 1901, improved dramatically in 1903, finishing second in the National League pennant race. John J. McGraw, who became manager midway through the 1902 season, was responsible for the team's dramatic turnaround. He built the Giants into one of the decade's dominating teams, relying on its powerful pitchers, Joe McGinnity and Christy Matthewson. McGinnity led the league in wins in 1900 and 1904, as did Matthewson in 1909. Although McGraw refused to play the Boston Red Sox in the 1904 World Series, the Giants defeated the Philadelphia Athletics, four games to one, for the world championship in 1905. Matthewson, the undisputed star of the 1905 World Series, hurled three shutouts against Philadelphia. Matthewson, moreover, did much to improve the public image of baseball players. Unlike most of his peers, the Bucknell College graduate neither smoked nor drank, and conducted himself as a gentleman at all times.

Philadelphia. Although soundly defeated by the New York Giants in the 1905 World Series, the Philadelphia Athletics ranked as one of the best American League clubs of the 1900s. Connie Mack, who managed the Athletics from 1901 to 1950, brought respectability to baseball and conducted himself as a gentleman on and off the field. In contrast to the pugnacious McGraw, he earned the affection as well as the respect of his players. He assembled some of the decade's best talent, and his players often led the league in several areas. In 1901 Napoleon Lajoie led American League batters with a

Honus Wagner sliding home

.405 average and 13 home runs. Other Philadelphia home run leaders included Ralph Seybold in 1902 with 16 and Harry Davis, who belted 38 homers from 1904 through 1907. Topsy Hartsell stole 54 bases in 1902, and Danny Hoffmann stole 46 in 1905. The often temperamental Rube Waddell led American League pitchers with 23 wins in 1902 and 27 in 1905, as did Eddie Plank with 19 in 1906.

Chicago Cubs. In 1906 the Chicago Cubs won the first of three consecutive National League pennants. Since 1903 the Cubs had been a contender for the league title but had fallen short under manager Frank Selee. Midway through the 1905 season, club owner Charlie W. Murphy appointed Frank Chance, the Cubs' first baseman, as manager. Chance, who continued to play first base, led the Cubs to records of 116–36 in 1906, 107–45 in 1907, and 99–61 in 1908. Individually, he led the league in stolen bases and runs in 1906. Chicago's success also rested upon the superb pitching of Ed Ruelbach, who led the league in wins from 1906 to 1908. Although the Cubs lost the 1906 World Series, four games to one, to the Chicago White Sox, they became the first team to win consecutive World Series titles in 1907 and 1908.

Detroit. Chicago's consecutive World Series titles came at the expense of the Detroit Tigers, who captured three consecutive American League pennants from 1907 to 1909. In 1907 Hugh Jennings became manager of the Tigers, a team that had never finished higher than third place in the American League pennant race. In his first year he brought the Tigers from sixth to first place, with a record of 92 wins and 58 losses. Detroit boasted records of 90–63 in 1908 and 98–54 in 1909. Detroit's strength came from the hitting and base-running talents of Ty Cobb and the pitching acumen of Bill Donovan and George Mullin. Cobb led the league in batting average in 1907, 1908, and 1909; home runs in 1909; and stolen bases in 1907 and 1909. Donovan led the league in wins in 1907, as did Mullin in 1909.

Ty Cobb rounding a base

Sources:

Bill James, *The Bill James Historical Baseball Abstract* (New York: Villard Books, 1988);

Benjamin G. Rader, *Baseball: A History of America's Game* (Urbana & Chicago: University of Illinois Press, 1992);

David Quentin Voigt, *American Baseball: From the Gentleman's Sport to the Commissioner System* (University Park & London: Pennsylvania State University Press, 1992).

BASEBALL: SEGREGATION

A "Gentlemanly" Game. By 1900 major league baseball, like most American institutions, was racially segregated. The roots of this separatism may be traced to the 1867 decision of the National Association of Base Ball Players (NABBP), the ruling organization of amateur baseball, to bar African American players and teams. Maintaining that only whites could uphold the "gentlemanly character" of amateur baseball, the NABBP argued that excluding blacks would prevent racial resentment and avoid a "rupture on political grounds." Professional baseball teams, however, valued winning games more than underscoring racial differences and signed contracts with skilled African American players. In 1872 a professional team in New Castle, Pennsylvania, signed John "Bud" Fowler to play second base. Although Fowler is recognized as the first black to play professional baseball, Moses Fleetwood Walker was the first to play in the major leagues. Toledo of the American Association

Rube Foster (third from left) with the team formed by the Royal Poinciana Hotel, Palm Beach, Florida, in 1905

signed Walker as a catcher in 1883. White baseball fans, especially those in the South, did not share major league team owners' appreciation for black baseball talent, however. In 1884 the Toledo manager received a letter threatening to "mob Walker" if he accompanied the team to play in Richmond, Virginia, the capital of the former Confederacy. Walker did not make the trip to Richmond, as a broken rib sustained in an earlier game prevented him from traveling with the team.

The Color Line Is Drawn. Team owners decided to draw the color line against African Americans in 1887. In that year a white player on the Syracuse team of the International League refused to pose for the team picture because of a black teammate. In response International League owners decided to discontinue signing African Americans, though they permitted existing players to remain on the teams. Following the ruling of the International League, Adrian "Cap" Anson, manager of the Chicago White Sox, refused to let his team play an exhibition game against Newark of the International League because Newark planned to start George Stovey, a black pitcher. Stovey did not play because he became "sick" before the start of the game. Later that year Anson prevented the New York Giants from signing a contract with Stovey. In reporting the Stovey story, a Newark newspaper observed that "if anywhere in the world the social

barriers are broken down, it is on the baseball field. There many men of low birth and poor breeding are the idols of the rich and cultured; the best man is he who plays best." Major league owners, however, did not share that sentiment and by the end of the 1880s, had released their African American players and agreed not to sign any more to contracts.

Rise of African American Teams and Leagues. African Americans began to form their own professional baseball teams and leagues in the late 1880s. The first black club was the Cuban Giants, formed in 1885 by Frank Thompson, the head waiter of the Argyle Hotel at Babylon, Long Island. The team, composed mostly of the Argyle's waiting staff, chose the name Cuban Giants because they believed they would be treated with more respect if the public did not think they were Americans. In 1887 the League of Colored Baseball Clubs organized with teams in Boston, New York, Philadelphia, Washington, Pittsburgh, Norfolk, Cincinnati, Baltimore, and Louisville. It folded within a year because many of the league's teams could not afford to travel between cities. In 1888 the Cuban Giants defeated the Pittsburgh Keystones in the first Colored Championships of America. A reporter for the *Sporting News* observed that "there are players among these colored men that are equal to any white men on the ball field. If you don't think so, go and see the Cuban Giants play. This club would play a favorable game against such clubs as the New Yorks or the Chicagos." The Cubans continued to dominate black baseball through the 1890s.

The 1900s. African American baseball in the 1900s produced some outstanding players and teams. The Philadelphia Giants, the top African American club of the decade, was organized in 1902 by Solomon White and Harry Smith and owned by white businessman Walter Schlicter. The Giants' main rival was the Cuban X-Giants, also from Philadelphia. In 1903 the Cuban X-Giants defeated the Giants four games to one for the East Colored Championships in a series that saw the Giants' Dan McClelland pitch the first perfect game by an African American. The segregation of professional baseball and the hostility of most whites toward African Americans did lead some players to leave the United States for Cuba. The Cuban Stars and the Havana Stars were the island's leading teams, and they often traveled to the United States to play other African American teams. In 1906 the Cuban teams became part of the International League of Independent Professional Baseball Clubs, which included two white teams, as well as three other African American clubs. Actually a front for Nat Strong, a white bookmaker who had ties to major league club owners, the International League enjoyed some success. On 3 September 1906 the Philadelphia Giants won the International League's pennant before ten thousand spectators, at that date the largest crowd to witness an African American baseball game.

Rube Foster. One of the most outstanding and influential African American players of the 1900s was Andrew "Rube" Foster. The son of a Texas minister, Foster began pitching for the Waco Yellow Jackets after completing eighth grade in 1892. In 1902 he won 51 games, including an exhibition victory over Rube Waddell of the Philadelphia Athletics, who led the American League in pitching by winning 27 games that year. From this feat, Foster acquired the nickname "Rube," which remained with him throughout his life. In that same year he joined the Chicago Union Giants and pitched briefly for that club until joining a white semiprofessional team in Ostego, Michigan. Foster pitched at Ostego for less than a year before returning to African American baseball, joining the Cuban X-Giants in Philadelphia in 1903. That season he won 54 games and lost only one, leading the Cubans to victory in the African American championship. He pitched for the Philadelphia Giants the following year and led the team to the African American pennant. A salary dispute caused Foster to leave Philadelphia and join the Leland Giants in Chicago in 1907, where he enjoyed great success as a player-manager. In 1909 a broken leg kept him out of the playoffs and his team lost the series. In 1910 the Leland Giants roared back to the top of African American baseball, posting a remarkable record of 128 wins and 6 losses and winning the championship.

Sources:

Arthur R. Ashe Jr., *A Hard Road to Glory: A History of the African American Athlete, 1618–1918* (New York: Amistead Press, 1993);

Robert W. Petersen, *Only the Ball Was White* (Englewood Cliffs, N.J.: Prentice-Hall, 1970).

BASKETBALL

A New Game. In the fall of 1891 Dr. Luther Halsey Gulick, the director of physical education at the International Young Men's Christian Association Training School in Springfield, Massachusetts, asked one of his instructors, James Naismith, to develop a new indoor game to replace the gymnastics and calisthenics routinely practiced during the winter months. After studying the attributes of lacrosse, football, rugby, and soccer, Naismith created a game in which players would bounce and pass a soccer ball from one teammate to another and score points by tossing the ball into a suspended goal. The concept for the game came to him from watching rugby players spending the winter months throwing rugby balls into boxes. Since he did not have boxes to use for goals, he obtained two peach baskets and hung them from the railing around the YMCA gymnasium, ten feet above the floor. In December 1891 Naismith developed thirteen rules for the new game, which received an unenthusiastic response from his students, who had tired of their instructor's experimentation with new games that fall. "I asked the boys to try it once as a favor to me," Naismith recalled. "They started, and after the ball was first thrown up there was no need for further coaxing." Although some students wanted to name the new game "Naismith Ball," their modest instructor settled on a simpler suggestion: "basket-ball."

From the YMCA to the AAU. Basketball quickly spread throughout the YMCAs of New England and the Northeast. The organization used the game as a promotional tool to increase membership, as an intramural recreational activity, and as a competitive extramural game. Competition between YMCAs became so intense that it threatened the mission of the organization to promote spiritual growth. The YMCAs attempted to regulate basketball through the establishment of separate basketball leagues, but the organizations were soon undermined by professionalism, which, according to YMCA director Gulick, "resulted in men of lower character going into the game, for men of serious purpose in life do not care to go into that kind of thing." In 1896 the YMCA turned to the Amateur Athletic Union (AAU) for help in regulating the extramural basketball leagues and, especially, curbing the tendency toward professionalism. The AAU gained control of basketball by exercising editorial control over its official rules, which had been published by the A.G. Spalding and Brothers Company in 1894, and by establishing uniform play according to those rules through the establishment of leagues and sponsorship of regional and national championships. To be eligible for regional and national championships, basketball teams

RISE OF WOMEN'S BASKETBALL

During the 1900s basketball became the most pervasive sport for women in American colleges and universities. In 1892, soon after James Naismith created basketball at the YMCA Training School in Springfield, Massachusetts, Senda Berenson as director of physical training introduced the game to the women of Smith College in nearby Northampton, Massachusetts. Although acknowledging basketball as the one game that had "helped to develop the athletic spirit in women more than any other," she thought that the game played under Naismith's rules was too rough for women. Berenson, whose concept of female physical activity was in sharp contrast to Victorian notions of restraint, still preferred a more orderly game. She formulated rules that prohibited snatching the ball away from opponents, holding the ball more than three seconds, or dribbling it more than three times. To prevent overexertion and the domination of skilled players, Berenson divided the court into three sections and assigned players to each section. In 1899 she and representatives of Radcliffe, Oberlin, and the Boston Normal School of Gymnastics formed the Women's Basketball Rules Committee, which codified women's basketball rules and had them published by the A.G. Spalding Company. Although Smith defeated Bryn Mawr, 4–3, in the first intercollegiate women's basketball game in 1901, Berenson stressed intramural over intercollegiate games because they facilitated greater student participation in physical training and stressed the social and cooperative rather than the competitive aspects of sports. Women's basketball continued to be played under her rules until the 1960s with minimal modifications.

Source: Ronald A. Smith, "The Rise of Basketball for Women in Colleges," *Canadian Journal of History of Sport and Physical Education*, 1 (December 1970): 18–36.

Dr. James Naismith, the inventor of basketball

teams. A month later, the first game played between five-man teams resulted in the University of Chicago defeating the University of Iowa YMCA, 15–12. Teams in the Northeast took the lead in the development of intercollegiate basketball leagues in the 1900s, with the establishment of the Eastern League, composed of Yale, Harvard, Columbia, Cornell, and Princeton. The formation of the Eastern League especially drew criticism from the AAU, because the conduct of Yale and Harvard bordered on professionalism, as the schools benefited from gate receipts and paid coaches. Despite threats from the AAU to ban the University of Pennsylvania from amateur play, Penn joined the Eastern League in 1905. In opposition to the AAU, that same year the Eastern League and the University of Chicago of the Western League drew up a separate set of college basketball rules, the *Official Collegiate Guide*. In 1908 Chicago defeated Penn in a two-game national championship series, which the *Spalding Guide* described as showing "crowds in Philadelphia and Chicago what a good, wholesome, sportsmanlike game basketball is." In 1909 the basketball rules committee of the Eastern and Western Leagues joined the National Collegiate Athletic Association, an organization formed in 1905 to reform college football, to standardize college basketball rules and distinguish them from those of the AAU.

Professional Basketball. Professional basketball began in the late 1890s, as independent teams, particularly in

had to register with the AAU, whose leagues and championship play emerged first in New York in 1898 and then spread to other cities across the nation. New York hosted the first AAU national basketball championship in 1908, while Chicago staged the second in 1909.

College. Colleges and universities throughout the Midwest and Northeast quickly embraced basketball, establishing teams, leagues, and rules. On 9 February 1895 the Minnesota School of Agriculture and Mining defeated Hamline College, 9–3, in the first intercollegiate game. This game, however, was played with nine-man

Philadelphia, resisted the control of the AAU. After gaining control of amateur basketball in 1896, the AAU attempted to standardize the game, eliminate rough play, and require teams to pay registration fees to the organization. Philadelphia teams, which played a rough style of basketball, objected to paying registration fees to the AAU and formed a rival organization, the Eastern Amateur Basketball Association (EABA) in 1898, to accomplish the goals of the AAU without the registration fees. The real reason for the EABA, however, was to promote professionalism, as managers and players feared the AAU would follow through on its threat to disrupt their money-making schemes. In 1899 the EABA became the National League of Professional Basketball (NLPB), with its primary function to make sure that owners and players would honor team contracts. Before the establishment of the NLPB, owners would raid teams for the best players, and players would jump teams for better pay. After the 1903 season, the NLPB folded because it could not control these abuses. From 1903 to 1909 the American League, established by *Reach Guide* editor William J. Scheffers, governed professional basketball. Professional teams in western Pennsylvania and eastern Ohio formed the Central League in 1906. In the 1900s, however, professional basketball languished behind other sports in its appeal to masses of spectators.

Sources:

Albert G. Applin II, "From Muscular Christianity to the Market Place: The History of Men's and Boys' Basketball in the United States, 1891–1957," dissertation, University of Massachusetts, 1982;

Neil D. Issacs, *All the Moves: A History of College Basketball* (New York: Harper & Row, 1984).

James J. Jeffries, the century's first heavyweight champion, held the crown from 1899 until his retirement in 1904.

BOXING

Boxing's Brutal Legacy. In the 1900s boxing, or prizefighting, still held much of its nineteenth-century character. For much of the century pugilists had fought under the London, or Broughton, Rules, with bare fists, battering each other through endless rounds until only one combatant remained standing. Offended by the sport's brutality and its association with blood sports such as cockfighting, as well as crime, gambling, drinking, and prostitution, Victorian society instituted strict prohibitions against it. Although illegal, prizefights were held in back rooms of saloons, on secluded riverboats, and in isolated frontier towns. In 1890 New Orleans legalized prizefighting under the rules formulated in 1867 by the marquess of Queensbury, an English aristocrat and sportsman. Aimed at reducing boxing's brutality, these rules required the use of gloves, prohibited wrestling holds, limited rounds to three minutes, and provided for ten-second knockouts. In 1892 New Orleans held the first heavyweight championship under these rules between James J. Corbett and John L. Sullivan, who had held the heavyweight title since 1882. Corbett knocked out Sullivan in the twenty-first round and became the first heavyweight champion under the Queensbury Rules.

With Corbett's victory the bare-knuckle era in prizefighting came to an end. Adoption of the Queensbury Rules, however, did not immediately curb boxing's brutality, since the rules did not limit the number of rounds in a bout. The sport remained illegal in most of the country until the 1920s.

Heavyweights. In the 1900s, as throughout boxing history, the heavyweight division garnered the most attention from aficionados. In 1897 Corbett lost the title to Robert Fitzsimmons, a lean but powerful Englishman, who held the title until 1899, when James J. Jeffries, a former Ohio iron worker, knocked him out in eleven rounds at New York's Coney Island. The bout was Jeffries's thirteenth professional fight; no fighter before him had won the heavyweight crown with less ring experience. On several occasions between 1900 and 1903 Jeffries defended his title against challenges from both Corbett and Fitzsimmons. In 1904 Jeffries retired from boxing, vacating the heavyweight crown. On 3 July 1905 Marvin Hart, the son of a Kentucky farmer, defeated Jack Root, the former middleweight champion, for the heavyweight crown. Denied recognition as the world heavyweight champion by sportswriters because he had not defeated the previous titleholder, Hart fought the leading

Jack Johnson easily defeated Canadian Tommy Burns to become the first African American heavyweight champion.

contender, Tommy Burns, in 1906. Burns, a French Canadian, won a twenty-round decision.

African Americans Enter the Ring. Prior to 1900 several African Americans had gained notoriety as bareknuckle fighters; the most outstanding of these pugilists was Tom Molyneux, a freed Virginia slave, who had defeated the English champion Tom Cribbs in 1810. The leading white prizefighters refused to confront their counterparts of African heritage in the ring. Sullivan, for example, successfully avoided fighting Peter Jackson, a powerful African Australian, who was considered the leading heavyweight contender. In 1903 Jack Johnson emerged as a contender for the heavyweight title, but Jeffries, and later Hart, refused to fight him. Burns, however, fought Johnson on 26 December 1908 in Sydney, Australia, where the African American won a fourteen-round decision to become the first world heavyweight champion of African descent. For most white American boxing fans, a black heavyweight champion was intolerable, and they began looking for an able white contender. On 4 July 1910 Jeffries came out of retirement, only to become one of several "Great White Hopes" to fall victim to Johnson's powerful blows. Johnson would hold the title until suffering a twenty-six-round knockout by Jess Willard on 5 April 1915 in Havana, Cuba.

Joe Walcott, Joe Gans, and the Dixie Kid. The 1900s witnessed the rise of other champion African American pugilists. Joe Walcott, Aaron "Dixie Kid" Brown, and Billy "Honey" Mellody dominated the welterweight division. Walcott, a West Indies emigrant who began boxing professionally in 1890, established himself as a leading contender for the world welterweight title with wins over former titlist Billy Smith. On 18 December 1901 Walcott captured the world welterweight title by knocking out defending champion Rube Ferns. On 30 April 1904 he lost the title to the Dixie Kid on a disqualification after twenty rounds. Twelve days later they fought to a twenty-round draw, and the Dixie Kid retained the title. Later in the year Brown vacated the welterweight title, having surpassed the 147-pound weight limit. Walcott, the top contender, assumed the welterweight crown and fought Joe Gans on 30 September 1904. Since the bout ended in a draw, Walcott remained the champion. In 1906 he lost the title to Mellody, who lost to Mike Sullivan the following year. Although he failed to win the welterweight title, Gans, reportedly the son of African American baseball player Joseph Butts, held the lightweight title from 1902 to 1908. In 1905 he contracted tuberculosis but successfully defended his title until suffering a seventeenth-round knockout by Oscar "Battling" Nelson on 4 July 1908 in San Francisco. Gans retired from the ring in 1909.

The flying wedge, here beginning with a center snap, sometimes proved to be a fatal formation for opponents.

Other Divisions. In 1903 Lou Houseman, a Chicago newspaperman and boxing promoter, suggested the creation of the light heavyweight division with a weight limit of 175 pounds. He advocated this new division because Jack Root, whom he managed, had outgrown the middleweight division but was still too light for the heavyweight division. On 22 April 1903 Houseman arranged for Root to fight Charles "Kid" McCoy to determine the first titleholder of the new weight class. Root defeated McCoy easily and held the light heavyweight title until relinquishing it on 4 July to George Gardner, who knocked him out in the twelfth round. Gardner held the title five months, when former heavyweight champion Fitzsimmons won on points after twenty rounds. On 20 December 1905 Jack O'Brien knocked Fitzsimmons out in a thirteen-round bout and held the title until 1912. Tommy Ryan dominated the middleweight division for much of the 1900s, holding the title from 1897 to 1907. Upon his retirement in 1907 Ryan vacated the title, and Stanley Ketchel fought and defeated Billy Papke to claim it. Abe Attell, also known as the "Little Hebrew," dominated the featherweight division from 1905 to 1912.

Sources:

Nat Fleischer and Sam Andre, *A Pictorial History of Boxing,* revised edition (New York: Carol, 1993);

Elliot J. Gorn, *The Manly Art: Bare-Knuckle Prize Fighting in America* (Ithaca, N.Y.: Cornell University Press, 1986);

Jeffrey T. Sammons, *Beyond the Ring: The Role of Boxing in American Society* (Urbana & Chicago: University of Illinois Press, 1988).

COLLEGE FOOTBALL: COACHES, PLAYERS, AND TEAMS

The Rise of College Football. By 1900 football had become well established as the principal sport in American colleges and universities. After Rutgers defeated Princeton 6 goals to 4 in history's first collegiate football game on 6 November 1869, the sport spread from the Northeast to the Midwest, West, and South. In the Northeast, Yale University, led by former player and unofficial coach Walter Camp, dominated the game. Yale won 197 and lost only 9 games during the 1880s and 1890s, holding opponents scoreless in 1888, 1891, and 1892. In the Midwest the University of Michigan started playing football in 1879 but briefly abandoned the game in 1882, after losing several games to the powerful eastern schools. Michigan resumed football in 1883 and became the region's powerhouse. With the inauguration of an annual game between Stanford and the University of California, Berkeley, in 1892, football caught on in the West as well. Southern colleges and universities took up the game in the 1880s and 1890s, but a dominating team did not emerge in that region until the rise of Vanderbilt in the 1900s and 1910s.

Ivy League. Throughout the 1900s the teams from the Northeast, particularly the Ivy League, continued to dominate college football. Teams from Yale (1900, 1907, and 1909), Princeton (1903 and 1906), and the University of Pennsylvania (1904 and 1908) captured national titles. Although Harvard boasted an undefeated season in 1901 and defeated Yale in its season finale, 22–0, the Crimson lost national championship recognition to an undefeated Michigan team. In 1904 Pennsylvania scored 222 points and held opponents to a single field goal on the way to a 12–0 season and the national title. Princeton and Yale, each with ten wins and no losses, met for the deciding national title match in 1906. After a brutal, scoreless game, Princeton received the nod as national champion. Although Harvard contended for the national title several times throughout the 1900s, its time did not arrive until 1910, after Percy Haughton became coach in 1908. A former Cornell football standout and an innovative coach, Haughton blended speed, deception, and power to lead the Crimson to national titles in 1910, 1912, and 1913. Harvard won 71, lost 7, and tied 5 games from 1908 to 1916. Another Cornell gridiron graduate, Glenn "Pop" Warner, became coach at the Carlisle Indian School in Pennsylvania and challenged the dominance of the Ivy League. After handing Pennsylvania its only loss of the season, Carlisle lost its next game to Princeton, spoiling an otherwise undefeated season in 1907.

Michigan. The 1900s witnessed the rise to national prominence of college football in the Midwest, with the University of Michigan setting the standard of play. One of several midwestern universities that organized the Western Conference in 1895 (later known as the Big Ten), the first intercollegiate organization to supervise college athletics, Michigan in 1901 and 1902 managed to take the national championship away from the Ivy League. Michigan's success throughout the 1900s hinged upon the contributions of Fielding Yost, who coached the Wolverines from 1901 to 1926, compiling a career record of 165–29–10. Yost, a former West Virginia football player, arrived at Michigan after successful coaching stints at Ohio Wesleyan, Nebraska, Kansas, and Stanford. At Stanford he also coached San Jose Teachers College, where he discovered William M. Heston, a talented offensive back. Yost persuaded Heston to play for Michigan, where he could also attend law school. From 1901 to 1904 Heston scored 93 touchdowns and averaged 113 yards rushing per game. He provided the muscle behind Yost's "point-a-minute" teams, which outscored opponents by an astonishing 2,830 to 30 points from 1901 to 1905. Often lining up into offensive formations without a huddle, Michigan scored relentlessly with its indomitable running attacks. With the introduction of the forward pass in 1906, Yost employed a more balanced

MICHIGAN'S POINT-A-MINUTE RECORD

From 1901 to 1905 Fielding Yost's "point-a-minute" Michigan football teams scored 2,821 points to their opponents' 42. Michigan would have gone undefeated during these years except for a 2–0 loss to Chicago in the last game of the 1905 season.

Year	Wins	Losses	Ties	Michigan	Opponents
1901	11	0	0	550	0
1902	11	0	0	644	12
1903	11	0	1	565	6
1904	10	0	0	567	22
1905	12	1	0	495	2
Total	55	1	1	2,821	42

Source: Frank G. Menke, *The Encyclopedia of Sports*, fourth revised edition (New York: A. S. Barnes, 1969).

offensive strategy, utilizing long passes and short punts to supplement the running game.

The Chicago Challenge. Besides Michigan, the other midwestern university to earn national championship acclaim in the decade was Chicago in 1905. Another of the founding institutions of the Western Conference, Chicago was the home of the outstanding coach Amos Alonzo Stagg, a Yale graduate and member of the first Walter Camp All-American football team in 1889. He studied physical education under James Naismith at the YMCA Training School before joining Chicago as an associate professor of physical culture and director of athletics in 1892. Stagg became a full professor in 1900 and was the first athletic coach to have academic status in a major university. The innovative Stagg transformed the game by introducing the center snap, the huddle, the lateral pass, the man-in-motion, the onside kick, the T formation, the placekick, and the fake kick. His leading player was Walter Eckersall, who from 1903 to 1906 led the Maroons to a record of 31–4–2. An all-around performer, Eckersall's outstanding performances included his drop-kicking five field goals against Illinois and Nebraska and his returning punts 107 and 106 yards for touchdowns against Texas and Wisconsin. The highlight of Chicago's undefeated 1905 season came with a 2–0 defeat of Michigan on Thanksgiving Day, when a Michigan runner was tackled in the end zone after catching an Eckersall punt.

Football in the South and West. By the late 1900s the caliber of college football in the South and the West began to catch up with that of the Northeast and the Midwest. In 1904 Dan McGugin, who played guard at Michigan from 1901 to 1903, became the football coach at Vanderbilt University. Under McGugin, Vanderbilt

ARMY-NAVY FOOTBALL

One of the oldest and best-known rivalries in college athletics is between Army and Navy. Except in the years 1894 to 1898, 1909, 1917, and 1918, Army and Navy have met each year since 1890, when Navy defeated Army, 24–0, at West Point. In the 1900s Army won five of their nine games.

Year	Army	Navy
1900	7	11
1901	11	5
1902	22	8
1903	40	5
1904	11	0
1905	6	6
1906	0	10
1907	0	6
1908	6	4

Source: Frank G. Menke, *The Encyclopedia of Sports*, fourth revised edition (New York: A. S. Barnes, 1969).

Character of College Football. College football began as a student-centered activity on the campuses of a few private northeastern colleges. By the turn of the century, however, the game had evolved into a nationwide commercial spectacle, controlled by college and university administrators, and played more for spectator enjoyment and college prestige than player satisfaction. From this transformation came an emphasis upon winning, recruitment of players, abuses of eligibility, intense training schedules, professional coaching, and deliberate violence. The brutality of the game, which often resulted in injury and death, nearly led to football's demise. While some journalists, college presidents, and politicians called for the game's abolition, others such as R. Tait McKenzie, the director of physical education at the University of Pennsylvania, urged reform, recognizing the "training in presence of mind, audacity, courage, and endurance of pain and fatigue" that football provided young men.

Professional Coaches. The rise of football powerhouses, such as Harvard, Carlisle, and Michigan, demonstrated how important winning had become to colleges. One factor in the winning calculus was the professional coach, who often received a salary greater than those of the most esteemed professors, despite not being a regular member of the university staff. Coaches, such as Pop Warner of Carlisle, imposed strict discipline and a strenuous training regimen upon their teams. Warner required his players to run five miles each morning, practice three hours in the afternoon, and be in bed by 6:00. Although the players abhorred the regimen, they basked in the adoration lavished upon them by the fans on Saturday afternoons. Harvard, eager to reverse its dismal record against Ivy League rival Yale, hired Percy Haughton as its first professional football coach in 1908. Before Haughton's tenure, Harvard players had received haphazard instruction on the game, as coaches rarely agreed on basic fundamentals. Haughton implemented a chain of command, in which his orders reached the players through a hierarchy of assistants and the team captain. He strictly controlled the team, cursing and physically disciplining those players who refused to abide by the Haughton system. In preparation for each game he emphasized physical conditioning and mastering basic skills, training that enabled Harvard to defeat Yale every year except one from 1908 to 1916.

Recruitment and Eligibility Abuses. Another often abused factor in the development of a winning football program was the recruitment of eligible and academically qualified players. Before joining Michigan in 1901, Fielding Yost coached successful teams at Kansas and Stanford. The star player of his undefeated Kansas squad in 1899 already had played football for five years at West Virginia University. At Stanford, Yost recruited a player with questionable academic credentials who flunked out of the university. "Yost carried him to Michigan," ex-

captured ten Southern Intercollegiate Athletic Association championships (1904–1907, 1910–1912, and 1921–1923). In 1904 Vanderbilt enjoyed an undefeated season and led the nation in scoring, outpointing opponents 474 to 4. In 1905, 1906, 1907, 1911, 1912, 1915, 1916, and 1926 McGugin's teams would have enjoyed perfect seasons had they not lost or tied one game in each season. In California the highlight of the college football season was the annual game between Stanford and California. In 1902 the directors of the Tournament of Roses Festival in Pasadena decided to hold a football game as part of their celebration. They invited Michigan to play Stanford in what would later become known as the Rose Bowl. Michigan, however, routed Stanford 49–0, thus ending the Rose Bowl until 1916. The University of Washington in Seattle, however, ranked as the most successful West Coast team of the 1900s and 1910s. From 1908 to 1916 the Huskies compiled a fifty-six-game winning streak, although a few of their victories came against high school teams.

Sources:

Allison Danzig, *The History of American Football: Its Great Teams, Players, and Coaches* (Englewood Cliffs, N.J.: Prentice-Hall, 1956);

Ivan Kaye, *Good Clean Violence: A History of College Football* (Philadelphia: Lippincott, 1973).

PROFESSIONAL FOOTBALL

While college football developed into a national spectacle during the late nineteenth and early twentieth centuries, professional football was being organized and played on local and regional levels. In Pittsburgh the Allegheny Athletic Association and the Pittsburgh Athletic Club organized professional teams in the early 1890s. In 1892 the Allegheny AA hired Pudge Heffelfinger, a three-time All-American at Yale University, to play against archrival Pittsburgh AC. The Allegheny AA paid him $500 after he scooped up a fumble and ran for a touchdown to win the game. Football teams throughout western Pennsylvania continued to hire former Ivy League All-Americans throughout the 1890s and 1900s. In 1902 the Philadelphia Athletics and the Philadelphia Phillies baseball teams organized professional football teams in Philadelphia and Pittsburgh, creating what they called the National Football League, which folded after one season.

Professional football also developed in Ohio during the 1900s. In 1903 the Massillon Tigers defeated the Akron Indians for the Ohio state championship. Massillon, which had signed four former Pittsburgh players to its roster that year, won the state championship in 1904, 1905, and 1906. In 1904 Charles Folley became the first African American professional football player when he joined the Shelby Blues Athletic Club. The Canton Bulldogs formed in 1905, acquiring Willie Heston, the outstanding offensive back from the University of Michigan. Although Canton lost to Massillon in the Ohio state championship in 1905, the Bulldogs handed the Tigers their first loss in three years in 1906. Massillon, however, defeated Canton in the championship later that year. A Massillon newspaper charged Canton coach Blondy Wallace with throwing the 1906 championship game. Canton denied the charges, maintaining that Massillon only wanted to ruin the club's reputation before their final game with Latrobe, Pennsylvania. Although Massillon could not prove that Canton had indeed thrown the game, it so tarnished Canton's name that virtually no one attended the Latrobe game. The scandal ruined professional football in Ohio until the mid 1910s.

Source: David S. Neft, Richard M. Cohen, and Rick Korch, *The Football Encyclopedia: The Complete History of Professional Football from 1892 to the Present* (New York: St. Martins Press, 1994).

THE PORTAGE LAKERS AND THE INTERNATIONAL HOCKEY LEAGUE

In 1903 George L. "Jack" Gibson, a dentist in Houghton, Michigan, organized the International Hockey League, the world's first professional hockey organization. His team, the Portage Lakers, won the league championship from 1904 to 1907. In their first year the Portage Lakers won twenty-four of twenty-six games. Considered to be one of history's greatest hockey teams, the Portage Lakers challenged Stanley Cup winners, the Ottawa Silver Seven in 1905 and the Montreal Wanderers in 1906, to championship series, but both Canadian teams refused to contest the American club from the coal fields of northern Michigan.

Source: Dan Diamond and Joseph Romain, *Hockey Hall of Fame: The Official History of the Game and Its Greatest Stars* (New York: Doubleday, 1988).

companied Yost to Michigan to play football and attend law school, played football for seven years as a Wolverine, only four of which were as a student. The desire for a successful football program that would surpass those of the Northeast institutions led Michigan faculty to support Yost's recruitment practices, keep his players eligible, and pay him well. In 1906 the Western Conference introduced rules that restricted player eligibility to three years, limited competition to undergraduates, and required coaches to be regular members of the university staff and receive a salary commensurate with their professional rank. In 1908 Michigan withdrew over the enforcement of these rules, which it believed were established by the conference to diminish the university's football prowess.

Brutality. The real crisis in college football was not over the salary of coaches or the eligibility of players but over the violent character of the sport. With the introduction of the line of scrimmage and an emphasis on running to gain a certain number of yards in a limited number of plays in the 1880s, football teams developed mass-momentum offensive formations, which directed a tight assembly of players, protecting a ball carrier, into the heart of the defense. The most effective of these mass-momentum plays was the flying wedge, introduced by Harvard against Yale in 1892, in which two groups of linemen formed a "V" to shield the ball carrier on kickoff returns. Injuries and even death resulted from such plays, since football players wore only the most rudimentary protective gear or none at all. The death of a University of Georgia player in 1897 inspired the Georgia legislature to pass a law banning football, though it was promptly vetoed by the state's governor. In that same year Marquette University dropped the sport because of its lack of "moral scruples." In 1905 *The Nation* quoted the dean of the

plained the *School Review,* "where he has become the center of the strong team which is the pride of Michigan." Former Stanford standout Willie Heston, who ac-

University of Chicago Divinity School in condemning football as "a boy-killing, education-prostituting, gladiatorial sport."

The Call to Reform. Before the start of the 1905 college football season President Theodore Roosevelt invited select alumni, faculty, and the coaches of Harvard, Princeton, and Yale to the White House, "to persuade them to teach men to play football honestly." Although some at the conference wished to completely reform the rules of the game and curb its increasingly commercial character, others, such as Walter Camp of Yale, the architect of American football and chairman of the Intercollegiate Rules Committee, insisted on minor changes that would not disturb the game's status quo. The delegates presented Roosevelt with a resolution promising to "eliminate unnecessary roughness, holding, and foul play." Nevertheless, the 1905 season proved to be as brutal as those which preceded it, as 18 players died and 159 were seriously injured. The death of a Union College player in a game against New York University led Henry B. McCracken, the chancellor of New York University, to organize a series of conferences to initiate fundamental reforms in the conduct of college football. These meetings in December 1905, which excluded Walter Camp and other members of the Intercollegiate Rules Committee whom McCracken held responsible for the current crisis in college football, resulted in the creation of the Intercollegiate Athletic Association (IAA).

Revolution of 1906. In 1906 the IAA and the Intercollegiate Rules Committee agreed to form a single organization. From this organization new rules emerged to reduce the brutality of the game and promote spectator appeal. One was a new rule that gave teams three attempts to gain ten yards, instead of five yards, for a first down. Reformers hoped that the additional yardage requirement would discourage mass-momentum plays for short yardage gains. The rules committee also approved the forward pass but placed restrictions on its use, such as a fifteen-yard penalty for an incomplete pass. These rule changes resulted in an even more conservative style of play. Most teams did not even mount offensive attacks, instead choosing to kick on first down, hoping to take advantage of a mistake by the other team. Scoring came from kicking. Moreover, the brutality of the game was not much abated: in 1909, eight college players lost their lives on the playing field. In 1910 the rules committee limited the offensive line to seven players, allowed the ball to cross the scrimmage line at any point in the air, and eliminated the penalty for an incomplete pass. The death and injury rate did not significantly decrease until the introduction of protective equipment in the 1910s.

Sources:

Guy Maxton Lewis, "The American Intercollegiate Football Spectacle, 1869–1917," dissertation, University of Maryland, 1964;

Benjamin G. Rader, *American Sports: From the Age of Folk Games to the Age of Spectators* (Englewood Cliffs, N.J.: Prentice-Hall, 1983);

Ronald A. Smith, *Sports and Freedom: The Rise of Big Time College Athletics* (New York & Oxford: Oxford University Press, 1988).

GOLF

The Game in America. Americans began playing golf after the American Revolution, with two of the earliest clubs established in Charleston, South Carolina, in 1786, and Savannah, Georgia, in 1795. Between the War of 1812 and the Civil War, Americans showed little interest in golf, and not until the 1880s did significant numbers of Americans start playing the game again. In 1887 Joseph M. Fox, a member of the Merion Cricket Club in Philadelphia, and John Reid, a Scottish immigrant and executive of an ironwork in Yonkers, New York, organized the nation's first modern golf club, named St. Andrews after the historic club in Scotland. In 1891 William K. Vanderbilt hired Willie Dunn, a noted Scottish golfer, to build Shinnecock Hills, the first professionally designed course, near Southampton, Long Island, where New York's wealthy elite had summer homes. The Shinnecock Hills Golf Club became the model for clubs throughout the country. By the mid 1890s rich golfers easily could follow the seasons, playing clubs in the Northeast during the spring and summer and the South during the fall and winter. In 1894 both St. Andrews and the Newport Club, in Rhode Island, held national championship tournaments.

Rise of the United States Golf Association. In 1894 the Amateur Golf Association (AGA) was formed to administer and standardize the game. Later that year the AGA changed its name to the United States Golf Association (USGA). The five charter-member clubs were St. Andrews, Newport, Shinnecock Hills, the Chicago Golf Club, and the Brookline Country Club in Massachusetts. On 22 December 1894 Henry O. Tallmadge, the secretary of the St. Andrews Club, held a conference of USGA officials to establish a site for a single national championship. They decided to hold both an amateur and an open championship tournament at the Newport Club in October 1895. Charles Blair McDonald won the 1895 USGA amateur title over Laurence Curtis, who, according to the *New York Herald*, "was not in any way in the game against McDonald, for he had a low short drive compared to a long well directed drive of his opponent." The first U.S. Open was won by Horace Rawlins, the Newport assistant pro, against nine other professionals and an amateur. A $50 gold medal and $150 cash accounted for his winnings. By 1895 there were seventy-five golfing clubs in the United States. By the late 1890s golf had acquired such an elite following that *Outing* reported it as "a sport restricted to the richer classes of the country."

The Influence of Harry Vardon. Despite golf's somewhat limited popular appeal, the number of clubs in the nation grew to exceed a thousand by the turn of the century. In 1900 the three-time British Open champion and top-ranked player in the world, Harry Vardon of Great Britain, toured the United States, playing in a series of exhibition matches sponsored by the A.G. Spalding and Brothers sporting goods firm to promote its new golf ball, the Vardon Flyer. Despite his fame and his

Craftsmen in 1900 nicking and painting gutta-percha golf balls, which were soon superseded by rubber-centered balls

victory in the 1900 U.S. Open at Chicago, Vardon's promotional campaign for the golf ball that bore his name was not considered a success by the Spalding company. The Vardon Flyer was an outmoded gutta-percha ball, inferior to the recently introduced rubber-centered ball. Vardon's tour, however, did succeed in further promoting golf in the United States.

Early U.S. Open Champions. In the 1900s foreign-born golfers dominated the United States Open. Willie Anderson, a Scottish immigrant, won four Open titles (1901 and 1903–1905). His feat of winning three consecutive titles has yet to be surpassed or equaled in this century. Alex Smith, the 1906 Open champion, was one of five Scottish-born brothers who gained prominence in American golfing circles during the 1900s and 1910s. He defeated his brother Willie with a combined score of 295 in 1906, the first sub-300 U.S. Open performance. Smith, who became one of golf's greatest instructors, developed Jerome D. Travers, one of the leading amateurs and professionals of the late 1900s and 1910s, as well as Glenna Collett, the leading female golfer of the 1920s and 1930s. George Sargent surpassed Smith's record total of 295 with a 290 performance in 1909.

The Decade's Leading Amateurs. Among the decade's top amateur golfers, Walter J. Travis was perhaps the most remarkable. A native Australian, Travis immigrated to the United States in 1885 and did not start playing golf until the age of thirty-five. He played his first golf match in 1896 and won his first tournament in 1898. Travis lost the U.S. amateur title to Findlay Douglas in 1898 and 1899 but defeated him for the title in 1900 and 1901. After winning a third national amateur championship in 1903, he became the first foreigner to capture the British amateur title in 1904. Travis made up for his lack of power with aggressive and accurate play and exceptional putting. In 1901 he published the popular guide *Practical Golf* and, in 1905, started the magazine *American Golfer*. Amateur golf had greater appeal for most Americans than open play because many of the leaders, besides Travis, were American-born. Smith's protégé, Travers, one of Travis's chief competitors, won consecutive amateur titles in 1907 and 1908 as well as in 1912 and 1913. He also captured the New York Metropolitan Amateur Tournament five times between 1906 and 1913. Like Travis, Travers authored several articles and three books on golf.

Rise of Women's Golf. Golf, like tennis, offered women the opportunity for high-level competition. In 1894 the British Ladies' Golf Union held the first women's golf championship. The USGA held the first women's amateur championship at the Meadowbrook Club on Long Island in November 1895. Mrs. Charles S. Brown won that inaugural event. The first player to dominate women's golf in the United States was Beatrix Hoyt, who won three consecutive amateur titles from

Walter J. Travis, the top U.S. amateur golfer at the beginning of the century

The first U.S. Davis Cup team: Malcolm Whitman, Dwight Davis, and Holcombe Ward

1896 to 1898. She won her first title at the age of sixteen and retired from golf at the age of twenty-one. Genevieve Hecker won two consecutive amateur championships from 1900 to 1901. Dorothy Campbell of Scotland, who won the amateur title twice in 1909 and 1910, became the first woman to win the American and British amateur titles in the same year in 1909.

Sources:

Will Grimsley, *Golf: Its History, People and Events* (Englewood Cliffs, N.J.: Prentice-Hall, 1966);

John M. Ross, ed., *Golf Magazine's Encyclopedia of Golf* (New York: Harper & Row, 1979);

Herbert Warren Wind, *The Story of American Golf: Its Champions and its Championships* (New York: Knopf, 1975).

LAWN TENNIS

A Family Pastime. Although the first recorded game of lawn tennis in America was played 8 October 1874 at Camp Apache, near Tucson, Arizona, Mary Ewing Outerbridge, a New York socialite, is credited with introducing the game to the United States. In 1874, during her annual winter vacation in Bermuda, she observed British army officers hitting a rubber ball across a net stretched across a frashly mowed lawn with implements strung with catgut. Intrigued by the game, she purchased a box of tennis equipment and brought it back to the United States, whereupon customs agents confiscated the unrecognizable items. Emilius Outerbridge, an influential family member prominent in the shipping business, succeeded in getting the tennis accoutrements into the country. Soon thereafter, the Staten Island Cricket and Baseball Club, which Mary's brother Eugenius directed, set up a tennis court in the corner of the cricket field. For nearly a year tennis was an Outerbridge family pastime. As other club members began learning and playing the game, the club devoted one day a week exclusively to it. Tennis, however, did not spread across the nation solely from the Staten Island Cricket and Baseball Club. The game had similar beginnings in Boston, Philadelphia, New Orleans, and San Francisco.

Social Aspects of Tennis. Throughout the late nineteenth and early twentieth centuries, tennis, or lawn tennis, as it was called until the late 1960s, was played and enjoyed almost exclusively by the wealthy. Despite its social stratification, the game did not place any boundaries on gender, as both men and women, separately and together, participated at all levels of ability. In contrast to football, baseball, and other "manly" sports, in which the gender lines were clearly drawn, tennis projected a delicate and effeminate image to some men. In 1878, for example, when several members of the Harvard crew abandoned the sport for tennis, a *Harvard Crimson* editorialist wrote: "Is it not a pity that serious athletes should be set aside by able-bodied men for a game that is at best intended for a seaside pastime? The game is well enough for lazy or weak men, but men who have rowed or taken part in a nobler sport should blush to be seen playing Lawn Tennis." Paul Gallico, one of the leading sportswriters of the 1920s, remembered that during his childhood in early-twentieth-century New York, boys carrying tennis rackets would be met with greetings such as "Deuce, darling," or "Forty-love, dear."

Birth of the USLTA. Despite the effeminate connotations attached to tennis, many men took up the sport, including Dr. James Dwight, who organized one of the nation's earliest tennis tournaments at Nahant, Massachusetts, in 1876 and the United States Lawn Tennis Association (USLTA) in 1881, serving as its president from 1882 to 1884 and from 1893 to 1911. Under the aegis of the USLTA, the men's singles and doubles championships started in 1881, the women's singles and doubles championships in 1887, and the mixed doubles in 1894. From 1881 to 1886 Dwight ranked as the nation's second-best singles player behind his half cousin, Richard D. Sears, who won a then-record seven consecutive men's singles titles from 1881 to 1887. Dwight teamed with Sears to win the doubles championship from 1882 to 1884 and from 1886 to 1887. The 1900s witnessed the rise of one of the twentieth century's most dominating players, William A. Larned, who won the singles title in 1901 and 1902 and from 1907 to 1911, becoming the second player to win seven national championships. Other men's singles champions of the 1900s included Malcolm D. Whitman from 1899 to 1900; Hugh L. Doherty of England, the first foreign USLTA singles champion in 1903; Holcombe Ward in 1904; Beals C. Wright in 1905; and William J. Clothier in 1906.

Rise of the Davis Cup. During the 1880s and 1890s tennis had an international flair, as British players competed regularly in the USLTA championships and Americans played in Wimbledon, the British national championship. In the 1900s international competition increased with the development of the International Lawn Tennis Challenge Cup tournament, better known simply as the Davis Cup tournament. The silver cup awarded to the tournament champion was donated by Dwight F. Davis, the son of a wealthy Saint Louis banker and merchant. Ranked as the second-best men's singles player in 1899 and 1900, Davis captured the 1899 national college men's singles championship as a Harvard junior. After a successful California tennis tour in 1899 with Whitman, Ward, and Wright, Davis decided that an officially sanctioned international tennis competition, especially one that would exploit the already established Anglo-American rivalry, would promote and enhance the

May Sutton, who caused an uproar at the 1905 Wimbledon matches when she wore a white tennis dress that rose almost two inches above her ankles

reputation of the sport. His format for the three-day tournament, which has not changed since, included two singles matches the first day and a doubles competition the second day, followed by two singles contests on the final day of competition. A point was awarded for each victory, with a team needing three points to win a round. The United States, led by Davis, defeated the British in the first two Challenge Cup tournaments in 1900 and 1902. Britain won the tournament from 1903 to 1906. In

1907 Britain lost the Davis Cup to Australia, which defended its possession until 1912, when Britain reclaimed the title.

Women's Tennis. Tennis at the beginning of the century was one of the few sports that provided women with the opportunity for national and international competition. Ellen F. Hansell, the first USLTA women's singles champion in 1887, was followed by the first two-time champion, Bertha L. Townsend, from 1888 to 1889. Juliette P. Atkinson ranked as the top woman of the 1890s, winning the singles title in 1895 and from 1897 to 1898. An outstanding doubles player as well, Atkinson combined for the doubles championship with Helen R. Helwig from 1894 to 1895, Elisabeth H. Moore in 1896, Kathleen Atkinson from 1897 to 1898, Myrtle McAteer in 1901, and Marion Jones in 1902. Jones, who captured the singles championship in 1899 and 1902, also earned the bronze medal in the 1900 Olympic Games. Moore won the USLTA title three times — in 1901, 1903, and 1905. May G. Sutton, the daughter of a British naval officer, became the first American woman to capture the Wimbledon singles title, in 1905 and again in 1907. She won the USLTA singles title in 1904.

Sources:

E. Digby Baltzell, *Sporting Gentlemen: Men's Tennis from the Age of Honor to the Cult of the Superstar* (New York: Free Press, 1995);

Allison Danzig and Peter Schwed, eds., *The Fireside Book of Tennis* (New York: Simon & Schuster, 1972);

Will Grimsley, *Tennis: Its History, People and Events* (Englewood Cliffs, N.J.: Prentice-Hall, 1971).

Baron Pierre de Coubertin led the effort to revive the Olympic Games.

OLYMPICS: THE 1900 GAMES

Revival. In the 1890s Baron Pierre de Coubertin, a wealthy French aristocrat, revived the Olympic Games. Interest in the Olympic Games, which had last been contested in 776 B.C., had increased significantly since the early 1880s, after a team of German archaeologists unearthed the ruins of Olympia, the site of the ancient Greek athletic festival. In 1894 Coubertin held a conference in Paris to establish an organization to govern the Olympic Games and the principles upon which to restore them. From this conference emerged the International Olympic Committee (IOC), with Coubertin as its secretary-general, and an accord that the games would be held in a different city every four years, that only modern sports would be contested, and that only amateur adult males would be allowed to compete. In 1895 the IOC selected Athens to host the first modern Olympic Games in 1896. Greek athletes dominated the games, winning a total of 47 medals. America, second to Greece, garnered 19 medals, of which 16 came in track and field alone.

Paris Granted the Games. Following the conclusion of the inaugural Olympic Games in Athens, many officials and athletes, including the Americans, petitioned the IOC to hold the games permanently in Athens. Coubertin, however, upheld the principle that the games would be held in a different city every four years, insisting that the next Olympiad should take place in Paris. Ironically, many French athletic organizations opposed Paris as a site for the Olympics, and the French government demonstrated less than enthusiastic support for the idea. Coubertin, however, persuaded the government to sponsor the games as part of the Paris Exposition, which had already been planned for 1900. The Olympics became a sideshow to the exposition, as exposition organizers renamed the games the International Meeting of Physical Training and Sport and spread the competition across two months. France's poor preparation for the games prompted Caspar Whitney, an American Olympic Committee official, to remark that France's lack of knowledge of sports "would fill volumes." Moreover, the rudeness of French government officials toward Coubertin strengthened his belief that state involvement in sport resulted in "impotence and mediocrity."

Americans. Despite France's inept handling of the Olympic Games, the nation emerged as the unofficial team champion, winning 103 medals. The United States, in second place, garnered 53 medals, 41 in track and field. Americans won all but three of twenty-three track-and-field events, establishing seven Olympic records and two world records. Alvin C. Kraenzlein won gold medals in the 60-meter dash, 110- and 200-meter hurdles, and the

Alvin Kraenzlein won four individual gold medals in track and field in the 1900 Olympics.

Ray Ewry won gold medals in the standing jump events in each of the four Olympics held during the decade.

long jump. His performances resulted in a world record of 7 seconds in the 60 meters and Olympic records of 15.4 seconds in the 110-meter hurdles and 23′ 6 3/4" in the long jump. Maxwell Long won the 400 meters in an Olympic record of 49.4 seconds. After winning the high jump in an Olympic record of 6′ 2 3/4", Irving Baxter won the pole vault and placed second in the standing high jump, standing long jump, and standing triple jump. Ray Ewry won all three standing jumps and established a world record of 5′ 5" in the standing high jump. Richard Sheldon, who established an Olympic record of 46′ 3 1/4" in the shot put, led an American sweep of the medals in that event. John Flanagan, an Irish American New York City policeman and world-record holder in the hammer throw, led an American sweep of the medals in that event as well.

Sabbath Controversy. Several American track-and-field performers, leading contenders in the 400 and 1,500 meters, high jump, long jump, and pole vault, refused to participate because their events were held on a Sunday. They asked French officials to reschedule the contests for the next day, which happened to be 14 July, Bastille Day, the most revered of French holidays. French officials politely denied the Americans' request. The outcomes of the pole vault and the long jump competitions were perhaps most affected by this decision. After Bascom Johnson, Charles Dvorak, and Daniel Horton, the American pole-vault entrants, refused to participate in the event, Baxter, who had just won the high jump, was persuaded to represent the United States in the event, which he won with a height of 10′ 10". A second pole-vault competition was held days later, according to the French, "to appease the indignant visitors from across the sea." Horton won the competition in 11′ 3 3/4" and Dvorak took second in, 11′ 1 3/4". Meyer Prinstein, the world-record holder in the long jump, won the silver medal in the event based on his previous day's qualifying performance of 23′ 6 1/4". A Jewish athlete, he joined his Christian teammates in their boycott of the sabbath day events. Days later, Prinstein returned to win the triple jump in an Olympic record of 47′ 5 3/4".

Women Participate in the Games. One of the original principles upon which the modern Olympic Games were established in 1894 was that only adult amateur males would participate. In 1900, however, eleven women participated in golf and lawn tennis. Golfer Margaret Abbott became the first American woman to win an Olympic gold medal. Abbott, a Chicago socialite, was living in Paris with her mother, Mary Ives Abbott, a literary editor and novelist, so that she could study art. According to Abbott, she won "because all the French girls apparently misunderstood the nature of the game . . . and turned up to play in high heels and tight skirts." Pauline Whitier and Daria Pratt garnered the silver and bronze medals, respectively, in golf. Marion Jones, the daughter of U.S. Sen. John Percival Jones of Nevada and the 1899 USLTA singles champion, won the bronze medal in lawn tennis.

Sources:

John Findling and Kim Pelle, eds., *The Historical Dictionary of the Olympic Games* (Westport, Conn.: Greenwood Press, 1996);

Allen Guttmann, *The Olympics: A History of the Modern Games* (Urbana & Chicago: University of Illinois Press, 1992);

David Wallechinsky, *The Complete Book of the Olympics* (New York: Penguin, 1988).

OLYMPICS: THE 1904 GAMES

Saint Louis Gets the Games. In 1893 Coubertin toured the United States to garner support for the revival of the Olympic Games. He had attended the Chicago Columbian Exposition that year and was impressed by the enterprise and efficiency of the city. In 1899 William Rainey Harper, the president of the University of Chicago, expressed interest in having Chicago host the Olympics. With Coubertin's support the IOC awarded Chicago the 1904 Olympic Games. The city, however, lost its enthusiasm for holding the games, and Saint Louis, which planned to hold a World's Fair in 1904 to celebrate the centennial of the Louisiana Purchase, expressed interest. The IOC, following a 14–2 decision, awarded the Olympics to Saint Louis in 1902. Hoping to avoid the poor preparations of the last Olympiad, Coubertin asked James E. Sullivan, the president of the American Athletic Union, to manage the preparations for the games. Coubertin also asked Theodore Roosevelt to preside as the president of the games, but the American president declined the offer, citing his responsibilities in Washington.

An American Affair. Twelve nations sent at least one representative to the Olympics, and of the 554 athletes who participated, 432 were Americans. Many teams declined to journey to the nation's Midwest, which many foreigners perceived as a savage wilderness. As a result, Americans dominated the games, winning 238 of 300 medals. As in the previous two Olympiads, Americans dominated track and field. Chicagoan James Lightbody set a world record of 4:05.4 in the 1,500 meters and an Olympic record of 1:56 in the 800 meters. In leading a sweep of the medals in the shot put, Ralph Rose established a world record of 48′ 7″. Ray Ewry, who defended his Olympic titles in the three standing jumps, set a world record of 11′ 4 7/8″ in the standing long jump. In addition to winning the 400-meter hurdles, Harry Hillman, a twenty-two-year-old New York bank teller, established Olympic records of 24.6 seconds in the 200-meter hurdles and 49.2 seconds in the 400 meters. Meyer Prinstein defended his Olympic title in the triple jump and won the long jump in an Olympic record of 24′. Archibald Hahn, the "Milwaukee Meteor," won the 60, 100, and 200 meters. His 200-meter performance resulted in an Olympic record of 21.6 seconds. In defense of his hammer throw title, John Flanagan established an Olympic record of 170′ 4″. George Poage, third-place finisher in the 200- and 400-meter hurdles, became the first African American Olympic medalist.

American Domination. Besides track and field, Americans dominated boxing, gymnastics, rowing, tennis, and wrestling. American boxers swept all medals awarded in five weight classes. Oliver Kirk, who won both the bantamweight and featherweight divisions, remains the only Olympic boxer to have achieved that feat. Anton Heida, of the Philadelphia Turner Society, won three gold and two silver medals and led an American sweep of medals in gymnastics. The strength of these gymnasts, many of whom were of German descent, reflected the long tradition of German gymnastic societies,

THE 1906 INTERIM GAMES

Greek Olympic officials and many of the participants in the 1896 Olympic Games petitioned the International Olympic Committee (IOC) to hold the Olympic Games in Athens permanently. Although Baron Pierre de Coubertin rejected the proposal, insisting that the games would be held in a different city every four years, other IOC officials searched for a compromise. At its 1901 meeting the IOC addressed the Greek question and considered a proposal that Athens and another city alternately host the Olympic Games every two years. Coubertin remained opposed to the idea, suggesting that if the Greeks had to hold a quadrennial athletic event they should call it the Panhellenic Games to distinguish it from the Olympic Games. IOC officials, however, overruled Coubertin, whose authority as secretary-general had been weakened by the problems associated with the 1900 games, and proclaimed that Athens would host the Olympic Games in 1906.

Twenty nations sent 884 athletes to participate in the 1906 Olympic Games. France won the unofficial team championship, collecting 40 medals. Greece finished second with 34 medals, and the United States took third with 27, 20 of which were won in track and field. Several performers defended the titles they had won two years earlier in Saint Louis: Archie Hahn won the 100 meters; James Lightbody, the 1,500 meters; Meyer Prinstein, the long jump; Martin Sheridan, the discus; and Ray Ewry, the standing high jump and standing long jump. Paul Pilgrim of the New York Athletic Club won both the 400 and 800 meters. His victories came as a pleasant surprise to the United States, since he had not officially qualified for the Olympic team and was allowed to compete only because he paid his way to Athens. Despite Coubertin's disapproval of the 1906 Olympic Games, the event was an organizational success for the Greeks, who hoped that Athens would become the permanent site for the modern Olympic Games. Although the IOC discussed the possibility of holding the Olympic Games in Athens in 1910 and 1914, political problems in the Balkans intervened. After World War I the debate over Athens as a permanent site for the Olympic Games flagged but was resumed during the Cold War when several Olympic Games were marred by political demonstrations and boycotts.

Source: John Findling and Kim Pelle, eds., *The Historical Dictionary of the Olympic Games* (Westport, Conn.: Greenwood Press, 1996).

or Turnverein, in American sport. George Eyser, of the Saint Louis Concordia Turnverein, won two gold, one silver, and one bronze medal in gymnastics despite having a wooden leg. The overwhelming superiority of American gymnasts in 1904 was due, in part, to having the AAU gymnastic championships serve as the Olympic events. American male gymnasts would not enjoy the same Olympic success until 1984, when the Soviet Union boycotted the games in Los Angeles. American wrestlers, who swept fifteen medals in five events, also hailed from many of those same Turner societies. American swimmers, who encountered strong competition from the British and the Hungarians, nevertheless established a tradition of dominating the freestyle events, as Charles Daniels finished first in the 200 and 400 meters, second in the 100 meters, and third in the 50 meters. In archery, the only event held for women, Americans swept the accolades.

Anthropological Days. The 1904 Olympics were not without controversy, however. On 12 and 13 August Olympic organizers held the Anthropological Days, during which many indigenous Asians, Africans, and Americans were rounded up from the sideshows of the Exposition and asked to demonstrate their native games and compete in modern Western contests. Promoters of the racist theories of the day pointed to the poor performances of these "savages" in the Western games as evidence of their inferiority. "In no place but America would have one dared place such events on the program," remarked Coubertin in response to the Anthropological Days.

Sources:

John Findling and Kim Pelle, eds., *The Historical Dictionary of the Olympic Games* (Westport, Conn.: Greenwood Press, 1996);

Allen Guttmann, *The Olympics: A History of the Modern Games* (Urbana & Chicago: University of Illinois Press, 1992);

David Wallechinsky, *The Complete Book of the Olympics* (New York: Penguin, 1988).

OLYMPICS: THE 1908 GAMES

London. In 1904 the IOC designated Rome as the host of the 1908 Olympic Games. Although Berlin was a strong contender for the games, Coubertin remarked that he "desired Rome only because I wanted Olympism, after its return from the excursion to utilitarian America to don once again the sumptuous toga, woven of art and philosophy, in which I had always wanted to clothe her." The Rome Olympic organizers had grand plans for the 1908 games, which were to include automobile races at Milan, boxing and wrestling in the Colosseum, and yachting in the Bay of Naples. Rome, however, declined to hold the games after its organizing committee dissolved over personality disputes and Mount Vesuvius erupted, claiming two thousand lives in 1906. London, which planned to hold the Franco-British Exposition in 1908, persuaded the IOC to award it the games.

Shot-put champion Ralph Rose, the American flag bearer in the 1908 Olympic opening ceremonies who refused to dip the flag to the English king

New Management. Despite its association with a World's Fair, the 1908 Olympics marked an improvement in management and bureaucratic organization. London erected a new seventy-thousand-seat stadium and adopted metric distances for athletic events. The distance of the marathon, however, was set at the English calibration of 26 miles, 385 yards, the distance from the start at Windsor Palace to the finish at the stadium. The British Olympic Association also clarified the definition of an amateur athlete as someone who had never earned money from sports, and entrusted national and international sports federations with the task of enforcing the standard in selection of national teams, though the British organization reserved the right to resolve eligibility questions. Finally, the British limited nations to three entries per event and established firm entry deadlines.

Protest. Political discontent, especially over Irish independence from Britain, tarnished the 1908 Olympics. Britain prevented Irish athletes from competing as a separate team under their own flag. Protest over British treatment of the Irish Olympians came not so much from the Irish but from the Americans, many of whom were Irish immigrants or of Irish descent. America's most striking protest came during the opening ceremonies, when, during the parade of nations, Ralph Rose, the defending Olympic shot-put champion and world-record holder, refused to dip the Stars and Stripes before the king of England. Martin Sheridan, an Irish immigrant and defending Olympic discus champion, later explained to the shocked British press that "This flag dips to no earthly King!" No American flag bearer since Rose has

John Hayes was awarded the gold medal in the 1908 Olympic marathon after Dorando Pietri was disqualified.

spectively, established world records of 15.0 seconds and 55.0 seconds in the 110-meter and 400-meter hurdles. Olympic record performances of 2:55:18 came in the marathon from Johnny Hayes; 6′ 3″ in the high jump from Harry Porter; 12′ 2″ in the pole vault from Edward Cooke; 24′ 6 1/2″ in the long jump from Frank Irons; 134′ 2″ in the discus throw from Sheridan; and 170′ 4″ in the hammer throw from John Flanagan. In the 1,600-meter medley relay (200, 200, 400, 800), 400-meter specialist John Taylor became the first African American Olympic gold medalist.

Biased Officiating. The abundant medal harvest by the British resulted, in part, from biased officiating by the host nation, which sparked many protests from France, Canada, Italy, Sweden, and the United States. One of the most controversial decisions came in the 400 meters. Four runners, John C. Carpenter, William Robbins, and John Taylor of the United States and Wyndham Halswelle of Great Britain, competed in the final. Anticipating team tactics from the Americans, officials stood trackside every twenty meters to observe the Yanks. In the homestretch Halswelle attempted to pass Carpenter, who ran wide to block him. Officials stopped the race, and after a bitter argument, which resulted in the disqualification of Carpenter, they agreed that the race would be rerun two days later. Only Halswelle competed in the rerun, as Taylor and Robbins refused to compete in protest over Carpenter's disqualification. In response to the furor over British officiating, the IOC ruled that Olympic officiating would become international in 1912.

Sources:

John Findling and Kim Pelle, eds., *The Historical Dictionary of the Olympic Games* (Westport, Conn.: Greenwood Press, 1996);

Allen Guttmann, *The Olympics: A History of the Modern Games* (Urbana & Chicago: University of Illinois Press, 1992);

David Wallechinsky, *The Complete Book of the Olympics* (New York: Penguin, 1988).

RISE OF THE MARATHON

Invention of a Footrace. An influential figure in the revival of the Olympic Games was Michel Breal, a French classicist and historian, who insisted that the athletic program include an endurance footrace. Although the longest race held in ancient Olympia was about three miles, what Breal had in mind was a race of 40 kilometers, to celebrate the feat of Pheidippides, a Greek soldier, who ran that distance from Marathon to Athens to announce the Greek triumph over Persia in 490 B.C. "If the Organizing Committee of the Athens Olympics would be willing to revive the famous run of the Marathon soldier as part of the program of the Games," Breal wrote Coubertin, "I would be glad to offer a prize for this Marathon race." Coubertin presented the idea to the Greeks, who with a deep sense of history and national pride embraced the offer. The event would be called the marathon, and the prize, as promised by Breal, would be a gold cup. The Greeks, in hopes of a national victory in

dipped the flag before a foreign or domestic head of state during Olympic opening ceremonies.

Americans Dominate Track and Field. Britain, the unofficial team champion, won 147 medals, many in events discontinued in recent Olympiads. The United States, in second place, garnered 47 medals. As they had in the previous Olympiads, Americans dominated track and field, winning nine of twenty-seven events, more than any other single nation. Ten of their victories resulted in three world and seven Olympic track-and-field records. Melvin Sheppard set a world record of 1:52.8 in the 800 meters and an Olympic record of 4:03.4 in the 1,500 meters. Forrest Smithson and Charles Bacon, re-the marathon, held two races over the proposed Olympic course, from Marathon to the Olympic stadium in Athens, several weeks before the games. Spiridon Louis, who finished fifth in the second practice race, won the 1896 Olympic Games marathon in less than three hours.

Boston and American Origins of the Marathon. Although the only American entrant in the inaugural Olympic marathon dropped out after 14 miles, interest in the race was great among Olympic team members, many of whom hailed from the Boston Athletic Association (BAA). The BAA decided to hold a marathon that following spring, on Patriot's Day, to honor the famous ride of Paul Revere. The New York City Knickerbocker Athletic Club upstaged the BAA, however, by holding the first marathon in the United States on 20 September 1896. John J. McDermott, who won the New York Marathon, also won the inaugural Boston Marathon the following year. Although the New York Marathon was a onetime affair, the Boston Marathon became an annual Patriot's Day sporting event. Throughout the decade the Boston Marathon grew in popularity, drawing runners from throughout the northeastern United States and Canada. In 1903 John C. Lorden of Cambridge, Massachusetts, became the first local runner to win the Boston Marathon. Timothy Ford, a self-confident and superbly conditioned eighteen-year-old, became the youngest champion in 1906. He passed an exhausted David Kneeland in the final mile and won by six seconds. Thomas Longboat, an Onondaga Indian from Toronto, became the first runner to average less than six minutes per mile for the 24.7 mile course in 1907.

Saint Louis Olympics Encourages the Race. The 1904 Olympic Games in Saint Louis furthered the development of marathon running in the United States. Since few foreign athletes journeyed to Saint Louis for the games, the top contenders in the marathon were Americans. Thomas J. Hicks, the second-place finisher in the Boston Marathon that year, won the race, which was held, according to David E. Martin and Roger Gynn, in history's "most devastating marathon environment." The Saint Louis course, which included seven hills, followed mostly unpaved, dusty, gravel roads. A choking cloud of dust and exhaust fumes from automobiles that accompanied the runners for much of the race resulted in the death of one competitor. In the last 10 kilometers of the race, Hicks, who had nearly succumbed to the stifling conditions (made worse by 90° heat), received several sponge baths and took several sips of a strychnine sulfate, egg white, and brandy concoction. Hicks led an American sweep of the medals, as Albert Corey, an up-and-coming competitor from Chicago, took second, and Arthur Newton, the fifth-place marathon finisher in the 1900 Olympic Games, took third. Saint Louis, as a result of the Olympic race, inaugurated an annual marathon in 1905 that continued for several years. Inspired by Corey's silver medal performance, the Illinois Athletic Club organized an annual marathon in Chicago in 1905. A rivalry developed between the runners of these midwestern races, who occasionally ventured to compete in Boston.

Impact of the 1908 Olympic Marathon. The outcome of the 1908 Olympic marathon resulted in a controversial victory for Irish American John J. Hayes. In the final mile of the race, Italian Dorando Pietri, followed closely by Hayes, surged ahead of South African Charles Hefferon. Upon entering the stadium Pietri, disoriented from fatigue, turned in the wrong direction for the final lap around the track. After officials pointed him in the right direction, they assisted the Italian throughout the final 400 meters, as he staggered and fell several times. With Hayes quickly closing on Pietri, officials carried Pietri across the finish line and declared him the winner. The assistance provided Pietri by the British not only violated Olympic rules but reflected their biased officiating, especially against the Americans, whose protest of the Italian's victory was upheld by the IOC. Pietri, who relinquished his gold medal to Hayes, received a gold cup, similar to that awarded Spiridon Louis in the 1896 Olympic marathon, from Queen Alexandra. Praise for the Italian runner also came from Arthur Conan Doyle, author of the Sherlock Holmes stories, who wrote: "No Roman of prime ever has borne himself better; the breed is not yet extinct." Upon returning to America Hayes received a hero's welcome and congratulations from President Theodore Roosevelt, who exclaimed, "This is fine, fine, and I am so glad that a New York boy won it."

Professional Races. The end of the decade witnessed a boom in marathon racing, especially at the professional level, as race promoters were eager to profit from the interest in marathon running resulting from the rivalry between Hayes and Pietri after the 1908 Olympic Games. Between November 1908 and April 1909, eight professional marathon races, many indoors, were held in the Northeast and Midwest. Pietri, who then went only by the name Dorando, competed in five of the eight races. The first race, held at Madison Square Garden in New York in November 1908, was billed as a rematch between Hayes and Dorando. In defeating the American, the Italian remarked that "his triumph confirmed the claim that he would have won the race in England at the Olympic Games but for the interference of the officials." Within the next two months Dorando raced three more times. Twice in Saint Louis he lost to Thomas Longboat, the 1907 Boston Marathon champion; in Chicago he easily defeated Albert Corey. New York City, however, became the hotbed for professional marathon races, with Longboat, Hayes, Matthew Maloney, and Englishman Alf Shrubb dominating the events. On 3 April 1909 the most lucrative race, with a purse of more than $10,000, was held at the Polo Grounds. Bookmakers freely took bets on the field of six, which included Dorando, Hayes, Longboat, Maloney, Shrubb, and Henri St. Yves, a waiter from France and marathon novice. St. Yves, who won the race by more than five minutes, "killed off Longboat and Shrubb at 21 and 25 miles and raced the three other competitors into such a state that they were unable to cause him the slightest worry or anxiety for the first twenty miles." On 1 May 1909 the Frenchman won another high stakes marathon at the Polo Grounds, collecting $5,000, or half of the entire purse.

Source:
David Martin and Roger Gynn, *The Marathon Footrace: Performers and Performances* (Springfield, Ill.: C.C. Thomas, 1979).

HEADLINE MAKERS

WILLIE ANDERSON

1880-1910

GOLF CHAMPION

Son of Greenskeeper. Willie Anderson, the first golfer to win four U.S Open titles, was the son of Tom Anderson, a Scottish immigrant, who worked as a greenskeeper. Willie and his brother, Tom Jr., learned how to play golf from their father, and both became professionals. A muscular man, with strong shoulders and forearms, Anderson developed a game characterized by a smooth swing and superb concentration. After finishing second in his first U.S. Open in 1897, losing the championship by a single stroke to Joe Lloyd, he placed third in 1898, fifth in 1899, and a distant eleventh in 1900.

U.S. Open Champion. Anderson captured his first U.S. Open title in 1901, defeating Alex Smith by one stroke in a playoff round at the difficult Myopia Hunt Club in South Hamilton, Massachusetts. After a fifth-place finish in 1902, he captured three consecutive U.S Opens from 1903 to 1905. Although Bobby Jones and Ben Hogan each have also won four U.S. Open titles, Anderson remains the only competitor to have won three consecutive tournaments. Of these victories, the closest was a two-stroke triumph over David Brown in 1903. After using the original gutta-percha ball in his first U.S. Open win, Anderson turned to the newer Haskell rubber-core ball for his three consecutive titles.

America's Best Golfer. Although Anderson failed to win another U.S. Open after 1905, he compiled one of golf's best records and earned more money than any prior professional. He led the 1906 Open after the first round, but an 84 in the second round spoiled his opportunity for a fourth consecutive triumph; he finished fourth in the Open in 1908 and 1909. Anderson captured four consecutive Western Opens, then ranked as the country's sec-

ond most prestigious golf tournament, from 1906 to 1909. His Western Open score of 288 was then history's best for four 18-hole rounds (71–73–72–72). In 1906 Anderson reportedly earned the highest salary in the game.

A Country Club Pro. Anderson became the head professional at the Philadelphia Country Club in 1910, that year's site of the U.S. Open, in which he finished eleventh. After his thirtieth birthday that year, he suddenly died. Although the cause of death has never been made public, it was believed to have been from arteriosclerosis. A charter member of the PGA Hall of Fame, Anderson is also a member of the World Golf Hall of Fame.

Sources:
Len Elliot and Barbara Kelley, *Who's Who in Golf* (New York, 1976);

Ross Goodner, *Golf's Greatest: The Legendary Hall of Famers* (Norwalk, Conn., 1978).

WALTER CAMP

1859-1925

FOOTBALL COACH

Father of American Football. Walter Camp, who was associated with football at Yale University from 1876 to 1910, first as a player and then as a coach, is considered the "Father of American Football." He was the son of Leverett and Ellen Camp, and his father served as a schoolmaster in New Haven, Connecticut. After attending the Hopkins Grammar School in New Haven, Camp enrolled at Yale University and graduated in 1880. He stayed on at Yale to study medicine for two years. In 1882 Camp started working for the Manhattan Watch Company and became president of the company in 1903. In 1888 he married Alice Graham Sumner, the sister of William Graham Sumner, an eminent Yale sociologist and outspoken proponent of social Darwinism.

Innovator. Camp played football at Yale from 1876 to 1882, the final two years as a medical student. In 1876 he played halfback in the first Harvard-Yale game. As the team captain for the next three years, Camp developed rule changes that cast the foundation of modern American football. One of his first innovations was to reduce the number of players on the field for each team from fifteen to eleven. In 1880 he proposed replacing the rugby scrum with the scrimmage. Whereas the scrum led to constant turnover of the ball from team to team, the scrimmage encouraged the undisputed possession of the ball by one team. The scrimmage brought order to the game and encouraged the development of rational strategy and team formations. The scrimmage, however, made it possible for one team to control the ball for the entire game, so in 1882 Camp proposed the downs system, in which the team was given three downs to advance the ball five yards (later four downs to move the ball ten yards) or relinquish possession of the ball. Under the downs system, lines marking five-yard increments were chalked across the playing field, thus producing the gridiron effect upon the field. Camp also instituted the present point system for touchdowns (6), field goals (3), and safeties (2). As secretary of the intercollegiate football rules convention from 1877 to 1906, he influenced the development of college football nationwide.

Unofficial Coach. From the mid 1880s to about 1910, Camp served as an unofficial advisory coach to the Yale football team. Because he could not attend the team's daily practice sessions due to his work at the watch company, Camp analyzed its progress from detailed notes taken by his wife. In the evenings Camp would meet with the team captain and other key players, suggesting improvements and formulating game-winning strategy. His role as advisory coach provided continuity to the Yale football program. During Camp's association with the team, as a player and coach from 1876 to 1909, Yale established an astonishing record, losing only fourteen games. As graduate athletic adviser and paid treasurer of the Yale Financial Union, Camp contributed stability to the entire Yale athletic program.

Commercialization. A savvy businessman, Camp sold college athletics to a ready public. He applied his business acumen to college athletics in producing both victories and spectator interest. His most successful device in promoting college football to the public was the annual All-American Team, which he first instituted in 1889, personally selecting the outstanding players from colleges and universities nationwide. Camp also successfully promoted the game through his prolific publication. In addition to editing the annual *Spalding's Official Intercollegiate Football Guide,* he authored hundreds of newspaper and magazine articles.

Response to Brutality. Despite football's popularity, it was a violent and at times a deadly sport. In the 1890s Camp spearheaded an investigation of the brutality in college football, publishing his findings in *Football Facts and Figures* (1894). Camp maintained that regardless of its hazards, football was a benefit both physically and mentally to the men who played it. In 1894 the intercollegiate football rules committee, under Camp's direction, eliminated many of the dangerous mass plays, including the flying wedge, which resulted in injury and death. In 1905 the death toll in college football rose so dramatically that President Theodore Roosevelt convened a meeting of representatives from football's Big Three — Yale, Harvard, and Princeton — at the White House to devise a strategy to reform the game. Camp, as one of the representatives from Yale, took the lead at the conference and scripted a statement, acceptable to Roosevelt, which promised to "eliminate unnecessary roughness, holding, and foul play." Reluctant to reform football, the conservative Camp opposed the forward pass rule agreed upon by the Intercollegiate Football Rules Committee in 1906. With the growing power of the National Collegiate Athletic Association, Camp soon lost the control over college football that he had enjoyed since the 1880s.

Withdrawal. After 1910 Camp withdrew from most aspects of Yale's athletic program. When the United States entered the First World War, he directed the U.S. Navy Training Camps Physical Development Program and created a popular "Daily Dozen" exercise program. Camp remained active on the football rules committee until 1925, when he died of a heart attack at the rules committee meeting that year. On 3 November 1928 the Walter Camp Memorial Gateway was dedicated at the Yale Bowl to the man who more than any single person developed American football.

Sources:

Richard Borkowski, "Life and Contributions of Walter Camp to American Football," dissertation, Temple University, 1979;

Harford Powel Jr., *Walter Camp: The Father of American Football* (Freeport, N.Y.: Books for Libraries Press, 1970).

CHARLES M. DANIELS

1885-1973

SWIMMING CHAMPION

Innovator of the American Crawl. Charles M. Daniels, who emerged as the nation's foremost swimmer at the 1904 Olympic Games in Saint Louis, initiated America's twentieth-century dominance in the sport. At Saint Louis he won the 200- and 400-meter freestyle events, after finishing second to Zoltan Halmay of Hungary in the 100 meters. In 1905 a loss to J. Scott Leary marked a turning point in Daniels's career. Leary defeated Daniels with the Australian crawl, using a two-beat kick. Daniels adopted the Australian crawl but modified the kick to six beats. His new stroke, which became known as the American crawl, helped Daniels to win a record thirty-three individual American Amateur Athletic Union (AAU) indoor and outdoor titles from 1904 to 1911 at distances ranging from 50 yards to a mile.

America's Best Olympic Swimmer. Daniels secured America's hegemony in men's Olympic swimming at the 1906 and 1908 Olympic Games. He won the 100-meter freestyle and defeated Hungary's Halmay both times, establishing a world record of 1:05.6 in 1908. In all Daniels won a record four gold, one silver, and two bronze medals in the Olympic Games. His bronze medals came in the 50-yard freestyle in 1904 and the 4x200-meter freestyle relay in 1908. Daniels's record of four swimming gold medals stood until 1968, when Don Schollander won his fifth gold medal in the 4x200-meter freestyle relay in Mexico City.

World Records. During the 1900s Daniels's name dominated the record books at distances ranging from 25 yards to a mile. On 26 February 1906 he became the first American to swim 100 yards in a 25-yard pool in less than one minute, equaling the world record of 57.6 seconds. On 23 March 1906 he set a world record of 56.0 seconds for the 100-meter freestyle. He lowered the world record in the 100-meter freestyle to 55.4 seconds in 1907 and to 54.8 seconds in 1910.

Legacy. Daniels retired from swimming soon after setting the 1910 world record for the 100-yard freestyle. He went on to become an outstanding amateur golfer and the New York Athletic Club bridge and squash champions. More than any other swimmer of the early twentieth century, Daniels helped establish America's dominance in his sport, especially in the 100-meter freestyle, an event ever since ruled by American swimmers.

Source:
Francois Oppenheim, *The History of Swimming* (North Hollywood, Cal., 1970).

JACK JOHNSON

1878-1946

BOXING CHAMPION

Son of a Former Slave. Jack Johnson, the first African American heavyweight champion, was born in Galveston, Texas, the son of Henry and Tina Johnson. His father, a former slave, worked as a porter and a janitor. Despite their lack of formal education, Johnson's parents encouraged their six children to pursue learning and provided a stable, religious home life for them. Johnson completed the fifth grade in elementary school before going to work in the cotton fields and assisting his father as a janitor. He later worked as a stevedore at the Galveston shipyards and as a stable boy in a carriage shop. Walter Lewis, his boss at the carriage shop, was a former prizefighter who taught Johnson how to box. He honed his skills in the "battle royals," degrading staged fights between black youths, and in private clubs before entering the professional ring in 1897.

Early Professional Career. Johnson's first major bout came against Joe Choynsky, a noted Polish Jewish heavyweight on 25 February 1901. Choynsky knocked out Johnson in the third round, and the fight resulted in a three-week jail sentence for both fighters because boxing was illegal in Texas. Despite this defeat, Johnson developed into one of the leading contenders for the world heavyweight title, but the leading white fighters, including the champion, James J. Jeffries, refused to fight him because of his race. Although Johnson participated in several interracial contests, most of his bouts were against less skilled black fighters. He supplemented his income from boxing with stints as an impromptu speaker and vaudeville performer, developing his own show, in which he sang, danced, and played the fiddle and harmonica. After defeating Denver Ed Martin for the unofficial black world heavyweight championship in 1903, he fought throughout England and Australia, developing an international reputation.

World Heavyweight Champion. In 1905 Jeffries retired from boxing and left the world heavyweight championship vacant without any serious contenders for the title. Marvin Hart gained the title but lost it to Canadian Tommy Burns in 1906. Johnson became the leading contender for the heavyweight title and met Burns on 26 December 1908 for the championship in Sydney, Australia. Burns, who believed black boxers were inherently cowards, was no match for the powerful Johnson. The 6-foot, 200-pound Johnson taunted and toyed with the 5' 7", 175-pound Burns. Referees ended the bout in the fourteenth round, declaring Johnson the heavyweight champion. The fight carried a lucrative purse of $40,000, with $35,000 going to Burns and $5,000 to Johnson.

Racial Resentment. For most white Americans recognizing a black as the world heavyweight champion was intolerable since the title personified physical and athletic superiority. White resentment toward Johnson intensified as several "Great White Hopes" failed to win back the title. On 4 July 1910 Jeffries returned to the ring against Johnson, who brutally thrashed the former champion. The outcome of the fight resulted in a nationwide white backlash against blacks and a crusade to banish boxing. White indignation toward Johnson intensified following the champion's marriage to Etta Terry Duryea, a white, in 1911. After her suicide in 1912 he married Lucille Cameron, another white. His interracial marriages received condemnation from both the black and white press and led to the passage of laws banning interracial marriages in several states. Determined to punish Johnson for his social and sexual transgressions, federal authorities prosecuted him for violating the Mann Act, a federal law forbidding the interstate transportation of women for immoral purposes. Despite his innocence, an all-white jury convicted the champion, who fled to France to avoid incarceration.

Johnson's Downfall. After Johnson successfully defended his title in exile in 1913, his career deteriorated to giving boxing and wrestling demonstrations throughout England and France. On 5 April 1915 Johnson met Jess Willard for the world heavyweight title in Havana, Cuba. After twenty-six rounds of brutal slugging in the blazing sun, Willard knocked out the champion. Although Johnson claimed that the fight was fixed, it seems likely that the aged and poorly conditioned Johnson lost a fair fight. The former champion remained in exile in Spain and Mexico before surrendering to federal authorities at the United States–Mexico border in 1920. After serving a yearlong sentence in Leavenworth, Johnson returned to the ring and fought a few professional fights before retiring from the sport in 1921 at age forty-three. In later life he gave boxing exhibitions, dabbled in several business ventures, and authored a fanciful autobiography. Speeding through Raleigh, North Carolina, on 10 June 1946 to attend the Joe Louis–Billy Conn heavyweight rematch, Johnson died in a crash when he lost control of his automobile.

Sources:

Al-Tony Gimore, *Bad Nigger! The National Impact of Jack Johnson* (Port Washington, N.Y.: Kennikat Press, 1975);

Randy Roberts, *Papa Jack: Jack Johnson and the Era of White Hopes* (New York: Free Press, 1983);

Jeffrey T. Sammons, *Beyond the Ring: The Role of Boxing in American Society* (Urbana & Chicago: University of Illinois Press, 1988).

ALVIN KRAENZLEIN

1876-1928

TRACK-AND-FIELD CHAMPION

Hurdling Innovator. Alvin Kraenzlein is one of the pivotal figures in the development of track and field. Historians of the sport recognize him as the father of straight-lead-leg hurdling (in which the first leg over the hurdle is kept straight and parallel to the ground). Hurdlers continue to employ this technique, which permits the athlete to clear the barriers without breaking stride. Although Arthur C. M. Croome of Great Britain first attempted the straight-lead-leg style in 1886, Kraenzlein perfected the technique. The style probably came naturally to him because of his sprinting and long-jumping skills. Kraenzlein in the 1900 Olympic Games won gold medals in four individual events, a feat that has never been equaled. (While Jesse Owens in 1936 and Carl Lewis in 1984 collected four gold medals apiece, one of each man's medals came in a relay event.)

High School Superstar. Kraenzlein was born in Milwaukee, the son of Augusta and John G. Kraenzlein, a brewer. He demonstrated all-around track-and-field skill during his senior year at Milwaukee's East Side High School in 1895. In a meet against crosstown rival West Side High School, Kraenzlein won the 100- and 220-yard dashes, 120-yard high hurdles, 220-yard low hurdles, high jump, long jump, and shot put. In the Wisconsin Interscholastic Championships that year, he nearly duplicated that performance, capturing first places in the 100-yard dash, 120-yard high hurdles, 220-yard low hurdles, high jump, and shot put.

University of Wisconsin Trackman. Kraenzlein entered the University of Wisconsin to study engineering in 1895. He continued to dominate track-and-field competition, winning the 220-yard low hurdles and the high jump and placing second in the 100-yard dash and shot put at the 1896 freshman-sophomore track-and-field meet. In 1897 Kraenzlein established an indoor world record of 36.6 seconds in the 300-yard low hurdles. He also won the 220-yard low hurdles and the high jump in the 1897 Intercollegiate Athletic Conference Championship, leading the University of Wisconsin to the team title. As a member of the Chicago Athletic Club, he captured the 1897 Amateur Athletic Union title in the 220-yard low hurdles.

University of Pennsylvania Standout. Kraenzlein left Wisconsin for the University of Pennsylvania in 1898, where he came under the tutelage of Michael Murphy, the nation's leading track-and-field coach, and developed into the world's leading hurdler. After establishing an indoor world record of 6.0 seconds for the 50-yard high hurdles in 1898, he captured both the 120-yard high hurdles and 220-yard low hurdles at the AAU Championships in 1898 and 1899 and at the Intercollegiate American Amateur Athletic Association (IC4A) Championships in 1898, 1899, and 1900. His 1898 AAU victory in the 120-yard high hurdles resulted in a world record of 15.2 seconds, and his IC4A triumph in the 220-yard low hurdles that year produced a world record of 23.6 seconds, a time that stood as the global standard for nearly twenty-five years. Kraenzlein also succeeded in the long jump, establishing a world record of 24' 3 1/2" in 1899. He won the long jump in both the AAU and IC4A Championships, improving the world record by one inch in the latter. Moreover, he won the AAU and IC4A 100-yard dash titles in 1899 and 1900, respectively. As captain of the Penn track-and-field team in 1900, he scored a record 18 points in the IC4A Championship, leading Penn to its fourth consecutive team title.

Olympic Champion. In 1900 Penn's championship track-and-field team was one of several college teams that represented the United States in the Olympic Games at Paris. Before arriving in Paris, Penn competed in the British Amateur Athletic Association (BAAA) Championships in London. Kraenzlein captured BAAA titles in the 120-yard high hurdles and the long jump. His winning time in the hurdles of 15.4 seconds marked a world record for grass tracks. At the Olympic Games Kraenzlein won his four gold medals in the 60-meter dash (7.0

seconds), 110-meter high hurdles (15.4 seconds), 200-meter low hurdles (25.4 seconds), and the long jump (23' 6 3/4"). His winning performances in each event established new Olympic records.

Coaching Career. After the 1900 Olympic Games Kraenzlein retired from athletic competition. Having graduated from the University of Pennsylvania with a degree in dentistry that year, he returned to Milwaukee and established a practice. Kraenzlein also managed the Milwaukee Athletic Association. He returned to Philadelphia in 1902 to wed Claudine Gilman, whom he had met at the University of Pennsylvania. Kraenzlein continued to practice dentistry in Philadelphia until 1906, when he became the track-and-field coach at Mercersburg Academy. In 1910 he became an assistant professor of physical training and track-and-field coach at the University of Michigan. Among the athletes he mentored at Michigan, the most notable was Ralph Craig, who captured Olympic titles in both the 100 and 200 meters in 1912. In 1913 the German imperial government signed Kraenzlein to a five-year, $50,000 contract to prepare the German Olympic team for the 1916 Olympic Games, scheduled to be held in Berlin. However, the outbreak of World War I canceled the German games. Kraenzlein returned to the United States and served in the army as a physical training specialist. After the war he worked as an assistant track-and-field coach at Penn. Kraenzlein's final years were spent coaching young boys at various summer camps and the trackmen of the Havana (Cuba) Golf and Tennis Club in the winter. In late 1927 he suffered from pleurisy and died early in 1928 from endocarditis.

Source:
Roberto Quercetani, *A World History of Track and Field Athletics* (New York: Oxford University Press, 1964).

WILLIAM LARNED

1872-1926

TENNIS CHAMPION

The Century's First Champion. William Larned ranks as the twentieth century's first great tennis champion. From 1901 to 1902 and from 1907 to 1911 he captured the United States Lawn Tennis Association (USLTA) men's singles title seven times, equaling the record established by Richard Sears in the 1880s. Only Bill Tilden, during the 1920s, has matched the record shared by Sears and Larned. The son of a wealthy New York landowner and lawyer, Larned attended but did not graduate from Cornell University. In 1890 he won the intercollegiate tennis singles championship.

A Complete Player. Larned's game was characterized by precise footwork, balance, ease, and grace, except when nervousness or annoyance marred his concentration. His service and volleys were powerful and accurate. Larned frustrated his opponents with forehands and backhands to the corners. Although easily distracted throughout the 1890s, his temperament and concentration improved throughout the 1900s, and from 1907 to 1911 he dominated the major events. Besides his seven USLTA triumphs, Larned won most of the prestigious northeastern tournaments and ten of his fifteen Davis Cup matches. He also reached the Wimbledon quarterfinals twice. Plagued by rheumatoid arthritis, Larned retired after the 1911 Davis Cup.

Outdoorsman. Independently wealthy, Larned devoted his time to outdoor recreation, sports, travel, and adventure. He pitched on his high school baseball team, captained a New York ice hockey team, golfed, shot rifles, rode horses, and eventually piloted airplanes. In 1898 he served in the Spanish-American War as one of Roosevelt's Rough Riders. In Cuba he contracted the rheumatic fever that was to recur in later years and hamper his tennis game. He served on the executive committee of the USLTA from 1899 to 1916 and, during World War I, commanded Army Air Force personnel in England. After the war he gained a seat on the New York Stock Exchange.

Deteriorating Health. Larned's health declined through the 1920s, and he relinquished his New York Stock Exchange seat in 1922. That year he also formed the Dayton Steel Racquet Company to manufacture a steel tennis racket that he designed. In 1924 Larned suffered a nervous breakdown and contracted spinal meningitis, which left him partially paralyzed. Unable to endure his disability, he committed suicide in 1926 at the New York Knickerbocker Club. In 1927 a tablet was placed in his honor at the tennis stadium in Forest Hills, New York, which read: "Modest — courageous — a True Sportsman — ever loyal to the highest ideals."

Sources:
E. Digby Baltzell, *Sporting Gentleman: Men's Tennis: From the Days of Honor to the Cult of the Superstar* (New York: Free Press, 1995);

Will Grimsley, *Tennis: Its History, People and Events* (Englewood Cliffs, N.J.: Prentice-Hall, 1971).

HONUS WAGNER

1874-1955

BASEBALL PLAYER

The Flying Dutchman. One of baseball's greatest shortstops, Honus Wagner earned the nickname of "The Flying Dutchman" because of his Germanic heritage and great speed. John Peter Wagner was one of five sons and four daughters of Katrina and Peter Wagner, a coal miner. At age twelve Wagner began working in the coal mines and steel mills of western Pennsylvania. He learned to play baseball on a sandlot team with his brothers and mastered each position. "While Wagner was the greatest shortstop," remarked New York Giants manager John J. McGraw, "he could have been the number one player at any position he might have selected."

A Decade of Dominance. Wagner ranked as the most dominating offensive player of the 1900s. After playing for the National League's Louisville Colonels for two years, he joined the Pittsburgh Pirates in 1899, where he remained until he retired. Throughout his twenty-one-year career he never batted below .300, and he led the National League in batting average in 1900, 1903, 1904, 1906 to 1909, and 1911. During the 1900s Wagner also led the NL twice in hits and runs scored, three times in triples, five times in stolen bases, six times in slugging, and eight times in doubles. With a lifetime batting average of .329 and a slugging average of .469, he compiled 10,247 at bats, 1,740 runs scored, 1,732 RBIs, 3,430 hits, 651 doubles, 252 triples, 101 home runs, and 722 stolen bases.

Clash with Cobb. When Louisville owner Barney Dreyfuss became president of the Pittsburgh Pirates in 1899, he brought Wagner with him. Pittsburgh, led by Wagner's batting average of .381, began to dominate the National League in 1900, winning the pennant from 1901 to 1903 and again in 1909, when Forbes Field opened. While Wagner's Pirates lost to Boston in the 1903 World Series, the club defeated Detroit in a seven-game series in 1909. Wagner outplayed Detroit's Ty Cobb, batting .333 to Cobb's .231 and stealing four more bases. An attempt by Cobb to steal second base resulted in Wagner tagging the Georgian out with such force that three stitches were needed to close a gash in Cobb's lip.

Manager and Coach. After Dreyfuss fired Jimmy Callahan in 1917, Wagner became manager of the Pittsburgh Pirates. He soon resigned, however, after leading the club to one win and four losses. After finishing the season as a player, Wagner, age forty-three, retired from Major League Baseball after twenty-one years. He opened a sporting goods store in Pittsburgh, coached baseball and basketball at Carnegie Tech (now Carnegie-Mellon University), and served as the Pennsylvania state legislature sergeant at arms. Wagner, who was one of the original inductees to the Baseball Hall of Fame in 1936, managed the Pirates from 1933 to 1951.

Sources:

Bill James, *Bill James Historical Baseball Abstract* (New York: Villard Books, 1988);

David Quentin Voigt, *American Baseball: From the Commissioners to Continental Expansion* (University Park & London: Pennsylvania State University Press, 1992).

PEOPLE IN THE NEWS

On 30 April 1904 **Aaron L. "Dixie Kid" Brown** defeated Joe Walcott for the world welterweight boxing championship. In late 1904 he outgrew the welterweight title and fought successfully as a middleweight.

From 1899 to 1901 **Dwight F. Davis** captured three consecutive United States Lawn Tennis Association doubles championships. In 1901 he initiated the Davis Cup tennis tournament between the United States and Great Britain.

Playing in the "deadball era," **Harry H. Davis**, of the Philadelphia Athletics, led the American League in home runs for four consecutive seasons, with 10 in 1904, 8 in 1905, 12 in 1906, and 8 in 1907.

In 1904 **Norman Dole** became the first pole vaulter to clear twelve feet, with a vault of 12' 1 1/2".

From 1903 to 1906 **Walter Eckersall** led the University of Chicago football team to a 31–4–2 record through the execution of brilliant strategy, dropkicking, punting, blocking, and tackling.

Competing in the standing high jump, standing long jump, and standing triple jump, **Ray Ewry** won a total of ten Olympic gold medals from 1900 to 1908.

From 1897 to 1909 **John Flanagan** dominated the hammer throw, winning seven Amateur Athletic Union titles and three Olympic gold medals and setting eight world records, with a lifetime best throw of 184' 8".

In 1904 **Henry Ford**, founder of the Ford Motor Company, established a land motor speed record of 91.37 MPH. Throughout the decade he developed race cars, including the Model T that won the transcontinental race from New York to Seattle in 1909.

George Gaidzik won the first three national platform diving championships from 1909 to 1911.

From 1902 to 1908 **Joe Gans** held the world lightweight boxing title. Regarded as the greatest lightweight ever, Gans recorded 120 victories, 8 losses, 10 draws, and 18 no-decisions.

From 1906 to 1917 **Frank Gotch** held the American professional wrestling championship, posting a career record of 394 wins and 6 losses.

Archie Hahn, who equaled the world record of 9.8 seconds in the 100-yard dash in 1901, won Amateur Athletic Union titles in the 100-yard dash in 1903 and the 220-yard dash in 1903 and 1905. In the 1904 Olympic Games he won the 60-, 100-, and 200-meter dashes; in 1908 he defended his Olympic title in the 100 meters.

In 1908 **Johnny Hayes** won the first Olympic marathon contested at the now-standard distance of 26.2 miles.

From 1901 to 1904 University of Michigan halfback **Willie Heston** scored 93 touchdowns and averaged 113 yards rushing per game in leading the Wolverines to a record of 43 wins, 0 losses, and 1 tie.

Harry Hillman captured Amateur Athletic Union titles in the 220-yard low hurdles in 1904 and 1906 and the 440-yard dash in 1903 and 1908. In the 1904 Olympic Games he won gold medals in the 200-meter low hurdles, 400-meter intermediate hurdles, and 400-meter dash, setting a world record of 49.2 seconds.

On 9 June 1899 **James J. Jeffries** knocked out Bob Fitzsimmons for the world heavyweight boxing title. He retired in 1905, though he returned to the ring to challenge Jack Johnson, who soundly defeated him to retain the heavyweight title in 1910.

In 1901 **Byron Bancroft "Ban" Johnson,** president of the Western League, organized the American Baseball League as a rival to the National League and served as its president, secretary, and treasurer from 1901 to 1927.

Napoleon Lajoie, who played for the Philadelphia Athletics and the Cleveland Indians, led the American League in batting average in 1901 (.405), 1903 (.355), and 1904 (.381). He was the home run leader in 1901 with 13.

Sam Leever of the Pittsburgh Pirates led National League pitchers in 1901 with 19 wins, 6 losses; in 1903 with 25 wins, 7 losses; and in 1905 with 20 wins, 5 losses.

Joe McGinnity of the New York Giants led National League pitchers in 1900 with 20 wins, 6 losses. He was the top winner in 1904 with 35 wins, 8 losses.

As manager of the New York Giants **John McGraw** directed his team to the National League pennant in 1904 and 1905. After refusing to play the Boston Red Sox in the 1904 World Series, his team won the world title in 1905, defeating the Philadelphia Athletics.

Elisabeth H. Moore won the United States Lawn Tennis Association singles title in 1896, 1903, and 1905; doubles in 1896 and 1903; and mixed doubles in 1902 and 1904. In 1907 she captured the first indoor singles championship and in 1908 the indoors doubles championship.

On 20 December 1905 **Philadelphia Jack O'Brien** knocked out Bob Fitzsimmons for the world light heavyweight boxing championship. He retired as the champion in 1912, never having to defend the title.

At the 1904 Olympic Games in Saint Louis **George Poage** of the University of Wisconsin and the Milwaukee Athletic Club became the first African American Olympic medalist, winning bronze medals in the 200- and 400-meter hurdles.

Meyer Prinstein captured Amateur Athletic Union long jump titles in 1898, 1902, and 1906. In the 1900 Olympic Games he won the silver medal in the long jump and the gold medal in the triple jump. Besides defending his Olympic title in the triple jump in 1904, Prinstein also captured the long jump. He won the long jump as well in the 1906 Olympic Games.

Harry C. Pulliam served as president of baseball's National League from 1903 to 1909.

From 1907 to 1910 **Ralph Rose** won the Amateur Athletic Union shot put title. He won the Olympic shot put title in 1904 and 1908. In putting the shot 51′ in 1909 he became the first man to go beyond 50′. Rose garnered the silver medal in both the shot put and discus throw in the 1912 Olympic Games.

Pitcher **Ed Ruelbach** of the Chicago Cubs led the National League in victories with 19 wins, 4 losses in 1906; 17 wins, 4 losses in 1907; and 24 wins, 7 losses in 1908.

From 1904 to 1908 **Adolph George Schultz** excelled as an interior lineman for the University of Michigan.

Mel Sheppard captured the Amateur Athletic Union 880-yard dash in 1906, 1907, 1908, 1911, and 1912.

He won gold medals in the 800 meters and the 1,500 meters in the 1908 Olympic Games and a silver medal in the 800 meters in 1912. Sheppard established a world record of 1:52.8 for 800 meters in the 1908 Olympic Games.

Martin Sheridan reigned as the Amateur Athletic Union champion in the discus throw in 1904, 1906, 1907, and 1911. He won the discus throw in the 1904, 1906, and 1908 Olympic Games. From 1902 to 1911 Sheridan set nine world records in the discus, with the last measuring 141′ 4″.

Amos Alonzo Stagg, the football coach at the University of Chicago (1900–1932), led his team to an undefeated season and a national championship in 1905. In his career Stagg compiled 255 victories and developed four undefeated teams as well as eleven All-Americans.

In 1904 sixteen-year-old **May G. Sutton** became the youngest winner of the United States Lawn Tennis Association women's singles title. As the top-ranked American throughout the decade, she won the Wimbledon singles title in 1905, becoming the first American, male or female, to win the British championship.

On 18 December 1901 **Joe Walcott** knocked out Rube Ferns for the world welterweight boxing championship. Although he lost the title to the Dixie Kid in 1904, he claimed it again after Kid outgrew the title later that year. He lost the title to Honey Mellody in 1906.

In 1906 seventy-year-old **Edward P. Weston** walked from New York City to San Francisco in one hundred days. In 1907 he completed the return trip in seventy days.

Jimmy Winkfield, riding His Eminence in 1901 and Alan-a-Dale in 1902, became the first jockey to win two consecutive Kentucky Derbys and the last African American jockey to win the Derby.

From 1901 to 1905 **Fielding Yost,** the football coach at the University of Michigan, led the Wolverines on a 56-game winning streak.

From 1890 to 1911 **Cy Young** won 508 games, with ten twenty-win seasons and five seasons of thirty or more wins.

AWARDS

1900

Kentucky Derby, Horse Racing — Lieutenant Gibson (Jimmy Boland, jockey)

Collegiate Football National Champion — Yale University, 12–0

U.S.G.A. Amateur Championship — Walter J. Travis

U.S.G.A. Open Championship — Harry Vardon

U.S.G.A. Women's Amateur Championship — Frances C. Griscom

U.S. Lawn Tennis Association Men's Singles Championship — Malcolm D. Whitman

U.S. Lawn Tennis Association Women's Singles Championship — Myrtle McTeer

1901

Kentucky Derby, Horse Racing — His Eminence (Jimmy Winkfield, jockey)

Collegiate Football National Champion — University of Michigan 11–0

U.S.G.A. Amateur Championship — Walter J. Travis

U.S.G.A. Open Championship — Willie Anderson

U.S.G.A. Women's Amateur Championship — Genevieve Hecker

U.S. Lawn Tennis Association Men's Singles Championship — William A. Larned

U.S. Lawn Tennis Association Women's Singles Championship — Elisabeth H. Moore

1902

Kentucky Derby, Horse Racing — Alan-a-Dale (Jimmy Winkfield, jockey)

Collegiate Football National Champion — University of Michigan, 11–0

U.S.G.A. Amateur Championship — L. N. James

U.S.G.A. Open Championship — Laurie Auchterlonie

U.S.G.A. Women's Amateur Championship — Genevieve Hecker

U.S. Lawn Tennis Association Men's Singles Championship — William A. Larned

U.S. Lawn Tennis Association Women's Singles Championship — Marion Jones

1903

Major League Baseball World Series — Boston Red Sox (American League), 5 vs. Pittsburgh Pirates (National League), 3

Kentucky Derby, Horse Racing — Judge Himes (Hal Booker, jockey)

Collegiate Football National Champion — Princeton University, 11–0

U.S.G.A. Amateur Championship — Walter J. Travis

U.S.G.A. Open Championship — Willie Anderson

U.S.G.A. Women's Amateur Championship — Bessie Anthony

U.S. Lawn Tennis Association Men's Singles Championship — Hugh L. Doherty (England)

U.S. Lawn Tennis Association Women's Singles Championship — Elisabeth H. Moore

1904

Major League Baseball World Series — no World Series held between New York Giants (National League) and Boston Red Sox (American League)

Kentucky Derby, Horse Racing — Elwood (Frankie Prior, jockey)

Collegiate Football National Champion — University of Pennsylvania 12–0

U.S.G.A. Amateur Championship — H. Chandler Egan

U.S.G.A. Open Championship — Willie Anderson

U.S.G.A. Women's Amateur Championship — Georgiana Bishop

U.S. Lawn Tennis Association Men's Singles Championship — Holcombe Ward

U.S. Lawn Tennis Association Women's Singles Championship — May G. Sutton

1905

Major League Baseball World Series — New York Giants (National League), 4 vs. Philadelphia Athletics (American League), 1

Kentucky Derby, Horse Racing — Agile (Jack Martin, jockey)

Collegiate Football National Champion — University of Chicago 11–0

U.S.G.A. Amateur Championship — H. Chandler Egan

U.S.G.A. Open Championship — Willie Anderson

U.S.G.A. Women's Amateur Championship — Pauline Mackay

U.S. Lawn Tennis Association Men's Singles Championship — Beals C. Wright

U.S. Lawn Tennis Association Women's Singles Championship — Elisabeth H. Moore

1906

Major League Baseball World Series — Chicago White Sox (American League), 4 vs. Chicago Cubs (National League), 1

Kentucky Derby, Horse Racing — Sir Huon (Roscoe Troxler, jockey)

Collegiate Football National Champion — Princeton University 9–0–1

U.S.G.A. Amateur Championship — E. M. Byers

U.S.G.A. Open Championship — Alex Smith

U.S.G.A. Women's Amateur Championship — Harriot S. Curtis

U.S. Lawn Tennis Association Men's Singles Championship — William J. Clothier

U.S. Lawn Tennis Association Women's Singles Championship — Helen Homans

1907

Major League Baseball World Series — Chicago Cubs (National League), 4 vs. Detroit Tigers (American League), 0

Kentucky Derby, Horse Racing — Pink Star (Andy Minder, jockey)

Collegiate Football National Champion — Yale University 9–0–1

U.S.G.A. Amateur Championship — Jerome D. Travers

U.S.G.A. Open Championship — Alex Ross

U.S.G.A. Women's Amateur Championship — Margaret Curtis

U.S. Lawn Tennis Association Men's Singles Championship — William A. Larned

U.S. Lawn Tennis Association Women's Singles Championship — Evelyn Sears

1908

Major League Baseball World Series — Chicago Cubs (National League), 4 vs. Detroit Tigers (American League), 1

Kentucky Derby, Horse Racing — Stone Street (Arthur Pickens, jockey)

Collegiate Football National Champion — University of Pennsylvania 11–0

U.S.G.A. Amateur Championship — Jerome D. Travers

U.S.G.A. Open Championship — Fred McLeod

U.S.G.A. Women's Amateur Championship — Kate C. Harley

U.S. Lawn Tennis Association Men's Singles Championship — William A. Larned

U.S. Lawn Tennis Association Women's Singles Championship — Mrs. Maud Bargar-Wallach

1909

Major League Baseball World Series — Pittsburgh Pirates (National League), 4 vs. Detroit Tigers (American League), 3

Kentucky Derby, Horse Racing — Wintergreen (Vincent Powers, jockey)

Collegiate Football National Champion — Yale University 10–0

U.S.G.A. Amateur Championship — R. A. Gardner

U.S.G.A. Open Championship — George Sargent

U.S.G.A. Women's Amateur Championship — Dorothy Campbell

U.S. Lawn Tennis Association Men's Singles Championship — William A. Larned

U.S. Lawn Tennis Association Women's Singles Championship — Hazel V. Hotchkiss

DEATHS

Louis R. Browning, 44, outfielder who played from 1882 to 1894 in the American Association, principally for Louisville, compiling the fourth highest lifetime batting average (.355) in baseball history, 10 September 1905.

Charles G. Buffington, 46, one of baseball's premier pitchers who from 1882 to 1892 won 231 games against 151 losses, with seven 20-win seasons and a 2.96 ERA, 23 September 1907.

Henry Chadwick, 83, journalist and promoter of baseball who popularized the British origins of baseball, 20 April 1908.

John Gibson Clarkson, 48, pitcher principally for the Chicago White Sox and the Boston Beaneaters from 1884 to 1887, 326–177 with a 2.81 ERA, 4 February 1909.

Edward James Delahanty, 36, played from 1887 to 1903 for Philadelphia of the National League, Cleveland of the Player's League, and Washington of the American League and compiled history's seventh best lifetime batting average (.346), 2 July 1903.

Frederick C. Dunlap, 43, second baseman, 1 December 1902.

William Buckingham Ewing, 47, catcher principally for the New York Giants, recognized as the first to crouch behind home plate, 20 October 1906.

J. Malcolm Forbes, 59, successful thoroughbred race-horse breeder and yachtsman who won the 1885 America's Cup, 19 February 1904.

James Francis Galvin, 46, one of baseball's greatest pitchers, played from 1879 to 1892, principally for Buffalo and Pittsburgh of the National League, 7 March 1902.

Michael Joseph Griffin, 43, considered the best center fielder from 1887 to 1898, played with Baltimore of the American Association, Philadelphia of the Player's Association, and Brooklyn of the National League, 10 April 1908.

Herman C. Long, 43, shortstop from 1887 to 1903 for Kansas City of the American Association and Boston of the National League, 17 September 1909.

Pierre Lorillard, 67, horse breeder and owner, who successfully raced American horses in England and France, 7 July 1901.

Richard J. Pearce, 72, shortstop from 1856 to 1877, the last two years for Saint Louis of the National League, 18 September 1908.

Harry Clay Pulliam, 40, president of the National League from 1902 to 1909, 9 July 1909.

Frank Gibson Selee, 50, baseball manager, principally with Boston of the National League (1890–1901), 5 July 1909.

Charles Sylvester Stahl, 34, outfielder for the Boston National League club (1897–1900) as well as the Boston American League franchise (1901–1906), 28 March 1907.

Ezra Ballou Sutton, 56, versatile major league infielder and outfielder from 1872 to 1888, 20 June 1907.

John Taylor, 24, first African American to win a gold medal in the Olympics, in the 1,600-meter medley relay in 1908, 2 December 1908.

Bertha Louise Townsend Toulmin, 40, United States Lawn Tennis Association women's singles champion from 1888 to 1889, 12 May 1909.

Robert Wyndham Walden, 61, jockey, won the Preakness seven times (1875, 1878–1882, and 1888), 28 April 1905.

PUBLICATIONS

Adrian C. Anson, *A Ball Player's Career* (Chicago: Era, 1900);

Ralph Henry Barbour, *For the Honor of the School: A Story of School Life and Interscholastic Sport* (New York: Appleton, 1900);

Senda Berenson, *Line Basket Ball or Basketball for Women* (New York: American Sports, 1901);

Samuel Crowther and Arthur Ruhl, *Rowing and Track Athletics* (New York: Macmillan, 1905);

Michael Donovan, *The Roosevelt I Knew: Ten Years of Boxing with the President — and Other Memories of Famous Fighting Men* (New York: B. W. Dodge, 1909);

Charles Dryden, *The Champion Athletics* (Philadelphia, 1905);

Harry Ellard, *Baseball in Cincinnati: A History* (Cincinnati, Ohio: Johnson & Hardin, 1907);

E. J. Giannini, *Rowing* (New York: American Sports, 1909);

Luther Halsey Gulick, *Physical Education for Muscular Exercise* (Philadelphia: P. Blakiston, 1904);

George T. Hepbron, *How to Play Basketball* (New York: American Sports, 1904);

Lucille Eaton Hill, *Athletic and Out-Door Sports for Women* (New York: Macmillan, 1903);

Felix Klien, *In the Land of the Strenuous Life* (Chicago: McClurg, 1905);

Life and Fights of John L. Sullivan (London: Health & Strength, 1909);

Barrett O'Hara, *From Figg to Johnson: A Complete History of the Heavyweight Championship* (Chicago: Blossom Book Bourse, 1909);

J. Parmly Paret, ed., *The Women's Book of Sports* (New York: Appleton, 1901);

Francis C. Richter, *A Brief History of Baseball* (Philadelphia: Sporting Life Publication, 1909);

Theodore Roosevelt, *The Strenuous Life: Essays and Addresses* (Philadelphia: Gebbie, 1903);

F. A. Schmidt and Eustace H. Miles, *The Training of the Body* (New York: Dutton, 1901);

T. P. Sullivan, *Humorous Stories of the Ball Field* (Chicago: M. Donohue, 1903);

Walter J. Travis, *Practical Golf* (New York & London: Harper, 1901);

Charles E. Trevathan, *The American Thoroughbred* (New York: Macmillan, 1905);

Fielding Harris Yost, *Football for Player and Spectator* (Ann Arbor: University of Michigan, 1905);

American Golfer, periodical;

American Physical Education Review, periodical;

Baseball Magazine, periodical;

Illustrated Outdoor News, periodical;

Illustrated Sporting News, periodical;

Mind and Body, periodical;

Napoleon Lajoie's Official Base Ball Guide, periodical;

Official Golf Guide, periodical;

Outing, periodical;

Physical Culture, periodical;

Reach's Official Base Ball Guide, periodical;

Sol White's Official Base Ball Guide, periodical;

Spalding's Annual Baseball Record, periodical;

Spalding's Official Base Ball Guide, periodical;

Sporting Life, periodical;

Sporting News, periodical.

GENERAL REFERENCES

GENERAL

Frederick Lewis Allen, *The Big Change: America Transforms Itself* (New York: Harper, 1952);

Daniel Boorstin, *The Americans: The Democratic Experience* (New York: Vintage, 1973);

Sean Dennis Cashman, *America in the Age of Titans* (New York: New York University Press, 1988);

Mary Kupiec Cayton, Elliott J. Gorn, and Peter T. Williams, eds., *Encyclopedia of American Social History*, 3 volumes (New York: Scribners, 1993);

John Chambers II, *The Tyranny of Change: America in the Progressive Era, 1900–1917* (New York: St. Martin's Press, 1992);

Chronicle of the Twentieth Century (Mount Kisco, N.Y.: Chronicle, 1987);

John Milton Cooper Jr., *Pivotal Decades: The United States, 1900–1920* (New York, 1990);

John W. Dodds, *Everyday Life in Twentieth Century America* (New York: Putnam, 1965);

Richard Hofstadter, *The Age of Reform: From Bryan to FDR* (New York: Vintage, 1955);

Gabriel Kolko, *The Triumph of Conservatism* (New York: Free Press, 1963);

Irving S. Kull and Nell M. Kull, eds., *An Encyclopedia of American History*, revised and updated by Stanley H. Friedelbaum (New York: Popular Library, 1965);

Charles D. Lowery and John F. Marszalek, eds., *Encyclopedia of African-American Civil Rights: From Emancipation to the Present* (Westport, Conn.: Greenwood Press, 1992);

Iwan W. Morgan and Neil A. Wynn, *America's Century: Perspectives on U.S. History Since 1900* (New York: Holmes & Meier, 1993);

Thomas J. Schlereth, *Victorian America: Transformations in Everyday Life, 1876–1915* (New York: HarperCollins, 1991);

Barbara Sicherman and Carol Hurd Green, with Ilene Kantrov and Harriette Walker, eds., *Notable American Women: The Modern Period, A Biographical Dictionary* (Cambridge, Mass.: Harvard University Press, 1980);

Statistical History of the United States from Colonial Times to the Present (Stamford, Conn.: Fairfield, 1965);

Mark Sullivan, *Our Times* (New York: Scribners, 1930);

This Fabulous Century (New York: Time-Life Books, 1988);

James Trager, *The People's Chronology*, revised edition (New York: Holt, Rinehart & Winston, 1994);

Claire Walter, *Winners: The Blue Ribbon Encyclopedia of Awards* (New York: Facts On File, 1982);

Robert Wiebe, *The Search for Order, 1877–1920* (New York: Hill & Wang, 1967);

Leigh Carol Yuster and others, eds., *Ulrich's International Periodicals Directory: A Classified Guide to Current Periodicals, Foreign and Domestic, 1986–1987*, twenty-fifth edition, 2 volumes (New York & London: R. R. Bowker, 1986).

ARTS

Daniel Aaron, *Writers on the Left* (New York: Harcourt, Brace & World, 1961);

Gayle Addison Jr., *Oak and Ivy: A Biography of Paul Laurence Dunbar* (Garden City, N.Y.: Anchor/Doubleday, 1971);

H. H. Arnason, *History of Modern Art: Painting • Sculpture • Architecture* (Englewood Cliffs, N.J.: Prentice-Hall / New York: Abrams, 1968);

John I. H. Baur, ed., *New Art in America: Fifty Painters of the 20th Century* (Greenwich, Conn.: New York Graphic Society, 1957);

Nina Baym and others, *The Norton Anthology of American Literature*, fourth edition, volume 2 (New York: Norton, 1994);

Alfred L. Bernheim and Sarah Harding, *The Business of the Theatre: An Economic History of the American Theatre, 1750–1932* (New York: Benjamin Blom, 1932);

Walter Blair and Hamlin Hill, *America's Humor* (New York: Oxford University Press, 1978);

Eileen Bowser, *The Transformation of Cinema* (New York: Scribners, 1990);

Paul S. Boyer, *Purity in Print* (New York: Scribners, 1968);

Oscar G. Brockett and Robert R. Findlay, *Century of Innovation: A History of European and American Theatre and Drama Since 1870* (Englewood Cliffs, N.J.: Prentice-Hall, 1984);

Ann Charters, *Nobody: The Story of Bert Williams* (New York: Macmillan, 1970);

Joseph Csida and June Bundy Csida, *American Entertainment: A Unique History of Show Business* (New York: Watson-Guptill, 1978);

Susan Curtis, *Dancing to a Black Man's Tune: A Life of Scott Joplin* (Columbia: University of Missouri Press, 1994);

Isadora Duncan, *The Art of the Dance*, edited by Sheldon Cheney (New York: Theatre Arts, 1928);

Eleanor Dwight, *Edith Wharton, An Extraordinary Life* (New York: Abrams, 1994);

Emory Elliott, ed., *Columbia Literary History of the United States* (New York: Columbia University Press, 1988);

Lewis Erenberg, *Steppin' Out: New York Nightlife and the Transformation of American Culture, 1890–1930* (Westport, Conn.: Greenwood Press, 1981);

David Ewen, *All the Years of American Popular Music* (Englewood Cliffs, N.J.: Prentice-Hall, 1977);

Philip Furia, *The Poets of Tin Pan Alley: A History of America's Great Lyricists* (New York: Oxford University Press, 1990);

William H. Gerdts, *American Impressionism* (New York: Abbeville Press, 1984);

Horace Gregory and Marza Zaturensha, *A History of American Poetry, 1900–1940* (New York: Harcourt, Brace, 1946);

Katrina Hazzard-Gordon, *Jookin': The Rise of Social Dance Formations in African-American Culture* (Philadelphia: Temple University Press, 1990);

William Innes Homer, *Alfred Stieglitz and the Photo-Secession* (New York: Little, Brown, 1983);

Paul Kuritz, *The Making of Theatre History* (Englewood Cliffs, N.J.: Prentice Hall, 1988);

Paul Lauter, *The Heath Anthology of American Literature*, volume 2 (Lexington, Mass.: Heath, 1990);

R. W. B. Lewis, *Edith Wharton: A Biography* (New York: Harper & Row, 1975);

Richard Lingeman, *Theodore Dreiser: An American Journey* (London: John Wiley & Sons, 1993);

Glenn Loney, *20th Century Theatre*, volume 1 (New York: Facts On File, 1983);

Ethan Madden, *Better Foot Forward: The History of American Musical Theater* (New York: Grossman, 1976);

Paul Magriel, *Chronicles of American Dance* (New York: Holt, 1948);

Gerald Mast, *A Short History of the Movies*, revised by Bruce F. Kawin (New York: Macmillan, 1992);

Henry F. May, *The End of American Innocence*, revised edition (New York: Columbia University Press, 1992);

Walter Meserve, *An Outline History of American Drama* (New York: Feedback Theatre Books & Prospero Press, 1994);

Thomas L. Morgan and William Barlow, *From Cakewalks to Concert Halls: An Illustrated History of African-American Popular Music from 1895 to 1930* (Washington, D.C.: Elliott & Clark, 1992);

Charles Musser, *Before the Nickelodeon: Edwin S. Porter and the Edison Manufacturing Company* (Berkeley: University of California Press, 1991);

Musser, *The Emergence of Cinema* (New York: Scribners, 1990);

David Perkins, *A History of Modern Poetry: From the 1890s to the High Modernist Mode* (Cambridge, Mass.: Harvard University Press, 1976);

Christina Peterson, *Alfred Stieglitz's Camera Notes* (New York: Norton, 1993);

Peter Quartermain, ed., *American Poets, 1880–1945*, series 1–3; *Dictionary of Literary Biography*, volumes 45, 48, and 54 (Detroit: Bruccoli Clark/Gale Research, 1986–1987);

Walter B. Rideout, *The Radical Novel in the United States 1900–1954* (Cambridge, Mass.: Harvard University Press, 1956);

Barbara Rose, *American Art Since 1900* (New York: Praeger, 1968);

Louis D. Rubin Jr., ed., *The History of Southern Literature* (Baton Rouge: Louisiana State University Press, 1985);

Nancy Lee Chalfa Ruyter, *Reformers and Visionaries: The Americanization of the Art of Dance* (New York: Dance Horizons, 1979);

Ruth St. Denis, *An Unfinished Life: An Autobiography* (New York: Harper, 1939);

Maxine Schwartz Seller, ed., *Ethnic Theatre in the United States* (Westport, Conn.: Greenwood Press, 1983);

Andrew Sinclair, *Jack: A Biography* (New York: Harper & Row, 1977);

Anthony Slide, *The Encyclopedia of Vaudeville* (Westport, Conn.: Greenwood Press, 1994);

Eric L. Smith, *Bert Williams: A Biography of the Black Comedian* (Jefferson, N.C. & London: McFarland, 1992).

BUSINESS AND THE ECONOMY

Norman Beasley, *Main Street Merchant: The Story of the J.C. Penney Company* (New York: Whittlesey House, 1948);

Ernest L. Bogart and Donald L. Kemmerer, *Economic History of the American People* (New York: Longmans, Green, 1942);

Richard O. Boyer and Herbert M. Morais, *Labor's Untold Story* (Pittsburgh: UERMWA, 1955);

John Brooks, *The Autobiography of American Business* (Garden City, N.Y.: Doubleday, 1974);

Andrew Carnegie, *Autobiography* (Boston: Houghton Mifflin, 1920);

Carnegie, *The Gospel of Wealth and Other Timely Essays* (New York: Century, 1900);

Vincent P. Carosso, *The Morgans: Private International Bankers* (Cambridge, Mass.: Harvard University Press, 1988);

Frank Barkley Copley, *Frederick W. Taylor: Father of Scientific Management,* volumes 1 and 2 (New York: Kelley, 1969);

Melvyn Dubofsky, *We Shall Be All: A History of the Industrial Workers of the World* (Chicago: Quadrangle, 1969);

Foster Rhea Dulles, *Labor in America: A History* (New York: Crowell, 1949);

Henry Ford, *My Life and Work* (Garden City, N.Y.: Doubleday, Page, 1922);

Joshua Freeman and others, *Who Built America? Working People and the Nation's Economy, Politics, Culture, and Society,* volume 2 (New York: Pantheon, 1992);

Great Stories of American Businessmen (New York: American Heritage Publishing, 1972);

Big Bill Haywood, *Bill Haywood's Book: The Autobiography* (New York: International, 1929);

Robert Hessen, *Steel Titan: The Life of Charles M. Schwab* (New York: Oxford University Press, 1975);

Robert Lacy, *Ford: The Men and the Machine* (Boston: Little, Brown, 1986);

Andrew Mellon, *Taxation: The People's Business* (New York: Macmillan, 1924);

David Montgomery, *The Fall of the House of Labor: The Workplace, the State, and American Labor Activism, 1865–1925* (Cambridge: Cambridge University Press, 1987);

Gareth Morgan, *Images of Organization* (Newbury Park, Cal.: Sage, 1986);

Margaret Myers, *A Financial History of the United States* (New York: Columbia University Press, 1970);

Allan Nevins, *Ford: The Times, The Man, The Company* (New York: Scribners, 1954);

Harvey O'Connor, *Mellon's Millions: The Biography of a Fortune* (New York: Day, 1993);

J. C. Penney, *Fifty Years with the Golden Rule* (New York: Harper, 1950);

Penney, *View from the Next Decade: Jottings from a Merchant's Daybook* (New York: Nelson, 1960);

Glenn Porter, *The Rise of Big Business, 1860–1910* (New York: Crowell, 1973);

Edwin C. Rozwenc, ed., *Roosevelt, Wilson and the Trusts* (Boston: Heath, 1950);

Herbert Satterlee, *J. Pierpont Morgan: An Intimate Portrait* (New York: Macmillan, 1939);

Philip Taft, *Organized Labor in American History* (New York: Harper & Row, 1964);

Frederick Winslow Taylor, *Principles of Scientific Management* (New York: Harper, 1911);

Joseph Frazier Wall, *Andrew Carnegie* (New York: Oxford University Press, 1970).

EDUCATION

James D. Anderson, *The Education of Blacks in the South, 1860–1935* (Chapel Hill: University of North Carolina Press, 1988);

Howard K. Beale, *A History of Freedom of Teaching in American Schools,* Report of the Commission on the Social Studies, American Historical Association, part 16 (New York & Chicago: Scribners, 1941);

Barbara Beatty, *Preschool Education in America: The Culture of Young Children from the Colonial Era to the Present* (New Haven: Yale University Press, 1995);

Selma Cantor Berrol, *Julia Richman: A Notable Woman* (Philadelphia: Balch Institute Press, 1993);

Randolph S. Bourne, *The Gary Schools* (Cambridge: MIT Press, 1970);

Robert H. Bremner, *American Philanthropy* (Chicago: University of Chicago Press, 1960);

H. Warren Button and Eugene F. Provenzo Jr., *History of Education and Culture in America* (Englewood Cliffs, N.J.: Prentice-Hall, 1983);

Robert L. Church and Michael W. Sedlak, *Education in the United States: An Interpretive History* (New York: Free Press, 1976);

Lawrence A. Cremin, *American Education: The Metropolitan Experience, 1876–1980* (New York: Harper & Row, 1988);

Cremin, *The Transformation of the School: Progressivism in American Education, 1876–1957* (New York: Vintage, 1964);

Charles William Dabney, *Universal Education in the South* (Chapel Hill: University of North Carolina Press, 1936);

Howard A. Dawson and M. C. S. Noble Jr., *Handbook on Rural Education: Factual Data on Rural Education, Its Social and Economic Backgrounds* (Washington, D.C.: National Education Association of the United States, Department of Rural Education, 1961);

Eliot (New York: Oxford University Press, 1972);

Raymond B. Fosdick, *The Story of the Rockefeller Foundation* (New Brunswick: Transaction Publishers, 1989);

Patricia Albjerg Graham, *S.O.S.: Sustain Our Schools* (New York: Hill & Wang, 1992);

Margaret A. Haley, *Battleground: The Autobiography of Margaret A. Haley,* edited by Robert L. Reid (Urbana: University of Illinois Press, 1982);

Louis R. Harlan, *Booker T. Washington: The Wizard of Tuskegee, 1901–1915* (New York: Oxford University Press, 1983);

Harlan, *Separate and Unequal: Public School Campaigns and Racism in the Southern Seaboard States, 1901–1915* (Chapel Hill: University of North Carolina Press, 1958);

Richard Hofstadter and Wilson Smith, *American Higher Education: A Documentary History,* 2 volumes (Chicago: University of Chicago Press, 1961);

Helen Lefkowitz Horowitz, *Campus Life: Undergraduate Cultures from the End of the Eighteenth Century to the Present* (Chicago: University of Chicago Press, 1987);

Horowitz, *The Power and Passion of M. Carey Thomas* (New York: Knopf, 1994);

Henry James, *Charles W. Eliot: President of Harvard University, 1869–1909* (Boston: Houghton Mifflin, 1930);

Thomas James, *Public versus Nonpublic Education in Historical Perspective* (Stanford, Cal.: Institute for Research on Educational Finance and Governance, School of Education, Stanford University, 1982);

Geraldine Jonich, *The Sane Positivist: A Biography of Edward L. Thorndike* (Middletown, Conn.: Wesleyan University Press, 1968);

Clarence J. Karier, *Roots of Crisis: American Education in the Twentieth Century* (Chicago: Rand, McNally, 1973);

Herbert M. Kliebard, *The Struggle for the American Curriculum, 1893–1958* (New York: Routledge & Kegan Paul, 1987);

Edward A. Krug, *The Shaping of the American High School* (New York: Harper & Row, 1964);

Ellen Condliffe Lagemann, *The Politics of Knowledge: The Carnegie Corporation, Philanthropy, and Public Policy* (Chicago: University of Chicago Press, 1989);

Lagemann, *Private Power for the Public Good: A History of the Carnegie Foundation for the Advancement of Teaching* (Middletown, Conn.: Wesleyan University Press, 1983);

Marvin Lazerson, ed., *American Education in the Twentieth Century: A Documentary History* (New York: Teachers College Press, Columbia University, 1987);

David Levering Lewis, *W.E.B. Du Bois: Biography of a Race, 1868–1919* (New York: Holt, 1993);

Christopher J. Lucas, *American Higher Education: A History* (New York: St. Martin's Press, 1994);

Robert A. Margo, *Race and Schooling in the South, 1880–1950: An Economic History* (Chicago: University of Chicago Press, 1990);

James McLachlan, *American Boarding Schools: A Historical Study* (New York: Scribners, 1970);

Neil R. McMillen, *Dark Journey: Black Mississippians in the Age of Jim Crow* (Urbana: University of Illinois Press, 1989);

Samuel Eliot Morison, *The Development of Harvard University Since the Inauguration of President Eliot, 1869–1929* (Cambridge, Mass.: Harvard University Press, 1930);

Majorie Murphy, *Blackboard Unions: The AFT and the NEA, 1900–1980* (Ithaca, N.Y.: Cornell University Press, 1990);

Joel Perlmann, *Ethnic Differences: Schooling and Social Structure Among the Irish, Italians, Jews and Blacks in an American City, 1880–1935* (New York: Cambridge University Press, 1988);

John D. Pulliam, *History of Education in America,* third edition (Columbus, Ohio: Merrill, 1986);

Maxine Schwartz Seller, ed., *Women Educators in the United States, 1820–1993: A Bio-Bibliographical Sourcebook* (Westport, Conn.: Greenwood Press, 1994);

Vivian Trow Thayer, *Formative Ideas in American Education, from the Colonial Period to the Present* (New York: Dodd, Mead, 1965);

Ridgely Torrance, *The Story of John Hope* (New York: Macmillan, 1948);

David B. Tyack, *The One Best System: A History of American Urban Education* (Cambridge, Mass.: Harvard University Press, 1974);

Tyack and Elizabeth Hansot, *Managers of Virtue: Public School Leadership in America, 1820–1980* (New York: Basic Books, 1982);

Rena L. Vassar, *Social History of American Education* (Chicago: Rand, McNally, 1965);

Laurence R. Veysey, *The Emergence of the American University* (Chicago: University of Chicago Press, 1965);

Warren Weaver, *U.S. Philanthropic Foundations: Their History, Structure, Management, and Record* (New York: Harper & Row, 1967);

Arthur Zilversmit, *Changing Schools: Progressive Education Theory and Practice, 1930–1960* (Chicago: University of Chicago Press, 1993).

FASHION

Victor Arwas, *Glass: Art Nouveau to Art Deco* (New York: Abrams, 1987);

Michael Batterberry and Ariane Batterberry, *Mirror, Mirror: A Social History of Fashion* (New York: Holt, Rinehart & Winston, 1977);

Helen L. Brockman, *The Theory of Fashion Design* (New York: Wiley, 1965);

John Burchard and Albert Bush-Brown, *The Architecture of America: A Social and Cultural History* (Boston: Atlantic Monthly/Little, Brown, 1961);

Stephen Calloway, *Twentieth-Century Decoration: The Domestic Interior from 1900 to the Present Day* (London: Weidenfeld & Nicolson, 1988);

Calloway and Elizabeth Cromley, eds., *The Elements of Style* (New York: Simon & Schuster, 1991);

The Changing American Woman: Two Hundred Years of American Fashion (New York: Fairchild, 1976);

Clifford Edward Clark Jr., *The American Family Home, 1800–1960* (Chapel Hill: University of North Carolina Press, 1986);

Carl W. Condit, *The Chicago School of Architecture* (Chicago: University of Chicago Press, 1964);

Mila Contini, *Fashion: From Ancient Egypt to the Present Day* (New York: Odyssey, 1965);

Diana de Marly, *Fashion for Men: An Illustrated History* (New York: Holmes & Meier, 1985);

de Marly, *The History of Haute Couture, 1850–1950* (New York: Holmes & Meier, 1980);

Maryanne Dolan, *Vintage Clothing, 1880–1960: Identification and Value Guide* (Florence, Ala.: Books Americana, 1984);

Elizabeth Ewing, *History of Twentieth Century Fashion*, revised and updated edition (London: Batsford, 1992; Lanham, Md.: Barnes & Noble, 1992);

Jonathan L. Fairbanks and Elizabeth Bidwell Bates, *American Furniture: 1620 to the Present* (New York: Marek, 1981);

Madeleine Ginsburg, *Victorian Dress in Photographs* (New York: Holmes & Meier, 1982);

William Dudley Hunt Jr., *Encyclopedia of American Architecture* (New York: McGraw-Hill, 1980);

Edgar R. Jones, *Those Were the Good Old Days: A Happy Look at American Advertising, 1880–1930* (New York: Simon & Schuster, 1989);

Sandra Ley, *Fashion for Everyone: The Story of Ready-to-Wear, 1870–1970* (New York: Scribners, 1975);

Valerie Lloyd, *McDowell's Directory of Twentieth Century Fashion* (Englewood Cliffs, N.J.: Prentice-Hall, 1985);

Diane Maddex, ed., *Master Builders: A Guide to Famous American Architects* (Washington, D.C.: Preservation Press, 1985);

Virginia McAlester and Lee McAlester, *A Field Guide to American Houses* (New York: Knopf, 1992);

Caroline Rennolds Milbank, *New York Fashion: The Evolution of American Style* (New York: Thames & Hudson, 1989);

Mary Jane Pool, ed., *20th-Century Decorating, Architecture & Gardens: 80 Years of Ideas & Pleasure from House & Garden* (New York: Holt, Rinehart & Winston, 1980);

Meyric R. Rogers, *American Interior Design: The Traditions and Development of Domestic Design from Colonial Times to the Present* (New York: Norton, 1947);

Leland M. Roth, *A Concise History of American Architecture* (New York: Icon Editions/Harper & Row, 1979);

Mary Shaw Ryan, *Clothing: A Study in Human Behavior* (New York: Holt, Rinehart & Winston, 1966);

O. E. Schoeffler and William Gale, *Esquire's Encyclopedia of 20th Century Men's Fashion* (New York: McGraw-Hill, 1973);

Marion Sichel, *History of Men's Costume* (London: Batsford, 1984);

C. Ray Smith, *Interior Design in 20th Century America: A History* (New York: Harper & Row, 1986);

Donald Stowell and Erin Wertenberger, *A Century of Fashion 1865–1965* (Chicago: Encyclopaedia Britannica, 1987);

Jane Trahey, *The Mode in Costume* (New York: Scribners, 1958);

Trahey, ed., *Harper's Bazaar: One Hundred Years of the American Female* (New York: Random House, 1967);

Robert Twombly, *Frank Lloyd Wright: His Life and His Architecture* (New York: Wiley, 1978);

Anne V. Tyrrell, *Changing Trends in Fashion: Patterns of the Twentieth Century 1900–1970* (London: Batsford, 1986);

Marcus Whiffen and Frederick Koeper, *American Architecture, 1607–1976* (Cambridge: MIT Press, 1981).

GOVERNMENT AND POLITICS

Edward L. Ayers, *The Promise of the New South: Life After Reconstruction* (New York: Oxford University Press, 1992);

Richard C. Bain and Judith H. Parris, *Convention Decisions and Voting Records*, second edition (Washington, D.C.: Brookings Institution, 1973);

Robert W. Cherny, *A Righteous Cause: The Life of William Jennings Bryan* (Boston: Little, Brown, 1985);

Paolo E. Coletta, *The Presidency of William Howard Taft* (Lawrence: University Press of Kansas, 1973);

Congressional Quarterly's Guide to U.S. Elections, second edition (Washington, D.C.: Congressional Quarterly, 1985);

Lewis L. Gould, *The Presidency of Theodore Roosevelt* (Lawrence: University Press of Kansas, 1991);

William Henry Harbaugh, *Power and Responsibility: The Life and Times of Theodore Roosevelt* (New York: Farrar, Straus & Cudahy, 1961);

Louis R. Harlan, *Booker T. Washington: The Making of a Black Leader, 1856–1901* (New York: Oxford University Press, 1972);

Harlan, *Booker T. Washington: The Wizard of Tuskegee, 1901–1915* (New York & Oxford: Oxford University Press, 1983);

William Keylor, *The Twentieth-Century World: An International History* (New York: Oxford University Press, 1984);

Lawrence W. Levine, *Defender of the Faith* (Cambridge, Mass.: Harvard University Press, 1965);

Arthur M. Schlesinger Jr., ed., *History of American Presidential Elections 1789–1968*, 3 volumes (New York: Chelsea House/McGraw-Hill, 1971);

Schlesinger ed., *History of U.S. Political Parties* (New York: Chelsea House, 1973);

Andrew Sinclair, *Era of Excess: A Social History of the Prohibition Movement* (New York: Harper & Row, 1962);

David P. Thelen, *Robert M. La Follette and the Insurgent Spirit* (Boston: Little, Brown, 1976);

Booker T. Washington, *Up from Slavery: An Autobiography* (New York: Doubleday, Page, 1901).

LAW AND JUSTICE

Henry J. Abraham, *Justices and Presidents: A Political History of Appointments to the Supreme Court* (New York: Oxford University Press, 1985);

Liva Baker, *The Justice from Beacon Hill: the Life and Times of Oliver Wendell Holmes, Jr.* (New York: HarperCollins, 1991);

Ruth Bordin, *Frances Willard: A Biography* (Chapel Hill: University of North Carolina Press, 1986);

Bordin, *Women and Temperance: The Quest for Power and Liberty, 1873–1900* (Chapel Hill: University of North Carolina Press, 1981);

Clare Cushman, ed., *The Supreme Court Justices: Illustrated Biographies, 1789–1993* (Washington, D.C.: Congressional Quarterly, 1993);

Philip S. Foner, *History of the Labor Movement in the United States, volume 4: The Industrial Workers of the World, 1905–1917* (New York: International Publishers, 1965);

Foner, *The Spanish-Cuban-American War and the Birth of American Imperialism, volume 2: 1898–1902* (New York: Monthly Review Press, 1972);

Steven R. Fox, *Blood and Power: Organized Crime in the Twentieth Century* (New York: Morrow, 1989);

Fox, *The Guardian of Boston: William Monroe Trotter* (New York: Atheneum, 1970);

John Hope Franklin and Alfred A. Moss Jr., *From Slavery to Freedom: A History of African Americans* (New York: McGraw-Hill, 1994);

George Fredrickson, *The Black Image in the White Mind: The Debate on Afro-American Character and Destiny, 1817–1914* (Middletown, Conn.: Wesleyan University Press, 1971);

Laurence M. Friedman, *A History of American Law* (New York: Simon & Schuster, 1985);

J. C. Furnas, *The Life and Times of the Late Demon Rum* (New York: Putnam, 1965);

John A. Garraty, ed., *Quarrels That Have Shaped the Constitution* (New York: Harper & Row, 1962);

Gerald Gunther, *Learned Hand: The Man and the Judge* (New York: Knopf, 1994);

Samuel Hendel, *Charles Evans Hughes and the Supreme Court* (New York: King's Crown, 1951);

John Higham, *Strangers in the Land: Patterns of American Nativism* (New Brunswick: Rutgers University Press, 1955);

Morton J. Horwitz, *The Transformation of American Law, 1870–1960: The Crisis of Legal Orthodoxy* (Cambridge, Mass.: Harvard University Press, 1992);

Alfred H. Kelly, Winifred Harbison, and Herman Belz, *The American Constitution: Its Origins and Development*, sixth edition (New York: Norton, 1983);

Paul Kens, *Judicial Power and Reform Politics: The Anatomy of Lochner vs. New York* (Lawrence: University Press of Kansas, 1990);

Richard Kluger, *Simple Justice: The History of Brown v. Board of Education and Black America's Struggle for Equality* (New York: Knopf, 1975);

Gerald Langford, *The Murder of Stanford White* (Indianapolis: Bobbs-Merrill, 1962);

Charles Larsen, *The Good Fight: The Life and Times of Ben B. Lindsey* (Chicago: Quadrangle, 1972);

Max Lerner, ed., *The Mind and Faith of Justice Holmes* (Boston: Little, Brown, 1943);

John Charles Livingston, *Clarence Darrow for the Defense* (New York: Garland, 1988);

Walter Lord, *The Good Years: From 1900 to the First World War* (New York: Harper, 1960);

Alpheus T. Mason, *Brandeis: A Free Man's Life* (New York: Viking, 1946);

Richard O'Connor, *Courtroom Warrior: The Combative Career of William Travers Jerome* (Boston: Little, Brown, 1963);

Nell Irvin Painter, *Standing at Armageddon: The United States 1877–1919* (New York: Norton, 1987);

Ruth Rosen, *Lost Sisterhood: Prostitution in America, 1900–1918* (Baltimore: Johns Hopkins University Press, 1982);

David J. Rothman, *Conscience and Convenience: The Asylum and its Alternatives in Progressive America* (Boston: Little, Brown, 1980);

Jacqueline Jones Royster, *The Anti-Lynching Campaign of Ida B. Wells, 1892–1900* (New York: St. Martin's Press, 1996);

Irving Stone, *Clarence Darrow for the Defense* (Garden City, N.Y.: Doubleday, Doran, 1941);

Kevin Tierney, *Darrow: A Biography* (New York: Crowell, 1979).

LIFESTYLES AND SOCIAL TRENDS

Mimi Abramovitz, *Regulating the Lives of Women* (Boston: South End Press, 1988);

Burton Benedict, *The Anthropology of World's Fairs* (Berkeley: University of California Press, 1983);

Paul Boyer, *Urban Masses and Moral Order in America, 1820–1920* (Cambridge, Mass.: Harvard University Press, 1978);

David Brody, *Workers in Industrial America: Essays on the Twentieth-Century Struggle* (New York: Oxford University Press, 1980);

John Whiteclay Chambers II, *The Tyranny of Change: America in the Progressive Era, 1890–1920* (New York: St. Martin's Press, 1980);

Norman H. Clark, *Deliver Us From Evil: An Interpretation of American Prohibition* (New York: Norton, 1976);

Allen F. Davis, *American Heroine: The Life and Legend of Jane Addams* (New York: Oxford University Press, 1973);

Davis, *Spearheads for Reform: The Social Settlements and the Progressive Movement, 1890–1914* (New York: Oxford University Press, 1967);

Melvin Dubofsky, *Industrialism and the American Worker, 1865–1920* (Arlington Heights, Ill.: Harlan Davidson, 1985);

Robert Fishman, *Bourgeois Utopias: The Rise and Fall of Suburbia* (New York: Basic Books, 1987);

Eleanor Flexner, *Century of Struggle: The Woman's Rights Movement in the United States* (Cambridge, Mass.: Harvard University Press, 1959);

Stephen R. Fox, *The American Conservation Movement: John Muir and His Legacy* (Madison: University of Wisconsin Press, 1981);

John Hope Franklin and Alfred A. Moss Jr., *From Slavery to Freedom: A History of African Americans* (New York: McGraw-Hill, 1994);

Franklin Starr and Isidore Starr, *The Negro in Twentieth Century America* (New York: Random House, 1967);

Joshua Freeman and others, *Who Built America? Working People and the Nation's Economy, Politics, Culture, and Society* (New York: Pantheon, 1992);

J. C. Furnas, *Great Times: An Informal Social History of the United States* (New York: Putnam, 1974);

James R. Green, *The World of the Worker: Labor in Twentieth-Century America* (New York: Hill & Wang, 1980);

Samuel P. Hays, *Conservation and the Gospel of Efficiency* (Cambridge, Mass.: Harvard University Press, 1959);

John Higham, *Strangers in the Land: Patterns of American Nativism, 1860–1925* (New York: Atheneum, 1955);

Kenneth Jackson, *Crabgrass Frontier: The Suburbanization of the United States* (New York: Oxford University Press, 1985);

Jacqueline Jones, *Labor of Love, Labor of Sorrow: Black Women, Work and the Family from Slavery to the Present* (New York: Basic Books, 1985);

John F. Kasson, *Amusing the Millions: Coney Island at the Turn of the Century* (New York: Hill & Wang, 1978);

Alice Kessler-Harris, *Out to Work: A History of Wage-Earning Women in the United States* (New York: Oxford University Press, 1982);

Alan Kraut, *The Huddled Masses: The Immigrant in American Society, 1880–1921* (Arlington Heights, Ill.: Harlan Davidson, 1982);

Ann J. Lane, *To Herland and Beyond: The Life and Work of Charlotte Perkins Gilman* (New York: Pantheon, 1990);

William Leach, *Land of Desire: Merchants, Power, and the Rise of a New American Culture* (New York: Random House, 1993);

Mark Edward Lender and James Kirby Martin, *Drinking in America* (New York: Free Press, 1987);

Peter J. Ling, *America and the Automobile: Technology, Reform and Social Change* (Manchester, U.K.: Manchester University Press, 1990);

Arthur S. Link and Richard L. McCormick, *Progressivism* (Arlington Heights, Ill.: Harlan Davidson, 1983);

Steven Mintz and Susan Kellogg, *Domestic Revolutions: A Social History of American Family Life* (New York: Free Press, 1988);

David Montgomery, *The Fall of the House of Labor* (New York: Cambridge University Press, 1987);

Roderick Nash, *Wilderness and the American Mind* (New Haven: Yale University Press, 1967);

Rosalind Rosenberg, *Divided Lives: American Women in the Twentieth Century* (New York: Hill & Wang, 1992);

Robert W. Rydell, *World of Fairs: The Century-of-Progress Expositions* (Chicago: University of Chicago Press, 1993);

Paul Sann, *Fads, Follies and Delusions of the American People* (New York: Bonanza Books, 1968);

Virginia Scharff, *Taking the Wheel: Women and the Coming of the Motor Age* (New York: Free Press, 1991);

Gary Scharnhorst, *Charlotte Perkins Gilman* (Boston: Twayne, 1985);

Mel Scott, *American City Planning Since 1890* (Berkeley: University of California Press, 1969);

Kathryn Kish Sklar, *Florence Kelley and Women's Political Culture: Doing the Nation's Work, 1820–1940* (New Haven: Yale University Press, 1992);

Susan Strasser, *Never Done: A History of American Housework* (New York: Pantheon, 1982);

James Thorpe, *Henry Edwards Huntington: A Biography* (Berkeley: University of California Press, 1994);

Robert H. Wiebe, *The Search for Order, 1877–1920* (New York: Hill & Wang, 1967);

C. Vann Woodward, *The Strange Career of Jim Crow*, third revised edition (New York: Oxford University Press, 1974).

MEDIA

Stephen Becker, *Comic Art in America* (New York: Simon & Schuster, 1959);

Meyer Berger, *The Story of the New York Times: 1851–1951* (New York: Simon & Schuster, 1951);

Kathleen Brady, *Ida Tarbell: Portrait of a Muckraker* (New York: Putnam, 1984);

David Mark Chalmers, *The Muckrake Years* (New York: Van Nostrand, 1974);

Susan J. Douglas, *Inventing American Broadcasting, 1899–1922* (Baltimore: Johns Hopkins University Press, 1987);

Roy S. Durstine, *This Advertising Business* (New York: Scribners, 1928);

Peter Dzwonkoski, ed., *American Literary Publishing Houses, 1900–1980: Trade and Paperback; Dictionary of Literary Biography*, volume 46 (Detroit: Bruccoli Clark/Gale Research, 1986);

Edwin Emery and Michael Emery, *The Press and America: An Interpretive History of the Mass Media*, fourth edition (Englewood Cliffs, N.J.: Prentice-Hall, 1978);

Louis Filler, *The Muckrakers* (University Park: Pennsylvania State University Press, 1976);

Ellen Fitzpatrick, *Muckraking: Three Landmark Articles* (New York: Bedford Books/St. Martin's Press, 1994);

Roland Gelatt, *The Fabulous Phonograph: From Edison to Stereo* (New York: Appleton-Century, 1966);

Sally Foreman Griffith, *Hometown News: William Allen White and the Emporia Gazette* (New York: Oxford University Press, 1989);

Justin Kaplan, *Lincoln Steffens, A Biography* (New York: Simon & Schuster, 1974);

Sidney Kobre, *Development of American Journalism* (Dubuque, Iowa: Braun, 1969);

Richard Marschall, *America's Great Comic Strip Artists* (New York: Abbeville Press, 1989);

Sally M. Miller, ed., *The Ethnic Press in the United States: A Historical Analysis and Handbook* (Westport, Conn.: Greenwood Press, 1987);

Michael Macdonald Mooney, *Evelyn Nesbit and Stanford White: Love in the Gilded Age* (New York: Morrow, 1976);

Frank Luther Mott, *American Journalism: A History, 1690–1960*, third edition (New York: Macmillan, 1962);

Theodore Peterson, *Magazines in the Twentieth Century* (Urbana: University of Illinois Press, 1956);

Jerry Robinson, *The Comics: An Illustrated History of Comic Strip Art* (New York: Putnam, 1974);

Madelon Golden Schlipp and Sharon M. Murphy, *Great Women of the Press* (Carbondale: Southern Illinois University Press, 1983);

Michael Schudson, *Discovering the News: A Social History of American Newspapers* (New York: Basic Books, 1978);

Gilbert Seldes, *Lords of the Press* (New York: Messner, 1938);

W. A. Swanberg, *Citizen Hearst* (New York: Scribners, 1961);

John Tebbel, *Between Covers: The Rise and Transformation of Book Publishing in America* (New York: Oxford University Press, 1987);

Tebbel, *The Compact History of the American Newspaper* (New York: Hawthorn Books, 1963);

Tebbel, *A History of Book Publishing in the United States*, volume 2: *The Expansion of an Industry, 1865–1919* (New York & London: R. R. Bowker, 1975).

MEDICINE AND HEALTH

Ruth J. Abram, ed., *Send Us a Lady Physician: Women Doctors in America, 1835–1920* (New York: Norton, 1985);

Barbara Bates, *Bargaining for Life: A Social History of Tuberculosis, 1876–1938* (Philadelphia: University of Pennsylvania Press, 1992);

William Bennett Bean, *Walter Reed: A Biography* (Charlottesville: University Press of Virginia, 1982);

James Bordley and A. McGehee Harvey, *Two Centuries of American Medicine, 1776–1976* (Philadelphia: Saunders, 1976);

Allan M. Brandt, *No Magic Bullet: A Social History of Venereal Disease in the United States Since 1880* (New York: Oxford University Press, 1985);

James G. Burrow, *AMA: Voice of American Medicine* (Baltimore: Johns Hopkins University Press, 1963);

James H. Cassedy, *Medicine in America: A Short History* (Baltimore: Johns Hopkins University Press, 1991);

John Duffy, *The Healers: The Rise of the Medical Establishment* (New York: McGraw-Hill, 1976); republished as *The Healers: A History of American Medicine* (Urbana: University of Illinois Press, 1979);

E. W. Etheridge, *The Butterfly Caste: A Social History of Pellagra in the South* (Westport, Conn.: Greenwood Press, 1972);

John Ettling, *The Germ of Laziness: Rockefeller Philanthropy and Public Health in the New South* (Cambridge, Mass.: Harvard University Press, 1981);

Morris Fishbein, *A History of the American Medical Association, 1847–1947* (Philadelphia: Saunders, 1947);

Abraham Flexner, *Medical Education in the United States and Canada: A Report to the Carnegie Foundation for the Advancement of Teaching* (New York: Carnegie Foundation, 1910);

John M. Gibson, *Physician to the World: The Life of General William C. Gorgas* (Tuscaloosa: University of Alabama Press, 1989);

Susan E. Lederer, *Subjected to Science: Human Experimentation in America before the Second World War* (Baltimore: Johns Hopkins University Press, 1995);

John Parascandola, *The Development of American Pharmacology: John J. Abel and the Shaping of a Discipline* (Baltimore: Johns Hopkins University Press, 1992);

D. A. Roe, *A Plague of Corn: The Social History of Pellagra* (Ithaca: Cornell University Press, 1973);

Michael E. Teller, *The Tuberculosis Movement: A Public Health Campaign in the Progressive Era* (Westport, Conn.: Greenwood Press, 1988);

Steven Charles Wheatleys, *The Politics of Philanthropy: Abraham Flexner and Medical Education* (Madison: University of Wisconsin Press, 1988).

RELIGION

Aaron I. Abell, *American Catholicism and Social Action: A Search for Social Justice, 1865–1950* (Garden City, N.Y.: Hanover House, 1960);

Sydney E. Ahlstrom, *A Religious History of the American People* (New Haven: Yale University Press, 1972);

Catherine L. Albanese, *America: Religions and Religion*, second edition (Belmont, Cal.: Wadsworth, 1992);

Gay Wilson Allen, *William James: A Biography* (New York: Viking, 1967);

Robert Mapes Anderson, *Vision of the Disinherited: The Making of American Pentecostalism* (Peabody, Mass.: Hendrickson, 1979);

Norman Bentwich, *Solomon Schechter: A Biography* (Cambridge: Cambridge University Press, 1938);

Jay P. Dolan, *The American Catholic Experience* (Garden City, N.Y.: Doubleday, 1985);

Jacob H. Dorn, *Washington Gladden: Prophet of the Social Gospel* (Columbus: Ohio State University Press, 1967);

Edwin Scott Gaustad, *A Religious History of America*, revised edition (San Francisco: HarperCollins, 1990);

C. Carlyle Haaland, "Shinto and Indigenous Chinese Religion," in *Encyclopedia of the American Religious Experience*, edited by Charles H. Lippy and Peter Williams (New York: Scribners, 1988);

William R. Hutchinson, *The Modernist Impulse in American Protestantism* (Cambridge, Mass.: Harvard University Press, 1976);

Jehovah's Witnesses: Proclaimers of God's Kingdom (Brooklyn: Watch Tower Bible & Tract Society of New York, 1993);

George M. Marsden, *Fundamentalism and American Culture: The Shaping of Twentieth Century Evangelicalism, 1870–1925* (New York: Oxford University Press, 1980);

Martin E. Marty, *Modern American Religion, Volume 1: The Irony of It All, 1893–1919* (Chicago: University of Chicago Press, 1986);

J. Gordon Melton, ed., *Religious Leaders of America* (Detroit: Gale Research, 1991);

William R. Miller, ed., *Contemporary American Protestant Thought, 1900–1970* (Indianapolis: Bobbs-Merrill, 1973);

Rene Noorbergen, *Ellen G. White: Prophet of Destiny* (New Canaan, Conn.: Keats, 1972);

Marvin O'Connell, *John Ireland and the American Catholic Church* (Saint Paul: Minnesota Historical Society Press, 1988);

M. James Penton, *Apocalypse Delayed: The Story of Jehovah's Witnesses* (Toronto: University of Toronto Press, 1985);

Charles S. Prebish, "Buddhism," in *Encyclopedia of the American Religious Experience*, edited by Charles H. Lippy and Peter Williams (New York: Scribners, 1988);

Ernest Sandeen, *The Roots of Fundamentalism: British and American Millenarianism, 1800–1930* (Chicago: University of Chicago Press, 1970);

Robert David Thomas, *"With Bleeding Footsteps": Mary Baker Eddy's Path to Religious Leadership* (New York: Knopf, 1994);

Timothy P. Weber, *Living in the Shadow of the Second Coming: American Premillennialism, 1875–1982* (Grand Rapids, Mich.: Academie Books, 1983);

P. W. Wilson, *General Evangeline Booth of the Salvation Army* (New York: Scribners, 1948).

SCIENCE AND TECHNOLOGY

Gleason L. Archer, *History of Radio to 1926* (New York: American Historical Society, 1938);

Saul Benison, A. Clifford Barger, and Elin L. Wolfe, *Walter B. Cannon: The Life and Times of a Young Scientist* (Cambridge, Mass.: Harvard University Press, 1987);

Roger E. Bilstein, *Flight in America: From the Wrights to the Astronauts* (Baltimore: Johns Hopkins University Press, 1984);

Peter J. Bowler, *The Mendelian Revolution* (Baltimore: Johns Hopkins University Press, 1989);

Frank Donovan, *Wheels for a Nation* (New York: Crowell, 1965);

Peter Dreyer, *A Gardener Touched with Genius: The Life of Luther Burbank* (Berkeley: University of California Press, 1985);

James J. Flink, *America Adopts the Automobile, 1895–1910* (Cambridge: MIT Press, 1970);

Henry Ford, *My Life and Work* (Garden City, N.Y.: Doubleday, 1922);

Robert Freidel and Paul Israel, *Edison's Electric Light: Biography of an Invention* (New Brunswick, N.J.: Rutgers University Press, 1987);

Thomas F. Glick, ed., *The Comparative Reception of Relativity* (Dordrecht, Netherlands: D. Reidel, 1987);

Nathan G. Hale Jr., *Freud and the Americans: The Beginnings of Psychoanalysis in the United States, 1876–1917* (New York: Oxford University Press, 1971);

J. Gordon Hayes, *Robert Edwin Peary: A Record of his Explorations, 1886–1909* (London: Grant Richards, 1929);

William Herbert Hobbs, *Peary* (New York: Macmillan, 1936);

Fred Howard, *Wilbur and Orville: A Biography of the Wright Brothers* (New York: Knopf, 1987);

Matthew Josephson, *Edison: A Biography* (New York: McGraw-Hill, 1959);

Rebecca R. Joslin, *Chasing Eclipses: The Total Solar Eclipses of 1905, 1914, 1925* (Boston: Walton, 1925);

Ronald R. Kline, *Steinmetz: Engineer and Socialist* (Baltimore: Johns Hopkins University Press, 1992);

Robert E. Kohler, *Lords of the Fly: Drosophila Genetics and the Experimental Life* (Chicago: University of Chicago Press, 1994);

Kohler, *Partners in Science: Foundations and Natural Scientists, 1900–1945* (Chicago: University of Chicago, 1991);

Robert Lacey, *Ford: The Men and the Machine* (Boston: Little, Brown, 1986);

André Milliard, *Edison and the Business of Invention* (Baltimore: Johns Hopkins University Press, 1990);

Samuel Alfred Mitchell, *Eclipses of the Sun* (New York: Columbia University Press, 1923);

T. H. Morgan, *The Genetics of Drosophila* (The Hague: M. Nijhoff, 1925);

Richard Knowles Morris, *John P. Holland, Inventor of the Modern Submarine* (Annapolis, Md.: United States Naval Institute, 1966);

Philip L. Pauly, *Controlling Life: Jacques Loeb and the Engineering Idea in Biology* (Berkeley: University of California Press, 1990);

Nathan Reingold and Ida H. Reingold, *Science in America* (Chicago: University of Chicago Press, 1981);

Dorothy Ross, *G. Stanley Hall: The Psychologist as Prophet* (Chicago: University of Chicago Press, 1972);

Loyd S. Swenson Jr., *The Ethereal Aether: A History of the Michelson-Morley-Miller Aether-Drift Experiments, 1880–1930* (Austin: University of Texas Press, 1972);

Wynn Wachhorst, *Thomas Alva Edison: An American Myth* (Cambridge: MIT Press, 1981);

Robert Wohl, *A Passion for Wings: Aviation and the Western Imagination, 1908–1918* (New Haven: Yale University Press, 1994);

Helen Wright, *Explorer of the Universe: A Biography of George Ellery Hale*, second edition (Woodbury, N.Y.: American Institute of Physics, 1994).

SPORTS

Arthur R. Ashe Jr., *A Hard Road to Glory: A History of the African American Athlete, 1618–1918* (New York: Amistead Press, 1993);

E. Digby Baltzell, *Sporting Gentlemen: Men's Tennis from the Age of Honor to the Cult of the Superstar* (New York: Free Press, 1995);

Allison Danzig, *The History of American Football: Its Great Teams, Players, and Coaches* (Englewood Cliffs, N.J.: Prentice-Hall, 1956);

Danzig and Peter Schwed, eds., *The Fireside Book of Tennis* (New York: Simon & Schuster, 1972);

Len Elliot and Barbara Kelley, *Who's Who in Golf* (New York, 1976);

John Findling and Kim Pelle, eds., *The Historical Dictionary of the Olympic Games* (Westport, Conn.: Greenwood Press, 1996);

Nat Fleischer and Sam Andre, *A Pictorial History of Boxing*, revised edition (New York: Carol, 1993);

Al-Tony Gimore, *Bad Nigger! The National Impact of Jack Johnson* (Port Washington, N.Y.: Kennikat Press, 1975);

Ross Goodner, *Golf's Greatest: The Legendary Hall of Famers* (Norwalk, Conn., 1978);

Elliot J. Gorn, *The Manly Art: Bare-Knuckle Prize Fighting in America* (Ithaca, N.Y.: Cornell University Press, 1986);

Will Grimsley, *Golf: Its History, People and Events* (Englewood Cliffs, N.J.: Prentice-Hall, 1966);

Grimsley, *Tennis: Its History, People and Events* (Englewood Cliffs, N.J.: Prentice-Hall, 1971);

Allen Guttmann, *The Olympics: A History of the Modern Games* (Urbana & Chicago: University of Illinois Press, 1992);

Neil D. Issacs, *All the Moves: A History of College Basketball* (New York: Harper & Row, 1984);

Bill James, *The Bill James Historical Baseball Abstract* (New York: Villard, 1988);

Ivan Kaye, *Good Clean Violence: A History of College Football* (Philadelphia: Lippincott, 1973);

David Martin and Roger Gynn, *The Marathon Footrace: Performers and Performances* (Springfield, Ill.: Thomas, 1979);

François Oppenheim, *The History of Swimming* (North Hollywood, Cal., 1970);

Robert W. Petersen, *Only the Ball Was White* (Englewood Cliffs, N.J.: Prentice-Hall, 1970);

Harford Powell Jr., *Walter Camp: The Father of American Football* (Freeport, N.Y.: Books for Libraries Press, 1970);

Roberto Quercetani, *A World History of Track and Field Athletics* (New York: Oxford University Press, 1964);

Benjamin G. Rader, *American Sports: From the Age of Folk Games to the Age of Spectators* (Englewood Cliffs, N.J.: Prentice-Hall, 1983);

Rader, *Baseball: A History of America's Game* (Urbana & Chicago: University of Illinois Press, 1992);

Randy Roberts, *Papa Jack: Jack Johnson and the Era of White Hopes* (New York: Free Press, 1983);

John M. Ross, ed., *Golf Magazine's Encyclopedia of Golf* (New York: Harper & Row, 1979);

John Rousmaniere, *America's Cup Book, 1851–1983* (New York: Norton, 1983);

Jeffrey T. Sammons, *Beyond the Ring: The Role of Boxing in American Society* (Urbana & Chicago: University of Illinois Press, 1988);

Ronald A. Smith, *Sports and Freedom: The Rise of Big Time College Athletics* (New York & Oxford: Oxford University Press, 1988);

David Quentin Voigt, *American Baseball: From the Gentleman's Sport to the Commissioner System* (University Park & London: Pennsylvania State University Press, 1992);

David Wallechinsky, *The Complete Book of the Olympics* (New York: Penguin, 1988);

A. B. C. Whipple, *The Racing Yachts* (Alexandria, Va.: Time-Life Books, 1978);

Herbert Warren Wind, *The Story of American Golf: Its Champions and its Championships* (New York: Knopf, 1975).

CONTRIBUTORS

ARTS	JANE GERHARD *Brown Uiversity* CYNTHIA MCCOWN *Beloit College*
BUSINESS AND THE ECONOMY	LISA MCNARY *Capital University* STEVE MELLUM *Capital University*
EDUCATION	KEITH WHITESCARVER *Ohio University*
FASHION	JANE GERHARD *Brown University*
GOVERNMENT AND POLITICS	JAMES G. LEWIS *Florida State University*
LAW AND JUSTICE	ROBERT J. ALLISON *Suffolk University*
LIFESTYLES AND SOCIAL TRENDS	ALANA J. ERICKSON *Columbia University* DAVID MCLEAN *Santa Barbara, California* JAMES G. LEWIS *Florida State University*
MEDIA	NANCY BERNHARD *Somerville, Massachussetts*
MEDICINE AND HEALTH	A. J. WRIGHT *University of Alabama at Birmingham*
RELIGION	DAVID MCLEAN *Santa Barbara, California* MONICA SIEMS *University of California, Santa Barbara*
SCIENCE AND TECHNOLOGY	THOMAS GLICK *Boston University*
SPORTS	ADAM HORNBUCKLE *Alexandria, Virginia*

INDEX OF PHOTOGRAPHS

GENERAL INDEX

Alessandro, Antionetta Pisanelli 54
Alexander, Charles 340
"Alexander, Don't You Love Your Baby No More?" 24
Alexander's Magazine 340
Alexanderson, Ernst F. W. 340, 465, 479
Alexandra, Queen of Greece 518
Alger, Horatio 35, 472
Alger, Russell A. 250
Allegheny Athletic Association 508
Allegheny College 364
Allen, Gracie 53
Allen, Timothy Field 481
Allen University 165
Allison, William Boyd 224, 250, 293
All's Well That Ends Well (movie) 28
Alphonse and Gaston series 20
An Alpine Echo 31
Altgeld, John Peter 265, 293
Amalgamated Association of Street Railway Employees 88
Amateur Golf Association (AGA) 509
The Ambassadors (James) 22, 49
America 494
America Is Worth Saving 65
The American (James) 49
American Academy of Mechanical Engineers 104
American Amateur Athletic Union (AAU) 490, 501–503, 515–516, 521–522, 525–526
American & Continental Tobacco 258
American Anti-Boycott Association 89
American Anti-Saloon League (ASL) 318
American Antivivisection Society 453
American Association (baseball) 496, 499, 529
American Association for Cancer Research 375
American Association of Universities 154
American Automobile Association (AAA) 169
American Baptist Home Missionary Society 157
American Bar Association 260–261, 288, 290, 294
American Baseball League 525
American Bell Telephone Company 88

American Bowling Congress 486
American Breeders' Association 459, 470
American Breeders' Magazine 460
American Can Company 88
American Cereal Company 119
American Civic Federation 431
American Civil War 55, 58, 63, 70, 98, 101, 118, 139, 147, 157, 163, 218, 225, 244, 250, 263, 266, 279, 294–295, 306, 311, 327, 331, 345, 361–362, 368–369, 377, 380, 382, 384, 391–392, 397–398, 408, 410–411, 424, 429, 451, 459, 481, 496, 509
American Cyanamid Company 88
American Economic Association 332
American Fabian 326
American Federation of Arts 126
American Federation of Catholic Societies 402
American Federation of Labor (AFL) 80, 88, 97, 104, 106, 116, 123, 226, 237, 239, 261, 287, 315, 321
American Federation of Musicians 20
American Genetic Association 460
American Golfer 510
American Historical Association 290, 334
American Home Economics Association 125
American Humane Society 384
The American Idea (Cohan) 31
American Impressionism 29, 36–39, 74, 77
American Industries 83
American Institute of Architects 188, 190
American Institute of Electrical Engineers 477
American Journal of Mathematics 477
American Journal of Psychology 475
American Labor Party 325
American Labor Union 106
American Ladies Tailors Association 172
American League (baseball) 486–492, 496–499, 501, 503, 525, 527–529
American Lung Association 390
American Magazine 340, 364
American Medical Association (AMA) 98, 353, 372, 374, 376–380, 384–385, 394, 397, 399, 453

— Bureau of Investigation 395
— Committee on Medical Legislation 380
— Council on Medical Education 380
— Council on Pharmacy and Chemistry 380
— Council on the Defense of Medical Research 376, 384
— Special Committee on Reorganization 379
American Medicine 395
American Musician and Art Journal 69
American Olympic Committee 513
American Power Boat Association 487
American Psychological Association 475
American Railway Union (ARU) 109, 264
American Red Cross 304
American Revolution 106, 240, 380, 468, 509
American School Hygiene Association 124
American Social Hygiene Committee 155
American Society for Clinical Investigation 375
American Society for Pharmacology and Experimental Therapeutics 392
American Society for the Prevention of Cruelty to Animals 384, 453
American Society of Anesthesiologists 374
American Society of Biological Chemists 374, 392
American Society of Mechanical Engineers 143
American Society of Newspaper Editors 366
American Soldier in Love and War 22
American Steel Foundries 115
American Sugar Refining Company 118
American Telephone and Telegraph Company 471
American Tobacco Company 215, 258
An American Tragedy (Dreiser) 65, 84, 90
American Unitarian Association 440
American Weekly 362
Americanism 413, 431

Avenging a Crime, or, Burned at the Stake 24

Aviation 61, 82, 85–86, 88, 90, 111, 303–304, 306, 446–448, 450–452, 468, 478–479, 482

The Awakening (Chopin) 76

An Awful Skate 28

Aycock, Charles B. 153

Ayer, Harriet Hubbard 334

Ayres, Leonard P. 149

Azora (Paine) 23

Azusa Street Apostolic Faith Mission, Los Angeles 406, 436–437

B

B. W. Huebsch (publishing house) 339

Babb, Cook and Willard (architectural firm) 168

Babcock, Dr. James 376, 386

Babes In Toyland (Herbert) 23, 46

Babette (Scheff) 75

Babies' Milk Fund Association 374

Bacon, Charles 517

Bacon, Robert 112

"The Bad Man" — A Tale of the West" 28

Baden-Powell, Sir Robert 125

Baekeland, Leo Hendrik 304, 479

Baer, George F. 91–92

Bagley, William C. 124, 162

Bailey, James Anthony 76, 118

Bailey, Liberty Hyde 459

Bailly, Leon 189

Bakelite plastic 304

Baker, Abigail 428

Baker, Albert 428

Baker, George Pierce 23, 46, 124, 162

Baker, Harvey Humphrey 290

Baker, Mark 428

Baker, Ray Stannard 223, 276, 315, 339–341, 343, 359, 363–364, 366

Baker, Dr. Sara Josephine 375, 395

Baker Car Company 183

Baldwin, Simeon E. 290

Balin, Charles D. 117

Ball, Ernest R. 25, 27, 63

Ballinger, Richard 206, 243

Ballinger-Pinchot Affair of 1909–1910 206, 243

Baltimore Evening Times 338

Baltimore Orioles 486

Bancroft, Dr. Frederick Jones 397

Bandanaland (Cook, Dunbar, Williams, and Walker) 46

Bandini bungalow, Pasadena 169

The Bandit King 28

Bangs, Frank C. 334

"A Banjo Song" (Dunbar) 66

The Bank 26

Bank of England 94, 112

Bankers Trust 93

Baptist Social Union 282

Baptist Temple, Philadelphia 402

Bar Association of New York 294

Barber, George F. 182

The Barber of Sevilla (movie) 24

Barbour, Nelson H. 434

Bardeen, C. W. 125

Bargain Fiend; or, Shopping A La Mode 28

Bargar-Wallach, Mrs. Maud 528

Barker, Dr. L. F. 388

Barker, Wharton 196

Barnard, Henry 164

Barnard, Kate 290

Barnes, Justus D. 22

Barnett, Ferdinand Lee 365

Barney, Charles T. 93

Barnum and Bailey Circus 22, 76, 118

Barnum's Trunk 24

Barrett, Samuel A. 144

Barrie, J. M. 43, 74

The Barrier (Beach) 29

Barrill, Edward N. 355

Barron, Charles Walker 366

Barrymore, Ethel 20, 47, 74, 76, 273

Barrymore, Georgianna Drew 47

Barrymore, John 47, 74, 76

Barrymore, Lionel 47, 76

Barrymore, Maurice 47, 76

Barsotti, Charles 350

Bartholdi, Frédéric-Auguste 25, 76

Bartholow, Dr. Roberts 397

Baseball Hall of Fame 524

Basilica of Saint Mary, Minneapolis 432

Basis: A Journal of Citizenship 369

Bassett, Ebenezer Don Carlos 164

Bate, William B. 250

Bateham, Josephine Abiah Penfield Cushman 334, 440

Bates, Blanche 47, 74

Battle Creek College (later Andrews University) 438

Battle Creek Sanitarium. *See* Western Health Reform Institute.

Battle Creek Toasted Corn Flake Company 117

Battle of Chancellorsville 252

Battle of Mafeking 18

Battle of New Market 252

Battle of Second Manassas 252

The Battle of the Slum 367

The Battleground (Glasgow) 21, 156

Baum, L. Frank 18, 46

Baxter, Irving 514

Bay Area Style 181

Bayes, Nora 30, 32

Baylor University 46

Beach, Rex 27, 29

Beaumont, Clarence 498

"Bedelia" 23, 62

Bedell, Harriet M. 162

Beebe, Joseph A. 440

Beecher, Henry Ward 293, 325, 407

"Beef trust" 202, 215, 259, 280

Beers, Clifford Whittingham 375

Beheading a Chinese Prisoner 18

Behind the Scenes 29

Behr, Hans Herman 481

Beilhart, Jacob 402, 440

Belasco, David 22, 26, 42, 44, 47, 74

Belasco-Stuyvesant Theater, New York City 32

Bell, Alexander Graham 451–452, 472, 475, 479, 481

Bell, Alexander Melville 481

Bell, Clark 389

Bell, Mifflin E. 192

Bell, Gen. Sherman 96

Bellamy, Edward 326

Bellevue Hospital Medical College 393–394

Bellew, Kyrle 20–21

Bellows, George 30–31, 38, 68

Belmont, Alva Erskine Smith Vanderbilt 333

Ben-Hur (Wallace) 35, 77, 253

Benjamin, Robert Charles O'Hara 293

Bennett, Edward H. 185

Bennett Cup (aviation) 490

Benny, Jack 53

Benson, Frank 37

Benz, Karl 456

Berea College v. *Kentucky* 125

Berenson, Senda 493, 502

Berkman, Alexander 290, 327

Berle, Milton 53

Berlin, Irving 28, 30–31, 40

Bermuda Race (yachting) 489

Bernard, Claude 452

Bernard, Pierre 438

Bernhardt, Sarah 19, 74

Brick, Abraham L. 250

The Bride of the Lamermoor 31

Bridgman, Percy W. 462

Brill, A. A. 463

Brinton, Dr. John Hill 397

Brisbane, Arthur 338, 352, 361–362

British Amateur Athletic Association Championships 522

British Army 511

British Blondes (dance troupe) 77

British Ladies Golf Union 510

British Museum 435

British Olympic Association 516

British Open Golf Championship 509

Broadway Magazine 65

Brokaw, Irving 489

Bronco Buster (Remington) 40

Brookline, Mass., Police Court 290

Brookline Country Club, Mass. 509

Brooklyn Bridge 301

Brooklyn Dodgers 486, 497

Brooklyn Eagle 367–368, 434

Brooklyn Tabernacle 434

Brooks, William Keith 481

Brosius, Marriott 250

Brother Against Brother 31

Brotherhood of Locomotive Firemen 109

Brotherhood of the New Life 440

Brown, Aaron "Dixie Kid" 488, 504, 525–526

Brown, Mrs. Charles S. 510

Brown, Dr. Charlotte Amanda Blake 397

Brown, David 487, 519

Brown, Grace 84–85, 90–91

Brown, Hallie 66

Brown, Henry 259, 271, 273

Brown, John 252, 324

Brown, Percy 479

Brown, William H. 494

Brown University 157, 282

Brown v. *Board of Education* 314

Brownfield, John 257

Brownfield v. *South Carolina* 257

Browning, Louis R. 529

Brownsville Affair 228, 238, 259, 267, 302, 313, 405

Bruce, James 135

Bruce, Patrick Henry 68

Brush, Alanson Partridge 171

Brush Car Company 171

Bryan, Elizabeth Baird 240

Bryan, Vincent P. 21, 25, 191

Bryan, Sen. William J. 250

Bryan, William Jennings 30, 196–197, 205, 209, 225, 232–233, 235, 237–241, 270, 286–287, 362, 365

Bryn Mawr College 122, 159–160, 307, 460, 502

Bubonic plague 372, 387–388

Buck, Henry 23

Buck, Richard 23

Bucknell College 498

Buck's Stove and Range Company 260, 265, 287

Buddhism 411–413

Buddhist Churches of America 412

Buddhist Mission of North America 412

The Budget 440

Buffalo Harvard Club 155

Buffalo World's Fair of 1901. *See* Pan-American Exposition of 1901, Buffalo.

Buffington, Charles G. 529

Buick, David D. 457

Buick Motor Car Company 101, 117, 170–171, 457

Bulger, Harry 301

The Bulwark (Dreiser) 65

Bunau-Varilla, Phillipe 213

Bunnell, Lafayette Houghton 481

Bunsen School, Belleville, Ill. 122

Bunyan, John 27, 259, 344

Burbank, Luther 304, 459, 470–471

Burbank, Maj. Nathaniel 361

Burdock's Blood Bitters 352

The Burglar's Slide for Life 25

Burk, Henry 250

Burke, Martha Jane. *See* Calamity Jane.

Burke, Robert E. 250

Burlington Railroad 99, 102, 215

Burnett, Frances Hodgson 29

Burnham, Daniel Hudson 24, 168, 170–171, 179, 185, 187

Burnham and Root (architectural firm) 179, 185

Burns, George 53

Burns, Tommy 490, 492, 504, 521

Burroughs, Nannie Helen 402, 410

Burton, Theodore E. 303

Busey, Dr. Samuel Clagett 397

Bushnell, David 468

Bushnell, Horace 417, 430

Buster Brown and His Dog Tige series 24

Butler, Nicholas Murray 162–163, 324

Butler Brothers 103

Butterick patterns 175

Butts, Joseph 504

"By the Light of the Silvery Moon" 31

By the Light of the Soul (Freeman) 27, 51

Byers, E. M. 528

Byrnes, James F. 387

C

C. M. Clark (publishing house) 338

Cabbages and Kings (Henry) 24

Cable, George Washington 66

Cable cars 84

Cabot, Godfrey Lowell 290

Cabrini, Mother Francis Xavier 438

Cadillac Motor Car Company 101, 110, 117, 169, 171, 174, 457

Caesar's Column (Donnelly) 293, 334

Caffrey, James J. 486

Cahan, Abraham 52, 339, 350, 360–361

Cahill, Thaddeus 446, 448, 479

Cake Walking Horse 20

Calamity Jane 334

California Chronicle-Examiner 355

California Fish Patrol 70

California Gold Rush of 1849 187

California Institute of Technology 474

California Nationalist 326

The Call of the Wild (London) 22, 35, 50, 70

Callahan, Jimmy 524

Callahan, T. M. 113

Calumet Building, Chicago 185

Calumet Mining Company 119

Cambridge University 435

Camera Notes 37, 39

Camera Work 23, 37, 39

Cameron, Lucille 521

Cameron, Robert 419

Camille 76

Camnitz, Howie 498

Camp, Ellen 519

Camp, Leverett 519

Camp, Walter 505, 509, 519–520

Camp Apache, Ariz. 511

Campbell, Dorothy 511, 528

Campbell, Ira 436

Campbell, James Edwin 66

Corwin, G. H. 29

Cosmopolitan 26, 35, 70, 224, 343, 362

Costello, Maurice 60

Cotton States and International Exposition, Atlanta 141, 247

Cottrell, Frederick G. 479

Coubertin, Baron Pierre de 493, 513–517

Couche Dance on the Midway 19

Coughlin, "Bath Tub" John 217

Council of African Affairs 325

Council on Medical Education 374–375, 385

Councill, William Hooper 164

The Count of Monte Cristo 29, 44

The Country of the Pointed Firs (Jewett) 76

The County Chairman (Ade) 45

Covan, Willie 42

Covello, Leonard 144

Covington, Dr. Benjamin J. 380

The Cowboy Escapade 29

Cowboys and Indians 24

Cowles, Gardner 366

Cox, Jacob D. 250

Coxhead, Ernest 169, 181

Craftsman Workshops, Syracuse, N.Y. 182

Craig, Ralph 523

Craig, Thomas 481

Craig, William 248

Cramer, Malinda Elliott 440

Cramp, Dr. Arthur Joseph 394–395

Crane, Stephen 18, 50, 76, 343, 345, 368

Crapsey, Dr. Algernon S. 416, 438

Crawford, F. Marion 28

Crayono 28

Cree tribe 441

Creek tribe 441

Creelman, James 352

The Creole Show 61

Crétin, Joseph 431

Cribbs, Tom 504

Crile, George Washington 395

The Crisis 268, 325

Critique Philosophique 433

Crocker, Sewall K. 169, 300

Croft, George W. 250

Croly, David 368

Croly, Herbert 283, 333, 338, 368

Croly, Jane Cunningham (Jennie June) 334, 368

Crome, Arthur C. M. 522

Cromwell, William Nelson 358

"Cross of Gold" speech (Bryan) 240–241

Crothers, Rachel 45

Crowdy, William Saunders 440

Crucial Instances (Wharton) 72

The Cruise of the Dazzler (London) 70

The Cruise of the Snark (London) 71

Crump, Rosseau O. 250

Cuban Constitution 198, 256, 271, 295

Cuban Giants 500–501

Cuban Revolution of 1959 271

Cuban Stars 501

Cuban X-Giants 501

Cuba's Struggle Against Spain (Lee) 251

Cubberly, Ellwood P. 133

Cubism 38

"Cuddle Up A Little Closer" 30

Cuforhedake Brane-Fude 385

Cummings, Amos J. 250, 368

Cuneo, Joan 301, 333

Curie, Marie 43

Curran, John J. 438

Currency Act of 1900 256

"Curtain" (Dunbar) 66

Curtis, Cyrus H. K. 343, 351, 366

Curtis, Harriot S. 528

Curtis, Laurence 509

Curtis, Margaret 528

Curtis Publishing Company Building, Philadelphia 189

Curtiss, Glenn 451–452, 479, 490

Cushing, John 494

Cushman, Francis W. 250

Cushney, Dr. Arthur Robertson 372

Cuyler, Rev. Theodore Ledyard 334

Cycle and Automobile 100, 170

The Cynic's Word Book (Bierce) 27

Czolgosz, Leon 198, 256, 290, 299, 327, 338

D

D. E. Loewe and Company 99

D. H. Burnham and Company 185

DaCosta, Dr. Jacob Mendez 397

"Daddy's Little Girl" 25

Daggett, Collin M. 368

Daimler, Gottlieb 456

Dally, Clarence 473

Daly, Arnold 44

Daly, Thomas Augustin 49

Daly, William D. 250

Dana, Dr. Israel Thorndike 397

Danbury hatters 260, 264–265, 287

Danbury Hatters Case. *See Loewe* v. *Lawlor.*

Daniel Boone; or, Pioneer Days in America 26

Daniels, Charles M. 489, 516, 520–521

Danks, H. P. 63

Dante Alighieri 350

Darby, John Nelson 420

The Darling of the Gods 22

Darrow, Clarence 92, 97–98, 111, 241, 265, 272–274, 294

Darwin, Charles 449, 459, 461, 470, 474, 482

Darwinism 326, 409, 416, 461, 475

A Daughter of the Snows (London) 21

Daughters of the American Revolution (DAR) 134, 323

Davenport, Homer 351–352

Davenport-Lander, Jean Margaret 76

Davey, Robert C. 250

David Harum (Westcott) 35

Davidson, Arthur 117

Davidson, Walter 117

Davidson, William 117

Davies, Arthur Bowen 30, 38, 68

Davis, Collin 30

Davis, Cushman K. 250

Davis, Dwight F. 512, 525

Davis, Edward 67

Davis, Harry 26, 303, 499, 525

Davis, Henry Gassaway 202, 235

Davis, Jessie Bartlett 76

Davis, Nathan Smith 334, 397

Davis, Noah 334

Davis, Richard Harding 346

Davis, Stuart 68

Davis Cup Tennis Tournament 486–487, 493, 512, 523, 525

Davison, Henry P. 93

Dawson, Percy 453

Day, Thomas F. 495

Day, Thomas Fleming 489

Day, William Howard 164

Day, William Rufus 257, 273

Dayton Herald 66

Dayton Steel Racquet Company 523

Dayton-Wright Aircraft Company 479

Daytona Literary and Industrial Institute 123, 162

DDT 391

"Drawing the Line in Mississippi" (political cartoon) 81, 103

Dream of a Rarebit Fiend 26, 57, 72

Dreamland, Coney Island 308–309

Drebbel, Cornelius 468

Dreiser, Helen Patges Richardson 65

Dreiser, Paul. *See* Dresser, Paul.

Dreiser, Sallie White 64

Dreiser, Theodore 18, 33, 35, 38, 50, 64–65, 68, 76, 62, 84, 90

Dresser, Paul 25, 60, 62, 64, 76

Dressler, Marie 46

Dreyfuss, Barney 524

Dropsie College for Hebrew and Cognate Learning 405

The Drunkard's Reformation 60

Du Bois, Mary 324

Du Bois, W. E. B. 23, 34, 123, 141–143, 158, 228, 247, 259, 267–268, 289, 301, 304, 314, 324–325, 340–341, 404

Dubois-Reymond, Emil 474

Dumas, Alexander 54

Dunbar, Joshua 65

Dunbar, Matilda 65

Dunbar, Paul Laurence 18–19, 21–22, 24, 35, 46, 49, 65–66, 76

Duncan, Isadora 26, 41–43, 67, 74

Dundy, Elmer "Skip" 308–309

Dunlap, Frederick C. 529

Dunn, Willie 509

Dunne, Edward F. 156

Dunne, Finley Peter 18–19, 21, 27, 50, 271, 340, 343, 366

Dunraven, Lord. *See* Wyndham-Quin, Windham Thomas, Earl of Dunraven.

Dunwell, Charles T. 250

Dunwoody, Gen. Henry 465

Dupont 446

Durant, William Crapo 101, 117, 170–171, 191, 457

Durham, William 436

Duryea, Charles E. 171, 183

Duryea, Etta Terry 521

Duryea brothers 457

Dutton (publishing house) 345

Dvorak, Charles 514

Dwight, Dr. James 512

"Dynamite Rag" 62

E

E. C. Knight Company 214, 279

E. F. Hutton and Company 117

Eakins, Thomas 36, 68

The Earl and the Girl (musical) 26

The Easiest Way (Walter) 32, 45

East Colored Championships (baseball) 501

East London Revival Society 427

East Side High School, Milwaukee 522

Eastern Amateur Basketball Association (EABA) 503

Eastern Association of Vaudeville Managers 20, 55

Eastern League (basketball) 502

Eastlake, Charles Locke 181

Eastman, Charles Alexander 24, 28, 31, 52

Eastman, Elaine Goodale 31, 52

Eastman, George 338

Eastman, Dr. Joseph 397

Eastman Kodak Company 18, 338, 352

Eaton, Edith Maude (Sui Sin Far) 31, 34, 52

Eaton, Walter Pritchard 48

Eaton, Winifred (Onoto Watanna) 53

Eckersall, Walter 506, 525

Ecole Centrales des Arts et Manufactures, Paris 187

Ecole des Beaux Arts, Paris 68, 178, 187–188

Ecumenism 416–417

Eddy, Asa Gilbert 429

Eddy, Mary Baker 341, 428–429

Edgar Thomson Steel Workers 114

Edison, Thomas Alva 30, 43, 56, 71, 74, 300, 356, 446–448, 450, 456, 462, 465–466, 472–473, 477–480

Edison Electric Company 472

Edison Illuminating Company 456

Edison motion picture company 18–20, 22, 24–26, 28–31, 56–57, 60, 71–72

Edison Phonographs 40

Edison Portland Cement Company 462

Editor and Publisher 338

"The Editor's Easy Chair" (Howells) 50

Edsall, Dr. David Linn 375

The Education of Henry Adams (Adams) 28

Education of Women (Thomas) 160

Educational Alliance, New York City 159

Educational Review 122, 125

Edward VII of Great Britain 73, 168, 177, 359, 447, 465, 494

Edward, Prince of Wales. *See* Edward VII of Great Britain.

Edwards, Gus 18, 25, 27–28, 30–31, 191

Egan, Gladys 31

Egan, H. Chandler 527–528

Eggleston, Edward 164

Eickemeyer and Osterheld Company 477

Eiffel Tower 471

The Eight 30, 38–39, 67–69

Einstein, Albert 447, 450, 455, 461–462, 476, 478

Einthoven, Willem 447

Electric Boat Company 469

Electric Theater, Los Angeles 57

Electrical Vehicle Company 82

Electrical World and Engineering 466

Elementary Principles in Statistical Mechanics (Gibbs) 479

Elephants Shooting the Chutes at Luna Park 24

Eliot, Charles W. 125–126, 137, 139, 152, 154–155, 160, 377, 385, 406

Eliot, T. S. 35, 162

Elkins, Stephen 257

Elkins, William Lukens 118

Elkins Act of 1903 81, 85, 98, 100, 200, 216, 248, 257

Ellen Scripps House, La Jolla, Cal. 186

Ellis, Havelock 464

Elmira Gazette 351, 366

Elmira Star 351, 366

The Elms, Newport, R.I. 168

Elmslie, George Grant 181

Eltinge, Julian 53

Elwell, Dr. John Johnson 397

Elwood (racehorse) 488, 527

Ely, Richard T. 425

Emerald Necklace, Boston 334

Emerson, Ralph Waldo 35, 220, 357

Emory University 123

Empire dress 170–171, 173

Employers' Liability Act of 1908 85, 260–261

Emporia Gazette 351, 365

Encyclopedia Africana 325

Encyclopedia of Physical Culture 394

Engels, Friedrich 329

Engineering Magazine 143

Harper, William Rainey 163, 515
Harper (publishing house) 345
Harper's Bazaar 326, 362
Harper's Monthly 35, 50, 366
Harper's Weekly 66, 89, 343, 368
"Harrigan" 28
Harriman, Edward Henry 118, 215, 237, 278–279, 283, 328
Harris, Arthur 267
Harris, Charles K. 19
Harris, Dr. H. F. 373, 386
Harris, Joel Chandler 21, 76, 347, 368
Harris, John P. 303
Harris, Nathaniel Harrison 294
Harris, Paul Percy 301
Harris, Thomas Lake 440
Harris, William Torrey 124, 163–164, 334
Harrison, Benjamin 244, 251, 294
Harrison, Henry Baldwin 294
Harrison, Job 196
Harrison, Dr. Ross G. 375, 479
Hart, Albert Bushnell 125
Hart, Joseph 20
Hart, Marvin 488, 503–504, 521
Harte, Bret 32, 76, 343, 368
Hartley, Marsden 39
Hartman, Samuel Brubaker 395
Hartsell, Topsy 499
The Harvard Classics 137
Harvard Crimson 512
Harvard Monthly 123
Harvard University 35, 46, 48, 124–126, 137–138, 146, 152, 154–155, 160–162, 164, 228, 244, 288–289, 324, 362, 377, 384–385, 406, 416, 432–433, 453, 460, 463, 474, 479–480, 488, 492, 502, 506–509, 512, 520
— Divinity School 416, 425
— Graduate School of Business Administration 125, 139
— Harvard Annex (later Radcliffe College) 155
— Harvard College 142
— Law School 288, 291
— Lawrence Scientific School 187, 432
— Lowell Lectures 476
— Medical School 372, 381, 432, 453
— Observatory 473
— Radcliffe College 23, 25, 46, 155, 333, 502
— School of Education 155
— Stadium 487

— Theatre Collection 19
Haselbock, Joe 281
Haskell, Charles N. 239
Hassam, Childe 37
Hastings, Samuel Dexter 294, 334
Hatcher, John Bell 481
Hauerbach, Otto 30
Haughton, Percy 506–507
Hauptmann, Gerhart 55
Havana Golf and Tennis Club, Cuba 523
Havana Stars 501
Havemeyer, Henry Osborne 118
Havez, Jean 25
Hawkes, Dr. E. Zeh 375
Hawley, James H. 97, 272
Hawthorne, Nathaniel 68
Hay, John 66, 196–197, 201, 210, 251
Hay–Bunau-Varilla Treaty 201, 214, 234
Hay-Herrán Treaty 200, 213
Hay-Pauncefote Treaty 198–199, 213
Hayden, Scott 23
Hayes, John J. 489, 493, 517–518, 525
Hayes, Rutherford B. 472
The Haymarket (Sloan) 29
Haywood, William D. "Big Bill" 83–84, 96–98, 106, 109–111, 259–260, 265, 272–274, 291
"He Done Me Wrong, or, the Death of Bill Bailey" 24
Health, or How to Live (White) 437
Healy, Eliza (Sister Mary Magdalene) 403
Healy, James Augustine 440
Hearst, Phoebe Apperson 188
Hearst, William Randolph 26, 34, 235, 239, 283, 287, 338, 341, 348–349, 351–353, 355, 357, 360–363, 388
Hearst Mines Building, Berkeley 181
Hearst syndicate 349
The Heart is the Teacher (Covello) 144
Heart of Darkness (Conrad) 21
The Heart of Happy Hollow (Dunbar) 24
"Heart of My Heart" 28
Heaviside, Oliver 480
Hebrew Union College 441
Heckcr, Genevieve 511, 527
Hedda Gabler (Ibsen) 27
Heffelfinger, Pudge 508

Hefferon, Charles 518
Heflin, J. Thomas 248
Heida, Anton 515
"Heidelberg Stein Song" 46
Heikes, Rollo O. "Pop" 486
Heinze, F. Augustus 93
Hektoen, Dr. Ludvig 372, 374
Held, Anna 46
"Hello Central, Give Me Heaven, For My Mama's There" 19
Helmholtz, Hermann von 474–475
Helmuth, Dr. William Tod 398
Helwig, Helen R. 513
Hemingway, Ernest 35, 70
Henderson, David Bremner 225, 294
Henderson, Dr. Yandell 376
Henri, Robert 30, 38–39, 67–69
Henry, O. 24, 27–29, 343, 347
Henry, Patrick 294
Henry, William Wirt 294
Henry E. Huntington Library and Art Gallery 328
Henry Street Settlement, New York City 315–317
Hepburn Act of 1906 84, 98, 203, 216, 237, 239, 259, 340
Herald of the Morning 434
Herald Square Theater, New York City 31
Herbert, Victor 23, 25, 46, 63
Herland (Gilman) 327
Hernandez-Villalongin Company 54
Herne, James A. 76
The Hero of Liao-Yang 24
Herreshoff, Nathanael 495–496
Herrick, Clarence Luther 481
Herring, Alexander 452
Herrold, Charles D. "Doc" 341
Herron, George D. 425, 438
Hershey company 88
Hertz, Heinrich 464
Herzl, Theodor 405, 415
The Hessian Renegades 60
Heston, Willie 506, 508, 525
Hetch Hetchy Valley, Yosemite National Park 222, 243
Heurtley, Arthur 190
Heurtley House, Chicago 190
Hewitt, Abram Stevens 118, 244, 251
Heyburn Bill of 1906 83, 98
Hiawatha (Taylor) 24, 31
Hicks, Thomas J. 518
Higgins, Edward J. 428

International Order of the King's Daughters and Sons 440

International Rule (yachting) 496

International Young Men's Christian Association Training School 501

International Zionist Congress of 1905 404

"The Internationale" 67

Interstate Commerce Act of 1887 84, 98, 200, 203, 214–216, 238

Interstate Commerce Commission (ICC) 84–85, 98, 100, 215–216, 237, 248, 259, 263, 278, 293

Intolerance 60

Introduction to the Theory of Mental and Social Measurements (Thorndike) 161

Ireland, Archbishop John 404, 409, 414, 430–432

Ireland, Ward Stone 302

Irish Americans 236

The Iron Heel (London) 29, 71

Irons, Frank 517

Iroquois Theatre, Chicago 24, 53, 56, 201, 300

Irwin, Will 356

Isabella Building, Chicago 187

Islam 406

Isthmian Canal Act (Spooner Act) 199

Itala Car Company 172

Italian Immigrant (Stella) 39

"I've Got Rings on My Fingers" 63

Ives, Charles 20, 33, 63

J

J. C. Penney Company 88

J. P. Morgan and Company 93, 112, 358

Jackson, Andrew 241

Jackson, Dr. Horatio Nelson 169, 300

Jackson, Peter 504

Jackson, Sheldon 441

Jackson, Gen. Stonewall 398

Jacobsen v. *Massachusetts* 258

The Jailbird and How He Flew 26

James, Edward Christopher 294

James, Henry 19, 21–22, 24, 35, 49–50, 70, 72, 345, 432

James, Henry Sr. 432

James, L. N. 527

James, William 123, 161, 324, 332, 403, 409, 432–433, 453–454, 463, 474, 479

Jamestown Tercentennial Exposition of 1907 189, 191, 303, 308

Jane Cable (McCutcheon) 28

Janney, O. Edward 291

Japanese Americans 84, 203, 211, 229, 412–413

Jarvis, Anna M. 303

Jazz Singer 472

Jefferson, Joseph 22, 47, 76

Jefferson, Thomas 265

Jeffries, James J. 487, 503–504, 521, 525

Jehovah's Witnesses 407, 409, 418, 433

Jellinek, Adolph 435

Jenkins, Tom 489

Jenks, Dr. Edward Watrous 398

Jenney, Mundie, and Jensen (architectural firm) 187

Jenney, William Le Baron 173, 179, 185, 187–188, 192

Jennie Gerhardt (Dreiser) 65

Jennings, Hugh 499

Jennings Seminary, Aurora, Ill. 331

Jensen, Elmer C. 187

Jensen, Jens 185

Jerome, William 23

Jerome, William Travers 261, 269, 284, 291

Jesus and the Social Question (Peabody) 425

Jesus Christ 410, 416, 418–423, 429, 434, 437–438

Jewett, Sarah Orne 35, 51, 76, 344

Jewish Daily Forward 52, 339, 350, 360–361

Jewish Orphanage, Cleveland 192

The Jewish State (Herzl) 405, 415

Jewish Theological Seminary, New York City 403, 415, 415, 435

Jim Crow laws 140–141, 219, 227, 247, 259, 313, 406, 410

Joan of Arc 74

Johannsen, Wilhelm 449, 459

John Barleycorn (London) 70

John D. and the Reporter 28

John Deere and Company 118

John P. Holland Torpedo Boat Company 468

John the Baptist 75

John Worthy School, St. Charles, Ill. 292

Johns Hopkins University 122, 154, 160, 164, 386, 392, 394–396, 398, 450, 474, 479, 482

— Hospital 373

— Medical School 374–375, 381–382, 385, 452–453

Johnson, Andrew 293

Johnson, Bascom 514

Johnson, Byron Bancroft "Ban" 486, 492, 496–497, 525

Johnson, Ed 276

Johnson, Eldridge 74

Johnson, Henry 521

Johnson, Hiram 220, 248

Johnson, J. Rosamond 18–19, 21, 23, 27, 47, 61

Johnson, Jack 490, 492, 504, 521–522, 525

Johnson, James Weldon 19, 47, 61, 267

Johnson, John G. 279

Johnson, Jonathan Eastman 76

Johnson, Joseph French 331

Johnson, Lucy Bagby 294

Johnson, Marietta Pierce 163

Johnson, Martin N. 251

Johnson, Tina 521

Johnson, Tom 218, 286

Johnson and Callahan stores 113

Johnson Brothers 55, 61

Johnson Wax Company Administration Building, Racine, Wis. 190

Johnston, Mary 345

Jokes and their Relation to the Unconscious (Freud) 448

Jolson, Al 53, 55, 472

Jones, Benjamin Franklin 118

Jones, Bobby 519

Jones, Charles F. 291

Jones, Charles Price 405

Jones, John Luther "Casey" 19, 80

Jones, John Percival 514

Jones, Marion 513–514, 527

Jones, Mary Harris "Mother" 106, 291

Jones, Samuel "Golden Rule" 218–219

Jones, Samuel Porter 334, 441

Jones, Sisserietta 61

Jones, "Captain" William R. 114

Jones and Laughlin Steel Company 118

Joplin, Robert 69

Joplin, Scott 23, 33, 62–63, 69–70, 299

Joplin, Will 69

Jordan, David Starr 122, 130

Jose, Richard 24, 63

Joseph, Chief of the Nez Perce tribe 334

La Lanne, Jack 394
Lamb, Arthur J. 18, 21, 27
Lamb, Bessie 76
Lamb, Joseph 62, 69
Lancaster Academy 470
Lanchester, Frederick W. 446
Land of Little Rain (Austin) 51
Landis, Kenesaw Mountain 216, 248, 291
Lane, Dr. Levi Cooper 398
Langdell, Christopher Columbus 164
Langley, Samuel P. 447, 451, 482
Langmuir, Irving 471
Langtry, Lily 189
"Largo" 340, 360
Larkin Company Administration Building, Buffalo, N.Y. 180
Larned, William A. 487, 512, 523, 527–528
Lasker, Albert 346
Lassiter, Francis R. 251
"The Last Leaf" (Henry) 28
The Last of the Plainsmen (Grey) 29
Latell, Alfred 53
Lathrop, Julia 302
Latimer, Asbury C. 251
The Launching of the USS "Connecticut" 25
Laura Comstock's Bag-Punching Dog 19
Laurie, Annie (Winifred Black) 341, 348–349, 354–355
Lauste, Eugène 27
Lawrence, Florence 28, 30
Lawrenceville Preparatory School 147
Lawson, Ernest 30, 38, 68
Lawson House, Berkeley 188
Lazarus, Emma 23
Lazear, Dr. Jesse William 398, 482
Lea, Luke 291
Leach, Thomas W. 498
League of Colored Baseball Clubs 500
Leary, J. Scott 520
Leary, John 118
"Leaves from the Mental Portfolio of a Eurasian" (Eaton) 31, 53
Leaves of Grass (Whitman) 68
Leconte, Joseph 482
Lee, Fitzhugh 251
Lee, Rebecca 380
Lee, Robert E. 251
Lee, Stephen D. 251
Leever, Sam 498, 525
Leffingwell, Dr. Albert T. 384

Lehar, Franz 29
Lehigh Zinc Company 119
Lehman, Emmanuel 118
Lehman, Eugene Heitler 23
Lehman Brothers and Company 118
Leland, Henry Martyn 110, 169, 174, 191
Leland Giants 501
Lenard, Philipp 448
Lenin, Vladimir Ilyich 67, 111
Lenin Peace Prize 325
Lenox, Jean 25
Pope Leo XII 292, 403
Leonard, Eddie 23
Lesley, J. Peter 482
Lester, Rufus E. 251
"Letters from the Earth" (Twain) 35
Leukemia 398
Lewis, Carl 522
Lewis, Gilbert N. 462
Lewis, Walter 521
Lewis, William Henry 289, 291
Lewis and Clark Centennial Exposition of 1905, Portland 61, 301, 308
Lewy, Israel 435
"Liberty of Contract" (Pound) 288
Liberty Theater, New York City 27
Libman, Dr. Emanuel 374
Library of Congress 66
Library of Congress — Reading Room 66
Lick Observatory, Cal. 455, 482
Lieutenant Gibson (racehorse) 486, 527
Life 22, 177, 356
The Life of an American Fireman (Porter) 71
The Life of Christ 26
The Life of George Washington 31
The Life of Moses 31
"Lift Every Voice and Sing" (J. W. & J. R. Johnson) 18, 62
Lightbody, James 515
Lighthouse, the New York Association for the Blind 163
Li'l Gal (Dunbar) 66
Lincoln, Abraham 247, 251, 253, 268, 305, 313, 363–364
Lincoln, Charles M. 354
Lincoln Hospital, Durham, N.C. 380
"Lincoln, the Man of the People" (Markham) 49
Lincoln Theater, New York City 69

Lindsey, Ben B. 285–286
"A Line o' Type or Two" (Taylor) 367
Lingard, William H. 19
The Lion and the Mouse (Klein) 45
Lippincott, Sara Jane Clarke (Grace Greenwood) 368
Lippincott's 368
Lipton, Sir Thomas 494–496
Lister, Joseph 377
Little, Frances 28
"The Little Church Around the Corner" 28
Little Citizens (Kelly) 163
Little Galleries of the Photo-Secession. *See* 291 galleries.
Little Johnny Jones (Cohan) 74
"Little Nemo in Slumberland" (McKay) 302
"Little Orphan Annie" (Riley) 49
The Little Shepherd of Kingdom Come (Fox) 35
Littleton, Martin 269
Livermore, Mary Ashton Rice 334, 398
A Living Wage (Ryan) 405, 425
Living Way 365
Livingston College 113
Lloyd, Henry Demarest 251, 294, 334, 368
Lloyd, Joe 519
Lloyd, John Uri 395
Lochner, Joseph 274, 287
Lochner v. New York 83, 99, 202, 259, 264, 274–275, 281, 287
Locke, Alain 124
Lockhart, Charles 118
Lodge, George Cabot 35
Lodge, Henry Cabot 244
Lodge, Oliver 450, 464
Loeb, Jacques 458–459
Loew, Marcus 54
Loewe, Dietrich E. 264
Loewe v. Lawlor 85, 99, 204, 260, 265
Logan, Olive 76
London, Bessie 71
London, Jack 21–22, 24–25, 29, 31, 35, 50–51, 70–71, 117, 343
London, John 70
London Daily Illustrated Mirror 25
London Rules (boxing) 503
London Tabernacle 434
London World's Fair. *See* Franco-British Exposition of 1908, London.
The Lone Highwayman 26

Marinetti, Filippo 75

Marion, Frank 22

Markham, Edwin 49

Markle, John 92

Marks, Josephine Preston Peabody 45

Marmon Car Company 169

The Marne (Wharton) 73

Marquette University 508

Marquis, Don 344

Married for Millions 26

The Marrow of Tradition (Chesnutt) 19, 52, 290

Marsh, Benjamin F. 251

Marsh, Mae 60

Marshall Field and Company 118–119

Marshall Field and Company Building, Chicago 171, 179

Martin, David E. 518

Martin, Denver Ed 521

Martin, Dr. Franklin Henry 395

Martin, Glenn 452

Martin, Jack 488, 528

Martin and Seig's Mastodon Minstrels 73

Martin Beck's Orpheum 54

Martin Eden (London) 31, 71

Martin House, Buffalo, New York 170

Marvin, Arthur 18

Marvin, Ross G. 355, 482

Marx, Karl 329, 425

Marxism 41, 106

"Mary White" (White) 365

"Mary's A Grand Old Name" 25, 61

Mary's Wonderful Stomach Remedy 389

The Masher 28

Mason, Charles H. 405–406, 436

Mason, John 301

Masonic Temple, Chicago 185

Masonic Temple, Cleveland 192

Massachusetts Board of Education 164

Massachusetts Board of Health, Lunacy, and Charity 293

Massachusetts Commission on Industrial and Technical Education 124

Massachusetts General Hospital 382, 463

Massachusetts Hospital School for Crippled Children 395

Massachusetts Institute of Technology (MIT) 154, 164, 186, 188, 462, 473–474

Massachusetts Metaphysical College 429

Massachussetts Conference on Charities 291

Massillon Tigers 508

Masterson, William B. "Bat" 367

Matas, Dr. Rudolph 395

Mathews, Brander 48

Mathews, George A. 192

Mathews, Shailer 417

Le Matin 489

The Matinee Idol 28

Matisse, Henri 39

Matthews, James Newton 66

Matthewson, Christy 498

Maude's Naughty Little Brother 18

Maxwell, James Clerk 462

Maybeck, Bernard 173, 181, 187–188

Mayo, Dr. Charles H. 382

Mayo, Dr. William W. 382

Mayo Clinic. *See* St. Mary's Hospital.

McAdoo, William Gibbs 300

McAteer, Myrtle 513

McCabe, Charles Cardwell 441

McCall, John Augustine 118

McCall's 344

McCall's patterns 175

McCarthy, Joseph 325

McCaw, Dr. James Brown 398

McCaw, Walter Drew 395

McClellan, George 261

McClelland, Dan 501

McClennan, Dr. Alonzo C. 380

McClintic-Marshall Construction Company 111

McClung, Clarence E. 460, 480

McClure, Frank 347

McClure, Samuel S. 359, 364

McClure Phillips (publishing house) 338

McClure's 21, 35, 70, 136, 218, 241, 286, 338–340, 343, 359–361, 363–366, 389

McComas, Louis Emory 294

McCormack, Joseph N. 379

McCormack Institute for Infectious Diseases 373

McCormick, Cyrus Hall Jr. 117

McCoy, Bessie 31

McCoy, Charles "Kid" 487, 505

McCracken, Henry B. 509

McCray v. *United States* 258

McCutcheon, George Barr 28

McCutcheon, Ross 22

McCutcheon, Wallace 18, 22, 25–26, 29, 59, 75

McDermott, John J. 518

McDonald, Charles Blair 509

McElwain, William Howe 118

McFadden, Mary 393

McFadden, William 393

McGee, Dr. Anita Newcomb 396

McGiffert, Arthur Cushman 418

McGinnity, Joe "Iron Man" 486, 498

McGraw, John J. 488, 497–498, 524, 526

McGraw-Hill Book Company 88

McGugin, Dan 506–507

McGuire, Dr. Hunter Holmes 398

McIver, Charles D. 148, 164

McKay, Gordon 118

McKay, Winsor 302–303

McKean, William V. 367–368

McKeesport [Pa.] *News* 338

McKelway, St. Clair 367

McKenna, Joseph 273

McKenzie, Dr. Robert Tait 375, 507

McKesson, Dr. E. I. 375

McKim, Mead, and White (architectural firm) 182, 298

McKinley, William 19, 80–81, 196–198, 208, 210, 215, 223–225, 227, 229–233, 236–237, 241, 243–245, 251, 256, 266, 279, 286, 290, 294, 299, 308, 327, 338, 351–352, 365, 396

McLaurin, Anselm J. 252

McLeod, Fred 490, 528

McMillan, James 252

McPharlan, James 97

McQuaid, Bernard J. 431

McTeague (Norris) 76

McTeer, Myrtle 527

Mead Pulp and Paper 88

Meadowbrook Golf Club, Long Island, New York 510

Meat Inspection Act of 1906 84, 98, 203, 217, 259, 302, 340, 374

Mechanic's Savings Bank 117

"Mechanical Jurisprudence" (Pound) 288

Medical Association of the State of Alabama 398

Medical Diagnosis (DaCosta) 397

The Medical Follies 394

Medical Record 395

Medical Society of Virginia 398

New York Post 453

New York Public Service Commission 283

New York School of Art 39, 68

New York Society for the Prevention of Crime 261

New York Society for the Suppression of Vice 65

New York State
— Assembly 203, 220, 244
— Commission on Immigration 285
— Court of Appeals 261
— Supreme Court 287

New York Stock Exchange 523

New York Sun 270, 356, 367–369

New York Telegraph 367

New York Theater 32

The New York Times 20, 32, 66, 168, 171, 338, 340, 342, 347–349, 354–356, 359, 368, 379, 415, 439, 489

New York Tribune 362, 367

New York University 509

New York University Settlement 315

New York World 282–283, 342, 348, 353–354, 356–359, 362–363, 367

New York World Building, Manhattan 363

New York Yacht Club 494–496

New York Yankees 497

New Yorker Staats-Zeitung 350, 368

Newcomb, Simon 482

Newell, Frederick 221

Newlands, Francis G. 330

Newlands Act of 1902. *See* National Reclamation Act of 1902.

Newport Golf Club, Rhode Island 509

Newspaper Enterprise Association 339

Newton, Arthur 518

Newton, Isaac 477

Newtonian physics 461, 476

Nez Perce tribe 334

Niagara Movement 247, 259–261, 268, 289, 301, 314, 324, 341, 404

Nicene Creed 416

Nicholson, Eliza 361

Nicholson, Nick 28

Nickelodeons 26–27, 34, 54, 57, 301, 303–304

Niedecken, George 181

Nielson, Ada 76

The Nigger 47

Nkrumah, Kawme 325

Nobel Prizes 20
— for Chemistry 448–449
— for Medicine or Physiology 448, 458
— for Physics 447–449, 462, 476
— Peace Prize 202, 211, 324

"Nobody" 74

Non-Partisan Women's Christian Temperance Union 335

Nordenfeldt, Thorsten 468

Norris, Frank 19, 22, 31, 35, 50–51, 60, 64, 68, 76

Norse Sonatas (MacDowell) 63

North, Charles Edward 396

North American Shinto Church 413

North Carolina State Normal and Industrial College 147

North Congregational Church, Springfield, Mass. 430

North Dakota Tuberculosis Association 376

Northern Pacific Railroad 99, 102, 215, 256, 278–279

Northern Securities Company 81, 99, 102, 199, 215, 234, 256–258, 279–280

Northern Securities v. *United States* 82, 89, 99, 102, 201, 258, 275, 278–279

Northwestern University 288, 329, 331, 403, 416
— Business School 139

Norton, J. Pease 374

Norworth, Jack 28, 30

Nostromo (Conrad) 24

Nostrums and Quackery and Pseudo-Medicine (Cramp) 394

Nott, Dr. Josiah 391, 394

Novocain 301

Novy, Dr. Frederick George 373, 388

Noyes, Crosby S. 368

The Numerical Bible (Grant) 440

Nutting, June Wallace 301

O

"O Holy Night" 340, 360

Oakland Car Company 101, 117

Oberlin College 163, 268, 502

The Object and Manner of Our Lord's Return (Russell) 434

O'Brien, Dr. A. P. 387

O'Brien, Philadelphia Jack 488, 505, 526

O'Brien, Sara 134

Observations by Mr. Dooley (Dunne) 21

Ochs, Adolph S. 338, 348–349, 354

O'Connell, Denis 430–431

The Octopus (Norris) 19, 51, 76

"An Ode in Time of Hesitation" (Moody) 19

"Ode to Ethiopia" (Dunbar) 66

Odell, Benjamin 283

Oelrichs, Mrs. Hermann 169

"Of Mr. Booker T. Washington and Others" (Du Bois) 142

Of One Blood, or, The Hidden Self (Hopkins) 22

Official Collegiate Guide (basketball) 502

Ogden, Robert C. 147

Oh! That Limburger 26

Ohio State Supreme Court 295

Ohio State University College of Law 295

O'Keeffe, Georgia 39

Oklahoma Constitution 204, 260, 303, 318

Olcott, Chauncey 63

"Old Home Rag" 62

Old Indian Days (Eastman) 28, 52

Old Indian Legends (Bonnin) 19

Old Isaacs the Pawnbroker 29

Old Madame and Other Stories (Spofford) 18, 51

Old Washington (Spofford) 27, 51

Olds, Ransom Eli 168, 170, 183, 457

Olds Motor Works 101, 110, 117, 168–170, 174, 184, 457

Oliver, Henry William 118

Oliver, James 118

Oliver, Joe "King" 63

Oliver Chilled Plow Works 118

Olmsted, Frederick Law 334

Olmsted, Frederick Law Jr. 186

Olmsted, John Charles 186

Olney, Richard 263

Olympic Games
— 1896 513, 515, 518
— 1900 486, 513–514, 518, 522–523, 526
— 1904 107, 488, 515–516, 518, 520, 525–526
— 1906 489, 515, 517, 521, 526
— 1908 490, 493, 516–518, 521, 525–526
— 1910 515
— 1912 526
— 1914 515
— 1916 523

West Side High School, Milwaukee 522

West Virginia University 507

Westchester Cup (polo) 490

Westcott, Edward 35

Western Association. *See* American League (baseball).

Western Association of Writers 66

Western Conference (football) 506, 508

Western Electric 472

Western Federation of Miners (WFM) 82–83, 97–98, 106, 111, 264, 272

Western Health Reform Institute (later the Battle Creek Sanitarium) 437

Western Justice 28

Western League (baseball) 492, 496, 525

Western League (basketball) 502

Western Open Golf Tournament 519

Western Reserve University 161, 475

Western Theological Seminary, Chicago 404

Western Union 472

Westinghouse Electric 466

Weston, Edward P. 490, 526

Weston and Barnes (songwriters) 63

Wharton, Edith 21, 24–25, 28–29, 49, 72–73, 345–346

Wharton, Joseph 119

What a Pipe Did 28

What Diantha Did 326–327

"What You Gonna Do When the Rent Comes 'Round" 25

"What's the Matter with Kansas?" (White) 365

The Wheel of Life (Glasgow) 28

Wheeler, Benjamin 123, 139

Wheeler, J. R. 130

Wheeler, Joseph 253

When Women Vote 28

Whilomville Stories (Crane) 18

"When Irish Eyes Are Smiling" 63

When Malindy Sings (Dunbar) 66

Whistler, James McNeill 36, 39, 77

White, Alma 403

White, Clarence 39

White, Edward Douglass 273

White, Ellen Gould Harmon 418, 437–438

White, Emerson Elbridge 165

White, Henry 437

White, James 18–19, 59, 437–438

White, Dr. Joseph H. 388

White, Maunsel 115

White, Rollin H. 168, 183

White, Solomon 501

White, Stanford 57, 77, 169, 182, 192, 268–269, 341, 353–354

White, Stephen Mallory 295

White, Walter 325

White, William Allen 340, 351, 365

White, William Jefferson 157

White Fang (London) 25, 35

White House Conference on the Care of Dependent Children (1909) 291, 304

White Rats (actors' union) 54

White Sewing Machine Company 168, 183

The White Terror and the Red (Cahan) 52

White Wing 452

Whitehead, Dr. William Riddick 399

Whitier, Pauline 514

Whitman, Malcolm D. 512, 527

Whitman, Walt 63, 68, 188

Whitney, Caspar 513

Whitney, Gertrude Vanderbilt 28

Whittier, John Greenleaf 35

The Whole Dam Family and the Dam Dog 25, 57

Who's Who in America 338

"Why Did I Pick a Lemon in the Garden of Love" 61

"Why Teaching Repels Men" (Bardeen) 125

Whyte, William Pinkney 253

The Widow and the Only Man 24

Wiggin, Kate Douglas 22, 28, 345

Wigwam Evenings (Eastman and Eastman) 31, 52

Wilberforce University 324

Wild West Show 18

Wilde, Oscar 29, 75

Wiley, Ariosto A. 253

Wiley, Harvey W. 385

Wilhelm II of Germany 211

"The Will to Believe" (James) 433

The Will to Believe and Other Essays On Popular Philosophy (James) 433

"Will You Love Me in December as You Do in May?" 25

Willard, Frances E. 427

Willard, Jess 504

Willard, Josiah Flint (Josiah Flynt) 369

Williams, Bert 18, 34, 46, 55, 61, 73–74, 300

Williams, Dr. Daniel H. 380

Williams, Henry 25, 27

Williams, Marshall Jay 295

Williams, Samuel W. 204

Williams, Walter 341

Williams, William Carlos 31

Williams College 430, 474

Williamsburg Bridge, New York City 299

Williamson, Dr. John M. 387

Willits, Ward W. 190

Willits House, Highland Park, Ill. 190

Wilson, Edmund B. 460, 480

Wilson, Dr. Frank P. 387

Wilson, Dr. Louis Blanchard 374

Wilson, William Lyne 295

Wilson, Woodrow 112, 123, 137–138, 224–225, 241–242, 245, 287, 289, 334, 393, 428, 471

Wilson Acton Hotel, La Jolla, Cal. 186

Wimbledon tennis tournament 488, 493, 512–513, 523

Windsor Palace, London 516

The Wings of the Dove (James) 21

Winkfield, Jimmy 486–487, 526–527

Winona, A Tale of Negro Life in the South (Hopkins) 21

Winter, William 48

Wintergreen (racehorse) 490, 528

Wirt, William 125, 143

"Wisconsin Idea" (Van Hise) 123, 130–131, 241

Wisconsin Interscholastic Championships 522

Wisconsin News 362

The Wisdom of Ben Sira (Schechter) 435

Wise, Isaac Mayer 441

Wise, Richard A. 253

Wishnieweski, Lazare 329

Wister, Owen 21, 25, 27, 35, 52

With Her in Outland (Gilman) 327

Wittenmyer, Annie Turner 335, 441

"Wizard of Menlo Park" 472

The Wizard of Oz (musical) 23, 46

Wolf, Lucien 435

The Wolf (Norris) 50

Wollstein, Dr. Martha 382

Woman's Medical College of Pennsylvania 381